West Academic Publishing's Emeritus Advisory Board

JESSE H. CHOPER
Professor of Law and Dean Emeritus
University of California, Berkeley

LARRY D. KRAMER
President, William and Flora Hewlett Foundation

JAMES J. WHITE
Robert A. Sullivan Emeritus Professor of Law
University of Michigan

West Academic Publishing's Law School Advisory Board

MARK C. ALEXANDER
Arthur J. Kania Dean and Professor of Law
Villanova University Charles Widger School of Law

JOSHUA DRESSLER
Distinguished University Professor Emeritus
Michael E. Moritz College of Law, The Ohio State University

MEREDITH J. DUNCAN
Professor of Law
University of Houston Law Center

RENÉE McDONALD HUTCHINS
Dean & Professor of Law
University of Maryland Carey School of Law

RENEE KNAKE JEFFERSON
Joanne and Larry Doherty Chair in Legal Ethics &
Professor of Law, University of Houston Law Center

ORIN S. KERR
William G. Simon Professor of Law
University of California, Berkeley

JONATHAN R. MACEY
Professor of Law,
Yale Law School

DEBORAH JONES MERRITT
Distinguished University Professor,
John Deaver Drinko/Baker & Hostetler Chair in Law Emerita
Michael E. Moritz College of Law, The Ohio State University

ARTHUR R. MILLER
University Professor and Chief Justice Warren E. Burger Professor of
Constitutional Law and the Courts, New York University

GRANT S. NELSON
Professor of Law Emeritus, Pepperdine University
Professor of Law Emeritus, University of California, Los Angeles

A. BENJAMIN SPENCER
Dean & Trustee Professor of Law
William & Mary Law School

STATE CONSTITUTIONAL LAW
THE MODERN EXPERIENCE

Fourth Edition

■ ■ ■

Jeffrey S. Sutton
Chief Judge
United States Court of Appeals for the Sixth Circuit

Stephen R. McAllister
E.S. & Tom W. Hampton Professor of Law
University of Kansas School of Law

Randy J. Holland
The Late Former Justice
Delaware Supreme Court

Jeffrey M. Shaman
Vincent de Paul Professor of Law Emeritus
DePaul University College of Law

AMERICAN CASEBOOK SERIES®

The publisher is not engaged in rendering legal or other professional advice, and this publication is not a substitute for the advice of an attorney. If you require legal or other expert advice, you should seek the services of a competent attorney or other professional.

American Casebook Series is a trademark registered in the U.S. Patent and Trademark Office.

© 2010 Thomson Reuters
© 2016, 2020 LEG, Inc. d/b/a West Academic
© 2023 LEG, Inc. d/b/a West Academic
     860 Blue Gentian Road, Suite 350
     Eagan, MN 55121
     1-877-888-1330

West, West Academic Publishing, and West Academic are trademarks of West Publishing Corporation, used under license.

Printed in the United States of America

ISBN: 978-1-68561-533-8

In memory of and with fondness toward our friend and late co-author, the Honorable Randy J. Holland (1947–2022), a long-standing Justice of the Delaware Supreme Court.

The Co-Authors also Dedicate This Book as Follows:

Jeffrey S. Sutton
To Peggy Sutton,
Nathaniel, John, and Margaret

Stephen McAllister
To,
Emma, Mara, Fiona, Brett, Isabel, and Sofia

FOREWORD

State Constitutional Law – The Modern Experience
Foreword by E. Norman Veasey*

As is the case with the weather, lawyers often talk about the constitutions of the various states, but seldom do anything about that subject. Most of the American cases and literature focus on the United States Constitution. State constitutional law is often neglected, but it is a vibrant and significant feature of our jurisprudence. Justice Randy J. Holland, Judge Jeffrey S. Sutton, Professor Stephen R. McAllister and Professor Jeffrey M. Shaman have breathed new life into the subject with this outstanding, scholarly casebook.

Lawyers take an oath upon admission to the bar to support the United States Constitution and the constitution of their states of admission. *See, e.g.*, Rule 54, Rules of the Supreme Court of Delaware ("I do solemnly swear (or affirm) that I will support the Constitution of the United States and the Constitution of the State of Delaware."). But can a lawyer be true to this solemn oath if she has not studied state constitutional law or been examined on her state constitution? Perhaps she can "catch up" in practice with some "on the job training," as the need arises. But that is not a particularly professional approach. This new, epic work on state constitutional law should become an important basis for law school curricula. Moreover, state constitutional law should be considered as a bar examination topic.

The framers of the United States constitution adopted a "constitutionally mandated balance of power between the States and the Federal Government to ensure the protection of our fundamental liberties." *Atascadero State Hosp. v. Scanlon*, 473 U.S. 234, 242 (1985) (quoting *Garcia v. San Antonio Metro. Transit Auth.*, 469 U.S. 528 (Powell, J., dissenting)). The preservation of diversity in the legal and governmental systems of each state was expressly contemplated when the United States constitution was framed and adopted. *See* Randy J. Holland, *State Constitutions: Purpose and Function*, 69 Temp. L. Rev. 989, 998–99 (1996). State constitutions are a source of rights independent of the Federal Constitution and may be applied by state courts to grant more extensive protection for individual rights than is recognized under the Federal Constitution.

Under the system of dual sovereignty that exists in this nation, a state court is free to interpret its own state constitution in any way it determines, provided it does not contravene federal law. While the Supremacy Clause of the Federal Constitution makes federal law supreme to state law, so long as state constitutional protection does not fall below the federal floor,

---

* Chief Justice (Ret.), Delaware Supreme Court (1992–2004).

a state court may interpret its own state constitution as it chooses, irrespective of federal constitutional law. Although decisions of the United States Supreme Court concerning constitutional issues are entitled to respect and may provide guidance on constitutional matters, they are not binding on a state court as it interprets its own state constitutional guarantees. A state court is free as a matter of its own law to grant more expansive rights than those afforded by federal law. The expansion beyond federally guaranteed individual liberties by a state constitution is attributable to a variety of reasons: differences in textual language, legislative history, pre-existing state law, structural differences, matters of particular concern, and state traditions.

As Judge Sutton, one of the co-authors of this work, has written, "lawyers and clients have two chances, not one, to invalidate dubious state or local action. They may invoke the United States Constitution or that State's Constitution to strike the law. Yet that is not what most lawyers do." Jeffrey S. Sutton, *Why Teach—and Why Study—State Constitutional Law*, 34 Okla. City U.L. Rev. 165, 166 (2009). A lawyer challenging police action or a dubious state statute should welcome the leverage of two arrows in her quiver.

Indeed, lawyers *should*, in many cases, frame their attacks on the constitutions of both sovereigns. Why? "State constitutional law not only gives the client two chances to win, it will also give the client a *better* chance to win." *Id.* at 173. There are many reasons cited by Judge Sutton showing this to be true, but one overarching reason is that a state supreme court's decision that rests on its application of the state constitution is the last word in the case and cannot be countermanded by the United States Supreme Court. As the late Supreme Court Justice William Brennan has written, "Moreover, the state decisions not only cannot be overturned by, they indeed are not even reviewable by, the Supreme Court of the United States." William J. Brennan, Jr., *State Constitutions and the Protection of Individual Rights*, 90 Harv. L. Rev. 489, 501 (1977). This principle is based on the established doctrine that "if a state ground is independent and adequate to support a judgment, the U.S. Supreme Court has no jurisdiction at all over the decision despite the presence of federal issues." *Id.* at 501 n.80.

The law concerning unreasonable searches and seizures reflects differing standards between federal and state constitutions and a labyrinth of factual situations. *See United States v. Cortez*, 449 U.S. 411, 417 (1981). A case in point is the 1999 Delaware Supreme Court decision in *Jones v. State*, 745 A.2d 856 (Del. 1999). There the Court held—arguably in the face of contrary federal and Delaware decisions under the United States Constitution adjudicating similarly worded provisions—that the police did not have a reasonable and articulable basis to make a stop of the defendant and the seizure of controlled substances on his person.

In *Jones* the Court framed the issue as "whether the search and seizure language in the Delaware Constitution means the same thing as the United States Supreme Court's construction of *similar* language in the United States Constitution." *Id.* at 495. The Court then analyzed a number of historical references, including those where similar terms had been used, with differing results. *Id.* at 495–506. Noting that the law concerning unreasonable searches and seizures "reflects differing standards between federal and state constitutions and a labyrinth of factual situations," the Court held:

> If an officer attempts to seize someone before possessing reasonable and articulable suspicion, that person's actions stemming from the attempted seizure may not be used to manufacture the suspicion the police lacked initially.

Id. at 855–56.

State constitutional law, like its federal counterpart, is not limited to issues involving the common law or individual rights. Numerous other areas of law involve the application of state constitutions. The structure and power of state and local governments, the state judicial system, taxation, public finance, and public education are all affected by a state's constitutions and its interpretation. "From the inception of the American republic, federal and state constitutional traditions have been distinct." James E. Henretta, *Foreword: Rethinking the State Constitutional Tradition*, 22 Rutgers L.J. 819, 819–26, 836–39 (1991). The United States Constitution has retained its original character as a document that fixed the basic structure of government and allocated power among its three branches. State constitution-making and amending has been a recurring process within the broader political, social, economic, and historical contexts of time and place. A.E. Dick Howard, *The Values of Federalism*, 1 New Eur. L. Rev. 241, 145-46 (1993); Lewis B. Kaden, *Politics, Money, and State Sovereignty: The Judicial Role*, 79 Colum. L. Rev. 847, 853–57 (1979). *See also* Robert P. Stoker, Reluctant Partners (1991).

This new, richly documented and superbly analyzed casebook by such distinguished legal scholars is destined to be the seminal authority in this vitally important field. For some lawyers, a system of dual sovereignty means that litigants will have two opportunities, not just one, to invalidate a state law or otherwise halt state action. And for others, our federal system makes state courts accountable for properly interpreting their own constitutions, without regard to whether those interpretations increase or decrease individual liberty and without regard to whether they follow or break from decisions of the U.S. Supreme Court. But for all lawyers, the independence of the sovereignty of the states makes the study and effective use of state constitutional law an imperative in the twenty-first century.

SUMMARY OF CONTENTS

FOREWORD v
TABLE OF CONTENTS xiii
TABLE OF CASES xxiii
TABLE OF AUTHORITIES xxxi
EXPLANATORY NOTE.. xxxv
ACKNOWLEDGEMENTS xxxv
PERMISSION TO REPRINT xxxv

CHAPTER I
INTRODUCTION.. 1

CHAPTER II
DUAL SOVEREIGNTY: THE INTERRELATION OF THE STATE AND FEDERAL CONSTITUTIONS 9
   A. INTRODUCTION 9
   B. THE SOURCES AND NATURE OF FEDERAL AND STATE POWERS 9
      1. Exclusive Federal Powers 9
      2. Exclusive State Powers 33
      3. Overlapping and Shared Powers 34
   C. LIMITATIONS ON FEDERAL POWER 39
      1. The Anti-Commandeering Principle 39
      2. Immunity from Suits under Federal Law 44
   D. FEDERAL LIMITATIONS ON STATE POWER 58
      1. Article VI – The Supremacy Clause 58
      2. Article IV 64

CHAPTER III
THEORIES BY WHICH STATE COURTS MAY CONSTRUE STATE CONSTITUTIONS DIFFERENTLY FROM THEIR FEDERAL COUNTERPARTS ... 77
   A. SIMILARLY WORDED GUARANTEES... 78
   B. DIFFERENTLY WORDED PROVISIONS... 98
   C. STATE GUARANTEES MAY OFFER MORE OR FEWER PROTECTIONS THAN THEIR FEDERAL COUNTERPARTS 110
   D. INDEPENDENT AND ADEQUATE STATE GROUNDS: STATE COURT RULINGS THAT ADDRESS FEDERAL AND STATE BASES FOR DECISION.. 113
   E. SEQUENCING: THE ORDER IN WHICH STATE COURTS RESOLVE RELATED STATE AND FEDERAL CLAIMS AND THE PRIORITY GIVEN TO EACH 124

CHAPTER IV
EQUALITY 133
   A. INTRODUCTION 133
   B. RACIAL CLASSIFICATIONS 134
   C. GENDER-BASED CLASSIFICATIONS 148
   D. AGE-BASED CLASSIFICATIONS 153
   E. SEXUAL-ORIENTATION CLASSIFICATIONS 162
   F. ECONOMIC CLASSIFICATIONS.. 164

CHAPTER V
REPRESENTATION AND VOTING 177
   A. INTRODUCTION 177
   B. CREATING ELECTION DISTRICTS 179
   C. REGULATING ELECTIONS 221

    1. Voter ID Litigation 222
    2. Mail-In Voting 235
    3. The Role of a State "Legislature" in Regulating Elections 241

CHAPTER VI
DUE PROCESS OF LAW 251
    A. INTRODUCTION 251
    B. PROCEDURAL GUARANTEES 252
    C. REPRODUCTIVE AUTONOMY 258
    D. THE RIGHT OF INTIMATE ASSOCIATION 287
    E. CIVIL UNION 304
    F. MARRIAGE 314
    G. THE RIGHTS OF BODILY INTEGRITY AND DOMESTIC PRIVACY 334
    H. VESTED RIGHTS 346

CHAPTER VII
CRIMINAL PROCEDURE 351
    A. RIGHT TO JURY TRIAL 351
    B. SELF-INCRIMINATION 363
    C. RIGHT TO COUNSEL 377
    D. CONFRONTATION – FACE TO FACE 381
    E. DUTY TO PRESERVE EVIDENCE 384
    F. DOUBLE JEOPARDY 392
    G. CRUEL AND UNUSUAL PUNISHMENT 396
    H. POST-CONVICTION RELIEF 405

CHAPTER VIII
SEARCH AND SEIZURE 409
    A. INTRODUCTION 409
    B. PROBABLE CAUSE 409
    C. GOOD FAITH EXCEPTION TO WARRANT REQUIREMENT 418
    D. AUTOMATIC STANDING 437
    E. WARRANT REQUIREMENT 443
    F. PHYSICAL SEIZURE OF AN INDIVIDUAL BY POLICE ... 459
    G. WARRANTLESS AUTOMOBILE SEARCH 465
    H. *MIRANDA* VIOLATION – PHYSICAL EVIDENCE EXCLUDED 476

CHAPTER IX
PROPERTY RIGHTS 483
    A. INTRODUCTION 483
    B. WHAT IS PROPERTY? 483
    C. TAKINGS PROVISIONS AND THE *KELO* STORY 486
    D. WHAT IS "JUST COMPENSATION"? 508
    E. OTHER PROPERTY-RELATED RIGHTS UNDER STATE CONSTITUTIONS 513

CHAPTER X
RELIGION CLAUSES 535
    A. FREEDOM OF RELIGION 535
    B. ESTABLISHMENT OF RELIGION 555
        1. Background 555
        2. Cases 560

CHAPTER XI
SCHOOL FUNDING CLAUSES 595
    A. INTRODUCTION 595

B. EQUAL PROTECTION DECISIONS 597
  C. ADEQUACY DECISIONS 607
  D. SCHOOL UNIFORMITY CLAUSES... 627
  E. TEACHER TENURE 632
  F. REMEDY 637

CHAPTER XII
CIVIL REMEDIES: THE RIGHT TO A REMEDY AND OPEN COURTS; THE RIGHT TO A JURY TRIAL; SEPARATION OF POWERS; OTHER POSSIBLE CLAIMS .. 651
  A. INTRODUCTION AND HISTORICAL BACKGROUND............................ 651
  B. CASES DEFINING THE RIGHT TO A REMEDY/OPEN COURTS 659
  C. JURY TRIAL RIGHTS (AND OTHER POTENTIAL CHALLENGES) UNDER STATE CONSTITUTIONS – ARE STATUTORY DAMAGES CAPS CONSTITUTIONAL?.. 683
  D. IS THERE AN AFFIRMATIVE RIGHT TO A STATE REMEDY? 692

CHAPTER XIII
OTHER STATE INDIVIDUAL RIGHTS 701
  A. PRIVACY... 701
  B. FREE SPEECH AND EXPRESSION 706
  C. CIVIL JURY TRIAL 718
  D. RIGHT TO BEAR ARMS 727
  E. ENVIRONMENTAL RIGHTS 748
  F. CRIME VICTIMS' RIGHTS.. 754
  G. RIGHT TO HUNT AND FISH 761
  H. NATURAL OR INALIENABLE RIGHTS 766
  I. UNENUMERATED RIGHTS... 766

CHAPTER XIV
LEGISLATIVE PROCESS PROVISIONS WITH NO FEDERAL COUNTERPARTS 767
  A. INTRODUCTION 767
  B. SINGLE SUBJECT AND CLEAR TITLE RULES 768
  C. PUBLIC PURPOSE REQUIREMENTS 790

CHAPTER XV
ORGANIZATION OF STATE GOVERNMENTS 809
  A. INTRODUCTION 809
  B. LEGISLATIVE POWER... 809
    1. Introduction.. 809
    2. Term Limits for State and Local Officials 810
    3. Legislative Process and Procedures 816
  C. EXECUTIVE POWER 824
    1. The Selection and Organization of the Executive 824
    2. The "Line Item" Veto Power 841
  D. JUDICIAL POWER 850
    1. The Selection of Judges 850
    2. Justiciability in State Courts... 865
    3. Certified Questions 901
    4. State Limitations on Judicial Tenure and Service 906
  E. SEPARATION OF POWERS 909

CHAPTER XVI
ADMINISTRATIVE LAW.. 925
  A. INTRODUCTION 925
  B. NONDELEGATION 926

C. JUDICIAL DEFERENCE TO ADMINISTRATIVE AGENCIES 958

Chapter XVII
LOCAL GOVERNMENTS 975
   A. CASES INVALIDATING STATE LAWS ON HOME RULE GROUNDS 978
   B. CASES REJECTING HOME-RULE CHALLENGES TO STATE LAWS 996
   C. LOCAL SEPARATION-OF-POWERS DISPUTES 1018

Chapter XVIII
AMENDMENT AND REVISION OF STATE CONSTITUTIONS 1027
   A. INTRODUCTION 1027
   B. ALTERING STATE CONSTITUTIONS 1029
   C. INITIATIVE 1041
   D. CONSTITUTIONAL CONVENTION – REQUIRED FOR COMPLETE
      REVISION 1045
   E. PROCEDURAL REQUIREMENTS 1050
   F. CONSTITUTIONAL COMMISSIONS 1059
   G. LEGISLATING BY VOTER INITIATIVE 1065

Index 1073

TABLE OF CONTENTS

FOREWORD v
SUMMARY OF CONTENTS ix
TABLE OF CASES xxiii
TABLE OF AUTHORITIES xxxi
EXPLANATORY NOTE... xxxv
ACKNOWLEDGEMENTS xxxv
PERMISSION TO REPRINT xxxv

CHAPTER I
INTRODUCTION.. 1

CHAPTER II
DUAL SOVEREIGNTY: THE INTERRELATION OF THE STATE AND FEDERAL CONSTITUTIONS 9
   A. INTRODUCTION 9
   B. THE SOURCES AND NATURE OF FEDERAL AND STATE POWERS 9
      1. Exclusive Federal Powers 9
         GONZALES v. RAICH 10
         NOTE... 21
         NFIB v. SEBELIUS 22
         CITY OF BOERNE v. FLORES 27
      2. Exclusive State Powers 33
      3. Overlapping and Shared Powers 34
         UNITED STATES v. LOPEZ.. 35
   C. LIMITATIONS ON FEDERAL POWER 39
      1. The Anti-Commandeering Principle 39
         PRINTZ v. UNITED STATES.. 39
         NOTE... 44
      2. Immunity from Suits under Federal Law 44
         ALDEN v. MAINE 45
         FRANCHISE TAX BOARD OF CALIFORNIA v. HYATT.............. 51
         NOTE... 57
   D. FEDERAL LIMITATIONS ON STATE POWER 58
      1. Article VI – The Supremacy Clause 58
         U.S. TERM LIMITS, INC. v. THORNTON...................................... 58
         GREGORY v. ASHCROFT.. 62
      2. Article IV 64
         COYLE v. SMITH... 65
         NOTE... 68
         LUTHER v. BORDEN.. 69
         PACIFIC STATES TELEPHONE & TELEGRAPH CO. v. OREGON 73

CHAPTER III
THEORIES BY WHICH STATE COURTS MAY CONSTRUE STATE CONSTITUTIONS DIFFERENTLY FROM THEIR FEDERAL COUNTERPARTS... 77
   A. SIMILARLY WORDED GUARANTEES... 78
         SITZ v. DEPARTMENT OF STATE POLICE 80
         NOTES... 83
         STATE v. HEMPELE 84
         STATE v. WRIGHT 88
         NOTE... 93
         BLUM v. MERRELL DOW PHARMACEUTICALS, INC. 93
         NOTES... 98
   B. DIFFERENTLY WORDED PROVISIONS... 98

   RACING ASSOCIATION OF CENTRAL IOWA v. FITZGERALD 99
   NOTES 103
   STATE v. JORDEN 103
   STATE v. MIXTON 105
 C. STATE GUARANTEES MAY OFFER MORE OR FEWER PROTECTIONS
   THAN THEIR FEDERAL COUNTERPARTS 110
   STATE v. SCOTTIZE DANYELLE BROWN 111
   NOTE 113
 D. INDEPENDENT AND ADEQUATE STATE GROUNDS: STATE COURT
   RULINGS THAT ADDRESS FEDERAL AND STATE BASES FOR
   DECISION 113
   OHIO v. ROBINETTE (Ohio 1995) 115
   OHIO v. ROBINETTE (U.S. 1996) 117
   OHIO v. ROBINETTE (Ohio 1997) 120
   NOTES 123
 E. SEQUENCING: THE ORDER IN WHICH STATE COURTS RESOLVE
   RELATED STATE AND FEDERAL CLAIMS AND THE PRIORITY GIVEN
   TO EACH 124
   Jeffrey S. Sutton, *What Does—and Does Not—Ail State Constitutional
    Law* 127

CHAPTER IV
EQUALITY 133
 A. INTRODUCTION 133
   Jeffrey M. Shaman, *Equality and Liberty in The Golden Age of State
    Constitutional Law* 133
 B. RACIAL CLASSIFICATIONS 134
   SHEFF v. O'NEILL 134
   NOTE 140
   MALABED v. NORTH SLOPE BOROUGH 141
   NOTES 147
 C. GENDER-BASED CLASSIFICATIONS 148
   *COMMONWEALTH v. PENNSYLVANIA INTERSCHOLASTIC ATHLETIC
    ASSOCIATION* 148
   NOTE 150
   STATE v. RIVERA 151
   NOTES 153
 D. AGE-BASED CLASSIFICATIONS 153
   DRISCOLL v. CORBETT 153
   NOTES 156
   ARNESON v. STATE 158
 E. SEXUAL-ORIENTATION CLASSIFICATIONS 162
   GARTNER v. IOWA DEPARTMENT OF PUBLIC HEALTH 162
 F. ECONOMIC CLASSIFICATIONS 164
   AFSCME IOWA COUNCIL 61 v. STATE 164
   NOTE 175

CHAPTER V
REPRESENTATION AND VOTING 177
 A. INTRODUCTION 177
 B. CREATING ELECTION DISTRICTS 179
   LEAGUE OF WOMEN VOTERS OF P.A. v. PENNSYLVANIA 183
   NOTES 192
   HARPER v. HALL 193

       JOHNSON v. WISCONSIN ELECTIONS COMMISSION 199
       HARKENRIDER v. HOCHUL 206
       NOTES.. 210
       NORTH CAROLINA STATE CONFERENCE v. MOORE 211
       NOTE.. 221
   C. REGULATING ELECTIONS 221
      1. Voter ID Litigation... 222
       LEAGUE OF WOMEN VOTERS OF WISCONSIN EDUCATION NETWORK
         v. WALKER 222
       MILWAUKEE BRANCH OF THE NAACP v. WALKER.............................. 227
       NOTE.. 233
       MARTIN v. KOHLS... 233
      2. Mail-In Voting 235
       McLINKO v. DEPARTMENT OF STATE 235
       NOTES.. 241
      3. The Role of a State "Legislature" in Regulating Elections 241
       ARIZONA STATE LEGISLATURE v. ARIZONA INDEP. REDISTRICTING
         COMM'N.. 241
       NOTES.. 250

CHAPTER VI
DUE PROCESS OF LAW 251
   A. INTRODUCTION 251
   B. PROCEDURAL GUARANTEES 252
       STATE v. VEALE 252
       M.E.K. v. R.L.K. 255
   C. REPRODUCTIVE AUTONOMY 258
       DAVIS v. DAVIS.. 258
       NOTE.. 264
       In re T.W. 265
       NOTE.. 267
       HODES & NAUSER, MDs, P.A. v. SCHMIDT 267
       NOTE.. 279
       PLANNED PARENTHOOD OF THE HEARTLAND, INC. v. REYNOLDS ex
         rel. STATE 280
   D. THE RIGHT OF INTIMATE ASSOCIATION 287
       STATE v. SAUNDERS... 287
       NOTE.. 293
       COMMONWEALTH v. WASSON 294
       NOTE.. 304
   E. CIVIL UNION 304
       BAKER v. STATE 304
       NOTES.. 313
   F. MARRIAGE 314
       GOODRIDGE v. DEPARTMENT OF PUBLIC HEALTH 314
       NOTES.. 330
   G. THE RIGHTS OF BODILY INTEGRITY AND DOMESTIC PRIVACY 334
       Matter of FARRELL 334
       KRISCHER v. McIVER 337
       RAVIN v. STATE 341
       NOTES.. 345
   H. VESTED RIGHTS.. 346
       MITCHELL v. ROBERTS... 346

Chapter VII
CRIMINAL PROCEDURE ... 351
- A. RIGHT TO JURY TRIAL ... 351
  - *CLAUDIO v. STATE* ... 351
  - NOTES ... 360
  - *SMITH v. ISAKSON* ... 362
- B. SELF-INCRIMINATION ... 363
  - *COMMONWEALTH v. MOLINA* ... 364
  - NOTES ... 371
  - *ELLIOTT v. GEORGIA* ... 372
- C. RIGHT TO COUNSEL ... 377
  - *STATE v. McADAMS* ... 377
  - NOTES ... 381
- D. CONFRONTATION – FACE TO FACE ... 381
  - *COMMONWEALTH v. LUDWIG* ... 381
  - NOTES ... 384
- E. DUTY TO PRESERVE EVIDENCE ... 384
  - *HAMMOND v. STATE* ... 384
  - NOTES ... 391
- F. DOUBLE JEOPARDY ... 392
  - *PEOPLE v. ARANDA* ... 392
  - NOTES ... 396
- G. CRUEL AND UNUSUAL PUNISHMENT ... 396
  - *WASHINGTON v. GREGORY* ... 396
  - *STATE v. SANTIAGO* ... 399
  - NOTES ... 405
- H. POST-CONVICTION RELIEF ... 405
  - *BROWN v. BOOKER* ... 405
  - NOTES ... 408

Chapter VIII
SEARCH AND SEIZURE ... 409
- A. INTRODUCTION ... 409
- B. PROBABLE CAUSE ... 409
  - *PEOPLE v. GRIMINGER* ... 409
  - *STATE v. TUTTLE* ... 412
  - NOTES ... 418
- C. GOOD FAITH EXCEPTION TO WARRANT REQUIREMENT ... 418
  - *STATE v. KOIVU* ... 418
  - *COMMONWEALTH v. EDMUNDS* ... 423
  - NOTES ... 436
- D. AUTOMATIC STANDING ... 437
  - *STATE v. LAMB* ... 437
  - *STATE v. BULLOCK* ... 439
  - NOTE ... 443
- E. WARRANT REQUIREMENT ... 443
  - *STATE v. EARLS* ... 443
  - *STATE v. BRYANT* ... 450
  - *STATE v. LEONARD* ... 454
  - NOTES ... 458
- F. PHYSICAL SEIZURE OF AN INDIVIDUAL BY POLICE ... 459
  - *STATE v. BEAUCHESNE* ... 459

| NOTES   464
G.   WARRANTLESS AUTOMOBILE SEARCH   465
     STATE v. CORA   465
     STATE v. VILLELA   469
     NOTES   470
     STATE v. ARREOLA-BOTELLO   471
H.   *MIRANDA* VIOLATION – PHYSICAL EVIDENCE EXCLUDED   476
     STATE v. PETERSON   476
     NOTES   481

CHAPTER IX
PROPERTY RIGHTS 483
A.   INTRODUCTION   483
B.   WHAT IS PROPERTY?   483
     TEXAS SOUTHERN UNIVERSITY v. VILLARREAL   484
C.   TAKINGS PROVISIONS AND THE *KELO* STORY   486
     CITY OF NORWOOD v. HORNEY   487
     BD. OF CTY. COMM'RS OF MUSKOGEE CNTY. v. LOWERY   494
     GOLDSTEIN v. NEW YORK STATE URBAN DEV. CORP.   498
     NOTES   507
D.   WHAT IS "JUST COMPENSATION"?   508
     *BAYOU BRIDGE PIPELINE, LLC v. 38.00 ACRES, MORE OR LESS,
        LOCATED IN ST. MARTIN PARISH, ET AL.*   509
     NOTE   513
E.   OTHER PROPERTY-RELATED RIGHTS UNDER STATE
     CONSTITUTIONS   513
     PATEL v. TEXAS DEP'T OF LICENSING   513
     *TEXAS DEPARTMENT OF STATE HEALTH SERVICES v. CROWN
        DISTRIBUTING LLC*   527

CHAPTER X
RELIGION CLAUSES 535
A.   FREEDOM OF RELIGION   535
     EMPLOYMENT DIVISION v. SMITH   536
     NOTES   538
     CITY OF BOERNE v. FLORES   539
     NOTES   540
     HUMPHREY v. LANE   541
     ATTORNEY GENERAL v. DESILETS   543
     NOTES   545
     BARR v. CITY OF SINTON   546
     CATHOLIC CHARITIES OF THE DIOCESE OF ALBANY v. SERIO   551
     NOTES   554
B.   ESTABLISHMENT OF RELIGION   555
     1. Background   555
         Mark Edward DeForrest, *An Overview and Evaluation of State Blaine
            Amendments: Origins, Scope, and First Amendment Concerns*   555
     2. Cases   560
         TRINITY LUTHERAN CHURCH OF COLUMBIA, INC. v. COMER   560
         *FREEDOM FROM RELIGION FOUND. v. MORRIS CNTY. BD. OF
            CHOSEN FREEHOLDERS*   563
         TAYLOR v. TOWN OF CABOT   567
         NOTES   570
         ZELMAN v. SIMMONS-HARRIS   570

JACKSON v. BENSON 572
NOTE 575
*TAXPAYERS FOR PUBLIC EDUCATION v. DOUGLAS CNTY. SCHOOL
    DISTRICT* 575
CAIN v. HORNE 581
MEREDITH v. PENCE 584
NOTES 587
MOSES v. RUSZKOWSKI 587
NOTE 593

CHAPTER XI
SCHOOL FUNDING CLAUSES 595
  A. INTRODUCTION 595
  B. EQUAL PROTECTION DECISIONS 597
      HORNBECK v. SOMERSET COUNTY BOARD OF EDUCATION 598
      HORTON v. MESKILL 600
      VINCENT v. VOIGHT 603
      NOTE 606
  C. ADEQUACY DECISIONS 607
      EDGEWOOD INDEPENDENT SCHOOL DISTRICT v. KIRBY 608
      DeROLPH v. STATE (Ohio 1997) 611
      DeROLPH v. STATE (Ohio 2001) 615
      NOTE 618
      *COLUMBIA FALLS ELEMENTARY SCHOOL DISTRICT NO. 6 v.
        STATE* 618
      ABBOTT v. BURKE 620
      NOTES 623
      *CITIZENS FOR STRONG SCHOOLS, INC. v. FLORIDA STATE BOARD OF
        EDUCATION* 623
      NOTES 627
  D. SCHOOL UNIFORMITY CLAUSES 627
      BUSH v. HOLMES 628
  E. TEACHER TENURE 632
      VERGARA v. CALIFORNIA 632
  F. REMEDY 637
      HOKE COUNTY BOARD OF EDUCATION v. STATE 637
      CLAREMONT SCHOOL DISTRICT v. GOVERNOR 642
      *NEELEY v. WEST ORANGE-COVE CONSOLIDATED INDEPENDENT
        SCHOOL DISTRICT* 648
      NOTE 650

CHAPTER XII
CIVIL REMEDIES: THE RIGHT TO A REMEDY AND OPEN COURTS; THE RIGHT TO A JURY TRIAL; SEPARATION OF POWERS; OTHER POSSIBLE CLAIMS .. 651
  A. INTRODUCTION AND HISTORICAL BACKGROUND 651
      Shannon M. Roesler, *The Kansas Remedy by Due Course of Law Provision:
        Defining a Right to a Remedy* 652
      KENTUCKY v. CLAYCOMB 653
  B. CASES DEFINING THE RIGHT TO A REMEDY/OPEN COURTS 659
      MELLO v. BIG Y FOODS, INC. 659
      *YANAKOS v. UNIVERSITY OF PITTSBURGH MEDICAL CENTER, ET
        AL.* 661
      McINTOSH v. MELROE CO. 669
      NOTES 673

       LANEY v. FAIRVIEW CITY 673
       TINDLEY v. SALT LAKE CITY SCHOOL DISTRICT 679
       NOTES... 682
  C. JURY TRIAL RIGHTS (AND OTHER POTENTIAL CHALLENGES) UNDER STATE CONSTITUTIONS – ARE STATUTORY DAMAGES CAPS CONSTITUTIONAL?.. 683
       HILBURN v. ENERPIPE LTD. 683
       McCLAY v. AIRPORT MANAGEMENT SERVICES, LLC............. 686
  D. IS THERE AN AFFIRMATIVE RIGHT TO A STATE REMEDY? 692
       FIELDS v. MELLINGER.. 692
       NOTES... 698

CHAPTER XIII
OTHER STATE INDIVIDUAL RIGHTS 701
  A. PRIVACY... 701
       YORK v. WAHKIAKUM SCHOOL DISTRICT NO. 200................ 701
       NOTE... 706
  B. FREE SPEECH AND EXPRESSION 706
       FASHION VALLEY MALL v. NLRB 707
       NOTE... 712
       STATE v. STUMMER... 713
       NOTES... 718
  C. CIVIL JURY TRIAL... 718
       SOFIE v. FIBREBOARD CORP. 719
       NOTE... 723
       McCOOL v. GEHRET.. 723
       NOTES... 727
  D. RIGHT TO BEAR ARMS 727
       ROCKY MOUNTAIN GUN OWNERS v. POLIS............................ 727
       JANE DOE v. WILMINGTON HOUSING AUTHORITY 732
       STATE v. MISCH 740
       NOTES... 746
  E. ENVIRONMENTAL RIGHTS 748
       PENNSYLVANIA ENVIRONMENTAL DEFENSE FOUND. v.
         COMMONWEALTH... 748
       NOTES... 753
  F. CRIME VICTIMS' RIGHTS.. 754
       STATE v. STROM.. 754
       STATE v. DAMATO-KUSHEL 756
       NOTES... 760
  G. RIGHT TO HUNT AND FISH 761
       CABOT v. THOMAS 761
       NOTE... 766
  H. NATURAL OR INALIENABLE RIGHTS 766
  I. UNENUMERATED RIGHTS 766

CHAPTER XIV
LEGISLATIVE PROCESS PROVISIONS WITH NO FEDERAL COUNTERPARTS 767
  A. INTRODUCTION 767
  B. SINGLE SUBJECT AND CLEAR TITLE RULES 768
       Martha J. Dragich, *State Constitutional Restriction on Legislative Procedure:*
         Rethinking the Analysis of Original Purpose, Single Subject, and Clear
         Title Challenges.. 768

GREGORY v. SHURTLEFF	774
KOUSSA v. ATTORNEY GENERAL	779
BURNS v. CLINE	782
NOTE	785
TURNBULL v. FINK	785
NOTE	789

C. PUBLIC PURPOSE REQUIREMENTS 790
- *MAREADY v. CITY OF WINSTON-SALEM* 790
- *HOPPER v. CITY OF MADISON* 798
- *TOWN OF BELOIT v. COUNTY OF ROCK* 802

CHAPTER XV
ORGANIZATION OF STATE GOVERNMENTS 809

A. INTRODUCTION 809
B. LEGISLATIVE POWER 809
  1. Introduction 809
  2. Term Limits for State and Local Officials 810
     - *HOERGER v. SPOTA* 810
     - *TELLI v. BROWARD COUNTY* 812
     - *KEMP ET AL. v. GONZALEZ ET AL* 814
     - NOTES 816
  3. Legislative Process and Procedures 816
     - *OPINION OF THE JUSTICES* 816
     - *MARKWELL v. COOKE* 819

C. EXECUTIVE POWER 824
  1. The Selection and Organization of the Executive 824
     - *PERDUE v. BAKER* 826
     - NOTE 830
     - *STATE v. STEPHENS* 831
     - *DUNLEAVY v. THE ALASKA LEGISLATIVE COUNCIL* 838
  2. The "Line Item" Veto Power 841
     - *ST. JOHN'S WELL CHILD & FAMILY CTR. v. SCHWARZENEGGER* 842
     - *JACKSON v. SANFORD* 845
     - *HOMAN v. BRANSTAD* 847
     - NOTES 850

D. JUDICIAL POWER 850
  1. The Selection of Judges 850
     - Judith L. Maute, *Selecting Justice in State Courts: The Ballot Box or the Backroom?* 851
     - NOTES 855
     - *BROWN v. GIANFORTE* 857
  2. Justiciability in State Courts 865
     - *GREGORY v. SHURTLEFF* 865
     - *BENSON v. McKEE* 868
     - *COUEY v. ATKINS* 873
     - *In re GUARDIANSHIP OF TSCHUMY* 876
     - *BERRY v. CRAWFORD* 881
     - *In re ABBOTT* 885
     - *BURT v. SPEAKER OF THE HOUSE OF REPRESENTATIVES* 889
     - *STATE OF KANSAS ex rel. MORRISON v. SEBELIUS* 891
     - *OPINION OF THE JUSTICES* 894
  3. Certified Questions 901
     - *LEHMAN BROTHERS v. SCHEIN* 901

        HALEY v. UNIVERSITY OF TENNESSEE-KNOXVILLE 904
    4. State Limitations on Judicial Tenure and Service 906
        CANTRELL v. STATE 906
  E. SEPARATION OF POWERS 909
        STATE ex rel. JUSTICE v. KING 909
        In re REQUEST FOR ADVISORY OPINION FROM HOUSE OF
            REPRESENTATIVES 919

CHAPTER XVI
ADMINISTRATIVE LAW 925
  A. INTRODUCTION 925
  B. NONDELEGATION 926
        A.L.A. SCHECHTER POULTRY CORP. v. UNITED STATES 926
        NOTE 930
        GUNDY v. UNITED STATES 930
        NOTES 934
        McNEILL v. STATE 934
        In re CERTIFIED QUESTIONS FROM U.S. DISTRICT COURT 936
        ASKEW v. CROSS KEY WATERWAYS 944
        NOTE 949
        GUILLOU v. STATE OF NEW HAMPSHIRE, DIVISION OF MOTOR
            VEHICLES 949
        TEXAS BOLL WEEVIL ERADICATION FOUNDATION, INC. v.
            LEWELLEN 950
        NOTE 956
        In re PETITION TO TRANSFER TERRITORY FROM HIGH SCHOOL
            DISTRICT NO. 6, LAME DEER, ROSEBUD COUNTY, TO HIGH
            SCHOOL DISTRICT NO. 1, HARDIN, BIG HORN COUNTY 957
  C. JUDICIAL DEFERENCE TO ADMINISTRATIVE AGENCIES 958
        CHEVRON v. NATURAL RESOURCES DEFENSE COUNCIL 958
        NOTE 961
        TETRA TECH v. WISCONSIN DEPARTMENT OF REVENUE 961
        NOTE 968
        KING v. MISSISSIPPI MILITARY DEPARTMENT 968
        PUBLIC WATER SUPPLY CO., INC. v. DIPASQUALE 970
        NOTE 973

CHAPTER XVII
LOCAL GOVERNMENTS 975
  A. CASES INVALIDATING STATE LAWS ON HOME RULE GROUNDS 978
        CITY OF DAYTON v. STATE 979
        NOTE 986
        DWAGFYS MANUFACTURING, INC. v. CITY OF TOPEKA 986
        COOPERATIVE HOME CARE, INC. v. CITY OF ST. LOUIS 990
  B. CASES REJECTING HOME-RULE CHALLENGES TO STATE LAWS 996
        CITY OF LAREDO v. LAREDO MERCHANTS ASSOCIATION 996
        ORTIZ v. COMMONWEALTH OF PENNSYLVANIA 1001
        BASS v. CITY OF EDMONDS 1004
        STATE ex rel. BRNOVICH v. CITY OF TUSCON 1006
        NOTES 1014
  C. LOCAL SEPARATION-OF-POWERS DISPUTES 1018
        N.Y. STATEWIDE COAL. OF HISPANIC CHAMBERS OF COMMERCE v.
            N.Y.C. DEP'T OF HEALTH & MENTAL HYGIENE 1019
        NOTES 1022

Chapter XVIII
AMENDMENT AND REVISION OF STATE CONSTITUTIONS 1027
   A. INTRODUCTION 1027
   B. ALTERING STATE CONSTITUTIONS 1029
        Anne Permaloff, *Methods of Altering State Constitutions* 1029
   C. INITIATIVE 1041
        Ronald M. George, *The Perils of Direct Democracy: The California
        Experience* 1041
        NOTES 1045
   D. CONSTITUTIONAL CONVENTION – REQUIRED FOR COMPLETE
      REVISION 1045
        *CITIZENS PROTECTING MICHIGAN'S CONSTITUTION v. SECRETARY
        OF STATE* 1045
   E. PROCEDURAL REQUIREMENTS 1050
        STATE ex rel. VOTERS FIRST v. OHIO BALLOT BD. 1051
        SAVE OUR VOTE v. BENNETT 1055
   F. CONSTITUTIONAL COMMISSIONS 1059
        Peter J. Galie & Christopher Bopst, *The Constitutional Commission in New
        York: A Worthy Tradition* 1059
        NOTE 1065
   G. LEGISLATING BY VOTER INITIATIVE 1065
        CARTER v. LEHI CITY 1065

INDEX 1073

TABLE OF CASES

Principal cases are in bold type. Non-principal cases are in roman type. References are to Pages.

Abbeville Cnty. Sch. Dist. v. South Carolina, 767 S.E.2d 157 (S.C. 2014), 627, 650
Abbott v. Burke, 971 A.2d 989 (N.J. 2009), **620**, 623
Abbott, In re, 628 S.W.3d 288 (Tex. 2021), **885**
Abdul-Alazim v. Superintendent, Massachusetts Correctional Institution, Cedar Junction, 778 N.E.2d 946 (Mass. 2002), 545
AFSCME Iowa Council 61 v. State, 928 N.W.2d 21 (Iowa 2019), **164**
Albright v. Oliver, 510 U.S. 266 (1994), 699
Alden v. Maine, 527 U.S. 706 (1999), 44, **45**
Am. Atheists, Inc. v. City of Detroit Downtown Dev. Auth., 567 F.3d 278 (6th Cir. 2009), 126
Anderson v. Town of Durham, 895 A.2d 944 (Me. 2006), 587
Arizona State Legislature v. Arizona Indep. Redistricting Comm'n, et al., 135 S. Ct. 2652 (2015), **241**
Arizona v. Gant, 445 U.S. 332 (2009), 6
Arneson v. State, 864 P.2d 1245 (Mont. 1993), **158**
Askew v. Cross Key Waterways, 372 So.2d 913 (Fla. 1978), **944**
Attorney General v. Desilets, 636 N.E.2d 233 (Mass. 1994), **543**
A.L.A. Schechter Poultry Corp. v. United States, 295 U.S. 495 (1935), **926**
Baehr v. Lewin, 852 P.2d 44 (Haw. 1993), 313
Baehr v. Miike (Haw. 1996), 313
Badgley v. Walton, 10 A.3d 469 (Vt. 2010), 158
Bailey v. County of Shelby, 188 S.W.3d 539 (Tenn. 2006), 816
Baker v. Nelson, 409 U.S. 810 (1972), 6
Baker v. State, 744 A.2d 864 (Vt. 1999), **304**
Barr v. City of Sinton, 295 S.W.2d 287 (Tex. 2009), **546**
Bass v. City of Edmonds, 508 P.3d 172 (Wash. 2022), **1004**
Bayou Bridge Pipeline, LLC v. 38.00 Acres, More or Less, Located in St. Martin Parish, et al., 320 So.3d 1054 (La. 2021), **509**
Bd. of Cnty. Comm'rs of Muskogee Cnty. v. Lowery, 136 P.3d 639 (Okla. 2006), 5, **494**
Benson v. McKee, 273 A.3d 121 (R.I. 2022), **868**
Berger v. N.C. State Conf. v. NAACP, 142 S. Ct. 2191 (2022), 831

Berry v. Crawford, 990 N.E.2d 410 (Ind. 2013), **881**
B.H. v. State, 645 So.2d 987 (Fla. 1994), 949
Blum v. Merrell Dow Pharmaceuticals, Inc., 626 A.2d 537 (Pa. 1993), 93, **727**
Bowers v. Hardwick, 478 U.S. 186 (1986), 304
Brackett v. Civil Service Comm'n, 850 N.E.2d 533 (Mass. 2006), 147
Brigham v. State, 889 A.2d 715 (Vt. 2005), 627
Britt v. State, 681 S.E.2d 320 (N.C. 2009), 746
Brown v. Bd. of Educ. of Topeka, 349 U.S. 294, 301 (1955), 595
Brown v. Bd. of Educ., 347 U.S. 483 (1954), 140, 595
Brown v. Booker, 826 S.E.2d 304 (Va. 2019), **405**
Brown v. Gianforte, 488 P.3d 548 (Mont. 2021), **857**
Burns v. Cline, 382 P.3d 1048 (Okla. 2016), **782**
Burt v. Speaker of the House of Representatives, 243 A.3d 609 (N.H. 2021), **889**
Burwell v. Hobby Lobby, 134 S. Ct. 2751 (2014), 554
Bush v. Holmes, 919 So.2d 392 (Fla. 2006), **628**
Bush v. Schiavo, 885 So.2d 321 (Fla. 2004), 949
Cabot v. Thomas, 514 A.2d 1034 (Vt. 1986), **761**
Cain v. Horne, 202 P.3d 1178 (Ariz. 2009), **581**
California v. Greenwood, 486 U.S. 35 (1988), 458
California v. Hodari D., 499 U.S. 621 (1991), 98
Camacho v. State, 75 P.3d 370 (Nev. 2003), 470
Cameron v. EMW Women's Surgical Ctr., 142 S. Ct. 1002 (2022), 831
Campbell Cnty. Sch. Dist. v. State, 181 P.3d 43 (Wyo. 2008), 650
Cantrell v. State (La. 2020), **906**
Cantwell v. Connecticut, 310 U.S. 296 (1940), 535
Caplan v. Town of Acton, 92 N.E.3d 691 (Mass. 2018), 560
Caperton v. A.T. Massey Coal Co., 556 U.S. 868 (2009), 855
Carson v. Makin, 142 S. Ct. 1987 (2022), 593

xxiii

Carter v. Lehi City, 269 P.3d 141 (Utah 2012), **1065**
Catholic Charities of the Diocese of Albany v. Serio, 859 N.E.2d 459 (Ct. App. N.Y. 2006), **551**
Certified Questions from Dist. Court, In re, 958 N.W.2d 1 (Mich. 2020), **936**
Chevron, U.S.A., Inc. v. Natural Resources Defense Council, 467 U.S. 837 (1984), **958**
Child v. Lomax, 188 P.3d 1103 (Nev. 2008), 816
Chisholm v. Georgia, 2 U.S. 419 (1793), 44
Church of the Lukumi Babalu Aye, Inc. v. Hialeah, 508 U.S. 520 (1993), 538
Citizens Arizona Chamber of Commerce & Indus. v. Kiley, 399 P.3d 80 (2017), 785
Citizens for Strong Sch., Inc. v. Fla. State Bd. of Educ., 262 So.3d 127 (Fla. 2019), **623**
Citizens Protecting Michigan's Constitution v. Secretary of State, 503 Mich. 42 (2018), **1045**
City of Boerne v. Flores, 521 U.S. 507 (1997), **27, 539**
City of Clinton v. Cedar Rapids & Missouri River R.R. Co., 24 Iowa 544 (1869), 1015
City of Dayton v. State, 87 N.E.3d 176 (Ohio 2017), **979**
City of Laredo v. Laredo Merchants Ass'n, 550 S.W.3d 586 (Tex. 2018), **996**
City of Norwood v. Horney, 853 N.E.2d 1115 (Ohio 2006), **487**
City of Memphis v. Hargett, 414 S.W.3d 88 (Tenn. 2013), 233
City of Philadelphia v. New Jersey, 437 U.S. 617 (1978), 10
City of Toledo v. State, 130 N.E.3d 341 (Ohio Ct. App. 2019), 986
Claremont Sch. Dist. v. Governor, 794 A.2d 744 (N.H. 2002), **642**
Claudio v. State, 585 A.2d 1278 (Del. 1991), **351**
Clinton v. City of New York, 524 U.S. 417 (1998), 841
Coalition for Adequacy & Fairness in Sch. Funding, Inc. v. Chiles, 680 So.2d 400 (Fla. 1996), 627
Columbia Falls Elementary Sch. Dist. No. 6 v. State, 109 P.3d 257 (Mont. 2005), **618**
Commonwealth v. Armendola, 550 N.E.2d 1221 (Mass. 1990), 443
Commonwealth v. Bonadio, 415 A.2d 47 (Pa. 1980), 293
Commonwealth v. Edmunds, 586 A.2d 887 (Pa. 1991), **423**
Commonwealth v. Johnson, 86 A.3d 182 (2014), 436

Commonwealth v. Ludwig, 594 A.2d 281 (Pa. 1991), **381**
Commonwealth v. Martin, 827 N.E.2d 198 (Mass. 2005), 481
Commonwealth v. Mavredakis, 725 N.E.2d 169 (Mass. 2000), 381
Commonwealth v. Molina, 104 A.3d 430 (Pa. 2013), **364**
Commonwealth v. Pennsylvania Interscholastic Association, 334 A.2d 839 (Pa. 1975), **148**
Commonwealth v. Wasson, 842 S.W.2d 487 (Ky. 1992), **294**
Commonwealth v. White, 910 A.2d 648 (Pa. 2006), 361
Conn. Coal. For Justice in Educ. Funding, Inc. v. Rell, 176 A.3d 28 (Conn. 2018), 627
Cooperative Home Care, Inc v. City of St. Louis, 514 S.W.3d 571 (Mo. 2017), **990**
Couey v. Atkins, 355 P.3d 866 (Or. 2015), **873**
Coyle v. Smith, 221 U.S. 559 (1911), **65**
Crawford v. Bd. of Educ., 551 P.2d 28 (Cal. 1976), 141
Cutter v. Wilkinson, 544 U.S. 709 (2005), 540
Davids v. New York, 74 N.Y.S.3d 228 (N.Y. App. Div. 2018), 632
Davis v. Bandemer, 478 U.S. 109 (1986), 180
Davis v. Davis, 842 S.W.2d 588 (Tenn. 1992), **258**
Davis v. South Dakota, 804 N.W.2d 618 (S.D. 2011), 627
Democratic Party of Georgia, Inc. v. Perdue, 707 S.E.2d 67 (Ga. 2011), 233
DeRolph v. State, 677 N.E.2d 733 (Ohio 1997), **611**, 627
DeRolph v. State, 754 N.E.2d 1184 (Ohio 2001), **615**
DeRolph v. State, 758 N.E.2d 1113 (Ohio 2001), 618
DeRolph v. State, 780 N.E.2d 529 (Ohio 2002), 618
DiRaimo v. City of Providence, 714 A.2d 554 (R.I. 1998), 718
District of Columbia v. Heller, 554 U.S. 570 (2008), 746
Donahoe v. Richards, 38 Me. 376 (1854), 967
Dool v. Burke, 497 F. App'x 782 (10th Cir. 2012), 856, 857
Dorsey v. State, 716 A.2d 807 (Del. 2000), 682
D.P. v. State, 705 So.2d 593 (Fla. 1997), **171**
Driscoll v. Corbett, 69 A.3d 197 (Pa. 2013), **153**, 156
Duncan v. Louisiana, 391 U.S. 145 (1968), 683, 718
Dunleavy v. Alaska Legislative Council, 498 P.3d 608 (Alaska 2021), **838**

Dupree v. Alma Sch. Dist. No. 30, 651 S.W.2d 90 (Ark. 1983), 597
Dwagfys Manufacturing, Inc. v. City of Topeka, 443 P.3d 1052 (Kan. 2019), **986**
Edgewood Indep. Sch. Dist. v. Kirby, 777 S.W.2d 391 (Tex. 1989), 3, **608**
Elliot v. Georgia, 824 S.E.2d 265 (2019), 371, **372**
Employment Div., Dep't of Human Res. of Oregon v. Smith, 494 U.S. 872 (1990), 5, **536**
Espinoza v. Mont. Dep't of Revenue, 140 S. Ct. 224 (2020), 593
Everson v. Bd. of Educ., 330 U.S. 1 (1947), 535
Ex parte James, 836 So.2d 813 (Ala. 2002), 627
Fashion Valley Mall v. National Labor Relations Bd., 172 P.3d 742 (Cal. 2007), **707**
F.C. III, In re, 2 A.3d 1201 (Pa. 2010), 126
Fields v. Mellinger, 851 S.E.2d 789 (W. Va. 2020), **692**
Forslund v. Minnesota, 924 N.W.2d 25 (Minn. Ct. App. 2019), 632
Fulton v. City of Philadelphia, 141 S. Ct. 1868 (2021), 554
Franchise Tax Bd. Of Cal. v. Hyatt, 136 S. Ct. 1277 (2016), 44, **51**
Freedom From Religion Found. v. Morris Cnty. Bd. of Chosen Freeholders, 181 A.3d 992 (N.J. 2018), 560, **563**
Gannon v. Kansas, 319 P.3d 1196 (Kan. 2014), 627, 650
Garcia v. San Antonio Metropolitan Transit Auth., 469 U.S. 528 (1985), 10
Garcia v. Siffrin Residential Ass'n, 407 N.E.2d 1369 (Ohio 1980), 979
Gartner v. Iowa Dep't of Pub. Health, 830 N.W.2d 335 (Iowa 2013), **162**
Guardianship of Tschumy, In re, 853 N.W.2d 728 (Minn. 2014), **876**
Gill v. Whitford, 138 S. Ct. 1916 (2016), 234
Glisson v. City of Marion, 720 N.E.2d 1034 (1999), 754
Gonzales v. O Centro Espirita Beneficente Uniao do Vegetal, 546 U.S. 418 (2006), 554
Gonzales v. Raich, 545 U.S. 1 (2005), **10**
Goldstein v. New York State Urban Dev. Corp., 921 N.E.2d 165 (2009), **498**
Goodridge v. Dep't of Public Health, 798 N.E.2d 941 (Mass. 2003), 6, **314**
Gore v. State, 599 So.2d 978 (Fla. 1992), 761
Graham v. Connor, 490 U.S. 386 (1989), 699
Gregory v. Ashcroft, 501 U.S. 452 (1991), **62**, 906
Gregory v. Shurtleff, 299 P.3d 1098 (Utah 2013), **774, 865**

Griffin v. Crane, 716 A.2d 1029 (Md. 1998), 153
Grutter v. Bollinger, 539 U.S. 306 (2003), 147
Guillou v. Div. of Motor Vehicles, 503 A.2d 838 (N.H. 1986), **949**
Gundy v. United States, 139 S. Ct. 2116 (2019), **930**
Haley v. University of Tennessee-Knoxville, 188 S.W.3d 518 (Tenn. 2006), **904**
Hammerschmidt v. Boone County, 877 S.W.2d 98 (Mo. 1994), 789
Hammond v. State, 569 A.2d 81 (Del. 1989), **384**
Hans v. Louisiana, 134 U.S. 1 (1890), 44
Harkenrider v. Hochul (N.Y. 2022), **206**
Harper v. Hall, 380 N.C. 317 (N.C. 2022), **193**
Herring v. State, 805 A.2d 872 (Del. 2002), 361
Hi Voltage Wire Works, Inc. v. San Jose, 12 P.3d 1068 (Cal. 2000), 147
Highland Farms Dairy v. Agnew, 300 U.S. 608 (1937), 809
Hilburn v. Enerpipe Ltd., 442 P.3d 509 (Kan. 2019), **683**, 723
Hines v. State, 30 N.E.3d 1216 (Ind. 2015), 396
Hoerger v. Spota, 997 N.E.2d 1229, 21 N.Y.3d 549 (2013), **810**
Hodes & Nauser, MDS, P.A. v. Schmidt, 440 P.3d 461 (Kan. 2019), **267**
Hoffman v. Reagan, 429 P.3d 70 (2018), 785
Hoke Cnty. Bd. of Educ. v. State, 599 S.E.2d 365 (N.C. 2004), **637**
Hollingsworth v. Perry, 133 S. Ct. 265 (2013), 332
Holt v. Hobbs, 135 S. Ct. 853 (2015) 546, 554
Homan v. Branstad, 812 N.W.2d 623 (Iowa 212), **847**
Hope Clinic for Women, Ltd. v. Flores, 991 N.E.2d 745 (Ill. 2013), 125
Hopper v. City of Madison, 256 N.W.2d 139 (Wis. 1977), **798**
Hornbeck v. Somerset Cnty. Bd. of Educ., 458 A.2d 758 (Md. 1983), **598**
Horton v. Meskill, 376 A.2d 359 (Conn. 1977), 597, **600**
Hulit v. State, 982 S.W.d 431 (Tex. Crim. App. 1998), 458
Humphrey v. Lane, 728 N.E.2d 1039 (Ohio 2000), 5, **541**
Idaho Schools for Equal Educational Opportunity, Inc. v. Evans, 850 P.2d 724 (Idaho 1993), 627
Israel v. West Virginia Secondary Schools Activities Comm'n, 388 S.E.2d 480 (W. Va. 1989), 150
Jackson v. Benson, 578 N.W.2d 602 (Wis. 1998), **572**

Jackson v. Pasadena City Sch. Dist., 382 P.2d 878 (Cal. 1963), 141

Jackson v. Sanford, 731 S.E.2d 722 (S.C. 2011), **845**

Jane Doe v. Wilmington Housing Auth., 88 A.3d 654 (Del. 2014), **732**

Johnson v. Wis. Elections Comm'n, 399 Wis.2d 623 (Wis. 2021), **199**

Jones v. Delaware, 745 A.2d 856 (Del. 1999), 98

Joye v. Hunterdon Cent. Reg'l High Sch. Bd. of Educ., 826 A.2d 624 (N.J. 2003), 706

Kansas v. Nebraska & Colorado, 135 S. Ct. 1042 (2015), 39

Kelo v. City of New London, 545 U.S. 469 (2005), 5

Kemp et al. v. Gonzalez et al., 849 S.E.2d 667 (Ga. 2020), **814**

Kentucky v. Claycomb, 566 S.W.3d 202 (Ky. 2018), **653**

Kentucky v. Dennison, 65 U.S. (24 How.) 66 (1861), 64

King v. Miss. Military Dep't, 245 So.3d 404 (Miss. 2018), **968**

Koussa v. Attorney General, 188 N.E.3d 510 (Mass. 2022), **779**

Krischer v. McIver, 697 So.2d 97 (Fla. 1997), **337**

Knick v. Twp. of Scott, 139 S. Ct. 2162 (2019), 508

Lake View Sch. Dist. No. 25 of Phillips Cnty. v. Huckabee, 220 S.W.3d 645 (Ark. 2005), 627

Laney v. Fairview City, 57 P.3d 1007 (Utah 2002), **673**

Lawrence v. Texas, 539 U.S. 558 (2003), 304

League of Women Voters of Fla. v. Detzner, 172 So.3d 363 (Fla. 2015), 210

League of Women Voters of Indiana v. Rokita, 929 N.E.2d 758 (Ind. 2010), 233

League of Women Voters of Pa. v. Pennsylvania, 178 A.3d 737 (Pa. 2018), 3, **183**

League of Women Voters of Wis., 851 N.W.2d 302 (Wis. 2014), **222**

Leandro v. State, 488 S.E.2d 249 (N.C. 1997), 627

Lehman Brothers v. Schein, 416 U.S. 386 (1974), **901**

Lewis E. v. Spagnolo, 710 N.E.2d 798 (Ill. 1999), 627

Lloyd Corp. v. Tanner, 407 U.S. 551 (1972), 712

Lobato v. Colorado, 304 P.3d 1132 (Colo. 2013), 627

Lochner v. New York, 198 U.S. 45 (1905), 513

Luther v. Borden, 7 How. 1 (1849), 33, **69**

Maddux v. Blagojevich, 911 N.E.2d 979 (Ill. 2009), 157

Malabed v. North Slope Borough, 70 P.3d 416 (Alaska 2003), **141**

Marbury v. Madison, 5 U.S. (1 Cranch) 137 (1803), 77

Maready v. City of Winston-Salem, 467 S.E.2d 615 (N.C. 1996), **790**

Marriages Cases, In re, 183 P.3d 384 (Cal. 2008), 332

Martin v. Kohls, 444 S.W.3d 844 (Ark. 2014), **233**

Massey v. Secretary of State, 579 N.W.2d 862 (Mich. 1998), 816

Masterpiece Cakeshop v. Colo. Civil Rights Comm'n, 138 S. Ct. 1719 (2018), 570

Matter of Farrell, 529 A.2d 404 (N.J. 1987), **334**

Markwell v. Cooke, 482 P.3d 422 (Colo. 2021), **819**

McClay v. Airport Management Services, LLC, 596 S.W.3d 686 (Tenn. 2020), **686**

McCool v. Gehret, 657 A.2d 269 (Del. 1995), **723**

McDonald v. City of Chicago, 561 U.S. 742 (2010), 6, 35

McIntosh v. Melroe Co., 729 N.E.2d 972 (Ind. 2000), **669**

McLinko v. Dep't of State, 279 A.3d 539 (Pa. 2022), **235**

McNeill v. State, 375 P.3d 1022 (Nev. 2016), **934**

M.E.K. v. R.L.K., 921 So.2d 787 (Fla. App. 2006), **255**

Mello v. Big Y Foods, Inc., 826 A.2d 1117 (Conn. 2003), **659**

Meredith v. Pence, 984 N.E.2d 1213 (Ind. 2013), **584**

Michigan v. Goldston, 682 N.W.2d 479 (Mich. 2004), 436

Michigan v. Long, 463 U.S. 1032 (1983), 114, 124

Miller v. Alabama, 567 U.S. 460 (2012), 405

Milwaukee Branch of the NAACP v. Walker, 851 N.W.2d 262 (Wis. 2014), **227**

Minneapolis & St. Louis R.R. v. Bombolis, 241 U.S. 211 (1916), 683, 719

Mitchell v. Roberts, 469 P.3d 901 (Utah 2020), **346**

Mont. Envt'l Info. Ctr. v. Dep't of Envt'l Quality, 988 P.2d 1236 (Mont. 1999), 754

Moran v. Burbine, 475 U.S. 412 (1986), 381

Moses v. Ruszkowski, 458 P.3d 406 (N.M. 2018), **587**

Murphy v. NCAA, 138 S. Ct. 1461 (2018), 44

National Federation of Indep. Businesses v. Sebelius, 567 U.S. 519 (2012), 21, **22**

Nebraska Coalition for Educational Equity & Adequacy v. Heineman, 731 N.W.2d 164 (Neb. 2007), 627

Neeley v. West Orange-Cove Consol. Indep. Sch. Dist., 176 S.W.3d 746 (Tex. 2005), **648**

New Mexico v. Crane, 329 P.3d 689 (N.M. 2014), 93

New State Ice Co. v. Liebmann, 285 U.S. 262 (1932), 4

New York v. Belton, 453 U.S. 454 (1981), 6

N.C. State Conference v. Moore, 876 S.E.2d 513 (N.C. 2022), **211**

N.Y. Statewide Coal. of Hispanic Chambers of Commerce v. N.Y.C. Dep't of Health & Mental Hygiene, 16 N.E.3d 538 (N.Y. 2014), 956, **1019**

Obergefell v. Hodges, 135 S. Ct. 2584 (2015), 6, 333

O'Connor v. Bd. of Educ. of Sch. Dist. No. 23, 645 F.2d 578 (7th Cir. 1981), 151

Ohio v. Robinette, 519 U.S. 33 (1996), **117**

Ohio v. Robinette, 653 N.E.2d 695 (Ohio 1995), **115**

Ohio v. Robinette, 685 N.E.2d 762 (Ohio 1997), **120**

Oklahoma Educ. Ass'n v. State, 158 P.3d 1058 (Okla. 2007), 627

Olevik v. State, 806 S.E.2d 505 (Ga. 2017), 371

Opinion of the Justices, 274 A.3d 269 (Del. 2022), **894**

Opinion of the Justices, 608 A.2d 202 (N.H. 1992), 362

Opinion of the Justices, 842 A.2d 816 (N.H. 2003), **816**

Opinion of the Justices to the Senate, 802 N.E.2d 565 (Mass. 2004), 331

Ortiz v. Commonwealth of Pennsylvania, 681 A.2d 152 (Pa. 1996), **1001**

Pacific States Tel. & Tel. v. Oregon, 223 U.S. 118 (1912), 73, 241

Panama Refining Co. v. Ryan, 293 U.S. 388 (1935), 926

Patel v. Texas Dep't of Licensing, 469 S.W.3d 69 (Tex. 2015), **513**

Pauley v. Kelly, 255 S.E.2d 859 (W. Va. 1979), 597

Paynter v. State, 797 N.E.2d 1225 (N.Y. 2003), 650

Pa. Envt'l Def. Found. v. Commonwealth, 161 A.3d 911 (Pa. 2017), **748**

Penneast Pipeline Co. v. New Jersey, 141 S. Ct. 2244 (2021), 57

Pennsylvanians Against Gambling Expansion Fund, Inc. v. Commonwealth, 877 A.2d 383 (Pa. 2005), 790

People v. Aranda, 437 P.3d 845 (Cal. 2019), **392**

People v. Collins, 475 N.W.2d 684 (Mich. 1991), 126

People v. Griminger, 524 N.E.2d 409 (N.Y. 1988), **409**

People v. Hurlbut, 24 Mich. 44 (1871), 1016

People v. Superior Court, 774 P.2d 769 (Cal. 1989), 718

Perdue v. Baker, 586 S.E.2d 606 (Ga. 2003), **826**

Perry v. Brown, 671 F.3d 1052 (9th Cir. 2012), 332

Perry v. Schwarzenegger, 704 F. Supp. 2d 921 (N.D. Cal. 2010), 332

Petition to Transfer Territory from High Sch. Dist. No. 6 Lame Deer, Rosebud Cnty., to High Sch. Dist. No. 1, Hardin, Big Horn Cnty., In re, 15 P.3d 447 (Mont. 2000), **957**

Phillips v. Washington Legal Foundation, 524 U.S. 156, 164 (1998), 483

Pierce v. State, 171 P.3d 525 (Wyo. 2007), 471

Planned Parenthood of the Heartland, Inc. v. Reynolds ex rel. State, 975 N.W.2d 710 (Iowa 2022), **280**

Printz v. United States, 521 U.S. 898 (1997), **39**

PruneYard Shopping Ctr. v. Robins, 447 U.S. 74 (1980), 712

Public Water Supply Co., Inc. v. DiPasquale, 735 A.2d 378 (Del. 1999), **970**

Puerto Rico v. Branstad, 483 U.S. 219 (1987), 65

Racing Ass'n of Cent. Iowa v. Fitzgerald, 675 N.W.2d 1 (Iowa 2004), **99**

Ramos v. Louisiana, 140 S. Ct. 1390 (2020), 34, 362, 683

Ravin v. State, 537 P.2d 494 (Alaska 1975), **341**

Republican Party of Minnesota v. White, 536 U.S. 765 (2002), 855

Request for Advisory Opinion from House of Representatives, In re, 961 A.2d 930 (R.I. 2008), **919**

Right to Choose v. Byrne, 450 A.2d 925 (N.J. 1982), 125

Roberto D.B., In re, 923 A.2d 115 (Md. 2007), 264

Rocky Mountain Gun Owners v. Polis, 467 P.3d 314 (Colo. 2020), **737**

Rodriguez v. San Antonio Indep. Sch. Dist., 337 F. Supp. 280 (W.D. Tex. 1971), 595, 596

Robins v. PruneYard Shopping Ctr., 592 P.2d 341, 347 (Cal. 1979), 712

Romer v. Evans, 517 U.S. 620 (1996), 68

Ross v. State, 925 A.2d 489 (Del. 2007), 464

Rucho v. Common Cause, 139 S. Ct. 2484 (2019), 3

San Antonio Indep. Sch. Dist. v. Rodriguez, 411 U.S. 1 (1973), 3

San Francisco Unified Sch. Dist. v. Johnson, 479 P.2d 669 (Cal. 1971), 141

Save Our Vote v. Bennett, 291 P.3d 342 (Ariz. 2013), **1055**

Schuette v. Coalition to Defend Affirmative Action, 134 S. Ct. 1623 (2014), 147

Seeley v. State, 940 P.2d 604 (Wash. 1997), 345

Seminole Tribe of Fla. v. Florida, 517 U.S. 44 (1996), 44

Serrano v. Priest, 5 Cal.3d 584 (Cal. 1971), 595

Sheff v. O'Neill, 678 A.2d 1267 (Conn. 1996), **134**, 140

Sherbert v. Verner, 374 U.S. 398 (1963), 538

Simmons-Harris v. Goff, 711 N.E.2d 203 (Ohio 1999), 587

Sitz v. Dep't of State Police, 506 N.W.2d 209 (Mich. 1993), **80**, 83–84

Smallfoot v. State, 272 P.3d 314 (2012), 126

Smith v. Isakson, 962 N.W.2d 594 (N.D. 2021), **362**

Sofie v. Fibreboard Corp., 771 P.2d 711 (Wash. 1989), **719**

South Dakota v. Dole, 483 U.S. 203 (1987), 22

St. John's Well Child and Family Ctr. v. Schwarzenegger, 239 P.3d 651 (Cal. 2010), **842**

State ex rel. Brnovich v. City of Tucson, 399 P.3d 663 (Ariz. 2017), **1006**

State ex rel. Justice v. King, 852 S.E.2d 292 (W. Va. 2020), **909**

State of Kansas ex rel. Morrison v. Sebelius, 179 P.3d 366 (Kan. 2008), **891**

State ex rel. Rear Door Bookstore v. Tenth Dist. Court of Appeals, 588 N.E.2d 116 (Ohio 1992), 126

State ex rel. Voters First v. Ohio Ballot Bd., 978 N.E.2d 119 (Ohio 2012), **1051**

State ex rel. Warren v. Nusbaum, 208 N.W.2d 780 (Wis. 1973), 768

State of Kansas ex rel. Stephan v. Finney, 836 P.2d 1169 (Kan. 1992), 825

State v. Arreola-Botello, 451 P.3d 939 (Or. 2019), **471**

State v. Badger, 450 A.2d 336 (Vt. 1982), 125

State v. Ball, 471 A.2d 347 (N.H. 1983), 125

State v. Bauder, 924 A.2d 38 (Vt. 2007), 458, 471

State v. Birchard, 5 A.3d 879 (Vt. 2010), 471

State v. Beauchesne, 868 A.2d 972 (N.H. 2005), **459**, 464

State v. Boland, 800 P.2d 1112 (Wash. 1990), 458

State v. Bryant, 950 A.2d 467 (Vt. 2008), **450**

State v. Bullock, 901 P.2d 61 (Mont. 1995), **439**

State v. Cadman, 476 A.2d 1148 (Me. 1984), 124

State v. Coe, 679 P.2d 359 (Wash. 1984), 125

State v. Cora, 167 A.3d 633 (N.H. 2017), **465**

State v. Damato-Kushel, 173 A.3d 357 (Conn. 2017), **756**

State v. Dupuis, 197 A.3d 343 (Vt. 2018), 458

State v. Earls, 70 A.3d 630 (N.J. 2013), **443**

State v. Erickson, 574 P.2d 1 (Alaska 1978), 345

State v. Evans, 150 P.3d 105 (Wash. 2007), 443

State v. Farris, 849 N.E.2d 985 (Ohio 2006), 481

State v. Gness, 85 A.3d 382 (N.H. 2014), 125

State v. Goss, 834 A.2d 316 (N.H. 2003), 458

State v. Harrington, 222 P.3d 92 222 P.3d 92 (Wash. 2009), 464

State v. Hempele, 576 A.2d 793 (N.J. 1990), **84**

State v. Horwitz, 191 So.3d 429 (Fla. 2016), 371

State v. Jenkins, 3 A.3d 806 (Conn. 2010), 126

State v. Jorden, 156 P.3d 893 (Wash. 2007), **103**

State v. Knapp, 700 N.W.2d 899 (Wis. 2005), 481

State v. Koivu, 272 P.3d 483 (Idaho 2012), **418**

State v. Lamb, 95 A.3d 123 (N.J. 2014), **437**

State v. Leonard, 943 N.W.2d 149 (Minn. 2020), **454**

State v. Lewis, 789 N.E.2d 195 (Ohio 2003), 618

State v. Lien, 441 P.3d 185 (Or. 2019), 458

State v. Mallan, 950 P.2d 178 (Haw. 1998), 345

State v. McAdams, 193 So.3d 824 (Fla. 2016), **377**

State v. McCormick, 494 S.W.3d 673 (Tenn. 2016), 464

State v. Misch, 256 A.3d 519 (Vt. 2019), **740**

State v. Mixton, 478 P.3d 1227 (Ariz. 2021), **105**

State v. Neil, 958 A.2d 1173 (Vt. 2008), 458

State v. Peterson, 923 A.2d 585 (Vt. 2007), **476**

State v. Purcell, 203 A.3d 542 (Conn. 2019), 381

State v. Rivera, 612 P.2d 526 (Haw. 1980), **151**

State v. Roache, 803 A.2d 572 (N.H. 2002), 381

State v. Sanchez, 350 P.3d 1169 (N.M. 2015), 125

State v. Santiago, 122 A.3d 1 (Conn. 2015), **399**

State v. Saunders, 381 A.2d 333 (N.J. 1977), 287

State v. Saunders, 992 P.2d 951 (Utah 1999), 361

State v. Scottize Danyelle Brown, 930 N.W.2d 840 (Iowa 2019), **111**

State v. Short, 851 N.W.2d 474 (Iowa 2014), 84, 126

State v. Stephens (Tex. Crim. App. 2021), **831**

State v. Stevens, 367 N.W.2d 788 (Wis. 1985), 126

State v. Stoddard, 537 A.2d 446 (Conn. 1988), 381

State v. Strom, 921 N.W.2d 660 (N.D. 2019), **754**

State v. Stummer, 194 P.3d 1043 (Ariz. 2008), **713**

State v. Tsujimura, 400 P.3d 500, 314 (Haw. 2017), 371

State v. Tuttle, 515 S.W.3d 282 (Tenn. 2017), **412**

State v. Veale, 972 A.2d 1009 (N.H. 2009), **252**

State v. Villela, 450 P.3d 170 (Wash. 2019), **469**

State v. Vondehn, 236 P.3d 691 (Or. 2010), 481

State v. Williams, 185 S.W.3d 311 (Tenn. 2006), 464

State v. Wright, 961 N.W.2d 396 (Iowa 2021), **88**

State v. Young, 957 P.2d 681 (Wash. 1998), 464

Stepp v. Cottrell on behalf of Estate of Cottrell, 874 S.E.2d 700 (W. Va. 2022), 699

Sterling v. Cupp, 625 P.2d 123 (Or. 1981), 125

Supreme Court of New Hampshire v. Piper, 470 U.S. 274 (1985), 64

Swanner v. Anchorage Equal Rights Comm'n, 874 P.2d 274 (Alaska 1994), 546

Sweezy v. New Hampshire, 354 U.S. 234 (1957), 809

Taxpayers for Public Educ. v. Douglas Cnty. Sch. Dist., 351 P.3d 461 (Colo. 2015), **575**

Taylor v. Town of Cabot, 178 A.3d 313 (Vt. 2017), 560, **567**

Teigen v. Wisconsin Elections Comm'n, 976 N.W.2d 519 (Wis. 2022), 241

Telli v. Broward County, 94 So.3d 504 (Fla. 2012), **812**

Tennessee v. Marshall, 859 S.W.2d 289 (Tenn. 1993), 718

Tetra Tech v. Wisconsin Dep't of Revenue, 914 N.W.2d 21 (Wisc. 2018), **961**

Texas Boll Weevil Eradication Found., Inc. v. Lewellen, 952 S.W.2d 454 (Tex. 1997), **950**

Texas Dep't of State Health Services v. Crown Distributing LLC, 647 S.W.3d 648 (Tex. 2022), **527**

Texas Southern University v. Villarreal, 620 S.W.3d 899 (Tex. 2021), **484**

Timbs v. Indiana, 139 S. Ct. 682 (2019), 35

Tindley v. Salt Lake City Sch. Dist., 116 P.3d 295 (Utah 2005), **679**

Torres v. Texas Dep't of Public Safety, 142 S.Ct. 2455 (2022), 57

Town of Beloit v. County of Rock, 657 N.W.2d 344 (Wis. 2003), **802**

Town of Greece v. Galloway, 134 S. Ct. 1811 (2014), 6

Trinity Lutheran Church of Columbia, Inc. v. Comer, 137 S. Ct. 2012 (2017), 113, **560**

Tully v. City of Wilmington, 810 S.E.2d 208 (N.C. 2018), 767

Turnbull v. Fink, 668 A.2d 1370 (Del. 1995), **785**

T.W., In re, 551 So.2d 1186 (Fla. 1989), **265**

T.J.S., In re, 54 A.3d 263 (N.J. 2012), 153

United States v. Calandra, 414 U.S. 338 (1974), 436

United States v. Lopez, 514 U.S. 549 (1995), **35**

United States v. Patane, 542 U.S. 630 (2004), 476

U.S. Term Limits, Inc. v. Thornton, 514 U.S. 779 (1995), 1, 58, 810

Utah v. Walker, 267 P.3d 210 (Utah 2011), 436

Vergara v. California, 209 Cal. Rptr. 3d 558 (2016), **632**

Village of Lindale v. State, 706 N.E.2d 1227 (Ohio 1999), 979

Vincent v. Voight, 614 N.W.2d 388 (Wis. 2000), **603**

Walker v. Sauvinet, 92 U.S. 90 (1876), 443

Washakie Cnty. Sch. Dist. No. One v. Herschler, 606 P.2d 310 (Wyo. 1980), 597

Washington v. Gregory, 427 P.3d 621 (Wash. 2018), **396**

Weinschenk v. State, 203 S.W.3d 201 (Mo. 2006), **233**

West Jefferson v. Robinson, 205 N.E.2d 382 (Ohio 1965), 979

William Penn Sch. Dist. v. Pa. Dep't Educ., 170 A.3d 414 (Pa. 2017), 627

Williams-Yulee v. Florida Bar, 135 S. Ct. 1656 (2015), 855

Williamson Cnty. Reg'l Planning Comm'n v. Hamilton Bank of Johnson City, 473 U.S. 172 (1985), 508

Yanakos v. University of Pittsburg Medical Ctr., et al., 218 A.3d 1214 (Pa. 2019), **661**

York v. Wahkiakum Sch. Dist. No. 200, 178 P.3d 995 (Wash. 2008), **701**

Zelman v. Simmons-Harris, 536 U.S. 639 (2002), **570**

Ziglar v. Abbasi, 137 S. Ct. 1843 (2017), 698

TABLE OF AUTHORITIES

Books and Articles

Amar, Akhil Reed, *America's Constituion: A Biography* (Random House 2005) 177
Barron, David J., *The Promise of Cooley's City: Traces of Local Constituitonalism*, 147 Pa. L. Rev. 487 (1999) 1017, 1023
Barron, David J., *Reclaiming Home Rule*, 116 Harv. L. Rev. 487 (2003).....................................1025
Bayard, James A., *A Brief Exposition of the Constitution of the United States* (2d ed. 1838).......883, 1029
Bernstein, Richard B., & Jerome Agel, *Amending America* (Times Books 1993) 1029
Blocher, Joseph, *Reverse Incorporation of State Constitutional Law*, 84 S. Cal. L. Rev. 323 (2011) 125
Brady, Maureen E., *The Damagings Clauses*, 104 Va. L. Rev. 341 (2018)...................................513
Brady, Maureen E., *Property's Ceiling: State Courts and the Expansion of Takings Clause Property*, 102 Va. L. Rev. 1167 (2016) 513
Briffault, Richard, *Election Law Localism and Democracy*, 100 N.C. L. Rev. 1421 (2022) 250
Briffault, Richard, *The Item Veto In State Courts*, 66 Temp. L. Rev. 1171 (1993).......................850
Briffault, Richard, *The Challenge of the New Preemption*, 70 Stan. Rev. 1995 (2011).....1018, 1025
Briffault, Richard et al., *Principles of Home Rule for the Twenty-First Century*, National League of Cities (Feb. 12, 2020) 1024, 1025
Calabresi, Steven G., *The Fatally Flawed Theory of the Unbundled Executive*, 93 Minn. L. Rev. 1696 (2009) 825
Carmella, Angela C., *State Constitutional Protection of Religious Exercise: An Emerging Post-Smith Jurisprudence*, 1993 B.Y.U. L. Rev. 277 (1993)..536
Coester, Adam, *Dillon's Rule or Not? National Association of Counties* (Jan. 2004) 1015
Cooley, Thomas M., *A Treatise on the Constitutional Limitations Which Rest Upon the Legislative Power of the States of the American Union* (1868)..251
Davidson, Nestor M., *Cooperative Localism: Federal-Local Collaboration in an Era of State Sovereignty*, 93 Va. L. Rev. 959 (2007) 1025
Davidson, Nestor M., *Localist Administrative Law*, 126 Yale L.J. 564 (2017)..............................956
DeForrest, Mark Edward, *An Overview and Evaluation of State Blaine Amendments: Origins, Scope, and First Amendment Concerns*, 26 Harv. J. L. & Pub. Pol'y 551 (2003) 555
Diller, Paul, *Intrastate Preemeption*, 87 B.U. L. Rev. 1113 (2007)..1024
Dinan, John, *State Constitutional Amendments and American Constitutionalism*, 41 Okla. City U. L. Rev. 27 (2016)..1065
Dinan, John, *State Constitutional Initiative Process and Governance in the Twenty-First Century*, 12 Chap. L. Rev. 61 (2016)...1065
Dinan, John, *State Constitutional Politics* (Chicago 2018).............................977, 1017, 1018, 1028
Dillon, John F., *The Law of Municipal Corporations* (2d Rev. Ed. James Cockroft & Co. 1873) 1015
Dragich, Martha J., *State Constitutional Restriction on Legislative Procedure: Rethinking the Analysis of Original Purpose, Single Subject, and Clear Title Challenges*, 38 Harv. J. Legis. 103 (2001) 768
Foley, Edward B., *Ballot Battles: The History of Disputed Elections in the United States* (Oxford 2015)...250
Friesen, Jennifer, *State Constitutional Law: Litigating Individual Rights, Claims and Defenses* (2006) 332, 701
Fritz, Mechthild, *Religion in a Federal System: Diversity Versus Uniformity*, 38 Kan. L. Rev. 39 (1989) 535
Galie, Peter J. & Christopher Bopst, *The Constitutional Commission in New York: A Worthy Tradition*, 64 Alb. L. Rev. 1285 (2001) 1059
Gardner, James A., *The Failed Discourse of State Constitutionalism*, 90 Mich. L. Rev. 761 (1992) 124
Gentithes, Michael, *Gobbledygook: Political Questions, Manageability, & Partisan Gerrymandering*, 105 Iowa L. Rev. 1081 (2020) 250

George, Ronald M., *Remarks by California's Chief Justice, Ronald M. George, to the American Academy of Arts & Sciences* (Oct.10, 2009)..........1041
Gerkin, Heather, *Foreword: Federalism All the Way Down*, 124 Harv. L. Rev. 4 (2010)..........1025
Ginsburg, Douglas H. & Steven Menashi, *Our Illiberal Administrative Law*, 10 N.Y.U. J.L. & Liberty 475 (2016)..........926
Goldberg, John C. P., *The Constitutional Status of Tort Law: Due Process and the Right to a Law for the Redress of Wrongs*, 115 Yale L.J. 524 (2005)..........683
Goldenziel, Jill, *Blaine's Name in Vain?: State Constitutions, School Choice, and Charitable Choice*, 83 Denv. U. L. Rev. 57 (2005)..........535
Graves, W. Brooke, *State Constitutional Law: A Twenty-Five Year Summary*, 8 Wm. & Mary L. Rev. 1 (1966)..........1028
Grofman, Bernard & Jonathan R. Cervas, *Can State Courts Cure Partisan Gerrymandering: Lessons from* League of Women Voters of Pennsylvania v. Commonwealth of Pennsylvania *(2018)*, 17 Election L.J. 264 (2018)..........192
Hall, Kermit L., *"'Mostly Anchor and Little Sail': The Evolution of American State Constitutions"* in *Toward a Usable Past: Liberty Under State Constitutions* (Paul Finkelman & Stephen E. Gottlieb eds., U. Ga. 1991)..........1028, 1029
Henkin, Louis, *"Selective Incorporation" in the Fourteenth Amendment*, 73 Yale L.J. 74 (1963) 982
Henretta, James A., *Foreword: Rethinking the State Constitutional Tradition*, 22 Rutgers L.J (1991)..........1028
Hoffman, Jonathan M., *Questions Before Answers: The Ongoing Search to Understand the Origins of the Open Courts Clause*, 32 Rutgers L.J. 1005 (2001)..........683
Holliday, Winston David, Jr., *Tipping the Balance of Power: A Critical Survey of the Gubernatorial Line Item Veto*, 50 S.C. L. Rev. 503 (1999)..........850
Iuliano, Jason & Keith E. Whittington, *The Nondelegation Doctrine: Alive and Well*, 93 Notre Dame L. Rev. 619 (2017)..........926, 973
Kemerer, Frank R., *The Constitutional Dimension of School Vouchers*, 3 Tex F. on C.L. & C.R. 137 (1998)..........587
Klapper, Rudy, *The Falcon Cannot Hear the Falconer: How California's Initiative Process Is Creating an Untenable Constitution*, 48 Loy. L.A.L. Rev. 755 (2015)..........1045
Klinghoffer, Judith Apter & Lois Elkis, *"The Petticoat Electors": Women's Suffrage in New Jersey, 1776-1807*, 12(2) J. Early Republic 159 (1992)..........177
Kosklea, Alice, Comment, *Victim's Rights Amendments: An Irresistible Political Force Transforms the Criminal Justice System*, 34 Idaho L. Rev. 157 (1997)..........760

LaCroix, Alison L., *The Ideological Origins of American Federalism* (Harvard 2010)..........9
Linde, Hans A., *Due Process of Lawmaking*, 55 Neb. L. Rev. 197 (1976)..........124
Linde, Hans A., *Without "Due Process": Unconstitutional Law in Oregon*, 49 Or. L. Rev. 125 (1970)..........124
Lutz, Donald S., *Toward a Theory of Constitutional Amendment*, 88 Am. Pol. Sci. Rev. 355 (1994) 1028, 1029
Maute, Judith L., *Selecting Justice in State Courts: The Ballot Box or the Backroom?* 41 S. Tex. L. Rev. 1197 (2000)..........851
Mazo, Eugene D., *Finding Common Ground on Voter ID Laws*, 49 U. Mem. L. Rev. 1233 (2019) 250
McAllister, Stephen R., *A* Marbury v. Madison *Moment on the Eve of the Civil War: Chief Judge Roger Taney and the* Kentucky v. Dennison *Case*, 14 The Green Bag 2d 405 (2011)..........64
McConnell, Michael W., *The Origins and Historical Understanding of Free Exercise of Religion*, 103 Harv. L. Rev. 1409 (1990)..........535
McUsic, Molly S., *The Future of* Brown v. Board of Education: *Economic Integration of The Public Schools*, 117 Harv. L. Rev. 1334 (2004)..........597
O'Connor, Sandra Day, *Judicial Independence and Civics Education*, Utah Bar Journal, Sept./Oct. 2009, at 10..........855
O'Connor, Sandra Day, *The Threat to Judicial Independence*, The Wall Street Journal, Sept. 27, 2006, at A18..........855

Ortner, Daniel, *The End of Deference: How States Are Leading a (Sometimes Quiet) Revolution Against Administrative Deference Doctrines* (March 11, 2020) 973

Pappas, Michael, *No Two-Stepping in the Laboratories: State Deference Standards and Their Implications for Improving the* Cheveron *Doctrine*, 39 McGeorge L. Rev. 977 (2008) 973

Permaloff, Anne, *Altering State Constitutions*, 33 Cumb. L. Rev. 217 (2003) 1029

Philipson, Jon M., *Second-Order Logrolling: The Impact of Direct Legislative Amendments to State Constitutions*, 41 Nova L. Rev. 23 (2016) 1065

Proacaccini, Francesca Lina, *Partisan Gerrymandering: State Courts Come to Bat on the Free-Speech Issue of Our Day*, 2 Md. B.J. 128 (2020) 250

Razel, Timothy A., Note, *Dying to Get Away with It: How the Abatement Doctrine Thwarts Justice—And What Should be Done Instead*, 75 Fordham L. Rev. 2193 (2007) 760

Rebell, Michael A., "Educational Adequacy, Democracy, and the Courts," *in* National Research Council, *Achieving High Educational Standards for All: Conference Summary* (Timothy Ready et al. eds. 2002) 597

Roesler, Shannon M., *The Kansas Remedy by Due Course of Law Provision: Defining a Right to a Remedy*, 47 Kan. L. Rev. 655 (1999) 652

Rossi, James, *Institutional Design and the Lingering Legacy of Antifederalist Separation of Powers Ideas in the States*, 52 Vand. L. Rev. 1167 (1999) 926

Rossi, James, *Dual Constitutions and Constitutional Duels: Separation of Powers and State Implementation of Federally-Inspired Regulatory Programs and Standards*, 46 Wm. & Mary L. Rev. 1343 (2005) 973

Ruud, Millard H., *No Law Shall Embrace More Than One Subject*, 42 Minn. L. Rev. 389 (1958). 767

Saiger, Aaron, Chevron *and Deference in State Administrative Law*, 83 Fordham L. Rev. 555 (2014) 973

Scharff, Erin, *Hyper Preemption: A Reordering of the State-Local Relationship*, 106 Geo. L.J. 1469 (2018) 1025

Schleicher, David, *Federalism and State Democracy*, 95 Tex. L. Rev. 763 (2017) 1024

Schuman, David, *The Right To A Remedy*, 65 Temp. L. Rev. 1197 (1992) 683

Seifter, Miriam, *Gubernatorial Administration*, 131 Harv. L. Rev. 484 (2017) 973

Seifter, Miriam, *Further From the People? The Puzzle of State Administration*, 93 N.Y.U. L. Rev. 107 (2018) 973

Seifter, Miriam, *Understanding State Agency Independence*, 117 Mich. L. Rev. 1537 (2019) 973

Shaman, Jeffrey M., *Equality and Liberty in the Golden Age of State Constitutional Law* (2008) 133, 304, 332, 768

Shaman, Jeffrey M., *On the 100th Anniversary of* Lochner v. New York, 72 Tenn. L. R. 455 (2005) 251

Shaw, John W., *Principled Interpretations of State Constitutional Law—Why Don't the 'Primacy' States Practice What They Preach?* 54 U. Pitt. L. Rev. 1019 (1993) 124, 125

Somin, Ilya, *The Grasping Hand:* Kelo v. City of New London *and the Limits of Eminent Domain* (Univ. of Chi. 2015) 487

Sutton, Jeffrey S., *51 Imperfect Solutions: States and the Making of American Constitutional Law* (Oxford 2018) 7, 111, 597

Sutton, Jeffrey S., *A Response to Justice Goodwin Liu*, 128 Yale L.J. Forum 936 (2019) 34

Sutton, Jeffrey S., *Courts as Change Agents: Do We Want More—Or Less?* 127 Harv. L. Rev. 1419 (2014) 623

Sutton, Jeffrey S., *San Antonio Independent School District v. Rodriguez and Its Aftermath*, 94 Va. L. Rev. 1963 (2008) 78, 486, 596, 597

Sutton, Jeffrey S., *What Does—and Does Not—Ail State Constitutional Law*, 59 Kan. L. Rev. 687 (2011) 127

Sutton, Jeffrey S., *Who Decides?: States as Laboratories of Constitutional Experimentation* (Oxford 2021) 7, 768, 973, 978, 979, 1027

Sutton, Nathaniel C., *Lockstepping Through Stop-and-Frisk: A Call to Independently Assess* Terry v. Ohio *Under State Law*, 107 Va. L. Rev. 369 (2021) 437

Tarr, G. Alan, *Constitutional Politics in the States, Contemporary Controversies and Historical Patterns* (Greenwood Press 1996) 1028

Thompson, Barton H., Jr., "The Environment and Natural Resources," *in State Constitutions in the 21st Century* (G. Alan Tarr & Robert E. Williams eds. 2006) 767
Viteritti, Joseph P., *Blaine's Wake: School Choice, The First Amendment, and State Constitutional Law*, 22 Harv. J. L. & Pub. Pol'y 657 (1998) 587
Weinstein-Tull, Justin, *Election Law Federalism*, 114 Mich. L. Rev. 747 (2016) 250
Williams, Robert F., *State Constitutional Law: Cases and Materials* (1993) 1028, 1029
Zackin, Emily, *Looking for Rights in All the Wrong Places: Why State Constitutions Contain America's Positive Rights* (Princeton 2013) 623
Zitter, Jay M., Annotation, *Validity, Construction, and Application of State Constitutional or Statutory Victims' Bill of Rights*, 91 A.L.R.5th 343 § 2[a] (2008) 760

Other Sources

Ariz. Enabling Act, 36 Stat. 569 (1910) 69
Comprehensive Drug Abuse Prevention and Control Act of 1970, Pub. L. 91-513, 84 Stat. 1236 (1970) 346
Letter from Thomas Jefferson to Samuel Kercheval (July 12, 1816), *in* Thomas Jefferson, *Writings* (Library of America 1984) 1027
Magna Carta 251
N.M. Enabling Act, 36 Stat. 558 (1910) 69
Okla. Enabling Act, 34 Stat. 269 (1906) 69
The Federalist No. 17 (Hamilton) 975
The Federalist No. 49 (Madison) 1027
Utah Enabling Act, 28 Stat. 108 (1894) 69
4 William Blackstone, *Commentaries* 706

EXPLANATORY NOTE

The key objective in putting together the fourth edition of this case book has been to present a wide variety of materials in an accessible, streamlined, and engaging way. To that end, we have edited the opinions to remove unnecessary discussions, to eliminate unilluminating citations and internal quotations, and to omit nearly all footnotes. As a general rule, we have eliminated ellipses and removed brackets from the excerpted opinions and other quoted text, and have not used ellipses or brackets of our own to show when sentences or paragraphs or words have been eliminated or modified for ease of understanding. Through it all, the critical point is that we have created these abridged opinions to facilitate teaching an important subject, not to make legal research easier and above all not for the purpose of using the opinions as citations or quotations in legal pleadings. Before citing *any* of these materials, lawyers should consult the original opinion or article or other source.

ACKNOWLEDGEMENTS

For this fourth edition, special thanks go to Cassidy Bee, Nathan Dahlstrom, Chris Deucher, and Jacob Felicetty, who provided invaluable research assistance throughout.

PERMISSION TO REPRINT

The introductions to Chapter 5 (Representation and Voting) and Chapter 17 (Local Governments) borrow heavily from the introductions to Chapters 8 and 9 in *Who Decides? States as Laboratories of Constitutional Experimentation* (Oxford 2021). The authors and publishers gratefully acknowledge permission to use excerpts from the following:

Mark Edward DeForrest, *An Overview and Evaluation of State Blaine Amendments: Origins, Scope, and First Amendment Concerns*, 26 Harv. J. L. & Pub. Pol'y. 551 (2003);

Martha J. Dragich, *State Constitutional Restriction on Legislative Procedure: Rethinking the Analysis of Original Purpose, Single Subject, and Clear Title Challenges*, 38 Harv. J. Legis. 103 (2001);

Peter J. Galie and Christopher Bopst, *The Constitutional Commission in New York: A Worthy Tradition*, 64 Alb. L. Rev. 1285 (2001);

Judith L. Maute, *Selecting Justice in State Courts: The Ballot Box or the Backroom?* 40 S. Tex. L. Rev. 1197 (2000);

Anne Permaloff, *Altering State Constitutions*, 33 Cumb. L. Rev. 217 (2003);

Shannon M. Roesler, *The Kansas Remedy By Due Course Of Law Provision: Defining A Right To A Remedy*, 47 Kan. L. Rev. 655 (1999);

Jeffrey M. Shaman, *Equality and Liberty in the Golden Age of State Constitutional Law* (Oxford 2008);

Jeffrey S. Sutton, *Why Teach—and Why Study—State Constitutional Law*, 34 Okla. City Univ. L. Rev. 165 (2009);

Jeffrey S. Sutton, San Antonio Independent School District v. Rodriguez *and Its Aftermath*, 94 Va. L. Rev. 1963 (2008).

Jeffrey S. Sutton, *51 Imperfect Solutions: States and the Making of American Constitutional Law* (Oxford 2018).

Jeffrey S. Sutton, *Who Decides? States as Laboratories of Constitutional Experimentation* (Oxford 2021).

STATE CONSTITUTIONAL LAW
THE MODERN EXPERIENCE

Fourth Edition

Chapter I

INTRODUCTION

All law schools in this country offer a course called "Constitutional Law," and virtually all of these courses (and textbooks) teach just half of the story. They teach the course from the perspective of the Federal Constitution, infrequently mentioning, much less explaining, the role of the State Constitutions in our system of government and laws. In one sense, that is quite understandable; it is difficult enough to teach all of *federal* constitutional law in a full-year course. In another sense, it is a missed opportunity, as too many students never learn the full story.

When the Framers "split the atom of sovereignty," *U.S. Term Limits, Inc. v. Thornton*, 514 U.S. 779, 838 (1995) (Kennedy, J., concurring), they created a dual system of government, one with two sets of sovereigns for every corner of the country, not just one. It is an American innovation, one of the few ideas the Framers could have patented because no government yet had tried it, no political philosopher had ever proposed it, and none of the existing state governments needed it. The American experiment launched a governmental structure with horizontal separation of powers (dividing the executive, legislative, and judicial branches at the national level) *and* vertical separation of powers (dividing the national and the state governments).

In this country, we thus have fifty-one Constitutions—fifty-one charters of government that simultaneously empower and constrain: that give two sets of sovereigns in any one location in the country the power to regulate most areas of American life, and that limit those regulations through individual-liberty guarantees and other constraints on the legislative and executive branches. To understand *American* constitutional law, one cannot study federal constitutional law by itself or for that matter state constitutional law by itself. A full understanding of the one cannot be understood without an appreciation of the other. To think otherwise about the matter is akin to taking a course on civil procedure without learning that there are state court procedures as well as federal ones. American constitutional law, like American procedural law, covers both.

Although it is not the objective of this textbook to cover *all* of American constitutional law—to cover the subject from the perspective of all of its federal and state counterparts—it is our mission to correct the imbalance. Our focus is the fifty State Constitutions, yet our method of presentation emphasizes the interrelation of the two sets of constitutions, frequently explaining how the U.S. Constitution deals with an issue before explaining how the State Constitutions handle it or in some instances explaining how the State Constitutions contain provisions that have no parallel in the U.S. Constitution.

As with most textbooks about torts, property, and contracts, this casebook is not parochial. It uses decisions from courts throughout the country. It does not focus on the Constitution or cases from any one State but surveys the most interesting and thoughtful and up-to-date cases from all of the States.

The book covers several basic topics. The first substantive chapter sets the framework. It explains the interrelation of the State and Federal Constitutions: where federal power is exclusive, where state power is exclusive, and where the two overlap. The next substantive chapter introduces a key theme of the book. It explains why and how state courts may construe guarantees in their own constitutions differently from identical or similarly worded guarantees in the Federal Constitution—whether by giving the local guarantees more *or* less protection than their federal counterparts.

The next several chapters, the heart of the textbook, apply these principles to a variety of individual-rights guarantees in the State Constitutions, including chapters devoted to equal protection, due process, voting rights, criminal procedure, property rights, the religion clauses, and school funding. Some of the state guarantees, as the student will see, have exact counterparts in the U.S. Constitution and indeed often were the models for the first eight provisions of the federal Bill of Rights. Others have similarities to their federal cousins. This section of the book ends with a chapter concerning state constitutional guarantees that have no counterparts in the U.S. Constitution and sometimes are unique to one State or another. Among them are single-subject requirements, clear-title rules, and public-purpose requirements.

The book then shifts from individual rights to structure. It devotes a long chapter to the branches of state government, delving into the grants of authority to each division of state government and the various limitations placed on that power. Several state innovations, including term limits for state legislatures, a plural executive, the line-item veto, judicial elections, and advisory opinions, all take a prominent place. What follows is a chapter on a consequential aspect of separation of powers, what sometimes looks like a merger of powers: administrative law. Here the comparison between the federal and state models is especially revealing, as many state courts, often in contrast to their federal brethren, have not hesitated to adopt a vibrant nondelegation doctrine and to place limits on deference to administrative agencies tasked with implementing state laws. The penultimate chapter introduces an increasingly salient topic in American law: the role of local governments. Here we see federalism within federalism. Just as federal and state power sometimes conflict, so the same can happen between state and local governments, as state courts and state legislatures take shifting approaches to "home rule." The last chapter addresses an issue of considerable import: the relatively easy amendment process for most State Constitutions, which usually require just a majority vote and often permit direct democracy, constitutional initiatives proposed by the people themselves. It might be said that the U.S. Constitution is too difficult to amend, and the State Constitutions are too easy to amend, and we will consider the impact of this juxtaposition on the appropriate role of the state and federal courts in developing American constitutional law.

Why take a class on state constitutional law? A lawyer's duty to a client is a good place to start. Our fifty-one constitutions place two potential sets of constitutional limitations on the validity of every state and local law. Lawyers are problem solvers, and when a state or local law stands in the way of a client's objective, it generally will matter little to the client whether the lawyer manages to invalidate the law on federal or state grounds. A constitutional claimant needs to win just once. No State permits a law invalidated under its constitution to be enforced; and the Supremacy Clause of the U.S. Constitution prohibits any State from enforcing laws invalidated under the U.S. Constitution. A necessary consequence of a system of dual sovereignty is that it permits dual claims of unconstitutionality. One reason to study state constitutional law, then, is simple: Lawyers are paid to solve problems for their clients, and one way to do that is to win cases. Lawyers paid to help a client win a case will have some explaining to do if they fail to consider taking two shots, rather than just one, to invalidate a state or local law. No one wants a lawyer who is *half-equipped* to win a case.

State constitutional law not only gives the client two chances to win, but in some settings it may give the client a *better* chance to win. The U.S. Supreme Court is at a disadvantage relative to the state courts when it comes to defining constitutional rights and crafting constitutional remedies in many areas of the law. Because the Supreme Court must announce rights and remedies for fifty States, one National Government, and roughly 330 million people, it is more constrained than a state supreme court addressing a difficult problem for one State and, say, fifteen million people. That reality begins to explain why, as you will read in Chapter XI, the U.S. Supreme Court might reject a constitutional challenge to Texas's system for funding public education, but the Texas Supreme Court later would grant relief in a similar challenge filed under the Texas Constitution. *Compare San Antonio Indep. Sch. Dist. v. Rodriguez*, 411 U.S. 1 (1973), *with Edgewood Indep. Sch. Dist. v. Kirby*, 777 S.W.2d 391 (Tex. 1989). And that reality may explain why, as you will read in Chapter V, the U.S. Supreme Court might reject a constitutional challenge to partisan gerrymandering of electoral districts but the Pennsylvania Supreme Court would grant relief in a like-minded challenge filed under the Pennsylvania Constitution. *Compare Rucho v. Common Cause*, 139 S. Ct. 2484 (2019), *with League of Women Voters of Pennsylvania v. Pennsylvania*, 178 A.3d 737 (Pa. 2018). In some settings, the challenge of imposing a constitutional solution on the whole country at once will increase the likelihood that federal constitutional law will be under-enforced or that a "federalism discount" will be applied to the right. State courts face no such problem in construing their own constitutions.

State courts also have a freer hand in doing something the Supreme Court cannot: customizing interpretations of a general constitutional guarantee to account for local conditions, history, and culture. The Alaska Supreme Court might gauge privacy issues differently from other States or for that matter the U.S. Supreme Court. The Montana Supreme Court might gauge property rights and gun-possession rights differently from other States or the U.S. Supreme Court. Or the Utah and Maryland Supreme Courts might gauge free-exercise rights differently from other state courts given their histories. State constitutional law respects, indeed embraces, differences between and among the States by allowing fifty constitutions to be interpreted differently to account for these differences in culture, geography, and tradition. In state constitutional law, as in state legislation, the States may be "laboratories of experimentation." *See New State Ice Co. v. Liebmann*, 285 U.S. 262, 311 (1932) (Brandeis, J., dissenting).

State constitutional law also holds promise as a way to facilitate the development of *federal* constitutional law. For far too long, we have lived in a top-down constitutional world, in which the U.S. Supreme Court announces a ruling, and the state supreme courts move in lockstep in construing the counterpart guarantees of their own constitutions. Why not do the reverse? That is the way other areas of the law traditionally have developed, be it tort, property, or contract law. In these settings, the state courts are the vanguard—the first ones to decide whether to embrace or reject innovative legal claims. Over time, the market of common law decisions identifies winners and losers. An opinion by Cooley, Cardozo or Traynor (or Kruger or Liu or Markman, to say nothing of many others) might become the benchmark, after which other state courts opt to follow that view or variations on it. Or the state courts might go their separate ways. In either event, the federal courts profit from the experience, as they can choose whether to federalize the issue *after* learning the strengths and weaknesses of the competing ways of addressing a problem.

Once the student learns that State Constitutions are documents of independent force—that the meaning of state guarantees is a matter for the state courts, not the U.S. Supreme Court, to resolve—it opens up a new way of thinking about constitutional law. By the second or third year of law school, most students come to appreciate that many constitutional issues do not lend themselves to one-size-fits-all solutions. It is one thing to apply the requirement that the President be thirty-five years of age, U.S. Const. art. II, § 1, cl. 5, or a requirement that the Governor of a State be thirty years of age, Ala. Const. art. V, § 117. But it is quite another to decipher what the more-generalized individual-liberty guarantees—say, "due" process or "free" speech or "unreasonable" search and seizure—mean when they appear in the State and Federal Constitutions.

As to these vexing areas of the law, the state courts may adopt their own interpretations of parallel (or somewhat parallel) guarantees found in their own constitutions. When difficult areas of constitutional litigation arise, why assume that the U.S. Supreme Court is the only supreme court in the country capable of offering an insightful solution to a challenging problem? Four distinct levels of scrutiny—rational basis, rational basis plus, intermediate, or strict—may be the best way to assess equal-protection claims, but serial tiers of review are hardly the self-evident way or the text-ordained way for handling such claims. Rational-basis review may be the best way to assess free-exercise challenges to neutral, generally applicable laws as a matter of national constitutional law, *see Emp't Div. v. Smith*, 494 U.S. 872, 878–79 (1990), but the same may not be true for each state constitution, *see Humphrey v. Lane*, 728 N.E.2d 1039, 1043 (Ohio 2000). A modest standard for enforcing the Takings Clause may work for national taking-of-property claims, *see Kelo v. City of New London*, 545 U.S. 469, 483 (2005), but it is by no means clear that every State should embrace the same approach in addressing similar challenges under its own constitution, *see Bd. of Cty. Comm'rs v. Lowery*, 136 P.3d 639, 652 (Okla. 2006). The more difficult the constitutional question, as these cases show, the more indeterminate the answer may be. In these settings, it may be appropriate to have fifty-one imperfect solutions rather than one imperfect solution—particularly when imperfection may be something we have to live with in a given area.

In some cases, the *only* way a lawyer can win a case is through the State Constitution because it is the only constitution with a provision on point. State constitutions have a variety of clauses found nowhere in the U.S. Constitution: right-to-remedy clauses, single-subject clauses, uniform-law clauses, public-purpose clauses, to name a few. And some state constitutions have exotic clauses found in few, if any, other state constitutions. The Ohio Constitution, for example, bars the taxation of food sold for human consumption, *see* Ohio Const. art. XII, § 13, and the Alaska Constitution generally forbids the creation of any "exclusive right or special privilege of fishery" within Alaskan waters, Alaska Const. art. VIII, § 15.

If ever there were a propitious time for thinking twice about the meaning of American constitutional law—its federal and state components—now may be it. Many of the most ground-breaking constitutional disputes of the day are being waged in the state courts under the State Constitutions. Whether it is abortion, gerrymandering, voting regulations, school funding, property rights, criminal procedure, religious liberties, or other modern rights disputes, the state courts in recent years have gone from being civil-rights followers to leaders. There is, indeed, a softer side to federalism: A loss in the U.S. Supreme Court no longer inevitably foreshadows a loss in the state courts when the claim is premised on a state constitutional counterpart. As many of these debates confirm, state constitutional litigation can proceed without waiting for, or worrying about, the shadow of federal constitutional law.

Often, indeed, there is a synergy between federal and state constitutional law. It is difficult to imagine *Obergefell v. Hodges*, 135 S. Ct. 2584 (2015), without *Goodridge v. Department of Public Health*, 798 N.E.2d 941 (Mass. 2003). The U.S. Supreme Court recognized as much in *Obergefell*. In establishing a right to same-sex marriage in the Fourteenth Amendment and in overruling its decision in *Baker v. Nelson*, 409 U.S. 810 (1972), the Court noted that "the highest courts of many States have contributed to this ongoing dialogue in decisions interpreting their own State Constitutions." *Obergefell*, 135 S. Ct. at 2597. Something similar happened in *Arizona v. Gant*, 556 U.S. 332 (2009), a case about searches incident to arrest. There too the U.S. Supreme Court overruled a prior decision (*New York v. Belton*, 453 U.S. 454 (1981)), and there too the Court recognized that many state courts had not followed *Belton* in construing comparable guarantees in their own constitutions. *Gant*, 556 U.S. at 347 n.8. The influence of state constitutional law on federal constitutional law, moreover, affects originalists and living constitutionalists alike. For originalists, the meaning of the early state constitutions often provides the best evidence of what the Federal Constitution means, particularly when (as is so often the case) the latter was modeled after the former. *See Town of Greece v. Galloway*, 134 S. Ct. 1811 (2014) (construing the First and Fourteenth Amendments); *McDonald v. City of Chicago*, 561 U.S. 742 (2010) (construing the Second and Fourteenth Amendments). For living constitutionalists, developments in state constitutional law often provide the best evidence of evolving social norms. *See Obergefell*.

Of special interest in many States have been recent debates about abortion, electoral redistricting, and gun regulations. As to abortion and redistricting, the U.S. Supreme Court's decisions in *Rucho* in 2019 and *Dobbs v. Jackson Women's Health Organization* in 2022 squarely placed the spotlight on the States. Whether through constitutional amendments, state legislative initiatives, or state court decisions, the people in each State have had to fend for themselves in deciding how they will handle these vexing issues. As to gun regulation, the U.S. Supreme Court's decision in *New York State Rifle & Pistol Association v. Bruen* in 2022 takes some local authority away from the States but still leaves plenty of room for regulation and state court decision making in the area.

As all of this suggests and as the rest of the book confirms, no lawyer in the twenty-first century can be a good advocate without appreciating the possibility—the value—of raising state constitutional claims when representing a client. Ask students why they went to law school, and you will find a common answer among most of them: the opportunity to make a difference in the great issues of the day. No lawyer can take advantage of these opportunities without understanding state constitutional law. That is especially so when one accounts for the number of cases filed in the state courts each year: roughly 40 to 50 million versus roughly 400,000 in the federal courts. If one focuses just on the most important cases to liberty, the criminal cases, the difference is roughly 17 million versus 70,000. Anyone interested in improving the American justice system cannot ignore the state courts. If the rule of law does not exist there, it does not exist. *See generally* Jeffrey S. Sutton, *51 Imperfect Solutions: States and the Making of American Constitutional Law* (Oxford 2018); Jeffrey S. Sutton, *Who Decides?: States as Laboratories of Constitutional Experimentation* (Oxford 2021).

CHAPTER II

DUAL SOVEREIGNTY: THE INTERRELATION OF THE STATE AND FEDERAL CONSTITUTIONS

A. INTRODUCTION

Federalism is a head scratcher in some ways. How could two governments simultaneously have authority over the same territory and *both* call themselves sovereign? The paradox is not directly answered by the U.S. Constitution because the Framers never define the concept of federalism. This American contribution to political theory instead grows out of numerous federal constitutional provisions that carve out some separate federal powers, some separate state powers, and some overlapping powers. The history of the development of American federalism could occupy a full book in its own right. *See, e.g.*, Alison L. LaCroix, *The Ideological Origins of American Federalism* (Harvard 2010).

Rather than take on that task, this chapter focuses on the provisions in the U.S. Constitution that tend to bear most directly on state constitutional law. It is divided into three sections. The first section examines the federal constitutional sources of the relationship between the state and federal governments, with a focus on the powers exclusive to the federal government, the powers exclusive to the States, and the powers shared by the two sovereigns. The second section looks at limitations on the federal government's power vis-à-vis the States, focusing on two of the most frequently litigated: the anti-commandeering principle and state sovereign immunity. The third section explores Articles IV and VI of the U.S. Constitution. Article VI contains the all-important Supremacy Clause, which establishes that properly enacted federal law preempts all contrary state law, including state constitutional law. Article IV addresses the States' role in the federal system and contains numerous provisions that affect the content of state constitutional law.

B. THE SOURCES AND NATURE OF FEDERAL AND STATE POWERS

1. Exclusive Federal Powers

a. Article I, § 8

Article I, § 8, of the Federal Constitution enumerates the majority of Congress's powers, many of which are exclusive in nature. Some of the exclusive powers include the power to establish rules of naturalization and immigration, regulate bankruptcy, coin money, establish post offices, protect intellectual property through patent, copyright, and trademark laws, create the lower federal courts, regulate and punish piracy, declare war, raise and support an army and a navy, and acquire property for the federal government's use.

Some Article I powers are theoretically exclusive, but in practice end up overlapping with traditional state police powers. The best example of this phenomenon is Congress's Article I power to regulate commerce "among the several states." At the outset, one could have envisioned a future in which Congress alone had the power to regulate interstate commerce and Congress alone had the power to preempt any state laws that interfered with interstate commerce or that otherwise affected it. Over time, the Supreme Court developed an "implied," "negative," or "dormant" commerce doctrine that preempts state police-power regulations. Call it what you will that, the doctrine initially permitted the Court to invalidate state laws that intruded on Congress's exclusive power to regulate interstate commerce and eventually covered laws that, in the Court's view, discriminated against out-of-state interests or unduly burdened interstate commerce. The Court invokes this doctrine in the absence of any act of Congress either expressly or implicitly requiring such federal preemption. As a practical matter, the dormant commerce power imposes a substantial limit on the States' efforts to regulate in many areas that might seem to fall under the States' traditional police power. *See, e.g.*, *City of Philadelphia v. New Jersey*, 437 U.S. 617 (1978) (invalidating New Jersey's ban on the importation of "most solid or liquid waste which originated outside the state" under the dormant commerce power).

As the nature of "commerce" in the country has changed, the U.S. Supreme Court has struggled to identify the lines between the States' traditional police powers that remain exclusive and those that overlap with federal power. In some contexts, the Court has abandoned any effort to limit Congress's power over interstate commerce insofar as a law is challenged as intruding into the States' sovereignty and government activities. *See, e.g.*, *Garcia v. San Antonio Metropolitan Transit Auth.*, 469 U.S. 528 (1985).

Another potentially important Article I, § 8, power is the Necessary and Proper Clause, which along with the commerce power received attention in *Gonzales v. Raich*, 545 U.S. 1 (2005).

i. The Commerce Power and the Necessary and Proper Clause

GONZALES v. RAICH
545 U.S. 1 (2005)

STEVENS, J.

California is one of at least nine States that authorize the use of marijuana for medicinal purposes. The question presented in this case is whether the power vested in Congress by Article I, § 8, of the Constitution "to make all Laws which shall be necessary and proper for carrying into Execution" its authority to "regulate Commerce with foreign Nations, and among the several States" includes the power to prohibit the local cultivation and use of marijuana in compliance with California law.

In 1996, California voters passed Proposition 215, now codified as the Compassionate Use Act of 1996. The proposition was designed to ensure that "seriously ill" residents of the State have access to marijuana for medical purposes, and to encourage Federal and State Governments to take steps toward ensuring the safe and affordable distribution of the drug to patients in need. The Act creates an exemption from criminal prosecution for physicians, as well as for patients and primary caregivers who possess or cultivate marijuana for medicinal purposes with the recommendation or approval of a physician.

Respondents brought this action against the Attorney General of the United States and the head of the DEA seeking injunctive and declaratory relief prohibiting the enforcement of the federal Controlled Substances Act (CSA) to the extent it prevents them from possessing, obtaining, or manufacturing cannabis for their personal medical use. Respondents claimed that enforcing the CSA against them would violate the Commerce Clause.

Shortly after taking office in 1969, President Nixon declared a national "war on drugs." As the first campaign of that war, Congress set out to enact legislation that would consolidate various drug laws on the books into a comprehensive statute, provide meaningful regulation over legitimate sources of drugs to prevent diversion into illegal channels, and strengthen law enforcement tools against the traffic in illicit drugs. That effort culminated in the passage of the Comprehensive Drug Abuse Prevention and Control Act of 1970.

Title II of that Act repealed most of the earlier antidrug laws in favor of a comprehensive regime to combat the international and interstate traffic in illicit drugs. The main objectives of the CSA were to conquer drug abuse and to control the legitimate and illegitimate traffic in controlled substances. Congress was particularly concerned with the need to prevent the diversion of drugs from legitimate to illicit channels.

To effectuate these goals, Congress devised a closed regulatory system making it unlawful to manufacture, distribute, dispense, or possess any controlled substance except in a manner authorized by the CSA. The CSA categorizes all controlled substances into five schedules. The drugs are grouped together based on their accepted medical uses, the potential for abuse, and their psychological and physical effects on the body.

In enacting the CSA, Congress classified marijuana as a Schedule I drug. This preliminary classification was based, in part, on the recommendation of the Assistant Secretary of HEW "that marihuana be retained within schedule I at least until the completion of certain studies now underway." Schedule I drugs are categorized as such because of their high potential for abuse, lack of any accepted medical use, and absence of any accepted safety for use in medically supervised treatment. These three factors, in varying gradations, are also used to categorize drugs in the other four schedules. For example, Schedule II substances also have a high potential for abuse which may lead to severe psychological or physical dependence, but unlike Schedule I drugs, they have a currently accepted medical use. By classifying marijuana as a Schedule I drug, as opposed to listing it on a lesser schedule, the manufacture, distribution, or possession of marijuana became a criminal offense, with the sole exception being use of the drug as part of a Food and Drug Administration preapproved research study.

Respondents argue that the CSA's categorical prohibition of the manufacture and possession of marijuana as applied to the intrastate manufacture and possession of marijuana for medical purposes pursuant to California law exceeds Congress' authority under the Commerce Clause.

In assessing the validity of congressional regulation, none of our Commerce Clause cases can be viewed in isolation. As charted in considerable detail in *United States v. Lopez* (1995), our understanding of the reach of the Commerce Clause, as well as Congress' assertion of authority thereunder, has evolved over time. The Commerce Clause emerged as the Framers' response to the central problem giving rise to the Constitution itself: the absence of any federal commerce power under the Articles of Confederation. For the first century of our history, the primary use of the Clause was to preclude the kind of discriminatory state legislation that had once been permissible. Then, in response to rapid industrial development and an increasingly interdependent national economy, Congress "ushered in a new era of federal regulation under the commerce power," beginning with the enactment of the Interstate Commerce Act in 1887, and the Sherman Antitrust Act in 1890.

Cases decided during that "new era," which now spans more than a century, have identified three general categories of regulation in which Congress is authorized to engage under its commerce power. First, Congress can regulate the channels of interstate commerce. Second, Congress has authority to regulate and protect the instrumentalities of interstate commerce, and persons or things in interstate commerce. Third, Congress has the power to regulate activities that substantially affect interstate commerce. Only the third category is implicated in the case at hand.

Our case law firmly establishes Congress' power to regulate purely local activities that are part of an economic "class of activities" that have a substantial effect on interstate commerce. In *Wickard v. Filburn* (1942), we upheld the application of regulations promulgated under the Agricultural Adjustment Act of 1938, which were designed to control the volume of wheat moving in interstate and foreign commerce in order to avoid surpluses and consequent abnormally low prices. The regulations established an allotment of 11.1 acres for Filburn's 1941 wheat crop, but he sowed 23 acres, intending to use the excess by consuming it on his own farm. Filburn argued that even though we had sustained Congress' power to regulate the production of goods for commerce, that power did not authorize "federal regulation of production not intended in any part for commerce but wholly for consumption on the farm." Justice Jackson's opinion for a unanimous Court rejected this submission. He wrote:

> The effect of the statute before us is to restrict the amount which may be produced for market and the extent as well to which one may forestall resort to the market by producing to meet his own needs. That appellee's own contribution to the demand for wheat may be trivial by itself is not enough to remove him from the scope of federal regulation where, as here, his contribution, taken together with that of many others similarly situated, is far from trivial.

Wickard thus establishes that Congress can regulate purely intrastate activity that is not itself "commercial," in that it is not produced for sale, if it concludes that failure to regulate that class of activity would undercut the regulation of the interstate market in that commodity.

The similarities between this case and *Wickard* are striking. Like the farmer in *Wickard*, respondents are cultivating, for home consumption, a fungible commodity for which there is an established, albeit illegal, interstate market. Just as the Agricultural Adjustment Act was designed "to control the volume of wheat moving in interstate and foreign commerce in order to avoid surpluses" and consequently control the market price, a primary purpose of the CSA is to control the supply and demand of controlled substances in both lawful and unlawful drug markets. In *Wickard*, we had no difficulty concluding that Congress had a rational basis for believing that, when viewed in the aggregate, leaving home-consumed wheat outside the regulatory scheme would have a substantial influence on price and market conditions. Here too, Congress had a rational basis for concluding that leaving home-consumed marijuana outside federal control would similarly affect price and market conditions.

More concretely, one concern prompting inclusion of wheat grown for home consumption in the 1938 Act was that rising market prices could draw such wheat into the interstate market, resulting in lower market prices. The parallel concern making it appropriate to include marijuana grown for home consumption in the CSA is the likelihood that the high demand in the interstate market will draw such marijuana into that market. While the diversion of homegrown wheat tended to frustrate the federal interest in stabilizing prices by regulating the volume of commercial transactions in the interstate market, the diversion of homegrown marijuana tends to frustrate the federal interest in eliminating commercial transactions in the interstate market in their entirety. In both cases, the regulation is squarely within Congress' commerce power because production of the commodity meant for home consumption, be it wheat or marijuana, has a substantial effect on supply and demand in the national market for that commodity.

Nonetheless, respondents suggest that *Wickard* differs from this case in three respects: (1) the Agricultural Adjustment Act, unlike the CSA, exempted small farming operations; (2) *Wickard* involved a "quintessential economic activity"—a commercial farm—whereas respondents do not sell marijuana; and (3) the *Wickard* record made it clear that the aggregate production of wheat for use on farms had a significant impact on market prices.

The fact that Filburn's own impact on the market was "trivial by itself" was not a sufficient reason for removing him from the scope of federal regulation. That the Secretary of Agriculture elected to exempt even smaller farms from regulation does not speak to his power to regulate all those whose aggregated production was significant, nor did that fact play any role in the Court's analysis. Moreover, even though Filburn was indeed a commercial farmer, the activity he was engaged in—the cultivation of wheat for home consumption—was not treated by the Court as part of his commercial farming operation. And while it is true that the record in the *Wickard* case itself established the causal connection between the production for local use and the national market, we have before us findings by Congress to the same effect.

In assessing the scope of Congress' authority under the Commerce Clause, we stress that the task before us is a modest one. We need not determine whether respondents' activities, taken in the aggregate, substantially affect interstate commerce in fact, but only whether a "rational basis" exists for so concluding. Given the enforcement difficulties that attend distinguishing between marijuana cultivated locally and marijuana grown elsewhere, and concerns about diversion into illicit channels, we have no difficulty concluding that Congress had a rational basis for believing that failure to regulate the intrastate manufacture and possession of marijuana would leave a gaping hole in the CSA. Thus, as in *Wickard*, when it enacted comprehensive legislation to regulate the interstate market in a fungible commodity, Congress was acting well within its authority to "make all Laws which shall be necessary and proper" to "regulate Commerce among the several States." That the regulation ensnares some purely intrastate activity is of no moment. As we have done many times before, we refuse to excise individual components of that larger scheme.

To support their contrary submission, respondents rely heavily on two of our more recent Commerce Clause cases. In their myopic focus, they overlook the larger context of modern-era Commerce Clause jurisprudence preserved by those cases. Moreover, even in the narrow prism of respondents' creation, they read those cases far too broadly.

Those two cases, of course, are *Lopez* and *United States v. Morrison* (1994). As an initial matter, the statutory challenges at issue in those cases were markedly different from the challenge respondents pursue in the case at hand. Here, respondents ask us to excise individual applications of a concededly valid statutory scheme. In contrast, in both *Lopez* and *Morrison*, the parties asserted that a particular statute or provision fell outside Congress' commerce power in its entirety. This distinction is pivotal for we have often reiterated that "where the class of activities is regulated and that class is within the reach of federal power, the courts have no power to excise, as trivial, individual instances of the class."

At issue in *Lopez* was the validity of the Gun-Free School Zones Act of 1990, which was a brief, single-subject statute making it a crime for an individual to possess a gun in a school zone. The Act did not regulate any economic activity and did not contain any requirement that the possession of a gun have any connection to past interstate activity or a predictable impact on future commercial activity. Distinguishing our earlier cases holding that comprehensive regulatory statutes may be validly applied to local conduct that does not, when viewed in isolation, have a significant impact on interstate commerce, we held the statute invalid. We explained:

> Section 922(q) is a criminal statute that by its terms has nothing to do with commerce or any sort of economic enterprise, however broadly one might define those terms. Section 922(q) is not an essential part of a larger regulation of economic activity, in which the regulatory scheme could be undercut unless the intrastate activity were regulated. It cannot, therefore, be sustained under our cases upholding regulations of activities that arise out of or are connected with a commercial transaction, which viewed in the aggregate, substantially affects interstate commerce.

The statutory scheme that the Government is defending in this litigation is at the opposite end of the regulatory spectrum. As explained above, the CSA, enacted in 1970 as part of the Comprehensive Drug Abuse Prevention and Control Act, was a lengthy and detailed statute creating a comprehensive framework for regulating the production, distribution, and possession of five classes of "controlled substances." Our opinion in *Lopez* casts no doubt on the validity of such a program.

Nor does this Court's holding in *Morrison*. The Violence Against Women Act of 1994 created a federal civil remedy for the victims of gender-motivated crimes of violence. The remedy was enforceable in both state and federal courts, and generally depended on proof of the violation of a state law. Despite congressional findings that such crimes had an adverse impact on interstate commerce, we held the statute unconstitutional because, like the statute in *Lopez*, it did not regulate economic activity. We concluded that "the noneconomic, criminal nature of the conduct at issue was central to our decision" in *Lopez*, and that our prior cases had identified a clear pattern of analysis: "Where economic activity substantially affects interstate commerce, legislation regulating that activity will be sustained."

Unlike those at issue in *Lopez* and *Morrison*, the activities regulated by the CSA are quintessentially economic. The CSA is a statute that regulates the production, distribution, and consumption of commodities for which there is an established, and lucrative, interstate market. Prohibiting the intrastate possession or manufacture of an article of commerce is a rational (and commonly utilized) means of regulating commerce in that product. Because the CSA is a statute that directly regulates economic, commercial activity, our opinion in *Morrison* casts no doubt on its constitutionality.

SCALIA, J., concurring in the judgment.

I agree with the Court's holding that the Controlled Substances Act may validly be applied to respondents' cultivation, distribution, and possession of marijuana for personal, medicinal use. I write separately because my understanding of the doctrinal foundation on which that holding rests is, if not inconsistent with that of the Court, at least more nuanced.

Since *Perez v. United States* (1971), our cases have mechanically recited that the Commerce Clause permits congressional regulation of three categories: (1) the channels of interstate commerce; (2) the instrumentalities of interstate commerce, and persons or things in interstate commerce; and (3) activities that "substantially affect" interstate commerce. The first two categories are self-evident, since they are the ingredients of interstate commerce itself. *See Gibbons v. Ogden* (1824). The third category, however, is different in kind, and its recitation without explanation is misleading and incomplete.

It is *misleading* because, unlike the channels, instrumentalities, and agents of interstate commerce, activities that substantially affect interstate commerce are not themselves part of interstate commerce, and thus the power to regulate them cannot come from the Commerce Clause alone. Rather, as this Court has acknowledged since at least *United States v. Coombs* (1838), Congress's regulatory authority over intrastate activities that are not themselves part of interstate commerce (including activities that have a substantial effect on interstate commerce) derives from the Necessary and Proper Clause. And the category of "activities that substantially affect interstate commerce," is *incomplete* because the authority to enact laws necessary and proper for the regulation of interstate commerce is not limited to laws governing intrastate activities that substantially affect interstate commerce. Where necessary to make a regulation of interstate commerce effective, Congress may regulate even those intrastate activities that do not themselves substantially affect interstate commerce.

Today's principal dissent objects that, by permitting Congress to regulate activities necessary to effective interstate regulation, the Court reduces *Lopez* and *Morrison* to little "more than a drafting guide." I think that criticism unjustified. Unlike the power to regulate activities that have a substantial effect on interstate commerce, the power to enact laws enabling effective regulation of interstate commerce can only be exercised in conjunction with congressional regulation of an interstate market, and it extends only to those measures necessary to make the interstate regulation effective. As *Lopez* itself states, and the Court affirms today, Congress may regulate noneconomic intrastate activities only where the failure to do so "could undercut" its regulation of interstate commerce. This is not a power that threatens to obliterate the line between "what is truly national and what is truly local."

Lopez and *Morrison* affirm that Congress may not regulate certain "purely local" activity within the States based solely on the attenuated effect that such activity may have in the interstate market. But those decisions do not declare noneconomic intrastate activities to be categorically beyond the reach of the Federal Government. Neither case involved the power of Congress to exert control over intrastate activities in connection with a more comprehensive scheme of regulation; *Lopez* expressly disclaimed that it was such a case, and *Morrison* did not even discuss the possibility that it was.

And there are other restraints upon the Necessary and Proper Clause authority. As Chief Justice Marshall wrote in *McCulloch v. Maryland* (1819), even when the end is constitutional and legitimate, the means must be "appropriate" and "plainly adapted" to that end. Moreover, they may not be otherwise "prohibited" and must be "consistent with the letter and spirit of the constitution." These phrases are not merely hortatory. For example, cases such as *Printz v. United States* (1997) and *New York v. United States* (1992) affirm that a law is not "*proper* for carrying into Execution the Commerce Clause" "when it violates a constitutional principle of state sovereignty."

The application of these principles to the case before us is straightforward. In the CSA, Congress has undertaken to extinguish the interstate market in Schedule I controlled substances, including marijuana. The Commerce Clause unquestionably permits this. The power to regulate interstate commerce "extends not only to those regulations which aid, foster and protect the commerce, but embraces those which prohibit it."

By this measure, I think the regulation must be sustained. Not only is it impossible to distinguish "controlled substances manufactured and distributed intrastate" from "controlled substances manufactured and distributed interstate," but it hardly makes sense to speak in such terms. Drugs like marijuana are fungible commodities. As the Court explains, marijuana that is grown at home and possessed for personal use is never more than an instant from the interstate market—and this is so whether or not the possession is for medicinal use or lawful use under the laws of a particular State. Congress need not accept on faith that state law will be effective in maintaining a strict division between a lawful market for "medical" marijuana and the more general marijuana market.

Finally, neither respondents nor the dissenters suggest any violation of state sovereignty of the sort that would render this regulation "inappropriate"—except to argue that the CSA regulates an area typically left to state regulation. That is not enough to render federal regulation an inappropriate means. At bottom, respondents' state-sovereignty argument reduces to the contention that federal regulation of the activities permitted by California's Compassionate Use Act is not sufficiently necessary to be "necessary and proper" to Congress's regulation of the interstate market. I cannot agree.

O'CONNOR, J., dissenting.

We enforce the "outer limits" of Congress' Commerce Clause authority not for their own sake, but to protect historic spheres of state sovereignty from excessive federal encroachment and thereby to maintain the distribution of power fundamental to our federalist system of government. One of federalism's chief virtues, of course, is that it promotes innovation by allowing for the possibility that "a single courageous State may, if its citizens choose, serve as a laboratory; and try novel social and economic experiments without risk to the rest of the country."

This case exemplifies the role of States as laboratories. The States' core police powers have always included authority to define criminal law and to protect the health, safety, and welfare of their citizens. Exercising those powers, California (by ballot initiative and then by legislative codification) has come to its own conclusion about the difficult and sensitive question of whether marijuana should be available to relieve severe pain and suffering. Today the Court sanctions an application of the federal Controlled Substances Act that extinguishes that experiment, without any proof that the personal cultivation, possession, and use of marijuana for medicinal purposes, if economic activity in the first place, has a substantial effect on interstate commerce and is therefore an appropriate subject of federal regulation. In so doing, the Court announces a rule that gives Congress a perverse incentive to legislate broadly pursuant to the Commerce Clause—nestling questionable assertions of its authority into comprehensive regulatory schemes—rather than with precision.

In *Lopez*, our decision about whether gun possession in school zones substantially affected interstate commerce turned on four considerations. First, we observed that our "substantial effects" cases generally have upheld federal regulation of economic activity that affected interstate commerce, but that § 922(q) was a criminal statute having "nothing to do with commerce or any sort of economic enterprise." In this regard, we also noted that "§ 922(q) is not an essential part of a larger regulation of economic activity, in which the regulatory scheme could be undercut unless the intrastate activity were regulated. It cannot, therefore, be sustained under our cases upholding regulations of activities that arise out of or are connected with a commercial transaction, which viewed in the aggregate, substantially affects interstate commerce." Second, we noted that the statute contained no express jurisdictional requirement establishing its connection to interstate commerce.

Third, we found telling the absence of legislative findings about the regulated conduct's impact on interstate commerce. We explained that while express legislative findings are neither required nor, when provided, dispositive, findings "enable us to evaluate the legislative judgment that the activity in question substantially affects interstate commerce, even though no such substantial effect is visible to the naked eye." Finally, we rejected as too attenuated the Government's argument that firearm possession in school zones could result in violent crime which in turn could adversely affect the national economy. The Constitution, we said, does not tolerate reasoning that would "convert congressional authority under the Commerce Clause to a general police power of the sort retained by the States." Later in *Morrison*, we relied on the same four considerations to hold that § 40302 of the Violence Against Women Act of 1994 exceeded Congress' authority under the Commerce Clause.

In my view, the case before us is materially indistinguishable from *Lopez* and *Morrison* when the same considerations are taken into account.

We would do well to recall how James Madison, the father of the Constitution, described our system of joint sovereignty to the people of New York: "The powers delegated by the proposed Constitution to the federal government are few and defined. Those which are to remain in the State governments are numerous and indefinite. The powers reserved to the several States will extend to all the objects which, in the ordinary course of affairs, concern the lives, liberties, and properties of the people, and the internal order, improvement, and prosperity of the State." The Federalist No. 45 (Madison).

Relying on Congress' abstract assertions, the Court has endorsed making it a federal crime to grow small amounts of marijuana in one's own home for one's own medicinal use. This overreaching stifles an express choice by some States, concerned for the lives and liberties of their people, to regulate medical marijuana differently. If I were a California citizen, I would not have voted for the medical marijuana ballot initiative; if I were a California legislator I would not have supported the Compassionate Use Act. But whatever the wisdom of California's experiment with medical marijuana, the federalism principles that have driven our Commerce Clause cases require that room for experiment be protected in this case.

THOMAS, J., dissenting.

Respondents Diane Monson and Angel Raich use marijuana that has never been bought or sold, that has never crossed state lines, and that has had no demonstrable effect on the national market for marijuana. If Congress can regulate this under the Commerce Clause, then it can regulate virtually anything—and the Federal Government is no longer one of limited and enumerated powers.

Respondents' local cultivation and consumption of marijuana is not "Commerce among the several States." By holding that Congress may regulate activity that is neither interstate nor commerce under the Interstate Commerce Clause, the Court abandons any attempt to enforce the Constitution's limits on federal power. The majority supports this conclusion by invoking, without explanation, the Necessary and Proper Clause. Regulating respondents' conduct, however, is not "necessary and proper for carrying into Execution" Congress' restrictions on the interstate drug trade. Thus, neither the Commerce Clause nor the Necessary and Proper Clause grants Congress the power to regulate respondents' conduct.

The majority holds that Congress may regulate intrastate cultivation and possession of medical marijuana under the Commerce Clause, because such conduct arguably has a substantial effect on interstate commerce. The majority's decision is further proof that the "substantial effects" test is a "rootless and malleable standard" at odds with the constitutional design.

The majority's treatment of the substantial effects test is malleable, because the majority expands the relevant conduct. By defining the class at a high level of generality (as the intrastate manufacture and possession of marijuana), the majority overlooks that individuals authorized by state law to manufacture and possess medical marijuana exert no demonstrable effect on the interstate drug market. The majority ignores that whether a particular activity substantially affects interstate commerce—and thus comes within Congress' reach on the majority's approach—can turn on a number of objective factors, like state action or features of the regulated activity itself. For instance, here, if California and other States are effectively regulating medical marijuana users, then these users have little effect on the interstate drug trade.

The substantial effects test is easily manipulated for another reason. This Court has never held that Congress can regulate noneconomic activity that substantially affects interstate commerce. To evade even that modest restriction on federal power, the majority defines economic activity in the broadest possible terms as "the production, distribution, and consumption of commodities." This carves out a vast swath of activities that are subject to federal regulation. If the majority is to be taken seriously, the Federal Government may now regulate quilting bees, clothes drives, and potluck suppers throughout the 50 States. This makes a mockery of Madison's assurance to the people of New York that the "powers delegated" to the Federal Government are "few and defined," while those of the States are "numerous and indefinite."

The majority prevents States like California from devising drug policies that they have concluded provide much-needed respite to the seriously ill. It does so without any serious inquiry into the necessity for federal regulation or the propriety of "displacing state regulation in areas of traditional state concern." The majority's rush to embrace federal power "is especially unfortunate given the importance of showing respect for the sovereign States that comprise our Federal Union." Our federalist system, properly understood, allows California and a growing number of other States to decide for themselves how to safeguard the health and welfare of their citizens. I would affirm the judgment of the Court of Appeals.

NOTE

The U.S. Supreme Court has added other limits to the reach of the Commerce Clause and the Necessary and Proper Clause. In *NFIB v. Sebelius*, 567 U.S. 519, 520 (2012), the Court held that Congress's power to "*regulate* commerce" does not encompass the power to "compel individuals to *become* active in commerce by purchasing a product, on the ground that their failure to do so affects interstate commerce." At the same time, the Court rejected the argument that the individual mandate to purchase insurance could be justified under the Necessary and Proper Clause. It reasoned that the mandate "was not a 'proper' means for making those reforms effective," because it permitted "Congress to reach beyond the natural limit of its authority and draw within its regulatory scope those who otherwise would be outside of it."

ii. The Spending Power

The first clause of Article I, § 8, obliquely mentions a source of power that modern Congresses have used in many settings to enact significant legislation. It's the "spending power," placed in air quotes because the phrase does not appear in the U.S. Constitution. What the Constitution does say is that Congress has the power to "lay and collect Taxes, Duties, Imposts and Excises, to pay the Debts and provide for the common Defence and general Welfare of the United States." U.S. Const. art. I, § 8. As construed by the U.S. Supreme Court, this authority permits Congress to devote federal money to a variety of uses while imposing on the recipients of those federal funds a range of requirements. The Court has described the power as analogous to a "contract" between a State that receives the federal funds and the federal government that disburses the funds and imposes conditions on their use. Because the spending power operates like a take-it-or-leave-it contract, the terms and conditions of which each State may accept or reject, it permits Congress to regulate the States and the People in ways that the

Commerce Clause and other sources of authority would not allow it to do directly.

The Supreme Court's defining case about the scope of the Spending Power for many years was *South Dakota v. Dole*, 483 U.S. 203 (1987). It upheld a federal program that required States that accepted certain highway funds to raise their minimum drinking age to 21 or else lose a portion of the federal funds. The following case is a more recent and dramatic example of Congress linking substantial new conditions imposed on the States with massive amounts of federal funding—funding the States would have lost had they declined to embrace and implement the expansion of the Medicaid program that Congress sought to implement.

NFIB v. SEBELIUS
567 U.S. 519 (2012)

ROBERTS, C.J.

The second provision of the Affordable Care Act directly challenged here is the Medicaid expansion. Enacted in 1965, Medicaid offers federal funding to States to assist pregnant women, children, needy families, the blind, the elderly, and the disabled in obtaining medical care. In order to receive that funding, States must comply with federal criteria governing matters such as who receives care and what services are provided at what cost. By 1982 every State had chosen to participate in Medicaid. Federal funds received through the Medicaid program have become a substantial part of state budgets, now constituting over 10 percent of most States' total revenue.

The Affordable Care Act expands the scope of the Medicaid program and increases the number of individuals the States must cover. For example, the Act requires state programs to provide Medicaid coverage to adults with incomes up to 133 percent of the federal poverty level, whereas many States now cover adults with children only if their income is considerably lower, and do not cover childless adults at all. The Act increases federal funding to cover the States' costs in expanding Medicaid coverage, although States will bear a portion of the costs on their own. If a State does not comply with the Act's new coverage requirements, it may lose not only the federal funding for those requirements, but all of its federal Medicaid funds.

Along with their challenge to the individual mandate, the state plaintiffs in the Eleventh Circuit argued that the Medicaid expansion exceeds Congress's constitutional powers. The Court of Appeals unanimously held that the Medicaid expansion is a valid exercise of Congress's power under the Spending Clause. And the court rejected the States' claim that the threatened loss of all federal Medicaid funding violates the Tenth Amendment by coercing them into complying with the Medicaid expansion.

The States contend that the Medicaid expansion exceeds Congress's authority under the Spending Clause. They claim that Congress is coercing the States to adopt the changes it wants by threatening to withhold all of a State's Medicaid grants, unless the State accepts the new expanded funding and complies with the conditions that come with it. This, they argue, violates the basic principle that the "Federal Government may not compel the States to enact or administer a federal regulatory program."

There is no doubt that the Act dramatically increases state obligations under Medicaid. The current Medicaid program requires States to cover only certain discrete categories of needy individuals—pregnant women, children, needy families, the blind, the elderly, and the disabled. There is no mandatory coverage for most childless adults, and the States typically do not offer any such coverage. The States also enjoy considerable flexibility with respect to the coverage levels for parents of needy families. On average States cover only those unemployed parents who make less than 37 percent of the federal poverty level, and only those employed parents who make less than 63 percent of the poverty line.

The Medicaid provisions of the Affordable Care Act, in contrast, require States to expand their Medicaid programs by 2014 to cover *all* individuals under the age of 65 with incomes below 133 percent of the federal poverty line. The Act also establishes a new "essential health benefits" package, which States must provide to all new Medicaid recipients—a level sufficient to satisfy a recipient's obligations under the individual mandate. The Affordable Care Act provides that the Federal Government will pay 100 percent of the costs of covering these newly eligible individuals through 2016. In the following years, the federal payment level gradually decreases, to a minimum of 90 percent. In light of the expansion in coverage mandated by the Act, the Federal Government estimates that its Medicaid spending will increase by approximately $100 billion per year, nearly 40 percent above current levels.

The Spending Clause grants Congress the power "to pay the Debts and provide for the general Welfare of the United States." We have long recognized that Congress may use this power to grant federal funds to the States, and may condition such a grant upon the States' "taking certain actions that Congress could not require them to take." Such measures "encourage a State to regulate in a particular way, and influence a State's policy choices." The conditions imposed by Congress ensure that the funds are used by the States to "provide for the general Welfare" in the manner Congress intended.

At the same time, our cases have recognized limits on Congress's power under the Spending Clause to secure state compliance with federal objectives. "We have repeatedly characterized Spending Clause legislation as much in the nature of a *contract*." The legitimacy of Congress's exercise of the spending power "thus rests on whether the State voluntarily and knowingly accepts the terms of the contract." Respecting this limitation is critical to ensuring that Spending Clause legislation does not undermine the status of the States as independent sovereigns in our federal system. That system "rests on what might at first seem a counter-intuitive insight, that freedom is enhanced by the creation of two governments, not one." For this reason, "the Constitution has never been understood to confer upon Congress the ability to require the States to govern according to Congress' instructions." Otherwise the two-government system established by the Framers would give way to a system that vests power in one central government, and individual liberty would suffer.

Permitting the Federal Government to force the States to implement a federal program would threaten the political accountability key to our federal system. "Where the Federal Government directs the States to regulate, it may be state officials who will bear the brunt of public disapproval, while the federal officials who devised the regulatory program may remain insulated from the electoral ramifications of their decision." Spending Clause programs do not pose this danger when a State has a legitimate choice whether to accept the federal conditions in exchange for federal funds. In such a situation, state officials can fairly be held politically accountable for choosing to accept or refuse the federal offer. But when the State has no choice, the Federal Government can achieve its objectives without accountability, just as in *New York* and *Printz*. Indeed, this danger is heightened when Congress acts under the Spending Clause, because Congress can use that power to implement federal policy it could not impose directly under its enumerated powers.

Congress may attach appropriate conditions to federal taxing and spending programs to preserve its control over the use of federal funds. In the typical case we look to the States to defend their prerogatives by adopting "the simple expedient of not yielding" to federal blandishments when they do not want to embrace the federal policies as their own. The States are separate and independent sovereigns. Sometimes they have to act like it.

The States, however, argue that the Medicaid expansion is far from the typical case. They object that Congress has "crossed the line distinguishing encouragement from coercion" in the way it has structured the funding: Instead of simply refusing to grant the new funds to States that will not accept the new conditions, Congress has also threatened to withhold those States' existing Medicaid funds. The States claim that this threat serves no purpose other than to force unwilling States to sign up for the dramatic expansion in health care coverage effected by the Act.

Given the nature of the threat and the programs at issue here, we must agree. We have upheld Congress's authority to condition the receipt of funds on the States' complying with restrictions on the use of those funds, because that is the means by which Congress ensures that the funds are spent according to its view of the "general Welfare." Conditions that do not here govern the use of the funds, however, cannot be justified on that basis. When, for example, such conditions take the form of threats to terminate other significant independent grants, the conditions are properly viewed as a means of pressuring the States to accept policy changes.

In *South Dakota v. Dole* (1987), we considered a challenge to a federal law that threatened to withhold five percent of a State's federal highway funds if the State did not raise its drinking age to 21. The Court found that the condition was "directly related to one of the main purposes for which highway funds are expended—safe interstate travel." At the same time, the condition was not a restriction on how the highway funds—set aside for specific highway improvement and maintenance efforts—were to be used.

We accordingly asked whether "the financial inducement offered by Congress" was "so coercive as to pass the point at which pressure turns into compulsion." By "financial inducement" the Court meant the threat of losing five percent of highway funds; no new money was offered to the States to raise their drinking ages. We found that the inducement was not impermissibly coercive, because Congress was offering only "relatively mild encouragement to the States." We observed that "all South Dakota would lose if she adheres to her chosen course as to a suitable minimum drinking age is 5%" of her highway funds. In fact, the federal funds at stake constituted less than half of one percent of South Dakota's budget at the time. In consequence, "we concluded that the encouragement to state action was a valid use of the spending power." Whether to accept the drinking age change "remained the prerogative of the States not merely in theory but in fact."

In this case, the financial "inducement" Congress has chosen is much more than "relatively mild encouragement"—it is a gun to the head. Section 1396c of the Medicaid Act provides that if a State's Medicaid plan does not comply with the Act's requirements, the Secretary of Health and Human Services may declare that "further payments will not be made to the State." A State that opts out of the Affordable Care Act's expansion in health care coverage thus stands to lose not merely "a relatively small percentage" of its existing Medicaid funding, but *all* of it. Medicaid spending accounts for over 20 percent of the average State's total budget, with federal funds covering 50 to 83 percent of those costs. In addition, the States have developed intricate statutory and administrative regimes over the course of many decades to implement their objectives under existing Medicaid. It is easy to see how the *Dole* Court could conclude that the threatened loss of less than half of one percent of South Dakota's budget left that State with a "prerogative" to reject Congress's desired policy, "not merely in theory but in fact." The threatened loss of over 10 percent of a State's overall budget, in contrast, is economic dragooning that leaves the States with no real option but to acquiesce in the Medicaid expansion.

Here, the Government claims that the Medicaid expansion is properly viewed merely as a modification of the existing program because the States agreed that Congress could change the terms of Medicaid when they signed on in the first place. The Government observes that the Social Security Act, which includes the original Medicaid provisions, contains a clause expressly reserving "the right to alter, amend, or repeal any provision" of that statute. So it does. But "if Congress intends to impose a condition on the grant of federal moneys, it must do so unambiguously." A State confronted with statutory language reserving the right to "alter" or "amend" the pertinent provisions of the Social Security Act might reasonably assume that Congress was entitled to make adjustments to the Medicaid program as it developed. Congress has in fact done so, sometimes conditioning only the new funding, other times both old and new.

The Medicaid expansion, however, accomplishes a shift in kind, not merely degree. The original program was designed to cover medical services for four particular categories of the needy: the disabled, the blind, the elderly, and needy families with dependent children. Previous amendments to Medicaid eligibility merely altered and expanded the boundaries of these categories. Under the Affordable Care Act, Medicaid is transformed into a program to meet the health care needs of the entire nonelderly population with income below 133 percent of the poverty level. It is no longer a program to care for the neediest among us, but rather an element of a comprehensive national plan to provide universal health insurance coverage.

As we have explained, "though Congress's power to legislate under the spending power is broad, it does not include surprising participating States with post-acceptance or retroactive conditions." A State could hardly anticipate that Congress's reservation of the right to "alter" or "amend" the Medicaid program included the power to transform it so dramatically.

The Court in *Steward Machine Co. v. Collector of Internal Revenue* (1937) did not attempt to "fix the outermost line" where persuasion gives way to coercion. The Court found it "enough for present purposes that wherever the line may be, this statute is within it." We have no need to fix a line either. It is enough for today that wherever that line may be, this statute is surely beyond it. Congress may not simply "conscript state agencies into the national bureaucratic army," and that is what it is attempting to do with the Medicaid expansion.

b. Fourteenth Amendment Enforcement Powers

Section 5 of the Fourteenth Amendment grants Congress the power to enforce the Privileges or Immunities, Due Process, and Equal Protection Clauses of the Fourteenth Amendment by "appropriate legislation." The Supreme Court has wrestled with how expansive the Section 5 power is and what judicially definable limits confine it. The following case illustrates those challenges.

CITY OF BOERNE v. FLORES
521 U.S. 507 (1997)

KENNEDY, J.

A decision by local zoning authorities to deny a church a building permit was challenged under the Religious Freedom Restoration Act of 1993. The case calls into question the authority of Congress to enact RFRA. We conclude the statute exceeds Congress' power.

Situated on a hill in the city of Boerne, Texas, some 28 miles northwest of San Antonio, is St. Peter Catholic Church. Built in 1923, the church's structure replicates the mission style of the region's earlier history. The church seats about 230 worshippers, a number too small for its growing parish. Some 40 to 60 parishioners cannot be accommodated at some Sunday masses. In order to meet the needs of the congregation the Archbishop of San Antonio gave permission to the parish to plan alterations to enlarge the building.

A few months later, the Boerne City Council passed an ordinance authorizing the city's Historic Landmark Commission to prepare a preservation plan with proposed historic landmarks and districts. Under the ordinance, the commission must preapprove construction affecting historic landmarks or buildings in a historic district.

Soon afterwards, the Archbishop applied for a building permit so construction to enlarge the church could proceed. City authorities, relying on the ordinance and the designation of a historic district denied the application. The Archbishop relied upon RFRA as one basis for relief from the refusal to issue the permit. The District Court concluded that by enacting RFRA Congress exceeded the scope of its enforcement power under § 5 of the Fourteenth Amendment. The court certified its order for interlocutory appeal and the Fifth Circuit reversed, finding RFRA to be constitutional.

Congress enacted RFRA in direct response to the Court's decision in *Employment Division v. Smith* (1990). There, we considered a Free Exercise Clause claim brought by members of the Native American Church who were denied unemployment benefits when they lost their jobs because they had used peyote. Their practice was to ingest peyote for sacramental purposes, and they challenged an Oregon statute of general applicability which made use of the drug criminal. In evaluating the claim, we declined to apply the balancing test set forth in *Sherbert v. Verner* (1963), under which we would have asked whether Oregon's prohibition substantially burdened a religious practice and, if it did, whether the burden was justified by a compelling government interest. We stated:

> Government's ability to enforce generally applicable prohibitions of socially harmful conduct cannot depend on measuring the effects of a governmental action on a religious objector's spiritual development. To make an individual's obligation to obey such a law contingent upon the law's coincidence with his religious beliefs, except where the State's interest is compelling, contradicts both constitutional tradition and common sense.

The application of the *Sherbert* test, the *Smith* decision explained, would have produced an anomaly in the law, a constitutional right to ignore neutral laws of general applicability.

Four Members of the Court disagreed. They argued the law placed a substantial burden on the Native American Church members so that it could be upheld only if the law served a compelling state interest and was narrowly tailored to achieve that end. Justice O'Connor concluded Oregon had satisfied the test, while Justice Blackmun, joined by Justice Brennan and Justice Marshall, could see no compelling interest justifying the law's application to the members.

These points of constitutional interpretation were debated by Members of Congress in hearings and floor debates. Many criticized the Court's reasoning, and this disagreement resulted in the passage of RFRA.

RFRA prohibits "government" from "substantially burdening" a person's exercise of religion even if the burden results from a rule of general applicability unless the government can demonstrate the burden "(1) is in furtherance of a compelling governmental interest; and (2) is the least restrictive means of furthering that compelling governmental interest." The Act's mandate applies to any "branch, department, agency, instrumentality, and official (or other person acting under color of law) of the United States," as well as to any "State, or subdivision of a State." The Act's universal coverage is confirmed by the fact that RFRA "applies to all Federal and State law, and the implementation of that law, whether statutory or otherwise, and whether adopted before or after RFRA's enactment." In accordance with RFRA's usage of the term, we shall use "state law" to include local and municipal ordinances.

Under our Constitution, the Federal Government is one of enumerated powers. The judicial authority to determine the constitutionality of laws, in cases and controversies, is based on the premise that the "powers of the legislature are defined and limited; and that those limits may not be mistaken, or forgotten, the constitution is written." *Marbury v. Madison* (1803).

Congress relied on its Fourteenth Amendment enforcement power in enacting the most far-reaching and substantial of RFRA's provisions, those which impose its requirements on the States. The Fourteenth Amendment provides, in relevant part:

> Section 1. No State shall make or enforce any law which shall abridge the privileges or immunities of citizens of the United States; nor shall any State deprive any person of life, liberty, or property, without due process of law, nor deny to any person within its jurisdiction the equal protection of the laws.
>
> Section 5. The Congress shall have power to enforce, by appropriate legislation, the provisions of this article.

All must acknowledge that § 5 is "a positive grant of legislative power" to Congress. Legislation which deters or remedies constitutional violations can fall within the sweep of Congress' enforcement power even if in the process it prohibits conduct which is not itself unconstitutional and intrudes into "legislative spheres of autonomy previously reserved to the States."

It is also true, however, that "as broad as the congressional enforcement power is, it is not unlimited." In assessing the breadth of § 5's enforcement power, we begin with its text. Congress has been given the power "to enforce" the "provisions of this article." We agree with respondent, of course, that Congress can enact legislation under § 5 enforcing the constitutional right to the free exercise of religion. The "provisions of this article," to which § 5 refers, include the Due Process Clause of the Fourteenth Amendment. Congress' power to enforce the Free Exercise Clause follows from our holding in *Cantwell v. Connecticut* (1940) that the "fundamental concept of liberty embodied in the Fourteenth Amendment's Due Process Clause embraces the liberties guaranteed by the First Amendment."

Congress' power under § 5, however, extends only to "enforcing" the provisions of the Fourteenth Amendment. The Court has described this power as "remedial." The design of the Amendment and the text of § 5 are inconsistent with the suggestion that Congress has the power to decree the substance of the Fourteenth Amendment's restrictions on the States. Legislation which alters the meaning of the Free Exercise Clause cannot be said to be enforcing the Clause. Congress does not enforce a constitutional right by changing what the right is. It has been given the power "to enforce," not the power to determine what constitutes a constitutional violation. Were it not so, what Congress would be enforcing would no longer be, in any meaningful sense, the "provisions of the Fourteenth Amendment."

While the line between measures that remedy or prevent unconstitutional actions and measures that make a substantive change in the governing law is not easy to discern, and Congress must have wide latitude in determining where it lies, the distinction exists and must be observed. There must be a congruence and proportionality between the injury to be prevented or remedied and the means adopted to that end. Lacking such a connection, legislation may become substantive in operation and effect. History and our case law support drawing the distinction, one apparent from the text of the Amendment.

Respondent contends that RFRA is a proper exercise of Congress' remedial or preventive power. The Act, it is said, is a reasonable means of protecting the free exercise of religion as defined by *Smith*. It prevents and remedies laws which are enacted with the unconstitutional object of targeting religious beliefs and practices. To avoid the difficulty of proving such violations, it is said, Congress can simply invalidate any law which imposes a substantial burden on a religious practice unless it is justified by a compelling interest and is the least restrictive means of accomplishing that interest. If Congress can prohibit laws with discriminatory effects in order to prevent racial discrimination in violation of the Equal Protection Clause, then it can do the same, respondent argues, to promote religious liberty.

While preventive rules are sometimes appropriate remedial measures, there must be a congruence between the means used and the ends to be achieved. The appropriateness of remedial measures must be considered in light of the evil presented. Strong measures appropriate to address one harm may be an unwarranted response to another, lesser one.

A comparison between RFRA and the Voting Rights Act is instructive. In contrast to the record which confronted Congress and the Judiciary in the voting rights cases, RFRA's legislative record lacks examples of modern instances of generally applicable laws passed because of religious bigotry. The history of persecution in this country detailed in the hearings mentions no episodes occurring in the past 40 years. This lack of support in the legislative record, however, is not RFRA's most serious shortcoming. Judicial deference, in most cases, is based not on the state of the legislative record Congress compiles but "on due regard for the decision of the body constitutionally appointed to decide." As a general matter, it is for Congress to determine the method by which it will reach a decision.

Regardless of the state of the legislative record, RFRA cannot be considered remedial, preventive legislation, if those terms are to have any meaning. RFRA is so out of proportion to a supposed remedial or preventive object that it cannot be understood as responsive to, or designed to prevent, unconstitutional behavior. It appears, instead, to attempt a substantive change in constitutional protections. Preventive measures prohibiting certain types of laws may be appropriate when there is reason to believe that many of the laws affected by the congressional enactment have a significant likelihood of being unconstitutional. Remedial legislation under § 5 "should be adapted to the mischief and wrong which the Fourteenth Amendment was intended to provide against."

RFRA is not so confined. Sweeping coverage ensures its intrusion at every level of government, displacing laws and prohibiting official actions of almost every description and regardless of subject matter. RFRA's restrictions apply to every agency and official of the Federal, State, and local Governments. RFRA applies to all federal and state law, statutory or otherwise, whether adopted before or after its enactment. RFRA has no termination date or termination mechanism. Any law is subject to challenge at any time by any individual who alleges a substantial burden on his or her free exercise of religion.

The reach and scope of RFRA distinguish it from other measures passed under Congress' enforcement power, even in the area of voting rights. In *South Carolina v. Katzenbach* (1966), the challenged provisions were confined to those regions of the country where voting discrimination had been most flagrant, and affected a discrete class of state laws, *i.e.*, state voting laws. Furthermore, to ensure that the reach of the Voting Rights Act was limited to those cases in which constitutional violations were most likely (in order to reduce the possibility of overbreadth), the coverage under the Act would terminate "at the behest of States and political subdivisions in which the danger of substantial voting discrimination has not materialized during the preceding five years." The provisions restricting and banning literacy tests, upheld in *Katzenbach v. Morgan* (1966) and *Oregon v. Mitchell* (1970), attacked a particular type of voting qualification, one with a long history as a "notorious means to deny and abridge voting rights on racial grounds." In *City of Rome v. United States* (1980), the Court rejected a challenge to the constitutionality of a Voting Rights Act provision which required certain jurisdictions to submit changes in electoral practices to the Department of Justice for pre-implementation review. The requirement was placed only on jurisdictions with a history of intentional racial discrimination in voting. Like the provisions at issue in *South Carolina v. Katzenbach*, this provision permitted a covered jurisdiction to avoid preclearance requirements under certain conditions and, moreover, lapsed in seven years. This is not to say, of course, that § 5 legislation requires termination dates, geographic restrictions, or egregious predicates. Where, however, a congressional enactment pervasively prohibits constitutional state action in an effort to remedy or to prevent unconstitutional state action, limitations of this kind tend to ensure Congress' means are proportionate to ends legitimate under § 5.

The stringent test RFRA demands of state laws reflects a lack of proportionality or congruence between the means adopted and the legitimate end to be achieved. If an objector can show a substantial burden on his free exercise, the State must demonstrate a compelling governmental interest and show that the law is the least restrictive means of furthering its interest. Claims that a law substantially burdens someone's exercise of religion will often be difficult to contest. Requiring a State to demonstrate a compelling interest and show that it has adopted the least restrictive means of achieving that interest is the most demanding test known to constitutional law. If "compelling interest really means what it says, many laws will not meet the test. The test would open the prospect of constitutionally required religious exemptions from civic obligations of almost every conceivable kind." Laws valid under *Smith* would fall under RFRA without regard to whether they had the object of stifling or punishing free exercise. Even assuming RFRA would be interpreted in effect to mandate some lesser test, say, one equivalent to intermediate scrutiny, the statute nevertheless would require searching judicial scrutiny of state law with the attendant likelihood of invalidation. This is a considerable congressional intrusion into the States' traditional prerogatives and general authority to regulate for the health and welfare of their citizens.

The substantial costs RFRA exacts, both in practical terms of imposing a heavy litigation burden on the States and in terms of curtailing their traditional general regulatory power, far exceed any pattern or practice of unconstitutional conduct under the Free Exercise Clause as interpreted in *Smith*. Simply put, RFRA is not designed to identify and counteract state laws likely to be unconstitutional because of their treatment of religion. In most cases, the state laws to which RFRA applies are not ones which will have been motivated by religious bigotry.

When Congress acts within its sphere of power and responsibilities, it has not just the right but the duty to make its own informed judgment on the meaning and force of the Constitution. This has been clear from the early days of the Republic. In 1789, when a Member of the House of Representatives objected to a debate on the constitutionality of legislation based on the theory that "it would be officious" to consider the constitutionality of a measure that did not affect the House, James Madison explained that "it is incontrovertibly of as much importance to this branch of the Government as to any other, that the constitution should be preserved entire. It is our duty." Were it otherwise, we would not afford Congress the presumption of validity its enactments now enjoy.

Our national experience teaches that the Constitution is preserved best when each part of the Government respects both the Constitution and the proper actions and determinations of the other branches. When the Court has interpreted the Constitution, it has acted within the province of the Judicial Branch, which embraces the duty to say what the law is. When the political branches of the Government act against the background of a judicial interpretation of the Constitution already issued, it must be understood that in later cases and controversies the Court will treat its precedents with the respect due them under settled principles, including *stare decisis*, and contrary expectations must be disappointed. RFRA was designed to control cases and controversies, such as the one before us; but as the provisions of the federal statute here invoked are beyond congressional authority, it is this Court's precedent, not RFRA, which must control.

It is for Congress in the first instance to "determine whether and what legislation is needed to secure the guarantees of the Fourteenth Amendment," and its conclusions are entitled to much deference. Congress' discretion is not unlimited, however, and the courts retain the power, as they have since *Marbury v. Madison*, to determine if Congress has exceeded its authority under the Constitution. Broad as the power of Congress is under the Enforcement Clause of the Fourteenth Amendment, RFRA contradicts vital principles necessary to maintain separation of powers and the federal balance. The judgment of the Court of Appeals sustaining the Act's constitutionality is reversed.

2. Exclusive State Powers

a. Organization of State Governments

The U.S. Constitution does not purport to limit or direct the organization of state governments once admitted to the Union, save through the Article IV promise that the United States shall guarantee to every State a "Republican Form" of government. But the Court, in cases like *Luther v. Borden* (1849), excerpted below in section C of this chapter, has left it to Congress and the President to enforce the guarantee, if it is to be enforced at all. The Supreme Court also has not required the state governments to follow federal separation of powers principles. So it is that a State may structure its legislative branch however it wishes (such as by creating a unicameral legislature), give its Governor a variety of powers denied the President of the United States, (such as by giving its Governor a line item veto), and generally structure its state court system as it wishes (such as by using elections to select state court judges). All in all, the federal Constitution has little to say about the organization of state governments and the powers given the various branches and officials or for that matter the powers given to cities and other local governments.

b. Traditional Police Powers

The States, unlike the federal government, are the repository of traditional police powers, understood as the general authority to enact laws relating to the public health, safety, welfare, and morals. In talking about the States' regulatory authority, then, the constitutional question generally is not whether they have the authority to pass a law but whether a state constitutional guarantee prohibits it. By contrast, Congress must point to an enumerated power in the U.S. Constitution before it has any power to regulate.

The result is that the States, not the federal government, are responsible for most criminal law, domestic relations law, tort law, property law, contract law, commercial law, and many other areas of law. No doubt, the U.S. Supreme Court's expansion of the commerce power has led Congress to regulate in areas once thought exclusively or largely the province of the States. But even when that has happened, as with criminal law for example, the bulk of the law in this area remains state law and the bulk of the criminal prosecutions remain state prosecutions. One measure of the difference in state regulatory and federal regulatory authority is the number of cases filed in each system. For every case filed in a federal court, there are scores of cases filed in the state courts. *See* Jeffrey S. Sutton, *A Response to Goodwin Liu*, 128 Yale L.J. Forum 936, 942 (2019) (responding to Goodwin Liu, *State Courts and Constitutional Structure*, 128 Yale L.J. 1174 (2019)).

3. Overlapping and Shared Powers

a. Individual Liberties

The framers of the early state constitutions were the architects of the first individual liberties in this country. The revolutionary era state constitutions in turn served as the models for the Bill of Rights that James Madison introduced in the first session of Congress. At the outset, and indeed for roughly the first 150 years of our history, each type of Constitution—the federal and the state—generally limited just one type of government, with a given state constitution limiting the government of that State, and with the federal constitution limiting the federal government. Just as the Commerce Clause started out as creating exclusive spheres of regulatory power, so did most of the early state and federal constitutional individual rights guarantees. And just as the Court eventually construed the Commerce Clause to permit overlapping regulatory authority, so the same has happened with respect to many individual rights.

The creation and growth of the federal incorporation doctrine transformed individual-rights litigation. The doctrine relies on the Due Process Clause of the Fourteenth Amendment and its application to state conduct to "incorporate" against the States nearly all of the individual liberties protected by the federal Bill of Rights, save for the right to an indictment by a grand jury. Long ago, the Supreme Court held that the Bill of Rights by its terms restricts only the federal government. But following the Civil War, Reconstruction, and the adoption of the Fourteenth Amendment, the argument was made that "due process of law" necessarily should include the protections of the Bill of Rights, for example liberties like freedom of speech and religion, the right to bear arms, freedom from unreasonable searches and seizures, the privilege against self-incrimination, the right to counsel and to a jury trial in criminal cases, and freedom from cruel and unusual punishments. Over time, the Supreme Court has held that nearly all of the Bill of Rights' protections apply to the States. *See Ramos v. Louisiana*, 140 S. Ct. 1390 (2020) (incorporating the Sixth Amendment's requirement that criminal jury verdicts be unanimous); *Timbs v. Indiana*, 139 S. Ct. 682 (2019) (incorporating the Eighth Amendment's Excessive Fines Clause); *McDonald v. Chicago*, 561 U.S. 742 (2010) (incorporating the Second Amendment); *id.* at 764 n.12 (noting that the Court has already incorporated "almost all of" the rights guaranteed by the First, Fourth, Fifth, Sixth, and Eighth Amendments).

When a Bill of Rights protection applies to the States through the Due Process Clause, the Supremacy Clause prevents the States from giving such liberties *less* protection than the federal provision requires if an individual brings a federal claim. That reality, however, generally does not limit the States in interpreting their own constitutional provisions that may be analogous, or identical, to federal provisions. They may interpret the state provisions to provide *more or less* protection than the counterpart federal guarantee, as we elaborate in Chapter III.

b. Criminal Law

The States need no justification for enacting criminal laws other than that such laws serve the general health, welfare, safety and morals of their citizens. It is a core aspect of the States' traditional police powers to enact and enforce such laws. The federal government, by contrast, is not given any general power to enact criminal laws. It instead must point to powers in Article I, § 8 or elsewhere that justify the creation of federal crimes or that in combination with the Necessary and Proper Clause will support such legislation. Perhaps the most frequently invoked federal power to justify the enactment of criminal laws is the power of Congress to regulate commerce "among the several States." Expansive federal use of this power has caused some controversy and resulted in some important Supreme Court decisions in recent years. An important example follows.

UNITED STATES v. LOPEZ
514 U.S. 549 (1995)

REHNQUIST, C.J.

In the Gun-Free School Zones Act of 1990, Congress made it a federal offense "for any individual knowingly to possess a firearm at a place that the individual knows, or has reasonable cause to believe, is a school zone." The Act neither regulates a commercial activity nor contains a requirement that the possession be connected in any way to interstate commerce. We hold that the Act exceeds the authority of Congress "to regulate Commerce among the several States."

On March 10, 1992, respondent, who was then a 12th-grade student, arrived at Edison High School in San Antonio, Texas, carrying a concealed .38-caliber handgun and five bullets. Acting upon an anonymous tip, school authorities confronted respondent, who admitted that he was carrying the weapon. He was arrested and charged under Texas law with firearm possession on school premises. The next day, the state charges were dismissed after federal agents charged respondent by complaint with violating the Gun-Free School Zones Act of 1990.

A federal grand jury indicted respondent on one count of knowing possession of a firearm at a school zone, in violation of § 922(q). Respondent moved to dismiss his federal indictment on the ground that § 922(q) "is unconstitutional as it is beyond the power of Congress to legislate control over our public schools." The District Court denied the motion, concluding that § 922(q) "is a constitutional exercise of Congress' well-defined power to regulate activities in and affecting commerce, and the business of elementary, middle and high schools affects interstate commerce." The District Court found Lopez guilty of violating § 922(q), and sentenced him to six months' imprisonment and two years' supervised release. The Court of Appeals reversed respondent's conviction holding that the statute is invalid as beyond the power of Congress under the Commerce Clause.

We start with first principles. The Constitution creates a Federal Government of enumerated powers. As James Madison wrote: "The powers delegated by the proposed Constitution to the federal government are few and defined. Those which are to remain in the State governments are numerous and indefinite." The Federalist No. 45 (Madison). This constitutionally mandated division of authority "was adopted by the Framers to ensure protection of our fundamental liberties." The commerce power "is the power to regulate; that is, to prescribe the rule by which commerce is to be governed. This power, like all others vested in Congress, is complete in itself, may be exercised to its utmost extent, and acknowledges no limitations, other than are prescribed in the constitution."

Even the Court's modern-era precedents, which have expanded congressional power under the Commerce Clause, confirm that this power is subject to outer limits. We have identified three broad categories of activity that Congress may regulate under its commerce power. First, Congress may regulate the use of the channels of interstate commerce. Second, Congress is empowered to regulate and protect the instrumentalities of interstate commerce, or persons or things in interstate commerce, even though the threat may come only from intrastate activities. Finally, Congress' commerce authority includes the power to regulate those activities having a substantial relation to interstate commerce, *i.e.*, those activities that substantially affect interstate commerce.

We now turn to consider the power of Congress, in the light of this framework, to enact § 922(q). The first two categories of authority may be quickly disposed of: § 922(q) is not a regulation of the use of the channels of interstate commerce, nor is it an attempt to prohibit the interstate transportation of a commodity through the channels of commerce; nor can § 922(q) be justified as a regulation by which Congress has sought to protect an instrumentality of interstate commerce or a thing in interstate commerce. Thus, if § 922(q) is to be sustained, it must be under the third category as a regulation of an activity that substantially affects interstate commerce.

First, § 922(q) is a criminal statute that by its terms has nothing to do with "commerce" or any sort of economic enterprise, however broadly one might define those terms. Section 922(q) is not an essential part of a larger regulation of economic activity, in which the regulatory scheme could be undercut unless the intrastate activity were regulated. It cannot, therefore, be sustained under our cases upholding regulations of activities that arise out of or are connected with a commercial transaction, which viewed in the aggregate, substantially affects interstate commerce.

Second, § 922(q) contains no jurisdictional element which would ensure, through case-by-case inquiry, that the firearm possession in question affects interstate commerce.

Third, although as part of our independent evaluation of constitutionality under the Commerce Clause we of course consider legislative findings, and indeed even congressional committee findings, regarding effect on interstate commerce, the Government concedes that "neither the statute nor its legislative history contains express congressional findings regarding the effects upon interstate commerce of gun possession in a school zone." We agree with the Government that Congress normally is not required to make formal findings as to the substantial burdens that an activity has on interstate commerce. But to the extent that congressional findings would enable us to evaluate the legislative judgment that the activity in question substantially affected interstate commerce, even though no such substantial effect was visible to the naked eye, they are lacking here.

The Government's essential contention, *in fine*, is that we may determine here that § 922(q) is valid because possession of a firearm in a local school zone does indeed substantially affect interstate commerce. The Government argues that possession of a firearm in a school zone may result in violent crime and that violent crime can be expected to affect the functioning of the national economy in two ways. First, the costs of violent crime are substantial, and, through the mechanism of insurance, those costs are spread throughout the population. Second, violent crime reduces the willingness of individuals to travel to areas within the country that are perceived to be unsafe. The Government also argues that the presence of guns in schools poses a substantial threat to the educational process by threatening the learning environment. A handicapped educational process, in turn, will result in a less productive citizenry. That, in turn, would have an adverse effect on the Nation's economic well-being.

We pause to consider the implications of the Government's arguments. The Government admits, under its "costs of crime" reasoning, that Congress could regulate not only all violent crime, but all activities that might lead to violent crime, regardless of how tenuously they relate to interstate commerce. Similarly, under the Government's "national productivity" reasoning, Congress could regulate any activity that it found was related to the economic productivity of individual citizens: family law (including marriage, divorce, and child custody), for example. Under the theories that the Government presents it is difficult to perceive any limitation on federal power, even in areas such as criminal law enforcement or education where States historically have been sovereign. Thus, if we were to accept the Government's arguments, we are hard pressed to posit any activity by an individual that Congress is without power to regulate.

Although Justice Breyer argues that acceptance of the Government's rationales would not authorize a general federal police power, he is unable to identify any activity that the States may regulate but Congress may not. Justice Breyer posits that there might be some limitations on Congress' commerce power, such as family law or certain aspects of education. These suggested limitations, when viewed in light of the dissent's expansive analysis, are devoid of substance.

For instance, if Congress can, pursuant to its Commerce Clause power, regulate activities that adversely affect the learning environment, then, *a fortiori*, it also can regulate the educational process directly. Congress could determine that a school's curriculum has a "significant" effect on the extent of classroom learning. As a result, Congress could mandate a federal curriculum for local elementary and secondary schools because what is taught in local schools has a significant "effect on classroom learning," and that, in turn, has a substantial effect on interstate commerce.

Admittedly, a determination whether an intrastate activity is commercial or noncommercial may in some cases result in legal uncertainty. But so long as Congress's powers are interpreted as having judicially enforceable outer limits, legislation under the Commerce Clause always will engender "legal uncertainty."

These are not precise formulations, and in the nature of things they cannot be. But we think they point the way to a correct decision of this case. The possession of a gun in a local school zone is in no sense an economic activity that might, through repetition elsewhere, substantially affect any sort of interstate commerce. Respondent was a local student at a local school; there is no indication that he had recently moved in interstate commerce, and there is no requirement that his possession of the firearm have any concrete tie to interstate commerce.

To uphold the Government's contentions here, we would have to pile inference upon inference in a manner that would bid fair to convert congressional authority under the Commerce Clause to a general police power of the sort retained by the States. Admittedly, some of our prior cases have taken long steps down that road, giving great deference to congressional action. The broad language in these opinions has suggested the possibility of additional expansion, but we decline here to proceed any further. To do so would require us to conclude that the Constitution's enumeration of powers does not presuppose something not enumerated, and that there never will be a distinction between what is truly national and what is truly local. This we are unwilling to do.

c. Interstate Compacts – Article I, § 10, cl. 3

An interesting example of overlapping federal and state powers is found in Article I, § 10, cl. 3, which declares that "No State shall, without the Consent of Congress enter into any Agreement or Compact with another State." States, of course, do enter into agreements with each other, and sometimes such agreements are essential, for example in resolving a boundary dispute or allocating water rights in interstate rivers. Congress must give its blessing to such agreements and thus has some leverage to influence the nature and substance of such agreements. Disputes under such compacts sometimes are resolved in original jurisdiction proceedings in the U.S. Supreme Court. *See, e.g.*, *Kansas v. Nebraska and Colorado*, 135 S. Ct. 1042 (2015) (resolving disputed issues between States under the Republican River Compact).

C. LIMITATIONS ON FEDERAL POWER

1. The Anti-Commandeering Principle

PRINTZ v. UNITED STATES
521 U.S. 898 (1997)

SCALIA, J.

The question presented in these cases is whether certain interim provisions of the Brady Handgun Violence Prevention Act, commanding state and local law enforcement officers to conduct background checks on prospective handgun purchasers and to perform certain related tasks, violate the Constitution.

The Gun Control Act of 1968 (GCA), establishes a detailed federal scheme governing the distribution of firearms. It prohibits firearms dealers from transferring handguns to any person under 21, not resident in the dealer's State, or prohibited by state or local law from purchasing or possessing firearms. It also forbids possession of a firearm by, and transfer of a firearm to, convicted felons, fugitives from justice, unlawful users of controlled substances, persons adjudicated as mentally defective or committed to mental institutions, aliens unlawfully present in the United States, persons dishonorably discharged from the Armed Forces, persons who have renounced their citizenship, and persons who have been subjected to certain restraining orders or been convicted of a misdemeanor offense involving domestic violence.

In 1993, Congress amended the GCA by enacting the Brady Act. The Act requires the Attorney General to establish a national instant background-check system by November 30, 1998, and immediately puts in place certain interim provisions until that system becomes operative. Under the interim provisions, a firearms dealer who proposes to transfer a handgun must first: (1) receive from the transferee a statement (the Brady Form), containing the name, address, and date of birth of the proposed transferee along with a sworn statement that the transferee is not among any of the classes of prohibited purchasers; (2) verify the identity of the transferee by examining an identification document; and (3) provide the "chief law enforcement officer" (CLEO) of the transferee's residence with notice of the contents (and a copy) of the Brady Form. With some exceptions, the dealer must then wait five business days before consummating the sale, unless the CLEO earlier notifies the dealer that he has no reason to believe the transfer would be illegal.

The Brady Act creates two significant alternatives to the foregoing scheme. A dealer may sell a handgun immediately if the purchaser possesses a state handgun permit issued after a background check, or if state law provides for an instant background check. In States that have not rendered one of these alternatives applicable to all gun purchasers, CLEOs are required to perform certain duties. When a CLEO receives the required notice of a proposed transfer from the firearms dealer, the CLEO must "make a reasonable effort to ascertain within 5 business days whether receipt or possession would be in violation of the law, including research in whatever State and local recordkeeping systems are available and in a national system designated by the Attorney General." The Act does not require the CLEO to take any particular action if he determines that a pending transaction would be unlawful; he may notify the firearms dealer to that effect, but is not required to do so. If, however, the CLEO notifies a gun dealer that a prospective purchaser is ineligible to receive a handgun, he must, upon request, provide the would-be purchaser with a written statement of the reasons for that determination. Moreover, if the CLEO does not discover any basis for objecting to the sale, he must destroy any records in his possession relating to the transfer, including his copy of the Brady Form. Under a separate provision of the GCA, any person who "knowingly violates the section of the GCA amended by the Brady Act shall be fined under this title, imprisoned for not more than 1 year, or both."

Petitioners Jay Printz and Richard Mack, the CLEOs for Ravalli County, Montana, and Graham County, Arizona, respectively, filed separate actions challenging the constitutionality of the Brady Act's interim provisions. In each case, the District Court held that the provision requiring CLEOs to perform background checks was unconstitutional, but concluded that that provision was severable from the remainder of the Act, effectively leaving a voluntary background-check system in place. A divided panel of the Court of Appeals for the Ninth Circuit reversed, finding none of the Brady Act's interim provisions to be unconstitutional.

The Brady Act purports to direct state law enforcement officers to participate, albeit only temporarily, in the administration of a federally enacted regulatory scheme. Petitioners here object to being pressed into federal service, and contend that congressional action compelling state officers to execute federal laws is unconstitutional. Because there is no constitutional text speaking to this precise question, the answer to the CLEOs' challenge must be sought in historical understanding and practice, in the structure of the Constitution, and in the jurisprudence of this Court.

The Government observes that statutes enacted by the first Congresses required state courts to record applications for citizenship, to transmit abstracts of citizenship applications and other naturalization records to the Secretary of State, and to register aliens seeking naturalization and issue certificates of registry. Other statutes of that era apparently or at least arguably required state courts to perform functions such as resolving controversies between a captain and the crew of his ship concerning the seaworthiness of the vessel, hearing the claims of slave owners who had apprehended fugitive slaves and issuing certificates authorizing the slave's forced removal to the State from which he had fled, taking proof of the claims of Canadian refugees who had assisted the United States during the Revolutionary War, and ordering the deportation of alien enemies in times of war.

These early laws establish, at most, that the Constitution was originally understood to permit imposition of an obligation on state *judges* to enforce federal prescriptions, insofar as those prescriptions related to matters appropriate for the judicial power. That assumption was perhaps implicit in one of the provisions of the Constitution, and was explicit in another. In accord with the so-called Madisonian Compromise, Article III, § 1, established only a Supreme Court, and made the creation of lower federal courts optional with the Congress-even though it was obvious that the Supreme Court alone could not hear all federal cases throughout the United States. And the Supremacy Clause announced that "the Laws of the United States shall be the supreme Law of the Land; and the Judges in every State shall be bound thereby." It is understandable why courts should have been viewed distinctively in this regard; unlike legislatures and executives, they applied the law of other sovereigns all the time. The principle underlying so-called "transitory" causes of action was that laws which operated elsewhere created obligations in justice that courts of the forum State would enforce. The Constitution itself, in the Full Faith and Credit Clause, generally required such enforcement with respect to obligations arising in other States.

We do not think the early statutes imposing obligations on state courts imply a power of Congress to impress the state executive into its service. Indeed, it can be argued that the numerousness of these statutes, contrasted with the utter lack of statutes imposing obligations on the States' executive (notwithstanding the attractiveness of that course to Congress), suggests an assumed *absence* of such power.

It is incontestable that the Constitution established a system of "dual sovereignty." *Gregory v. Ashcroft* (1991). Although the States surrendered many of their powers to the new Federal Government, they retained "a residuary and inviolable sovereignty." The Federalist No. 39. This is reflected throughout the Constitution's text, including (to mention only a few examples) the prohibition on any involuntary reduction or combination of a State's territory; the Judicial Power Clause, and the Privileges and Immunities Clause, which speak of the "Citizens" of the States; the amendment provision, Article V, which requires the votes of three-fourths of the States to amend the Constitution; and the Guarantee Clause, which "presupposes the continued existence of the states and those means and instrumentalities which are the creation of their sovereign and reserved rights." Residual state sovereignty was also implicit, of course, in the Constitution's conferral upon Congress of not all governmental powers, but only discrete, enumerated ones, which implication was rendered express by the Tenth Amendment's assertion that "the powers not delegated to the United States by the Constitution, nor prohibited by it to the States, are reserved to the States respectively, or to the people."

This separation of the two spheres is one of the Constitution's structural protections of liberty. The power of the Federal Government would be augmented immeasurably if it were able to impress into its service—and at no cost to itself—the police officers of the 50 States.

The dissent perceives a simple answer in that portion of Article VI which requires that "all executive and judicial Officers, both of the United States and of the several States, shall be bound by Oath or Affirmation, to support this Constitution," arguing that by virtue of the Supremacy Clause this makes "not only the Constitution, but every law enacted by Congress as well," binding on state officers, including laws requiring state-officer enforcement. The Supremacy Clause, however, makes "Law of the Land" only "Laws of the United States which shall be made in Pursuance of the Constitution," so the Supremacy Clause merely brings us back to the question discussed earlier, whether laws conscripting state officers violate state sovereignty and are thus not in accord with the Constitution.

Finally, and most conclusively in the present litigation, we turn to the prior jurisprudence of this Court. When we were at last confronted squarely with a federal statute that unambiguously required the States to enact or administer a federal regulatory program, our decision should have come as no surprise. At issue in *New York v. United States* (1992) were the so-called "take title" provisions of the Low-Level Radioactive Waste Policy Amendments Act of 1985, which required States either to enact legislation providing for the disposal of radioactive waste generated within their borders, or to take title to, and possession of, the waste–effectively requiring the States either to legislate pursuant to Congress's directions, or to implement an administrative solution. We concluded that Congress could constitutionally require the States to do neither. "The Federal Government," we held, "may not compel the States to enact or administer a federal regulatory program."

The Government contends that *New York* is distinguishable on the following ground: Unlike the "take title" provisions invalidated there, the background-check provision of the Brady Act does not require state legislative or executive officials to make policy, but instead issues a final directive to state CLEOs.

The dissent makes no attempt to defend the Government's basis for distinguishing *New York*, but instead advances what seems to us an even more implausible theory. The Brady Act, the dissent asserts, is different from the "take title" provisions invalidated in *New York* because the former is addressed to individuals—namely, CLEOs—while the latter were directed to the State itself. That is certainly a difference, but it cannot be a constitutionally significant one. While the Brady Act is directed to "individuals," it is directed to them in their official capacities as state officers; it controls their actions, not as private citizens, but as the agents of the State. To say that the Federal Government cannot control the State, but can control all of its officers, is to say nothing of significance. By resorting to this, the dissent not so much distinguishes *New York* as disembowels it.

We held in *New York* that Congress cannot compel the States to enact or enforce a federal regulatory program. Today we hold that Congress cannot circumvent that prohibition by conscripting the State's officers directly. The Federal Government may neither issue directives requiring the States to address particular problems, nor command the States' officers, or those of their political subdivisions, to administer or enforce a federal regulatory program. It matters not whether policymaking is involved, and no case-by-case weighing of the burdens or benefits is necessary; such commands are fundamentally incompatible with our constitutional system of dual sovereignty.

NOTE

The U.S. Supreme Court has since held that, under the anti-commandeering doctrine, Congress could not prohibit States from legalizing sports betting. *See Murphy v. Nat'l Collegiate Athletic Ass'n*, 138 S. Ct. 1461 (2018). The Professional and Amateur Sports Protection Act made it illegal for a State to "authorize by law" gambling based on sporting events, with a narrow exception for laws already in effect at, or adopted within one year of, the statute's enactment in 1992. The Act did not, however, make sports betting itself illegal. New Jersey legalized certain sports betting schemes in specific locations across the state in 2012, running afoul of the law. The Court explained that enjoining New Jersey's new betting scheme was unconstitutional because the Act's operative provision "unequivocally dictates what a state legislature may and may not do" in violation of the anti-commandeering principle. The Court rejected the argument that the Act simply (and validly) preempted state law. Because the federal government did not itself regulate the conduct in question, it could not force the States to do so in its place.

2. Immunity from Lawsuits under Federal Law

The Eleventh Amendment provides that "the Judicial power of the United States shall not be construed to extend to any suit in law or equity, commenced or prosecuted against one of the United States by Citizens of another State, or by Citizens or Subjects of any Foreign State." Although there is general agreement that this amendment was a reaction to the Supreme Court's decision in *Chisholm v. Georgia*, 2 U.S. 419 (1793), permitting a suit by a citizen of South Carolina to proceed in federal court over Georgia's objections, there is disagreement about the scope of the constitutional immunity the Eleventh Amendment recognizes.

The Supreme Court long ago decided that the immunity is not limited to the diversity jurisdiction language of the amendment, and instead protects the States more broadly. *See Hans v. Louisiana*, 134 U.S. 1 (1890) (holding that the immunity also bars a citizen from suing her own State). In recent years, the Court has held that Congress cannot abrogate the States' immunity from suit using its powers under Article I, irrespective of whether the suit is brought in federal court, *Seminole Tribe of Fla.* v. *Florida*, 517 U.S. 44 (1996), or state court, *Alden v. Maine*, 527 U.S. 706 (1999). More recently, the Court held that, as a matter of federal constitutional law, States are immune from a lawsuit in the courts of another State. *See Franchise Tax Bd. of Cal. v. Hyatt*, 139 S. Ct. 1485 (2019).

ALDEN v. MAINE
527 U.S. 706 (1999)

KENNEDY, J.

In 1992, petitioners, a group of probation officers, filed suit against their employer, the State of Maine, in the United States District Court for the District of Maine. The officers alleged the State had violated the overtime provisions of the Fair Labor Standards Act of 1938 (FLSA) and sought compensation and liquidated damages. We hold that the powers delegated to Congress under Article I of the United States Constitution do not include the power to subject nonconsenting States to private suits for damages in state courts. We decide as well that the State of Maine has not consented to suits for overtime pay and liquidated damages under the FLSA.

The Eleventh Amendment makes explicit reference to the States' immunity from suits "commenced or prosecuted against one of the United States by Citizens of another State, or by Citizens or Subjects of any Foreign State." We have, as a result, sometimes referred to the States' immunity from suit as "Eleventh Amendment immunity." The phrase is convenient shorthand but something of a misnomer, for the sovereign immunity of the States neither derives from, nor is limited by, the terms of the Eleventh Amendment. Rather, as the Constitution's structure, its history, and the authoritative interpretations by this Court make clear, the States' immunity from suit is a fundamental aspect of the sovereignty which the States enjoyed before the ratification of the Constitution, and which they retain today (either literally or by virtue of their admission into the Union upon an equal footing with the other States) except as altered by the plan of the Convention or certain constitutional Amendments.

Although the Constitution establishes a National Government with broad, often plenary authority over matters within its recognized competence, the founding document "specifically recognizes the States as sovereign entities." Various textual provisions of the Constitution assume the States' continued existence and active participation in the fundamental processes of governance. The limited and enumerated powers granted to the Legislative, Executive, and Judicial Branches of the National Government, moreover, underscore the vital role reserved to the States by the constitutional design. Any doubt regarding the constitutional role of the States as sovereign entities is removed by the Tenth Amendment, which, like the other provisions of the Bill of Rights, was enacted to allay lingering concerns about the extent of the national power. The Amendment confirms the promise implicit in the original document: "The powers not delegated to the United States by the Constitution, nor prohibited by it to the States, are reserved to the States respectively, or to the people."

The federal system established by our Constitution preserves the sovereign status of the States in two ways. First, it reserves to them a substantial portion of the Nation's primary sovereignty, together with the dignity and essential attributes inhering in that status. The States "form distinct and independent portions of the supremacy, no more subject, within their respective spheres, to the general authority than the general authority is subject to them, within its own sphere." The Federalist No. 39.

Second, even as to matters within the competence of the National Government, the constitutional design secures the founding generation's rejection of "the concept of a central government that would act upon and through the States" in favor of "a system in which the State and Federal Governments would exercise concurrent authority over the people who were, in Hamilton's words, the only proper objects of government." In this the Founders achieved a deliberate departure from the Articles of Confederation: Experience under the Articles had "exploded on all hands" the "practicality of making laws, with coercive sanctions, for the States as political bodies."

The States thus retain "a residuary and inviolable sovereignty." The Federalist No. 39. They are not relegated to the role of mere provinces or political corporations, but retain the dignity, though not the full authority, of sovereignty.

The Court has been consistent in interpreting the adoption of the Eleventh Amendment as conclusive evidence "that the decision in *Chisholm* was contrary to the well-understood meaning of the Constitution," and that the views expressed by Hamilton, Madison, and Marshall during the ratification debates, and by Justice Iredell in his dissenting opinion in *Chisholm v. Georgia* (1793), reflect the original understanding of the Constitution. In accordance with this understanding, we have recognized a "presumption that no anomalous and unheard-of proceedings or suits were intended to be raised up by the Constitution—anomalous and unheard of when the constitution was adopted." As a consequence, we have looked to "history and experience, and the established order of things," rather than "adhering to the mere letter" of the Eleventh Amendment, in determining the scope of the States' constitutional immunity from suit.

Following this approach, the Court has upheld States' assertions of sovereign immunity in various contexts falling outside the literal text of the Eleventh Amendment. In *Hans v. Louisiana* (1890), the Court held that sovereign immunity barred a citizen from suing his own State under the federal-question head of jurisdiction. The Court was unmoved by the petitioner's argument that the Eleventh Amendment, by its terms, applied only to suits brought by citizens of other States: Later decisions rejected similar requests to conform the principle of sovereign immunity to the strict language of the Eleventh Amendment in holding that nonconsenting States are immune from suits brought by federal corporations, foreign nations, or Indian tribes, and in concluding that sovereign immunity is a defense to suits in admiralty, though the text of the Eleventh Amendment addresses only suits "in law or equity."

These holdings reflect a settled doctrinal understanding, consistent with the views of the leading advocates of the Constitution's ratification, that sovereign immunity derives not from the Eleventh Amendment but from the structure of the original Constitution itself. The Eleventh Amendment confirmed, rather than established, sovereign immunity as a constitutional principle; it follows that the scope of the States' immunity from suit is demarcated not by the text of the Amendment alone but by fundamental postulates implicit in the constitutional design.

In this case we must determine whether Congress has the power, under Article I, to subject nonconsenting States to private suits in their own courts. As the foregoing discussion makes clear, the fact that the Eleventh Amendment by its terms limits only "the Judicial power of the United States" does not resolve the question. To rest on the words of the Amendment alone would be to engage in the type of ahistorical literalism we have rejected in interpreting the scope of the States' sovereign immunity since the discredited decision in *Chisholm*.

While the constitutional principle of sovereign immunity does pose a bar to federal jurisdiction over suits against nonconsenting States, this is not the only structural basis of sovereign immunity implicit in the constitutional design. Rather, "there is also the postulate that States of the Union, still possessing attributes of sovereignty, shall be immune from suits, without their consent, save where there has been a surrender of this immunity in the plan of the convention." This separate and distinct structural principle is not directly related to the scope of the judicial power established by Article III, but inheres in the system of federalism established by the Constitution. In exercising its Article I powers Congress may subject the States to private suits in their own courts only if there is "compelling evidence" that the States were required to surrender this power to Congress pursuant to the constitutional design.

In light of history, practice, precedent, and the structure of the Constitution, we hold that the States retain immunity from private suit in their own courts, an immunity beyond the congressional power to abrogate by Article I legislation.

The constitutional privilege of a State to assert its sovereign immunity in its own courts does not confer upon the State a concomitant right to disregard the Constitution or valid federal law. The States and their officers are bound by obligations imposed by the Constitution and by federal statutes that comport with the constitutional design. We are unwilling to assume the States will refuse to honor the Constitution or obey the binding laws of the United States. The good faith of the States thus provides an important assurance that "this Constitution, and the Laws of the United

States which shall be made in Pursuance thereof shall be the supreme Law of the Land."

Sovereign immunity, moreover, does not bar all judicial review of state compliance with the Constitution and valid federal law. Rather, certain limits are implicit in the constitutional principle of state sovereign immunity.

The first of these limits is that sovereign immunity bars suits only in the absence of consent. Many States, on their own initiative, have enacted statutes consenting to a wide variety of suits. The rigors of sovereign immunity are thus "mitigated by a sense of justice which has continually expanded by consent the suability of the sovereign." Nor, subject to constitutional limitations, does the Federal Government lack the authority or means to seek the States' voluntary consent to private suits.

The States have consented, moreover, to some suits pursuant to the plan of the Convention or to subsequent constitutional Amendments. In ratifying the Constitution, the States consented to suits brought by other States or by the Federal Government. A suit which is commenced and prosecuted against a State in the name of the United States by those who are entrusted with the constitutional duty to "take Care that the Laws be faithfully executed" differs in kind from the suit of an individual: While the Constitution contemplates suits among the members of the federal system as an alternative to extralegal measures, the fear of private suits against nonconsenting States was the central reason given by the Founders who chose to preserve the States' sovereign immunity. Suits brought by the United States itself require the exercise of political responsibility for each suit prosecuted against a State, a control which is absent from a broad delegation to private persons to sue nonconsenting States.

We have held also that in adopting the Fourteenth Amendment, the people required the States to surrender a portion of the sovereignty that had been preserved to them by the original Constitution, so that Congress may authorize private suits against nonconsenting States pursuant to its § 5 enforcement power. By imposing explicit limits on the powers of the States and granting Congress the power to enforce them, the Amendment "fundamentally altered the balance of state and federal power struck by the Constitution." When Congress enacts appropriate legislation to enforce this Amendment, federal interests are paramount, and Congress may assert an authority over the States which would be otherwise unauthorized by the Constitution.

The second important limit to the principle of sovereign immunity is that it bars suits against States but not lesser entities. The immunity does not extend to suits prosecuted against a municipal corporation or other governmental entity which is not an arm of the State. Nor does sovereign immunity bar all suits against state officers. Some suits against state officers are barred by the rule that sovereign immunity is not limited to suits which name the State as a party if the suits are, in fact, against the State. The rule, however, does not bar certain actions against state officers for injunctive or declaratory relief. Even a suit for money damages may be prosecuted against a state officer in his individual capacity for unconstitutional or wrongful conduct fairly attributable to the officer himself, so long as the relief is sought not from the state treasury but from the officer personally.

The principle of sovereign immunity as reflected in our jurisprudence strikes the proper balance between the supremacy of federal law and the separate sovereignty of the States. Established rules provide ample means to correct ongoing violations of law and to vindicate the interests which animate the Supremacy Clause. That we have, during the first 210 years of our constitutional history, found it unnecessary to decide the question presented here suggests a federal power to subject nonconsenting States to private suits in their own courts is unnecessary to uphold the Constitution and valid federal statutes as the supreme law.

This case at one level concerns the formal structure of federalism, but in a Constitution as resilient as ours form mirrors substance. Congress has vast power but not all power. When Congress legislates in matters affecting the States, it may not treat these sovereign entities as mere prefectures or corporations. Congress must accord States the esteem due to them as joint participants in a federal system, one beginning with the premise of sovereignty in both the central Government and the separate States. Congress has ample means to ensure compliance with valid federal laws, but it must respect the sovereignty of the States.

In an apparent attempt to disparage a conclusion with which it disagrees, the dissent attributes our reasoning to natural law. We seek to discover, however, only what the Framers and those who ratified the Constitution sought to accomplish when they created a federal system. We appeal to no higher authority than the Charter which they wrote and adopted. Theirs was the unique insight that freedom is enhanced by the creation of two governments, not one. We need not attach a label to our dissenting colleagues' insistence that the constitutional structure adopted by the Founders must yield to the politics of the moment. Although the Constitution begins with the principle that sovereignty rests with the people, it does not follow that the National Government becomes the ultimate, preferred mechanism for expressing the people's will. The States exist as a refutation of that concept. In choosing to ordain and establish the Constitution, the people insisted upon a federal structure for the very purpose of rejecting the idea that the will of the people in all instances is expressed by the central power, the one most remote from their control. The Framers of the Constitution did not share our dissenting colleagues' belief that the Congress may circumvent the federal design by regulating the States directly when it pleases to do so, including by a proxy in which individual citizens are authorized to levy upon the state treasuries absent the States' consent to jurisdiction.

The case before us depends upon these principles. The State of Maine has not questioned Congress' power to prescribe substantive rules of federal law to which it must comply. Despite an initial good-faith disagreement about the requirements of the FLSA, it is conceded by all that the State has altered its conduct so that its compliance with federal law cannot now be questioned. The Solicitor General of the United States has appeared before this Court, however, and asserted that the federal interest in compensating the States' employees for alleged past violations of federal law is so compelling that the sovereign State of Maine must be stripped of its immunity and subjected to suit in its own courts by its own employees. Yet, despite specific statutory authorization, the United States apparently found the same interests insufficient to justify sending even a single attorney to Maine to prosecute this litigation. The difference between a suit by the United States on behalf of the employees and a suit by the employees implicates a rule that the National Government must itself deem the case of sufficient importance to take action against the State; and history, precedent, and the structure of the Constitution make clear that, under the plan of the Convention, the States have consented to suits of the first kind but not of the second. The judgment of the Supreme Judicial Court of Maine is Affirmed.

SOUTER, J., dissenting.

In *Seminole Tribe of Fla. v. Florida*, a majority of this Court invoked the Eleventh Amendment to declare that the federal judicial power under Article III of the Constitution does not reach a private action against a State, even on a federal question. In the Court's conception, however, the Eleventh Amendment was understood as having been enhanced by a "background principle" of state sovereign immunity (understood as immunity to suit), that operated beyond its limited codification in the Amendment, dealing solely with federal citizen-state diversity jurisdiction. To the *Seminole Tribe* dissenters, of whom I was one, the Court's enhancement of the Amendment was at odds with constitutional history and at war with the conception of divided sovereignty that is the essence of American federalism.

Today's issue arises naturally in the aftermath of the decision in *Seminole Tribe*. The Court holds that the Constitution bars an individual suit against a State to enforce a federal statutory right under the Fair Labor Standards Act of 1938, when brought in the State's courts over its objection. In thus complementing its earlier decision, the Court of course confronts the fact that the state forum renders the Eleventh Amendment beside the point, and it has responded by discerning a simpler and more straightforward theory of state sovereign immunity than it found in *Seminole Tribe*: a State's sovereign immunity from all individual suits is a "fundamental aspect" of state sovereignty "confirmed" by the Tenth Amendment. As a consequence, *Seminole Tribe*'s contorted reliance on the Eleventh Amendment and its background was presumably unnecessary; the Tenth would have done the work with an economy that the majority in *Seminole Tribe* would have welcomed. Indeed, if the Court's current reasoning is correct, the Eleventh Amendment itself was unnecessary. Whatever Article III may originally have said about the federal judicial power, the embarrassment to the State of Georgia occasioned by attempts in federal court to enforce the State's war debt could easily have been avoided if only the Court that decided *Chisholm v. Georgia* had understood a State's inherent, Tenth Amendment right to be free of any judicial power, whether the court be state or federal, and whether the cause of action arise under state or federal law.

The sequence of the Court's positions prompts a suspicion of error, and skepticism is confirmed by scrutiny of the Court's efforts to justify its holding. There is no evidence that the Tenth Amendment constitutionalized a concept of sovereign immunity as inherent in the notion of statehood, and no evidence that any concept of inherent sovereign immunity was understood historically to apply when the sovereign sued was not the font of the law. Nor does the Court fare any better with its subsidiary lines of reasoning, that the state-court action is barred by the scheme of American federalism, a result supposedly confirmed by a history largely devoid of precursors to the action considered here. The Court's federalism ignores the accepted authority of Congress to bind States under the FLSA and to provide for enforcement of federal rights in state court. The Court's history simply disparages the capacity of the Constitution to order relationships in a Republic that has changed since the founding.

On each point the Court has raised it is mistaken, and I respectfully dissent from its judgment.

FRANCHISE TAX BOARD OF CALIFORNIA v. HYATT
139 S. Ct. 1485 (2019)

THOMAS, J.

This case, now before us for the third time, requires us to decide whether the Constitution permits a State to be sued by a private party without its consent in the courts of a different State. We hold that it does not and overrule our decision to the contrary in *Nevada v. Hall* (1979).

In the early 1990s, respondent Gilbert Hyatt earned substantial income from a technology patent for a computer formed on a single integrated circuit chip. Although Hyatt's claim was later canceled, his royalties in the interim totaled millions of dollars. Prior to receiving the patent, Hyatt had been a long-time resident of California. But in 1991, Hyatt sold his house in California and rented an apartment, registered to vote, obtained insurance, opened a bank account, and acquired a driver's license in Nevada. When he filed his 1991 and 1992 tax returns, he claimed Nevada—which collects no personal income tax—as his primary place of residence.

Petitioner Franchise Tax Board of California, the state agency responsible for assessing personal income tax, suspected that Hyatt's move was a sham. Thus, in 1993, the Board launched an audit to determine whether Hyatt underpaid his 1991 and 1992 state income taxes by misrepresenting his residency. In the course of the audit, employees of the Board traveled to Nevada to conduct interviews with Hyatt's estranged family members and shared his personal information with business contacts. In total, the Board sent more than 100 letters and demands for information to third parties. The Board ultimately concluded that Hyatt had not moved to Nevada until April 1992 and owed California more than $10 million in back taxes, interest, and penalties.

Hall's determination that the Constitution does not contemplate sovereign immunity for each State in a sister State's courts misreads the historical record and misapprehends the "implicit ordering of relationships within the federal system necessary to make the Constitution a workable governing charter and to give each provision within that document the full effect intended by the Framers." As Chief Justice Marshall explained, the Founders did not state every postulate on which they formed our Republic—"we must never forget, that it is a constitution we are expounding." And although the Constitution assumes that the States retain their sovereign immunity except as otherwise provided, it also fundamentally adjusts the States' relationship with each other and curtails their ability, as sovereigns, to decline to recognize each other's immunity.

After independence, the States considered themselves fully sovereign nations. As the Colonies proclaimed in 1776, they were "Free and Independent States" with "full Power to levy War, conclude Peace, contract Alliances, establish Commerce, and to do all other Acts and Things which Independent States may of right do." Under international law, then, independence "entitled" the Colonies "to all the rights and powers of sovereign states."

"An integral component" of the States' sovereignty was "their immunity from private suits." This fundamental aspect of the States' "inviolable sovereignty" was well established and widely accepted at the founding. As Alexander Hamilton explained:

> It is inherent in the nature of sovereignty not to be amenable to the suit of an individual without its consent. This is the general sense and the general practice of mankind; and the exemption, as one of the attributes of sovereignty, is now enjoyed by the government of every State in the Union.

The Founders believed that both "common law sovereign immunity" and "law-of-nations sovereign immunity" prevented States from being amenable to process in any court without their consent. The common-law rule was that "no suit or action can be brought against the king, even in civil matters, because no court can have jurisdiction over him." According to the founding era's foremost expert on the law of nations, "it does not belong to any foreign power to take cognisance of the administration of another sovereign, to set himself up for a judge of his conduct, and to oblige him to alter it." The sovereign is "exempt from all foreign jurisdiction."

The founding generation thus took as given that States could not be haled involuntarily before each other's courts. This understanding is perhaps best illustrated by a preratification example. In 1781, a creditor named Simon Nathan tried to recover a debt that Virginia allegedly owed him by attaching some of its property in Philadelphia. James Madison and other Virginia delegates to the Confederation Congress responded by sending a communique to Pennsylvania requesting that its executive branch have the action dismissed. As Madison framed it, the Commonwealth's property could not be attached by process issuing from a court of "any other State in the Union." To permit otherwise would require Virginia to "abandon its Sovereignty by descending to answer before the Tribunal of another Power." The court agreed and refused to grant Nathan the writ of attachment.

The Founders were well aware of the international-law immunity principles behind this case. Federalists and Antifederalists alike agreed in their preratification debates that States could not be sued in the courts of other States. One Federalist, who argued that Article III would waive the States' immunity in federal court, admitted that the waiver was desirable because of the "impossibility of calling a sovereign state before the jurisdiction of another sovereign state." Two of the most prominent Antifederalists—Federal Farmer and Brutus—disagreed with the Federalists about the desirability of a federal forum in which States could be sued, but did so for the very reason that the States had previously been "subject to no such actions" in any court and were not "obliged" "to answer to an individual in a court of law." They found it "humiliating and degrading" that a State might have to answer "the suit of an individual."

In short, at the time of the founding, it was well settled that States were immune under both the common law and the law of nations. The Constitution's use of the term "States" reflects both of these kinds of traditional immunity. And the States retained these aspects of sovereignty, "except as altered by the plan of the Convention or certain constitutional Amendments."

One constitutional provision that abrogated certain aspects of this traditional immunity was Article III, which provided a neutral federal forum in which the States agreed to be amenable to suits brought by other States. "The establishment of a permanent tribunal with adequate authority to determine controversies between the States, in place of an inadequate scheme of arbitration, was essential to the peace of the Union." As James Madison explained during the Convention debates, "there can be no impropriety in referring such disputes" between coequal sovereigns to a superior tribunal.

The States, in ratifying the Constitution, similarly surrendered a portion of their immunity by consenting to suits brought against them by the United States in federal courts. "While that jurisdiction is not conferred by the Constitution in express words, it is inherent in the constitutional plan." Given that "all jurisdiction implies superiority of power," the only forums in which the States have consented to suits by one another and by the Federal Government are Article III courts.

The Antifederalists worried that Article III went even further by extending the federal judicial power over controversies "between a State and Citizens of another State." They suggested that this provision implicitly waived the States' sovereign immunity against private suits in federal courts. But "the leading advocates of the Constitution assured the people in no uncertain terms" that this reading was incorrect. According to Madison:

> A federal court's jurisdiction in controversies between a state and citizens of another state is much objected to, and perhaps without reason. It is not in the power of individuals to call any state into court. The only operation it can have, is that, if a state should wish to bring a suit against a citizen, it must be brought before the federal court. This will give satisfaction to individuals, as it will prevent citizens, on whom a state may have a claim, being dissatisfied with the state courts.

John Marshall echoed these sentiments:

> With respect to disputes between a state and the citizens of another state, its jurisdiction has been decried with unusual vehemence. I hope no gentleman will think that a state will be called at the bar of the federal court. The intent is, to enable states to recover claims of individuals residing in other states. I contend this construction is warranted by the words.

Not long after the founding, however, the Antifederalists' fears were realized. In *Chisholm v. Georgia* (1793), the Court held that Article III allowed the very suits that the "Madison-Marshall-Hamilton triumvirate" insisted it did not. That decision precipitated an immediate "furor" and "uproar" across the country. Congress and the States accordingly acted swiftly to remedy the Court's blunder by drafting and ratifying the Eleventh Amendment.

The Eleventh Amendment provides: "The Judicial power of the United States shall not be construed to extend to any suit in law or equity, commenced or prosecuted against one of the United States by Citizens of another State, or by Citizens or Subjects of any Foreign State." The

Eleventh Amendment confirmed that the Constitution was not meant to "raise up" any suits against the States that were "anomalous and unheard of when the Constitution was adopted." Although the terms of that Amendment address only "the specific provisions of the Constitution that had raised concerns during the ratification debates and formed the basis of the *Chisholm* decision," the "natural inference" from its speedy adoption is that "the Constitution was understood, in light of its history and structure, to preserve the States' traditional immunity from private suits." We have often emphasized that "the Amendment is rooted in a recognition that the States, although a union, maintain certain attributes of sovereignty, including sovereign immunity. In proposing the Amendment, "Congress acted not to change but to restore the original constitutional design." The "sovereign immunity of the States," we have said, "neither derives from, nor is limited by, the terms of the Eleventh Amendment."

Consistent with this understanding of state sovereign immunity, this Court has held that the Constitution bars suits against nonconsenting States in a wide range of cases.

Despite this historical evidence that interstate sovereign immunity is preserved in the constitutional design, Hyatt insists that such immunity exists only as a "matter of comity" and can be disregarded by the forum State. He reasons that, before the Constitution was ratified, the States had the power of fully independent nations to deny immunity to fellow sovereigns; thus, the States must retain that power today with respect to each other because "nothing in the Constitution or formation of the Union altered that balance among the still-sovereign states." Like the majority in *Hall*, he relies primarily on our early foreign immunity decisions. For instance, he cites *Schooner Exchange v. McFaddon* (1812), in which the Court dismissed a libel action against a French warship docked in Philadelphia because, under the law of nations, a sovereign's warships entering the ports of a friendly nation are exempt from the jurisdiction of its courts. But whether the host nation respects that sovereign immunity, Chief Justice Marshall noted, is for the host nation to decide, for "the jurisdiction of a nation within its own territory is necessarily exclusive and absolute" and "is susceptible of no limitation not imposed by itself." Similar reasoning is found in *The Santissima Trinidad* (1822), where Justice Story noted that the host nation's consent to provide immunity "may be withdrawn upon notice at any time, without just offence."

The problem with Hyatt's argument is that the Constitution affirmatively altered the relationships between the States, so that they no longer relate to each other solely as foreign sovereigns. Each State's equal dignity and sovereignty under the Constitution implies certain constitutional "limitations on the sovereignty of all of its sister States." One such limitation is the inability of one State to hale another into its courts without the latter's consent. The Constitution does not merely allow States to afford each other immunity as a matter of comity; it embeds interstate sovereign immunity within the constitutional design. Numerous provisions reflect this reality.

To begin, Article I divests the States of the traditional diplomatic and military tools that foreign sovereigns possess. Specifically, the States can no longer prevent or remedy departures from customary international law because the Constitution deprives them of the independent power to lay imposts or duties on imports and exports, to enter into treaties or compacts, and to wage war.

Article IV also imposes duties on the States not required by international law. The Court's Full Faith and Credit Clause precedents, for example, demand that state-court judgments be accorded full effect in other States and preclude States from "adopting any policy of hostility to the public Acts" of other States. States must also afford citizens of each State "all Privileges and Immunities of Citizens in the several States" and honor extradition requests upon "Demand of the executive Authority of the State" from which the fugitive fled. Foreign sovereigns cannot demand these kinds of reciprocal responsibilities absent consent or compact. But the Constitution imposes them as part of its transformation of the States from a loose league of friendship into a perpetual Union based on the "fundamental principle of equal sovereignty among the States."

The Constitution also reflects implicit alterations to the States' relationships with each other, confirming that they are no longer fully independent nations. For example, States may not supply rules of decision governing "disputes implicating their conflicting rights." Thus, no State can apply its own law to interstate disputes over borders, water rights, or the interpretation of interstate compacts. The States would have had the raw power to apply their own law to such matters before they entered the Union, but the Constitution implicitly forbids that exercise of power because the "interstate nature of the controversy makes it inappropriate for state law to control." Some subjects that were decided by pure "political power" before ratification now turn on federal "rules of law."

Interstate sovereign immunity is similarly integral to the structure of the Constitution. Like a dispute over borders or water rights, a State's assertion of compulsory judicial process over another State involves a direct conflict between sovereigns. The Constitution implicitly strips States of any power they once had to refuse each other sovereign immunity, just as it denies them the power to resolve border disputes by political means. Interstate immunity, in other words, is "implied as an essential component of federalism."

Hyatt argues that we should find no right to sovereign immunity in another State's courts because no constitutional provision explicitly grants that immunity. But this is precisely the type of "ahistorical literalism" that we have rejected when "interpreting the scope of the States' sovereign immunity since the discredited decision in *Chisholm*." In light of our constitutional structure, the historical understanding of state immunity, and the swift enactment of the Eleventh Amendment after the Court departed from this understanding in *Chisholm*, "it is not rational to suppose that the sovereign power should be dragged before a court." Indeed, the spirited historical debate over Article III courts and the immediate reaction to *Chisholm* make little sense if the Eleventh Amendment were the only source of sovereign immunity and private suits against the States could already be brought in "partial, local tribunals." Nor would the Founders have objected so strenuously to a neutral federal forum for private suits against States if they were open to a State being sued in a different State's courts. Hyatt's view thus inverts the Founders' concerns about state-court parochialism.

Moreover, Hyatt's ahistorical literalism proves too much. There are many other constitutional doctrines that are not spelled out in the Constitution but are nevertheless implicit in its structure and supported by historical practice—including, for example, judicial review, intergovernmental tax immunity, executive privilege, executive immunity, and the President's removal power. Like these doctrines, the States' sovereign immunity is a historically rooted principle embedded in the text and structure of the Constitution.

Nevada v. Hall is irreconcilable with our constitutional structure and with the historical evidence showing a widespread preratification understanding that States retained immunity from private suits, both in their own courts and in other courts. We therefore overrule that decision. Because the Board is thus immune from Hyatt's suit in Nevada's courts, the judgment of the Nevada Supreme Court is reversed, and the case is remanded for proceedings not inconsistent with this opinion.

NOTE

Rarely does a Term or two go by without the U.S. Supreme Court addressing a new sovereign immunity question. Here are the most recent ones. *See Penneast Pipeline Company v. New Jersey* (2021) (actions filed by natural gas companies under the federal Natural Gas Act to condemn state-affected rights of way do not violate state sovereign immunity); *Torres v. Texas Dep't of Public Safety* (2022) (in ratifying the U.S. Constitution, the States agreed that their sovereignty would yield to the national power to raise and support the Armed Forces and thus Congress could authorize private damages lawsuits against nonconsenting States under the Uniformed Services Employment and Reemployment Rights Act).

D. FEDERAL LIMITATIONS ON STATE POWER

1. Article VI – The Supremacy Clause

Article VI may contain the most important provision of all with respect to the effect of federal law on the States. The Supremacy Clause declares:

> This Constitution, and the Laws of the United States which shall be made in pursuance thereof; and all Treaties made, or which shall be made, under the Authority of the United States, shall be the supreme Law of the Land; and the Judges in every State shall be bound thereby, any Thing in the Constitution or Laws of any State to the Contrary notwithstanding.

The Supremacy Clause is bolstered by Article VI, clause 3's mandate that "the Members of the several State Legislatures, and all executive and judicial Officers, both of the United States and of the several States, shall be bound by Oath or Affirmation, to support this Constitution."

The two clauses make clear that federal law has primacy over state law, including state constitutions, when a conflict emerges between a federal law (whether constitutional, statutory, or even regulatory) and a state law. Although this general preemption principle is easy to state, it is not always easy to apply, as the next case shows.

a. Federal Preemption of State Law

U.S. TERM LIMITS, INC. v. THORNTON
514 U.S. 779 (1995)

STEVENS, J.

The Constitution sets forth qualifications for membership in the Congress of the United States. Article I, § 2, cl. 2, which applies to the House of Representatives, provides: "No Person shall be a Representative who shall not have attained to the Age of twenty five Years, and been seven Years a Citizen of the United States, and who shall not, when elected, be an Inhabitant of that State in which he shall be chosen."

Article I, § 3, cl. 3, which applies to the Senate, similarly provides: "No Person shall be a Senator who shall not have attained to the Age of thirty Years, and been nine Years a Citizen of the United States, and who shall not, when elected, be an Inhabitant of that State for which he shall be chosen."

Today's cases present a challenge to an amendment to the Arkansas State Constitution that prohibits the name of an otherwise-eligible candidate for Congress from appearing on the general election ballot if that candidate has already served three terms in the House of Representatives or two terms in the Senate. Such a state-imposed restriction is contrary to the "fundamental principle of our representative democracy," embodied in the Constitution, that "the people should choose whom they please to govern them." Allowing individual States to adopt their own qualifications for congressional service would be inconsistent with the Framers' vision of a uniform National Legislature representing the people of the United States.

At the general election on November 3, 1992, the voters of Arkansas adopted Amendment 73 to their State Constitution. Proposed as a "Term Limitation Amendment," its preamble stated:

> The people of Arkansas find and declare that elected officials who remain in office too long become preoccupied with reelection and ignore their duties as representatives of the people. Entrenched incumbency has reduced voter participation and has led to an electoral system that is less free, less competitive, and less representative than the system established by the Founding Fathers. Therefore, the people of Arkansas, exercising their reserved powers, herein limit the terms of elected officials.

The limitations in Amendment 73 apply to three categories of elected officials. Section 3, the provision at issue in these cases, applies to the Arkansas Congressional Delegation. It provides:

> (a) Any person having been elected to three or more terms as a member of the United States House of Representatives from Arkansas shall not be certified as a candidate and shall not be eligible to have his/her name placed on the ballot for election to the United States House of Representatives from Arkansas.
>
> (b) Any person having been elected to two or more terms as a member of the United States Senate from Arkansas shall not be certified as a candidate and shall not be eligible to have his/her name placed on the ballot for election to the United States Senate from Arkansas.

On November 13, 1992, respondent Bobbie Hill, on behalf of herself, similarly situated Arkansas "citizens, residents, taxpayers and registered voters," and the League of Women Voters of Arkansas, filed a complaint in the Circuit Court for Pulaski County, Arkansas, seeking a declaratory judgment that § 3 of Amendment 73 is "unconstitutional and void." The State of Arkansas, through its Attorney General, intervened as a party defendant in support of the amendment. Several proponents of the amendment also intervened, including petitioner U.S. Term Limits, Inc.

Petitioners argue that the Constitution contains no express prohibition against state-added qualifications, and that Amendment 73 is therefore an appropriate exercise of a State's reserved power to place additional restrictions on the choices that its own voters may make. We disagree for two independent reasons. First, we conclude that the power to add qualifications is not within the "original powers" of the States, and thus is not reserved to the States by the Tenth Amendment. Second, even if States possessed some original power in this area, we conclude that the Framers intended the Constitution to be the exclusive source of qualifications for Members of Congress, and that the Framers thereby "divested" States of any power to add qualifications.

Contrary to petitioners' assertions, the power to add qualifications is not part of the original powers of sovereignty that the Tenth Amendment reserved to the States. Petitioners' Tenth Amendment argument misconceives the nature of the right at issue because that Amendment could only "reserve" that which existed before. With respect to setting qualifications for service in Congress, no such right existed before the Constitution was ratified. Electing representatives to the National Legislature was a new right, arising from the Constitution itself.

Even if we believed that States possessed as part of their original powers some control over congressional qualifications, the text and structure of the Constitution, the relevant historical materials, and, most importantly, the "basic principles of our democratic system" all demonstrate that the Qualifications Clauses were intended to preclude the States from exercising any such power and to fix as exclusive the qualifications in the Constitution. In light of the Framers' evident concern that States would try to undermine the National Government, they could not have intended States to have the power to set qualifications.

The right to choose representatives belongs not to the States, but to the people. From the start, the Framers recognized that the "great and radical vice" of the Articles of Confederation was "the principle of LEGISLATION for STATES or GOVERNMENTS, in their CORPORATE or COLLECTIVE CAPACITIES, and as contradistinguished from the INDIVIDUALS of whom they consist." The Federalist No. 15 (Hamilton). Thus the Framers, in perhaps their most important contribution, conceived of a Federal Government directly responsible to the people, possessed of direct power over the people, and chosen directly, not by States, but by the people. The Framers implemented this ideal most clearly in the provision, extant from the beginning of the Republic, that calls for the Members of the House of Representatives to be "chosen every second Year by the People of the several States." Following the adoption of the Seventeenth Amendment in 1913, this ideal was extended to elections for the Senate. The Congress of the United States, therefore, is not a confederation of nations in which separate sovereigns are represented by appointed delegates, but is instead a body composed of representatives of the people.

Petitioners argue that, even if States may not add qualifications, Amendment 73 is constitutional because it is not such a qualification, and because Amendment 73 is a permissible exercise of state power to regulate the "Times, Places and Manner of holding Elections."

In our view, Amendment 73 is an indirect attempt to accomplish what the Constitution prohibits Arkansas from accomplishing directly. We must, of course, accept the state court's view of the purpose of its own law: We are thus authoritatively informed that the sole purpose of § 3 of Amendment 73 was to attempt to achieve a result that is forbidden by the Federal Constitution. Indeed, it cannot be seriously contended that the intent behind Amendment 73 is other than to prevent the election of incumbents.

Petitioners make the related argument that Amendment 73 merely regulates the "Manner" of elections, and that the amendment is therefore a permissible exercise of state power under Article I, § 4, cl. 1 to regulate the "Times, Places and Manner" of elections. We cannot agree.

A necessary consequence of petitioners' argument is that Congress itself would have the power to "make or alter" a measure such as Amendment 73. That the Framers would have approved of such a result is unfathomable. The Framers were particularly concerned that a grant to Congress of the authority to set its own qualifications would lead inevitably to congressional self-aggrandizement and the upsetting of the delicate constitutional balance. Petitioners would have us believe, however, that even as the Framers carefully circumscribed congressional power to set qualifications, they intended to allow Congress to achieve the same result by simply formulating the regulation as a ballot access restriction under the Elections Clause. We refuse to adopt an interpretation of the Elections Clause that would so cavalierly disregard what the Framers intended to be a fundamental constitutional safeguard.

The merits of term limits, or "rotation," have been the subject of debate since the formation of our Constitution, when the Framers unanimously rejected a proposal to add such limits to the Constitution. The cogent arguments on both sides of the question that were articulated during the process of ratification largely retain their force today. Over half the States have adopted measures that impose such limits on some offices either directly or indirectly, and the Nation as a whole, notably by constitutional amendment, has imposed a limit on the number of terms that the President may serve. Term limits, like any other qualification for office, unquestionably restrict the ability of voters to vote for whom they wish. On the other hand, such limits may provide for the infusion of fresh ideas and new perspectives, and may decrease the likelihood that representatives will lose touch with their constituents. It is not our province to resolve this longstanding debate.

We are, however, firmly convinced that allowing the several States to adopt term limits for congressional service would effect a fundamental change in the constitutional framework. Any such change must come not by legislation adopted either by Congress or by an individual State, but rather—as have other important changes in the electoral process—through the amendment procedures set forth in Article V. The Framers decided that the qualifications for service in the Congress of the United States be fixed in the Constitution and be uniform throughout the Nation. That decision reflects the Framers' understanding that Members of Congress are chosen by separate constituencies, but that they become, when elected, servants of the people of the United States. They are not merely delegates appointed by separate, sovereign States; they occupy offices that are integral and essential components of a single National Government. In the absence of a properly passed constitutional amendment, allowing individual States to craft their own qualifications for Congress would thus erode the structure envisioned by the Framers, a structure that was designed, in the words of the Preamble to our Constitution, to form a "more perfect Union."

b. Limits on Federal Preemption – The Clear Statement Rule

GREGORY v. ASHCROFT
501 U.S. 452 (1991)

O'CONNOR, J.

Article V, § 26, of the Missouri Constitution provides that "all judges other than municipal judges shall retire at the age of seventy years." We consider whether this mandatory retirement provision violates the federal Age Discrimination in Employment Act of 1967 and whether it comports with the federal constitutional prescription of equal protection of the laws.

The ADEA makes it unlawful for an "employer" "to discharge any individual" who is at least 40 years old "because of such individual's age." The term "employer" is defined to include "a State or political subdivision of a State." Petitioners work for the State of Missouri. They contend that the Missouri mandatory retirement requirement for judges violates the ADEA.

As every schoolchild learns, our Constitution establishes a system of dual sovereignty between the States and the Federal Government. This Court also has recognized this fundamental principle. The Constitution created a Federal Government of limited powers. "The powers not delegated to the United States by the Constitution, nor prohibited by it to the States, are reserved to the States respectively, or to the people." The States thus retain substantial sovereign authority under our constitutional system. The Federal Government holds a decided advantage in this delicate balance: the Supremacy Clause. As long as it is acting within the powers granted it under the Constitution, Congress may impose its will on the States. Congress may legislate in areas traditionally regulated by the States. This is an extraordinary power in a federalist system. It is a power that we must assume Congress does not exercise lightly.

The present case concerns a state constitutional provision through which the people of Missouri establish a qualification for those who sit as their judges. This provision goes beyond an area traditionally regulated by the States; it is a decision of the most fundamental sort for a sovereign entity. Through the structure of its government, and the character of those who exercise government authority, a State defines itself as a sovereign. "It is obviously essential to the independence of the States, and to their peace and tranquility, that their power to prescribe the qualifications of their own officers should be exclusive, and free from external interference, except so far as plainly provided by the Constitution."

Congressional interference with this decision of the people of Missouri would upset the usual constitutional balance of federal and state powers. For this reason, "it is incumbent upon the federal courts to be certain of Congress' intent before finding that federal law overrides" this balance. We explained recently:

> If Congress intends to alter the usual constitutional balance between the States and the Federal Government, it must make its intention to do so unmistakably clear in the language of the statute. Congress should make its intention clear and manifest if it intends to pre-empt the historic powers of the States.

This plain statement rule is nothing more than an acknowledgment that the States retain substantial sovereign powers under our constitutional scheme, powers with which Congress does not readily interfere.

These cases stand in recognition of the authority of the people of the States to determine the qualifications of their most important government officials. It is an authority that lies at "the heart of representative government." It is a power reserved to the States under the Tenth Amendment and guaranteed them by that provision of the Constitution under which the United States "guarantees to every State in this Union a Republican Form of Government."

In 1974, Congress extended the substantive provisions of the ADEA to include the States as employers. At the same time, Congress amended the definition of "employee" to exclude all elected and most high-ranking government officials.

Governor Ashcroft contends that the exclusion of certain public officials also excludes judges, like petitioners, who are appointed to office by the Governor and are then subject to retention election. Governor Ashcroft relies on the plain language of the statute: It exempts persons appointed "at the policymaking level." The Governor argues that state judges, in fashioning and applying the common law, make policy. Missouri is a common law state. The common law, unlike a constitution or statute, provides no definitive text; it is to be derived from the interstices of prior opinions and a well-considered judgment of what is best for the community.

The statute refers to appointees "on the policymaking level," not to appointees "who make policy." It may be sufficient that the appointee is in a position requiring the exercise of discretion concerning issues of public importance. This certainly describes the bench, regardless of whether judges might be considered policymakers in the same sense as the executive or legislature.

Nonetheless, "appointee at the policymaking level," particularly in the context of the other exceptions that surround it, is an odd way for Congress to exclude judges; a plain statement that judges are not "employees" would seem the most efficient phrasing. But in this case we are not looking for a plain statement that judges are excluded. We will not read the ADEA to cover state judges unless Congress has made it clear that judges are *included*. This does not mean that the Act must mention judges explicitly, though it does not. Rather, it must be plain to anyone reading the Act that it covers judges. In the context of a statute that plainly excludes most important state public officials, "appointee on the policymaking level" is sufficiently broad that we cannot conclude that the statute plainly covers appointed state judges. Therefore, it does not.

2. Article IV

Article IV of the U.S. Constitution concerns the role of the States in the federal system. Among other guarantees, it contains the Full Faith and Credit Clause, the Privileges and Immunities Clause, and the Extradition Clause, all of which essentially mandate interstate comity—a kind of Golden Rule for the States. Article IV also gives Congress the power to admit new States into the union and guarantees to the States a "republican form of government," U.S. Const. art. IV, § 4.

a. Full Faith and Credit

Section 1 of Article IV provides that "Full Faith and Credit shall be given in each State to the public Acts, Records, and judicial Proceedings of every other State." Complex questions can and do arise about what judgments of one State must be accorded legal recognition by another State.

b. Privileges and Immunities

Section 2 of Article IV declares that the "Citizens of each State shall be entitled to all Privileges and Immunities of Citizens in the several States." This Privileges and Immunities Clause (as distinct from the Privileges or Immunities Clause of the Fourteenth Amendment) essentially establishes a non-discrimination principle that protects non-residents in each State. *See, e.g., Supreme Court of New Hampshire v. Piper*, 470 U.S. 274 (1985).

c. Extradition

Article IV, § 2 also provides that a fugitive "who shall flee from Justice, and be found in another State, shall on Demand of the executive Authority of the State from which he fled, be delivered up, to be removed to the State having Jurisdiction of the Crime." The Extradition Clause was the subject of a fascinating Supreme Court decision on the eve of the Civil War, *see Kentucky v. Dennison*, 65 U.S. 66 (1861); Stephen R. McAllister, *A* Marbury v. Madison *Moment on the Eve of the Civil War: Chief Judge Roger Taney and the* Kentucky v. Dennison *Case*, 14 The Green Bag 2d 405 (2011), which led the courts to play a limited role in enforcing the clause for over 125 years. Eventually, the Supreme Court overruled the

Dennison case and expanded the courts' ability to require extradition in *Puerto Rico v. Branstad*, 483 U.S. 219 (1987).

d. Congressional Power to Admit New States

The first clause of Article IV, § 3, provides that "New States may be admitted by the Congress into this Union." This provision has been understood to mean that Congress may impose substantive conditions on new States, requiring, for example, the inclusion of particular provisions or prohibitions in a State's constitution as a condition for admission to the Union. The following case applies this principle.

COYLE v. SMITH
221 U.S. 559 (1911)

LURTON, J.

This is a writ of error to the supreme court of Oklahoma to review the judgment of that court upholding a legislative act of the state, providing for the removal of its capital from Guthrie to Oklahoma City.

The question reviewable under this writ of error, if any there be, arises under the claim set up by the petitioner, and decided against him, that the Oklahoma act of December 29, 1910, providing for the immediate location of the capital of the state at Oklahoma City, was void as repugnant to the enabling act of Congress of June 16, 1906, under which the state was admitted to the Union. The second section is lengthy and deals with the organization of a constitutional convention, and concludes in these words: "The capital of said state shall temporarily be at the city of Guthrie and shall not be changed therefrom previous to Anno Domini nineteen hundred and thirteen; but said capital shall, after said year, be located by the electors of said state at an election to be provided for by the legislature." The twenty second and last section, applicable to Oklahoma, reads thus: "That the constitutional convention provided for herein shall by ordinance irrevocably accept the terms and conditions of this act."

The Oklahoma Constitution as framed contains nothing as to the location of the state capital; but the convention which framed it adopted a separate ordinance in these words:

> Enabling act accepted by ordinance irrevocable. Be it ordained by the constitutional convention for the proposed state of Oklahoma, that said constitutional convention do, by this ordinance irrevocable, accept the terms and conditions of an act of the Congress of the United States, entitled, "An Act to Enable the People of Oklahoma and the Indian Territory to Form a Constitution and State Government, and be Admitted into the Union on an Equal Footing with the Original States."

The only question for review by us is whether the provision of the enabling act was a valid limitation upon the power of the state after its admission, which overrides any subsequent state legislation repugnant thereto.

The power to locate its own seat of government, and to determine when and how it shall be changed from one place to another, and to appropriate its own public funds for that purpose, are essentially and peculiarly state powers. That one of the original thirteen states could now be shorn of such powers by an act of Congress would not be for a moment entertained. The question, then, comes to this: Can a state be placed upon a plane of inequality with its sister states in the Union if the Congress chooses to impose conditions which so operate, at the time of its admission? The argument is, that while Congress may not deprive a state of any power which it *possesses*, it may, as a condition to the admission of a new state, constitutionally restrict its authority, to the extent, at least, of suspending its powers for a definite time in respect to the location of its seat of government. This contention is predicated upon the constitutional power of admitting new states to this Union, and the constitutional duty of guaranteeing to "every state in this Union a republican form of government."

The power of Congress in respect to the admission of new states is found in the third section of the fourth article of the Constitution. That provision is that, "new states may be admitted by the Congress into this Union." The only expressed restriction upon this power is that no new state shall be formed within the jurisdiction of any other state, nor by the junction of two or more states, or parts of states, without the consent of such states, as well as of the Congress. But what is this power? It is not to admit political organizations which are less or greater, or different in dignity or power, from those political entities which constitute the Union.

The definition of "a state" is found in the powers possessed by the original states which adopted the Constitution—a definition emphasized by the terms employed in all subsequent acts of Congress admitting new states into the Union. The first two states admitted into the Union were the states of Vermont and Kentucky, one as of March 4, 1791, and the other as of June 1, 1792. No terms or conditions were exacted from either. Each act declares that the state is admitted "as a new and *entire member* of the United States of America." Even stronger was the declaration upon the admission in 1796 of Tennessee as the third new state, it being declared to be "one of the United States of America," "on an equal footing with the original states in all respects whatsoever"—phraseology which has ever since been substantially followed in admission acts, concluding with the Oklahoma act, which declares that Oklahoma shall be admitted "on an equal footing with the original states."

The power is to admit "new states into *this* Union." "This Union" was and is a union of states, equal in power, dignity, and authority, each competent to exert that residuum of sovereignty not delegated to the United

States by the Constitution itself. To maintain otherwise would be to say that the Union, through the power of Congress to admit new states, might come to be a union of states unequal in power, as including states whose powers were restricted only by the Constitution, with others whose powers had been further restricted by an act of Congress accepted as a condition of admission.

The argument that Congress derives from the duty of "guaranteeing to each state in this Union a republican form of government," power to impose restrictions upon a new state which deprive it of equality with other members of the Union, has no merit. It may imply the duty of such new state to provide itself with such state government, and impose upon Congress the duty of seeing that such form is not changed to one anti-republican, but it obviously does not confer power to admit a new state which shall be any less a state than those which compose the Union.

We come now to the question as to whether there is anything in the decisions of this court which sanctions the claim that Congress may, by the imposition of conditions in an enabling act, deprive a new state of any of those attributes essential to its equality in dignity and power with other states.

As to requirements in such enabling acts as relate only to the contents of the Constitution for the proposed new state, little needs to be said. The constitutional provision concerning the admission of new states is not a mandate, but a power to be exercised with discretion. From this alone it would follow that Congress may require, under penalty of denying admission, that the organic law of a new state at the time of admission shall be such as to meet its approval. A Constitution thus supervised by Congress would, after all, be a Constitution of a state, and as such subject to alteration and amendment by the state after admission. Its force would be that of a state Constitution, and not that of an act of Congress.

So far as this court has found occasion to advert to the effect of enabling acts as affirmative legislation affecting the power of new states after admission, there is to be found no sanction for the contention that any state may be deprived of any of the power constitutionally possessed by other states, as states, by reason of the terms in which the acts admitting them to the Union have been framed.

The plain deduction from the Court's cases is that when a new state is admitted into the Union, it is so admitted with all of the powers of sovereignty and jurisdiction which pertain to the original states, and that such powers may not be constitutionally diminished, impaired, or shorn away by any conditions, compacts, or stipulations embraced in the act under which the new state came into the Union, which would not be valid and effectual if the subject of congressional legislation after admission.

It may well happen that Congress should embrace in an enactment introducing a new state into the Union legislation intended as a regulation of commerce among the states, or with Indian tribes situated within the limits of such new state, or regulations touching the sole care and disposition of the public lands or reservations therein, which might be upheld as legislation within the sphere of the plain power of Congress. But in every such case such legislation would derive its force not from any agreement or compact with the proposed new state, nor by reason of its acceptance of such enactment as a term of admission, but solely because the power of Congress extended to the subject, and therefore would not operate to restrict the state's legislative power in respect of any matter which was not plainly within the regulating power of Congress.

No such question is presented here. The legislation in the Oklahoma enabling act relating to the location of the capital of the state, if construed as forbidding a removal by the state after its admission as a state, is referable to no power granted to Congress over the subject, and if it is to be upheld at all, it must be implied from the power to admit new states. If power to impose such a restriction upon the general and undelegated power of a state be conceded as implied from the power to admit a new state, where is the line to be drawn against restrictions imposed upon new states?

Has Oklahoma been admitted upon an equal footing with the original states? If she has, she, by virtue of her jurisdictional sovereignty as such a state, may determine for her own people the proper location of the local seat of government. She is not equal in power to them if she cannot.

In *Lane County v. Oregon* (1868), Chief Justice Chase said:

> The people of the United States constitute one nation, under one government; and this government, within the scope of the powers with which it is invested, is supreme. On the other hand, the people of each state compose a state, having its own government, and endowed with all the functions essential to separate and independent existence. The states disunited might continue to exist. Without the states in union there could be no such political body as the United States.

To this we may add that the constitutional equality of the states is essential to the harmonious operation of the scheme upon which the Republic was organized. When that equality disappears we may remain a free people, but the Union will not be the Union of the Constitution.

NOTE

Congress occasionally has insisted on a particular provision being included in a new State's constitution as a condition of admission to the Union. One notable example is an anti-polygamy provision in several western state constitutions. *See* Ariz. Const. art. XX, par. 2; Idaho Const. art. I, § 4; N.M. Const. art. XXI, § 1; Okla. Const. art. I, § 2; Utah Const. art. III, § 1; *Romer v Evans*, 517 U.S. 620, 648–49 (1996) (Scalia, J., dissenting) ("The Constitutions of the States of Arizona, Idaho, New

Mexico, Oklahoma, and Utah contain provisions stating that polygamy is "forever prohibited."). The United States Congress *required* the inclusion of these antipolygamy provisions in the Constitutions of Arizona, New Mexico, Oklahoma, and Utah, as a condition of their admission to statehood. *See* Arizona Enabling Act, 36 Stat. 569 (1910); New Mexico Enabling Act, 36 Stat. 558 (1910); Oklahoma Enabling Act, 34 Stat. 269 (1906); Utah Enabling Act, 28 Stat. 108 (1894). For Arizona, New Mexico, and Utah, the Enabling Acts required that the antipolygamy provisions be "irrevocable without the consent of the United States and the people of said State." Congress also required many States to include Blaine Amendments, which prohibited the use of state resources to support churches and other religious entities, in their state constitutions as a condition of admission to the union. The history of the Blaine Amendments and the controversies that arise under them are discussed in Chapter X.

e. The Guarantee Clause

Article IV, § 4, known as the Republican Government Clause or Guarantee Clause, potentially could influence the States and the contents of state constitutions. The Guarantee Clause declares that the "United States shall guarantee to every State in this Union a Republican Form of Government." The U.S. Supreme Court to date has not given the provision substantive content. It instead has treated claims under the Clause as raising nonjusticiable, political questions beyond the competence of the courts to resolve. Enforcement of the Clause has been left to Congress.

LUTHER v. BORDEN
48 U.S. 1 (1849)

TANEY, C.J.

This case has arisen out of the unfortunate political differences which agitated the people of Rhode Island in 1841 and 1842. It is an action of trespass brought by Martin Luther, the plaintiff in error, against Luther M. Borden and others for breaking and entering the plaintiff's house. The defendants justify upon the ground that large numbers of men were assembled in different parts of the State for the purpose of overthrowing the government by military force, and were actually levying war upon the State; that, in order to defend itself from this insurrection, the State was declared by competent authority to be under martial law; that the plaintiff was engaged in the insurrection; and that the defendants, being in the military service of the State, by command of their superior officer, broke and entered the house and searched the rooms for the plaintiff, who was supposed to be there concealed, in order to arrest him, doing as little damage as possible. The plaintiff replied that the trespass was committed by the defendants of their own proper wrong, and without any such cause.

The evidence offered by the plaintiff and the defendants and the questions decided by the Circuit Court, and brought up by the writ of error, are not such as commonly arise in an action of trespass. The existence and authority of the government under which the defendants acted was called in question; and the plaintiff insists that, before the acts complained of were committed, that government had been displaced and annulled by the people of Rhode Island, and that the plaintiff was engaged in supporting the lawful authority of the State, and the defendants themselves were in arms against it.

This is a new question in this court, and certainly a very grave one; and at the time when the trespass is alleged to have been committed, it had produced a general and painful excitement in the State, and threatened to end in bloodshed and civil war.

The evidence shows that the defendants, in breaking into the plaintiff's house and endeavouring to arrest him, as stated in the pleadings, acted under the authority of the government which was established in Rhode Island at the time of the Declaration of Independence, and which is usually called the charter government. For when the separation from England took place, Rhode Island did not, like the other States, adopt a new constitution, but continued the form of government established by the charter of Charles the Second in 1663; making only such alterations, by acts of the legislature, as were necessary to adapt it to their condition and rights as an independent State. It was under this form of government that Rhode Island united with the other States in the Declaration of Independence, and afterwards ratified the Constitution of the United States and became a member of this Union; and it continued to be the established and unquestioned government of the State until the difficulties took place which have given rise to this action.

For some years previous to the disturbances of which we are now speaking, many of the citizens became dissatisfied with the charter government, and particularly with the restriction upon the right of suffrage. Memorials were addressed to the legislature upon this subject, urging the justice and necessity of a more liberal and extended rule. But they failed to produce the desired effect. And thereupon meetings were held and associations formed by those who were in favor of a more extended right of suffrage, which finally resulted in the election of a convention to form a new constitution to be submitted to the people for their adoption or rejection. This convention was not authorized by any law of the existing government. It was elected at voluntary meetings, and by those citizens only who favored this plan of reform; those who were opposed to it, or opposed to the manner in which it was proposed to be accomplished, taking no part in the proceedings. The persons chosen as above mentioned came together and framed a constitution, by which the right of suffrage was extended to every male citizen of twenty-one years of age, who had resided in the State for one year, and in the town in which he offered to vote, for six months, next preceding the election. The convention also prescribed the manner in which this constitution should be submitted to the decision of the people, permitting everyone to vote on that question who was an American citizen, twenty-one years old, and who had a permanent residence or home in the State.

Upon the return of the votes, the convention declared that the constitution was adopted and ratified by a majority of the people of the State. The charter government did not, however, admit the validity of these proceedings, nor acquiesce in them. On the contrary, when this new constitution was communicated to the governor, and by him laid before the legislature, it passed resolutions declaring all acts done for the purpose of imposing that constitution upon the State to be an assumption of the powers of government, in violation of the rights of the existing government and of the people at large; and that it would maintain its authority and defend the legal and constitutional rights of the people.

But, notwithstanding the determination of the charter government, and of those who adhered to it, to maintain its authority, Thomas W. Dorr, who had been elected governor under the new constitution, prepared to assert the authority of that government by force, and many citizens assembled in arms to support him. The charter government thereupon passed an act declaring the State under martial law, and at the same time proceeded to call out the militia, to repel the threatened attack and to subdue those who were engaged in it. In this state of the contest, the house of the plaintiff, who was engaged in supporting the authority of the new government, was broken and entered in order to arrest him. The defendants were, at the time, in the military service of the old government, and in arms to support its authority.

The plaintiff contends that the charter government was displaced, and ceased to have any lawful power, after the organization, in May, 1842, of the government which he supported, and although that government never was able to exercise any authority in the State, nor to command obedience to its laws or to its officers, yet he insists that it was the lawful and established government, upon the ground that it was ratified by a large majority of the male people of the State of the age of twenty-one and upwards.

The Circuit Court instructed the jury that the charter government and laws under which the defendants acted were, at the time the trespass is alleged to have been committed, in full force and effect as the form of government and paramount law of the State, and constituted a justification of the acts of the defendants.

Certainly, the question which the plaintiff proposed to raise by the testimony he offered has not heretofore been recognized as a judicial one in any of the State courts. Undoubtedly the courts of the United States have certain powers under the Constitution and laws of the United States which do not belong to the State courts. But the power of determining that a State government has been lawfully established, which the courts of the State disown and repudiate, is not one of them. Upon such a question the courts of the United States are bound to follow the decisions of the State tribunals, and must therefore regard the charter government as the lawful established government during the time of this contest.

Moreover, the Constitution of the United States, as far as it has provided for an emergency of this kind, and authorized the general government to interfere in the domestic concerns of a State, has treated the subject as political in its nature, and placed the power in the hands of that department. The fourth section of the fourth article of the Constitution of the United States provides that the United States shall guarantee to every State in the Union a republican form of government, and shall protect each of them against invasion; and on the application of the legislature or of the executive (when the legislature cannot be convened) against domestic violence.

Under this article of the Constitution it rests with Congress to decide what government is the established one in a State. For as the United States guarantee to each State a republican government, Congress must necessarily decide what government is established in the State before it can determine whether it is republican or not. And when the senators and representatives of a State are admitted into the councils of the Union, the authority of the government under which they are appointed, as well as its republican character, is recognized by the proper constitutional authority. And its decision is binding on every other department of the government, and could not be questioned in a judicial tribunal.

Congress, by the act of February 28, 1795, provided, that, "in case of an insurrection in any State against the government thereof, it shall be lawful for the President of the United States, on application of the legislature of such State or of the executive (when the legislature cannot be convened), to call forth such number of the militia of any other State or States, as may be applied for, as he may judge sufficient to sufficient to suppress such insurrection."

By this act, the power of deciding whether the exigency had arisen upon which the government of the United States is bound to interfere, is given to the President. He is to act upon the application of the legislature or of the executive, and consequently he must determine what body of men constitute the legislature, and who is the governor, before he can act. The fact that both parties claim the right to the government cannot alter the case, for both cannot be entitled to it. If there is an armed conflict, like the one of which we are speaking, it is a case of domestic violence, and one of the parties must be in insurrection against the lawful government. And the President must, of necessity, decide which is the government, and which party is unlawfully arrayed against it.

After the President has acted and called out the militia, is a Circuit Court of the United States authorized to inquire whether his decision was right? If the judicial power extends so far, the guarantee contained in the Constitution of the United States is a guarantee of anarchy, and not of order. No one, we believe, has ever doubted the proposition, that, according to the institutions of this country, the sovereignty in every State resides in the people of the State, and that they may alter and change their form of government at their own pleasure. But whether they have changed it or not by abolishing an old government, and establishing a new one in its place, is a question to be settled by the political power.

PACIFIC STATES TELEPHONE & TELEGRAPH CO. v. OREGON
223 U.S. 118 (1912)

WHITE, C.J.

We premise by saying that while the controversy which this record presents is of much importance, it is not novel. It is important, since it calls upon us to decide whether it is the duty of the courts or the province of Congress to determine when a state has ceased to be republican in form, and to enforce the guaranty of the Constitution on that subject. It is not novel, as that question has long since been determined by this court conformably to the practice of the government from the beginning to be political in character, and therefore not cognizable by the judicial power, but solely committed by the Constitution to the judgment of Congress.

The case is this: In 1902 Oregon amended its Constitution. This amendment, while retaining an existing clause vesting the exclusive legislative power in a general assembly consisting of a senate and a house of representatives, added to that provision the following: 'But the people reserve to themselves power to propose laws and amendments to the Constitution, and to enact or reject the same at the polls, independent of the legislative assembly, and also reserve power at their own option to approve or reject at the polls any act of the legislative assembly.' Specific means for the exercise of the power thus reserved was contained in further clauses authorizing both the amendment of the Constitution and the enactment of laws to be accomplished by the method known as the initiative and that commonly referred to as the referendum. In 1903 detailed provisions for the carrying into effect of this amendment were enacted by the legislature.

By resort to the initiative in 1906, a law taxing certain classes of corporations was submitted, voted on, and promulgated by the governor in 1907 as having been duly adopted. By this law telephone and telegraph companies were taxed, by what was qualified as an annual license, 2 percent upon their gross revenue derived from business done within the state. Penalties were provided for nonpayment, and methods were created for enforcing payment in case of delinquency.

The Pacific States Telephone & Telegraph Company, an Oregon corporation engaged in business in that state, made a return of its gross receipts, as required by the statute, and was accordingly assessed 2 per cent upon the amount of such return. The suit which is now before us was commenced by the state to enforce payment of this assessment and the statutory penalties for delinquency. The company challenged the tax assessment, lost, and appealed to the Supreme Court.

The assignments of error are numerous. The entire matters covered by each and all of them in the argument, however, are reduced to six propositions, which really amount to but one. In other words, the propositions of alleged error each and all proceed alone upon the theory that the adoption of the initiative and referendum destroyed all government republican in form in Oregon. Before immediately considering the text of § 4 of article IV, in order to uncover and give emphasis to the anomalous and destructive effects upon both the state and national governments which the adoption of the proposition implies, let us briefly fix the inconceivable expansion of the judicial power and the ruinous destruction of legislative authority in matters purely political which would necessarily be occasioned by giving sanction to the doctrine which underlies and would be necessarily involved in sustaining the propositions contended for.

We shall not stop to consider the text of Article IV, § 4, to point out how absolutely barren it is of support for the contentions sought to be based upon it, since the repugnancy of those contentions to the letter and spirit of that text is so conclusively established by prior decisions of this court as to cause the matter to be absolutely foreclosed. In view of the importance of the subject, the apparent misapprehension on one side and seeming misconception on the other, suggested by the argument as to the full significance of the previous doctrine, we do not content ourselves with a mere citation of the cases, but state more at length than we otherwise would the issues and the doctrine expounded in the leading and absolutely controlling case, *Luther v. Borden* (1849).

The fundamental doctrines thus so lucidly and cogently announced by the court, speaking through Mr. Chief Justice Taney in *Luther*, have never been doubted or questioned since, and have afforded the light guiding the orderly development of our constitutional system from the day of the deliverance of that decision up to the present time. It is indeed a singular misconception of the nature and character of our constitutional system of government to suggest that the settled distinction between judicial authority over justiciable controversies and legislative power as to purely political questions tends to destroy the duty of the judiciary in proper cases to enforce the Constitution. The suggestion but results from failing to distinguish between things which are widely different; that is, the legislative duty to determine the political questions involved in deciding whether a state government republican in form exists, and the judicial power and ever-present duty whenever it becomes necessary, in a controversy properly submitted, to enforce and uphold the applicable provisions of the Constitution as to each and every exercise of governmental power.

How better can the broad lines which distinguish these two subjects be pointed out than by considering the character of the defense in this very case? The defendant company does not contend here that it could not have been required to pay a license tax. It does not assert that it was denied an opportunity to be heard as to the amount for which it was taxed, or that there was anything inhering in the tax or involved intrinsically in the law which violated any of its constitutional rights. If such questions had been raised, they would have been justiciable, and therefore would have required the calling into operation of judicial power. Instead, however, of doing any of these things, the attack on the statute here made is of a wholly different character. Its essentially political nature is at once made manifest by understanding that the assault which the contention here advanced makes is not on the tax as a tax, but on the state as a state. It is addressed to the framework and political character of the government by which the statute levying the tax was passed. It is the government, the political entity, which (reducing the case to its essence) is called to the bar of this court, not for the purpose of testing judicially some exercise of power, assailed on the ground that its exertion has injuriously affected the rights of an individual because of repugnancy to some constitutional limitation, but to demand of the state that it establish its right to exist as a state, republican in form.

As the issues presented, in their very essence, are, and have long since by this court been, definitely determined to be political and governmental, and embraced within the scope of the powers conferred upon Congress, and not, therefore, within the reach of judicial power, it follows that the case presented is not within our jurisdiction, and the writ of error must therefore be, and it is, dismissed for want of jurisdiction.

Chapter III

THEORIES BY WHICH STATE COURTS MAY CONSTRUE STATE CONSTITUTIONS DIFFERENTLY FROM THEIR FEDERAL COUNTERPARTS

In this chapter, we develop one of the main themes of the textbook: the reasons why state courts might choose to construe a guarantee in their own constitutions differently from a related guarantee in the U.S. Constitution. Before discussing what state courts might do in this respect, it is worth remembering why they may do it. The Supremacy Clause of the U.S. Constitution says that the "Constitution of the United States shall be the supreme Law of the Land" and makes "the Judges in every State bound thereby," notwithstanding any "Thing in the Constitution of any State to the Contrary." U.S. Const. art. VI. The Clause amounts to a conflict-of-laws provision. Much as the U.S. Constitution governs when it conflicts with a federal statute, *see Marbury v. Madison* (1803), so the Supremacy Clause establishes that federal law governs when it conflicts with a state statute or state constitution. In establishing that federal law trumps contrary state law, however, the Supremacy Clause does nothing to limit the force of state law in the absence of a relevant federal provision or decision. That means the state supreme courts not only have the final say over the meaning of their own constitutions, but they also have the final say over the "constitutional" limitations in the State to the extent those limitations exceed any floor set by the U.S. Constitution.

Another way to think about it is this: A litigant challenging the validity of a state or local law may seek relief under the federal or the relevant state constitution. The Framers established a government that features two sets of sovereigns over any given part of the country, that produced fifty-one constitutions, and that, in the end, places two constitutional limitations on the validity of most state and local laws. The constitutional claimant needs to win just once, and a victory under the one invalidates a local law no less than a victory under the other. One upshot of a federal system of dual sovereignty is that it permits dual claims of unconstitutionality.

To say that a state supreme court *may* invalidate a law under its constitution, however, is not to say that it *should*. The key point of this chapter is to offer reasons why state courts in some areas have charted different paths from the U.S. Supreme Court in construing identical or related constitutional guarantees. The chapter breaks down into five parts. The first considers the reasons why a state court might choose to construe an identically worded guarantee in its own constitution differently from a parallel provision in the U.S. Constitution. The second part considers the state courts' treatment of uniquely worded guarantees. The third part considers two related topics: (1) why a state court might choose not to chart a separate path from the federal constitutional baseline and (2) how one determines whether a state court has relied on an independent and adequate state law ground and thereby insulated its ruling from review by the U.S. Supreme Court. The fourth part explains that state courts may construe their constitutions to provide more *or* less protection than their federal counterparts. The fifth part addresses a sequencing question that state courts face in resolving every case that raises a state and federal constitutional claim: Which answer comes first? Should the state courts resolve the state claim before resolving the related federal claim? Or should they resolve the federal claims first? Through it all, should the state courts presume that the U.S. Supreme Court's resolution of a federal constitutional claim is presumptively correct when construing similar state guarantees? The chapter is a prelude to the next several chapters of the casebook, which develop these themes in the context of specific areas of constitutional law, such as equal protection, voting, due process, property rights, criminal procedure, and many others.

A. SIMILARLY WORDED GUARANTEES

Why might a state supreme court construe an individual-rights guarantee of its state constitution differently from one found in the U.S. Constitution and do so even when the guarantees parallel each other word for word? There are several reasons.

Scope of jurisdiction. The U.S. Supreme Court faces geographical and jurisdictional challenges that the state courts do not. Because the Supreme Court must announce rights and remedies for fifty States, one National Government and 330 million people, it is far more constrained than a state supreme court addressing a difficult problem for one State and ten million people. All U.S. Supreme Court Justices, no matter the president who appointed them or the worldview they embrace, are sensitive to the risks of issuing rulings that prevent the democratic processes from working in fifty-one different jurisdictions.

New constitutional rights not only require the articulation of a new constitutional theory, they also require the management of a new constitutional right. All judges worry about the next case when they identify a new constitutional right. But U.S. Supreme Court Justices have more to worry about than state court judges in view of the breadth of their jurisdiction and the wider variety of circumstances that each new right will confront. In some settings, the challenge of imposing a constitutional solution on the whole country at once will increase the likelihood that federal constitutional law will be under-enforced or that a "federalism discount" will be applied to the right. Jeffrey S. Sutton, San Antonio Independent School District v. Rodriguez *and Its Aftermath*, 94 Va. L. Rev. 1963, 1979 (2008). State courts face no such problem in construing their own constitutions.

A mistaken or an ill-conceived constitutional decision is also easier to correct at the state level than it is at the federal level. Not only do the state courts have a narrower jurisdiction and smaller populations that their decisions will affect, but the people at the state level have other remedies at their disposal: an easier constitutional amendment process and, for better or worse, judicial elections in most States. In some settings, these considerations will give state courts more room to innovate—to be the familiar "laboratories of experimentation" that Justice Brandeis envisioned.

Local conditions and traditions. State courts also have a freer hand to do something the Supreme Court cannot: to allow local conditions and traditions to affect their interpretation of a constitutional guarantee and the remedies imposed to implement that guarantee. In one State, the right to privacy may warrant greater protection than in another. In a rural State, individual property rights and the right to bear arms may warrant greater protection than in a State with large suburban and urban populations. Free exercise concerns may resonate differently in some States than in others. And the right to equal protection, and its application to the definition of marriage, may be viewed differently in some States than in others. State constitutional law respects these distinct traditions by allowing the fifty state constitutions to be interpreted differently to account for these differences in culture, geography, and history. Through it all, the counterpart guarantees of the U.S. Constitution provide a potential floor in each of these areas.

Indeterminate questions. Another reason why the state courts might not follow the federal courts in construing identical constitutional guarantees is that the legal and equitable complexities of many issues do not lend themselves to one-size-fits-all solutions. Some constitutional issues do not readily submit to a clear answer, and indeterminate legal questions often lead to indeterminate legal answers. The federal courts might apply a balancing test in construing a liberty guarantee, while the state courts might apply a bright-line rule or might adopt a balancing test but balance the competing interests differently. The federal courts might adopt an originalist approach in construing a guarantee, while the state courts might embrace a living constitutionalist approach to the same language. Another protection might be construed in a pragmatic way in the federal courts but construed in a formalistic way in a state court. The more indeterminate the answer to a legal question the more one should expect federal and state court judges of good will, faced with distinct geographical limitations on their power, to construe similar language differently.

Disagreement with the U.S. Supreme Court. In some cases, the state court's analysis comes to nothing more than an analytical or policy-based objection to the federal precedent. While these cases may be influenced by the above factors, the theme that dominates the state court's ruling is a fundamental disagreement with the National Court's interpretation of similar language. A system of dual sovereignty contemplates, tolerates, and ultimately embraces state and federal differences of opinion.

In the cases that follow, and in the chapters that follow, ask yourself why the state courts chose to construe the guarantees of their constitutions differently from the similarly worded guarantees of the U.S. Constitution.

SITZ v. DEPARTMENT OF STATE POLICE
506 N.W.2d 209 (Mich. 1993)

BOYLE, J.

The case before us concerns a challenge to the use of sobriety checkpoints by the Michigan State Police. The United States Supreme Court held that the checkpoint scheme does not constitute a violation of the Fourth Amendment of the United States Constitution. On remand from that Court, a two-judge majority of the Michigan Court of Appeals determined that sobriety checkpoints violate art. 1, § 11 of the Michigan Constitution. Because there is no support in the constitutional history of Michigan for the proposition that the police may engage in warrantless and suspicionless seizures of automobiles for the purpose of enforcing the criminal law, we hold that sobriety check points violate art. 1, § 11 of the Michigan Constitution.

The first sobriety checkpoint operation was conducted at Dixie Highway and Gretchen Road in Saginaw County on May 17 and 18, 1986. The Saginaw County Sheriff's Department cooperated in the operation which lasted from about 11:45 p.m. to 1:00 a.m. One hundred twenty-six vehicles passed through the checkpoint in that time, with an average delay to motorists of twenty-five seconds or less. Two drivers were retained for sobriety field tests; one was arrested for driving while under the influence of alcohol. A third driver drove through the checkpoint without stopping, was pulled over by an officer in an observation vehicle, and was arrested for driving under the influence.

The U.S. Supreme Court held that the Michigan sobriety checkpoint program did not violate the Fourth Amendment of the United States Constitution: "In sum, the balance of the State's interest in preventing drunken driving, the extent to which this system can reasonably be said to advance that interest, and the degree of intrusion upon individual motorists who are briefly stopped, weighs in favor of the state program. We therefore hold that it is consistent with the Fourth Amendment."

During the decade of United States Supreme Court jurisprudence "commonly characterized as the criminal law revolution of the Warren Court," the Supreme Court "rapidly extended the reach of various constitutional provisions applicable to the criminal justice process."

Subsequent decisions of the Burger Court were characterized by some commentators as pulling back from, suspending, or weakening the scope of constitutional protections, including the specific guarantees of the Bill of Rights.

Awakened to the potential for a reappraisal of claims based on state constitutional grounds, members of the Michigan bar joined their colleagues across the country in pressing claims seeking interpretations of state law that provided more expansive criminal procedure protections than those recognized under federal law. By 1983, the number of rights-expansive claims based on state law had proliferated to the point that guidance from this Court was deemed both appropriate and necessary.

Thus, in *People v. Nash* (Mich. 1983), the Court conducted the first modern-day comprehensive survey of the circumstances surrounding the creation of Const. 1963, art. 1, § 11 to determine whether our constitution required a higher level of search and seizure protection than the Fourth Amendment of the United States Constitution. Our conclusion in *Nash*, that "the history of Const. 1963, art. 1, § 11, and its plain import, suggest that its further expansion should occur only when there is a compelling reason to do so" was intended to clarify for the bench and bar that claims that art. 1, § 11 should be interpreted more expansively than the Fourth Amendment must rest on more than a disagreement with the United States Supreme Court.

Our analysis in *Nash* began by noting that the federal and state constitutional provisions that forbid unreasonable searches and seizures are nearly identical.[1]

The judiciary of this state is not free to simply engraft onto art. 1, § 11 more "enlightened" rights than the framers intended. By the same token, we may not disregard the guarantees that our constitution confers on Michigan citizens merely because the United States Supreme Court has withdrawn or not extended such protection.

---

[1] U.S. Const. amend. IV provides:

The right of the people to be secure in their persons, houses, papers, and effects, against unreasonable searches and seizures, shall not be violated, and no Warrants shall issue, but upon probable cause, supported by Oath or affirmation, and particularly describing the place to be searched, and the persons or things to be seized.

Const. 1963, art. 1, § 11 provides:

The person, houses, papers and possessions of every person shall be secure from unreasonable searches and seizures. No warrant to search any place or to seize any person or things shall issue without describing them, nor without probable cause, supported by oath or affirmation. The provisions of this section shall not be construed to bar from evidence in any criminal proceeding any narcotic drug, firearm, bomb, explosive or any other dangerous weapon, seized by a peace officer outside the curtilage of any dwelling house in this state.

The Michigan Declaration of Rights, like the federal Bill of Rights, is "drawn to restrict governmental conduct and to provide protection from governmental infringement and excesses." When there is a clash of competing rights under the state and federal constitutions, the Supremacy Clause, art. VI, cl. 2, dictates that the federal right prevails. Where a right is given to a citizen under federal law, it does not follow that the organic instrument of state government must be interpreted as conferring the identical right. Nor does it follow that where a right given by the federal constitution is not given by a state constitution, the state constitution offends the federal constitution. It is only where the organic instrument of government purports to deprive a citizen of a right granted by the federal constitution that the instrument can be said to violate the constitution.

Thus, appropriate analysis of our constitution does not begin from the conclusive premise of a federal floor. Indeed, the fragile foundation of the federal floor as a bulwark against arbitrary action is clearly revealed when, as here, the federal floor falls below minimum state protection. As a matter of simple logic, because the texts were written at different times by different people, the protections afforded may be greater, lesser, or the same.

As long ago as 1889, the justices of this Court stated:

> Personal liberty, which is guaranteed to every citizen under our Constitution and laws, consists of the right of locomotion—to go where one pleases, and when, and to do that which may lead to one's business or pleasure, only so far restrained as the rights of others may make it necessary for the welfare of all other citizens. One may travel along the public highways or in public places; and while conducting themselves in a decent and orderly manner, disturbing no other, and interfering with the rights of no other citizens, there, they will be protected under the law, not only in their persons, but in their safe conduct. The Constitution and the laws are framed for the public good, and the protection of all citizens, from the highest to the lowest; and no one may be restrained of his liberty, unless he has transgressed some law.

Our commitment to the protection of liberty was further demonstrated when the Supreme Court of Michigan adopted an exclusionary rule in 1919, forty-two years before it was mandated by federal law. Moreover, this Court's "historical general power to construe the constitutional provision relating to searches and seizures," has been extended to the seizure and search of vehicles.

The history of our jurisprudence conclusively demonstrates that, in the context of automobile seizures, we have extended more expansive protection to our citizens than that extended in *Sitz*. This Court has never recognized the right of the state, without any level of suspicion whatsoever, to detain members of the population at large for criminal investigatory purposes. Nor has Michigan completely acquiesced to the judgment of "politically accountable officials" when determining reasonableness in such a context. In these circumstances, the Michigan Constitution offers more protection than the United States Supreme Court's interpretation of the Fourth Amendment.

This Court showed a marked hostility toward the use of a license check as a pretext to investigate criminal activity. In *People ex rel. Attorney General v. Lansing Municipal Judge* (Mich. 1950), we stressed:

> It will be said that no legislature would go so far as to dry up the entire stream of constitutional immunity. But it is not the genius of our system that the constitutional rights of persons shall depend for their efficacy upon legislative benevolence. Rather, the courts are charged with the solemn obligation of erecting around those rights, in adjudicated cases, a barrier against legislative or executive invasion.

The Michigan Constitution has historically treated searches and seizures for criminal investigatory purposes differently than those for regulatory or administrative purposes. These administrative or regulatory searches and seizures have traditionally been regarded as "reasonable" in a constitutional sense. However, seizures with the primary goal of enforcing the criminal law have generally required some level of suspicion, even if that level has fluctuated over the years.

We do not suggest that in a different context we might not reach a similar result under the balancing test of reasonableness employed in *Sitz*. Indeed, our precedent regarding automobiles implicitly incorporates a balancing test that is inherent in assessing the reasonableness of warrantless searches and seizures. We hold only that the protection afforded to the seizures of vehicles for criminal investigatory purposes has both an historical foundation and a contemporary justification that is not outweighed by the necessity advanced. Suspicionless criminal investigatory seizures, and extreme deference to the judgments of politically accountable officials is, in this context, contrary to Michigan constitutional precedent.

NOTES

1. Consider the following excerpts from the U.S. Supreme Court's decision in *Sitz* remanding the case to the Michigan Supreme Court:

> Conversely, the weight bearing on the other scale—the measure of the intrusion on motorists stopped briefly at sobriety checkpoints—is slight. We reached a similar conclusion as to the intrusion on motorists subjected to a brief stop at a highway checkpoint for detecting illegal aliens. We see virtually no difference between the levels of intrusion on law-abiding motorists from the brief stops necessary to the effectuation of these two types of checkpoints, which to the average motorist would seem identical save for the nature of the questions the checkpoint officers might ask. The trial court and the Court of Appeals, thus, accurately gauged the "objective" intrusion, measured by the duration of the seizure and the intensity of the investigation, as minimal.
>
> The balance of the State's interest in preventing drunken driving, the extent to which this system can reasonably be said to advance that interest, and the degree of intrusion upon individual motorists who are briefly stopped, weighs in favor of

the state program. We therefore hold that it is consistent with the Fourth Amendment.

Mich. Dep't of State Police v. Sitz, 496 U.S. 444, 451–52, 455 (1990).

Did the state court simply balance these interests differently? Did it rely on traditions unique to Michigan? Did it simply disagree with the U.S. Supreme Court?

2. One reason that state courts often follow U.S. Supreme Court decisions in construing their own constitutional guarantees is the benefit of uniformity—one standard for state court judges to use and one standard for state officials to follow. But as Justice Appel on the Iowa Supreme Court has pointed out, such efficiencies may not be consistent with our unique system of federalism: "it is doubtful that uniformity is a constitutional value in a federal system. Indeed, diversity of constitutional analysis is baked into the constitutional cake where states retain sovereign authority over questions not delegated to the federal government by the United States Constitution." *State v. Short*, 851 N.W.2d 474, 487 (Iowa 2014).

STATE v. HEMPELE
576 A.2d 793 (N.J. 1990)

CLIFFORD, J.

The issue in these appeals, argued together, is the constitutionality of warrantless seizures and searches of garbage bags left on the curb for collection.

In *State v. Hempele*, a confidential source informed the state police that defendants, Conrad D. Hempele and Sharon Hempele, were distributing illicit drugs from their home at 303 Mill Street in Belvidere. The informant claimed to have seen fifty pounds of marijuana in Conrad's bedroom.

On the basis of that information, a trooper seized the trash sitting in front of 303 Mill Street six months later. 303 Mill Street is one of about ten attached row houses, each with its own front entrance. A short stairway runs from each row house to an eight-foot-wide sidewalk abutting the street. The seized trash was next to the flight of stairs leading to 303 Mill Street. Two weeks later the trooper again seized the garbage in front of the Hempeles' home. On both occasions the trooper removed white plastic trash bags from a plastic garbage can and took the bags to the State Police Tri-Man Unit, where, without a warrant, he opened them and analyzed their contents. He discovered traces of marijuana, cocaine, and methamphetamine in the trash.

A search warrant for defendants' home issued on the basis of the informant's tip and the evidence found in the garbage. When the subsequent search turned up controlled substances and drug paraphernalia, the Hempeles were indicted for drug offenses.

We consider first whether the garbage searches in these two cases violated the United States Constitution.

In *California v. Greenwood* (1988), the United States Supreme Court held that the fourth amendment does not prohibit unreasonable searches and seizures of garbage left for collection in an area accessible to the public. The Supreme Court held that the warrantless searches of Greenwood's garbage "would violate the Fourth Amendment only if respondents had manifested a subjective expectation of privacy in their garbage that society accepts as objectively reasonable." Ruling that a privacy expectation in garbage is not reasonable, the Court rejected the defendants' argument.

The Court decided that people lose any reasonable expectation of privacy in their trash by leaving it in bags alongside the street, because such garbage is vulnerable to an unscrupulous person or scavenging animal. Furthermore, garbage is placed on the curb for the specific purpose of having a third party remove it. The defendants should have realized that the trash collector might look through the garbage or allow another person to do so. The Court added that the fourth amendment does not protect what a person knowingly exposes to the public because "the police cannot reasonably be expected to avert their eyes from evidence of criminal activity that could have been observed by any member of the public."

Having decided that an expectation of privacy in trash left for collection in an area accessible to the public is unreasonable, the Court found it unnecessary to determine whether the defendants had manifested a subjective expectation of privacy. The warrantless garbage searches did not violate the fourth amendment.

Under *Greenwood* the issue is whether the garbage was left at a location "accessible to the public." The Hempeles left their garbage at a location accessible to the public. They cannot escape the force of *Greenwood*.

We now determine whether the New Jersey Constitution protects curbside garbage from unreasonable searches and seizures. Despite the similarity between the text of article I, paragraph 7 of the New Jersey Constitution and the text of the fourth amendment, we have found on several occasions that the former "affords our citizens greater protection against unreasonable searches and seizures than does the fourth amendment."

For most of our country's history, the primary source of protection of individual rights has been state constitutions, not the federal Bill of Rights. The genius of federalism is that the fundamental rights of citizens are protected not only by the United States Constitution but also by the laws of each of the states. The system may be untidy on occasion, but that untidiness invests it with "a vibrant diversity." "As tempting as it may be to harmonize results under the state and federal constitutions, federalism contemplated that state courts may grant greater protection to individual rights if they choose."

Cognizant of the diversity of laws, customs, and mores within its jurisdiction, the United States Supreme Court is necessarily "hesitant to impose on a national level far-reaching constitutional rules binding on each and every state." The Supreme Court must be especially cautious in fourth-amendment cases. When determining whether a search warrant is necessary in a specific circumstance, the Court must take note of the disparity in warrant-application procedures among the several states, and must consider whether a warrant requirement in that situation might overload the procedure in any one state. In contrast, we are fortunate to have in New Jersey a procedure that allows for the speedy and reliable issuance of search warrants based on probable cause. A warrant requirement is not so great a burden in New Jersey as it might be in other states.

The Supreme Court itself has implied that garbage searches are an appropriate issue on which state courts may rise above "the lowest common denominator." In holding that the fourth amendment does not protect garbage, the Court suggested that "individual States may surely construe their own constitutions as imposing more stringent constraints on police conduct than does the Federal Constitution."

In determining the reasonableness of an expectation of privacy in curbside garbage left for collection, we start from the premise that "expectations of privacy are established by general social norms." The "ultimate question" is whether, if garbage searches are "permitted to go unregulated by constitutional restraints, the amount of privacy and freedom remaining to citizens would be diminished to a compass inconsistent with the aims of a free and open society." With that question in mind, we first examine whether it is reasonable for a person to want to keep the contents of his or her garbage private.

Clues to people's most private traits and affairs can be found in their garbage. "Almost every human activity ultimately manifests itself in waste products and any individual may understandably wish to maintain the confidentiality of his refuse." A plethora of personal information can be culled from garbage:

> A single bag of trash testifies eloquently to the eating, reading, and recreational habits of the person who produced it. A search of trash, like a search of the bedroom, can relate intimate details about sexual practices, health, and personal hygiene. Like rifling through desk drawers or intercepting phone calls, rummaging through trash can divulge the target's financial and professional status, political affiliations and inclinations, private thoughts, personal relationships, and romantic interests.

Most people seem to have an interest in keeping such matters private; few publicize them voluntarily. Undoubtedly many would be upset to see a neighbor or stranger sifting through their garbage, perusing their discarded mail, reading their bank statements, looking at their empty pharmaceutical bottles, and checking receipts to see what videotapes they rent. The

California Supreme Court commented that it could "readily ascribe many reasons why residents would not want their castaway clothing, letters, medicine bottles or other telltale refuse and trash to be examined by neighbors or others. Half truths leading to rumor and gossip may readily flow from an attempt to read the contents of another's trash." *People v. Edwards* (Cal. 1969) (garbage left inside curtilage is constitutionally protected).

Like the fourth amendment, article I, paragraph 7 "provides protection to the owner of every container that conceals its contents from plain view." There is no "constitutional distinction between worthy and unworthy containers." "Paper bags, locked trunks, lunch buckets, and orange crates" all receive the same treatment. A privacy expectation does not depend on the value or quality of the container.

The critical issue is whether the container conceals its contents from plain view. Because ordinary opaque garbage bags conceal their contents from plain view, the presumption is that an expectation of privacy in the contents is reasonable.

The New Jersey Constitution "requires the approval of an impartial judicial officer based on probable cause before most searches may be undertaken." "Any warrantless search is *prima facie* invalid." Those principles certainly apply to opaque containers.

Once the protections of article I, paragraph 7 apply, a lower expectation of privacy is not a sufficient basis on which to carve out an exception to the warrant and probable-cause requirement. We can dispense with that requirement "only in those exceptional circumstances in which special needs, beyond the normal need for law enforcement, make the warrant and probable cause requirement impracticable." If a "special need" does exist, we can then make an exception to the requirement only after we "balance the nature and quality of the intrusion on the individual's constitutional interests against the importance of the governmental interests alleged to justify the intrusion."

Thus, even if garbage searches are only "minimally intrusive" of a person's privacy, the warrant and probable-cause requirement for garbage searches can be scrapped only if a special government interest significantly outweighs those privacy interests.

Because we find no special state interest that makes the warrant requirement impracticable, we hold that the State must secure a warrant based on probable cause in order to search garbage bags left on the curb for collection.

In summary, article I, paragraph 7 applies to the search but not to the seizure of a garbage bag left on the curb for collection. Law-enforcement officials need no cause to seize the bag, but they must have a warrant based on probable cause to search it.

Our decision today does not follow the course set by the Supreme Court because "we are persuaded that the equities so strongly favor protection of a person's privacy interest that we should apply our own standard rather than defer to the federal provision." We are aware that our ruling conflicts not only with *California v. Greenwood* but also with the holdings of virtually every other court that has considered this issue. Although the weight of the cited authority is impressive, our thorough consideration of the issue leads us to record our respectful disagreement with those courts that have reached a result contrary to ours.

We do concur, however, in the observation that there is no "unique New Jersey state attitude about garbage." Our differences with the cited authority rest on other grounds. As the trial court in *Pasanen* so eloquently put it, "the trouble with those cases is that they are flatly and simply wrong as the matter of the way people think about garbage." Garbage can reveal much that is personal. We do not find it unreasonable for people to want their garbage to remain private and to expect that it will remain private from the meddling of the State.

Article I, paragraph 7 confers "as against the government, the right to be let alone—the most comprehensive of rights and the right most valued by civilized men." Permitting the police to pick and poke their way through garbage bags to peruse without cause the vestiges of a person's most private affairs would be repugnant to that ideal. A free and civilized society should comport itself with more decency.

STATE v. WRIGHT
961 N.W.2d 396 (Iowa 2021)

McDONALD, J.

"Decency, security, and liberty alike demand that government officials shall be subjected to the same rules of conduct that are commands to the citizen." We are tasked in this case of determining whether this bedrock constitutional principle prohibits a peace officer engaged in general criminal investigation without a warrant from taking a citizen's opaque trash bags left outside for collection, opening the trash bags, and rummaging through the papers and effects contained therein.

Nicholas Wright lives in Clear Lake. Like most municipalities, Clear Lake regulates the "storage, collection and disposal of solid waste" to protect the "health, safety and welfare" of its residents. The city restricts the manner in which residents can dispose of waste. The city requires "the owner or occupant of the premises served" to set out the solid waste containers for collection once per week "at the curb or alley line." The city limits who may access and collect solid waste to licensed and contracted collectors. The city makes it "unlawful for any person to take or collect any solid waste which has been placed out for collection on any premises, unless such person is an authorized solid waste collector." Violation of this ordinance is punishable by a fine.

Despite the ordinance making it unlawful for any person (other than an authorized collector) to take solid waste placed out for collection, Officer Brandon Heinz, on three occasions, during the dark of night, without probable cause or a warrant, went into the alley behind Wright's residence to take Wright's garbage bags and search through them to "obtain information about what Mr. Wright may have been doing inside his house." More specifically, Officer Heinz was "looking for anything related to drug activity." Heinz focused his criminal investigation on Wright based on information from Deputy Tami Cavett. She informed Heinz that a male nicknamed "Beef" was selling drugs and lived near a local bar. Through the course of his investigation, Heinz discovered Wright went by the nickname "Beef" and lived three blocks from the bar.

The Iowa Constitution provides, "this Constitution shall be the supreme law of the state, and any law inconsistent therewith, shall be void." The Iowa Constitution provides any law—without regard to its source—inconsistent therewith "shall be void." None of the departments of our state government are authorized—by bill, order, rule, judicial decision, or otherwise—to make law or legalize conduct infringing upon the minimum rights guaranteed in the Iowa Constitution. We "must provide at a minimum the degree of protection the constitution afforded when it was adopted."

In determining the minimum degree of protection the constitution afforded when adopted, we generally look to the text of the constitution as illuminated by the lamp of precedent, history, custom, and practice.

This court is the final arbiter of the meaning of the Iowa Constitution. While we give respectful consideration to the decisions of the United States Supreme Court in its interpretation of parallel provisions of the Federal Constitution, we have a duty to independently interpret the Iowa Constitution. Our duty to independently interpret the Iowa Constitution holds even "though the two provisions may contain nearly identical language and have the same general scope, import, and purpose." On questions of state constitutional law, the Supreme Court "is, in law and in fact, inferior in authority to the courts of the States."

Our duty of independent interpretation is truly independent. Federal constitutional law is not a framework or "floor" that dictates the required doctrine or minimum content of the state constitution. "However useful that floor-ceiling metaphor may be, it obscures the larger truth that the level of protection of rights under the state constitutions can be the same as, higher than, or lower than that provided by the federal constitution."

In claims arising under the Iowa Constitution, the right question is thus not whether the Iowa Constitution should be interpreted more stringently or less stringently than its federal counterpart. "This court is free to interpret our constitution to provide less or more protection than the Federal Constitution."

Article I, section 8 of the Iowa Constitution provides:

> The right of the people to be secure in their persons, houses, papers and effects, against unreasonable seizures and searches shall not be violated; and no warrant shall issue but on probable cause, supported by oath or affirmation, particularly describing the place to be searched, and the persons and things to be seized.

At the time of America's founding, the prohibition against "unreasonable" seizures and searches had a particular meaning. John Adams first introduced the term "unreasonable" into search and seizure law in his draft of the 1780 Massachusetts Constitution. "Adams's authorship reveals that 'unreasonable' was derived from Sir Edward Coke's earlier use of 'against reason' as a synonym for inherent illegality or unconstitutionality."

The Fourth Amendment did not refer to reasonableness in a relativistic, balancing sense. "Originally, the word 'unreasonable' in the Fourth Amendment likely meant 'against reason'—as in 'against the reason of the common law.'" Justice Story, in his leading treatise on the Federal Constitution, stated the prohibition against unreasonable seizures and searches "is little more than the affirmance of a great constitutional doctrine of the common law."

The original understanding of article I, section 8 is in accord with the original understanding of the Fourth Amendment. As we long ago explained, "the term 'unreasonable' in the constitutions of the States, has allusion to what had been practiced before our revolution, and especially to general search warrants, in which the person, place or thing was not described."

Consistent with this understanding, we have long held that a peace officer engaged in general criminal investigation acted unreasonably and unlawfully when he trespassed against a citizen without first obtaining a warrant based on probable cause.

Iowa adhered to this original understanding of article I, section 8 until the era of incorporation of the Bill of Rights into the Fourteenth Amendment. Although not compelled to construe article I, section 8 to follow the Supreme Court's construction of the Fourth and Fourteenth Amendments, this court nonetheless began to do so. As a consequence, this court's jurisprudence changed rather dramatically in conjunction with changes in the Supreme Court's jurisprudence. The Supreme Court moved away from the original understanding of the Fourth Amendment right in two significant respects. First, the Court imposed a modern, relativistic meaning on the word "unreasonable." Second, in *Katz v. United States* (1967), the Court refocused the inquiry from common law trespass to the aggrieved party's reasonable expectation of privacy.

In recent years, this court has moved away from the lockstep approach and taken a more historical approach in interpreting article I, section 8.

This court and the Supreme Court's return to the historical understandings of seizure and search jurisprudence, to some degree, was born of necessity. Current Fourth Amendment jurisprudence is a mess. While *Katz* became "'the basis of a new formula of fourth amendment coverage,' it can hardly be said that the Court produced clarity where theretofore there had been uncertainty. If anything, the exact opposite has occurred."

"Fourth Amendment jurisprudence is in flux." There are competing, inconsistent doctrines governing seizure and search law—the original meaning, the "touchstone" of reasonableness, and the "lodestar" of *Katz*. Given the uncertainty and lack of clarity in federal search and seizure jurisprudence, we conclude it is no longer tenable to follow federal precedents in lockstep. Article I, section 8, as originally understood, was meant to provide the same protections as the Fourth Amendment, as originally understood, but the Supreme Court's interpretation and construction of the Fourth Amendment has deviated from the text and original meaning. Respectful consideration of the Supreme Court's precedents does not require adherence to federal doctrine that members of that great Court, other jurists, and commentators all acknowledge departs from the text and original meaning of the constitutional prohibition against unreasonable seizures and searches.

A survey of the relevant text, history, and precedents shows article I, section 8's prohibition against unreasonable searches and seizures was tied to common law trespass. In light of that understanding, we hold a peace officer engaged in general criminal investigation acts unreasonably under article I, section 8 when the peace officer commits a trespass against a citizen's house, papers, or effects without first obtaining a warrant based "on probable cause, supported by oath or affirmation, particularly describing the place to be searched, and the persons and things to be seized."

We now directly address Wright's claim that Officer Heinz violated his state constitutional right under article I, section 8. Wright has two separate and distinct bases for challenging the warrantless seizures and searches. First, relying on the common law understanding of seizure and search law, Wright argues Heinz physically trespassed on Wright's property and thus the warrantless search violated article I, section 8. Second, relying on the expectation-of-privacy approach to seizure and search law, Wright argues Heinz violated article I, section 8 by invading Wright's expectation of privacy in his garbage bags. It is the State's burden to prove that a warrantless search or seizure is constitutional.

We first consider whether Heinz's conduct amounted to a seizure or search within the meaning of article I, section 8. There is no evidence these terms were terms of art at the time of the founding. "No literal or mechanical approach should be adopted in determining what may constitute a search and seizure." We thus give the words their fair and ordinary meaning.

It is apparent Heinz seized the garbage bags and papers and effects contained therein under any fair and ordinary definition of the term seizure. "A 'seizure' of property occurs when there is some meaningful interference" with the property.

It is equally apparent Heinz engaged in a search when he opened the garbage bags and rummaged through them. "When the Fourth Amendment was adopted, as now, to 'search' meant 'to look over or through for the purpose of finding something; to explore; to examine by inspection; as, to search the house for a book; to search the wood for a thief.'" Historical legal dictionaries defined a search as an examination "with a view to the discovery of contraband or illicit or stolen property, or some evidence of guilt to be used in the prosecution of a criminal action for some crime or offense with which he is charged," or an examination conducted for the "purpose of discovering proof of his guilt in relation to some crime or misdemeanor of which he is accused." Here, Heinz testified he opened the garbage to "obtain information about what Mr. Wright may have been doing inside his house" and obtain evidence "related to drug activity." A constitutional search occurs whenever the government commits a physical trespass against property, even where de minimis, conjoined with "an attempt to find something or to obtain information."

For the purposes of determining whether a seizure or search occurred, it is not relevant whether Wright had an expectation of privacy in the garbage bags or the contents.

We next address whether the items Heinz seized and searched were protected papers and effects within the meaning of article I, section 8. The word papers is self-explanatory, but the word effects requires some explanation. The modern understanding of the term effects is "movable property; goods." This is consistent with the original understanding. "The Framers would have understood the term 'effects' to be limited to personal, rather than real, property."

We have little trouble concluding the property at issue is protected within the meaning of article I, section 8. Opaque garbage bags are containers, and containers are an "effect" as originally understood. The fact that the containers happen to be garbage bags rather than, say, expensive luggage, is not of constitutional consequence. There is no "constitutional distinction between 'worthy' and 'unworthy' containers." "Even though such a distinction perhaps could evolve in a series of cases in which paper bags, locked trunks, lunch buckets, and orange crates were placed on one side of the line or the other, the central purpose of the Fourth Amendment forecloses such a distinction." In addition, Heinz opened the garbage bags and searched through the contents. The contents included other personal property, including two pieces of mail addressed to Wright. Letters are certainly papers. Further, "letters are in the general class of effects," and "warrantless searches of such effects are presumptively unreasonable."

We next address whether Heinz's conduct constituted a trespass thus making the warrantless search unconstitutional under article I, section 8. At the time of the founding, trespass was a broad concept that encompassed far more than physical intrusions into or on real or personal property. "Trespass, in its largest and most extensive sense, signified any transgression or offence against the law of nature, of society, or of the country in which we live; whether it related to a man's person, or his property." Within the meaning of article I, section 8, an officer acts unreasonably when, without a warrant, the officer physically trespasses on protected property or uses means or methods of general criminal investigation that are unlawful, tortious, or otherwise prohibited. Otherwise prohibited conduct includes means and methods of general criminal investigation that violate a citizen's reasonable expectation of privacy as articulated in our cases adopting the *Katz* standard.

We hold Officer Heinz conducted an unreasonable search and seizure in violation of article I, section 8 of the Iowa Constitution when he acted without a search warrant and removed opaque trash bags from waste bins set out for collection behind a residence, took possession of the trash bags, transported them to a different location, opened the bags, and searched through the contents.

NOTE

The Iowa Supreme Court's decision in *Wright* confirms that *Hempele* does not turn on any "unique New Jersey state attitude about garbage," to quote the New Jersey Supreme Court. The New Mexico Supreme Court also adopted a similar approach in the context of trash left at a motel. *See New Mexico v. Crane*, 329 P.3d 689 (N.M. 2014) (holding that individual had "a reasonable expectation of privacy in garbage left out for collection in a motel dumpster" under the New Mexico Constitution).

BLUM v. MERRELL DOW PHARMACEUTICALS, INC.
626 A.2d 537 (Penn. 1993)

NIX, C.J.

The issue before this Court is whether Article I, Section 6 of the Pennsylvania Constitution entitles a party who demands a twelve person jury to a verdict from a jury of twelve persons. For the reasons that follow, we affirm the Superior Court Order and hold that Section 6 of Article I of the Pennsylvania Constitution entitles a party who properly demands a twelve person jury to a verdict from a jury of twelve persons.

Our starting point must be the decision of the United States Supreme Court in *Williams v. Florida* (1970). In *Williams*, the Supreme Court departed from a long history of requiring a twelve person jury as a necessary ingredient of the Sixth Amendment guarantee of trial by jury in all criminal cases. The Supreme Court in *Williams* concluded that the "twelve man panel is not a necessary ingredient of trial by jury, and that Florida's refusal to impanel more than six members provided for by Florida law did not violate Williams' Sixth Amendment rights as applied to the states through the Fourteenth Amendment." We must now determine whether the *Williams*, *Colgrove* and *Ballew* trilogy, which allows trial by less than twelve member juries in civil cases, is properly part of the jurisprudence of this Commonwealth, by virtue of Section 6 of Article I of the Pennsylvania Constitution.

This Court has emphasized that, in interpreting a provision of the Pennsylvania Constitution, we are not bound by the decisions of the United States Supreme Court which interpret similar federal constitutional provisions. In *Commonwealth v. Edmunds* (Pa. 1991), Mr. Justice Cappy, writing for the majority of the Court, established the following four-part framework which we consider in analyzing our State Constitution:

> Litigants must brief and analyze at least the following four factors:
>
> 1) text of the Pennsylvania Constitutional provision;
>
> 2) history of the provision, including Pennsylvania case law;
>
> 3) related case law from other states;
>
> 4) policy considerations, including unique issues of state and local concern, and applicability within modern Pennsylvania jurisprudence.

The text of Section 6 of Article I of the Pennsylvania Constitution provides as follows:

> Trial by jury shall be as heretofore and the right thereof remain inviolate. The General Assembly may provide, however, by law, that a verdict may be rendered by not less than five-sixths of the jury in any civil case.

On its face, Article I, Section 6 preserves the following two things: the right to trial by jury shall be as heretofore; and the right to trial by jury remains inviolate. The Seventh Amendment to the United States Constitution, although worded differently, is similar to the Pennsylvania provision. On its face, the Seventh Amendment provides the right to trial by jury is preserved and no fact tried by a jury shall be otherwise reexamined other than according to the rules of common law. Although worded differently, both provisions retain the right to trial by jury in civil cases where it existed at common law. Therefore, we must undertake an examination of the history of Section 6 of Article I of our Constitution to determine the meaning of that provision and to decide whether our constitutional scheme is the same as the Federal Constitution or requires a verdict from a twelve member jury in a civil case when a demand for a twelve member jury is properly made.

Before discussing any case law, however, we must give an overview of the concept of juries of twelve members throughout this Commonwealth's history. The Superior Court in this case gave an excellent overview of the twelve member jury concept in this Commonwealth. The Superior Court stated:

> The concept of juries of twelve in this Commonwealth has its origin in a document introduced and adopted in Pennsylvania in 1682 by William Penn and known as "Laws Agreed Upon in England."
>
> Penn's other writings discussed the evolution of the jury and his belief that it was a "fundamental" part of the government and important to a free society. However, "nowhere did he endeavor to explain why a jury required *twelve* members to fulfill its purpose."
>
> One commentator has observed:
>
>> Penn's own writings and deeds appear to show that his commitment to twelve-member juries was not based on any reasoned notion that twelve was required to assure fairness, but instead stemming from his adherence to traditional common law principles that required twelve member juries.
>
> Likewise, there is little information available that casts any light on the intent of the framers of the Pennsylvania Constitution of 1776 regarding the size of juries. The same can be said with regard to the Constitutional Conventions of 1790 and 1838. As for the 1873 Convention, discussion was had on the deletion of the unanimity requirement and the elimination of the term "heretofore." Some saw no problem with this since they *equated a trial by jury with a jury of twelve men*, whereas others believed excising the word "heretofore" would pave the way for a jury of "three or five or seven or less than twelve as a constitutional jury." The proposal was defeated without explanation.

The framers at Pennsylvania's 1968 Convention did not consider the jury provision at all, believing that it was beyond their jurisdiction to affect that right. Even so, our first Constitution of 1776 contained verbiage which has survived and appears in the present-day Article I, section 6. *E.g.*, the 1776 Constitution declared that "trials by jury shall be as *heretofore*." The Constitution of 1790, and the amended ones of 1838, 1873 and 1968, adopted substantially the same provision. Their language was "trial by jury shall be as *heretofore*, the right thereof remain inviolate."

As the Superior Court stated, all of our Constitutions have had the identical language, that being "trial by jury shall be as heretofore." The following language was added to Section 6 of Article I of our Constitution by amendment on May 18, 1971:

> The General Assembly may provide, however, by law, that a verdict may be rendered by not less than five-sixths of the jury in a civil case.

Every Constitution of this Commonwealth has guaranteed to the parties a verdict from a jury of twelve persons where the parties would have had that right at common law. The Constitution, beginning in 1776, has always provided that "trial by jury shall be as heretofore." As stated above, our history and our case law evidence that that language, "trial by jury shall be as heretofore," was understood to guarantee a jury of twelve persons. Thus, Appellants' statement that there is no rationale in 1991 for following *Smith* and the other cases which commented upon the "heretofore" language in our earlier Constitutions is incorrect.

Appellants also argue, assuming *arguendo* that a right to a twelve person jury exists, the 1971 Pennsylvania Constitution and the subsequently enacted five-sixths rule allow that a decision by ten of twelve jurors constitutes "the verdict of the jury" and it "shall have the same effect as a unanimous verdict of the jury." Therefore, Appellants aver that the decision of ten jurors is always constitutionally sufficient and no constitutional right in this appeal could have been violated where eleven of eleven jurors agree on a verdict.

When the people of this Commonwealth amended Section 6 of Article I of our Constitution in 1971, authorizing the General Assembly to provide for a verdict by not less than five-sixths of the jury in any civil case, they reaffirmed the constitutional right to a jury of twelve persons. A provision of the Constitution will be interpreted, not in a strained or technical manner, but as understood by the people who adopted it. As previously discussed, in this Commonwealth "trial by jury shall be as heretofore" has always required a jury of twelve persons. When the people of this Commonwealth approved the May 18, 1971 amendment to Section 6 of Article I, they understood the reference to "the jury in any civil case" to be to a jury of twelve persons. Thus, the people of this Commonwealth amended only the unanimity feature and reaffirmed that a jury is made up of twelve persons.

The third element we will analyze is the case law from other jurisdictions. Subsequent to the United States Supreme Court decisions, a number of states other than Pennsylvania confronted the issue of whether their state constitutions require a twelve person jury.

Most significantly, after the United States Supreme Court decision in *Williams*, the Supreme Court of Rhode Island, in an advisory opinion to the Senate, held that the jury referred to in Section 15 of Article I of the Rhode Island Constitution requires a panel of twelve. After a thorough analysis of Rhode Island's constitutional history, that court reasoned:

> Although the Supreme Court in *Williams* described the common-law requirement that a petit jury be composed of precisely twelve people as an "historical accident," the Court obviously could not share this observation made in June 1970 with the framers and adopters of the Rhode Island Constitution. Accident or not, it is our firm belief that in 1842 when the draftsmen and the voters said that the right to a jury trial was to remain inviolate, they were extending to an accused, or

any litigant who might be entitled to a jury trial, the immutable right to have his case considered in the courts of this state by petit jury composed of exactly twelve persons.

Thus, the Rhode Island Supreme Court, after analyzing its case law and constitutional history, went above the minimum standards set forth by the United States Supreme Court in *Williams* and determined that, under the Rhode Island Constitution, a jury is composed of twelve members.

We similarly conclude that, because of Pennsylvania's history and case law, a jury must be composed of twelve persons where that right existed at common law and the demand for a twelve person jury is properly made. If this Court changed a right that had been understood and guaranteed to the people of this Commonwealth for over 200 years, we would be breaching our duty to speak the will of the people of this Commonwealth. We refuse to breach that duty by allowing a jury to be composed of less than twelve jurors. Only the people of this Commonwealth, by constitutional amendment, may make such a change.

The last prong of the *Edmunds* test is an examination of policy considerations and their applicability within modern Pennsylvania jurisprudence. One policy consideration Appellants request us to consider is the financial burden a jury of twelve persons presents for this Commonwealth.

We find that the most substantial policy consideration is that the people of this Commonwealth have understood since our first Constitution was adopted in 1776 that a "trial by jury" meant a jury composed of twelve persons. Given that understanding of the constitutional right, it is not for the legislative, executive, or judicial branch to change that right; rather, it is exclusively left to the people of this Commonwealth to amend the twelve member jury requirement if they desire that change.

Our constitutional history and case law mandate that we refrain from adopting the United States Supreme Court analysis in *Williams*, *Colgrove*, and *Ballew*, which held that verdicts from juries of less than twelve did not violate the Federal Constitution. This Court is under a duty to guarantee that the intent of the people of this Commonwealth in adopting the Pennsylvania Constitution is carried forward. We are convinced that, when Pennsylvania adopted its first Constitution in 1776, the framers assumed that a jury meant twelve persons. This Court has repeatedly adopted that view. Therefore, even though Section 6 of Article I of the Pennsylvania Constitution does not explicitly state that a jury is constituted of twelve members, our constitutional history and case law make it apparent that "trial by jury" means a jury of twelve persons.

NOTES

1. The Pennsylvania and U.S. Constitutions both preserve the right to "trial by jury." Why does the state court take a different tack in interpreting this language? Does the state court embrace any aspects of the relevant federal decisions?

2. The Delaware Supreme Court, like many state supreme courts, has adopted criteria for determining whether a state constitutional guarantee offers greater protection than a similarly worded federal guarantee. In *Jones v. Delaware*, 745 A.2d 856, 864–65 (Del. 1999), the Court in an opinion by Chief Justice Veasey used the following criteria in deciding to give the State's search-and-seizure guarantee more protection than the U.S. Supreme Court provided in *California v. Hodari D.*, 499 U.S. 621 (1991):

> (1) Textual Language—A state constitution's language may itself provide a basis for reaching a result different from that which could be obtained under federal law.
>
> (2) Constitutional History—Whether or not the textual language of a given provision is different from that found in the federal Constitution, legislative history may reveal an intention that will support reading the provision independently of federal law.
>
> (3) Preexisting State Law—Previously established bodies of state law may also suggest distinctive state constitutional rights. State law is often responsive to concerns long before they are addressed by constitutional claims.
>
> (4) Structural Differences—Differences in structure between the federal and state constitutions might also provide a basis for rejecting the constraints of federal doctrine at the state level. The United States Constitution is a grant of enumerated powers to the federal government. Our State Constitution, on the other hand, serves only to limit the sovereign power which inheres directly in the people and indirectly in their elected representatives.
>
> (5) Matters of Particular State Interest or Local Concern—A state constitution may also be employed to address matters of peculiar state interest or local concern.
>
> (6) State Traditions—A state's history and traditions may also provide a basis for the independent application of its constitution.
>
> (7) Public Attitudes—Distinctive attitudes of a state's citizenry may also furnish grounds to expand constitutional rights under state charters. While we have never cited this criterion in our decisions, courts in other jurisdictions have pointed to public attitudes as a relevant factor in their deliberations.

B. DIFFERENTLY WORDED PROVISIONS

When the language of a state constitutional guarantee differs materially from its federal counterpart, the state courts have an additional reason for construing their constitutions differently. That, however, does not diminish the force of the earlier considerations: the scope of jurisdiction of the two courts; the effect of local history (including the history and purpose of the state constitutional provision), local traditions, and local customs; the difficulty of answering some constitutional questions; and the potential for disagreement between the two courts. In the following cases, consider the impact of the difference in language between the state and federal guarantees on the courts' decisions relative to the role of these other considerations.

RACING ASSOCIATION OF CENTRAL IOWA v. FITZGERALD
675 N.W.2d 1 (Iowa 2004)

TERNUS, J.

When this case was initially before our court, we held that a statute taxing gross gambling receipts generated at racetracks at a rate nearly twice the rate imposed on gross gambling receipts generated on riverboats violated the United States Constitution and the Iowa Constitution. On certiorari to the United States Supreme Court, that part of our decision holding the statute violated the Equal Protection Clause of the United States Constitution was reversed. The Supreme Court then remanded the case "for further proceedings not inconsistent with its opinion." Although this court's ruling that the statute also violated the equality provision contained in the Iowa Constitution was not reviewed by the Supreme Court, we take the opportunity on remand to reconsider our prior decision on the state constitution claim in light of the Court's ruling on the federal constitution issue.

After giving due consideration to the Court's analysis and decision, we find no basis to change our earlier opinion that the differential tax violates article I, section 6 of the Iowa Constitution. Therefore, we reverse the trial court's contrary ruling and remand this case for a determination of the appropriate relief.

This action was commenced by the appellant, Racing Association of Central Iowa (RACI), to enjoin the collection of that portion of taxes it was required to pay on adjusted gross receipts from gambling in excess of the tax charged to "excursion boats" on such receipts. RACI claimed the tax was unconstitutional under the Equal Protection Clauses of the United States and Iowa Constitutions.

The tax statute challenged by these parties imposes a tax "on the adjusted gross receipts received annually from gambling games." The maximum rate is twenty percent. The statute has an exception, however, for the "adjusted gross receipts from gambling games at racetrack enclosures." The tax rate on racetrack gambling receipts began at twenty-two percent in 1997, and has automatically increased by two percent each year to a maximum rate of thirty-six percent in 2004.

In our first consideration of this case, we held this differential tax violated the Equal Protection Clause of the United States Constitution and article I, section 6 of the Iowa Constitution.[2]

It is this court's constitutional obligation as the highest court of this sovereign state to determine whether the challenged classification violates Iowa's constitutional equality provision. While the Supreme Court's judgment on the constitutionality of Iowa's disparate tax rates under the federal Equal Protection Clause is persuasive, it is not binding on this court as we evaluate this law under the Iowa Constitution.

The Supreme Court has stated that the Equal Protection Clause "is essentially a direction that all persons similarly situated should be treated alike." Whether this ideal has been met in the context of economic legislation is determined through application of the rational basis test. In its consideration of the case at hand, the Court described the rational basis test as follows:

> The Equal Protection Clause is satisfied so long as there is a plausible policy reason for the classification, the legislative facts on which the classification is apparently based rationally may have been considered to be true by the governmental decisionmaker, and the relationship of the classification to its goal is not so attenuated as to render the distinction arbitrary or irrational.

The Court has in the past more succinctly stated this standard as "whether the classifications drawn in a statute are reasonable in light of its purpose." It was this enunciation of the rational basis test that our court said in *Bierkamp v. Rogers* (Iowa 1980) was appropriate for analyzing a claim based on the Iowa equality provision found in article I, section 6 of the Iowa Constitution.

Based on these principles, this court must first determine whether the Iowa legislature had a valid reason to treat racetracks differently from riverboats when taxing the gambling revenue of these businesses. Moreover, the claimed state interest must be *"realistically conceivable."* Our court must then decide whether this reason has a basis in fact. Finally, we must consider whether the relationship between the classification, *i.e.*, the differences between racetracks and excursion boats, and the purpose of the classification is so weak that the classification must be viewed as arbitrary.

Our examination of this statute must also be guided by the general legal principles that control a court's review of the constitutionality of a legislative enactment. These tenets are well established. "Statutes are

---

[2] The United States Constitution provides that no state shall "deny to any person within its jurisdiction the equal protection of the laws." U.S. Const. amend. 14. In contrast, article I, section 6 of the Iowa Constitution states: "All laws of a general nature shall have a uniform operation; the general assembly shall not grant to any citizen, or class of citizens, privileges or immunities, which, upon the same terms shall not equally belong to all citizens."

cloaked with a strong presumption of constitutionality." Therefore, a person challenging a statute shoulders a heavy burden of rebutting this presumption. This burden includes the task of negating every reasonable basis that might support the disparate treatment. These rigorous standards have not, however, prevented this court from finding economic and social legislation in violation of equal protection provisions. Our prior cases illustrate that, although the rational basis standard of review is admittedly deferential to legislative judgment, "it is not a toothless one" in Iowa. Indeed, this court's meaningful review of social and economic legislation is mandated by our constitutional obligation to safeguard constitutional values by ensuring all legislation complies with those values.

Although the State has advanced several reasons for the legislative classification challenged in this case, we focus our discussion primarily on those found satisfactory by the Supreme Court, as that is the reason for our reconsideration of the state constitutional claim. The Supreme Court viewed the issue as whether there was "rational support for the 20 percent/36 percent differential." It then concluded "that difference" was helpful to the riverboats because it (1) "encouraged the economic development of river communities and promoted riverboat history"; (2) "protected the reliance interests of riverboat operators" who were accustomed to a twenty percent tax rate; and (3) "aided the financial position of the riverboats." We will address each suggested purpose separately.

Our court does not accept the economic development of river communities and the promotion of riverboat history as a rational basis for the legislature's distinction between excursion boats and racetracks. Although these are laudable legislative goals, "the legislative facts on which the classification is apparently based cannot rationally be considered to be true by the governmental decisionmaker," as required by the Court's articulation of the rational basis test. We note initially that excursion boat gambling was never anticipated as solely a "river" activity so as to promote "river communities." When the legislature authorized gambling on "excursion boats" in 1989, it was envisioned that these boats would be located on inland waters, such as lakes and reservoirs, as well as on the Mississippi River and Missouri River, the historical location of riverboats. Moreover, there is nothing peculiar about racetracks that prevents their location in river cities. In fact, two of the three communities in which racetracks are located—Dubuque and Council Bluffs—are river communities. The Dubuque racetrack is actually on an island in the Mississippi River. On the other hand, the excursion boat docked near Osceola, Iowa, is moored on a lake, not a river, and is certainly not located in a river community. In addition, one river community—Council Bluffs—has both a racetrack and an excursion boat, only blocks apart. So, to justify the differential tax treatment of these enterprises on the supposed connection of excursion boats to river communities and riverboat history and the absence of such a connection by racetracks is illogical.

We acknowledge "the overinclusive-underinclusive dichotomy is usually applied only as part of a strict scrutiny analysis." But our court has stated, in holding legislation violative of the state constitution under the rational basis test, "that as a classification involves extreme degrees of overinclusion and underinclusion in relation to any particular goal, it cannot be said to reasonably further that goal." That is precisely the case here insofar as the differential tax is based on the promotion of river communities and riverboat history. Thus, this legislative purpose cannot withstand review under the rational basis standard.

Even if this court were to take a more expansive view of potential legislative purposes and assume the general assembly sought to promote economic development in general, the taxing scheme still suffers from an irrational classification. There is nothing in the record, nor is it a matter of common knowledge, that excursion boats are a superior economic development tool as compared to racetracks. To the contrary, it appears that both types of gambling enterprises have the potential to enhance the economic climate of the communities in which they are located. If we presume the legislature thought the promotion of gambling was in the economic interests of the general public, then we find no rational basis for distinguishing between gambling that takes place on a floating casino and gambling that occurs at a land-based casino. Regardless of the relative number of such establishments or the size of the city in which they are to be found, excursion boats and racetracks contribute in the same manner to the economy of the local area: they are both gambling enterprises generating gambling receipts that are indistinguishable in terms of the economic benefits to the local community.

Our decision today is a difficult one because we have great respect for the legislature. Notwithstanding our preference to defer to its judgment, we declare the differential tax at issue here invalid under the Iowa Constitution because we are convinced the classifications lack a rational basis in the constitutional sense. Because we are keenly aware of the legislature's constitutional role to make decisions of a policy and political nature, we have not lightly undertaken today's decision. Nonetheless, "our obligation not to interfere with the legislature's right to pass laws is no higher than our obligation to protect the citizens from discriminatory class legislation violative of the constitutional guaranty of equality of all before the law." Consequently, we decline the opportunity to alter our prior decision that the statutory exception to the twenty percent tax rate on gambling receipts violates article I, section 6 of the Iowa Constitution.

NOTES

1. Does the Iowa Supreme Court apply the same equal protection test as the U.S. Supreme Court or a different test?

2. Do you think the U.S. Supreme Court would find the Iowa Supreme Court's most recent decision convincing? Might the Iowa Supreme Court's recent explanation alter the U.S. Supreme Court's analysis under federal law?

STATE v. JORDEN
156 P.3d 893 (Wash. 2007)

BRIDGE, J.

Timothy Jorden appeals his conviction for unlawful possession of cocaine. On March 15, 2003, a Pierce County deputy sheriff conducted a random warrant check of the Golden Lion Motel's guests via the guest registry and discovered Jorden's presence at the Lakewood motel as well as the fact of two outstanding warrants for Jorden's arrest. Deputy sheriffs then entered Jorden's motel room in order to arrest him for the outstanding warrants. Upon entering the room, officers saw cocaine in plain view. Jorden contends that the random check of the motel registry revealing his whereabouts constitutes a violation of his privacy rights under article I, section 7 of the Washington State Constitution.

The Pierce County Sheriff's Department takes part in the "Lakewood Crime-Free Hotel Motel Program." The program offers assistance to motels and hotels that have a history of significant criminal activity, providing training on methods of crime reduction. The program also encourages officers to review the guest registries of hotels and motels on a random basis and without individualized or particularized suspicion. Officers often conduct random criminal checks of the names in guest registries at motels with reputations for frequent criminal activity. When checking into a participating motel, guests are advised that a valid identification is required for check-in and that the identification information is kept on file, but the guests are not told of the possibility for random, suspicionless searches of the registry by law enforcement.

Article I, section 7 of the Washington Constitution provides that "no person shall be disturbed in his private affairs, or his home invaded, without authority of law." "It is well established that article I, section 7 qualitatively differs from the Fourth Amendment and in some areas provides greater protections than does the federal constitution." We must therefore determine "whether article I, section 7 affords enhanced protection in the particular context." Accordingly, we must determine whether that heightened protection is available in these circumstances to Jorden.

Article I, section 7 protects against warrantless searches of a citizen's private affairs. Therefore, a warrantless search is per se unreasonable unless it falls under one of Washington's recognized exceptions. Here, the State does not argue the motel registry review falls into one of the exceptions, but argues that the information in the registry is not a private affair and thus there was no search triggering article I, section 7 protection.

Private affairs are those "interests which citizens of this state have held, and should be entitled to hold, safe from government trespass." In determining whether a certain interest is a private affair deserving article I, section 7 protection, a central consideration is the *nature* of the information sought—that is, whether the information obtained via the governmental trespass reveals intimate or discrete details of a person's life.

In addition, this court has also considered whether there are historical protections afforded to the perceived interest. And, where the perceived interest involves the gathering of personal information by the government, this court has also considered the purpose for which the information sought is kept, and by whom it is kept.

Our most important inquiry then becomes whether a random and suspicionless search of a guest registry reveals intimate details of one's life. We first consider that here there is more information at stake than simply a guest's registration information: an individual's very presence in a motel or hotel may in itself be a sensitive piece of information. There are a variety of lawful reasons why an individual may not wish to reveal his or her presence at a motel. As the amicus American Civil Liberties Union points out, couples engaging in extramarital affairs may not wish to share their presence at the hotel with others, just as a closeted same-sex couple forced to meet at the motel also would not. The desire for privacy may extend to business people engaged in confidential negotiations or celebrities seeking respite from life in the public eye. One could also imagine a scenario, as Jorden's trial attorney pointed out during the motion to suppress, where a domestic violence victim flees to a hotel in hopes of remaining hidden from an abuser.

Additionally, we note the sensitivity of the registry information in and of itself. Not only does it reveal one's presence at the motel, it may also reveal co-guests in the room, divulging yet another person's personal or business associates. Thus, it appears that the information gleaned from random, suspicionless searches of a guest registry may indeed provide "intimate details about a person's activities and associations."

Therefore, the information contained in a motel registry—including one's whereabouts at the motel—is a private affair under our state constitution, and a government trespass into such information is a search. We hesitate to allow a search of a citizen's private affairs where the government cannot express at least an individualized or particularized suspicion about the search subject or present a valid exception to a warrantless search. A random, suspicionless search is a fishing expedition, and we have indicated displeasure with such practices on many occasions.

Consequently, we hold that the practice of checking the names in a motel registry for outstanding warrants without individualized or particularized suspicion violated the defendant's article I, section 7 rights.

We are not insensitive to the difficulties facing law enforcement in ensuring our motels and hotels remain relatively crime-free, but as a practical matter our holding does not unduly restrict the investigative powers of the police. Random, suspicionless registry checks are but one part of the Lakewood Crime-Free Hotel Motel Program. Law enforcement may continue to randomly run checks of the license plates of cars parked at the motels, provide training to motel owners, and encourage motel owners to be watchful of behavior evincing criminal activity. Reports of such observations may engender the requisite individualized suspicion that is notably missing from current program techniques.

Information contained in a motel registry constitutes a private affair under article I, section 7 of the Washington State Constitution because it reveals sensitive, discrete, and private information about the motel's guest. Absent a valid exception to the prohibition against warrantless searches, random viewing of a motel registry violates article I, section 7 of the Washington State Constitution. The evidence obtained from the registry of the Golden Lion Motel, which led officers to Jorden's room, was obtained through unlawful means and should have been excluded.

STATE v. MIXTON
478 P.3d 1227 (Ariz. 2021)

LOPEZ, J.

We consider whether the Fourth Amendment to the United States Constitution or article 2, section 8 of the Arizona Constitution requires law enforcement officials to secure a judicially-authorized search warrant or order to obtain either (1) a user's Internet Protocol ("IP") address or (2) subscriber information the user voluntarily provides to an Internet Service Provider ("ISP") as a condition or attribute of service. We hold that neither the federal nor the Arizona Constitution requires a search warrant or court order for such information and that law enforcement officials may obtain IP addresses and ISP subscriber information with a lawful federal administrative subpoena.

The Fourth Amendment does not apply to IP addresses or subscriber information under the third-party doctrine, and this information is not a "private affair" under the Private Affairs Clause. Thus, the state lawfully obtained this information with a valid federal administrative subpoena.

BOLICK, J., dissenting.

We are now in the second century of Arizona statehood, yet this is the first time the Court has given more than cursory consideration to the meaning of the private affairs clause of article 2, section 8 of the Arizona Constitution. That provision has no analogue in the federal constitution and was clearly intended to provide additional and forceful protections to Arizonans against government intrusions into their private affairs. Because the majority interprets the private affairs clause in lockstep with the less-protective Fourth Amendment as construed by the United States Supreme Court, thereby draining the meaning expressed in the clause and intended by its architects, we respectfully dissent.

As Arizona was the forty-eighth state, its framers "had the opportunity to ponder more than 100 years of United States history before penning their own constitution, allowing them to adopt or adjust provisions employed by the federal government or other states to meet Arizona's needs." In some instances, the framers concluded they could not improve upon the federal constitutional framers' handiwork; in others, they sought to add greater protections of individual rights and constraints on government power.

In particular, as this Court has recognized, our constitution's Declaration of Rights is the "main formulation of rights and privileges conferred on Arizonans." Thus, it is our duty to "first consult our constitution" whenever a right it "guarantees is in question." As former Chief Justice Rebecca Berch observed, "had the framers merely intended to mirror the guarantees found in the Federal Bill of Rights, they could have simply adopted the first eight amendments of the U.S. Constitution. But records of Arizona's convention clearly show that the framers did not always agree with the language or implementation of the Federal Bill of Rights."

Whereas the vast majority of state constitutions have provisions that roughly parallel the language of the Fourth Amendment, only two—ours and Washington State's, whose provisions are identical—deliberately chose to depart from the Fourth Amendment's language in favor of a distinct provision encompassing a protection for private affairs.

Rather than accord independent vitality to a protection of individual rights in our constitution, the majority urges that we should extol "the value in uniformity with federal law when interpreting and applying the Arizona Constitution." Uniformity is certainly a value, and when all other things are equal, uniformity may be preferable to divergence. But where the Constitution's framers made deliberate effort to distinguish our state constitutional protections from the narrower confines of the federal constitution, our failure to credit and enforce our constitution's language and intent inevitably means that those protections will not have their intended effect. *See* Ruth V. McGregor, *Recent Developments in Arizona State Constitutional Law*, 35 ARIZ. ST. L.J. 265, 276 (2003) ("None of the opinions from our court provide any in-depth analysis of the reasons we have so often opted for a goal of uniformity.").

Indeed, the Supreme Court has recognized that an "interest in uniformity does not outweigh the general principle that States are independent sovereigns with plenary authority to make and enforce their own laws as long as they do not infringe on federal constitutional guarantees." The states' authority to make distinct rules of criminal procedure, the Court remarked, "is not otherwise limited by any general, undefined federal interest in uniformity. Nonuniformity is, in fact, an unavoidable reality in a federalist system of government."

A comparison of the words of the Fourth Amendment and those chosen by the framers of article 2, section 8 underscore the stark differences:

> The right of the people to be secure in their persons, houses, papers, and effects, against unreasonable searches and seizures, shall not be violated, and no Warrants shall issue, but upon probable cause, supported by Oath or affirmation, and particularly describing the place to be searched, and the persons or things to be seized.

U.S. Const. amend. IV.

> No person shall be disturbed in his private affairs, or his home invaded, without authority of law.

Ariz. Const. art. 2, § 8.

The protection of "private affairs" is nowhere found in the Fourth Amendment. Indeed, a right to privacy—based not on express constitutional text but on "penumbras, formed by emanations"—would not be found in the federal constitution for another 53 years. Its express inclusion in a 1912 state constitution strongly suggests that the framers had a significant protection in mind, one whose omission in the federal constitution they found wanting.

Moreover, by its terms, the Fourth Amendment is limited to "persons, houses, papers, and effects," which are protected only against "unreasonable searches and seizures." By contrast, the scope of "private affairs" under article 2, section 8 is broader on its face, and the protection is categorical.

And our constitutional language was not chosen randomly. The delegates to the constitutional convention considered language parallel to the Fourth Amendment, but instead adopted language containing the private affairs clause from the Washington Constitution. In other words, the language of article 2, section 8 was *deliberately chosen as an alternative* to the language of the Fourth Amendment.

In rejecting language echoing the Fourth Amendment, Arizona's constitutional framers changed existing Arizona law. The Arizona territory was governed by the Howell Code, which contained a provision nearly identical to the Fourth Amendment. Once statehood was achieved, the new constitution's architects abandoned that approach in favor of the broader, express privacy provision of article 2, section 8. And when a legislature amends a provision by making a significant change in language, we presume it intended a different meaning.

All of which invites the question: if the framers wanted to craft language that would be enforced on its own terms, how could they have better done so than to reject one set of words and deliberately adopt another? Under such circumstances, we should be loath to interpret the language the framers chose in lockstep with language the framers consciously rejected, and indeed, not only as it was interpreted in 1912 but as the Supreme Court has construed it many years later.

That the framers meant our constitutional language to have independent vitality necessarily follows from the fact that when our constitution was adopted, the Fourth Amendment was not yet applicable to the states through incorporation under the Fourteenth Amendment. Thus, our Declaration of Rights was meant to provide the solitary protection for individual liberty against the state. As former Chief Justice Ruth McGregor has observed, because the Bill of Rights did not yet apply to the states, "the drafters of our state constitution could not have operated under the assumption that interpretations of the federal constitution would control the rights guaranteed citizens under the state constitution."

And the dominant school of state constitutional interpretation at the time was originalism, so the framers likely expected their handiwork to be interpreted on its own terms rather than through federal court interpretations of a different constitution. Our early cases specified that the purpose of rules of interpretation is to arrive at the intent of the framers.

This Court frequently has interpreted provisions of our state constitution more broadly than their federal counterparts, and sensibly, we have done so especially where the language is different. Thus, we have repeatedly held that our speech protection is broader than that accorded by the First Amendment. Likewise, our courts have construed the broader language of article 2, section 17 of the Arizona Constitution to provide greater protection against eminent domain than does the Fifth Amendment's takings clause as construed by the Supreme Court. By contrast, where the state constitutional language parallels that of the Bill of Rights, we have tended to construe it in tandem with Supreme Court interpretations of the federal constitutional provision.

These cases, juxtaposed against the Court's decision today, leave us in a curious and perplexing place. On the one hand, this Court has construed the home invasion provision of article 2, section 8 more broadly than the Fourth Amendment and has rejected Supreme Court doctrines inconsistent with that clause, even though both provisions protect homes. By contrast, the majority here subsumes the private affairs clause within the Supreme

Court's interpretation of the Fourth Amendment, even though the Fourth Amendment does not on its face protect against government intrusions into private affairs. By what principle does it do so? We are left to ponder not only that, but by what standard we will determine when to give independent meaning to our state constitutional language in other contexts. By our lights, we should at least do so where the language is conspicuously different, and certainly where (as here) no analogous provision exists in the federal constitution. Otherwise, the necessary consequence is to diminish constitutional protections.

We should not follow that long and winding road of Fourth Amendment jurisprudence to its uncharted destination. When the constitutions converge, it makes sense to take Supreme Court decisions into account and place value on uniform application. But where the language of the two constitutions differs—and especially where our provision does not appear in the federal constitution in any manner—relying on the Supreme Court to determine our constitutional meaning deprives our citizens of the precious freedoms their forebears proclaimed when they embraced a wider conception of liberty than the federal constitution. After all, U.S. Supreme Court justices do not take an oath to uphold the Arizona Constitution. But we do.

"Private affairs" was a commonly used term during the period preceding our constitution's adoption, and the protection of private affairs was a major preoccupation of contemporary legislatures, courts, and scholars. A review of these efforts concludes that "'mind your own business' was an eleventh commandment in nineteenth century America."

In particular, Americans in the twilight of the Nineteenth and dawn of the Twentieth Centuries sought to keep what was private from becoming public. A major concern was preventing the disclosure of private information when third parties, such as telegraph operators, were entrusted with transmission or delivery and the "messages were necessarily read by the operators who sent and received them." Similarly, Congressman James Garfield championed legislation against disclosure of census information, so that an individual's "private affairs, the secrets of his family and his business," would not be revealed. The shielding of tax returns, in the words of the newspaper *The Nation*, protected "the 'natural and inalienable right' of everybody to keep his affairs to himself." Courts likewise protected the confidentiality of certain public records to prevent making "public men's private affairs."

These examples illustrate that "private affairs" were understood in the early Twentieth Century to broadly encompass both personal and business matters, even if transmitted through third parties, thus making Arizona's constitutional provision irreconcilable with the later-emerging federal "third-party" doctrine allowing any information divulged to a third party to be obtained by the government without a warrant.

The protection of private affairs was also reflected in local concerns. In 1912, the year our constitution was adopted, the *Arizona Republican* editorialized against a proposal to disclose the names of their subscribers, condemning it as a "perniciously inquisitorial" effort to gain access to "private business affairs and financial affairs." That same year, the newspaper warned against congressional investigations of alleged monopolies because "attacks upon corporate credit and private affairs ought to be deprecated." It appears clear that the common meaning of "private affairs" in statehood-era Arizona encompassed the type of business transactions that would be swept up by the third-party doctrine many decades later.

The majority asserts that a "clear consensus" of state courts hold that their state constitutions do not protect IP addresses or ISP subscriber information. Unfortunately, those decisions do little to aid us, for none of the constitutions at issue contains a private affairs clause. Applying the language and intent of our state constitutional provision, rather than decisions more than a half-century later applying markedly different constitutional language, we conclude that the data here is protected by article 2, section 8's private affairs clause and may be obtained by the government only with authority of law.

We entrust private information to third parties every day: every time we use a credit card, provide our Social Security number, use a security card reader, mail a saliva sample to a genetics lab, make a bank deposit or withdrawal, use a password to enter a website, or even send an email. Even under a reasonable expectation of privacy analysis, "people often do reasonably expect that information they entrust to third parties, especially information subject to confidentiality agreements, will be kept private." Indeed, sharing such information often is a precondition to engaging in commerce. The majority points to the widespread third-party data collection on the internet, but that observation is simply irrelevant as the private affairs clause restricts government action. The notion that anything one must share for purposes of voluntary transactions is thereby subject to government inspection would eviscerate any meaningful notion of privacy.

C. STATE GUARANTEES MAY OFFER MORE OR FEWER PROTECTIONS THAN THEIR FEDERAL COUNTERPARTS

As one of us has pointed out:

> State courts have authority to construe their own constitutional provisions however they wish. Nothing compels the state courts to imitate federal interpretations of the liberty and property guarantees in the U.S. Constitution when it comes to the rights guarantees found in their own constitutions, even guarantees that match the federal ones letter for letter. As long as a state court's interpretation of its own constitution does not violate a federal requirement, it will

stand, and, better than that, it will be impervious to challenge in the U.S. Supreme Court.

State constitutions create independent limits on state and local power, limits that may do more or less than their counterpart guarantees in the Federal Constitution.

Jeffrey S. Sutton, *51 Imperfect Solutions: States and the Making of American Constitutional Law* 16, 173 (Oxford 2018).

STATE v. SCOTTIZE DANYELLE BROWN
930 N.W.2d 840 (Iowa 2019)

McDONALD, J. concurring.

Scottize Brown failed to establish a violation of her rights arising under the Federal or Iowa Constitutions, and the district court did not err in denying Brown's motion to suppress. I thus concur in Justice Christensen's opinion affirming Brown's conviction and sentence. I write separately to address Brown's argument that the Federal Constitution sets the floor for claims arising under the Iowa Constitution.

The fundamental premise of this court's most recent jurisprudence in the area of state constitutional law has been that "although this court cannot interpret the Iowa Constitution to provide *less* protection than that provided by the United States Constitution, the court is free to interpret our constitution as providing *greater* protection for our citizens' constitutional rights." Pursuant to this premise, this court has treated the Iowa Constitution as a one-way ratchet to provide only greater rights and remedies than a parallel provision of the United States Constitution. The fundamental premise of our recent jurisprudence is not sound. This court is free to interpret our constitution to provide less or more protection than the Federal Constitution.

The conclusion that this court can interpret the Iowa Constitution to provide less or more protection than a parallel provision of the Federal Constitution is inherent in the federal system. The Bill of Rights, in and of itself, applies only to the federal government. The Supreme Court is the final arbiter of the meaning of the Federal Constitution. In contrast, the Iowa Constitution applies to the state government. This court is the final arbiter of the meaning of the Iowa Constitution. In determining the meaning of state constitutional law, this court has a duty to independently determine the meaning of the Iowa Constitution. This is true whether we interpret the Iowa Constitution to provide less or more protection than the Federal Constitution.

Brown's contention that the incorporation doctrine dictates the minimum required content of state constitutional law misapprehends the incorporation doctrine. Incorporation did not change the substantive content of state constitutional law; it changed the substantive content of federal constitutional law. Specifically, the Supreme Court held the Due Process Clause of the Fourteenth Amendment incorporated most of the Bill of Rights. "Incorporated Bill of Rights guarantees are enforced against the States under the Fourteenth Amendment according to the same standards that protect those personal rights against federal encroachment." Pursuant to the Supremacy Clause, this court is bound to apply the Supreme Court's Fourteenth Amendment jurisprudence to resolve claims arising under the Fourteenth Amendment. The Supreme Court's Fourteenth Amendment jurisprudence does not dictate the substance of the state law or the remedy for any violation of the same.

Certainly, as a matter of federal law, state courts are bound not to apply any rule which is inconsistent with decisions of the Supreme Court; the Supremacy Clause of the Federal Constitution clearly embodies this mandate. It would be a mistake, however, to view federal law as a floor for state constitutional analysis; principles of federalism prohibit the Supreme Court from dictating the content of state law. In other words, state courts are not required to incorporate federally-created principles into their state constitutional analysis; the only requirement is that in the event of an irreconcilable conflict between federal law and state law principles, the federal principles must prevail.

Such courts must undertake an independent determination of the merits of each claim based solely on principles of state constitutional law. If the state court begins its analysis with the view that the federal practice establishes a "floor," the state court is allowing a federal governmental body—the United States Supreme Court—to define, at least in part, rights guaranteed by the state constitution.

I thus conclude this court has a duty to independently interpret the Iowa Constitution. This court discharges that duty by looking to the text of the document through the prism of our precedent, tradition, and custom. This court's interpretation of the Iowa Constitution may be the same as the Supreme Court's interpretation of a parallel provision of the Federal Constitution. This court's interpretation of the Iowa Constitution may be different than the Supreme Court's interpretation of a parallel provision of the Federal Constitution. But this court's interpretation of the Iowa Constitution is not dictated by the Supreme Court's precedents under the incorporation doctrine of the Federal Constitution.

"Metaphors in law are to be narrowly watched, for starting as devices to liberate thought, they end often by enslaving it." This has been true of the floor–ceiling metaphor. "However useful that floor-ceiling metaphor may be, it obscures the larger truth that the level of protection of rights under the state constitutions can be the same as, higher than, or lower than that provided by the federal constitution." The failure of the metaphor has caused this court to undertake its interpretive function with a results-oriented approach that has created distortions in Iowa legal doctrine.

While there may be reasons why this court would want to adopt the exclusionary rule for violations of the Iowa Constitution, many of which are discussed in *State v. Cline* (Iowa 2001), it was incorrect to say *Mapp v. Ohio* (1961) compelled this court to do so.

This special concurrence is not intended as a call to arms to find less or more protection of individual rights under the Iowa Constitution as compared to the United States Constitution. Instead, it is a call to determine the meaning of the Iowa Constitution without an interpretive predisposition that the Iowa Constitution must, as a matter of law, be interpreted to provide only greater protection than the United States Constitution. In this particular case, I concur with my colleagues that neither the United States Constitution nor the Iowa Constitution provides Brown with any relief and that her conviction should be affirmed.

NOTE

Unless carefully "watched," metaphors can slay. The U.S. Constitution indeed sets a "floor" of protected conduct when a *federal* claim is brought. But it does not set a floor when it comes to the meaning of the 50 State Constitutions. If a State is free not to have an equal protection clause at all, as is true in many state constitutions, it follows that a state high court is free to construe its own equal protection clause to provide less protection than the federal counterpart. Those inclined toward metaphors might consider a different one in this setting. Try this: the state and federal constitutions operate like two sets of elevators, each with stops at different floors, some going up, some going down, each with different baselines. The only exception is a modest one—that a state court's interpretation of a state constitutional provision, say a state establishment clause, cannot violate a separate federal guarantee, say the federal free exercise guarantee. *See Trinity Lutheran Church of Columbia, Inc. v. Comer*, 137 S. Ct. 2012 (2017). But that problem arises infrequently.

D. INDEPENDENT AND ADEQUATE STATE GROUNDS: STATE COURT RULINGS THAT ADDRESS FEDERAL AND STATE BASES FOR DECISION

Given the reality that the state courts may construe a constitutional guarantee in their own constitutions more broadly than one found in the U.S. Constitution, lawyers often will raise both grounds in challenging the validity of a state or local law. When that happens, at least two issues arise: Will the state court rely on just one constitutional guarantee or both of them? And, if it relies on both of them, or at least precedents from both jurisdictions, how will the reviewing court—the U.S. Supreme Court—

know whether the state court has relied on an independent and adequate state ground, which is insulated from review, or on a federal ground, which is open to review? The answers to both questions have strategic consequences. The losing litigant, for example, will want to show that the state court decision turns on federal law, so that it may seek review in the U.S. Supreme Court. Otherwise, the case is over—unless the litigant can convince the people of the State to amend the state constitution.

In *Michigan v. Long*, 463 U.S. 1032 (1983), the Court provided guidance on these issues. It created a clear-statement rule to the effect that, unless the state court expressly says otherwise, the U.S. Supreme Court would presume that a state court decision dealing with federal and state law issues was based on federal law. Here is how the Court put it:

> Accordingly, when, as in this case, a state court decision fairly appears to rest primarily on federal law, or to be interwoven with the federal law, and when the adequacy and independence of any possible state law ground is not clear from the face of the opinion, we will accept as the most reasonable explanation that the state court decided the case the way it did because it believed that federal law required it to do so. If a state court chooses merely to rely on federal precedents as it would on the precedents of all other jurisdictions, then it need only make clear by a plain statement in its judgment or opinion that the federal cases are being used only for the purpose of guidance, and do not themselves compel the result that the court has reached. In this way, both justice and judicial administration will be greatly improved. If the state court decision indicates clearly and expressly that it is alternatively based on bona fide separate, adequate, and independent grounds, we, of course, will not undertake to review the decision.

Despite this directive from *Michigan v. Long*, state court cases continue to arise in which the ground of decision remains unclear. The next set of decisions presents a case study of this problem—by examining three decisions concerning the same traffic stop, two by the Ohio Supreme Court and one by the U.S. Supreme Court. *Ohio v. Robinette* also considers the other half of the issue this chapter introduces: Why state courts sometimes *resist* relying on independent and adequate state law grounds, even when they have the authority to do so and even when they are expressly told in a given case that they have that authority.

In *Robinette*, the courts dealt with a traffic stop governed by the Fourth Amendment and a virtually identical state guarantee. Section 14 of Article I of the Ohio Constitution provides: "The right of the people to be secure in their persons, houses, papers, and possessions, against unreasonable searches and seizures shall not be violated; and no warrant shall issue, but upon probable cause, supported by oath or affirmation, particularly describing the place to be searched, and the person and things to be seized." The Fourth Amendment, similarly, provides: "The right of the people to be secure in their persons, houses, papers, and effects, against unreasonable searches and seizures, shall not be violated, and no Warrants shall issue, but upon probable cause, supported by oath or affirmation, and particularly describing the place to be searched, and the persons or things to be seized."

OHIO v. ROBINETTE
653 N.E.2d 695 (Ohio 1995)

PFEIFER, J.

The issue in this case is whether the evidence used against Robinette was obtained through a valid search. We find that the search was invalid since it was the product of an unlawful seizure. We also use this case to establish a bright-line test, requiring police officers to inform motorists that their legal detention has concluded before the police officer may engage in any consensual interrogation.

In order to justify any investigative stop, a police officer "must be able to point to specific and articulable facts which, taken together with the rational inferences from those facts, reasonably warrant that intrusion." Absent any additional articulable facts arising after the stop is made, the police officer must tailor his detention of the driver to the original purpose of the stop.

In this case, Newsome certainly had cause to pull over Robinette for speeding. The question is when the validity of that stop ceased. Newsome testified that from the outset he never intended to ticket Robinette for speeding. When Newsome returned to Robinette's car after checking Robinette's license, every aspect of the speeding violation had been investigated and resolved. All Newsome had to do was to issue his warning and return Robinette's driver's license.

Instead, for no reason related to the speeding violation, and based on no articulable facts, Newsome extended his detention of Robinette by ordering him out of the vehicle. Newsome retained Robinette's driver's license and told Robinette to stand in front of the cruiser. Newsome then returned to the cruiser and activated the video camera in order to record his questioning of Robinette regarding whether he was carrying any contraband in the vehicle.

When the motivation behind a police officer's continued detention of a person stopped for a traffic violation is not related to the purpose of the original, constitutional stop, and when that continued detention is not based on any articulable facts giving rise to a suspicion of some separate illegal activity justifying an extension of the detention, the continued detention constitutes an illegal seizure.

The entire chain of events, starting when Newsome had Robinette exit the car and stand within the field of the video camera, was related to the questioning of Robinette about carrying contraband. Newsome asked Robinette to step out of his car for the sole purpose of conducting a line of questioning that was not related to the initial speeding stop and that was not based on any specific or articulable facts that would provide probable cause for the extension of the scope of the seizure of Robinette, his passenger and his car. Therefore the detention of Robinette ceased being legal when Newsome asked him to leave his vehicle.

However, this case contains a unique feature: Robinette consented to the search of his vehicle during the illegal seizure. Because Robinette's consent was obtained during an illegal detention, his consent is invalid unless the state proves that the consent was not the product of the illegal detention but the result of an independent act of free will. The burden is on the state to prove that the consent to search was voluntarily given. The factors used in consideration of whether the consent is sufficiently removed from the taint of the illegal seizure include the length of time between the illegal seizure and the subsequent search, the presence of intervening circumstances, and the purpose and flagrancy of the circumstances.

In this case there was no time lapse between the illegal detention and the request to search, nor were there any circumstances that might have served to break or weaken the connection between one and the other. The sole purpose of the continued detention was to illegally broaden the scope of the original detention. Robinette's consent clearly was the result of his illegal detention, and was not the result of an act of will on his part. Given the circumstances, Robinette felt that he had no choice but to comply.

This case demonstrates the need for this court to draw a bright line between the conclusion of a valid seizure and the beginning of a consensual exchange. A person has been seized for the purposes of the Fourth Amendment when a law enforcement officer, by means of physical force or show of authority, has in some way restrained his liberty such that a reasonable person would not feel free to walk away.

The transition between detention and a consensual exchange can be so seamless that the untrained eye may not notice that it has occurred. The undetectability of that transition may be used by police officers to coerce citizens into answering questions that they need not answer, or to allow a search of a vehicle that they are not legally obligated to allow.

The present case offers an example of the blurring between a legal detention and an attempt at consensual interaction. Even assuming that Newsome's detention of Robinette was legal through the time when Newsome handed back Robinette's driver's license, Newsome then said, "One question *before you get gone*: are you carrying any illegal contraband in your car?" Newsome tells Robinette that before he leaves Newsome wants to know whether Robinette is carrying any contraband. Newsome does not ask if he may ask a question, he simply asks it, implying that Robinette must respond before he may leave. The interrogation then continues. Robinette is never told that he is free to go or that he may answer the question at his option.

Most people believe that they are validly in a police officer's custody as long as the officer continues to interrogate them. The police officer retains the upper hand and the accouterments of authority. That the officer lacks legal license to continue to detain them is unknown to most citizens, and a reasonable person would not feel free to walk away as the officer continues to address him.

We are aware that consensual encounters between police and citizens are an important, and constitutional, investigative tool. However, citizens who have not been detained immediately prior to being encountered and questioned by police are more apt to realize that they need not respond to a police officer's questions. A "consensual encounter" immediately following a detention is likely to be imbued with the authoritative aura of the detention. Without a clear break from the detention, the succeeding encounter is not consensual at all.

Therefore, we are convinced that the right, guaranteed by the federal and Ohio Constitutions, to be secure in one's person and property requires that citizens stopped for traffic offenses be clearly informed by the detaining officer when they are free to go after a valid detention, before an officer attempts to engage in a consensual interrogation. Any attempt at consensual interrogation must be preceded by the phrase "At this time you legally are free to go" or by words of similar import.

While the legality of consensual encounters between police and citizens should be preserved, we do not believe that this legality should be used by police officers to turn a routine traffic stop into a fishing expedition for unrelated criminal activity. The Fourth Amendment to the federal Constitution and Section 14, Article I of the Ohio Constitution exist to protect citizens against such an unreasonable interference with their liberty.

OHIO v. ROBINETTE
519 U.S. 33 (1996)

REHNQUIST, C.J.

We are here presented with the question whether the Fourth Amendment requires that a lawfully seized defendant must be advised that he is "free to go" before his consent to search will be recognized as voluntary. We hold that it does not.

We have long held that the "touchstone of the Fourth Amendment is reasonableness." Reasonableness, in turn, is measured in objective terms by examining the totality of the circumstances.

In applying this test we have consistently eschewed bright-line rules, instead emphasizing the fact-specific nature of the reasonableness inquiry. Thus, in *Florida v. Royer* (1983), we expressly disavowed any "litmus-paper test" or single "sentence or paragraph rule," in recognition of the "endless variations in the facts and circumstances" implicating the Fourth Amendment. Then, in *Michigan v. Chesternut* (1988), when both parties urged "bright-line rules applicable to all investigatory pursuits," we rejected both proposed rules as contrary to our "traditional contextual approach." And again, in *Florida v. Bostick* (1991), when the Florida Supreme Court adopted a *per se* rule that questioning aboard a bus always constitutes a seizure, we reversed, reiterating that the proper inquiry necessitates a consideration of "all the circumstances surrounding the encounter."

We have previously rejected a *per se* rule very similar to that adopted by the Supreme Court of Ohio in determining the validity of a consent to search. In *Schneckloth v. Bustamonte* (1973), it was argued that such a consent could not be valid unless the defendant knew that he had a right to refuse the request. We rejected this argument: "While knowledge of the right to refuse consent is one factor to be taken into account, the government need not establish such knowledge as the *sine qua non* of an effective consent." And just as it "would be thoroughly impractical to impose on the normal consent search the detailed requirements of an effective warning," so too would it be unrealistic to require police officers to always inform detainees that they are free to go before a consent to search may be deemed voluntary.

GINSBURG, J., concurring in the judgment.

I write separately because it seems to me improbable that the Ohio Supreme Court understood its first-tell-then-ask rule to be the Federal Constitution's mandate for the Nation as a whole. "A State is free *as a matter of its own law* to impose greater restrictions on police activity than those this Court holds to be necessary upon federal constitutional standards." But ordinarily, when a state high court grounds a rule of criminal procedure in the Federal Constitution, the court thereby signals its view that the Nation's Constitution would require the rule in all 50 States. Given this Court's decisions in consent-to-search cases such as *Schneckloth v. Bustamonte* and *Florida v. Bostick*, however, I suspect that the Ohio Supreme Court may not have homed in on the implication ordinarily to be drawn from a state court's reliance on the Federal Constitution. In other words, I question whether the Ohio court thought of the strict rule it announced as a rule for the governance of police conduct not only in Miami County, Ohio, but also in Miami, Florida.

Formerly, the Ohio Supreme Court was "reluctant to use the Ohio Constitution to extend greater protection to the rights and civil liberties of Ohio citizens" and had usually not taken advantage of opportunities to "use the Ohio Constitution as an independent source of constitutional rights." Recently, however, the state high court declared: "The Ohio Constitution is a document of independent force. As long as state courts provide at least as much protection as the United States Supreme Court has provided in its interpretation of the federal Bill of Rights, state courts are unrestricted in according greater civil liberties and protections to individuals and groups."

The first-tell-then-ask rule seems to be a prophylactic measure not so much extracted from the text of any constitutional provision as crafted by the Ohio Supreme Court to reduce the number of violations of textually guaranteed rights. In *Miranda v. Arizona* (1966), this Court announced a similarly motivated rule as a minimal national requirement without suggesting that the text of the Federal Constitution required the precise measures the Court's opinion set forth. Although all parts of the United States fall within this Court's domain, the Ohio Supreme Court is not similarly situated. That court can declare prophylactic rules governing the conduct of officials in Ohio, but it cannot command the police forces of sister States. The very ease with which the Court today disposes of the federal leg of the Ohio Supreme Court's decision strengthens my impression that the Ohio Supreme Court saw its rule as a measure made for Ohio, designed to reinforce in that State the right of the people to be secure against unreasonable searches and seizures.

The Ohio Supreme Court's syllabus and opinion, however, were ambiguous. Under *Long*, the existence of ambiguity regarding the federal- or state-law basis of a state-court decision will trigger this Court's jurisdiction. *Long* governs even when, all things considered, the more plausible reading of the state court's decision may be that the state court did not regard the Federal Constitution alone as a sufficient basis for its ruling.

It is incumbent on a state court, therefore, when it determines that its State's laws call for protection more complete than the Federal Constitution demands, to be clear about its ultimate reliance on state law. Similarly, a state court announcing a new legal rule arguably derived from both federal and state law can definitively render state law an adequate and independent ground for its decision by a simple declaration to that effect. A recent Montana Supreme Court opinion on the scope of an individual's privilege against self-incrimination includes such a declaration:

> While we have devoted considerable time to a lengthy discussion of the application of the Fifth Amendment to the United States Constitution, it is to be noted that this holding is also based separately and independently on the defendant's right to remain silent pursuant to Article II, Section 25 of the Montana Constitution.

An explanation of this order meets the Court's instruction in *Long* that "if the state court decision indicates clearly and expressly that it is alternatively based on bona fide separate, adequate, and independent grounds, this Court will not undertake to review the decision."

On remand, the Ohio Supreme Court may choose to clarify that its instructions to law enforcement officers in Ohio find adequate and independent support in state law, and that in issuing these instructions, the court endeavored to state dispositively only the law applicable in Ohio. To avoid misunderstanding, the Ohio Supreme Court must itself speak with the clarity it sought to require of its State's police officers. The efficacy of its endeavor to safeguard the liberties of Ohioans without disarming the State's police can then be tested in the precise way Our Federalism was designed to work.

OHIO v. ROBINETTE
685 N.E.2d 762 (Ohio 1997)

LUNDBERG STRATTON, J.

The first issue that we must determine is whether this court's prior holding should be reaffirmed under the adequate and independent ground of the Constitution of the state of Ohio.

When the United States Supreme Court incorporated the federal Bill of Rights into the Fourteenth Amendment, the United States Constitution became the primary mechanism to safeguard an individual's rights. As a result, state court litigation of constitutional issues was based primarily upon the authority of the United States Constitution.

However, more recently, there has been a trend for state courts to rely on their own constitutions to provide broader protection for individual rights, independent of protections afforded by the United States Constitution. A state may impose greater restrictions on police activity pursuant to its own state constitution than is required by federal constitutional standards. This movement toward enforcing state constitutions independently has been called the "New Federalism."

Despite this wave of New Federalism, where the provisions are similar and no persuasive reason for a differing interpretation is presented, this court has determined that protections afforded by Ohio's Constitution are coextensive with those provided by the United States Constitution.

The language of Section 14, Article I of the Ohio Constitution and the Fourth Amendment is virtually identical. Accordingly, this court has interpreted Section 14, Article I of the Ohio Constitution as affording the same protection as the Fourth Amendment. In *Nicholas v. Cleveland* (Ohio 1932), the Court, in comparing the Fourth Amendment and Section 14, Article I of the Ohio Constitution, stated:

> While we are not bound by federal decisions upon this feature of the case, since the Bill of Rights in the Constitution of the United States is in almost the exact language of that found in our own, the reasoning of the United States court upon this aspect of the case should be very persuasive. The state courts, however, with practical unanimity, have adopted the same principle as the federal courts.

Thus, case law indicates that, consistent with *Robinette II*, we should harmonize our interpretation of Section 14, Article I of the Ohio

Constitution with the Fourth Amendment, unless there are persuasive reasons to find otherwise.

We will first determine whether Robinette's stop and continued detention were justified. It is undisputed that Officer Newsome's act of stopping Robinette was justified because Robinette was speeding. We also find that Newsome's instruction for Robinette to exit the vehicle was also justified because it was a traffic stop. Once Newsome administered the warning for speeding to Robinette, the reason for the stop ended.

However, Newsome continued to detain Robinette pursuant to a drug interdiction policy. The drug interdiction policy required police officers to ask persons detained during a traffic stop whether they had any contraband and then to ask to search the vehicle.

Royer and *Brown* set out a standard whereby police officers, under certain circumstances, may briefly detain an individual without reasonably articulable facts giving rise to suspicion of criminal activity, if the detention promotes a legitimate public concern, *e.g.*, removing drunk drivers from public roadways or reducing drug trade.

In the case at bar, we find that, pursuant to *Royer* and *Brown*, Officer Newsome was justified in briefly detaining Robinette in order to ask him whether he was carrying any illegal drugs or weapons pursuant to the drug interdiction policy, because such a policy promotes the public interest in quelling the drug trade.

The next issue for our determination is whether the continued detention of Robinette after this point was lawful.

If during the initial detention to ask the contraband question, the officer ascertained reasonably articulable facts giving rise to a suspicion of criminal activity, the officer may then further detain and implement a more in-depth investigation of the individual. For example, at a sobriety checkpoint, an officer who detects slurred speech would be justified in detaining the individual to perform a field test.

In the case at bar, Newsome did not have any reasonably articulable facts or individualized suspicion to justify Robinette's further detention in order to ask to search his car. Accordingly, Newsome was not justified in detaining Robinette in order to ask for and execute an intrusive search.

Even though we have determined that Newsome unlawfully detained Robinette to ask for permission to search his car, our analysis is not complete. Voluntary consent, determined under the totality of the circumstances, may validate an otherwise illegal detention and search.

Robinette argues that retention of *Robinette I*'s "free to go" rule would provide predictability in determining whether an individual consented to a search. We find that Robinette's conclusion is based on an oversimplified approach to the issue of consent.

In sum, every search situation is unique unto itself and no set of fixed rules will be sufficient to cover every situation. For that reason, *Bustamonte* utilized the totality-of-the-circumstances test to determine when consent is voluntary. Such a test serves both interests of allowing police to legitimately investigate under varying circumstances while protecting individuals from unreasonable searches and seizures.

In the case at bar, Officer Newsome stopped Robinette for driving sixty-nine miles per hour in a forty-five-mile-per-hour construction zone. Officer Newsome asked Robinette to step to the rear of his (Robinette's) car, which was in front of the patrol car. Newsome returned to his patrol car and turned on a video camera. Newsome gave Robinette a verbal warning *and advised Robinette that he was letting him off with only a verbal warning. But without any break in the conversation* and still in front of the camera, Newsome then asked Robinette, "One question before you get gone: are you carrying any illegal contraband in your car? Any weapons of any kind, drugs, anything like that?" Robinette denied having any contraband in the car. Newsome then immediately asked Robinette if he could search the car. Robinette hesitated, looked at his car, then back at the officer, then nodded his head. Newsome commenced a lengthy search of Robinette's car. During the search Newsome recovered some marijuana and a pill. Robinette was charged with drug abuse.

At the suppression hearing, Robinette provided the following testimony pertaining to the search:

> Q And did Newsome indicate to you that at that time when he returned from activating the video camera that he was giving you a warning and that you were free to go?
>
> A Yes, he did.
>
> Q And then at that time, I think, as the tape will reflect, the officer asked you some questions about did you have any weapons of any kind, drugs, anything like that. Do you recall that question?
>
> A Yes.
>
> Q Did you in fact feel that you were free to leave at that point?
>
> A I thought I was.
>
> Q The officer then asked if he could search your vehicle. What went through your mind at that point in time?
>
> A Uhm, I was still sort of shocked and I-I thought-I just automatically said yes.
>
> Q Did-did you feel that you could refuse the officer?
>
> A No.

Newsome's words did not give Robinette any indication that he was free to go, but rather implied just the opposite—that Robinette was *not free* to go until he answered Newsome's additional questions. The timing of Newsome's immediate transition from giving Robinette the warning for speeding into questioning regarding contraband and the request to search is troubling.

When these factors are combined with a police officer's superior position of authority, any reasonable person would have felt compelled to submit to the officer's questioning. While Newsome's questioning was not expressly coercive, the circumstances surrounding the request to search made the questioning impliedly coercive. Even the state conceded, at an oral argument before the United States Supreme Court, that an officer has discretion to issue a ticket rather than a warning to a motorist if the motorist becomes uncooperative. From the totality of the circumstances, it appears that Robinette merely submitted to "a claim of lawful authority" rather than consenting as a voluntary act of free will. Under *Royer*, this is not sufficient to prove voluntary compliance.

We are very mindful that police officers face the enormous and difficult task of fighting crime. Furthermore, we explicitly continue to recognize that officers may conduct checkpoint-type questioning and consensual searches, and may progress to further detention and investigation when individualized suspicion of criminal activity arises during questioning based on reasonably articulable facts. But allowing police officers to do their jobs must be balanced against an individual's right to be free from unreasonable searches. At some point, individual rights must prevail. This is just such a case.

Accordingly, we find that Section 14, Article I of the Ohio Constitution affords protections that are coextensive with those provided by the Fourth Amendment and, therefore, the Ohio Constitution does not require a police officer to inform an individual, stopped for a traffic violation, that he or she is free to go before the officer may attempt to engage in a consensual interrogation. Further, under Section 14, Article I of the Ohio Constitution, we find that the totality-of-the circumstances test is controlling in an unlawful detention to determine whether permission to search a vehicle is voluntary. Once an individual has been unlawfully detained by law enforcement, for his or her consent to be considered an independent act of free will, the totality of the circumstances must clearly demonstrate that a reasonable person would believe that he or she had the freedom to refuse to answer further questions and could in fact leave.

Therefore, pursuant to the totality of the circumstances, we find that Robinette did not voluntarily consent to allow Newsome to search his automobile. As a result, the evidence collected in that search is inadmissible.

NOTES

1. Did the second Ohio Supreme Court decision satisfy *Michigan v. Long*? In other words, does it establish an adequate and independent state law ground? If not, why not?

2. As for the merits, why did the Ohio Supreme Court choose to align the interpretation of its "unreasonable searches and seizures" protection with the similarly worded federal guarantee? Was the initial bright-line rule indefensible as a matter of state law? How was it different from the U.S. Supreme Court's bright-line rule for applying the Fifth Amendment under *Miranda*? What explains the state supreme court's second decision?

E. SEQUENCING: THE ORDER IN WHICH STATE COURTS RESOLVE RELATED STATE AND FEDERAL CLAIMS AND THE PRIORITY GIVEN TO EACH

Michigan v. Long, 463 U.S. 1032 (1983), answers one question but leaves open another. After the decision, it is clear that the U.S. Supreme Court will presume that the resolution of state court cases involving federal and state claims turns on federal law unless the state court expressly relies on state law in resolving the claim. But *Michigan v. Long* does not tell state courts whether to prioritize the federal or the related state constitutional argument in resolving dual-claim disputes. That question has led to a vigorous debate among courts and academics about the appropriate sequence for resolving each claim and the proper weight given U.S. Supreme Court decisions in resolving related state court claims. There are two main approaches to dual-claim cases that appear in the casebooks and the legal literature.

The first goes by the name of the "primacy" approach. It treats state constitutions as the first line of defense in guarding individual liberties and the U.S. Constitution as a backstop in the event the state guarantee does not protect the individual. It requires state courts to resolve the state claims first and to reach the federal claims only if the court does not grant relief based on the state constitution. Another way of putting it is that the "state courts should approach their state constitutions just as the U.S. Supreme Court would approach the federal Constitution—as a unique and highly significant document with a meaning that can and must be derived through independent analysis of the document itself." James A. Gardner, *The Failed Discourse of State Constitutionalism*, 90 Mich. L. Rev. 761, 774 (1992). The leading proponent of the primacy approach is Hans Linde, who argued in favor of it as an academic and later put the theory into practice as a Justice on the Oregon Supreme Court. *See* Hans A. Linde, *Due Process of Lawmaking*, 55 Neb. L. Rev. 197 (1976); Hans A. Linde, *Without "Due Process": Unconstitutional Law in Oregon*, 49 Or. L. Rev. 125 (1970). In addition to Oregon, other state supreme courts, including Maine and New Hampshire, have used the primacy approach. John W. Shaw, *Principled Interpretations of State Constitutional Law—Why Don't the 'Primacy' States Practice What They Preach?* 54 U. Pitt. L. Rev. 1019, 1025–26 (1993). *See, e.g., State v. Cadman*, 476 A.2d 1148, 1150 (Me. 1984); *State v. Gness*, 85 A.3d 382, 384–85 (N.H. 2014) ("We first address the defendant's claim under the state constitution and rely upon federal law only to aid our analysis."); *State v. Ball*, 471 A.2d 347, 350-51 (N.H. 1983); *Sterling v. Cupp*, 625 P.2d 123 (Or. 1981). Two States apply a variation on this school of thought, the "dual sovereignty" approach, which starts with the state constitution but does not end there; it proceeds to resolve the federal claim independently regardless of whether the court grants relief on the state claim. *See* Shaw, *Principled Interpretations*, *supra*, at 2028; *see also, e.g., State v. Coe*, 679 P.2d 353 (Wash. 1984); *State v. Badger*, 450 A.2d 336, 346–47 (Vt. 1982).

The second theory goes by a name only an academic would love, the "interstitial" approach, but just as well might be called the "secondary" approach. It treats the U.S. Constitution as the key guardian of individual rights and the state constitutions as supplemental add-on sources of individual rights. It tells state courts in dual-claim cases to resolve the federal claim first and to reach the state claim only if the court denies relief under the federal claim and, even then, to give considerable deference to U.S. Supreme Court decisions in construing the state constitution. The New Mexico Supreme Court is one of many state courts that follow this approach:

> Under the interstitial approach, the court asks first whether the right being asserted is protected under the federal constitution. If it is, then the state constitutional claim is not reached. If it is not, then the state constitution is examined. A state court adopting this approach may diverge from federal precedent for three reasons: a flawed federal analysis, structural differences between state and federal government, or distinctive state characteristics.

State v. Sanchez, 350 P.3d 1169, 1174 (N.M. 2015); *see also, e.g., Hope Clinic for Women, Ltd. v. Flores*, 991 N.E.2d 745 (Ill. 2013) ("When the language of the provisions within our state and federal constitutions is nearly identical, departure from the United States Supreme Court's construction of the provision will generally be warranted only if we find in the language of our constitution, or in the debates and the committee reports of the constitutional convention, something which will indicate that the provisions of our constitution are intended to be construed differently than are similar provisions in the Federal Constitution."); *Right to Choose v. Byrne*, 450 A.2d 925 (N.J. 1982). Most state supreme courts follow the "secondary" approach or variations on it. Joseph Blocher, *Reverse Incorporation of State Constitutional Law*, 84 S. Cal. L. Rev. 323, 339 (2011) ("To this day, most state courts adopt federal constitutional law as their own. Bowing to the nationalization of constitutional discourse, they tend to follow whatever doctrinal vocabulary is used by the United States Supreme Court, discussed in the law reviews, and taught in the law schools.")

Once a state court opts not to give its constitutional guarantee a meaning independent of the federal counterpart, it tends to proceed in "lockstep" with U.S. Supreme Court decisions construing the linguistically similar guarantee. *See, e.g., State v. Jenkins*, 3 A.3d 806, 839 (Conn. 2010) (holding that "the Connecticut constitution does not provide criminal defendants with greater protections than does the federal constitution in the context of unrelated questioning, including requests for consent to search, made during routine traffic stops"); *State v. Stevens*, 367 N.W.2d 788, 796–97 (Wis. 1985) (holding that search of garbage left out for collection did not violate Wisconsin or Federal Constitutions); *see also People v. Collins*, 475 N.W.2d 684, 691 (Mich. 1991) (stating that the Michigan constitutional provision prohibiting "unreasonable searches and seizures" should "be construed to provide the same protection as that secured by the Fourth Amendment, absent compelling reason to impose a different interpretation"); *State ex rel. Rear Door Bookstore v. Tenth Dist. Court of Appeals*, 588 N.E.2d 116, 123 (Ohio 1992) (declining to find greater free speech guarantees in the Ohio Constitution than the Federal Constitution); *In re F.C. III*, 2 A.3d 1201, 1212 (Pa. 2010) ("We find the due process rights implicated herein under our Constitution to be equal to those under the Fourteenth Amendment of the United States Constitution."); *cf. Am. Atheists, Inc. v. City of Detroit Downtown Dev. Auth.*, 567 F.3d 278, 301 (6th Cir. 2009) (holding that, under Michigan law, the establishment clauses of the Michigan and Federal Constitutions should be interpreted the same way).

A practical consideration affects all dual-claim cases. Unless the parties independently analyze and brief the state constitutional claim, the state court often will be forced to rely on federal law in resolving the state and federal claims. A short coda at the end of an appellate brief to the effect that, if the state court denies relief under the federal claim, it should grant relief under the state constitution, is not apt to convince state courts to take state constitutional claims seriously. Here is an example of how one court dealt with the problem:

> Although Smallfoot challenges the district court's suppression ruling under both Article I, section 4 of the Wyoming Constitution and the Fourth Amendment to the United States Constitution, he does not provide any legal analysis that the outcome under the Wyoming Constitution would differ from the federal constitution. Smallfoot's state constitutional argument consists of nothing more than recitation of a passage from *O'Boyle v. State* and an assertion that "the warrantless entry and search of his residence was not reasonable under all the circumstances." This Court has consistently declined, as a matter of policy, to consider a state constitutional claim in the absence of a sufficient argument supporting "adequate and independent state grounds."

Smallfoot v. State, 272 P.3d 314, 318 (Wyo. 2012); *see also State v. Short*, 851 N.W.2d 474, 491 (Iowa 2014) ("Notwithstanding the development of independent state constitutional law, in many cases lawyers do not advocate an Iowa constitutional standard different from the generally accepted federal standard. As a matter of prudence, we have adopted the approach in these cases that we will utilize the general standard urged by the parties, but reserve the right to apply the standard in a fashion different from the federal caselaw.").

Here is one perspective on the risks of the secondary approach and the lockstepping that often goes with it.

Jeffrey S. Sutton, *What Does—and Does Not—Ail State Constitutional Law*
59 Kan. L. Rev. 687 (2011)

Some state courts diminish their constitutions by interpreting them in lockstep with the Federal Constitution, occasionally at the beck and call of the state constitution itself.[1] The issue arises when the Federal Constitution and a state constitution contain an identical or similarly worded guarantee and a litigant invokes both of them, by arguing, say, that an arrest violates the federal and state prohibitions on "unreasonable searches and seizures." There is no reason to think, as an interpretive matter, that constitutional guarantees of independent sovereigns, even guarantees with the same or similar words, must be construed the same. Still less is there reason to think that a highly generalized guarantee, such as a prohibition on "unreasonable" searches, would have just one meaning for a range of differently situated sovereigns. Yet in my experience, state and federal courts frequently handle such cases by considering the federal constitutional claim first, after which they summarily announce that the state provision means the same thing.

Why the meaning of a federal guarantee proves the meaning of an independent state guarantee is rarely explained and often seems inexplicable. If the court decisions of another sovereign ought to bear on the inquiry, those of a sister state should have more to say about the point. State constitutions are more likely to share historical and cultural similarities. They necessarily will cover smaller jurisdictions. And in almost all instances they will be construing individual-liberty guarantees that

---

[1] *See* Fla. Const. art. I, §§ 12, 17 (requiring that Florida courts construe the state constitutional right against unlawful searches, seizures, and excessive punishments "in conformity with" the Fourth and Eighth Amendments, respectively, as interpreted by the U.S. Supreme Court); *cf.* Cal. Const. art. I, § 7(a) ("A person may not be denied equal protection of the laws; provided, that nothing imposes upon the State any obligations or responsibilities which exceed those imposed by the Equal Protection Clause of the 14th Amendment to the United States Constitution with respect to the use of pupil school assignment or pupil transportation."); *Raven v. Deukmejian*, 801 P.2d 1077, 1089 (Cal. 1990) (striking down a section of Proposition 115 that prevented state courts from construing the California constitution to afford greater rights to criminal defendants than the Federal Constitution).

originated in state constitutions, not the Federal Constitution,[2] and they indeed will be exercising a power—judicial review—that originated in state constitutional law, not in *Marbury v. Madison*.[3]

Why borrow in particular from the larger, far larger, jurisdiction? Federalism considerations may lead the United States Supreme Court to underenforce (or at least not to overenforce) constitutional guarantees in view of the number of people affected (over 300 million) and the range of jurisdictions implicated (one national government, fifty states, and thousands of local governments). No state supreme court, by contrast, has any reason to apply a "federalism discount" to its decisions, making it odd for state courts to rely exclusively on the meaning of the Federal Constitution in construing their own.

State court decisions of this type not only seem to be prioritizing the wrong decisions in determining the meaning of their own constitutions, but they also seem to be inverting the right sequence for considering state and federal arguments. Federal constitutional avoidance principles would suggest that the state guarantee ought to be considered first. If the state supreme court grants relief to the claimant on the state ground and provides a clear statement that it is doing so, the case is over, and the need to construe the federal constitutional provision disappears with it. No version of the constitutional avoidance doctrine to my knowledge says that courts should consider the claim arising from the larger sovereign before they consider the claim arising from the smaller one.

The nature of a federal constitutional claim points in the same direction. At issue is whether state action violates the Federal Constitution. If the state constitution prohibits the law or conduct at issue, however, there is no work for the Federal Constitution to do. Why not consider that point first, not as a matter of exhaustion, but as a matter of potentially eliminating any ultra vires state action at all and sparing the need to consider the federal claim in

---

[2] *See, e.g.*, William J. Brennan, Jr., *State Constitutions and the Protection of Individual Rights*, 90 Harv. L. Rev. 489, 501 (1977) ("Prior to the adoption of the federal Constitution, each of the rights eventually recognized in the federal Bill of Rights had previously been protected in one or more state constitutions."); Randy J. Holland, *State Constitutions: Purpose and Function*, 69 Temp. L. Rev. 989, 997 (1996) ("State Declarations of Rights were the primary origin and model for the provisions set forth in the Federal Bill of Rights."); Gordon S. Wood, *Foreword: State Constitution-Making in the American Revolution*, 24 Rutgers L.J. 911, 911 (1993) ("The office of our governors, the bicameral legislatures, tripartite separation of powers, bills of rights, and the unique use of constitutional conventions were all born during the state constitution-making period between 1775 and the early 1780s, well before the federal constitution of 1787 was created.").

[3] Joseph Blocher, *Reverse Incorporation of State Constitutional Law*, 84 S. Cal. L. Rev. 323, 334 (2011).

the process? By deciding the federal claim first, state courts engage in federal constitutional aggrandizement, not avoidance, and they risk diminishing their state constitutions in the process. By doing the reverse, they claim the rightful independence of their state constitutions.

In defense of the state (and federal) courts that take this path, explanations abound. As a matter of history, state constitutional law may have been all that mattered in the country's first 150 years, at least from the perspective of an individual-rights claimant. *See Barron ex rel. Tiernan v. Mayor of Baltimore*, 32 U.S. 243 (1833). But the incorporation of most of the Bill of Rights beginning in the 1920s started to change that, and the expansion of federal constitutional protections in the 1950s and 1960s completed the transformation. After the breakthroughs of the Warren Court revolution, who could blame state courts and advocates for relegating state constitutional claims to second-class treatment, if indeed to any treatment at all? A tradition of jurisprudence premised on the predominance of federal rights may not be easy to undo. Even though twenty-first century state courts are as apt to be constitutional innovators as federal courts, decades of state court precedents remain on the books paralleling the federal precedents or at least starting their analyses with them.

Efficiencies also may make a difference. Keep in mind that, by one count, ninety-five percent of the disputes resolved by courts in this country are filed in the state courts, as opposed to the federal ones. Just one of those courts, the California Supreme Court, resolved thirty-seven state constitutional law disputes in 2005, while the United States Supreme Court resolved thirty federal constitutional law disputes that same year. All of this makes it understandable that state courts would keep up with their burgeoning dockets by sticking to the calf-path rather than diverging from it.

Also daunting is the reality, at least the one I have experienced, that many advocates do not press the state arguments on an independent basis. What is argued is not a ground-up assessment of the independent meaning of the state guarantee, premised on its language, its history, or early understandings of its meaning. The point urged instead is that the state courts should construe the state guarantee differently because they can, not because they must, or because the dissent rather than the majority in a U.S. Supreme Court case has the better of the (federal) arguments.

This is the one respect in which Justice Brennan's boundary-crossing 1977 article, *State Constitutions and the Protection of Individual Rights*, 90 Harv. L. Rev. 489, delivered less than it could have for the development of state constitutional law. With the waning of civil rights victories brought by the end of the Warren Court and the beginning of the Burger Court, Justice Brennan pressed the state courts to fortify the breach, to grant relief by another name: a state constitution. "It may not be wide of the mark," he said, "to suppose that state courts discern, and disagree with, a trend in recent opinions of the United States Supreme Court to pull back from, or at least suspend for the time being, the application of the federal Bill of Rights and the restraints of the due process and equal protection clauses of the fourteenth amendment." State courts, he thus urged, "cannot rest when they have afforded their citizens the full protections of the federal Constitution," but should grant relief under their own constitutions instead.

In one respect, Justice Brennan was right. Constitutional claimants should prefer two arrows in their quiver—two chances, not just one, to invalidate a state or local law. But the messenger and the message may have helped to perpetuate, if not to create, two damaging myths.

The messenger may have prompted state court advocates and judges to misperceive this option as designed only to be a liberal ratchet, to give just some rights but not others a second chance in the state courts. Yet as shown above, independent state courts (and legislatures) often have protected a range of rights, whether involving liberty, equality, or property, whether before or after the federal courts entered the picture. That the state constitutions provide a second avenue for invalidating a local law says nothing about what kind of law should be, or will be, challenged.

The message pushed one feature of state constitutional law (the authority of the states to construe their constitutions differently) at the expense of another (an independent basis for doing so). The suggested inquiry was not whether state constitutional law demanded a different answer from federal constitutional law based on language, context, and history; it was that, if there is a will, there is now a new way for granting relief. Instead of urging first-principle inquiries into the meaning of the state provisions, the article urged state courts to side with the dissenters in debates already held at the United States Supreme Court—under federal law no less. While state court judges and advocates assuredly have the authority to invoke dissents rather than majority opinions of the United States Supreme Court in construing their own constitutions, heavy reliance on debates about the meaning of a federal guarantee are not apt to dignify the state constitutions as independent sources of law.

The Brennan article thus helped advance state constitutional law in one sense: by reminding advocates, through a prominent Supreme Court Justice, that once-forgotten state constitutional protections remain on the books and that they provide an alternative theory for relief. But in a state constitutional law equivalent of Stockholm syndrome, the article may have advanced the unfortunate myth that federal constitutional law remains front and center—the first line of inquiry—leaving state constitutional law as the quintessential argument of last resort.

Some say that federal claims should be resolved first in cases presenting federal and state contentions because state courts cannot construe their constitutions to offer less protection than the federal guarantee. That is wrong. State courts remain free to construe their constitutional guarantees to offer as little protection as they think appropriate, and only a constitutional amendment can alter that decision. Some state courts have said as much.[4] The only thing state courts cannot do is ignore the independent federal claim. It may be true that a state constitutional ruling that asks less of the government than existing federal constitutional law requires will not impact the parties before the court. But that is not a moot point. Once a state court establishes the interrelation between the two guarantees, it has established that no state constitutional inquiry is needed, a not-unhelpful development for future litigants and courts.

That also is a not-insignificant development for the United States Supreme Court, as it manages and assesses decisions of its own. Some state court rulings directly implicate the meaning of a federal guarantee, such as the Eighth Amendment's prohibition on "cruel and unusual punishments."[5] And some state court rulings may help to inform the original meaning of language in the Federal Constitution that first appeared in the state constitutions or may provide pragmatic reasons for following or steering clear of an approach embraced by the states.[6] Why live in a "top-down constitutional world" when we have the option of allowing the states to be the "vanguard—the first ones to decide whether to embrace or reject innovative legal claims"—and allowing the United States Supreme Court, informed by these experiences, to decide whether to federalize the issue. In a process that Professor Blocher calls "reverse incorporation," the United States Supreme Court remains free, whether on pragmatic or originalist grounds, to learn from and, if appropriate, borrow from the states' experiences.

Perhaps some fear confusion in the bar if the state courts de-link the two constitutional inquiries. After all, the United States Supreme Court's multi-decade experiment with dueling standards for Bill of Rights guarantees applicable to the state and federal governments did not end well, as the Court ultimately collapsed the two. But is confusion really a problem for a single state? If the state courts treat the two guarantees as distinct, the bench,

---

[4] *See, e.g., State v. Kennedy*, 666 P.2d 1316, 1323 (Or. 1983) ("A state's view of its own guarantee may indeed be less stringent, in which case the state remains bound to whatever is the contemporary federal rule.").

[5] *See Roper v. Simmons*, 543 U.S. 551, 574 (2005); *Atkins v. Virginia*, 536 U.S. 304, 312 (2002); *Penry v. Lynaugh*, 492 U.S. 302, 330–31 (1989); *Stanford v. Kentucky*, 492 U.S. 361, 369 (1989); Blocher, *supra* note 3, at 378.

[6] *See District of Columbia v. Heller*, 554 U.S. 570, 580 n.6, 583 n.7, 584-86, 590 n.13 (2008); *New York Times Co. v. Sullivan*, 376 U.S. 254, 280 (1964); *Davis v. Massachusetts*, 167 U.S. 43 (1897); Blocher, *supra* note 3, at 371, 382.

bar, law enforcement, and citizenry still will have to pay attention to just one standard: the more far-reaching of the two.

In the final analysis, there assuredly are historical and practical explanations for linking the meaning of federal and state guarantees and for prioritizing consideration of the federal ones. But continuing to do so in 2011 as a matter of course is increasingly difficult to justify and, worse, all the more likely to deepen the inertia-driven groove that already exists.

CHAPTER IV

EQUALITY

A. INTRODUCTION

Jeffrey M. Shaman, *Equality and Liberty in The Golden Age of State Constitutional Law* **1–5 (2008)**

Equality is a principle that enjoys a long history in state constitutional law. Some of the earliest state constitutions, the oldest political documents in America, proclaimed: "All men are born equally free and independent, and have certain inherent and indefeasible rights." Pa. Const. of 1776, art. I, § 1. *See also* Va. Const. of 1776, Bill of Rights, § 1 ("All men are by nature equally free and independent."). Today, that sentiment can still be found in a number of state constitutions, but it is more likely to be expressed as: "All people are created equal and are entitled to equal rights and opportunity under the law." Wis. Const. art. I, § 1 (1982). A number of the early state constitutions also contained provisions prohibiting the granting of unequal privileges or immunities. These provisions, too, along with their close counterparts banning special entitlements, can be found in many state constitutions today. After the Civil War and the enactment in the Federal Constitution of the Fourteenth Amendment guaranteeing equal protection of the laws to all persons, some states were moved to follow suit by adding equal protection clauses to their constitutions when the opportunity arose. The civil rights movement of the 1950s and 60s inspired some states to add provisions to their constitutions prohibiting discrimination against persons in the exercise of their civil rights. And after the Equal Rights Amendment (ERA) prohibiting discrimination on the basis of sex failed to gain passage at the federal level, some states adopted their own versions of the ERA. Long before the conception of the ERA, it is worth adding, Utah and Wyoming enacted state constitutional provisions guaranteeing equal civil, political, and religious rights and privileges for "male and female citizens."

Furthermore, in a number of state constitutions there are provisions that grant specialized protection for various kinds of equality. For instance, a few state constitutions provide for "free and equal elections." There are provisions in three state constitutions that expressly bar segregation. The Alaska constitution states that "No exclusive right or special privilege of fishery shall be created or authorized in the natural waters of the State." Some state constitutions expressly prohibit certain forms of discrimination in the private sector as well as the public one.

Some state constitutions contain a combination of equality provisions, creating a comprehensive mandate for equal treatment under the law. The Connecticut Constitution offers a good example:

> All men when they form a social compact, are equal in rights; and no man or set of men are entitled to exclusive public emoluments or privileges from the community. No person shall be denied the equal protection of the law nor be subjected to segregation or discrimination in the exercise or enjoyment of his or

her civil or political rights because of religion, race, color, ancestry, national origin, sex or physical or mental disability.

At the other end of the spectrum, some state constitutions contain no language expressly addressing equality or only briefly refer to it. Even in these settings, the state high courts may construe other language in the constitutions, say a due process guarantee, to encompass an equality imperative. The Maryland Court of Appeals, for example, has ruled that although the Maryland Declaration of Rights does not contain an express equal protection clause, the concept of equal protection is embodied in the due process article of the Declaration of Rights. Similarly, the West Virginia Supreme Court of Appeals has held that, although the phrase "equal protection" is not found in the state constitution, the principle of equality is an integral part of the state's constitutional law, inherent in the due process clause of the West Virginia Bill of Rights. And the Minnesota Supreme Court has recognized that the law of the land provision in the Minnesota Bill of Rights embraces principles of equality synonymous with the Equal Protection Clause of the Fourteenth Amendment to the Federal Constitution.

B. RACIAL CLASSIFICATIONS

SHEFF v. O'NEILL
678 A.2d 1267 (Conn. 1996)

PETERS, C.J.

The public elementary and high school students in Hartford suffer daily from the devastating effects that racial and ethnic isolation, as well as poverty, have had on their education. Federal constitutional law provides no remedy for their plight. The principal issue in this appeal is whether, under the unique provisions of our state constitution, the state, which already plays an active role in managing public schools, must take further measures to relieve the severe handicaps that burden these children's education. The issue is as controversial as the stakes are high. We hold today that the needy schoolchildren of Hartford have waited long enough. The constitutional imperatives contained in article eighth, § 1, and article first, §§ 1 and 20, of our state constitution entitle the plaintiffs to relief. At the same time, the constitutional imperative of separation of powers persuades us to afford the legislature, with the assistance of the executive branch, the opportunity, in the first instance, to fashion the remedy that will most appropriately respond to the constitutional violations that we have identified.

The stipulation of the parties and the trial court's findings establish the following relevant facts. Statewide, in the 1991–92 school year, children from minority groups constituted 25.7 percent of the public school population. In the Hartford public school system in that same period, 92.4 percent of the students were members of minority groups, including, predominantly, students who were either African-American or Latino. Fourteen of Hartford's twenty-five elementary schools had a white student enrollment of less than 2 percent. The Hartford public school system currently enrolls the highest percentage of minority students in the state. In the future, if current conditions continue, the percentage of minority students in the Hartford public school system is likely to increase rather than decrease. Although enrollment of African-American students in the twenty-one surrounding suburban towns has increased by more than 60 percent from 1980 to 1992, only seven of these school districts had a minority student enrollment in excess of 10 percent in 1992. Because of the negative consequences of racial and ethnic isolation, a more integrated public school system would likely be beneficial to all schoolchildren.

A majority of the children who constitute the public school population in Hartford come from homes that are economically disadvantaged, that are headed by a single parent and in which a language other than English is spoken. The percentage of Hartford schoolchildren at the elementary level who return to the same school that they attended the previous year is the lowest such percentage in the state. Such socioeconomic factors impair a child's orientation toward and skill in learning and adversely affect a child's performance on standardized tests. The gap in the socioeconomic status between Hartford schoolchildren and schoolchildren from the surrounding twenty-one suburban towns has been increasing. The performance of Hartford schoolchildren on standardized tests falls significantly below that of schoolchildren from the twenty-one surrounding suburban towns.

The state has not intentionally segregated racial and ethnic minorities in the Hartford public school system. Except for a brief period in 1868, no students in Connecticut have intentionally been assigned to a public school or to a public school district on the basis of race or ethnicity. There has never been any other manifestation of de jure segregation either at the state or the local level. In addition to various civil rights initiatives undertaken by the legislature from 1905 to 1961 to combat racial discrimination, the state board of education was reorganized, during the 1980s, to concentrate on the needs of urban schoolchildren and to promote diversity in the public schools. Since 1970, the state has supported and encouraged voluntary plans for increasing interdistrict diversity.

The state has nonetheless played a significant role in the present concentration of racial and ethnic minorities in the Hartford public school system. Although intended to improve the quality of education and not racially or ethnically motivated, the districting statute that the legislature enacted in 1909 is the single most important factor contributing to the present concentration of racial and ethnic minorities in the Hartford public school system. The districting statute and the resultant school district boundaries have remained virtually unchanged since 1909. The districting statute is of critical importance because it establishes town boundaries as the dividing line between all school districts in the state.

The defendants maintain that the plaintiffs are not entitled to judicial relief because the educational disparities of which they complain do not result from the requisite state action. The plaintiffs claim that the state bears responsibility to correct the constitutional violations alleged in their complaint because of the state's failure to "take corrective measures to ensure that its Hartford public schoolchildren receive an equal educational opportunity." That failure is actionable, according to the plaintiffs, because of the state's knowledge of the racial and ethnic isolation in the Hartford schools, combined with the state's extensive involvement in the operations of Connecticut's public schools and the impact of state statutes mandating school attendance within statutorily defined school districts. The defendants maintain, to the contrary, that the state's constitutional duty to provide for the elementary and secondary education of Connecticut schoolchildren is triggered only by state action that is alleged to be intentional state misconduct.

The defendants' argument, derived largely from principles of federal constitutional law, founders on the fact that article eighth, § 1, and article first, §§ 1 and 20, impose on the legislature an affirmative constitutional obligation to provide schoolchildren throughout the state with a substantially equal educational opportunity. It follows that, if the legislature fails, for whatever reason, to take action to remedy substantial inequalities in the educational opportunities that such children are being afforded, its actions and its omissions constitute state action.

The affirmative constitutional obligation that we recognized in *Horton I* and *Horton III*, and reaffirmed recently in *Moore v. Ganim*, was not premised on a showing that the legislature had played an active role in creating the inequalities that the constitution requires it to redress. In *Horton I*, we determined that the state's educational financing scheme was unconstitutional even though it was facially nondiscriminatory and even though the disparities resulting therefrom had not been created intentionally by the legislature. These constitutionally unacceptable disparities developed, instead, "from the circumstance that over the years there had arisen a great disparity in the ability of local communities to finance local education," and from the legislature's failure to consider "the financial capability of each municipality." In declaring this statutory scheme unconstitutional in *Horton I*, and in requiring further remedial action in *Horton III*, we necessarily determined that the state's failure adequately to address school funding inequalities constituted the state action that is the constitutional prerequisite for affording judicial relief.

The claims now before us likewise implicate the legislature's affirmative constitutional obligation to provide a substantially equal educational opportunity to all of the state's schoolchildren. The plaintiffs document the existence of an extensive statutory system developed in response to the legislature's plenary authority over state public elementary and secondary schools. As a general matter, the plaintiffs challenge the failure of the legislature to address continuing unconstitutional inequities resulting, de facto, from that scheme. The failure adequately to address the racial and ethnic disparities that exist among the state's public school districts is not different in kind from the legislature's failure adequately to address the "great disparity in the ability of local communities to finance local education" that made the statutory scheme at issue in *Horton I* unconstitutional in its application.

The defendants urge us to follow federal precedents that concededly require, as a matter of federal constitutional law, that claimants seeking judicial relief for educational disparities pursuant to the equal protection clause of the fourteenth amendment to the United States constitution must prove intentional governmental discrimination against a suspect class. According to the defendants, because the plaintiffs raise claims of unconstitutional disparities in educational opportunities on the basis of severe racial and ethnic imbalances among school districts, the plaintiffs, too, must prove intentional state action.

For two reasons, we are not persuaded that we should adopt these precedents as a matter of state constitutional law. First and foremost, the federal cases start from the premise that there is no right to education under the United States constitution. Our Connecticut constitution, by contrast, contains a fundamental right to education and a corresponding affirmative state obligation to implement and maintain that right. Second, the federal cases are guided by principles of federalism as "a foremost consideration in interpreting any of the pertinent constitutional provisions under which a court examines state action." Principles of federalism, however, do not restrict our constitutional authority.

In summary, under our law, which imposes an affirmative constitutional obligation on the legislature to provide a substantially equal educational opportunity for all public schoolchildren, the state action doctrine is not a defense to the plaintiffs' claims of constitutional deprivation. The state had ample notice of ongoing trends toward racial and ethnic isolation in its public schools, and indeed undertook a number of laudable remedial efforts that unfortunately have not achieved their desired end. The fact that the legislature did not affirmatively create or intend to create the conditions that have led to the racial and ethnic isolation in the Hartford public school system does not, in and of itself, relieve the defendants of their affirmative obligation to provide the plaintiffs with a more effective remedy for their constitutional grievances.

Since *Horton I*, it is common ground that the state has an affirmative constitutional obligation to provide all public schoolchildren with a substantially equal educational opportunity. Any infringement of that right must be strictly scrutinized. The issue presented by this case is whether the state has fully satisfied its affirmative constitutional obligation to provide a substantially equal educational opportunity if the state demonstrates that it has substantially equalized school funding and resources. For the purposes of the present litigation, we decide only that the scope of the constitutional obligation expressly imposed on the state by article eighth, § 1, is informed by the constitutional prohibition against segregation contained in article first, § 20. Reading these constitutional provisions conjointly, we conclude that the existence of extreme racial and ethnic isolation in the public school system deprives schoolchildren of a substantially equal educational opportunity and requires the state to take further remedial measures.

The affirmative constitutional obligation of the state to provide a substantially equal educational opportunity, which is embodied in article eighth, § 1, differs in kind from most constitutional obligations. Organic documents only rarely contain provisions that explicitly require the state to act rather than to refrain from acting. Nothing in the description of the relevant legal landscape in any of our cases suggests that the constitutional right that we articulated in *Horton I* was limited to school financing.

For Connecticut schoolchildren, the scope of the state's constitutional obligation to provide a substantially equal educational opportunity is informed and amplified by the highly unusual provision in article first, § 20, that prohibits segregation not only indirectly, by forbidding discrimination, but directly, by the use of the term "segregation." The section provides in relevant part: "No person shall be denied the equal protection of the law nor be subjected to segregation or discrimination because of race or ancestry."

The express inclusion of the term "segregation" has independent constitutional significance. The addition of this term to the text of our equal protection clause distinguishes this case from others in which we have found a substantial equivalence between our equal protection clause and that contained in the United States constitution. Fundamental principles of constitutional interpretation require that "effect must be given to every part of and each word in our constitution." In other cases, we have held that, insofar as article first, § 20, differs textually from its federal counterpart, its judicial construction must reflect such a textual distinction.

The issue before us, therefore, is what specific meaning to attach to the protection against segregation contained in article first, § 20, in a case in which that protection is invoked as part of the plaintiff school-children's fundamental affirmative right to a substantially equal educational opportunity under article eighth, § 1. In concrete terms, this issue devolves into the question of whether the state has a constitutional duty to remedy the educational impairment that results from segregation in the Hartford public schools, even though the conditions of segregation that contribute to such impairment neither were caused by nor are perpetuated by invidious intentional conduct on the part of the state.

Linguistically, the term "segregation" in article first, § 20, which denotes "separation," is neutral about segregative intent. The section prohibits segregation that occurs "because of religion, race, color, ancestry, national origin, sex or physical or mental disability," without specifying the manner in which such a causal relationship must be established.

Whatever this language may portend in other contexts, we are persuaded that, in the context of public education, in which the state has an affirmative obligation to monitor and to equalize educational opportunity, the state's awareness of existing and increasing severe racial and ethnic isolation imposes upon the state the responsibility to remedy "segregation because of race or ancestry." We therefore hold that, textually, article eighth, § 1, as informed by article first, § 20, requires the legislature to take affirmative responsibility to remedy segregation in our public schools, regardless of whether that segregation has occurred de jure or de facto.

Sound principles of public policy support our conclusion that the legislature's affirmative constitutional responsibility for the education of all public schoolchildren encompasses responsibility for segregation to which the legislature has contributed, even unintentionally. The parties agree, as the trial court expressly found, that racial and ethnic segregation is harmful, and that integration would likely have positive benefits for all children and for society as a whole. Further, as the trial court also expressly found, the racial and ethnic isolation of children in the Hartford schools is likely to worsen in the future.

In light of the complexities of developing a legislative program that would respond to the constitutional deprivation that the plaintiffs had established, we concluded, in *Horton I*, that further judicial intervention should be stayed "to afford the General Assembly an opportunity to take appropriate legislative action." Prudence and sensitivity to the constitutional authority of coordinate branches of government counsel the same caution in this case.

In staying our hand, we do not wish to be misunderstood about the urgency of finding an appropriate remedy for the plight of Hartford's public schoolchildren. Every passing day denies these children their constitutional right to a substantially equal educational opportunity. Every passing day shortchanges these children in their ability to learn to contribute to their own well-being and to that of this state and nation. We direct the legislature and the executive branch to put the search for appropriate remedial measures at the top of their respective agendas. We are confident that with energy and good will, appropriate remedies can be found and implemented in time to make a difference before another generation of children suffers the consequences of a segregated public school education.

BORDEN, J., dissenting.

I agree that racial and ethnic isolation in our public schools is harmful—both to those races and ethnic groups that are so isolated and to the other races and ethnic groups from whom they are isolated. I also agree with the majority's statement, based upon the trial court's finding, that the racial and ethnic isolation of Hartford's schoolchildren is likely to worsen in the future. I agree, furthermore, that racial and ethnic integration of our public schools would be beneficial for all children and society in general. These points of agreement rest on the notions that, as the majority recognizes, schools are important socializing institutions that bear a central responsibility for imparting our shared democratic values to our children, and that the opportunity for children of different races, ethnic backgrounds, economic levels and social groups to get to know each other in school is important if they are to understand and respect each other. Finally, I agree with the majority that the health of the economy of our state requires an educated workforce, which includes "the urban poor as an integral part of our future economic strength." Thus, I agree with the majority on the importance in our state of finding a way to cross the racial divide.

The majority, however, has transformed a laudable educational philosophy into a constitutional mandate. Thus, the majority has used this court's power to interpret the constitution in order to mandate a vast and unprecedented social experiment. It is a bedrock principle of our system of government that the legislative branch is the source of the fundamental public policy of the state, and that the courts may invalidate such a policy only where it is established beyond a reasonable doubt that it violates a constitutional right. Not only does the majority fail even to give lip service to this principle, the majority violates it.

NOTE

In *Brown v. Board of Education* (1954), the U.S. Supreme Court ruled that racial segregation in public schools violated the Equal Protection Clause of the United States Constitution. In that landmark decision and others adhering to its principles, the Supreme Court rendered classifications based on race constitutionally suspect and subject to strict judicial scrutiny. Since then, litigation concerning racial discrimination has occurred primarily in the federal courts and has been predominantly a matter of federal constitutional law. Even in this area, as *Sheff v. O'Neill* reveals, state constitutional provisions may provide more protection than the Federal Constitution.

Some years after *Brown*, the Supreme Court drew a distinction between *de jure* and *de facto* racial segregation, ruling that the latter amounted to a violation of the Equal Protection Clause only when based on intentional racial discrimination. In California, the state supreme court ruled otherwise, holding in a series of cases that the California equal protection clause prohibited *de facto* as well as *de jure* racial segregation in public schools and that state officials had an affirmative obligation to eradicate all forms of racial segregation in public schools. *Jackson v. Pasadena City Sch. Dist.* (Cal. 1963); *San Francisco Unified Sch. Dist. v. Johnson* (Cal. 1971); *Crawford v. Bd. of Educ.* (Cal. 1976). In these cases, the California high court took the position that, even in the absence of intentional discriminatory conduct, the state constitution required the elimination of racial segregation in public schools. The force of these rulings, though, was undermined by a ballot initiative that amended the state constitution. In contrast, no action has been taken to overrule *Sheff v. O'Neill*.

MALABED v. NORTH SLOPE BOROUGH
70 P.3d 416 (Alaska 2003)

BRYNER, J.

In 1997 the North Slope Borough enacted an ordinance that creates a mandatory preference for hiring, promoting, transferring, and reinstating Native Americans in borough government employment. The current version of the preference extends to all Native American applicants who are minimally qualified or meet most minimum job requirements and can meet the remaining requirements during their probationary period of employment; for purposes of the preference, "Native American" is defined to include any person belonging to an Indian tribe under federal law.

The borough enacted this preference after a study of economic conditions showed that the Native American population within the borough, specifically the resident Inupiat Eskimos, was both underemployed and earning substantially less money than borough residents of other races.

Article I, section 1, of the Alaska Constitution guarantees equal protection, providing that "all persons are equal and entitled to equal rights, opportunities, and protection under the law." In addition, Article I, section 3, of the Alaska Constitution categorically prohibits discrimination based on race or national origin: "No person is to be denied the enjoyment of any civil or political right because of race, color, creed, sex, or national origin." The legislature implemented these provisions in part by enacting the Alaska Human Rights Act, which prohibits employment discrimination based on race or national origin, and AS 29.20.630, which specifically prohibits Alaska's municipalities—including home rule municipalities like the North Slope Borough—from engaging in racial and national origin discrimination. In recognition of these requirements, the borough's charter itself prohibits these forms of discrimination: "No person may be discriminated against in any borough employment because of race, age, color, political or religious affiliation, or national origin."

Relying on these provisions, Malabed argues that the borough's hiring preference adopts a racial classification or, alternatively, a classification based on national origin, in violation of the Alaska Constitution. The borough responds by denying that its preference uses a race-conscious classification; instead, the borough insists, the preference adopts a well-accepted and constitutionally permissible political classification based on membership in federally recognized tribes. In advancing this argument, the borough relies chiefly on *Morton v. Mancari* (1974).

In *Mancari* the Supreme Court upheld a Bureau of Indian Affairs employment preference for hiring and promoting Native Americans within the BIA. Several non-Native American employees challenged the preference, arguing that the 1972 Equal Employment Opportunity Act had repealed the BIA's statutory authority to grant hiring preferences to Native Americans and that the preference amounted to invidious racial discrimination in violation of their Fifth Amendment due process rights. But the Court found that Congress had not repealed the BIA's authority to prefer Native Americans in hiring. And after analyzing the unique historical relationship between the federal government and Native Americans, the Court concluded that the preference was not only not invidious racial discrimination but was not based on race at all.

The Court pointed out that the disputed BIA preference applied only to members of federally recognized tribes and excluded many individuals who were racially Native American. Noting the "unique legal status of Indian tribes under federal law" and the BIA's special interest in furthering Native American self-government, the Court held that the hiring preference was "reasonably and directly related to a legitimate, nonracially based goal."

Assuming for present purposes that the borough's ordinance reflects this kind of political classification and does not discriminate on the basis of race, the ordinance might avoid problems with the Alaska Constitution's bar against racial discrimination. But the political nature of the classification would not necessarily insulate the ordinance from Malabed's equal protection challenge. For the borough, unlike the BIA in *Mancari*, has no obvious governmental interest, as a borough, in furthering Native American self-government; and Native Americans have no explicitly established "unique legal status" under borough law, as *Mancari* found them to have under federal law. Given these disparities between federal and local law, the legitimacy of the borough's hiring preference as a political classification is less apparent than the legitimacy of the BIA's hiring preference in *Mancari*. We must therefore consider whether the ordinance's ostensibly political lines discriminate in a way that offends the Alaska Constitution's guarantee of equal protection.

We have long recognized that our Constitution's equal protection clause affords greater protection to individual rights than the U.S. Constitution's Fourteenth Amendment. To implement Alaska's more stringent equal protection standard, we have adopted a three-step, sliding-scale test that places a progressively greater or lesser burden on the state, depending on the importance of the individual right affected by the disputed classification and the nature of the governmental interests at stake: first, we determine the weight of the individual interest impaired by the classification; second, we examine the importance of the purposes underlying the government's action; and third, we evaluate the means employed to further those goals to determine the closeness of the means-to-end fit.

To determine how the borough's hiring preference fares under this standard, we begin by considering the importance of the individual interests implicated by the preference. Here, the borough's hiring preference impairs Malabed's right to seek and obtain employment in his profession. Under similar circumstances, we have declared the right to employment to be an important right. In *State, Departments of Transportation & Labor v. Enserch Alaska Construction, Inc.* (Alaska 1989), we reviewed an equal protection challenge to an Alaska statute that provided hiring preferences to residents of economically distressed zones for employment on public works projects. A contractor building a road for the state challenged the preference as a violation of Alaska equal protection. Addressing the first step of Alaska's three-step analysis, we held that the "right to engage in an economic endeavor within a particular industry is an important right for state equal protection purposes."

In the second part of the equal protection analysis we consider the borough's interests, asking whether it had important and legitimate reasons to adopt the hiring preference. The borough offers several reasons supporting its ordinance: reducing unemployment of the largest group of unemployed borough residents—Inupiat Eskimos; strengthening the borough's economy; and training its workforce. But we found comparable governmental interests insufficient in *Enserch*. There the state tried to establish an important and legitimate governmental interest by arguing that the challenged hiring preference reduced unemployment, remedied social harms resulting from chronic unemployment, and assisted economically disadvantaged residents. Though acknowledging these interests as important, we found them to be illegitimate because they favored one class of Alaskans over another. Here, as in *Enserch*, it might seem that "this conclusion essentially ends our inquiry." But the borough nevertheless claims a special interest in preferring to hire Native Americans.

We reject the notion that the Alaska Constitution radiates implied guardianship powers allowing the state or its boroughs to treat Alaska Natives as if they were wards. To be sure, the United States Supreme Court has recognized implied powers in the United States Constitution that allow Congress broad latitude to legislate on behalf of Native Americans. The borough reasons that the Alaska Constitution must implicitly grant parallel powers to state and municipal governments. But the federal government's implied powers spring directly from the express powers granted to Congress in the United States Constitution's Indian Commerce and Treaty clauses.

In contrast to the federal constitution's provisions dealing with Indian tribes, the Alaska Constitution includes no provisions authorizing state action regarding Alaska Natives and so grants no express powers from which implied powers could arise. To the extent that the Alaska Constitution implies anything concerning the state's relations with Alaska Natives, then, it mirrors the constitutional drafters' well-recognized desire to treat Alaska Natives like all other Alaska citizens. The Alaska Constitution thus implies nothing that would give the borough a legitimate interest in enacting the disputed preference.

We by no means suggest that boroughs are categorically barred from adopting hiring preferences. Nor do we suggest that all state or local legislation pertaining to Alaska Natives or tribal governments should be assumed to establish suspect classifications presumptively barred by equal protection. Our focus is considerably narrower: we simply hold, in keeping with *Enserch*, that the borough has no legitimate basis to claim a general governmental interest in enacting hiring preferences favoring one class of citizens over others; and we find that the borough has failed to identify any source of a legitimate, case-specific governmental interest in the preference it actually adopted—a hiring preference favoring Native Americans. Because the borough is a political subdivision of Alaska, its legitimate sphere of municipal interest lies in governing for all of its people; preferring the economic interests of one class of its citizens at the expense of others is not a legitimate municipal interest, regardless of whether we view its ordinance as drawing distinctions founded on political status or race.

The last step of equal protection analysis under the Alaska Constitution examines the nexus between the state's asserted interests and the means selected to implement those interests. As previously mentioned, even when the state acts for important and legitimate reasons, its action must bear a close connection to those interests to justify impairing an important individual right. Here, of course, because we have found no legitimate borough interest supporting the challenged preference, we need not dwell on the closeness of its means-to-end fit. But a brief comment on the issue is nevertheless important to establish an alternative basis for our equal protection ruling.

For even assuming that the borough had legitimate and important interests in enacting a hiring preference favoring Native Americans, its preference is not closely related to attaining those interests. Addressing a similar situation in *Enserch*, we found a hiring preference in favor of residents of economically distressed areas unconstitutional under Alaska's equal protection guarantee in part because the fit between the preference and its objective was not sufficiently close. We noted that the preference failed to "prioritize relief for those areas most affected by nonresident employment" and that it set no meaningful limits on the state's power to declare any part of Alaska economically distressed at any time.

Here, the nexus between the borough's preference and its stated goals is insufficiently close for comparable reasons. The primary interest asserted by the borough lies in reducing Native American unemployment. But when viewed in light of this purpose, the borough's hiring preference is stunningly broad: it extends borough-wide and to all aspects of borough employment; is potentially limitless in duration; covers not only hiring but also promotions, transfers, and reinstatements; and applies absolutely— even to the extent of requiring Native American applicants without minimum qualifications to be hired over qualified non-Native applicants. Because the borough advances no particular reasons to justify these sweeping provisions, it fails to establish a close fit between its goals and its actions.

We conclude that the borough's hiring preference violates the Alaska Constitution's guarantee of equal protection because the borough lacks a legitimate governmental interest to enact a hiring preference favoring one class of citizens at the expense of others and because the preference it enacted is not closely tailored to meet its goals.

MATTHEWS, J., concurring.

I agree with the opinion of the court that the borough hiring preference violates the equal rights clause of the Alaska Constitution and with much of the court's reasoning. But I prefer to address directly the question whether the ordinance discriminates on the basis of race. I believe that it does, for the reasons that follow.

Inupiat Eskimos are a racial rather than a tribal group. The ordinance frankly acknowledges that its goal is to benefit them. In a prefatory clause the ordinance states "that its purpose in establishing an employment preference for Native Americans is to employ and train its Inupiat Eskimo residents in permanent, full-time positions." Another clause sounds the same theme: "Whereas, to increase the employment of Inupiat Eskimos, the North Slope Borough would like to give an employment preference to Native Americans." Similarly, the implementation plan for the ordinance expressly states that its purpose is to employ Inupiat Eskimo residents. Further, at oral argument counsel for the borough explained that one reason the term "Native American" was defined in terms of tribal membership was that it served to distinguish eligible Native Americans from others who are not eligible for benefits under the preference ordinance even though they may have some Native American ancestors. Tribal membership was thus used as a convenient mechanism to describe bona fide Native Americans.

Based on the above we can say with confidence that the purpose of the ordinance was to discriminate on the basis of race. Because by the express terms of the civil rights clause of the Alaska Constitution race is a suspect category, the ordinance must be subjected to strict scrutiny in order to determine whether it is permissible under the equal rights and civil rights clauses. But even if there were no clear indicators of an intent to discriminate on the basis of race, I believe that strict scrutiny would still be required because tribal membership is not only a political category but a racial one.

I reach the conclusion that state or municipal laws that grant individual benefits differentially based on tribal membership should be subject to strict scrutiny for a number of reasons. As noted, this is how we treat all race-based classifications. Further, strict scrutiny is well designed to ensure that laws remain race-neutral, as contemplated by the framers of the Alaska Constitution. This case illustrates that tribal membership readily lends itself to use as a proxy for a racial classification and as a pretext for racial discrimination. An effective tool is necessary to prevent these abuses. In addition, strict scrutiny is the approach taken by some federal courts in tribal classification cases when construing the equal protection clause of the Fourteenth Amendment to the federal constitution. Since the federal constitution contains provisions authorizing legislation on behalf of Native Americans, while the Alaska Constitution presumptively prohibits such legislation, it follows that stronger reasons exist for using the strict scrutiny method for state constitutional questions than for those arising under the federal constitution.

Although strict scrutiny review presents a high barrier, it is a barrier that may be overcome in deserving cases. It is impossible to categorize the kinds of cases that might pass strict scrutiny review. But a federal law calling on the state to give preferential treatment to tribal members would almost certainly present a compelling justification for state legislation. On balance, I believe that strict scrutiny properly accommodates the state's strong interest in preventing discrimination on the basis of race and its relatively rare and limited need to act adjunctively with the federal government in programs that favor tribal members over other state citizens.

The present ordinance does not survive strict scrutiny review. As the opinion of the court establishes, the borough had no legitimate interest, much less a compelling one, in adopting the preference.

NOTES

1. In *Brackett v. Civil Service Commission* (Mass. 2006), the Massachusetts High Court upheld an affirmative action program designed to increase the hiring and promotion of women and minorities in the state civil service. In upholding the program, the Court took the position that the standard for equal protection analysis under the Massachusetts Declaration of Rights was the same as the standard under the Federal Constitution. Following the federal standard, the court ruled that the program was justified as a means of remedying the continuing effects of past racial and gender discrimination, and therefore did not violate either the Massachusetts or Federal Constitution.

2. In recent years, three states—California, Michigan, and Washington—have amended their constitutions to prohibit affirmative action programs. The California Constitution, for example, now provides that:

> The state shall not discriminate against, or grant preferential treatment to, any individual or group on the basis of race, sex, color, ethnicity, or national origin in the operation of public employment, public education, or public contracting.

After passage of this provision, the Supreme Court of California found that it was contravened by an outreach program that required contractors bidding on city projects to employ a specified percentage of minority and female subcontractors. *Hi Voltage Wire Works, Inc. v. San Jose* (Cal. 2000).

After the U.S. Supreme Court upheld Michigan Law School's race-conscious admission program in *Grutter v. Bollinger* (2003), Michigan citizens put on the ballot "Proposal 2," and voters approved it by a margin of 58 percent to 42 percent. This enactment became Article I, § 26, of the Michigan Constitution, and provides as follows:

> (1) The University of Michigan, Michigan State University, Wayne State University, and any other public college or university, community college, or school district shall not discriminate against, or grant preferential treatment to, any individual or group on the basis of race, sex, color, ethnicity, or national origin in the operation of public employment, public education, or public contracting.
>
> (2) The state shall not discriminate against, or grant preferential treatment to, any individual or group on the basis of race, sex, color, ethnicity, or national origin in the operation of public employment, public education, or public contracting.
>
> (3) For the purposes of this section 'state' includes, but is not necessarily limited to, the state itself, any city, county, any public college, university, or community college, school district, or other political subdivision or governmental instrumentality of or within the State of Michigan not included in sub-section 1.

In *Schuette v. Coalition to Defend Affirmative Action* (2014), the U.S. Supreme Court upheld Proposal 2, rejecting the plaintiffs' *federal* equal protection challenge. Proposal 2 thus is valid and effectively bans the use of affirmative action by state educational institutions in Michigan.

C. GENDER-BASED CLASSIFICATIONS

COMMONWEALTH v. PENNSYLVANIA INTERSCHOLASTIC ATHLETIC ASS'N
334 A.2d 839 (Pa. Commw. Ct. 1975)

BLATT, J.

On November 13, 1973 the Commonwealth of Pennsylvania, acting through its Attorney General initiated suit against the Pennsylvania Interscholastic Athletic Association (PIAA) by filing a complaint in equity in this Court. The PIAA is a voluntary unincorporated association whose members include every public senior high school in this Commonwealth, except for those in Philadelphia. It also includes some public junior high schools as well as some private schools. The PIAA regulates interscholastic competition among its members in the following sports: football, cross-country, basketball, wrestling, soccer, baseball, field hockey, lacrosse, gymnastics, swimming, volleyball, golf, tennis, track, softball, archery and badminton.

The complaint here specifically challenges the constitutionality of this by law: "Girls shall not compete or practice against boys in any athletic contest." The Commonwealth asserts that this provision violates both the equal protection clause of the Fourteenth Amendment to the United States Constitution and also Article I, Section 28 of the Pennsylvania Constitution, the Equal Rights Amendment, in that it denies to female student athletes the same opportunities which are available to males to practice for and compete in interscholastic sports.

Article I, Section 28 of the Pennsylvania Constitution provides:

> Equality of rights under the law shall not be denied or abridged in the Commonwealth of Pennsylvania because of the sex of the individual.

Since the adoption of the ERA in the Commonwealth of Pennsylvania, the courts of this state have unfailingly rejected statutory provisions as well as case law principles which discriminate against one sex or the other. In *Conway v. Dana* (Pa. 1974) the court cast aside the presumption which had previously existed to the effect that the father, because of his sex, must accept the principal burden of financial support of minor children. The court there indicated that support is the equal responsibility of both parents and that, in light of the ERA, the courts must now consider the property, income, and earning capacity of both in order to determine their respective obligations.

In *Hopkins v. Blanco* (Pa. 1974) the court extended to the wife the right to recover damages for loss of consortium, a right previously available only to the husband. The court there stated: "The obvious purpose of the Amendment was to put a stop to the invalid discrimination which was based on the sex of the person. The Amendment gave legal recognition to what society had long recognized, that men and women must have equal status in today's world."

Most recently in *Henderson v. Henderson* (Pa. 1974) the section of the Divorce Law which permitted only the wife to receive alimony pendente lite, counsel fees and expenses was ruled unconstitutional. The court in broad terms proclaimed:

> The thrust of the Equal Rights Amendment is to insure equality of rights under the law and to eliminate sex as a basis for distinction. The sex of citizens of this Commonwealth is no longer a permissible factor in the determination of their legal rights and legal responsibilities. The law will not impose different benefits or different burdens upon the members of a society based on the fact that they may be man or woman.

Commonwealth v. Butler (Pa. 1974), filed on the same day as Henderson, held unconstitutional the provision of the Muncy Act which prevented trial courts from imposing a minimum sentence on women convicted of a crime. Only male criminals were subject to the minimum sentence provision.

The PIAA seeks to justify the challenged By-Law on the basis that men generally possess a higher degree of athletic ability in the traditional sports offered by most schools and that because of this, girls are given greater opportunities for participation if they compete exclusively with members of their own sex. This attempted justification can obviously have no validity with respect to those sports for which only one team exists in a school and that team's membership is limited exclusively to boys. Presently a girl who wants to compete interscholastically in that sport is given absolutely no opportunity to do so under the challenged By-Law. Although she might be sufficiently skilled to earn a position on the team, she is presently denied that position solely because of her sex. Moreover, even where separate teams are offered for boys and girls in the same sport, the most talented girls still may be denied the right to play at that level of competition which their ability might otherwise permit them. For a girl in that position, who has been relegated to the "girls' team," solely because of her sex, equality under the law has been denied.

The notion that girls as a whole are weaker and thus more injury-prone, if they compete with boys, especially in contact sports, cannot justify the By-Law in light of the ERA. Nor can we consider the argument that boys are generally more skilled. The existence of certain characteristics to a greater degree in one sex does not justify classification by sex rather than by the particular characteristic. If any individual girl is too weak, injury-prone, or unskilled, she may, of course, be excluded from competition on that basis but she cannot be excluded solely because of her sex without regard to her relevant qualifications. We believe that this is what our Supreme Court meant when it said in *Butler* that "sex may no longer be accepted as an exclusive classifying tool."

Although the Commonwealth in its complaint seeks no relief from discrimination against female athletes who may wish to participate in football and wrestling, it is apparent that there can be no valid reason for excepting those two sports from our order in this case.

NOTE

The federal Equal Rights Amendment, which would have prohibited the denial or abridgement of rights on account of sex, failed to gain passage as an amendment to the Federal Constitution, falling just two states short of the three-quarters requirement of Article V. However, between 1970 and 1978, fifteen states adopted constitutional amendments modeled on the ERA. They joined three other states—California, Utah, and Wyoming—whose constitutions have contained provisions expressly banning sexual discrimination since the late 1800s. By now, twenty state constitutions include equality provisions that expressly prohibit discrimination on the basis of sex.

In most states whose constitutions contain a provision expressly proscribing discrimination on the basis of sex, the courts take a strong stance against gender discrimination. The Supreme Court of Washington has taken an especially forceful stance regarding its ERA:

> The ERA absolutely prohibits discrimination on the basis of sex and is not subject to even the narrow exceptions permitted under traditional "strict scrutiny." The ERA mandates equality in the strongest of terms and absolutely prohibits the sacrifice of equality for any state interest, no matter how compelling.

A few courts in other states take a nearly absolutist approach to the ERA by ruling that classifications based on gender are prohibited except when necessitated by physical differences between the sexes. Most states that have adopted the ERA, however, take the position that the ERA elevates gender to a suspect classification calling for strict judicial scrutiny of any law that classifies persons on the basis of sex. In one or two states that have adopted a version of the ERA, the courts use an intermediate level of scrutiny to assess gender classifications.

In states whose constitutions do not contain a provision expressly barring sex discrimination, the courts tend to follow the federal approach of using intermediate scrutiny to review classifications based on gender. Some of these states have found that intermediate scrutiny can be an effective means to combat sexual discrimination. For example, in West Virginia, which has not adopted the ERA, the state supreme court used intermediate scrutiny in ruling that the state due process clause, which encompasses an equal protection principle, was violated by a regulation barring girls from playing on high school baseball teams. *Israel v. West Virginia Secondary Schools Activities Comm'n* (W. Va. 1989). In striking down the regulation, the court stated that the purpose of the equal protection principle was "to avoid this type of artificial distinction based solely on gender."

Intermediate scrutiny, though, has its limits, and occasionally is used to uphold gender classifications that might be struck down under strict scrutiny. For instance, in *O'Connor v. Board of Education of School District No. 23* (7th Cir. 1981), the court employed intermediate scrutiny in upholding a junior high school regulation barring girls from playing on the boys' interscholastic basketball team. Although there was a separate girls' basketball team, it functioned at a lower level of competition than the boys' team and therefore did not offer an equivalent opportunity for the development of athletic skills. Given the substantial disparity between the girls' and boys' teams, it is questionable whether the regulation could have survived strict scrutiny.

STATE v. RIVERA
612 P.2d 526 (Haw. 1980)

OGATA, J.

Appellant was convicted of first degree rape. The applicable statute was amended as of June 26, 1979 and as we understand appellant he would have no equal protection challenge to the new statute. The purpose of the amendment was to restate the statutory provisions in gender-neutral terms. Appellant challenges the constitutionality of HRS § 707-730 prior to its amendment, and claims that, by its terms, it denied him the equal protection of the law by punishing only men and no women, and protecting only women and no men, thus violating the equal protection guarantees of the Fourteenth Amendment of the United States Constitution and Article I, Section 4 of the Hawaii State Constitution and the equal rights amendment, Article I, Section 21, of the Hawaii State Constitution (ERA).

To withstand judicial scrutiny under the equal protection clause, a sex-based distinction must serve governmental objectives and must be substantially related to achievement of those objectives. Under this principle, the question is whether the sex-based classification in the former rape law served an important governmental objective and was substantially related to achievement of that objective. We find that it plainly met the test.

Although the statute sets up a gender-based classification by defining rape as an offense which can be committed only by a male, it reflects a legislative judgment as to the degree of harm posed to potential victims of nonconsensual intercourse. "While we recognize that it is possible for females to commit a sex offense which might be deemed rape, the fact remains that historically and generally rape is a crime committed by males against females." *Moore v. Cowan* (6th Cir. 1977). The legislature chose to selectively deal with the act of forced intercourse by men upon women as a more significant societal problem where the need for proscription was clearest. Protecting women from nonconsensual intercourse is an important legislative objective. And a law which punishes males for nonconsensual intercourse with women against their will is substantially related to that objective. Appellant's contentions might be more persuasive if he had provided us with empirical data tending to show that female rapes of males presented a social problem. In *West Coast Hotel Co. v. Parrish* (1937), the United States Supreme Court restated the principle that "if the law presumably hits the evil where it is most felt, it is not to be overthrown because there are other instances to which it might have been applied." We are dealing with a criminal sex offense statute. We are not dealing with an overbroad generalization based on sex which is entirely irrelevant to any difference between men and women or which demeans the ability or status of the affected class. The courts have been reluctant in striking down criminal sex laws and all have upheld rape statutes against constitutional challenges.

Appellant claims that because the Hawaii State Constitution specifically enumerates sex along with race, religion and ancestry, this specific enumeration requires a more stringent test than that required by the Fourteenth Amendment. Moreover, the ERA, which, by its terms forbids classifications based on sex, is said to necessitate a judicial standard of review at least as high as "strict scrutiny."

Not even the ERA, however, forbids all classifications. "The fundamental legal principle underlying the ERA is that the law must deal with particular attributes of individuals." A classification based on a physical characteristic unique to one sex is not an impermissible under- or over-inclusive classification because the differentiation is based on the unique presence of a physical characteristic in one sex and not based on an averaging of a trait or characteristic which exists in both sexes. Two frequently cited examples are laws relating to wet nurses, which would apply to all or some women but no men; or laws regulating sperm donation which would apply to all or some men, but no women.

Rape was defined as a male engaging in "sexual intercourse, by forcible compulsion, with a female." A sex-based distinction existed in the former rape statute but the differentiation in treatment was based upon unique physical characteristics of men and women and the unique characteristics justified the classification. Insofar as rape was defined as forced intercourse by a male with a female, it was based on a physiological characteristic unique to males. Furthermore, as the court stated in *Finley v. State* "hymen and uterine injury to female rape victims, the possibility of pregnancy, and the physiological difficulty of a woman forcing a man to have sexual intercourse with her all suggest a justification for the sexual distinction." It has also been said that "so long as the law deals only with a characteristic found in all (or some) women but no men, or in all (or some) men but no women, it does not ignore individual characteristics found in both sexes." The statute neither denied equal rights to men nor did it violate the ERA.

NOTES

1. In *Griffin v. Crane* (Md. 1998), the Maryland Court of Appeals (the highest court in Maryland) held that a trial court's custody decision based on the daughter's "need for a female hand" violated that State's ERA. The court reasoned that "the Amendment's broad, sweeping mandatory language" was an "expression of Maryland's commitment to equal rights for men and women and of its intention to alter traditional attitudes" around family matters when determining those rights. Justice McAuliffe's dissent objected to the scope of the majority's decision and its interpretation of the trial judge's remarks. He emphasized that the judge's conclusion that the daughter would be better off with her mother reflected his assessment of "this mother and this daughter, not some stereotypical figures."

2. *In Re T.J.S.* (N.J. 2012), interpreted New Jersey's Equal Protection Clause more narrowly. The case concerned the New Jersey Parentage Act, which gives an infertile married man the right to become the natural father of a child conceived when his wife is artificially inseminated with the sperm of another man, but does not provide a comparable right to an infertile married woman. By a vote of 3-3 the Supreme Court of New Jersey left in place a lower court decision upholding the Act against a claim that it violated the equal protection requirement of the New Jersey Constitution.

D. AGE-BASED CLASSIFICATIONS

DRISCOLL v. CORBETT
69 A.3d 197 (Pa. 2013)

SAYLOR, J.

By way of background, in 1967–68, a limited constitutional convention was convened with the approval of Pennsylvania voters. Its purpose was to consider certain proposed changes to the state charter, including changes to Article V, which pertains to the judiciary. The proposed revisions that emerged from the various committees and subcommittees were subject to public hearings and provided to the full convention for debate and amendment. They were adopted by the convention in March 1968, and ratified by the electorate of Pennsylvania on April 23, 1968.

Article V of the Pennsylvania Constitution was completely rewritten and, as such, effectively replaced Article V of the Constitution of 1874. One feature of the new Article V was a mandate that Pennsylvania jurists retire at a specific age. In particular, Section 16(b), as adopted in 1968, stated: "Justices, judges and justices of the peace shall be retired upon attaining the age of seventy years."

Approximately twenty years after the 1967–68 constitutional convention, several judges challenged the validity of Section 16(b)'s age-based retirement mandate on federal and state constitutional grounds. The challenges, which were resolved in *Gondelman v. Commonwealth* (Pa. 1989), were unsuccessful on both grounds. Two years later, the United States Supreme Court rejected a similar challenge to a mandatory retirement provision of the Missouri Constitution, pursued under federal constitutional principles. *See Gregory v. Ashcroft* (1991).

This year, several groups of Pennsylvania jurists have sought to renew the attack on Article V, Section 16(b) via multiple legal actions commenced in both federal and state courts. The judges lodged complaints relating that they were elected, and then retained, to ten-year judicial terms, and that the named Commonwealth officials' enforcement of Section 16(b) would require them to retire against their will prior to the expiration of those terms.

In advancing their equal protection claim, Petitioners initially rely on Article I, Section 1 of the state charter, which lists as inherent and indefeasible rights the enjoyment and defense of foundational freedoms— the right to life and liberty, the acquisition, possession and protection of property and reputation, and the pursuit of happiness. (This wording is substantively unchanged from the provision as it appeared in the 1776 Pennsylvania Constitution.) Their arguments accept, however, that their right to equal protection derived from this and other constitutional provisions may be qualified by the government—and no less the people— via the use of certain classifications. They proceed to advocate a heightened level of scrutiny of the age-based classification involved, and, failing this, they contend Section 16(b) does not satisfy the most liberal threshold for constitutional compliance, namely, the rational-basis test.

We reject the effort to secure heightened review. First and foremost, as related above, any judicial review for constitutional compliance internal to the foundational document must be highly deferential. Here, Petitioners seek to employ heightened scrutiny to regulate the people themselves in the exercise of their "inalienable and indefeasible" right to amend their constitution as they see fit. In such circumstances, we are persuaded by the reasoning in *Gregory* disposing of a similar challenge to a state constitutional retirement mandate for Missouri judges.

In view of the manifest need to balance the constitutionally grounded right of citizens to equal protection of the laws, against the people's indefeasible right to amend their governing charter as they see fit, we would reject Petitioners' contention that the age-related basis for the classification implicates a heightened level of scrutiny, even if it were conceded that such elevated review should obtain, under the state Constitution, relative to similar age restrictions contained in an act of the General Assembly.

Much of Petitioners' argumentation is based on the premise that most judges are able to function as skilled jurists past the age of 70, and that changes in longevity render the retirement mandate unreasonable by current standards. In their complaints, as well, Petitioners alleged that the state pension system would benefit if the retirement mandate were to be lifted. Petitioners overlook that "the wisdom of the policy behind legislative enactments is generally not the concern of the court," as we are only charged with assessing legality. As to legality, we do not believe Section 16(b) "is so unrelated to the achievement of any combination of legitimate purposes that we can only conclude that the people's actions were irrational." Thus, although we have no doubt that many individual judges would be capable of serving with distinction beyond their mandatory retirement date—and while the service of the present Petitioners and of many other Pennsylvania jurists reaching age 70 is honored and appreciated—there are systemic goals that are rationally related to valid governmental and societal interests.

Petitioners' final argument is that the retirement provision violates their due process rights under the Pennsylvania Constitution. Judges have no property interest conferred by their election or retention in serving as commissioned jurists past the date set by the Constitution for their retirement. *Firing v. Kephart* (Pa. 1976) leaves little doubt on this point, as it concluded that judges who reach the constitutional retirement age are not elected to "regular" terms—i.e., six years in the case of a justice of the peace, or ten years in the case of judges and Supreme Court Justices—but instead, to terms that expire early due to the mandatory retirement provision. Since the Constitution provides for mandatory retirement at age 70, the Constitution does not itself provide for the election of any judge for any term that extends beyond the age of 70.

Petitioners' due process argument rests on the premise that they have a more general right, protected by due process norms reflected in Article I, to pursue their chosen profession. While *Nixon v. Commonwealth* (Pa. 2003), indicated that the right to pursue a lawful occupation is, indeed, protected from undue infringement under Article I, Section 1, it also clarified that strict judicial scrutiny is only required vis-à-vis legislation that affects fundamental rights (such as the right to marry, the right to privacy, and the right to procreate), whereas rational basis review is applicable to laws that impinge upon rights that are not fundamental. Further, *Nixon* clarified that the right to pursue a particular occupation is not fundamental.

In summary, there is colorable merit to Petitioners' position that, theoretically at least, there is some possibility that a constitutional amendment might impinge on inherent, inalienable rights otherwise recognized in the Constitution itself. Nevertheless, we do not believe that the charter's framers regarded an immutable ability to continue in public service as a commissioned judge beyond seventy years of age as being within the scope of the inherent rights of mankind. Rather, in view of the people's indefeasible right to alter their government as they think proper through amending its basic charter, the mandatory retirement provision for judicial officers is subject to deferential, rational basis review under both equal protection and due process, and it satisfies that standard. Therefore, although certain societal circumstances may have changed since 1968 when the challenged provision was added to the Constitution—and, indeed, some of the original justifications for mandatory retirement may not have reflected the most fair or even the most beneficial public policy—the proper approach of conforming the Constitution more closely with Petitioners' vision of how experiential changes should be taken into account is to pursue further amendment to the Pennsylvania Constitution.

EAKIN, J., concurring.

I write separately to suggest another, more structural justification of age limitations for judicial service, beyond the presumption of mental decay. I acknowledge such justification is not needed to resolve this challenge, but offer it only to impugn petitioners' premise that mental acuity is the sole rationale for this constitutional provision.

The Pennsylvania Constitution is designed to assure the judiciary a measure of independence not given to the other branches of government in order to insulate it from political pressure. For instance, terms of office are not merely two years, or four years, but an expansive ten years. Once elected, common pleas and appellate judges do not face contested reelections or partisan opponents—they only face the electorate via a "yes or no" retention vote. Furthermore, Article II, § 8 establishes a legislator's compensation may not be increased during a term; in contrast, § 16(a) assures a jurist's compensation will not be decreased during a term in retaliation for decisions made.

Jurists are thus uniquely positioned and sequestered in various ways to protect their impartiality and independence—vital bulwarks of our governmental system. However, such sequestration has a counterpoint, for too much immunity risks usurpation of power, which the tripartite structure was designed to prevent. If the power of independence is given, it is hardly imprudent to put some concrete limit on that power. A time-based limit does nothing to threaten judicial independence, but simply creates terminal points at which the power will pass to others. Thus, § 16(b) seems to me a legitimate and considered constitutional strategy to establish a temporal limit on judicial service, regardless of past or current perceptions of one's ability to perform competently beyond any given age.

NOTES

1. *Driscoll v. Corbett* dealt with a mandatory retirement provision that was enacted as an amendment to the Pennsylvania Constitution. The Court embraced a "highly deferential" approach to judicial review, principally because it was dealing with a state constitutional amendment approved by the electorate of the state "in the exercise of their inalienable and indefeasible right to amend their constitution as they see fit." Accordingly,

the Court declined to reconsider the factual assumption underlying the amendment that, as a general matter, the intellectual ability of judges diminishes at age 70. In acquiescing to that assumption, the Court dismissed the plaintiff's assertion that most judges are able to function as skilled jurists past the age of 70 and that changes in longevity render the retirement mandate unreasonable by current standards. The Court took the position that a constitutional amendment that was valid at its inception does not become invalid due to changes that have occurred with the passage of time. In the Court's view, the proper channel for persons who believe that the underlying policies of a constitutional amendment are no longer viable due to new evidence or changed circumstances is an appeal to the General Assembly and the citizenry.

Do you agree that a constitutional amendment that is valid when first enacted does not become invalid due to changes that have occurred with the passage of time? Is the same true about a statutory provision? Suppose that the Pennsylvania retirement mandate for judges was a statutory provision rather than a constitutional one; should the Court be more willing to re-examine the assumption that the intellectual ability of judges diminishes at age 70? Should the Court be more willing to consider the possibility that, given changes in longevity, mandatory retirement at age 70 is no longer reasonable?

The Court says that the proper channel for persons who believe that the underlying policies of a constitutional amendment are no longer viable is an appeal to the General Assembly and the citizenry. Article XI of the Pennsylvania Constitution states that the Constitution may be amended by a majority vote of both chambers of the General Assembly in two consecutive sessions, followed by approval of the electorate. Although the Constitution makes no mention of constitutional conventions as a means of amendment, the state has held five such conventions, most recently in 1968.

2. In his concurring opinion, Justice Eakin suggested an alternative justification for age limitations on judicial service, namely, to counterbalance the degree of judicial independence that judges possess by virtue of various constitutional safeguards that insulate them from the political process. While Justice Eakin believes that judicial independence is vital to our governmental system, he maintains that mandatory retirement is a proper means of setting a temporal limit on the exercise of judicial authority in order to curb the possible abuse of judicial independence. Given that judges in Pennsylvania are elected to ten-year terms, after which they may be voted out of office in a "yes or no" retention election, is mandatory retirement necessary as an additional time-based limit of judicial authority?

3. In *Maddux v. Blagojevich* (Ill. 2009), the Supreme Court of Illinois struck down a state statute mandating the retirement of judges at age 75. Although the state constitution contained a provision authorizing the

General Assembly to provide by law for the retirement of judges at a prescribed age, the court nonetheless found that the statute in question violated the constitutional requirement of equal protection of the laws. In striking down the statute, the court noted that it mandated retirement of judges at 75 while other persons 75 and older could run for and hold judicial office:

> There is no rational basis upon which the legislature can prevent 75-year-old or older *former judges* from running in an election, but not citizens 75 years old or older *who were never judges* when the disqualifying characteristic is age. If the legitimate state interest is to insure a "vigorous judiciary," the classification we describe above cannot be deemed rationally related to that purpose. We stress again that if age defines ability (and both the constitutional and legislative history indicate that it was believed that it does), either *all* those 75 years of age or older are unfit or they are not. No presumption of constitutionality could save legislation like this that so blatantly violates equal protection.
>
> The judicial article allows for the General Assembly to enact mandatory judicial retirement legislation; however, the plain language of the specific legislation that has been enacted pursuant to the constitution violates equal protection. Moreover, as it is written, it allows certain judges to avoid mandatory retirement. This court is mindful that restraint is called for when presented with challenges to the constitutionality of legislation enacted pursuant to a specific grant of constitutional authority. But we cannot be reluctant to invalidate legislation that either goes beyond the specific grant of authority or is otherwise inconsistent with our constitution.

4. In *Badgley v. Walton* (Vt. 2010) the Supreme Court of Vermont ruled that a law requiring all public safety officers to retire at the age of 55 did not violate the common benefits clause of the Vermont Constitution. Adopting a deferential approach, the court concluded that the mandatory retirement law bore a reasonable and just relationship to the legitimate state interest of having a police force that is mentally and physically capable of performing its tasks. While admitting that the law was to some degree an overinclusive means of accomplishing its purpose, the court nonetheless ruled that the law was not so overinclusive as to violate the common benefits clause. The court acknowledged that there were many strong policy arguments for abandoning the mandatory retirement law or raising the retirement age, but the court thought those arguments were more appropriately addressed to the legislature than to the judiciary.

ARNESON v. STATE
864 P.2d 1245 (Mont. 1993)

McDONOUGH, J.

This is an appeal from the decision of the District Court of the First Judicial District, Lewis and Clark County, concluding that § 19-20-711, MCA) is unconstitutional to the extent that it employed an unreasonable classification in violation of the equal protection clause of the Montana Constitution, Article II, Section 4. We affirm.

In 1989, the legislature passed Chapter 115 Session Laws of 1989 which, for its purpose, provided for a post-retirement adjustment increase in the pensions of the beneficiaries of the Teachers' Retirement System. The law provided that to be eligible for the adjustment, retirees or their beneficiaries must be 55 years of age or older; or, irrespective of age, receive disability or survivorship benefits.

The respondent's benefit was derived from her mother, who was a member of the Teachers' Retirement System, and who had reached retirement age and retired. The mother selected the retirement option that would permit benefits to be paid to her for her lifetime and upon her death continue through the life of her beneficiary (respondent). The mother died shortly after her retirement and the respondent began receiving the benefits. The respondent is 31 years of age. Being under 55 years of age, she did not receive the adjustment. However, if her mother had continued to work and died while working, the respondent would be considered a survivor and would receive the adjustment even though she was 31 years of age.

This statute, under the equal protection question, does not come under the strict scrutiny test because strict scrutiny of a legislative classification is required only when the classification impermissibly interferes with the exercise of a fundamental right or operates to a peculiar disadvantage of a suspect class. Here the respondent is not a member of a suspect class nor is a fundamental right involved.

The respondent urges us to adopt the middle-level scrutiny test. The middle-level scrutiny test has been recently applied by the U.S. Supreme Court in discussing cases involving such things as gender, alienage and illegitimacy, but the court has specifically refused to invoke it involving age and has applied the rational test thereto. We have previously declined to apply the middle tier scrutiny test to an "age plus" classification, absent a constitutionally based benefit. We also decline to apply it here. The District Court applied the lowest level of scrutiny, the rational basis test, which determines whether the classification is rationally related to furthering a legitimate state purpose. We will also apply the rational basis test.

The purpose of this law is to grant to the Retirement System beneficiaries, retirees' survivors, and the disabled, an amount to alleviate the eroding effect of inflation on their pension. Both the survivor of an employee and the beneficiary of an employee who has retired, are subject to the effect of inflation. But the classification as to who is to receive the post-retirement adjustment does not include the respondent who is the beneficiary of a former employee who had retired. As a result, this legislation is "under inclusive." This differentiation does not create a reasonable classification between such ultimate adult survivor and adult beneficiary. They are both similarly situated with respect to the purpose of this law.

The respondent states that there is no possible purpose which can be conceived to justify such a classification considering the overall purpose of the legislation of post-retirement adjustment to compensate for inflation. The respondent contends no distinction should be made between a beneficiary of a retired employee and the beneficiary of an employee who died while working when the beneficiaries are both under the age of 55. We agree.

We are unable to find any rational relationship to the purpose of the legislation for the establishment of such a classification. It is wholly arbitrary and an example of the legislature picking and choosing who will receive benefits. Such a classification must distinguish one class from another taking into consideration the purpose of the statute.

The granting of a post-retirement adjustment does not come within the approach of considering whether the enactment is experimental or piecemeal, and therefore applying the legislation to one phase of the problem and not affecting others. As we stated above, the legislature cannot arbitrarily pick and choose. The appellant has made such an argument on a money saving basis, but even if the governmental purpose is to save money, it cannot be done on a wholly arbitrary basis. The classification must have some rational relationship to the purpose of the legislation. There is nothing in the record or by conjecture which would justify the differentiation here.

There is no reasonable basis to the classification which permits an adult beneficiary of a disabled or deceased member to receive the adjustment regardless of age, and deny the adult beneficiary of a deceased service retiree who retired under voluntary or involuntary circumstances the adjustment because the beneficiary is under 55 years of age. The constitutional defect of the statute as applied to respondent is revealed when it is reviewed in light of its practical application. We conclude that its application to this respondent whereby the classification excludes her from receiving the post-retirement adjustment, is unconstitutional and in violation of Article II, Section 4 of the Montana Constitution.

TRIEWEILER, J., concurring.

I rejoice at the majority's re-discovery of the rights provided for in the Equal Protection Clause of Article II, Section 4, of Montana's Constitution. However, I find it peculiar that nowhere in the majority's opinion is any mention made of the majority's decision in *Stratemeyer v. MACO Workers' Compensation Trust* (Mont. 1993). Perhaps that is because the result in this case cannot be reconciled with the majority's decision in *Stratemeyer*. That is because under *Stratemeyer* there is no legislative classification which won't satisfy the toothless rational basis test.

This same majority held in *Stratemeyer* that even where no rational basis for a legislative classification is established by the Legislature or proven in district court, this Court can speculate about why the Legislature acted as it did, and that speculation can serve as the basis for overcoming a constitutional challenge. This Court went on to add that even when the State offers no evidence to justify a legislative classification, a person challenging the legislation has the burden of proving that there is no rational basis. In other words, under the *Stratemeyer* decision, a citizen victimized by legislative discrimination has to, first of all, imagine every conceivable basis for that discrimination about which this Court might speculate and then somehow disprove it. This Court then went on in *Stratemeyer* to conclude that a justification for the classification at issue in that case could have been the Legislature's intention to save money, even though there was no evidence in the record that the classification would save money. This Court held that:

> The exclusion of mental claims rationally relates to the *possible goal* of reducing costs and having a viable program for the State and the enrolled employers and employees in the workers' compensation field.

Certainly, by that standard the classification in this case passes any rational basis test. Who can dispute that discriminating against beneficiaries under a certain age "relates to the possible goal of reducing costs" for the teachers' retirement system?

I, of course, have no regard for the *Stratemeyer* decision. I would not follow it and will urge its early demise at every opportunity. The majority, however, has neither followed it, distinguished it, nor overruled it. Therefore, its decision in this case is both legally and intellectually inconsistent.

I believe that the right to be free from discrimination based on age is a significant enough right that classifications based on age warrant middle-tier scrutiny. A need exists to develop a meaningful middle-tier analysis. Equal protection of law is an essential underpinning of this free society. The old rational basis test allows government to discriminate among classes of people for the most whimsical reasons.

According to the laws of Montana, age is a "sensitive" if not "suspect" basis for classification. To hold otherwise would be to ignore the import of the Montana Human Rights Act which provides that "the right to be free from discrimination because of age is recognized as and declared to be a civil right." I would hold that statutory classifications based upon age involve a sensitive basis for classification and warrant a middle-tier test for determining whether they violate the Equal Protection Clause.

E. SEXUAL-ORIENTATION CLASSIFICATIONS

GARTNER v. IOWA DEPARTMENT OF PUBLIC HEALTH
830 N.W.2d 335 (Iowa 2013)

WIGGINS, J.

The first clause in article I, section 1 states: "All men and women are, by nature, free and equal." We have also used article I, section 6 to determine if a statute violates equal protection guarantees under the state constitution. Article I, section 6 provides: "All laws of a general nature shall have a uniform operation; the general assembly shall not grant to any citizen, or class of citizens, privileges or immunities, which, upon the same terms shall not equally belong to all citizens."

The Gartners argue the refusal of the Department to list both of the spouses in a lesbian marriage on the birth certificate of a child born during marriage classifies a person based on sex and sexual orientation under the Iowa Constitution. The Department contends the refusal only classifies individuals based on sex. Nonetheless, the Department concedes that even if we classify the refusal on sex, an intermediate level of scrutiny applies.

In *Varnum v. Brien* (Iowa 2013), we rejected the argument that the Defense of Marriage Act classified individuals based on sex and analyzed the classification based on sexual orientation. The legislature's purposeful use of "husband" in section 144.13(2) does not allow married lesbian couples to have the nonbirthing spouse's name on the birth certificate when one of the spouses in that relationship gives birth to the child. Therefore, as in *Varnum*, the refusal to list the nonbirthing lesbian spouse on the child's birth certificate "differentiates implicitly on the basis of sexual orientation."

Under *Varnum*, a sexual-orientation-based classification is subject to a heightened level of scrutiny under the Iowa Constitution. Heightened scrutiny requires the State to show the statutory classification is substantially related to an important governmental objective. Accordingly, we must evaluate whether the governmental objectives proffered by the State are important and whether the statutory classification substantially relates to those objectives.

Our construction of the statute is the same as the Department's. The plain language of the statute requires the Department to put a husband's name on the birth certificate if a married opposite-sex couple has a child born during the marriage and if the couple used an anonymous sperm donor to conceive the child. Thus, the statute treats married lesbian couples who conceive through artificial insemination using an anonymous sperm donor differently than married opposite-sex couples who conceive a child in the same manner. We must analyze this differential treatment to determine if it is substantially related to an important governmental objective.

The Department enumerates three objectives supporting section 144.13(2)'s differing treatment of married, lesbian and opposite-sex couples. Specifically, the Department argues the government has an interest in the accuracy of birth certificates, the efficiency and effectiveness of government administration, and the determination of paternity.

First, we understand that ensuring the accuracy of birth records for identification of biological parents is a laudable goal. However, the present system does not always accurately identify the biological father. When a married opposite-sex couple conceives a child using an anonymous sperm donor, the child's birth certificate reflects the male spouse as the father, not the biological father who donated the sperm. In that situation, the Department is not aware the couple conceived the child by an anonymous sperm donor.

The Department next asserts the refusal to apply the presumption of parentage to nonbirthing spouses in lesbian marriages serves administrative efficiency and effectiveness. However, when couples use an anonymous sperm donor, there will be no rebuttal of paternity. Moreover, even when couples conceive without using an anonymous sperm donor, there is no showing in the record that the presumption of paternity in opposite-sex marriages is rebutted in a significant number of births.

The Department concedes its interest in administrative efficiency and effectiveness is present when the Department puts the father on the birth certificate of a child born during the marriage of an opposite-sex couple. This efficiency is lost if the law is not applied equally to married lesbian couples. It is more efficient for the Department to list, presumptively, the nonbirthing spouse as the parent on the birth certificate when the child is born, rather than to require the Department to issue a birth certificate with only one spouse's name on the certificate and then later, after an adoption is complete, reissue the certificate. These realities demonstrate that the disparate treatment of married lesbian couples is less effective and efficient, and that some other unarticulated reason, such as stereotype or prejudice, may explain the real objective of the State.

The third proffered reason for the Department's action is the government's interest in establishing paternity to ensure financial support of the child and the fundamental legal rights of the father. When a lesbian couple is married, it is just as important to establish who is financially responsible for the child and the legal rights of the nonbirthing spouse. As we said in *Varnum*:

> Same-sex couples are in committed and loving relationships, many raising families, just like heterosexual couples. Moreover, official recognition of their status provides an institutional basis for defining their fundamental relational rights and responsibilities, just as it does for heterosexual couples. Society benefits, for example, from providing same-sex couples a stable framework within which to raise their children and the power to make health care and end-

of-life decisions for loved ones, just as it does when that framework is provided for opposite-sex couples.

It is important for our laws to recognize that married lesbian couples who have children enjoy the same benefits and burdens as married opposite-sex couples who have children. By naming the nonbirthing spouse on the birth certificate of a married lesbian couple's child, the child is ensured support from that parent and the parent establishes fundamental legal rights at the moment of birth. Therefore, the only explanation for not listing the nonbirthing lesbian spouse on the birth certificate is stereotype or prejudice. The exclusion of the nonbirthing spouse on the birth certificate of a child born to a married lesbian couple is not substantially related to the objective of establishing parentage.

We find the presumption of parentage statute violates equal protection under the Iowa Constitution as applied to married lesbian couples. However, we are not required to strike down the statute because our obligation is to preserve as much of a statute as possible, within constitutional restraints. Accordingly, instead of striking section 144.13(2) from the Code, we will preserve it as to married opposite-sex couples and require the Department to apply the statute to married lesbian couples.

F. ECONOMIC CLASSIFICATIONS

AFSCME IOWA COUNCIL 61 v. STATE
928 N.W.2d 21 (Iowa 2019)

WATERMAN, J.

This appeal presents constitutional challenges to the 2017 amendments to the Public Employment Relations Act. The amendments ended payroll deductions for union dues and narrowed the scope of mandatory collective bargaining topics for bargaining units comprised of less than thirty percent "public safety employees," defined to include most police officers and firefighters. The new classifications result in many public employees losing significant statutory bargaining rights compared to other public employees with arguably similar jobs. A public employee union and several of its members filed this action against the State of Iowa and the Public Employment Relations Board (PERB) seeking injunctive and declaratory relief. The plaintiffs allege the amendments violate the equal protection clause of the Iowa Constitution.

We begin by reviewing the statute in place before the 2017 amendments to put the constitutional challenges in context. In 1974, after public employees engaged in multiple strikes, the Iowa legislature enacted the Public Employment Relations Act (PERA). PERA sought to create an orderly system of collective bargaining for public employees by establishing rules and procedures and by prohibiting strikes. PERA permitted, but did not require, public employees to join a public employee organization (union). Employees could vote to select a union to represent them. An employee who joined a union had the option to pay dues through automatic payroll deductions. Once employees selected a union, PERA required the union and public employer to bargain in good faith on these topics: wages, hours, vacations, insurance, holidays, leaves of absence, shift differentials, overtime compensation, supplemental pay, seniority, transfer procedures, job classifications, health and safety matters, evaluation procedures, procedures for staff reduction, in-service training and other matters mutually agreed upon. If a public employer and union were unable to reach an agreement on these mandatory topics, PERA established a procedure for resolving the impasse through mediation and binding arbitration.

On February 17, the Governor signed House File 291 into law. The amendments altered the scope of mandatory collective bargaining and arbitration and eliminated payroll deductions for all union dues. House File 291 gave public employees different bargaining rights depending on whether they are part of a bargaining unit with at least thirty percent "public safety employees." Public safety employees are defined to include

 a. A sheriff's regular deputy.
 b. A marshal or police officer of a city, township, or special-purpose district or authority who is a member of a paid police department.
 c. A member, except a non-peace officer member, of the division of state patrol, narcotics enforcement, state fire marshal, or criminal investigation, including but not limited to a gaming enforcement officer, who has been duly appointed by the department of public safety in accordance with section 80.15.
 d. A conservation officer or park ranger as authorized by section 456A.13.
 e. A permanent or full-time fire fighter of a city, township, or special-purpose district or authority who is a member of a paid fire department.
 f. A peace officer designated by the department of transportation under section 321.477 who is subject to mandated law enforcement training.

Not included in the statutory definition of public safety employees are university police, probation or parole officers, fraud bureau investigation officers, airport firefighters, corrections officers, and emergency medical service providers.

If a union represents a bargaining unit with at least thirty percent public safety employees, it may exercise broad bargaining rights on behalf of all of its members, including those who are not public safety employees. The union continues to have the right to bargain and, in the event of an impasse, the right to mediate and arbitrate with public employers on the following mandatory topics: wages, hours, vacations, insurance, holidays, leaves of absence, shift differentials, overtime compensation, supplemental pay, seniority, transfer procedures, job classifications, health and safety matters, evaluation procedures, procedures for staff reduction, in-service training, grievance procedures for resolving any questions arising under the agreement, and other matters mutually agreed upon.

In sharp contrast, for unions representing a bargaining unit with less than thirty percent public safety employees, House File 291 limited mandatory bargaining and, in the event of an impasse, mediation and arbitration, to the subject of "base wages and other matters mutually agreed upon." The amendment specifies that these subjects "shall be interpreted narrowly and restrictively." The amendments allow public employers to voluntarily bargain over formerly mandatory topics. Longevity pay, shift differentials, and overtime compensation are still *permissive* subjects of bargaining. This leaves it up to the state or local government or school board whether to negotiate on these matters. Public employees, like all citizens in our state, have the ability to affect those decisions. A unit of state government, a municipality, or a school board that wishes to negotiate on these matters with the employee organization is free to do so. But the union may not bargain over "insurance, leaves of absence for political activities, supplemental pay, transfer procedures, evaluation procedures, procedures for staff reduction, and subcontracting public services."

Article I, section 6 of the Iowa Constitution provides, "All laws of a general nature shall have a uniform operation; the general assembly shall not grant to any citizen, or class of citizens, privileges or immunities, which, upon the same terms shall not equally belong to all citizens." Iowa's equal protection clause "is essentially a direction that all persons similarly situated should be treated alike."

Even in the zealous protection of the constitution's mandate of equal protection, courts must give respect to the legislative process and presume its enactments are constitutional. We understand that Iowa's tripartite system of government requires the legislature to make difficult policy choices, including distributing benefits and burdens amongst the citizens of Iowa. In this process, some classifications and barriers are inevitable. As a result, courts pay deference to legislative decisions when called upon to determine whether the Iowa Constitution's mandate of equality has been violated by legislative action.

Here, House File 291 distinguishes first between public safety employees and all other public employees, and second between bargaining units comprised of at least thirty percent public safety employees and all other bargaining units. The parties agree that rational basis review applies to the plaintiffs' equal protection challenge. The rational basis test is a "very deferential standard. Plaintiffs bear "the heavy burden of showing the statute unconstitutional and must negate every reasonable basis upon which the classification may be sustained." The rational basis test defers to the legislature's prerogative to make policy decisions by requiring only a plausible policy justification, mere rationality of the facts underlying the decision and, again, a merely rational relationship between the classification and the policy justification.

In *Racing Ass'n. of Cent. Iowa v. Fitzgerald* (Iowa 2004) (*RACI*), we made clear that actual proof of an asserted justification was not necessary, but the court would not simply accept it at face value and would examine it to determine whether it was credible as opposed to specious. Since *RACI* was decided, we have continued to uphold legislative classifications based on judgments the legislature could have made, without requiring evidence or "proof" in either a traditional or nontraditional sense. The district court found that the valid, realistically conceivable purpose for House File 291 was a concern for labor peace, especially among public safety employees. The State also asserts that another purpose was the unique health and safety concerns public safety employees face. We consider each justification.

1. *Labor peace rationale.* The plaintiffs argue that House File 291's legislative history belies the labor peace justification because no one mentioned this justification during the recorded legislative debates as a reason for amending PERA. The plaintiffs also argue that House File 291's definition of public safety employees includes employees who would not be crucial to maintaining labor peace, such as park rangers, DOT motor vehicle enforcement officers, fire marshals, and gaming enforcement officers, while excluding employees who may be necessary to maintain peace during a strike, including university police officers and other emergency medical service providers. The plaintiffs note that police officers already routinely enforce laws against union members, neighbors, friends, and even other police officers. Finally, the plaintiffs argue that the labor peace rationale is belied by the fact that there has not been a strike since PERA was enacted in 1974.

The plaintiffs also argue that even if a labor peace rationale could support House File 291, the law is so overinclusive and underinclusive "it cannot reasonably be said to further that goal." The plaintiffs contend that the thirty percent threshold ignores the bargaining unit's size, and some cities could have entire police forces that do not have expanded bargaining rights. These public safety employees would not have the same incentive to avoid strikes. The plaintiffs give examples of the effect House File 291 has on public safety employees. For example, plaintiffs identify a number of populous counties including Tama (population 17,337), Fayette (population 20,257), Delaware (population 17,403), Dubuque (population 97,125), Harrison (population 14,265), and Black Hawk (population 133,455) in which sheriff's deputies are unable to exercise the broad collective bargaining rights guaranteed to public safety employees in House File 291 because they are in bargaining units made up of less than thirty percent public safety employees. Yet deputies from comparably populated counties such as Floyd (population 15,960), Woodbury (population 102,782), Cedar (population 18,340), Webster (population 37,071), and Washington (population 22,247) are able to exercise broad collective bargaining rights under House File 291. Plaintiffs argue this extreme arbitrariness is not justified by any of the purported rationales of House File 291.

We hold that maintaining labor peace is a valid, realistically conceivable purpose and has a basis in fact. The legislature could reasonably have found that giving public safety employees expanded bargaining rights would discourage them from engaging in strikes or sick-outs. It is true that there have been no strikes of public employees in Iowa since PERA was enacted in 1974. But it is also true that until 2017 there had never been legislation substantially curtailing the collective bargaining rights of Iowa public employees. Iowa legislators in 2017 could consider what happened several years earlier in Wisconsin to see that labor unrests and strikes may result when legislative amendments curtail public union bargaining rights. Wisconsin public employees staged mass protests in 2011, occupying the rotunda of the state capitol with great media fanfare.

Even assuming a strike is improbable, reasonable legislators could also be rationally concerned that public employees who experience a reduction in collective bargaining rights will be more likely to experience low morale and labor unrest. Labor unrest short of a strike could reasonably be considered by legislators to contribute to instability in the public sector workforce. Other jurisdictions have experienced incidents of civil disobedience through sickouts by public employees and "Blue Flu" by law enforcement in response to less desirable terms and conditions of employment. The State cites numerous news articles about police officers in New York City, Memphis, Tennessee, Selma, Alabama and East Orange, New Jersey calling in sick in large numbers in order to protest issues such as unsafe conditions, low pay, and lack of benefits.

We agree with the district court that legislative facts readily available to Iowa lawmakers support concerns that labor unrest among police could undermine public safety, if not through strikes, then through reduced initiative or "blue flu." Historically, police officers in other states have used strategies such as the blue flu to protest labor conditions and policy changes. The district court aptly observed that in Iowa "the potential for 'Blue Flu' or some other exhibition of labor unrest short of a strike is realistically conceivable."

Against that backdrop, Iowa legislators in 2017 could rationally decide to extend more beneficial negotiating rights to bargaining units comprised of at least thirty percent public safety employees. The public safety rationale need not be voiced during the floor debates over House File 291 or proven with evidence. Iowa legislators individually and collectively can have multiple or mixed motives. Courts applying rational basis review do not take testimony from senators or representatives. Our rational basis review is purposefully limited and does not include evidentiary fact-finding on the motives of individual legislators or validity of the labor peace rationale. A State, moreover, has no obligation to produce evidence to sustain the rationality of a statutory classification. "The problems of government are practical ones and may justify, if they do not require, rough accommodations—illogical, it may be, and unscientific."

2. Health and safety rationale. The main rationale advanced during the legislative debates on House File 291 centered on the health and safety risks that public safety employees face on the job. Because of these risks, legislators determined that public safety employees should retain broader bargaining rights. This rationale provides another ground for upholding the classifications in House File 291.

We note that on November 2, 2016, just over three months before the enactment of House File 291, two police officers were fatally shot in their squad cars in Des Moines and Urbandale, respectively. And the preceding summers, five police officers were gunned down in Dallas, Texas, and another three officers were shot dead two weeks later in Baton Rouge, Louisiana. These legislative facts provided vivid reminders to the Iowa General Assembly of the dangers police face on the job. While this appeal was under submission, a firefighter died in the line of duty in Clinton, Iowa, with another firefighter seriously injured. It is inarguable that the legislature could rationally conclude public safety employees face significantly greater risks to their health and safety than other public employees.

3. The thirty percent threshold. In our view, the foregoing authorities make clear the Iowa Constitution permits the State to treat public safety employees differently from other public employees and to treat bargaining units comprised of at least thirty percent public safety employees better than bargaining units with a smaller percentage. The plaintiffs nevertheless argue that the thirty percent threshold itself is unconstitutional, even if the labor peace and public safety rationales would permit preferential treatment of a bargaining unit comprised solely of public safety employees. The State responds that the legislative classifications reflect the current reality that local government bargaining units in Iowa happen to be comprised of a mix of public safety employees and other employees. The State notes it would be impractical to segregate for collective bargaining purposes public safety employees and other employees with different employers and unions. The plaintiffs fail to persuasively rebut that State's showing of the practical problems with interunit collective bargaining. Nor do the plaintiffs suggest a different, higher threshold that concededly passes constitutional muster. Ten percent? Forty percent? Ninety percent? Perhaps in plaintiffs' view preferential treatment can be allowed only for public safety employees isolated in their own bargaining unit with no one else, as in Wisconsin.

It is not the court's role under our separation of powers to redraw the legislature's chosen thirty percent threshold. The Seventh Circuit recognized that "defining the class of persons subject to a regulatory requirement requires that some persons who have an almost equally strong claim to favored treatment be placed on different sides of the line and this is a matter for legislative, rather than judicial, consideration." We reiterate that "for legislation to be violative of the Iowa Constitution under the rational basis test, the classification must involve *extreme* degrees of overinclusion and underinclusion in relation to any particular goal." We hold that the thirty percent threshold is not so extremely overinclusive or underinclusive as to flunk our deferential rational basis review.

CADY, C.J., dissenting.

The majority opinion finds a rational basis to justify the disparate treatment in this case from the special need to protect the public against the potential harm of labor unrest by public safety employees and to give special protection to public safety employees from the health and safety risks they face on the job. The premise is that public safety is a vital concern in Iowa and this concern supports special laws that give greater bargaining rights to public safety employees than other public employees to help keep them on the job, instead of engaging in strikes or becoming injured and unable to perform their jobs.

The problem with the law is not its purpose or justification to discriminate, but how the general assembly failed to apply this purpose in articulating the law. Instead of treating public employees differently by dividing them into one group of public safety employees and another group of other public employees, the general assembly passed a law giving different rights to public employees based on their membership in a collective bargaining agreement. The problem is that bargaining units in Iowa contain both public safety employees and other public employees. Thus, while the law purported to put public safety employees in a separate class based on a valid purpose, it created classifications by using bargaining units and permitted the bargaining units to contain up to seventy percent of persons who are not public safety employees. This means the statute enacted ended up giving many public employees rights of public safety employees and denied many public safety employees those rights.

This type of line drawing falls far too short of our constitution's demands. While line drawing can never be clean and can present a variety of obstacles, this case is not even close to a fair delineation. Moreover, there is simply no reason why the general assembly could not have drawn the lines to eliminate the unconstitutional distinctions. The law cannot purport to give needed special protection to one group of people and then allow that group to be populated by up to seventy percent of other people not included within the purpose. This approach is a bad fit and destroys the justification for the law.

If the line drawing needed to accomplish the stated purpose in this case were difficult to do, as it can be in some cases, leeway would exist. But, in truth, there is no reason it cannot be done in this case.

APPEL, J., dissenting.

I begin with a discussion of the remarkable classification system created by the law. It identifies an oddball group of public employees and throws them into the burlap grab bag labeled "public safety employees." Then, some of those within the grab bag are denied privileges that others receive. And some public employees not within the grab bag receive the benefits denied to a portion of public safety employees, while others do not. Perplexing, I know. The classification system is illogical. The identification of public safety employees is made not on the basis of an employee's duties or functions, but rather by the title an employee holds. In some respects, the "public safety" grab bag is astonishingly inclusive. The grab bag was stretched astoundingly wide. It accommodates park rangers, gaming enforcement officers, and peace officers designated by the department of transportation.

But then, it excludes employees with obvious public safety responsibilities. The grab bag has no room for university police who, just like other police officers, are law enforcement officers, are trained and certified by the Iowa Law Enforcement Academy, and engage in law enforcement and emergency response alongside other city police officers. Airport firefighters are excluded even though they too work alongside the firefighters designated as public safety employees by House File 291. The law also excludes others, like parole officers and fraud bureau investigators, who work in unpredictable environments with broad arrest powers and the obligation to respond to emergencies. And none of our state's corrections officers, jailers, and emergency medical service providers are considered public safety employees. Yet all of those public employees work in "protection occupations."

As is evident, the statutory classification of public safety employees is obviously remarkably overinclusive and underinclusive. I think it very doubtful that the classification of public safety employees makes much sense, but we are not done with the irrationalities of the statute. This is because classification as a public safety employee does not even determine whether a public employee gets the benefits of collective bargaining granted to some and denied others. Under House File 291, full collective bargaining rights are provided to all state employees in bargaining units with at least thirty percent public safety employees. In such a unit, the thirty percent public safety employees get the benefit of representatives who have the ability to collectively bargain fully over wages and a list of other terms and conditions of employment. But so do the remaining seventy percent of non-"public safety employees" in the bargaining unit. Thus, in a unit with thirty percent public safety employees, a supermajority of the beneficiaries are not public safety employees! If the law is designed to target public safety employees for preferential treatment, it is way, way overbroad.

And yet, once again, it is also underinclusive. What about a bargaining unit with twenty-nine percent public safety employees? Those public safety employees, along with their colleagues in the bargaining unit, are out in the cold. For instance, we are told that the police officers serving the City of Guttenberg, along with the police and fire departments of the City of Decorah, are all relegated to disfavored status under House File 291. So too are the deputy sheriffs of Humboldt County, even though the county sheriffs and Humboldt police officers serve side-by-side and share equipment. Thus, the set of public safety employees benefiting from the statute is doubly underinclusive. The definition of "public safety employees" is underinclusive, and then only some public safety employees are doled out benefits based solely on whether the employee happens to fall within a given type of bargaining unit.

What kind of statute is this? Notably, the parties have failed to identify a similar statute anywhere at any time. House File 291 is unlike the recent legislation passed in Wisconsin because, under the Wisconsin law, all those designated as public safety employees receive broader collective bargaining rights and all those who are not so designated do not receive those rights. Make no mistake, House File 291 is really odd.

The State has suggested two purposes for House File 291—labor peace and the health and safety of public safety employees. Neither provides a basis for sustaining this statute. I begin with the purported purpose of labor peace. First, the historical record is striking. No one claims that there has ever been a strike of any public employees, let alone public safety employees, since the enactment of the Public Employment Relations Act over forty years ago. Further, no one claims that such a strike has been seriously threatened.

Second, as plaintiffs point out, labor peace was not a rationale for the law asserted by any Iowa legislators during the floor debate. That is striking. If there was truly a risk to public safety that a strike by public safety employees would create, surely the legislators would have said so. The fact that avoiding strikes was not even mentioned in the debates further suggests a lack of basis in fact.

Third, for forty years, draconian sanctions have been in place in the event any public employee contemplated striking. The sanctions can include imprisonment for six months; daily individual fines of $500; daily union fines of $10,000; termination from employment and ineligibility for public employment for one year; decertification of union and one-year waiting period for recertification; injunctions; contempt; and "any other legal or equitable remedy or penalty." The existence and effectiveness of the sanctions undermine the State's argument that labor peace is a purpose of the discriminatory treatment in House File 291.

In Iowa, we "examine the credibility of the asserted factual basis for the challenged classification rather than simply accepting it at face value." Based on the history, the lack of justification in legislative debates, and the existence of strong sanctions already addressing the problem, I conclude that the labor peace rational fails that test.

As an alternative, the State generally claims that the health and safety of certain endangered public employees could be a legitimate end for the law. No one questions the general proposition that promoting the health and safety of employees is a legitimate state interest. But to the extent House File 291 provides nebulous health and safety benefits apparently arising from robust collective bargaining rights, what is the rationale for denying those benefits to other public safety employees under the statute? It seems odd to suggest that *some* public safety employees are entitled to the health and safety benefits afforded by robust collective bargaining and benefits and others are not. Why, say, are park rangers entitled to the health and safety benefits of robust collective bargaining while corrections officers are not?

I now turn to the question of whether there is a rational relationship between the purported goals of the statute and the means chosen by the legislature. If labor peace were the goal, why aren't corrections staff, or parole officers, or university police officers, or healthcare workers, provided the benefits of the statute? Other states deal with the potential of strikes in inclusive ways. If House File 291 is designed to prevent strikes that would jeopardize public safety, it is remarkably underinclusive.

Conversely, is there anything in the record suggesting that public safety employees included in the House File 291 grab bag have threatened to strike? And if they have, have they threatened to strike more frequently or more intensively than the corrections officials and university police? Is there anything in the record suggesting that a strike by gaming enforcement officers would be a threat to public safety? And could it be of the same magnitude as a strike by the many police and fire departments left out in the cold by the thirty percent threshold? Moreover, is the danger of a strike by non-"public safety employees" in a favored bargaining unit somehow of such concern that they, too, need special bargaining rights? These questions, of course, must be answered in the negative, and reveal the arbitrariness and extreme overinclusion of the classifications.

Most importantly, perhaps, is the absence of a rational connection between doling benefits and preventing strikes. Does the record, or any legislative facts, show that only some public safety employees—*i.e.*, those in unions in which they comprise more than thirty percent of members—need special benefits *to convince them not to break the law* and strike? Or that, unless they are doled out special benefits, police officers in those units will refuse to do their duty in the face of others breaking the law and striking? Are public safety employees in units in which they comprise less than thirty percent of members somehow better able to resist lawbreaking? Or are those public safety employees less important to public safety?

The classifications in House File 291 are arbitrary if the goal was labor peace. There is no relationship between the classifications, which feature extreme degrees of overinclusion and underinclusion, and labor peace. And the linchpin of the argument advanced in favor of the law—public safety employees might strike in the face of criminal penalty if they are not granted special status—is specious. In the face of such irrationality, I would not uphold the oddball classifications in House File 291.

I now turn to the question of whether the classifications in House File 291 may be supported as health and safety measures. In my view, the slicing and dicing in House File 291 bears no rational connection to protecting health and safety of public employees exposed to greater risks. In short, the law confers privileges on some public employees and withholds them from others without regard to whether the persons actually face greater danger. It also does not consider whether the privileges are rationally related to protecting health and safety.

The legislature's choice of who may be allowed greater collective bargaining rights is grievously underinclusive towards achieving a goal of protecting health and safety of public employees exposed to danger. Why omit university police officers, corrections officers, jailers, emergency medical service providers, airport firefighters, and others from the category of public safety employees? The record shows that many employees in these jobs, especially corrections officers and university police officers, face similar or greater risks than those classified as public safety employees. Psychiatric aides and medical technicians, according to the record, are approximately four times as likely to be injured on the job as are police officers and approximately 150 times as likely to be injured on the job as firefighters. Meanwhile, the number of road safety workers killed in Iowa exceeds the number of police killed in the line of duty.

The statute, of course, is also overinclusive if the goal is to protect health and safety of those exposed to greater danger. Why allow supermajorities of non-"public safety employees" to access those benefits? There is no rational explanation. Further, the limitations on bargaining applicable to the two groups are numerous, and in almost every respect, divorced from health and safety. For instance, House File 291 gives units with thirty percent public safety employees greater rights than other units in arbitrating over wages. What rational connection is there between a cap on the wages that an arbitrator may award to some bargaining units and the health and safety of a portion of the members of other bargaining units? There is none.

NOTE

In the companion case to *AFSCME*, *Iowa State Education Ass'n v. State* (Iowa 2019), the Iowa Supreme Court upheld another provision of the 2017 Amendments ending payroll deductions for union dues while still allowing payroll deductions for dues or contributions to other organizations that also had been challenged as violating the state equal protection clause. The majority opinion, again written by Justice Waterman, reiterated the understanding of rationality review articulated in his previous opinion and adhered to the extremely deferential version of rationality review articulated there. Thus, Justice Waterman concluded that the provision ending payroll deductions for union dues survived rationality review:

> The plaintiffs concede, as they must, that the State is not constitutionally required to provide payroll deductions at all. Rather, the plaintiffs contend that once the State allows voluntary payroll deductions for charitable contributions or dues for other professional organizations, the equal protection clause requires the State to also allow payroll deductions for union dues. Yet the plaintiffs and their amicus cite no decisions holding it is unconstitutional to disallow voluntary payroll deductions for union dues while allowing deductions for other organizations. To the contrary, the United States Supreme Court and other appellate courts have rejected equal protection challenges to enactments or policies eliminating payroll deductions for union dues while allowing payroll deductions for nonunion organizations.
>
> As the district court correctly concluded, "The fiscal interests of the government are routinely accepted as a rational basis for legislative activity that is viewed as a cost-saving measure for the public." The legislature could rationally choose to stop helping unions collect dues through payroll deductions. The Iowa Constitution does not require public employers to collect dues for the very unions that sit across the bargaining table negotiating at arms' length for higher wages and costlier employee benefits at taxpayer expense. The State argued that "collective bargaining is expensive, disruptive, and not in the best interest of citizens." We agree with the district court "that the concerns of the legislature regarding the cost of collective bargaining provide a rational basis for making the classification concerning the payroll deduction." The district court noted the plaintiffs did not challenge the factual basis for the legislature's cost-saving premise, which the court accepted as a matter of "common knowledge."
>
> We hold the payroll deduction prohibition survives Iowa's rational basis review. Public employees do not have a constitutional right to payroll deductions for union dues. There is no constitutional equal protection violation merely because voluntary automatic payroll deductions continue for charities or organizations that do not target the public fisc. Employees remain free to retain their union membership and to pay their union dues directly. House File 291 reflects lawful policy choices by the legislature.

CHAPTER V

REPRESENTATION AND VOTING

A. INTRODUCTION

Throughout American history, the people have tried to make legislatures more representative. Most familiar, and much needed, were extensions of the suffrage, eventually guaranteeing to all men and women eighteen and over the right to vote. Many of these efforts eventually ended in federal laws: federal constitutional amendments and the 1965 Voting Rights Act. The states had a key role in launching many of these changes. The admission of Vermont and Kentucky to the Union paved the way for eliminating property requirements for voting, with Georgia and Delaware soon following their leads. New York and New England set the example of extending the franchise to African Americans and other racial minorities. The early nineteenth century saw Jacksonian sentiments take root in many states, spreading some of these electoral reforms and others too. With one passing caveat, states in the West and Midwest that entered the Union in the last half of the nineteenth century led the effort to extend the right to vote to women, an effort that culminated in the Nineteenth Amendment in 1920. Akhil Reed Amar, *America's Constitution: A Biography* 421-22 (2005). New Jersey, the caveat, allowed women to vote from 1776 to roughly 1807. Judith Apter Klinghoffer & Lois Elkis, *"The Petticoat Electors": Women's Suffrage in New Jersey, 1776-1807*, 12(2) J. Early Republic 159, 159-160 (1992).

It is tempting to think of these developments as part of a single federal-centric story. That's understandable given how many of these provisions eventually made their way into U.S. constitutional amendments: the Fourteenth Amendment (apportionment and race), the Fifteenth (race), the Seventeenth (popular election of U.S. senators), the Nineteenth (gender), the Twenty-Fourth (no poll tax), and the Twenty-Sixth (18 and over). That is a federal story to be certain. But even then, these federal constitutional amendments still amount to a form of representation-enhancing federalism. No amendment becomes part of the U.S. Constitution without the approval of three-quarters of the states. Efforts to change the U.S. Constitution often start as local stories and sometimes end as federal ones. But the state-federal story about extending the right to vote, important as it is, is not the focus of this chapter.

The focus instead is on two modern challenges: (1) drawing electoral districts in a fair manner and (2) regulating elections in a fair way. After each decennial census, the Federal Constitution requires the states to draw new legislative districts for state and congressional elections. What often happens is partisan gerrymandering, the time-honored, if scorned, practice of drawing legislative districts to favor incumbents. Gerrymandering raises a knotty division-of-powers problem that has been with us from the beginning of the Republic. It implicates unique features of American federalism because state legislatures draw state *and* federal electoral districts and because attempts to curb it involve state and federal law and state and federal actors.

State regulation of the time and manner of elections raises problems of its own. To start, it grows out of federal constitutional responsibilities imposed on the states. Under Article I, Section 4 of the U.S. Constitution, the "Times, Places and Manner of holding Elections for Senators and Representatives, shall be prescribed in each State by the Legislature thereof." That leaves state legislatures with responsibility to set their own election regulations for state and federal elections, whether with respect to the places and manner offered to exercise the franchise or with respect to requirements for casting a ballot. It is the rare election cycle that does not see considerable state litigation over these issues.

In addition to the U.S. Constitution, most state constitutions have provisions, often many provisions, with respect to who can vote and how. Many state constitutions explicitly make the right to vote a constitutional right. *See, e.g.*, Kan. Const. Art. V § 1 ("Suffrage – Qualification of Electors. Every citizen of the United States who has attained the age of eighteen years and who resides in the voting area in which he or she seeks to vote shall be deemed a qualified elector."); N.M. Const. Art. VII § 1 ("Every person who is a qualified elector pursuant to the constitution and laws of the United States and a citizen thereof shall be qualified to vote in all elections in New Mexico."); N.Y. Const. Art. II § 1 ("Every citizen shall be entitled to vote at every election for all officers elected by the people and upon all questions submitted to the vote of the people provided that such citizen is eighteen years of age or over and shall have been a resident of this state, and of the county, city, or village for thirty days next preceding an election."); Pa. Const. Art. VII § 1 ("Every citizen 21 years of age, possessing the following qualifications, shall be entitled to vote at all elections."); Haw. Const. Art. II § 1 ("Every citizen of the United States who shall have attained the age of eighteen years, have been a resident of this State not less than one year next preceding the election and be a voter registered as provided by law, shall be qualified to vote in any state or local election.").

Many state constitutions, frequently based on amendments in recent years, contain provisions that limit gerrymandering during redistricting. For example, both the Ohio and Florida Constitutions prohibit redistricting on a partisan basis. Ohio Const. Art. XI § 6(A) ("No general assembly district plan shall be drawn primarily to favor or disfavor a political party."); Fla.

Const. Art. III § 20(a) ("No apportionment plan or individual district shall be drawn with the intent to favor or disfavor a political party or an incumbent."); *see also, e.g.*, Cal. Const. Art. XXI §2(e) ("The place of residence of any incumbent or political candidate shall not be considered in the creation of a map. Districts shall not be drawn for the purpose of favoring or discriminating against an incumbent, political candidate, or political party."); N.Y. Const. Art. III § 4(c)(5) ("Districts shall not be drawn for the purpose of favoring or disfavoring incumbents or other particular candidates or political parties."); Wash. Const. Art. II § 43(5) ("The commission's plan shall not be drawn purposely to favor or discriminate against any political party or group."). On top of that, state constitutions contain other unique voting and election-related provisions. *See, e.g.*, Kan. Const. Art V § 7 ("Electors, during their attendance at elections, and in going to and returning therefrom, shall be privileged from arrest in all cases except felony or breach of the peace."); Ark. Const. Art. III § 7 ("No soldier, sailor, or marine, in the military or naval service of the United States, shall acquire a residence by reason of being stationed on duty in this State."); Ala. Const. § 191 ("It shall be the duty of the legislature to pass adequate laws giving protection against the evils arising from the use of intoxicating liquors at all elections."); La. Const. Art. 11 § 4 ("No public funds shall be used to urge any elector to vote for or against any candidate or proposition, or be appropriated to a candidate or political organization. This provision shall not prohibit the use of public funds for dissemination of factual information relative to a proposition appearing on an election ballot.").

With this background and foundation in place, let's turn to the two topics central to this chapter: the creation of election districts and the regulation of elections.

B. CREATING ELECTION DISTRICTS

Once the American people chose a government that featured representative legislatures and once they opted not to select all representatives based on statewide elections, there was no escaping the need to draw district lines for some elections. But there is no inherently fixed and geographically fair way to draw district lines. Whether it is geographical landmarks, like mountains and rivers, or the eventual creation of local government units, like cities and counties, none of them could provide fixed markers for legislative maps that would suit all future circumstances. Shifts in population can transform a representative district into an unrepresentative one, making the dynamic demographics of our restless country a constant challenge. These realities come with a federalism component of the national constitution. It not only delegates to the states the power to set the terms and rules for elections to state legislatures, but it also does the same for the members of Congress, whether the House of Representatives or the Senate. The U.S. Constitution also allocates representatives to the states based on population, and the states elect those representatives based on election districts created within each state. Whether legislatures draw district lines in incumbent-leaning ways, party-leaning ways, or largely neutral ways, the decisions have rippling stakes for control of all houses of the state legislatures and the House of Representatives.

Under the U.S. Supreme Court's decisions in *Baker v. Carr* (1962) and *Reynolds v. Sims* (1964), the states are obligated to redraw state and federal district lines after each decennial census to ensure that they meet the one-person-one-vote requirements of the Fourteenth Amendment. The imperative of regular redistricting creates room for mischief, giving the legislators an excuse—in truth a mandate—to draw new lines on a regular basis with all of the individual-capacity self-interest and official-capacity self-interest that go with it. Keep in mind that ensuring that each legislative district within a state has the same number of voters does not prevent gerrymandering. And requiring the legislature to redraw districts every ten years creates decennial opportunities for partisan gerrymandering—and perhaps more covert gerrymandering because the legislators can say the U.S. Supreme Court made them do it.

The federal side of the story about efforts to tamp down extreme partisan gerrymandering took more than three decades and required several High Court decisions. In 1986, the U.S. Supreme Court first addressed the question of whether political gerrymandering—drawing district lines to favor one political party over the other—presented a cognizable constitutional claim in *Davis v. Bandemer*, 478 U.S. 109. Competing intuitions underscored the claim. In one direction, an equal protection challenge to a "political gerrymander" sounded odd given that gerrymandering had always had a political component to it. In the other direction, the one-person-one-vote mandate at some point could become a silent guarantee if a political party, while superficially honoring the rule, nonetheless made it very difficult to elect candidates from one party or the other. The Court gave half a loaf. It agreed that a political gerrymandering challenge under the Equal Protection Clause raised a justiciable question—one the federal courts could resolve—but declined to say more.

Vieth v. Jubelirer, decided in 2004, confirmed the vexing complexities of creating a judicially enforceable right in this area. At issue was whether Pennsylvania's congressional districts, drawn to favor Republican candidates, violated equal protection. The three-judge district court dismissed the claim, and the Supreme Court affirmed the decision without agreeing on the right approach. A four-vote plurality, written by Justice Scalia, took the position that the federal courts had no business, and no basis for, assessing political gerrymandering claims and that *Bandemer* should be overruled. Three separate dissents, joined by four justices, suggested three distinct standards for resolving political gerrymandering claims. Justice Kennedy concurred in the judgment. "A decision ordering the correction of all election district lines drawn for partisan reasons," he worried, "would commit federal and state courts to unprecedented intervention in the American political process." At the same time, he "would not foreclose all possibility of judicial relief if some limited and precise rationale were found to correct an established violation of the Constitution in some redistricting cases." For the next fifteen years, the Court's gerrymandering jurisprudence clung to this fine line, creating considerable suspense over whether a political gerrymander would ever be sufficiently extreme to justify federal judicial involvement.

In 2019, the Court gave an answer in *Rucho v. Common Cause*, which involved two partisan gerrymanders, not one. Republicans led the district-redrawing effort in North Carolina, and Democrats led the effort in Maryland. Writing for a unified five-justice majority, Chief Justice Roberts wrote that the political question doctrine deprived federal courts of jurisdiction to handle partisan gerrymandering claims. He acknowledged what everyone accepted, that these congressional districting maps were "highly partisan, by any measure." But the highly partisan underpinnings of a constitutional claim did not prove that it was "of a Judiciary Nature" in the words of James Madison. "Sometimes," he wrote, "the judicial department has no business entertaining the claim of unlawfulness—because the question is entrusted to one of the political branches or involves no judicially enforceable rights" that are discernible. "Aware of electoral districting problems," he observed, the Framers "settled on a characteristic approach, assigning the issue to the state legislatures, expressly checked and balanced by the Federal Congress." While that reality has not prohibited the Court from resolving refusal-to-reapportion claims or race-based claims, it has "proved far more difficult" to identify enforceable standards for political gerrymandering claims. "To hold that legislators cannot take partisan interests into account when drawing district lines would essentially countermand the Framers' decision to entrust districting to political entities." Once it's accepted that some politics will go into reapportionment, it becomes difficult to identify how much is "too much." And the most likely measure of "too much"—reversions to proportional representation—is not the measure the Constitution imposes. Such claims are based on the mistaken "conviction that the greater the departure from proportionality, the more suspect an apportionment plan becomes." In the absence of a request for proportional representation, "plaintiffs inevitably ask the courts to make their own political judgment about how much representation particular political parties *deserve*—based on the votes of their supporters—and to rearrange the challenged districts to achieve that end." That requires federal courts "to apportion political power as a matter of fairness," something they are not "equipped" to do, in part because "it is not even clear what fairness looks like in this context." Should the focus be on creating more competitive races, more safe seats, or greater use of traditional criteria, such as "maintaining political subdivisions, keeping communities of interest together, and protecting incumbents"? The trade-offs between these and other values turn on "political" value judgments, not "legal" determinations. It is only *after* determining an acceptable measure of fairness that a court can determine "How much is too much?" and "At what point does permissible partisanship become unconstitutional?" Nor did the Court's one-person-one-vote cases require a different conclusion. "It hardly follows from the principle that each person must have an equal say in the election of representatives that a person is entitled to have his political party achieve representation in some way commensurate to its share of statewide support." He then explained that the states had adopted many reforms to address extreme gerrymandering, and Congress eventually could do the same.

Justice Kagan's dissent lamented the "politics of polarization and dysfunction" left in place by the Court's decision. As she saw it, *Baker v. Carr* charted the path for resolving the political question concerns raised by the Court and, if followed, would have allowed the Court to correct a despairing problem in American democracy—that too often gerrymandering allows politicians and interest groups to "cherry pick" their voters. Even as more sophisticated computer technology allowed political parties to gerrymander with more precision than at any time in the past, she thought technology could help the federal courts sort out what gerrymanders went "too far" based on a state's own acknowledged reapportionment priorities. Accepting the difficulty of refining some constitutional principles in this area, she thought it easy enough to decide *these* cases given the egregiousness of the gerrymanders. And she found the majority's belief that state courts could help solve partisan gerrymandering while federal courts could not "perplexing." "If [state courts] can develop and apply neutral and manageable standards to identify unconstitutional gerrymanders," she asked, "why couldn't we?"

Unlike many landmark U.S. Supreme Court cases in modern times, just two opinions came out of the case. Both reveal two justices at the top of their game. As for their dueling positions about the role of the states in addressing the partisan dysfunction caused by partisan gerrymandering, there's no better way to gauge the situation than to look at the state court opinions in the area. What's complex in federal court is no less complex in state court. The first state court decision comes before *Rucho*. The others come after it.

LEAGUE OF WOMEN VOTERS OF PA. v. PENNSYLVANIA
178 A.3d 737 (Pa. 2018)

TODD, J.

It is a core principle of our republican form of government "that the voters should choose their representatives, not the other way around." In this case, Petitioners allege that the Pennsylvania Congressional Redistricting Act of 2011 does the latter, infringing upon that most central of democratic rights—the right to vote. Specifically, they contend that the 2011 Plan is an unconstitutional partisan gerrymander. While federal courts have, to date, been unable to settle on a workable standard by which to assess such claims under the federal Constitution, we find no such barriers under our great Pennsylvania charter. The people of this Commonwealth should never lose sight of the fact that, in its protection of essential rights, our founding document is the ancestor, not the offspring, of the federal Constitution. We conclude that, in this matter, it provides a constitutional standard, and remedy, even if the federal charter does not. Specifically, we hold that the 2011 Plan violates Article I, Section 5—the Free and Equal Elections Clause—of the Pennsylvania Constitution.

Pennsylvania's Constitution, when adopted in 1776, was widely viewed as "the most radically democratic of all the early state constitutions." Indeed, our Constitution, which was adopted over a full decade before the United States Constitution, served as the foundation—the template—for the federal charter. Our autonomous state Constitution, rather than a "reaction" to federal constitutional jurisprudence, stands as a self-contained and self-governing body of constitutional law, and acts as a wholly independent protector of the rights of the citizens of our Commonwealth.

Article I, Section 5 of the Pennsylvania Constitution, entitled "Elections," is contained within the Pennsylvania Constitution's "Declaration of Rights," which is an enumeration of the fundamental individual human rights possessed by the people of this Commonwealth that are specifically exempted from the powers of Commonwealth government to diminish. This section provides: Elections shall be free and equal; and no power, civil or military, shall at any time interfere to prevent the free exercise of the right of suffrage. This clause first appeared, albeit in different form, in our Commonwealth's first organic charter of governance adopted in 1776, 11 years before the United States Constitution was adopted. By contrast, the United States Constitution—which furnishes no explicit protections for an individual's electoral rights, nor sets any minimum standards for a state's conduct of the electoral process—does not contain, nor has it ever contained, an analogous provision.

The broad text of the first clause of this provision mandates clearly and unambiguously, and in the broadest possible terms, that *all* elections conducted in this Commonwealth must be "free and equal." In accordance with the plain and expansive sweep of the words "free and equal," we view them as indicative of the framers' intent that all aspects of the electoral process, to the greatest degree possible, be kept open and unrestricted to the voters of our Commonwealth, and, also, conducted in a manner which guarantees, to the greatest degree possible, a voter's right to equal participation in the electoral process for the selection of his or her representatives in government. Thus, Article I, Section 5 guarantees our citizens an equal right, on par with every other citizen, to elect their representatives. Stated another way, the actual and plain language of Section 5 mandates that all voters have an equal opportunity to translate their votes into representation. This interpretation is consistent with both the historical reasons for the inclusion of this provision in our Commonwealth's Constitution and the meaning we have ascribed to it through our case law.

We turn now to the question of what measures should be utilized to assess a dilution claim under the Free and Equal Elections Clause of the Pennsylvania Constitution. Neither Article I, Section 5, nor any other provision of our Constitution, articulates explicit standards which are to be used in the creation of congressional districts. However, since the inclusion of the Free and Equal Elections Clause in our Constitution in 1790, certain neutral criteria have, as a general matter, been traditionally utilized to guide the formation of our Commonwealth's legislative districts in order to prevent the dilution of an individual's vote for a representative in the General Assembly. These standards place the greatest emphasis on creating representational districts that both maintain the geographical and social cohesion of the communities in which people live and conduct the majority of their day-to-day affairs, and accord equal weight to the votes of residents in each of the various districts in determining the ultimate composition of the state legislature.

Significantly, the framers of the 1790 constitution who authored the Free and Equal Elections Clause also included a mandatory requirement therein for the legislature's formation of state senatorial districts covering multiple counties, namely that the counties must adjoin one another. Also, the architects of that charter expressly prohibited the division of any county of the Commonwealth, or the City of Philadelphia, in the formation of such districts. Thus, as preventing the dilution of an individual's vote was of paramount concern to that august group, it is evident that they considered maintaining the geographical contiguity of political subdivisions, and barring the splitting thereof in the process of creating legislative districts, to afford important safeguards against that pernicious prospect.

In the eight-plus decades after the 1790 Constitution became our Commonwealth's fundamental plan of governance, many problems arose from the corruption of the political process by well-heeled special interest groups who rendered our representative democracy deeply dysfunctional by weakening the power of an individual's vote through their selection, and financial backing in the electoral process, of representatives who exclusively served their narrow interests and not those of the people as a whole. One of the methods by which the electoral process was manipulated by these interest groups to attain those objectives was the practice of gerrymandering, popular revulsion of which became one of the driving factors behind the populace's demand for the calling of the 1873 Constitutional Convention.

As noted by an eminent authority on Pennsylvania constitutional law, by the time of that convention, gerrymandering was regarded as "one of the most flagrant evils and scandals of the time, involving notorious wrong to the people and open disgrace to republican institutions." Although the delegates to that convention did not completely eliminate this practice through the charter of governance which they adopted, and which the voters subsequently approved, they nevertheless included significant protections against its occurrence through the explicit adoption of certain requirements which all state legislative districts were, thereafter, required to meet: (1) the population of such districts must be equal, to the extent possible; (2) the district that is created must be comprised of compact and contiguous geographical territory; and (3) the district respects the boundaries of existing political subdivisions contained therein, such that the district divides as few of those subdivisions as possible. Given the great concern of the delegates over the practice of gerrymandering occasioned by their recognition of the corrosive effects on our entire democratic process through the deliberate dilution of our citizenry's individual votes, the focus on these neutral factors must be viewed, then, as part of a broader effort by the delegates to that convention to establish "the best methods of representation to secure a just expression of the popular will." Consequently, these factors have broader applicability beyond setting standards for the drawing of electoral districts for state legislative office.

The utility of these requirements to prevent vote dilution through gerrymandering retains continuing vitality, as evidenced by our present Constitution, adopted in 1968. In that charter, these basic requirements for the creation of senatorial districts were not only retained, but, indeed, were expanded by the voters to govern the establishment of election districts for the selection of their representatives in the state House of Representatives.

Because these factors are deeply rooted in the organic law of our Commonwealth, and continue to be the foundational requirements which state legislative districts must meet under the Pennsylvania Constitution, we find these neutral benchmarks to be particularly suitable as a measure in assessing whether a congressional districting plan dilutes the potency of an individual's ability to select the congressional representative of his or her choice, and thereby violates the Free and Equal Elections Clause. In our judgment, they are wholly consistent with the overarching intent of the framers of the 1790 Constitution that an individual's electoral power not be diminished through any law which discriminatorily dilutes the power of his or her vote, and, thus, they are a measure by which to assess whether the guarantee to our citizenry of "free and equal" elections promised by Article, I, Section 5 in the selection of their congressional representative has been violated. Because the character of these factors is fundamentally impartial in nature, their utilization reduces the likelihood of the creation of congressional districts which confer on any voter an unequal advantage by giving his or her vote greater weight in the selection of a congressional representative as prohibited by Article I, Section 5. Thus, use of these objective factors substantially reduces the risk that a voter in a particular congressional district will unfairly suffer the dilution of the power of his or her vote.

Moreover, rather than impermissibly lessening the power of an individual's vote based on the geographical area in which the individual resides—which, as explained above, Article I, Section 5 also prohibits—the use of compactness, contiguity, and the maintenance of the integrity of the boundaries of political subdivisions maintains the strength of an individual's vote in electing a congressional representative. When an individual is grouped with other members of his or her community in a congressional district for purposes of voting, the commonality of the interests shared with the other voters in the community increases the ability of the individual to elect a congressional representative for the district who reflects his or her personal preferences. This approach inures to no political party's benefit or detriment. It simply achieves the constitutional goal of fair and equal elections for all of our Commonwealth's voters.

Consequently, we adopt these measures as appropriate in determining whether a congressional redistricting plan violates the Free and Equal Elections Clause of the Pennsylvania Constitution. Therefore, an essential part of such an inquiry is an examination of whether the congressional districts created under a redistricting plan are "composed of compact and contiguous territory; as nearly equal in population as practicable; and which do not divide any county, city, incorporated town, borough, township, or ward, except where necessary to ensure equality of population."

We recognize that other factors have historically played a role in the drawing of legislative districts, such as the preservation of prior district lines, protection of incumbents, or the maintenance of the political balance which existed after the prior reapportionment. However, we view these factors to be wholly subordinate to the neutral criteria of compactness, contiguity, minimization of the division of political subdivisions, and maintenance of population equality among congressional districts. These neutral criteria provide a "floor" of protection for an individual against the dilution of his or her vote in the creation of such districts.

When, however, it is demonstrated that, in the creation of congressional districts, these neutral criteria have been subordinated, in whole or in part, to extraneous considerations such as gerrymandering for unfair partisan political advantage, a congressional redistricting plan violates Article I, Section 5 of the Pennsylvania Constitution. This standard does not require a showing that the creators of congressional districts intentionally subordinated these traditional criteria to other considerations in the creation of the district in order for it to violate Article I, Section 5; rather, it is sufficient to establish a violation of this section to show that these traditional criteria were subordinated to other factors. The overarching objective of this provision of our constitution is to prevent dilution of an individual's vote by mandating that the power of his or her vote in the selection of representatives be equalized to the greatest degree possible with all other Pennsylvania citizens.

In the three elections since the 2011 Plan was enacted, Democrats have won the same five districts, and Republicans have won the same 13 districts. In the 2012 election, Democrats won five congressional districts with an average of 76.4% of the vote in each, whereas Republicans won the remaining 13 congressional districts with an average 59.5% of the vote in each, and, notably, Democrats earned a statewide share of 50.8% of the vote, an average of 50.4% per district, with a median of 42.8% of the vote, whereas Republicans earned only a statewide share of 49.2% of the vote. In the 2014 election, Democratic candidates again won five congressional races, with an average of 73.6% of the vote in each, whereas Republicans again won 13 congressional districts, with an average of 63.4% of the vote in each. In 2014, Democrats earned a 44.5% statewide vote share in contested races, whereas Republicans earned a 55.5% statewide vote share in contested races, with a 54.1% statewide share vote in the aggregate. In the 2016 election, Democrats again won those same five congressional districts, with an average of 75.2% of the vote in each and a statewide vote share of 45.9%, whereas Republicans won those same 13 districts with an average of 61.8% in each and a statewide vote share of 54.1%. In short, in the last three election cycles, the partisan distribution has been as follows:

Year	Districts	Democratic Seats	Republican Seats	Democratic Vote Percentage	Republican Vote Percentage
2012	18	5	13	50.8%	49.2%
2014	18	5	13	44.5%	55.5%
2016	18	5	13	45.9%	54.1%

Perhaps the most compelling evidence concerning the 2011 Plan derives from the expert testimony of Dr. Jowei Chen, an expert in the areas of redistricting and political geography. As detailed above, Dr. Chen created two sets of 500 computer-simulated Pennsylvania redistricting plans, the first of which—Simulated Set 1—employed the traditional redistricting criteria of population equality, compactness, contiguousness, and political-subdivision integrity—*i.e.*, a simulation of the potential range of redistricting plans attempting to apply the traditional redistricting criteria. Dr. Chen's Simulated Set 1 plans achieved population equality and contiguity; had a range of Reock Compactness Scores from approximately .31 to .46, which was significantly more compact than the 2011 Plan's score of .278; and had a range of Popper–Polsby Compactness Scores from approximately .29 to .35, which was significantly more compact than the 2011 Plan's score of .164. Further, his simulated plans generally split between 12–14 counties and 40–58 municipalities, in sharp contrast to the 2011 Plan's far greater 28 county splits and 68 municipality splits. In other words, all of Dr. Chen's Simulated Set 1 plans, which were, again, a simulation of the potential range of redistricting plans attempting to apply the traditional redistricting criteria, were more compact and split fewer political subdivisions than the 2011 Plan, establishing that a process satisfying these traditional criteria would not lead to the 2011 Plan's adoption. Thus, Dr. Chen unsurprisingly opined that the 2011 Plan subordinated the goals of compactness and political-subdivision integrity to other considerations. Dr. Chen's testimony in this regard establishes that the 2011 Plan did not primarily consider, much less endeavor to satisfy, the traditional redistricting criteria.

Dr. Chen's testimony in this regard comports with a lay examination of the Plan, which reveals tortuously drawn districts that cause plainly unnecessary political-subdivision splits. In terms of compactness, a rudimentary review reveals a map comprised of oddly shaped, sprawling districts which wander seemingly arbitrarily across Pennsylvania, leaving 28 counties, 68 political subdivisions, and numerous wards, divided among as many as five congressional districts, in their wakes. Significantly, these districts often rend municipalities from their surrounding metropolitan areas and quizzically divide small municipalities which could easily be incorporated into single districts without detriment to the traditional redistricting criteria. As Dr. Kennedy explained below, the 7th Congressional District, pictured above, has been referred to as resembling "Goofy kicking Donald Duck," and is perhaps chief among a number of rivals in this regard, ambling from Philadelphia's suburbs in central Montgomery County, where it borders four other districts, south into Delaware County, where it abuts a fifth, then west into Chester County, where it abuts another district and travels northwest before jutting out in both northerly and southerly directions into Berks and Lancaster Counties. Indeed, it is difficult to imagine how a district as Rorschachian and sprawling, which is contiguous in two locations only by virtue of a medical facility and a seafood/steakhouse, respectively, might plausibly be referred to as "compact." Moreover, in terms of political subdivision splits, the 7th Congressional District splits each of the five counties in its path and some 26 separate political subdivisions between multiple congressional districts. In other words, the 7th Congressional District is itself responsible for 17% of the 2011 Plan's county splits and 38% of its municipality splits.

The 7th Congressional District, however, is merely the starkest example of the 2011 Plan's overall composition. As pictured above, and as discussed below, many of the 2011 Plan's congressional districts similarly sprawl through Pennsylvania's landscape, often contain "isthmuses" and "tentacles," and almost entirely ignore the integrity of political subdivisions in their trajectories. Although the 2011 Plan's odd shapes and seemingly arbitrary political subdivision splits are not themselves sufficient to conclude it is not predicated on the traditional redistricting factors, Dr. Chen's cogent analysis confirms that these anomalous shapes are neither necessary to, nor within the ordinary range of, plans generated with solicitude toward applying traditional redistricting considerations.

In sum, we conclude that the evidence detailed above and the remaining evidence of the record as a whole demonstrates that Petitioners have established that the 2011 Plan subordinates the traditional redistricting criteria in service of achieving unfair partisan advantage, and, thus, violates the Free and Equal Elections Clause of the Pennsylvania Constitution. Such a plan, aimed at achieving unfair partisan gain, undermines voters' ability to exercise their right to vote in free and "equal" elections if the term is to be interpreted in any credible way. An election corrupted by extensive, sophisticated gerrymandering and partisan dilution of votes is not "free and equal." In such circumstances, a "power, civil or military," to wit, the General Assembly, has in fact "interfered to prevent the free exercise of the right of suffrage."

Having set forth why the 2011 Plan is constitutionally infirm, we turn to our January 22, 2018 Order which directed a remedy for the illegal plan. Our Court initially invited our sister branches—the legislative and executive branches—to take action, through the enactment of a remedial congressional districting plan; however, recognizing the possibility that the legislature and executive would be unwilling or unable to act, we indicated in our Order that, in that eventuality, we would fashion a judicial remedial plan. Should the Pennsylvania General Assembly choose to submit a congressional districting plan that satisfies the requirements of the Pennsylvania Constitution, it shall submit such plan for consideration by the Governor on or before February 9, 2018. If the Governor accepts the

General Assembly's congressional districting plan, it shall be submitted to this Court on or before February 15, 2018. Should the General Assembly not submit a congressional districting plan on or before February 9, 2018, or should the Governor not approve the General Assembly's plan on or before February 15, 2018, this Court shall proceed expeditiously to adopt a plan based on the evidentiary record developed in the Commonwealth Court. In anticipation of that eventuality, the parties shall have the opportunity to be heard; to wit, all parties and intervenors may submit to the Court proposed remedial districting plans on or before February 15, 2018.

BAER, J., concurring in part and dissenting in part.

I join the Majority's conclusion that the 2011 Plan violates the Pennsylvania Constitution. Moreover, I concur with the Majority's erudite explication of the Free and Equal Election Clause and the Court's ultimate conclusion that the 2011 Plan violates the rights protected by that provision.

In conformity with the other dissenting justices, I dissent from the portions of the Majority Opinion supporting the remainder of the January 22nd Order, which enjoin the use of the 2011 Plan for the 2018 election cycle and set forth a procedure for implementing a new map for the May 2018 primary. In my view, the Court's remedy threatens the separation of powers dictated by Article I, Section 4 of the United States Constitution by failing to allow our sister branches sufficient time to legislate a new congressional districting map, potentially impinges upon the due process rights of the parties at bar as well as other interested parties, and foments unnecessary confusion in the current election cycle.

SAYLOR, C.J., dissenting.

The Supreme Court of the United States has emphasized that redistricting is committed to the political branch and is inherently political. Given the political character of redistricting, the pervading question relating to partisan considerations, with which courts have had great difficulty, is "how much is too much?" Rather than engaging this question in these conventional terms, the majority proceeds to overlay factors delineated by the Pennsylvania Constitution in relation to state-level reapportionment upon congressional redistricting. Since these considerations are not constitutional commands applicable to congressional redistricting, the majority's approach amounts to a non-textual, judicial imposition of a prophylactic rule.

In this regard, it is significant that the majority's new rule is overprotective, in that it guards not only against intentional discrimination, but also against legislative prioritization of any factor or factors other than those delineated in Article II, Section 16, including legitimate ones. Significantly, such additional factors include other traditional districting criteria appropriate to political consideration—such as the preservation of communities of interest, avoidance of pitting incumbents against each other, and maintenance of the core of prior district lines. I do not dispute that prophylactic rules may be legitimate in certain contexts. But they are, by their nature, vulnerable to claims of illegitimacy. The consideration of whether this sort of rule should be imposed by the judiciary upon a process committed by the federal Constitution to another branch of government seems to me to require particular caution and restraint.

Quite clearly, the character of redistricting, and concomitant separation-of-powers concerns, warrant special caution on the part of the judiciary in considering regulation and intervention. From my point of view, the majority opinion fails to sufficiently account for the fundamental character of redistricting, its allocation under the United States Constitution to the political branch, and the many drawbacks of constitutionalizing a non-textual judicial rule. For my own part, I would abide by the Court's previous determination, in the redistricting setting, that the Free and Equal Elections Clause provides no greater protection than the state charter's Equal Protection Clauses, which have been deemed coterminous with the protection provided by the United States Constitution. I find that the majority's focus on a limited range of traditional districting factors allocates too much discretion to the judiciary to discern violations in the absence of proof of intentional discrimination. Instead, I believe that, under the state and federal charters, the discretion belongs to the Legislature, which should be accorded appropriate deference and comity, as reflected in the majority's initial articulation of the presumption of constitutionality and the heavy burden borne by challengers.

I appreciate that the recommended factual findings of Judge Brobson of the Commonwealth Court suggest that the Court may be faced with a scenario involving extreme partisan gerrymandering. Were the present process an ordinary deliberative one, I would proceed to sift through the array of potential standards to determine if there was one which I could conclude would be judicially manageable. In my judgment, however, the acceptance of Petitioners' entreaty to proceed with extreme exigency presents too great of an impingement on the deliberative process to allow for a considered judgment on my part in this complex and politically charged area of the law.

MUNDY, J., dissenting.

Today the Majority announces that the Pennsylvania Congressional Redistricting Act of 2011 clearly, plainly and palpably violates the Pennsylvania Constitution on the basis of the Free and Equal Elections Clause. The Majority concedes, "neither Article 1, Section 5, nor any other provision of our Constitution, articulates explicit standards which are to be used in the creation of congressional districts." Nevertheless, the Majority holds that "certain neutral criteria" are to be utilized in drawing congressional districts in this Commonwealth.

Recognizing that the Pennsylvania Constitution does not articulate explicit standards to be used in the creation of congressional districts, the Majority fashions a three part test: "(1) the population of such districts must be equal, to the extent possible; (2) the district that is created must be comprised of compact and contiguous geographical territory, and (3) the district respects the boundaries of existing political subdivisions contained therein, such that the district divides as few of those subdivisions as possible." These vague judicially created "neutral criteria" are now the guideposts against which all future congressional redistricting maps will be evaluated, with this Court as the final arbiter of what constitutes too partisan an influence.

I also have grave concerns about the Majority's remedy. I agree with the Majority that we have the authority to direct the legislative and executive branches of our government to draw new maps to remedy any violation of law. However, I am troubled by the Majority's decision to strike down the 2011 congressional map on the eve of the 2018 midterm election. I further share the concerns expressed by the dissenting opinion of Chief Justice Saylor and the dissenting portion of the concurring and dissenting opinion of Justice Baer that this is a political process the General Assembly should be afforded the full opportunity and adequate time to address.

NOTES

1. When the 2011 Pennsylvania Plan was enacted, Republicans controlled both houses of the Pennsylvania General Assembly and a Republican was Governor of the state. In the 2014 election, the Republicans retained control of the General Assembly, and a Democrat was elected Governor. After invalidating the 2011 Plan, the Pennsylvania Supreme Court invited the General Assembly to draw up a remedial districting plan acceptable to the new Governor. Republicans and Democrats were unable to reach an agreement on a new plan. The Court received a number of separate plans from Republican and Democratic leaders, but none of them proved satisfactory. Ultimately, the Court adopted a plan of its own drawn up by the Court's consultant, a law professor from Stanford Law School. *See* Bernard Grofman & Jonathan R. Cervas, *Can State Courts Cure Partisan Gerrymandering: Lessons from* League of Women Voters of Pennsylvania v. Commonwealth of Pennsylvania (2018), 17 Election L.J. 264 (2018).

2. In his dissenting opinion, Chief Justice Saylor says that, because redistricting is committed to the political branch and is inherently political in nature, judicial review in this area requires restraint and deference to the legislature. That position later became the view of the U.S. Supreme Court in *Rucho*. But *Rucho*'s interpretation of the U.S. Constitution did not then, and would not now, foreclose the Pennsylvania Supreme Court from

continuing to rely on *its* Constitution to identify this judicially enforceable right. *League of Women Voters* ruled that the 2011 Plan violated the Free and Equal Elections Clause contained in the Declaration of Rights of the Pennsylvania Constitution. Other state constitutions contain similar guarantees, as the following cases, all decided after *Rucho*, show.

HARPER v. HALL
380 N.C. 317 (N.C. 2022)

HUDSON, J.

Today, we answer this question: does our state constitution recognize that the people of this state have the power to choose those who govern us, by giving each of us an equally powerful voice through our vote? Or does our constitution give to members of the General Assembly unlimited power to draw electoral maps that keep themselves and our members of Congress in office as long as they want, regardless of the will of the people, by making some votes more powerful than others? We hold that our constitution's Declaration of Rights guarantees the equal power of each person's voice in our government through voting in elections that matter.

In North Carolina, we have long understood that our constitution's promise that "all elections shall be free" means that every vote must count equally. As early as 1875, this Court declared it "too plain for argument" that the General Assembly's malapportionment of election districts "is a plain violation of fundamental principles." Likewise, this Court has previously held that judicial review was appropriate in legislative redistricting cases to enforce the requirements of the state constitution, even when doing so means interpreting state constitutional provisions more expansively than their federal counterparts.

While partisan gerrymandering is not a new tool, modern technologies enable mapmakers to achieve extremes of imbalance that, "with almost surgical precision," undermine our constitutional system of government. Indeed, the programs and algorithms now available for drawing electoral districts have become so sophisticated that it is possible to implement extreme and durable partisan gerrymanders that can enable one party to effectively guarantee itself a supermajority for an entire decade, even as electoral conditions change and voter preferences shift. Fortunately, the technology that makes such extreme gerrymanders possible likewise makes it possible to reliably evaluate the partisan asymmetry of such plans and review the extent to which they depart from and subordinate traditional neutral redistricting principles.

Partisan gerrymandering creates the same harm as malapportionment, which has previously been held to violate the state constitution: some peoples' votes have more power than others. But a legislative body can only reflect the will of the people if it is elected from districts that provide one person's vote with substantially the same power as every other person's vote. In North Carolina, a state without a citizen referendum process and where only a supermajority of the legislature can propose constitutional amendments, it is no answer to say that responsibility for addressing partisan gerrymandering is in the hands of the people, when they are represented by legislators who are able to entrench themselves by manipulating the very democratic process from which they derive their constitutional authority.

Here, the General Assembly enacted districting maps for the United States Congress, the North Carolina House of Representatives, and the North Carolina Senate that subordinated traditional neutral redistricting criteria in favor of extreme partisan advantage by diluting the power of certain people's votes. Despite finding that these maps were "extreme partisan outliers," "highly non-responsive" to the will of the people, and "incompatible with democratic principles," the three-judge panel below allowed the maps to stand because it concluded that judicial action "would be usurping the political power and prerogatives" of the General Assembly.

We emphatically disagree. Although the task of redistricting is primarily delegated to the legislature, it must be performed "in conformity with the State Constitution." It is thus the solemn duty of this Court to review the legislature's work to ensure such conformity using the available judicially manageable standards. Today, we hold that the enacted maps violate several rights guaranteed to the people by our state constitution.

Our dissenting colleagues have overlooked the fundamental reality of this case. Rather than stepping outside of our role as judicial officers and into the policymaking realm, here we are carrying out the most fundamental of our sacred duties: protecting the constitutional rights of the people of North Carolina from overreach by the General Assembly. Rather than passively deferring to the legislature, our responsibility is to determine whether challenged legislative acts, although presumed constitutional, encumber the constitutional rights of the people of our state. Here, our responsibility is to determine whether challenged apportionment maps encumber the constitutional rights of the people to vote on equal terms and to substantially equal voting power.

We must act as a Court to make sure that the rights of the people are treated with proper respect. In so doing, we are protecting the individual rights of voters to cast votes that matter equally, as guaranteed by our constitution in article I, sections 10, 12, 14, and 19:

Sec. 10. Free elections.

All elections shall be free.

Sec. 12. Right of assembly and petition.

The people have a right to assemble together to consult for their common good, to instruct their representatives, and to apply to the General Assembly for redress of grievances.

Sec. 14. Freedom of speech and press.

Freedom of speech and of the press are two of the great bulwarks of liberty and therefore shall never be restrained, but every person shall be held responsible for their abuse.

Sec. 19. Law of the land; equal protection of the laws.

No person shall be denied the equal protection of the laws.

We ground our decision in the text, structure, history, and intent of these provisions from the Declaration of Rights.

Despite the dissenters' repeated assertions, we seek neither proportional representation for members of any political party, nor to guarantee representation to any particular group. We are only upholding the rights of individual voters as guaranteed by our state constitution.

In this opinion, we give as much direction as appropriate to the General Assembly while fully respecting their authority to proceed first in the effort to draw maps that meet constitutional standards. Should they be unable to do so or if they produce maps that fail to protect the constitutional rights of the people, the trial court may select maps by the process it deems best, subject to our review.

However, simply because the U.S. Supreme Court has concluded partisan gerrymandering claims are nonjusticiable in federal courts, it does not follow that they are nonjusticiable in North Carolina courts, as Chief Justice Roberts himself noted in *Rucho*. 139 S. Ct. at 2507 ("Provisions in state statutes and state constitutions can provide standards and guidance for state courts to apply.").

Under North Carolina law, courts will not hear "purely political questions." This Court has recognized two criteria of political questions: (1) where there is "a textually demonstrable constitutional commitment of the issue" to the "sole discretion" of a "coordinate political department"; and (2) those questions that can be resolved only by making "policy choices and value determinations."

The constitution vests the responsibility for apportionment of legislative districts in the General Assembly under article II of our state constitution. Article II provides: "The General Assembly shall revise the senate districts and the apportionment of Senators among those districts." Legislative Defendants contend that "a delegation of a political task to a single political branch of government impliedly forecloses the other branches of government from undertaking that task" and that these provisions evidence such a textual commitment. This argument—that gerrymandering claims are categorically nonjusticiable because reapportionment is committed to the sole discretion of the General Assembly—is flatly inconsistent with our precedent.

This case does not ask us to remove all discretion from the redistricting process. The General Assembly will still be required to make choices regarding how to reapportion state legislative and congressional districts in accordance with traditional neutral districting criteria that will require legislators to exercise their judgment. Rather, this case asks how constitutional limitations in our Declaration of Rights limit the General Assembly's power to apportion districts.

More fundamentally, Legislative Defendants' argument that the textual grant of a power to a "political" branch is sufficient to render exercise of that power unreviewable strikes at the foundation stone of our state's constitutional caselaw—*Bayard v. Singleton*, (N.C. 1787). In *Bayard*, the courts of North Carolina first asserted the power and duty of judicial review of legislative enactments for compliance with the North Carolina Constitution, and to strike down laws in conflict therewith. In holding that we had the power of judicial review we specifically reasoned that if "members of the General Assembly" could violate some constitutional rights, "they might with equal authority, not only render themselves the Legislators of the State for life, without any further election of the people, but from thence transmit the dignity and authority of legislation down to their heirs male forever." It was out of concern for the very possibility that the legislature might intercede in the elections for their own office, which our constitution delegates the legislature power over, in contravention of the constitutional rights of the people to elect their own representatives that led this Court to assert the power of judicial review. To conclude that the mere commitment of the apportionment power in article II to the General Assembly renders its apportionment decisions unreviewable would require us to betray our most fundamental constitutional duty.

In determining whether plaintiffs' claims would require the court to make "policy choices and value determinations," we must determine whether the Declaration of Rights of the North Carolina Constitution prohibits partisan gerrymandering and, if so, whether the application of those claims would require such determinations. The Declaration of Rights preceded the constitution, and hence the rights reserved by the people preceded the division of power among the branches therein. "The relationship is not that exhibited by the U.S. Constitution with its appended Bill of Rights, the latter adding civil rights to a document establishing the basic institutions of government. Instead, North Carolina's declaration of rights is logically, as well as chronologically, prior to the constitutional text." John V. Orth & Paul M. Newby, *The North Carolina Constitution* (2013).

Article I, section 2 of the North Carolina Constitution establishes that "all political power is vested in and derived from the people," that "all government of rights originates from the people," and "is founded upon their will only." Furthermore, article I, section 1 of the constitution provides that "all persons are created equal." Subsequent constitutional provisions within the Declaration of Rights, including the free elections clause, the equal protection clause, the free speech clause, and the freedom of assembly clause, protect fundamental rights of the people in order to ensure, among other things, that their government is indeed "founded upon their will only."

We hold that claims of partisan gerrymandering are justiciable under the North Carolina Constitution. Although the primary responsibility for redistricting is constitutionally delegated to the General Assembly, this is not a delegation of unlimited power; the exercise of this power is subject to restrictions imposed by other constitutional provisions, including the Declaration of Rights.

We also hold that the General Assembly infringes upon voters' fundamental rights when, on the basis of partisan affiliation, it deprives a voter of his or her right to substantially equal voting power, as established by the free elections clause and the equal protection clause in our Declaration of Rights. We hold it also constitutes viewpoint discrimination and retaliation based on protected political activity in violation of the free speech clause and the freedom of assembly clause in our Declaration of Rights. When a redistricting plan creates such an infringement of fundamental rights, strict scrutiny must be applied to determine whether the plan is nevertheless narrowly tailored to advance a compelling governmental interest.

We reverse the trial court's judgment and remand this case to that court to oversee the redrawing of the maps by the General Assembly or, if necessary, by the court. The General Assembly shall now have the opportunity to submit new congressional and state legislative districting plans that satisfy all provisions of the North Carolina Constitution. It is the sincere hope of this Court that these new maps ensure that the channeling of "political power" from the people to their representatives in government through elections, the central democratic process envisioned by our constitutional system, is done on equal terms so that ours is a "government of right" that "originates from the people" and speaks with their voice.

NEWBY, C.J., dissenting.

How should a constitution be interpreted? Should its meaning be fixed or changing? If changing, to whom have the people given the task of changing it? When judges change the meaning of a constitution, does this undermine public trust and confidence in the judicial process? Traditionally, honoring the constitutional role assigned to the legislative branch, this Court has stated that acts of the General Assembly are presumed constitutional and deserving of the most deferential standard of review: To be unconstitutional, an act of the General Assembly must violate an explicit provision of our constitution beyond a reasonable doubt. We have recognized that our constitution allows the General Assembly to enact laws unless expressly prohibited by its text. This approach of having a fixed meaning and a deferential standard of review ensures a judge will perform his or her assigned role and not become a policymaker.

With this decision, unguided by the constitutional text, four members of this Court become policymakers. They wade into the political waters by mandating their approach to redistricting. They justify this activism because their understanding of certain constitutional provisions has "evolved over time." They lament that the people have not placed a provision in our constitution for a "citizen referendum" and use the absence of such a provision to justify their judicial activism to amend our constitution. The majority says courts must protect constitutional rights. This is true. Courts are not, however, to judicially amend the constitution to create those rights. As explicitly stated in our constitution, the people alone have the authority to alter our foundational document, and the people have the final say.

The majority cites *Bayard* in an effort to support its contention that judicial interference is necessary here "to prevent legislators from permanently insulating themselves from popular will." But *Bayard*, rightly understood, was simply about the authority of the Court to declare unconstitutional a law which violated an *express* provision of the constitution. It was not about limiting the General Assembly's authority to make discretionary political decisions within its express authority. *Bayard* involved a pointed assault on a clearly expressed and easily discernible *individual* right in the 1776 constitution, the right to a trial by jury "in all controversies at Law respecting Property." There the court weighed the General Assembly's ability to enact a statute that abolished the right to a jury trial for property disputes—for some citizens in some instances—in direct contradiction of the express text of the constitution.

Thus, the holding of *Bayard* is easily understood: A statute cannot abrogate an express provision of the constitution because the constitution represents the fundamental law and express will of the people; it is the role of the judiciary to perform this judicial review. The *Bayard* holding, however, does not support the proposition that this Court has the authority to involve itself in a matter that is both constitutionally committed to the General Assembly and lacking in manageable legal standards. Thus, the uncontroverted standard of review asks whether plaintiffs have shown that the challenged statutes, presumed constitutional, violate an express provision of the constitution beyond a reasonable doubt.

The majority inserts a requirement of "partisan fairness" into our constitution. Under the majority's newly created policy, any redistricting that diminishes or dilutes an individual's vote on the basis of partisanship is unconstitutional. This outcome results in a statewide proportionality standard. According to the majority, when groups of voters of "equal size" exist within a state, elections should result in an equal amount of representatives.

Recognizing that there is no explicit constitutional provision supporting its position, the majority resorts to an evolving understanding to support its expansive approach. Undoubtedly, Article I, Sections 1 and 2, are bedrock constitutional principles, recognizing that all are created equal and endowed with God-given rights and acknowledging that all political power originates and is derived from the people. Neither provision speaks expressly to limitations on the General Assembly's authority to redistrict. Undeterred, however, the majority reads into our constitution a proportionality requirement which appears to be more akin to the European parliamentary system, rather than the American system. Furthermore, the "will of the people" is expressed in the words of our constitution. The best way to honor the "will of the people" is to interpret the constitution as written and as the drafters intended. At no point in 1776, 1835, 1868, or 1971 did the drafters or refiners intend for the selected provisions of the Declaration of Rights to limit the legislature's authority to redistrict.

The majority defines "partisan advantage" as "achieving a political party's advantage across a map incommensurate with its level of statewide voter support." The majority also defines "political fairness" as "the effort to apportion to each political party a share of seats commensurate with its level of statewide support." These definitions demonstrate the majority's desire to judicially amend our constitution to include a requirement of statewide proportional representation.

JOHNSON v. WISCONSIN ELECTIONS COMMISSION
399 Wis.2d 623 (Wis. 2021)

BRADLEY, REBECCA, J.

The Wisconsin Constitution requires the legislature "to apportion and district anew the members of the senate and assembly, according to the number of inhabitants" after each census conducted under the United States Constitution every ten years. Wis. Const. art. IV, § 3. In fulfilling this responsibility, the legislature draws maps reflecting the legislative districts across the state. Every census invariably reveals population changes within legislative districts, and the legislature must satisfy the constitutional requirement that each district contain approximately equal numbers of people by developing new maps, which are subject to veto by the governor. When this occurs, courts are often asked to step in and draw the maps.

This year, the legislature drew maps, the governor vetoed them, and all parties agree the existing maps, enacted into law in 2011, are now unconstitutional because shifts in Wisconsin's population around the state have disturbed the constitutionally guaranteed equality of the people's representation in the state legislature and in the United States House of Representatives. We have been asked to provide a remedy for that inequality. Some parties to this action further complain that the 2011 maps reflect a partisan gerrymander favoring Republican Party candidates at the expense of Democrat Party candidates, and ask us to redraw the maps to allocate districts equally between these dominant parties, although no one asks us to assign districts to any minor parties in proportion to their share of Wisconsin's electoral vote.

The United States Supreme Court recently declared there are no legal standards by which judges may decide whether maps are politically "fair." *Rucho v. Common Cause* (2019). We agree. The Wisconsin Constitution requires the legislature—a political body—to establish the legislative districts in this state. Just as the laws enacted by the legislature reflect policy choices, so will the maps drawn by that political body. Nothing in the constitution empowers this court to second-guess those policy choices, and nothing in the constitution vests this court with the power of the legislature to enact new maps. Our role in redistricting remains a purely judicial one, which limits us to declaring what the law is and affording the parties a remedy for its violation.

In this case, the maps drawn in 2011 were enacted by the legislature and signed into law by the governor. Their lawfulness was challenged in a federal court, which upheld them (subject to a slight adjustment to comply with federal law). In 2021, those maps no longer comply with the constitutional requirement of an equal number of citizens in each legislative district, due to shifts in population across the state. This court will remedy that malapportionment, while ensuring the maps satisfy all other constitutional and statutory requirements. Claims of political unfairness in the maps present political questions, not legal ones. Such claims have no basis in the constitution or any other law and therefore must be resolved through the political process and not by the judiciary.

Four Wisconsin voters filed a petition for leave to commence an original action in this court following the release of the results of the 2020 census. Claiming to live in malapportioned congressional and state legislative districts, they have asked us to declare the existing maps violate the "one person, one vote" principle embodied in Article IV, Section 3 of the Wisconsin Constitution. They also have asked us to enjoin the Wisconsin Elections Commission from administering congressional and state legislative elections until the political branches adopt redistricting plans. Because the legislature and the governor reached an impasse, the Wisconsin voters request a mandatory injunction, remedying what all parties agree are unconstitutional plans by making only those changes necessary for the maps to comport with the one person, one vote principle while satisfying other constitutional and statutory mandates (a "least-change" approach).

We hold: (1) redistricting disputes may be judicially resolved only to the extent necessary to remedy the violation of a justiciable and cognizable right protected under state or federal law; (2) the partisan makeup of districts does not implicate any justiciable or cognizable right; and (3) this court will confine any judicial remedy to making the minimum changes necessary in order to conform the existing congressional and state legislative redistricting plans to constitutional and statutory requirements. The existing maps were passed by the legislature and signed by the governor. They survived judicial review in federal court. Revisions are now necessary only to remedy malapportionment produced by population shifts made apparent by the decennial census. Because the judiciary lacks the lawmaking power constitutionally conferred on the legislature, we will limit our remedy to achieving compliance with the law rather than imposing policy choices.

Both federal and state laws regulate redistricting. Article I, Section 2 of the United States Constitution requires members of the House of Representatives to be chosen "by the People of the several states." The United States Supreme Court construed this section to mean "that as nearly as is practicable one man's vote in a congressional election is to be worth as much as another's."

As a matter of federal constitutional law, the one person, one vote principle applies more forcefully to congressional districts than to state legislative districts. The United States Supreme Court declared: "There is no excuse for the failure to meet the objective of equal representation for equal numbers of people in congressional districting other than the practical impossibility of drawing equal districts with mathematical precision." "Population alone" is the "sole criterion of constitutionality in congressional redistricting." For congressional districts, even less than a one percent difference between the population of the largest and smallest districts is constitutionally suspect.

The Equal Protection Clause, as applied to state legislative districts, imposes a less exacting one person, one vote principle. Consistent with principles of federalism, states have limited flexibility to pursue other legitimate policy objectives, such as "maintaining the integrity of various political subdivisions" and keeping "compact districts of contiguous territory."

Federal statutes also govern redistricting. 2 U.S.C. § 2c prohibits multimember congressional districts. The Voting Rights Act prohibits the denial or abridgment of the right to vote on account of race, color, or membership in a language minority group, which implicates redistricting practices. It provides, in relevant part:

> (a) No voting qualification or prerequisite to voting or standard, practice, or procedure shall be imposed or applied by any State or political subdivision in a

manner which results in a denial or abridgement of the right of any citizen of the United States to vote on account of race or color, or in contravention of the guarantees set forth in section 10303(f)(2), which protects language minority groups, of this title, as provided in subsection (b).

(b) A violation of subsection (a) is established if, based on the totality of circumstances, it is shown that the political processes leading to nomination or election in the State or political subdivision are not equally open to participation by members of a class of citizens protected by subsection (a) in that its members have less opportunity than other members of the electorate to participate in the political process and to elect representatives of their choice. The extent to which members of a protected class have been elected to office in the State or political subdivision is one circumstance which may be considered: Provided, that nothing in this section establishes a right to have members of a protected class elected in numbers equal to their proportion in the population.

52 U.S.C. § 10301. The "dispersal" of a minority group among several districts can render the group an "ineffective" voting bloc. Such a result may violate the VRA, even if the map drawers lacked discriminatory intent.

The first section in the Wisconsin Constitution's Declaration of Rights states: "All people are born equally free and independent, and have certain inherent rights; among these are life, liberty and the pursuit of happiness; to secure these rights, governments are instituted, deriving their just powers from the consent of the governed." This section enshrines a first principle of our nation's founding: "The only source of political power is in the people; they are sovereign, that is to say, the aggregate community, the accumulated will of the people, is sovereign."

Article I, Section 1 of the Wisconsin Constitution has nothing to say about partisan gerrymanders. "The idea that partisan gerrymandering undermines popular sovereignty because the legislature rather than the people selects representatives is rhetorical hyperbole masked as constitutional argument. When legislatures draw districts, they in no way select who will occupy the resulting seats." Voters retain their freedom to choose among candidates irrespective of how district lines are drawn.

Contriving a partisan gerrymandering claim from the text of the Wisconsin Constitution would require us to indulge a fiction—that partisan affiliation is permanent and invariably dictates how a voter casts every ballot. Of course, political affiliation "is not an immutable characteristic, but may shift from one election to the next." "Voters can—and often do—move from one party to the other." Not only is political affiliation changeable, but self-identified partisans can—and do—vote for a different party's candidates.

If the constitution were misinterpreted to make changeable characteristics relevant factors in evaluating redistricting plans, "we fail to see why it demands only a partisan political mix." "Why would a Constitution that never mentions political parties, much less Republicans and Democrats, grant special status to partisan identity?" If we opened the floodgates, what would stop claims seeking proportional representation for "gun owners" or "vegetarians"? Nothing distinguishes partisan affiliation from hundreds—perhaps thousands—of other variables. Dispositively, none of these factors is mentioned in the text of the constitution.

The constitutional confines of our judicial authority must guide our exercise of power in affording the Petitioners a remedy for their claims. The existing maps were adopted by the legislature, signed by the governor, and survived judicial review by the federal courts. Treading further than necessary to remedy their current legal deficiencies would intrude upon the constitutional prerogatives of the political branches and unsettle the constitutional allocation of power.

For the paramount purpose of preserving liberty, the Wisconsin Constitution embodies a structural separation of powers among the three branches of government, restraining this court from exercising anything but judicial power. This court's precedent declares that the legislature's enactment of a redistricting plan is subject to presentment and a gubernatorial veto. If the legislature and the governor reach an impasse, the judiciary has a duty to remedy the constitutional defects in the existing plan. But a duty to remedy a constitutional deficiency is not a prerogative to make law.

Because our power to issue a mandatory injunction does not encompass rewriting duly enacted law, our judicial remedy "should reflect the least change" necessary for the maps to comport with relevant legal requirements. Using the existing maps "as a template" and implementing only those remedies necessary to resolve constitutional or statutory deficiencies confines our role to its proper adjudicative function, ensuring we fulfill our role as apolitical and neutral arbiters of the law.

Many intervenors have argued the 2011 maps entrenched a Republican Party advantage, so using them as a starting point perpetuates a partisan gerrymander. In other words, these intervenors argue we must tip the partisan balance to benefit one party in order to avoid accusations of partisanship. We reject this demand to "simply undo the work of one political party for the benefit of another." Endeavoring to rebalance the allocation of districts between the two major parties would be a nonjudicial exercise of partisanship by the court. While the application of neutral standards inevitably benefits one side or the other in any case, it does not place our thumb on any partisan scale.

"Putting courts into politics, and compelling judges to become politicians, in many jurisdictions has almost destroyed the traditional respect for the Bench." A least-change approach safeguards the long-term institutional legitimacy of this court by removing us from the political fray and ensuring we act as judges rather than political actors.

The judiciary has been repeatedly subject to "purely political attacks" by people who "did not get the result from the court they wanted." These often partisan onslaughts threaten the "institutional legitimacy" of the judiciary, which, in turn, threatens the "rule of law" itself. By utilizing the least-change approach, we do not endorse the policy choices of the political branches; rather, we simply remedy the malapportionment claims. Manufacturing a standard of political "fairness" by which to draw legislative maps in accordance with the subjective preferences of judges would refashion this court as a committee of oligarchs with political power superior to both the legislature and the governor. Judges must refuse to become "philosopher kings empowered to 'fix' things according to the dictates of what we fancy is our superior insight."

HAGEDORN, J., concurring.

To the extent feasible, a court's role in redistricting should be modest and restrained. We are not the branch of government assigned the constitutional responsibility to "apportion and district anew" after each decennial census; the legislature is. The job of the judiciary is to decide cases based on the law. Here, the laws passed in 2011 establishing legislative and congressional districts cannot govern future elections as written due to population shifts. Accordingly, our role is appropriately limited to altering current district boundaries only as needed to comply with legal requirements. The majority opinion so concludes, and I join it in almost all respects.

Where the political process has failed and modified maps are needed before the next election, the court's function is to formulate a remedy—one tailored toward fixing the legal deficiencies. The majority opinion asserts that only legal requirements may be considered in constructing a fitting remedy. That is not quite correct. Legal standards establish the need for a remedy and constrain the remedies we may impose, but they are not the only permissible judicial considerations when constructing a proper remedy. For example, one universally recognized redistricting criterion is communities of interest. It is not a legal requirement, but it may nonetheless be an appropriate, useful, and neutral factor to weigh. Suppose we receive multiple proposed maps that comply with all relevant legal requirements, and that have equally compelling arguments for why the proposed map most aligns with current district boundaries. In that circumstance, we still must exercise judgment to choose the best alternative. Considering communities of interest (or other traditional redistricting criteria) may assist us in doing so. In other words, while a remedy must be tailored to curing legal violations, a court is not necessarily limited to considering legal rights and requirements alone when formulating a remedy.

This does not mean our remedial powers are without guardrails. And this is where the dissent errs. The dissent argues we can take over the responsibility of the legislature entirely, discard policy judgments we don't like, and craft a new law from scratch consistent with our own policy concerns. The reader should look past pleas for fairness and see this for what it is: a claim of dangerously broad judicial power to fashion state policy.

The majority opinion aptly explains that our judicial role forecloses this; our remedial powers are not so unbounded. It is appropriate for us to start with the laws currently on the books because they were passed in accordance with the constitutional process and reflect the policy choices the people made through their elected representatives. Our task is therefore rightly focused on making only necessary modifications to accord with legal requirements.

DALLET, J., dissenting.

Redistricting is an "inherently political and legislative—not judicial—task," even when judges do it. That is one reason why I said that the federal courts, composed of judges insulated from partisan politics by lifetime appointments, are best suited to handle redistricting cases. But now that we have stepped out of our traditional judicial role and into the "the political thicket" of redistricting, it is vital that this court remain neutral and nonpartisan. The majority all but guarantees that we cannot. First, the majority adopts 2011's "sharply partisan" maps as the template for its "least-change" approach. And second, it effectively insulates future maps from being challenged as extreme partisan gerrymanders. The upshot of those two decisions—neither of which is politically neutral—is to elevate outdated partisan choices over neutral redistricting criteria.

The majority/lead opinion's adoption of a "least-change" approach to evaluating or crafting remedial maps does not "remove us from the political fray and ensure we act as judges rather than political actors." It does the opposite, inserting the court directly into politics by ratifying outdated partisan political choices. In effect, a least-change approach that starts with the 2011 maps nullifies voters' electoral decisions since then. In that way, adopting a least-change approach is an inherently political choice. Try as it might, the majority is fooling no one by proclaiming its decision is neutral and apolitical.

To be sure, there may be limited circumstances in which a least-change approach is appropriate. For example, when a court is redrawing maps based on a prior court-drawn plan, it may make sense to make fewer changes since the existing maps should already reflect neutral redistricting principles. Another situation where minimizing changes may be appropriate is when a court finds localized problems with a plan validly enacted through the political process.

Here, however, we are dealing with neither of those situations. We are adopting statewide maps to replace a 2011 plan that the parties all agree is now unconstitutional. But more to the point, the 2011 map was enacted using a "sharply partisan methodology" by a legislature no longer in power and a governor whom the voters have since rejected. The partisan character of the 2011 maps is evident both in the process by which they were drawn—"under a cloak of secrecy," totally excluding the minority political party—and in their departure from neutral traditional redistricting criteria.

It is one thing for the current legislature to entrench a past legislature's partisan choices for another decade. It is another thing entirely for this court to do the same. For starters, the least-change approach is not the "neutral standard" the majority/lead opinion portrays it as. Rather, applying that approach to 2011's maps affirmatively perpetuates the partisan agenda of politicians no longer in power. It doesn't matter which political party benefits from the 2011 maps, only that we cannot start with them and maintain judicial neutrality. Moreover, a least-change approach risks entrenching 2011's partisan agenda in future redistricting cycles. If the party that benefits from the maps adopted in this case controls only the legislature for the next redistricting cycle, it has every incentive to ensure an impasse. After all, an impasse will result in the court changing the maps as little as possible—thus preserving that party's hold on power. The point is, the least-change approach is anything but a "neutral standard."

HARKENRIDER v. HOCHUL
(N.Y. 2022)

DIFIORE, C.J.

In 2014, the People of the State of New York amended the State Constitution to adopt historic reforms of the redistricting process by requiring, in a carefully structured process, the creation of electoral maps by an Independent Redistricting Commission (IRC) and by declaring unconstitutional certain undemocratic practices such as partisan and racial gerrymandering. No one disputes that this year, during the first redistricting cycle to follow adoption of the 2014 amendments, the IRC and the legislature failed to follow the procedure commanded by the State Constitution. A stalemate within the IRC resulted in a breakdown in the mandatory process for submission of electoral maps to the legislature. The legislature responded by creating and enacting maps in a nontransparent manner controlled exclusively by the dominant political party—doing exactly what they would have done had the 2014 constitutional reforms never been passed. The primary questions before us are whether this failure to follow the prescribed constitutional procedure warrants invalidation of the legislature's congressional and state senate maps and whether there is record support for the determination of both courts below that the district lines for congressional races were drawn with an unconstitutional partisan intent. We answer both questions in the affirmative and therefore declare the congressional and senate maps void. As a result, judicial oversight is required to facilitate the expeditious creation of constitutionally conforming maps for use in the 2022 election and to safeguard the constitutionally protected right of New Yorkers to a fair election.

Following receipt of the results of the 2020 federal census, the redistricting process began in New York—the first opportunity for district lines to be drawn under the new IRC procedures established by the 2014 constitutional amendments. Due to shifts in New York's population, the state lost a congressional seat and other districts were malapportioned, undisputedly rendering the 2012 congressional apportionment—developed by a federal court following a legislative impasse—unconstitutional and necessitating the drawing of new district lines. Throughout 2021, the IRC held the requisite public hearings, gathering input from stakeholders and voters across the state to inform their composition of redistricting maps. In December 2021 and January 2022, however, negotiations between the IRC members deteriorated and the IRC, split along party lines, was unable to agree upon consensus maps.

As a result of their disagreements, the IRC submitted, as a first set of maps, two proposed redistricting plans to the legislature—maps from each party delegation—as is constitutionally permitted if a single consensus map fails to garner sufficient votes. The legislature voted on this first set of plans without amendment as required by the Constitution and rejected both plans. The legislature notified the IRC of that rejection, triggering the IRC's obligation to compose—within 15 days—a second redistricting plan for the legislature's review. On January 24, 2022—the day before the 15-day deadline but more than one month before the February 28, 2022 deadline—the IRC announced that it was deadlocked and, as a result, would not present a second plan to the legislature. Within a week, the Democrats in the legislature—in control of both the senate and assembly—composed and enacted new congressional, senate, and assembly redistricting maps, undisputedly without any consultation or participation by the minority Republican Party. On February 3rd, the Governor signed into law this new redistricting legislation, which also superseded the two percent limitation imposed in 2012 on the legislature's authority to amend IRC plans.

In addition to the procedural amendments, in 2014, the People also amended the New York State Constitution to include certain substantive limitations on redistricting, including an express prohibition on partisan gerrymandering, commanding that "districts shall not be drawn to discourage competition or for the purpose of favoring or disfavoring incumbents or other particular candidates or political parties." This amendment was made in recognition that the practice of partisan gerrymandering "jeopardizes the ordered working of our Republic, and of the democratic process" and, "at its most extreme, the practice amounts to rigging elections."

In this case, petitioners asserted that, along with being procedurally flawed, the 2022 congressional map enacted by the legislature violates the constitutional provision prohibiting partisan gerrymandering. To prevail on such a claim, petitioners bore the burden of proving beyond a reasonable doubt that the congressional districts were drawn with a particular impermissible intent or motive—that is, to "discourage competition" or to "favor or disfavor incumbents or other particular candidates or political parties." Such invidious intent could be demonstrated directly or circumstantially through proof of a partisan process excluding participation by the minority party and evidence of discriminatory results.

The trial court found by "clear evidence and beyond a reasonable doubt that the congressional map was unconstitutionally drawn with political bias" to "significantly reduce" the number of competitive districts. The Appellate Division affirmed, similarly drawing an inference of invidious partisan purpose based on "evidence of the largely one-party process used to enact the 2022 congressional map, a comparison of the 2022 congressional map to the 2012 congressional map, and the expert opinion of Sean P. Trende" that "the 2022 congressional map was drawn to discourage competition and favor democrats."

The enactment of the congressional and senate maps by the legislature was procedurally unconstitutional, and the congressional map is also substantively unconstitutional as drawn with impermissible partisan purpose, leaving the state without constitutional district lines for use in the 2022 primary and general elections. The parties dispute the proper remedy for these constitutional violations, with the State respondents arguing no remedy should be ordered for the 2022 election cycle because the election process for this year is already underway. In other words, the State respondents urge that the 2022 congressional and senate elections be conducted using the unconstitutional maps, deferring any remedy for a future election. We reject this invitation to subject the People of this state to an election conducted pursuant to an unconstitutional reapportionment.

Our State Constitution both requires expedited judicial review of redistricting challenges and authorizes the judiciary to "order the adoption of, or changes to, a redistricting plan" in the absence of a constitutionally viable legislative plan. Where, as here, legislative maps have been determined to be unenforceable, we are left in the same predicament as if no maps had been enacted. Prompt judicial intervention is both necessary and appropriate to guarantee the People's right to a free and fair election.

We are cognizant of the logistical difficulties involved in preparing for and executing an election—and appreciate that rescheduling a primary election impacts administrative officials, candidates for public office, and the voters themselves. Like the courts below, however, we are not convinced that we have no choice but to allow the 2022 primary election to proceed on unconstitutionally enacted and gerrymandered maps. With judicial supervision and the support of a neutral expert designated a special master, there is sufficient time for the adoption of new district lines. Although it will likely be necessary to move the congressional and senate primary elections to August, New York routinely held a bifurcated primary until recently, with some primaries occurring as late as September.

Nearly a century and a half ago, we wrote that "the Constitution is the voice of the people speaking in their sovereign capacity, and it must be heeded." Thirty years later, we relied on that fundamental principle to conclude that "a legislative apportionment act cannot stand as a valid exercise of discretionary power by the legislature when it is manifest that the constitutional provisions have been disregarded because any other determination by the courts might result in the constitutional standards being broken down and wholly disregarded." Today, we again uphold those constitutional standards by adhering to the will of the People of this State and giving meaningful effect to the 2014 constitutional amendments.

We therefore remit the matter to the Supreme Court which, with the assistance of the special master and any other relevant submissions shall adopt constitutional maps with all due haste.

TROUTMAN, J., dissenting in part.

I agree with the majority that petitioners have standing, and I further agree with the majority's holding that the 2022 congressional and state senate redistricting plans were not enacted by the legislature in compliance with the constitutional process. However, I dissent as to the majority's advisory opinion on the substantive issue of whether the plans constitute political gerrymandering and as to the remedy.

The State Constitution requires that any redistricting plan must be initiated by the Independent Redistricting Committee. Once this Court holds that the 2022 plans were unconstitutionally enacted and must be stricken on that threshold basis, it should not then step out of its judicial role to further opine on the purely academic issue of whether the 2022 congressional map failed to comply with these substantive requirements. The 2022 plans, which the majority concludes are void ab initio, are no longer substantively at issue, nor can the majority seriously claim them to be so. Furthermore, although the majority purports to provide "necessary guidance to inform the development of a new congressional map on remittal," the majority's opinion provides no such guidance. Its conclusion, based on affirmed findings of fact that the congressional map was drawn with partisan intent, is not illuminating in the least because the majority does not engage in the kind of careful district-specific analysis that might provide any practical guidance to an actual mapmaker. By opining on this academic issue, the majority renders "an inappropriate advisory opinion" by "prospectively declaring the redistricting invalid on additional constitutional grounds."

Given the procedural violation flowing from the breakdown in the constitutional process, we must fashion a remedy that matches the error. The Constitution contemplates that a court may be "required to order the adoption of a redistricting plan as a remedy for a violation of law." This Court should order the legislature to adopt either of the two plans that the IRC has already approved. Those plans show significant areas of bipartisan consensus among the IRC commissioners. The boundaries of the districts of Upstate New York, in particular, are nearly identical between the two plans and similar to those in the procedurally infirm plan enacted by the legislature. Given the existence of these IRC-approved plans, there is no need for a redistricting plan to be crafted out of whole cloth and adopted by a court. Rather, the legislature should be ordered to adopt one of the IRC-approved plans on a strict timetable.

Yet the remedy ordered by the majority takes the ultimate decision-making authority out of the hands of the legislature and entrusts it to a single trial court judge. Moreover, it may ultimately subject the citizens of this State, for the next 10 years, to an electoral map created by an unelected individual, with no apparent ties to this State, whom our citizens never envisioned having such a profound effect on their democracy. That is simply not what the people voted for when they enacted the constitutional provision at issue.

NOTES

1. In 2010, the voters of Florida approved the Fair Districts Amendment to the state Constitution, expressly designed to eliminate partisan political gerrymandering. *See* Fla. Const. art. III, § 20(a). The amendment forbids the Florida legislature from drawing a redistricting plan or an individual district with the "intent to favor or disfavor a political party or an incumbent." In *League of Women Voters of Florida v. Detzner*, 172 So.3d 363 (2015), the Supreme Court of Florida refused to enforce a legislative redistricting plan on the ground that the state legislature acted with an improper intent in violation of the Fair Districts Amendment. Other states have enacted constitutional amendments creating commissions mandated to devise district election maps that eliminate political favoritism. *See* Colo. Const. art. V, Cong. & Legis. Apportionments, §§ 44, 46; Mich. Const. art. IV, §6; Wash. Const. art. II, § 43; Idaho Code Ann. § 17-1501 to 08; Cal. Const. Art. XXI § 2.

2. The next case deals with a distinct remedial problem. At stake is not how a court should oversee the redrawing of new election districts for future elections. It is whether to honor laws enacted by a legislature whose members were elected by improperly drawn lines.

NORTH CAROLINA STATE CONFERENCE v. MOORE
876 S.E.2d 513 (N.C. 2022)

EARLS, J.

This case involves completely unprecedented circumstances that give rise to a novel legal issue directly implicating two fundamental principles upon which North Carolina's constitutional system of government is predicated: the principles of popular sovereignty and democratic self-rule. The issue is whether legislators elected from unconstitutionally racially gerrymandered districts possess unreviewable authority to initiate the process of changing the North Carolina Constitution, including in ways that would allow those same legislators to entrench their own power, insulate themselves from political accountability, or discriminate against the same racial group who were excluded from the democratic process by the unconstitutionally racially gerrymandered districts.

In the final week of the final regular legislative session preceding the 2018 general election, a General Assembly that was composed of a substantial number of legislators elected from districts that the United States Supreme Court had conclusively determined to have resulted from unconstitutional racial gerrymandering enacted legislation presenting six constitutional amendments to North Carolina voters. Some of these measures passed in the General Assembly by notably narrow margins. By this time, it had already been established that twenty-eight legislative districts were drawn in a manner that violated the Equal Protection Clause of the United States Constitution, and many other districts had also already been redrawn to remedy this unconstitutional racial gerrymander. The two amendments at issue in this case—the Tax Cap Amendment and the Voter ID Amendment—cleared the required three-fifths supermajority threshold by one and two votes in the House and by four and three votes in the Senate, respectively. Both amendments were ultimately ratified by a majority of North Carolina voters. In that same election, conducted using newly drawn legislative districts, the voters denied to any political party a three-fifths supermajority in either the North Carolina House or Senate.

What is extraordinary about these events is not that a legislative body was composed in part of legislators elected from unconstitutional districts. That has occurred on numerous occasions in recent years just in North Carolina alone. Rather, what makes this case so unique is that the General Assembly, acting with the knowledge that twenty-eight of its districts were unconstitutionally racially gerrymandered and that more than two-thirds of all legislative districts needed to be redrawn to achieve compliance with the Equal Protection Clause, chose to initiate the process of amending the state constitution at the last possible moment prior to the first opportunity North Carolinians had to elect representatives from presumptively constitutional legislative districts. Indeed, neither of the parties, nor any of the amici curiae, have identified a single previous instance of a legislative body composed of a substantial number of legislators elected from unconstitutional districts attempting to exercise powers relating to the passage of constitutional amendments after it had been conclusively established that numerous districts were unconstitutional.

The precise legal question before us is whether a General Assembly composed of a substantial number of legislators elected due to unconstitutional gerrymandering may exercise the sovereign power delegated by the people of North Carolina to the legislature under article XIII, section 4 of the North Carolina Constitution, which authorizes the General Assembly to propose constitutional amendments "if three-fifths of all the members of each house shall adopt an act submitting the proposal to the qualified voters of the State for their ratification or rejection." The broader question is whether there are any limits on the authority of legislators elected due to unconstitutional racial gerrymandering to alter or abolish "the fundamental law of the State that defines the form and concept of our government." These questions cut to the core of our constitutional system of government: if legislators who assumed power in a manner inconsistent with constitutional requirements possess unreviewable authority to initiate the process of altering or abolishing the constitution, then the fundamental principle that all political power resides with and flows from the people of North Carolina would be threatened.

We conclude that article I, sections 2 and 3 of the North Carolina Constitution impose limits on these legislators' authority to initiate the process of amending the constitution under these circumstances. Nonetheless, we also conclude that the trial court's order in this case invalidating the two challenged amendments swept too broadly. Because the legislators elected due to unconstitutional racial gerrymandering retained the authority needed to avoid "chaos and confusion in government," the trial court should have considered whether invalidating both the Voter ID Amendment and the Tax Cap Amendment was necessary "upon balancing the equities" of the situation.

In particular, the trial court should have examined as a threshold matter whether the legislature was composed of a sufficient number of legislators elected from unconstitutionally gerrymandered districts—or from districts that were made possible by the unconstitutional gerrymander—such that the votes of those legislators could have been decisive in passing the challenged enactments. If not, no further inquiry is necessary, and the challenged amendments must be left undisturbed. In this case, however, the record is clear that votes of legislators from unconstitutionally gerrymandered districts could have been decisive. Therefore, the trial court needed to also consider three additional questions: whether there was a substantial risk that each challenged constitutional amendment would (1) immunize legislators elected due to unconstitutional racial gerrymandering from democratic accountability going forward; (2) perpetuate the continued exclusion of a category of voters from the democratic process; or (3) constitute intentional discrimination against the same category of voters discriminated against in the reapportionment process that resulted in the unconstitutionally gerrymandered districts.

The North Carolina Constitution itself provides guidance to this Court when we are called upon to interpret constitutional provisions protecting the people of North Carolina's fundamental rights: "A frequent recurrence to fundamental principles is absolutely necessary to preserve the blessings of liberty." This "solemn warning" has long informed our interpretation of the "fundamental guarantees" contained in our constitution's Declaration of Rights. Thus, in examining plaintiff's claim, we begin and end with the principles codified in numerous provisions of our constitution that function as the beating heart of North Carolina's system of government: the principles of popular sovereignty and democratic self-rule.

Under our constitution, "all political power is vested in and derived from the people; all government of right originates from the people, is founded upon their will only, and is instituted solely for the good of the whole." Our constitution also reserves to the "people of this State the inherent, sole, and exclusive right of altering or abolishing their Constitution and form of government." These provisions of the North Carolina Constitution express and safeguard the people of North Carolina's "revolutionary faith in popular sovereignty" as the theory of government that best promotes the liberty and equality of all persons. In short, they establish that there is no source of political power other than the people of North Carolina; nobody but the people of North Carolina possess the authority to redefine the purpose and structure of North Carolina's system of government.

In the system of government our constitution prescribes, the legislature "represents the untrammeled will of the people" and "the expression of the people's will can only be made by legislation." Yet there is no legislative power independent of the people. Instead, the constitution defines and structures political processes that allow individuals to assume offices to which the people of North Carolina have delegated sovereign power. These processes enable the "sovereign power" to be "exercised by the People's representatives in the General Assembly," but at all times the sovereign power "resides with the people." The legitimacy of any individual officer's claim to exercise sovereign power depends upon the legitimacy of the process by which that individual came to assume the office to which sovereign power has been delegated.

Consistent with the principles of popular sovereignty and democratic self-rule, only the people can change the way sovereign power is allocated and exercised within North Carolina's system of government. And, through their constitution, the people assigned the General Assembly a vital role in the amendment process. Specifically, the constitution authorizes the General Assembly to initiate the process of enacting constitutional amendments by "adopting an act submitting the proposed constitutional amendments to the qualified voters of the State for their ratification or rejection," provided that "three-fifths of all the members of each house shall adopt the act." It is undisputed that three-fifths of the members of each house adopted acts submitting the proposals to add the Voter ID and Tax Cap Amendments to the North Carolina Constitution, and that a majority of voters ratified both amendments in 2018. The sole question before us is whether the legislators who passed the bills submitting these two amendments to the voters could validly exercise the authority conferred upon the legislature by the people.

Before examining the legislators' authority to initiate the process of amending the North Carolina Constitution, we note the argument that this question is practically irrelevant because a majority of North Carolina voters ratified the Voter ID and Tax Cap Amendments. This argument has some superficial appeal: if what matters is safeguarding our constitutional commitment to popular sovereignty and democratic self-rule, the fact that a majority of voters approved the challenged amendments could indicate that the amendments reflected the people's will.

First, this argument overlooks the fact that constitutional provisions defining the procedures elected officials must utilize in order to exercise the people's sovereign power reflect the people's conscious choices regarding how, and under what circumstances, their power may be exercised by elected representatives. These choices have meaning—they reflect the people's best efforts to structure a political system that would facilitate effective governance without fostering tyranny.

Second, embracing this argument would also flagrantly ignore the purpose of the people's choice to structure the amendment process to require something more than ratification by the voters. The legislative supermajority requirement is not a mere procedural nicety; it is a means of safeguarding the system of government created in the North Carolina Constitution by ensuring that the people's fundamental law is not altered or abolished rashly in response to the whims of a particular moment.

We next consider the status of the legislators who were elected from districts that were either unconstitutionally racially gerrymandered or from districts that needed to be redrawn to cure those racial gerrymanders. The crux of the parties' dispute centers on competing assertions regarding those individuals' entitlement to exercise power assigned to the legislature and the status of the acts they undertook post-*Covington*. Our resolution of this dispute requires us to interpret and apply cases defining three categories of individuals who purport to hold elected offices established by the North Carolina Constitution: de jure officers, de facto officers, and usurpers.

A de jure officer is one who "exercises the office as a matter of right." To be a de jure officer, an individual must (1) "possess the legal qualifications for the office in question;" (2) "be lawfully chosen to such office;" and (3) have been "qualified to perform the duties of such office." De jure officers may legitimately exercise all the powers assigned to an office because they have assumed office in accordance with all legal requirements.

It would be reasonable to presume that any individual other than a de jure officer lacks the capacity to exercise the authority assigned to a governmental office. However, this Court long ago concluded that such a rule would lead to chaos, undermine the orderly administration of government, and unfairly burden individuals who reasonably relied on the acts of apparent officeholders. Under the common law de facto officer doctrine, an individual "who occupies an office under some color of right, and for the time being performs its duties with public acquiescence, though having no right in fact" may exercise the powers attendant to that office in ways that bind third parties and the public. A paradigmatic example of a de facto officer is someone who is validly elected to an office, but who is later determined to have been ineligible to assume that office for failure to satisfy all legal prerequisites for holding office. Until it is conclusively determined that the officeholder is not a de jure officer, the officeholder is a de facto officer whose acts "are valid in law in respect to the public whom he represents and to third persons with whom he deals officially."

Still, not all individuals who claim to hold an office may exercise the powers of that office. North Carolina law recognizes a third category of putative officeholders: usurpers. In contrast to a de facto officer who "goes into office under color of authority," a usurper is an individual "who takes possession of an office without any authority." Essentially, a usurper is someone who purports to exercise the powers of an office that the individual has no legitimate claim to hold, provided that the invalidity of the putative officeholder's claim is readily apparent to the public.

The status of these legislators after *Covington* was decided is less certain. Plaintiff argues that these legislators were nothing more than usurpers, such that the Voter ID and Tax Cap Amendments are necessarily void. Legislative Defendants argue that, at a minimum, these legislators remained de facto officers who were entitled to exercise all the powers assigned to the legislature. Our cases, and cases from other jurisdictions, do not conclusively answer this question.

Plaintiff's argument that legislators elected from unconstitutionally racially gerrymandered districts became usurpers is straightforward. To validly hold an office established by the North Carolina Constitution, an individual must assume that office in a manner consistent with the legal requirements of the United States and North Carolina Constitutions. If the individual assumes office in a manner inconsistent with those legal requirements, that individual is not a de jure officer. Plaintiff contends that once it is conclusively (and publicly) determined that an individual lacks a valid claim to an office, that individual becomes a usurper.

The problem with this theory is that it invites the exact problem the de facto officer doctrine was created to avoid: the chaos and confusion that would result from declaring that the people lacked any representatives empowered to exercise any legislative authority for more than a year. Conceptually, plaintiff has no answer to the question of why, if its theory is correct, any actions undertaken by the challenged legislators post-*Covington* can be upheld.

Historically, legislators who were determined to have been elected as a result of an unconstitutional apportionment have been permitted to continue serving in office until after the conclusion of the next general election. There is also a longstanding public policy against leaving public offices vacant.

But while the de facto officer doctrine is properly invoked to stave off the possibility of "endless confusion and expense," it does not change the fact that individuals exercising the power of an office assumed that office through unlawful means. Reflexively applying the de facto officer doctrine runs the risk of degrading the importance of the constitutionally prescribed processes through which individuals assume governmental office.

In sum, legislators elected due to unconstitutional racial gerrymandering did not lack any colorable claim to exercise the powers delegated to the legislature. Actions undertaken by these legislators are presumptively valid as the actions of de facto officers. But we are unconvinced that recognizing the challenged legislators' status as de facto officers compels the conclusion that these legislators possessed the authority to initiate the process of amending the North Carolina Constitution. The de facto officer doctrine is a creation of the common law, introduced for prudential and practical reasons in response to issues that arise when a putative officeholder exercises the powers of an office. Although we agree that the de facto officer doctrine applies in this case, we conclude that we must define its scope in view of the interests the doctrine was designed to advance.

The same prudential considerations do not justify applying the de facto officer doctrine to completely shield proposed constitutional amendments from collateral review when some number of legislators who voted on the amendment had already been determined to lack de jure status. The North Carolina Constitution itself draws a distinction between ordinary legislation and legislation initiating the process of altering or abolishing North Carolina's fundamental law. The constitution imposes heightened procedural requirements for enacting constitutional amendments precisely because the people did not wish to see their fundamental law altered or abolished in response to everyday exigencies. Preserving de facto legislators' authority to initiate the amendment process in all circumstances is not only unnecessary to achieve the doctrine's goal of preventing chaos and maintaining the orderly administration of government, but it is also contrary to the theory and structure of government enacted by the North Carolina Constitution.

Constitutional amendments can work dramatic changes to our system of government that cannot easily be revisited. The people's power to alter or abolish the North Carolina Constitution is limited only by the United States Constitution under the terms of the Supremacy Clause. Unlike ordinary legislation, a new constitutional amendment can fundamentally change or repudiate then-existing constitutional provisions and principles. If a legislator's de facto authority is unlimited, legislators who do not lawfully represent the will of the people could exercise legislative powers to evade democratic accountability and entrench themselves and their chosen policies by redefining how the people's sovereign power is allocated and exercised.

For example, legislators could present a proposed amendment constitutionalizing a particular policy alongside another amendment providing that, going forward, the constitution can only be amended with the unanimous consent of all legislators and approval by a ninety-nine percent majority of voters. Legislators could present a proposed amendment overruling a judicial decision conclusively establishing that the districts they were elected from violated the North Carolina Constitution and extending their own terms in office. Legislators could present a proposed amendment targeting a group of citizens who had been unconstitutionally excluded from the democratic process with particular burdens or devaluing the voice of that same group of citizens in the political process.

We believe the trial court was correct to draw a distinction between ordinary legislation on the one hand and legislation initiating the process of amending the North Carolina Constitution on the other. Still, further inquiry is needed before invalidating a challenged constitutional amendment. Given the risk of confusion that may arise when a court retroactively examines a constitutional amendment that has recently been approved by a majority of North Carolina voters, a constitutional amendment enacted by a legislature composed of unconstitutionally elected members should only be invalidated when the threat to popular sovereignty and democratic self-rule is substantial. While the North Carolina Constitution demands that courts scrutinize legislation proposing constitutional amendments when the authority of legislators to do so is challenged, prudential considerations demand that courts exercise "this most important and delicate power of holding legislation invalid" only when doing so is clearly necessary. A court must consider the following questions when determining whether to apply the de facto officer doctrine to uphold legislation proposing constitutional amendments enacted under these circumstances.

First, as a threshold matter, a court must consider whether the votes of legislators who were elected as a result of unconstitutional gerrymandering were potentially decisive. This inquiry is necessary because it is individual *legislators* whose claim to office is constitutionally deficient; the *legislature* as a whole has not lost its authority to exercise the people's sovereign power. When a sufficient number of legislators elected in a manner consistent with the constitution approve a bill, there is little reason to doubt that the bill reflects the will of the people as expressed by individuals properly authorized to exercise the powers delegated to the legislature.

In this case, there is no doubt that the votes of legislators elected as a result of unconstitutional gerrymandering could have been decisive. Approving a bill to present a constitutional amendment to the voters requires a supermajority of three-fifths, and Legislative Defendants do not challenge the trial court's finding that "curing the widespread and sweeping racial gerrymander required that over two-thirds of the North Carolina House and Senate districts be redrawn." It is indisputable that plaintiff will satisfy this threshold inquiry. Nonetheless, under different circumstances—for example, if the bills proposing the amendments had passed by a margin larger than the number of legislators who were not de jure officers—no further inquiry would be required, and the prudential considerations justifying the de facto officer doctrine would require leaving the legislature's actions undisturbed.

However, when as in this case the unconstitutionally elected legislators were sufficient in number to be decisive in the vote on a bill proposing a constitutional amendment, three further factors must be examined to determine if a challenged constitutional amendment so gravely threatens principles of popular sovereignty and democratic self-rule as to require retroactive invalidation. Courts must consider whether there is a substantial risk that a challenged constitutional amendment will immunize legislators from democratic accountability going forward or perpetuate the ongoing exclusion of a category of voters from the political process. When either of these situations occur, a legislature that did not fully represent the people of North Carolina has sought to entrench itself by redefining who "the people" are and how they govern themselves—the legislature has attempted to legitimate and perpetuate an otherwise legally deficient claim to exercise the people's political power and, in the process, sought to preempt the people's capacity to reassert their will consistent with the terms of their fundamental law. Under these circumstances, judicial intervention is necessary in light of "the importance of giving effect to already stated expressions of the popular will."

Thus, when the votes of legislators elected due to an unconstitutional gerrymander could have been decisive in enacting a bill proposing a constitutional amendment, courts must assess whether there is a substantial risk that the challenged amendment will (1) immunize legislators from democratic accountability; (2) perpetuate the ongoing exclusion of a category of voters from the political process; or (3) intentionally discriminate against a particular category of citizens who were also discriminated against in the political process leading to the legislators' election. If any of these factors are present, then the balance of equities requires the court to invalidate the challenged amendment. If these factors are not present—or if the legislators elected due to an unconstitutional gerrymander were not so numerous as to be potentially decisive in the vote to put a proposed amendment to the people—the challenged amendment must be left in place.

Although the questions raised in this appeal are novel, the answers can be found in the principles that are the foundation of North Carolina's system of government as expressed in multiple provisions of the North Carolina Constitution, the people's fundamental law. The people have reserved to themselves the power to amend or replace these principles and provisions. While they have assigned the legislature a role in the amendment process, the potentially transformative consequences of amendments that could change basic tenets of our constitutional system of government warrant heightened scrutiny of amendments enacted through a process that required the participation of legislators whose claim to represent the people's will has been disputed. Consistent with these constitutional principles and provisions, we conclude that acts proposing constitutional amendments passed by a legislature composed of a substantial number of legislators elected from unconstitutionally racially gerrymandered legislative districts, after the unlawfulness of those districts has been conclusively established, are not automatically shielded by application of the de facto officer doctrine.

BERGER, J., dissenting.

At issue today is not what our constitution says. The people of North Carolina settled that question when they amended the constitution to include the Voter ID and Tax Cap Amendments. These amendments were placed on the November 2018 ballot by the constitutionally required three-fifths majority in the legislature. On November 6, 2018, the citizens of North Carolina voted overwhelmingly to approve the North Carolina Voter ID Amendment and the North Carolina Income Tax Cap Amendment. More than 2,000,000 people, or 55.49% of voters, voted in favor of Voter ID, while the Tax Cap Amendment was approved by more than 57% of North Carolina's voters.

Instead, the majority engages in an inquiry that is judicially forbidden— what *should* our constitution say? The majority concedes that constitutional procedures were followed, yet they invalidate more than 4.1 million votes and disenfranchise more than 55% of North Carolina's electorate. Unwilling to accept the results of a procedurally sound election that enshrined the Voter ID and Tax Cap Amendments in our state constitution, the majority nullifies the will of the people and precludes governance by the majority.

Voiding constitutional authority is far more egregious than picking and choosing which category of laws to invalidate. Striking at the very heart of our form of government, the majority unilaterally reassigns constitutional duties and declares that the will of the judges is superior to the will of the people of North Carolina. At what point does the seizure of popular sovereignty by this Court violate the federal constitution?

One could argue that this Court has circumvented the will of the people and subverted our republican form of government guaranteed in Article IV, Section 4 of the United States Constitution through its "systematic frustration of the will of a majority of the electorate of the State." In Federalist No. 39, James Madison stated that a republic is "a government which derives all its powers directly or indirectly from the great body of the people, and is administered by persons holding their offices during pleasure, for a limited period, or during good behavior." Anti-Federalist author Centinel stated that, in a republican government, "the people are the sovereign, and their sense or opinion is the criterion of every public measure. When this ceases to be the case, the nature of the government is changed."

More than eighty years ago, this Court rejected as nonjusticiable the same argument plaintiffs ask us to address today. Specifically, this Court declined to interject itself in such a dispute, and we noted that the General Assembly's knowing failure to abide by constitutional directives in apportionment did not prevent the legislature from performing constitutional functions designated exclusively to that branch.

It is ironic that the majority finds the ultimate safeguard for the will of the people to be four individuals on this Court, not the more than 4.1 million votes cast for the Voter ID and Tax Cap Amendments. The gatekeeping function for inclusion of any such proposals into our constitution rests solely with the people and the political process, not this Court.

A governmental official either has the authority to act, or he does not. Consistent with this fact, well-established judicial doctrines have emerged. Specifically, courts have recognized instances in which governmental officials maintain the full power of their office, and other occasions when individuals attempt to occupy an office but have no power to act. The former may be either de jure or de facto officers; the latter are known as usurpers. None of these recognized legal distinctions, however, have ever limited or hybridized legislative power as the majority does here. Imagining its creation as the "best" for the situation at hand, the majority excises from legislative authority those actions it deems out of the "ordinary."

Even assuming that the members of the 2018 General Assembly were not de jure officers, those legislators certainly possessed full de facto authority. "A *de facto* officer may be defined as one whose title is not good in law, but who is in fact in the unobstructed possession of an office and discharging its duties in full view of the public, in such manner and under such circumstances as not to present the appearance of being an intruder or usurper." A de facto officer's official acts are categorically valid, even if that individual is found to lack de jure legal authority.

This decision is a radical departure from mere judicial review as this Court expands its reach beyond constitutional guardrails and unilaterally amends the constitution. The majority restructures power constitutionally designated to the legislature, plainly violates the principles of non-justiciability, and wrests popular sovereignty from the people. The sober people of this state will be left to wonder why, if they amended the constitution, those provisions are not in effect. The negative fallout of today's decision will be felt most by the people of this state and the confidence they have in this institution. Sadly, they will experience the chaos and confusion courts seek to avoid.

NOTE

As the majority acknowledges, the North Carolina Supreme Court's 4-3 decision charts a new remedial path in gerrymandering litigation. It creates the possibility that some actions of a legislature—here the initiation and subsequent passage of two constitutions amendments—could be retroactively undone, It remains to be seen what the state trial court will do on remand and what further appellate review will bring. Could similar modifications of the de facto officer doctrine apply in other settings, including later challenges to statutes enacted by an improperly elected legislature? Should the majority's approach apply to the 18 or so States that (unlike North Carolina) permit initiatives—constitutional amendments proposed by the people and democratically approved directly by them? Is there anything to the dissent's claim that the Court's interpretation of the North Carolina Constitution violates the U.S. Constitution? If so, on what ground? We return to the issue at the end of this chapter.

C. REGULATING ELECTIONS

The States in the twenty-first century first began proposing and adopting "voter-ID laws" and, to a lesser extent, "proof of U.S. citizenship" laws as requirements for voting. In *Crawford v. Marion County Election Board* (2008), the U.S. Supreme Court rejected federal challenges to an Indiana law requiring photo identification to vote. The Court determined that the burdens on voters to obtain a photo ID were relatively minimal compared to the state's interest in ensuring the integrity of its elections. In *Crawford*'s aftermath, there have been battles over the requirements of state constitutions in this area, now the key potential constitutional limit on voter ID laws and related requirements. What follows are decisions coming down on both sides of the issue.

1. Voter ID Litigation

LEAGUE OF WOMEN VOTERS OF WISCONSIN EDUCATION NETWORK v. WALKER
851 N.W.2d 302 (Wis. 2014)

ROGGENSACK, J.

The League of Women Voters of Wisconsin Education Network and its president bring a facial challenge to the state's voter-identification law under the Wisconsin Constitution. We conclude that the legislature did not exceed its authority under Article III of the Wisconsin Constitution when it required electors to present acceptable photo identification. Since 1859, we have held that "it is clearly within the legislature's province to require any person offering to vote to furnish such proof as it deems requisite that he is a qualified elector." The requirement to present photo identification also comes within the legislature's authority to enact laws providing for the registration of electors under Article III because the identification is the mode by which election officials verify that a potential voter is the elector listed on the registration list.

Act 23 requires an elector to present one of nine acceptable forms of photo identification in order to vote. Generally stated, these include: Wisconsin Department of Transportation (DOT) issued driver's license; DOT issued photo identification card; United States uniformed service identification card; United States passport; United States naturalization certificate issued within two years preceding the election; federally recognized Wisconsin Native American tribe's identification card; Wisconsin university or college student identification card; and a citation or notice of driver's license suspension.

If an elector does not present acceptable identification on the day of the election in which he or she offers to vote, the elector may cast a provisional ballot. However, the provisional ballot will be counted only if the elector presents identification at the polling location before 4:00 p.m. on the day of the election or at the office of the municipal clerk or board of election commissioners by the following Friday.

The qualifications of an elector entitled to vote are set out in Article III, Section 1 of the Wisconsin Constitution. Article III, Section 2 of the Wisconsin Constitution addresses implementation of voting rights through legislation. Those two sections are the focus of our review and they provide in their entirety:

> Electors. Section 1. Every United States citizen age 18 or older who is a resident of an election district in this state is a qualified elector of that district.
>
> Implementation. Section 2. Laws may be enacted:
>
> (1) Defining residency.
>
> (2) Providing for registration of electors.
>
> (3) Providing for absentee voting.
>
> (4) Excluding from the right of suffrage persons:
>
> (a) Convicted of a felony, unless restored to civil rights.
>
> (b) Adjudged by a court to be incompetent or partially incompetent, unless the judgment specifies that the person is capable of understanding the objective of the elective process or the judgment is set aside.
>
> (5) Subject to ratification by the people at a general election, extending the right of suffrage to additional classes.

The League's major argument is that the law is unconstitutional because being required to present photo identification is an additional elector qualification beyond what is listed in Article III, Section 1. As provided in full above, Section 1 requires that an elector be a United States citizen, at least 18 years of age, a resident of Wisconsin and a resident of the district in which the elector offers to vote.

We agree with the League that the legislature cannot add to these qualifications for electors. As we have explained "the persons who may exercise the right of suffrage and the day of election are fixed by the constitution." However, we also noted that "these provisions are not and were never intended to be self-executing or exclusive of regulation in other respects. The power to prescribe the manner of conducting elections is clearly within the province of the legislature."

The League agrees that the legislature has the authority to pass laws that allow election officials to ascertain whether a potential voter possesses the constitutional qualifications required of an elector. As the League acknowledges, this includes the ability to require a potential voter to identify himself or herself in some fashion, thereby answering the question, "Are you who you say you are, a constitutionally qualified elector?"

The focus of the League's argument is that the law's presentation requirement goes beyond such authority because it "bars constitutionally qualified voters from voting." This argument fails for several reasons.

Under the League's proposed logic, "virtually any requirement placed on voters would be an unconstitutional and impermissible additional 'qualification.'" Stated otherwise, if the League were correct, mode and manner requirements for voting would not be permissible because the State could not enforce them.

This conclusion is bolstered by other ways in which an elector who fails to comply with indisputably valid election laws can lose the opportunity to vote. For example, an elector who fails to arrive at a polling location on time can lose his right to vote in that election. Therefore, although the elector is a United States citizen, over the age of 18, and a resident of the election district in which he or she offers to vote, if the elector does not arrive at a polling place between the hours of 7 a.m. and 8 p.m., and is not voting absentee, the elector may lose his right to vote in that election. The same holds true for an elector who fails to arrive at the correct polling place. Yet none of these laws that affect the manner of voting can be seriously characterized as additional elector qualifications.

Our decision is supported by the decisions of courts in other jurisdictions that have considered whether the requirement of presenting photo identification prior to voting is an additional elector qualification. For example, in *City of Memphis v. Hargett* (Tenn. 2013), the Tennessee Supreme Court considered the same constitutional challenge the League presents to us. The court began by reviewing the Tennessee Constitution, which required that "one must be at least eighteen years of age, a United States citizen, a Tennessee resident and registered to vote."

In rejecting the contention that the photo identification requirement imposed by the Tennessee law was an additional voter qualification, the court concluded that "the photo ID requirement is more properly classified as a regulation pertaining to an existing voting qualification." The court explained that photo identification was merely a "mode of ascertaining" whether the potential voter possessed the necessary constitutional qualifications to vote.

In *Democratic Party of Ga. v. Perdue* (2011), the Georgia Supreme Court addressed whether requiring the presentation of government-issued photo identification to identify qualified voters was an additional voter qualification. The court explained that the right to vote is guaranteed by the Georgia Constitution, and it cannot be denied or taken away by legislative enactment. However, the legislature may prescribe "reasonable regulations as to how these qualifications shall be determined." The court concluded that photo identification was "a reasonable procedure for verifying that the individual appearing to vote in person is actually the same person who registered to vote."

In *League of Women Voters of Ind., Inc. v. Rokita* (Ind. 2010), the Indiana Supreme Court rejected the additional qualification contention. The court first explained that the legislature could "not by statutory enactment add a substantive qualification to the right to vote." However, the court further explained that "[r]equiring qualified voters to present a specified form of identification is not in the nature of such a personal, individual characteristic or attribute but rather functions merely as an election regulation to verify the voter's identity."

Although none of the state constitutions is word for word identical with

Article III, Section 1 of the Wisconsin Constitution, the reasoning of all three supreme courts is consistent with our own. Accordingly, we now turn to Article III, Section 2, which expressly permits the legislature to provide for registration of voters.

In addition to the authority to "require any person offering to vote to furnish such proof as it deems requisite that he is a qualified elector," the legislature may pass five types of election-related laws. One of those enumerated types are laws that "provide for registration of electors."

The court of appeals succinctly summarized the current registration system as follows: Election officials compile registration information into "poll lists" for use at polling places, containing "the full name and address of each registered elector." Thus, poll lists memorialize who is registered to vote in a given election in a given voting district and they play a critical role in the voting process. When a potential voter arrives at the polling place for his or her residence in a given election, he or she "shall state his or her full name and address" to election officials, who "shall verify that the name and address" provided match the name and address on the poll list.

Requiring an elector to identify himself or herself by stating his or her full name and address is unquestionably part of the registration process. After all, there would be no point to compiling a list of registered electors if there were no means by which to ascertain if the person offering to vote was an elector appearing on the list. Identification of registered voters by a government-issued photo identification is the mode of identification that the legislature has chosen.

Based on the League's arguments before us, we can see no meaningful grounds on which to distinguish the photo identification requirement from the requirement that an elector state his or her full name and address in order to verify that it matches the registration list. Both requirements permit use of registration lists to verify at the polling place that the potential voter is registered. An elector who fails to comply with either procedure cannot vote. Furthermore, the League does not rely on the difficulty and inconvenience of procuring an acceptable form of identification. Therefore, the ease with which most electors will be able to state their names and addresses is not relevant to our decision in this case.

We conclude that the League has failed to prove Act 23 unconstitutional beyond a reasonable doubt.

ABRAHAMSON, C.J., dissenting.

"Who are to be the electors? Not the rich, more than the poor; not the learned, more than the ignorant; not the haughty heirs of distinguished names, more than the humble sons of obscurity and unpropitious fortune. The electors are to be the great body of the people of the United States." The Federalist No. 57 (James Madison).

Today the court follows not James Madison—for whom Wisconsin's capital city is named—but rather Jim Crow—the name typically used to refer to repressive laws used to restrict rights, including the right to vote, of African–Americans.

Indeed the majority opinion in *NAACP v. Walker* brings the specter of Jim Crow front and center. It invalidates costs incurred by a qualified Wisconsin voter to obtain an Act 23 photo ID as an illegal de facto poll tax.

The right to vote is "a fundamental political right, because it is preservative of all rights." When an individual who is qualified under the Wisconsin Constitution goes to the polls to vote, no legislative action may prevent that person from casting a ballot: "An act of the legislature which deprives a person of the right to vote, although he has every qualification which the constitution makes necessary, cannot be sustained." *State ex rel. Knowlton v. Williams* (Wis. 1856).

Yet under the majority opinion, an individual who has fulfilled every requirement to vote—he or she is a citizen of the United States, is a resident of Wisconsin, is over the age of 18, and is registered—can nonetheless be denied the right to vote for failing to produce a government-issued photo identification enumerated in Act 23, such as a driver's license, a State identification card, a military identification card, a United States passport, certain certificates of United States naturalization, an identification by a federally recognized tribe, or certain university and college identification cards.

The State may require verification of the identity of the voter, but Act 23 severely restricts and limits the form of identification that enables a qualified voter to cast a ballot. Rather than merely verify identity, Act 23's requirement conditions the right to vote on possession of a restricted list of identifying documents; no other form of proof of identity than an Act 23 photo ID allows a qualified voter to verify identity and cast a ballot. By restricting verification of identity to only certain government-issued photo IDs, Act 23 does not condition the right to vote on *verification of identity*. Instead, Act 23 conditions the right to vote on *production of a particular identity card*. Requiring a specific photo ID is an additional qualification on the right to vote, and is therefore impermissible under the Wisconsin Constitution.

Without any evidence that in-person voter impersonation is a problem in Wisconsin, the voting restrictions that the majority opinion approves today give Wisconsin the most restrictive voting laws in America, laws that systematically disenfranchise entire classes of individuals who are without the required Act 23 photo ID. For example, an estimated 23 percent of persons aged 65 and over do not have a Wisconsin driver's license or other Act 23 photo ID.

Qualified and registered Wisconsin individuals who voted in the last election may be barred from voting in the next election under the majority opinions in *NAACP* and this case unless they obtain an Act 23 photo ID. Their vote now depends upon possession of a specific ID, not their constitutional qualifications or their identity. The possession of an Act 23 photo ID may be further contingent on the discretion of an agency administrator who determines whether they can obtain an Act 23 photo ID.

The *NAACP* majority opinion avers that it cures the unconstitutional imposition of these costs and fees through its "saving construction" of Wis. Admin. Code § Trans 102.15(3)(b)–(c). But that is not "a cure for the constitutional defect."

First, the *NAACP* majority opinion provides no process for an individual to demonstrate that he or she is "constitutionally 'unable'" to obtain the necessary documentation required. The *NAACP* majority opinion appears to leave discretion in the hands of the Department of Transportation administrator and his or her designees but provides no guidance to the Department of Transportation or to the public about proper procedures and the rights of qualified voters. Second, the section of administrative regulations that the *NAACP* majority opinion "construes" to cure Act 23's constitutional defects appears to apply only to documents regarding proof of name and date of birth, not to other documentation required to obtain an Act 23 photo ID. A naturalization certificate required to prove citizenship or a marriage certificate required to prove identity may require payments to a government agency; these documents are not covered by the *NAACP* majority opinion's "saving" regulation. Third, fees and costs other than fees paid directly to government agencies may be required to obtain an Act 23 photo ID. These costs are similarly unaddressed and unresolved and may be invidious discrimination.

Thus, although the *NAACP* majority opinion appears to deem invalid any fees and costs paid to any government agency necessary for documentation to obtain an Act 23 photo ID, its supposed "saving construction" of the administrative regulations fails to cure the myriad variety of costs that Act 23 imposes on individuals attempting to obtain the photo ID necessary to exercise the right to vote. The *NAACP* majority opinion invalidates the unconstitutional imposition of some de facto poll taxes as part of Act 23, but leaves other de facto poll taxes, fees, and costs intact.

MILWAUKEE BRANCH OF THE NAACP v. WALKER
851 N.W.2d 262 (Wis. 2014)

ROGGENSACK, J.

Plaintiffs contend that Act 23 is invalid because "it would severely burden a significant number of qualified voters but is not reasonably necessary or designed to deter fraud or otherwise effect an important government interest." Plaintiffs identify burdens of time, inconvenience and costs associated with Act 23.

In *League of Women Voters of Wisconsin Education Network, Inc. v. Walker*, also released today, we concluded that requiring an elector to present acceptable photo identification in order to vote is not an additional elector qualification. In the present case, we conclude that the burdens of time and inconvenience associated with obtaining photo identification are not undue burdens on the right to vote.

We conclude, as did the United Stated Supreme Court in *Crawford v. Marion County Election Board,* that "the inconvenience of making a trip to a state motor vehicle office, gathering the required documents, and posing for a photograph surely does not qualify as a substantial burden on the right to vote." Furthermore, photo identification is a condition of our times where more and more personal interactions are being modernized to require proof of identity with a specified type of photo identification. With respect to these familiar burdens, which accompany many of our everyday tasks, we conclude that Act 23 does not constitute an undue burden on the right to vote. Payment to a government agency, however, is another story.

Act 23 provides that the DOT "may not charge a fee to an applicant for the initial issuance, renewal, or reinstatement of an identification card" when "the applicant requests that the identification card be provided without charge for purposes of voting." On its face, then, the law prohibits a government or its agencies from requiring any elector, rich or poor, to pay a fee as a condition to obtaining a DOT photo identification card to vote. The mandate of Act 23 is consistent with the Wisconsin tradition of "jealously guarding and protecting" the fundamental right to vote.

Plaintiffs produced evidence at trial that, in the course of obtaining a DOT photo identification card for voting, government agencies charged them fees to obtain supporting documents for their applications. A common example is a birth certificate, which is satisfactory proof of name, date of birth and citizenship, and can cost $20 to obtain. The requirement for such documents arose under administrative rules that implement Act 23.

In order to resolve the conflict between Act 23 and Wis. Admin. Code § Trans 102.15(3)(a), we interpret the administrative rules and explain that the discretion of the Division of Motor Vehicles (DMV) administrators must be exercised in a constitutionally sufficient manner. Such exercise of discretion requires the issuance of DOT photo identification cards for voting without requiring documents for which an elector must pay a fee to a government agency. Our conclusion employs a saving construction of the regulation, conforms to Act 23's mandate and relieves a severe burden on the right to vote that would otherwise exist.

The record provides extensive testimony about trips to DMV offices by individuals who sought to obtain acceptable photo identification for voting.

Some of these trips were at quite a distance and many trips were repeats because either the line to obtain a photo identification card was too long or the applicant did not have the documents that DMV required in order to issue a photo identification card. Some witnesses testified that they had spent in excess of six hours in their efforts.

No one who testified thought the process of obtaining a DOT photo identification card was easy. However, all were successful, except two applicants, Ruthelle R. Frank and Ricky T. Lewis. They were unable to obtain photo identification cards because of problems with their birth certificates that may require court action to correct.

Few cases have parsed the constitutional significance of time and inconvenience burdens on the right to vote. However, *Crawford* did, to some extent, when it considered the burden that "life's vagaries" can impose and noted that:

> A photo identification requirement imposes some burdens on voters that other methods of identification do not share. For example, a voter may lose his photo identification, may have his wallet stolen on the way to the polls, or may not resemble the photo in the identification because he recently grew a beard.

Crawford also went on to explain that "the inconvenience of making a trip to a state motor vehicle office, gathering the required documents, and posing for a photograph surely does not qualify as a substantial burden on the right to vote, or even represent a significant increase over the usual burdens of voting." We agree with that assessment.

Moreover, we note that photo identification is, to some extent, a condition of our times. Many important personal interactions are being modernized to require proof of identity with photo identification. For example, years ago, driver licenses did not require a photograph of the licensee; now Wisconsin driver licenses do. Photo identification is now required to purchase a firearm, to board a commercially operated airline flight, to enter some federal buildings and to obtain food stamps. Photo identification is often required to obtain a book from a public library, to cash a check, to purchase alcoholic beverages, to be admitted to many places of employment and to be seen by one's own physician for a personal appointment. Elector identification is certainly as important an identification as any of the above examples.

The federal government also has directed states to require photo identification in circumstances where the federal government was not involved in the past. For example, the REAL ID Act of 2005 sets forth requirements for state driver licenses wherein underlying documents are required to obtain or renew a driver's license in a state that has implemented the REAL ID Act, as Wisconsin has. As inconvenient as it may be, photo identification is here to stay. It is a fact of life to which we all have to adjust.

We do not minimize the difficulties that some who applied for Act 23–

acceptable photo identification have encountered in the past or will encounter in the future. However, the time and inconvenience incurred are not severe burdens on the right to vote. In many cases, these familiar burdens are no more of an imposition than is the exercise of the franchise itself, which can involve waiting in long lines and traveling distances in order to personally cast a ballot on election day.

In addition, we note that the NAACP and Voces are two of Wisconsin's most conscientious and capable organizations in regard to encouraging and facilitating voting. They will know what documentation DMV requires to issue DOT photo identification cards for voting and will work to assure that members of the African–American and Latino communities will be well prepared for their trips to DMV. NAACP and Voces have seen the power that the voting booth can give to their communities and will continue to work to assure that all eligible voters have the opportunity to exercise their franchise.

We now turn to the other burden that the plaintiffs identified and the circuit court found, which are the costs incurred in obtaining a DOT-issued photo identification card for voting. Some costs involved payments for transportation to DMV offices or time taken from work. They are not costs paid to a government agency nor are they regulated by Act 23. In some respects, they are similar to those costs incurred in casting an in-person ballot. They are not a severe burden on the right to vote.

Plaintiffs also provided evidence of payments to government agencies to obtain documents required by DMV to issue DOT photo identification cards to vote. Plaintiffs do not employ the term "poll tax" in regard to those payments and we do not define them as poll taxes. Plaintiffs assert, however, that those payments are an unconstitutional burden on the right to vote. Because other jurisdictions have characterized payments to government agencies to obtain documents necessary to voting as a de facto poll tax and because there are compelling reasons to assure that Wisconsin does not impose an unconstitutional fee as a condition of voting, we interpret Act 23 with both characterizations in mind.

Act 23 provides that DOT "may not charge a fee to an applicant for the initial issuance, renewal, or reinstatement of an identification card" when "the applicant requests that the identification card be provided without charge for purposes of voting." This provision prohibits DOT from causing any elector, rich or poor, to pay a fee as a condition to voting.

However, plaintiffs incurred costs due to payments to government agencies for documents that DMV required in order to issue DOT photo identification cards for voting. These costs were not paid to DOT or its division, DMV; they were paid to other government agencies. One example of such a cost is the payment for certified copies of birth certificates that DMV has required as proof of name, date of birth and citizenship.

Other state supreme courts have examined claims that fees paid to state agencies to obtain documents required as part of the application process for state photo identification cards violated electors' constitutional rights. For example, in *In re Request for Advisory Opinion Regarding Constitutionality of 2005 PA 71,* the Michigan Supreme Court considered a facial challenge to a Michigan statute that required potential voters to identify themselves with a government-issued photo identification card. As part of its discussion, the court examined whether ancillary charges for documents necessary to obtaining the required photo identification card operated as a de facto poll tax that violated the Michigan Constitution or United States Constitution.

In concluding that the Michigan statute was not a de facto poll tax, the court explained:

> The statute does not condition the right to vote on the payment of any fee. A voter who does not otherwise possess adequate photo identification is not required to incur the costs of obtaining photo identification as a condition of voting. Instead, a voter may simply sign an affidavit in the presence of an election inspector. Nothing in the statute contemplates that a voter is required to incur any costs in the execution of an affidavit.

In *City of Memphis v. Hargett,* the Tennessee Supreme Court considered a Tennessee statute that required, with limited exceptions, electors to provide photographic proof of identity. Under the Tennessee law, an elector who attempted to vote in person, but was unable to produce valid evidence of identification and did not fall within the exceptions to the law, may cast a provisional ballot, which would be counted if the voter presented valid proof of identity within two days after the election.

Two voters presented non-compliant photo identifications issued by the City of Memphis and cast provisional ballots when their identifications were not accepted. Those voters and the City then challenged the statute, bringing both facial and as-applied constitutional challenges. In upholding the constitutionality of the Tennessee statute against the challenges, part of which contended that the law amounted to a de facto poll tax, the court pointed out that:

> This state's Act contains an exception for any in-person voter who "is indigent and unable to obtain proof of identification without payment of a fee." By its plain language, this provision exempts from the photo ID requirement any voter unable to pay the fees needed to obtain valid evidence of identification, *including any fee associated with the documentation necessary to obtain a "free" photo ID card* pursuant to section 55–50–336(g)(1). Because of this provision, we cannot endorse the Plaintiffs' characterization of the photo ID requirement as a poll tax.

There, indigency operated as an exception to payment of direct and ancillary fees while preserving the right to vote.

The voter identification laws of Michigan, Tennessee and Indiana all included a provision by which a voter could cast a ballot without paying money to a government agency. Act 23 similarly provides that DOT "may not charge a fee to an applicant for the initial issuance, renewal, or reinstatement of an identification card" when "the applicant requests that the identification card be provided without charge for purposes of voting."

Requiring payment to a government agency to obtain a DOT photo identification card for voting puts the administrative regulation on a collision course with Act 23's directive that DOT "may not charge a fee." It also would be a severe burden on the right to vote.

Why is this burden severe? The usual payment of $20 for a certified copy of a birth certificate is modest and does not approach the sizeable costs parsed in other cases that bear on voting.

The modest fees for documents necessary to prove identity would be a severe burden on the constitutional right to vote not because they would be difficult for some to pay. Rather, they would be a severe burden because the State of Wisconsin may not enact a law that requires any elector, rich or poor, to pay a fee of any amount to a government agency as a precondition to the elector's exercising his or her constitutional right to vote.

Given our conclusion that it would be contrary to Act 23 and a severe burden on the right to vote if an elector were obligated to pay a fee to a government agency in order to obtain documents required for a DOT photo identification card to vote, we now consider whether a saving construction that is consistent with the statutory mandate and the Wisconsin constitution is possible. If a saving construction of the administrative rule preserves the constitutionality of the statute, we will employ it.

Here, Wis. Admin. Code § Trans 102.15(3)(a) requires documents for "Proof of Name and Date of Birth," that other statutes, such as Wis. Stat. § 69.22, require payment to provide. This creates a conflict with Act 23's directive to provide DOT photo identification cards for voting without charge.

However, DMV administrators have discretion under Wis. Admin. Code § Trans 102.15(3)(b) to excuse the failure to provide documents when DOT photo identification cards for voting are requested. Because the exercise of a DMV administrator's discretion has constitutional ramifications when a DOT photo identification card for voting is requested, we note that we are obliged to choose the interpretation of Wis. Admin. Code § Trans 102.15(3)(b) that does not conflict with the Wisconsin Constitution.

Stated otherwise, to invoke an administrator's discretion in the issuance of a DOT photo identification card to vote, an elector: (1) makes a written petition to a DMV administrator as directed by Wis. Admin. Code § Trans 102.15(3)(b) set forth above; (2) asserts he or she is "unable" to provide documents required by § Trans 102.15(3)(a) without paying a fee to a government agency to obtain them; (3) asserts those documents are "unavailable" without the payment of such a fee; and (4) asks for an exception to the provision of § Trans 102.15(3)(a) documents whereby proof of name and date of birth that have been provided are accepted. § Trans 102.15(3)(b) and (c). Upon receipt of a petition for an exception, the administrator, or his or her designee, shall exercise his or her discretion in a constitutionally sufficient manner.

We conclude that the burdens of time and inconvenience associated with obtaining Act 23–acceptable photo identification are not severe burdens on the right to vote and do not invalidate the law. The burdens of time and inconvenience of obtaining Act 23–acceptable photo identification are in many respects no more of an imposition than is casting an in-person ballot on election day. Furthermore, photo identification is a condition of our times where more and more personal interactions are being modernized to require proof of identity with a specified type of photo identification before proceeding.

The payments at issue arise under Wisconsin administrative rules that implement Act 23. Therefore, we construed those rules and explained how the discretion of the DMV administrator must be exercised in a constitutionally sufficient manner. Such exercise of discretion requires the issuance of DOT photo identification cards for voting without requiring documents for which a fee continues to be charged by a government agency. In so doing, we employ a saving construction of Wis. Admin. Code § Trans 102.15(3)(b) and relieve the severe burden that would otherwise exist due to costs levied by government agencies.

Because Act 23 does not place a severe burden on the exercise of the franchise, we apply rational basis scrutiny and conclude that Act 23 is reasonably related to the State's significant interests.

NOTE

In addition to the Wisconsin cases, several state supreme courts have rejected state constitutional challenges to voter identification laws. *See, e.g., City of Memphis v. Hargett*, 414 S.W.3d 88 (Tenn. 2013); *Democratic Party of Georgia v. Perdue*, 707 S.E.2d 67 (Ga. 2011); and *League of Women Voters of Ind., Inc. v. Rokita*, 929 N.E.2d 758 (Ind. 2010). Two decisions that upheld such challenges are *Martin v. Kohls*, 444 S.W.2d 844 (Ark. 2014), and *Weinshenk v. Missouri*, 203 S.W.3d 201 (Mo. 2006). Here is the *Martin* decision.

MARTIN v. KOHLS
444 S.W.2d 844 (Ark. 2014)

CORBIN, J.

On March 19, 2013, both houses of the Arkansas General Assembly passed Act 595, which required Arkansas residents to provide "proof of identity" when voting at the polls. Act 595 is entitled, "AN ACT TO REQUIRE THAT A VOTER PROVIDE PROOF OF IDENTITY WHEN VOTING; TO PROVIDE FOR THE ISSUANCE OF A VOTER IDENTIFICATION CARD; AND FOR OTHER PURPOSES." Specifically, section 1 of Act 595 requires proof of identity in the form of a voter-identification card or a document or identification card showing the voter's name and photo issued by the United States, the State of Arkansas, or an accredited postsecondary educational institution in Arkansas with an expiration date. Section 1 of Act 595 provides a list of such acceptable documentation.

The challengers claim that Act 595 (1) added a new and unconstitutional qualification to the right to vote in violation of article 3, section 1, of the Arkansas Constitution and (2) impaired the right to vote in violation of article 3, section 2, of the Arkansas Constitution.

Section 1 of article 3 of the Arkansas Constitution provides as follows:

Except as otherwise provided by this Constitution, any person may vote in an election in this state who is:

(1) A citizen of the United States;

(2) A resident of the State of Arkansas;

(3) At least eighteen (18) years of age; and

(4) Lawfully registered to vote in the election.

Act 595, as enacted, states that "any person desiring to vote in this state shall present proof of identity to the election official when appearing to vote in person either early or at the polls on election day." Specifically, section 1 of Act 595 provides the definition of "proof of identity" as follows:

(i) A voter identification card under § 7–5–322; or

(ii) A document or identification card that:

(a) Shows the name of the person to whom the document was issued;

(b) Shows a photograph of the person to whom the document was issued;

(c) Is issued by the United States, the State of Arkansas, or an accredited postsecondary educational institution in the State of Arkansas; and

(d) If displaying an expiration date:

(1) Is not expired; or

(2) Expired no more than four (4) years before the date of the election in which the person seeks to vote.

Further, section 1 lists acceptable documentation, which includes such items as a driver's license, photo-identification card, and a United States passport, that satisfy the proof-of-identity requirement.

For approximately 150 years, this court has remained steadfast in its adherence to the strict interpretation of the requisite voter qualifications articulated in the Arkansas Constitution. In *Rison v. Farr,* Farr's ballot was refused when he declined to subscribe to a statutory oath that he would support the Constitution of the United States and the Constitution of Arkansas; that he had not voluntarily borne arms against the United States or Arkansas; and that he had not aided, directly or indirectly, the Confederate authorities since April 18, 1864. We rejected this requirement, holding that, as a prerequisite to voting, the statutory oath prescribed by the Arkansas General Assembly was in direct conflict with the Arkansas Constitution.

This proposition was reaffirmed years later in *Faubus v. Miles*. In *Faubus,* the Arkansas General Assembly passed legislation to establish a system of voter registration "purporting to substitute a 'free' poll tax (for registration purposes) in lieu of a poll tax for which the voter has paid $1.00." A citizen and taxpayer filed suit challenging the constitutionality of the act, and the chancellor declared the act unconstitutional. On appeal, this court held as follows:

> It is our conclusion that the legislature has no power, in state elections to substitute said "free" poll tax for the poll tax required by Amendment 8 which provides that the voters "shall exhibit a poll tax receipt or other evidence that they have *paid* their poll tax." To hold otherwise would be to approve a subterfuge for evading the letter and the spirit of a plain constitutional provision.

Applying our well-established precedent to the present case, Act 595 cannot survive a constitutional facial challenge. Here, the Arkansas General Assembly's passage of Act 595 requires an Arkansas voter to provide a "voter identification card" or "a document or identification card." However, Act 595's added requirement of providing a proof of identity as a prerequisite to voting runs afoul of article 3, section 1, of the Arkansas Constitution. Section 1 of article 3 plainly states that any person may vote in an election who is (1) a U.S. citizen, (2) an Arkansas resident, (3) eighteen years of age, and (4) lawfully registered to vote in the election before voting in an Arkansas election. These four qualifications set forth in our state's constitution simply do not include any proof-of-identity requirement.

We adhere to the framers' intent to require the foregoing four qualifications of voters in an Arkansas election and nothing more. To hold otherwise would disenfranchise Arkansas voters and would negate "the object sought to be accomplished" by the framers of the Arkansas Constitution. Therefore, we hold that Act 595 requiring proof of identity is unconstitutional on its face and imposes a requirement that falls outside the ambit of article 3, section 1, of the Arkansas Constitution.

2. **Mail-In Voting**

McLINKO v. DEPARTMENT OF STATE
279 A.3d 539 (Pa. 2022)

DONOHUE, J.

This is a case that is steeped in the history of this Commonwealth and the development of its Constitution. More than one hundred years ago, this Court recognized that our Constitution mandates that elections be free and equal, but that "the power to regulate elections is a legislative one, which has been exercised by the General Assembly since the foundation of the government." Before the Court now is a question of whether the General Assembly overstepped the bounds of this power and violated our Constitution when it enacted legislation that allows for universal mail-in voting. For the reasons that follow, we find no constitutional violation.

The 2019 legislation at issue is commonly referred to as Act 77. For the first time it allowed all qualified voters to cast their vote by mail. Prior to Act 77's enactment, a voter was required to establish that he or she fit the criteria of an absentee voter to be able to cast a ballot by mail. Absentee voting has a long history in the Commonwealth, dating to 1864. At the time of its inception, only otherwise qualified voters who were not present in their election districts on Election Day because of active military duty were allowed to cast an absentee ballot. Both the categories of qualified voters who are permitted to cast absentee ballots and the methods for casting absentee ballots have changed over the intervening century and a half. However, since 1963, a qualified voter has been able to receive and return an absentee ballot through the mail. Act 77's universal mail-in provisions extended the ability to receive and return a ballot through the mail to the electorate without the excuse of absenteeism.

The overarching basis for this constitutional challenge is the *Chase* Court's interpretation of the term "offer to vote," which it interpreted to mean that a vote must be cast in person. The phrase has appeared in all iterations of the elections article of our Charter since 1838 including its current version.

The meaning ascribed by the *Chase* and *Lancaster City* Court to the phrase "offer to vote"—that the Constitution requires in-person voting—cannot be reconciled with the text of Article VII, Section 1, which at the time of the passage of Act 77 provided:

> Every citizen 21 years of age, possessing the following qualifications, shall be *entitled to vote* at all elections subject, however, to such laws requiring and regulating the registration of electors as the General Assembly may enact.
>
> 1. He or she shall have been a citizen of the United States at least one month.
>
> 2. He or she shall have resided in the State 90 days immediately preceding the election.
>
> 3. He or she shall have resided in the election district where he or she shall *offer to vote* at least 60 days immediately preceding the election, except that if qualified *to vote* in an election district prior to removal of residence, he or she may, if a resident of Pennsylvania, *vote* in the election district from which he or she removed his or her residence within 60 days preceding the election.

The rationale for the *Chase* Court's imposition of an in-person voting requirement was the need for other voters in a voting district to verify the bona fides of an individual appearing to cast a ballot. The Constitution it was interpreting was drafted at a time when there were no voter registration laws and, arguably, the only way to verify an individual's qualifications to vote in an election district was to allow his neighbors to identify him as qualified. This lack of verifiable qualifications to vote ended with the passage of registration laws.

Since the enactment of the Election Code in 1937, voters are required to prove their identities and qualifications prior to casting a vote. The Commonwealth relies on the Statewide Uniform Registry of Electors, which is "a single, uniform integrated computer system" that "contains a database of all registered electors in this Commonwealth." In order to register, voters submit to the Department of State their personal information, including their name, address, party affiliation, part of their Social Security number, and driver's license or state ID number.

We therefore conclude that neither *Chase* nor *Lancaster City* supports the conclusion that "offer to vote" creates in-person ballot-casting as a voter qualification in Article VII, Section 1 of the Pennsylvania Constitution in effect when Act 77 was enacted. Rather, the phrase "offer to vote" is a descriptive term, used to define the election district residency requirement found in Article VII, Section 1(3).

Having established that Section 1 does not require electors to submit their ballots in person at their polling location, it remains that submitting a ballot in person is a method by which electors may vote. Article VII, Section 4, unchanged since 1901, provides "all elections by the citizens shall be by ballot or by such other method as may be prescribed by law: Provided, that secrecy in voting be preserved."

Based on the use of such broad language, the General Assembly is authorized, pursuant to Section 4, to prescribe any process by which electors may vote. The amendment did not limit the relevant methods of casting a vote to ballot or voting machine, as were relevant at the time of its passage, but instead provided that the General Assembly could enact laws establishing "other methods" for elections by citizens, subject only to the requirement that the method preserve secrecy in voting. However, the requirement that secrecy must be preserved cannot alone inform the legislature as to what methods it may prescribe, only that those methods must maintain this secrecy. This was, and continues to be, the sole restriction found in Section 4.

Act 77 prescribed another method for elections. By application, universal mail-in voters pre-qualify to cast a ballot in their election district and request mail-in ballots, and return the completed slip to their respective county board of elections for canvassing. Nothing in Article VII, Section 4 dictates how an elector must deliver their vote for canvassing and nothing in Article VII, Section 1 requires a qualified elector to deliver a vote in person, i.e., to manually deliver the ballot to a designated official. The Constitution does not restrain the legislature from designing a method of voting in which votes can be delivered by mail by qualified electors for canvassing. Thus, pursuant to Section 4, the legislature has the authority to provide that votes can be cast by mail by all qualified electors.

MUNDY, J., dissenting.

The majority opinion takes an approach that, if not ahistorical, is at best historically selective. Its most glaring omission is its failure to come to grips with the fact that the Pennsylvania Constitution's election-related provisions have been amended on numerous occasions in the 160 years since this Court first explained that by default it requires in-person voting, and in none of those instances have the people of this Commonwealth sought to eliminate, alter, or clarify the textual basis for that ruling as it appears in our organic law. The majority also emphasizes the popularity of the legislation under review and the care with which it was debated. None of these observations has any relevance to the issue before this Court. Legislation inconsistent with our state Charter cannot gain validity through popular sentiment or careful drafting. The Constitution stands as a bulwark against the passions of the moment, and it can only be altered in the careful manner that it prescribes.

To find authorization for universal no-excuse, mail-in balloting, the majority relies almost exclusively on Section 4 of Article VII. That provision indicates elections "shall be by ballot or by such other method as may be prescribed by law" so long as ballot secrecy is maintained. But that language does not speak to the issue before this Court, as there is no dispute that mail-in voting under Act 77 is "by ballot." The ballot is mailed in, rather than completed in person at the polling place, but it is still a ballot. Given the meaning of the word "other," Section 4's reference to "other methods" plainly pertains to non-ballot methods—most notably when the provision was added to the Constitution in 1901, voting machines. It is true, as the majority emphasizes, that this language is broad enough to encompass other methods besides voting machines, including methods not yet invented. My point here is that those other methods cannot include mail-in ballots because, as noted, they must be "other" than ballots. As a consequence, Section 4's reference to "other methods" cannot accurately be understood the way the majority interprets it, as authorizing mail-in ballots. To the contrary, Section 4, standing alone, is neutral on the question of whether the ballots used in an election must be completed at the polling place, or whether they may instead be completed elsewhere and delivered by mail.

I also cannot support a reading of Article VII where everything that is not expressly prohibited is presumed to be permissible, and thereby treat all contrary authority from this Court as either *dicta* or insufficiently reasoned. Perhaps it is possible in some instances to say that an election-related constitutional provision which states the Legislature "shall" do something leaves open the possibility that it "may" do other things not mentioned. But that example is devoid of context, *i.e.*, information concerning the assumptions, the prior communications, and the prior course of conduct of the parties involved. More important, it does not align with the historical understanding of the Constitution's absentee-voting provisions, and it cannot be taken literally, as to do so would mean the Legislature, for example, has the authority to permit ten-year-old Nebraska residents to vote in Pennsylvania elections because it states Pennsylvania residents who are over 21 years old (now 18 years old by virtue of the United States Constitution) "shall be entitled to vote," but it does not expressly prohibit younger persons or non-residents from voting.

To understand why "shall" in this context and others within Article VII often carries an implication of exclusivity, it is important to recognize the unique role voting plays in a viable democracy, and that individuals will sometimes seek to corrupt the electoral process for political ends. It goes without saying that, without election integrity, democracy is no more than a façade, and a cynical one at that. The very word democracy assumes both the availability of the franchise and its integrity, neither concept being more or less important than the other.

It is self-evident that the *integrity* of electoral actions becomes more difficult to verify when they are undertaken at a distance and outside of public scrutiny: not only is fraud more difficult to detect, but the voter lacks contemporaneous assistance from election officials and so there is a greater chance for honest mistakes. Thus, the concept of mail-in ballots was virtually unknown during the early years of this Republic.

In Pennsylvania the concept of a defined place for voting has always had special prominence. The majority recognizes as much but relies on advances in voter registration schemes to suggest this need no longer exists. Even assuming the need for in-person verification is diminished or no longer exists, the originally intended meaning still applies unless and until the text has been repealed, amended, or clarified, which it has not. If the phrase "offer to vote" were inserted into the Constitution for the first time today, we might interpret it differently. But it was inserted in 1838 and should be construed according to what it meant at that time. *Chase* was decided close in time to when the provision was first included in the Constitution, and the authoring Justice participated in the constitutional convention that adopted it. The relevant constitutional text remains unchanged, and the explanation in *Chase* is so clear, that the majority must resort to demoting it through disparaging language by referring to it as an "incidental interpretation" resulting in *dicta*, and criticizing a later decision which employed the established principle of *stare decisis* as having "slavishly" adhered to precedent.

With the *Chase* decision in the books, the people of Pennsylvania amended the Constitution in 1864 to allow for absentee voting by soldiers. Notably, the people did not see fit to alter, delete, or clarify the phrase, "offer to vote"; instead, they added a section specifically giving soldiers the right to cast absentee ballots.

Our Court discussed this amendment in *Lancaster City*, a decision in which *Chase*'s status as binding precedent was cemented. In *Lancaster City*, this Court addressed whether persons other than soldiers could constitutionally be permitted to vote absentee. The Court recognized, as a general precept, that the Constitution requires an elector to tender his or her vote in person, as set forth in *Chase*, and that this rule was consistent with the view taken in "many other states during the Civil War period, where like constitutional requirements existed."

Twenty-five years after *Lancaster City*, the people of this Commonwealth expanded the privilege of absentee voting to war veterans whose injuries made them unavoidably absent from their county of residence on election day. This time, instead of directly granting a right to such persons, the Constitution was amended to authorize the General Assembly to "provide a manner" for such voting, and this provision was modified eight years later to include electors who could not vote in person due to illness or physical disability. Two years after that, Section 1 of Article VIII was changed to permit residents to vote in their old election district if they had moved less than 60 days before the election.

The history of absentee voting in Pennsylvania confirms that the electorate has always understood that any expansion of the franchise on an absentee basis can only be accomplished through an amendment to the Constitution.

Under Act 77, a person can apply by mail for a mail-in ballot to the Secretary of the Commonwealth or the county board of elections—which, notably, may be situated outside of the voter's election district—and then mail the ballot in from anywhere in the world to the county board of elections. As the voter will not have taken any action at all in the election district, it follows that he or she cannot have "offered to vote" in that district. The majority's interpretation thus renders the phrase "offer to vote" of no practical effect, which is contrary both to long-established interpretive principles and to our precedent construing the same language.

When Article VII is viewed as a whole, within this context and in light of its history and the judicial construction of the phrase "offer to vote," the naming of certain classes of electors who are given the right to vote absentee necessarily implies that those are the only electors who may do so. It seems a stretch to conclude that the framers of the 1967 Constitution, in *guaranteeing* absentee voting to the identified classes, intended thereby to *cede control* over this delicate balance to the Legislature.

NOTES

1. Other States generally permit mail-in voting that is not tied to absentee qualifications. They include Florida, Georgia, Idaho, New Jersey, Oklahoma, Pennsylvania, and Virginia.

2. A recent Wisconsin Supreme Court decision struck down—on state statutory grounds only—two rules promulgated by the Wisconsin Elections Commission. One rule permitted municipal clerks and local election officers to establish ballot "drop boxes" to receive absentee ballots (rather than mailing the ballots), and provided such boxes should be "secure, locked" but could be "staffed or unstaffed, temporary or permanent." The other rule provided that a "family member or another person may return the ballot on behalf of the voter." The Wisconsin Supreme Court held that both rules violated state statutes generally requiring absentee voters to mail the ballot and providing strict limits on the use of alternative ballot return sites. *Teigen v. Wisconsin Elections Commission*, 976 N.W.2d 519 (Wisc. 2022).

3. The Role of a State "Legislature" in Regulating Elections

In *Pacific States Tel. & Tel. Co. v. Oregon* (1912), the U.S. Supreme Court held that the initiative process permitted by many state constitutions does not violate the Guarantee Clause, the federal constitutional provision that guarantees a "republican" form of government. But the decision leaves open a different question that arises from the increasing use of the initiative process in modern America: May a State use an initiative to curb partisan gerrymandering in federal elections by empowering a state commission to re-draw legislative districts? The answer turns not on the Guarantee Clause after *Pacific States* but on the meaning of the "Elections Clause" in Article I of the U.S. Constitution. That Clause permits the "Legislature" of each State to establish the "Times, Places, and Manner" of elections for federal senators and representatives. In a 5-4 decision, the U.S. Supreme Court held that Arizona's adoption of an initiative to deal with extreme partisan gerrymandering did not violate the Elections Clause.

ARIZONA STATE LEGISLATURE v. ARIZONA INDEP. REDISTRICTING COMM'N
135 S. Ct. 2652 (2015)

GINSBURG, J.

This case concerns an endeavor by Arizona voters to address the problem of partisan gerrymandering—the drawing of legislative district lines to subordinate adherents of one political party and entrench a rival party in power. "Partisan gerrymanders," this Court has recognized, "are incompatible with democratic principles." *Vieth v. Jubelirer* (2004). Even so, the Court in *Vieth* did not grant relief on the plaintiffs' partisan gerrymander claim. The plurality held the matter nonjusticiable.

In 2000, Arizona voters adopted an initiative, Proposition 106, aimed at "ending the practice of gerrymandering and improving voter and candidate participation in elections." Proposition 106 amended Arizona's Constitution to remove redistricting authority from the Arizona Legislature and vest that authority in an independent commission, the Arizona Independent Redistricting Commission (AIRC or Commission). After the 2010 census, as after the 2000 census, the AIRC adopted redistricting maps for congressional as well as state legislative districts.

The Arizona Legislature challenged the map the Commission adopted in January 2012 for congressional districts. Recognizing that the voters could control redistricting for state legislators, the Arizona Legislature sued the AIRC in federal court seeking a declaration that the Commission and its map for congressional districts violated the "Elections Clause" of the U.S. Constitution. That Clause, critical to the resolution of this case, provides:

> The Times, Places and Manner of holding Elections for Senators and Representatives, shall be prescribed in each State by the Legislature thereof; but the Congress may at any time by Law make or alter such Regulations.

Proposition 106, vesting redistricting authority in the AIRC, was adopted by citizen initiative in 2000. Aimed at "ending the practice of gerrymandering and improving voter and candidate participation in elections," Proposition 106 amended the Arizona Constitution to remove congressional redistricting authority from the state legislature, lodging that authority, instead, in a new entity, the AIRC. The AIRC convenes after each census, establishes final district boundaries, and certifies the new districts to the Arizona Secretary of State. The legislature may submit nonbinding recommendations to the AIRC, and is required to make necessary appropriations for its operation. The highest ranking officer and minority leader of each chamber of the legislature each select one member of the AIRC from a list compiled by Arizona's Commission on Appellate Court Appointments. The four appointed members of the AIRC then choose, from the same list, the fifth member, who chairs the Commission. A Commission's tenure is confined to one redistricting cycle; each member's time in office "expires upon the appointment of the first member of the next redistricting commission."

Holders of, or candidates for, public office may not serve on the AIRC, except candidates for or members of a school board. No more than two members of the Commission may be members of the same political party and the presiding fifth member cannot be registered with any party already represented on the Commission.

On January 17, 2012, the AIRC approved final congressional and state legislative maps based on the 2010 census. Less than four months later, on June 6, 2012, the Arizona Legislature filed suit in the United States District Court for the District of Arizona, naming as defendants the AIRC, its five members, and the Arizona Secretary of State. The Legislature sought both a declaration that Proposition 106 and congressional maps adopted by the AIRC are unconstitutional, and, as affirmative relief, an injunction against use of AIRC maps for any congressional election after the 2012 general election.

We hold that the Elections Clause permits the people of Arizona to provide for redistricting by independent commission. To restate the key question in this case, the issue centrally debated by the parties: Absent congressional authorization, does the Elections Clause preclude the people of Arizona from creating a commission operating independently of the state legislature to establish congressional districts? The history and purpose of the Clause weigh heavily against such preclusion, as does the animating principle of our Constitution that the people themselves are the originating source of all the powers of government.

We note, preliminarily, that dictionaries, even those in circulation during the founding era, capaciously define the word "legislature." Samuel Johnson defined "legislature" simply as "the power that makes laws." Thomas Sheridan's dictionary defined "legislature" exactly as Dr. Johnson did: "The power that makes laws." Noah Webster defined the term precisely that way as well. And Nathan Bailey similarly defined "legislature" as "the Authority of making Laws, or Power which makes them."

As to the "power that makes laws" in Arizona, initiatives adopted by the voters legislate for the State just as measures passed by the representative body do. As well in Arizona, the people may delegate their legislative authority over redistricting to an independent commission just as the representative body may choose to do.

The dominant purpose of the Elections Clause, the historical record bears out, was to empower Congress to override state election rules, not to restrict the way States enact legislation. As this Court explained in *Arizona v. Inter Tribal Council of Arizona, Inc.* (2013), the Clause "was the Framers' insurance against the possibility that a State would refuse to provide for the election of representatives to the Federal Congress."

The Clause was also intended to act as a safeguard against manipulation of electoral rules by politicians and factions in the States to entrench themselves or place their interests over those of the electorate. As Madison urged, without the Elections Clause, "whenever the State Legislatures had a favorite measure to carry, they would take care so to mould their regulations as to favor the candidates they wished to succeed."

Arguments in support of congressional control under the Elections Clause were reiterated in the public debate over ratification. While attention focused on potential abuses by state-level politicians, and the consequent need for congressional oversight, the legislative processes by which the States could exercise their initiating role in regulating congressional elections occasioned no debate. That is hardly surprising. Recall that when the Constitution was composed in Philadelphia and later ratified, the people's legislative prerogatives—the initiative and the referendum—were not yet in our democracy's arsenal. The Elections Clause, however, is not reasonably read to disarm States from adopting modes of legislation that place the lead rein in the people's hands.

The Arizona Legislature maintains that, by specifying "the Legislature thereof," the Elections Clause renders the State's representative body the sole "component of state government authorized to prescribe regulations for congressional redistricting." The Chief Justice, in dissent, agrees. But it is characteristic of our federal system that States retain autonomy to establish their own governmental processes. "Through the structure of its government, and the character of those who exercise government authority, a State defines itself as a sovereign." Arizona engaged in definition of that kind when its people placed both the initiative power and the AIRC's redistricting authority in the portion of the Arizona Constitution delineating the State's legislative authority.

This Court has "long recognized the role of the States as laboratories for devising solutions to difficult legal problems." Deference to state lawmaking "allows local policies more sensitive to the diverse needs of a heterogeneous society, permits innovation and experimentation, enables greater citizen involvement in democratic processes, and makes government more responsive by putting the States in competition for a mobile citizenry."

We resist reading the Elections Clause to single out federal elections as the one area in which States may not use citizen initiatives as an alternative legislative process. Nothing in that Clause instructs, nor has this Court ever held, that a state legislature may prescribe regulations on the time, place, and manner of holding federal elections in defiance of provisions of the State's constitution.

Banning lawmaking by initiative to direct a State's method of apportioning congressional districts would do more than stymie attempts to curb partisan gerrymandering, by which the majority in the legislature draws district lines to their party's advantage. It would also cast doubt on numerous other election laws adopted by the initiative method of legislating.

The people, in several States, functioning as the lawmaking body for the purpose at hand, have used the initiative to install a host of regulations governing the "Times, Places and Manner" of holding federal elections. For example, the people of California provided for permanent voter registration, specifying that "no amendment by the Legislature shall provide for a general biennial or other periodic reregistration of voters." The people of Ohio banned ballots providing for straight-ticket voting along party lines.

The people of Oregon shortened the deadline for voter registration to 20 days prior to an election. None of those measures permit the state legislatures to override the people's prescriptions. The Arizona Legislature's theory—that the lead role in regulating federal elections cannot be wrested from "the Legislature," and vested in commissions initiated by the people—would endanger all of them.

The list of endangered state elections laws, were we to sustain the position of the Arizona Legislature, would not stop with popular initiatives. Almost all state constitutions were adopted by conventions and ratified by voters at the ballot box, without involvement or approval by "the Legislature." Core aspects of the electoral process regulated by state constitutions include voting by "ballot" or "secret ballot," voter registration, absentee voting, vote counting, and victory thresholds. Again, the States' legislatures had no hand in making these laws and may not alter or amend them.

The importance of direct democracy as a means to control election regulations extends beyond the particular statutes and constitutional provisions installed by the people rather than the States' legislatures. The very prospect of lawmaking by the people may influence the legislature when it considers (or fails to consider) election-related measures. Turning the coin, the legislature's responsiveness to the people its members represent is hardly heightened when the representative body can be confident that what it does will not be overturned or modified by the voters themselves.

Invoking the Elections Clause, the Arizona Legislature instituted this lawsuit to disempower the State's voters from serving as the legislative power for redistricting purposes. But the Clause surely was not adopted to diminish a State's authority to determine its own lawmaking processes. Article I, § 4, stems from a different view. Both parts of the Elections Clause are in line with the fundamental premise that all political power flows from the people. So comprehended, the Clause doubly empowers the people. They may control the State's lawmaking processes in the first instance, as Arizona voters have done, and they may seek Congress' correction of regulations prescribed by state legislatures.

The people of Arizona turned to the initiative to curb the practice of gerrymandering and, thereby, to ensure that Members of Congress would have "a habitual recollection of their dependence on the people." The Federalist No. 57 (Madison). In so acting, Arizona voters sought to restore "the core principle of republican government," namely, "that the voters should choose their representatives, not the other way around." The Elections Clause does not hinder that endeavor.

ROBERTS, C.J., dissenting.

Just over a century ago, Arizona became the second State in the Union to ratify the Seventeenth Amendment. That Amendment transferred power to choose United States Senators from "the Legislature" of each State to "the people thereof." The Amendment resulted from an arduous, decades-long campaign in which reformers across the country worked hard to garner approval from Congress and three-quarters of the States.

What chumps! Didn't they realize that all they had to do was interpret the constitutional term "the Legislature" to mean "the people"? The Court today performs just such a magic trick with the Elections Clause. That Clause vests congressional redistricting authority in "the Legislature" of each State. An Arizona ballot initiative transferred that authority from "the Legislature" to an "Independent Redistricting Commission." The majority approves this deliberate constitutional evasion by doing what the proponents of the Seventeenth Amendment dared not: revising "the Legislature" to mean "the people."

The Court's position has no basis in the text, structure, or history of the Constitution, and it contradicts precedents from both Congress and this Court. The Constitution contains seventeen provisions referring to the "Legislature" of a State, many of which cannot possibly be read to mean "the people." Indeed, several provisions expressly distinguish "the Legislature" from "the People." This Court has accordingly defined "the Legislature" in the Elections Clause as *"the representative body* which makes the laws of the people."

The majority largely ignores this evidence, relying instead on disconnected observations about direct democracy, a contorted interpretation of an irrelevant statute, and naked appeals to public policy. Nowhere does the majority explain how a constitutional provision that vests redistricting authority in "the Legislature" permits a State to wholly exclude "the Legislature" from redistricting. Arizona's Commission might be a noble endeavor—although it does not seem so "independent" in practice—but the "fact that a given law or procedure is efficient, convenient, and useful will not save it if it is contrary to the Constitution." No matter how concerned we may be about partisanship in redistricting, this Court has no power to gerrymander the Constitution.

The majority begins by discussing policy. I begin with the Constitution. The Elections Clause provides:

> The Times, Places and Manner of holding Elections for Senators and Representatives, shall be prescribed in each State by the Legislature thereof; but the Congress may at any time by Law make or alter such Regulations, except as to the Places of chusing Senators.

The Elections Clause both imposes a duty on States and assigns that duty to a particular state actor: In the absence of a valid congressional directive to the contrary, States must draw district lines for their federal representatives. And that duty "shall" be carried out "in each State by the Legislature thereof."

In Arizona, however, redistricting is not carried out by the legislature. Instead, as the result of a ballot initiative, an unelected body called the Independent Redistricting Commission draws the lines. The key question in the case is whether the Commission can conduct congressional districting consistent with the directive that such authority be exercised "by the Legislature."

The majority concedes that the unelected Commission is not "the Legislature" of Arizona. The Court contends instead that the people of Arizona as a whole constitute "the Legislature" for purposes of the Elections Clause, and that they may delegate the congressional districting authority conferred by that Clause to the Commission. The majority provides no support for the delegation part of its theory, and I am not sure whether the majority's analysis is correct on that issue. But even giving the Court the benefit of the doubt in that regard, the Commission is still unconstitutional. Both the Constitution and our cases make clear that "the Legislature" in the Elections Clause is the representative body which makes the laws of the people.

The relevant question in this case is how to define "the Legislature" under the Elections Clause. The Court seems to conclude, based largely on its understanding of the "history and purpose" of the Elections Clause, that "the Legislature" encompasses any entity in a State that exercises legislative power. That circular definition lacks any basis in the text of the Constitution or any other relevant legal source.

The majority's textual analysis consists, in its entirety, of one paragraph citing founding era dictionaries. The majority points to various dictionaries that follow Samuel Johnson's definition of "legislature" as the "power that makes laws." The notion that this definition corresponds to the entire population of a State is strained to begin with, and largely discredited by the majority's own admission that "direct lawmaking by the people was virtually unknown when the Constitution of 1787 was drafted." Thus, even under the majority's preferred definition, "the Legislature" referred to an institutional body of representatives, not the people at large.

Any ambiguity about the meaning of "the Legislature" is removed by other founding era sources. "Every state constitution from the Founding Era that used the term legislature defined it as a distinct multimember entity comprised of representatives." The Federalist Papers are replete with references to "legislatures" that can only be understood as referring to representative institutions. Noah Webster's heralded American Dictionary of the English Language defines "legislature" as "the body of men in a state or kingdom, invested with power to make and repeal laws." It continues,

"The legislatures of most of the states in America consist of two houses or branches."

I could go on, but the Court has said this before. As we put it nearly a century ago, "Legislature" was "not a term of uncertain meaning when incorporated into the Constitution."

The unambiguous meaning of "the Legislature" in the Elections Clause as a representative body is confirmed by other provisions of the Constitution that use the same term in the same way. When seeking to discern the meaning of a word in the Constitution, there is no better dictionary than the rest of the Constitution itself. Our precedents new and old have employed this structural method of interpretation to read the Constitution in the manner it was drafted and ratified—as a unified, coherent whole.

The Constitution includes seventeen provisions referring to a State's "Legislature." Every one of those references is consistent with the understanding of a legislature as a representative body. More importantly, many of them are only consistent with an institutional legislature—and flatly incompatible with the majority's reading of "the Legislature" to refer to the people as a whole.

Start with the Constitution's first use of the term: "The House of Representatives shall be composed of Members chosen every second Year by the People of the several States, and the Electors in each State shall have the Qualifications requisite for Electors of the most numerous Branch of the State Legislature." This reference to a "Branch of the State Legislature" can only be referring to an institutional body, and the explicit juxtaposition of "the State Legislature" with "the People of the several States" forecloses the majority's proposed reading.

The next Section of Article I describes how to fill vacancies in the United States Senate: "if Vacancies happen by Resignation, or otherwise, during the Recess of the Legislature of any State, the Executive thereof may make temporary Appointments until the next Meeting of the Legislature, which shall then fill such Vacancies." The references to "the Recess of the Legislature of any State" and "the next Meeting of the Legislature" are only consistent with an institutional legislature, and make no sense under the majority's reading. The people as a whole (schoolchildren and a few unnamed others excepted) do not take a "Recess."

The list goes on. Article IV provides that the "United States shall guarantee to every State in this Union a Republican Form of Government, and shall protect each of them against Invasion; and on Application of the Legislature, or of the Executive (when the Legislature cannot be convened), against domestic Violence." It is perhaps conceivable that all the people of a State could be "convened"—although this would seem difficult during an "Invasion" or outbreak of "domestic Violence"—but the only natural reading of the Clause is that "the Executive" may submit a federal application when "the Legislature" as a representative body cannot be convened.

Each of these provisions offers strong structural indications about what "the Legislature" must mean. But the most powerful evidence of all comes from the Seventeenth Amendment. Under the original Constitution, Senators were "chosen by the Legislature" of each State, while Members of the House of Representatives were chosen "by the People." That distinction was critical to the Framers. As James Madison explained, the Senate would "derive its powers from the States," while the House would "derive its powers from the people of America."

Before long, reformers took up Wilson's mantle and launched a protracted campaign to amend the Constitution. That effort began in 1826, when Representative Henry Storrs of New York proposed—but then set aside—a constitutional amendment transferring the power to elect Senators from the state legislatures to the people. Over the next three quarters of a century, no fewer than 188 joint resolutions proposing similar reforms were introduced in both Houses of Congress.

At no point in this process did anyone suggest that a constitutional amendment was unnecessary because "Legislature" could simply be interpreted to mean "people." In fact, as the decades rolled by without an amendment, 28 of the 45 States settled for the next best thing by holding a popular vote on candidates for Senate, then pressuring state legislators into choosing the winner. All agreed that cutting the state legislature out of senatorial selection entirely would require nothing less than to "Strike out" the original words in the Constitution and "insert, 'elected by the people'" in its place.

Yet that is precisely what the majority does to the Elections Clause today—amending the text not through the process provided by Article V, but by judicial decision. The majority's revision renders the Seventeenth Amendment an 86-year waste of time, and singles out the Elections Clause as the only one of the Constitution's seventeen provisions referring to "the Legislature" that departs from the ordinary meaning of the term.

The constitutional text, structure, history, and precedent establish a straightforward rule: Under the Elections Clause, "the Legislature" is a representative body that, when it prescribes election regulations, may be required to do so within the ordinary lawmaking process, but may not be cut out of that process. Put simply, the state legislature need not be exclusive in congressional districting, but neither may it be excluded.

The majority shows greater concern about redistricting practices than about the meaning of the Constitution. I recognize the difficulties that arise from trying to fashion judicial relief for partisan gerrymandering. But our inability to find a manageable standard in that area is no excuse to abandon a standard of meaningful interpretation in this area. This Court has stressed repeatedly that a law's virtues as a policy innovation cannot redeem its inconsistency with the Constitution.

The people of Arizona have concerns about the process of congressional redistricting in their State. For better or worse, the Elections Clause of the Constitution does not allow them to address those concerns by displacing their legislature. But it does allow them to seek relief from Congress, which can make or alter the regulations prescribed by the legislature. And the Constitution gives them another means of change. They can follow the lead of the reformers who won passage of the Seventeenth Amendment. Indeed, several constitutional amendments over the past century have involved modifications of the electoral process. Unfortunately, today's decision will only discourage this democratic method of change. Why go through the hassle of writing a new provision into the Constitution when it is so much easier to write an old one out?

NOTES

1. The U.S. Supreme Court is not finished when it comes to construing the Elections Clause. In 2022, it granted a certiorari petition in the aforementioned case *Harper v. Hall*, under the new name *Moore v. Harper*, to review this question: "Whether a state's judicial branch may nullify the regulations governing the 'Manner of holding Elections for Senators and Representatives ... prescribed ... by the Legislature thereof,' and replace them with regulations of the state courts' own devising, based on vague state constitutional provisions purportedly vesting the state judiciary with power to prescribe whatever rules it deems appropriate to ensure a 'fair' or 'free' election." While *Arizona State Legislature* permits a redistricting commission created by a state initiative to draw new district lines in the State, it remains to be seen whether the federal High Court will permit the state court to alter state legislative election regulations premised on interpretations of state constitutional provisions.

2. For more information on this topic, see EDWARD B. FOLEY, BALLOT BATTLES: THE HISTORY OF DISPUTED ELECTIONS IN THE UNITED STATES (2015); Richard Briffault, *Election Law Localism and Democracy*, 100 N.C. L. Rev. 1421 (2022); Travis Crum, *Deregulated Redistricting*, 107 Cornell L. Rev. 359 (2021); Michael Gentithes, *Gobbledygook: Political Questions, Manageability, & Partisan Gerrymandering*, 105 Iowa L. Rev. 1081 (2020); Eugene D. Mazo, Finding Common Ground on Voter ID Laws, 49 U. Mem. L. Rev. 1233 (2019); Francesca Lina Proacaccini, *Partisan Gerrymandering: State Courts Come to Bat on the Free-Speech Issue of Our Day*, 2 Md. B.J. 128 (2020); Justin Weinstein-Tull, *Election Law Federalism*, 114 Mich. L. Rev. 747 (2016).

Chapter VI

DUE PROCESS OF LAW

A. INTRODUCTION

Conferred by King John on the meadow of Runnymede in the year 1215, the Magna Carta proclaimed:

> No Free man shall be taken or imprisoned, or be disseised of his Freehold, or Liberties, or free Customs, or be outlawed, or exiled, or any other wise destroyed; nor will we not pass upon him, nor condemn him, but by lawful judgment of his Peers, or by the Law of the land. We will sell to no man, we will not deny or defer to any man either Justice or Right.

The Magna Carta served as a model for the American colonies, many of which adopted laws based upon the great charter. Shortly after achieving independence, most of the new states enacted constitutional provisions prohibiting the deprivation of life, liberty, or property except by the "law of the land." In time, some states used different phrasing, prohibiting the deprivation of life, liberty, or property without "due process of law." Eventually, all of the states enacted either law of the land clauses or due process clauses as part of their state constitutions. According to Thomas Cooley, an eminent constitutional scholar of the late nineteenth century, whichever phrase was used, "the meaning was the same in every case." Thomas M. Cooley, *A Treatise on the Constitutional Limitations Which Rest upon the Legislative Power of the States of the American Union* 353 (1868).

At a minimum, the guarantee of due process of law requires the government to follow fair procedures before depriving anyone of life, liberty, or property. The principle applies to all manner of government proceedings, whether civil, criminal, or administrative. At its core, the principle of procedural due process requires notice and an opportunity to be heard in a fair proceeding. In some instances, the scope of protection afforded by procedural due process under a state constitution has been extended beyond that provided by the Federal Constitution.

Many courts have construed their due process clauses to include substantive components. Early in American history, some state and federal courts determined that due process of law required the invalidation of laws that arbitrarily divested persons of property rights. *See* Jeffrey M. Shaman, *On the 100th Anniversary of Lochner v. New York*, 72 Tenn. L. Rev. 455, 476–88 (2005). As support for substantive interpretations of due process, some state constitutions contain differently worded provisions directed to safeguarding life, liberty, or property. The Kentucky Constitution, for example, states: "Absolute and arbitrary power over the lives, liberty and property of freemen exists nowhere in a republic, not even in the largest majority." Ky. Const. Bill of Rights, § 2. In other States, protection for life, liberty, or property has been found implicit in constitutional provisions declaring that "all persons are by nature free and independent, and have certain natural and inalienable rights." N.J. Const. art I, § 1.

One feature of substantive due process that has generated considerable state court litigation is the right to privacy. State constitutional conceptions of the right of privacy first emerged in the early twentieth century, but then fell into quiescence for decades before being revived in the 1960s. In the meantime, the United States Supreme Court formulated a constitutional right of privacy under the Due Process Clause of the Fourteenth Amendment in *Griswold*. That line of decisions was eventually extended to cover the right to reproductive autonomy, certain family rights, and a right of intimate association, among others. But the foundations of the federal right to privacy have come under attack in recent years, most recently in the *Dobbs* decision, which overruled the *Roe* and *Casey* decisions. All of this has left considerable room for state court experimentation in these areas.

Some States have strengthened the right of privacy by placing it in their state constitutions. Five States—Alaska, California, Florida, Hawaii, and Montana—have amended their constitutions to expressly protect the right of privacy. These express provisions offer a sound textual basis for the expansion of privacy rights. In some States that do not have an express constitutional protection for privacy, the courts have used more generally worded provisions, such as a due process clause, to recognize and eventually enlarge the right of privacy.

B. PROCEDURAL GUARANTEES

STATE v. VEALE
972 A.2d 1009 (N.H. 2009)

HICKS, J.

The defendant, Scott W. Veale, appeals orders of the Superior Court relating to its finding that he is incompetent to stand trial. The relevant facts are as follows. The defendant is a real estate broker who has been involved in various land and logging disputes for many years. He was indicted in June 2003 for one count of timber trespass and one count of theft by unauthorized taking, after a property owner alleged that he cut and removed oak timber from the owner's property. The court appointed a public defender to represent the defendant. A second public defender entered an appearance to assist in the defense.

The attorney-client relationship deteriorated over the following months. The defendant believed that he owned the timber and the property. He also believed that local and State authorities prosecuted him as part of an ongoing conspiracy to deprive him of property rights. The public defender conferred with two real estate attorneys to determine whether the defendant's claim had merit. Both concluded that it did not. The defendant, however, continued to insist that the public defenders seek funds for a property survey. Eventually, the defendant accused the public defenders of being part of the conspiracy against him and his family. This severely impaired communication and the public defenders concluded that he was unable to assist in his defense. In July 2004, defense counsel filed a motion to determine competency. Dr. James Adams, a psychiatrist, examined the defendant in November 2004 and ultimately determined that, although the defendant suffered from a paranoid disorder, he was competent to stand trial. Defense counsel moved for, and were granted funds for, a second opinion. Dr. Philip Kinsler, a clinical and forensic psychologist, examined the defendant in March 2005 and concluded that he suffered from a delusional disorder and was incompetent. The defendant filed a *pro se* motion in July 2005 summarizing the breakdown of communication with his appointed counsel, outlining their disagreement over "the need for a mental evaluation," requesting a finding that such evaluation was unnecessary, and requesting new counsel.

The Superior Court held a competency hearing in September 2005, receiving testimony from each doctor. The State conducted the direct examination of Dr. Adams and cross-examination of Dr. Kinsler. The public defender conducted the direct examination of Dr. Kinsler and cross-examination of Dr. Adams. The court also made limited inquiry. The defendant was present at the hearing but did not testify. The court ultimately found the defendant incompetent to stand trial and ruled that he could not be restored to competency. The court later held a hearing on dangerousness, ruled that the defendant was not dangerous and granted the defendant's motion to dismiss the criminal charges.

We appointed the defendant's trial counsel to represent him on appeal and granted the appellate defender's motion to withdraw. The defendant appeals only the denial of his motion to vacate, arguing that he was denied due process in the competency determination. He cites the Due Process Clauses of the Fourteenth Amendment to the Federal Constitution and Part I, Article 15 of the State Constitution. We first address this argument under the State Constitution and cite federal opinions for guidance only.

Part I, Article 15 of the State Constitution provides, in relevant part: "No subject shall be deprived of his property, immunities, or privileges, put out of the protection of the law, exiled or deprived of his life, liberty, or estate, but by the judgment of his peers, or the law of the land." Law of the land in this article means due process of law. Our threshold determination in a procedural due process claim is "whether the challenged procedures concern a legally protected interest." Undoubtedly, the state constitutional right to due process protects defendants from standing trial if they are legally incompetent. The defendant's due process challenge, however, does not implicate this right. Indeed, the competency proceedings below resulted in a dismissal of the two indictments, and resulted in no confinement because the defendant was found not to be dangerous. The defendant grounds his due process challenge on the stigma attached to his reputation by virtue of the incompetency finding. He argues that, while the competency proceedings may have protected his right not to be tried if incompetent, they erroneously imposed upon him an "indelible stigma" affecting the exercise of various civil rights. It is through this lens that we consider his procedural due process challenge.

The State contends that the defendant's asserted reputational interest fails to trigger a due process analysis because he simply "speculates about a number of potential consequences that may or can flow from a finding of incompetence," rendering each "too speculative and remote to constitute the kind of liberty or property interest contemplated by the constitution."

The State would have a stronger argument if we had adopted the analysis in *Paul v. Davis* (1976), under our State Constitution. In *Paul*, the Supreme Court coined what would later be known as the "stigma plus" test. The Court noted that "the words liberty and property as used in the Fourteenth Amendment do not in terms single out reputation as a candidate for special protection." It narrowed its prior holding in *Wisconsin v. Constantineau* (1971), by concluding that defamation alone could not constitute an interest triggering due process protection. Instead, the Court read *Wisconsin* as recognizing a cognizable right warranting due process protection where reputational stigma exists in addition to state action altering or extinguishing "a right or status previously recognized by state law." In *Siegert v. Gilley* (1991), the Court extended the doctrine by requiring, in addition to the stigma, a contemporaneous tangible loss. We, however, have never adopted the stigma-plus test as the touchstone for procedural due process under the State Constitution. Although other cases have approached the issue, they have merely assumed that state constitutional due process attaches to a reputational right. Accordingly, the issue remains open under the State Constitution.

Although we do not necessarily agree with all of the scholarly criticism of the stigma-plus doctrine, we are mindful that constitutional scholars have not received the doctrine well. By requiring that a separate liberty or property interest accompany the reputational injury, the decision in *Paul* marked a drastic narrowing of its predecessors. In our view, *Paul* effectively relegates the reputational interest to insignificance because the separate injury would, itself, often invoke the Due Process Clause.

"Although in interpreting the New Hampshire Constitution we have often followed and agreed with the federal treatment of parallel provisions of the federal document, we never have considered ourselves bound to adopt the federal interpretations." In *Clark v. Manchester* (1973), we concluded that a probationary employee was not entitled to due process, in part, because he failed to show "that the governmental conduct likely will seriously damage his standing and associations in the community or impose a stigma upon the employee that will foreclose future opportunities to practice his chosen profession." In *Petition of Bagley* (1986), we stated that "the general rule is that a person's liberty may be impaired when governmental action seriously damages his standing and associations in the community." We also "recognized that the stigmatization that attends certain governmental determinations may amount to a deprivation of constitutionally protected liberty." Thus, we find ample support in our jurisprudence for the proposition that reputational stigma can, by itself, constitute a deprivation of liberty deserving due process.

Accordingly, we hold that competency determinations sufficiently implicate reputational interests to warrant the protection afforded by the State Due Process Clause. Guaranteeing some minimal process guards against the difficulty of undoing harm once visited upon a person's good name. In instances such as the present one, a person may not immediately suffer the more tangible effects of such a determination. We have long recognized that some forms of reputational harm can safely be assumed.

Having concluded that competency determinations can potentially damage the protected interest in reputation, we consider what process is required to protect that interest. In so doing, we balance three factors: First, the private interest that will be affected by the official action; second, the risk of an erroneous deprivation of such interest through the procedures used, and the probable value, if any, of additional or substitute procedural safeguards; and finally, the Government's interest, including the function involved and the fiscal and administrative burdens that the additional or substitute procedural requirement would entail.

After balancing the private interest here at issue; the risk of an erroneous deprivation of that interest through the procedures used, and the probable value of additional procedural safeguards; and the Government's interest, we conclude that due process does not require additional process under the State Constitution.

M.E.K. v. R.L.K.
921 So.2d 787 (Fla. App. 2006)

PLEUS, C.J.

The sole issue in this appeal is whether an indigent mother facing involuntary termination of parental rights in an adoption proceeding has a constitutional right to appointment of trial and appellate counsel. We believe she does and therefore reverse the order denying her counsel.

J.L.K. was born in September 2004. A month later, the Department of Children and Families sheltered J.L.K. with his maternal grandmother and initiated dependency proceedings based on allegations that his mother was unable to care for him. Prior to the adjudicatory hearing, J.L.K.'s grandmother moved to dismiss the dependency proceeding on the ground that she would file a separate adoption proceeding pursuant to Chapter 63 and would seek to have the mother's parental rights terminated as part of the adoption. The dependency court abated the dependency proceeding to allow the adoption to proceed.

In March 2005, the grandmother filed a petition for termination of parental rights pending adoption pursuant to Chapter 63 of the Florida Statutes. The lower court terminated the mother's parental rights by default after the mother failed to file a responsive pleading. She was incarcerated at the time. Subsequently, the mother's attorney in the dependency action filed a notice of appearance in the adoption action. He also filed an affidavit of indigency, motion to appoint counsel and motion to vacate the final judgment and set aside default. The mother's appellate attorney appealed the final judgment terminating her parental rights and also filed a motion in the lower court to appoint appellate counsel. The court denied the motions to appoint trial and appellate counsel in the adoption proceeding. The mother appealed this order as well. We consolidated these appeals and temporarily relinquished jurisdiction, after which the lower court approved the parties' stipulation to set aside the final judgment and reinstate the dependency proceedings. Based on this development, we acknowledged dismissal of appeal of the final judgment but agreed to proceed with the appeal of the order denying appointed counsel.

In a 1980 appeal of an order terminating parental rights, the Florida Supreme Court held that an indigent parent has a right under the Florida and United States Constitutions to appointed counsel in "proceedings involving the permanent termination of parental rights to a child."

A year later, in *Lassiter v. Dep't of Social Serv. of Durham County, N.C.* (1981), the U.S. Supreme Court held that the federal due process clause does not require appointed counsel in every state-initiated termination of a parental rights proceeding. Instead, it required trial courts to evaluate the need for counsel on a case-by-case basis. The court noted that it was only determining the minimum due process standard under the federal constitution and that many states have higher standards based on wise public policy. In *O.A.H. v. R.L.A.* (1998), the second district held that an indigent parent has a constitutional right to appointed counsel in a Chapter 63 involuntary adoption proceeding. It recently reaffirmed that holding in *In the Interest of M.C.* (2005). Both *O.A.H.* and *M.C.* are similar to the instant case in that they involved indigent parents who did not attend the final hearing in which their parental rights were terminated because they were incarcerated at the time.

In denying the mother's requests for appointed counsel, the lower court declined to follow *O.A.H.* or *M.C.*, stating:

> Ordinarily, the Court would be bound by precedent from another District Court of Appeal in the absence of contrary authority from the Fifth District Court of Appeal. However, the Court in this matter is bound by the U.S. Supreme Court decision in *Lassiter v. Department of Social Services of Durham County*, N.C.

We disagree with this reasoning. *Lassiter* addressed only the minimum due process requirements under the federal due process clause. The citizens of Florida are also protected by the due process clause in Article 1, section 9 of the Florida Constitution. In our federal system of jurisprudence, the United States Constitution establishes the minimum level of due process protections for all people, but state constitutions and laws may provide additional due process protections.

In the area of termination of parental rights, the Florida due process clause provides higher due process standards than the federal due process clause. Under the federal provision, *Lassiter* does not require appointment of counsel in every case. It only requires a case-by-case determination. But under the state due process clause, *D.B.* requires appointment of counsel in "proceedings involving the permanent termination of parental rights to a child." For these reasons, the lower court should have followed *O.A.H.* and *M.C.* rather than *Lassiter*.

Alternatively, the grandmother argues that even if the trial court was obligated to follow *O.A.H.*, this Court is free to disagree with it. She urges us to reject *O.A.H.*, claiming that it disregards the underlying reasons for appointing counsel and because its broad interpretation of state action creates a slippery slope that will obligate the state to provide counsel in many other types of civil cases. The grandmother is wrong on both counts. In *M.L.B.*, the United States Supreme Court rejected a similar slippery slope argument. *M.L.B.* involved the right of an indigent parent to have the state pay for a transcript of the hearing in an appeal of a private termination of parental rights case. Justice Thomas argued in dissent that extending due process protections found in criminal cases involving the loss of one's liberty to a civil case involving termination of parental rights would create a dangerous precedent used to extend such protections to other civil cases.

The majority rejected this argument, noting that termination of parental rights work "unique kind of deprivation" involving the "awesome authority of the State" to permanently destroy legal recognition of the parental relationship. Therefore, finding certain due process protections applicable in termination of parental rights cases could not be used as precedent to extend such protections to other civil cases. The same analysis is true in the instant case. Finding a right to counsel in a civil termination of parental rights case does not create a dangerous precedent for finding such a right in other civil cases because other civil cases do not involve the same unique deprivation of a fundamental right by the State.

The grandmother also argues that *O.A.H.* ignores the underlying reasons for appointing counsel. She instead urges us to apply the factors found in *Mathews v. Eldridge* (1976), for determining whether a right to counsel exists. However, *D.B.* makes clear that in the context of determining whether a right to appointed counsel exists in a case involving the parent-child relationship, Florida courts must weigh the factors enunciated in *Potvin v. Keller* (1975), not *Mathews*. Those factors include: (1) the potential length of parent-child separation, (2) the degree of parental restrictions on visitation, (3) the presence or absence of parental consent, (4) the presence or absence of disputed facts, and (5) the complexity of the proceeding in terms of witnesses and documents. The *D.B.* court further stated that in applying these factors, "counsel will always be required where permanent termination of custody might result, but where there is no threat of permanent termination of parental custody, the test should be applied on a case-by-case basis."

We therefore hold, as our sister courts have, that article 1, section 9 of the Florida Constitution mandates that counsel be appointed to an indigent parent in an involuntary termination of parental rights proceeding under Chapter 63.

C. REPRODUCTIVE AUTONOMY

DAVIS v. DAVIS
842 S.W.2d 588 (Tenn. 1992)

DAUGHTREY, J.

This appeal presents a question of first impression, involving the disposition of the cryogenically-preserved product of in vitro fertilization (IVF), commonly referred to in the popular press and the legal journals as "frozen embryos." The case began as a divorce action, filed by the appellee, Junior Lewis Davis, against his then wife, appellant Mary Sue Davis. The parties were able to agree upon all terms of dissolution, except one: who was to have "custody" of the seven "frozen embryos" stored in a Knoxville fertility clinic that had attempted to assist the Davises in achieving a much-wanted pregnancy during a happier period in their relationship.

Mary Sue Davis originally asked for control of the "frozen embryos" with the intent to have them transferred to her own uterus, in a post-divorce effort to become pregnant. Junior Davis objected, saying that he preferred to leave the embryos in their frozen state until he decided whether or not he wanted to become a parent outside the bounds of marriage. We note, in this latter regard, that their positions have already shifted: both have remarried and Mary Sue Davis (now Mary Sue Stowe) has moved out of state. She no longer wishes to utilize the "frozen embryos" herself, but wants authority to donate them to a childless couple. Junior Davis is adamantly opposed to such donation and would prefer to see the "frozen embryos" discarded.

At the outset, it is important to note the absence of two critical factors that might otherwise influence or control the result of this litigation: When the Davises signed up for the IVF program at the Knoxville clinic, they did not execute a written agreement specifying what disposition should be made of any unused embryos that might result from the cryopreservation process. Moreover, there was at that time no Tennessee statute governing such disposition, nor has one been enacted in the meantime. In addition, because of the uniqueness of the question before us, we have no case law to guide us to a decision in this case.

The essential dispute here is whether the parties will become parents. The Court of Appeals held in effect that they will become parents if they both agree to become parents. The Court did not say what will happen if they fail to agree. We conclude that the answer to this dilemma turns on the parties' exercise of their constitutional right to privacy.

The right to privacy is not specifically mentioned in either the federal or the Tennessee state constitution, and yet there can be little doubt about its grounding in the concept of liberty reflected in those two documents. In the Tennessee Constitution, the concept of liberty plays a central role. Article I, Section 8 provides:

> That no man shall be taken or imprisoned, or disseized of his freehold, liberties or privileges, or outlawed, or exiled, or in any manner destroyed or deprived of his life, liberty or property, but by the judgment of his peers or the law of the land.

Indeed, the notion of individual liberty is so deeply embedded in the Tennessee Constitution that it, alone among American constitutions, gives the people, in the face of governmental oppression and interference with liberty, the right to resist that oppression even to the extent of overthrowing the government. The relevant provisions establishing this distinctive political autonomy appear in the first two sections of Article I of the Tennessee Constitution, its Declaration of Rights:

> Section 1. All power inherent in the people-Government under their control.
>
> That all power is inherent in the people, and all free governments are founded on their authority, and instituted for their peace, safety, and happiness; for the advancement of those ends they have at all times, an inalienable and indefeasible right to alter, reform, or abolish the government in such manner as they may think proper.
>
> Section 2. Doctrine of nonresistance condemned.
>
> That government being instituted for the common benefit, the doctrine of non-resistance against arbitrary power and oppression is absurd, slavish, and destructive of the good and happiness of mankind.

Obviously, the drafters of the Tennessee Constitution of 1796 could not have anticipated the need to construe the liberty clauses of that document in terms of the choices flowing from in vitro fertilization procedures. But there can be little doubt that they foresaw the need to protect individuals from unwarranted governmental intrusion into matters such as the one now before us, involving intimate questions of personal and family concern. Based on both the language and the development of our state constitution, we have no hesitation in drawing the conclusion that there is a right of individual privacy guaranteed under and protected by the liberty clauses of the Tennessee Declaration of Rights.

Undoubtedly, that right to privacy incorporates some of the attributes of the federal constitutional right to privacy and, in any given fact situation, may also share some of its contours. As with other state constitutional rights having counterparts in the federal bill of rights, however, there is no reason to assume that there is a complete congruency. Here, the specific individual freedom in dispute is the right to procreate. In terms of the Tennessee state constitution, we hold that the right of procreation is a vital part of an individual's right to privacy. Federal law is to the same effect.

In construing the reach of the federal constitution, the United States Supreme Court has addressed the affirmative right to procreate in only two cases. In *Buck v. Bell* (1927), the Court upheld the sterilization of a "feebleminded white woman." However, in *Skinner v. Oklahoma* (1942), the Supreme Court struck down a statute that authorized the sterilization of certain categories of criminals. The Court described the right to procreate as "one of the basic civil rights of man," and stated that "marriage and procreation are fundamental to the very existence and survival of the race." In the same vein, the United States Supreme Court has said:

> If the right of privacy means anything, it is the right of the *individual*, married or single, to be free from unwarranted governmental intrusion into matters so fundamentally affecting a person as the decision whether to bear or beget a child. *Eisenstadt v. Baird* (1972).

That a right to procreational autonomy is inherent in our most basic concepts of liberty is also indicated by the reproductive freedom cases, *see, e.g.*, *Griswold v. Connecticut* (1965); and *Roe v. Wade* (1973), and by cases concerning parental rights and responsibilities with respect to children. *See, e.g.*, *Wisconsin v. Yoder* (1972); *Pierce v. Society of the Sisters of the Holy Names of Jesus and Mary* (1925); and *Bellotti v. Baird* (1979). In fact, in *Bellotti v. Baird*, the Supreme Court noted that parental autonomy is basic to the structure of our society because the family is "the institution by which we inculcate and pass down many of our most cherished values, moral and cultural."

The United States Supreme Court has never addressed the issue of procreation in the context of in vitro fertilization. Moreover, the extent to which procreational autonomy is protected by the United States Constitution is no longer entirely clear. For the purposes of this litigation it is sufficient to note that, whatever its ultimate constitutional boundaries, the right of procreational autonomy is composed of two rights of equal significance—the right to procreate and the right to avoid procreation. Undoubtedly, both are subject to protections and limitations.

The equivalence of and inherent tension between these two interests are nowhere more evident than in the context of in vitro fertilization. None of the concerns about a woman's bodily integrity that have previously precluded men from controlling abortion decisions is applicable here. We are not unmindful of the fact that the trauma (including both emotional stress and physical discomfort) to which women are subjected in the IVF process is more severe than is the impact of the procedure on men. In this sense, it is fair to say that women contribute more to the IVF process than men. Their experience, however, must be viewed in light of the joys of parenthood that is desired or the relative anguish of a lifetime of unwanted parenthood. As they stand on the brink of potential parenthood, Mary Sue Davis and Junior Lewis Davis must be seen as entirely equivalent gamete-providers.

It is further evident that, however far the protection of procreational autonomy extends, the existence of the right itself dictates that decisional authority rests in the gamete-providers alone, at least to the extent that their decisions have an impact upon their individual reproductive status. No other person or entity has an interest sufficient to permit interference with the gamete-providers' decision to continue or terminate the IVF process, because no one else bears the consequences of these decisions in the way that the gamete-providers do.

Further, at least with respect to Tennessee's public policy and its constitutional right of privacy, the state's interest in potential human life is insufficient to justify an infringement on the gamete-providers' procreational autonomy. The United States Supreme Court has indicated in *Webster*, and even in *Roe*, that the state's interest in potential human life may justify statutes or regulations that have an impact upon a person's exercise of procreational autonomy. This potential for sufficiently weighty state's interests is not, however, at issue here, because Tennessee's statutes contain no statement of public policy which reveals an interest that could justify infringing on gamete-providers' decisional authority over the preembryos to which they have contributed.

Tennessee's abortion statute reveals a public policy decision weighing the interests of living persons against the state's interest in potential life. At least during certain stages of a pregnancy, the personal interests of the pregnant woman outweigh the state's interests and the pregnancy may be terminated. Taken collectively, our statutes reflect the policy decision that, at least in some circumstances, the interest of living individuals in avoiding procreation is sufficient to justify taking steps to terminate the procreational process, despite the state's interest in potential life.

Certainly, if the state's interests do not become sufficiently compelling in the abortion context until the end of the first trimester, after very significant developmental stages have passed, then surely there is no state interest in these preembryos which could suffice to overcome the interests of the gamete-providers. The abortion statute reveals that the increase in the state's interest is marked by each successive developmental stage such that, toward the end of a pregnancy, this interest is so compelling that abortion is almost strictly forbidden. This scheme supports the conclusion that the state's interest in the potential life embodied by these four- to eight-cell preembryos (which may or may not be able to achieve implantation in a uterine wall and which, if implanted, may or may not begin to develop into fetuses, subject to possible miscarriage) is at best slight. When weighed against the interests of the individuals and the burdens inherent in parenthood, the state's interest in the potential life of these preembryos is not sufficient to justify any infringement upon the freedom of these individuals to make their own decisions as to whether to allow a process to continue that may result in such a dramatic change in their lives as becoming parents.

The unique nature of this case requires us to note that the interests of these parties in parenthood are different in scope than the parental interest considered in other cases. Previously, courts have dealt with the child-bearing and child-rearing aspects of parenthood. Abortion cases have dealt with gestational parenthood. In this case, the Court must deal with the question of genetic parenthood. We conclude, moreover, that an interest in avoiding genetic parenthood can be significant enough to trigger the protections afforded to all other aspects of parenthood. The technological fact that someone unknown to these parties could gestate these preembryos does not alter the fact that these parties, the gamete-providers, would become parents in that event, at least in the genetic sense. The profound impact this would have on them supports their right to sole decisional authority as to whether the process of attempting to gestate these preembryos should continue. This brings us directly to the question of how to resolve the dispute that arises when one party wishes to continue the IVF process and the other does not.

Resolving disputes over conflicting interests of constitutional import is a task familiar to the courts. In this case, the issue centers on the two aspects of procreational autonomy—the right to procreate and the right to avoid procreation. Beginning with the burden imposed on Junior Davis, we note that the consequences are obvious. Any disposition which results in the gestation of the preembryos would impose unwanted parenthood on him, with all of its possible financial and psychological consequences. The impact that this unwanted parenthood would have on Junior Davis can only be understood by considering his particular circumstances, as revealed in the record.

Junior Davis testified that he was the fifth youngest of six children. When he was five years old, his parents divorced, his mother had a nervous break-down, and he and three of his brothers went to live at a home for boys run by the Lutheran Church. Another brother was taken in by an aunt, and his sister stayed with their mother. From that day forward, he had monthly visits with his mother but saw his father only three more times before he died in 1976. Junior Davis testified that, as a boy, he had severe problems caused by separation from his parents. He said that it was especially hard to leave his mother after each monthly visit. He clearly feels that he has suffered because of his lack of opportunity to establish a relationship with his parents and particularly because of the absence of his father.

In light of his boyhood experiences, Junior Davis is vehemently opposed to fathering a child that would not live with both parents. Regardless of whether he or Mary Sue had custody, he feels that the child's bond with the non-custodial parent would not be satisfactory. He testified very clearly that his concern was for the psychological obstacles a child in such a situation would face, as well as the burdens it would impose on him. Likewise, he is opposed to donation because the recipient couple might divorce, leaving the child (which he definitely would consider his own) in a single-parent setting.

Balanced against Junior Davis's interest in avoiding parenthood is Mary Sue Davis's interest in donating the preembryos to another couple for implantation. Refusal to permit donation of the preembryos would impose on her the burden of knowing that the lengthy IVF procedures she underwent were futile, and that the preembryos to which she contributed genetic material would never become children. While this is not an insubstantial emotional burden, we can only conclude that Mary Sue Davis's interest in donation is not as significant as the interest Junior Davis has in avoiding parenthood. If she were allowed to donate these preembryos, he would face a lifetime of either wondering about his parental status or knowing about his parental status but having no control over it. He testified quite clearly that if these preembryos were brought to term he would fight for custody of his child or children. Donation, if a child came of it, would rob him twice—his procreational autonomy would be defeated and his relationship with his offspring would be prohibited.

The case would be closer if Mary Sue Davis were seeking to use the preembryos herself, but only if she could not achieve parenthood by any other reasonable means. We recognize the trauma that Mary Sue has already experienced and the additional discomfort to which she would be subjected if she opts to attempt IVF again. Still, she would have a reasonable opportunity, through IVF, to try once again to achieve parenthood in all its aspects—genetic, gestational, bearing, and rearing.

Further, we note that if Mary Sue Davis were unable to undergo another round of IVF, or opted not to try, she could still achieve the child-rearing aspects of parenthood through adoption. The fact that she and Junior Davis pursued adoption indicates that, at least at one time, she was willing to forego genetic parenthood and would have been satisfied by the child-rearing aspects of parenthood alone.

In summary, we hold that disputes involving the disposition of preembryos produced by in vitro fertilization should be resolved, first, by looking to the preferences of the progenitors. If their wishes cannot be ascertained, or if there is dispute, then their prior agreement concerning disposition should be carried out. If no prior agreement exists, then the relative interests of the parties in using or not using the preembryos must be weighed. Ordinarily, the party wishing to avoid procreation should prevail, assuming that the other party has a reasonable possibility of achieving parenthood by means other than use of the preembryos in question. If no other reasonable alternatives exist, then the argument in favor of using the preembryos to achieve pregnancy should be considered. However, if the party seeking control of the preembryos intends merely to donate them to another couple, the objecting party obviously has the greater interest and should prevail.

NOTE

In re Roberto D.B., 923 A.2d 115 (Md. 2007), presented the question of whether a woman who carried and gave birth to twins, but was genetically unrelated to them, must be listed on the birth certificate as the mother of the twins. The twins were conceived through in vitro fertilization when Roberto D.B., who was unmarried, provided his sperm to fertilize eggs from a donor. The fertilized eggs were then implanted in another woman to gestate in her womb. Eight months later, the woman gave birth to twins at a hospital in Silver Spring, Maryland. As required by law, the hospital provides information regarding births to the Maryland Division of Vital Records, which issues birth certificates. Unless a court orders otherwise, the hospital will report the gestational carrier as the "mother" of a child to the agency. The hospital followed this procedure. Roberto D.B. and the gestational carrier petitioned a circuit court to issue a birth certificate that did not list the gestational carrier as the children's mother. In the petition, they asked the court to declare that Roberto D.B. was the father of the children, and to authorize the hospital to report only the name of the father to the MDVR. Both parties claimed that they never intended the gestational carrier to exercise any parental rights over the children and that they agreed that her role in the lives of the children would end upon their birth. The circuit court refused to grant the petition, and an appeal was taken to the Maryland Court of Appeals, which ruled that the petition should be granted, allowing the gestational carrier's name to be deleted from the birth certificate.

The court's decision resulted from its construction of a state paternity statute that, as written, provided an opportunity for genetically unrelated males to avoid parentage, while genetically unrelated females did not have the same option. Because the state Equal Rights Amendment prohibited the granting of more rights to one sex than to the other, the court ruled that the paternity statute must be construed to allow genetically unrelated females to have the same right as genetically unrelated males to avoid parentage.

In re T.W.
551 So.2d 1186 (Fla. 1989)

SHAW, J.

The procedure that a minor must follow to obtain an abortion in Florida is set out in the parental consent statute and related rules. Prior to undergoing an abortion, a minor must obtain parental consent or, alternatively, must convince a court that she is sufficiently mature to make the decision herself or that, if she is immature, the abortion nevertheless is in her best interests. Pursuant to this procedure, T.W., a pregnant, unmarried, fifteen-year-old, petitioned for a waiver of parental consent under the judicial bypass provision on the alternative grounds that (1) she was sufficiently mature to give an informed consent to the abortion, (2) she had a justified fear of physical or emotional abuse if her parents were requested to consent, and (3) her mother was seriously ill and informing her of the pregnancy would be an added burden. The trial court, after appointing counsel for T.W. and separate counsel as guardian ad litem for the fetus, conducted a hearing within twenty-four hours of the filing of the petition.

The appeals court below found that the statute's judicial alternative to parental consent was unconstitutionally vague, permitting arbitrary denial of a petition. The court declared the entire statute invalid and ordered the petition dismissed. The guardian ad litem appealed.

Florida is unusual in that it is one of at least four states having its own express constitutional provision guaranteeing an independent right to privacy, and we opt to examine the statute first under the Florida Constitution. In 1980, Florida voters by general election amended our state constitution to provide:

> Every natural person has the right to be let alone and free from governmental intrusion into his private life except as otherwise provided herein. This section shall not be construed to limit the public's right of access to public records and meetings as provided by law.

We have said that the amendment provides "an explicit textual foundation for those privacy interests inherent in the concept of liberty which may not otherwise be protected by specific constitutional provisions." *Rasmussen v.*

South Fla. Blood Serv. (Fla. 1987). We have found the right implicated in a wide range of activities dealing with the public disclosure of personal matters. Florida courts have also found the right involved in a number of cases dealing with personal decisionmaking.

The privacy section contains no express standard of review for evaluating the lawfulness of a government intrusion into one's private life, and this Court when called upon, adopted the following standard:

> The right of privacy demands the compelling state interest standard. This test shifts the burden of proof to the state to justify an intrusion on privacy. The burden can be met by demonstrating that the challenged regulation serves a compelling state interest and accomplishes its goal through the use of the least intrusive means.

Florida's privacy provision is clearly implicated in a woman's decision of whether or not to continue her pregnancy. We can conceive of few more personal or private decisions concerning one's body that one can make in the course of a lifetime, except perhaps the decision of the terminally ill in their choice of whether to discontinue necessary medical treatment.

The decision whether to obtain an abortion is fraught with specific physical, psychological, and economic implications of a uniquely personal nature for each woman. The Florida Constitution embodies the principle that "few decisions are more personal and intimate, more properly private, or more basic to individual dignity and autonomy, than a woman's decision whether to end her pregnancy. A woman's right to make that choice freely is fundamental."

The next question to be addressed is whether this freedom of choice concerning abortion extends to minors. We conclude that it does, based on the unambiguous language of the amendment: The right of privacy extends to "every natural person." Minors are natural persons in the eyes of the law and "constitutional rights do not mature and come into being magically only when one attains the state-defined age of majority. Minors, as well as adults possess constitutional rights."

Common sense dictates that a minor's rights are not absolute; in order to overcome these constitutional rights, a statute must survive the stringent test announced in *Winfield v. Division of Pari-Mutuel Wagering* (Fla. 1985): The state must prove that the statute furthers a compelling state interest through the least intrusive means.

The challenged statute fails because it intrudes upon the privacy of the pregnant minor from conception to birth. Such a substantial invasion of a pregnant female's privacy by the state for the full term of the pregnancy is not necessary for the preservation of maternal health or the potentiality of life. However, where parental rights over a minor child are concerned, society has recognized additional state interests—protection of the immature minor and preservation of the family unit. For reasons set out below, we find that neither of these interests is sufficiently compelling under Florida law to override Florida's privacy amendment.

Under section 743.065, a minor may consent, without parental approval, to any medical procedure involving her pregnancy or her existing child—no matter how dire the possible consequences—except abortion. Under *In re Guardianship of Barry* (1984), this could include authority in certain circumstances to order life support discontinued for a comatose child. In light of this wide authority that the state grants an unwed minor to make life-or-death decisions concerning herself or an existing child without parental consent, we are unable to discern a special compelling interest on the part of the state under Florida law in protecting the minor only where abortion is concerned. We fail to see the qualitative difference in terms of impact on the well-being of the minor between allowing the life of an existing child to come to an end and terminating a pregnancy, or between undergoing a highly dangerous medical procedure on oneself and undergoing a far less dangerous procedure to end one's pregnancy. If any qualitative difference exists, it certainly is insufficient in terms of state interest.

We hold that section 390.001(4)(a), violates the Florida Constitution.

NOTE

In 1999, the Florida legislature enacted a statute requiring parental notification (rather than parental consent) before a minor could undergo an abortion. The statute provided for a judicial bypass in lieu of parental notification. Relying on its previous decision in *T.W.*, the Florida Supreme Court ruled that the statute was unconstitutional. *N. Fla. Women's Health and Counseling Servs., Inc. v. State* (Fla. 2003). In response, the state legislature proposed a constitutional amendment, adopted by the voters, that overruled *N. Fla Women's Health* by authorizing the legislature to require parental notification before a minor has an abortion so long as the legislature also establishes a procedure for judicial bypass of the notification requirement. Fla. Const. art. X, § 22. The amendment did not address parental consent and accordingly had no effect on the ruling in *T.W.*

HODES & NAUSER, MDs, P.A. v. SCHMIDT
440 P.3d 461 (Kan. 2019)

PER CURIAM

In 2015, the Kansas Legislature enacted S.B. 95, which prohibits physicians from performing an abortion method referred to in medical terms as Dilation and Evacuation (D & E) except when "necessary to preserve the life of the pregnant woman" or to prevent a "substantial and irreversible physical impairment of a major bodily function of the pregnant woman."

In this case, the Doctors provide abortions, including D & E procedures, in Kansas. They filed this action challenging S.B. 95 on behalf of themselves and their patients on June 1, 2015. They argued S.B. 95 prevents them from using the safest method for most second-trimester abortions—the D & E method. These restrictions, according to the Doctors, violate sections 1 and 2 of the Kansas Constitution Bill of Rights because they infringe on inalienable natural rights, specifically, the right to liberty.

A graphic description of the D & E procedure referred to in S.B. 95 is not necessary to resolving the legal issues before us. Although the detailed nature of the procedure may factor into the lower court's later decision on the full merits, at this temporary injunction stage the United States Supreme Court's description suffices. That Court explained the procedure involves "(1) dilation of the cervix; (2) removal of at least some fetal tissue using nonvacuum instruments; and (3) (after the 15th week) the potential need for instrumental disarticulation or dismemberment of the fetus or the collapse of fetal parts to facilitate evacuation from the uterus." *Stenberg v. Carhart* (2000). The Doctors argued that 95% of second-trimester abortions in the United States are performed using the D & E procedure.

We begin our analysis of the issue of whether the Kansas Constitution Bill of Rights protects a woman's right to decide whether to continue a pregnancy by comparing the text of section 1 and the Fourteenth Amendment. This comparison highlights that Kansans chose to protect their "inalienable natural rights," including their liberty. Our analysis leads us to the conclusion that section 1 of the Kansas Constitution Bill of Rights acknowledges rights that are distinct from and broader than the United States Constitution and that our framers intended these rights to be judicially protected against governmental action that does not meet constitutional standards. Among the rights is the right of personal autonomy. This right allows a woman to make her own decisions regarding her body, health, family formation, and family life—decisions that can include whether to continue a pregnancy.

A comparison of the text of section 1 of the Kansas Bill of Rights, which was part of the Kansas Constitution ratified by the territorial voters in October 1859, and the Fourteenth Amendment to the United States Constitution, which was ratified in 1868, reveals several differences in wording. Again, section 1 states: "All men are possessed of equal and inalienable natural rights, among which are life, liberty, and the pursuit of happiness." And the Fourteenth Amendment states, in relevant part, that no State can "deprive any person of life, liberty, or property, without due process of law; nor deny to any person within its jurisdiction the equal protection of the laws."

As this side-by-side comparison reveals, section 1 contains the following words not found in the Fourteenth Amendment: "All men are possessed of equal and inalienable natural rights." In fact, no provision of the United States Constitution uses the term "natural rights"—*i.e.*, "a right that is conceived as part of natural law and that is therefore thought to exist independently of rights created by government or society." This silence created an ambiguity as to whether rights other than those listed are protected by the United States Constitution. In contrast, the Kansas provision lists certain rights—life, liberty, and the pursuit of happiness—but indicates these are just among the natural rights Kansans possess.

The framers of the Kansas Constitution in 1859 were not alone in adopting a natural rights provision. William Hutchinson, who chaired the "Preamble and Bill of Rights" Committee of the Wyandotte Constitutional Convention that initially developed section 1, explained the history of natural rights declarations to the other Convention delegates when he submitted his committee's report, stating:

> It is a historical fact, that ever since the days of King John, when the magna charta (*sic*) in favor of British freedom was obtained by the English yeomanry, some declaration of rights similar to the one presented by us, has been common with the people of all countries; but it was not until 1776, when that memorable Declaration of ours came into existence, that the people cut loose from a narrow conception of humanity, and entered upon that broad field of human liberty. All the State Constitutions since that day down to that of the prospective State of Kansas, have contained a similar instrument, that becomes as it were the timbers of the building—the superstructure upon which the edifice of State must be erected.

By the time the Fourteenth Amendment to the United States Constitution was ratified in "1868, twenty-four of the thirty-seven state constitutions existing at that time, nearly a two-thirds majority, contained provisions guaranteeing inalienable, natural, or inherent rights of an unenumerated rights type. Thus, in 1868, approximately 67% of all Americans then living resided in states that constitutionally protected unenumerated individual liberty rights." These provisions in state constitutions, which are often referred to as "Lockean Natural Rights Guarantees," originated with the Virginia Declaration of Rights of 1776. The Virginia Declaration, principally drafted by George Mason, relies heavily on the philosophy of John Locke. In particular, Mason "endorsed the Lockean ideal that all men retain some of their natural rights after subscribing to the social compact, in contrast to the idea put forth by Thomas Hobbes and Jean-Jacques Rousseau that men surrender all their natural rights to the sovereign in exchange for security and public order." Mason's draft served not only as the model for many state constitutions but also for portions of the Declaration of Independence.

Returning to the language of section 1, after using the phrase "inalienable natural rights," it delineates three rights: life, liberty, and the pursuit of happiness. The framers made clear the list was not intended to be exhaustive—rather, the listed rights are "among" the inalienable natural rights recognized by the provision. Section 1's broad declaration that all men are entitled to a nonexhaustive list of inalienable natural rights clearly reveals that section 1 recognizes a distinct and broader category of rights than does the Fourteenth Amendment.

The State focuses on the omission of a due process clause from section 1 to argue the rights listed there are aspirational or hortatory and not enforceable or self-executing. The Kansas Constitution does include a due process provision, however: section 18 of the Bill of Rights. It states: "All persons, for injuries suffered in person, reputation or property, shall have remedy by due course of law." But the Wyandotte Convention delegates simply chose to separate the provisions acknowledging rights—for example, section 1—from the due process provision in section 18.

The broad wording of Kansas' section 1, with its unenumerated natural rights guarantee, was not unlike the natural rights guarantees in at least 14 other states' constitutions in place at the time of the Wyandotte Convention. Although the wording of each state's constitutional natural rights guarantee varied, the provisions shared three characteristics. They (1) "affirmed the freedom or equality of men (or both)"; (2) "guaranteed inalienable, inherent, or natural rights"; and (3) "guaranteed a right to enjoy life, liberty," property, the pursuit of happiness, or some combination of these words. Applying these provisions in cases decided before Kansas convened the 1859 Wyandotte Convention, the courts in many of these 14 states had enforced unenumerated rights through judicial orders. These cases provided a context for how these natural rights guarantees would have been viewed at the time of the Wyandotte Convention.

First, these cases "make it crystal clear that the Lockean Natural Rights Guarantees did mean *something*. They did not function as simply vague, preambular language but were instead applied with varying degrees of judicial vigor to decide some of the most challenging and controversial issues of the day." Second, the "state supreme courts applied the Lockean Natural Rights Guarantees to an enormous variety of topics, suggesting an understanding during this time that the Lockean Natural Rights Guarantees protected a vast range of unenumerated rights." For example, state supreme courts had invoked the rights guarantees in cases dealing with a number of civil and political rights, including: "(1) freedom of religion; (2) the right of marriage; (3) the involuntary confinement and transportation of the poor; (4) retroactive legislation; (5) the constitutionality of statutes imposing or exempting tort liability"; and (6) a variety of other issues that "show the far-reaching nature of the state court's consideration of liberty and natural or unalienable rights for a very broad range of fact patterns." So, contrary to the State's argument, at the time the Kansas Bill of Rights was written and ratified in 1859, provisions like section 1 were widely accepted as guaranteeing natural rights enforceable via court proceedings.

In the present case, the Doctors assert that the following natural rights underlie the right of a woman to decide whether to continue a pregnancy: personal autonomy and decision-making about issues that affect one's physical health, family formation, and family life. The natural right to personal autonomy has been recognized by the United States Supreme Court for more than 120 years. In 1891, the Supreme Court recognized that "no right is held more sacred, or is more carefully guarded, by the common law, than the right of every individual to the possession and control of his own person." At about that same time, future Supreme Court Justice Louis Brandeis wrote of the "general right of the individual to be let alone," which is a component of the "inviolate personality" of human beings.

Various state courts have reached the same conclusion as the United States Supreme Court. In Illinois, "under a free government at least, the free citizen's first and greatest right, which underlies all others—the right to the inviolability of his person, in other words, his right to himself—is the subject of universal acquiescence." New York's highest court has held: "Every human being of adult years and sound mind has a right to determine what shall be done with his own body." And the Florida Supreme Court has stated that "everyone has a fundamental right to the sole control of his or her person."

The Alaska Supreme Court has concluded that exercising control over one's body "involves the kind of decision-making that is necessary for civilized life and ordered liberty." And Mississippi's highest court has held: "Each of us has a right to the inviolability and integrity of our persons, a freedom to choose or a right of bodily self-determination, if you will." This court has recognized the same principles, stating: "Anglo-American law starts with the premise of thorough-going self determination. It follows that each man is considered to be master of his own body, and he may, if he be of sound mind, expressly prohibit the performance of life-saving surgery, or other medical treatment."

At the heart of a natural rights philosophy is the principle that individuals should be free to make choices about how to conduct their own lives, or, in other words, to exercise personal autonomy. Few decisions impact our lives more than those about issues that affect one's physical health, family formation, and family life. We conclude that this right to personal autonomy is firmly embedded within section 1's natural rights guarantee and its included concepts of liberty and the pursuit of happiness.

Denying a pregnant woman the ability to determine whether to continue a pregnancy would severely limit her right of personal autonomy. And abortion laws do not merely restrict a particular action; they can impose an obligation on an unwilling woman to carry out a long-term course of conduct that will impact her health and alter her life. Pregnancy often brings discomfort and pain and, for some, can bring serious illness and even death.

The list of ways the government's restriction on abortion can have an impact on a woman's ability to control her own body and the course of her life could continue at length. In summary, "the decision whether to obtain an abortion is fraught with specific physical, psychological, and economic implications of a uniquely personal nature for each woman." Other courts with natural rights constitutional guarantees similar to Kansas' have reached the same conclusion. Some have done so based on privacy, but others have reached the conclusion because of constitutional protections of inalienable natural rights such as liberty—guarantees like that in the Kansas Constitution Bill of Rights.

Recently the Iowa Supreme Court also has held that the Iowa Constitution's guarantee that "no person shall be deprived of life, liberty, or property, without due process of law," protects a woman's right to decide whether to continue a pregnancy. *Planned Parenthood v. Reynolds ex rel.* (Iowa 2018). The court wrote that "autonomy and dominion over one's body go to the very heart of what it means to be free." It characterized the right to decide whether to continue a pregnancy as "the right to shape, for oneself, without unwarranted governmental intrusion, one's own identity, destiny, and place in the world" and noted that "nothing could be more fundamental to the notion of liberty." It concluded that "under the Iowa Constitution, implicit in the concept of ordered liberty is the ability to decide whether to continue or terminate a pregnancy."

The natural right of personal autonomy recognized in these states' constitutions allows individuals to control their own bodies, to make health care decisions, and to make decisions about whether to bear or beget a child. Consistent with these and other states, today we hold our Kansas Constitution's drafters' and ratifiers' proclamation of natural rights applies to pregnant women.

The strict scrutiny standard has been applied in cases where the government has imposed restrictions on abortions. Initially, the United States Supreme Court applied the strict scrutiny standard in *Roe v. Wade* (1973) and its companion case, *Doe v. Bolton* (1973), to state statutes restricting access to medical procedures used to end a pregnancy. The Court adopted a different standard in *Planned Parenthood of Southeastern PA v. Casey* (1992)—a case that addressed restrictions on women's access to abortion. After reaffirming *Roe*'s conclusions on a woman's right to choose an abortion, the three authoring justices in *Casey* realigned the "other side of the equation, which is the interest of the State in the protection of potential life." Rather than the traditional strict scrutiny standard, the three justices adopted an "undue burden" standard for the State to meet.

This court has never adopted the undue burden standard. But it has tended to employ a Fourteenth Amendment based approach to challenges invoking both that amendment and section 1 of the Kansas Constitution Bill of Rights. Thus, the trial court and the six members comprising the Court of Appeals plurality predicted this court would adopt the undue burden standard. Several worthy reasons lead us to do otherwise and apply the strict scrutiny standard.

First, the undue burden standard has proven difficult to understand and apply. One troubling ambiguity has arisen regarding the level of judicial scrutiny the standard requires. At least one author has referred to the *Casey* standard as "a form of intermediate scrutiny." Under this standard, the State must show only an "important" interest in order to successfully defend the challenged legislation. Meanwhile, the Fifth Circuit has interpreted the undue burden test as a form of the rational basis test—*i.e.*, a standard of review even less demanding than intermediate scrutiny.

As further support for our adopting the strict scrutiny standard, we note it has been applied by a majority of other courts that have determined their state constitutions provide a right to decide whether to continue a pregnancy. Finally, and perhaps most importantly, we adopt the strict scrutiny standard because it is our obligation to protect (1) the intent of the Wyandotte Convention delegation and voters who ratified the Constitution and (2) the inalienable natural rights of all Kansans today. And the strict scrutiny test best protects those natural rights that we today hold to be fundamental. Simply put, the undue burden standard lacks the rigor demanded by the Kansas Constitution for protecting the right of personal autonomy at issue in this case.

Accepting the trial court's factual findings, we now ask the ultimate question before us in this appeal: Did the trial court abuse its discretion when it concluded that the Doctors were substantially likely to prevail on the merits of their claim? The trial court did not apply a strict scrutiny standard when answering this question. Applying the wrong legal standard constitutes an abuse of discretion. Nevertheless, when a trial court applies the wrong standard, remand for it to apply the correct standard is not always necessary. We conclude a remand is not necessary here because the result would be the same. The trial court and the Court of Appeals plurality held there was a substantial likelihood S.B. 95 could not survive the undue burden test, which in our view is a lesser standard.

Although we have responded to some points made by the dissent, we pause here to point out key distinctions between it and the majority opinion. The overriding difference between the opinions is the degree of importance and substance that each attaches to individual liberty. The majority holds that individuals enjoy constitutional protection against unwarranted government intrusion in their personal business, whereas the dissent leaves the individual nearly naked and defenseless, especially in the realm of individual sovereignty.

The dissent finds itself in a painful dilemma: It feels obligated to hold that government may intrude with impunity on the most fundamental of natural human rights, the right of personal autonomy—in particular, the right to make medical decisions about oneself; but it also wants to hold itself out as favoring constitutionally limited government power. In order to resolve this conflict, the dissent engages in a fantastic acrobatic midair twist. It contends that government should come from rights first, but then maintains that government should be largely unrestrained in exercising its power over the personal sovereignty of pregnant women. The dissent achieves this astonishing reversal by fervently arguing that the Kansas Constitution Bill of Rights was intended to protect the pre-political rights of Kansans. But that argument eventually leads, of course, to the same conclusion that the majority reaches.

As a consequence, the dissent is forced to mischaracterize the majority opinion. It attempts to portray the majority as paternalistic and authoritarian, endorsing government power at the expense of citizens' rights, e.g., personal autonomy. But it is the dissent who argues for a government largely unfettered by constitutional constraints, with the State deciding for the individual what is best for that individual. The dissent concedes that some state action may violate the protections of section 1 but only if such exercise of police power is completely arbitrary, irrational, or discriminatory. The dissent ultimately favors limited state powers that in reality have no practical limits. The dissent's vision of government and rights is one of regal government powers, powers that sweep away individual liberty in favor of a majoritarian dictate. In the dissent's view, the Kansas Constitution Bill of Rights is akin to a gentle reminder not to disturb liberty very much but with no legal consequences if government ignores that reminder.

We hold today that section 1 of the Kansas Constitution Bill of Rights protects all Kansans' natural right of personal autonomy, which includes the right to control one's own body, to assert bodily integrity, and to exercise self-determination. This right allows a woman to make her own decisions regarding her body, health, family formation, and family life—decisions that can include whether to continue a pregnancy.

Under our strict scrutiny standard, the State is prohibited from restricting that right unless it can show it is doing so to further a compelling government interest and in a way that is narrowly tailored to that interest. The Doctors have shown they are substantially likely to prevail on their claim that S.B. 95 does not meet this standard.

STEGALL, J., dissenting.

This case is not only about abortion *policy*—the most divisive social issue of our day—it is more elementally about the *structure* of our republican form of government. Which is to say, this case is about the proper conditions for just rule. At bottom, this case is about finding and drawing the sometimes elusive line between law and arbitrary exercises of power. Here we venture onto a battlefield as old as politics itself. The structural idea that gave birth to Kansas as a political community, which has achieved consensus support across most of our history, is that the proper conditions for just rule are met via *participatory consent to secure and promote the common welfare*. Today, a majority of this court dramatically departs from this consensus. Today, we hoist our sail and navigate the ship-of-state out of its firm anchorage in the harbor-of-common-good and onto the uncertain waters of the sea-of-fundamental-values. Today we issue the most significant and far-reaching decision this court has ever made. The majority's decision is so consequential because it fundamentally alters the structure of our government to magnify the power of the state—all while using that power to arbitrarily grant a regulatory reprieve to the judicially privileged act of abortion.

Reading today's majority opinion is a follow-the-white-rabbit experience. One is left feeling like Alice, invited by the Queen to believe "as many as six impossible things before breakfast." Carroll, *Through the Looking-Glass* 100 (1899). Indeed, the story told by the majority is a strange one. In it, all the luminaries of the western legal tradition— from Sir Edward Coke and William Blackstone to Edmund Burke and Thomas Jefferson— would celebrate and enshrine a right to nearly unfettered abortion access. Invoking the spirit of living constitutionalism (while avoiding its name), today's majority proceeds as follows. First, it contrives to find a "wide range of judicially enforceable though unenumerated rights" in section 1 of the Kansas Constitution Bill of Rights. Then it divines a "natural right" to abortion. And finally, it decides to review restrictions on that newly minted right according to one among varying levels of judicial "scrutiny" depending on its favored or disfavored classification.

In the end, our court holds the right to an abortion is "fundamental" under the Kansas Constitution and restrictions on that right are subject to the highest, strictest level of judicial review in a system of tiered scrutiny. Despite claiming to interpret section 1 of the Kansas Constitution Bill of Rights independent of the United States Constitution, the majority imposes a legal rubric that is indistinguishable from the "substantive due process" guarantees the 20th century United States Supreme Court found in the Fourteenth Amendment. Perhaps it is apropos—though macabre—that while reviewing a prohibition against human dismemberment we have fashioned a 20th century jurisprudence of fundamental rights and tiered scrutiny into a procrustean bed upon which we now force the Kansas Constitution Bill of Rights to lie.

Today's decision is a textbook case of unexplainable results. The majority misunderstands and misuses history; bolsters its rejection of Kansas law with factually unsupported allegations of prejudice; ignores even its own claim to be pursuing the "drafters' intent" as the "polestar" of constitutional interpretation; and in the end, can do no better than to fall back on federal substantive due process jurisprudence—complete with judicially favored rights and a byzantine system of tiered scrutiny.

The majority recognizes the influence of John Locke on the Declaration of Independence and thus on section 1 of our Bill of Rights. Tracing the language of section 1 all the way back to Locke's Second Treatise, the majority discovers a line that says "every Man has a *Property* in his own *Person*." This lonely line then becomes the springboard to a fundamental—nay absolute—right to abortion. Connecting these dots is difficult, to say the least. But it begins with the premise that Locke's Treatise announced a 21st-century-style list of fundamental rights. The premise is not just wrong, it is utterly foreign to Locke. Locke was less interested in delineating "rights" than he was in describing the contours of republican self-government.

Either section 1 is a fount of judicially discovered and preferred "fundamental" rights or it is a blanket guarantee to all Kansans of the *first* rights of republican self-government: the right to participatory consent to government for the benefit of the common welfare, on the one hand, and the right to otherwise be free from arbitrary, irrational, or discriminatory regulation that bears no reasonable relationship to the common welfare, on the other. Section 1 cannot be both. The former road alienates the people from the exercise of power and disembeds them from the political community. But this is the way the majority has decided to go.

If section 1 does not protect "fundamental" rights with the shield of "strict scrutiny" judicial review, is it necessarily a mere paper law—a glittering generality? No. Contrary to modern notions of "rational basis" review, the judicial inquiry demanded by section 1 would look to the actual legislative record rather than to hypothetical reasons or any possible imagined rationale. The test has occasionally been described as "rational basis with bite." As one judge recently put it, "this test is rational basis with bite, demanding actual *rationality*, scrutinizing the law's actual *basis*, and applying an actual *test*." On the one hand, it does not load "the dice—relentlessly—in government's favor," resulting in a "pass/fail" test that the "government never fails." On the other hand, it remains a deferential test—one that recognizes our Constitution vests the legislative branch of government with the institutional competence to consider competing interests and policy options, resulting in democratic judgment about the common welfare of all Kansans.

In sum, section 1 demands this "rational basis with bite" judicial inquiry. In order to be a constitutional exercise of power, *every* act of our Legislature must be rationally related to the furtherance or protection of the commonwealth. The lodestar of this test is, *"what have* the people *authorized to be done?"* The people have not authorized the State to act in arbitrary, irrational, or discriminatory ways. Applying the necessary deference, a court must examine the *actual* legislative record to determine the *real* purpose behind any law in question before it can conclude the law is within the limited constitutional grant of power possessed by the State.

Here I pause to observe that the majority's characterization of the judicial test I have set forth—the test section 1 demands *every* exercise of the State's police powers must satisfy—bears no resemblance to anything I have written here. The majority claims I am "dismissive" of the rights of citizens. The majority reads the limitations on the State's police power I describe as setting "too low a bar" and "allowing the State to intrude into all decisions about childbearing" and "our families." The original public meaning of section 1 is described as leaving citizens "naked and defenseless" against abusive state power. The majority suggests my approach grants "unrestrained" power to the State, "unfettered by constitutional constraints," which has "no practical limits" and allows the government to "intrude with impunity" against the individual. And finally, with an Atwoodian flourish, I stand accused of maintaining "that upon becoming pregnant, women relinquish virtually all rights of personal sovereignty in favor of the Legislature's determination of what is in the common good." All of which leads to the preposterous "presumption" that I would find "no constitutional conflicts" with state-mandated mass sterilization.

I am agog. I must know—*what* have my colleagues been reading? It cannot be anything I have written. In any case, I assure the reader this description of my view is a fabrication so flimsy it makes run-of-the-mill straw men appear as fairy tale knights by comparison.

So, is S.B. 95 a legitimate exercise of state police power? If the original meaning of section 1—and this court's prior mode of consistently applying section 1 as a police power provision—had carried the day here, I would be content to wait to answer that question. In the meantime, I would remand this case to the district court to apply the correct legal standard. On remand, the question for the parties to litigate, and the district court to resolve, would be whether S.B. 95 bears a reasonable relationship to the common welfare or is otherwise arbitrary, irrational, or discriminatory.

Unfortunately, history, reason, and original meaning have not carried the day. Hence, because the proper "rational basis with bite" test will otherwise go unapplied in today's context, I offer some thoughts on the general considerations a court *might* entertain if such a test was applied, with the caveat that sufficient facts have not been developed in the record to arrive at any definitive conclusions.

The stated goal of S.B. 95 is to protect Kansas unborn children from dismemberment abortion, or being "cut" "one piece at a time from the uterus." It is certainly reasonable to say the State could have a valid purpose in banning this brutal method of killing an unborn child. Shockingly, the majority hardly even *considers* the State's legitimate interest in protecting unborn life as a means of promoting and furthering the common welfare of our state.

This failure is glaring when contrasted with the State of Kansas' longstanding policy of protecting the unborn—even outside the abortion context. For instance, Kansas criminalizes homicides of the unborn; refuses to execute pregnant convicts; permits wrongful death actions for the unborn; gives no effect to a living will when the patient is pregnant; and provides for the representation of the unborn in trust and probate proceedings.

As explained at length above, section 1—properly understood—expresses a truth widely known and accepted at the time of Kansas' constitutional moment: pre-political individual sovereigns possess a natural and inalienable right to do "what they like." But that was only half the story. Just as important, Kansans understood the Declaration's language anticipated that such pre-political people desired to be more—they desired to be citizens. Such people came together and formed political communities by relinquishing however much of that individual sovereignty was necessary to obtain a "state"—that is, a common welfare secured for all.

Thus, the newly constituted State of Kansas exercised limited police power *in the name of* the pre-constitutional person who, by his or her implied consent, had agreed to be bound to police regulations so long as they were not irrational, arbitrary, or discriminatory, and were reasonably related to the furtherance of the common welfare. At our founding, Kansans understood the "old truth" embodied in section 1 to mean that every person would give up "enough control over his original rights to permit government to maintain an organized, stable, peaceful pattern of human relations."

The first Kansans understood the language of section 1 not only as an inherent limitation on the police power of the state, but also as legitimizing the political community itself, along with its "deliberative sense" of how to further the common welfare of all Kansans. The people's deliberative sense, when confined to the pursuit of the common welfare, creates a pragmatic and flexible counterweight to the absolute sovereignty of the Lockean pre-constitutional person. Such balance is the hallmark of our historic understanding of what makes a republican form of government. When pursued unilaterally, each version of "liberty" had proven inherently unstable. But when placed in creative equipoise, the two traditions achieved their most lasting expression in the Declaration and the explosion of republican governments it spawned. Thus, the natural rights theorists that so influenced the American founding "emphasized both individual rights and the common good as complementary rather than conflicting aspects of the human condition."

A more down-to-earth way to say the same thing—the Constitution announces and defines boundaries, not values. Or, if one must use the language and discourse of values, one might say those boundaries *are the values* the Constitution announces. And it is the courts' job to patrol boundaries, not to decide whether any particular enactment is consistent with "fundamental" or "substantive" values.

Thus, among the casualties of today's decision is the deliberative sense of our particular political community—constituted in 1861 as "Kansas"—concerning what best serves the common welfare of its people. Without that deliberative sense, the ground under the political community erodes. The loss of this self-reflective, deliberative sense of ourselves is felt keenly by citizens who perceive, even if dimly, that something of their political "essence" is being eliminated.

We have turned our constitutional structure on its head. Instead of a general limit on the police power of the state which constrains *every* exercise of that power, section 1 is now a "guarantee" of limited, preferred rights granted by the arbitrary power of a majority of judges on this court. Of course, this leaves in place the equally dangerous arbitrary power of the Legislature to act with impunity in any area not already occupied by this court.

At the outset, I noted that this case isn't just about the policy of abortion, it is more basically about the structure of our government. While true, this description fails to account for a strange but persistent symbiosis between the two. Abortion has become the judicially preferred policy tail wagging the structure of government dog. For the majority, the settled and carefully calibrated republican structure of our government must give way, at every turn, to the favored policy. But in my considered judgment, *constitutional structure* is the very thing securing and guaranteeing the *full range* of human liberty. History and reason suggest that those who, in the name of liberty, tear down that edifice will wind up out in the political elements, unsheltered and exposed to the cold wind of every arbitrary power. I dissent.

NOTE

In *Dobbs v. Planned Parenthood* (2022), the U.S. Supreme Court overruled its *Casey* and *Roe* decisions. Plenty of state court cases had previously determined, as the Kansas Supreme Court did, that their state constitutions already offered greater protection in this area than the Fourteenth Amendment did. Not long after the *Dobbs* decision, the people of Kansas had an opportunity to vote on whether to overrule by constitutional amendment the *Hodes & Nauser* decision. They rejected the proposed amendment. In the run up to *Dobbs* and in its aftermath, several States have placed amendments on the ballot to include a constitutional right to abortion. On top of that, considerable state court litigation has arisen over whether the existing guarantees in some state constitutions protect a right to abortion. However this story ends, it is likely to include considerable activity in the States.

PLANNED PARENTHOOD OF THE HEARTLAND, INC. v. REYNOLDS ex rel. STATE
975 N.W.2d 710 (Iowa 2022)

MANSFIELD, J.

In this case, we again consider the right to an abortion under the Iowa Constitution. In 2015, this court applied the federal *Casey* undue burden test under the Iowa Constitution. *See Planned Parenthood of the Heartland, Inc. v. Iowa Bd. of Med.* (*PPH I*) (Iowa 2015). We found that a statewide ban on telemedicine medication abortions, adopted by the board of medicine when it was otherwise approving the use of telemedicine, violated the Iowa Constitution. Notably, Planned Parenthood had wanted us to recognize a state constitutional right to abortion that was broader than the federal constitutional right. We did not reach that issue because we found the telemedicine ban was unconstitutional even under the federal undue burden test, a test that the State had conceded was applicable under the Iowa Constitution.

Three years later, in *Planned Parenthood of the Heartland v. Reynolds* (*PPH II*) (Iowa 2018), we confronted a mandatory 72-hour waiting period for abortion that the legislature had enacted in 2017. This time we rejected the undue burden test. Instead, we found that the Iowa Constitution—specifically, the due process clause—protected abortion as a fundamental right. We determined that the waiting period could not survive strict scrutiny under that test and struck it down as unconstitutional.

In 2020, in the waning hours of a legislative session that had been disrupted by COVID-19, the general assembly added a mandatory 24-hour waiting period for abortion to pending legislation limiting courts' ability to withdraw life-sustaining procedures. The 24-hour waiting period involved the same period of time that the United States Supreme Court had upheld in *Casey*. Yet Planned Parenthood sued successfully in district court to block the statute from taking effect.

Today, we decide only the issues that *the parties* have presented to us in the current procedural posture of the case. As to issue preclusion, we agree with the State that a 72-hour waiting period and a 24-hour waiting period are not identical. We also agree that issue preclusion does not bar a state's highest court from revisiting its decision on a broad question of constitutional law such as the right to an abortion. And, finally, we hold that any subsidiary fact-findings we made in *PPH II* occurred within a constitutional framework that placed every burden of persuasion and proof on the State. If we overrule that broad constitutional framework, as the State urges, the findings cannot have preclusive effect. Accordingly, after carefully considering the parties' arguments, we decide that *PPH II* can and should be overruled.

Although we overrule *PPH II*, and thus reject the proposition that there is a fundamental right to an abortion in Iowa's Constitution subjecting abortion regulation to strict scrutiny, we do not at this time decide what constitutional standard should replace it. As noted, in *PPH I*, we applied the undue burden test under our constitution when the State conceded that it applied. An amicus curiae argues that we should hold that the rational basis test applies to abortion regulations. But *the State* takes no such position; it simply asks that *PPH II* be overruled and stops there.

In addition, we are not blind to the fact that an important abortion case is now pending in the United States Supreme Court. *See Dobbs v. Jackson Women's Health Org* (2022). That case could alter the federal constitutional landscape established by *Roe* and *Casey*. While we zealously guard our ability to interpret the Iowa Constitution independently of the Supreme Court's interpretations of the Federal Constitution, the opinion in that case may provide insights that we are currently lacking.

Hence, all we hold today is that the Iowa Constitution is not the source of a fundamental right to an abortion necessitating a strict scrutiny standard of review for regulations affecting that right. For now, this means that the *Casey* undue burden test we applied in *PPH I* remains the governing standard. On remand, the parties should marshal and present evidence under that test, although the legal standard may also be litigated further.

Stare decisis—"to stand by things decided"—cautions us against overturning our past decisions. But stare decisis is not an "inexorable command." "Within a system of justice, courts cannot blindly follow the past. Instead, we are obligated to depart from past cases when they were erroneously decided." "It is our obligation to revisit a prior decision of our court if we conclude the previous decision is unsound." "Of course, stare decisis is a factor to consider. At the same time, we recognize that stare decisis is not always determinative. Otherwise, the law would be like a fly imprisoned in volcanic rock."

There are several reasons why stare decisis has less force here than it might in other contexts. First, *PPH II* was a constitutional decision. "Stare decisis has limited application in constitutional matters." "Constitutional cases tend to invoke a weak or less strict form of stare decisis, on the theory that only the courts can correct bad constitutional precedent, absent constitutional amendments. In other words, courts must be free to correct their own mistakes when no one else can."

Second, *PPH II* was decided only four years ago. It is certainly not "long-standing." It is not "well-established" or "settled."

Third, *PPH II* was overtly based on the notion of a "living" constitution. We "considered current prevailing standards that draw their meaning from the evolving standards that mark the progress of a maturing society." To the extent *PPH II* viewed constitutional interpretation as an evolutionary process rather than a search for fixed meaning, it is hard now to argue that the evolutionary process had to end as soon as *PPH II* was decided. Does the Iowa Constitution get to "live" until 2018, at which point it must stop living?

A group of distinguished law professors from the University of Iowa and Drake filed an amicus brief in this case on the subject of stare decisis. We respect their views, but we disagree with them.

The professors argue that a precedent should only be overruled when "stare decisis has lapsed"—that is, a sufficient time period has passed. In the professors' view, four years is not enough. Overruling a four-year-old precedent "would suggest that this Court had not deliberated adequately in 2018."

To be clear, we do not contend that the court failed to deliberate adequately in 2018. But we do not agree that every state supreme court decision is entitled to some minimum try-out period before it can be challenged.

We believe the views of Justice Amy Coney Barrett, who was writing at the time as a law professor, are worth quoting:

> To be sure, partisan politics are not a good reason for overturning precedent. But neither are they a good reason for deciding a case of first impression. One who believes that an overruling reflects votes cast based on political preference must believe that all cases (or at least all the hot-button ones) are decided that way, for there would be no reason for politics to taint reversals but not initial decisions. If all such decisions are based on politics, there is no reason why the precedent—itself thus tainted—is worthy of deference. (Nor, for that matter, would there be reason to accept the legitimacy of judicial review.) Basic confidence in the Supreme Court requires the assumption that, as a general matter, justices decide cases based on their honestly held beliefs about how the Constitution should be interpreted. If one is willing to make that assumption about the decision of cases

of first impression, one should also be willing to make it about the decision to overrule precedent.

Amy Coney Barrett, *Precedent and Jurisprudential Disagreement*, 91 Tex. L. Rev. 1711, 1729 (2013).

Doctrinally, *PPH II* stands virtually alone, both inside and outside Iowa. *PPH II* found a fundamental right to an abortion where others had not: in the due process clause as a right "implicit in the concept of ordered liberty." While some other state supreme courts have found a fundamental right to an abortion within their state constitution, as is discussed below, they have done so based on one or more substantive constitutional guarantees. Conversely, states that find a right to an abortion in a state constitutional due process clause have gone no further than the undue burden test.

In 2019, one year after *PPH II*, the Kansas Supreme Court recognized a fundamental constitutional right to an abortion. *Hodes & Nauser, MDs, P.A. v. Schmidt*. However, unlike our court, it relied on the inalienable rights clause while specifically *declining* to rely on the due process clause.

Elsewhere, the story is similar. Minnesota has recognized a fundamental right to an abortion under a combination of guarantees in the Minnesota Constitution. *Women of State of Minn. by Doe v. Gomez* (Minn. 1995). California has found a fundamental right to an abortion under California's constitutional privacy clause. *Am. Acad. of Pediatrics v. Lungren* (Cal. 1997). Likewise, Alaska has found a fundamental right to an abortion encompassed within the right to privacy in the Alaska Constitution. *Valley Hosp. Ass'n v. Mat-Su Coal. for Choice* (Alaska 1997); *see* Alaska Const. art. I, § 22 ("The right of the people to privacy is recognized and shall not be infringed."). Montana has found a fundamental right to an abortion based on a constitutional guarantee of individual privacy that has no counterpart in the Iowa Constitution. *Armstrong v. State* (Mont. 1999); *see* Mont. Const. art. II, § 10 ("The right of individual privacy is essential to the well-being of a free society and shall not be infringed without the showing of a compelling state interest."). Tennessee, until the court's decision was overturned by a constitutional amendment, likewise relied on various grants of rights within the Tennessee Constitution "more particularly stated than those stated in the federal Bill of Rights." *Planned Parenthood of Middle Tenn. v. Sundquist* (Tenn. 2000), *superseded by constitutional amendment*, Tenn. Const. art. I, § 36. New Jersey has found a fundamental right to an abortion within the "natural and unalienable rights" clause of the New Jersey Constitution. *Planned Parenthood of Cent. N.J. v. Farmer* (N.J. 2000). Florida has pinpointed a fundamental right to an abortion within Florida's constitutional right to privacy, which was added to the Florida Constitution in 1980 and which establishes the right of every person to "be let alone and free from governmental intrusion into one's private life." *Gainesville Woman Care, LLC v. State* (Fla. 2017).

Meanwhile, state courts focusing specifically on the due process clause have overwhelmingly found that the right to an abortion in the state constitution is no broader than the federal right (if it exists at all). *See, e.g.*, *Hope Clinic for Women, Ltd. v. Flores* (Ill. 2013) (finding a due process right to an abortion in the Illinois Constitution congruent with the federal right and rejecting the existence of a right to an abortion within the privacy clause); *Reprod. Health Servs. of Planned Parenthood of St. Louis Region, Inc. v. Nixon* (Mo. 2006) (en banc) (per curiam) (applying the due process clause of the Missouri Constitution as giving the same protection to a pregnant woman recognized by *Casey*); *Pro-Choice Miss. v. Fordice* (Miss. 1998) (en banc) (applying the undue burden test under the Mississippi Constitution and noting that "the abortion issue is much more complex than most cases involving privacy rights"); *Preterm Cleveland v. Voinovich* (Ohio Ct. App. 1993) ("We find no reason under the circumstances of this case to find that the Ohio Constitution confers upon a pregnant woman a greater right to choose whether to have an abortion or bear the child than is conferred by the United States Constitution, as explained in the plurality opinion of *Casey*."); *see also Planned Parenthood Ariz., Inc. v. Am. Ass'n of Pro-Life Obstetricians & Gynecologists* (Ariz. Ct. App. 2011) (applying the federal undue burden test under the Arizona Constitution even though it contains an express privacy clause); *Clinic for Women, Inc. v. Brizzi* (Ind. 2005) (holding that Indiana's inalienable rights clause provides protection similar to the *Casey* undue burden test); *Planned Parenthood League of Mass., Inc. v. Att'y Gen.* (Mass. 1997) (explaining that Massachusetts does not follow federal abortion precedent under the Massachusetts due process clause which has different wording, but the reviewing court does engage in balancing and does not require the state to advance a compelling state interest); *State v. Koome* (Wash. 1975) (en banc) (applying federal abortion precedent to strike down a Washington statute under both federal and state due process).

So, our point is: State courts recognizing broader, "fundamental" abortion rights have at least had textual grounds for doing so other than the due process clause.

McDERMOTT, J., concurring in part and dissenting in part.

I join almost all parts of the court's opinion. But I dissent from my colleagues' remand directing the district court to apply an "undue burden" standard, subject (apparently) to the standard being "litigated further" by the parties. In my view, we should emphatically reject—not recycle—*Casey*'s moribund undue burden test and instead direct the district court to apply the rational basis test to the plaintiffs' constitutional challenge.

A "fundamental right," as we apply that term in our constitutional analysis, doesn't simply mean "important." To qualify as a fundamental right, the alleged right at issue must objectively be "deeply rooted" in our "history and tradition" and "implicit in the concept of ordered liberty." Whether abortion is deeply rooted in our history and tradition determines whether it's a fundamental right and thus whether it's protected by the Iowa Constitution. It isn't for us, as justices on a court, to decide whether the Iowa Constitution *should* provide a right to abortion; we must decide whether the Iowa Constitution in fact *does* provide a right to abortion. "The rule of law is in unsafe hands when courts cease to function as courts and become organs for control of policy." Justice Robert H. Jackson, *The Struggle for Judicial Supremacy* 322 (1941).

An undue burden standard inevitably leaves courts unable to provide predictability, consistency, or coherence in its application. Regardless of outcome, the rule of law inevitably loses when courts are made to attempt the undue burden test's balancing act. We need not adopt it in Iowa, and we should not adopt it in Iowa.

Again, we already have coherent, well-established tiers of review that we routinely apply when analyzing whether a regulation infringes constitutional due process rights. The waiting period statute challenged in this case implicates no suspect classifications such as race, alienage, or national origin. And as discussed, abortion is not a fundamental right. When "no suspect class or fundamental right is at issue, we apply the rational basis test." The court should apply the rational basis test in analyzing the plaintiffs' challenge to the abortion regulation in this case.

Overruling a precedent always introduces some confusion. But we only magnify that confusion by requiring the district court to apply a nebulous test that practically demands that judges read in their own views instead of applying a time-tested standard with doctrinal stability as we find with the rational basis test. Even the most well-intentioned judge attempting to apply the undue burden standard will not be able to overcome "the underlying fact that the concept has no principled or coherent legal basis." As a constitutional test, it generates answers so subjective as to make Hermann Rorschach envious, presenting not so much an exercise in constitutional interpretation as imagination.

APPEL, J., dissenting.

"Liberty finds no refuge in a jurisprudence of doubt." Yet, by rejecting the holdings in a 5–2 majority decision in *Planned Parenthood of the Heartland v. Reynolds ex rel. State* decided only a few years ago, and punting the case back to the district court, the court creates a jurisprudence of doubt about a liberty interest of the highest possible importance to every Iowa woman of reproductive age.

This jurisprudence of doubt is troublesome for three reasons. First, in recent years, approximately one in four women of reproductive age have exercised reproductive autonomy by choosing an abortion. This jurisprudence of doubt will plainly impact many women and the men who support them. Second, the weight and depth of a woman's interest in reproductive autonomy involved in this case is so profound. As noted by Chief Justice Cady in *Planned Parenthood II*: "Autonomy and dominion over one's body go to the very heart of what it means to be free. At stake in this case is the right to shape, for oneself, without unwarranted governmental intrusion, one's own identity, destiny, and place in the world. Nothing could be more fundamental to the notion of liberty."

Third, this jurisprudence of doubt is entirely avoidable. The decision in *Planned Parenthood II* was dispositive when it was issued and should be dispositive today.

I would take a different path. I would affirm the holding of *Planned Parenthood II* that a woman's liberty interest in reproductive autonomy is a fundamental right under article I, section 9 of the Iowa Constitution; the State may regulate only upon a showing of compelling state interest and only if the regulation is narrowly tailored to advance that interest. Further, given the record presented, which is virtually the same as the record in *Planned Parenthood II*, I would find the 24-hour waiting period fails to pass constitutional muster under strict scrutiny review. But if we make the unfortunate choice of abandoning strict scrutiny, I would replace it, as a least harmful alternative, with an undue burden test "with teeth" to provide a woman's reproductive autonomy with as much constitutional protection as possible.

Constitutional liberties are often destroyed "not with a bang, but a whimper." I fear for the future of reproductive autonomy in Iowa. The majority today "casts into darkness the hopes and visions of every woman in this country who had come to believe that the Constitution guaranteed her the right to exercise some control over her unique ability to bear children."

For those who favor a woman's autonomy and personal freedom, this is an unwelcome development. A strong barrier to state interference in a woman's right to determine whether to have an abortion has been removed by the majority. And the right to abortion is left in a free fall. Make no mistake—reproductive rights are at great risk with this decision.

D. THE RIGHT OF INTIMATE ASSOCIATION

STATE v. SAUNDERS
381 A.2d 333 (N.J. 1977)

PASHMAN, J.

Defendant Charles Saunders was indicted along with Bernard Busby on charges of rape, assault with intent to rape and armed robbery. At trial both admitted to having had sexual intercourse with the two complainants, but insisted that the women had participated willingly in exchange for a promise that they would receive "reefers" (marijuana cigarettes) in return. The trial judge, on his own initiative, charged the jury that the defendants could be convicted of the "lesser included offense" of fornication if they were found not guilty on the other counts. The jury acquitted the defendants of the charges in the indictment and convicted them of fornication. In charging the jury, the judge defined the crime of fornication as "an act of illicit sexual intercourse by a man, married or single, with an unmarried woman."

Defendant asserts that the instant statute, N.J.S.A. 2A:110-1, is unconstitutional on its face since it generally seeks to outlaw conduct which the State has no power to prohibit. The right of privacy, upon which defendant bases his attack, is not explicitly mentioned in either the New Jersey or United States Constitutions. However, both documents have been construed to include such a right. On the federal level, the right was first recognized as being of constitutional stature by a majority of the Court in *Griswold v. Connecticut* (1965). Subsequent Supreme Court decisions have firmly established the constitutional nature of the right of privacy. In *Roe v. Wade* (1973), the Court found that the right of privacy encompassed a woman's decision whether or not to terminate a pregnancy. More recently the right has been recognized in the Court's decisions in *Carey v. Population Services International* (1977); *Whalen v. Roe* (1977); and *Paul v. Davis* (1976).

However, the precise scope of the interests protected by the right of privacy are not easily defined. As the Court noted in *Carey v. Population Services International*, the interests which have been held to fall within the protections of the right have been "personal" ones; they have included those "relating to marriage, *Loving v. Virginia* (1967); procreation, *Skinner v. Oklahoma* (1942); contraception, *Eisenstadt v. Baird* (1972); family relationships, *Prince v. Massachusetts* (1944); and child rearing and education, *Pierce v. Society of Sisters* (1925)."

Although the Court in *Carey* observed that the "decision whether or not to beget or bear a child is at the very heart of this cluster of constitutionally protected choices," we believe that the right of privacy is not confined to the private situations involved in each of these decisions. While *Carey* certainly emphasizes the importance of a person's choice regarding whether or not to have children, it indicates that the constitutional basis for the protection of such decisions is their relationship to individual autonomy. Mr. Justice Brennan observed that such personal choices concern "the most intimate of human activities and relationships," adding that "decisions whether to accomplish or to prevent conception are among the most private and sensitive."

This view of the right of privacy is consistent with the approach taken by this Court in our recent decision in *In re Quinlan* (1976). There we held, as a matter of State constitutional law, that this important right was broad enough to encompass the freedom to make a personal choice as to the continuance of artificial life-support mechanisms. Though Chief Justice Hughes noted for the Court that the right of privacy had theretofore been primarily associated with decisions involving contraception and family life, he also found that its underlying concern was with the protection of personal decisions, and that it might be included within "the class of what have been called rights of personality." Our *Quinlan* decision could not have been predicated on privacy grounds if the class of cognizable privacy interests was limited to personal decisions concerning procreative matters.

Any discussion of the right of privacy must focus on the ultimate interest (by) which protection the Constitution seeks to ensure the freedom of personal development. Whether one defines that concept as a "right to intimacy and a freedom to do intimate things," or "a right to the integrity of one's personality," the crux of the matter is that governmental regulation of private personal behavior under the police power is sharply limited. As Mr. Justice Brandeis stated so eloquently in his dissent in *Olmstead v. United States* (1928):

> The makers of our Constitution undertook to secure conditions favorable to the pursuit of happiness. They recognized the significance of man's spiritual nature, of his feelings and of his intellect. They knew that only a part of the pain, pleasure and satisfactions of life are found in material things. They sought to protect Americans in their beliefs, their thoughts, their emotions and their sensations. They conferred, as against the government, the right to be let alone the most valued by civilized men.

We conclude that the conduct statutorily defined as fornication involves, by its very nature, a fundamental personal choice. Thus, the statute infringes upon the right of privacy. Although persons may differ as to the propriety and morality of such conduct and while we certainly do not condone its particular manifestations in this case, such a decision is necessarily encompassed in the concept of personal autonomy which our Constitution seeks to safeguard.

We recognize that the conduct prohibited by this statute has never been explicitly treated by the Supreme Court as falling within the right of privacy. In fact, we note that this question has been specifically reserved by the Court. Nevertheless, our decision today is consistent with the tenor and thrust of the Court's more recent decisions. As we stated earlier, the Court in *Carey* and *Wade* underscored the inherently private nature of a person's decision to bear or beget children. It would be rather anomalous if such a decision could be constitutionally protected while the more fundamental decision as to whether to engage in the conduct which is a necessary prerequisite to child-bearing could be constitutionally prohibited. Surely, such a choice involves considerations which are at least as intimate and personal as those which are involved in choosing whether to use contraceptives. We therefore join with other courts which have held that such sexual activities between adults are protected by the right of privacy.

Finally, we note that our doubts as to the constitutionality of the fornication statute are also impelled by this Court's development of a constitutionally mandated "zone" of privacy protecting individuals from unwarranted governmental intrusion into matters of intimate personal and family concern. It is now settled that the right of privacy guaranteed under the Fourteenth Amendment has an analogue in our State Constitution. Although the scope of this State right is not necessarily broader in all respects, the lack of constraints imposed by considerations of federalism permits this Court to demand stronger and more persuasive showings of a public interest in allowing the State to prohibit sexual practices than would be required by the United States Supreme Court.

Yet our inquiry cannot end here. Having found that the statute impinges upon the fundamental right of privacy, we must go on to consider whether that impingement can be justified by some compelling state interest. In an attempt to justify the statute's infringement of protected rights, the State cites its interests in preventing venereal disease and an increase in the number of illegitimate children, and in protecting the marital relationship and public morals by preventing illicit sex.

Perhaps the strongest reason favoring the law is its supposed relationship to the furtherance of the State's salutary goal of preventing venereal disease. We do not question the State's compelling interest in preventing the spread of such diseases. Nor do we dispute the power of the State to regulate activities which may adversely affect the public health. However, we do not believe that the instant enactment is properly designed with that end in mind. First, while we recognize that the statute would substantially eliminate venereal diseases if it could successfully deter people from engaging in the prohibited activity, we doubt its ability to achieve that result. The risk of contracting venereal disease is surely as great a deterrent to illicit sex as the maximum penalty under this act: a fine of $50 and/or imprisonment in jail for six months. As the Court found in *Carey*, absent highly coercive measures, it is extremely doubtful that people will be deterred from engaging in such natural activities. The Court rejected the assertion that the threat of an unwanted pregnancy would deter persons from engaging in extramarital sexual activities. We conclude that the same is true for the possibility of being prosecuted under the fornication statute.

Furthermore, if the State's interest in the instant statute is that it is helpful in preventing venereal disease, we conclude that it is counter-productive. To the extent that any successful program to combat venereal disease must depend upon affected persons coming forward for treatment, the present statute operates as a deterrent to such voluntary participation. The fear of being prosecuted for the "crime" of fornication can only deter people from seeking such necessary treatment.

We similarly fail to comprehend how the State's interest in preventing the propagation of illegitimate children will be measurably advanced by the instant law. If the unavailability of contraceptives is not likely to deter people from engaging in illicit sexual activities, it follows that the fear of unwanted pregnancies will be equally ineffective.

The last two reasons offered by the State as compelling justifications for the enactment that it protects the marital relationship and the public morals by preventing illicit sex offer little additional support for the law. Whether or not abstention is likely to induce persons to marry, this statute can in no way be considered a permissible means of fostering what may otherwise be a socially beneficial institution. If we were to hold that the State could attempt to coerce people into marriage, we would undermine the very independent choice which lies at the core of the right of privacy. We do not doubt the beneficent qualities of marriage, both for individuals as well as for society as a whole. Yet, we can only reiterate that decisions such as whether to marry are of a highly personal nature; they neither lend themselves to official coercion or sanction, nor fall within the regulatory power of those who are elected to govern.

This is not to suggest that the State may not regulate, in an appropriate manner, activities which are designed to further public morality. Our conclusion today extends no further than to strike down a measure which has as its objective the regulation of private morality. To the extent the law serves as an official sanction of certain conceptions of desirable lifestyles, social mores or individualized beliefs, it is not an appropriate exercise of the police power.

Fornication may be abhorrent to the morals and deeply held beliefs of many persons. But any appropriate "remedy" for such conduct cannot come from legislative fiat. Private personal acts between two consenting adults are not to be lightly meddled with by the State. The right of personal autonomy is fundamental to a free society. Persons who view fornication as opprobrious conduct may seek strenuously to dissuade people from engaging in it. However, they may not inhibit such conduct through the coercive power of the criminal law. As aptly stated by Sir Francis Bacon, "the sum of behavior is to retain a man's own dignity without intruding on the liberty of others." The fornication statute mocks the dignity of both offenders and enforcers. Surely police have more pressing duties than to search out adults who live a so-called "wayward" life. Surely the dignity of the law is undermined when an intimate personal activity between consenting adults can be dragged into court and "exposed." More importantly, the liberty which is the birthright of every individual suffers dearly when the State can so grossly intrude on personal autonomy.

SCHREIBER, J., concurring.

I concur in the result reached by the Court but for different reasons. The majority relies heavily on recent United States Supreme Court decisions involving the right of privacy for its conclusion that the State cannot interfere with the conduct proscribed by the New Jersey fornication statute. I believe they have misgauged the scope of those decisions. For the reasons developed below, I would rest the invalidity of this statute squarely on the ground that it conflicts with Article I, par. 1 of the New Jersey Constitution:

> All persons are by nature free and independent, and have certain natural and unalienable rights, among which are those of enjoying and defending life and liberty and of pursuing and obtaining safety and happiness.

The rights of two adults to make personal decisions are inherent in their freedom of thought. Implementation of those decisions in pursuit of their concept of happiness manifests an exercise of human liberty. Whatever else may be said of happiness, it is best obtained in a climate of free decision where each individual has the choice of consenting or not to acts or events which may affect him. Different persons have differing spiritual and moral views and so long as their personal conduct does not affect others, individuals have freedom to think, decide and act as they see fit. This freedom is an aspect of their right of privacy. Private consensual sexual conduct represents an exercise of that right.

Unlike the United States Constitution, the New Jersey Constitution is not a grant of enumerated powers, but rather a limitation of the sovereign powers of the State vested in the Legislature. That legislative authority is circumscribed by constitutional provisions, including those expressed in Article I, par. 1. Although the Legislature, in exercising its powers, may incidentally affect the natural and unalienable rights of individuals to liberty and the pursuit of happiness which have been recognized in Article I, the validity of any statute directly limiting those rights should be carefully scrutinized in light of its legislative purposes.

At common law fornication was not a crime. As explained by Blackstone:

> In the year 1650, when the ruling power found it for their interest to put on the semblance of a very extraordinary strictness and purity of morals, not only incest and wilful adultery were made capital crimes; but also the repeated act of keeping a brothel, or committing fornication, were (upon a second conviction) made

felony without benefit of clergy. But at the restoration, when men, from an abhorrence of the hypocrisy of the late times, fell into a contrary extreme of licentiousness, it was not thought proper to renew a law of such unfashionable rigor. And these offences have been ever since left to the feeble coercion of the spiritual court, according to the rules of the canon law. 4 William Blackstone, *Commentaries* *64.

The State rationalizes that the fornication statute is justifiable as a means of preventing the spread of venereal disease and the birth of illegitimate children. As the majority indicates, these grounds are not persuasive. More importantly, there is no evidence that this statute was intended as anything but an attempt to regulate private morality.

The Legislature cannot infringe on the rights of individuals who in private and without affecting others adopt and live by standards which differ from those of society. It is only when the public interest would be substantially adversely affected by some exercise of the right of privacy or when the public interest would be otherwise substantially promoted by legislation that the Legislature may infringe upon that right.

CLIFFORD, J., dissenting.

I hold to the view that absent a compelling state interest the State may not regulate a person's private decisions which have merely incidental effects on others. In application that principle leads to the conclusion that if two people freely determine that they wish to have sexual relations in a setting inoffensive to and only incidentally affecting others, the State is without authority to interfere through the criminal process with that decision, despite the fact that such decision may be in violation of conventional community standards of morality. And that includes the grubby little exercise in self-gratification involved here.

But I think we need not, and I would not, get to the constitutional issue, at least not at this point. Rather I would call for the submission of briefs and further argument of counsel on the question whether fornication is a lesser included offense with respect to rape. For several reasons this is the desirable course.

First, there is the sound, oft-expressed principle that constitutional questions should not be reached and resolved unless absolutely imperative in the disposition of the litigation. Inasmuch as there may be another, non-constitutional basis for decision, we should heed that admonition and defer addressing the constitutional question here.

Additionally, the interests of the parties will be amply served by a decision on the narrower "lesser included offense" ground. If fornication is not included in rape, then defendant goes free; certainly Mr. Saunders' interests are fully vindicated, it being neither apparent nor even likely that he has any burning curiosity about, or yearning for resolution of, the constitutional dimensions of the controversy in which he finds himself embroiled. If fornication is a lesser included offense of the crime of rape, then that issue (not heretofore directly presented or authoritatively determined in this State) will have been put to rest, thereby clarifying the law. We would then proceed in the instant case to the constitutional question.

NOTE

In *Commonwealth v. Bonadio*, 415 A.2d 47 (Pa. 1980), the Supreme Court of Pennsylvania refused to enforce a statute that criminalized "deviate sexual intercourse" (defined as oral or anal sex) between persons who were not husband and wife. In the course of its opinion, the court explained that:

> The threshold question in determining whether the statute in question is a valid exercise of the police power is to decide whether it benefits the public generally. The state clearly has a proper role to perform in protecting the public from inadvertent offensive displays of sexual behavior, in preventing people from being forced against their will to submit to sexual contact, in protecting minors from being sexually used by adults, and in eliminating cruelty to animals. To assure these protections, a broad range of criminal statutes constitute valid police power exercises, including proscriptions of indecent exposure, open lewdness, rape, involuntary deviate sexual intercourse, indecent assault, statutory rape, corruption of minors, and cruelty to animals. The statute in question serves none of the foregoing purposes and it is nugatory to suggest that it promotes a state interest in the institution of marriage. The Voluntary Deviate Sexual Intercourse Statute has only one possible purpose: to regulate the private conduct of consenting adults. Such a purpose, we believe, exceeds the valid bounds of the police power while infringing the right to equal protection of the laws guaranteed by the Constitution of the United States and of this Commonwealth.
>
> With respect to regulation of morals, the police power should properly be exercised to protect each individual's right to be free from interference in defining and pursuing his own morality but not to enforce a majority morality on persons whose conduct does not harm others. "No harm to the secular interests of the community is involved in atypical sex practice in private between consenting adult partners." Model Penal Code § 207.5 Sodomy & Related Offenses Comment (Tent. Draft No. 4, 1955). Many issues that are considered to be matters of morals are subject to debate, and no sufficient state interest justifies legislation of norms simply because a particular belief is followed by a number of people, or even a majority. Indeed, what is considered to be "moral" changes with the times and is dependent upon societal background. Spiritual leadership, not the government, has the responsibility for striving to improve the morality of individuals. Enactment of the Voluntary Deviate Sexual Intercourse Statute, despite the fact that it provides punishment for what many believe to be abhorrent crimes against nature and perceived sins against God, is not properly in the realm of the temporal police power.
>
> The concepts underlying our view of the police power in the case before us were once summarized as follows by the great philosopher, John Stuart Mill, in his eminent and apposite work, *On Liberty* (1859):
>
>> The sole end for which mankind are warranted, individually or collectively, in interfering with the liberty of action of any of their number, is self-protection. The only purpose for which power can be

rightfully exercised over any member of a civilised community, against his will, is to prevent harm to others. His own good, either physical or moral is not a sufficient warrant. He cannot rightfully be compelled to do or forbear because it will be better for him to do so, because it will make him happier, because, in the opinions of others, to do so would be wise, or even right. These are good reasons for remonstrating with him, or reasoning with him, or persuading him, or entreating him, but not for compelling him, or visiting him with any evil in case he do otherwise. To justify that, the conduct from which it is desired to deter him must be calculated to produce evil to some one else. The only part of the conduct of any one, for which he is amenable to society, is that which concerns others. In the part which merely concerns himself, his independence is, of right, absolute. Over himself, over his own body and mind, the individual is sovereign.

COMMONWEALTH v. WASSON
842 S.W.2d 487 (Ky. 1992)

LEIBSON, J.

Jeffrey Wasson is charged with having solicited an undercover Lexington policeman to engage in deviate sexual intercourse. KRS 510.100 punishes "deviate sexual intercourse with another person of the same sex" as a criminal offense, and specifies "consent of the other person shall not be a defense." Nor does it matter that the act is private and involves a caring relationship rather than a commercial one. It is classified as a Class A misdemeanor.

The charges were brought in the Fayette District Court where appellee moved to dismiss the charge on grounds that a statute criminalizing deviate sexual intercourse between consenting adults of the same sex, even if the act is committed in the privacy of a home, violates the Kentucky Constitution as: (1) an invasion of a constitutionally protected right of privacy; and (2) invidious discrimination in violation of constitutionally protected rights to equal treatment.

The Fayette District Judge held the statute violated appellee's right of privacy, and dismissed the charge. The Commonwealth appealed to Fayette Circuit Court which affirmed, and further held this statute infringed upon equal protection guarantees found in the Kentucky Constitution. Once more the Commonwealth appealed, and, because of the constitutional issues involved, this Court granted transfer.

Both courts below decided the issues solely on state constitutional law grounds, and our decision today, affirming the judgments of the lower courts, is likewise so limited. Federal constitutional protection under the Equal Protection Clause was not an issue reached in the lower courts and we need not address it. *Bowers v. Hardwick*, 478 U.S. 186 (1986) held federal constitutional protection of the right of privacy was not implicated in laws penalizing homosexual sodomy. We discuss *Bowers* in particular, and federal cases in general, not in the process of construing the United States Constitution or federal law, but only where their reasoning is relevant to discussing questions of state law.

No language specifying "rights of privacy," as such, appears in either the Federal or State Constitution. The Commonwealth recognizes such rights exist, but takes the position that, since they are implicit rather than explicit, our Court should march in lock step with the United States Supreme Court in declaring when such rights exist. Such is not the formulation of federalism. On the contrary, under our system of dual sovereignty, it is our responsibility to interpret and apply our state constitution independently. We are not bound by decisions of the United States Supreme Court when deciding whether a state statute impermissibly infringes upon individual rights guaranteed in the State Constitution so long as state constitutional protection does not fall below the federal floor, meaning the minimum guarantee of individual rights under the United States Constitution as interpreted by the United States Supreme Court.

Contrary to popular belief, the Bill of Rights in the United States Constitution represents neither the primary source nor the maximum guarantee of state constitutional liberty. Our own constitutional guarantees against the intrusive power of the state do not derive from the Federal Constitution. The adoption of the Federal Constitution in 1791 was preceded by state constitutions developed over the preceding 15 years, and, while there is, of course, overlap between state and federal constitutional guarantees of individual rights, they are by no means identical. State constitutional law documents and the writings on liberty were more the source of federal law than the child of federal law. Thus, while we respect the decisions of the United States Supreme Court on protection of individual liberty, and on occasion we have deferred to its reasoning, certainly we are not bound to do so, and we should not do so when valid reasons lead to a different conclusion.

We are persuaded that we should not do so here for several significant reasons. First, there are both textual and structural differences between the United States Bill of Rights and our own, which suggest a different conclusion from that reached by the United States Supreme Court is more appropriate. More significantly, Kentucky has a rich and compelling tradition of recognizing and protecting individual rights from state intrusion in cases similar in nature, found in the Debates of the Kentucky Constitutional Convention of 1890 and cases from the same era when that Constitution was adopted. The judges recognizing that tradition in their opinions wrote with a direct, firsthand knowledge of the mind set of the constitutional fathers, upholding the right of privacy against the intrusive police power of the state.

Kentucky cases recognized a legally protected right of privacy based on our own constitution and common law tradition long before the United States Supreme Court first took notice of whether there were any rights of privacy inherent in the Federal Bill of Rights. The United States Supreme Court, defining the reach of the zone of privacy in terms of federal due process analysis, limits rights of privacy to "liberties that are deeply rooted in this Nation's history and tradition." Sodomy is not one of them. *Bowers* decides that rights protected by the Due Process Clauses in the Fifth and Fourteenth Amendments to the U.S. Constitution do not "extend a fundamental right to homosexuals to engage in acts of consensual sodomy."

Bowers decides nothing beyond this. But state constitutional jurisprudence in this area is not limited by the constraints inherent in federal due process analysis. Deviate sexual intercourse conducted in private by consenting adults is not beyond the protections of the guarantees of individual liberty in our Kentucky Constitution simply because "proscriptions against that conduct have ancient roots." Kentucky constitutional guarantees against government intrusion address substantive rights. The only reference to individual liberties in the Federal Constitution is the statement in the Preamble that one of the purposes in writing the Constitution is to "secure the Blessings of Liberty to ourselves and our Posterity." Similarly, the Kentucky Constitution has a Preamble:

> We, the people of the Commonwealth of Kentucky, grateful to Almighty God for the civil, political and religious liberties we enjoy, and invoking the continuance of these blessings, do ordain and establish this Constitution.

But the Kentucky Constitution of 1891 does not limit the broadly stated guarantee of individual liberty to a statement in the Preamble. It amplifies the meaning of this statement of gratitude and purpose with a Bill of Rights in 26 sections, the first of which states:

> § 1. All men are, by nature, free and equal, and have certain inherent and inalienable rights, among which may be reckoned:
>
>> First: The right of enjoying and defending their lives and liberties.
>>
>> Third: The right of seeking and pursuing their safety and happiness.
>
> § 2. Absolute and arbitrary power over the lives, liberty and property of freemen exists nowhere in a republic, not even in the largest majority.

The leading case on this subject is *Commonwealth v. Campbell* (Ky. 1909). At issue was an ordinance that criminalized possession of intoxicating liquor, even for "private use." Our Court held that the Bill of Rights in the 1891 Constitution prohibited state action thus intruding upon the "inalienable rights possessed by the citizens" of Kentucky. Our Court interpreted the Kentucky Bill of Rights as defining a right of privacy, even though the constitution did not say so in that terminology:

> Man in his natural state has the right to do whatever he chooses and has the power to do. When he becomes a member of organized society, under governmental regulation, he surrenders, of necessity, all of his natural right the exercise of which

is, or may be, injurious to his fellow citizens. This is the price that he pays for governmental protection, but it is not within the competency of a free government to invade the sanctity of the absolute rights of the citizen any further than the direct protection of society requires. It is not within the competency of government to invade the privacy of a citizen's life and to regulate his conduct in matters in which he alone is concerned, or to prohibit him any liberty the exercise of which will not directly injure society. Let a man therefore be ever so abandoned in his principles, or vicious in his practice, provided he keeps his wickedness to himself, and does not offend against the rules of public decency, he is out of the reach of human laws.

The Court concludes:

The theory of our government is to allow the largest liberty to the individual commensurate with the public safety, or, as it has been otherwise expressed, that government is best which governs least. Under our institutions there is no room for that inquisitorial and protective spirit which seeks to regulate the conduct of men in matters in themselves indifferent, and to make them conform to a standard, not of their own choosing, but the choosing of the lawgiver.

The right of privacy has been recognized as an integral part of the guarantee of liberty in our 1891 Kentucky Constitution since its inception. The *Campbell* case is overwhelming affirmation of this proposition:

We are of the opinion that it never has been within the competency of the Legislature to so restrict the liberty of this citizen, and certainly not since the adoption of the present 1891 Constitution. The Bill of Rights, which declares that among the inalienable rights possessed by the citizens is that of seeking and pursuing their safety and happiness, and that the absolute and arbitrary power over the lives, liberty, and property of freeman exists nowhere in a republic, not even in the largest majority, would be but an empty sound if the Legislature could prohibit the citizen the right of owning or drinking liquor, when in so doing he did not offend the laws of decency by being intoxicated in public.

At the time *Campbell* was decided, the use of alcohol was as much an incendiary moral issue as deviate sexual behavior in private between consenting adults is today. Prohibition was the great moral issue of its time.

Nor is the *Campbell* case an aberration. Subsequent cases cited and followed *Campbell*. In *Commonwealth v. Smith* (1915), the Court declared a statute unconstitutional that had led to Smith being arrested for drinking beer in the backroom of an office:

The power of the state to regulate and control the conduct of a private individual is confined to those cases where his conduct injuriously affects others. With his faults or weaknesses, which he keeps to himself, and which do not operate to the detriment of others, the state as such has no concern.

The holding in *Smith* is that "the police power may be called into play only when it is reasonably necessary to protect the public health, or public morals, or public safety." The implication is that immorality in private that does "not operate to the detriment of others," is placed beyond the reach of state action by the guarantees of liberty in the Kentucky Constitution.

In *Hershberg v. City of Barbourville* (1911), the Court declared an ordinance which purported to regulate cigarette smoking in such broad terms that it could be applied to persons who smoked in the privacy of their own home "unreasonably interfered with the right of the citizen to determine for himself such personal matters."

In the area of civil law, Kentucky has been in the forefront in recognizing the right of privacy. In 1909, our Court stepped outside traditional libel law and recognized invasion of privacy as a tort in *Foster-Milburn Co. v. Chinn*. Then in 1927, in *Brents v. Morgan*, our Court defined this emerging right as "the right to be left alone, that is, the right of a person to be free from unwarranted publicity, or the right to live without unwarranted interference by the public about matters with which the public is not necessarily concerned."

> The right of privacy is incident to the person and not to property. It is considered as a natural and an absolute or pure right springing from the instincts of nature. It is of that class of rights which every human being has in his natural state and which he did not surrender by becoming a member of organized society. The fundamental rights of personal security and personal liberty include the right of privacy, the right to be left alone. The right to enjoy life in the way most agreeable and pleasant, and the right of privacy is nothing more than a right to live in a particular way.

In the *Campbell* case our Court quoted at length from the "great work" On Liberty of the 19th century English philosopher and economist, John Stuart Mill. We repeat the quote in part:

> The only part of the conduct of anyone, for which he is amenable to society, is that which concerns others. In the part which merely concerns himself, his independence is, of right, absolute. The principle requires liberty of taste and pursuits; of framing the plan of our life to suit our own character; of doing as we like, subject to such consequences as may follow; without impediment from our fellow creatures, so long as what we do does not harm them, even though they should think our conduct foolish, perverse, or wrong.

Mill's premise is that "physical force in the form of legal penalties," *i.e.*, criminal sanctions, should not be used as a means to improve the citizen. The majority has no moral right to dictate how everyone else should live. Public indignation, while given due weight, should be subject to the overriding test of rational and critical analysis, drawing the line at harmful consequences to others. Modern legal philosophers who follow Mill temper this test with an enlightened paternalism, permitting the law to intervene to stop self-inflicted harm such as the result of drug taking, or failure to use seat belts or crash helmets, not to enforce majoritarian or conventional morality, but because the victim of such self-inflicted harm becomes a burden on society.

Based on the *Campbell* opinion, and on the Comments of the 1891 Convention Delegates, there is little doubt but that the views of John Stuart Mill, which were then held in high esteem, provided the philosophical underpinnings for the reworking and broadening of protection of individual rights that occurs throughout the 1891 Constitution.

We have recognized protection of individual rights greater than the federal floor in a number of cases, most recently: *Ingram v. Commonwealth* (1990), involving protection against double jeopardy and *Dean v. Commonwealth* (1989), involving the right of confrontation. Perhaps the most dramatic recent example of protection of individual rights under the state Constitution where the United States Supreme Court had refused to afford protection under the Federal Constitution, is *Rose v. Council for Better Educ., Inc.* (1989). In *Rose*, our Court recognized our Kentucky Constitution afforded individual school children from property poor districts a fundamental right to an adequate education such as provided in wealthier school districts, even though 16 years earlier the United States Supreme Court held the Federal Constitution provided no such protection in *San Antonio Independent School District v. Rodriguez* (1973). The United States Supreme Court found there was no constitutional, or fundamental, right to a particular quality of education which justified invoking the Equal Protection Clause of the Fourteenth Amendment. Our Court found a duty in the Kentucky constitutional requirement that the General Assembly "provide an efficient system of common schools."

We view the United States Supreme Court decision in *Bowers v. Hardwick* as a misdirected application of the theory of original intent. To illustrate: as a theory of majoritarian morality, miscegenation was an offense with ancient roots. It is highly unlikely that protecting the rights of persons of different races to copulate was one of the considerations behind the Fourteenth Amendment. Nevertheless, in *Loving v. Virginia* (1967), the United States Supreme Court recognized that a contemporary, enlightened interpretation of the liberty interest involved in the sexual act made its punishment constitutionally impermissible.

Certainly, the practice of deviate sexual intercourse violates traditional morality. But so does the same act between heterosexuals, which activity is decriminalized. Going one step further, all sexual activity between consenting adults outside of marriage violates our traditional morality. The issue here is not whether sexual activity traditionally viewed as immoral can be punished by society, but whether it can be punished solely on the basis of sexual preference.

We do not speculate on how the United States Supreme Court as presently constituted will decide whether the sexual preference of homosexuals is entitled to protection under the Equal Protection Clause of the Federal constitution. We need not speculate as to whether male and/or female homosexuals will be allowed status as a protected class if and when the United States Supreme Court confronts this issue. They are a separate and identifiable class for Kentucky constitutional law analysis because no class of persons can be discriminated against under the Kentucky Constitution. All are entitled to equal treatment, unless there is a substantial governmental interest, a rational basis, for different treatment. The statute before us is in violation of Kentucky constitutional protection in Section Three that "all men (persons), when they form a social compact, are equal," and in Section Two that "absolute and arbitrary power over the lives, liberty and property of free men (persons) exist nowhere in a republic, not even in the largest majority." We have concluded that it is "arbitrary" for the majority to criminalize sexual activity solely on the basis of majoritarian sexual preference, and that it denied "equal" treatment under the law when there is no rational basis, as this term is used in our Kentucky cases.

The Commonwealth has tried hard to demonstrate a legitimate governmental interest justifying a distinction but has failed. Many of the claimed justifications are simply outrageous: that "homosexuals are more promiscuous than heterosexuals, that homosexuals enjoy the company of children, and that homosexuals are more prone to engage in sex acts in public." The only proffered justification with superficial validity is that "infectious diseases are more readily transmitted by anal sodomy than by other forms of sexual copulation." But this statute is not limited to anal copulation, and this reasoning would apply to male-female anal intercourse the same as it applies to male-male intercourse. The growing number of females to whom AIDS has been transmitted is stark evidence that AIDS is not only a male homosexual disease. The only medical evidence in the record before us rules out any distinction between male-male and male-female anal intercourse as a method of preventing AIDS. The act of sexual contact is not implicated, per se, whether the contact is homosexual or heterosexual. In any event, this statute was enacted in 1974 before the AIDS nightmare was upon us. It was 1982 or 1983 before AIDS was a recognized diagnostic entity.

In the final analysis we can attribute no legislative purpose to this statute except to single out homosexuals for different treatment for indulging their sexual preference by engaging in the same activity heterosexuals are now at liberty to perform. By 1974 there had already been a sea change in societal values insofar as attaching criminal penalties to extramarital sex. The question is whether a society that no longer criminalizes adultery, fornication, or deviate sexual intercourse between heterosexuals, has a rational basis to single out homosexual acts for different treatment. Is there a rational basis for declaring this one type of sexual immorality so destructive of family values as to merit criminal punishment whereas other acts of sexual immorality which were likewise forbidden by the same religious and traditional heritage of Western civilization are now decriminalized? If there is a rational basis for different treatment it has yet to be demonstrated in this case. We need not sympathize, agree with, or even understand the sexual preference of homosexuals in order to recognize their right to equal treatment before the bar of criminal justice.

"Equal Justice Under Law," inscribed above the entrance to the United States Supreme Court, expresses the unique goal to which all humanity aspires. In Kentucky it is more than a mere aspiration. It is part of the "inherent and inalienable" rights protected by our Kentucky Constitution. Our protection against exercise of "arbitrary power over the liberty of freemen" by the General Assembly (Section Two) and our guarantee that all persons are entitled to "equal" treatment (in Section Three) forbid a special act punishing the sexual preference of homosexuals. It matters not that the same act committed by persons of the same sex is more offensive to the majority because Section Two states such "power exists nowhere in a republic, not even in the largest majority."

The purpose of the present statute is not to protect the marital relationship against sexual activity outside of marriage, but only to punish one aspect of it while other activities similarly destructive of the marital relationship, if not more so, go unpunished. Sexual preference and not the act committed, determine criminality, and is being punished. Simply because the majority, speaking through the General Assembly, finds one type of extramarital intercourse more offensive than another, does not provide a rational basis for criminalizing the sexual preference of homosexuals.

LAMBERT, J., dissenting.

The issue is not whether private homosexual conduct should be allowed or prohibited. The only question properly before this Court is whether the Constitution of Kentucky denies the legislative branch a right to prohibit such conduct. Nothing in the majority opinion demonstrates such a limitation on legislative prerogative.

To justify its view that private homosexual conduct is protected by the Constitution of Kentucky, the majority has found it necessary to disregard virtually all of recorded history, the teachings of the religions most influential on Western Civilization, the debates of the delegates to the Constitutional Convention, and the text of the Constitution itself. Rather than amounting to a decision based upon precedent as is suggested, this decision reflects the value judgment of the majority and its view that public law has no right to prohibit the conduct at issue here. The history and traditions of this Commonwealth are fully in accord with the Biblical, historical and common law view. Since at least 1860, sodomy has been a criminal offense in Kentucky and this fact was well known to the delegates at the time of the 1890 Constitutional Convention.

Embracing "state constitutionalism," a practice in vogue among many state courts as a means of rejecting the leadership of the Supreme Court of the United States, the majority has declared its independence from even the influence of this nation's highest court. The majority cannot, however, escape the logic and scholarship of *Bowers* which reached the conclusion that nothing in the Due Process Clause of the United States Constitution prevented a state from punishing sodomy as a crime. While I do not advocate the view that state courts should march in lock step with the Supreme Court of the United States, on those occasions when state courts depart from that Court's reasoned interpretations, it should be for compelling reasons, usually text or tradition, and only in clearly distinguishable circumstances, none of which are present here.

Perhaps the greatest mischief to be found in the majority opinion is in its discovery of a constitutional right which lacks any textual support. The majority has referred generally to the twenty-six sections in the Bill of Rights of the Kentucky Constitution and quoted § 1 First and Third and § 2. None of the sections cited or quoted contain an inkling of reference to rights of privacy or sexual freedom of any kind. This is conceded by the majority as follows: "No language specifying rights of privacy, as such, appears in either the Federal or State Constitution." The majority opinion is a departure from the accepted methodology of constitutional analysis which requires that text be the beginning point. The majority reasons that differences between the text of the Kentucky Constitution and the United States Constitution free this Court from federal influence, but it fails to explain its discovery of the rights announced here in the absence of any textual basis. This is a dangerous practice. When judges free themselves of constitutional text, their values and notions of morality are given free rein and they, not the Constitution, become the supreme law.

The major premise in the majority opinion is that the Constitution forbids any legal restriction upon the private conduct of adults unless it can be shown that such conduct is harmful to another. This view represents the essence of the philosophy of John Stuart Mill in his essay *On Liberty*. While espousing such a view, however, Mill recognized the difficulty of distinguishing that part of a person's life which affected only himself from that which affected others. He recognized that one who by deleterious vices harmed himself indirectly harmed others and that society suffered indirect harm by the mere knowledge of immoral conduct. Nevertheless, Mill clung to his philosophy by insisting that society was without *power* to punish gambling or drunkenness. He made a ringing defense of the right of persons so disposed to practice polygamy.

Unfortunately for the purposes of the majority, the philosophy of Mill and the views contained in the *Campbell* case, if logically applied, would necessarily result in the eradication of numerous other criminal statutes. For example, if majoritarian morality is without a role in the formulation of criminal law and the only standard is harm to another, all laws proscribing the possession and use of dangerous or narcotic drugs would fall. Likewise, incest statutes which proscribe sexual intercourse between persons of close kinship regardless of age or consent would be rendered invalid. Laws prohibiting cruelty to animals, the abuse of dead human bodies, suicide and polygamy would be held unconstitutional. Despite the majority's disingenuous departure from Mill based on "an enlightened paternalism" to prevent self-inflicted harm, many prevailing criminal statutes would nevertheless fail the "harm to another" test. While the majority of this Court manifestly sees the proposition otherwise, the Supreme Court of the United States has addressed the role of morality as a rationale to support criminal law and found no impediment.

> The law, however, is constantly based on notions of morality, and if all laws representing essentially moral choices are to be invalidated under the Due Process Clause, the courts will be very busy indeed.

From my study of this case, I have concluded that the privacy right found in the Constitution of Kentucky does not apply to claimed rights not remotely envisioned by the delegates to the Constitutional Convention or reasonably emerging from our history and traditions. As such, the right to determine whether sodomy should be a criminal offense belongs to the people through their elected representatives. We should not deprive the people of that right. As the majority has observed, many states have already decriminalized consensual sodomy. Appellee should take his case to the Kentucky General Assembly and let that branch of government say whether the crime shall remain or be abolished.

To resolve the equal protection issue, one must first review the statute, KRS 510.100. This Act is not limited in its application to persons who consider themselves homosexual nor is it limited to the male or female gender. Any person who engages in deviate sexual intercourse with another person of the same sex is in violation. The statute prohibits conduct and says nothing of the sexual preference or gender of the violator. There is nothing in the statute by which persons are classified and certainly nothing which accords unequal treatment to persons comprising a recognizable class on factors such as race, gender or ethnic origin.

As persons who engage in homosexual sodomy have never been held to constitute a suspect classification, to be upheld, the statute at issue need only satisfy the lowest level of judicial scrutiny and demonstrate that it bears a rational relationship to a legitimate legislative objective. Protection of public "health, safety and morality" was held to be such an objective in *Bosworth v. City of Lexington* (1930).

I conclude with the view that this Court has strayed from its role of interpreting the Constitution and undertaken to make social policy. This decision is a vast extension of judicial power by which four Justices of this Court have overridden the will of the Legislative and Executive branches of

Kentucky State Government and denied the people any say in this important social issue. No decision cited by the majority has ever gone so far and certainly none comes to mind. Where this slippery slope may lead is anybody's guess, but the ramifications of this decision will surely be profound.

NOTE

The majority opinion in *Wasson* discusses and rejects *Bowers v. Hardwick*, 478 U.S. 186 (1986), in which the United States Supreme Court upheld the constitutionality of a Georgia criminal law prohibiting sodomy and ruled that the Due Process Clause of the Federal Constitution does not protect the right of a consenting adult to engage in homosexual conduct. *Bowers* was decided by a 5–4 vote and was overruled seventeen years later in *Lawrence v. Texas*, 539 U.S. 558 (2003). In the seventeen-year interim between the two cases, courts in five states—one of which was Georgia—rejected both the reasoning and result of *Bowers*, ruling that criminal laws prohibiting adult consensual homosexual activity violated state constitutional provisions protecting the right of privacy. The first decision of a state supreme court to do so was *Wasson*. The five state decisions rejecting *Bowers* were acknowledged by the Supreme Court in *Lawrence* and apparently played some part in convincing the high Court to overrule *Bowers*. See Jeffrey M. Shaman, *Equality and Liberty in the Golden Age of State Constitutional Law* 215–22 (2008).

E. CIVIL UNION

BAKER v. STATE
744 A.2d 864 (Vt. 1999)

AMESTOY, C.J.

May the State of Vermont exclude same-sex couples from the benefits and protections that its laws provide to opposite-sex married couples? That is the fundamental question we address in this appeal, a question that the Court well knows arouses deeply-felt religious, moral, and political beliefs. Our constitutional responsibility to consider the legal merits of issues properly before us provides no exception for the controversial case. The issue before the Court, moreover, does not turn on the religious or moral debate over intimate same-sex relationships, but rather on the statutory and constitutional basis for the exclusion of same-sex couples from the secular benefits and protections offered married couples.

The Common Benefits Clause of the Vermont Constitution (Chapter I, Article 7) reads:

> That government is, or ought to be, instituted for the common benefit, protection, and security of the people, nation, or community, and not for the particular

emolument or advantage of any single person, family, or set of persons, who are a part only of that community.

Under the Clause, plaintiffs may not be deprived of the statutory benefits and protections afforded persons of the opposite sex who choose to marry. We hold that the State is constitutionally required to extend to same-sex couples the common benefits and protections that flow from marriage under Vermont law. Whether this ultimately takes the form of inclusion within the marriage laws themselves or a parallel "domestic partnership" system or some equivalent statutory alternative, rests with the Legislature. Whatever system is chosen, however, must conform with the constitutional imperative to afford all Vermonters the common benefit, protection, and security of the law.

Plaintiffs are three same-sex couples who have lived together in committed relationships for periods ranging from four to twenty-five years. Two of the couples have raised children together. Each couple applied for a marriage license from their respective town clerk, and each was refused a license as ineligible under the applicable state marriage laws.

Assuming that the marriage statutes preclude their eligibility for a marriage license, plaintiffs contend that the exclusion violates their right to the common benefit and protection of the law guaranteed by Chapter I, Article 7 of the Vermont Constitution. They note that in denying them access to a civil marriage license, the law effectively excludes them from a broad array of legal benefits and protections incident to the marital relation, including access to a spouse's medical, life, and disability insurance, hospital visitation and other medical decisionmaking privileges, spousal support, intestate succession, homestead protections, and many other statutory protections.

In considering this issue, it is important to emphasize at the outset that it is the Common Benefits Clause of the Vermont Constitution we are construing, rather than its counterpart, the Equal Protection Clause of the Fourteenth Amendment to the United States Constitution. It is altogether fitting and proper that we do so. Vermont's constitutional commitment to equal rights was the product of the successful effort to create an independent republic and a fundamental charter of government, the Constitution of 1777, both of which preceded the adoption of the Fourteenth Amendment by nearly a century. As we explained in *State v. Badger* (1982), "our constitution is not a mere reflection of the federal charter. Historically and textually, it differs from the United States Constitution. It predates the federal counterpart, as it extends back to Vermont's days as an independent republic. It is an independent authority, and Vermont's fundamental law."

The words of the Common Benefits Clause are revealing. While they do not, to be sure, set forth a fully-formed standard of analysis for determining the constitutionality of a given statute, they do express broad principles which usefully inform that analysis. Chief among these is the principle of inclusion. As explained more fully in the discussion that follows, the specific proscription against governmental favoritism toward not only groups or "sets of men," but also toward any particular "family" or "single man," underscores the framers' resentment of political preference of any kind. The affirmative right to the "common benefits and protections" of government and the corollary proscription of favoritism in the distribution of public "emoluments and advantages" reflect the framers' overarching objective "not only that everyone enjoy equality before the law or have an equal voice in government but also that everyone have *an equal share in the fruits of the common enterprise.*" Thus, at its core the Common Benefits Clause expressed a vision of government that afforded every Vermonter its benefit and protection and provided no Vermonter particular advantage.

We must ultimately ascertain whether the omission of a part of the community from the benefit, protection and security of the challenged law bears a reasonable and just relation to the governmental purpose. Consistent with the core presumption of inclusion, factors to be considered in this determination may include: (1) the significance of the benefits and protections of the challenged law; (2) whether the omission of members of the community from the benefits and protections of the challenged law promotes the government's stated goals; and (3) whether the classification is significantly underinclusive or overinclusive.

The principal purpose the State advances in support of excluding same-sex couples from the legal benefits of marriage is the government's interest in "furthering the link between procreation and child rearing." The State has a strong interest, it argues, in promoting a permanent commitment between couples who have children to ensure that their offspring are considered legitimate and receive ongoing parental support. The State contends, further, that the Legislature could reasonably believe that sanctioning same-sex unions "would diminish society's perception of the link between procreation and child rearing and advance the notion that fathers or mothers are mere surplusage to the functions of procreation and child rearing." The State argues that since same-sex couples cannot conceive a child on their own, state-sanctioned same-sex unions "could be seen by the Legislature to separate further the connection between procreation and parental responsibilities for raising children." Hence, the Legislature is justified, the State concludes, "in using the marriage statutes to send a public message that procreation and child rearing are intertwined."

Do these concerns represent valid public interests that are reasonably furthered by the exclusion of same-sex couples from the benefits and protections that flow from the marital relation? It is beyond dispute that the State has a legitimate and long-standing interest in promoting a permanent commitment between couples for the security of their children. It is equally undeniable that the State's interest has been advanced by extending formal public sanction and protection to the union, or marriage, of those couples considered capable of having children, i.e., men and women. And there is no doubt that the overwhelming majority of births today continue to result from natural conception between one man and one woman.

It is equally undisputed that many opposite-sex couples marry for reasons unrelated to procreation, that some of these couples never intend to have children, and that others are incapable of having children. Therefore, if the purpose of the statutory exclusion of same-sex couples is to "further the link between procreation and child rearing," it is significantly underinclusive. The law extends the benefits and protections of marriage to many persons with no logical connection to the stated governmental goal.

Furthermore, while accurate statistics are difficult to obtain, there is no dispute that a significant number of children today are actually being raised by same-sex parents, and that increasing numbers of children are being conceived by such parents through a variety of assisted-reproductive techniques.

Thus, with or without the marriage sanction, the reality today is that increasing numbers of same-sex couples are employing increasingly efficient assisted-reproductive techniques to conceive and raise children. The Vermont Legislature has not only recognized this reality, but has acted affirmatively to remove legal barriers so that same-sex couples may legally adopt and rear the children conceived through such efforts. The state has also acted to expand the domestic relations laws to safeguard the interests of same-sex parents and their children when such couples terminate their domestic relationship.

Therefore, to the extent that the state's purpose in licensing civil marriage was, and is, to legitimize children and provide for their security, the statutes plainly exclude many same-sex couples who are no different from opposite-sex couples with respect to these objectives. If anything, the exclusion of same-sex couples from the legal protections incident to marriage exposes their children to the precise risks that the State argues the marriage laws are designed to secure against. In short, the marital exclusion treats persons who are similarly situated for purposes of the law, differently.

The State also argues that because same-sex couples cannot conceive a child on their own, their exclusion promotes a "perception of the link between procreation and child rearing," and that to discard it would "advance the notion that mothers and fathers are mere surplusage to the functions of procreation and child rearing" Apart from the bare assertion, the State offers no persuasive reasoning to support these claims. Indeed, it is undisputed that most of those who utilize nontraditional means of conception are infertile married couples, and that many assisted-reproductive techniques involve only one of the married partner's genetic material, the other being supplied by a third party through sperm, egg, or embryo donation. The State does not suggest that the use of these technologies undermines a married couple's sense of parental responsibility, or fosters the perception that they are "mere surplusage" to the conception and parenting of the child so conceived. Nor does it even remotely suggest that access to such techniques ought to be restricted as a matter of public policy to "send a public message that procreation and child rearing are intertwined." Accordingly, there is no reasonable basis to conclude that a same-sex couple's use of the same technologies would undermine the bonds of parenthood, or society's perception of parenthood.

The question thus becomes whether the exclusion of a relatively small but significant number of otherwise qualified same-sex couples from the same legal benefits and protections afforded their opposite-sex counterparts contravenes the mandates of Article 7. We turn, accordingly, from the principal justifications advanced by the State to the interests asserted by plaintiffs.

As noted, in determining whether a statutory exclusion reasonably relates to the governmental purpose it is appropriate to consider the history and significance of the benefits denied. What do these considerations reveal about the benefits and protections at issue here? In *Loving v. Virginia*, (1967), the United States Supreme Court, striking down Virginia's anti-miscegenation law, observed that "the freedom to marry has long been recognized as one of the vital personal rights." The Court's point was clear; access to a civil marriage license and the multitude of legal benefits, protections, and obligations that flow from it significantly enhance the quality of life in our society.

The Supreme Court's observations in *Loving* merely acknowledged what many states, including Vermont, had long recognized. One hundred thirty-seven years before *Loving*, this Court characterized the reciprocal rights and responsibilities flowing from the marriage laws as "the natural rights of human nature." Decisions in other New England states noted the unique legal and economic ramifications flowing from the marriage relation. Early decisions recognized that a marriage contract, although similar to other civil agreements, represents much more because once formed, the law imposes a variety of obligations, protections, and benefits. As the Maine Supreme Judicial Court observed, the rights and obligations of marriage rest not upon contract, "but upon the general law of the State, statutory or common, which defines and prescribes those rights, duties and obligations. They are of law, not of contract." In short, the marriage laws transform a private agreement into a source of significant public benefits and protections.

While the laws relating to marriage have undergone many changes during the last century, largely toward the goal of equalizing the status of husbands and wives, the benefits of marriage have not diminished in value. On the contrary, the benefits and protections incident to a marriage license under Vermont law have never been greater. They include, for example, the right to receive a portion of the estate of a spouse who dies intestate and protection against disinheritance through elective share provisions, under 14 V.S.A. §§ 401-404, 551; preference in being appointed as the personal representative of a spouse who dies intestate, under 14 V.S.A. § 903; the right to bring a lawsuit for the wrongful death of a spouse, under 14 V.S.A. § 1492; the right to bring an action for loss of consortium, under 12 V.S.A. § 5431; the right to workers' compensation survivor benefits under 21 V.S.A. § 632; the right to spousal benefits statutorily guaranteed to public employees, including health, life, disability, and accident insurance, under 3 V.S.A. § 631; the opportunity to be covered as a spouse under group life insurance policies issued to an employee, under 8 V.S.A. § 3811; the opportunity to be covered as the insured's spouse under an individual health insurance policy, under 8 V.S.A. § 4063; the right to claim an evidentiary privilege for marital communications, under V.R.E. 504; homestead rights and protections, under 27 V.S.A. §§ 105-108, 141-142; the presumption of joint ownership of property and the concomitant right of survivorship, under 27 V.S.A. § 2; hospital visitation and other rights incident to the medical treatment of a family member, under 18 V.S.A. § 1852; and the right to receive, and the obligation to provide, spousal support, maintenance, and property division in the event of separation or divorce, under 15 V.S.A. §§ 751-752.

While other statutes could be added to this list, the point is clear. The legal benefits and protections flowing from a marriage license are of such significance that any statutory exclusion must necessarily be grounded on public concerns of sufficient weight, cogency, and authority that the justice of the deprivation cannot seriously be questioned. Considered in light of the extreme logical disjunction between the classification and the stated purposes of the law—protecting children and "furthering the link between procreation and child rearing"—the exclusion falls substantially short of this standard. The laudable governmental goal of promoting a commitment between married couples to promote the security of their children and the community as a whole provides no reasonable basis for denying the legal benefits and protections of marriage to same-sex couples, who are no differently situated with respect to this goal than their opposite-sex counterparts. Promoting a link between procreation and childrearing similarly fails to support the exclusion. We turn, accordingly, to the remaining interests identified by the State in support of the statutory exclusion.

The State asserts that a number of additional rationales could support a legislative decision to exclude same-sex partners from the statutory benefits and protections of marriage. The most substantive of the State's remaining claims relates to the issue of childrearing. It is conceivable that the Legislature could conclude that opposite-sex partners offer advantages in this area, although we note that child-development experts disagree and the answer is decidedly uncertain. The argument, however, contains a more fundamental flaw, and that is the Legislature's endorsement of a policy diametrically at odds with the State's claim. In 1996, the Vermont General Assembly enacted, and the Governor signed, a law removing all prior legal barriers to the adoption of children by same-sex couples. At the same time, the Legislature provided additional legal protections in the form of court-ordered child support and parent-child contact in the event that same-sex parents dissolved their "domestic relationship." In light of these express policy choices, the State's arguments that Vermont public policy favors opposite-sex over same-sex parents or disfavors the use of artificial reproductive technologies are patently without substance.

Finally, it is suggested that the long history of official intolerance of intimate same-sex relationships cannot be reconciled with an interpretation of Article 7 that would give state-sanctioned benefits and protection to individuals of the same sex who commit to a permanent domestic relationship. We find the argument to be unpersuasive for several reasons. First, to the extent that state action historically has been motivated by an animus against a class, that history cannot provide a legitimate basis for continued unequal application of the law. As we observed recently in *Brigham*, "equal protection of the laws cannot be limited by eighteenth-century standards." Second, whatever claim may be made in light of the undeniable fact that federal and state statutes—including those in Vermont—have historically disfavored same-sex relationships, more recent legislation plainly undermines the contention. In 1992, Vermont was one of the first states to enact statewide legislation prohibiting discrimination in employment, housing, and other services based on sexual orientation. Sexual orientation is among the categories specifically protected against hate-motivated crimes in Vermont. Furthermore, as noted earlier, recent enactments of the General Assembly have removed barriers to adoption by same-sex couples, and have extended legal rights and protections to such couples who dissolve their "domestic relationship."

Thus, viewed in the light of history, logic, and experience, we conclude that none of the interests asserted by the State provides a reasonable and just basis for the continued exclusion of same-sex couples from the benefits incident to a civil marriage license under Vermont law. Accordingly, in the faith that a case beyond the imagining of the framers of our Constitution may, nevertheless, be safely anchored in the values that infused it, we find a constitutional obligation to extend to plaintiffs the common benefit, protection, and security that Vermont law provides opposite-sex married couples. It remains only to determine the appropriate means and scope of relief compelled by this constitutional mandate.

We hold only that plaintiffs are entitled under Chapter I, Article 7, of the Vermont Constitution to obtain the same benefits and protections afforded by Vermont law to married opposite-sex couples. We do not purport to infringe upon the prerogatives of the Legislature to craft an appropriate means of addressing this constitutional mandate, other than to note that the record here refers to a number of potentially constitutional statutory schemes from other jurisdictions. These include what are typically referred to as "domestic partnership" or "registered partnership" acts, which generally establish an alternative legal status to marriage for same-sex couples, impose similar formal requirements and limitations, create a parallel licensing or registration scheme, and extend all or most of the same rights and obligations provided by the law to married partners. We do not intend specifically to endorse any one or all of the referenced acts, particularly in view of the significant benefits omitted from several of the laws.

Further, while the State's prediction of "destabilization" cannot be a ground for denying relief, it is not altogether irrelevant. A sudden change in the marriage laws or the statutory benefits traditionally incidental to marriage may have disruptive and unforeseen consequences. Absent legislative guidelines defining the status and rights of same-sex couples, consistent with constitutional requirements, uncertainty and confusion could result. Therefore, we hold that the current statutory scheme shall remain in effect for a reasonable period of time to enable the Legislature to consider and enact implementing legislation in an orderly and expeditious fashion.

The judgment of the superior court upholding the constitutionality of the Vermont marriage statutes under Chapter I, Article 7 of the Vermont Constitution is reversed.

JOHNSON, J., concurring in part and dissenting in part.

I concur with the majority's holding, but I respectfully dissent from its novel and truncated remedy, which in my view abdicates this Court's constitutional duty to redress violations of constitutional rights. I would grant the requested relief and enjoin defendants from denying plaintiffs a marriage license based solely on the sex of the applicants.

In 1948, when the California Supreme Court struck down a state law prohibiting the issuance of a license authorizing interracial marriages, the court did not suspend its judgment to allow the legislature an opportunity to enact a separate licensing scheme for interracial marriages. See *Perez v. Lippold* (granting writ of mandamus compelling county clerk to issue certificate of registry). Indeed, such a mandate in that context would be unfathomable to us today. Here, as in *Perez*, we have held that the State has unconstitutionally discriminated against plaintiffs, thereby depriving them of civil rights to which they are entitled. Like the Hawaii Circuit Court in *Baehr v. Miike* (1996), which rejected the State's reasons for excluding same-sex couples from marriage, we should simply enjoin the State from denying marriage licenses to plaintiffs based on sex or sexual orientation. That remedy would provide prompt and complete relief to plaintiffs and create reliable expectations that would stabilize the legal rights and duties of all couples.

During the civil rights movement of the 1960's, state and local governments defended segregation or gradual desegregation on the grounds that mixing the races would lead to interracial disturbances. The Supreme Court's "compelling answer" to that contention was "that constitutional rights may not be denied simply because of hostility to their assertion or exercise." Here, too, we should not relinquish our duty to redress the unconstitutional discrimination that we have found merely because of "personal speculations" or "vague disquietudes." While the laudatory goals of preserving institutional credibility and public confidence in our government may require elected bodies to wait for changing attitudes concerning public morals, those same goals require courts to act independently and decisively to protect civil rights guaranteed by our Constitution.

In our system of government, civil rights violations are remedied by courts, not because we issue "Holy Writ" or because we are "the only repository of wisdom." It is because the courts "must ultimately define and defend individual rights against government in terms independent of consensus or majority will." Today's decision, which is little more than a declaration of rights, abdicates that responsibility.

This case is undoubtedly one of the most controversial ever to come before this Court. Newspaper, radio and television media have disclosed widespread public interest in its outcome, as well as the full spectrum of opinion as to what that outcome should be and what its ramifications may be for our society as a whole. One line of opinion contends that this is an issue that ought to be decided only by the most broadly democratic of our governmental institutions, the Legislature, and that the small group of men and women comprising this Court has no business deciding an issue of such enormous moment. For better or for worse, however, this is simply not so. This case came before us because citizens of the state invoked their constitutional right to seek redress through the judicial process of a perceived deprivation under state law. The Vermont Constitution does not permit the courts to decline to adjudicate a matter because its subject is controversial, or because the outcome may be deeply offensive to the strongly held beliefs of many of our citizens. We do not have, as does the

Supreme Court of the United States, certiorari jurisdiction, which allows that Court, in its sole discretion, to decline to hear almost any case. To the contrary, if a case has been brought before us, and if the established procedures have been followed, as they were here, we must hear and decide it.

Moreover, we must decide the case on legal grounds. However much history, sociology, religious belief, personal experience or other considerations may inform our individual or collective deliberations, we must decide this case, and all cases, on the basis of our understanding of the law, and the law alone. This must be the true and constant effort of every member of the judiciary. That effort, needless to say, is not a guarantee of infallibility, nor even an assurance of wisdom. It is, however, the fulfillment of our pledge of office.

NOTES

1. In response to *Baker*, the Vermont legislature adopted a civil union law granting comprehensive legal benefits to same-sex couples. Ten years later, in 2009, the legislature enacted a law authorizing same-sex marriage, thereby making Vermont the first state to legalize same-sex marriage by statutory enactment without being required to do so by a court ruling. Following the decision in *Baker*, a number of states enacted laws authorizing same-sex civil unions.

2. The opinion in *Baker* mentions *Baehr v. Miike*, No. 91–1394, 1996 WL 694235 (Haw. Cir. Ct., Dec. 3, 1996), a lower court decision ruling that a law limiting marriage to opposite-sex couples violated the Hawaii Equal Protection Clause. Prior to that ruling, the Supreme Court of Hawaii had held that the law in question was presumptively unconstitutional unless the state could show that it was supported by a compelling state interest. *Baehr v. Lewin*, 852 P.2d 44 (Haw. 1993). On remand, the circuit court concluded that the law was not supported by a compelling state interest and was unconstitutional. However, that ruling was superseded by an amendment to the Hawaii Constitution providing that the legislature had the power to reserve marriage to opposite-sex couples. Haw. Const. art. I, § 23.

F. MARRIAGE

GOODRIDGE v. DEPARTMENT OF PUBLIC HEALTH
798 N.E.2d 941 (Mass. 2003)

MARSHALL, C.J.

Marriage is a vital social institution. The exclusive commitment of two individuals to each other nurtures love and mutual support; it brings stability to our society. For those who choose to marry, and for their children, marriage provides an abundance of legal, financial, and social benefits. In return it imposes weighty legal, financial, and social obligations. The question before us is whether, consistent with the Massachusetts Constitution, the Commonwealth may deny the protections, benefits, and obligations conferred by civil marriage to two individuals of the same sex who wish to marry. We conclude that it may not. The Massachusetts Constitution affirms the dignity and equality of all individuals. It forbids the creation of second-class citizens. In reaching our conclusion we have given full deference to the arguments made by the Commonwealth. But it has failed to identify any constitutionally adequate reason for denying civil marriage to same-sex couples.

We are mindful that our decision marks a change in the history of our marriage law. Many people hold deep-seated religious, moral, and ethical convictions that marriage should be limited to the union of one man and one woman, and that homosexual conduct is immoral. Many hold equally strong religious, moral, and ethical convictions that same-sex couples are entitled to be married, and that homosexual persons should be treated no differently than their heterosexual neighbors. Neither view answers the question before us. Our concern is with the Massachusetts Constitution as a charter of governance for every person properly within its reach. "Our obligation is to define the liberty of all, not to mandate our own moral code."

Whether the Commonwealth may use its formidable regulatory authority to bar same-sex couples from civil marriage is a question not previously addressed by a Massachusetts appellate court. It is a question the United States Supreme Court left open as a matter of Federal law in *Lawrence*, where it was not an issue. There, the Court affirmed that the core concept of common human dignity protected by the Fourteenth Amendment to the United States Constitution precludes government intrusion into the deeply personal realms of consensual adult expressions of intimacy and one's choice of an intimate partner. The Court also reaffirmed the central role that decisions whether to marry or have children bear in shaping one's identity. The Massachusetts Constitution is, if anything, more protective of individual liberty and equality than the Federal Constitution; it may demand broader protection for fundamental rights; and it is less tolerant of government intrusion into the protected spheres of private life.

Barred access to the protections, benefits, and obligations of civil marriage, a person who enters into an intimate, exclusive union with another of the same sex is arbitrarily deprived of membership in one of our community's most rewarding and cherished institutions. That exclusion is incompatible with the constitutional principles of respect for individual autonomy and equality under law.

The plaintiffs are fourteen individuals from five Massachusetts counties. As of April 11, 2001, the date they filed their complaint, the plaintiffs Gloria Bailey, sixty years old, and Linda Davies, fifty-five years old, had been in a committed relationship for thirty years; the plaintiffs Maureen Brodoff, forty-nine years old, and Ellen Wade, fifty-two years old, had been in a committed relationship for twenty years and lived with their twelve year old daughter; the plaintiffs Hillary Goodridge, forty-four years old, and Julie Goodridge, forty-three years old, had been in a committed relationship for thirteen years and lived with their five year old daughter; the plaintiffs Gary Chalmers, thirty-five years old, and Richard Linnell, thirty-seven years old, had been in a committed relationship for thirteen years and lived with their eight year old daughter and Richard's mother; the plaintiffs Heidi Norton, thirty-six years old, and Gina Smith, thirty-six years old, had been in a committed relationship for eleven years and lived with their two sons, ages five years and one year; the plaintiffs Michael Horgan, forty-one years old, and Edward Balmelli, forty-one years old, had been in a committed relationship for seven years; and the plaintiffs David Wilson, fifty-seven years old, and Robert Compton, fifty-one years old, had been in a committed relationship for four years and had cared for David's mother in their home after a serious illness until she died. The plaintiffs include business executives, lawyers, an investment banker, educators, therapists, and a computer engineer. Many are active in church, community, and school groups.

The plaintiffs alleged violation of the laws of the Commonwealth, including but not limited to their rights under arts. 1, 6, 7, 10, 12, and 16, and Part II, c. 1, § 1, art. 4, of the Massachusetts Constitution. The plaintiffs' claim that the marriage restriction violates the Massachusetts Constitution can be analyzed in two ways. Does it offend the Constitution's guarantees of equality before the law? Or do the liberty and due process provisions of the Massachusetts Constitution secure the plaintiffs' right to marry their chosen partner? In matters implicating marriage, family life, and the upbringing of children, the two constitutional concepts frequently overlap, as they do here. Much of what we say concerning one standard applies to the other.

We begin by considering the nature of civil marriage itself. Simply put, the government creates civil marriage. In Massachusetts, civil marriage is, and since pre-Colonial days has been, precisely what its name implies: a wholly secular institution. No religious ceremony has ever been required to validate a Massachusetts marriage.

Without question, civil marriage enhances the "welfare of the community." It is a "social institution of the highest importance." Civil marriage anchors an ordered society by encouraging stable relationships over transient ones. It is central to the way the Commonwealth identifies individuals, provides for the orderly distribution of property, ensures that children and adults are cared for and supported whenever possible from private rather than public funds, and tracks important epidemiological and demographic data.

Marriage also bestows enormous private and social advantages on those who choose to marry. Civil marriage is at once a deeply personal commitment to another human being and a highly public celebration of the ideals of mutuality, companionship, intimacy, fidelity, and family. "It is an association that promotes a way of life, not causes; a harmony in living, not political faiths; a bilateral loyalty, not commercial or social projects." Because it fulfils yearnings for security, safe haven, and connection that express our common humanity, civil marriage is an esteemed institution and the decision whether and whom to marry is among life's momentous acts of self-definition.

Tangible as well as intangible benefits flow from marriage. The marriage license grants valuable property rights to those who meet the entry requirements, and who agree to what might otherwise be a burdensome degree of government regulation of their activities. The benefits accessible only by way of a marriage license are enormous, touching nearly every aspect of life and death. The department states that "hundreds of statutes" are related to marriage and to marital benefits. With no attempt to be comprehensive, we note that some of the statutory benefits conferred by the Legislature on those who enter into civil marriage include, as to property: joint Massachusetts income tax filing; tenancy by the entirety (a form of ownership that provides certain protections against creditors and allows for the automatic descent of property to the surviving spouse without probate); extension of the benefit of the homestead protection (securing up to $300,000 in equity from creditors) to one's spouse and children; automatic rights to inherit the property of a deceased spouse who does not leave a will; the rights of elective share and of dower (which allow surviving spouses certain property rights where the decedent spouse has not made adequate provision for the survivor in a will); entitlement to wages owed to a deceased employee; eligibility to continue certain businesses of a deceased spouse; the right to share the medical policy of one's spouse; thirty-nine week continuation of health coverage for the spouse of a person who is laid off or dies; preferential options under the Commonwealth's pension system; preferential benefits in the Commonwealth's medical program,

MassHealth; access to veterans' spousal benefits and preferences; financial protections for spouses of certain Commonwealth employees (fire fighters, police officers, and prosecutors, among others) killed in the performance of duty; the equitable division of marital property on divorce; temporary and permanent alimony rights; the right to separate support on separation of the parties that does not result in divorce; and the right to bring claims for wrongful death and loss of consortium, and for funeral and burial expenses and punitive damages resulting from tort actions.

Exclusive marital benefits that are not directly tied to property rights include the presumptions of legitimacy and parentage of children born to a married couple; and evidentiary rights, such as the prohibition against spouses testifying against one another about their private conversations, applicable in both civil and criminal cases. Other statutory benefits of a personal nature available only to married individuals include qualification for bereavement or medical leave to care for individuals related by blood or marriage; an automatic "family member" preference to make medical decisions for an incompetent or disabled spouse who does not have a contrary health care proxy; the application of predictable rules of child custody, visitation, support, and removal out-of-State when married parents divorce; priority rights to administer the estate of a deceased spouse who dies without a will, and the requirement that a surviving spouse must consent to the appointment of any other person as administrator; and the right to interment in the lot or tomb owned by one's deceased spouse.

Where a married couple has children, their children are also directly or indirectly, but no less auspiciously, the recipients of the special legal and economic protections obtained by civil marriage. Notwithstanding the Commonwealth's strong public policy to abolish legal distinctions between marital and nonmarital children in providing for the support and care of minors, the fact remains that marital children reap a measure of family stability and economic security based on their parents' legally privileged status that is largely inaccessible, or not as readily accessible, to nonmarital children. Some of these benefits are social, such as the enhanced approval that still attends the status of being a marital child. Others are material, such as the greater ease of access to family-based State and Federal benefits that attend the presumptions of one's parentage.

It is undoubtedly for these concrete reasons, as well as for its intimately personal significance, that civil marriage has long been termed a "civil right." The United States Supreme Court has described the right to marry as "of fundamental importance for all individuals" and as "part of the fundamental right of privacy implicit in the Fourteenth Amendment's Due Process Clause."

Without the right to marry—or more properly, the right to choose to marry—one is excluded from the full range of human experience and denied full protection of the laws for one's "avowed commitment to an intimate and lasting human relationship." Because civil marriage is central to the lives of individuals and the welfare of the community, our laws assiduously protect the individual's right to marry against undue government incursion. Laws may not "interfere directly and substantially with the right to marry."

For decades, indeed centuries, in much of this country (including Massachusetts) no lawful marriage was possible between white and black Americans. That long history availed not when the Supreme Court of California held in 1948 that a legislative prohibition against interracial marriage violated the due process and equality guarantees of the Fourteenth Amendment, or when, nineteen years later, the United States Supreme Court also held that a statutory bar to interracial marriage violated the Fourteenth Amendment. As both *Perez* and *Loving* make clear, the right to marry means little if it does not include the right to marry the person of one's choice, subject to appropriate government restrictions in the interests of public health, safety, and welfare. In this case, as in *Perez* and *Loving*, a statute deprives individuals of access to an institution of fundamental legal, personal, and social significance—the institution of marriage—because of a single trait: skin color in *Perez* and *Loving*, sexual orientation here. As it did in *Perez* and *Loving*, history must yield to a more fully developed understanding of the invidious quality of the discrimination.

The Massachusetts Constitution protects matters of personal liberty against government incursion as zealously and often more so, than does the Federal Constitution, even where both Constitutions employ essentially the same language. That the Massachusetts Constitution is in some instances more protective of individual liberty interests than is the Federal Constitution is not surprising. Fundamental to the vigor of our Federal system of government is that "state courts are absolutely free to interpret state constitutional provisions to accord greater protection to individual rights than do similar provisions of the United States Constitution."

The individual liberty and equality safeguards of the Massachusetts Constitution protect both "freedom from" unwarranted government intrusion into protected spheres of life and "freedom to" partake in benefits created by the State for the common good. Both freedoms are involved here. Whether and whom to marry, how to express sexual intimacy, and whether and how to establish a family—these are among the most basic of every individual's liberty and due process rights. And central to personal freedom and security is the assurance that the laws will apply equally to persons in similar situations. "Absolute equality before the law is a fundamental principle of our own Constitution." The liberty interest in choosing whether and whom to marry would be hollow if the Commonwealth could, without sufficient justification, foreclose an individual from freely choosing the person with whom to share an exclusive commitment in the unique institution of civil marriage.

The Massachusetts Constitution requires, at a minimum, that the exercise of the State's regulatory authority not be "arbitrary or capricious." Under both the equality and liberty guarantees, regulatory authority must, at very least, serve "a legitimate purpose in a rational way"; a statute must "bear a reasonable relation to a permissible legislative objective." Any law failing to satisfy the basic standards of rationality is void.

The plaintiffs challenge the marriage statute on both equal protection and due process grounds. With respect to each such claim, we must first determine the appropriate standard of review. Where a statute implicates a fundamental right or uses a suspect classification, we employ "strict judicial scrutiny." For all other statutes, we employ the "rational basis test." For due process claims, rational basis analysis requires that statutes "bear a real and substantial relation to the public health, safety, morals, or some other phase of the general welfare." For equal protection challenges, the rational basis test requires that "an impartial lawmaker could logically believe that the classification would serve a legitimate public purpose that transcends the harm to the members of the disadvantaged class."

The department argues that no fundamental right or "suspect" class is at issue here, and rational basis is the appropriate standard of review. For the reasons we explain below, we conclude that the marriage ban does not meet the rational basis test for either due process or equal protection. Because the statute does not survive rational basis review, we do not consider the plaintiffs' arguments that this case merits strict judicial scrutiny.

The department posits three legislative rationales for prohibiting same-sex couples from marrying: (1) providing a "favorable setting for procreation"; (2) ensuring the optimal setting for child rearing, which the department defines as "a two-parent family with one parent of each sex"; and (3) preserving scarce State and private financial resources. We consider each in turn.

The judge in the Superior Court endorsed the first rationale, holding that "the state's interest in regulating marriage is based on the traditional concept that marriage's primary purpose is procreation." This is incorrect. Our laws of civil marriage do not privilege procreative heterosexual intercourse between married people above every other form of adult intimacy and every other means of creating a family. General Laws c. 207 contains no requirement that the applicants for a marriage license attest to their ability or intention to conceive children by coitus. Fertility is not a condition of marriage, nor is it grounds for divorce. People who have never consummated their marriage, and never plan to, may be and stay married. People who cannot stir from their deathbed may marry. While it is certainly true that many, perhaps most, married couples have children together (assisted or unassisted), it is the exclusive and permanent commitment of the marriage partners to one another, not the begetting of children, that is the sine qua non of civil marriage.

Moreover, the Commonwealth affirmatively facilitates bringing children into a family regardless of whether the intended parent is married or unmarried, whether the child is adopted or born into a family, whether assistive technology was used to conceive the child, and whether the parent or her partner is heterosexual, homosexual, or bisexual. If procreation were a necessary component of civil marriage, our statutes would draw a tighter circle around the permissible bounds of nonmarital child bearing and the creation of families by noncoital means. The attempt to isolate procreation as "the source of a fundamental right to marry," overlooks the integrated way in which courts have examined the complex and overlapping realms of personal autonomy, marriage, family life, and child rearing. Our jurisprudence recognizes that, in these nuanced and fundamentally private areas of life, such a narrow focus is inappropriate.

The "marriage is procreation" argument singles out the one unbridgeable difference between same-sex and opposite-sex couples, and transforms that difference into the essence of legal marriage. Like "Amendment 2" to the Constitution of Colorado, which effectively denied homosexual persons equality under the law and full access to the political process, the marriage restriction impermissibly "identifies persons by a single trait and then denies them protection across the board." In so doing, the State's action confers an official stamp of approval on the destructive stereotype that same-sex relationships are inherently unstable and inferior to opposite-sex relationships and are not worthy of respect.

The department's first stated rationale, equating marriage with unassisted heterosexual procreation, shades imperceptibly into its second: that confining marriage to opposite-sex couples ensures that children are raised in the "optimal" setting. Protecting the welfare of children is a paramount State policy. Restricting marriage to opposite-sex couples, however, cannot plausibly further this policy. "The demographic changes of the past century make it difficult to speak of an average American family. The composition of families varies greatly from household to household." Massachusetts has responded supportively to "the changing realities of the American family," and has moved vigorously to strengthen the modern family in its many variations. Moreover, we have repudiated the common-law power of the State to provide varying levels of protection to children based on the circumstances of birth. The "best interests of the child" standard does not turn on a parent's sexual orientation or marital status.

The department has offered no evidence that forbidding marriage to people of the same sex will increase the number of couples choosing to enter into opposite-sex marriages in order to have and raise children. There is thus no rational relationship between the marriage statute and the Commonwealth's proffered goal of protecting the "optimal" child rearing unit. Moreover, the department readily concedes that people in same-sex couples may be "excellent" parents. These couples (including four of the plaintiff couples) have children for the reasons others do—to love them, to care for them, to nurture them. But the task of child rearing for same-sex couples is made infinitely harder by their status as outliers to the marriage laws. While establishing the parentage of children as soon as possible is crucial to the safety and welfare of children, same-sex couples must undergo the sometimes lengthy and intrusive process of second-parent adoption to establish their joint parentage. While the enhanced income provided by marital benefits is an important source of security and stability for married couples and their children, those benefits are denied to families headed by same-sex couples. While the laws of divorce provide clear and reasonably predictable guidelines for child support, child custody, and property division on dissolution of a marriage, same-sex couples who dissolve their relationships find themselves and their children in the highly unpredictable terrain of equity jurisdiction. Given the wide range of public benefits reserved only for married couples, we do not credit the department's contention that the absence of access to civil marriage amounts to little more than an inconvenience to same-sex couples and their children. Excluding same-sex couples from civil marriage will not make children of opposite-sex marriages more secure, but it does prevent children of same-sex couples from enjoying the immeasurable advantages that flow from the assurance of "a stable family structure in which children will be reared, educated, and socialized."

No one disputes that the plaintiff couples are families, that many are parents, and that the children they are raising, like all children, need and should have the fullest opportunity to grow up in a secure, protected family unit. Similarly, no one disputes that, under the rubric of marriage, the State provides a cornucopia of substantial benefits to married parents and their children. The preferential treatment of civil marriage reflects the Legislature's conclusion that marriage "is the foremost setting for the education and socialization of children" precisely because it "encourages parents to remain committed to each other and to their children as they grow." It cannot be rational under our laws, and indeed it is not permitted, to penalize children by depriving them of State benefits because the State disapproves of their parents' sexual orientation.

The third rationale advanced by the department is that limiting marriage to opposite-sex couples furthers the Legislature's interest in conserving scarce State and private financial resources. The marriage restriction is rational, it argues, because the General Court logically could assume that same-sex couples are more financially independent than married couples and thus less needy of public marital benefits, such as tax advantages, or private marital benefits, such as employer-financed health plans that include spouses in their coverage.

An absolute statutory ban on same-sex marriage bears no rational relationship to the goal of economy. First, the department's conclusory generalization—that same-sex couples are less financially dependent on each other than opposite-sex couples—ignores that many same-sex couples, such as many of the plaintiffs in this case, have children and other dependents (here, aged parents) in their care. The department does not contend, nor could it, that these dependents are less needy or deserving than the dependents of married couples. Second, Massachusetts marriage laws do not condition receipt of public and private financial benefits to married individuals on a demonstration of financial dependence on each other; the benefits are available to married couples regardless of whether they mingle their finances or actually depend on each other for support.

The department suggests additional rationales for prohibiting same-sex couples from marrying, which are developed by some amici. It argues that broadening civil marriage to include same-sex couples will trivialize or destroy the institution of marriage as it has historically been fashioned. Certainly our decision today marks a significant change in the definition of marriage as it has been inherited from the common law, and understood by many societies for centuries. But it does not disturb the fundamental value of marriage in our society.

Here, the plaintiffs seek only to be married, not to undermine the institution of civil marriage. They do not want marriage abolished. They do not attack the binary nature of marriage, the consanguinity provisions, or any of the other gate-keeping provisions of the marriage licensing law. Recognizing the right of an individual to marry a person of the same sex will not diminish the validity or dignity of opposite-sex marriage, any more than recognizing the right of an individual to marry a person of a different race devalues the marriage of a person who marries someone of her own race. If anything, extending civil marriage to same-sex couples reinforces the importance of marriage to individuals and communities. That same-sex couples are willing to embrace marriage's solemn obligations of exclusivity, mutual support, and commitment to one another is a testament to the enduring place of marriage in our laws and in the human spirit.

We also reject the argument suggested by the department, and elaborated by some amici, that expanding the institution of civil marriage in Massachusetts to include same-sex couples will lead to interstate conflict. We would not presume to dictate how another State should respond to today's decision. But neither should considerations of comity prevent us from according Massachusetts residents the full measure of protection available under the Massachusetts Constitution. The genius of our Federal system is that each State's Constitution has vitality specific to its own traditions, and that, subject to the minimum requirements of the Fourteenth Amendment, each State is free to address difficult issues of individual liberty in the manner its own Constitution demands.

Several amici suggest that prohibiting marriage by same-sex couples reflects community consensus that homosexual conduct is immoral. Yet Massachusetts has a strong affirmative policy of preventing discrimination on the basis of sexual orientation.

The department has had more than ample opportunity to articulate a constitutionally adequate justification for limiting civil marriage to opposite-sex unions. It has failed to do so. The department has offered purported justifications for the civil marriage restriction that are starkly at odds with the comprehensive network of vigorous, gender-neutral laws promoting stable families and the best interests of children. It has failed to identify any relevant characteristic that would justify shutting the door to civil marriage to a person who wishes to marry someone of the same sex.

The marriage ban works a deep and scarring hardship on a very real segment of the community for no rational reason. The absence of any reasonable relationship between, on the one hand, an absolute disqualification of same-sex couples who wish to enter into civil marriage and, on the other, protection of public health, safety, or general welfare, suggests that the marriage restriction is rooted in persistent prejudices against persons who are (or who are believed to be) homosexual. "The Constitution cannot control such prejudices but neither can it tolerate them. Private biases may be outside the reach of the law, but the law cannot, directly or indirectly, give them effect." Limiting the protections, benefits, and obligations of civil marriage to opposite-sex couples violates the basic premises of individual liberty and equality under law protected by the Massachusetts Constitution.

We consider next the plaintiffs' request for relief. We preserve as much of the statute as may be preserved in the face of the successful constitutional challenge. Here, no one argues that striking down the marriage laws is an appropriate form of relief. Eliminating civil marriage would be wholly inconsistent with the Legislature's deep commitment to fostering stable families and would dismantle a vital organizing principle of our society. We face a problem similar to one that recently confronted the Court of Appeal for Ontario, the highest court of that Canadian province, when it considered the constitutionality of the same-sex marriage ban under Canada's Federal Constitution, the Charter of Rights and Freedoms (Charter). Canada, like the United States, adopted the common law of England that civil marriage is "the voluntary union for life of one man and one woman, to the exclusion of all others." In holding that the limitation of civil marriage to opposite-sex couples violated the Charter, the Court of Appeal refined the common-law meaning of marriage. We concur with this remedy, which is entirely consonant with established principles of jurisprudence empowering a court to refine a common-law principle in light of evolving constitutional standards.

We construe civil marriage to mean the voluntary union of two persons as spouses, to the exclusion of all others. This reformulation redresses the plaintiffs' constitutional injury and furthers the aim of marriage to promote stable, exclusive relationships. It advances the two legitimate State interests the department has identified: providing a stable setting for child rearing and conserving State resources. It leaves intact the Legislature's broad discretion to regulate marriage. We declare that barring an individual from the protections, benefits, and obligations of civil marriage solely because that person would marry a person of the same sex violates the Massachusetts Constitution.

GREANEY, J., concurring.

The right to marry is not a privilege conferred by the State, but a fundamental right that is protected against unwarranted State interference. This right is essentially vitiated if one is denied the right to marry a person of one's choice.

A comment is in order with respect to the insistence of some that marriage is, as a matter of definition, the legal union of a man and a woman. To define the institution of marriage by the characteristics of those to whom it always has been accessible, in order to justify the exclusion of those to whom it never has been accessible, is conclusory and bypasses the core question we are asked to decide. This case calls for a higher level of legal analysis. Precisely, the case requires that we confront ingrained assumptions with respect to historically accepted roles of men and women within the institution of marriage and requires that we reexamine these assumptions in light of the unequivocal language of art. 1, in order to ensure that the governmental conduct challenged here conforms to the supreme charter of our Commonwealth. I do not doubt the sincerity of deeply held moral or religious beliefs that make inconceivable to some the notion that any change in the common-law definition of what constitutes a legal civil marriage is now, or ever would be, warranted. But, as a matter of constitutional law, neither the mantra of tradition, nor individual conviction, can justify the perpetuation of a hierarchy in which couples of the same sex and their families are deemed less worthy of social and legal recognition than couples of the opposite sex and their families.

I am hopeful that our decision will be accepted by those thoughtful citizens who believe that same-sex unions should not be approved by the State. I am not referring here to acceptance in the sense of grudging acknowledgment of the court's authority to adjudicate the matter. My hope is more liberating. The plaintiffs are members of our community, our neighbors, our coworkers, our friends. As pointed out by the court, their professions include investment advisor, computer engineer, teacher, therapist, and lawyer. The plaintiffs volunteer in our schools, worship beside us in our religious houses, and have children who play with our children, to mention just a few ordinary daily contacts. We share a common humanity and participate together in the social contract that is the foundation of our Commonwealth. Simple principles of decency dictate that we extend to the plaintiffs, and to their new status, full acceptance, tolerance, and respect. We should do so because it is the right thing to do.

SPINA, J., dissenting.

What is at stake in this case is not the unequal treatment of individuals or whether individual rights have been impermissibly burdened, but the power of the Legislature to effectuate social change without interference from the courts. The power to regulate marriage lies with the Legislature, not with the judiciary. Today, the court has transformed its role as protector of individual rights into the role of creator of rights, and I respectfully dissent.

The marriage statutes do not impermissibly burden a right protected by our constitutional guarantee of due process implicit in art. 10 of our Declaration of Rights. There is no restriction on the right of any plaintiff to enter into marriage. Each is free to marry a willing person of the opposite sex. Substantive due process protects individual rights against unwarranted government intrusion. Today the court does not fashion a remedy that affords greater protection of a right. Instead, using the rubric of due process, it has redefined marriage.

Although this court did not state that same-sex marriage is a fundamental right worthy of strict scrutiny protection, it nonetheless deemed it a constitutionally protected right by applying rational basis review. Before applying any level of constitutional analysis there must be a recognized right at stake. Same-sex marriage, or the "right to marry the person of one's choice" as the court today defines that right, does not fall within the fundamental right to marry. Same-sex marriage is not "deeply rooted in this Nation's history," and the court does not suggest that it is. Except for the occasional isolated decision in recent years, same-sex marriage is not a right, fundamental or otherwise, recognized in this country. In this Commonwealth and in this country, the roots of the institution of marriage are deeply set in history as a civil union between a single man and a single woman. There is no basis for the court to recognize same-sex marriage as a constitutionally protected right.

The remedy that the court has fashioned both in the name of equal protection and due process exceeds the bounds of judicial restraint mandated by art. 30. The remedy that construes gender-specific language as gender-neutral amounts to a statutory revision that replaces the intent of the Legislature with that of the court. Article 30 permits the court to modify statutory language only if legislative intent is preserved. Here, the alteration of the gender-specific language alters precisely what the Legislature unambiguously intended to preserve, the marital rights of single men and women. Such a dramatic change in social institutions must remain at the behest of the people through the democratic process.

SOSMAN, J., dissenting.

Based on our own philosophy of child rearing, and on our observations of the children being raised by same-sex couples to whom we are personally close, we may be of the view that what matters to children is not the gender, or sexual orientation, or even the number of the adults who raise them, but rather whether those adults provide the children with a nurturing, stable, safe, consistent, and supportive environment in which to mature. Same-sex couples can provide their children with the requisite nurturing, stable, safe, consistent, and supportive environment in which to mature, just as opposite-sex couples do. It is therefore understandable that the court might view the traditional definition of marriage as an unnecessary anachronism, rooted in historical prejudices that modern society has in large measure rejected and biological limitations that modern science has overcome.

It is not, however, our assessment that matters. Conspicuously absent from the court's opinion today is any acknowledgment that the attempts at scientific study of the ramifications of raising children in same-sex couple households are themselves in their infancy and have so far produced inconclusive and conflicting results. Notwithstanding our belief that gender and sexual orientation of parents should not matter to the success of the child rearing venture, studies to date reveal that there are still some observable differences between children raised by opposite-sex couples and children raised by same-sex couples. Interpretation of the data gathered by those studies then becomes clouded by the personal and political beliefs of the investigators, both as to whether the differences identified are positive or negative, and as to the untested explanations of what might account for those differences. (This is hardly the first time in history that the ostensible steel of the scientific method has melted and buckled under the intense heat of political and religious passions.) Even in the absence of bias or political agenda behind the various studies of children raised by same-sex couples, the most neutral and strict application of scientific principles to this field would be constrained by the limited period of observation that has been available. Gay and lesbian couples living together openly, and official recognition of them as their children's sole parents, comprise a very recent phenomenon, and the recency of that phenomenon has not yet permitted any study of how those children fare as adults and at best minimal study of how they fare during their adolescent years. The Legislature can rationally view the state of the scientific evidence as unsettled on the critical question it now faces: are families headed by same-sex parents equally successful in rearing children from infancy to adulthood as families headed by parents of opposite sexes? Our belief that children raised by same-sex couples *should* fare the same as children raised in traditional families is just that: a passionately held but utterly untested belief. The Legislature is not required to share that belief but may, as the creator of the institution of civil marriage, wish to see the proof before making a fundamental alteration to that institution.

As a matter of social history, today's opinion may represent a great turning point that many will hail as a tremendous step toward a more just society. As a matter of constitutional jurisprudence, however, the case stands as an aberration. To reach the result it does, the court has tortured the rational basis test beyond recognition.

CORDY, J., dissenting.

The plaintiffs ground their contention that they have a fundamental right to marry a person of the same sex in a long line of Supreme Court decisions that discuss the importance of marriage. In context, all of these decisions and their discussions are about the "fundamental" nature of the institution of marriage as it has existed and been understood in this country, not as the court has redefined it today. Even in that context, its "fundamental" nature is derivative of the nature of the interests that underlie or are associated with it. An examination of those interests reveals that they are either not shared by same-sex couples or not implicated by the marriage statutes.

Supreme Court cases that have described marriage or the right to marry as "fundamental" have focused primarily on the underlying interest of every individual in procreation, which, historically, could only legally occur within the construct of marriage because sexual intercourse outside of marriage was a criminal act. Because same-sex couples are unable to procreate on their own, any right to marriage they may possess cannot be based on their interest in procreation, which has been essential to the Supreme Court's denomination of the right to marry as fundamental.

Supreme Court cases recognizing a right to privacy in intimate decision-making have also focused primarily on sexual relations and the decision whether or not to procreate, and have refused to recognize an "unlimited right" to privacy. Although some of the privacy cases also speak in terms of personal autonomy, no court has ever recognized such an open-ended right. "That many of the rights and liberties protected by the Due Process Clause sound in personal autonomy does not warrant the sweeping conclusion that any and all important, intimate, and personal decisions are so protected." Such decisions are protected not because they are important, intimate, and personal, but because the right or liberty at stake is "so deeply rooted in our history and traditions, or so fundamental to our concept of constitutionally ordered liberty" that it is protected by due process. Accordingly, the Supreme Court has concluded that while the decision to refuse unwanted medical treatment is fundamental because it is deeply rooted in our nation's history and tradition, the equally personal and profound decision to commit suicide is not because of the absence of such roots.

While the institution of marriage is deeply rooted in the history and traditions of our country and our State, the right to marry someone of the same sex is not. Unlike opposite-sex marriages, which have deep historic roots same-sex relationships, although becoming more accepted, are certainly not so "deeply rooted in this Nation's history and tradition" as to warrant such enhanced constitutional protection.

The burden of demonstrating that a statute does not satisfy the rational basis standard rests on the plaintiffs. It is a weighty one. "A reviewing court will presume a statute's validity, and make all rational inferences in favor of it. The Legislature is not required to justify its classifications, nor provide a record or finding in support of them." The statute "only needs to be supported by a conceivable rational basis."

It is difficult to imagine a State purpose more important and legitimate than ensuring, promoting, and supporting an optimal social structure within which to bear and raise children. At the very least, the marriage statute continues to serve this important State purpose.

The question we must turn to next is whether the statute, construed as limiting marriage to couples of the opposite sex, remains a rational way to further that purpose. Stated differently, we ask whether a conceivable rational basis exists on which the Legislature could conclude that continuing to limit the institution of civil marriage to members of the opposite sex furthers the legitimate purpose of ensuring, promoting, and supporting an optimal social structure for the bearing and raising of children. In considering whether such a rational basis exists, we defer to the decision-making process of the Legislature, and must make deferential assumptions about the information that it might consider and on which it may rely. We must assume that the Legislature (1) might conclude that the institution of civil marriage has successfully and continually provided this structure over several centuries; (2) might consider and credit studies that document negative consequences that too often follow children either born outside of marriage or raised in households lacking either a father or a mother figure, and scholarly commentary contending that children and families develop best when mothers and fathers are partners in their parenting; and (3) would be familiar with many recent studies that variously support the proposition that children raised in intact families headed by same-sex couples fare as well on many measures as children raised in similar families headed by opposite-sex couples; support the proposition that children of same-sex couples fare worse on some measures; or reveal notable differences between the two groups of children that warrant further study.

We must also assume that the Legislature would be aware of the critiques of the methodologies used in virtually all of the comparative studies of children raised in these different environments, cautioning that the sampling populations are not representative, that the observation periods are too limited in time, that the empirical data are unreliable, and that the hypotheses are too infused with political or agenda driven bias.

Taking all of this available information into account, the Legislature could rationally conclude that a family environment with married opposite-sex parents remains the optimal social structure in which to bear children, and that the raising of children by same-sex couples, who by definition cannot be the two sole biological parents of a child and cannot provide children with a parental authority figure of each gender, presents an alternative structure for child rearing that has not yet proved itself beyond reasonable scientific dispute to be as optimal as the biologically based marriage norm. Working from the assumption that recognition of same-sex marriages will increase the number of children experiencing this alternative, the Legislature could conceivably conclude that declining to recognize same-sex marriages remains prudent until empirical questions about its impact on the upbringing of children are resolved.

The fact that the Commonwealth currently allows same-sex couples to adopt, does not affect the rationality of this conclusion. The eligibility of a child for adoption presupposes that at least one of the child's biological parents is unable or unwilling, for some reason, to participate in raising the child. In that sense, society has "lost" the optimal setting in which to raise that child—it is simply not available. In these circumstances, the principal and overriding consideration is the "best interests of the child," considering his or her unique circumstances and the options that are available for that child. The objective is an individualized determination of the best environment for a particular child, where the normative social structure—a home with both the child's biological father and mother—is not an option. That such a focused determination may lead to the approval of a same-sex couple's adoption of a child does not mean that it would be irrational for a legislator, in fashioning statutory laws that cannot make such individualized determinations, to conclude generally that being raised by a same-sex couple has not yet been shown to be the absolute equivalent of being raised by one's married biological parents.

That the State does not preclude different types of families from raising children does not mean that it must view them all as equally optimal and equally deserving of State endorsement and support. For example, single persons are allowed to adopt children, but the fact that the Legislature permits single-parent adoption does not mean that it has endorsed single parenthood as an optimal setting in which to raise children or views it as the equivalent of being raised by both of one's biological parents. The same holds true with respect to same-sex couples—the fact that they may adopt children means only that the Legislature has concluded that they may provide an acceptable setting in which to raise children who cannot be raised by both of their biological parents. The Legislature may rationally permit adoption by same-sex couples yet harbor reservations as to whether parenthood by same-sex couples should be affirmatively encouraged to the same extent as parenthood by the heterosexual couple whose union produced the child.

There is no question that many same-sex couples are capable of being good parents, and should be (and are) permitted to be so. The policy question that a legislator must resolve is a different one, and turns on an assessment of whether the marriage structure proposed by the plaintiffs will, over time, if endorsed and supported by the State, prove to be as stable and successful a model as the one that has formed a cornerstone of our society since colonial times, or prove to be less than optimal, and result in consequences, perhaps now unforeseen, adverse to the State's legitimate interest in promoting and supporting the best possible social structure in which children should be born and raised. Given the critical importance of civil marriage as an organizing and stabilizing institution of society, it is eminently rational for the Legislature to postpone making fundamental changes to it until such time as there is unanimous scientific evidence, or popular consensus, or both, that such changes can safely be made.

While "the Massachusetts Constitution protects matters of personal liberty against government incursion as zealously, and often more so, than does the Federal Constitution," this case is not about government intrusions into matters of personal liberty. It is not about the rights of same-sex couples to choose to live together, or to be intimate with each other, or to adopt and raise children together. It is about whether the State must endorse and support their choices by changing the institution of civil marriage to make its benefits, obligations, and responsibilities applicable to them. While the courageous efforts of many have resulted in increased dignity, rights, and respect for gay and lesbian members of our community, the issue presented here is a profound one, deeply rooted in social policy, that must, for now, be the subject of legislative not judicial action.

NOTES

1. After *Goodridge*, the Massachusetts Senate requested an advisory opinion from the Massachusetts Supreme Judicial Court concerning the constitutionality of a bill pending before the legislature that would prohibit

same-sex couples from entering into marriage but allow them to form civil unions with all of the benefits, protections, rights and responsibilities of marriage. In response to the request, the court issued an opinion declaring that civil union was not an adequate substitute for marriage and that to continue to disallow same-sex marriage would be a violation of the state constitution. *Opinion of the Justices to the Senate*, 802 N.E.2d 565 (Mass. 2004). Here's an excerpt from the opinion:

> The same defects of rationality evident in the marriage ban considered in *Goodridge* are evident in, if not exaggerated by, Senate No. 2175. Segregating same-sex unions from opposite-sex unions cannot possibly be held rationally to advance or "preserve" what we stated in *Goodridge* were the Commonwealth's legitimate interests in procreation, child rearing, and the conservation of resources. Because the proposed law by its express terms forbids same-sex couples' entry into civil marriage, it continues to relegate same-sex couples to a different status. The holding in *Goodridge*, by which we are bound, is that group classifications based on unsupportable distinctions, such as that embodied in the proposed bill, are invalid under the Massachusetts Constitution. The history of our nation has demonstrated that separate is seldom, if ever, equal.
>
> The bill's absolute prohibition of the use of the word "marriage" by "spouses" who are the same sex is more than semantic. The dissimilitude between the terms "civil marriage" and "civil union" is not innocuous; it is a considered choice of language that reflects a demonstrable assigning of same-sex, largely homosexual, couples to second-class status. The denomination of this difference by the separate opinion of Justice Sosman as merely a "squabble over the name to be used" so clearly misses the point that further discussion appears to be useless. If, as the separate opinion posits, the proponents of the bill believe that no message is conveyed by eschewing the word "marriage" and replacing it with "civil union" for same-sex "spouses," we doubt that the attempt to circumvent the court's decision in *Goodridge* would be so purposeful. For no rational reason the marriage laws of the Commonwealth discriminate against a defined class; no amount of tinkering with language will eradicate that stain. The bill would have the effect of maintaining and fostering a stigma of exclusion that the Constitution prohibits. It would deny to same-sex "spouses" only a status that is specially recognized in society and has significant social and other advantages. The Massachusetts Constitution, as was explained in the *Goodridge* opinion, does not permit such invidious discrimination, no matter how well intentioned.
>
> We recognize that the pending bill palliates some of the financial and other concrete manifestations of the discrimination at issue in *Goodridge*. But the question the court considered in *Goodridge* was not only whether it was proper to withhold tangible benefits from same-sex couples, but also whether it was constitutional to create a separate class of citizens by status discrimination, and withhold from that class the right to participate in the institution of civil marriage, along with its concomitant tangible and intangible protections, benefits, rights, and responsibilities. Maintaining a second-class citizen status for same-sex couples by excluding them from the institution of civil marriage is the constitutional infirmity at issue. We are of the opinion that Senate No. 2175 violates the equal protection and due process requirements of the Constitution of the Commonwealth and the Massachusetts Declaration of Rights. The bill maintains an unconstitutional, inferior, and discriminatory status for same-sex

couples, and the bill's remaining provisions are too entwined with this purpose to stand independently.

2. In 2004, Massachusetts became the first state to allow same-sex marriage and in May of that year same-sex couples began to marry in Massachusetts. In 2007, the Massachusetts legislature voted to amend its constitution to define marriage as a union between a man and a woman. However, to be effective, constitutional amendments in Massachusetts must be re-approved a second time by the legislature and then submitted to the electorate for a statewide vote. After the initial vote on the amendment, the legislature had a change of heart and voted against the amendment, thereby allowing the continuation of same-sex marriage in the Commonwealth. *See* Jeffrey M. Shaman, *Equality and Liberty in the Golden Age of State Constitutional Law* 207 (2008).

3. Since *Goodridge*, other state high courts have addressed the issue of same-sex marriage, with varying results. Some state high courts, in disagreement with *Goodridge*, found nothing unconstitutional about laws limiting marriage to opposite-sex couples. Others, in agreement with *Goodridge*, struck down laws precluding same-sex marriage. *See* Jennifer Friesen, *State Constitutional Law: Litigating Individual Rights, Claims And Defenses* 2–106 (4th ed. 2006); *id.* 23–25 (4th ed. Supp. 2009). A similar pattern developed in the federal courts, with some federal courts upholding bans on same-sex marriage, and others striking them down.

4. In California, the state supreme court ruled that state laws precluding same-sex marriage violated the equal protection clause of the California Constitution, *In re Marriages Cases*, 183 P.3d 384 (Cal. 2008), but that decision was nullified by Proposition 8, a constitutional amendment adopted by the electorate stating that only marriage between a man and a woman is valid or recognized in California. Cal. Const. art. I, § 7.5. In turn, a federal district court in California ruled that Proposition 8 violated the Due Process and Equal Protection Clauses of the United States Constitution. *Perry v. Schwarzenegger*, 704 F. Supp. 2d 921 (N.D. Cal. 2010). State officials decided not to appeal the district court decision, but several backers of Proposition 8 who intervened in the case appealed to the United States Court of Appeals for the Ninth Circuit, which affirmed the district court decision. *Perry v. Brown*, 671 F.3d 1052 (9th Cir. 2012). However, the Court of Appeals decision was vacated by the United States Supreme Court on the ground that the interveners did not have standing to appeal the district court decision. *Hollingsworth v. Perry*, 133 S. Ct. 265 (2013). This left the ruling of the district court as the final ruling in the case.

5. At one time, 41 states had adopted statutory or constitutional provisions defining marriage as the union of a man and a woman, thereby precluding same-sex marriage. Friesen, *State Constitutional Law* 22–23 (4th ed. Supp. 2019). Over time, state legislatures began to enact laws authorizing same-

sex marriage. In some instances, these laws were submitted to the voters for their approval or disapproval in state referenda. In 2012 the voters in three states—Maine, Maryland, and Washington—voted in referenda to uphold legislation that had been enacted allowing same-sex marriage. In the same year, the voters of Minnesota rejected a constitutional amendment to prohibit same-sex marriage. The actions taken in these four states reversed a trend of public votes rejecting same-sex marriage; previously voters in 32 states had voted against same-sex marriage. By March of 2015, 37 states and the District of Columbia, either by legislation, public vote, or court decision, had recognized same-sex marriage.

6. In June 2015, the Supreme Court of the United States announced its decision in *Obergefell v. Hodges*, ruling that the right to marry is a fundamental right inherent in the liberty of the person and that under the Due Process and Equal Protection Clauses of the Fourteenth Amendment same-sex couples may not be denied the fundamental right to marry. The decision legalized same-sex marriage throughout the United States and required all states to issue marriage licenses to same-sex couples and to recognize same-sex marriages performed in other states.

In the Court's 5-4 decision, Justice Kennedy acknowledged that a significant number of States had recognized a right to same-sex marriage. Consistent with those decisions, he added:

> No Union is more profound than marriage, for it embodies the highest ideals of love, fidelity, devotion, sacrifice, and family. In forming a marital union, two people become greater than once they were. As some of the petitioners in these cases demonstrate, marriage embodies a love that may endure even past death. It would misunderstand these men and women to say they disrespect the idea of marriage. Their plea is that they do respect it, respect it so deeply that they seek to fund its fulfillment for themselves. Their hope is not to be condemned to live in loneliness, excluded from one of civilization's oldest institutions. They ask for equal dignity in the eyes of the law. The Constitution grants them that right.

In a dissenting opinion, Chief Justice Roberts made the following observation:

> Although the policy arguments for extending marriage to same-sex couples may be compelling, the legal arguments for requiring such an extension are not. The fundamental right to marry does not include a right to make a State change its definition of marriage. And a State's decision to maintain the meaning of marriage that has persisted in every culture throughout human history can hardly be called irrational. In short, our Constitution does not enact any one theory of marriage. The people of a State are free to expand marriage to include same-sex couples, or to retain the historic definition.

G. THE RIGHTS OF BODILY INTEGRITY AND DOMESTIC PRIVACY

Matter of FARRELL
529 A.2d 404 (N.J. 1987)

GARIBALDI, J.

Although we stated the general principle that competent informed patients have the right to decline life-sustaining treatment in both *In re Quinlan* (1976) and *In re Conroy* (1985), each of those cases involved an incompetent institutionalized patient. In this case we deal for the first time with the right of a competent, terminally ill adult patient living at home to withdraw a life-sustaining respirator.

Kathleen married Francis Farrell in 1969. They had two children. Prior to her illness, Mrs. Farrell worked as a keypunch operator. In November 1982, she began to experience symptoms associated with ALS, a disorder of the nervous system that results in degeneration of the victim's muscles. Although it eventually renders a patient incapable of movement, ALS does not impair the patient's mental faculties. The cause of the disease is unknown and there is no available treatment or cure. At the time of diagnosis, a victim's life expectancy even with life-sustaining treatment is usually one to three years.

After she became ill, Mrs. Farrell was admitted to a Philadelphia hospital where she underwent a tracheotomy and was connected to a respirator. In the autumn of 1983, she was released from the hospital because it could provide no further help for her condition. She returned home to live with her husband and their two teenage sons. Thereafter Mrs. Farrell was paralyzed and confined to bed in need of around-the-clock nursing care. Insurance covered all the expenses of this care.

In November 1985, after an experimental program that her husband characterized as "their last hope" had failed, Mrs. Farrell told him that she wanted to be disconnected from the respirator that sustained her breathing. Mr. Farrell told her doctor, John Pino, of her decision. The doctor advised Mrs. Farrell that she would die if her respirator were removed. Dr. Pino arranged for a psychologist, Dr. Jean Orost, to interview Mrs. Farrell. Dr. Orost determined that Mrs. Farrell was not clinically depressed and needed no psychiatric treatment. She concluded that Mrs. Farrell had made an informed, voluntary, and competent decision to remove the respirator. Dr. Orost continued to see Mrs. Farrell on a weekly basis from the time of their first interview in January 1986 until her death the following June.

On June 13, 1986, Francis Farrell filed a Chancery Division complaint seeking his appointment as Special Medical Guardian for his wife with specific authority to disconnect her respirator. He also sought a declaratory judgment that he and anyone who assisted him in disconnecting her respirator would incur no civil or criminal liability.

At the trial, Mrs. Farrell testified that she had discussed her decision to withdraw the respirator with her husband, their two sons, her parents, her sister, and her psychologist, Dr. Orost. These discussions had been upsetting but resulted in open and full communication among all the parties. Mrs. Farrell had also discussed the consequences of her decision with a respiratory specialist, Dr. Sollami. When Mrs. Farrell was asked why she had decided to disconnect her respirator and to let nature take its course, she responded, "I'm tired of suffering."

After closing arguments on June 23, 1986, the trial court granted all the relief that Mr. Farrell had requested, but stayed his order pending appellate review. On June 29, 1986, Mrs. Farrell died while still connected to the respirator. Despite her death, both the guardian ad litem and Mr. Farrell have urged us to address her case and formulate guidelines that might aid future patients, their loved ones, and their physicians in dealing with similar situations. Because of the extreme importance of the issue and the inevitability of cases like this one arising in the future, we agree to render a decision on the merits.

In resolving this case, as well as the two other cases we decide today, we build on the principles established in *Quinlan* and *Conroy*. Hence, we start by reaffirming the well-recognized common-law right of self-determination that "every human being of adult years and sound mind has a right to determine what shall be done with his own body." In *Conroy*, we stated that "the right of a person to control his own body is a basic societal concept, long recognized in the common law." We explained that the doctrine of "informed consent" was developed to protect the right to self-determination in matters of medical treatment. This doctrine prescribes the "duty of a physician to disclose to a patient information that will enable him to evaluate knowledgeably the options available and the risks attendant upon each before subjecting that patient to a course of treatment."

As medical technology has been advancing, the doctrine of informed consent has been developing. Thus, in *Conroy* we recognized the patient's right to give an informed refusal to medical treatment as the logical correlative of the right to give informed consent. We stated that "a competent adult person generally has the right to decline to have any medical treatment initiated or continued."

While we held that a patient's right to refuse medical treatment even at the risk of personal injury or death is primarily protected by the common law, we recognized that it is also protected by the federal and state constitutional right of privacy. Numerous other courts have upheld the right of a competent patient to refuse medical treatment even if that decision will hasten his or her death.

Nevertheless, the right to refuse life-sustaining medical treatment is not absolute. The state has at least four potentially countervailing interests in sustaining a person's life:

> preserving life, preventing suicide, safeguarding the integrity of the medical profession and protecting innocent third parties. When a party declines life-sustaining medical treatment, we balance the patient's common-law and constitutional rights against these four state interests. In this case, none of these interests, as we interpreted them in *Conroy*, nor their concert, outweighs Kathleen Farrell's rights to privacy and self-determination.

The state's interest in preserving life embraces "an interest in preserving the life of the particular patient, and an interest in preserving the sanctity of all life." Neither of those interests is compelling in this case. In *Conroy*, we decided that the value of life is desecrated not by a decision to refuse medical treatment but "by the failure to allow a competent human being the right of choice." Thus, "in cases that do not involve the protection of the actual or potential life of someone other than the decisionmaker, the state's indirect and abstract interest in preserving the life of the competent patient generally gives way to the patient's much stronger personal interest in directing the course of his own life."

The next two state interests that we consider in rejection-of-treatment cases, i.e., preventing suicide and safeguarding the integrity of the medical profession, are not threatened by Mrs. Farrell's decision. In *Conroy*, we determined that the State's interest in preventing suicide is "motivated by, if not encompassed within," its interest in preserving life. We explained that declining life sustaining medical treatment may not properly be viewed as an attempt to commit suicide. Refusing medical intervention merely allows the disease to take its natural course; if death were to eventually occur, it would be the result, primarily of the underlying disease, and not the result of a self-inflicted injury.

Courts in other jurisdictions have consistently agreed that refusal of life-supporting treatment does not amount to an attempt to commit suicide. Similarly, medical ethics create no tension in this case. Our review of well-established medical authorities finds them in unanimous support of the right of a competent and informed patient such as Mrs. Farrell to decline medical treatment. Health care standards are not undermined by the medical authorities that support the right to self-determination that we recognize today. Even as patients enjoy control over their medical treatment, health-care professionals remain bound to act in consonance with specific ethical criteria. We realize that these criteria may conflict with some concepts of self-determination. In the case of such a conflict, a patient has no right to compel a health-care provider to violate accepted professional standards.

Although Mrs. Farrell left behind two teenage sons, her case is manifestly distinguishable from those in which a parent could be forced to accept treatment because his or her prospect for recovery was good and the parent's death threatened the security of a child or children. Mrs. Farrell did not disregard her children's interest when she decided to withdraw the respirator. In fact, she based her decision in part on her recognition that her medical condition had already put them under extreme stress.

We hold that the state's interests did not outweigh Mrs. Farrell's right to withdraw her respirator.

KRISCHER v. McIVER
697 So.2d 97 (Fla. 1997)

GRIMES, J.

Charles E. Hall and his physician, Cecil McIver, M.D., filed suit for a declaratory judgment that section 782.08, which prohibits assisted suicide, violated the Privacy Clause of the Florida Constitution and the Due Process and Equal Protection Clauses of the Fourteenth Amendment to the United States Constitution. They sought an injunction against the state attorney from prosecuting the physician for giving deliberate assistance to Mr. Hall in committing suicide. Mr. Hall is thirty-five years old and suffers from acquired immune deficiency syndrome (AIDS) which he contracted from a blood transfusion. The court found that Mr. Hall was mentally competent and that he was in obviously deteriorating health, clearly suffering, and terminally ill.

At the outset, we note that the United States Supreme Court recently issued two decisions on the subject of whether there is a right to assisted suicide under the United States Constitution. In *Washington v. Glucksberg* (1997), the Court reversed a decision of the Ninth Circuit Court of Appeals which had held that the State of Washington's prohibition against assisted suicide violated the Due Process Clause. The Court reasoned that the asserted "right" to assistance in committing suicide was not a fundamental liberty interest protected by the Due Process Clause. In the second decision, the Court upheld New York's prohibition on assisted suicide against the claim that it violated the Equal Protection Clause. *Vacco v. Quill* (1997). The Court held that there was a logical and recognized distinction between the right to refuse medical treatment and assisted suicide and concluded that there were valid and important public interests which easily satisfied the requirement that a legislative classification bear a rational relation to some legitimate end.

The remaining issue is whether Mr. Hall has the right to have Dr. McIver assist him in committing suicide under Florida's guarantee of privacy contained in our constitution's declaration of rights. Florida has no law against committing suicide. However, Florida imposes criminal responsibility on those who assist others in committing suicide. Section 782.08, which was first enacted in 1868, provides in pertinent part that "every person deliberately assisting another in the commission of self murder shall be guilty of manslaughter." Thus, it is clear that the public policy of this state is opposed to assisted suicide.

Florida's position is not unique. Forty-five states that recognize the right to refuse treatment or unwanted life support have expressed disapproval of assisted suicide. As of 1994, thirty-four jurisdictions had statutes which criminalized such conduct. Since that date, at least seventeen state legislatures have rejected proposals to legalize assisted suicide.

In 1984, Governor Mario Cuomo convened the New York State Task Force on Life and the Law, a blue ribbon commission composed of doctors, ethicists, lawyers, religious leaders, and interested laypersons, with a mandate to develop public policy on a number of issues arising from medical advances. With respect to assisted suicide and euthanasia, the task force concluded as follows:

> In this report, we unanimously recommend that New York laws prohibiting assisted suicide and euthanasia should not be changed. In essence, we propose a clear line for public policies and medical practice between forgoing medical interventions and assistance to commit suicide or euthanasia. Decisions to forgo treatment are an integral part of medical practice; the use of many treatments would be inconceivable without the ability to withhold or to stop the treatments in appropriate cases. We have identified the wishes and interests of patients as the primary guideposts for those decisions.
>
> Assisted suicide and euthanasia would carry us into new terrain. American society has never sanctioned assisted suicide or mercy killing. We believe that the practices would be profoundly dangerous for large segments of the population, especially in light of the widespread failure of American medicine to treat pain adequately or to diagnose and treat depression in many cases. The risks would extend to all individuals who are ill. They would be most severe for those whose autonomy and well-being are already compromised by poverty, lack of access to good medical care, or membership in a stigmatized social group. The risks of legalizing assisted suicide and euthanasia for these individuals, in a health care system and society that cannot effectively protect against the impact of inadequate resources and ingrained social disadvantage, are likely to be extraordinary.

The Advocacy Center for Persons with Disability opposes the legalization of assisted suicide, either by judicial decision negating its prohibition or by legislative enactment. If assisted suicide is permitted in Florida, Floridians will be put on the so-called slippery slope of determining the relative value of life. Floridians with severe physical and mental disabilities, who are particularly vulnerable to being devalued as burdens of society, would be at grave risk.

This Court has also rendered several prior decisions declaring in various contexts that there is a constitutional privacy right to refuse medical treatment. Those cases recognized the state's legitimate interest in (1) the preservation of life, (2) the protection of innocent third parties, (3) the prevention of suicide, and (4) the maintenance of the ethical integrity of the medical profession. However, we held that these interests were not sufficiently compelling to override the patient's right of self-determination to forego life-sustaining medical treatment.

We cannot agree that there is no distinction between the right to refuse medical treatment and the right to commit physician-assisted suicide through self-administration of a lethal dose of medication. The assistance sought here is not treatment in the traditional sense. It is an affirmative act designed to cause death—no matter how well-grounded the reasoning behind it. Each of our earlier decisions involved the decision to refuse medical treatment and thus allow the natural course of events to occur.

In the instant case, Mr. Hall seeks affirmative medical intervention that will end his life on his timetable and not in the natural course of events. There is a significant difference between these two situations. As explained by the American Medical Association:

> When a life-sustaining treatment is declined, the patient dies primarily because of an underlying disease. The illness is simply allowed to take its natural course. With assisted suicide, however, death is hastened by the taking of a lethal drug or other agent. Although a physician cannot force a patient to accept a treatment against the patient's will, even if the treatment is life-sustaining, it does not follow that a physician ought to provide a lethal agent to the patient. The inability of physicians to prevent death does not imply that physicians are free to help cause death.

Measured by the criteria employed in our cases addressing the right to refuse medical treatment, three of the four recognized state interests are so compelling as to clearly outweigh Mr. Hall's desire for assistance in committing suicide. First, the state has an unqualified interest in the preservation of life. The state also has a compelling interest in preventing suicide. Finally, the state also has a compelling interest in maintaining the integrity of the medical profession.

We do not hold that a carefully crafted statute authorizing assisted suicide would be unconstitutional. Nor do we discount the sincerity and strength of the respondents' convictions. However, we have concluded that this case should not be decided on the basis of this Court's own assessment of the weight of the competing moral arguments. By broadly construing the privacy amendment to include the right to assisted suicide, we would run the risk of arrogating to ourselves those powers to make social policy that as a constitutional matter belong only to the legislature.

KOGAN, C.J., dissenting.

The notion of "dying by natural causes" contrasts neatly with the word "suicide," suggesting two categories readily distinguishable from one another. How nice it would be if today's reality were so simple. No doubt there once was a time when, for all practical purposes, the distinction was clear enough to all. But that was a time before today, before technology had crept into medicine, when dying was a far more inexorable process.

Medicine now has pulled the aperture separating life and death far enough apart to expose a limbo unthinkable fifty years ago, for which the law has no easy description. Dying no longer falls into the neat categories our ancestors knew. In today's world, we demean the hard reality of terminal illness to say otherwise.

The ability of medicine to intrude so profoundly into the act of dying has prompted a rising emphasis on the right of privacy, with its deep concern with self-determination. Since being added to the state Constitution in 1980, Florida's privacy right unquestionably has subtracted certain death-inducing actions from the category of "suicide" as defined at common law. Thus, in 1980, we upheld the decision of an individual suffering Lou Gehrig's disease to cease artificial respiration needed to keep him alive. In *Public Health Trust v. Wons* (1989), we upheld an individual's right to refuse a blood transfusion needed to save her life even though she had children, where refusal was based on religious beliefs. On similar facts, we reached the same conclusion *In re Dubreuil* (1993), where the State failed to establish the unfitness of the other parent to assume custody of the children. *In re Guardianship of Browning* (1990), we found that the right to refuse treatment could be asserted by a surrogate on behalf of a woman who was vegetative but not terminally ill, but who previously had indicated she wanted life support removed in such circumstances. All of these acts would have been suicide at common law, and the assistance provided by physicians would have been homicide. Today they are not.

Once Florida had set itself adrift from the common law definition, the problem that immediately arose—that has vexed our courts ever since—is where to draw the new dividing line between improper "suicide" and the emerging "right of self-determination" without simultaneously authorizing involuntary euthanasia. This is no simple task. The majority tries to fix the mark through scrutinizing the means by which dying occurs: Suicide thus is "active" death caused by a "death producing agent," whereas Floridians have a right to choose "passive" death through "natural causes." While language in our prior opinions can be read to support this view, I am not convinced this language can be stretched beyond the differing facts we previously faced.

The issue is different here. In cases of this type, we simply cannot focus on the means by which death occurs, but on the fact that the patient at the time in question has reached the death bed. That is the fact unique in this case that was not present in the earlier cases, and it is the reason why we must use a different analysis. A means-based test works well in the context of refusing medical treatment where life otherwise will continue. It does not work where there is no question death must occur, and must occur painfully.

To my mind, the right of privacy attaches with unusual force at the death bed. This conclusion arises in part from the privacy our society traditionally has afforded the death bed, but also from the very core of the right of privacy—the right of self-determination even in the face of majoritarian disapproval. What possible interest does society have in saving life when there is nothing of life to save but a final convulsion of agony? The state has no business in this arena. Terminal illness is not a portrait in blacks and whites, but unending shades of gray, involving the most profound of personal, moral, and religious questions. Many people can and do disagree over these questions, but the fact remains that it is the dying person who must resolve them in the particular case. And while we certainly cannot ignore the slippery-slope problem, we previously have established fully adequate standards to police the exercise of privacy rights in this context to ensure against abuse.

Finally, I cannot ignore the majority's statement that the issues in this case must be left to the legislature. Such a statement ignores fundamental tenets of our law. Constitutional rights must be enforced by courts even against the legislature's powers, and privacy in particular must be enforced even against majoritarian sentiment. Indeed, the overarching purpose of the Florida Declaration of Rights along with its privacy provision is to "protect each individual within our borders from the unjust encroachment of state authority—from whatever official source—into his or her life.

RAVIN v. STATE
537 P.2d 494 (Alaska 1975)

RABINOWITZ, C.J.

The constitutionality of Alaska's statute prohibiting possession of marijuana is put in issue in this case. We first address petitioner's contentions that his constitutionally protected right to privacy compels the conclusion that the State of Alaska is prohibited from penalizing the private possession and use of marijuana. Ravin's basic thesis is that there exists under the federal and Alaska constitutions a fundamental right to privacy, the scope of which is sufficiently broad to encompass and protect the possession of marijuana for personal use. Given this fundamental constitutional right, the State would then have the burden of demonstrating a compelling state interest in prohibiting possession of marijuana.

In Alaska this court has dealt with the concept of privacy on only a few occasions. One of the most significant decisions in this area is *Breese v. Smith* (1972), where we considered the applicability of the guarantee of "life, liberty, the pursuit of happiness" found in the Alaska Constitution, to a school hairlength regulation. Noting that hairstyles are a highly personal matter in which the individual is traditionally autonomous, we concluded that governmental control of personal appearance would be antithetical to the concept of personal liberty under Alaska's constitution. Subsequent to our decision in *Breese*, a right to privacy amendment was added to the Alaska Constitution. Article I, section 22 reads:

> The right of the people to privacy is recognized and shall not be infringed. The legislature shall implement this section.

The effect of this amendment is to place privacy among the specifically enumerated rights in Alaska's constitution. But this fact alone does not, in and of itself, yield answers concerning what scope should be accorded to this right of privacy. We have suggested that the right to privacy may afford less than absolute protection to "the ingestion of food, beverages or other substances." For any such protection must be limited by the legitimate needs of the State to protect the health and welfare of its citizens.

In our view, the right to privacy amendment to the Alaska Constitution cannot be read so as to make the possession or ingestion of marijuana itself a fundamental right. Nor can we conclude that such a fundamental right is shown by virtue of the analysis we employed in *Breese*. In that case, the student's traditional liberty pertaining to autonomy in personal appearance was threatened in such a way that his constitutionally guaranteed right to an education was jeopardized. Hairstyle, as emphasized in *Breese*, is a highly personal matter involving the individual and his body. Few would believe they have been deprived of something of critical importance if deprived of marijuana, though they would if stripped of control over their personal appearance. Therefore, if we were employing our former test, we would hold that there is no fundamental right, either under the Alaska or federal constitutions, either to possess or ingest marijuana.

The foregoing does not complete our analysis of the right to privacy issues. Ravin's right to privacy contentions are not susceptible to disposition solely in terms of answering the question whether there is a general fundamental constitutional right to possess or smoke marijuana. This leads us to a more detailed examination of the right to privacy and the relevancy of where the right is exercised. If there is any area of human activity to which a right to privacy pertains more than any other, it is the home. The importance of the home has been amply demonstrated in constitutional law. Among the enumerated rights in the federal Bill of Rights are the guarantee against quartering of troops in a private house in peacetime (Third Amendment) and the right to be "secure in their houses against unreasonable searches and seizures" (Fourth Amendment). The First Amendment has been held to protect the right to "privacy and freedom of association in the home." The Fifth Amendment has been described as providing protection against all governmental invasions "of the sanctity of a man's home and the privacies of life." The protection of the right to receive birth control information in *Griswold v. Connecticut* (1965), was predicated on the sanctity of the marriage relationship and the harm to this fundamental area of privacy if police were allowed to "search the sacred precincts of marital bedrooms." And in *Stanley v. Georgia* (1969), the Court emphasized the home as the situs of protected "private activities." The right to receive information and ideas was found in *Stanley* to take on an added dimension precisely because it was a prosecution for possession in the home. In a later case, the Supreme Court noted that *Stanley* was not based on the notion that the obscene matter was itself protected by a constitutional penumbra of privacy, but rather was a "reaffirmation that a man's home is his castle." At the same time the Court noted, "the Constitution extends special safeguards to the privacy of the home, just as it protects other special privacy rights such as those of marriage, procreation, motherhood, child rearing, and education." And as the Supreme Court pointed out, there exists a "myriad" of activities which may be lawfully conducted within the privacy and confines of the home, but may be prohibited in public.

In Alaska we have also recognized the distinctive nature of the home as a place where the individual's privacy receives special protection. This court has consistently recognized that the home is constitutionally protected from unreasonable searches and seizures, reasoning that the home itself retains a protected status under the Fourth Amendment and Alaska's constitution distinct from that of the occupant's person. The privacy amendment to the Alaska Constitution was intended to give recognition and protection to the home. Such a reading is consonant with the character of life in Alaska. Our territory and now state has traditionally been the home of people who prize their individuality and who have chosen to settle or to continue living here in order to achieve a measure of control over their own lifestyles which is now virtually unattainable in many of our sister states.

The home, then, carries with it associations and meanings which make it particularly important as the situs of privacy. Privacy in the home is a fundamental right, under both the federal and Alaska constitutions. We do not mean by this that a person may do anything at anytime as long as the activity takes place within a person's home. There are two important limitations on this facet of the right to privacy. First, we agree with the Supreme Court of the United States, which has strictly limited the *Stanley* guarantee to possession for purely private, noncommercial use in the home. And secondly, we think this right must yield when it interferes in a serious manner with the health, safety, rights and privileges of others or with the public welfare. No one has an absolute right to do things in the privacy of his own home which will affect himself or others adversely. Indeed, one aspect of a private matter is that it is private, that is, that it does not adversely affect persons beyond the actor, and hence is none of their business. When a matter does affect the public, directly or indirectly, it loses its wholly private character, and can be made to yield when an appropriate public need is demonstrated.

Thus, we conclude that citizens of the State of Alaska have a basic right to privacy in their homes under Alaska's constitution. This right to privacy would encompass the possession and ingestion of substances such as marijuana in a purely personal, non-commercial context in the home unless the state can meet its substantial burden and show that proscription of possession of marijuana in the home is supportable by achievement of a legitimate state interest.

The evidence which was presented at the hearing before the district court consisted primarily of several expert witnesses familiar with various medical and social aspects of marijuana use. Numerous written reports and books were also introduced into evidence. The justifications offered by the State to uphold AS 17.12.010 are generally that marijuana is a psychoactive drug; that it is not a harmless substance; that heavy use has concomitant risk; that it is capable of precipitating a psychotic reaction in at least individuals who are predisposed towards such reaction; and that its use adversely affects the user's ability to operate an automobile. The State relies upon a number of medical researchers who have raised questions as to the substance's effect on the body's immune system, on chromosomal structure, and on the functioning of the brain. On the other hand, in almost every instance of reports of potential danger arising from marijuana use, reports can be found reaching contradictory results. It appears that there is no firm evidence that marijuana, as presently used in this country, is generally a danger to the user or to others. But neither is there conclusive evidence to the effect that it is harmless. The one significant risk in use of marijuana which we do find established to a reasonable degree of certainty is the effect of marijuana intoxication on driving.

Given the evidence of the effect of marijuana on driving, an individual's right to possess or ingest marijuana while driving would be subject to the prohibition provided for in AS 17.12.010. However, given the relative insignificance of marijuana consumption as a health problem in our society at present, we do not believe that the potential harm generated by drivers under the influence of marijuana, standing alone, creates a close and substantial relationship between the public welfare and control of ingestion of marijuana or possession of it in the home for personal use. Thus we conclude that no adequate justification for the state's intrusion into the citizen's right to privacy by its prohibition of possession of marijuana by an adult for personal consumption in the home has been shown. The privacy of the individual's home cannot be breached absent a persuasive showing of a close and substantial relationship of the intrusion to a legitimate governmental interest. Here, mere scientific doubts will not suffice. The state must demonstrate a need based on proof that the public health or welfare will in fact suffer if the controls are not applied.

The state has a legitimate concern with avoiding the spread of marijuana use to adolescents who may not be equipped with the maturity to handle the experience prudently, as well as a legitimate concern with the problem of driving under the influence of marijuana. Yet these interests are insufficient to justify intrusions into the rights of adults in the privacy of their own homes. Further, neither the federal or Alaska constitution affords protection for the buying or selling of marijuana, nor absolute protection for its use or possession in public. Possession at home of amounts of marijuana indicative of intent to sell rather than possession for personal use is likewise unprotected.

In view of our holding that possession of marijuana by adults at home for personal use is constitutionally protected, we wish to make clear that we do not mean to condone the use of marijuana. The experts who testified below, including petitioner's witnesses, were unanimously opposed to the use of any psychoactive drugs. We agree completely. It is the responsibility of every individual to consider carefully the ramifications for himself and for those around him of using such substances. With the freedom which our society offers to each of us to order our lives as we see fit goes the duty to live responsibly, for our own sakes and for society's. This result can best be achieved, we believe, without the use of psychoactive substances.

NOTES

1. A few years after *Ravin*, the Alaska Supreme Court upheld the constitutionality of a criminal law prohibiting the use and possession of cocaine. *State v. Erickson*, 574 P.2d 1 (Alaska 1978). In upholding the law, the court ruled that the personal use and possession of cocaine in the home was not encompassed within the right of privacy. The court distinguished *Ravin* on the ground that cocaine, unlike marijuana, was shown by scientific evidence to be a serious hazard to health and welfare.

2. Courts in other states have declined to follow *Ravin*. The Supreme Court of Hawaii, for example, refused to allow a right to smoke marijuana, even in the home, even though Hawaii's constitution, like Alaska's, contains a provision expressly protecting the right of privacy. *State v. Mallan*, 950 P.2d 178 (Haw. 1998). The Hawaii high court repudiated *Ravin*, commenting that it was based, at least partially, on social and cultural factors unique to Alaska.

3. In *Seeley v. State*, 940 P.2d 604 (Wash. 1997), the Supreme Court of Washington refused to approve a right for a terminally ill cancer patient to smoke marijuana for medicinal purposes. The patient claimed that marijuana offered the most effective relief from the nausea and vomiting he suffered as a result of chemotherapy. Although the patient claimed only a limited right to smoke marijuana for medical treatment, the court rejected his claim:

This court has held that "the right to smoke marijuana is not fundamental to the American scheme of justice, it is not necessary to ordered liberty, and it is not within a zone of privacy." *State v. Smith* (Wash. 1980). Other federal and state courts have agreed that possession of marijuana is not a fundamental right guaranteed by the United States Constitution. However, Respondent contends the right infringed is not a general right to smoke marijuana but, rather, a right to have marijuana prescribed as his preferred medical treatment for the nausea and vomiting associated with chemotherapy.

Here, Respondent asserts a constitutionally protected interest in having his physician prescribe marijuana, an unapproved drug which is regulated as a Schedule I controlled substance, for medical treatment. Scientifically reliable evidence showed that currently available therapies are more effective and do not carry with them the same risks which are attributable to marijuana. This court and other federal and state courts have reviewed evidence similar to that which has been submitted in this case and have all upheld the constitutionality of marijuana's classification.

The challenged legislation involves conclusions concerning a myriad of complicated medical, psychological and moral issues of considerable controversy. We are not prepared on this limited record to conclude that the legislature could not reasonably conclude that marijuana should be placed in schedule I of controlled substances. It is clear not only from the record in this case but also from the long history of marijuana's treatment under the law that disagreement persists concerning the health effects of marijuana use and its effectiveness as a medicinal drug. The evidence presented by the Respondent is insufficient to convince this court that it should interfere with the broad judicially recognized prerogative of the legislature. Respondent has not shown that the legislative treatment of marijuana is "so unrelated" to the achievement of the legitimate purposes of the legislature or that "the facts have so far changed as to render the classification arbitrary and obsolete."

4. In 1996, California voters approved Proposition 215, making California the first state in the union to allow medical use of marijuana. Since then, a significant majority of states and the District of Columbia have enacted similar laws permitting the use of marijuana for medical purposes. In addition, a number of states and the District of Columbia have either legalized or decriminalized the personal use of marijuana for recreational purposes. Under federal law, marijuana remains classified as a Schedule I substance having a high potential for abuse and no medicinal value. Comprehensive Drug Abuse Prevention and Control Act of 1970, Pub. L. 91-513, 84 Stat. 1236 (1970). The use or possession of marijuana remains illegal under federal law.

H. VESTED RIGHTS

MITCHELL v. ROBERTS
469 P.3d 901 (Utah 2020)

LEE, J.

This case is before us on certification from the United States District Court for the District of Utah. In the underlying federal case Terry Mitchell asserts civil claims against Richard Warren Roberts. The claims arise out of allegations that Roberts sexually abused Mitchell in 1981 when she was sixteen years old. Mitchell alleges that the abuse took place in the course of interactions she had with Roberts related to a pending criminal action in which Roberts was a prosecuting attorney and Mitchell was a witness.

Mitchell concedes that each of her claims against Roberts had expired under the original statute of limitations. But she contends that her claims were revived when the legislature enacted Utah Code section 78B-2-308(7) in 2016. That statute provides that certain civil claims against perpetrators of sexual abuse may be asserted, even if "time barred as of July 1, 2016," if they are "brought within 35 years of the victim's 18th birthday, or within three years of the effective date of this Subsection (7), whichever is longer." And Mitchell asserts that her claims against Roberts were timely filed under this statute because they were brought within three years of its effective date.

Roberts has responded by challenging the legislature's authority to enact a statute reviving time-barred claims. And that response raises important questions of Utah law. Our case law has long questioned the authority of the legislature to revive a time-barred cause of action, but the nature and basis of any such limitation has not been clearly delineated. With that in mind, the federal court certified this case to us.

We hold that the Utah Legislature is constitutionally prohibited from retroactively reviving a time-barred claim in a manner depriving a defendant of a vested statute of limitations defense. This principle is well-rooted in our precedent, a point meriting respect as a matter of *stare decisis*. It is also confirmed by the extensive historical material presented to us by the parties in their supplemental briefs, which shows that the founding-era understanding of "due process" and "legislative power" forecloses legislative enactments that vitiate a "vested right" in a statute of limitations defense.

We resolve the questions certified to us on this basis. We do not do so lightly. We respect and consistently defer to the legislature's judgment on the broad range of policy matters committed to its discretion. And we acknowledge the reasonable policy basis for the judgment the legislature made in seeking to revive previously time-barred claims asserted by victims of child-sex abuse. The devastating effects of child-sex abuse can span a lifetime. And as the legislature has indicated, it may take "decades for children and adults to pull their lives back together and find the strength to face what happened to them"—particularly where (as is too often the case) "the perpetrator is a member of the victim's family" or a friend or confidant.

We would thus uphold the legislature's decision if the question went merely to the reasonableness of its policy judgment. But that is not the question presented for our review. We are asked instead to interpret and apply the terms of the Utah Constitution (in particular, the Due Process

Clause). We take a solemn oath to uphold that document—as ratified by the people who established it as the charter for our government, and as they understood it at the time of its framing. That understanding is controlling.

The original meaning of the constitution binds us as a matter of the rule of law. Its restraint on our power cannot depend on whether we agree with its current application on policy grounds. Such a commitment to originalism would be no commitment at all. It would be a smokescreen for the outcomes that we prefer.

Our laws are written down for a reason. And a key reason is to establish clear, fixed limits that the public may rely on—unless and until the law is repealed or amended by established procedures for doing so. The people of Utah retain the power to amend the Utah Constitution to alter the legislature's authority in this area if they see fit. But the document as it stands (and as originally understood) forecloses the legislature's power to enact legislation that retroactively vitiates a ripened statute of limitations defense.

Beginning in 1897 and continuing for over a century, this court has repeatedly stated that the legislature lacks the power to revive a plaintiff's claim in a manner that vitiates a "vested" right of a defendant. Our cases have been less than crystal clear in identifying a constitutional basis for this principle. But the "vested rights" limitation on the legislative power is firmly rooted in our case law. This limitation, moreover, has long been extended to the specific vested right asserted by Roberts—the right to retain a statute of limitations defense after a plaintiff's claim has expired under existing law.

The "vested rights" limitation set forth in our case law is also consistent with the original understanding of the Utah Constitution. Our legislature has broad, sweeping power. But that power is not boundless. It is circumscribed by a range of limitations in the state and federal constitutions. And an original understanding of "legislative power" and the state constitutional right to "due process" confirms the principle set forth in our longstanding case law.

The Due Process Clause is not "a free-wheeling constitutional license for courts to assure fairness on a case-by-case basis." It is a "constitutional standard measured by reference to 'traditional notions of fair play and substantial justice.'"

In the latter part of the nineteenth century the principle of due process was viewed at least in part through the lens of the separation of powers and the concept of vested rights. Due process thus flavored the original understanding of the "legislative power" throughout the country and specifically in Utah. And the original understanding of the ratifying public dictates our answer to the questions presented in this case.

In the era of the framing of the Utah Constitution, the public understood the principle of "due process," at least in part, as a matter relegating certain functions to the courts and not the legislature. Nathan S. Chapman & Michael W. McConnell, *Due Process As Separation of Powers*, 121 YALE L.J. 1672, 1781–82 (2012). The legislature was viewed as prohibited from exercising judicial functions—in interpreting and applying the law to the disposition of a case in which a party's rights or property were in dispute. "This meant the legislature could not retrospectively divest a person of vested rights that had been lawfully acquired under the rules in place at the time." *Id.* at 1782. The legislature "could enact general laws for the future, including the rules for acquisition and use of property, but it could not assume the 'judicial' power of deciding individual cases." *Id.* Retroactive divestment statutes were viewed as judicial in nature because these laws were backward looking and operated to deprive individuals of rights and property "acquired under the rules in place at the time" of acquisition. *Id.* at 1782. Thus, valid legislative acts, in contrast to retroactive divestment statutes, stated the law going forward rather than "determining specific applications of law or punishing past acts"—functions relegated to the judiciary. Because divestment statutes operated to confiscate or vitiate previously vested rights, the nineteenth-century public viewed these laws as "judicial decrees in disguise." And the public viewed such legislative encroachment into the domain of the judiciary as unconstitutional both as a matter of the principle of separation of powers itself and under the due process clause, which was understood as policing the division of powers between coordinate branches of government.

We have long looked to founding-era materials like the records of the constitutional convention in ascertaining the meaning of the Utah Constitution. The delegates' discussion at the ratification debates suggests that they understood retroactive interference with vested rights as a matter beyond the power of the legislature. These statements can be separated into two categories. In the first category, the delegates voiced opinions to the effect that even the constitution they were drafting could not operate to retroactively divest a vested right. The second category is comprised of statements suggesting that delegates viewed the due process clause they were drafting in accordance with the general nineteenth-century understanding, and that understanding of the state's due process clause prohibited retroactive legislative interference with vested rights.

Early Utahns viewed the guarantee of due process as a limitation on legislative power. They understood that the due process guarantee foreclosed legislative acts vitiating a person's vested rights.

A vested right is "a term of art with a specific, historical meaning." And by the time of the framing of the Utah Constitution, vested rights were a well-established class of property. Just a year prior to the drafting of the

Utah Constitution in 1895, this court's territorial antecedent defined a vested right as "title, legal and equitable, to the present and future enjoyment of property, or to the present enjoyment of a demand or a legal exemption from a demand." And "Thomas Cooley, the preeminent authority of the late nineteenth century on state constitutional matters," defined vested rights in similar terms in the 1870s: "a vested right is something more than such a mere expectation as may be based upon an anticipated continuance of the present general laws: it must have become a title, legal or equitable, to the present or future enjoyment of property, or to the present or future enforcement of a demand, or a legal exemption from a demand made by another." THOMAS M. COOLEY, A TREATISE ON THE CONSTITUTIONAL LIMITATIONS WHICH REST UPON THE LEGISLATIVE POWER OF THE STATES OF THE AMERICAN UNION 415 (3rd ed. 1874).

A ripened limitations defense seems to fit within this definition, since it is at least arguably "a legal exemption from a demand." *Id.* And that conclusion is confirmed by founding-era evidence on this precise question.

We can appreciate the moral impulse and substantial policy justifications for the legislature's decision to revive previously time-barred claims of victims of child sex abuse. Child sex abuse is a "massive national problem" whose devastating "effects often span a lifetime." For a variety of reasons, moreover, "the majority of child sexual abuse survivors do not disclose their abuse until adulthood." The legislature clearly had these concerns in mind in enacting Utah Code section 78B-2-308(7). And that judgment is an eminently reasonable one at a policy level.

The question presented for us, however, is not a matter of policy. We are asked to give voice to the limitations on our government established in the charter—the constitution—ratified by the voice of the people. The terms of that charter merit our respect unless and until they are amended or repealed.

We render our decision with this in mind. The problems presented in a case like this one are heart-wrenching. We have enormous sympathy for victims of child sex abuse. But our oath is to support, obey, and defend the constitution. And we find the constitution to dictate a clear answer to the question presented. The legislature lacks the power to retroactively vitiate a ripened statute of limitations defense under the Utah Constitution.

Chapter VII

CRIMINAL PROCEDURE

A. RIGHT TO JURY TRIAL

One of the foundations of the American legal system is the common law right to a trial by jury that existed in England prior to the Declaration of Independence. The right to a trial by jury in criminal cases is provided for in the constitutions of all fifty states. Traditionally, a jury consisted of twelve jurors who had to reach a unanimous verdict. But states differ on what aspects of a traditional jury their constitutions require them to preserve.

CLAUDIO v. STATE
585 A.2d 1278 (Del. 1991)

HOLLAND, J.

The defendants' claim of error presents a novel question in this jurisdiction. The defendants contend that the trial judge improperly substituted an alternate juror for a regular juror after the jury's deliberations had begun. Before the twelve jurors retired to deliberate on the guilt/innocence phase of the trial, the trial judge read his instructions to the twelve regular jurors and the three alternates. When the jury had not reached a verdict at 5:00 p.m., it was sequestered separately as required by title 11, section 4209(b) of the Delaware Code.

The jury began its deliberations at approximately 10:30 a.m. on December 1, 1987. During the first day of deliberations, the jury requested a view of the face of the defendant, Claudio. The trial judge acceded to this request. The twelve jurors and the three alternates were brought back into the courtroom to view Claudio. When the jury had not reached a verdict at 5:00 p.m., it was sequestered for the night.

During the night, one of the regular jurors became ill. The next morning, December 2, he was excused by the trial judge. The trial judge decided to replace the ill juror with one of the alternates, who had been separately sequestered during the first day of deliberations. Defense counsel moved for a mistrial. That motion was denied.

The judge asked the three alternates if they had discussed the case among themselves during their sequestration. The alternates stated they had not discussed the case. The trial judge then permitted the first alternate to become a member of the regular jury in place of the incapacitated juror. Thereafter, the trial judge gave a special instruction to the reconstituted jury. In particular, he instructed the jury to begin its deliberations anew and emphasized the importance of the alternate familiarizing herself with the views of the other eleven jurors.

The reconstituted jury began its deliberations at approximately 9:30 a.m. It deliberated until approximately 5:00 that evening, breaking only for lunch. The jury reconvened at approximately 10:00 a.m. on December 3. It deliberated until it took a break for lunch at noon. The jury continued deliberating after lunch. At approximately 2:00 p.m., the jury indicated that it had arrived at verdicts on all charges. Thus, the jury deliberated six-and-one-half hours prior to the substitution of the alternate juror and the reconstituted jury deliberated "anew" for approximately nine-and-one-half hours.

Claudio and Maymi also contend that the substitution of an alternate juror during the deliberative process violates their right to trial by jury, as it is guaranteed by the Delaware Constitution. The constitutions adopted by the original States and "the constitution of every State entering the Union thereafter, in one form or another," have protected the right to trial by jury in criminal cases. "The guarantees of jury trial in the Federal and State Constitutions reflect a *profound judgment* about the *way* in which law should be enforced and justice administered."

The Delaware Constitution is not a mirror image of the United States Constitution. The right to a trial by jury in the Delaware Constitution is not phrased identically to its corollary in the original federal Constitution or the federal Bill of Rights. A review of the history and origin of the right to trial by jury in the Delaware Constitution, *vis-a-vis* the history and origins of that right in the United States Constitution, reveals that the differences in phraseology between the Delaware and the federal right to trial by jury are not merely stylistic. There is, in fact, a significant substantive difference in that historic right, as it has been preserved for Delaware's citizens.

Delaware History of Jury Trials

The right to trial by jury which is provided for in the Delaware Constitution has a long and distinguished historical origin. "Jury trial came to America with English colonists and received strong support from them." The legal heritage from England was followed in the Delaware courts. It is probable that a jury was empaneled in Delaware as early as 1669. By 1675, trial by jury had become a fixed institution in Delaware.

The American colonies resented royal interference with the right to trial by jury. On October 14, 1774, the First Continental Congress declared:

> That the respective colonies are entitled to the common law of England, and more especially to the great and inestimable privilege of being tried by their peers of the vicinage, according to the course of that law.

The Declaration of Independence stated solemn objections to the King's "depriving us in many cases, of the benefits of Trial by Jury."

Following the signing of the Declaration of Independence on July 4, 1776, several states adopted their own constitutions, which included their own "bills of rights." A convention met in Delaware at New Castle on

August 27, 1776, to draft a Constitution for Delaware. One of the delegates to that convention was Richard Bassett. The importance of Richard Bassett's participation in framing Delaware's original Constitution, for the purpose of this case, will become apparent.

The Declaration of Rights and Fundamental Rules of the State of Delaware was adopted by the convention on September 11, 1776. Section 13 of that declaration provided: "That trial by jury of facts where they arise is one of the greatest securities of the lives, liberties, and estates of the people."

Shortly thereafter, the first Constitution of the State of Delaware was enacted on September 20, 1776. Article 25 of that first Delaware Constitution stated:

> *The common law of England*, as well as so much of the statute law as have been heretofore adopted in practice in this state, *shall remain in force*, unless they shall be altered by a future law of the Legislature; such parts only excepted as are repugnant to the rights and privileges contained in this constitution and the declaration of rights, & c. agreed to by this convention.

Thus, Delaware commenced its existence as an independent State with an unambiguous expression of its intention to perpetuate the right to trial by jury, as it had existed at common law, for its citizens.

During the Revolutionary War, the states governed themselves with virtual autonomy. After securing their freedom from England, the states were reluctant to subject themselves to any other central government, particularly one with substantial powers. Consequently, when the several independent states united following the American Revolutionary War, pursuant to the Articles of Confederation, each state's own sovereignty was made paramount to the national sovereignty. Moreover, since "the Articles of Confederation asserted no authority over individuals," it also afforded no individual protections. Therefore, Delaware's citizens continued to be protected by the Declaration of Fundamental Rights and the Constitution which had been adopted by Delaware in 1776.

Delaware and Debates on the Federal Right to Trial by Jury

When the Constitution of the United States was being considered for ratification in other states, one of the overriding concerns expressed by many was the effect that the presence of a strong central government and the absence of a federal Bill of Rights would have on fundamental rights which had existed at common law, *e.g.*, trial by jury. Article III of the proposed federal Constitution provided that "the Trial of all Crimes shall be by Jury; and such Trial shall be held in the State where the said Crimes shall have been committed." "The very scanty history of this provision in the records of the Constitutional Convention sheds little light either way on the intended correlation between Article III's jury and the features of the jury at common law." However, in John Dickinson's view, the provision in

Article III perpetuated the right to trial by jury as it had existed at common law.

In stating that view in 1788 and urging other states to follow Delaware's lead in ratifying the federal Constitution, John Dickinson described several aspects of the common law right to trial by jury in detail. Dickinson's understanding of Article III and the common law right to trial by jury is particularly instructive in this case.

> It seems highly probable, that those who would reject this labour of public love the proposed Constitution, would also have rejected the Heaven-taught institution of trial by jury, had they been consulted upon its establishment. Would they not have cried out, that there never was framed so detestable, so paltry, and so tyrannical a device for extinguishing freedom, and throwing unbounded domination into the hands of the king and barons, under a contemptible pretence of preserving it? "What! Why then is it insisted on; but because the fabricators of it know that it will, and intend that it shall reduce the people to slavery? Away with it—Freemen will never be enthralled by so insolent, so execrable, so pitiful a contrivance."
>
> Happily for us our ancestors thought otherwise. They were not so over-nice and curious, as to refuse blessing, because, they might possibly be abused.
>
> Trial by Jury is our birth-right; and tempted to his own ruin, by some seducing spirit, must be the man, who in opposition to the genius of United American, shall dare to attempt its subversion.
>
> In the proposed confederation, it is preserved inviolable in criminal cases, and cannot be altered in other respects, but when United America demands it.

Despite the assurances from John Dickinson and other Federalist writers, fears had continued to be expressed that Article III's provision failed to preserve *all of the common-law rights* to trial by jury, *e.g.*, the right to be tried by a "jury of the vicinage." That concern, as well as the desire "to preserve the right to jury in civil as well as criminal cases, furnished part of the impetus for introducing amendments to the Constitution that ultimately resulted in the jury trial provisions of the Sixth and Seventh Amendments."

When President George Washington gave his first annual message to Congress in 1789, he noted that demands for amendments to the United States Constitution were widespread. On June 8, 1789, not long after President Washington's first annual message to Congress, James Madison addressed the House of Representatives. The proposed amendments to the United States Constitution, which were described by Madison in that address, covered all of the provisions which eventually became the federal Bill of Rights.

The amendment relating to jury trial in criminal cases, as introduced by James Madison in the House, would have provided that: "The trial of all crimes shall be by an impartial jury of freeholders of the vicinage, with the requisite of unanimity for conviction, of the right of challenge, and other accustomed requisites." That Amendment passed the House in substantially the same form in which it was submitted. For the purpose of this case, it is important to note the common law form in which the right to trial by jury originally passed in the United States House of Representatives, since John Vining of Delaware was the Chairman of the House Committee Select which had studied Madison's proposals.

After more than a week of debate in the Senate, Madison's proposed amendment with regard to trial by jury was returned to the House in a considerably altered form. "The version that finally emerged from the Committee was the version that ultimately became the Sixth Amendment, ensuring an accused: the right to a speedy and public trial, by an impartial jury of the State and district wherein the crime shall have been committed, which district shall have been previously ascertained by law." The provisions spelling out such *common-law features* of the jury as "unanimity," or "the accustomed requisites" *were gone*. The "vicinage" requirement had been replaced by wording that reflected a compromise between broad and narrow definitions of that term. Thus, it was left to Congress to determine the actual size of the "vicinage" through the establishment of judicial districts. Significantly, one of Delaware's first two United States Senators during the time of this debate was Richard Bassett. Senator Bassett voted in favor of the common law right to trial by jury, as originally proposed by Madison and recommended by the House Committee Select, chaired by John Vining.

The United States Supreme Court has concluded that three significant features may be observed in the history of the enactment of the United States Constitution's jury trial provisions.

> First, even though the vicinage requirement was as much a feature of the common-law jury as was the twelve-man requirement, the mere reference to "trial by jury" in Article III was not interpreted to include that feature. Second, provisions that would have explicitly tied the "jury" concept to the "accustomed requisites" of the time were eliminated. Finally, contemporary legislative and constitutional provisions indicate that where Congress wanted to leave no doubt that it was incorporating existing common-law features of the jury system, it knew how to use express language to that effect.

Consequently, the United States Supreme Court has concluded that it is not "able to divine precisely what the word jury imported to the Framers, the First Congress, or the States in 1789. But there is absolutely no indication in the intent of the Framers of an explicit decision to equate the constitutional and common-law characteristics of the jury."

The debates about Madison's proposed amendments to the United States Constitution ended in 1791 with the adoption of the federal Bill of Rights. When the debates about the federal Bill of Rights were over, John Dickinson's interpretation of the phrase "trial by jury" in Article III, as preserving the common law right to trial by jury, had been proven incorrect. Moreover, despite the original urging of James Madison, the subsequent endorsement of that recommendation by the House Committee Select, chaired by Delaware's Congressman John Vining and the support of Senators, such as Delaware's Richard Bassett, the effort to preserve *all* of the common law rights to trial by jury in the federal Bill of Rights had not prevailed. Congress had made an express decision not to preserve all of the features of the common law right to trial by jury, when it could have done so in the Sixth and Seventh Amendments to the United States Constitution.

On September 8, 1791, the Delaware General Assembly called for a state constitutional convention. The Delaware Constitutional Convention "assembled at Dover, on Tuesday, November 29, 1791, and elected John Dickinson, president." Delaware's United States Senator, Richard Bassett, who had been a delegate to the state constitutional convention in 1776 was also a delegate to the Delaware Constitutional Convention in 1791.

John Dickinson's involvement in the debates about the right to trial by jury in Article III, during the ratification process of the United States Constitution in 1788, as well as Congressman John Vining's and Senator Richard Bassett's involvement with the debates on that subject, preceding the enactment of the federal Bill of Rights in 1791, provide important historical insight into what happened in 1791, when Delaware decided to amend its own Constitution. After the debates about the meaning of the term "trial by jury" in Article III and the provisions on that subject to be included in the federal Bill of Rights were finished, Delawareans, especially John Dickinson and Richard Bassett, were acutely aware of the need to set forth an intention to perpetuate fundamental rights, as they had existed at common law, in unambiguous language.

When the amendments to the United States Constitution, which had been proposed by Madison, were being discussed by the House of Representatives Committee Select, John Vining had urged "a plainness and simplicity of style on this and every other occasion, which should be easily understood." John Vining's advice was followed by Dickinson, Bassett, and the other delegates to the 1791 Delaware Constitutional Convention. When the convention concluded its work on December 31, 1791, its draft of the proposed Delaware Constitution provided that "trial by jury shall be as heretofore," *i.e.*, the provision in the 1776 Delaware Constitution perpetuating the guarantee of trial by jury as it existed at common law.

Thus, Delaware's unambiguous commitment to the preservation of the common law right to trial by jury was evidenced with a "simplicity of style." The draft was signed by the members of the Delaware Constitutional Convention on January 12, 1792. The signatures of the long-time champions of the common law right to trial by jury, John Dickinson and Richard Bassett, signify their satisfaction and approval of the provision that "trial by jury shall be as heretofore" in the December 31, 1791 draft. That draft was adopted, without change, as Delaware's Constitution later in 1792.

Delaware's constitutional commitment to continue to guarantee the right to trial by jury for its citizens, as it existed at common law, was expressly recognized in the arguments presented in the earliest reported decision to construe the phrase "trial by jury shall be as heretofore" in the Delaware Constitution of 1792:

> The Constitution is express that "trial by jury shall be as heretofore," plainly intending to secure both the form and the substance, the trial and the constitution of the jury.
>
> The framers of the Constitution of 1776 were aware of that importance, when they declared it to be a fundamental rule "that trial by jury of facts where they arise is one of the greatest securities of the lives, liberties and estates of the people." The provision in the present Constitution is stronger and more positive, "Trials by jury shall be as heretofore."
>
> A comparison of the Constitution or System of Government and Declaration of Rights of 1776 with the present Constitution will convince any one, if a doubt exists on the subject, that the Convention of 1792 had the old Constitution before them and made it in fact the groundwork of their labors; for many of its most important provisions are inserted in the present Constitution without the slightest variation even of the expressions, while other principles of the old system are adopted in language differing but little in its terms, and bearing precisely the same purport. The fourteenth section of the Declaration of Rights is made the seventh section of the first article of the present Constitution, with this important exception, that it is not provided in the latter, as in the former, that no person shall be found guilty without the unanimous consent of an impartial jury. But are we therefore to suppose that it was intended to vest the legislature with the power of enacting that a person accused of a criminal offense might be convicted upon the finding of a majority of a jury? By no means. It was considered that this principle was secured by the fourth section, which says that "trial by jury shall be as heretofore," and a repetition of it was deemed unnecessary.

Wilson v. Oldfield (1818).

The teaching of *Oldfield* was ratified and reaffirmed by this Court one hundred and fifty years later in *Fountain v. State* (1971):

> It is of course fundamental under our law that the verdict of a jury must be unanimous. This follows from article I, section 4 of the Delaware Constitution, providing that, "The right to trial by jury shall be as heretofore." This provision of our Constitution guarantees the right to trial by jury as it existed at common law. Unanimity of the jurors is therefore required to reach a verdict since such was the common law rule.

One year earlier, in 1970, the Delaware Constitution Revision Commission had written in its study commentary:

> Article I, section 4, of the present constitution deals with three distinct subjects: (1) Right of trial by jury in civil cases; (2) right of trial by jury in criminal cases; and (3) requirement, composition, and conduct of the grand jury. Since the three types of juries, including special juries, existed at common law, the 1792 Constitution's adoption of the right of trial by jury "as heretofore," and its carryover in successive constitutions to date, brings forward to the present day

reliance on the common law as to right of the petit jury in civil and criminal actions, the special jury in civil actions, and the grand jury. Because of this situation, reference must always be made to common law to properly interpret the meaning of the present constitution.

Article I, section 4 of the Delaware Constitution still provides that "trial by jury shall be as heretofore." This language has appeared in article I, section 4 of three successive Delaware constitutions—1792, 1831 and 1897. This language was left unchanged when article I, section 4 was amended as recently as 1984. This Court and the other courts of Delaware have always construed that provision in the Delaware Constitution as "guaranteeing the right to trial by jury as it existed at common law."

In *Williams v. Florida* (1970), when examining the federal Constitutional right to a jury trial, the United States Supreme Court stated:

> While "the intent of the Framers" is often an elusive quarry, the relevant constitutional history casts considerable doubt on the easy assumption in our past decisions that if a given feature existed in a jury at common law in 1789, then it was necessarily preserved in the Constitution.

After an extensive review of the history leading to the actual wording of the right to trial by jury in the federal Bill of Rights, the United States Supreme Court concluded:

> There is absolutely no indication in "the intent of the Framers" of an explicit decision to equate the constitutional and common-law characteristics of the jury.

Accordingly, the United States Supreme Court has turned to other than purely historical considerations to determine which features of the jury system, as it existed at common law, were preserved in the United States Constitution.

Conversely, it is untenable to conclude that the right to trial by jury in the Delaware Constitution means exactly the same thing as that right in the United States Constitution. The history of the right to trial by jury "as heretofore," which has remained unchanged in the Delaware Constitution since 1792, demonstrates an unambiguous intention to equate Delaware's constitutional right to trial by jury with the common law characteristics of that right. Consequently, all of the fundamental features of the jury system, as they existed at common law, have been preserved for Delaware's citizens. Therefore, the proper focus of any analysis of the right to trial by jury, as it is guaranteed in the Delaware Constitution, requires an examination of the common law.

At common law, when a member of a jury became ill or died during the trial, the jury was discharged. The other eleven members of the jury were then recalled along with another juror to complete the twelve. The parties were given their full complement of challenges and afforded the opportunity to use them against the reconstituted panel. Once a new jury was selected and sworn, the trial began anew. This was obviously a costly and time consuming process.

This Court and others have recognized the validity of implementing procedures which improve the operation of the jury system, as it existed at common law, *without* changing the fundamental common law features of right to trial by jury. For example, in an effort to save scarce judicial resources, statutes and court rules have been enacted which permit the selection of alternate jurors at the beginning of the trial when the regular jurors are selected. Delaware adopted a rule analogous to that used in the federal system. Superior Court Criminal Rule 24(c) permits the selection of up to four alternates along with the regular jury, to "replace jurors who, prior to the time the jury retires to consider its verdict, become or are found to be unable or disqualified to perform their duties."

The present procedure in the Superior Court, which provides for the simultaneous selection of regular and alternate jurors and allows alternate jurors to be substituted prior to the commencement of the jury's deliberations, is the functional equivalent of the common law system. The jurors and the alternates are assiduously instructed not to discuss the case until it has been submitted to them for deliberation.

The present practice preserves the common law system of submitting the case to twelve persons, who deliberate for the first time, only after all of the evidence has been presented. As one court has stated:

> There is no question that the provision for the substitution of alternate jurors prior to the submission of the case to the jury is constitutional. During the course of the trial the 12 regular jurors and the alternate jurors are treated similarly in all respects. And since the jurors are not permitted to discuss the case among themselves until it is submitted to them, there is no way in which the defendants' rights could be prejudiced if 1 or more of the 12 jurors are replaced by an alternate juror. Twelve jurors who hear the evidence and are in all respects treated as jurors participate in the deliberations and render a verdict.

In fact, the present procedure, pursuant to Superior Court Criminal Rule 24, which provides for the use of alternate jurors and their substitution prior to the commencement of the jury's deliberations has been upheld under the Delaware Constitution by this Court.

Although the substitution of an alternate juror prior to the commencement of the jury's deliberations is the functional equivalent of the practice at common law, the substitution of an alternate juror during the jury's deliberations is the antithesis of the practice at common law. At common law, the commencement of the jury's deliberative process marked a unique and inviolate stage of the trial proceeding. As one commentator notes:

> In 1354, we find among the Parliament Rolls a striking petition, "that hereafter when any people are at issue and the inquest is charged and sworn, all evidence which is to be said (*totes evidences que sont a dire*) be openly said at the bar, so that after the inquest departs with its charge, no justice or other person have conference (*parlance*) with them to move or procure the said inquest, but that they say the fact upon their own peril and oath." This petition was granted.

In the 18th century, Blackstone wrote:

> Our law has therefore wisely placed this strong and two-fold barrier, of a presentment and a trial by jury, between the liberties of the people, and the prerogative of the crown. The founders of the English law have with excellent forecast contrived, that the truth of every accusation, whether preferred in the shape of indictment, information, or appeal, should afterwards be confirmed by the unanimous suffrage of twelve of his equals and neighbours, indifferently chosen and superior to all suspicion.

Blackstone described the jury's deliberative process as follows:

> The jury, after the proofs are summed up, unless the case be very clear, withdraw from the bar to consider of their verdict: and, in order to avoid intemperance and causeless delay, are to be kept without meat, drink, fire, or candle, unless by the permission of the judge, till they are all unanimously agreed.

Thus, at common law, once it retired to consider its verdict, "the jury" was irrevocably constituted. The deliberative process was required to continue inviolate by those twelve persons "until they are all unanimously agreed."

All of the fundamental features of the right to trial by jury, as they existed at common law, have been preserved by the Delaware Constitution. This Court has expressly held that under the Delaware Constitution, unanimity of the jurors is required to reach a verdict since such was the common law rule. It has also been expressly recognized that the Delaware Constitution guarantees the common law right to a trial by a jury of twelve persons in a criminal proceeding. Similarly, the right to trial by jury at common law required a unanimous verdict by the same twelve jurors who retired to deliberate. Thus, that common law characteristic of the right to trial by jury in a criminal proceeding is guaranteed by the Delaware Constitution.

At common law, the rule was "if a juror becomes unable to serve after the jury retires to deliberate, a mistrial must be declared if one or both parties refuse to stipulate to a verdict delivered by a jury of less than twelve members." In this case, the substitution of an alternate juror during the deliberative process was in derogation of the common law. Consequently, it was contrary to defendants' right to trial by jury "as heretofore," which has been guaranteed by the Delaware Constitution since 1792.

NOTES

1. Prior to 1999, the Advisory Committee for the Federal Rules of Criminal Procedure rejected avoiding mistrials by amending Rule 24(c) to permit the substitution of alternates if a juror was dismissed during deliberations. The Advisory Committee noted, the old version of Rule 24(c) forbidding substitution of alternates was "grounded on the concern that after the case has been submitted to the jury, its deliberations must be private and inviolate." In 1999, however, the Advisory Committee changed its view. Rule 24(c) was amended to repeal the mandatory dismissal of alternate

jurors after the jury returns to consider its verdict and gives a judge discretionary authority to retain alternates during deliberation. If a juror is dismissed during deliberations, a judge may now substitute an alternate without the parties' stipulation. In supporting the rule change, the Advisory Committee recognized the practical problems of juror dismissal during long trials, stating that the availability of alternates for substitution during deliberations "might be especially appropriate in a long, costly, and complicated case." In order to "protect the sanctity of the deliberative process," the 1999 Rule 24(c) required a judge to insulate the alternates from the deliberating jurors and to instruct the jury to begin deliberations anew if an alternate was substituted.

2. In criminal cases, the Pennsylvania Constitution provides the prosecution "shall have the same right to trial by jury as does the accused." Pa. Const. art. I, § 6; *Commonwealth v. White*, 910 A.2d 648 (Pa. 2006) (prosecution asserted the right).

3. The Montana Constitution requires the state's consent to waive a jury trial in a criminal case. Mont. Const. art. II, § 26.

4. The Delaware Constitution provides that "judges shall not charge juries with respect to matters of fact, but may state the questions of fact in issue and declare the law." Del. Const. art. IV, § 19; *Herring v. State*, 805 A.2d 872, 876 (Del. 2002).

5. Some state constitutions not only specify the number of jurors required in a criminal proceeding but also distinguish between the number of jurors needed when the charged offense is either a felony or misdemeanor. Article I, § 16 of the California Constitution provides:

> In criminal actions in which a felony is charged, the jury shall consist of 12 persons. In criminal actions in which a misdemeanor is charged, the jury shall consist of 12 persons or a lesser number agreed on by the parties in open court.

6. Article VI, section 18(a) of the New York Constitution provides:

> The Legislature may provide that in any court of original jurisdiction a jury shall be composed of six or twelve persons, provided, however, that crimes prosecuted by indictment shall be tried by a jury composed of twelve persons, unless a jury trial has been waived as provided in section two article one of this constitution.

7. The New York Constitution specifies stringent requirements for the waiver of a jury trial in criminal cases that are not required under the United States Constitution, including that the defendant must personally sign a written waiver in open court before the judge.

8. The Utah Constitution requires "jury unanimity" as to a specific crime and as to each element of the crime. *State v. Saunders*, 992 P.2d 951 (Utah 1999).

9. The elimination of jury trial for offenses punishable by less than six months in jail violated the New Hampshire Constitution because the framers

intended to guarantee jury trial to all facing the possibility of incarceration. *Opinion of the Justices*, 608 A.2d 202 (N.H. 1992).

10. The Oregon Constitution is the only state constitution that allows for non-unanimous jury verdicts in criminal felony cases, excluding trials for first-degree murder. Or. Const. art. I, § 11. But this provision likely is no longer enforceable. *Ramos v. Louisiana*, 140 S. Ct. 1390 (2020) (holding that the Sixth Amendment requires a unanimous criminal jury in both state and federal court).

SMITH v. ISAKSON
962 N.W.2d 594 (N.D. 2021)

VANDEWALLE, J.

Eric Smith filed a petition for a writ of supervision after he was found guilty of violating a Bismarck ordinance restricting the use of public grounds without a permit. Smith argues he had a constitutional right to a jury trial for the offense. We grant the writ of supervision and remand the case back to the district court for a jury trial.

On August 2, 2020, Smith was operating a stand selling political merchandise promoting a presidential campaign in south Bismarck. Bismarck police officers responded after an employee of a nearby restaurant and Smith himself called dispatch. Smith claimed the restaurant employee removed his political flags from the area where he set up his stand. Officers discovered Smith's stand was located on a boulevard between the sidewalk and Washington Street. The City of Bismarck alleges officers informed Smith of the ordinance prohibiting commercial use of public grounds without a permit, and Smith continued to sell his merchandise.

On September 2, 2020, the City filed a summons and complaint against Smith in municipal court alleging he violated Bismarck City Ordinance § 10-05.1-01, which restricts the commercial use of public property. At his arraignment, Smith requested the action be removed from municipal court to district court for a jury trial. Municipal Judge Severin denied the request, stating Smith had "no right to jury trial." That same day, Smith filed a formal request to remove the case to district court for a jury trial. Smith later filed a motion requesting the removal. The municipal court denied Smith's request, stating Smith had no right to a jury trial for an infraction.

Smith argues he had a right to a jury trial under the North Dakota Constitution. "We may provide the citizens of our state, as a matter of state constitutional law, greater protection than the safeguards guaranteed in the Federal Constitution." Article I, Section 13 of the North Dakota Constitution states, "The right of trial by jury shall be secured to all, and remain inviolate." We have previously explained this constitutional provision is not absolute: "This provision neither enlarges nor restricts the right to a jury trial, but merely preserves the right as it existed at the time of the adoption of our constitution."

In this case, the City filed a summons and complaint in Bismarck municipal court alleging Smith violated Bismarck City Ordinance § 10-05.1-01. The ordinance states, "Except as authorized by this Chapter, no person, firm, or entity shall sell, offer, or expose for sale any food, goods, wares, or merchandise, upon any public street, alley, sidewalk, public right-of-way or other public grounds owned or controlled by the City." Bismarck City Ordinance § 10-05.1-01. A person can sell merchandise in these areas with a permit issued by the city traffic engineer. Selling merchandise in these areas without a permit is an infraction, and infractions carry the possibility of a one thousand dollar fine.

Although our previous decisions in *Brown* and *Riemers* did not recognize a right to a jury trial for an infraction, this case presents a unique circumstance where the state constitution preserved the right to a jury trial for the crime in 1889. At the time the state constitution was adopted, the Compiled Laws permitted cities to comprehensively regulate sales upon the streets and public places and license, tax, and regulate certain businesses. Potential penalties included fines up to one hundred dollars and the possibility of incarceration for three months. Due to the potential penalties, a jury trial was guaranteed for a violation of these ordinances in 1889. Similarly, today the City has regulated sales in public areas with Bismarck City Ordinance § 10-05.1-01. A violation of this ordinance carries the potential for a one thousand dollar fine.

In *Brown*, we concluded infractions did not carry the right to a jury trial because an infraction-level offense was "a new statutory category and procedure which did not exist at the time the constitution was adopted in 1889." However, like the ordinance at issue here, some actions labeled as infractions today were still outlawed in 1889, even though at the time they were categorized as felonies and misdemeanors. Rather than looking to the named categorization of the crime, we must look to the underlying historical nature of the act and the severity of a possible penalty to determine whether the right to a jury trial was preserved for the crime when the state constitution was adopted. Therefore, where the North Dakota Constitution and the Compiled Laws preserved a right to a jury trial for a crime in 1889, the constitution still provides a defendant the right to a jury trial for the crime today.

B. SELF-INCRIMINATION

The federal Fifth Amendment provides in part: "No person shall be compelled in any criminal case to be a witness against himself." Textual differences in about twenty state constitutions broaden the scope of the privilege beyond compelled testimonial evidence by providing that: "No person shall be compelled to give evidence against himself." *See* Conn. Const. art. I, § 8; *see also* Pa. Const. art. I, § 9 ("In all criminal prosecutions the accused cannot be compelled to give evidence against himself."). The origin of this wording was probably the Virginia provision, *see* Va. Const. art. I, § 8 (The accused "shall not be compelled in any criminal proceeding to give evidence against himself"), or the Massachusetts provision, *see* Mass. Const. pt. I, art. XII ("No subject shall be compelled to accuse, or furnish evidence against himself."). Other states adopted those models rather than the federal one. *See* Miss. Const. art. III, § 26 ("In all criminal prosecutions the accused shall not be compelled to give evidence against himself."); Tex. Const. art. I, § 19 (same).

COMMONWEALTH v. MOLINA
104 A.3d 430 (Pa. 2013)

BAER, J.

We granted review in this case to consider whether a defendant's right against self-incrimination, as protected by the federal and Pennsylvania constitutions, is violated when the prosecution utilizes a non-testifying defendant's pre-arrest silence as substantive evidence of guilt. After reviewing this issue of first impression, to which the United States Supreme Court has not definitively spoken, we agree with the Superior Court, as well as several of our sister courts, that the use of pre-arrest silence as substantive evidence of guilt violates a non-testifying defendant's constitutional rights. As discussed below, we would affirm the order of the Superior Court remanding for a new trial. However, given that the status of federal jurisprudence is uncertain, we base our holding upon the right against self-incrimination set forth in Article I, Section 9 of the Pennsylvania Constitution.

In this case, a jury convicted Michael Molina of third degree murder and related crimes resulting from the savage beating of Melissa Snodgrass, apparently as a result of drug debts owed by Victim to Defendant. On September 7, 2003, Victim told her mother, with whom she lived, that she was leaving the house to run some errands. When she did not return, Victim's mother reported her disappearance to the Missing Persons Unit of the Pittsburgh Police Department. Six months later, her decomposed remains were found under moldy clothing and other debris in the basement of a house in the Spring Garden section of Pittsburgh in which Michael Benintend, one of the prosecution's primary witnesses, resided during the relevant time period.

The issue presented to this Court requires consideration of the Missing Persons Unit detective's testimony and the prosecutor's closing arguments regarding the early days of the investigation into Victim's disappearance. Following a lead that Defendant was holding Victim against her will, the

Missing Persons Unit detective assigned to the case went to Defendant's house two days after Victim's disappearance. Pamela Deloe, a second primary prosecution witness, answered the door and asserted that neither Victim nor Defendant were at the house. Accordingly, the detective left her card and asked that Defendant call her. Later that day, Defendant called the detective.

The detective testified regarding the phone call from Defendant:

> I asked him—well, before I could even ask him if he was aware of Victim being missing, he stated to me that there were—that he didn't know where she was. It was out on the street that someone said that he was involved in her being missing and it wasn't him.

The detective then inquired as to when Defendant had last seen Victim. He initially responded that he had not seen her for a year and a half, but then he immediately contradicted his statement, claiming instead that he had not seen her for three months. Subsequent to this contradiction, the detective testified that she asked him to come to the police station to speak to her and he refused:

> A. Yes. After he stated that, I asked him if he could come into our office and sit down and talk with me about the case, and he refused. He said he refused to come in.
>
> Q. So this contact that you had with him was over the telephone. Is that what you're saying?
>
> A. Yes, it was over the telephone.

During closing argument, the prosecutor accentuated Defendant's refusal to go to the police station, and when defense counsel objected, the prosecutor stated before the jury that it was not improper to comment on Defendant's pre-arrest silence:

> Prosecutor: Look also at what happened in terms of the police investigation in this matter. Three days after this young lady goes missing, three days after she goes missing, detectives are already knocking on the defendant's door because of something they heard, maybe he was holding this person against their [sic] will, and he calls the police back and is very defensive. I mean, before a question's even asked, he denies any knowledge or any involvement with this young lady. He makes contradictory statements to the police about when's the last time that he saw her. First he says, "I saw her a year and a half ago." Then he says, "I saw her three months ago." But most telling, I think, is the fact that the officer invited him. "Well, come on down and talk to us. We want to ask you some more questions about this incident, your knowledge of this young lady," especially because he made these contradictory statements. And what happens? Nothing happens. He refuses to cooperate with the Missing Persons detectives. And why?
>
> Defense Counsel: Your Honor, I have to object to that. That's improper comment, absolutely improper.
>
> Prosecutor: Your Honor, pre-arrest silence is not improper comment at all.

In a brief sidebar discussion, defense counsel requested that the jury be instructed to disregard the statement, which the defense viewed as "absolutely improper;" "If somebody wants to assert their right not to cooperate and talk to the police, that cannot be commented upon." Notably, defense counsel did not seek a mistrial at this juncture. The prosecution responded "there's a sharp line drawn between pre-arrest silence and post-arrest silence." The court allowed the prosecution to proceed without issuing any instructions. The prosecutor further emphasized the silence following the sidebar, stating, "Factor that in when you're making an important decision in this case as well."

The jury found Defendant not guilty of first-degree murder but convicted him of third-degree murder and unlawful restraint based substantially on the eyewitness testimony of Benintend and Deloe, who claimed to have witnessed Defendant brutally beat Victim to death. The trial court sentenced him to twenty to forty years of imprisonment. Defendant appealed the judgment of sentence, raising four issues in his concise statement of issues presented on appeal, including the claim currently before this Court: whether the trial court erred in not sustaining the objection to the prosecution's reference to Defendant's pre-arrest silence and in not declaring a mistrial.

The Commonwealth filed a petition for allowance of appeal, and this Court granted review to consider whether "the Superior Court erred in ruling that the use by the Commonwealth of a non-testifying defendant's pre-arrest silence as substantive evidence of his guilt infringes upon his constitutional right to be free from self-incrimination?"

Turning to the issue upon which we granted review, the Commonwealth maintains that the Superior Court erred in concluding that the prosecutor's reference to Defendant's pre-arrest silence violated his right against self-incrimination. The Commonwealth claims that this Court has drawn a line of significance between pre- and post-arrest silence, and that the "privilege against self-incrimination" does not extend backward from the post-arrest period to cover the pre-arrest timeframe scrutinized herein.

We conduct Pennsylvania constitutional analysis consistently with the model set forth in *Commonwealth v. Edmunds* (Pa. 1991). "Under *Edmunds*, the Court should consider: the text of the relevant Pennsylvania Constitutional provision; its history, including Pennsylvania case law; policy considerations, including unique issues of state and local concern and the impact on Pennsylvania jurisprudence; and relevant cases, if any, from other jurisdictions."

A. Text

In considering the text of the provisions, we first look to their placement in the larger charter. The structure of the Pennsylvania Constitution highlights the primacy of Pennsylvania's protection of individual rights: "The very first Article of the Pennsylvania Constitution consists of the Pennsylvania Declaration of Rights, and the first section of that Article affirms, among other things, that all citizens have certain inherent and indefeasible rights." Moreover, our charter further protects the rights detailed in Article I in Section 25, providing, "To guard against transgressions of the high powers which we have delegated, we declare that everything in this article is excepted out of the general powers of government and shall forever remain inviolate." "Unlike the Bill of Rights of the United States Constitution which emerged as a later addendum in 1791, the Declaration of Rights in the Pennsylvania Constitution was an organic part of the state's original constitution of 1776, and appeared (not coincidentally) first in that document."

One of the rights protected in Article I is Section 9's right against self-incrimination. As is true of most of the provisions of the Pennsylvania Declaration of Rights, Section 9 was adopted in 1776 and served as a model for the protections provided by the Fifth Amendment of the United States Constitution as it predated the federal provision by fifteen years. Originally, the provision was worded to provide that no "man" can "be compelled to give evidence against himself," with the current wording adopted in 1838. Section 9 currently dictates, "In all criminal prosecutions, the accused cannot be compelled to give evidence against himself." This language is very similar to the Fifth Amendment, which provides: "no person shall be compelled in any criminal case to be a witness against himself." U.S. Const. amend. V. While we recognize that "no man" in the federal provision is arguably broader than "the accused" in Pennsylvania's section, we also observe that Pennsylvania's protection against being forced "to give evidence" is potentially more extensive than the federal protection against being "a witness against himself." Given the substantial similarity of the provisions, we do not find the textual differences dispositive. Moreover, "we are not bound to interpret the two provisions as if they were mirror images, even where the text is similar or identical." Indeed, we have previously found Section 9 to provide greater protection than the Fifth Amendment, despite the similar language. The Pennsylvania Constitution also historically contained two exceptions to the right against self-incrimination not present in the federal charter. In 1874, Article III, Section 32 and Article VIII, Section 10 (now renumbered Article VII, Section 8) were added to allow for compelled testimony regarding cases involving bribery or corrupt solicitations and contested elections, respectively. The provisions stated that testimony could be compelled but "such testimony shall not afterwards be used against the witness in any judicial proceedings except for perjury in giving such testimony." While these provisions provide specific exceptions for when testimony can be compelled, they do not guide our analysis of whether the protections of Section 9 apply to pre-arrest silence.

Given that the textual distinctions between Section 9 and the Fifth Amendment do not definitively speak to the issue before the Court, we find more persuasive our jurisprudence interpreting the provisions, which also incorporates underlying policy considerations.

B. History and Policy Considerations

We recognize that this Court has taken inconsistent stances in determining whether the right against self-incrimination under Section 9 exceeds the protections of the Fifth Amendment. At times, we have "stated that, except for the protection afforded by our Commonwealth's Constitution to reputation, the provision in Article I, § 9 which grants a privilege against self-incrimination tracks the protection afforded under the Fifth Amendment." Similarly, we opined generally that we should not extend rights under our Pennsylvania Constitution beyond those in the federal charter absent "a compelling reason to do so." In most of the cases where we have interpreted the rights as coextensive, however, we have indicated that the defendant failed to provide a convincing argument in favor of stronger protection under the Pennsylvania Constitution.

On several occasions, our Court has specifically concluded that the protections of Section 9 exceed those in its federal counterpart. Given the arguably contradictory holdings regarding the interaction between Section 9 and the Fifth Amendment, we must consider our precedent regarding the right against self-incrimination more broadly to determine whether Section 9 protects a defendant's decision to remain silent in the pre-arrest context.

1. General Right Against Self-Incrimination

Similar to the Fifth Amendment, Article I Section 9 dictates that the accused "cannot be compelled to give evidence against himself." We have acknowledged, however, the "inherent conflict" between the right against self-incrimination and our system's reliance on compelled testimony. While we have credited the "public's right to every man's evidence," our courts have emphasized the need for the protection against self-incrimination to avoid the "cruel trilemma of self-accusation, perjury or contempt" that faced those brought before tribunals such as the Star Chamber in England. Through forced confession, individuals had to choose whether to incriminate themselves, perjure themselves, or be held in contempt if they remained silent. As Dean Gormley has observed, "the prohibition against conviction by a process of inquisition is the crown jewel" of all rights afforded the accused under federal and state constitutions.

This Court has viewed the right against self-incrimination as protecting silence as well as overt self-incrimination. In *Commonwealth v. Dravecz* (Pa. 1967), Justice Musmanno explained how silence and self-incrimination are tied:

> Under common law and, of course, this was doubly true in medieval continental Europe, forced confessions were as common as they were cruel and inhuman. The framers of our Bill of Rights were too aware of the excesses possible in all governments, even a representative government, to permit the possibility that any

person under the protection of the United States flag could be forced to admit to having committed a crime. In order to make the protection hazard-proof, the framers went beyond coercion of confessions. They used the all-embracive language that no one could be compelled to be a witness against himself. What did the Trial Court in this case do but compel Dravecz to be a witness against himself? Dravecz had said nothing, yet because something was read to him, to which he made no comment, the prosecution insisted that Dravecz admitted guilt. If Dravecz could not be made a self-accusing witness by coerced answers, he should not be made a witness against himself by unspoken assumed answers.

Our Court took the occasion of the *Dravecz* case to further explore the ambiguity inherent in silence, recognizing that not all those accused of a crime immediately declare their innocence, but some may be made speechless by the accusation. Other courts, as did the Superior Court below, have similarly observed that innocent individuals accused of a crime may also remain silent for fear that their explanation will not be believed or to protect another.

2. Permitted Use of Silence as Impeachment Evidence or Fair Response

Under both state and federal precedent, the analysis changes dramatically once a defendant decides to testify because he has waived his right against self-incrimination: "His waiver is not partial; having once cast aside the cloak of immunity, he may not resume it at will, whenever cross-examination may be inconvenient or embarrassing." As the Supreme Court noted in *Jenkins v. Anderson* (1980), it would undermine the fundamental truth-seeking purpose of our adversary system to prevent the prosecution from questioning the validity of the defendant's testimony in an attempt to uncover fabricated defenses: "Once a defendant decides to testify, the interests of the other party and regard for the function of courts of justice to ascertain the truth become relevant, and prevail in the balance of considerations determining the scope and limits of the privilege against self-incrimination." Accordingly, the prosecution may impeach the testifying defendant with his prior statements, actions, or silence, regardless of whether the statements, actions, or silence occurred prior to or after the reading of *Miranda* rights or the defendant's arrest, if the defendant waives his right against self-incrimination by testifying.

The question of whether reference to a non-testifying defendant's pre-arrest silence violates the defendant's right against self-incrimination is now squarely before this Court. As discussed below, we conclude that the timing of the silence, whether it be pre- or post-arrest, or pre- or post-*Miranda* warnings, is not relevant to the question of whether a prosecutor's use of the silence as substantive evidence of guilt violates an individual's right against self-incrimination. While our courts have found the timing of a defendant's silence in relation to the provision of *Miranda* warnings to be extremely relevant to a defendant's due process rights, the underpinnings of the right against self-incrimination are not based on timing but on whether a person has been compelled to be a witness against himself at a criminal proceeding. Regardless of whether a forced confession is obtained prior to the official act of an arrest or after, it is not admissible at trial as it would result in the defendant being "compelled to give evidence against himself."

Moreover, allowing reference to a defendant's silence as substantive evidence endangers the truth-determining process given our recognition that individuals accused of a crime may remain silent for any number of reasons. As in this case, a defendant's silence in the face of police questioning is "insolubly ambiguous" as it could be indicative of a busy schedule, a distrust of authority, an unwillingness to snitch, as much as it is indicative of guilt. Nonetheless, jurors generally view silence as an indication of guilt.

Accordingly, we conclude that our precedent, and the policies underlying it, support the conclusion that the right against self-incrimination prohibits use of a defendant's pre-arrest silence as substantive evidence of guilt, unless it falls within an exception such as impeachment of a testifying defendant or fair response to an argument of the defense.

C. Other Jurisdictions

In addition to reviewing the text, history, and policies relating to the Pennsylvania constitutional provisions, under *Edmunds*, we also consider the opinions of our sister states. In so doing, our goal is not to create a "score card," but rather to consider whether the underlying logic of the decisions informs our analysis of the related Pennsylvania provision. We recognize that the First, Sixth, Seventh and Tenth Circuits have concluded that use of pre-arrest silence as substantive evidence of guilt is inadmissible as violative of the right against self-incrimination, while the Fifth, Ninth, and Eleventh have found no constitutional violation, reasoning that the defendant is not subject to government compulsion before he is arrested. Similarly, the question has divided state courts across the nation, through numerous, often fractured, decisions. Jurists on these courts have ably set forth the competing arguments surrounding the use of pre-arrest silence as substance evidence. We find all of these discussions insightful and helpful to our analysis. However, we ultimately base our decision on the Pennsylvania constitution and our precedent applying the right against self-incrimination.

After reviewing Article I, Section 9 of the Pennsylvania Constitution pursuant to *Edmunds*, we conclude that the factors weigh in favor of diverging from the currently asserted minimum standard of federal protection of the right against self-incrimination in regard to the use of pre-arrest silence as substantive evidence. Specifically, while we recognize the textual similarities with the Fifth Amendment, we conclude that the primacy of the Declaration of Rights to Pennsylvania's charter requires stronger protection of our liberties than under the federal counterpart. More significantly, we emphasize that, while this Court has often tracked federal jurisprudence in regard to the right against self-incrimination, we have interpreted Section 9 to provide a broader right on several occasions. Accordingly, we hold that Article I, Section 9 is violated when the prosecution uses a defendant's silence whether pre- or post-arrest as substantive evidence of guilt.

Turning to the facts of this case, we agree with the Superior Court that the prosecutor violated Defendant's Fifth Amendment right against self-incrimination when he emphasized Defendant's silence as "most telling," by asking "why" Defendant refused to cooperate with the detective, and then instructing the jury to "factor that in when you're making an important decision in this case as well." While the prosecutor's argument is not evidence, the prosecutor used the evidence referencing Defendant's silence to imply his guilt, in essence making him "a witness against himself by unspoken assumed answers." Accordingly, we hold that the prosecutor's use of the properly admitted evidence of Defendant's pre-arrest silence to infer guilt violates Article I, Section 9 of the Pennsylvania Constitution.

NOTES

1. Forty-eight States have a provision in their constitutions that provide for an individual right against self-incrimination. The States that do not have a self-incrimination clause in their constitutions are Iowa and New Jersey.

2. Colorado's constitution uses one popular formulation, stating that "no person shall be compelled to testify against himself in a criminal case." Colo. Const. art. II, § 18. Kansas's constitution provides that "no person shall be a witness against himself." Kan. Const. Bill of Rights, §10. Maine's constitution provides that "in all criminal prosecutions" "the accused shall not be compelled to furnish or give evidence against himself or herself." Me. Const. art. I, § 6.

3. In *State v. Horwitz*, 191 So.3d 429 (Fla. 2016), the Florida Supreme Court held that a non-testifying defendant's privilege against self-incrimination guaranteed under article I, section 9 of the Florida Constitution is violated when his or her pre-arrest, pre-*Miranda* silence is used against the defendant at trial as substantive evidence of the defendant's consciousness of guilt.

4. Hawaii has ruled that the use of a defendant's pre-arrest silence "that occurs at least as of the time of detention" as substantive proof of guilt is a violation of the right against compelled self-incrimination under the Hawaii Constitution. *State v. Tsujimura*, 400 P.3d 500, 314 (Haw. 2017).

5. The Georgia state constitutional protection against self-incrimination applies to more than mere testimony. It also protects against being forced to perform acts that generate incriminating evidence. *Olevik v. State*, 806 S.E.2d 505 (Ga. 2017). The next case excerpted below, *Elliott v. Georgia*, 824 S.E.2d 265 (Ga. 2019), extends this principle to a driver's refusal to take a roadside breath test.

ELLIOTT v. GEORGIA
824 S.E.2d 265 (Ga. 2019)

PETERSON, J.

The State is prosecuting Andrea Elliott for driving under the influence of alcohol. When Elliott was arrested, she refused to submit to a breath test. Georgia statutes allow the State to use her refusal against her in her criminal trial, and the State has sought to do precisely that.

The United States Supreme Court has held that the Fifth Amendment to the United States Constitution does not bar the State from using such a refusal, in part because the Fifth Amendment gives Elliott no right to refuse to act in the first place. But we have held—and hold again today—that the protection against compelled self-incrimination provided by Article I, Section I, Paragraph XVI of the Georgia Constitution does afford the right to refuse such a test. So Elliott argues to us that Paragraph XVI gives her the protection that the Fifth Amendment does not, and thus renders invalid the portions of the statutes allowing her refusal to be admitted against her. We agree.

The relevant facts are not in dispute. In August 2015, a police officer stopped Elliott after observing her commit several traffic violations, including a failure to maintain her lane. During the stop, Elliott admitted to consuming alcohol earlier that day. After smelling the odor of alcohol and observing several signs of impairment, including several clues during a field sobriety test, the officer arrested Elliott for DUI and other traffic offenses and read her the statutorily mandated implied consent notice. Elliott replied that she was overwhelmed and unsure of what was happening, so the officer explained why he stopped her, why he asked her to perform field sobriety tests, why he read her the implied consent notice following her arrest, and that a refusal to submit to a state-administered breath test could result in certain consequences, including that her refusal to submit might be offered into evidence against her at trial. Elliott refused to submit to a breath test and was taken to jail. She filed a motion to suppress her refusal to submit to a breath test, claiming that the introduction of that evidence at trial would violate her right against compelled self-incrimination under the Georgia Constitution.

We have often explained that we interpret the Georgia Constitution according to its original public meaning. And, of course, the Georgia Constitution that we interpret today is the Constitution of 1983; the original public meaning of that Constitution is the public meaning it had at the time of its ratification in 1982. But many of the provisions of the Constitution of 1983 first originated in an earlier Georgia constitution; unlike the United States, the State of Georgia has had ten constitutions since declaring independence from Great Britain. The meaning of those previous provisions is critical to understanding the meaning they carried at the time they were readopted. Paragraph XVI first appeared in the Constitution of 1877, and was carried forward without material change into the Constitutions of 1945, 1976, and now our current Constitution of 1983. Our focus on the original public meaning of this provision thus requires us to consider two interpretive principles that arise from the provision's multi-constitutional history, and a third principle that simply arises from the independent nature of state constitutions.

Original public meaning is an interpretive principle that we apply to each of our constitutions. Because the meaning of a previous provision that has been readopted in a new constitution is generally the most important legal context for the meaning of that new provision, and because we accord each of those previous provisions their own original public meanings, we generally presume that a constitutional provision retained from a previous constitution without material change has retained the original public meaning that provision had at the time it first entered a Georgia Constitution, absent some indication to the contrary. This presumption of constitutional continuity helps maintain the stability of Georgia's constitutional law, while still yielding when other considerations make clear that the people have changed the meaning of a provision.

When we consider the meaning of a provision of the United States Constitution, we faithfully apply the decisions of the United States Supreme Court as to the meaning of that provision. Such a faithful application is not an act of judgment on our part; it is an act of obedience. But when the provision we consider is a provision of the Georgia Constitution, our approach is different. When interpreting a provision of our Constitution that parallels a provision of the United States Constitution, we should take seriously decisions of the United States Supreme Court that have interpreted that parallel provision. And here, the federal self-incrimination clause of the Fifth Amendment, see U.S. Const. Amend. V ("No person shall be compelled in any criminal case to be a witness against himself."), is similar to the state self-incrimination clause of Paragraph XVI ("No person shall be compelled to give testimony tending in any manner to be self-incriminating."). But we owe those federal decisions no obedience when interpreting our own Constitution. "Questions of the construction of the State Constitution are strictly matters for the highest court of this State. The construction of similar federal constitutional provisions, though persuasive authority, is not binding on this State's construction of its own Constitution." And so it follows that "state constitutional provisions may, of course, confer greater protections than their federal counterparts, provided that such broader scope is rooted in the language, history, and context of the state provision. In the same way, a state constitution may also offer less rights than federal law, so long as it does not affirmatively violate federal law."

This is scarcely a Georgia-specific idea. State constitutional rights were "meant to be and remain genuine guarantees against misuse of the state's governmental powers, truly independent of the rising and falling tides of federal case law both in method and in specifics." *State v. Kennedy*, 666 P.2d 1316, 1323 (Or. 1983). *See also State v. Walker*, 267 P.3d 210, 216–27 (Utah 2011) (Lee, J., concurring); *Malyon v. Pierce County*, 935 P.2d 1272, 1281 n.30 (Wash. 1997); *Sitz v. Dep't of State Police*, 506 N.W.2d 209, 216–17 (1993); *Ex parte Tucci*, 859 S.W.2d 1, 32 n.34 (Tex. 1993) (Phillips, C.J., concurring); Jeffrey S. Sutton, *51 Imperfect Solutions: States and the Making of American Constitutional Law* 174–78 (Oxford 2018).

In order to understand the meaning of the constitutional right, we must understand the nature of that common-law right as it was understood in 1877. We must also determine if a consistent and definitive construction of the constitutional right now found in Paragraph XVI applies to the issues raised here, and, if so, whether we should presume that construction was carried forward into the Constitution of 1983.

Prior to the adoption of a provision on self-incrimination in the 1877 Constitution, Georgia courts described the right against compelled self-incrimination as forbidding a "man to accuse himself of any crime, or to furnish any evidence to convict himself of any crime." In *Marshall v. Riley* (Ga. 1849), this Court held that the right against compelled self-incrimination, based on the common law and "considered as one of our constitutional rights" (despite there being no such express state constitutional right at that time), applied in civil proceedings and protected a person from being compelled to answer interrogatories that would subject him to a penalty or forfeiture or punishment for a crime, "or have a tendency thereto." Just two years after this right received express protection in our state constitution, this Court construed that provision as barring a defendant from being "compelled to incriminate himself by acts or words."

In 1886, less than 10 years after passage of the 1877 Constitution, the United States Supreme Court unanimously held that compelling production of a defendant's private papers to be used as evidence against him was equivalent to compelling him to be a witness against himself in violation of the Fifth Amendment. *See Boyd v. United States* (1886).

Boyd was about the compelled production of existing documents, and said nothing about compelling a person to act. The United States Supreme Court later rejected the view that the Fifth Amendment protected affirmative acts, *see Holt v. United States*, 218 U.S. 245, 252–53 (1910), but for many years did not distinguish between spoken words and physical evidence reflecting written words.

From the middle of the nineteenth century through the middle of the twentieth century, at least nine states, including three of our neighboring states (Alabama, North Carolina, and Tennessee), concluded that defendants could not be compelled to perform affirmative acts that were incriminating; many of these jurisdictions cited their state constitutional provision or the common law.

Forty years after recognizing that affirmative acts were protected under the state's constitutional protection against compelled self-incrimination, the Oklahoma Criminal Court of Appeals held that the results of involuntary chemical testing in a DUI case would be inadmissible as violative of the state's constitutional self-incrimination clause that was "broad enough to encompass more than just oral testimony," and ruled that the court properly instructed the jury not to consider the results of the test if it found that the defendant did not voluntarily submit to such testing. Several years later, Utah reached a similar conclusion that its state's constitutional ban against compelled self-incrimination covered affirmative acts.

In the light of the history described above, the State's sweeping pronouncements that *Day* and *Calhoun* were uniquely out of step with the rest of the country are simply wrong. And though many jurisdictions have since abandoned their affirmative-acts standard in favor of a right that is limited to the present scope of the Fifth Amendment, the decisions of sister states cannot change the meaning of a preexisting provision of the Georgia Constitution.

Our opinion in *Aldrich* reaffirmed that the 1945 Constitution, which contained the same language as the 1877 Constitution, carried forward the principle enunciated in *Day* and its progeny; we cited or distinguished *Aldrich* in at least three other cases decided prior to the adoption of the 1976 Constitution.

In short, the compelled self-incrimination provision at issue, which has remained materially the same since the 1877 Constitution, has received a consistent and definitive construction from its inception through the ratification of the 1983 Constitution.

We find nothing sufficient to rebut the presumption that the 1983 Constitution incorporated this meaning and thus conclude that Paragraph XVI generally prohibits admission of a defendant's pretrial refusal to speak or act. And we conclude that OCGA §§ 40-5-67.1 (b) and 40-6-392 (d) violate the Georgia Constitution by allowing the admission of a defendant's refusal to submit to a breath test to prove that the defendant had been drinking alcohol.

Although the state constitutional provision at issue here is sometimes referred to as embodying a right against self-incrimination, by its text the 1877 Provision prohibited only "compelled" self-incrimination. Paragraph XVI also uses the term "compelled." "Compel" is generally defined as to "constrain" or "force" a person to do something. Just as asking a person to take a breath test, without more, is not compelling that person to do any act, admission of evidence of a defendant's refusal to submit to a breath test does not fit within a natural understanding of the word "compel."

But we do not read the text in isolation; rather, "we interpret a constitutional provision according to the original public meaning of its text," which requires considering its context. Where, as here, a constitutional provision incorporates a pre-existing right, the provision cannot be said to create that right—it merely secures and protects it. And where the right enshrined in the constitution was one found at common law, that constitutional right is understood with reference to the common law, absent some clear textual indication to the contrary. We thus proceed to consider pre-Revolution English common law on the right against compelled self-incrimination, then subsequent developments that provide important context for the original public meaning of the 1877 Provision.

The pre-Revolution English common-law right did not preclude admission of a defendant's refusal to incriminate herself or adverse inferences therefrom. But the second half of the nineteenth century was a time of great change in the American criminal justice system. And decisions of this Court in the years leading up to, and around the time of, the adoption of the 1877 Provision indicate a significant deviation from the common law of England on the question of whether a defendant's silence could be presented as evidence of guilt.

The historical record in the years leading up to and shortly after Georgia adopted the 1877 Provision lead us to conclude that it prohibited admission of a defendant's refusal to speak or act as evidence against him.

Of course, the 1877 Provision does not apply today; Paragraph XVI of the 1983 Constitution does. A constitutional provision—like Paragraph XVI—that is retained from a previous constitution without material change is strongly presumed to retain the original public meaning that provision had at the time it was first adopted. Thus, we presume that Paragraph XVI as it is found in the 1983 Constitution carries the same meaning as that of the 1877 Provision. Although not ironclad, this presumption is strong.

The State's remaining arguments, citing state statutes, general principles of state criminal law, and policy concerns, fail to appreciate the constitutional nature of the right at issue. We acknowledge that the State has a considerable interest in prosecuting DUI offenses (and thereby deterring others), and that our decision today may make that task more difficult. But the State also has a compelling interest in prosecuting murders, rapes, armed robberies, and a whole host of other serious crimes, and the right to be free from compelled self-incrimination does not wax or wane based on the severity of a defendant's alleged crimes.

This Court cannot change the Georgia Constitution, even if we believe there may be good policy reasons for doing so; only the General Assembly and the people of Georgia may do that. And this Court cannot rewrite statutes. This decision may well have implications for the continuing validity of the implied consent notice as applied to breath tests, but revising that notice is a power reserved to the General Assembly. Having considered the text of Paragraph XVI and the context in which it was enacted, as well as all of the arguments made by the parties and the amici, we conclude that Paragraph XVI precludes admission of evidence that a suspect refused to consent to a breath test. Consequently, we conclude that OCGA §§ 40-5-67.1 (b) and 40-6-392 (d) are unconstitutional to the extent that they allow a defendant's refusal to submit to a breath test to be admitted into evidence at a criminal trial.

C. RIGHT TO COUNSEL

STATE v. McADAMS
193 So.3d 824 (Fla. 2016)

LEWIS, J.

The Pasco County Sheriff's Office was notified that Lynda McAdams, the estranged wife of Respondent/Cross-Petitioner Michael McAdams, and her boyfriend/coworker, William Andrews, had been reported missing by concerned family members. On October 21, 2009, a detective responded to Lynda's home on Palomino Lake Drive in Dade City and, after observing her truck parked at the residence, conducted a welfare check at the house. He found the door unlocked and walked through the residence. No one was present. During the welfare check, the detective observed that the lid of the washing machine was open and a substance that appeared to be blood could be seen on the rim. Blood-stained clothing was inside the washing machine. The detective also observed latex gloves in the kitchen, along with rolls of duct tape. He departed the residence and notified a supervisor of his observations. McAdams was contacted, and he gave written consent for a search of the Palomino Lake Drive home. During the search, in addition to other items of interest, there appeared to be blood spatter on a wall, blood was discovered on clothing, and a bedroom door evidenced what appeared to be a bullet hole. A projectile was later recovered from the wall.

A different detective entered McAdams's separate residence in Spring Hill to perform a welfare check there with the consent of McAdams's father. When the detective walked through the garage, he observed a pair of blue-jean shorts that appeared to have blood on them. Further, a broken cell phone was found on a night stand and McAdams's father stated that it did not belong to McAdams. Law enforcement subsequently obtained a search warrant for the Spring Hill home. The warrant was executed at approximately 2:22 a.m. on October 23, and McAdams was not present. The shorts, a grey shirt, and a black belt were seized.

Later that morning, a detective with the Hernando County Sheriff's Office approached McAdams in the driveway of the Spring Hill home and asked if he would be willing to come to the sheriff's office to speak with detectives. McAdams understood that the detective was there because Lynda was missing and replied that he wanted to help. McAdams rode to the sheriff's office in the back of a deputy's vehicle, but he was not handcuffed. The detective specifically informed McAdams that he was not under arrest.

Upon his arrival at the Hernando County Sheriff's Office, McAdams was escorted to an interview room where he met with Pasco County Detectives Christensen and Arey. The encounter at the sheriff's office between McAdams and the detectives began at 11:55 a.m., and the interview was recorded in its entirety. During the majority of the interview, McAdams maintained that he did not know what happened to Lynda or Andrews. However, at 2:27 p.m., while McAdams was in the room with only Detective Arey, he commenced a confession in which he admitted that he fatally shot Lynda and Andrews on October 18, 2009. McAdams also confessed that he buried the bodies and discarded the weapon off a bridge. At 2:42 p.m., Detective Arey read McAdams the *Miranda* warnings. After receiving the warnings, McAdams continued to speak with Detective Arey, and he subsequently directed law enforcement to the bodies.

At 2:04 p.m., while McAdams was being interrogated by the Pasco County detectives in the Hernando office, and before the confession commenced, an attorney retained by McAdams's parents arrived at that office.

After determining that McAdams was being interrogated in the building, the deputy at the counter advised the attorney that it would not be possible to convey any information to the location where McAdams was being questioned by any means, including e-mail, telephone, a knock on the door, or even a note slipped under the door. Although the attorney stated: "I want all questioning to stop. I don't want anymore questioning to go on without my presence." He was not allowed to see or otherwise communicate with McAdams in any manner. Facing that insurmountable obstacle, the attorney departed from the sheriff's office at 2:17 p.m., just ten minutes before McAdams commenced his confession. McAdams was first informed about the presence of the attorney only after he directed the detectives to the burial site. On November 10, 2009, McAdams was indicted on two counts of first-degree murder.

McAdams subsequently filed a motion to suppress any statements made to law enforcement, any evidence obtained as a result of those statements, and any audio or video evidence that resulted from those statements.

McAdams asserted that he was in custody when he was questioned by Detectives Arey and Christensen, and they failed to read him the *Miranda* warnings. McAdams also contended that he was improperly denied access to his attorney, who was actually at the sheriff's office while he was being interrogated.

Both the State and McAdams petitioned for review of the certified question. For purposes of our analysis, we rephrase the question as follows:

> Under the Due Process Clause of the Florida Constitution, when must a person who is being questioned by law enforcement in a non-public location be notified that an attorney retained on his or her behalf is at the location and available to speak with him or her?

Three theories have been posited as to what is required under the Due Process Clause of the Florida Constitution when an attorney retained on behalf of an individual who is being questioned in a non-public area of a law enforcement office appears at the office. They are:

1) Absent some other outrageous conduct, no due process violation occurs under the Florida Constitution where the police fail to inform a person about the appearance of an attorney who has been retained on his or her behalf, even if he or she is in custody (the position taken by the State).

2) The Due Process Clause of the Florida Constitution requires a person to be informed about the appearance of an attorney who has been retained on his or her behalf once he or she is in custody (the holding of the Second District).

3) The Due Process Clause of the Florida Constitution requires a person to be informed about the appearance of an attorney who has been retained on his or her behalf regardless of whether he or she is in custody (the position taken by McAdams).

The State's theory simply does not lead to a practical application. Were this Court to adopt such a position, the police could routinely conceal from a suspect who is even in custody the fact that an attorney who has been retained on his or her behalf is at the law enforcement office and is available to speak with him or her. This application would constitute a complete departure from the conclusion of *Haliburton v. State* (Fla. 1987) (*Haliburton II*) that under the Florida Constitution, "police interference in the attorney-client relationship is the type of governmental misconduct on a matter of central importance to the administration of justice that the Due Process Clause prohibits."

Further, to adopt the interpretation of the State would inject uncertainty into the law. Questions would arise as to what type of conduct, coupled with the failure to inform the individual of the attorney's presence, would be sufficiently outrageous to rise to the level of a due process violation. No bright-line rule would exist for trial courts to apply or law enforcement officers to follow. Instead, outrageousness would be evaluated on a case-by-case basis, creating a substantial risk that trial courts would reach different conclusions on similar facts. This would muddy, rather than clarify, the level of conduct by law enforcement officers that is constitutionally permissible. Therefore, we reject the position advocated by the State.

Moreover, while *Haliburton II* involved a situation where the defendant was in custody, the present case demonstrates why it is also unworkable for the due process rights of an individual under the Florida Constitution to be contingent upon custodial status with regard to access to a retained attorney. It is clear that as soon as a retained attorney arrives at the law enforcement office, the questioning of the individual can intensify significantly with the goal of obtaining a confession. Here, within minutes of the arrival of the attorney at the Hernando County Sheriff's Office, the questioning of McAdams by the detectives became more pointed and aggressive. Detective Arey confronted McAdams with the blood and DNA evidence discovered at both of his residences. Further, Arey clearly conveyed to McAdams that law enforcement knew he was responsible for the disappearances of Lynda and Andrews. Although probable cause may have existed to arrest McAdams, Detective Arey continued to apply psychological pressure until McAdams confessed.

We conclude that the only way to properly protect the due process rights of citizens under the Florida Constitution is to implement a bright-line rule. Otherwise, determinations of when voluntary questioning evolves into custodial interrogation will spawn hundreds of thousands of dollars in costs or expenses and hours in litigation. Therefore, we now hold that when an individual is being questioned in a non-public area, and an attorney retained on his or her behalf arrives at the location, the Due Process Clause of the Florida Constitution requires that the police notify the individual of the attorney's presence and purpose. Pursuant to this holding, a person can no longer be deprived of the critical information that an attorney is present and available to provide legal advice based on pure police conjecture that the individual is not in custody. We also cannot allow law enforcement to refuse to interrupt an interview, as occurred here. Under the interpretation of the Due Process Clause of the Florida Constitution that we adopt today, it is the individual, rather than law enforcement, who is given the knowledge and power to decide whether to take advantage of the attorney's services.

In light of the foregoing, we hold that McAdams's right to due process under the Florida Constitution was violated when law enforcement officers failed to inform him that an attorney retained by his parents had arrived at the Hernando County Sheriff's Office and was available to assist him. Pursuant to this holding, the determinations of both the trial court and the Second District as to when McAdams had the right to be notified about the attorney were in error.

NOTES

1. The Connecticut Constitution requires, as a matter of due process, that police promptly inform a suspect of timely efforts by retained counsel to render assistance. *State v. Stoddard*, 537 A.2d 446 (Conn. 1988); *see also State v. Purcell*, 203 A.3d 542 (Conn. 2019).

2. The privilege against compelled self-incrimination in the Massachusetts and New Hampshire Constitutions required the rejection of *Moran v. Burbine*, 475 U.S. 412 (1986) (holding that the failure of police to inform a suspect of his attorney's efforts to reach him, where the attorney was retained by a relative without the suspect's knowledge, did not deprive him of his right to counsel or vitiate his *Miranda* waiver). *State v. Roache*, 803 A.2d 572 (N.H. 2002); *Commonwealth v. Mavredakis*, 725 N.E.2d 169 (Mass. 2000). Other states that have declined to follow *Moran* include Delaware, Illinois, Indiana, and New Jersey.

D. CONFRONTATION – FACE TO FACE

COMMONWEALTH v. LUDWIG
594 A.2d 281 (Pa. 1991)

ZAPPALA, J.

We granted review in this case to determine whether the use of closed circuit television testimony by an alleged child victim violates the confrontation clauses of the United States and Pennsylvania Constitutions. We hold that the confrontation clause of the Pennsylvania Constitution does not permit such infringement of a defendant's constitutional right to meet a witness face to face. The use of closed circuit television to transmit the testimony of the witness in this case violates the constitutional protection given to the defendant under article I, section 9 of the Pennsylvania Constitution.

On August 9, 1984, appellant was charged with rape, involuntary deviate sexual intercourse, incest, indecent assault, corrupting the morals of a minor, and endangering the welfare of children. The alleged victim of these crimes was appellant's five-year-old daughter. At the preliminary hearing, the victim testified that she did not remember what happened with appellant. The victim was unresponsive to further questioning, and the Commonwealth requested a continuance so that it could prepare a petition to the court seeking to use videotaped testimony at the preliminary hearing. The petition was filed by the Commonwealth, and a hearing held. At the hearing, the Commonwealth presented testimony of a psychologist to the effect that the victim had undergone "emotional freezing" at the preliminary hearing and that the condition could occur again. The psychologist also testified that the victim had become withdrawn following the incident, but was now making psychological progress. The psychologist was concerned that the progress might be impaired if the child was forced to testify in court in the physical presence of her father.

The court granted the Commonwealth's petition to the extent that it allowed the child to testify by way of closed circuit television. At the second preliminary hearing, the alleged victim did testify on closed circuit television and the evidence was deemed sufficient to hold the appellant for trial. Notwithstanding appellant's objection, the trial court allowed the same closed circuit television procedures to be employed during the trial itself.

A jury trial began on March 7, 1985. The child testified at the trial via closed circuit television from another room. The child's foster mother was permitted to sit next to the child while the child testified. Also in the room where the child was located was the video camera operator. The courtroom where the judge, prosecutor, defense counsel, appellant and jury were located was linked to the child by microphone. Although the child could not see the people in the courtroom, she could hear them and respond to their questions.

Article I, section 9 of our state constitution guarantees an accused the right to meet his accusers:

> In all criminal prosecutions the accused hath a right to be heard by himself and his counsel, to demand the nature and cause of the accusations against him, to meet the witnesses *face to face.* (emphasis added).

Unlike the Sixth Amendment to the United States Constitution, article 1, section 9 of the Pennsylvania Constitution specifically provides for a "face to face" confrontation. We have long held that in interpreting our Constitution we are not bound by the United States Supreme Court's interpretation of similar federal constitutional provisions.

Unlike its federal counterpart, article 1, section 9 of the Pennsylvania Constitution does not reflect a "preference" but clearly, emphatically and unambiguously requires a "face to face" confrontation. This distinction alone would require that we decline to adopt the United States Supreme Court's analysis and reasoning in *Maryland v. Craig* (1990). However, in addition, we have our own case law which mandates a "face to face" confrontation.

In *Commonwealth v. Russo* (Pa. 1957), we addressed the "face to face" requirement of article I, section 9 of our Constitution, stating:

> Many people possess the trait of being loose tongued or willing to say something behind a person's back that they dare not or cannot truthfully say to his face or under oath in a courtroom. It was probably for this reason, as well as to give the accused the right to cross-examine his accusers and thereby enable the jury to better determine the credibility of the Commonwealth's witnesses and the strength and truth of its case, that this important added protection was given to every person accused of crime. We have no right to disregard or (unintentionally) erode or distort any provision of the constitution, especially where, as here, its plain and simple language make its meaning unmistakably clear; indeed, because of the

times in which we live we have a higher duty than ever before to zealously protect and safeguard the constitution.

Although we were quite emphatic about the importance of this right, no right is absolute. Indeed, the right to confront an accuser is not without exception. In *Commonwealth v. Rodgers* (Pa. 1977), we permitted the prosecution to use preliminary hearing testimony of a witness at trial when that witness was unavailable. In *Commonwealth v. Stasko* (Pa. 1977), the prosecutor was permitted to use a videotape deposition of a witness unavailable for trial. In both instances, the original testimony was given in the presence of the defendant with the defendant having the opportunity to face and cross-examine his accuser. However, in each instance, the witnesses' subjective reactions to testifying in the presence of the accused were not a consideration.

Although we have recognized exceptions to the right to confront a witness, the policy reasons underlying those decisions are absent in this case. The witness in this case was neither unavailable nor subjected to cross-examination during prior testimony given in the presence of the accused. In fact, the trial judge instructed the jury that the victim was totally unaware of the existence of the trial itself: "We want the child to be as relaxed and casual and normal as possible and she doesn't really know that you are here in this setting. She doesn't really understand that this is all actually a trial. It probably has little significance to her."

Having diluted the significance of her testimony to that extent, it is questionable whether the victim would be testifying under the proper aura.

While we have recognized exceptions to the constitutional right of confrontation, we have done so only in those instances in which the accused has already had the opportunity to confront the witnesses against him face to face. We were satisfied that in those limited instances, the constitutional right to confront the witness had been afforded to the accused. Those decisions cannot be interpreted to permit restrictions on face to face confrontation where the right to confront the witness has *never* been afforded to the accused.

We are cognizant of society's interest in protecting victims of sexual abuse. However, that interest cannot be preeminent over the accused's constitutional right to confront the witnesses against him face to face. The record in this case does not disclose any conduct by the appellant during the proceedings that would give rise to the need to isolate the witness. The subjective fears of the witness, without more, are insufficient to restrict this important constitutional right. Since the trial court relied exclusively upon these fears, its actions cannot be affirmed. The appellant is entitled to face his accusers and the failure to protect that right was error. The appellant is therefore entitled to a new trial during which time the victim must testify in the courtroom before the judge, jury and appellant.

NOTES

1. Following the holding of the Supreme Court of Pennsylvania in *Commonwealth v. Ludwig*, article I, section 9 of the Pennsylvania Constitution was amended by replacing "meet face to face" with "be confronted by the witnesses against him." This amendment makes the language in the Pennsylvania Constitution the same as the United States Constitution. Article V, § 10(c) of the Pennsylvania Constitution was amended to provide the General Assembly with authority "to enact laws regarding the manner by which children may testify in criminal proceedings, including the use of videotaped depositions or testimony by closed-court television.

2. Seventeen state constitutions provide defendants with the express right "to meet face to face" the witnesses against them. The States are Arizona, Colorado, Delaware, Indiana, Kansas, Kentucky, Massachusetts, Missouri, Montana, Nebraska, New Hampshire, Ohio, Oregon, South Dakota, Tennessee, Washington, and Wisconsin.

3. The constitutions of Idaho, Nevada, and North Dakota do not contain a clause that guarantees the right to confrontation.

E. DUTY TO PRESERVE EVIDENCE

HAMMOND v. STATE
569 A.2d 81 (Del. 1989)

HOLLAND, J.

The defendant-appellant, George M. Hammond, III, was convicted on June 2, 1988, following a jury trial, of two counts of Vehicular Homicide in the First Degree. Hammond was sentenced on August 17, 1988. Hammond filed this appeal on August 18, 1988.

In this appeal, Hammond argues that the police negligently failed to gather and preserve evidence material to the preparation of his defense.

On July 25, 1986, at about 5:00 a.m., Hammond, then age eighteen, Keith Douglas Moore, and Leon Buddy Carter, were involved in a single-car accident. They were all occupants in an automobile which left the roadway and came to rest partially imbedded in the foundation of a townhouse that was under construction. The accident resulted in the deaths of Moore and Carter.

Officer William Wayne Walls of the City of Dover Police Department was one of the first persons to reach the accident scene. Walls testified as to what he saw when he arrived. Hammond was in the driver's seat of the vehicle, with his left shoulder against the left door, and his right shoulder against the driver's seat. Hammond's right leg, which was in a cast, was entangled between the accelerator and the brake pedal. Moore was also in the front seat area. Moore's head was on Hammond's chest and his feet were in the passenger's footwell. Carter was slumped over in the left rear seat.

Hammond testified in his own defense. His memory had been "hypnotically refreshed." Hammond stated that he graduated from high school on July 24, 1986, after completing summer courses. Following the graduation ceremony, Hammond and several friends celebrated at Scott William Kisters' apartment. Hammond, Carter, and Moore left Kister's apartment in the early morning hours of July 25, 1986, just prior to the accident. Hammond testified that they had all been drinking and that none of them were in "very good shape." He told the jury that Moore was driving Kisters' car at the time of the accident. According to Hammond's testimony, the force of the collision must have moved him and Moore about within the crash vehicle.

In support of his defense, Hammond presented testimony by Dr. George C. Govatos, a consulting engineer who was qualified as an accident reconstruction expert. Dr. Govatos testified about the kinematics of occupants in a crash vehicle, who are not wearing seatbelts. Dr. Govatos showed the jury a video tape of a test he had performed. The video tape depicted how the impact of a collision could cause the driver and the passenger to be thrown about and come to rest in each other's original seat. Dr. Govatos testified that an examination of the actual vehicle involved in the collision would have been important to his analysis because of the possibility of evidence in the interior of the vehicle that might have been left by the people as they were moved about by the collision, *e.g.*, hair, blood, pieces of clothing, or other physical evidence. Dr. Govatos testified that the existence of such evidence would have helped him to substantiate his opinion on the movement of Hammond and Moore within the crash vehicle. Dr. Govatos also testified that he would have needed the vehicle in order to determine whether mechanical failure could have caused or partially caused the collision.

The crash vehicle was not available to Dr. Govatos because the Dover police no longer had it in their possession when Hammond's attorney filed a discovery request on October 14, 1986. Although the crash vehicle had been towed from the scene and impounded, it was released by the Dover police on August 8, 1986. No evidence was collected from the vehicle by the Dover police before it was released. Hammond moved for a judgment of acquittal, or for a special instruction to the jury, as a result of the State's failure to preserve or to test the crash vehicle. The Superior Court denied both motions.

The first issue raised by Hammond on appeal is that the failure of the Dover police to preserve the crash vehicle itself or to gather evidence of blood, clothing, tissue, and fingerprints, from inside of the crash vehicle, violated his constitutionally guaranteed right of access to evidence. This

Court has recognized that the "obligation to preserve evidence is rooted in the due process provisions of the Fourteenth Amendment to the United States Constitution and the Delaware Constitution, article I, section 7." *Deberry v. State* (Del. 1983). The independent and alternative constitutional bases for our holding in *Deberry* is particularly significant in view of the subsequent development of the "access to evidence" doctrine in this Court and the United States Supreme Court. A review of the evolution of these precedents is not only instructive but necessary for a proper evaluation of Hammond's claim.

In *Deberry*, the question presented was "what relief is appropriate when the State had or should have had the requested evidence, but the evidence does not exist when the defense seeks its production?" In answering that inquiry, we held that claims of this type must be examined according to the following paradigm:

> 1) Would the requested material, if extant in the possession of the State at the time of the defense request, have been subject to disclosure under Criminal Rule 16 or *Brady*?
>
> 2) If so, did the government have a duty to preserve the material?
>
> 3) If there was a duty to preserve, was the duty breached, and what consequences should flow from a breach?

The consequences which should flow from a breach of the duty to preserve evidence are determined in accordance with a separate three-part analysis which considers:

> 1) the degree of negligence or bad faith involved;
>
> 2) the importance of the missing evidence considering the probative value and reliability of secondary or substitute evidence that remains available; and
>
> 3) the sufficiency of the other evidence produced at the trial to sustain the conviction.

In *Deberry*, we concluded "a claim that *potentially* exculpatory evidence was lost or destroyed by the State can only be decided after each element of the above analysis has been considered." In *Deberry*, we also noted, for future guidance, the "agencies that create rules for evidence preservation should broadly define discoverable evidence to include any material that *could* be favorable to the defendant."

The year following our decision in *Deberry*, the United States Supreme Court decided *California v. Trombetta* (1984). It held:

> Whatever duty the Constitution imposes on the States to preserve evidence, that duty must be limited to evidence that might be expected to play a significant role in the suspect's defense. To meet this standard of constitutional materiality, evidence must both possess an exculpatory value that was apparent before the evidence was destroyed, and be of such a nature that the defendant would be unable to obtain comparable evidence by other reasonably available means.

This Court has examined the "access to evidence" doctrine following *Trombetta*. In doing so, we have not limited our inquiry to *Trombetta*'s construction under the United States Constitution. Instead, we have held that "when a defendant claims that the State has failed to preserve evidence, by losing it after it has been gathered, the analysis which a Court must follow is set forth in *Deberry*."

The United States Supreme Court next decided *Arizona v. Youngblood* (1988). It held:

> The Due Process Clause of the Fourteenth Amendment, as interpreted in *Brady*, makes the good or bad faith of the State irrelevant when the State fails to disclose to the defendant material exculpatory evidence. But we think the Due Process Clause requires a different result when we deal with the failure of the State to preserve evidentiary material of which no more can be said than that it could have been subjected to tests, the results of which might have exonerated defendant. We therefore hold that unless a criminal defendant can show bad faith on the part of the police, failure to preserve potentially useful evidence does not constitute a denial of due process of law.

It appears that, as a matter of federal Constitutional law, the United States Supreme Court has developed a *hybrid approach* when a claim of denial of access to evidence is asserted. The principles of *Trombetta* are applicable to claims relating to a denial of access to *Brady* types of evidence. The "good faith" principles of *Youngblood* are applicable to allegations of a denial of access to potentially favorable types of evidence. However, in *Deberry*, in the event that *either* claim was made, this Court adopted a *unitary* approach.

In Hammond's case, the State has asked this Court to reconsider its decision in *Deberry*, in view of the holding in *Youngblood*. In *Deberry*, the conduct of the State was only one of three factors to be considered when potentially exculpatory evidence had not been preserved. The State argues that *Youngblood* has now established a *single* bright-line "good faith" test which should be applied by this Court in lieu of the *Deberry three-part analysis*, whenever a denial of access is asserted with respect to evidence that *could* be favorable to the defendant.

We remain convinced that fundamental fairness, as an element of due process, requires the State's failure to preserve evidence that could be favorable to the defendant "to be evaluated in the context of the entire record." When evidence has not been preserved, the conduct of the State's agents is a relevant consideration, but it is not determinative. Equally relevant is a consideration of the importance of the missing evidence, the availability of secondary evidence, and the sufficiency of the other evidence presented at trial. "There may well be cases which the defendant is unable to prove that the State acted in bad faith but in which the loss or destruction of evidence is nonetheless so critical to the defense as to make a criminal trial fundamentally unfair."

"Rules concerning preservation of evidence are generally matters of state, not federal constitutional law." We reaffirm our prior holdings, pursuant to the "due process" requirements of the Delaware Constitution. That analysis draws a balance between the nature of the State's conduct and the degree of prejudice to the accused. In general terms, if the duty to preserve evidence has been breached, a Delaware court must consider: "1) the degree of negligence or bad faith involved; 2) the importance of the missing evidence, considering the probative value and reliability of secondary or substitute evidence that remains available; and 3) the sufficiency of the other evidence used at trial to sustain conviction." We will examine Hammond's contentions in accordance with these principles.

The first step in a *Deberry* evaluation is to determine whether the crash vehicle, if extant in the possession of the State, would have been subject to disclosure under Superior Court Criminal Rule 16 or *Brady*? As we noted in *Deberry*, determining whether the crash vehicle would have been discoverable under *Brady* would be an artificial exercise, since it is no longer available for examination or testing. Therefore, we begin with the provisions of Rule 16.

"Under Superior Court Criminal Rule 16(b), a defendant need only show that an item may be material to the preparation of his defense to be discoverable." This Court has held in another homicide case, that the car which the defendants were using, when the victim was shot and killed, was clearly material to the defense and discoverable under Rule 16. A fortiori, the crash vehicle may clearly be material to the preparation of the defense of a person, such as Hammond, charged with vehicular homicide. Therefore, if the crash vehicle were in the possession of the State, it would have been discoverable under Superior Court Criminal Rule 16.

The second step in a *Deberry* evaluation requires an examination of the State's duty to preserve discoverable evidence. This Court has declined to prescribe the exact procedures that are necessary for the various law enforcement agencies in this State to follow, in order to fulfill their duties to preserve evidence. However, this Court has held that in fulfilling these duties, agencies should create rules for gathering and preserving evidence that are broad enough to include any material that could be favorable to a defendant. In *Deberry*, we observed:

> It is most consistent with the purposes of those safeguards to hold that the duty of disclosure attaches in some form once the Government has first gathered and taken possession of the evidence in question. Otherwise, disclosure might be avoided by destroying vital evidence before prosecution begins or before defendants hear of its existence. Only if evidence is carefully preserved during the early stages of investigation will disclosure be possible later.

We find that the police had a duty to gather and to preserve a crash vehicle which they knew was involved in a fatal accident, when criminal charges were pending and a criminal investigation was continuing.

The record reflects that the crash vehicle was "gathered." It was towed from the scene of the crime and impounded, at the direction of the Dover

Police Department, on July 25, 1986. However, the crash vehicle was not preserved. It was released on August 8, 1986. Although Hammond was arrested shortly after the accident, he was not indicted until September 3, 1986. Consequently, when Hammond's attorney filed a discovery request on October 14, 1986, pursuant to Criminal Rule 16, the Dover police no longer had possession of the crash vehicle. The record reflects that the duty to preserve the crash vehicle, at least until the defendant had a reasonable opportunity to inspect it, was breached in Hammond's case.

The final step in a *Deberry* evaluation requires a three-part analysis to determine the consequences which should flow from a breach of the duty to preserve evidence. The first factor to be considered is "the degree of negligence or bad faith involved." Hammond does not contend that the Dover police department released the crash vehicle in bad faith. Hammond does argue that the police were negligent.

The State argues that the police were not negligent in releasing the crash vehicle. When the police arrived, they found the bodies of the accident victims inside of the crash vehicle, in positions which indicated Hammond was the driver. At the hospital, Hammond told one of the investigating police officers that he was the driver. Under these conditions, the State argues that the police had no basis to believe that Hammond would deny being the driver or that the crash vehicle could be material to the preparation of his defense.

The State's argument is addressed to the good faith of the Dover police in releasing the crash vehicle. However, Hammond does not argue that the Dover police acted in bad faith. Hammond's position is that the police were negligent in not preserving the crash vehicle when he was charged with vehicular homicide, since the crash vehicle was the instrumentality of that crime. The Superior Court expressed concern "why a major piece of evidence would not be held at least a little bit longer to give the defendant a chance to look at it." We conclude that the Dover police should have preserved the crash vehicle, for a reasonable time, to permit its inspection by Hammond.

The second factor to be considered in this portion of a *Deberry/Bailey* evaluation is the importance of the missing evidence and the reliability of the secondary or substitute evidence that remains available. Hammond argues that the crash vehicle was important to his case for two separate reasons. First, because evidence of fingerprints, blood, hair, or torn clothing in the interior of the crash vehicle might have established that he was not the driver. Alternatively, because the crash vehicle could have been examined for mechanical failure as a cause of the accident, rather than driver negligence.

The secondary evidence which the State provided to Hammond consisted primarily of photographs of the crash vehicle. The maintenance records of the crash vehicle's owner were also available. Hammond contends that the secondary evidence, especially as it related to his ability to identify the driver, was not a satisfactory substitute. Hammond admits that his expert was able to prepare a video tape of a test, which supported his theory of the hypothetical movement of Hammond and Moore in the vehicle upon impact. However, Hammond argues that without either access to scientific test results or the opportunity to test the interior of the crash vehicle, he was unable to confirm his expert's opinion.

The police found no evidentiary value in the crash vehicle or its contents. In this case, once again, we decline to establish specific procedures which are necessary for law enforcement agencies in this State to fulfill the duty to gather and to preserve evidence. Nevertheless, assuming *arguendo* that there was no duty to gather and test evidence of the interior of the crash vehicle, the crash vehicle in a vehicular homicide should have been preserved. If the crash vehicle itself had been preserved, it would have been available to Hammond for testing. There was little, if any, probative value in the secondary evidence of the crash vehicle's interior that was made available to Hammond, *i.e.*, a single photograph.

The evidence obtained from the interior of the car included the following: torn pieces of clothing found in the car; pieces of car seat fabric; the brake and clutch pads; the steering wheel; test results from blood stains found in the car; test results from arm and head hairs found in the car; and numerous photographs taken from various angles at the scene and at the autobody shop.

The final factor in determining what consequences should flow from the State's breach of the duty to preserve evidence in a *Deberry* evaluation requires an examination of the sufficiency of the other evidence, which the State presented at trial. In Hammond's case, the State presented eyewitness testimony from another driver, who saw the crash vehicle pass him at a high rate of speed immediately prior to the collision. The record also reflects that the crash vehicle did not turn over and that all of its occupants remained inside. The crash vehicle became lodged in the foundation of a townhouse. Several persons reached the scene of the accident, almost immediately after it occurred. All of them testified that they saw Hammond in the driver's seat. Rescue workers testified that Hammond's leg was in a cast, which was wedged between the accelerator and the brake. The ambulance attendant testified that Hammond told him that he was driving, and that the accident occurred when the cast on his leg caused his foot to slip off of the brake pedal.

The question which must now be answered is what consequences should flow from the failure to preserve the crash vehicle. In the Superior Court, Hammond moved for dismissal or an instruction to the jury that the lost evidence, if available would be exculpatory in nature. In ruling on

Hammond's motions, the Superior Court stated it is "clear that the occupants were moved around in the car after the collision." Nevertheless, the Superior Court denied both of Hammond's motions because he had not shown that the evidence, which was not available, would have been conclusively exculpatory to the defendant.

The "conclusively exculpatory" standard, which was applied by the Superior Court, is obviously inconsistent with our holding in *Deberry*. Nevertheless, we find that the State's case against Hammond was strong. Hammond's trial for vehicular homicide, even in the absence of the crash vehicle, was not so fundamentally unfair that his prosecution should have been barred as a denial of due process. The Superior Court properly denied Hammond's motion to dismiss the State's case.

However, since the State must bear responsibility for the loss of evidence, Hammond was entitled to the inference that the crash vehicle, if available, would have been exculpatory. "Due process" required an appropriate instruction to the jury in a prosecution for vehicular homicide, in the absence of the preservation of the crash vehicle or of secondary evidence having a significant probative value. Such an instruction was given in *Arizona v. Youngblood*, even though no federal Constitutional right was found to have been violated.

More significantly, the trial judge instructed the jury: "If you find that the State has allowed to be destroyed or lost any evidence whose content or quality are in issue, you may infer that the true fact is against the State's interest." As a result, the uncertainty as to what the evidence might have proved was turned to the defendant's advantage.

We must now determine the effect of the Superior Court's failure to give such an instruction. Hammond's expert witness was able to prepare a video tape of a test supporting Hammond's theory of the hypothetical movement of the crash vehicle's occupants. Although Hammond's request for a jury instruction was denied, the Superior Court permitted Hammond's attorney to make "factual arguments" to the jury about the absence of the crash vehicle or any tests of its interior, and he did so forcefully. Given the strength of the State's case against Hammond, we are convinced beyond a reasonable doubt, that the Superior Court's failure to give a specific instruction was harmless error.

NOTES

1. States that have a higher due process standard than the *Arizona v. Youngblood* "bad faith test" under their state constitutions (*i.e.* States that adopt a *Hammond*-like test) are Alabama, Alaska, Connecticut, Hawaii, Massachusetts, Mississippi, Tennessee, Utah, Vermont, and West Virginia.

2. States that use a strict *Youngblood* standard are Kentucky, Idaho, and Minnesota.

F. DOUBLE JEOPARDY

PEOPLE v. ARANDA
437 P.3d 845 (Cal. 2019)

CORRIGAN, J.

Stone v. Superior Court (Cal. 1982) concluded that a court must accept a partial verdict of acquittal as to a charged greater offense when a jury has expressly indicated it has acquitted on that offense but has deadlocked on uncharged lesser included offenses. The question here is whether the *Stone* rule has been abrogated by the United States Supreme Court's decision in *Blueford v. Arkansas* (2012), which concluded that federal double jeopardy principles do not require a court to accept a partial verdict. We conclude the *Stone* rule survives as an interpretation of the state Constitution's double jeopardy clause.

Evidence was introduced that, on the night of December 1, 2009, defendant received texts from his girlfriend, 15-year-old Alexis C., asking for help because she feared her father was going to rape her as he had done before. Defendant went to her home and found her asleep in bed with her father. As defendant tried to take her out of the house, the father awakened and a fight ensued. During that confrontation, defendant fatally stabbed the father with an ice pick he had brought with him.

Defendant was charged with a single count of murder. At the close of evidence, the court instructed the jury on first degree murder, second degree murder, and voluntary manslaughter. The jury received "guilty" verdict forms for each offense and a single "not guilty" form.

On the third day of deliberations, the jury reported discussions had become hostile. After consulting with counsel, the court asked the foreperson "how things are going" and if the court could do anything to assist. The foreperson reported the jury was "at a stalemate" and explained: "So we've basically ruled out murder in the first degree. So then we moved to murder in the second degree. So we worked down to voluntary manslaughter, but there's still a couple that are still stuck on second degree." The foreperson later repeated that some jurors "are stuck on second degree and then went down to voluntary," but they were "working through it." Deliberations continued.

The next court day, defense counsel asked the jury be given a "not guilty" verdict form for first degree murder. The prosecutor objected. The foreperson asked to speak with the court and again reported the jury was at an impasse, explaining that one juror "thinks it's second degree," "and then we've got two that are on the side of voluntary. And then we've got nine that are not guilty." Outside the foreperson's presence, the prosecutor expressed his view that the jury was "hopelessly deadlocked." Defense counsel urged the jury was frustrated but not deadlocked. The court brought the panel into the courtroom to ask if anything would assist them. As they waited for the jury, counsel debated the defense request for a "not guilty" verdict form on first degree murder. The court denied the request, stating: "I don't want to change horses in midstream. We sent it in a certain way, and to change anything makes it seem like we're directing them as to which way to think, and I don't want to do that." After answering some questions about jury instructions, the court ordered the jury to deliberate for the remainder of the day, about 40 minutes. After that time expired, the jury returned, and the foreperson said they were "still at the same spot." The court asked whether "it's still basically nine to two to one," and the foreperson replied it was. The court concluded the jury was deadlocked and declared a mistrial.

The defense moved to dismiss the first degree murder allegation on double jeopardy grounds. Relying on *Stone*, defendant argued the court's failure to allow the jury to acquit him of first degree murder barred a retrial on that charge. Defendant also argued double jeopardy barred a trial on second degree murder and voluntary manslaughter as well. The court ultimately dismissed the first degree murder charge but declined to dismiss the lesser offenses.

Under the Fifth Amendment to the United States Constitution and article I, section 15, of the California Constitution, a person may not be twice placed in jeopardy for the same offense. This double jeopardy principle bars a second prosecution for the same crime after an acquittal or conviction. Even if a jury returns no verdict on a particular charge, retrial is only permitted in limited circumstances. "Retrial after discharge of a jury without manifest (in federal terminology) or legal necessity violates the protections afforded under both the federal and state constitutional double jeopardy clauses." Although "the failure of a jury to agree on a verdict is an instance of manifest necessity permitting retrial of the defendant," "granting an unnecessary mistrial bars retrial" under double jeopardy principles.

Stone held that "the trial court is constitutionally obligated to afford the jury an opportunity to render a partial verdict of acquittal on a greater offense when the jury is deadlocked only on an uncharged lesser included offense. Failure to do so will cause a subsequently declared mistrial to be without legal necessity." *Stone* was charged with a single count of murder. The jury was instructed on, and received guilty verdict forms for, first and second degree murder, and voluntary and involuntary manslaughter. It was given a single verdict form for acquittal on all charges, as well as a verdict form for "justifiable homicide." After seven days of deliberations, the foreman reported in open court that there were no votes for first or second degree murder but various votes for both forms of manslaughter and justifiable homicide. Each juror, in response to court inquiry, stated a belief that the jury was hopelessly deadlocked. The court denied defense counsel's request to accept a partial verdict of acquittal on murder and ordered further deliberations. After another day and a half of deliberations, the foreman again indicated that there were no votes for first or second degree murder and various votes for manslaughter and justifiable homicide. The court declared a mistrial and discharged the jury.

Stone reasoned there was no legal necessity for a mistrial as to murder and a partial verdict of acquittal could have been taken.

We conclude the *Stone* rule survives as an interpretation of California's double jeopardy clause. "The California Constitution is a document of independent force and effect that may be interpreted in a manner more protective of defendants' rights than that extended by the federal Constitution, as construed by the United States Supreme Court." The state double jeopardy clause was included in both the 1849 and 1879 California Constitutions long before the high court applied the federal clause to the states in *Benton v. Maryland* (1969). In 1974, as part of a broader constitutional revision, the voters retained the double jeopardy provision and added language that "rights guaranteed by this Constitution are not dependent on those guaranteed by the United States Constitution."

On several occasions, we have construed the state double jeopardy clause to be more protective than its federal counterpart. For example, *People v. Batts* concluded that double jeopardy principles not only barred a retrial after a prosecutor commits misconduct for the purpose of triggering a mistrial, the federal standard, but also if a prosecutor commits misconduct to thwart a reasonable prospect of acquittal. *People v. Henderson* (Cal. 1963) held that a defendant could not receive a more severe punishment on retrial after a successful appeal, a limitation not required by the federal double jeopardy clause. Similarly, *Cardenas v. Superior Court* (Cal. 1961) declined to follow high court authority and concluded that a mistrial declared without a defendant's consent barred a retrial even if the mistrial was declared for his "benefit."

Similarly here, nothing in the reasoning of the U.S. Supreme Court decision in *Blueford*, decided 30 years after *Stone*, suggests we should now abandon our long-established precedent. *Stone* observed that "one of the primary purposes of the double jeopardy protection is to prevent successive prosecutions for the same offense" and concluded that a procedure to accept a partial acquittal on a greater offense was necessary to prevent "seriously infringing on the defendant's double jeopardy interest in avoiding retrial for offenses on which he has been factually acquitted." *Stone* articulated a fairness rationale for its holding based upon our criminal procedure. As *Stone* explained, the Penal Code allows a prosecutor to charge an offense and all of its lesser included offenses in separate counts. Section 954 permits an accusatory pleading to charge "different statements of the same offense." Although, ordinarily, a defendant "may be convicted of any number of the offenses charged," "a judicially created exception to this rule prohibits multiple convictions based on necessarily included offenses."

Nothing in *Blueford*'s reasoning calls *Stone*'s analysis into question. As discussed, *Blueford* raised two primary concerns. First, *Blueford* suggested that a foreperson's report "was not a final resolution of anything" because "the fact that deliberations continued after the report deprives that report of the finality necessary to constitute an acquittal on the murder offenses." However, if, under the *Stone* rule, a jury is given verdict forms and given the option of rendering a unanimous verdict consistent with the foreperson's report, such a formalized verdict would be a final resolution of the issue. Second, *Blueford* observed that the high court has "never required a trial court, before declaring a mistrial because of a hung jury, to consider any particular means of breaking the impasse." However, in the *Stone* scenario, the jury has unanimously acquitted a defendant of a greater offense and it is at an "impasse" only as to which of several lesser offenses may have been committed. Accepting a unanimous, final verdict on the former has nothing to do with breaking an impasse on the latter, which can be retried.

"The determination whether there is a reasonable probability of agreement rests in the sound discretion of the trial court, based on consideration of all the factors before it." Here, there was an indication that the jury agreed defendant was not guilty of first degree murder. On three separate occasions over two court days, the jury foreperson reported that jurors were split between second degree murder, voluntary manslaughter, and a not guilty verdict. The foreperson said the jury had "ruled out" first degree murder and had "worked down to voluntary manslaughter, but there's still a couple that are still stuck on second degree." The next day, the foreperson gave a numerical split of one vote for second degree murder, two for voluntary manslaughter and nine for an acquittal. After further deliberations, the foreperson confirmed the split had not changed, and the court discharged the jury. That action was premature and unsupported by legal necessity.

Courts should be mindful of section 1164, subdivision (b), which expressly requires that "no jury shall be discharged until the court has verified on the record that the jury has either reached a verdict or has formally declared its inability to reach a verdict on all issues before it, including, but not limited to, the degree of the crime or crimes charged." The court failed to do so here with respect to first degree murder.

Defendant may not be retried for first degree murder but may be retried on the lesser included offenses of second degree murder and voluntary manslaughter. As *Stone* reasoned, an acquittal of a greater offense "does not bar a retrial for an offense necessarily included therein on which the jury is unable to agree, regardless of whether the lesser included offense is charged in a separate count." The jury's reported numerical split reflected it was deadlocked as to second degree murder and voluntary manslaughter. After two reports of a deadlock, the court instructed the jury to continue deliberating, but the jury remained at an impasse. The court acted well within its discretion by concluding no reasonable probability of agreement existed as to these counts.

NOTES

1. In 2015, the Indiana Supreme Court held that a defendant's conviction for battery was a violation of the state constitution's prohibition against double jeopardy. The court vacated the defendant's battery conviction but affirmed his criminal confinement conviction. *Hines v. State*, 30 N.E.3d 1216 (Ind. 2015).

2. The States without double jeopardy clauses are Connecticut, Maryland, Massachusetts, North Carolina, and Vermont.

G. CRUEL AND UNUSUAL PUNISHMENT

WASHINGTON v. GREGORY
427 P.3d 621 (Wash. 2018)

FAIRHURST, C.J.

The death penalty is invalid because it is imposed in an arbitrary and racially biased manner. While this particular case provides an opportunity to specifically address racial disproportionality, the underlying issues that underpin our holding are rooted in the arbitrary manner in which the death penalty is generally administered. The death penalty, as administered in our state, fails to serve any legitimate penological goal; thus, it violates article I, section 14 of our state constitution.

Gregory brought challenges under both the state and federal constitutions. We have "a duty, where feasible, to resolve constitutional questions first under the provisions of our own state constitution before turning to federal law." If we neglect this duty, we "deprive the people of their double security." "It is by now well established that state courts have the power to interpret their state constitutional provisions as more protective of individual rights than the parallel provisions of the United States Constitution."

Article I, section 14 of our state constitution provides, "Excessive bail shall not be required, excessive fines imposed, nor cruel punishment inflicted." Our interpretation of article I, section 14 "is not constrained by the Supreme Court's interpretation of the Eighth Amendment." The Washington State Constitution's cruel punishment clause often provides greater protection than the Eighth Amendment." Especially where the language of our constitution is different from the analogous federal provision, we are not bound to assume the framers intended an identical interpretation. The historical evidence reveals that the framers of the

Washington Constitution, article I, section 14 were of the view that the word "cruel" sufficiently expressed their intent, and refused to adopt an amendment inserting the word "unusual."

We have previously upheld the constitutionality of the death penalty under somewhat similar claims. However, "stability should not be confused with perpetuity," and major changes have taken place that support our decision to revisit the constitutionality of the death penalty. First, we have numerous additional trial reports for defendants convicted of aggravated murder that were not previously available to us or the defendants who made constitutional claims. Second, Gregory commissioned a statistical study based on the information in the trial reports to demonstrate that the death penalty is imposed in an arbitrary and racially biased manner.

In our conclusion, we afford great weight to Beckett's analysis and conclusions. After running various models, as requested by Commissioner Narda Pierce, Beckett summarized her findings regarding race:

"From December 1981 through May of 2014, special sentencing proceedings in Washington State involving Black defendants were between 3.5 and 4.6 times as likely to result in a death sentence as proceedings involving non-Black defendants after the impact of the other variables included in the model has been taken into account."

The most important consideration is whether the evidence shows that race has a meaningful impact on imposition of the death penalty. We make this determination by way of legal analysis, not pure science. At the very most, there is an 11 percent chance that the observed association between race and the death penalty in Beckett's regression analysis is attributed to random chance rather than true association. Just as we declined to require "precise uniformity" under our proportionality review, we decline to require indisputably true social science to prove that our death penalty is impermissibly imposed based on race.

This is consistent with constitutional legal analysis. For example, in *Furman v. Georgia* (1991), Justice Stewart explained that the death sentences before the court were "cruel and unusual in the same way that being struck by lightning is cruel and unusual. The petitioners are among a capriciously selected random handful upon whom the sentence of death has in fact been imposed." Justice Stewart did not need to compare the probability of being struck by lightning to the probability of being sentenced to death, nor did he need to rely on an expert's regression analysis to ensure that the petitioners were in fact randomly selected without any relation to other dependent variables. Similarly, Justice White explained what he believed to be "a near truism: that the death penalty could so seldom be imposed that it would cease to be a credible deterrent or measurably to contribute to any other end of punishment in the criminal justice system." He did not need to rely on an expert's calculation as to what point the rate at which the death penalty is imposed becomes low enough that potential murderers are no longer deterred from committing their intended crimes. Similarly, under the Sixth Amendment to the United States Constitution, ineffective assistance of counsel claimants must show deficient performance and prejudice, where prejudice entails a "reasonable probability that, but for counsel's unprofessional errors, the result of the proceeding would have been different." "A reasonable probability is a probability sufficient to undermine confidence in the outcome." We do not expect the defendant to present statistical evidence of the outcome of hypothetical trials with a more effective attorney and compare it to the original trial, controlling for all other variables. Lastly, in *State v. Santiago* (Conn. 2015), when deciding that the death penalty was unconstitutional, the Connecticut Supreme Court took judicial notice of scientific and sociological studies that were "not necessarily indisputably true" but were "more likely true than not true." Given the evidence before this court and our judicial notice of implicit and overt racial bias against black defendants in this state, we are confident that the association between race and the death penalty is not attributed to random chance.

When considering a challenge under article I, section 14, we look to contemporary standards and experience in other states. We recognize local, national, and international trends that disfavor capital punishment more broadly. When the death penalty is imposed in an arbitrary and racially biased manner, society's standards of decency are even more offended. Our capital punishment law lacks "fundamental fairness" and thus violates article I, section 14.

Given our conclusion that the death penalty is imposed in an arbitrary and racially biased manner, it logically follows that the death penalty fails to serve penological goals. The principal purposes of capital punishment are "retribution and deterrence of capital crimes by prospective offenders." Unless the death penalty "measurably contributes to one or both of these goals, it is nothing more than the purposeless and needless imposition of pain and suffering, and hence an unconstitutional punishment." "If the policy of this state is retribution for capital crimes, then it must be evenhanded."

Yet, the death penalty is not per se unconstitutional. We leave open the possibility that the legislature may enact a "carefully drafted statute," to impose capital punishment in this state, but it cannot create a system that offends constitutional rights. "The death penalty is constitutional only if it is properly constrained to avoid freakish and wanton application." The United States Supreme Court was "unwilling to say that there is any one right way for a State to set up its capital sentencing scheme." We agree. "To hold that the death penalty is per se unconstitutional would be to substitute our moral judgment for that of the people of Washington."

Under article I, section 14, we hold that Washington's death penalty is unconstitutional, as administered, because it is imposed in an arbitrary and racially biased manner. Given the manner in which it is imposed, the death penalty also fails to serve any legitimate penological goals. Pursuant to RCW 10.95.090, "if the death penalty established by this chapter is held to be invalid by a final judgment of a court which is binding on all courts in the state, the sentence for aggravated first degree murder shall be life imprisonment." All death sentences are hereby converted to life imprisonment.

STATE v. SANTIAGO
122 A.3d 1 (Conn. 2015)

PALMER, J.

Although the death penalty has been a fixture of Connecticut's criminal law since early colonial times, public opinion concerning it has long been divided. In 2009, growing opposition to capital punishment led the legislature to enact Public Acts 2009, No. 09-107, which would have repealed the death penalty for all crimes committed on or after the date of enactment but retained the death penalty for capital felonies committed prior to that date. Then-Governor M. Jodi Rell vetoed P.A. 09-107, however, and it did not become law. Three years later, in 2012, the legislature passed a materially identical act that prospectively repealed the death penalty and, this time, Governor Dannel P. Malloy signed it into law. During the public hearings on both P.A. 09-107 and P.A. 12-5, supporters argued that the proposed legislation represented a measured and lawful approach to the issue.

Others raised serious concerns, however, as to whether, following a prospective only repeal, the imposition of the death penalty would violate the state constitutional prohibition against cruel and unusual punishment. Perhaps most notably, Chief State's Attorney Kevin T. Kane, who serves as this state's chief law enforcement officer and represents the state in the present case, testified before the legislature that such a statute could not pass constitutional muster. Additionally, the Division of Criminal Justice submitted written testimony, in which it advised the legislature that a prospective only repeal would be a "fiction" and that, "in reality, it would effectively abolish the death penalty for anyone who has not yet been executed because it would be untenable as a matter of constitutional law. Any death penalty that has been imposed and not carried out would effectively be nullified."

In the present appeal, the defendant, Eduardo Santiago, raises similar claims, contending that, following the decision by the elected branches to abolish capital punishment for all crimes committed on or after April 25, 2012, it would be unconstitutionally cruel and unusual to execute offenders who committed capital crimes before that date. Upon careful consideration of the defendant's claims in light of the governing constitutional principles and Connecticut's unique historical and legal landscape, we are persuaded that, following its prospective abolition, this state's death penalty no longer comports with contemporary standards of decency and no longer serves any legitimate penological purpose. For these reasons, execution of those offenders who committed capital felonies prior to April 25, 2012, would violate the state constitutional prohibition against cruel and unusual punishment.

In December, 2000, Mark Pascual agreed to give the defendant a snowmobile from Pascual's repair shop if the defendant would kill the victim, Joseph Niwinski, for whose girlfriend Pascual had developed romantic feelings. That same month, with the assistance of Pascual and another friend, the defendant entered the victim's apartment and shot and killed the victim as he slept. The defendant was charged with, among other things, the capital felony of "murder committed by a defendant who is hired to commit the same for pecuniary gain."

Public Act 12-5 not only reflects this state's longstanding aversion to carrying out executions, but also represents the seminal change in the four century long history of capital punishment in Connecticut. Accompanying this dramatic departure are a host of other important developments that have transpired over the past several years. Historians have given us new chronicles of the history and devolution of the death penalty in Connecticut. Legal scholars have provided new understandings of the original meaning of the constitutional prohibition against cruel and unusual punishments. Social scientists repeatedly have confirmed that the risk of capital punishment falls disproportionately on people of color and other disadvantaged groups. Meanwhile, nationally, the number of executions and the number of states that allow the death penalty continue to decline, and convicted capital felons in this state remain on death row for decades with every likelihood that they will not be executed for many years to come, if ever.

Since this court first considered the constitutionality of capital punishment, we have recognized that, "in the area of fundamental civil liberties—which includes all protections of the declaration of rights contained in article first of the Connecticut constitution—we sit as a court of last resort. In such constitutional adjudication, our first referent is Connecticut law and the full panoply of rights Connecticut citizens have come to expect as their due."

It is by now well established that the constitution of Connecticut prohibits cruel and unusual punishments under the auspices of the dual due process provisions contained in article first, §§ 8 and 9. Those due process protections take as their hallmark principles of fundamental fairness rooted in our state's unique common law, statutory, and constitutional traditions. Although neither provision of the state constitution expressly references cruel or unusual punishments, it is settled constitutional doctrine that both of our due process clauses prohibit governmental infliction of cruel and unusual punishments.

In *State v. Geisler* (Conn. 1992), we identified six nonexclusive tools of analysis to be considered, to the extent applicable, whenever we are called on as a matter of first impression to define the scope and parameters of the state constitution: (1) persuasive relevant federal precedents; (2) historical insights into the intent of our constitutional forebears; (3) the operative constitutional text; (4) related Connecticut precedents; (5) persuasive precedents of other states; and (6) contemporary understandings of applicable economic and sociological norms, or, as otherwise described, relevant public policies.

The eighth amendment to the federal constitution establishes the minimum standards for what constitutes impermissibly cruel and unusual punishment. Specifically, the United States Supreme Court has indicated that at least three types of punishment may be deemed unconstitutionally cruel: (1) inherently barbaric punishments; (2) excessive and disproportionate punishments; and (3) arbitrary or discriminatory punishments. In *State v. Ross* (Conn. 1994), we broadly adopted, as a matter of state constitutional law, this federal framework for evaluating challenges to allegedly cruel and unusual punishments.

We first consider the preconstitutional roots of the freedom from cruel and unusual punishment in Connecticut. As early as 1672, our colonial code, which incorporated a quasi-constitutional statement of individual liberties, provided that, for bodily punishment, none shall be inflicted that are "Inhumane, Barbarous or Cruel." The 1672 code also differed from prior Connecticut statutes in that it (1) forbade the use of torture to extract confessions, (2) placed new restrictions on the use of corporal punishment, and (3) afforded novel procedural rights to criminal defendants, especially in capital cases.

In perhaps the most substantial scholarly account of the early legal traditions of the Connecticut colony, William K. Holdsworth offers a window into the original meaning of Connecticut's inceptive prohibition of cruel punishment. Holdsworth describes the years leading up to the adoption of the 1672 code as a key formative period in the colony's legal history. "The decade of 1662 through 1672 was a watershed in the early history of Connecticut," he explains, "a period of profound intellectual, social, economic, and political change that set the colony on a course of its own." During this period of "extraordinarily rapid and vital change," a new generation of leaders restructured the colony's political and judicial systems. The legislature "made fairer use of its juries, gave formal recognition to numerous civil liberties, displayed a greater awareness of individual rights, dealt less severely with most criminal offenders than before, and, either formally or in practice, reduced the penalties for several capital crimes." In the process, Connecticut's new leaders bequeathed to its citizens a "legacy of moderation."

"This unmistakable tendency toward judicial moderation in the use of physical punishments in the years 1662 through 1675 is all the more pronounced when we consider capital crimes and capital punishment." As public attitudes evolved, magistrates grew more reluctant to inflict capital punishment and came to believe that the death penalty should be reserved for only the most heinous and universally condemned offenses. It is apparent from this history that, long before the adoption of either the federal or state constitution, Connecticut citizens enjoyed a quasi-constitutional freedom from cruel punishment, one that reflected our unique social and political traditions and that far exceeded the protections recognized in England at the time. These protections were enshrined in Connecticut's early constitutional statutes and common law, and, from the start, were intimately tied to the principles of due process.

We next consider the historical circumstances leading up to the adoption of the state constitution in 1818. The late eighteenth and early nineteenth centuries witnessed the twilight of a premodern system of criminal justice in the United States. The rapid evolution in penology that occurred in the decades following the founding was especially pronounced in Connecticut. The late eighteenth and early nineteenth centuries in Connecticut witnessed a pronounced liberalization in public, legislative, and judicial attitudes toward crime and punishment. The period has been described as one characterized by penological reform, a broader commitment to human rights, and the first serious public questioning of the moral legitimacy of capital punishment. This time between the adoption of the federal and state constitutions also saw an emerging awareness of and compassion for "the fate of the condemned perpetrator." These changes coincided with the reopening of the newly established Newgate Prison in 1790, which provided the opportunity to impose incarceration as an alternative to more severe traditional punishments.

In summary, it is clear that, from the earliest days of the colonies, and extending until the adoption of the state constitution in 1818, the people of Connecticut saw themselves as enjoying significant freedoms from cruel and unusual punishment, freedoms that were safeguarded by our courts and enshrined in our state's pre-constitutional statutory and common law. That our history reveals a particular sensitivity to such concerns warrants our scrupulous and independent review of allegedly cruel and unusual practices and punishments, and informs our analysis thereof.

We next consider the relevant provisions of the state constitution. In light of our state's firm and enduring commitment to the principle that even those offenders who commit the most heinous crimes should not be subjected to inhumane, barbarous, or cruel punishment, the question naturally arises why the framers of the 1818 constitution decided to embed these traditional liberties in our dual due process clauses rather than in an express punishments clause. Although there is no indication that that question was debated during the 1818 constitutional convention, we find guidance in the broader legal history of turn of the century Connecticut.

Connecticut was among three of the original thirteen states that chose not to officially ratify the eighth amendment or, indeed, any of the first ten amendments to the federal constitution. In 1787, the state's representatives to the federal constitutional convention had argued vehemently against the need for a bill of rights. "In Connecticut, unlike those states that had recently been under the domination of royal and proprietary governors and appointed upper houses, limited government was taken for granted. Calvinist theory described limited government, Connecticut's Fundamental Orders of 1639 proclaimed it, the Connecticut Charter of 1662 established it, tradition demanded it, common law enforced it, and frequent elections guaranteed it." During the late eighteenth and early nineteenth centuries, for example, Connecticut courts routinely safeguarded the basic rights enshrined in the federal Bill of Rights on the basis of natural rights or common law, without the need for any formal constitutional sanction. Moreover, there was a particular fear in Connecticut that the adoption of a written bill of rights would imply, by negative inference, that citizens were no longer entitled to unenumerated protections long enshrined in the state's common law. "A strong statewide consensus, then, held that no bill of rights was necessary and, indeed, might even limit individual liberty."

Accordingly, in *Moore v. Ganim* (Conn. 1995), we "assumed that the framers believed that individuals would continue to possess certain natural rights even if those rights were not enumerated in the written constitution. On the basis of this assumption, we would not draw firm conclusions from the silence of the constitutional text. Rather, in determining whether unenumerated rights were incorporated into the constitution, we must focus on the framers' understanding of whether a particular right was part of the natural law, i.e., on the framers' understanding of whether the particular right was so fundamental to an ordered society that it did not require explicit enumeration. We can discern the framers' understanding, of course, only by examining the historical sources."

Turning to the next *Geisler* factor, namely, relevant Connecticut precedents, we write on a relatively blank slate with respect to cruel and unusual punishment. Nevertheless, since this court first recognized in *Ross* that our due process clauses independently prohibit cruel and unusual punishment, we have begun to carve out the broad contours of that prohibition. In *Ross* itself, as we have noted, we adopted the aforementioned federal framework for evaluating challenges to allegedly cruel and unusual punishments. Specifically, we recognized that, under the state constitution, whether a challenged punishment is cruel and unusual is to be judged according to the "evolving standards of human decency"; and that those standards are reflected not only in constitutional and legislative text, but also "in our history and in the teachings of the jurisprudence of our sister states as well as that of the federal courts." In *Ross*, we also rejected the theory that "article first, § 9, confers the authority to determine what constitutes cruel and unusual punishment solely on the Connecticut legislature and not on the courts." "Although we should exercise our authority with great restraint," we explained, "this court cannot abdicate its nondelegable responsibility for the adjudication of constitutional rights."

The unique structure and text of the Connecticut constitution of 1965, in which the freedom from cruel and unusual punishment is embedded in our dual due process clauses rather than in a distinct punishments clause, mean that sister state authority is less directly relevant than in cases in which we have construed other constitutional provisions. We do agree with our sister courts, however, that, under the state constitution, the pertinent standards by which we judge the fairness, decency, and efficacy of a punishment are necessarily those of Connecticut.

To summarize our analysis of the first five *Geisler* factors, when construing the state constitutional freedom from cruel and unusual punishment, we broadly adopt the framework that the federal courts have used to evaluate eighth amendment challenges. We apply this framework, however, with respect to the constitutional facts as they exist in Connecticut and mindful of our state's unique and expansive constitutional and preconstitutional history.

We take this opportunity to clarify that, although a sudden sea change in public opinion would be sufficient to demonstrate a constitutionally significant shift in contemporary standards of decency, such a dramatic shift is not necessary for us to recognize that a punishment has become repugnant to the state constitution. If the legally salient metaphor is the *evolution* of our standards of decency, then a gradual but inexorable extinction may be as significant as the sociological equivalent of the meteor that, it is believed, suddenly ended the reign of the dinosaurs. In any event, new insights into the history of capital punishment in Connecticut, in tandem with the legislature's 2012 decision to abolish the death penalty prospectively, persuade us that we now have not only a clear picture of the long, steady devolution of capital punishment in our state, and, indeed, throughout New England, but also a dramatic and definitive statement by our elected officials that the death penalty no longer can be justified as a necessary or appropriate tool of justice.

In conclusion, we are aware that the issue of whether the death penalty is an appropriate punishment for the most heinous crimes is one about which people of good faith continue to disagree. Nevertheless, our review of the five objective indicia that have been deemed relevant under both the federal and state constitutions compels the conclusion that, following the enactment of P.A. 12-5, Connecticut's capital punishment scheme no longer comports with our state's contemporary standards of decency. It therefore offends the state constitutional prohibition against excessive and disproportionate punishment.

NOTES

1. The prohibition on cruel and unusual punishment traces its origin to the English Bill of Rights of 1689. Its language appears almost verbatim in the Eighth Amendment to the United States Constitution.

2. A majority of the United States Supreme Court has held that the death penalty does not constitute cruel and unusual punishment.

3. The three States without a cruel and unusual punishment clause are Connecticut, Illinois and Vermont.

4. The United States Supreme Court's *Miller v. Alabama*, 567 U.S. 460 (2012) decision held that mandatory juvenile life without parole sentences were unconstitutional under the Eighth Amendment to the United States Constitution. It reasoned, that because a mandatory juvenile life without parole scheme did not consider the nature of youth and "children's diminished culpability and heightened capacity for change," it "poses too great a risk of disproportionate punishment." In response to *Miller*, the State of Washington's legislature enacted what is referred to as the *Miller*-fix statute. It requires sentencing courts to consider the *Miller* factors before sentencing a 16- or 17-year-old convicted of aggravated first degree murder to life without parole. The Supreme Court of Washington held that sentencing juvenile offenders to life without parole or early release constitutes cruel punishment and, therefore, the *Miller*-fix statute is unconstitutional, insofar as it allows such a sentence, under article I, section 14 of Washington Constitution.

H. POST-CONVICTION RELIEF

BROWN v. BOOKER
826 S.E.2d 304 (Va. 2019)

PER CURIAM

On May 25, 1970, Sherman Brown was convicted by a jury of the murder of a four-year-old child and was sentenced to death. This Court affirmed Brown's conviction, holding it was amply supported by the evidence, and affirmed his sentence. In 1973, after his death sentence was vacated as a result of *Furman v. Georgia* (1972), Brown was resentenced by a jury to life imprisonment.

In 2016, Brown filed a petition for a writ of actual innocence. We dismissed Brown's petition, holding the Court had no authority to issue a writ of actual innocence based on the DNA test results proffered by Brown, because the tests were conducted by a private laboratory and were not certified by the Commonwealth's Department of Forensic Science. Further, even if the Court were authorized to consider the private laboratory's results, Brown failed to prove by clear-and-convincing evidence that no rational factfinder would find him guilty of murder in light of the totality of the evidence before the Court.

Simultaneous with the filing of his petition for a writ of actual innocence, Brown submitted the present petition for a writ of habeas corpus. Brown asserts that new evidence, based on advances in forensic science, reveals flaws in hair and fiber evidence admitted at his trial and that new DNA evidence, the same evidence relied upon in his petition for a writ of actual innocence, exculpates him. Brown contends the admission of flawed hair and fiber evidence violated his right to a fair trial. Brown acknowledges his petition is untimely. However, Brown asserts that, if applied to him, this statutory limitation period would violate the bar against suspension of the writ of habeas corpus as set forth in the Suspension Clause of Article I, Section 9 of the Constitution of Virginia, because his claims are based on newly-discovered evidence and could not have been brought within the time permitted under the statute. We agree with Brown's concession that his petition is untimely under Code § 8.01-654(A)(2), but reject his argument that the limitation period violates the Suspension Clause and dismiss the petition.

Since 1998, Code § 8.01-654(A)(2) has provided that a habeas corpus petition attacking a criminal conviction or sentence, as here, must "be filed within two years from the date of final judgment in the trial court or within one year from either final disposition of the direct appeal in state court or the time for filing such appeal has expired, whichever is later." However, because Brown was convicted before July 1, 1998, when the statute became effective, he had until July 1, 1999, to file a timely petition for a writ of habeas corpus. Brown did not file his habeas petition until October 7, 2016, long after the limitation period expired.

Brown argues that the Suspension Clause bars application of the statute of limitations to his petition because his claims, based on allegedly newly discovered evidence, could not have been brought within the limitation period. Assuming without deciding that Brown's claims could not have been brought before the limitation period expired, we reject his argument that the statutory limitation period operates as a suspension of the writ of habeas corpus in contravention of Article I, Section 9 of the Constitution of Virginia.

The Suspension Clause states that "the privilege of the writ of habeas corpus shall not be suspended unless when, in cases of invasion or rebellion, the public safety may require." The Court has not previously addressed whether a particular statutory provision constitutes suspension of the writ. In addressing the issue now, we look to the limited subject matter to which habeas corpus review extended when our Suspension Clause was first adopted and conclude statutory limits on Brown's ability to raise his present claims are constitutional.

At common law, a "habeas court's role was most extensive in cases of pretrial and noncriminal detention, where there had been little or no previous judicial review of the cause for detention." As particularly relevant here, its use as a post-conviction remedy was limited to challenging the jurisdiction of the sentencing court. In England, the use of the writ for those "detained for criminal or supposed criminal matters was defined and regulated by the Habeas Corpus Act of 1679."

The writ was available in Virginia prior to 1830 but did not gain constitutional protection in Virginia until the Suspension Clause appeared as Article III, Section 11 of the Constitution of 1830. Although there "is little available evidence to cast light on the meaning of" the Clause by the time it was adopted, the scope of the writ, insofar as it lay to challenge the validity of a criminal conviction, remained as it did at common law, limited to challenging the jurisdiction of the sentencing court. As this Court explained:

> The writ of habeas corpus is not a writ of error. It deals, not with mere errors or irregularities, but only with such radical defects as render a proceeding absolutely void. It brings up the body of the prisoner with the cause of his commitment, and the court can inquire into the sufficiency of that cause; but, if he be detained in prison by virtue of a judgment of a court of competent jurisdiction, that judgment is in itself sufficient cause. An imprisonment under a judgment cannot be unlawful unless that judgment be an absolute nullity, and it is not a nullity if the court or magistrate rendering it had jurisdiction to render it.

Here, however, Brown challenges only the reliability of the evidence adduced at his trial—not the subject matter jurisdiction of the sentencing court to address his case—and he attempts to present new evidence which, he contends, shows he is actually innocent. The use of the writ to challenge non-jurisdictional claims of the sort alleged by Brown was unknown to the drafters of our Suspension Clause, and they could not have intended to protect a convicted prisoner's ability to raise them. Accordingly, Brown's inability to now question and present new evidence bearing on his factual guilt or innocence does not violate the Suspension Clause.

In so holding, we join numerous other states which have rejected similar challenges to their own limitation periods. Accordingly, the petition is dismissed.

NOTES

1. The constitutions of all fifty States prohibit the state legislature from suspending the writ of habeas corpus. The majority of these provisions include exceptions in cases of rebellion or invasion or to protect the public's safety.

2. A few States provide for an unqualified right to the writ of habeas corpus. For example, Vermont's constitution states: "the Writ of Habeas Corpus shall in no case be suspended. It shall be a writ issuable of right; and the General Assembly shall make provision to render it at a speedy and effectual remedy in all cases proper therefor." Vt. Const. ch. II, § 4.

CHAPTER VIII

SEARCH AND SEIZURE

A. INTRODUCTION

The prohibition on unreasonable searches and seizures in many state constitutions is almost identical to the Fourth Amendment of the United States Constitution. Nevada's constitution follows the typical formulation, stating that "the right of the people to be secure in their persons, houses, papers and effects against unreasonable seizures and searches shall not be violated." Nev. Const. art. I, § 18.

However, some state constitutions have textual differences that can be outcome determinative. *See, e.g.*, Haw. Const. art. I, § 7; N.Y. Const. art. I, § 12; La. Const. art. I, § 5. Missouri's constitution was amended in 2014 to reflect modern technological developments, holding that the people shall be secure in their persons, papers, homes, effects, and electronic communications and data from unreasonable searches and seizures. Mo. Const. art. I, § 15.

Under the Fourth Amendment, warrantless searches are *per se* unreasonable unless they fall within an exception to the warrant requirement. Some of the exceptions to the Fourth Amendment's warrant requirement are: frisks, inventory searches, searches incident to arrest, consensual searches, automobile searches, and searches under exigent circumstances. These and other exceptions are not always permitted in whole or in part by state constitutions.

State constitutions also have been construed to have standards that differ from the Fourth Amendment to determine probable cause and standing. The purpose, policy, and operation of the exclusionary rule under state constitutions is frequently different from the federal exclusionary rule.

B. PROBABLE CAUSE

PEOPLE v. GRIMINGER
524 N.E.2d 409 (N.Y. 1988)

TITONE, J.

The primary issue presented is whether the U.S. Supreme Court's *Aguilar-Spinelli* two-prong test, or its *Gates* totality-of-the-circumstances test, should be employed in determining the sufficiency of an affidavit submitted in support of a search warrant application. We conclude that, as a matter of State law, our courts should apply the *Aguilar-Spinelli* test.

Special agents of the United States Secret Service arrested a counterfeiting suspect, and, in the course of interrogation, he signed a detailed statement accusing defendant of keeping large quantities of marihuana and cocaine in his bedroom and adjacent attic. Consequently, one of the agents prepared an affidavit for a warrant to search defendant's home. According to the affidavit, a confidential informant known as source "A" observed substantial quantities of marihuana and quantities of cocaine in defendant's bedroom and attic on numerous occasions, saw defendant sell drugs on numerous occasions, and, as recently as seven days ago, "A" observed 150 to 200 pounds of marihuana in defendant's bedroom and adjacent attic. The affidavit further stated that, pursuant to a consent search, approximately four pounds of marihuana were found in a garbage can at defendant's residence.

Although the agent did not personally know the counterfeiting suspect, his affidavit said that the undisclosed informant was "a person known to your deponent." The agent also omitted the fact that the informant was under arrest when he provided this information. Based solely upon this affidavit, a Federal Magistrate issued the search warrant. On August 26, 1983, the warrant was executed by two Federal agents and six or seven Nassau County policemen. The search produced 10 ounces of marijuana, over $6,000 in cash and drug-related paraphernalia. Additionally, the Federal agents turned over the marijuana discovered during the consent search referred to in the warrant to Nassau County law enforcement officials.

Defendant was charged with two counts of criminal possession of marihuana, as well as with criminal sale of marihuana arising out of an unrelated May 1984 incident. Defendant sought to suppress the evidence obtained as a result of the August 26 search, but County Court denied the motion. Although the court found that the agent's affidavit failed to satisfy the "reliability" prong of the *Aguilar-Spinelli* test, it concluded that the *Gates* test should be applied in assessing the sufficiency of a search warrant. Under that test, the court determined that there was probable cause to issue the warrant.

Prior to *Illinois v. Gates* (1983), Federal courts applied the two-pronged *Aguilar-Spinelli* test in probable cause determinations when evaluating hearsay information from an undisclosed informant. Under this test, the application for a search warrant must demonstrate to the issuing Magistrate (i) the veracity or reliability of the source of the information, and (ii) the basis of the informant's knowledge. We adopted this standard as a matter of State constitutional law. In *Illinois v. Gates*, the United States Supreme Court altered its position and adopted the seemingly more relaxed "totality-of-the-circumstances approach."

In *People v. Johnson* (N.Y. 1985), this court expressly rejected the *Gates* approach for evaluating warrantless arrests. In *People v. Bigelow* (N.Y. 1985), although the People urged us to adopt the *Gates* test in the search warrant context, we found it unnecessary to decide the question, since "the People's evidence did not meet minimum standards of probable cause even if *Gates* was applied." This appeal squarely presents the issue left undecided in *Bigelow*. We are not persuaded, however, that the *Gates* approach provides a sufficient measure of protection, and we now hold that, as a matter of State constitutional law, the *Aguilar-Spinelli* two-prong test should be applied in determining whether there is a sufficient factual predicate upon which to issue a search warrant.

We reaffirm today, that in evaluating hearsay information, the Magistrate must find some minimum, reasonable showing that the informant was reliable and had a basis of knowledge. Our courts should not "blithely accept as true the accusations of an informant unless some good reason for doing so has been established." The *Aguilar-Spinelli* two-pronged inquiry has proven a satisfactory method of providing reasonable assurance that probable cause determinations are based on information derived from a credible source with firsthand information, and we are not convinced that the *Gates* test offers a satisfactory alternative.

The reasons advanced by the People in support of the *Gates* test are similar to those enunciated by the Supreme Court itself in *Illinois v. Gates*. They contend that the less stringent *Gates* test will encourage the use of warrants, a highly desirable goal. They assert that the *Aguilar-Spinelli* test has been applied in a rigid, inflexible manner to the detriment of law enforcement. The commonsense approach of *Gates*, posit the People, is a more reasonable rule of law, since the hypertechnical two-prong test places an unnecessary burden on law enforcement officers who are not lawyers, but rather public officials "acting under stress and often within the context of a volatile situation."

Although we agree with the People that the use of warrants should be encouraged, there is no reason to believe that police will refrain from obtaining a warrant merely because this State continues to apply the *Aguilar-Spinelli* test. With limited exceptions, carefully circumscribed by our courts, it is always incumbent upon the police to obtain a warrant before conducting a search. Furthermore, whether there was probable cause will generally be raised by the defendant at a suppression hearing. If a Magistrate has already determined that probable cause existed, great deference will be accorded that finding, resulting in far fewer suppression problems. This, in turn, results in a more efficient use of police resources; it is indeed wasteful to make an arrest or conduct a search without a warrant only to have those efforts invalidated by a suppression court.

Nor is the *Aguilar-Spinelli* test a hypertechnical approach to evaluating hearsay information. As we stated in *People v. Hanlon* (N.Y. 1975), "in the real world, we are confronted with search warrant applications which are generally not composed by lawyers in the quiet of a law library but rather by law enforcement officers who are acting under stress and often within the context of a volatile situation. Consequently such search warrant applications should not be read in a hypertechnical manner as if they were entries in an essay contest. On the contrary, they must be considered in the clear light of everyday experience and accorded all reasonable inferences."

In *People v. Johnson*, we recognized that the more structured "bright line" *Aguilar-Spinelli* test better served the highly desirable "aims of predictability and precision in judicial review of search and seizure cases," and that "the protection of the individual rights of our citizens is best promoted by applying State constitutional standards." We find this reasoning equally persuasive in cases involving search warrants. Given the deference paid to the Magistrate's probable cause finding, and given the somewhat subjective nature of the probable cause inquiry, the aims of predictability and precision are again well served by providing the Magistrate with *Aguilar-Spinelli's* concrete, structured guidelines. More importantly, this will also prevent the disturbance of the rights of privacy and liberty upon the word of an unreliable hearsay informant, a danger we perceive under the *Gates* totality-of-the-circumstances test.

STATE v. TUTTLE
515 S.W.3d 282 (Tenn. 2017)

CLARK, J.

We granted the State's appeal primarily to determine whether the intermediate appellate court erred in finding the search warrant affidavit insufficient to establish probable cause, and in doing so, to revisit the continuing vitality of *State v. Jacumin* (Tenn. 1989). In *Jacumin*, this Court refused to follow *Illinois v. Gates* (1983), which adopted a totality-of-the-circumstances analysis for determining whether an affidavit establishes probable cause for a search warrant, and instead embraced, as a matter of Tennessee constitutional law, another test derived from two earlier United States Supreme Court decisions, *Aguilar v. Texas* (1964) and *Spinelli v. United States* (1969). For the reasons explained herein, we overrule *Jacumin* and adopt the totality-of-the-circumstances analysis for determining whether an affidavit establishes probable cause for issuance of a warrant under Article I, section 7 of the Tennessee Constitution.

In 2012, the Maury County Grand Jury returned two separate indictments charging the defendant, Jerry Lewis Tuttle, with multiple offenses in connection with a drug trafficking conspiracy. The indictments were issued after officers executed a search warrant on April 24, 2012, for property located at 4571 Dugger Road, Culleoka, Tennessee, in Maury County. The property consisted of "5.77 acres," and the defendant resided in a mobile home on the property with his wife, Tammy A. Tuttle, who was the record owner of the property. The warrant authorized officers to search the defendant's "single wide mobile home gray in color with an attached wood constructed covered front porch" and "all outbuildings, outhouses and storage buildings, and all vehicles found thereon." Officers were authorized to seize "marijuana, all equipment, devices, records, computers and computer storage discs used for the purpose of producing, packaging, dispensing, delivering or obtaining controlled substances, or recording transactions involving controlled substances, and any indicia of ownership, dominion, or control over the premises to be searched."

When the warrant was executed, officers found, inside the residence, eight pounds of marijuana, almost a half an ounce of cocaine, and between $95,000 and $98,000 cash, in $100 and $50 bills, as well as multiple guns, a large scale capable of weighing items up to thirteen pounds, a small scale capable of weighing items up to two pounds, a money counter, a device used to grind marijuana into a powder, and a pipe and other items associated with smoking marijuana. Just outside the residence in the trunk of the defendant's Honda Civic, officers located a number of additional guns and an ammunition can containing $1,000,300 cash, all in $100 bills that were issued prior to the year 2000. Officers also located marijuana plants growing in an Igloo cooler and various items of personal property, including vehicles and farming equipment, believed to be derived from the defendant's involvement in drug trafficking.

Trooper Shawn Boyd, a Tennessee Highway Patrol officer, prepared the April 23, 2012 affidavit that resulted in the issuance of the April 24, 2012 search warrant allowing officers to search the 4571 Dugger Road property. When he prepared the affidavit, Trooper Boyd had worked as a THP officer for ten years and had been assigned to the Nashville Drug Enforcement Agency Task Force for two years.

At the pretrial suppression hearing, the defendant argued that the affidavit failed to establish probable cause because it lacked sufficient facts to establish a nexus between the drugs and the defendant's residence on the 4571 Dugger Road property.

In Tennessee, probable cause for issuance of a warrant is established by presenting "a sworn and written affidavit" to the magistrate. "To ensure that the magistrate exercises independent judgment, the affidavit must contain more than mere conclusory allegations by the affiant." The affidavit must include facts from which the neutral and detached magistrate may determine, upon examining the affidavit in a commonsense and practical manner, whether probable cause exists. When the affidavit seeks to establish probable cause for a search warrant, it must "set forth facts from which a reasonable conclusion might be drawn that the evidence is in the place to be searched." In other words, the affidavit must demonstrate a nexus between the criminal activity, the place to be searched, and the items to be seized. "The nexus between the place to be searched and the items to be seized may be established by the type of crime, the nature of the items, and the normal inferences where a criminal would hide the evidence."

This two-pronged test derives from two United States Supreme Court decisions—*Aguilar v. Texas* and *Spinelli v. United States*. However, in 1983 the United States Supreme Court abandoned the *Aguilar/Spinelli* test and adopted a totality-of-the-circumstances analysis for determining whether an affidavit that includes information from a criminal informant establishes probable cause. Six years after *Gates*, however, this Court declined to follow *Gates* and chose to retain the *Aguilar/Spinelli* test as a matter of Tennessee constitutional law. In the order granting the State's application for permission to appeal in this case, we directed the parties to brief and argue the issue of "whether this Court should revisit the continuing vitality of *State v. Jacumin*." We now take this opportunity to do so.

In *Aguilar*, the United States Supreme Court held that the magistrate reviewing a search warrant affidavit "must be informed of some of the underlying circumstances from which the informant concluded that the narcotics were where he claimed they were, and some of the underlying circumstances from which the officer concluded that the informant, whose identity need not be disclosed, was credible or his information reliable." Five years later, in *Spinelli*, the Supreme Court reiterated these requirements, but added that these prongs could be established through corroborating evidence. Therefore, under the *Aguilar/Spinelli* test the affidavit must include facts from which the magistrate may determine the informant's "basis of knowledge" and "veracity" or credibility, and if the information provided fails to establish either prong, corroborating evidence may make up the deficit.

The first prong of the *Aguilar/Spinelli* test—"basis of knowledge, is concerned with the question, how did the informant get the information? Its purpose is to prevent warrants from being issued based on conjecture or rumors. Generally speaking, facts and circumstances indicating that the information came from an informant who had obtained the information first-hand or by personal observation will satisfy this prong." This prong may also be satisfied when the informant provides "highly detailed" information "such that the magistrate could know that the informant was relating something more than casual rumor or reputation." The second prong of the test, veracity or credibility, "may be satisfied either by (1) demonstrating the informant's credibility or (2) by showing that the information is reliable." In other words, "the affiant must provide some concrete reason why the magistrate should believe the informant," although the "requisite volume or detail of information needed to establish the informant's credibility is not particularly great." Nevertheless, "each prong represents an independently important consideration that must be separately considered and satisfied or supplemented in some way."

The *Gates* Court rejected the proposition (embraced by *Jacumin*) "that these elements should be understood as entirely separate and independent requirements to be rigidly exacted in every case." The *Gates* Court held that *Aguilar* and *Spinelli* had been misinterpreted and applied in an overly rigid fashion. The Supreme Court declared that "rigid legal rules" are "ill-suited" to evaluate informants' tips, which, "like all other clues and evidence coming to a policeman on the scene, may vary greatly in their value and reliability." The *Gates* Court commented that the *Aguilar/Spinelli* test "had encouraged an excessively technical dissection of informants' tips, with undue attention being focused on isolated issues that cannot sensibly be divorced from the other facts presented to the magistrate."

The *Gates* Court theorized that "the type of scrutiny some courts had deemed appropriate" under the *Aguilar/Spinelli* test could actually discourage police officers from attempting to obtain warrants and encourage them to "resort to warrantless searches, with the hope of relying on consent or some other exception to the warrant clause that might develop at the time of the search." As a result, the *Gates* Court posited that the *Aguilar/Spinelli* test had served to frustrate the Court's preference for the warrant process, which was reflected in the standard of appellate review—whether the magistrate had a substantial basis for concluding that a search would uncover evidence of wrongdoing. "The rigorous inquiry" and "complex superstructure of evidentiary and analytical rules" that had developed around the two-pronged test could not be reconciled with the reality that "many warrants are—quite properly—issued on the basis of nontechnical, commonsense judgments of laymen applying a standard less demanding than those used in more formal legal proceedings."

The *Gates* Court also opined that the *Aguilar/Spinelli* test, when applied rigidly, "poorly served" the government's most basic function of providing for the security of individual citizens and property because an "anonymous tip seldom could survive a rigorous application" of the two-pronged test, even though "such tips, particularly when supplemented by independent police investigation, frequently contribute to the solution of otherwise perfect crimes." "While a conscientious assessment of the basis for crediting such tips is required by the Fourth Amendment, a standard that leaves virtually no place for anonymous citizen informants is not."

The *Gates* Court emphasized, however, "that an informant's veracity, reliability and basis of knowledge" remain "highly relevant in determining the value of his report" under the totality-of-the-circumstances analysis but "should be understood simply as closely intertwined issues that may usefully illuminate the commonsense, practical question whether there is probable cause to believe that contraband or evidence is located in a particular place."

> The task of the issuing magistrate is simply to make a practical, commonsense decision whether, given all the circumstances set forth in the affidavit before him, including the "veracity" and "basis of knowledge" of persons supplying hearsay information, there is a fair probability that contraband or evidence of a crime will be found in a particular place. And the duty of a reviewing court is simply to ensure that the magistrate had a substantial basis for concluding that probable cause existed.

The *Gates* Court was "convinced that this flexible, easily applied standard" would "better achieve the accommodation of public and private interests" required by the Fourth Amendment.

In declining six years later to follow *Gates*, the *Jacumin* Court characterized the totality-of-the-circumstances test as "inadequate as a test of probable cause." It held that the *Aguilar/Spinelli* standard, "if not applied hypertechnically," provides "a more appropriate structure for probable cause inquiries incident to the issuance of a search warrant than does *Gates*," and concluded that the *Aguilar/Spinelli* standard is "more in keeping with the specific requirement of Article I, section 7 of the Tennessee Constitution that a search warrant not issue without evidence of the fact committed." The *Jacumin* Court acknowledged that Article I, section 7 of the Tennessee Constitution had previously been interpreted as "identical in intent and purpose" with the Fourth Amendment and that the Court of Criminal Appeals had already applied *Gates* in several decisions. The *Jacumin* Court justified its decision to part company with *Gates* by referring to prior Tennessee decisions interpreting the open fields doctrine under the state constitution as "somewhat more restrictive than federal cases," and by pointing out that courts in a few other states, specifically Alaska, Massachusetts, Washington, and New York, also had declined to adopt the totality-of-the-circumstances analysis on state constitutional law grounds, describing it as "unacceptably shapeless and permissive," and "nebulous." Nevertheless, in subsequent decisions applying the *Aguilar/Spinelli* standard, this Court, like the *Gates* Court, has emphasized the role of corroboration:

> The credibility of the informant's information may also be buttressed by independent corroboration of its details. However, it is not necessary to corroborate every detail of the informant's information, or to "directly link the suspect to the commission of the crime." Corroboration of "only innocent aspects of the story" may suffice.

The overwhelming majority of states now apply the *Gates* totality-of-the-circumstances analysis for determining whether an affidavit establishes probable cause for issuance of a search warrant. Indeed, Tennessee is one of only a handful of states that still applies the two-pronged *Aguilar/Spinelli* test as a matter of state statutory or constitutional law. Having now reconsidered both tests, we conclude that the time has come to abandon the rigid *Aguilar/Spinelli* test and adopt the *Gates* totality-of-the-circumstances analysis. Overruling *Jacumin* and adopting the *Gates* totality-of-the-circumstances test is warranted for several reasons. First, the *Aguilar/Spinelli* test is often applied too rigidly. The decision of the intermediate appellate court in this appeal exemplifies the type of hypertechnical application that this Court warned against in *Jacumin*. For example, Mr. Davis, the criminal informant, described the drug trafficking organization (DTO) with which the defendant's son was involved, explained the basis of his own knowledge by admitting that he, too, had been involved with the same DTO, described the type and amount of drugs and the frequency of shipments to Tuttle's son, identified Tuttle's son from his driver's license photograph, provided law enforcement with the son's nickname, "Red," described the son's vehicle, described the area where the son resided near Nashville, and stated that the whole Tuttle family was involved in drug trafficking. Rather than seeking a search warrant based solely on the information Mr. Davis provided, law enforcement officials corroborated, in some fashion, almost every aspect of the information, including Mr. Davis's involvement with the DTO, the DTO's Tennessee client known as Red, the type of vehicle Tuttle's son drove, the location of his residence, the son's meetings with agents of the DTO near the 4571 Dugger Road property, at which Tuttle's son had previously concealed cash derived from the illegal drug trade, and even the family's previous involvement in the son's earlier drug trafficking activities.

Second, unlike the *Jacumin* Court, we have the benefit of years of experience applying *Jacumin* and have had the opportunity to review numerous cases from other jurisdictions applying *Gates*. Time has proven that the totality-of-the-circumstances analysis is not inadequate or too nebulous as a test for determining probable cause. Under *Gates*, "an informant's veracity, reliability, and basis of knowledge" remain "highly relevant in determining the value of his report." But by ensuring that these factors are not viewed as entirely separate prerequisites to probable cause, requiring rigid, formulistic, and technical analysis, *Gates* actually improves upon the *Aguilar/Spinelli* test.

Moreover, as the *Gates* Court explained, the totality-of-the-circumstances analysis is much more consistent with the nontechnical, commonsense approach courts already apply when determining whether probable cause exists. Indeed, although the *Jacumin* Court retained the *Aguilar/Spinelli* test, it expressly embraced the manner in which the *Gates* Court described the role of the magistrate in assessing probable cause, and we have reaffirmed this standard as the governing law in Tennessee.

Finally, it is certainly true, as the *Jacumin* Court recognized, that this Court has the authority to interpret the Tennessee Constitution differently than the federal constitution and has recognized that textual differences between federal and state constitutional provisions may support doing so. It is also true, as the *Jacumin* Court pointed out, that the text of Article I, section 7 differs from the text of the Fourth Amendment by precluding issuance of a warrant "without evidence of the fact committed." However, the *Jacumin* Court failed to recognize that the Fourth Amendment has also been interpreted as precluding issuance of a warrant unless facts, rather than conclusions, are presented to a magistrate to establish probable cause. Indeed, the *Gates* Court expressly reaffirmed this principle, stating, "sufficient information must be presented to the magistrate to allow that official to determine probable cause; his action cannot be a mere ratification of the bare conclusions of others." Therefore, over time the Fourth Amendment has been interpreted by federal courts in a manner that is entirely consistent with the text of Article I, section 7.

For all these reasons, we overrule *Jacumin*, insofar as it retained the *Aguilar/Spinelli* test, and adopt the *Gates* totality-of-the-circumstances analysis, which is, in our judgment and that of the vast majority of courts in other states, a sufficiently definite standard for assessing probable cause and much better suited to evaluating the practicalities that underlie the probable cause inquiry. We reiterate that, under the totality-of-the-circumstances analysis, the informant's basis of knowledge and veracity or credibility remain highly relevant considerations. Rather than separate and independent considerations, they "should be understood simply as closely intertwined issues that may usefully illuminate the commonsense, practical question whether there is probable cause to believe that contraband or evidence is located in a particular place." Thus, we will apply the *Gates* test to determine whether the affidavit sufficiently established probable cause for issuance of the warrant.

NOTES

1. The overwhelming majority of states now use the *Gates* totality-of-the-circumstances analysis for determining whether an affidavit establishes probable cause for issuance of a search warrant.

2. States that retain, as a matter of state law, the *Aguilar/Spinelli* test or a variant thereof include Alaska, Hawaii, Massachusetts, New Mexico, New York, Oregon, Vermont, and Washington.

3. The warrants clauses in the constitutions of Massachusetts, New Hampshire, and Vermont do not explicitly mention probable clause. *See* Mass. Const. pt. 1, art. XIV; N.H. Const. pt. 1, art. XIX; Vt. Const. ch. I, art. XI.

C. GOOD FAITH EXCEPTION TO WARRANT REQUIREMENT

STATE v. KOIVU
272 P.3d 483 (Idaho 2012)

EISMANN, J.

This is an appeal asking that we overrule *State v. Guzman* (Idaho 1992) and hold that the *Leon* good-faith exception to the exclusionary rule applies to violations of Article I, section 17, of the Idaho Constitution. Because the State has not shown any ground for doing so, we decline to overrule that case and affirm the order of the district court suppressing evidence obtained incident to an arrest pursuant to a wrongly issued warrant.

Randy Koivu was charged with the crime of possession of methamphetamine in Boundary County. He was found guilty of that crime, and on January 6, 2004, the district court sentenced him to five years in the custody of the Idaho Board of Correction, with three years fixed and two years indeterminate. The court suspended that sentence and placed Defendant on probation for four years. The terms of probation included that Defendant pay a fine of $500.00, court costs of $88.50, public defender reimbursement of $300.00, and restitution of $100.00. Defendant later violated the terms of his probation, and on November 1, 2005, the court entered an order revoking his probation and committing him to the custody of the Idaho Board of Correction. Defendant was released from prison on July 2, 2009.

On March 5, 2010, two sheriff deputies in neighboring Bonner County lawfully stopped a car for speeding. Defendant was the driver of the car. In running a background check of Defendant, the officers were informed that there was a warrant for his arrest out of Boundary County. Reasonably relying upon the validity of the warrant, the deputies arrested Defendant and transported him to the Bonner County jail. Defendant was arrested only because of the warrant; he could not have been arrested for speeding. While searching Defendant at the jail, a baggie of methamphetamine was discovered near his feet.

Article I, section 17, of the Idaho Constitution provides, "The right of the people to be secure in their persons, houses, papers and effects against unreasonable searches and seizures shall not be violated; and no warrant shall issue without probable cause shown by affidavit, particularly describing the place to be searched and the person or thing to be seized." The Idaho Constitution does not specify the remedy for a violation of this provision, nor does the Fourth Amendment to the Constitution of the United States.

In *Weeks v. United States* (1914), the United States Supreme Court held for the first time that evidence wrongfully seized by the federal government in violation of a criminal defendant's Fourth Amendment rights could not be used as evidence in the ensuing criminal prosecution. The Court stated that if evidence seized in violation of a defendant's Fourth Amendment rights could be used against him in a criminal prosecution, the protection of the Fourth Amendment would be of no value and it might as well be stricken from the Constitution.

> If letters and private documents can thus be seized and held and used in evidence against a citizen accused of an offense, the protection of the 4th Amendment, declaring his right to be secure against such searches and seizures, is of no value, and, so far as those thus placed are concerned, might as well be stricken from the Constitution. The efforts of the courts and their officials to bring the guilty to punishment, praiseworthy as they are, are not to be aided by the sacrifice of those great principles established by years of endeavor and suffering which have resulted in their embodiment in the fundamental law of the land.

However, the Court held that the Fourth Amendment did not apply to searches and seizures by city police because "its limitations reach the Federal government and its agencies."

Three and one-half decades later, the Court decided that the Fourth Amendment should apply to the States, and it used the Due Process Clause of the Fourteenth Amendment as the vehicle for doing so. *Wolf v. Colorado* (1949). However, the *Wolf* Court left to the individual States the right to decide whether exclusion of evidence or some other remedy should apply to Fourth Amendment violations. Thus, the Court held "that in a prosecution in a State court for a State crime the Fourteenth Amendment does not forbid the admission of evidence obtained by an unreasonable search and seizure." Under *Wolf*, the Fourth Amendment did not require any particular remedy for its violation. The Court stated that the exclusionary rule announced in *Weeks* "was not derived from the explicit requirements of the Fourth Amendment. The decision was a matter of judicial implication."

Twelve years later, the Court decided that the exclusionary rule should apply to the States. In *Mapp v. Ohio* (1961), the Court held that: (a) "extending the substantive protections of due process to all constitutionally unreasonable searches—state and federal—was logically and constitutionally necessary," (b) "to hold otherwise is to grant the right but in reality to withhold its privilege and enjoyment," and (c) "the exclusionary rule is an essential part of both the Fourth and Fourteenth Amendments." The Court also stated that reasons for extending the exclusionary rule to the states, included: (a) "the imperative of judicial integrity," (b) "nothing can destroy a government more quickly than its failure to observe its own laws, or worse, its disregard of the charter of its own existence," and (c) "it cannot lightly be assumed that, as a practical matter, adoption of the exclusionary rule fetters law enforcement." The *Mapp* Court held that the exclusionary rule was required by the Fourth Amendment. It stated, "The striking outcome of the *Weeks* case and those which followed it was the sweeping declaration that the Fourth Amendment, although not referring to or limiting the use of evidence in court, really forbade its introduction if obtained by government officers through a violation of the amendment." Thus, in *Mapp* the Court reversed direction and held that the exclusionary rule was a personal constitutional right.

The Court's view of the exclusionary rule later changed again. In *Stone v. Powell* (1976), the Court held that the exclusionary rule "is not a personal constitutional right," nor is it "calculated to redress the injury to the privacy of the victim of the search or seizure." Rather, "the primary justification for the exclusionary rule is the deterrence of police conduct that violates Fourth Amendment rights."

In *United States v. Leon* (1984), the Court adopted what became known as the *Leon* "good-faith" exception to the exclusionary rule under the Fourth Amendment. In *Leon*, the police had seized evidence acting in reasonable reliance on a search warrant, but the warrant was later determined to have been issued without probable cause. The Court held that the exclusionary rule would not apply to evidence obtained in objectively reasonable reliance on a subsequently invalidated search warrant. The Court also held that "the exclusionary rule is designed to deter police misconduct rather than to punish the errors of judges and magistrates."

The Court has since expanded the good-faith exception to include a search conducted in reasonable reliance upon a subsequently invalidated statute because legislators, like judges, are not the focus of the rule, *Illinois v. Krull* (1987); an arrest in reasonable reliance upon information that the arrestee had an outstanding warrant, where the warrant had been quashed but the court clerk had failed to notify the sheriff's office, because applying the exclusionary rule would not deter mistakes made by court employees, *Arizona v. Evans* (1995); an arrest in reasonable reliance upon the existence of an outstanding arrest warrant where the officer did not know that the warrant had been recalled due to the negligent failure of a sheriff's employee to update the computer database, *Herring v. United States* (2009); and to a search conducted in objectively reasonable reliance upon binding judicial precedent that was later overruled, *Davis v. United States* (2011).

In *Guzman*, the police had obtained evidence pursuant to a search warrant that was later declared invalid because the supporting affidavit alleged only conclusory statements of fact. The trial court applied the good-faith exception under *Leon* and refused to suppress the evidence. This Court declined to apply the good-faith exception to the exclusionary rule under Article I, section 17, of the Idaho Constitution. However, a majority did not agree upon the reasons for doing so. Justice Bistline, the author of *Guzman*, set forth his reasons for applying the exclusionary rule in Part V(A) of his opinion and his criticisms of the *Leon* good-faith exception in Parts V(B) and V(C). Justice Johnson concurred in Part V(A), while Justice McDevitt only concurred in the result in Part V. Chief Justice Bakes dissented, and Justice Boyle did not participate due to his resignation. Therefore, a majority rejected the good-faith exception, but a majority did not agree upon the reasons for doing so. Later, a unanimous Court stated that the Court had rejected applying the *Leon* good-faith exception to Article I, section 17, and that the *Guzman* decision would be applied retroactively to all cases that had not become final when *Guzman* was issued.

The State now asks us to revisit the *Leon* good-faith exception and overrule *Guzman*. We would also have to overrule *State v. Arregui* (Idaho 1927) and *State v. Rauch* (Idaho 1978) to the extent that they held that there were reasons supporting the exclusionary rule other than deterring unconstitutional searches and seizures that the law enforcement officers did not reasonably believe were lawful. We will ordinarily not overrule one of our prior opinions unless it is shown to have been manifestly wrong, or the holding in the case has proven over time to be unwise or unjust.

The State also asserts that "a review of the authority relied upon by the *Guzman* plurality does not support its analysis or results." It argues that "those cases clearly show that Idaho's exclusionary rule is co-extensive with the exclusionary rule as adopted and applied by the United States Supreme Court."

There is absolutely nothing in *Arregui* or any other authority relied upon by the *Guzman* Court that commits this Court to construe or apply Article I, section 17, in the same manner as the United States Supreme Court construes or applies the Fourth Amendment. "The Fourth Amendment and art. 1, section 17 are designed to protect a person's legitimate expectation of privacy, which society is prepared to recognize as reasonable." The similarity of language and purpose, however, does not require this Court to follow United States Supreme Court precedent in interpreting our own constitution." "Long gone are the days when state courts will blindly apply United States Supreme Court interpretation and methodology when in the process of interpreting their own constitutions."

The exclusionary rule is a judicially created remedy for searches and seizures that violate the Constitution. As shown above, courts have disagreed over the years as to whether there should be any remedy for such constitutional violations and, if so, whether it should focus upon redressing the wrong committed against the victim of the unconstitutional search or seizure or only upon deterring future violations of such constitutional rights by law enforcement officials. The holding in *Guzman* was that evidence obtained from a defendant pursuant to a warrant will not be admissible in the defendant's criminal trial if the warrant was issued without probable cause in violation of the Constitution. That holding is not manifestly wrong. It is identical to the holding in *Arregui* and is consistent with the holdings of other courts, including the United States Supreme Court.

The State contends that "the second flaw of Guzman is its contention that the *Leon* good-faith exception to the exclusionary rule is inimical to the values of exclusion unrelated to police deterrence." The State then argues why the *Leon* Court was right and the *Guzman* plurality was wrong. It also asserts that application of the exclusionary rule here would not deter police misconduct because the officers involved simply did what they were required to do—execute an arrest warrant.

This Court's rejection of the *Leon* good-faith exception in *Guzman* was supported by an independent exclusionary rule announced eighty-five years ago in *Arregui*. In *Arregui*, there was no claim of law enforcement misconduct. The officers relied upon the validity of a search warrant that was later held to be invalid due to the lack of a showing of probable cause in the affidavit upon which the warrant was issued. Likewise, in *State v. Oropeza* (Idaho 1976), evidence was suppressed for the same reason. When *Guzman* was decided, "Idaho had clearly developed an exclusionary rule as a constitutionally mandated remedy for illegal searches and seizures in addition to other purposes behind the rule such as recognizing the exclusionary rule as a deterrent for police misconduct."

In some instances, we have construed Article I, section 17, to provide greater protection than is provided by the United States Supreme Court's construction of the Fourth Amendment. "We provided greater protection to Idaho citizens based on the uniqueness of our state, our Constitution, and our long-standing jurisprudence." To overrule *Guzman* and hold that the exclusionary rule's sole purpose is to deter police misconduct, we would also have to overrule *Arregui*, which adopted the exclusionary rule in Idaho in a case in which there was no police misconduct. The State has not pointed to anything in the record showing that during the last eighty-five years *Arregui* has proved to be unwise or unjust. We therefore uphold the district court's order holding that the methamphetamine is not admissible into evidence because the Defendant's arrest pursuant to an invalid warrant of attachment violated his rights under Article I, section 17, of the Idaho Constitution.

COMMONWEALTH v. EDMUNDS
586 A.2d 887 (Pa. 1991)

CAPPY, J.

The issue presented to this court is whether Pennsylvania should adopt the "good faith" exception to the exclusionary rule as articulated by the United States Supreme Court in the case of *United States v. Leon* (1984). We conclude that a "good faith" exception to the exclusionary rule would frustrate the guarantees embodied in article I, section 8 of the Pennsylvania Constitution. Accordingly, the decision of the Superior Court is reversed.

The defendant in the instant case was found guilty after a non-jury trial on August 18, 1987, of criminal conspiracy, simple possession, possession with intent to deliver, possession with intent to manufacture and manufacture of a controlled substance. The conviction was premised upon the admission into evidence of marijuana seized at the defendant's property pursuant to a search warrant, after information was received from two anonymous informants.

The trial court held that the search warrant failed to establish probable cause that the marijuana would be at the location to be searched on the date it was issued. The trial court found that the warrant failed to set forth with specificity the date upon which the anonymous informants observed the marijuana. However, the trial court went on to deny the defendant's motion to suppress the marijuana. Applying the rationale of *Leon*, the trial court looked beyond the four corners of the affidavit, in order to establish that the officers executing the warrant acted in "good faith" in relying upon the warrant to conduct the search. In reaching this conclusion the trial court also decided that *Leon* permitted the court to undercut the language of Pennsylvania Rule of Criminal Procedure 2003, which prohibits oral testimony outside the four corners of the written affidavit to supplement the finding of probable cause.

Rule 2003 provides in relevant part:

(a) No search warrant shall issue but upon probable cause supported by one or more affidavits sworn to before the issuing authority. The issuing authority, in determining whether probable cause has been established, may not consider any evidence outside the affidavits.

(b) At any hearing on a motion for the return or suppression of evidence, or for the suppression of the fruits of the evidence obtained pursuant to a search warrant, no evidence shall be admissible to establish probable cause other than the affidavits provided for in paragraph (a).

The Superior Court in a divided panel decision affirmed the judgment of the trial court, specifically relying upon the decision of the United States Supreme Court in *Leon*. Allocatur was granted by this Court.

The pertinent facts can be briefly summarized as follows. On August 5, 1985, State Police Trooper Michael Deise obtained a warrant from a district magistrate to search a white corrugated building and curtilage on the property of the defendant. As the affidavit of probable cause is central to our decision, we will set it forth in full:

On the date of August 4, 1985, this affiant Michael D. Deise, Penna. State Police, was in contact by telephone with two anonymous Males who were and are members of the community where Louis R. Edmunds resides. Both anonymous males advised the affiant that while checking out familiar hunting areas off Rte. 31, east of Jones Mills and along the south side of Rte. 31. These men observed growing marijuana near a white corrugated building approximately 20 x 40 feet in a cleared off area. These men looked into the building and observed several plants that appeared to be marijuana. This affiant questioned both of these men as to their knowledge of marijuana. This affiant learned that one of these men saw growing marijuana numerous times while he was stationed in Viet Nam. The other male saw growing marijuana while at a police station. This affiant described a growing marijuana plant and its characteristics and they agreed that what they had viewed agreed with the description and also that it appeared to them to be marijuana as fully described by the affiant. The two males wish to remain anonymous for fear of retaliation or bodily harm. An anonymous male advised this affiant that Louis R. Edmunds lived there. Edmund's description being that of a white male in his middle thirties and he lived at the aforementioned location.

On the 5th of August, 1985, this affiant with the use of a State Police helicopter, flew over the described location and observed the white corrugated building in the mountain area and located as described by the two males. Also on this date this affiant drove past the Rte. 31 entrance and observed a mail box with "Edmunds 228" printed on it.

After obtaining the warrant from the local magistrate, Trooper Deise, accompanied by three other troopers, served the warrant upon the defendant at his residence. Though he did not place the defendant under arrest at this time, the trooper did advise him of his *Miranda* rights, and had him read the warrant. The trooper also explained to the defendant that the warrant was not for his residence, although the warrant itself included the residence. Rather, the trooper stated that the warrant was meant to relate to the white corrugated building, and that they were searching for marijuana in that building.

After producing the lease which indicated that the white corrugated building was in fact leased to Thomas Beacon, the defendant accompanied the troopers to the building, which was approximately one-quarter of a mile away, up a steep mountainous terrain, on a separate parcel of property owned by Edmunds. The record is devoid of evidence that there was marijuana growing outside the corrugated building. The defendant unlocked the door of the white building and entered with the troopers. Inside the building the troopers discovered seventeen growing marijuana plants, along with gardening implements, high-wattage lights, and a watering system. The marijuana was seized and the charges as recited above were brought against the defendant.

As a preliminary matter, we concur with the inevitable conclusion of the trial court and the Superior Court that probable cause did not exist on the face of the warrant. In *Commonwealth v. Conner* (Pa. 1973), this Court made clear that a search warrant is defective if it is issued without reference to the time when the informant obtained his or her information. Coupled with Rule 2003, which mandates that courts in Pennsylvania shall not consider oral testimony outside the four corners of the written affidavit to supplement the finding of probable cause for a search warrant, we are compelled to conclude that the affidavit of probable cause and warrant were facially invalid. As the Superior Court candidly stated, the affidavit in question "did not contain facts from which the date of the hunters' observations could be determined."

The sole question in this case, therefore, is whether the Constitution of Pennsylvania incorporates a "good faith" exception to the exclusionary rule, which permits the introduction of evidence seized where probable cause is lacking on the face of the warrant.

Put in other terms, the question is whether the federal *Leon* test circumvents the acknowledged deficiencies under Pennsylvania law, and prevents the suppression of evidence seized pursuant to an *invalid search warrant*. For the reasons that follow, we conclude that it does not.

Our starting point must be the decision of the United States Supreme Court in *Leon*. In *Leon*, the Supreme Court in 1984 departed from a long history of exclusionary rule jurisprudence dating back to *Weeks v. United States* (1914) and *Mapp v. Ohio* (1961). The Court in *Leon* concluded that the Fourth Amendment does not mandate suppression of illegally seized evidence obtained pursuant to a constitutionally defective warrant, so long as the police officer acted in good faith reliance upon the warrant issued by a neutral and detached magistrate.

We must now determine whether the good-faith exception to the exclusionary rule is properly part of the jurisprudence of this

Commonwealth, by virtue of article 1, section 8 of the Pennsylvania Constitution. In concluding that it is not, we set forth a methodology to be followed in analyzing future state constitutional issues which arise under our own Constitution.

This Court has long emphasized that, in interpreting a provision of the Pennsylvania Constitution, we are not bound by the decisions of the United States Supreme Court which interpret similar (yet distinct) federal constitutional provisions.

As Mr. Chief Justice Nix aptly stated in *Commonwealth v. Sell* (1983), the federal constitution establishes certain minimum levels which are "equally applicable to the state constitutional provision." However, each state has the power to provide broader standards, and go beyond the minimum floor which is established by the federal Constitution.

The United States Supreme Court has repeatedly affirmed that the states are not only free to, but also encouraged to engage in independent analysis in drawing meaning from their own state constitutions. Indeed, this is a positive expression of the jurisprudence which has existed in the United States since the founding of the nation. Alexander Hamilton, lobbying for the ratification of the United States Constitution in the Federalist Papers over two hundred years ago, made clear that the Supremacy Clause of the Federal Constitution was never designed to overshadow the states, or prevent them from maintaining their own pockets of autonomy.

Here in Pennsylvania, we have stated with increasing frequency that it is both important and necessary that we undertake an independent analysis of the Pennsylvania Constitution each time a provision of that fundamental document is implicated. Although we may accord weight to federal decisions where they "are found to be logically persuasive and well reasoned, paying due regard to precedent and the policies underlying specific constitutional guarantees," we are free to reject the conclusions of the United States Supreme Court so long as we remain faithful to the minimum guarantees established by the United States Constitution.

The recent focus on the "New Federalism" has emphasized the importance of state constitutions with respect to individual rights and criminal procedure. As such, we find it important to set forth certain factors to be briefed and analyzed by litigants in each case hereafter implicating a provision of the Pennsylvania constitution. The decision of the United States Supreme Court in *Michigan v. Long* (1983), now requires us to make a "plain statement" of the adequate and independent state grounds upon which we rely, in order to avoid any doubt that we have rested our decision squarely upon Pennsylvania jurisprudence. Accordingly, as a general rule, it is important that litigants brief and analyze at least the following four factors: (1) text of the Pennsylvania constitutional provision; (2) history of the provision, including Pennsylvania case law; (3) related case law from other states; (4) policy considerations, including unique issues of state and local concern, and applicability within modern Pennsylvania jurisprudence.

Depending upon the particular issue presented, an examination of related federal precedent may be useful as part of the state constitutional analysis, not as binding authority, but as one form of guidance. However, it is essential that courts in Pennsylvania undertake an independent analysis under the Pennsylvania Constitution. Utilizing the above four factors, and having reviewed *Leon*, we conclude that a "good faith" exception to the exclusionary rule would frustrate the guarantees embodied in article I, section 8 of our Commonwealth's constitution.

The text of article 1, section 8 of the Pennsylvania Constitution provides as follows:

> The people shall be secure in their persons, houses, papers and possessions from unreasonable searches and seizures, and no warrant to search any place or to seize any person or things shall issue without describing them as nearly as may be, nor without probable cause, supported by oath or affirmation subscribed to by the affiant.

Although the wording of the Pennsylvania Constitution is similar in language to the Fourth Amendment of the United States Constitution, we are not bound to interpret the two provisions as if they were mirror images, even where the text is similar or identical. Thus, we must next examine the history of article I, section 8, in order to draw meaning from that provision and consider the appropriateness of a "good faith" exception to the exclusionary rule in the Pennsylvania constitutional scheme.

We have made reference, on repeated occasions, to the unique history of article 1, section 8, as well as other provisions of the Pennsylvania Constitution. As we noted in *Sell*: "Constitutional protection against unreasonable searches and seizures existed in Pennsylvania more than a decade before the adoption of the federal Constitution, and fifteen years prior to the promulgation of the Fourth Amendment."

Perhaps the extent of the untapped history of the Pennsylvania Constitution should be underscored. Pennsylvania's Constitution was adopted on September 28, 1776, a full ten years prior to the ratification of the United States Constitution. Like the constitutions of Virginia, New Jersey, Maryland, and most of the original 13 Colonies, Pennsylvania's Constitution was drafted in the midst of the American Revolution, as the first overt expression of independence from the British Crown. The Pennsylvania Constitution was therefore meant to reduce to writing a deep history of unwritten legal and moral codes which had guided the colonists from the beginning of William Penn's charter in 1681. Unlike the Bill of Rights of the United States Constitution which emerged as a later addendum in 1791, the Declaration of Rights in the Pennsylvania Constitution was an organic part of the state's original constitution of 1776, and appeared (not coincidentally) first in that document.

Thus, contrary to the popular misconception that state constitutions are somehow patterned after the United States Constitution, the reverse is true. The federal Bill of Rights borrowed heavily from the Declarations of Rights contained in the constitutions of Pennsylvania and other colonies. For instance, the Pennsylvania Declaration of Rights was the "direct precursor" of the freedom of speech and press. The Delaware Declaration of Rights prohibited quartering of soldiers and ex-post facto laws. North Carolina's Declaration of Rights provided a number of protections to the criminally accused—the right to trial by jury, the privilege against self-incrimination, and others—which later appeared in the United States Constitution.

With respect to article 1, section 8 of the present Pennsylvania Constitution, which relates to freedom from unreasonable searches and seizures, that provision had its origin prior to the Fourth Amendment, in Clause 10 of the original Constitution of 1776. Specifically, the original version of the search and seizure provision reads as follows:

> The people have a right to hold themselves, their houses, papers and possessions free from search and seizure, and therefore warrants without oaths or affirmations first made, affording sufficient foundation for them, and whereby any officer or messenger may be commanded or required to search suspected places, or to seize any person or persons, his or their property, not particularly described, are contrary to that right and ought not be granted.

The above provision was reworded at the time the Pennsylvania Constitution was revised extensively in 1790, and reappeared as article 1, section 8. The modern version of that provision has remained untouched for two hundred years, with the exception of the words "subscribed to by the affiant," which were added by the Constitutional Convention of 1873.

The requirement of probable cause in this Commonwealth thus traces its origin to its original Constitution of 1776, drafted by the first convention of delegates chaired by Benjamin Franklin. The primary purpose of the warrant requirement was to abolish "general warrants," which had been used by the British to conduct sweeping searches of residences and businesses, based upon generalized suspicions. Therefore, at the time the Pennsylvania Constitution was drafted in 1776, the issue of searches and seizures unsupported by probable cause was of utmost concern to the constitutional draftsmen.

Moreover, as this Court has stated repeatedly in interpreting article 1, section 8, that provision is meant to embody a strong notion of privacy, carefully safeguarded in this Commonwealth for the past two centuries. As we stated in *Sell:* "The survival of the language now employed in article 1, section 8 through over 200 years of profound change in other areas demonstrates that the paramount concern for privacy first adopted as part of our organic law in 1776 continues to enjoy the mandate of the people of this Commonwealth."

The history of article I, section 8, thus indicates that the purpose underlying the exclusionary rule in this Commonwealth is quite distinct from the purpose underlying the exclusionary rule under the Fourth Amendment, as articulated by the majority in *Leon*.

The United States Supreme Court in *Leon* made clear that, in its view, the *sole purpose* for the exclusionary rule under the Fourth Amendment was to deter police misconduct. The *Leon* majority also made clear that, under the Federal Constitution, the exclusionary rule operated as "a judicially created remedy designed to safeguard Fourth Amendment rights generally through its deterrent effect, rather than a personal constitutional right of the party aggrieved."

This reinterpretation differs from the way the exclusionary rule has evolved in Pennsylvania since the decision of *Mapp v. Ohio* in 1961 and represents a shift in judicial philosophy from the decisions of the United States Supreme Court dating back to *Weeks v. United States*.

Like many of its sister states, Pennsylvania did not adopt an exclusionary rule until the United States Supreme Court's decision in *Mapp* required it to do so. However, at the time the exclusionary rule was embraced in Pennsylvania, we clearly viewed it as a constitutional mandate. This interpretation was in keeping with a long line of federal cases, beginning with *Weeks* in 1914, which viewed the exclusionary rule as a necessary corollary to the prohibition against unreasonable searches and seizures.

As one commentator noted in piecing together the history of the exclusionary rule: "Deterrence, now claimed to be the primary ground for exclusion, seems to have had no substantial place in any of these conceptions of the practice."

During the first decade after *Mapp*, our decisions in Pennsylvania tended to parallel the cases interpreting the Fourth Amendment. However, beginning in 1973, our case law began to reflect a clear divergence from federal precedent. The United States Supreme Court at this time began moving toward a metamorphosed view, suggesting that the purpose of the exclusionary rule "is not to redress the injury to the privacy of the search victim, but rather to deter future unlawful police conduct." At the same time this Court began to forge its own path under article I, section 8 of the Pennsylvania Constitution, declaring with increasing frequency that article I, section 8 of the Pennsylvania Constitution embodied a strong notion of privacy, notwithstanding federal cases to the contrary. In *Commonwealth v. Platou* (Pa. 1973) and *Commonwealth v. DeJohn* (Pa. 1979), we made explicit that "the right to be free from unreasonable searches and seizures contained in article I, section 8 of the Pennsylvania Constitution is tied into the implicit right to privacy in this Commonwealth." In *DeJohn*, we specifically refused to follow the United States Supreme Court's decision in *United States v. Miller* (1976), which had held that a citizen had no standing to object to the seizure of his or her bank records.

From *DeJohn* forward, a steady line of case law has evolved under the Pennsylvania Constitution, making clear that article I, section 8 is unshakably linked to a right of privacy in this Commonwealth.

As Mr. Justice Flaherty noted in *Denoncourt v. Commonwealth* (Pa. 1983), echoing the wisdom of Justice Brandeis over 60 years ago: "The makers of our Constitution undertook to secure conditions favorable to the pursuit of happiness. They conferred, as against the government, the right to be let alone—the most comprehensive of rights and the right most valued by civilized men."

Most recently, in *Commonwealth v. Melilli* (Pa. 1989), this Court cited with approval the decision of the Superior Court in *Commonwealth v. Beauford* (Pa. Super. Ct. 1984), holding that article I, section 8 of the Pennsylvania Constitution was offended by the installation of a pen register device without probable cause. Mr. Justice Papadakos, in rejecting the holding of the United States Supreme Court in *Smith v. Maryland* (1979), emphasized that "article I, section 8 of the Pennsylvania Constitution may be employed to guard *individual privacy* rights against unreasonable searches and seizures more zealously than the federal government does under the Constitution of the United States by serving as an independent source of supplemental rights." Mr. Justice Papadakos went on to conclude that, because a pen register "is the equivalent of a search warrant in its operative effect where the intrusion involves a violation of a privacy interest," the affidavit and order "must comply with the requirements of probable cause required under Pennsylvania Rules of Criminal Procedure Chapter 2000."

Thus, the exclusionary rule in Pennsylvania has consistently served to bolster the twin aims of article I, section 8; to-wit, the safeguarding of privacy and the fundamental requirement that warrants shall only be issued upon probable cause. As this Court explained in *Commonwealth v. Miller* (Pa. 1986):

> The linch-pin that has been developed to determine whether it is appropriate to issue a search warrant is the test of probable cause. It is designed to protect us from unwarranted and even vindictive incursions upon our privacy. It insulates from dictatorial and tyrannical rule by the state, and preserves the concept of democracy that assures the freedom of its citizens. This concept is second to none in its importance in delineating the dignity of the individual living in a free society.

Whether the United States Supreme Court has determined that the exclusionary rule does not advance the Fourth Amendment purpose of deterring police conduct is irrelevant. Indeed, we disagree with that Court's suggestion in *Leon* that we in Pennsylvania have been employing the exclusionary rule all these years to deter police corruption. We flatly reject this notion. We have no reason to believe that police officers or district justices in the Commonwealth of Pennsylvania do not engage in "good faith" in carrying out their duties. What is significant, however, is that our Constitution has historically been interpreted to incorporate a strong right of privacy, and an equally strong adherence to the requirement of probable cause under article 1, section 8. Citizens in this Commonwealth possess such rights, even where a police officer in "good faith" carrying out his or her duties inadvertently invades the privacy or circumvents the strictures of probable cause. To adopt a "good faith" exception to the exclusionary rule, we believe, would virtually emasculate those clear safeguards which have been carefully developed under the Pennsylvania Constitution over the past 200 years.

A number of states other than Pennsylvania have confronted the issue of whether to apply a "good faith" exception to the exclusionary rule, under their own constitutions, in the wake of *Leon*.

The highest courts of at least two states—Arkansas and Missouri—have seemingly embraced the good faith exception under their own constitutions. Intermediary appellate courts in at least four other states—Indiana, Kansas, Maryland and Louisiana—have indicated their acceptance of the "good faith" exception. In virtually all of those states embracing the "good-faith" exception under their own constitutions, however, the reasoning is a simple affirmation of the logic of *Leon*, with little additional state constitutional analysis.

On the other hand, the highest courts of at least four states—New Jersey, New York, North Carolina and Connecticut—have chosen to reject the "good-faith" exception under their own constitutions, with more detailed analysis of state constitutional principles. The intermediate appellate courts of at least four additional states—Tennessee, Wisconsin, Michigan, and Minnesota—have likewise eschewed the logic of *Leon* under their own state constitutions.

A mere scorecard of those states which have accepted and rejected *Leon* is certainly not dispositive of the issue in Pennsylvania. However, the logic of certain of those opinions bears upon our analysis under the Pennsylvania Constitution, particularly given the unique history of article 1, section 8.

In this respect, we draw support from other states which have declined to adopt a "good faith" exception, particularly New Jersey, Connecticut and North Carolina. In *State v. Novembrino* (N.J. 1987), the New Jersey Supreme Court found that the "good faith" exception to the exclusionary rule was inconsistent with the New Jersey Constitution, because it would undermine the requirement of probable cause. Although New Jersey, like Pennsylvania, had no exclusionary rule in place prior to *Mapp v. Ohio* in 1961, the New Jersey Court found that it had become "imbedded" in the jurisprudence under that state's constitution. As the New Jersey court wrote in *Novembrino*:

> The exclusionary rule, by virtue of its consistent application over the past twenty-five years, has become an integral element of our state-constitutional guarantee that search warrants will not issue without probable cause. Its function is not merely to deter police misconduct. The rule also serves as the indispensable mechanism for vindicating the constitutional right to be free from unreasonable searches.

Similarly, the Connecticut Supreme Court—which most recently rejected the good faith exception on August 7, 1990—concluded that the purpose of the exclusionary rule under article I, section 7 of the Connecticut Constitution, was to "preserve the integrity of the warrant issuing process as a whole." Thus, when evidence was suppressed under this provision due to a defective warrant, "the issuing authority is not being punished for a mistake, but is, rather, being informed that a constitutional violation has taken place and is also being instructed in how to avoid such violations in the future."

More directly on point, the North Carolina Supreme Court in *State v. Carter* (N.C. 1988) rejected the "good faith" exception to the exclusionary rule, noting the importance of the *privacy rights* flowing from the search and seizure provision in the North Carolina Constitution. The court in *Carter* emphasized the need to preserve the integrity of the judiciary in North Carolina, in excluding illegally seized evidence when such important rights of the citizenry were at stake. Wrote the North Carolina Supreme Court:

> The exclusionary sanction is indispensable to give effect to the constitutional principles prohibiting unreasonable search and seizure. We are persuaded that the exclusionary rule is the only effective bulwark against governmental disregard for constitutionally protected privacy rights. Equally of importance in our reasoning, we adhere to the rule for the sake of maintaining the integrity of the judicial branch of government.

We similarly conclude that, given the strong right of privacy which inheres in article 1, section 8, as well as the clear prohibition against the issuance of warrants without probable cause, or based upon defective warrants, the good faith exception to the exclusionary rule would directly clash with those rights of citizens as developed in our Commonwealth over the past 200 years. To allow the judicial branch to participate, directly or indirectly, in the use of the fruits of illegal searches would only serve to undermine the integrity of the judiciary in this Commonwealth. From the perspective of the citizen whose rights are at stake, an invasion of privacy, in good faith or bad, is equally as intrusive. This is true whether it occurs through the actions of the legislative, executive or the judicial branch of government.

We recognize that, in analyzing any state constitutional provision, it is necessary to go beyond the bare text and history of that provision as it was drafted 200 years ago, and consider its application within the modern scheme of Pennsylvania jurisprudence. An assessment of various policy considerations, however, only supports our conclusion that the good faith exception to the exclusionary rule would be inconsistent with the jurisprudence surrounding article 1, section 8.

First, such a rule would effectively negate the judicially created mandate reflected in the Pennsylvania Rules of Criminal Procedure, in Rules 2003, 2005 and 2006. Specifically, Rule 2003 relates to the requirements for the issuance of a warrant, and provides in relevant part:

> (a) No search warrant shall issue but upon probable cause supported by one or more affidavits sworn to before the issuing authority. The issuing authority, in determining whether probable cause has been established, may not consider any evidence outside the affidavits.
>
> (b) At any hearing on a motion for the return or suppression of evidence, or for suppression of the fruits of evidence, obtained pursuant to a search warrant, no evidence shall be admissible to establish probable cause other than the affidavits provided for in paragraph (a).

Rule 2003 serves to underscore the incongruity of adopting a good faith exception to the exclusionary rule in Pennsylvania. Although Rule 2003 is not constitutionally mandated by article 1, section 8, as *Milliken* correctly explains, it reflects yet another expression of this Court's unwavering insistence that probable cause exist before a warrant is issued, and only those facts memorialized in the written affidavit may be considered in establishing probable cause, in order to eliminate any chance of incomplete or reconstructed hindsight. It is true, as *Milliken* summarizes, that the history of article 1, section 8 does not itself prohibit the use of oral testimony to establish probable cause, outside the four corners of the warrant. Nonetheless, we have chosen to adopt that Rule as an administrative matter, and that Rule has now stood in Pennsylvania for 17 years.

In the instant case, probable cause—as defined under Pennsylvania law—is lacking. Two lower courts have so held; we concur. Applying the federal *Leon* test would not only frustrate the procedural safeguards embodied in Rule 2003, but would permit the admission of illegally seized evidence in a variety of contexts where probable cause is lacking, so long as the police officer acted in "good faith." In *Leon* itself, probable cause was absent entirely, yet illegally seized evidence was admitted into evidence.

We cannot countenance such a wide departure from the text and history of article 1, section 8, nor can we permit the use of a "good faith" exception to effectively nullify Pennsylvania Rule of Criminal Procedure 2003. Our Constitution requires that warrants shall not be issued except upon probable cause. We have specifically adopted Rule 2003 for the purpose of confining the probable cause inquiry to the written affidavit and warrant, in order to avoid any doubt as to the basis for probable cause. We decline to undermine the clear mandate of these provisions by slavishly adhering to federal precedent where it diverges from two hundred years of our own constitutional jurisprudence.

A second policy consideration which bolsters our conclusion is that the underlying premise of *Leon* is still open to serious debate. Although it is clear that the exclusionary rule presents some cost to society, in allowing "some guilty defendants go free," the extent of the costs are far from clear. A number of recent studies have indicated that the exclusion of illegally seized evidence has had a marginal effect in allowing guilty criminals to avoid successful prosecution. Indeed, the *Leon* decision itself indicates relatively low statistics with respect to the impact of the exclusionary rule in thwarting legitimate prosecutions. Equally as important, the alternative to the exclusionary rule most commonly advanced—*i.e.*, allowing victims of improper searches to sue police officers directly—has raised serious concern among police officers.

A third policy consideration which compels our decisions is that, given the recent decision of the United States Supreme Court in *Illinois v. Gates* (1983) adopting a "totality of the circumstances test" in assessing probable cause, there is far less reason to adopt a "good faith" exception to the exclusionary rule. We have adopted *Gates* as a matter of Pennsylvania law in the recent case of *Commonwealth v. Gray* (Pa. 1985). As a number of jurists have pointed out, the flexible *Gates* standard now eliminates much of the prior concern which existed with respect to an overly rigid application of the exclusionary rule.

Finally, the dangers of allowing magistrates to serve as "rubber stamps" and of fostering "magistrate-shopping," are evident under *Leon*. As the instant case illustrates, police officers and magistrates have historically worked closely together in this Commonwealth. Trooper Deise and District Justice Tlumac prepared the warrant and affidavit with Trooper Deise dictating the affidavit while the magistrate typed it verbatim.

There is no suggestion here that Trooper Deise and District Justice Tlumac acted other than in utmost "good faith" when preparing the warrant. Nevertheless, we are mindful of the fact that both state and federal interpretations of the Fourth Amendment require a warrant to be issued by a "neutral and detached magistrate," because as Mr. Justice Papadakos noted, there is a requirement of "an independent determination of probable cause." The reason for this requirement is evident. Would the District Justice act as nothing more than an adjunct of the police department, there would be no opportunity for *review* of the warrant prior to its issuance, and hence, a search warrant would be nothing more than the police's own determination of whether probable cause exists. We cannot countenance such a policy as it clearly runs afoul of our historically based system of government; which requires three *independent* branches.

It must be remembered that a District Justice is not a member of the executive branch—the police—but a member of the judiciary. By falling within the judicial branch of government, the District Justice is thus charged with the responsibility of being the *disinterested* arbiter of disputes and is charged further with acting as the bulwark between the police and the rights of citizens. Unless and until a magistrate independently determines there is probable cause, no warrant shall issue.

This is not to say that we distrust our police or district justices; far from it. We, in fact, have no doubt that police officers and district justices in Pennsylvania are intelligent, committed and independent enough to carry out their duties under the scheme which has evolved over the past thirty years, in order to safeguard the rights of our citizens.

However, requiring "neutral and detached magistrates" furthers the twin aims of safeguarding privacy and assuring that no warrant shall issue but upon probable cause. As such, we see no reason to eliminate this requirement, for if we did, we would eviscerate the purpose of requiring warrants prior to searches. As one member of the Mississippi Supreme Court noted in a similar vein: "If it ain't broke, don't fix it."

Thirty years ago, when the exclusionary rule was first introduced, police officers were perhaps plagued with ill-defined, unarticulated rules governing their conduct. However, the past thirty years have seen a gradual sharpening of the process, with police officers adapting well to the exclusionary rule.

The purpose of Rule 2003 is not to exclude *bona fide* evidence based upon technical errors and omissions by police officers or magistrates. Rather, Rule 2003 is meant to provide support for the probable cause requirement of article I, section 8 of the Pennsylvania Constitution by assuring that there is an objective method for determining when probable cause exists, and when it does not.

In the instant case, the evidence seized from defendant Edmunds was the product of a constitutionally defective search warrant. Article I, section 8 of the Pennsylvania Constitution does not incorporate a "good faith" exception to the exclusionary rule. Therefore, the marijuana seized from the white corrugated building, the marijuana seized from Edmund's home, and the written and oral statements obtained from Edmunds by the troopers, must be suppressed. We base our decision strictly upon the Pennsylvania Constitution; any reference to the United States Constitution is merely for guidance and does not compel our decision.

Justice Brandeis, in his eloquent dissent in *Olmstead v. United States* (1928), reminded us over a half-century ago:

> In a government of laws, existence of the government will be imperiled if it fails to observe the law scrupulously. Our government is the potent, the omnipresent teacher. For good or for ill, it teaches the whole people by its example. Crime is

contagious. If the Government becomes a lawbreaker, it breeds contempt for law; it invites every man to become a law unto himself; it invites anarchy.

Although the exclusionary rule may place a duty of thoroughness and care upon police officers and district justices in this Commonwealth, in order to safeguard the rights of citizens under article I, section 8, that is a small price to pay, we believe, for a democracy.

NOTES

1. In *Leon*, the United States Supreme Court characterized the adoption of the federal exclusionary rule in *Calandra* as a prophylactic measure to deter police conduct and not as a holding that was required by the Fourth Amendment. *United States v. Calandra*, 414 U.S. 338 (1974). This construction permits the Court to recognize exceptions like the "good faith" exception in *Leon*.

2. The rationale in *Leon* has been adopted by the majority of state courts in construing state constitutions. *See, e.g., Michigan v. Goldston*, 682 N.W.2d 479 (Mich. 2004).

3. A significant number of States, however, have rejected *Leon* as a matter of state constitutional law. Among them are: Arizona, Connecticut, Delaware, Georgia, Hawaii, Idaho, Iowa, Massachusetts, New Hampshire, New Jersey, New Mexico, New York, Oregon, Pennsylvania, Vermont, and Washington.

4. The California and Florida Constitutions have been amended to prohibit any state constitutional exclusionary rule, beyond what is required for violations of the Fourth Amendment. *See* Cal. Const. art. I, § 28(d); Fla. Const. art. I, § 12. Therefore, the California and Florida Constitutions required the adoption of *Leon* because the search and seizure provisions in both constitutions must be construed in lockstep with the Fourth Amendment.

5. The concurrence by Justice Lee in *Utah v. Walker*, 267 P.3d 210, 216–27 (Utah 2011), shows that a state court may reject the exclusionary rule—at least under its own constitution—a theory that would make it unnecessary to consider whether the *Leon* good-faith exception applies.

6. Applying *Edmunds*, the Pennsylvania Supreme Court held that the good faith exception would not be adopted for the purpose of admitting physical evidence seized incident to an arrest based solely on an expired arrest warrant. *Commonwealth v. Johnson*, 86 A.3d 182 (Pa. 2014).

7. "Fifty-two years ago, in *Terry v. Ohio*, the United States Supreme Court upheld stop-and-frisk under the Fourth Amendment. At that time, stop-and-frisk had provoked substantial disagreement at the state level—leading to divergent opinions and repeat litigation. But after *Terry*, the state courts became silent. Since 1968, every state court has lockstepped with *Terry* in interpreting its own constitutional provisions. This presents a puzzle, since

state courts are free to provide more expansive (or less expansive) rights protections in interpreting their own state constitutions. And in other contexts, they have not been shy in doing so. In roughly a quarter of the Supreme Court's Fourth Amendment cases, state courts have read their state guarantees to exceed the U.S. Constitution's protections. Too often, stop-and-frisk has eroded trust between police and local communities. It has contributed to concerns about systemic racism. It has 'humiliated' countless Americans. It has played a part in the deaths of Eric Garner, Michael Brown, and Freddie Gray, sparking nationwide unrest. And yet, state courts continue to lockstep—parroting *Terry* under their unique constitutional commands. This is hardly desirable. The 'double security' of dual sovereignty is premised on state experimentation and creativity. When the U.S. Supreme Court fails to safeguard individual rights, state courts and state constitutions have the option and the obligation to consider whether to step in with more expansive protections. So far, they do not seem to be doing that. Over the past few decades, state courts have been increasingly touted as guardians of individual liberty. In *American Legion v. American Humanist Association*, Justice Kavanaugh observed that the Supreme Court 'is not the only guardian of individual rights in America' because state courts 'possess authority to safeguard individual rights above and beyond the rights secured by the U.S. Constitution.' More recently, then-Judge Amy Coney Barrett testified before Congress and made a similar argument: 'Many states interpret their versions of the Fourth Amendment or other provisions to be even more protective of rights than is the United States Constitution.' 'We allow those differences to flourish,' she later added. State courts, it is said, can 'step into the breach' and serve as 'first responders in addressing innovative rights claims.' This Note proposes a change in perspective: that litigants challenge stop-and-frisk under state law. It also lays the groundwork for such challenges. It examines the history of stop-and-frisk at the state level before *Terry*. It analyzes the *Terry* litigation, relying especially on the NAACP's briefing, which accurately predicted stop-and-frisk's perverse potential. And it synthesizes this analysis into three arguments that should be raised against stop-and-frisk under state law." Nathaniel C. Sutton, *Lockstepping Through Stop-and-Frisk: A Call to Independently Assess* Terry v. Ohio *Under State Law*, 107 Va. L. Rev. 639 (2021) (excerpt quoted from this article).

D. AUTOMATIC STANDING

STATE v. LAMB
95 A.3d 123 (N.J. 2014)

CUFF, J.

This appeal involves the validity of a warrantless consent search of a house. An investigation of a reported shooting in another part of town led Pennsville police to the house in which police knew defendant Michael W.

Lamb had resided at one time. When police arrived, defendant's stepfather emphatically informed police that they were not welcome on his property or in his house.

While defendant's stepfather informed police that they could not enter his home, defendant's girlfriend appeared at the door and left the house. She supplied information to police that provided probable cause for defendant's arrest and confirmed his presence in the house.

Later, defendant's stepfather agreed to leave the house. Soon thereafter, defendant left the house at the insistence of his mother. She remained in the house with three children between the ages of eight months and nine years and a loaded gun.

Defendant's mother permitted police officers to enter the house and agreed to a search of the room where her son and his girlfriend were staying. Police located a loaded handgun and ammunition similar to the equipment used in the earlier shooting.

We conclude that the consent to search provided by defendant's mother was knowing, voluntary, and valid. The absence of defendant and his stepfather from the home permitted defendant's mother to provide or withhold consent. Furthermore, the initial opposition expressed by defendant's stepfather was no longer effective once he was not physically present in his home.

Under the totality of the circumstances, we hold that the warrantless search of defendant's bedroom was solidly anchored to the knowing and voluntary consent to search given by defendant's mother.

Defendant filed a motion to suppress the evidence seized from his bedroom. Defendant argued that his mother's will had been overborne by police. He emphasized that she was frightened and believed she had no choice but to consent to a search of her house. Under the circumstances, defendant insisted that her consent to search was not voluntary.

Under the automatic standing rule, virtually all defendants have standing to contest a search or seizure by police where they have either "a proprietary, possessory or participatory interest in either the place searched or the property seized," or if "possession of the seized evidence at the time of the contested search is an essential element of guilt." In this way, our courts have construed the New Jersey Constitution as affording New Jersey citizens greater protection against unreasonable searches and seizures than accorded under the United States Constitution.

The conclusion that a defendant has automatic standing to challenge a search on state constitutional grounds is independent of and unrelated to whether that defendant has a reasonable expectation of privacy in the place searched or item seized. The automatic standing rule's purpose is to avoid the need to sacrifice a defendant's Fifth Amendment rights and admit to criminal activity in order to assert his Fourth Amendment rights to challenge the search or seizure.

Here, defendant clearly had a possessory interest in the property seized. Possession of the handgun is an essential element of several offenses faced by defendant. Therefore, under New Jersey law, defendant has automatic standing to challenge the search and seizure of the firearm and ammunition.

STATE v. BULLOCK
901 P.2d 61 (Mont. 1995)

TRIEWEILER, J.

The defendants, Eddie Peterson and Bill Bullock, were charged in Jefferson County Justice Court with unlawfully killing a game animal and possession of an unlawfully killed animal. The Justice Court suppressed all of the State's evidence pertaining to Peterson, and dismissed the charges against Bullock. The State appealed to the District Court for a trial *de novo*. On appeal, the District Court denied the defendants' motions to dismiss and to suppress evidence. Peterson then pled guilty to unlawfully killing a game animal; Bullock pled guilty to unlawfully possessing a game animal; and both defendants reserved their right to appeal the District Court's order denying their motions to dismiss and suppress evidence. Following two orders by this Court which remanded this case to the District Court for further proceedings, we affirm the District Court's order which denied the defendants' motion to dismiss, and reverse the District Court's order which denied the defendants' motion to suppress evidence.

At about 6:30 a.m. on October 31, 1991, while returning home from work, Chuck Wing observed what he estimated was a large six or seven point antlered bull elk on Boulder Hill near Boulder, Montana. He recognized that the elk was in Hunting District 380 where hunters were allowed to shoot only "spikes" unless they had a special permit. As Wing observed the elk, he heard a gunshot, saw the elk fall, and observed two men and a boy standing near a pickup truck in the vicinity of the fallen elk. He believed the pickup belonged to defendant Eddie J. Peterson. He then observed the three people drag the elk to the truck and load it without field-dressing it. Wing reported the incident to Jefferson County Sheriff Tom Dawson, who, in turn, relayed the information to Game Warden Chris Anderson, an employee of the Montana Department of Fish, Wildlife, and Parks. Anderson traveled from Helena to Boulder that morning to investigate the incident.

Anderson first interviewed Wing who related the above information. He then drove to Peterson's home in Boulder, but Peterson was not at home. Anderson returned to the sheriff's office where he learned that Peterson had a cabin in Basin Creek. Rather than try to give directions, Dawson agreed to accompany him to the cabin. To reach Peterson's cabin, it is necessary to travel approximately seven miles on a one-lane forest service road which is bounded by forest on both sides. At least one sign along that road indicates that the road is bordered by private property and advises the public to remain on the road.

Peterson's property is separated from the road by a fence. There is a gate which provides access to his property from the forest service road. "No Trespassing" signs are posted on trees on each side of the gate. His cabin is located at the end of a private road 334 feet from the forest service road. Between the forest service road and Peterson's cabin, the terrain is slightly elevated in a way that conceals Peterson's cabin and the other structures on his property. He moved his cabin beyond the hill at an earlier time so that it would not be evident to passersby.

When Anderson and Dawson reached Peterson's property, the gate was open. They entered the property through the gate and drove approximately 180 feet down Peterson's private road. As they descended the crest of the hill between his cabin and the forest service road, they first observed a large bull elk hanging from a tree in an area about 126 feet from Peterson's cabin. The elk could not be seen from the public road, nor was there evidence that it could be seen from any other public location. Peterson testified that the elk was hanging between his cabin, several vehicles, and a guest sleeping cabin.

The parties agreed that, in the past, anyone who wished to enter Peterson's property or drive on his private road had called to ask permission. In fact, the Jefferson County Sheriff's Office had done so a few days earlier prior to conducting a search for lost hunters. On the date in question, neither Dawson nor Anderson asked or received permission to be on Peterson's property. Neither had they secured a search warrant, in spite of the fact that Anderson testified in Justice Court that he believed there was probable cause that a crime had been committed, that Peterson was involved, and that Peterson still possessed evidence of that crime.

At the hearing held in the District Court pursuant to the defendants' motion to suppress, there was disagreement about exactly what Anderson and Dawson did after observing the elk hanging near Peterson's cabin. However, in stipulations filed with the court earlier, the parties agreed that after observing the elk, Anderson and Dawson went over to examine it. After conducting the examination, Anderson then requested that Peterson take him and Dawson to the place where the elk was killed. Peterson did so, but at the site where the law enforcement officers were taken, there were no elk tracks—only a pile of the elk's entrails. It was apparent to Anderson that the elk had not been killed at that location.

Anderson then confronted Peterson with the information he had received from Wing. Peterson provided him with an explanation that ultimately was found to be inaccurate. Bullock was then questioned, provided responses consistent with Peterson's, and declined the State's offer of immunity in exchange for testimony that would incriminate Peterson.

The following day, Anderson returned to Peterson's cabin and confiscated the elk carcass.

On November 8, 1991, Peterson was charged in Jefferson County Justice Court with unlawfully killing a game animal. Bullock was charged with possession of an unlawfully killed animal. Both defendants pled not guilty to those charges.

The State contends that Bullock has no standing to challenge the legality of the State's entry onto and search of Peterson's land because he had no ownership interest in that land. It contends that pursuant to this Court's recent decisions in *State v. Gonzales* (Mont. 1988) and *State v. Powers* (Mont. 1988), a party must have some interest in the property searched before he or she can contest the admissibility of evidence gathered during the search.

Bullock responds that he was charged with possessing the elk carcass seized from Peterson's property, and that under our prior decisions, that possessory interest was sufficient to establish standing.

We agree that the State construes our prior decisions regarding standing too narrowly.

Even after the United States Supreme Court retreated from its "automatic standing" rule in cases where a defendant is charged with illegal possession of some item in *United States v. Salvucci* (1980), we held that ownership of the property searched is not necessary to establish standing to object to the legality of a search in *State v. Isom* (Mont. 1982). We stated:

> Notwithstanding the limitations placed on *Jones v. United States* (1960), the Court in *Rakas v. Illinois* (1978), and again in *Salvucci*, emphasized that ownership is not a key element in determining standing. The test for standing is not to be based on distinctions out of property and tort law: "In defining the scope of that interest, we adhere to the view expressed in *Jones* and echoed in later cases that arcane distinctions in property and tort law between guests, licensees, invitees, and the like ought not to control." The controlling view, then, seems to be that expressed in *Mancusi v. DeForte* (1968), in which the Court said that the *Katz* test of "legitimate expectation of privacy makes it clear that capacity to claim the protection of the Fourth Amendment depends not upon a property right in the invaded place, but upon whether the area was one in which there was a reasonable expectation of freedom from governmental intrusion."

Following this rationale, we concluded in *Isom* that a defendant who was a guest in his uncle's home at the time that it was searched had standing to object to the government search of that home, even though he had no ownership interest in the premises.

We have since held in both *Gonzales* and *Powers* that a possessory interest in either the premises searched *or the property seized* is sufficient to establish standing. However, we have never modified nor reversed our position in *Isom*.

Other states which have held that a possessory interest in the items seized is sufficient to establish standing to challenge the legality of a search or the property's seizure, have adopted automatic standing rules on independent state grounds where the defendant is charged with unlawfully possessing that item.

For example, in *State v. Alston* (N.J. 1981), the defendants were passengers in a vehicle from which weapons were seized during a search of the vehicle. They were later charged with unlawful possession of the weapons. Pursuant to the defendants' motion, the evidence was suppressed by the trial court, based on the illegality of the police search. On appeal, the state contended that the defendant passengers had no standing to challenge the legality of the search of the vehicle, despite their possessory interest in the weapons which had been seized.

After reviewing the United States Supreme Court's decisions on standing, including *Salvucci*, that court noted an inconsistency in the federal law which appeared to allow prosecutors to assert contradictory positions: "That the defendant possessed the contraband property for the purposes of proving criminal liability, but that he had insufficient possessory interest in the property for the purposes of defending the legality of the search and seizure." The court pointed out that a basic principle of American federalism confers on state courts the power to afford citizens of each state greater protection against unreasonable searches and seizures than may be required by the Supreme Court's interpretation of the Fourth Amendment, and on that basis, concluded that the *Salvucci* decision afforded inadequate protection against unreasonable searches and seizures.

Finally, the New Jersey Supreme Court concluded that based on its rule of standing which provided that "a criminal defendant is entitled to bring a motion to suppress evidence obtained in an unlawful search and seizure if he has a proprietary, possessory, or participatory interest in either the place searched or the property seized," it would retain the automatic standing rule where a defendant is charged with an offense in which possession of the seized evidence at the time of the contested search is an essential element of guilt. It adopted reasoning from former Justice Thurgood Marshall that:

> the automatic standing rule is a salutary one which protects the rights of defendants and eliminates the wasteful requirement of making a preliminary showing of standing in pretrial proceedings involving possessory offenses, where the charge itself alleges an interest sufficient to support a Fourth Amendment claim.

Other states have also adopted the rule of automatic standing for crimes of possession.

We agree with the reasoning in *Alston*. Based on independent state grounds pursuant to article II, section 11 of the Montana Constitution, we hold that when the charge against the defendant includes an allegation of a possessory interest in the property which is seized, the defendant has standing to object to the prosecutorial use of that evidence based on either the unlawful search of the location where it was found, or its unlawful seizure.

Since Bullock was accused by the State of unlawfully possessing the elk carcass which was found on Peterson's property, we conclude, based on our prior decisions and the logical application of those decisions as set forth above, that he had standing to object to the State's search of Peterson's property and seizure of that carcass.

NOTE

In *United States v. Salvucci*, 448 U.S. 83 (1980), the United States Supreme Court abolished the automatic standing rule for purposes of the Fourth Amendment. As in Montana and New Jersey, a minority of state constitutions are still construed to provide automatic standing for defendants charged with possession of an item seized, without requiring the defendant to assert an ownership or possessory interest. They include Louisiana, Massachusetts, New Hampshire, Pennsylvania, Vermont and Washington. *See, e.g., Commonwealth v. Armendola*, 550 N.E.2d 121 (Mass. 1990); *State v. Evans*, 150 P.3d 105 (Wash. 2007).

E. WARRANT REQUIREMENT

STATE v. EARLS
70 A.3d 630 (N.J. 2013)

RABNER, C.J.

Advances in technology offer great benefits to society in many areas. At the same time, they can pose significant risks to individual privacy rights. This case highlights both principles as we consider recent strides in cell-phone technology. New improvements not only expand our ability to communicate with one another and access the Internet, but the cell phones we carry can also serve as powerful tracking devices able to pinpoint our movements with remarkable precision and accuracy.

In this appeal, we consider whether people have a constitutional right of privacy in cell-phone location information. Cell phones register or identify themselves with nearby cell towers every seven seconds. Cell providers collect data from those contacts, which allows carriers to locate cell phones on a real-time basis and to reconstruct a phone's movement from recorded data. Those developments, in turn, raise questions about the right to privacy in the location of one's cell phone.

Historically, the State Constitution has offered greater protection to New Jersey residents than the Fourth Amendment. Under settled New

Jersey law, individuals do not lose their right to privacy simply because they have to give information to a third-party provider, like a phone company or bank, to get service. In addition, New Jersey case law continues to be guided by whether the government has violated an individual's reasonable expectation of privacy.

Applying those principles here, we note that disclosure of cell-phone location information, which cell-phone users must provide to receive service, can reveal a great deal of personal information about an individual. With increasing accuracy, cell phones can now trace our daily movements and disclose not only where individuals are located at a point in time but also which shops, doctors, religious services, and political events they go to, and with whom they choose to associate. Yet people do not buy cell phones to serve as tracking devices or reasonably expect them to be used by the government in that way. We therefore find that individuals have a reasonable expectation of privacy in the location of their cell phones under the State Constitution.

We also recognize that cell-phone location information can be a powerful tool to fight crime. That data will still be available to law enforcement officers upon a showing of probable cause. To be clear, the police will be able to access cell-phone location data with a properly authorized search warrant. If the State can show that a recognized exception to the warrant requirement applies, such as exigent circumstances, then no warrant is needed.

Having a clear set of rules serves two key goals. It protects legitimate privacy interests and also gives guidance to law enforcement officials who carry out important public safety responsibilities. Because today's decision creates a new rule of law that would disrupt the administration of justice if applied retroactively, the rule will apply to this defendant and prospective cases only.

The issue before the Court arises in the case of a burglary investigation. In an effort to locate the target and his girlfriend, whose safety was in question, the police obtained cell-phone location information from T-Mobile on three occasions during the same evening—without first getting a court order or a warrant.

We draw the following facts from testimony at the suppression hearing in this case. In January 2006, Detective William Strohkirch of the Middletown Township Police Department was investigating a series of residential burglaries. After a victim told Strohkirch that a cell phone stolen from his home was still active, a court-ordered trace of the phone led the police to a bar in Asbury Park. Strohkirch and two other officers found an individual at the bar with the phone, and they arrested him. He told the police that his cousin, defendant Thomas Earls, had sold him the phone. He added that defendant had been involved in residential burglaries and kept the proceeds in a storage unit that either defendant or his former girlfriend, Desiree Gates, had rented.

At some point on January 26, 2006, the police filed a complaint against defendant for receiving stolen property and obtained an arrest warrant. Strohkirch then began to search for defendant and Gates to ensure her safety and to execute the warrant.

In an effort to locate them, the police contacted T-Mobile, a cell-phone service provider, at about 6:00 p.m. At three different times that evening, T-Mobile provided information about the location of a cell phone the police believed defendant had been using. First, at around 8:00 p.m., T-Mobile told the police that the cell phone in question was in the "general location" of Highway 35 in Eatontown. The police searched the area but did not find defendant or Gates.

Second, at about 9:30 p.m., the police again contacted T-Mobile, which reported that the cell phone was being used in the area of Routes 33 and 18 in Neptune. The police searched that area in response but did not find defendant. Finally, after the police called T-Mobile at around 11:00 p.m., the carrier reported that a cell-site tower in the area of Route 9 in Howell had been used. At no point did the police seek a warrant for the three traces.

Local police departments assisted Strohkirch throughout the evening. At around midnight, the Howell Police Department located defendant's car at the Caprice Motel on Route 9 in Howell. A local officer stayed in the area to watch the car. Meanwhile, Strohkirch and Detective Deickman of the Middletown Police drove to the motel together. When they arrived at about 1:00 a.m., the officer on site reported that he had not seen any movement and that all of the motel rooms were dark.

At about 3:00 a.m., two hours after Strohkirch and Deickman first arrived at the motel, two police officers from Middletown arrived. At that point, Deickman spoke with a clerk in the motel office who confirmed where Gates and defendant were staying. Deickman called their room from the clerk's office to ask Gates to come outside. When defendant and Gates opened the door, the police arrested him. The police saw a flat-screen television and several pieces of luggage on the floor of the room. Inside a closed dresser drawer, the police found a pillowcase tied in a knot.

The police brought defendant and the items to headquarters, where defendant signed consent-to-search forms. Inside the luggage, the police found stolen property and marijuana. The pillowcase contained stolen jewelry.

Defendant filed a motion to suppress. After a three-day hearing, the trial court upheld the seizure of evidence from the storage unit and the motel room, except for the contents of the pillowcase. The court also denied defendant's motion to suppress evidence seized from his car and apartment.

Our focus in this appeal is on defendant's arrest, based on the location of the cell phone, and the resulting consequences.

Defendant argues that he had a reasonable expectation of privacy in his cell-phone location information and that a warrant was therefore needed before law enforcement officials could access that information. He submits that technology now allows law enforcement to track the location of cell phones in an intrusive, continuous manner and thereby threatens to erode protected privacy rights. Defendant argues that the traditional distinction between public and private realms is no longer valid because cell-phone tracking monitors a person's movements in and out of both areas.

A basic cell phone operates like a scanning radio. Cell phones use radio waves to communicate between a user's handset and a telephone network. To connect with the local telephone network, the Internet, or other wireless networks, cell-phone providers maintain an extensive network of cell sites, or radio base stations, in the geographic areas they serve.

Whenever a cell phone is turned on, it searches for a signal and automatically registers or identifies itself with the nearest cell site—the one with the strongest signal. The process is automatic. Cell phones re-scan every seven seconds, or whenever the signal strength weakens, even when no calls are made. Cell phones can be tracked when they are used to make a call, send a text message, or connect to the Internet—or when they take no action at all, so long as the phone is not turned off. Today, cell-phone providers can pinpoint the location of a person's cell phone with increasing accuracy. In some areas, carriers can locate cell-phone users within buildings, and even within "individual floors and rooms within buildings."

A recent decision of the United States Supreme Court that rests on principles of trespass has altered the landscape somewhat. *United States v. Jones* (2012) held that the physical installation of a GPS device on a car amounted to a Fourth Amendment search and required a warrant. Federal officers had attached a GPS tracking device to a car, without a valid warrant, and pinpointed the car's movements to within 50 to 100 feet for nearly one month.

The Court unanimously found a violation of the Fourth Amendment but split on the underlying basis. The majority opinion by Justice Scalia, joined by Chief Justice Roberts and Justices Kennedy, Thomas, and Sotomayor, held that the installation of the device constituted a trespass on private property. The decision did not address whether the defendant had a reasonable expectation of privacy that was violated when the police monitored the device.

Article I, Paragraph 7 of the New Jersey Constitution is nearly identical to the Fourth Amendment. Despite the similarity in language, the protections against unreasonable searches and seizures "are not always coterminous." On a number of occasions, this Court has found that the State

Constitution provides greater protection against unreasonable searches and seizures than the Fourth Amendment.

At the outset, we note that an individual's privacy interest under New Jersey law does not turn on whether he or she is required to disclose information to third-party providers to obtain service. Just as customers must disclose details about their personal finances to the bank that manages their checking accounts, cell-phone users have no choice but to reveal certain information to their cellular provider. That is not a voluntary disclosure in a typical sense; it can only be avoided at the price of not using a cell phone.

When people make disclosures to phone companies and other providers to use their services, they are not promoting the release of personal information to others. Instead, they can reasonably expect that their personal information will remain private. For those reasons, we have departed from federal case law that takes a different approach.

Beyond the question of third-party disclosure, we have examined the expectation of privacy that people reasonably have in various types of personal information. In *State v. Hunt* (N.J. 1982), this Court observed that people are "entitled to assume that the telephone numbers they dial in the privacy of their home will be recorded solely for the telephone company's business purposes" and not for law enforcement. As the Court explained, a list of phone numbers dialed "easily could reveal the identities of the persons and the places called, and thus reveal the most intimate details of a person's life."

Similarly, in *State v. McAllister* (N.J. 2005), the Court noted that bank records "reveal many aspects of a depositor's personal affairs, opinions, habits and associations. Indeed, the totality of bank records provides a virtual current biography."

More recently, in *State v. Reid* (N.J. 2008), we found that Internet "subscriber information alone can tell a great deal about a person. With a complete listing of IP addresses, one can track a person's Internet usage" and learn where they shop, what political organizations they find interesting, their health concerns, and more.

We also noted how integrally connected all three areas are to essential activities of everyday life. As to each, we found that the State Constitution protects the privacy interest at stake.

We consider the expectation of privacy that should be accorded the location of a cell phone in that context. Using a cell phone to determine the location of its owner can be far more revealing than acquiring toll billing, bank, or Internet subscriber records. It is akin to using a tracking device and can function as a substitute for 24/7 surveillance without police having to confront the limits of their resources. It also involves a degree of intrusion that a reasonable person would not anticipate. Location information gleaned from a cell-phone provider can reveal not just where people go—which doctors, religious services, and stores they visit—but also the people and groups they choose to affiliate with and when they actually do so. That information cuts across a broad range of personal ties with family, friends, political groups, health care providers, and others. In other words, details about the location of a cell phone can provide an intimate picture of one's daily life.

Modern cell phones also blur the historical distinction between public and private areas because cell phones emit signals from both places. In this case, defendant was located in a motel room, not on a public highway. Yet law enforcement had no way of knowing in advance whether defendant's cell phone was being monitored in a public or private space. Cell-phone location information, thus, does more than simply augment visual surveillance in public areas.

Finally, cell-phone use has become an indispensable part of modern life. The hundreds of millions of wireless devices in use each day can often be found near their owners—at work, school, or home, and at events and gatherings of all types. And wherever those mobile devices may be, they continuously identify their location to nearby cell towers so long as they are not turned off.

We analyze those considerations under the State's search-and-seizure jurisprudence. We are required to focus on reasonable expectation of privacy concerns.

As a general rule, the more sophisticated and precise the tracking, the greater the privacy concern. The question before the court, then, is informed by changes in technology, because they affect the level of detail that telephone companies can relay to law enforcement. To be sure, the degree of information available through cell-phone tracking has grown with each passing year. As discussed above, in 2006, cell phones could be tracked to within a one-mile radius or less of the nearest cell tower. Today, that distance has narrowed to the point that cell phones can be pinpointed with great precision—to within feet in some instances. That information is updated every seven seconds through interactions with cell towers, whether the phone is in public or private space. As noted, that continuous process can reveal a great deal of private information about a person's life.

Viewed from the perspective of a reasonable expectation of privacy, what was problematic in 2006 is plainly invasive today. We are not able to draw a fine line across that spectrum and calculate a person's legitimate expectation of privacy with mathematical certainty—noting each slight forward advance in technology. Courts are not adept at that task. Instead, our focus belongs on the obvious: cell phones are not meant to serve as tracking devices to locate their owners wherever they may be. People buy cell phones to communicate with others, to use the Internet, and for a growing number of other reasons. But no one buys a cell phone to share detailed information about their whereabouts with the police. That was true in 2006 and is equally true today. Citizens have a legitimate privacy interest in such information. Although individuals may be generally aware that their phones can be tracked, most people do not realize the extent of modern tracking capabilities and reasonably do not expect law enforcement to convert their phones into precise, possibly continuous tracking tools.

Law and practice have evolved in this area in response to changes in technology. In 2010, a new statute required that police get a court order for cell-site information on a showing of less than probable cause: "specific and articulable facts showing that there are reasonable grounds to believe that the record or other information is relevant and material to an ongoing criminal investigation." The statute contains an exception for location information for mobile devices when a "law enforcement agency believes in good faith that an emergency involving danger of death or serious bodily injury to the subscriber or customer" exists. Moreover, as discussed further below, the Attorney General reports that in recent years, many law enforcement officers have obtained warrants based on probable cause before gathering information about the location of a cell phone. We credit the Attorney General's office for that approach.

For the reasons discussed, we conclude that Article I, Paragraph 7 of the New Jersey Constitution protects an individual's privacy interest in the location of his or her cell phone. Users are reasonably entitled to expect confidentiality in the ever-increasing level of detail that cell phones can reveal about their lives. Because of the nature of the intrusion, and the corresponding, legitimate privacy interest at stake, we hold today that police must obtain a warrant based on a showing of probable cause, or qualify for an exception to the warrant requirement, to obtain tracking information through the use of a cell phone.

By providing greater clarity to the law in this area, we strive to meet two aims: to protect the reasonable expectation of privacy that cell-phone users have and, at the same time, to offer clear guidance to law enforcement officials so they may carry out important tasks in the interest of public safety. Both the public and the police will be better served by a clear set of rules. To be sure, law enforcement officials will still be able to turn to cell-phone providers to obtain location information, as long as such requests are accompanied by a warrant issued by a neutral magistrate and supported by probable cause. We emphasize that no warrant is required in emergency situations or when some other exception to the warrant requirement applies.

Our ruling today is based solely on the State Constitution. We recognize that *Jones* and *Smith*, to the extent they apply, would not require a warrant in this case.

STATE v. BRYANT
950 A.2d 467 (Vt. 2008)

SKOGLUND, J.

The issue on this appeal from a conviction for cultivation of marijuana is whether the warrantless aerial scrutiny of defendant's yard, for the purpose of detecting criminal activity by the occupant of the property, violated privacy rights secured by the Vermont Constitution. We hold that Vermont citizens have a constitutional right to privacy that ascends into the airspace above their homes and property. The warrantless aerial surveillance in this case violated that constitutionally protected privacy right. Accordingly, we reverse.

Defendant was charged with felony possession and cultivation of marijuana. He moved to suppress from evidence the marijuana plants discovered growing by his house, alleging a violation of chapter I, article 11 of the Vermont Constitution. The trial court denied the motion. A jury convicted defendant on the cultivation charge, but not on the possession charge. Defendant appeals from the trial court's denial of his motion to suppress. We reverse.

Defendant argues that an unconstitutional aerial surveillance of his property resulted in the issuance of a search warrant that led to the discovery of defendant's marijuana cultivation. At a hearing on the motion to dismiss, the following facts were found by the court or were uncontested. Defendant lives in a remote area on a wooded hill in the town of Goshen, in Addison County. The property is accessible by a locked gate on a Forest Service road to which only defendant, his partner, and the Forest Service have keys. Beyond the gate, the dirt road passes defendant's homestead and continues a short distance into the National Forest, where the road dead-ends. Where the road cuts across defendant's property, the Forest Service has a restricted right-of-way. Defendant has posted prominent no-trespassing signs around his property. Prior to the aerial surveillance, defendant told a local forest official that he did not want the Forest Service or anyone else trespassing on his land.

The local forest official suspected that defendant was responsible for marijuana plants that were reportedly growing in the National Forest (not on defendant's property) because he found defendant's insistence on privacy to be "paranoid." The forest official suggested to the State Police that a Marijuana Eradication Team (MERT) flight over defendant's property might be a good idea. MERT is an anti-drug program, and MERT flights are executed by the Vermont State Police in cooperation with the Army National Guard. A state trooper, scheduled to do a MERT flight, was given the information identifying the defendant's residence as a good target. On August 7, 2003, the state trooper and an Army National Guard pilot flew in a National Guard helicopter to the Goshen area. Having previously located the site on a map, the trooper directed the pilot to defendant's property, where two plots of marijuana were observed growing about 100 feet from the house.

Defendant introduced testimony of several people who witnessed the flight. One witness, who was working outside at the time of the flyover, described the helicopter as being at twice the height of her house, or approximately 100 feet above ground level. She testified that the noise was "deafening." She observed the helicopter spend "a good half-hour" in the area of defendant's residence, where it circled "very low down to the trees."

After the flight, the state trooper prepared an application for a search warrant based solely on his observation during the aerial surveillance of what he believed to be marijuana plants. In the application, the trooper characterized the surveillance as having been from "an aircraft at least 500 feet above the ground." The warrant was issued and executed, and three marijuana plots were discovered by defendant's home.

Based on the evidence presented at the suppression hearing, the court found that the helicopter circled defendant's property for approximately fifteen to thirty minutes, well below 500 feet in altitude, and at times as low as 100 feet above the ground. Although both the trooper and the pilot testified that the helicopter remained at least 500 feet off the ground at all times, the court did not find their testimony to be credible. The court further found that pilots doing MERT flights in Vermont are told to stay at least 500 feet above the ground and that, according to a National Guard pilot who testified for the State, the reason MERT pilots are so directed is to avoid invasions of privacy.

The court, however, denied defendant's motion, holding that defendant had no reasonable expectation of privacy from the sky. The court reasoned that, while helicopter flights over one's property in rural Vermont might be infrequent, a reasonable person would still assume that such flights will happen. The court concluded that the police surveillance was not so intrusive as to violate the Vermont Constitution. We disagree and reverse.

Article 11 of the Vermont Constitution protects the people's right to be free "from unreasonable government intrusions into legitimate expectations of privacy." When government conducts a warrantless search, the law presumes that the intrusion is unreasonable. The aerial surveillance at issue in this case was warrantless, and therefore presumptively unreasonable. Thus, the sole issue in this case is whether the aerial surveillance constitutes a search under article 11 of Vermont's Constitution.

An article 11 search occurs when the government intrudes into "areas or activities" that are the subject of "legitimate expectations of privacy." Under article 11, the question of whether an individual has a legitimate expectation of privacy "hinges on the essence of underlying constitutional values—including respect for both private, subjective expectations and public norms." Therefore, in order to invoke article 11 protection, a person must "exhibit an actual (subjective) expectation of privacy that society is prepared to recognize as reasonable." In other words, article 11 requires an individual to have "conveyed an expectation of privacy in such a way that a reasonable person would conclude that he sought to exclude the public." "Whether the steps taken are adequate for this purpose will depend on the specific facts of each case."

We have often noted the "significance of the home as a repository of heightened privacy expectations," and have deemed those heightened expectations legitimate. Therefore, although we have disagreed amongst ourselves about the extent to which circumstances may alter the general rule, government intrusions into the home are searches for purposes of article 11 even if an individual fails to take affirmative steps to convey his expectation of privacy.

A home's curtilage—the "area outside the physical confines of a house into which the privacies of life may extend"—merits "the same constitutional protection from unreasonable searches and seizures as the home itself." However, relying on the principle that there is no invasion of privacy—and therefore no search—when government observes that which is willingly exposed to the public, we have consistently held that an individual must take affirmative steps to protect his privacy in his curtilage and his "open fields"—the real property beyond his curtilage. Government does conduct a search when it intrudes onto open fields that a reasonable person would expect to be private. Fences, gates, and no-trespassing signs generally suffice to apprise a person that the area is private.

In this case, we consider whether surveillance from an Army helicopter, circling at 100 feet over defendant's home and garden for fifteen to thirty minutes for the purpose of detecting contraband, violated his legitimate expectations of privacy. Whether and when aerial surveillance constitutes a search are questions that we have not squarely confronted before. We decide this case solely on Vermont Constitutional grounds, but may be guided by decisions of our sister states and the United States Supreme Court on similar questions. We begin our analysis with a survey of those decisions.

The United States Supreme Court has decided three aerial-surveillance cases; the Court ruled in each that the surveillance at issue was not a search within the meaning of the Fourth Amendment. For the reasons explained below, we find minimal guidance in these decisions.

It is our opinion that many of the factors relied on by our sister states and the U.S. Supreme Court in *Florida v. Riley* (1989) are relevant to evaluating the legitimacy of privacy expectations under article 11 in the context of the aerial surveillance at issue in this case. The legitimacy of an individual's expectation of privacy is a broad question of "private, subjective expectations and public norms." When we declined to adopt the federal open-fields doctrine in *State v. Kirchoff* (Vt. 1991), we recognized that Vermonters normally expect their property to remain private when posted as such. We have also recognized that Vermonters normally have high expectations of privacy in and around their homes. Therefore, we think it is also likely that Vermonters expect—at least at a private, rural residence on posted land—that they will be free from intrusions that interrupt their use of their property, expose their intimate activities, or create undue noise, wind, or dust.

We are also persuaded that the legality of the altitude at which aerial surveillance takes place can be relevant to the determination of whether an individual has a legitimate expectation of privacy in his real property. Indeed, the citizens of Vermont likely expect that law enforcement personnel as well as other air travelers will abide by safety rules and other applicable laws and regulations when flying over their homes. However, it simply does not follow that whether a member of the public is abiding by the law in occupying a particular spot in the public airspace is an adequate test of whether government surveillance from that same spot is constitutional. Therefore, we disagree with those courts that would use the legality of an aircraft's position alone to evaluate the constitutionality of the surveillance conducted aboard it.

In any event, at least on the facts of this case, no one factor need act as a litmus test of constitutionality, because the surveillance at issue here was a patent violation of defendant's legitimate expectations of privacy. We understand that our abstention from drawing a bright line that makes the legality or frequency of flights at certain altitudes a quick index to the constitutionality of aerial surveillance gives limited guidance to trial courts and law enforcement personnel in the context of other cases. But we are not presented with other cases; we are presented only with this case. In this case, defendant has demonstrated that he has a subjective expectation of privacy in his back yard. He has taken precautions to exclude others from his back yard by posting his land and by communicating to a local forest official that he did not want people trespassing on his land.

The overriding function of article 11 is to protect personal privacy and dignity against unwarranted intrusion by the state. It requires that the state temper its efforts to apprehend criminals with a concern for the impact of its methods on our fundamental liberties. Principles established in cases such as this delineate the extent to which official intrusion into the privacy of any citizen will be constitutionally permissible.

In *Johnson v. United States* (1948), the Supreme Court wrote that the Fourth Amendment reflects a choice that our society should be one in which citizens "dwell in reasonable security and freedom from surveillance." With technological advances in surveillance techniques, the privacy-protection question is no longer whether police have physically invaded a constitutionally protected area. Rather, the inquiry is whether the surveillance invaded a constitutionally protected legitimate expectation of privacy. In this case, the targeted, low-level helicopter surveillance by the police of activities in an enclosed backyard is not consistent with that expectation—not without a warrant.

It may be easy to forget, especially in view of current concerns over drug abuse in our society, that the scope of article 11's protection "does not turn on whether the activity disclosed by a search is illegal or innocuous." The interest protected by article 11, like the Fourth Amendment, "is the expectation of the ordinary citizen, who has never engaged in illegal conduct in his life." In his dissent in *United States v. White* (1971), Justice Harlan reasoned that the scope of constitutional protection must reflect "the impact of a practice on the sense of security that is the true concern of the constitution's protection of privacy." We agree. We protect defendant's marijuana plots against such surveillance so that law-abiding citizens may relax in their backyards, enjoying a sense of security that they are free from unreasonable surveillance.

The aerial surveillance in this case was a warrantless search forbidden by the Vermont Constitution. The warrant authorizing the subsequent search of defendant's premises for marijuana plants was obtained solely on the basis of the aerial observations. The evidence seized upon executing the warrant should therefore have been excluded from defendant's trial. Since the error was clearly prejudicial, his conviction must be overturned.

STATE v. LEONARD
943 N.W.2d 149 (Minn. 2020)

HUDSON, J.

The State charged appellant John Thomas Leonard with check forgery based on evidence that law enforcement officers discovered in his hotel room. Leonard moved to suppress the State's evidence. He argued, among other things, that the officers violated Article I, Section 10 of the Minnesota Constitution when they examined the hotel guest registry, which led them to his room, without the officers having any individualized suspicion of criminal activity.

We hold that the law enforcement officers conducted a search under Article I, Section 10 of the Minnesota Constitution when they examined the guest registry. We hold further that law enforcement officers must have at least a reasonable, articulable suspicion to search a guest registry.

Law enforcement officers arrived at a Bloomington hotel on August 14, 2015, for a hotel interdiction. The officers were not responding to a particular call. Without a warrant and without any individualized suspicion of criminal activity, the officers told the clerk on duty that they wanted to examine the guest registry and to be provided with the name of any guest who paid in cash. Hotels and all other overnight lodging establishments are required to keep these guest registries under the hotel guest registry statutes. Specifically, the hotel guest registry statutes require all lodging establishments to collect each guest's name and address, vehicle information, and the names and addresses of any travel companions. Guests must provide this information to the hotel, and hotel operators must make this information available to law enforcement. Both hotel guests and hotel operators must comply with their statutory duties under threat of misdemeanor prosecution.

The clerk complied with the officers' request to examine the guest registry and alerted them that a man had checked into a room for six hours and paid in cash. The officers used the guest registry to identify this man as Leonard. The officers then ran a background check and found that Leonard had prior arrests for, among other things, drugs, firearms, and fraud. Based on this information, the officers developed an individualized suspicion that Leonard was involved in criminal activity and decided to conduct a "knock and talk" at the door of Leonard's hotel room. When Leonard heard the officers knock, he opened the door and gave them limited consent to search the room, but withheld access to his laptop, cell phone, and a file folder where several checks were visible. The officers subdued Leonard through a physical struggle after he tried to flee. After securing a search warrant, the officers discovered over $2,000 worth of suspicious checks paid to the order of "Spencer Alan Hill," over $5,000 in cash, and check-printing paper.

The Minnesota Constitution protects the "right of the people to be secure in their persons, houses, papers, and effects against unreasonable searches and seizures." Under Article I, Section 10, a search occurs when law enforcement intrudes upon an individual's subjective expectation of privacy that society is prepared to recognize as reasonable. Leonard has the burden to establish that he has a protectable right under the Minnesota Constitution.

Whether a guest has a reasonable expectation of privacy in the highly sensitive location information found in a guest registry under Article I, Section 10 is an issue of first impression. In such cases, we can look to other jurisdictions for guidance.

In *State v. Jorden* (Wash. 2007), the Supreme Court of Washington held that the Washington Constitution afforded individuals a reasonable expectation of privacy in their guest registry information because "an individual's very presence in a motel or hotel may in itself be a sensitive piece of information." The court noted that the anonymity of hotels may provide necessary space for people engaged in consensual—but deeply private—relationships or confidential business negotiations, for celebrities, and for people experiencing domestic violence who hope to "remain hidden from an abuser."

We find the reasoning in *Jorden* persuasive. Imagine instead that Leonard had stayed overnight at the hotel to attend a political or religious conference in the hotel ballroom, or that he had stayed overnight before a medical appointment in hopes of keeping a diagnosis private. In these examples, the guest's highly sensitive location information is revealed, regardless of what actually occurred in the hotel room. That such information would be accessible to the government through a fishing expedition, where the hotel guest was a stranger to law enforcement before the officers' random search, offends our core constitutional principles. The particular role that hotels play in society makes a guest's presence at that location sensitive information that warrants privacy protections. To conclude otherwise would deprive Minnesotans of rights that we have the duty to safeguard.

Simply put, we think that most Minnesotans would be surprised and alarmed if the sensitive location information found in the guest registries at hotels, motels, or RV campsites was readily available to law enforcement without any particularized suspicion of criminal activity. Exercising our responsibility to safeguard for the people of Minnesota the protections afforded in our Constitution, we now hold that hotel guests have a reasonable expectation of privacy in the sensitive location information found in guest registries.

We also agree with Leonard that the court of appeals erred in applying the third-party doctrine. Under this doctrine, a defendant loses a reasonable expectation of privacy in information upon disclosure to a third party. It relies on the long-standing and unchallenged principle that "what a person knowingly exposes to the public is not a subject of Fourth Amendment protection." In applying this doctrine to Leonard's disclosure under the hotel registry statutes, the court of appeals failed to consider that Leonard's disclosure transformed his otherwise public data into sensitive location information that society is prepared to recognize as a reasonable privacy interest.

Critical to our analysis is the meaning of public exposure. Society views most third-party institutions as places in which private affairs are not conducted or exposed. But some third-party institutions are generally considered private (e.g., a doctor's examination room or a lawyer's office). Thus, sharing private information in these spaces does not destroy someone's reasonable expectation of privacy, but rather contributes to its private character. Although a guest registry includes seemingly public information—a name and address—the act of recording this information in the guest registry creates sensitive location information because a hotel is a place where people engage in a variety of already described legal, but often deeply private, activities. The dissent ignores this distinction and lists several examples in which individuals likely understand and accept that their name and address is public, such as on a mailed envelope or in public school directory information. But none of these examples create sensitive location information.

GILDEA, C.J., dissenting.

The majority holds that the police conducted an unconstitutional search when they obtained Leonard's name and address from a registry at a hotel where Leonard rented a room for six hours. I disagree. Because Leonard did not have a reasonable expectation of privacy in his name and address, and because the majority's decision conflicts with our precedent interpreting the Minnesota Constitution, I dissent.

The threshold question in any case where a defendant claims that police conducted an unlawful search is whether the defendant had a reasonable expectation of privacy in the item searched. In this case, the item searched was the guest registry where the police found Leonard's name and address. The majority does not focus on Leonard's name and address but instead grounds its result in concerns over the privacy interests Leonard had in his activities inside of the hotel room. But those interests are not at issue in this case because Leonard gave consent for the police to enter and search his hotel room. Rather, we must decide whether Leonard had a reasonable expectation of privacy in his name and address in the hotel registry.

There is nothing in the record to suggest—much less prove—that Leonard exhibited a subjective expectation of privacy in his name and address. As far as I can tell, Leonard willingly gave his name and address to the hotel when he arrived and asked to rent a room. Relevant precedent from the United States Supreme Court confirms that where the defendant willingly gives his information to a third party, the defendant no longer has an expectation of privacy in the information given to the third party.

Even if Leonard harbored any expectation of privacy in his name and address prior to the disclosure, his decision to disclose his name and address to the hotel ended his expectation of privacy. That conclusion should be the end of this case.

But even if Leonard exhibited a subjective expectation of privacy, requiring us to consider the second step of the reasonable-expectation-of-privacy analysis, I would still affirm the court of appeals because Leonard has not demonstrated that any expectation of privacy in his name and address is reasonable.

As a threshold matter, the statutes at issue in this case, which required the hotel to collect Leonard's name and address as part of the registration process to rent a hotel room, were enacted in 1937. For the past 80 years in Minnesota, law enforcement officers have been able to obtain names and addresses from hotel registries. This long history confirms that police did nothing unusual here, and informs us on what society is prepared to protect as reasonable.

Moreover, name and address information is widely available in many public formats. Government records containing an individual's name and address include real estate sale documents and voter data. In addition to government records, phone books containing the names, addresses, and telephone numbers of individuals residing in a given municipality have existed for more than 100 years. And citizens put millions of pieces of mail containing their names and addresses through the postal system every day.

In this day and age, most individuals know and expect their names and addresses to be easily discoverable. Because names and addresses are publicly available in so many different ways in our society, I would hold that there is no reasonable expectation of privacy in an individual's name and address.

NOTES

1. The Vermont Constitution has been construed consistently as having a strong preference for warrants, *i.e.*, "one of the essential checks on unrestrained government determined by the framers to be necessary to the preservation of individual freedom." *State v. Bauder*, 924 A.2d 38 (Vt. 2007). Under article 11 of the Vermont Constitution, police must get a search warrant before searching a closed container unless "exceptional" circumstances—risk of undue delay, destruction of evidence, or danger to officers—make getting a warrant impracticable. *State v. Neil*, 958 A.2d 1173 (Vt. 2008); *see also State v. Dupuis*, 197 A.3d 343 (Vt. 2018) (warrant required to enter land to enforce hunting laws). Interestingly, article I, section 9 of the Texas Constitution "contains no requirement that a seizure or search be authorized by a warrant, and that a search or seizure that is otherwise reasonable will not be found to be in violation of that section because it was not authorized by a warrant." *Hulit v. State*, 982 S.W.2d 431 (Tex. Crim. App. 1998).

2. The United States Supreme Court has held that there is no reasonable expectation of privacy in garbage left in a public place with intent to disregard it. Thus, there was no Fourth Amendment search when police officers inspected the contents of opaque plastic bags left out for garbage collection. *California v. Greenwood*, 486 U.S. 35 (1988). Although most state constitutions have been construed to permit a warrantless search of trash that has been left out for collection, some state constitutions require a warrant. *See State v. Lien*, 441 P.3d 185 (Or. 2019); *State v. Goss*, 834 A.2d 316 (N.H. 2003). *Greenwood* was also rejected on the basis of the greater privacy protection provided by the text in article I, section 7 of the Washington Constitution. *See State v. Boland*, 800 P.2d 1112 (Wash. 1990).

F. PHYSICAL SEIZURE OF AN INDIVIDUAL BY POLICE

STATE v. BEAUCHESNE
868 A.2d 972 (N.H. 2005)

DUGGAN, J.

Following a bench trial on stipulated facts, the defendant, John Beauchesne, was convicted of possession of cocaine, possession of marijuana, and resisting detention. On appeal, he challenges his convictions for possession of cocaine and marijuana, arguing that the Superior Court erroneously denied his motion to suppress the cocaine and marijuana. The defendant does not challenge his conviction for resisting detention. We reverse and remand.

On September 27, 2002, Detective Peter Morelli of the Derry Police Department was on duty patrolling downtown Derry. Detective Morelli was in an unmarked cruiser, wearing street clothes and "on the lookout for 'drug crime.'" Although Detective Morelli testified that he previously had investigated drug transactions in the area he was patrolling, he also testified that a drug transaction was no more likely to occur there than any other area in Derry.

At approximately 6:30 p.m., Detective Morelli observed two men standing in an alley off Railroad Avenue. One man was straddling a bike. The defendant was facing the man on the bike. Detective Morelli saw the defendant hand something small and "unidentifiable" to the man straddling the bike, then turn and walk toward the street.

Believing that he had just witnessed a drug transaction, Detective Morelli stopped and exited his cruiser, made eye contact with the defendant and motioned for the defendant to approach him. The defendant did not respond and walked away. Detective Morelli then yelled to the defendant, identifying himself as a police officer and ordering the defendant to stop. The defendant again did not respond and continued walking away.

Detective Morelli followed the defendant on foot. When he saw that the defendant was running away, Detective Morelli again yelled that he was a police officer and ordered the defendant to stop. The defendant continued to run and Detective Morelli followed him. Detective Morelli eventually caught up with the defendant and attempted to grab him. The defendant, however, fell to the ground. During his fall, the defendant either dropped or threw a plastic bag containing a green vegetative matter, which Detective Morelli was able to identify immediately as marijuana. Detective Morelli then fell over the defendant.

Detective Morelli arrested the defendant for resisting detention and possessing marijuana. Detective Morelli subsequently searched the defendant's person and discovered a quantity of cocaine.

The defendant moved to suppress the cocaine and marijuana obtained as a result of the seizure because Detective Morelli lacked reasonable, articulable suspicion when he first ordered the defendant to stop. The trial court denied the motion, ruling that under *California v. Hodari D.* (1991), the defendant was not seized until he "fell and thus submitted to the detective's show of authority," at which time Detective Morelli had reasonable, articulable suspicion that the defendant had committed a crime.

On appeal, the defendant argues that the trial court erred in ruling that, under part I, article 19 of the State Constitution, the defendant was not seized until he submitted to Detective Morelli's show of authority. To that end, the defendant argues that we should not adopt the holding in *Hodari D.*, which requires submission to a show of authority, for determining when a seizure occurs under the State Constitution. In addition, the defendant argues that because he was seized for State constitutional purposes when Detective Morelli ordered him to stop, the trial court erred in denying his motion to suppress the cocaine and marijuana because the detective lacked reasonable, articulable suspicion at the time of the seizure.

The defendant argues that he was subject to an unlawful seizure because Detective Morelli lacked reasonable suspicion when he first ordered the defendant to stop. Accordingly, the defendant argues that the trial court erred in denying his motion to suppress the cocaine and marijuana as fruits of the unlawful seizure.

It is well settled that "in order for a police officer to undertake an investigatory stop, the officer must have a reasonable suspicion—based on specific, articulable facts taken together with rational inferences from those facts—that the particular person stopped has been, is, or is about to be, engaged in criminal activity." An investigatory stop is a very limited seizure. Thus, in deciding whether Detective Morelli conducted a lawful investigatory stop, we must conduct a two-step inquiry. First, we must determine when the defendant was seized. Second, we must determine whether, at that time, Detective Morelli possessed a reasonable suspicion that the defendant was, had been or was about to be engaged in criminal activity.

The crux of this appeal is the determination of when, under part I, article 19 of the State Constitution, the defendant was seized. The defendant argues that, for State constitutional purposes, he was seized when Detective Morelli first ordered him to stop. The State, relying upon the holding in *Hodari D.*, argues that the defendant was seized when he fell and submitted to Detective Morelli's show of authority.

Not all interactions between the police and citizens involve a seizure of the person. "A seizure does not occur simply because a police officer approaches an individual and asks a few questions." This is true "so long as a reasonable person would feel free to disregard the police and go about his business." Indeed, the police may request to examine the individual's identification or for consent to search the individual or his belongings. The person stopped, however, is not obliged to answer and the police may not convey a message that compliance with their request is required. Moreover, unless the police officer has reasonable suspicion, the person approached may not be detained.

An interaction between a police officer and a citizen becomes a seizure, however, when a reasonable person believes he or she is not free to leave. This occurs when an officer, by means of physical force or show of authority, has in some way restrained the liberty of the person. Circumstances indicating a "show of authority" might include the threatening presence of several officers, the display of a weapon by an officer, some physical touching of the person, or the use of language or tone of voice indicating that compliance with the officer's request might be compelled. The analysis is an objective one, requiring a determination of whether the defendant's freedom of movement was sufficiently curtailed by considering how a reasonable person in the defendant's position would have understood his situation.

In *Hodari D.*, the United States Supreme Court addressed the "narrow question whether, with respect to a show of authority, a seizure occurs even though the subject does not yield." In that case, two police officers on patrol in a high-crime area observed four or five youths, including the defendant, huddled around a car parked at the curb. When the youths saw the police car approach, they ran. One of the officers exited the car and pursued the defendant on foot. As the officer neared, the defendant tossed away what was later determined to be crack cocaine. The Court concluded that the defendant was not seized when the police officer was pursuing him and, thus, the cocaine was admissible because he had not yet been seized when he discarded it. Rather, relying primarily upon the dictionary definition of seizure and the common law of arrest, the Court held that:

> The word "seizure" readily bears the meaning of a laying on of hands or application of physical force to restrain movement, even when it is ultimately unsuccessful. ("She seized the purse-snatcher, but he broke out of her grasp.") It does not remotely apply, however, to the prospect of a policeman yelling "Stop, in the name of the law!" at a fleeing form that continues to flee. That is no seizure.

Accordingly, the Court held that a seizure "requires either physical force or, where that is absent, submission to the assertion of authority."

Several States have considered whether to adopt the holding in *Hodari D.* for determining when a seizure occurs under their respective state constitutions. Numerous state courts have rejected *Hodari D.* on state constitutional grounds. The Supreme Court of Tennessee summarized the "extensive criticisms" of *Hodari D.* as follows:

> First, the majority's analysis in *Hodari D.* represents a marked departure from the standard the Supreme Court adopted in *United States v. Mendenhall* (1980), *i.e.*,

that a seizure occurs when "in view of all of the circumstances surrounding the incident, a reasonable person would have believed he was not free to leave." Second, the majority's analysis fails to apply common law principles under which an arrest would not be distinguished from an attempted arrest in determining whether a person has been seized. Third, the majority's analysis is flawed for practical reasons and is subject to potential abuse by officers who pursue a subject without reasonable suspicion and use a flight or refusal to submit to authority as reason to execute an arrest or search.

Of the States that have adopted *Hodari D.* under their state constitutions, many do so noting that they do not have a history of providing greater privacy protection to their citizens than the Federal Constitution.

In contrast, we have recognized that our State Constitution incorporates a strong right of privacy and provides greater protection for individual rights than the Federal Constitution. Accordingly, we are persuaded by the reasoning of those States that have declined to adopt the holding in *Hodari D.* for determining when a seizure occurs as a matter of State constitutional law.

We have held that part I, article 19, provides greater protection for individual rights than does the Fourth Amendment. Indeed, we have recognized that "our Constitution has historically been interpreted to incorporate a strong right of privacy." In *Canelo*, for instance, we adopted the exclusionary rule under the State Constitution because it served to deter police misconduct and "to redress the injury to the privacy of the search victim." We also declined to adopt a good faith exception to the exclusionary rule because it was "incompatible with and detrimental to our citizens' strong right of privacy inherent in part I, article 19."

Likewise, the *Hodari D.* rule is incompatible with the guarantees of part I, article 19. As the Massachusetts Supreme Judicial Court aptly noted:

> Stops provoke constitutional scrutiny because they encumber a person's freedom of movement. Pursuit that appears designed to effect a stop is no less intrusive than a stop itself. Framed slightly differently, a pursuit, which, objectively considered, indicates to a person that he would not be free to leave the area (or to remain there) without first responding to a police officer's inquiry, is the functional equivalent of a seizure, in the sense that the person being pursued is plainly the object of an official assertion of authority, which does not intend to be denied, and which infringes considerably on the person's freedom of action.

Because of the intrusiveness of a police officer's assertion of authority, requiring police officers to possess reasonable suspicion prior to asserting their authority is necessary to adequately protect individual rights under the State Constitution. Thus, under part I, article 19 of the State Constitution, a police officer must possess reasonable suspicion before taking an action that would communicate to a reasonable person that he or she is not free to leave.

Our holding today is supported by sound practical and policy reasons. First, focusing the definition of seizure on the police officer's conduct, and not the individual's conduct, results in the same State constitutional implications for similar police conduct. In this case, for example, Detective

Morelli's conduct of identifying himself as a police officer and ordering the defendant to stop is the same, whether or not the defendant submitted to the officer's show of authority. It would be an anomaly to hold that the officer's conduct was a seizure had the defendant submitted, but because the defendant did not submit, the same conduct by the officer was not a seizure. If the officer's attempt to detain the defendant lacks reasonable suspicion, it is unlawful whether or not the defendant submits to the show of authority. Thus, by defining the moment a seizure occurs by the police officer's conduct, "the police can determine in advance whether the conduct contemplated will implicate the state constitution."

Second, constitutional protections become "meaningful only when it is assured that at some point the conduct of those charged with enforcing the laws can be subjected to the more detached, neutral scrutiny of a judge who must evaluate the reasonableness of a particular search or seizure." The *Mendenhall* test achieves this goal by providing an objective standard for judicial review of the seizure. Thus, our holding allows courts to continue to objectively evaluate the reasonableness of the police officer's actions, not the defendant's reaction. Third, we do not write on a blank slate for defining when a seizure occurs. An analysis that focuses exclusively on the conduct of the police is, as several state courts have pointed out, consistent with the well-settled definition of seizure in *Mendenhall*. In *State v. Quezada* (N.H. 1996), a police officer called to the defendant, "Hey, you, stop," and after the defendant did not respond, called out again, "Hey, I want to speak to you." One of the key factors in our analysis of whether a seizure occurred was that the officer used "language indicating that compliance was not optional." We thus concluded that, "given the late hour, the absence of other citizens in the vicinity, the presence of two uniformed police officers, and the language of the officer's requests, no reasonable person would have believed he was free to ignore the officer and simply walk away." In holding that there was a sufficient "show of authority" to effect a seizure, our analysis focused upon the officer's actions and the other surrounding circumstances. The defendant's reaction was not a part of our seizure analysis.

Finally, our holding serves to effectuate the goal of the exclusionary rule to deter police misconduct. Indeed, one of the primary criticisms of the holding in *Hodari D.* is that it is subject to potential abuse. Thus, because the police are not required to possess reasonable suspicion prior to asserting their authority under *Hodari D.*, that rule "will encourage unlawful displays of force that will frighten countless innocent citizens into surrendering whatever privacy rights they may still have."

Having determined when a seizure occurs under part I, article 19, we must now determine when the defendant was seized. As stated above, a seizure occurs only when a reasonable person believes he is not free to leave because the officer, by means of physical force or show of authority, has in some way restrained the liberty of the person. The analysis is an objective one, requiring a determination of whether the defendant's freedom of movement was sufficiently curtailed by considering how a reasonable person in the defendant's position would have understood his situation.

In this case, although Detective Morelli was in an unmarked cruiser and wearing street clothes, he yelled to the defendant, identified himself as a police officer and ordered the defendant to stop. Detective Morelli then pursued the defendant on foot, again identifying himself as a police officer and ordering the defendant to stop. In view of all the circumstances, the encounter transcended a mere request to communicate. Given Detective Morelli's repeated identification of himself as a police officer and his orders to stop, no reasonable person would have believed he was free to ignore the officer and simply walk away. Thus, the defendant was seized when Detective Morelli first identified himself as a police officer and ordered the defendant to stop.

NOTES

1. Under the New Hampshire Constitution "a seizure occurs when an officer, by means of physical force or show of authority, has in some way restrained the liberty of the person." *State v. Beauchesne*, 868 A.2d 972 (N.H. 2005).

2. The Tennessee Supreme Court held that a defendant was seized, for purposes of the state constitution, "at the moment when the officer pulled up behind the defendant's stopped vehicle and activated his blue emergency lights." *State v. Williams*, 185 S.W.3d 311 (Tenn. 2006); *see State v. McCormick*, 494 S.W.3d 673 (Tenn. 2016) (officers' actions in parking on the roadway behind defendant's vehicle with his lights activated and opening the door to the car and attempting to rouse defendant after taps on the window failed to rouse him were well within the community caretaking exception under Tenn. Const. art. I, § 7).

3. A seizure does not occur under article I, section 6 of the Delaware Constitution when uniformed officers follow a walking pedestrian and request to speak to him, without doing anything more. *Ross v. State*, 925 A.2d 489 (Del. 2007).

4. The rationale of *Hodari D.* was held to be contrary to the unique language in article I, section 8 of the Washington Constitution that restricts police invasions of privacy: "No person shall be disturbed in his private affairs, or his home invaded, without authority of law." *State v. Young*, 957 P.2d 681 (Wash. 1998); *see also State v. Harrington*, 222 P.3d 92 (Wash. 2009) (initiating conversation with defendant was not unlawful, but social contact with defendant by officer escalated into an illegal seizure under state constitution).

G. WARRANTLESS AUTOMOBILE SEARCH

STATE v. CORA
167 A.3d 633 (N.H. 2017)

HICKS, J.

The State appeals an order of the Superior Court granting the motion filed by the defendant, Daniel Jesus Cora, to suppress all evidence obtained from the warrantless entry by the police into his vehicle. On appeal, the State contends that the police were allowed to enter the vehicle without a warrant either under the federal automobile exception to the warrant requirement, which the State asks that we adopt under the State Constitution, or because the defendant had a diminished expectation of privacy in the interior space of his vehicle that is visible to the public. Under the federal automobile exception, police officers, with probable cause to search "a lawfully stopped vehicle," may conduct a warrantless search "of every part of the vehicle and its contents that may conceal the object of the search."

The State urges us to overrule our decision in *State v. Sterndale* (N.H. 1995), in which we declined to adopt, under Part I, Article 19 of the State Constitution, the federal automobile exception to the warrant requirement as articulated in *United States v. Ross* (1982) and other Supreme Court cases. Alternatively, the State asks that we conclude that *Sterndale* has been abrogated by our decision in *State v. Goss* (N.H. 2003), and that we adopt a "slightly more narrow exception" to the warrant requirement based upon the defendant's diminished expectation of privacy in the "publicly visible areas of his car."

We decline to overrule *Sterndale*. However, we agree with the State that *Sterndale* has been abrogated by *Goss*, at least in part, and that its abrogation requires that we re-evaluate whether to adopt an automobile exception to our warrant requirement. We now recognize a limited automobile exception to the warrant requirement pursuant to which the police do not need to obtain a warrant to enter an automobile when the vehicle has been lawfully stopped while in transit and the police have probable cause to believe that a plainly visible item in the vehicle is contraband.

In this case, the police did not need a warrant before entering the defendant's vehicle because the vehicle was subject to a lawful traffic stop, and the police had probable cause to believe that the baggie and cigarette, which were plainly visible, were drugs.

The trial court found, or the record establishes, the following facts. The defendant's vehicle was pulled over by Manchester Police Officer Day because it ran a red light and "cut off" Day's cruiser. The defendant was the driver of the vehicle and had two passengers with him. While Day spoke with the defendant, he noticed the odor of fresh marijuana. Day returned to his cruiser, ran a license check on the defendant, and requested that another officer assist him. When the other officer, Officer Horn, arrived on the scene, Day asked the defendant to exit the vehicle while Horn spoke with the passenger sitting in the front seat. Day told the defendant that he smelled marijuana in the automobile. The defendant admitted that he sometimes smoked marijuana inside his vehicle. When Day advised the defendant that the marijuana smelled fresh, the defendant admitted that there were a "couple roaches" in the vehicle. Day asked the defendant to consent to a search of the automobile; the defendant declined to do so.

Meanwhile, Horn asked the passenger sitting in the front seat to get out of the vehicle. From outside the vehicle, Horn saw that near the doorjamb of the front passenger side of the vehicle were a "tied-off baggie" containing a brown, powdery substance and a "cigarette" containing a leafy, green substance. Horn called Day's attention to the items. Based upon his training and expertise, Day believed that the baggie contained heroin and that the cigarette contained marijuana. Day seized the baggie and cigarette from the vehicle.

The defendant was charged with one misdemeanor and one felony count of possession of a controlled drug. Before trial, he moved to suppress all evidence obtained from Day's warrantless entry into his vehicle.

Part I, Article 19 of the New Hampshire Constitution protects an individual from "all unreasonable searches and seizures of his person, his houses, his papers, and all his possessions." "A warrantless search is per se unreasonable and invalid unless it comes within one of a few recognized exceptions." "Absent a warrant, the burden is on the State to prove that the search was valid pursuant to one of these exceptions."

One exception to the warrant requirement is the plain view exception, which authorizes the police to seize an item. In order for an item's warrantless seizure to be justified under the plain view exception: (1) the item must be in plain view; (2) the officer must not have violated the constitution "in arriving at the place from which the evidence could be plainly viewed"; and (3) the officer "must also have a lawful right of access to the object itself." In addition, the incriminating nature of the item seized must be "immediately apparent," which means that, at the time of the seizure, the police must have probable cause to believe that the item seized constitutes incriminating evidence. Because the items at issue are drugs, there is no requirement that the officers' view of them be inadvertent.

The State argues that the officers were allowed to enter the defendant's vehicle either under the federal automobile exception to the warrant requirement, which the State urges us to adopt, or under a narrower exception because the defendant had a diminished expectation of privacy in the interior space of his vehicle that is visible to the public. The State argues that we must either overrule *Sterndale* and adopt the federal automobile exception or conclude that *Sterndale* was abrogated by our adoption of the expectation of privacy analysis in *Goss* and adopt our own, more limited automobile exception. The defendant counters that *Sterndale* remains good law and that our decision in *Goss* does not undermine it. Alternatively, the defendant argues that the police in this case lacked authority to enter his vehicle without a warrant because doing so either interfered with his reasonable expectation of privacy or constituted a trespass.

In analyzing how *Goss* affected *Sterndale*, we begin by examining *Sterndale*. The defendant in *Sterndale* was subject to a traffic stop, and then arrested and placed in the back of a police cruiser. Following the arrest, the police officer returned to the defendant's vehicle and observed a brown paper bag. The officer leaned into the automobile, opened the paper bag, and found four clear, plastic bags containing what he believed to be marijuana. The trial court suppressed the contents of the brown paper bag.

On appeal, the State argued that the officer's search was justified as a search incident to arrest, under the exigent circumstances exception to the warrant requirement, and under the federal automobile exception to that requirement, which the State asked us to adopt. We rejected the State's search incident to arrest argument and declined to consider its exigent circumstances argument because the State had not preserved it for our review.

We also rejected the State's invitation to adopt, under Part I, Article 19 of the State Constitution, the federal automobile exception as articulated in such decisions as *Ross*. We stated that we did not find convincing the Court's two justifications for that exception: (1) that there is a "reduced expectation of privacy" in an automobile; and (2) that an automobile presents exigent circumstances because it is "readily mobile" and "could be moved beyond the reach of the police." We found the privacy justification unpersuasive because, at that time, we had not expressly adopted an expectation of privacy test under the State Constitution. We found the exigent circumstances rationale unpersuasive because we disagreed with the theory that "every automobile, due to its mobility, serves to justify governmental intrusion into the vehicle." We observed that some vehicles, such as the towed vehicle in *Camargo*, are not mobile. In those situations, we noted, the police may avoid incurring the risk that a vehicle will be moved by assigning an officer to guard it while a warrant is obtained.

Less than a decade later, in 2003, we decided *Goss*. As the State asserts, our adoption of the expectation of privacy analysis in *Goss* "changed the calculus that must be applied in determining whether a warrantless search was unreasonable."

Consistent with our decision in *Goss*, we now agree with the Supreme Court that there is a diminished expectation of privacy, generally, in automobiles. As the United States Supreme Court has "repeatedly recognized, the expectation of privacy in an automobile is significantly different from the traditional expectation of privacy and freedom in one's residence." The diminished protection "accorded automobiles derives from their continual exposure to public scrutiny." As the Court has explained, there is a diminished expectation of privacy in an automobile because "a car has little capacity for escaping public scrutiny. It travels public thoroughfares where both its occupants and its contents are in plain view." Moreover, "every operator of a motor vehicle must expect that the State, in enforcing its regulations, will intrude to some extent upon that operator's privacy." Therefore, we agree with the Supreme Court that there is a diminished expectation of privacy in an automobile.

The State contends that because we adopted an expectation of privacy analysis in *Goss*, we should, therefore, recognize the federal automobile exception under our State Constitution. We disagree.

We believe that the federal automobile exception is too broad. Under the federal automobile exception, police officers, with probable cause to search "a lawfully stopped vehicle," may conduct a warrantless search "of every part of the vehicle and its contents that may conceal the object of the search." We believe, however, that there can be "a reasonable expectation of privacy in certain areas of the interior of an automobile otherwise placed in the public view." Courts in other jurisdictions, for instance, have found that such an expectation exists "in those areas which would be otherwise free from observation except by physical intrusion of some sort," such as "the trunk, the glove compartment, closed containers in the interior, and in most cases, the area under the seats." In *State v. Elison* (Mont. 2000), for instance, the court concluded that the defendant had an actual expectation of privacy in items stowed behind the seat in his automobile and that his actual expectation was reasonable. The court explained that "when a person takes precautions to place items behind or underneath seats, in trunks or glove boxes, or uses other methods of ensuring that those items may not be accessed and viewed without permission, there is no obvious reason to believe that any privacy interest with regard to those items has been surrendered simply because those items happen to be in an automobile."

Accordingly, we reject the State's invitation to adopt the federal automobile exception under the State Constitution. However, we take this opportunity to recognize a more limited automobile exception to our warrant requirement. Under that more limited exception, the police need no warrant to enter an automobile when: (1) the vehicle has been stopped in transit pursuant to a lawful stop; and (2) the police have probable cause to believe that a plainly visible item in the vehicle is contraband.

We believe that this limited automobile exception is a legitimate extension of our decision in *Goss*. We further believe that it "correctly balances the need to search against the invasion which the search entails, and, thus heeds our constitution's proscription against unreasonable searches." Whereas the privacy expectations of an individual in his or her automobile are "considerably diminished, the governmental interests at stake are substantial." The government has a well-recognized "need to seize readily movable contraband." "Effective law enforcement would be appreciably impaired without the ability to" enter the plainly visible interior of a lawfully stopped vehicle when the police have probable cause to believe that there is contraband in that area. Moreover, when an automobile is stopped in transit, there is a "risk that the contraband will be permanently lost while a warrant is obtained."

In the instant case, because the defendant's vehicle was stopped in transit pursuant to a lawful stop and because the police had probable cause to believe that plainly visible items in the vehicle were contraband, they needed no warrant before entering the vehicle.

STATE V. VILLELA
450 P.3d 170 (Wash. 2019)

GONZALEZ, J.

Our state constitution protects our right to privacy. Under our constitution, the State and its agents may not disturb our "private affairs without authority of law." "Authority of law" generally means a warrant issued by a neutral magistrate or a long-standing exception to the warrant requirement.

We are asked today whether the legislature has created "authority of law," as understood in our constitution, by passing RCW 46.55.360. Under this law, officers are required to impound a vehicle any time they arrest its driver for driving under the influence. This impound is mandatory, regardless of whether the vehicle is safely off the roadway or whether another person is able to safely drive it away. Our constitution cannot be amended by statute, and while the legislature can give more protection to constitutional rights through legislation, it cannot use legislation to take that protection away.

Late one night in January 2018, Sergeant Paul Snyder stopped a jeep driven by Joel Villela for speeding. Sergeant Snyder smelled alcohol on Villela's breath and, after Villela declined a roadside field sobriety test, arrested him on suspicion of driving while under the influence of intoxicants. Sergeant Snyder also impounded Villela's jeep under RCW 46.55.360. Following the dictates of the statute, Sergeant Snyder did not consider whether there was a reasonable alternative to impounding Villela's jeep, such as releasing it to one of Villela's two passengers.

After the jeep was impounded, Sergeant Snyder did an inventory search of its contents. Sergeant Snyder found sandwich bags, digital scales, black cloth, pipes, and $340 in cash, all of which he believed was associated with drug dealing. A search incident to arrest discovered cocaine on Villela himself. Villela was charged with DUI and possession with intent to deliver controlled substances.

"The right to be free from searches by government agents is deeply rooted in our nation's history and law, and it is enshrined in our state and national constitutions." *State v. Day* (Wash. 2007). "Generally, officers of the State must obtain a warrant before intruding into the private affairs of others, and we presume that warrantless searches violate both constitutions." *Id.* However, "that presumption can be rebutted if the State shows a search fell within certain 'narrowly and jealously drawn exceptions to the warrant requirement.'" *Id.*

We use a two-step analysis to determine whether article I, section 7 has been violated. First, we "determine whether the action complained of constitutes a disturbance of one's private affairs." If so, we turn to the second step: "whether authority of law justifies the intrusion." "The 'authority of law' required by article I, section 7 is a valid warrant unless the State shows that a search or seizure falls within one of the jealously guarded and carefully drawn exceptions to the warrant requirement."

We have long held that under article I, section 7, authority of law to impound a vehicle after the driver has been arrested exists in two circumstances. First, a vehicle may be impounded on probable cause that it contains evidence of a crime. Second, a vehicle may be impounded when there is "'reasonable and proper justification for such impoundment.'" "The reasonableness of a search or seizure must be decided in light of the facts and circumstances of the case." "The police officer does not have to exhaust all possible alternatives, but must consider reasonable alternatives." Thus, an impound is lawful under article I, section 7 only if, in the judgment of the impounding officer, it is reasonable under the circumstances and there are no reasonable alternatives. Since the officer did not make that judgment, the impound was unlawful under our state constitution.

RCW 46.55.360 waives what our constitution requires before a car may be seized: either probable cause or a long-standing exception to the warrant requirement, such as community caretaking. In addition, in the absence of probable cause, a car may be impounded only after individualized consideration of reasonable alternatives. Since the officer did not do that individualized consideration and since there was no probable cause to seize the vehicle, the seizure was unlawful. Therefore, the fruits of the inventory search must be suppressed

NOTES

1. Under the Nevada Constitution, "there must exist both probable cause and exigent circumstances for police to conduct a warrantless search of an automobile incident to a lawful custodial arrest." *Camacho v. State*, 75 P.3d 370, 373–74 (Nev. 2003).

2. Under the Wyoming Constitution, a warrantless non-consensual search of a vehicle incident to the defendant's arrest was unreasonable when the operator was arrested for driving with a suspended license and was handcuffed outside the vehicle. *Pierce v. State*, 171 P.3d 525 (Wyo. 2007).

3. Under the Vermont Constitution, the police may not search a vehicle without a warrant after the driver has been arrested, handcuffed, and placed in a police car, unless there is a reasonable need to preserve evidence of a crime or protect the police officer's safety. *State v. Bauder*, 924 A.2d 38 (Vt. 2007); *accord State v. Birchard*, 5 A.3d 879 (Vt. 2010); *see also State v. Snapp*, 275 P.3d 289 (Wash. 2012).

STATE v. ARREOLA-BOTELLO
451 P.3d 939 (Or. 2019)

NELSON, J.

We consider the constitutionally permissible scope of a traffic stop under Article I, section 9, of the Oregon Constitution. Defendant was lawfully stopped for failing to signal a turn and a lane change. During the stop, while defendant was searching for his registration and proof of insurance, the officer asked him about the presence of guns and drugs in the vehicle, and requested consent to search the vehicle. Defendant consented, and during the search, the officer located a controlled substance. Defendant contends that the officer expanded the permissible scope of the traffic stop when he asked about the contents of the vehicle and requested permission to search it because those inquiries were not related to the purpose of the stop. The trial court erred in denying defendant's motion to suppress.

Officer Faulkner of the Beaverton Police Department observed defendant's vehicle change lanes and turn without signaling. Faulkner initiated his patrol car's overhead lights, and defendant pulled over. Faulkner approached defendant's vehicle and requested his driver's license, registration, and proof of insurance. Defendant was able to immediately produce his license but spent about three to four additional minutes searching for his registration and proof of insurance.

While defendant was searching, Faulkner asked him questions. Defendant, who primarily speaks Spanish, was having difficulty understanding the questions in English. At the beginning of the traffic stop, a passenger in the vehicle helped interpret Faulkner's questions, but she left after Faulkner told her that she was free to do so. Faulkner asked defendant about the presence of weapons, drugs, or other illegal items in the vehicle and requested consent to search the vehicle. Defendant responded, "Sure, okay," and consented to the search. During the search, Faulkner located a small package on the floor between the driver's seat and the door. Faulkner examined the package, found it to be consistent with drug packaging, and observed a substance in the package that he believed was methamphetamine. Faulkner placed defendant under arrest.

Article I, section 9, establishes "the right of the people to be secure in their persons, houses, papers, and effects, against unreasonable search, or seizure." For purposes of Article I, section 9, a seizure occurs when (1) a police officer intentionally and significantly interferes with an individual's liberty or freedom of movement; or (2) a reasonable person, under the totality of the circumstances, would believe that his or her liberty or freedom of movement has been significantly restricted. In those circumstances, Article I, section 9, protects a person's liberty or freedom of movement by defining the authority of law enforcement officers in their encounters with citizens.

However, not all encounters between law enforcement officers and citizens implicate Article I, section 9. This court has previously identified three general types of police-citizen encounters and has categorized them according to the requirements for their initiation by law enforcement. One type of encounter is a "mere conversation," or a "non-coercive encounter," and it does not involve any restraint on the liberty of an individual or his or her freedom of movement, and is not a seizure under Article I, section 9. On the other end of the spectrum, an arrest is recognized as a "seizure" under Article I, section 9, and requires probable cause. This case involves a traffic stop, which falls somewhere in between: This court has recognized that, when a motorist is stopped for a traffic infraction, that stop implicates Article I, section 9, because: "In contrast to a person on the street, who may unilaterally end an officer-citizen encounter at any time, the reality is that a motorist stopped for a traffic infraction is legally obligated to stop at an officer's direction and to interact with the officer, and therefore is not free unilaterally to end the encounter and leave whenever he or she chooses."

As our cases demonstrate, Article I, section 9, limits not only when a stop may be made, but also the purpose for which it is conducted. A stop that is reasonable for a limited investigatory purpose is not necessarily reasonable for all purposes, and we see no reason to distinguish between the activities that law enforcement officers conduct during such a stop and the questions that they ask; both must be reasonably related to the purpose that permits the officer to stop an individual in the first place. If we were to hold otherwise, then an officer who lacks a warrant, probable cause, or even reasonable suspicion of criminal activity, could stop an individual for a minor traffic offense, and, during that stop, conduct a criminal investigation anyway, making meaningless the rule which requires an officer to have reasonable suspicion before stopping an individual to conduct a criminal investigation. Thus, when determining whether a stop that was reasonable at the outset has become unreasonable, we must consider the totality of its circumstances, not only its duration.

In sum, we conclude that, for the purposes of Article I, section 9, all investigative activities, including investigative inquiries, conducted during a traffic stop are part of an ongoing seizure and are subject to both subject-matter and durational limitations. Accordingly, an officer is limited to investigatory inquiries that are reasonably related to the purpose of the traffic stop or that have an independent constitutional justification. Put simply, an "unavoidable lull" does not create an opportunity for an officer to ask unrelated questions, unless the officer can justify the inquiry on other grounds.

We realize that our decision precludes officers from asking certain investigative questions during investigatory stops—those unrelated to the purpose of the investigation and without independent constitutional justification. But that is as the constitution requires and, for statutory purposes, what the legislature intends. *See* ORS 131.615(3)(a) (officer's inquiries during traffic stop reasonable only if limited to the "immediate circumstances that arouse the officer's suspicion"). Given the near necessity of driving today, it is certainly not uncommon for a citizen to be lawfully stopped for a minor traffic violation. If, after stopping an individual based on probable cause that the individual committed a traffic offense, an officer may inquire into criminal activity without reasonable suspicion of a specific crime, an officer will have less of an incentive to develop the requisite reasonable suspicion of that crime which ordinarily would be required to stop the individual for a temporary criminal investigation. By applying subject-matter limitations to investigative activities and questioning, Article I, section 9, ensures that officers do not turn minor traffic violations into criminal investigations without a constitutional basis for doing so.

With that understanding of Article I, section 9, we conclude, in this case, that Faulkner's questioning and request to search defendant's vehicle violated Article I, section 9. Although Faulkner had probable cause to believe that defendant had committed a traffic infraction when he failed to signal a turn and, therefore, was permitted to stop defendant to investigate that infraction, Faulkner then asked questions that were not reasonably related to that investigation and exceeded its lawful scope. Faulkner stopped defendant for failing to use a turn signal, but then inquired about the possession of guns or controlled substances. The record does not demonstrate that the latter questioning was reasonably related to the investigation of the former investigation. The investigation of defendant's failure to signal a turn may have warranted questions about whether or why defendant acted or failed to take that action, other questions or actions reasonably related to that inquiry, or other questions or actions reasonably necessary to the issuance of a warning or a citation, such as questions to address reasonable officer-safety concerns. But, here, the state does not claim any such connections or concerns, and the record does not support the notion that any exist.

In addition, if there were evidence that, during the stop, Faulkner had learned facts giving rise to reasonable suspicion that defendant had engaged or was about to engage in criminal conduct, an expanded investigation could have been justified. But here, Faulkner did not testify to any particularized suspicion that defendant had weapons, controlled substances, or any other contraband in his vehicle. To the contrary, Faulkner testified that he asks such questions every time he makes a stop.

GARRETT, J., dissenting.

This court has held that, in ordinary police-citizen encounters (that is, encounters that are not seizures), police may engage citizens in "mere conversation" and generally ask questions of them without implicating Article I, section 9. We have also held that, because a traffic stop is a seizure, police may continue the traffic stop for only so long as the basis for that seizure exists; thus, police may not extend the stop with questioning, "mere conversation," or other activities unrelated to the original basis for the stop, unless they have an independent and constitutionally sufficient basis to continue the detention for such activities.

The question left unanswered until today is what subject matter restrictions, if any, apply to police activity that is not related to the original basis for the traffic stop but that also does *not* cause any prolongation of the stop. The Court of Appeals has addressed the issue and concluded that, so long as unrelated activity occurs during an "unavoidable lull" in the traffic stop, such activity effects no greater restriction on liberty than was already in place. Therefore, it is of no constitutional import.

That "unavoidable lull" rule is consistent with the decisions of this court that have defined a "seizure" for purposes of Article I, section 9, to occur "when either (1) a police officer intentionally and significantly interferes with the person's freedom of movement; or (2) the person believes, in an objectively reasonable manner, that his or her liberty of movement has been so restricted." Simply put, when an officer's question unnecessarily extends a traffic stop, that question represents an additional interference with that liberty interest and may therefore require an additional justification. But if a person has already been seized as a result of a lawful traffic stop, and the length of the stop is *not* extended, then questioning on unrelated matters does not cause any additional interference with the person's freedom of movement.

Today, the majority rejects the "unavoidable lull" rule, concluding that, unless they have independent constitutional justification, police are prohibited from engaging in activity or inquiring into any matters unrelated to the original basis of the stop, even if such activity does not extend the stop. Thus, if an officer observes behavior during a traffic stop that causes the officer to be concerned about past, present, or future criminal activity, but the officer does not yet possess enough information that would support an objectively reasonable suspicion or pose officer-safety concerns, then the officer may not ask questions or take other steps to investigate. That limitation does not govern police-citizen interactions in other contexts. Indeed, it will only partly govern police-citizen interactions in *this* context—the surprising result of the majority's decision is that, during a lull, an officer may make inquiries of the passenger of a stopped car but be absolutely forbidden from asking the same questions of the driver.

There may be sound reasons for such a rule. I dissent from today's decision because those reasons have not been adequately explained, and, as a result, today's decision raises significant questions without providing an analytical framework that will help lower courts answer them.

The majority bypasses crucial steps in the analysis by interpreting this court's precedents to have already decided the key question. According to the majority, we have already held that "an officer's investigative *activities*" during a traffic stop must be "reasonably related to the purpose of the stop or have independent constitutional justification," and today's decision simply addresses the "narrow question" of whether an officer's "inquiries" are treated any differently. That is not an accurate statement of our case law. Our past statements considering whether an officer's activities were reasonably related to the purpose of a traffic stop arose in the context of considering whether the officer had unlawfully *extended* the stop. The statements on which the majority relies can be correctly understood only in that context.

Because we have never held that all investigative activity during a traffic stop must have constitutional justification regardless of whether it extends the stop, we have never addressed what that actually means, which will pose difficulties for police trying to understand this rule and for trial courts trying to apply it. What constitutes investigative activity? We know from today's decision that a request for consent to search goes too far. But does the majority's rule encompass less invasive interaction, or activity that involves no interaction with the driver at all, such as a warrants check? If an officer develops an intuition, on the basis of training and experience, that something is not right, but lacks enough information to have a reasonable suspicion of criminal activity, may the officer engage the driver in "mere conversation" in the hope of eliciting additional useful information? If not, what *can* an officer do during a ten-minute wait? And if so, may that conversation include questions—or are questions off limits because they are "inquiries"? May the officer use the unavoidable lull to contact colleagues to see if they know anything about the driver, or take other steps to gather information from outside sources?

It is not clear how those questions are to be answered. It is clear, however, that the majority's new rule means that, during an unavoidable lull in a traffic investigation, police officers must avoid engaging in at least some of the ordinary police work that they routinely perform in other settings.

H. *MIRANDA* VIOLATION – PHYSICAL EVIDENCE EXCLUDED

The United States Supreme Court held that physical evidence uncovered as a result of *Miranda* violations need not be suppressed. *United States v. Patane*, 542 U.S. 630 (2004). A contrary result has been reached under some state constitutions.

STATE v. PETERSON
923 A.2d 585 (Vt. 2007)

DOOLEY, J.

The issue in this case is the scope of the exclusionary rule in criminal cases, specifically, whether physical evidence obtained as a result of a violation of defendant's *Miranda* rights must be excluded at trial. We conclude that under chapter I, article 10 of the Vermont Constitution and the Vermont exclusionary rule, physical evidence obtained in violation of *Miranda* rights must be suppressed. We reverse in part and remand.

Defendant James Peterson appeals the denial of two suppression motions. Both involve a core set of undisputed facts. Defendant was looking for his girlfriend and drove his car next to a police vehicle so that he and the officer could speak out of their windows. Upon speaking to defendant, the officer smelled marijuana through the vehicle window. During the conversation, defendant admitted that he had been convicted of a drug offense and that he had a marijuana "roach" in his vehicle. The officer then asked defendant to exit the vehicle, which he did.

The officer patted defendant down; he found no weapons, but smelled the odor of marijuana emanating from the front pocket of defendant's sweatshirt. The officer patted the pocket and, feeling nothing, used his flashlight to look inside the pocket, where he saw green flakes of marijuana plant. When asked, defendant admitted he had picked the marijuana earlier that day from a plant or two he had at home for personal use. The officer then asked defendant for consent to search both his vehicle and his home; defendant consented to these searches both verbally and in writing. The written consent form identified defendant's residence to be searched as "3141 Jersey St. & property" in Panton, Vermont.

After searching defendant's vehicle and finding a burned marijuana cigarette as well as a blanket smelling of marijuana, the officer and a state police trooper proceeded to defendant's residence. Defendant was placed in handcuffs for protection of the police, but was advised by the officer that he was not under arrest. The handcuffs were removed upon arrival at defendant's residence and were intermittently taken on and off while the officers conducted the home search. During the home search, the officer located a garbage bag containing a significant amount of marijuana and marijuana paraphernalia. Defendant led the officers to one marijuana plant growing behind his house.

Upon completion of the home search, the officer informed defendant that they would proceed to the Vergennes Police Department for processing. He placed defendant in handcuffs and instructed him to walk in front of the officer. During the walk, the officer expressed that he doubted so much marijuana came from just one plant, and asked defendant whether he had other marijuana plants. He did not inform defendant of his *Miranda* rights. Defendant eventually admitted to the existence of other plants. The officer asked defendant to show him the other plants, and the two men walked through a wooded area with high brush to a plot where twenty-seven growing plants were located. The plot where the twenty-seven plants were growing is not on, nor visible from, defendant's property.

As a result of the search, the police charged defendant with felony possession of more than twenty-five plants of marijuana and felony possession of marijuana consisting of an aggregate weight of one pound or more. Defendant moved to suppress "all evidence obtained by Vermont Law Enforcement Officials subsequent to his being taken into custody," asserting the officers in question violated his rights to be free from self-incrimination and unlawful search and seizure under both the Vermont and United States Constitutions. Defendant's primary argument was that the police had engaged in custodial interrogation, but failed to give defendant the required warnings under *Miranda v. Arizona* (1966), and that the finding of the twenty-seven marijuana plants was the result of the unwarned interrogation. The State responded primarily that the search was pursuant to defendant's consent.

Following the testimony and argument on the motion, the court *sua sponte* requested that the parties brief the impact of *United States v. Patane* (2004). After receiving the additional briefing, the court denied defendant's motion to suppress, basing its denial on *Patane*. The court concluded that defendant was in custody at the time he was questioned about possible additional marijuana plants, and as such was entitled to *Miranda* warnings at that time prior to further interrogation. Since it was undisputed that the police did not give defendant *Miranda* warnings, the court held that any statements made after defendant was in custody were made in response to interrogation that violated *Miranda*. The court denied the motion to suppress the twenty-seven plants, however, under *Patane*, which held that physical evidence uncovered as a result of a *Miranda* violation need not be suppressed. The court rejected defendant's additional argument that *Patane* is not good law under the Vermont Constitution.

Following the decision, defendant entered into a conditional plea of guilty allowing him to appeal the denial of his motion to suppress. The issue defendant raises on appeal is whether the twenty-seven marijuana plants must be suppressed.

We, therefore, consider the legality of the use of the twenty-seven marijuana plants as evidence and whether we will follow *United States v. Patane* under the Vermont Constitution.

Patane involved an arrest of a convicted felon for violating an abuse prevention order. Without completing *Miranda* warnings, the arresting officer asked the defendant whether he had a gun because gun possession was illegal for a felon, and there was a report that the defendant had a gun. Under persistent questioning, the defendant told the officer that he had a gun in his bedroom and gave permission to retrieve it. When the defendant was charged with illegally possessing a firearm, he moved to suppress the gun as the fruit of a confession given as a result of a custodial interrogation without *Miranda* warnings.

A majority of the United States Supreme Court concluded that the gun was admissible, but it did so in two separate opinions that differed in part. The plurality opinion written by Justice Thomas and joined by Chief Justice Rehnquist and Justice Scalia held:

> The *Miranda* rule is a prophylactic employed to protect against violations of the Self-Incrimination Clause. The Self-Incrimination Clause, however, is not implicated by the admission into evidence of the physical fruit of a voluntary statement. Accordingly, there is no justification for extending the *Miranda* rule to this context. And just as the Self-Incrimination Clause primarily focuses on the criminal trial, so too does the *Miranda* rule. The *Miranda* rule is not a code of police conduct, and police do not violate the Constitution (or even the *Miranda* rule, for that matter) by mere failures to warn. For this reason, the exclusionary rule articulated in cases such as *Wong Sun* does not apply.

The plurality went on to explain that because prophylactic rules "sweep beyond the actual protections of the Self-Incrimination Clause, any further extension of these rules must be justified by its necessity for the protection of the actual right against compelled self-incrimination." It concluded that a "blanket suppression rule could not be justified by reference to the Fifth Amendment goal of assuring trustworthy evidence or by any deterrence rationale," and that such a rule would therefore violate the Court's requirement that it maintain "the closest possible fit between the Self-Incrimination Clause and any rule designed to protect it."

The concurring opinion of Justices Kennedy and O'Connor accepted part of the plurality's rationale. They concluded that admission of the gun did "not run the risk of admitting into trial an accused's coerced incriminating statements against himself" and went on to state:

> In light of the important probative value of reliable physical evidence, it is doubtful that exclusion can be justified by a deterrence rationale sensitive to both law enforcement interests and a suspect's rights during an in-custody interrogation.

Three of the dissenters, Justices Souter, Stevens and Ginsburg, defined the issue as "whether courts should apply the fruit of the poisonous tree doctrine lest we create an incentive for the police to omit *Miranda* warnings before custodial interrogation." They concluded that the majority decision created an "unjustifiable invitation to law enforcement officers to flout *Miranda* when there may be physical evidence to be gained." Justice Breyer joined the dissent except where the failure to give *Miranda* warnings "was in good faith."

In examining whether we should follow *Patane* under the Vermont Constitution, we start with the context of our decision. The right against self-incrimination is guaranteed in the Fifth Amendment to the United States Constitution, which prohibits compelling a criminal defendant to "be a witness against himself." Equivalently, article 10 of the Vermont Constitution prohibits compelling a person "to give evidence against oneself." We have held, with respect to adults, that "the article 10 privilege against self-incrimination and that contained in the Fifth Amendment are synonymous." Consistent with this view, we have held that evidence gathered in violation of the prophylactic rules established in *Miranda* is also a violation of article 10. We have not, however, gone beyond *Miranda* and found a violation of the principles of that decision where the United States Supreme Court has not done so.

If this case involved the substance of *Miranda*, for example, the nature of the warnings or the circumstances under which they must be given, the State would have a strong argument that our precedents require that we not go beyond the limits in the decisions of the United States Supreme Court. This, however, is a case in which the district court found a violation of *Miranda* under accepted principles and defendant made a confession to an additional crime under custodial interrogation, a confession that is inadmissible under *Miranda*. The issue is the scope of the remedy for the *Miranda* violation, and on this point our precedents take a different view from that of the United States Supreme Court.

A starting point for examination of this question is *State v. Brunelle*, (Vt. 1987), where we addressed whether we would follow the U.S. Supreme Court's decisions in *Harris v. New York* (1971), and *United States v. Havens* (1980). These decisions allowed the prosecution to impeach a criminal defendant who testifies with statements taken in violation of *Miranda*. We rejected these decisions under the Vermont Constitution because they are inconsistent with the right under article 10 of a defendant "to be heard by himself and his counsel." We held instead that the prosecution can impeach with the suppressed evidence only where "a defendant has testified on direct examination to facts contradicted by previously suppressed evidence bearing directly on the crime charged." Although *Brunelle* is based primarily on a defendant's right to testify, the decision explained its relationship to the right against self-incrimination and *Miranda*. As discussed above, it held that a violation of *Miranda* was also a violation of the article 10 right against self-incrimination. Accordingly, the Court described *Brunelle* as "a limited exception to *State v. Badger* (Vt. 1982), which held that evidence obtained in violation of the Vermont Constitution, or as a result of a violation, cannot be admitted at trial as a matter of state law." *Brunelle* necessarily holds that the broad exclusionary rule of *Badger* applies to *Miranda* violations.

Badger is itself an important precedent because it applied a locally-created exclusionary rule to *Miranda* violations to suppress physical evidence, there the defendant's clothing. *Badger* found a violation of article 10 based in part on a failure to give *Miranda* warnings and an invalid waiver under *Miranda*, although it did not explicitly hold that a violation of *Miranda* was a violation of article 10. It went on to develop the broad exclusionary rule for such a violation, because:

> Introduction of such evidence at trial eviscerates our most sacred rights, impinges on individual privacy, perverts our judicial process, distorts any notion of fairness, and encourages official misconduct.

With respect to the clothing at issue, it held that "the seizure of the clothing is too directly connected to the illegal confession to allow" its admission.

We note that the three state supreme courts that have analyzed *Patane* under their state constitutions have concluded that they cannot adopt it because it undercuts the enforcement of *Miranda*. In *Commonwealth v. Martin* (Mass. 2005), the Massachusetts Supreme Judicial Court refused to follow *Patane* in enforcing *Miranda* rights through article 12 of the Declaration of Rights of the Massachusetts Constitution. The court agreed with the observation of Justice Souter, dissenting in *Patane*, that the decision added "an important inducement for interrogators to ignore the *Miranda* rule" and created "an unjustifiable invitation to law enforcement officers to flout *Miranda* when there may be physical evidence to be gained." It concluded: "To apply the *Patane* analysis to the broader rights embodied in article 12 would have a corrosive effect on them, undermine the respect we have accorded them, and demean their importance to a system of justice chosen by the citizens of Massachusetts in 1780." Thus, it followed earlier decisions in which it had rejected United States Supreme Court rulings weakening the applicability of *Miranda*.

In *State v. Knapp* (Wis. 2005), the Wisconsin Supreme Court reached the same conclusion under article I, section 8 of the Wisconsin Constitution in a case where the evidence showed that the police had intentionally violated *Miranda*. It relied on the loss of deterrence, the discouragement of police misconduct, and the need to preserve judicial integrity, in deciding to reject *Patane*.

The decisions in *Martin* and *Knapp* were followed under section 10, article I of the Ohio Constitution by the Ohio Supreme Court in *State v. Farris* (Ohio 2006). Again, the main rationale is the reduction in deterrence of *Miranda* violations:

> We believe that to hold otherwise would encourage law-enforcement officers to withhold *Miranda* warnings and would thus weaken section 10, article I of the

Ohio Constitution. In cases like this one, where possession is the basis for the crime and physical evidence is the keystone of the case, warning suspects of their rights can hinder the gathering of evidence. When physical evidence is central to a conviction and testimonial evidence is not, there can arise a virtual incentive to flout *Miranda*. We believe that the overall administration of justice in Ohio requires a law-enforcement environment in which evidence is gathered in conjunction with *Miranda*, not in defiance of it.

We agree with the analysis and result reached in each of these cases.

For the above reasons, we conclude that we will not follow *United States v. Patane* under article 10 of the Vermont Constitution and our exclusionary rule. Physical evidence gained from statements obtained under circumstances that violate *Miranda* is inadmissible in criminal proceedings as fruit of the poisonous tree. Since it is undisputed that the marijuana plants were such fruit in this case, the district court erred in failing to suppress them.

NOTES

1. The constitutions of Oregon and Wisconsin also require the exclusion of evidence seized as a result of a *Miranda* violation. *See State v. Knapp*, 700 N.W.2d 899 (Wis. 2005); *State v. Vondehn*, 236 P.3d 691 (Or. 2010).

2. Under the self-incrimination clause in article I, section 10 of the Ohio Constitution, only evidence "obtained as the direct result of statements made in custody without the benefit of a *Miranda* warning should be excluded." *State v. Farris*, 849 N.E.2d 985 (Ohio 2006).

3. The Massachusetts Supreme Court held that evidence received as the result of a defendant's pre-warning statement to police had to be suppressed as the "fruit" of the detective's unlawful questioning, to safeguard the Massachusetts Constitution's privilege against self-incrimination. *Commonwealth v. Martin*, 827 N.E.2d 198 (Mass. 2005).

CHAPTER IX

PROPERTY RIGHTS

A. INTRODUCTION

Generally speaking, there is no such thing as property without law. And the law that usually counts—that creates and defines property rights—is state law. "Because the U.S. Constitution protects rather than creates property interests, the existence of a property interest is determined by reference to existing rules or understandings that stem from an independent source such as state law." *Phillips v. Wash. Legal Found.*, 524 U.S. 156, 164 (1998).

This chapter begins with an example of an intangible claimed property interest, in which a law student dismissed after his first year due to low grades, argues that he had a protected property right under the state constitution to continue his legal education. The heart of the chapter addresses a state constitutional provision that protects property rights and that has a direct federal counterpart. Most, if not all, state constitutions contain a "takings clause" that parallels the Taking Clause in the Fifth Amendment of the U.S. Constitution. Interpretation of these guarantees has led to a story of dynamic federalism, with state courts and legislatures reacting negatively to a U.S. Supreme Court decision—the *Kelo* decision—that interpreted the federal takings clause in favor of broad governmental power to take private property. Although the terms of the state and federal takings clauses generally mirror each other, the interpretation of many state takings provisions varies considerably from the U.S. Supreme Court's interpretation of the federal counterpart. A final case in this section demonstrates that some state takings provisions differ significantly from the Fifth Amendment's language, potentially leading to different and more favorable results for landowners.

The chapter concludes with two Texas Supreme Court decisions in which the Justices debate how much protection state constitutions should provide to economic rights and interests, including under substantive due process protections. One case involves licensing regulations of "eyebrow threaders" that require hundreds of hours of instruction. The other case raises overarching questions about the protection of substantive due process under state constitutions and the proper way to look for such protection.

B. WHAT IS PROPERTY?

For due process purposes, not all "property" is tangible. The U.S. Supreme Court began recognizing protected interests such as continued employment rights, continued public assistance, the right to continue attending public schools under the Fifth and Fourteenth Amendments in the

1970s, and many state courts have done the same under their state constitutions. The next case presents a modern example.

TEXAS SOUTHERN UNIVERSITY v. VILLARREAL
620 S.W.3d 899 (Tex. 2021)

BUSBY, J.

In this case, we address whether a state university's dismissal of a student for poor academic performance implicates a liberty or property interest protected by the Texas Constitution's guarantee of due course of law. Texas Southern University's Thurgood Marshall School of Law dismissed Ivan Villarreal after one year because he did not maintain the required 2.0 grade point average. Villarreal sued the School, alleging claims for breach of contract and deprivation of his liberty and property without due course of law.

We hold that an academic dismissal from higher education carries insufficient stigma to implicate a protected liberty interest. And assuming without deciding that Villarreal had a protected property right in his continuing education, the procedures followed by the School in connection with his dismissal were constitutionally adequate.

Ivan Villarreal entered Thurgood Marshall School of Law in August 2014. He completed his first year with a 1.976 grade point average. The School's Student Rules and Regulations handbook includes a non-waivable requirement that a first-year student maintain an average of at least 2.0 to continue in the program. Villarreal was dismissed for failing to meet this requirement.

Villarreal sued the School as well as the dean and other faculty members in their official and personal capacities. He asserted a claim for breach of contract against the School, and he contended that the School and the faculty members violated his substantive and procedural rights under the due course of law clause of the Texas Constitution. The defendants contended that Villarreal lacked any constitutionally protected interest to support viable ultra vires claims under the due course of law clause.

Although there are factual disputes here regarding the School's cheating investigation, the parties agree on the facts relevant to our disposition of this case: Villarreal's grade point average was below a 2.0 at the conclusion of his first year; he filed multiple petitions seeking grade changes and reinstatements that were denied; and he was eligible to re-enroll after two years.

The Texas Constitution provides that "[n]o citizen of this State shall be deprived of life, liberty, property, privileges or immunities, or in any manner disfranchised, except by the due course of the law of the land." Tex. Const. art. I, § 19. To determine whether a governmental action violates the due course of law guarantee, we engage in a two-step inquiry. First, does the plaintiff have a liberty, property, or other enumerated interest that is entitled to protection? Second, if a protected interest is implicated, did the government defendant follow due course of law in depriving the plaintiff of that interest?

Turning to substantive due course of law, Villarreal contends that the Student Rules and Regulations and the money he spent on tuition confer a property right to continued graduate education that the Texas Constitution protects against arbitrary or capricious deprivation. Because our Constitution does not recognize higher education as a fundamental right, however, Villarreal's alleged property right does not fall within any substantive protection provided by the due course of law clause.

"Not every property right is entitled to the protection of substantive due process. While property interests are protected by procedural due process even though the interest is derived from state law rather than the Constitution, substantive due process rights are created only by the Constitution," and "the history of substantive due process counsels caution and restraint" in recognizing such rights. In particular, "a state-law contract right bears little resemblance to the fundamental liberty interests" the U.S. Supreme Court has "viewed as implicitly protected" by the federal due process clause.

We need not address today the extent to which the Texas Constitution's due course of law clause may provide similar substantive protection for fundamental rights because we have held that higher education is not such a right. Unlike the U.S. Constitution, our Texas Constitution is quite lengthy and frequently amended. (The U.S. Constitution has a mere 4,543 words and has been amended only twenty-seven times since 1789. In contrast, the Texas Constitution contains approximately 86,000 words and has been amended nearly 500 times since 1876.)

When Texans want to provide substantive constitutional protection for educational rights, they are not shy about saying so expressly. For example, Article VII section 1 imposes on the Legislature "the duty to establish and make suitable provision for the support and maintenance of an efficient system of public free schools." Tex. Const. art. VII, § 1. But in *Richards v. League of United Latin American Citizens* (Tex. 1993), we rejected the argument that this provision made "higher education a fundamental right secured by the Texas Constitution."

If the people of Texas want a fundamental right to higher education, they can create one by amending our Constitution. It is not our role as judges to adopt such a right for them. As a matter of Texas constitutional law, therefore, we decline to recognize substantive protections for educational rights that emanate implicitly from the due course of law clause.

For these reasons, we conclude that Villarreal is not entitled to substantive due course of law protection for any property right in his continued education, and that he received the procedural protections due in connection with his dismissal. Therefore, Villarreal's allegations do not establish that the School deprived him of a protected property interest without due course of law.

C. TAKINGS PROVISIONS AND THE *KELO* STORY

Most state constitutions prohibit the government from taking private property for public use unless just compensation is paid. The U.S. Constitution imposes a similar restraint, declaring "nor shall private property be taken for public use without just compensation." U.S. Const. amend. V. In *Kelo v. City of New London* (2005), the Supreme Court rejected a takings challenge to a city's plan for transferring certain private property obtained through eminent domain to private developers, because the plan served a *public purpose* (redeveloping blighted or less valuable property for more valuable uses) and thus satisfied the "public use" requirement.

The *Kelo* decision prompted responses in many States, with only a handful of States failing to take any action following *Kelo*. In most States, there was strong objection to the notion that taking private property for redevelopment—as opposed to doing so, say, to build schools or public buildings or roads—was constitutional. Some States responded with legislation, others with constitutional amendments, and some with court decisions favorable to property owners. As one co-author of this book puts it,

> over the last several years, through state legislation, state constitutional amendments and state-court decisions, property-rights advocates have made considerable gains—perhaps obtaining as much as, if not more than, a favorable *Kelo* decision could have offered them. As of today, most States have enacted legislation addressing issues of public use and eminent domain. Seven States have limited the public purposes for which eminent domain is acceptable. Nine States have enacted laws expressly limiting the States' power to exercise eminent domain. Five others have adopted variations on these themes. Some States have sought to reduce the potential abuse of eminent domain by developing procedural changes, requiring state agencies to make stronger showings of public use, requiring agencies to create redevelopment plans, and setting notice and offer requirements to prevent "stealth" condemnation. In other States, court rulings prompted the changes. In 2006, the Ohio and Oklahoma Supreme Courts extended their state constitutional protections against eminent domain beyond the federal baseline by holding that economic benefit alone does not constitutionally justify the exercise of eminent domain. Only a handful of States have not enacted legislation in the wake of *Kelo*.

Jeffrey S. Sutton, San Antonio Independent School District v. Rodriguez *And Its Aftermath*, 94 Va. L. Rev. 1963, 1984–85 (2008).

As Professor Ilya Somin has pointed out, some of the state legislative responses may be more cosmetic than real. Ilya Somin, *The Grasping Hand:* Kelo v. City of New London *and the Limits of Eminent Domain* (U. Chi. 2015). Of course, the more cosmetic those changes, the more one would expect a new federal challenge to these practices to arise, whether to overrule *Kelo* or to cut back on it. So far, that has not happened.

What follows are several state decisions that reject, modify, or follow the *Kelo* rule, and in the end illustrate the variety of state responses to *Kelo*.

CITY OF NORWOOD v. HORNEY
853 N.E.2d 1115 (Ohio 2006)

O'CONNOR, J.

We decide the constitutionality of a municipality's taking of an individual's property by eminent domain and transferring the property to a private entity for redevelopment. In doing so, we must balance two competing interests of great import in American democracy: the individual's rights in the possession and security of property and the sovereign's power to take private property for the benefit of the community.

Appropriation cases often represent more than a battle over a plot of cold sod in a farmland pasture or the plat of municipal land on which a building sits. For the individual property owner, the appropriation is not simply the seizure of a house. It is the taking of a home—the place where ancestors toiled, where families were raised, where memories were made. Fittingly, appropriations are scrutinized by the people and debated in their institutions.

In reviewing an appropriation similar to that at issue here, a sharply divided United States Supreme Court recently upheld the taking over a federal Fifth Amendment challenge mounted by individual property owners. *Kelo v. New London* (2005). Although it determined that the Federal Constitution did not prohibit the takings, the court acknowledged that property owners might find redress in the states' courts and legislatures, which remain free to restrict such takings pursuant to state laws and constitutions.

In response to that invitation in *Kelo*, Ohio's General Assembly unanimously enacted 2005 Am.Sub.S.B. No. 167. The legislature expressly noted in the Act its belief that as a result of *Kelo*, "the interpretation and use of the state's eminent domain law could be expanded to allow the taking of private property that is not within a blighted area, ultimately resulting in ownership of that property being vested in another private person in violation of Sections 1 and 19 of Article I, Ohio Constitution."

The appellants' property was appropriated by the city of Norwood after the city determined that the appellants' neighborhood was a "deteriorating area," as that term is defined in the provisions governing appropriations in the Codified Ordinances of the City of Norwood. Although, as we shall discuss below, we have held that a city may take a slum, blighted, or deteriorated property for redevelopment, and suggested that the taking is proper even when the city transfers the appropriated property to a private party for redevelopment, we have never been asked whether a city may appropriate property that the city determines is in an area that may deteriorate in the future.

We hold that although economic factors may be considered in determining whether private property may be appropriated, the fact that the appropriation would provide an economic benefit to the government and community, standing alone, does not satisfy the public-use requirement of Section 19, Article I of the Ohio Constitution.

The city of Norwood is a modern urban environment. Surrounded by the city of Cincinnati, Norwood was once home to several manufacturing plants and businesses that provided a substantial tax base for the municipality. Despite that industrial component, Norwood was, and for many remains, a desirable place to live. Norwood's neighborhoods were composed of traditional single-family houses and duplexes that provided homes to generations of families and many individuals.

Over the past 40 years, however, Norwood underwent many changes. Like many municipalities in Ohio, Norwood's industrial base eroded, taking with it tax dollars vital to the city. Municipal jobs and many services were eliminated, and the city is millions of dollars in debt. Though the financial outlook of Norwood has been altered greatly over the years, perhaps the most significant change for our purposes here is the physical nature of the city itself.

In the 1960s, property was appropriated from the appellants' neighborhood and used in the construction of a major highway—Interstate 71—through Cincinnati. In the neighborhoods affected, numerous homes were razed and front yards diminished in order to make way for the access roads and ramps to the highway. The streets became busier, creating safety problems for residents who had to back onto busy roadways from their driveways. Residential roads that once ran between major thoroughfares were bisected by the new highway, creating dead-end streets.

Over time, businesses arose in places where houses once stood. The neighborhood became less residential and more commercial. Other changes in the neighborhood's character followed. Traffic increased dramatically due to motorists seeking the highway and businesses in the area. Noise increased, and light pollution became more prevalent.

A private, limited-liability company, Rookwood Partners, entered discussions with Norwood about redeveloping the appellants' neighborhood. The preliminary plans for the development call for the construction of more than 200 apartments or condominiums and over 500,000 square feet of office and retail space (all of which would be owned by Rookwood), as well as two large public-parking facilities (which would be owned by Norwood) with spaces for more than 2,000 vehicles. The city expects the redeveloped area to result in nearly $2,000,000 in annual revenue for Norwood.

Norwood, operating with a deficit, was unable to fix the problems or redevelop the appellants' neighborhood on its own. Discussions between Norwood and Rookwood culminated in a redevelopment contract in which Rookwood agreed to reimburse the city for the expenses of the project, including the costs arising from any need to use eminent domain to appropriate the property necessary for the project.

Rookwood preferred that Norwood acquire the property needed for the project through eminent domain, but Norwood resisted. It encouraged Rookwood to purchase the property through voluntary sales of homes and businesses, without the city's intervention.

Rookwood was largely successful; it secured acquisition agreements from a substantial majority of the owners of the property necessary to complete the project. The appellants, however, refused to sell.

Because the appellants refused to sell their property, Rookwood asked Norwood to appropriate the appellants' properties and transfer them to Rookwood. Rookwood, in turn, agreed to raze the existing structures (including the appellants' homes), reconfigure the streets, and redevelop the area.

Norwood used funds provided by Rookwood to retain a consulting firm, Kinzelman Kline Grossman (KKG), to prepare an urban-renewal study of the appellants' neighborhood. The study concluded that the construction of I-71 and ensuing conversion of residential and industrial properties to commercial use had led to significant, negative changes in Norwood. Despite acknowledging that many homes were in fair to good condition, KKG concluded that the neighborhood was a "deteriorating area" as that term is defined in the Norwood Code. KKG further determined that the neighborhood would continue to deteriorate and that there would be "continuing piecemeal conversion" of residences to businesses that could be detrimental to the area.

After public hearings and town meetings were held and the local planning commission recommended approval of the redevelopment plan, Norwood City Council passed a series of ordinances adopting the plan and authorizing the mayor to enter the redevelopment agreement with Rookwood and to appropriate the appellants' property. The city then filed complaints against the appellants to appropriate their properties.

The rights related to property, *i.e.*, to acquire, use, enjoy, and dispose of property, are among the most revered in our law and traditions. Indeed, property rights are integral aspects of our theory of democracy and notions of liberty. Believed to be derived fundamentally from a higher authority and natural law, property rights were so sacred that they could not be entrusted lightly to "the uncertain virtue of those who govern." As such, property rights were believed to supersede constitutional principles. In light of such notions of property rights, it is not surprising that the founders of our state expressly incorporated individual property rights into the Ohio Constitution in terms that reinforced the sacrosanct nature of the individual's "inalienable" property rights, Section 1, Article I, which are to be held forever "inviolate."

Ohio has always considered the right of property to be a fundamental right. There can be no doubt that the bundle of venerable rights associated with property is strongly protected in the Ohio Constitution and must be trod upon lightly, no matter how great the weight of other forces.

There is an inherent tension between the individual's right to possess and preserve property and the state's competing interests in taking it for the communal good. Mindful of that friction and the potential for misuse of the eminent-domain power, James Madison's proposed draft of the Takings Clause included two equitable limitations on its use that were eventually incorporated into the Fifth Amendment: the "public use" requirement and the "just compensation" rule. The amendment confirms the sovereign's authority to take, but conditions the exercise of that authority upon satisfaction of two conjunctive standards: that the taking is for a "public use" and that "just compensation" for the taking is given to the owner.

Similarly, almost every state constitution eventually included provisions related to eminent-domain powers. Both the Northwest Ordinance and the Ohio Constitution recognized the state's right to take property from an individual, but conditioned the right to take on the equitable considerations of just compensation and public use. Section 19, Article I requires that the taking be necessary for the common welfare and, to "insure that principle of natural justice," that the persons deprived of their property will be compensated for "every injury resulting from this act," "every infringement on their property rights," and "every injurious interference with the control of their own property."

It is axiomatic that the federal and Ohio constitutions forbid the state to take private property for the sole benefit of a private individual, even when just compensation for the taking is provided. A sine qua non of eminent domain in Ohio is the understanding that the sovereign may use its appropriation powers only upon necessity for the common good.

However, the concept of public use has been malleable and elusive. While broad conceptualizations of public use evolved during the first decades of the 20th century, civic and government leaders became increasingly concerned with living conditions in urban areas and the array of social problems caused by the lack of adequate and safe, affordable housing in cities. The federal government eventually enacted sweeping legislation in an attempt to ameliorate some of those concerns. These modern urban-renewal and redevelopment efforts fostered the convergence of the public-health police power and eminent domain.

In this paradigm, the concept of public use was altered. Rather than furthering a public benefit by appropriating property to *create* something needed in a place where it did not exist before, the appropriations power was used to *destroy* a threat to the public's general welfare and well-being: slums and blighted or deteriorated property.

Historic notions equating physical, moral, and social illnesses with slums and blighted areas were reinforced. The term "blight" itself, borrowed from science and connoting an organism that promotes disease, became synonymous with urban decay, and courts were soon invoking the language of disease. Almost all courts, including this one, have consistently upheld takings that seized slums and blighted or deteriorated private property for redevelopment, even when the property was then transferred to a private entity, and continue to do so. These rulings properly employed an elastic public-use analysis to promote eminent domain as an answer to clear and present public-health concerns, permitting razing and "slum clearance."

Although there is merit in the notion that deference must be paid to a government's determination that there is sufficient evidence to support a taking in a case in which the taking is for a use that has previously been determined to be a public use, that deferential review is not satisfied by superficial scrutiny. To the contrary, it remains an essential and critical aspect in the analysis of any proposed taking.

There can be no doubt that our role—though limited—is a critical one that requires vigilance in reviewing state actions for the necessary restraint, including review to ensure that the state takes no more than that necessary to promote the public use, and that the state proceeds fairly and effectuates takings without bad faith, pretext, discrimination, or improper purpose. Thus, our precedent does not demand rote deference to legislative findings in eminent-domain proceedings, but rather, it preserves the courts' traditional role as guardian of constitutional rights and limits. Accordingly, "questions of public *purpose* aside, whether proposed condemnations are consistent with the Constitution's public use requirement is a constitutional question squarely within the Court's authority."

A court's independence is critical, particularly when the authority for the taking is delegated to another or the contemplated public use is dependent on a private entity. In such cases, the courts must ensure that the grant of authority is construed strictly and that any doubt over the propriety of the taking is resolved in favor of the property owner.

Similarly, when the state takes an individual's private property for transfer to another individual or to a private entity rather than for use by the state itself, the judicial review of the taking is paramount. A primordial purpose of the public-use clause is to prevent the legislature from permitting the state to take private property from one individual simply to give it to another. Although we have permitted economic concerns to be considered in addition to other factors, such as slum clearance, when determining whether the public-use requirement is sufficient, we have never found economic benefits alone to be a sufficient public use for a valid taking. We decline to do so now.

We hold that an economic or financial benefit alone is insufficient to satisfy the public-use requirement of Section 19, Article I. In light of that holding, any taking based solely on financial gain is void as a matter of law, and the courts owe no deference to a legislative finding that the proposed taking will provide financial benefit to a community.

The takings in the instant cases were based solely on a finding that the neighborhood was a deteriorating area. But what notice does the term "deteriorating area" give to an individual property owner?

As defined by the Norwood Code, a "deteriorating area" is not the same as a "slum or blighted or deteriorated area," the standard typically employed for a taking. And here, of course, there was no evidence to support a taking under that standard. To the contrary, the buildings in the neighborhood were generally in good condition and the owners were not delinquent in paying property taxes. There is no suggestion that the area was vermin-infested or subject to high crime rates or outbreaks of disease, or otherwise posed an impermissible risk to the larger community.

Some of the factors upon which the court relied, such as diversity of ownership, could apply to many neighborhoods. And although the term commonly appears in eminent-domain cases and regulations, it is susceptible of many meanings and to manipulation.

Moreover, diversity of ownership is a factor of questionable weight. As seems to have been the case here, diversity of ownership is typically considered to be a negative factor for a neighborhood because it purportedly impedes development. Yet Rookwood was able to secure virtually every property owner's assent to sale without any apparent difficulty. Thus, though diversity of ownership may be a factor to consider in determining whether an area is deteriorated, it is not a compelling one.

In essence, "deteriorating area" is a standardless standard. Rather than affording fair notice to the property owner, the Norwood Code merely recites a host of subjective factors that invite ad hoc and selective enforcement—a danger made more real by the malleable nature of the public-benefit requirement. We must be vigilant in ensuring that so great a power as eminent domain, which historically has been used in areas where the most marginalized groups live, is not abused.

As important, the standard for "deteriorating area" defined in the Norwood Code is satisfied not just upon a finding that a neighborhood *is* deteriorating or *will* deteriorate, but is also satisfied by a finding that it " *is in danger of* deteriorating into a blighted area." The statutory definition, therefore, incorporates not only the existing condition of a neighborhood, but also extends to what that neighborhood might become. But what it *might* become may be no more likely than what *might not* become. Such a speculative standard is inappropriate in the context of eminent domain, even under the modern, broad interpretation of "public use."

A fundamental determination that must be made before permitting the appropriation of a slum or a blighted or deteriorated property for redevelopment is that the property, because of its existing state of disrepair or dangerousness, poses a threat to the public's health, safety, or general welfare. Although we adhere to a broad construction of "public use," we hold that government does not have the authority to appropriate private property based on mere belief, supposition, or speculation that the property may pose such a threat in the future. To permit a taking of private property based solely on a finding that the property is deteriorating or in danger of deteriorating would grant an impermissible, unfettered power to the government to appropriate.

We therefore hold that the term "deteriorating area" cannot be used as a standard for a taking, because it inherently incorporates speculation as to the future condition of the property into the decision on whether a taking is proper rather than focusing that inquiry on the property's condition at the time of the proposed taking.

Because Norwood may not justify its taking of appellants' property on either the basis that the neighborhood was deteriorating or on the basis that the redeveloped area would bring economic value to the city, there is no showing that the taking was for public use. Our conclusion is not altered by the amount of compensation offered to the property owners in this case, even if it was in excess of the fair market value of their property. Though the questions of just compensation and public use are both critical in an eminent-domain analysis, they must be assessed and satisfied independently. Here, there is not an adequate showing that the takings were for a public use.

BD. OF CTY. COMM'RS OF MUSKOGEE CTY. v. LOWERY
136 P.3d 639 (Okla. 2006)

LAVENDER, J.

The issues in the present cause are as follows: (1) whether the County's exercise of eminent domain in the instant cases is for public use in accordance with Article 2, § 23 and Article 2, § 24 of the Oklahoma Constitution and (2) whether the County's taking for purposes of economic development of Muskogee County constitutes "public purposes" within the meaning of 27 O.S.2001 § 5 to support such a taking.

Plaintiff/Appellee County initiated condemnation proceedings against Defendant/Landowners for the purpose of acquiring temporary and permanent right-of-way easements for the installation of three water pipelines. Two of the proposed water pipelines ("the Eagle Pipeline") would solely serve Energetix, a privately owned electric generation plant, which was proposed for construction in Muskogee County. By way of the Eagle Pipeline, Energetix's proposed operations would require a maximum of 8,000,000 gallons of water daily for use in cooling towers associated with the operation of an 825 megawatt natural gas-fired power plant.

Energetix proposed to build the third water pipeline ("the Water District Pipeline") on behalf of the Rural Water District No. 5 pursuant to a contract which expressly provided for Energetix's agreement to build this pipeline at no cost to the Water District "as part of the consideration to induce certain property owners to grant private easements for the Eagle Pipeline." The Water District Pipeline was intended to serve residents of the Water District who were not currently being served and to enhance current water service to residents of the Water District, who were receiving it.

Landowners filed an answer and counterclaim in each case seeking declaratory and injunctive relief on the basis that the County's proposed taking was an unlawful taking of private property for private use and private purpose of the private company, Energetix, in violation of 27 O.S.2001 § 5 and the eminent domain provisions contained within both the Oklahoma Constitution and the U.S. Constitution.

The Report of Commissioners was thereafter filed, which provided the takings were for a public purpose and established the amount of just compensation to be awarded to Landowners for their respective properties. Landowners filed their respective Exceptions to the Commissioners' Report, objecting primarily on the basis that the takings were not for a valid public purpose, but rather an unlawful taking of private property for private purpose.

The trial court ultimately agreed with the County and entered an Order confirming the takings in these cases. Landowners appealed, and the COCA reversed and remanded, holding that the takings in the instant cases were unlawful in that they were for the direct benefit of a private company and not for "public purposes" as required.

The County sought to condemn Landowners' private property pursuant to its general eminent domain power. Additionally, we are guided by the applicable general federal constitutional and state constitutional eminent domain provisions, including and perhaps most notably our special provision concerning the taking of private property. Article 2, § 23 provides as follows: "No private property shall be taken or damaged for private use, with or without compensation, unless by consent of the owner, except for private ways of necessity, or for drains and ditches across lands of others for agricultural, mining, or sanitary purposes, in such manner as may be prescribed by law."

Our Constitution further generally provides "private property shall not be taken or damaged for public use without just compensation." That constitutional provision additionally states "in all cases of condemnation of private property for public or private use, the determination of the character of the use shall be a judicial question." The law is clear that "private property may not be taken or damaged by the condemning agency unless the taking or damage is necessary for the accomplishment of a lawful public purpose." We have used the terms "public use" and "public purpose" interchangeably in our analysis of our state constitutional eminent domain provisions, and we therefore view these terms as synonymous.

It is settled law that the constitutional eminent domain provisions "are not grants of power, but limitations placed upon the exercise of government power." The framers of the Oklahoma Constitution recognized "that to protect both life and property is the first duty of government." In keeping with these principles, we have determined the government's power of eminent domain "lies dormant in the state until the Legislature by specific enactment designates the occasion, modes and agencies by which it may be placed in operation."

As a general rule, we construe our state constitutional eminent domain provisions "strictly in favor of the owner and against the condemning party." Additionally, Oklahoma eminent domain statutes must conform to the restrictions placed on the exercise of such power by the Oklahoma constitutional eminent domain provisions. If we were to construe "public purpose" so broadly as to include economic development within those terms, then we would effectively abandon a basic limitation on government power by "washing out any distinction between private and public use of property-and thereby effectively deleting the words for public use from the constitutional provisions limiting governmental power of eminent domain." In our view, the power of eminent domain should be exercised with restraint and we therefore construe the term "public purpose" narrowly.

The County's primary argument is that the general eminent domain statute authorizes its exercise of eminent domain for the sole purpose of economic development (*i.e.*, increased taxes, jobs and public and private investment in the community) because economic development constitutes a "public purpose" within the meaning of the statute as well as the state constitutional eminent domain provisions.

We recognize the general rule that where legal relief is available on alternative, non-constitutional grounds, we avoid reaching a determination on the constitutional basis. However, the circumstances of this case lead us to the conclusion that it is necessary for us to reach a constitutional determination in addition to our statutory determination. Here, the two determinations are intertwined. The analysis under both the applicable eminent domain statute and under the state constitutional provisions turns on the identical determination of the meaning of the term "public purpose," which we have previously noted is synonymous with "public use" as provided in the Oklahoma Constitution.

Considering the fact that the proposed Eagle Pipeline would be solely dedicated to the purpose of serving a private entity to enable its construction and operation in energy production, it is clear that the County in this case urges a broad interpretation of "public purposes." While arguing the construction of the plant will serve a public purpose by significantly enhancing the economic development of Muskogee County through increased taxes, jobs and public and private investment, the County urges our adoption of a rule, which has been applied in other jurisdictions that the exercise of eminent domain for purposes of economic development alone (in the absence of blight) satisfies the constitutional "public use" or "public purpose" requirement. We recognize that the U.S. Supreme Court recently upheld in *Kelo* a city's exercise of eminent domain power in furtherance of an economic development plan, holding that economic development satisfied the "public use" restriction in the Fifth Amendment's Takings Clause and finding the city's economic development plan served a "public purpose."

The U.S. Supreme Court expressly limited its holding in *Kelo* as follows: "this Court's authority, however, extends only to determining whether the City's proposed condemnations are for a public use within the meaning of the Fifth Amendment to the Federal Constitution." Notably, the Court in *Kelo* additionally expressly provided as follows:

> We emphasize that nothing in our opinion precludes any State from placing further restrictions on its exercise of the takings power. Indeed, many states already impose "public use" requirements that are stricter than the federal baseline. Some of these requirements have been established as a matter of state constitutional law, while others are expressed in state eminent domain statutes that carefully limit the grounds upon which takings may be exercised.

Contrary to the Connecticut statute applicable in *Kelo*, which expressly authorized eminent domain for the purpose of economic development, we note the absence of such express Oklahoma statutory authority for the exercise of eminent domain in furtherance of economic development in the absence of blight. The statute at issue in the instant cases is a general grant of power that permits condemnation "in like manner as railroad companies, for highways, rights-of-way, building sites, cemeteries, public parks and other public purposes." County here seeks a broad, expansive interpretation of the term "public purpose" to permit the exercise of eminent domain pursuant to the County's general statutory power of eminent domain. However, we have already rejected such a broad interpretation of "public purpose" and have held that "a municipality is not possessed with an unfettered discretion to condemn property for economic redevelopment projects outside of the scope of statutory schemes that the Legislature has provided for removal of blighted property." Accordingly, we hold that economic development alone does not constitute a public purpose and therefore, does not constitutionally justify the County's exercise of eminent domain. Pursuant to our own narrow requirements in our constitutional eminent domain provisions, we view the transfer of property from one private party to another in furtherance of potential economic development or enhancement of a community in the absence of blight as a purpose, which must yield to our greater constitutional obligation to protect and preserve the individual fundamental interest of private property ownership.

We determine that our state constitutional eminent domain provisions place more stringent limitation on governmental eminent domain power than the limitations imposed by the Fifth Amendment of the U.S. Constitution. We join other jurisdictions, including Arizona, Arkansas, Florida, Illinois, South Carolina, Michigan, and Maine, which have reached similar determinations on state constitutional grounds. Other states have similarly restricted the government's eminent domain power through state statute.

While the Takings Clause of the U.S. Constitution provides "nor shall private property be taken for public use without just compensation," the Oklahoma Constitution places further restrictions by expressly stating "no private property shall be taken or damaged *for private use*, with or without compensation." That constitutional provision additionally expressly lists the exceptions for common law easements by necessity and drains for agricultural, mining and sanitary purposes. The proposed purpose of economic development, with its incidental enhancement of tax and employment benefits to the surrounding community, clearly does not fall within any of these categories of express constitutional exceptions to the general rule against the taking of private property for private use. To permit the inclusion of economic development alone in the category of "public use" or "public purpose" would blur the line between "public" and "private" so as to render our constitutional limitations on the power of eminent domain a nullity. If property ownership in Oklahoma is to remain what the framers of our Constitution intended it to be, this we must not do.

EDMONDSON, J., dissenting.

The Court's decision reflects an understandable sensitivity to the United States Supreme Court's recent approval in *Kelo v. City of New London* of a municipal exercise of eminent domain to take unblighted private residential property and deliver it to a private business in anticipation of public benefits to be derived solely from economic development.

In Oklahoma, our State Constitution extends greater protection to private property than does the Federal Constitution, as the majority opinion ably demonstrates. It also mandates that no private property be taken without just compensation.

However, I do not believe our greater measure of safety for private property was intended to deny non-riparian neighbors access to state water resources; particularly when the water is abundant, access can be achieved merely by taking an easement and is essential to the neighbor's survival, and the purpose is, as here, to expand electrical power resources in an economy in which energy is in critically short supply.

No one should be denied access to public water resources unless it is demonstrated that the access would impair the welfare of the public itself. New generation of electrical power is legislatively favored though it be by a private company and marketed directly to a private consumer, because it contributes to the national energy pool and to the ultimate benefit and security of the public.

GOLDSTEIN v. NEW YORK STATE URBAN DEV. CORP.
921 N.E.2d 164 (N.Y. 2009)

LIPPMAN, C.J.

We are asked to determine whether respondent's exercise of its power of eminent domain to acquire petitioners' properties for purposes of the proposed land use improvement project, known as Atlantic Yards, would be in conformity with certain provisions of our State Constitution. We answer in the affirmative.

On December 8, 2006, respondent Empire State Development Corporation (ESDC) issued a determination pursuant to Eminent Domain Proceedings Law (EDPL) § 204, finding that it should use its eminent domain power to take certain privately owned properties located in downtown Brooklyn for inclusion in a 22-acre mixed-use development proposed, and to be undertaken, by private developer Bruce Ratner and the real estate entities of which he is a principal, collectively known as the Forest City Ratner Companies (FCRC).

The project is to involve, in its first phase, construction of a sports arena to house the NBA Nets franchise, as well as various infrastructure improvements—most notably reconfiguration and modernization of the Vanderbilt Yards rail facilities and access upgrades to the subway transportation hub already present at the site. The project will also involve construction of a platform spanning the rail yards and connecting portions of the neighborhood now separated by the rail cut. Atop this platform are to be situated, in a second phase of construction, numerous high rise buildings and some eight acres of open, publicly accessible landscaped space. The 16 towers planned for the project will serve both commercial and residential purposes. They are slated to contain between 5,325 and 6,430 dwelling units, more than a third of which are to be affordable either for low and or middle income families.

The project has been sponsored by respondent ESDC as a "land use improvement project" within the definition of Urban Development Corporation Act, upon findings that the area in which the project is to be situated is "substandard and insanitary" or, in more common parlance, blighted. It is not disputed that the project designation and supporting blight findings are appropriate with respect to more than half the project footprint, which lies within what has, since 1968, been designated by the City of New York as the Atlantic Terminal Urban Renewal Area (ATURA). To the south of ATURA, however, and immediately adjacent to the Vanderbilt Rail Yard cut, are two blocks and a fraction of a third which, although within the project footprint, have not previously been designated as blighted. FCRC has purchased many of the properties in this area, but there remain some that it has been unsuccessful in acquiring, whose transfer ESDC now seeks to compel in furtherance of the project, through condemnation. In support of its exercise of the condemnation power with respect to these properties, some of which are owned by petitioners, ESDC, based on studies conducted by a consulting firm retained by FCRC, has made findings that the blocks in which they are situated possess sufficient indicia of actual or impending blight to warrant their condemnation for clearance and redevelopment and that the proposed land use improvement project will, by removing blight and creating in its place the above-described mixed-use development, serve a "public use, benefit or purpose."

Petitioners' initial challenge to ESDC's determination authorizing condemnation of their properties was made in a timely federal court action. The gist of that action was that the disputed condemnation was not supported by a public use and thus violated the Fifth Amendment of the Federal Constitution. Petitioners' federal claims were rejected by the Federal District Court, and the judgment dismissing the complaint was affirmed by the Second Circuit. Within six months, petitioners commenced the present proceeding in the Appellate Division and alleged that the proposed taking was not for a "public use" but for the benefit of a private party and thus would be in violation of article I, § 7(a) of the New York State Constitution.

The Appellate Division found for respondent on the merits. It observed that, while the State Constitution, literally read and in its early construction, permitted the taking of property only for "public use," "public use" had since come to be understood as entailing no more than a dominant public purpose. The Court noted that it was well established that the eradication of blight was such a public purpose and found that ESDC's blight findings were supported by the area studies contained in the administrative record.

Turning now to the merits, petitioners first contend that the determination authorizing the condemnation of their properties for the Atlantic Yards project is unconstitutional because the condemnation is not for the purpose of putting their properties to "public use" within the meaning of article I, § 7(a) of the State Constitution—which provides that "private property shall not be taken for public use without just compensation"—but rather to enable a private commercial entity to use their properties for private economic gain with, perhaps, some incidental public benefit. The argument reduces to this: that the State Constitution has from its inception, in recognition of the fundamental right to privately own property, strictly limited the availability of condemnation to situations in which the property to be condemned will actually be made available for public use, and that, with only limited exceptions prompted by emergent public necessity, the State Constitution's takings clause, unlike its federal counterpart, has been consistently understood literally, to permit a taking of private property only for "public use," and not simply to accomplish a public purpose.

Even if this gloss on this State's takings laws and jurisprudence were correct—and it is not—it is indisputable that the removal of urban blight is a proper, and, indeed, constitutionally sanctioned, predicate for the exercise of the power of eminent domain. It has been deemed a "public use" within the meaning of the State's takings clause at least since *Matter of New York City Housing Authority v. Muller* (N.Y. 1936) and is expressly recognized by the Constitution as a ground for condemnation. Article XVIII, § 1 of the State Constitution grants the Legislature the power to "provide in such manner, by such means and upon such terms and conditions as it may prescribe for the clearance, replanning, reconstruction and rehabilitation of substandard and insanitary areas," and section 2 of the same article provides "for and in aid of such purposes, notwithstanding any provision in any other article of this constitution, the legislature may grant the power of eminent domain to any public corporation." Pursuant to article XVIII, respondent

ESDC has been vested with the condemnation power by the Legislature and has here sought to exercise the power for the constitutionally recognized public purpose or "use" of rehabilitating a blighted area.

Petitioners maintain that the blocks at issue are not, in fact, blighted and that the allegedly mild dilapidation and inutility of the property cannot support a finding that it is substandard and insanitary within the meaning of article XVIII. They are doubtless correct that the conditions cited in support of the blight finding at issue do not begin to approach in severity the dire circumstances of urban slum dwelling described by the *Muller* court in 1936, and which prompted the adoption of article XVIII at the State Constitutional Convention two years later. We, however, have never required that a finding of blight by a legislatively designated public benefit corporation be based upon conditions replicating those to which the Court and the Constitutional Convention responded in the midst of the Great Depression. To the contrary, in construing the reach of the terms "substandard and insanitary" as they are used in article XVIII—and were applied in the early 1950s to the Columbus Circle area upon which the New York Coliseum was proposed to be built—we observed:

> Of course, none of the buildings are as noisome or dilapidated as those described in Dickens' novels or Thomas Burke's *Limehouse* stories of the London slums of other days, but there is ample evidence in this record to justify the determination of the city planning commission that a substantial part of the area is "substandard and insanitary" by modern tests.

And, subsequently, in *Yonkers Community Dev. Agency v. Morris* (N.Y. 1975), in reviewing the evolution of the crucial terms' signification and permissible range of application, we noted:

> Historically, urban renewal began as an effort to remove "substandard and insanitary" conditions which threatened the health and welfare of the public, in other words "slums," whose eradication was in itself found to constitute a public purpose for which the condemnation powers of government might constitutionally be employed. Gradually, as the complexities of urban conditions became better understood, it has become clear that the areas eligible for such renewal are not limited to "slums" as that term was formerly applied, and that, among other things, economic underdevelopment and stagnation are also threats to the public sufficient to make their removal cognizable as a public purpose.

It is important to stress that lending precise content to these general terms has not been, and may not be, primarily a judicial exercise. Whether a matter should be the subject of a public undertaking—whether its pursuit will serve a public purpose or use—is ordinarily the province of the Legislature, not the Judiciary, and the actual specification of the uses identified by the Legislature as public has been largely left to quasi-legislative administrative agencies. It is only where there is no room for reasonable difference of opinion as to whether an area is blighted, that judges may substitute their views as to the adequacy with which the public purpose of blight removal has been made out for that of the legislatively designated agencies; where, as here, "those bodies have made their finding, not corruptly or irrationally or baselessly, there is nothing for the courts to do about it, unless every act and decision of other departments of government is subject to revision by the courts."

It is quite possible to differ with ESDC's findings that the blocks in question are affected by numerous conditions indicative of blight, but any such difference would not, on this record, in which the bases for the agency findings have been extensively documented photographically and otherwise on a lot-by-lot basis, amount to more than another reasonable view of the matter; such a difference could not, consonant with what we have recognized to be the structural limitations upon our review of what is essentially a legislative prerogative, furnish a ground to afford petitioners relief.

It may be that the bar has now been set too low—that what will now pass as "blight," as that expression has come to be understood and used by political appointees to public corporations relying upon studies paid for by developers, should not be permitted to constitute a predicate for the invasion of property rights and the razing of homes and businesses. But any such limitation upon the sovereign power of eminent domain as it has come to be defined in the urban renewal context is a matter for the Legislature, not the courts. Properly involved in redrawing the range of the sovereign prerogative would not be a simple return to the days when private property rights were viewed as virtually inviolable, even when they stood in the way of meeting compelling public needs, but a re-weighing of public as against private interests and a reassessment of the need for and public utility of what may now be out-moded approaches to the revivification of the urban landscape. These are not tasks courts are suited to perform. They are appropriately situated in the policy-making branches of government.

The dissenter, after thoughtful review of the evolution of the concept of public use—an evolution that even he acknowledges has sapped the concept of much of its limiting power—urges that there remains enough left in it to require that this case be decided differently. We cannot agree. The Constitution accords government broad power to take and clear substandard and insanitary areas for redevelopment. In so doing, it commensurately deprives the Judiciary of grounds to interfere with the exercise.

While there remains a hypothetical case in which we might intervene to prevent an urban redevelopment condemnation on public use grounds—where "the physical conditions of an area might be such that it would be irrational and baseless to call it substandard or insanitary"—this is not that case. The dissenter looks at the "Blight Study" contained in the administrative record and sees only a "normal and pleasant residential neighborhood," but others, it would appear not irrationally, have come to very different conclusions. This is not a record that affords the purchase necessary for judicial intrusion. The situation in the end is remarkably like *Kaskel* where the Court said:

> Plaintiff does not dispute with defendants as to the condition of these properties or of the whole area. He is simply opposing his opinion and his judgment to that of public officials, on a matter which must necessarily be one of opinion or judgment, that is, as to whether a specified area is so substandard or insanitary, or both, as to justify clearance and redevelopment under the law. It is not seriously contended by anyone that, for an area to be subject to those laws, every single building therein must be below civilized standards. The statute (and the Constitution), like other similar laws, contemplates that clearing and redevelopment will be of an entire area, not of a separate parcel, and, surely, such statutes would not be very useful if limited to areas where every single building is substandard.

Here too, all that is at issue is a reasonable difference of opinion as to whether the area in question is in fact substandard and insanitary. This is not a sufficient predicate for us to supplant respondent's determination.

SMITH, J., dissenting.

The good news from today's decision is that our Court has not followed the lead of the United States Supreme Court in rendering the "public use" restriction on the Eminent Domain Clause virtually meaningless. The bad news is that the majority is much too deferential to the self-serving determination by Empire State Development Corporation (ESDC) that petitioners live in a "blighted" area, and are accordingly subject to having their homes seized and turned over to a private developer. I do not think the record supports ESDC's determination, and I therefore dissent.

Article I, § 7(a) of the State Constitution says: "Private property shall not be taken for public use without just compensation."

The words "public use" embody an important protection for property owners. They prevent the State from invoking its eminent domain power as a means of transferring property from one private owner to another who has found more favor with state officials, or who promises to use the land in a way more to the State's liking. They do not require that all takings result in public ownership of the property, but they do ordinarily require that, if the land is transferred to private hands, it be used after the taking in a way that benefits the public directly. A recognized exception permits the transfer of "blighted" land to private developers without so strict a limitation on its subsequent use, but that exception is applicable only in cases in which the use of the land by its original owner creates a danger to public health and safety.

These principles are established by two centuries of New York cases. A line of 19th century decisions made clear that the State could not use the eminent domain power to transfer property from one private owner to another, unless the use to which the second owner put the property would be "public" in some meaningful sense. In the 20th century, an era friendlier to government and less friendly to private property, this rule was diluted, but our cases do not justify the conclusion that the public use limitation was abandoned or rendered trivial. Rather, the 20th century cases created what may be called a "blight exception" to the public use limitation. The critical question on this appeal is whether that exception applies, a question that can be better understood after a more detailed description of the way our "public use" law has developed.

In the early 19th century, New York judges debated whether the eminent domain power could ever be used to transfer property from one private owner to another. Later cases make clear that this debate was settled in favor of the Chancellor's view that certain uses of property by private parties—*e.g.*, for "turnpike and other roads, railways, canals, ferries and bridges"—could be considered public, but that takings in which land was transferred to private hands would be strictly limited to situations in which the public nature of the use was clear. In *Matter of Niagara Falls & Whirlpool Ry. Co.* (N.Y. 1888), we said: "The right of the state to authorize the condemnation of private property for the construction of railroads and to delegate the power to take proceedings for that purpose to railroad corporations, has become an accepted doctrine of constitutional law and is not open to debate." But we held that the proposed taking in the *Niagara* case, which was for a railroad that would serve "the sole purpose of furnishing sightseers during about four months of the year," was not for a public use.

Under the 19th century understanding of public use, the taking at issue in this case would certainly not be permitted. It might be possible to debate whether a sports stadium open to the public is a "public use" in the traditional sense, but the renting of commercial and residential space by a private developer clearly is not.

Our 20th century cases, while not all consistent and containing some confusing language, are best read as modifying, rather than nullifying or abandoning, the established public use limitation. A series of cases upheld takings for what was variously characterized as slum clearance, removal of blight, or correction of unsafe, unsanitary or substandard housing conditions. While these cases undoubtedly expanded the old understanding of public use, they did not establish the general proposition that property may be condemned and turned over to a private developer every time a state agency thinks that doing so would improve the neighborhood.

Muller approved a taking of property where "unsanitary and substandard housing conditions" were found to exist. We observed:

> The public evils, social and economic of such conditions, are unquestioned and unquestionable. Slum areas are the breeding places of disease which take toll not only from denizens, but, by spread, from the inhabitants of the entire city and State. Juvenile delinquency, crime and immorality are there born, find protection and flourish. Enormous economic loss results directly from the necessary

expenditure of public funds to maintain health and hospital services for afflicted slum dwellers and to war against crime and immorality. Indirectly there is an equally heavy capital loss and a diminishing return in taxes because of the areas blighted by the existence of the slums.

Muller did not involve transfer to an ordinary private developer: the property in question was to be rented by the City, or by "limited dividend corporations," to people of low income. In *Muller*, we reiterated the essential principle of the public use limitation:

> Nothing is better settled than that the property of one individual cannot, without his consent, be devoted to the private use of another, even when there is an incidental or colorable benefit to the public. The facts here present no such case. The public is seeking to take the defendant's property and to administer it as part of a project conceived and to be carried out in its own interest and for its own protection.

Murray, unlike *Muller*, did involve a taking from which a purely private company "may ultimately reap a profit." The need to remedy "conditions in those blighted urban areas where slums exist," conditions that "affect the health, safety and welfare of the public," furnished the reason for upholding the taking.

Our later decision in *Yonkers Community Development* does seem to adopt a rather loose interpretation of "substandard" conditions that would justify a taking, but it also says that "courts are required to be more than rubber stamps in the determination of the existence of substandard conditions" and that "in order to utilize the public purpose attached to clearance of substandard land, such clearance must be the primary purpose of the taking, not some other public purpose, however laudable it might be." In *Yonkers*, we found that the agency had not provided factual support for its claim that the land to be taken was substandard, but held that the landowners had failed to raise this issue properly by their pleadings.

The most troubling cases cited by ESDC are *Cannata v. City of New York* (N.Y. 1962) and *Courtesy Sandwich Shop, Inc. v. Port of N.Y. Auth.* (N.Y. 1963), which can be read to support an interpretation of "public use" that would permit the transfer by eminent domain of almost anyone's property to a private entity if a state agency thinks the area would benefit from "redevelopment." These cases, however, must be understood in historical context. They were decided after the United States Supreme Court had adopted, in *Berman v. Parker* (1954), a "broad and inclusive" definition of public use, to include any "object within the authority of Congress." *Berman*, as later cases confirmed, eviscerated the "public use" limitation of the United States Constitution. And at the time of the *Cannata* and *Courtesy Sandwich Shop* decisions, our Court had not adopted the practice, which later became common, of interpreting our state Constitution to afford broader protection to individual rights and liberties than the federal Constitution does. I would view *Cannata* and *Courtesy Sandwich Shop* as mistakenly following *Berman's* lead, and would limit them to their facts or simply reject them.

The majority does not wholly reject what I have said in this dissent. Indeed, the majority seems to accept the premise that the Eminent Domain Clause of the New York Constitution has independent vitality, and may offer more protection to property owners than its federal counterpart. I am pleased that the majority does not follow the Supreme Court's decisions in *Berman*, *Midkiff* and *Kelo*, which equate "public use" in the Constitution with public purpose, thus leaving governments free to accomplish by eminent domain any goal within their general power to act. Where I part company with the majority is in its conclusion that we must defer to ESDC's determination that the properties at issue here fall within the blight exception to the public use limitation.

It is clear to me from the record that the elimination of blight, in the sense of substandard and unsanitary conditions that present a danger to public safety, was never the bona fide purpose of the development at issue in this case. Indeed, blight removal or slum clearance, which were much in vogue among the urban planners of several decades ago, have waned in popularity. It is more popular today to speak of an "urban landscape"—the words used by Bruce Ratner to describe his "vision" of the Atlantic Yards development in a public presentation in January 2004.

According to the petition in this case, when the project was originally announced in 2003 the public benefit claimed for it was economic development-job creation and the bringing of a professional basketball team to Brooklyn. Petitioners allege that nothing was said about "blight" by the sponsors of the project until 2005; ESDC has not identified any earlier use of the term. In 2005, ESDC retained a consultant to conduct a "blight study." In light of the special status accorded to blight in the New York law of eminent domain, the inference that it was a pretext, not the true motive for this development, seems compelling.

It is apparent from a review of ESDC's blight study that its authors faced a difficult problem. Only the northern part of the area on which Atlantic Yards is to be built can fairly be described as blighted. But the southern part of the project area, where petitioners live, has never been part of ATURA and appears, from the photographs and the descriptions contained in ESDC's blight study, to be a normal and pleasant residential community.

ESDC's consultants did their best. Proceeding lot by lot through the area in which petitioners live, they were able to find that a number of buildings were not in good condition; petitioners claim that this results in large part from the fact that Ratner's plan to acquire the properties and demolish the buildings had been public knowledge for years when the blight study was conducted. Choosing their words carefully, the consultants concluded that the area of the proposed Atlantic Yards development, taken as a whole, was "characterized by blighted conditions." They did not find, and it does not appear they could find, that the area where petitioners live is a blighted area or slum of the kind that prompted 20th century courts to relax the public use limitation on the eminent domain power.

The majority opinion acknowledges that the conditions ESDC relies on here "do not begin to approach in severity the dire circumstances of urban slum dwelling" contemplated by the cases that developed the blight exception. The majority concludes, however, that determining whether the area in question is really blighted is not "primarily a judicial exercise." In doing so, I think, the majority loses sight of the nature of the issue.

The determination of whether a proposed taking is truly for public use has always been a judicial exercise. The right not to have one's property taken for other than public use is a constitutional right like others. It is hard to imagine any court saying that a decision about whether an utterance is constitutionally protected speech, or whether a search was unreasonable, or whether a school district has been guilty of racial discrimination, is not primarily a judicial exercise. While no doubt some degree of deference is due to public agencies and to legislatures, to allow them to decide the facts on which constitutional rights depend is to render the constitutional protections impotent.

The whole point of the public use limitation is to prevent takings even when a state agency deems them desirable. To let the agency itself determine when the public use requirement is satisfied is to make the agency a judge in its own cause. I think that it is we who should perform the role of judges, and that we should do so by deciding that the proposed taking in this case is not for public use.

NOTES

1. Why might some state courts be more or less protective of property rights in the context of eminent domain? Could geography or population influence how a court reads a state constitutional takings provision?

2. Can you make arguments for and against a state court reading the state constitution's takings clause differently from the federal Takings Clause? Will different readings cause headaches for local governments, local developers, or national developers?

3. Should state courts interpret the state constitutions to restrict the power of eminent domain, or should that decision be left to each State's political processes, whether the legislature or a public referendum? Some state constitutions expressly provide that "the question whether the contemplated use be really public shall be a judicial question, and determined as such without regard to any legislative assertion that the use is public." Colo. Const. art. II, § 15; *see* Okla. Const. art. II, § 24 ("In all cases of

condemnation of private property for public or private use, the determination of the character of the use shall be a judicial question"); Wash. Const. art. I, § 16 (same language as the Colorado provision quoted above). Does requiring judicial determinations ensure greater protection of property rights?

4. Are courts the only or even the best protectors of property rights? Some states responded to the concerns *Kelo* raised by adopting stricter *procedural requirements* for takings that were not for a traditional public use. *See, e.g.*, Fla. Const. art. X, § 6(c) ("Private property taken by eminent domain on or after January 2, 2007, may not be conveyed to a natural person or private entity except as provided by general law passed by a three-fifths vote of the membership of each house of the Legislature.") Others adopted a flat prohibition that would appear to leave little, if any, room for court interpretation. *See, e.g.*, N.H. Const. pt. 1, art. 12-a ("No part of a person's property shall be taken by eminent domain and transferred, directly or indirectly, to another person if the taking is for the purpose of private development or other private use of the property.").

5. What are the consequences of providing greater protection to property owners under the state constitutions than the federal Takings Clause provides?

6. A recent development in the federal courts may affect the processing of federal and state takings claims. In *Williamson County Regional Planning Comm'n v. Hamilton Bank of Johnson City*, 473 U.S. 172 (1985), the Supreme Court created a nearly irrebuttable preference for assessing federal takings claim in state court first. It ruled that a property owner whose land has been taken by a local government does not suffer a Fifth Amendment violation—and so may not bring a federal takings claim in federal court—until the state courts have denied the claim for just compensation under state law. In 2019, the U.S. Supreme Court changed course in *Knick v. Township of Scott*, 139 S. Ct. 2162 (2019). It overruled the exhaustion requirement of *Williamson County* and held that a federal takings claimant may bring the claim in federal court at the outset. It remains to be seen how many federal claimants now will seek recourse initially in federal court.

D. WHAT IS "JUST COMPENSATION"?

The Fifth Amendment to the U.S. Constitution does not define what amounts to "just compensation," though the focus would appear to be on the value of the property the government has taken. The state constitutional provisions that mirror the Fifth Amendment's language would seem to indicate the same result. But not all state constitutional takings provisions are so short or generally stated. The following case offers another illustration of a key premise of this textbook—that the diligent lawyer should always consult the relevant state constitution when seeking to solve a client's problem.

BAYOU BRIDGE PIPELINE, LLC v. 38.00 ACRES, MORE OR LESS, LOCATED IN ST. MARTIN PARISH, ET AL.
320 So.3d 1054 (La. 2021)

GENOVESE, J.

This case involves whether an award of attorney fees and other litigation costs to defendant landowners in an expropriation proceeding may be upheld under current law. For the following reasons, we concur and affirm the court of appeal's award to defendants; however, we find that the basis of the award is vested in the Louisiana Constitution of 1974 rather than statutory law.

The facts in this case arise out of the construction of the Bayou Bridge Pipeline, which carries crude oil from Lake Charles to St. James, Louisiana. As part of the project, Bayou Bridge Pipeline, LLC ("BBP"), sought to acquire servitudes on the property of various landowners. The specific piece of property at the center of this litigation is approximately 38 acres of land in St. Martin Parish. Prior to reaching servitude agreements with all individuals with an ownership interest in this parcel of land, BBP began pipeline construction.

Peter Aaslestad, one of the property owners, filed suit against BBP. It stipulated that it would remain off the property as of September 10, 2018. However, the pipeline construction was more than 90% complete at that time.

Meanwhile, in late July 2018, after it had begun construction on the property, BBP filed expropriation litigation against hundreds of property owners with whom servitude agreements could not be reached, including Mr. Aaslestad, Katherine Aaslestad, and Theda Larson Wright. In response, defendants filed an action against BBP, alleging BPP trespassed on their property and violated due process by proceeding with construction of the pipeline prior to a judgment of expropriation.

The matter proceeded to a trial wherein the trial court granted BBP's petition for expropriation, finding the expropriation served a public and necessary purpose. The trial court also granted defendants' demand, finding that BBP trespassed on defendants' property prior to obtaining permission or legal authority. The trial court ultimately awarded each defendant $75.00 for the expropriation and another $75.00 in trespass damages.

Defendants appealed. Ultimately, the court of appeal found that although defendants could not challenge the amount of the trespass award, they were entitled to damages for due process violations. Finally, the court of appeal found defendants are entitled to attorney fees and other litigation costs pursuant to a Louisiana statute but remanded the matter for a hearing to determine the reasonable amounts of each.

BBP thereafter sought writs in this Court, arguing that the court of appeal erred in awarding defendants attorney fees and expert witness costs. Alternatively, BBP averred that the present action does not involve a proceeding "for compensation for the taking of property."

Louisiana Revised Statutes 13:5111(A) provides, in relevant part, as follows:

> A court of Louisiana rendering judgment for the plaintiff, in a proceeding brought against the state of Louisiana, a parish, or municipality or other political subdivision or an agency of any of them, for compensation for the taking of property by the defendant, other than through an expropriation proceeding, shall determine and award to the plaintiff, as part of the costs of court, such sum as will, in the opinion of the court, compensate for reasonable attorney fees actually incurred because of such proceeding.

By its plain language, the statute does not allow for an award of attorney fees in this case, as it involves expropriation by a private entity. Specifically, we find that BBP is not an "agency" of the state. Therefore, each party's arguments regarding whether or not this statute applies will not be addressed. Instead, we find that the Louisiana Constitution of 1974 does provide the legal authority and basis to uphold the award of attorney fees and litigation costs.

The Louisiana Constitution of 1974 requires that landowners be compensated "to the full extent" of their loss, which "shall include, but not be limited to, the appraised value of the property and all costs of relocation, inconvenience, and any other damages actually incurred by the owner because of the expropriation." La. Const. Art. I, § IV(B)(5). This article applies to both public and private entities and was amended in the Constitution of 1974 in order to encompass costs of litigation and attorney fees. Additionally, this Court has previously held that La. Const. Art. I, § IV allows landowners to seek compensation for land already taken or damaged by a "governmental or private entity" exercising the power of eminent domain. Furthermore, regardless of the specific procedural posture of the case, i.e., whether the proceeding is an expropriation matter (where the damage to property is anticipated) or an inverse taking (where the damage to the property occurred before suit was filed), "one thing that both actions have in common is our state constitution".

BBP argues that La. Const. art. I, § IV's "just compensation" clause does not provide for an award of attorney fees in expropriation or taking actions. It cites *Rivet v. State Dep't of Transp. and Dev.* (La. 2001), wherein this Court stated in dicta that "attorney's fees have traditionally been regarded as being distinct from the compensation due to the landowner. BPP notes that, in *Rivet*, the landowners brought an inverse condemnation action after the state appropriated their property without bringing an expropriation action. The trial court awarded the landowners approximately $3 million in just compensation, plus a 25% attorney fee and expert witness fees. After a remand from this Court on the amount of attorney fees originally awarded, the trial court awarded $237,500 in attorney fees, but thereafter granted a new trial on the attorney fee issue on the ground that Mr. Rivet would have to pay the difference between the initial amount awarded herein by the Court and the amount of attorney fees due per his contract. Thus, he would not be in the same position that he was in prior to the condemnation, and he would therefore not have been compensated to the full extent of his loss. Since he would not have been compensated to the full extent of his loss, he would have been denied his rights as guaranteed by the Louisiana Constitution. This Court found that the trial court's granting of a new trial was erroneous because the court's original attorney fee award of $237,500 was not "contrary to the law and evidence." The Court found that the trial court "fell into error" with respect to its concern that an attorney fee award in an amount that did not compensate the plaintiffs for the full amount they owed their attorney (in this case, 25% of the total award) would violate the "just compensation" clause. This Court reasoned that: (1) as stated above, attorney fees "have traditionally been regarded as being distinct from the compensation due to the landowner"; and, (2) "it is well settled that courts may inquire as to the reasonableness of attorney fees as part of their prevailing, inherent authority to regulate the practice of law." BBP argues that *Rivet* demonstrates that this Court rejected the argument that the "just compensation" clause of the Louisiana Constitution governs the issue of attorney fees in the expropriation/takings context.

In addressing *Rivet*, defendants note that the ruling does not explicitly state whether or to what extent La. Const. art. I, § IV(B)(5) is intended to include attorney fees and legal costs in the compensation awarded for a taking. They argue instead that this Court simply held that the amount of attorney fees to be awarded to compensate a landowner for the full extent of their loss is within the discretion of the trial court. Defendants aver that *Rivet*'s reliance on statutory provisions as the sole authority for its reasoning that "[a]ttorney's fees have traditionally been regarded as being distinct from the compensation due to the landowner" reinforces the premise that the statutes regulating attorney fees in takings cases give effect to, and should be applied to be consistent with, the constitutional compensation requirement.

While this Court has generally acknowledged that attorney fee awards are governed by statute or contract, we have also noted that there are exceptions to this rule. We agree with defendants that *Rivet* is inapplicable because it does not address the fundamental question presented herein: whether the Louisiana Constitution permits any award of attorney fees and litigation costs separate from any statutory authority explicitly authorizing an award of attorney fees and costs. We find that it does. Thus, under the specific facts of this case, we find sufficient support in the Louisiana Constitution to uphold the awards of attorney fees and costs.

WEIMER, C.J., concurring.

I agree that the Louisiana Constitution of 1974 provides a basis for upholding the award of attorney fees and litigation costs. I write separately only to highlight the history surrounding La. Const. art. I, § 4, which fully supports the majority's decision.

Article I, § 4(B)(5) provides:

> In every expropriation or action to take property pursuant to the provisions of this Section, a party has the right to trial by jury to determine whether the compensation is just, and the owner shall be compensated to the full extent of his loss. Except as otherwise provided in this Constitution, the full extent of loss shall include, but not be limited to, the appraised value of the property and all costs of relocation, inconvenience, and any other damages actually incurred by the owner because of the expropriation.

The language "the owner shall be compensated to the full extent of his loss" was included as part of the 1974 revision to the Louisiana Constitution. Previously, the 1921 constitution gave the landowner the right to "just and adequate compensation."

It has long been recognized, including by this court, that the 1974 constitution significantly expanded the concept of compensation by adding to the expropriation provision the requirement that the owner be compensated to the "full extent of his loss." While this court has not previously addressed whether "full extent of his loss" encompasses attorney fees, scholarly commentary from Professor Lee Hargrave and commentary from Louis Jenkins, a member of the House of Representatives and a delegate at the constitutional convention, undoubtedly support the holding in this case that attorney fees can be awarded.

Professor Hargrave explained:

> The history of Section 4 reveals a desire to increase the level of compensation beyond that provided by existing state law. The change from the 1921 Constitution's language ("just and adequate compensation") to the new phrase ("compensated to the full extent of his loss") was deliberate, prompted by a belief on the part of the sponsors that inadequate awards have been provided under existing law. The new formula comes from the 1972 Montana Constitution, and was stated by the committee in comments as "intended to permit the owner whose property has been taken to remain in equivalent financial circumstances after the taking."

Explaining his proposal, Delegate Louis Jenkins indicated it would even extend to costs of litigation and attorney fees: "And even if you win, you are going to lose, because of the cost of going to court, hiring an attorney, which you'll have to pay. So this would attempt to take into account that fact." Mr. Jenkins also related the purpose and intent of changing the constitutional language:

> The amount of compensation to be paid when property is taken is not merely "just compensation" as that term has been understood under the fifth and fourteenth amendments of the Federal Constitution and the 1921 State Constitution. Instead, the owner must be compensated "to the full extent of his loss." This is intended to include things "which, perhaps, in the past may have been considered damnum absque injuria, such as cost of removal, attorney fees, inconvenience, loss of aesthetic value or business profits and so forth.

NOTE

Professor Molly Brady has done fruitful work in uncovering the history of state damagings and takings clauses. In one article, she shows how the damagings clauses were meant to remedy perceived inequities created by a strict application of federal and state takings clauses, namely the failure to recognize a taking when a public works project devalued property without physically invading it. *See* Maureen E. Brady, *The Damagings Clauses*, 104 Va. L. Rev. 341 (2018). In an earlier article, she explains how state courts may, and in the past have, expanded the kinds of property interests eligible for federal or state takings protection. *See* Maureen E. Brady, *Property's Ceiling: State Courts and the Expansion of Takings Clause Property*, 102 Va. L. Rev. 1167 (2016).

E. OTHER PROPERTY-RELATED RIGHTS UNDER STATE CONSTITUTIONS

State constitutions also may recognize greater economic "liberty" interests than the U.S. Constitution guarantees—say by granting relief to state claims similar to the federal claims that the U.S. Supreme Court rejected in *Lochner v. New York*, 198 U.S. 45 (1905). A variety of state constitutional provisions may justify such relief, and sometimes state supreme courts may disagree with U.S. Supreme Court doctrine in the course of doing so. The following cases, both from Texas, offer fascinating examples of the situation—and include thoughtful discussions of how state courts should determine whether a state constitution protects substantive due process in the first place.

PATEL v. TEXAS DEP'T OF LICENSING
469 S.W.3d 69 (Tex. 2015)

JOHNSON, J.

In this declaratory judgment action several individuals practicing commercial eyebrow threading and the salon owners employing them assert that, as applied to them, Texas's licensing statutes and regulations violate the Texas Constitution's due course of law provision. They claim that most of the 750 hours of training Texas requires for a license to practice commercial eyebrow threading are not related to health and safety or what threaders actually do. The State concedes that over 40% of the required hours are unrelated, but maintains that the licensing requirements are nevertheless constitutional.

Eyebrow threading is a grooming practice mainly performed in South Asian and Middle Eastern communities. It involves the removal of eyebrow hair and shaping of eyebrows with cotton thread. "Threading," as it is most commonly known, is increasingly practiced in Texas on a commercial basis. Threaders tightly wind a single strand of cotton thread, form a loop in it with their fingers, tighten the loop, and then quickly brush the thread along the skin of the client, trapping unwanted hair in the loop and removing it. In 2011, commercial threading became regulated in Texas when the Legislature categorized it as a practice of "cosmetology."

In order to legally practice cosmetology in Texas a person must hold either a general operator's license or, in certain instances, a more limited but easier-to-obtain esthetician license. Licensing requirements for general operators include completing a minimum of 1,500 hours of instruction in a licensed beauty culture school and passing a state-mandated test. Requirements for an esthetician license include completing a minimum of 750 hours of instruction in an approved training program and passing a state-mandated test. Commercial eyebrow threaders must have at least an esthetician license.

The Texas Department of Licensing and Regulation, which is governed by the Texas Commission of Licensing and Regulation, is charged with overseeing individuals and businesses that offer cosmetology services. The executive director of TDLR is authorized to impose administrative fines of as much as $5,000 per violation, per day.

In late 2008 and early 2009, TDLR inspected Justringz—a threading business with kiosk locations in malls across Texas—and found Nazira Nasruddin Momin and Vijay Lakshmi Yogi performing eyebrow threading without licenses. TDLR issued Notices of Alleged Violations to them for the unlicensed practice of cosmetology. Minaz Chamadia was also performing threading at Justringz without a license, but she was not cited by TDLR.

Ashish Patel and Anverali Satani own threading salons named Perfect Browz. The State has not taken any administrative action related to Perfect Browz. Satani is the sole owner of another threading business, Browz and Henna. TDLR inspected and investigated Browz and Henna on the basis of complaints filed against it. Although Satani received two warnings for Browz and Henna employing unlicensed threaders, the Department did not issue a Notice of Alleged Violation.

In December 2009, Patel, Satani, Momin, Chamadia, and Yogi brought suit against TDLR, its executive director, the Commission, and the Commission's members pursuant to the Uniform Declaratory Judgments Act seeking declaratory and injunctive relief. The Threaders alleged that the cosmetology statutes and administrative rules issued pursuant to those statutes were unreasonable as applied to eyebrow threading and violated their constitutional right "to earn an honest living in the occupation of one's choice free from unreasonable governmental interference." They specifically sought declaratory judgment that, as applied to them, the cosmetology statutes and associated regulations violate the privileges and immunities and due course guarantees of Article I, § 19 of the Texas Constitution.

In this Court the Threaders argue that (1) the real and substantial test governs substantive due process challenges to statutes and regulations affecting economic interests when the challenges are brought under Article I, § 19 of the Texas Constitution; (2) the cosmetology statutes and rules are unconstitutional as applied to the Threaders because they have no real and substantial connection to a legitimate governmental objective; and (3) even if rational basis review is the correct constitutional test, the statutes and regulations are unconstitutional as applied to the Threaders.

The State contends that (4) there is no real difference between the "real and substantial" and "rational relationship" tests for due process concerns; and (5) threading raises public health concerns, implicating valid governmental concerns.

Article I, § 19 of the Texas Constitution provides that

No citizen of this State shall be deprived of life, liberty, property, privileges or immunities, or in any manner disfranchised, except by the due course of the law of the land.

We have at least twice noted that Texas courts have not been entirely consistent in the standard of review applied when economic legislation is challenged under Section 19's substantive due course of law protections. The Threaders go beyond those two cases. They assert that courts considering as-applied substantive due process challenges under Section 19 have mixed and matched three different standards of review through the years. They label those standards as: (1) real and substantial, (2) rational basis including consideration of evidence, and (3) no-evidence rational basis.

The Threaders argue that the first referenced standard—"real and substantial"—is one in which the reviewing court considers whether (1) the legislative purpose for the statute is a proper one, (2) there is a real and substantial connection between that purpose and the language of the statute as the statute functions in practice, and (3) the statute works an excessive or undue burden on the person challenging the statute in relation to the statutory purpose. They argue that the distinguishing characteristic of cases employing the standard is that the courts using it consider evidence concerning both the government's purpose for a law and the law's real-world impact on the challenging party.

The Threaders recognize that the real and substantial test affords less deference to legislative judgments than does the federal rational basis standard. But they point to cases in which this Court specifically said or implied that certain language in the Texas Constitution affords more protection than comparable text in the federal Constitution. They claim that twenty other states utilize the "real and substantial" test.

The Threaders present the second standard—"rational basis including consideration of evidence." Courts applying this test, the Threaders posit, lean heavily on the federal rational basis test and often weigh evidence—including expert testimony—to determine the purpose of a law and whether the law enacted to effect that purpose is reasonable.

The Threaders reference the third standard as "no evidence rational basis." Under the no-evidence version of the rational basis test, they argue, economic regulations do not violate Section 19 if they have any conceivable justification in a legitimate state interest, regardless of whether the justification is advanced by the government or "invented" by the reviewing court, and evidence "seldom" matters.

The Threaders say both the "real and substantial" and "rational basis including consideration of evidence" standards have two prongs, with the first being the primary difference between them. The first prong of the real and substantial standard, they maintain, is whether the challenged statute or regulation has a real and substantial connection to a legitimate governmental objective. They contrast that test with the rational basis including consideration of evidence standard, which they argue is more lenient and favorable toward the government because it asks only whether a statute or regulation arguably *could* bear some rational relationship to a legitimate governmental objective. They further maintain that for both standards the second prong is whether, on balance, the challenged statute or rule imposes an arbitrary or unduly harsh burden on the challenger in light of the government's objective.

The Declaration of Rights of the 1836 Texas Constitution included three rights guaranteeing "due course of law" or the "due course of the law of the land": (1) the sixth, which prevented an accused in a criminal proceeding from being "deprived of life, liberty, or property, but by due course of law"; (2) the eleventh, which provided that an injured person "shall have remedy by due course of law"; and (3) the seventh, which provided that "no citizen shall be deprived of privileges, outlawed, exiled, or in any manner disenfranchised, except by due course of the law of the land."

In 1845, a group of delegates met to draft and propose Texas's first state constitution. The committee responsible for drafting the Bill of Rights proposed including two due course of law clauses—not the three clauses in the Declaration of Rights of the 1836 Texas Constitution. One of the suggested clauses protected an injured party's right to have "remedy by due course of law." The other clause incorporated the criminal due course of law protections from Section 6 of the Republic's Declaration of Rights into a composite due course guarantee: "No citizen of this state shall be deprived of life, liberty, property, or privileges, outlawed, exiled, or in any manner disenfranchised, except by due course of the law of the land." Thus, the committee's proposal added "life, liberty, property" to the existing due course of law guarantee, while removing the same phrase from the protections for the criminally accused. The proposal also added "of this state" after the word "citizen." The proposal was ratified as Article I, § 16 of the Texas Constitution of 1845.

The language in the Due Course of Law Clause was not changed in the Texas Constitutions adopted in 1861, 1866, and 1869. But the Constitutional Convention of 1875 reexamined the clause and proposed changing it to its current language. The proposals were adopted, resulting in the clause reading as it now does.

Texas judicial decisions in the nineteenth and early twentieth century indicated that the Texas Due Course of Law Clause and the federal Due Process Clause were nearly, if not exactly, coextensive. Such decisions generally tracked the thinking expressed by this Court in *Mellinger v. City of Houston* (Tex. 1887), where the Court held that Article I, § 19 was not violated under the facts of that case because of the United States Supreme Court's interpretation of the Fourteenth Amendment in a similar case. During this period, Texas courts frequently addressed whether a legislative enactment was a proper exercise of the governmental unit's police power, examining justifications for the enactment and typically relying on decisions from the United States Supreme Court as guidance. Occasionally, Texas courts mentioned that a proper review involved examining the enactment for a "real or substantial" relationship to the government's police power interest in public health, morals, or safety—a standard consistent with decisions of the United States Supreme Court.

As to federal due process standards, this period before 1935 is sometimes referred to as the "*Lochner* period" in reference to the United States Supreme Court's decision in *Lochner v. New York*. The Court remained within the bounds charted by *Lochner* for several years. Basically, then, during the "*Lochner* era," substantive due process was a touchstone by which courts analyzed both the purpose and the effect of governmental economic regulation by scrutinizing them with a somewhat equivocal deference to the legislative body's pronounced purpose for a law and its choice of the method embodied in the law to achieve that purpose. The federal landscape changed in 1938. In *United States v. Carolene Products Co.*, the Supreme Court pronounced that

> regulatory legislation affecting ordinary commercial transactions is not to be pronounced unconstitutional unless in the light of the facts made known or generally assumed it is of such a character as to preclude the assumption that it rests upon some rational basis.

Texas courts were faced with the question of whether, after *Carolene Products*, to stay the course as to prior decisions interpreting Article I, § 19's due course of law provision, or follow the lead of the United States Supreme Court as to the Fourteenth Amendment's Due Process Clause. That is, Texas courts had to decide whether "due process of law," as used in the Fourteenth Amendment, and "due course of law of the land," as used in Article I, § 19 of the Texas Constitution, remained "in nearly if not all respects, practically synonymous," or whether the meaning of the Texas Constitution remained the same as it had been earlier interpreted because the Constitution's language had not been amended through the political process.

Following the lead of our prior jurisprudence, we conclude that the Texas due course of law protections in Article I, § 19, for the most part, align with the protections found in the Fourteenth Amendment to the United States Constitution. But, that having been said, the drafting, proposing, and adopting of the 1875 Constitution was accomplished shortly after the United States Supreme Court decision in the *Slaughter-House Cases* by which the Court put the responsibility for protecting a large segment of individual rights directly on the states. Given the temporal legal context, Section 19's substantive due course provisions undoubtedly were intended to bear at least some burden for protecting individual rights that the United States Supreme Court determined were not protected by the federal Constitution. That burden has been recognized in various decisions of Texas courts for over one hundred and twenty-five years. We continue to do so today: the standard of review for as-applied substantive due course challenges to economic regulation statutes includes an accompanying consideration as reflected by cases referenced above: whether the statute's effect as a whole is so unreasonably burdensome that it becomes oppressive in relation to the underlying governmental interest.

In sum, statutes are presumed to be constitutional. To overcome that presumption, the proponent of an as-applied challenge to an economic regulation statute under Section 19's substantive due course of law requirement must demonstrate that either (1) the statute's purpose could not arguably be rationally related to a legitimate governmental interest; or (2) when considered as a whole, the statute's actual, real-world effect as applied to the challenging party could not arguably be rationally related to, or is so burdensome as to be oppressive in light of, the governmental interest.

The Threaders do not contend that the State's licensing of the commercial practice of cosmetology is not rationally related to a legitimate governmental interest. But they strongly urge that the number of hours of training required to obtain even an esthetician license has an arbitrary and unduly burdensome effect as applied to them because the 750–hour requirement has no rational connection to reasonable safety and sanitation requirements, which the State says are the interests underlying its licensing of threaders.

One argument the Threaders make, which at its core challenges the rationality of *any* required training, is that the unlicensed practice of eyebrow threading is simply not a threat to public health and safety. In support of the argument they reference their expert witness who submitted a report addressing all of the available medical literature on eyebrow threading, as well as her own empirical analysis of the technique's safety. Based on her investigation and professional experience with eyebrow threading, the expert concluded that threading is safe and, from a medical perspective, requires nothing more than basic sanitation training.

But the Threaders' expert also raised public health concerns during her testimony. She testified that threading may lead to the spread of highly contagious bacterial and viral infections, including flat warts, skin-colored lesions known as mulluscum contagiosum, pink eye, ringworm, impetigo, and staphylococcus aureus, among others. She also agreed that failure to utilize appropriate sanitation practices—for example, proper use of disposable materials, cleaning of work stations, effective hand-washing techniques, and correct treatment of skin irritations and abrasions—can further expose threading clients to infection and disease.

Moving beyond the argument that threading does not pose health risks to begin with, the Threaders contend that as many as 710 of the required 750 training hours for an esthetician license are not related to properly training threaders in hygiene and sanitation, considering the activities they actually perform. The State argues that the Threaders greatly exaggerate the number of unrelated hours, but concedes that as many as 320 of the curriculum hours are not related to activities threaders actually perform.

The fact that approximately 58% of the minimum required training hours are arguably relevant to the activities threaders perform, while 42% of the hours are not, is determinative of the aspect of the second prong of the as-applied standard which asks whether the effect of the requirements as a whole could be rationally related to the governmental interest. They could be. But the percentage must also be considered along with other factors, such as the quantitative aspect of the hours represented by that percentage and the costs associated with them when determining the other aspect of the second prong—whether the licensing requirements as a whole are so burdensome as to be oppressive to the Threaders. Where the number of hours required and the associated costs are low, the ratio of required hours to arguably relevant hours is less important as to the burdensome question. But its importance increases as the required hours increase. For example, if the statute and Commission's rules required ten hours of training for a threader to be licensed and 58 percent, or 5.8 hours, were arguably relevant to what threaders do, the burden of the irrelevant hours would weigh less heavily in determining whether the effect of the requirements as a whole on aspiring threaders is oppressive. In the case of the Threaders, however, the large number of hours not arguably related to the actual practice of threading, the associated costs of those hours in out-of-pocket expenses, and the delayed employment opportunities while taking the hours makes the number highly relevant to whether the licensing requirements as a whole reach the level of being so burdensome that they are oppressive.

The admittedly unrelated 320 required training hours, combined with the fact that threader trainees have to pay for the training and at the same time lose the opportunity to make money actively practicing their trade, leads us to conclude that the Threaders have met their high burden of proving that, as applied to them, the requirement of 750 hours of training to become licensed is not just unreasonable or harsh, but it is so oppressive that it violates Article I, § 19 of the Texas Constitution.

WILLETT, J., concurring.

> *To understand the emotion which swelled my heart as I clasped this money, realizing that I had no master who could take it from me—<u>that it was mine—that my hands were my own</u>, and could earn more of the precious coin. I was not only a freeman but a free-working man, and no master Hugh stood ready at the end of the week to seize my hard earnings.*

Frederick Douglass's irrepressible joy at exercising his hard-won freedom captures just how fundamental—and transformative—economic liberty is. Self-ownership, the right to put your mind and body to productive enterprise, is not a mere luxury to be enjoyed at the sufferance of governmental grace, but is indispensable to human dignity and prosperity.

Texans are doubly blessed, living under two constitutions sharing a singular purpose: to secure individual freedom, the essential condition of human flourishing. In today's age of staggering civic illiteracy—when 35 percent of Americans cannot correctly name a single branch of government—it is unsurprising that people mistake majority rule as America's defining value. But our federal and state charters are not, contrary to popular belief, about "democracy"—a word that appears in neither document, nor in the Declaration of Independence. Our enlightened 18th- and 19th-century Founders, both federal and state, aimed higher, upended things, and brilliantly divided power to enshrine a *promise* (liberty), not merely a *process* (democracy).

One of our constitutions (federal) is short, the other (state) is long—like *really* long—but both underscore liberty's primacy right away. The federal Constitution, in the first sentence of the Preamble, declares its mission to "secure the Blessings of Liberty." The Texas Constitution likewise wastes no time, stating up front in the Bill of Rights its paramount aim to recognize and establish "the general, great and essential principles of liberty and free government." The point is unsubtle and undeniable: Liberty is not *provided* by government; liberty *preexists* government. It is not a gift from the sovereign; it is our natural birthright. Fixed. Innate. Unalienable.

> *Democracy is two wolves and a lamb voting on what to have for lunch. Liberty is a well-armed lamb contesting the vote.*

This case concerns the timeless struggle between personal freedom and government power. Do Texans live under a presumption of liberty or a presumption of restraint? The Texas Constitution confers power—but even more critically, it constrains power. What *are* the outer-boundary limits on government actions that trample Texans' constitutional right to earn an honest living for themselves and their families? Some observers liken judges to baseball umpires, calling legal balls and strikes, but when it comes to restrictive licensing laws, just how generous is the constitutional strike zone? Must courts rubber-stamp even the most nonsensical encroachments on occupational freedom? Are the most patently farcical and protectionist restrictions nigh unchallengeable, or are there, in fact, judicially enforceable limits?

This case raises constitutional eyebrows because it asks building-block questions about constitutional architecture—about how we as Texans govern ourselves and about the relationship of the citizen to the State. This case concerns far more than whether Ashish Patel can pluck unwanted hair with a strand of thread. This case is fundamentally about the American Dream and the unalienable human right to pursue happiness without curtsying to government on bended knee. It is about whether government can connive with rent-seeking factions to ration liberty unrestrained, and whether judges must submissively uphold even the most risible encroachments.

I recognize the potential benefits of licensing: protecting the public and preventing charlatanism. I also recognize the proven benefits of constitutional constraints: protecting the public and preventing collectivism. Invalidating irrational laws does not beckon a Dickensian world of run-amok frauds and pretenders. The Court's view is simple, and simply stated:

Laws that impinge your constitutionally protected right to earn an honest living must not be preposterous.

By contrast, the dissents see government power in the economic realm as infinitely elastic, and thus limited government as entirely fictive, troubling since economic freedom is no less vulnerable to majoritarian oppression than, say, religious freedom—perhaps more so. Exalting the reflexive deference championed by Progressive theorists like Justice Oliver Wendell Holmes, Jr., the dissents would seemingly uphold even the most facially protectionist actions.

The Texas Constitution enshrines structural principles meant to advance individual freedom; they are not there for mere show. Our Framers opted for constitutional—that is, *limited*—government, meaning majorities don't possess an untrammeled right to trammel. The State would have us wield a rubber stamp rather than a gavel, but a written constitution is mere meringue if courts rotely exalt majoritarianism over constitutionalism, and thus forsake what Chief Justice Marshall called their "painful duty"—"to say, that such an act was not the law of the land."

To be sure, the Capitol, not this Court, is the center of policymaking gravity, and judges are lousy second-guessers of the other branches' economic judgments. Lawmakers' policy-setting power is unrivaled—but it is not unlimited. Preeminence does not equal omnipotence. Politicians decide if laws pass, but courts decide if those laws pass muster. Cases stretching back centuries treat economic liberty as constitutionally protected—we crossed that Rubicon long ago—and there is a fateful difference between active judges who defend rights and activist judges who concoct rights. If judicial review means *anything*, it is that judicial restraint does not allow *everything*. The rational-basis bar may be low, but it is not subterranean.

I support the Court's "Don't Thread on Me" approach: Threaders with no license are less menacing than government with unlimited license.

This case lays bare a spirited debate raging in legal circles, one that conjures legal buzzwords and pejoratives galore: activism vs. restraint, deference vs. dereliction, adjudication vs. abdication. The rhetoric at times seems overheated, but the temperature reflects the stakes. It concerns the most elemental—if not elementary—question of American jurisprudence: the proper role of the judiciary under the Constitution.

Judicial duty requires courts to act judicially by adjudicating, not politically by legislating. So when *is* it proper for a court to strike down legislative or executive action as unconstitutional? There are people of goodwill on both sides, and as this case demonstrates, it seems a legal Rorschach test, where one person's "judicial engagement" is another person's "judicial usurpation."

This much is clear: Spirited debates over judicial review have roiled America since the Founding, from *Marbury v. Madison* (1803), to *Worcester v. Georgia* (1832) (against which President Jackson bellowed, "John Marshall has made his decision—now let him enforce it."), to the late 19th and early 20th centuries, when Progressives opposed judicial enforcement of economic liberties, all the way to present-day battles over the Patient Protection and Affordable Care Act. In the 1920s and 1930s, liberals began backing judicial protection of *non*economic rights, while resisting similar protection for property rights and other economic freedoms. The Progressives' preference for judicial nonintervention was later embraced by post-New Deal conservatives like Judge Bork. The judicial-review debate, both raucous and reasoned, is particularly pitched today within the broader conservative legal movement. A prominent fault line has opened on the right between traditional conservatives who champion majoritarianism and more liberty-minded theorists who believe robust judicial protection of economic rights is indispensable to limited government.

Today's case arises under the *Texas* Constitution, over which we have final interpretive authority, and nothing in its 60,000-plus words requires judges to turn a blind eye to transparent rent-seeking that bends government power to private gain, thus robbing people of their innate right–antecedent to government—to earn an honest living. Indeed, even if the Texas Due Course of Law Clause mirrored perfectly the federal Due Process Clause, that in no way binds Texas courts to cut-and-paste federal rational-basis jurisprudence that long post-dates enactment of our own constitutional provision, one more inclined to freedom.

The test adopted today bears a passing resemblance to "rational basis"-type wording, but this test is rational basis with bite, demanding actual *rationality*, scrutinizing the law's actual *basis*, and applying an actual *test*. In my view, the principal dissent is unduly diffident, concluding the threading rules, while "excessive" and "obviously too much" are not "clearly arbitrary." If these rules are not arbitrary, then the definition of "arbitrary" is itself arbitrary. Without discussing (or even citing) recent federal cases striking down nonsensical licensing rules under the supine federal test, the dissents sever "rational" from "rational basis," loading the dice—relentlessly—in government's favor. Their test is tantamount to no test at all; at most it is pass/fail, and government never fails.

No man is allowed to be a judge in his own cause, because his interest would certainly bias his judgment, and, not improbably, corrupt his integrity.

Anyone acquainted with human nature understands, as Madison did, that when people, or branches of government, are free to judge their own actions, nothing is prohibited. The Court recognizes that Texans possess a basic liberty under Article I, Section 19 to earn a living. And to safeguard that guarantee, the Court adopts a test allergic to nonsensical government encroachment. I prefer authentic judicial scrutiny to a rubber-stamp exercise that stacks the legal deck in government's favor.

My views are simply stated:

1. The economic-liberty test under Article I, Section 19 of the Texas Constitution is more searching than the minimalist test under the Fourteenth Amendment to the United States Constitution.

Even under the lenient rational-basis test—"the most deferential of the standards of review"—the would-be threaders should win this case. It is hard to imagine anything more irrational than forcing people to spend thousands of dollars and hundreds of hours on classes that teach everything they don't do but nothing they actually do. Not one of the 750 required hours of cosmetology covers eyebrow threading. Government-mandated barriers to employment should actually bear some meaningful relationship to reality.

The dissents would subordinate concrete scrutiny to conjectural scrutiny that grants a nigh-irrebuttable presumption of constitutionality. It is elastic review where any conceivable, theoretical, imaginary justification suffices. In my view, Texas judges should instead conduct a genuine search for truth—*as they do routinely in countless other constitutional areas*—asking "What is government actually up to?" When constitutional rights are imperiled, Texans deserve actual scrutiny of actual assertions with actual evidence.

- Should Texas courts reflexively accept disingenuous or smokescreen explanations for the government's actions? No.
- Is government allowed to prevail with purely illusory or pretextual justifications for a challenged law? No.
- Must citizens negate even purely hypothetical justifications for the government's infringement of liberty? No.
- Are Texas courts obliged to jettison their truth-seeking duty of neutrality and help government contrive post hoc justifications? No.

Texas judges should discern whether government is seeking a constitutionally valid end using constitutionally permissible means. And they should do so based on real-world facts and without helping government invent after-the-fact rationalizations. I believe the Texas Constitution requires an earnest search for truth, not the turn-a-blind-eye approach that prevails under the federal Constitution.

2. The Texas Constitution narrows the difference in judicial protection given to "fundamental" rights (like speech or religion) and so-called "non-fundamental" rights (like the right to earn a living).

The jurisprudential fact of the matter is that courts are more protective of some constitutional guarantees than others. One bedrock feature of 20th-century jurisprudence, starting with the U.S. Supreme Court's New Deal-era decisions, was to relegate economic rights to a more junior-varsity echelon of constitutional protection than "fundamental" rights. Nothing in the federal or Texas Constitutions requires treating certain rights as "fundamental" and devaluing others as "non-fundamental" and applying different levels of judicial scrutiny, but it is what it is: Economic liberty gets less constitutional protection than other constitutional rights.

But "economic" and "noneconomic" rights indisputably overlap. As the U.S. Supreme Court has recognized, freedom of speech would be meaningless if government banned bloggers from owning computers. Economic freedom is indispensable to enjoying other freedoms—for example, buying a Facebook ad to boost your political campaign. A decade (and three days) ago in *Kelo v. City of New London* (2005), the landmark takings case that prompted a massive national backlash, Justice Thomas's dissent lamented the bias against economic rights this way: "Something has gone seriously awry with this Court's interpretation of the Constitution. Though citizens are safe from the government in their homes, the homes themselves are not."

Kelo is indeed illustrative, as the rational-basis test applies in eminent-domain cases, too, notwithstanding the assurance in footnote four of *Carolene Products* that alleged violations of the Bill of Rights deserve heightened scrutiny. Even though the Fifth Amendment explicitly protects property, the U.S. Supreme Court has supplanted the *Carolene Products* bifurcation with rational-basis deference in takings cases. The *Kelo* Court stressed its "longstanding policy of deference to legislative judgments," and its unwillingness to "second-guess" the city's determination as to "what public needs justify the use of the takings power." Justice O'Connor's scathing dissent, her final opinion on the Court, forcefully accused her colleagues of shirking their constitutional duty.

I would not have Texas judges condone government's dreamed-up justifications (or dream up post hoc justifications themselves) for interfering with citizens' constitutional guarantees. As in other constitutional settings, we should be neutral arbiters, not bend-over-backwards advocates for the government. Texas judges weighing state constitutional challenges should scrutinize government's *actual* justifications for a law—what policymakers *really* had in mind at the time, not something they dreamed up after litigation erupted. And judges should not be obliged to concoct speculative or far-fetched rationalizations to save the government's case.

3. Texas courts need not turn a blind eye to the self-evident reasons why an increasing number of Texans need a government permission slip to work in their chosen field.

Today's decision recognizes another key contributor to the irrationalities afflicting occupational licensing: the hard-wired inclination to reduce competition. This metabolic impulse—Human Nature 101—has always existed.

Courts need not be oblivious to the iron political and economic truth that the regulatory environment is littered with rent-seeking by special-interest factions who crave the exclusive, state-protected right to pursue their careers. Again, smart regulations are indispensable, but nonsensical regulations inflict multiple burdens—on consumers (who pay more for goods and services, or try to do the work themselves), on would-be entrepreneurs (who find market entry formidable, if not impossible), on lower-income workers (who can't break into entry-level trades), and on the wider public (who endure crimped economic growth while enjoying no tangible benefit whatsoever).

While baseball may be the national pastime of the citizenry, dishing out special economic benefits to certain in-state industries remains the favored pastime of state and local governments.

Governments are "instituted among Men" to "secure" preexisting, "unalienable Rights." Our federal and Texas Constitutions are charters of liberty, not wellsprings of boundless government power. Madison adroitly divided political power because he prized a "We the People" system that extolled citizens over a monarchical system of rulers and subjects. The trick was to give government its requisite powers while structurally hemming in that power so that fallible men wouldn't become as despotic as the hereditary monarchs they had fled and fought.

Economic liberty is "deeply rooted in this Nation's history and tradition," and the right to engage in productive enterprise is as central to individual freedom as the right to worship as one chooses. Indeed, Madison declared that "protection" of citizens' "faculties of acquiring property" is the "first object of government," and admonished that a government whose "arbitrary restrictions" deny citizens "free use of their faculties, and free choice of their occupations" was "not a just government." When it comes to occupational licensing—often less about protecting the public than about bestowing special privileges on political favorites—government power has expanded unchecked. But government doesn't get to determine the reach of its own power, something that subverts the original constitutional design of limited government. The Texas Constitution imposes limits, and imposes them intentionally. Bottom line: Police power cannot go unpoliced.

I believe judicial passivity is incompatible with individual liberty and constitutionally limited government. Occupational freedom, the right to earn a living as one chooses, is a nontrivial constitutional right entitled to nontrivial judicial protection. People are owed liberty by virtue of their very humanity—"endowed by their Creator," as the Declaration affirms. And while government has undeniable authority to regulate economic activities to protect the public against fraud and danger, freedom should be the general rule, and restraint the exception.

The Founders understood that a "limited Constitution" can be preserved "no other way than through the medium of courts of justice, whose duty it must be to declare all acts contrary to the manifest tenor of the Constitution void. Without this, all the reservations of particular rights or privileges would amount to nothing." Judicial duty—"so arduous a duty," Hamilton called it—requires courts to be "bulwarks of a limited Constitution against legislative encroachments," including holding irrational anticompetitive actions unconstitutional. Such is life in a constitutional republic, which exalts constitutionalism over majoritarianism precisely in order to tell government "no." That's the paramount point, to tap the brakes rather than punch the gas.

The Court today rejects servility in the economic-liberty realm, fortifying protections for Texans seeking what Texans have always sought: a better life for themselves and their families. There remains, as Davy Crockett excitedly wrote his children, "a world of country to settle."

TEXAS DEPARTMENT OF STATE HEALTH SERVICES v. CROWN DISTRIBUTING LLC
647 S.W.3d 648 (Tex. 2022)

BOYD, J.

The Texas Constitution guarantees that "No citizen of this State shall be deprived of life, liberty, property, privileges or immunities, or in any manner disfranchised, except by the due course of the law of the land." TEX. CONST. art. I, § 19. The plaintiffs in this case assert that this guarantee invalidates a new Texas law that prohibits the processing and manufacturing of smokable hemp products.

The federal Agriculture Improvement Act of 2018—commonly referred to as the 2018 Farm Bill—classified "hemp" as an agricultural product and generally authorized each state to decide whether and how to regulate it within the state's borders. The bill delegated to the U.S. Department of Agriculture the responsibility for approving each state's hemp-regulation plan and for implementing a federal plan for any state that elects not to adopt its own. Although "marihuana" remains a Schedule 1 substance under the federal Controlled Substances Act, the 2018 Farm Bill excludes "hemp" and hemp products that are cultivated, produced, and sold in compliance with federal regulations and the relevant state's federally approved plan.

The Texas hemp plan generally permits Texans to cultivate, process, manufacture, sell, and purchase hemp and hemp-containing products within the state. But as an exception to this otherwise broad authorization, the plan expressly prohibits the "processing" or "manufacturing" of hemp-containing products "for smoking."

The plaintiffs in this case are Texas-based entities that manufacture, distribute, and sell hemp products—including smokable hemp products—in Texas. They filed this suit against the Texas Department of State Health Services, seeking a declaration that section 443.204(4) and rule 300.104 violate the Texas Constitution's due-course clause.

The Hemp Companies assert that the state's ban against the manufacturing and processing of smokable hemp products in Texas violates the Texas Constitution's due-course clause because the ban has no rational connection to any possible governmental interest and its real-world effect is so burdensome as to be oppressive in light of any governmental interest. They rely in particular on our decision in *Patel v. Texas Department of Licensing and Regulation* (Tex. 2015) (holding that state licensing requirements for commercial eyebrow threading were "so burdensome that they are oppressive").

To decide this case, we need not determine precisely what constitutes a "common occupation" or a "lawful calling." Nor must we decide how or whether Texas's due-course clause protects all such occupations or callings. It is enough to observe that the due-course clause, like its federal counterpart, has never been interpreted to protect a right to work in fields our society has long deemed "inherently vicious and harmful." Historically, for example, gambling and racetrack ownership were not "one of life's common occupations," and the desire to make a living by owning such an enterprise does not fall within the "liberty" or "property" interests the due-process and due-course clauses protect.

Similarly, some occupational interests exist only because the government has created them or made them available. For due-process and due-course purposes, such an interest is properly characterized as a form of "property" interest. But to be constitutionally protected, a property interest must be "vested." When an interest "is predicated upon the anticipated continuance" of an existing law and is "subordinate to" the legislature's right to change the law and "abolish" the interest, the interest is not vested.

So, for example, because the right to operate a charter school "rests entirely on the Legislature's decision to continue the [charter-school] system," a charter-school operator has no vested property interest in its charter. Similarly, a government-issued permit to operate a private club that sells alcohol "is not a vested property right but is a privilege that is granted and enjoyed subject to regulations prescribed by the Legislature." As "a general rule," constitutional due-process protections do not "extend" to such privileges.

Ultimately, the Hemp Companies complain that Texas law does not permit them to manufacture or process products that Texas law prohibited for nearly a century. The legislature's recent decision to adopt a "new framework" that permits the possession and use of those products, and even allows the manufacture and processing of similar products, does not transform the Hemp Companies' desire to produce products that the law still prohibits them from producing into a constitutionally protected interest. Considering the long history of the state's extensive efforts to prohibit and regulate the production and use of the *Cannabis sativa L.* plant, we conclude that the manufacture of smokable hemp products is neither a liberty interest nor a vested property interest the due-course clause protects. It is, instead, "purely a personal privilege" that the people's elected representatives in the legislature may grant or withdraw as they see fit.

YOUNG, J., concurring.

The Texas Constitution refers not to "due process" but to "the due course of the law of the land." The Court today "conclude[s] that the due-course clause does not protect the interest that the plaintiffs assert," and I agree. But what *does* that clause protect—and how does it do so? We still do not really know, even as we approach the sesquicentennial of our current Constitution. To the extent we have a due-course framework, it is that the due-course clause means what the federal due-process clause means . . . except when it means something else.

As I see it, this Court's cases about the relationship between the federal and state clauses fall into three general categories:

- First, this Court has explicitly said that § 19 is "without meaningful distinction" from the Fourteenth Amendment's due-process guarantee.
- Second, many cases have treated § 19 and the Fourteenth Amendment as the same without expressly saying so or appearing to give any thought to the question.
- Third, we have recognized the possibility of independent meaning—in two cases, nearly a century apart.

I fear that our repeated equation of due course and due process, intoned so often without any thought or analysis at all, leaves us without mooring. "A grave threat to independent state constitutions is lockstepping: the tendency of some state courts to diminish their constitutions by interpreting them in reflexive imitation of the federal courts' interpretation of the Federal Constitution." Yet it surely also is a "grave threat" to our Constitution to resolutely *insist* on there being a difference if none was intended. Perhaps that is a *graver* threat, since judicial imposition of distinction that lacks any historical or textual support is an encroachment on the rights of the People and the other branches.

One way or other, though, a reasoned decision about the due-course clause's scope will have to come, and soon. In anticipation of such a case, I describe one potential resolution: the possibility that the due-course clause was written to be an important procedural limitation yet not a freestanding font of substantive rights. This reading may be consistent both with precedent and text; it may have the additional benefit of allowing the Court to *use* rather than to discard our precedents equating federal due process and Texas due course.

Under the due-course-clause-as-procedural-limitation approach, it may well be that our 1876 due-course clause was meant to encapsulate the same principles as the 1868 federal due-process clause. In truth, it is easy to imagine that those who ratified the 1876 Constitution expected this result, and there is some real evidence of it beyond this Court's precedents.

Even if the People of Texas thought that the two provisions meant the same thing at the outset, I suspect that the People intended our clause to keep that meaning fixed, regardless of what federal courts might eventually say about the due-process clause. For the due-course clause to mean today what it meant in 1876 should seem normal, not odd. The consistent meaning of unchanged legal texts should be a common feature of all legal enactments, not just constitutions.

Thus, even if Texans in 1876 thought that they could enshrine federal due-process values into our Constitution, it does not follow that the due-course clause must forever march to the beat of the U.S. Supreme Court's drum. It was foreseeable in 1876 that the U.S. Supreme Court might take a constitutional detour; must the Texas Constitution go along for the ride? I doubt it. The opposite is more likely true. The value in locking down the original meaning of the due-process clause within the due-course clause would be as a hedge against the possibility that the federal understanding of the federal due-process clause would go astray. If Texas courts must resolutely interpret the Texas due-course clause to follow every federal fad, though, this hedge would be illusory. Why even have a due-course clause if its meaning must yo-yo up and down with the changing views of any five U.S. Supreme Court Justices? Nothing useful could come from such mimicry.

But as Chief Judge Sutton has put it, state courts "may interpret their own constitutions to provide less protection than the US Constitution offers." Jeffrey S. Sutton, *Who Decides?: States As Laboratories of Constitutional Experimentation* 141 (2021). Even in the context of a state constitutional provision that adopts the original meaning of a federal provision, that principle would suggest rejecting the ratchet approach in which state constitutions must have *at least* the substantive scope that the Supreme Court claims for the federal Constitution, or perhaps more. In such a "skewed market," "state courts innovate only in granting *more rights* under their constitutions. The only way in which state court federalism helps the country is when state courts engage constitutional rights in both directions, registering respectful disagreement with some federal decisions and creating prompts for new decisions." *Id.* at 142.

Staying the course on the original meaning of the due-process clause would make sense if we conclude that those who framed and ratified our Constitution never viewed the judiciary as empowered to change settled constitutional understandings. How much less likely would Texans in 1876 have delegated such power to Justices of the U.S. Supreme Court?

Even if the due-course clause meant to embody the original meaning of the Fourteenth Amendment's due-process clause, at least two further serious questions arise. First, what did those who ratified the Texas Constitution in 1876 think that they were getting by locking down the federal due-process guarantee? With full recognition of how fraught and contested that question is, I will continue the hypothesis for present purposes: that due process, and thus due course, had a primarily procedural import in 1876.

Second, and relatedly, if the 1876 enactment anticipated a powerful yet purely procedural role for the due-course clause, what would that mean for our law—and for our liberty? At first blush, one might assume a substantial change. I am less sure of that.

One can readily agree that Texans have inalienable rights, whether included in a constitution or not. Then-Justice Willett's elegant and stirring concurrence in *Patel* provides a wonderful defense of the inherent rights of us all. Texans tend to think of rights being "recognized," not "granted," by our Constitution. The real question, however, concerns the lawful role for *judges*. Basic to our system is the principle that judicial power is limited to what the People have delegated to the judiciary. The judiciary, while certainly different from the policymaking branches, is still part of the government. And like every other part of the government, the judiciary derives *all* its powers from the People alone. The People adopted the due-course clause and created a judicial system to enforce it. *If* the People placed only procedural protections within that clause, the judiciary would have no proper authority to say otherwise.

But the citizens of our State have many other tools at their disposal, including other ways to authorize judges to vindicate individual liberties. A procedural understanding of due course, in other words, hardly means that the Texas Constitution could not robustly protect liberty. To think that liberty can only come from judicially mining substantive rights from the spare phrase "due course of the law of the land" is an impoverished view of liberty and of our Constitution.

Quite unlike the federal Constitution, our State's Constitution already contains a rich repository of carefully written, detailed, well-known, expressly stated, unambiguous individual liberties. Freedom of speech, freedom of worship, protection from searches and seizures—all of these and more are provided with much greater detail than their federal analogues. Our People continue to add to the Constitution, too—eight more amendments last year, and two more just last month. "Our Texas Constitution is quite lengthy and frequently amended. When Texans want to provide substantive constitutional protection, they are not shy about saying so expressly." Our Framers provided for these amendments. Thus, our Constitution also recognizes far lesser-known rights, like public beach access and the right to hunt and fish. The People added this hunting-and-fishing right to our Constitution's Bill of Rights only six-and-a-half years ago, illustrating how active they are in articulating the rights that Texas courts must enforce.

Under these circumstances, our distinct Texas constitutional tradition seems to provide some evidence that the judiciary exists to protect rights that are textually expressed, but *not* to discover new ones in the due-course clause itself. A tradition in which judges dispense rights from comparatively vague texts is not self-evidently more pro-liberty than a tradition in which the People themselves decisively stand at the helm.

With greater specificity comes greater clarity about *when* the judiciary should act. A robust role for the judiciary, like the one described in *Patel* by Justice Willett, can be every bit as powerful—perhaps more—when the judiciary uses concrete provisions that directly protect liberty.

If the hypothesis that the original meaning of "due course" (and "due process") was primarily procedural is right, *saying so* could advance our law's clarity and predictability, not to mention the core principles of self-government. Our federal experience, with its comparative paucity of textually expressed rights, has led to an instinctive resort to due-process-type litigation. Such litigation prioritizes *judge*-centered questions (like what deeper truths might be lurking within the textually vague phrase "due course"). Moving away from that instinct would lead toward *text*-centered questions about the meaning of the Texas Constitution's many and varied substantive provisions. It would also encourage the People to remain vigilant about governing themselves rather than assuming that courts will supply any desired deficiency.

Or, I cheerfully recognize, perhaps all of that is wrong. Maybe something quite different should be the true doctrine of our due-course clause. In other words, we have a lot of work to do. It is fortunate that today's case does not require us to plumb these depths. But we must be prepared for the arrival of cases that demand far more from us. To that end, I turn, finally, to some of the tools that will help us discern the proper meaning of the due-course clause.

Perhaps most importantly, the history of the clause in our Constitution warrants careful assessment. Neither this Court nor the larger legal community were strangers to the phrase "due course" when the 1876 Constitution came into force. That phrase was common enough, not least because it was part of our prior Constitutions. Examining the use of that phrase in the time leading to the current Constitution's ratification may provide considerable persuasive force even if it is not necessarily dispositive.

Moreover, any investigation into the original public meaning of "due course of law" must acknowledge that the 1876 Constitution uses that phrase *twice* in the Bill of Rights. Section 13 provides that "all courts shall be open, and every person for an injury done him, in his lands, goods, person or reputation, shall have remedy by due course of law." Indeed, *every* Texas Constitution since 1836 has included not just one but at least two "due course" clauses—the Texas Republic's Constitution used "due course" *three* times. Before we finally resolve what § 19's due-course clause means, we should at least ask if the use of that exact phrase only six sections earlier within the same Bill of Rights may shed any meaningful light.

Other states' constitutions frequently have used the phrase "due course." There appears to be evidence that our Framers and Ratifiers consciously drew from and sought to remain basically consistent with this larger body of law. Treatises like Cooley's surveyed many cases from other jurisdictions; our (and other states') courts then used those treatises and cases. Particularly those sources in common use by Texas courts may help reflect the prevailing understanding of how due-course provisions properly operated. Usage drawn from English law's references to "due course" will likely be informative, too.

What came soon *after* enactment may also point to the original meaning. Cases, treatises, and legal publications could help sketch the then-new text's contours. Even if the text proves indeterminate, settled post-enactment practice may prove instructive.

Such methods of analyzing the text are, of course, by no means exhaustive. And as to them or others, advocates need not start from scratch. Scholars have been working to unravel the knotted meaning of "due process," "due course," and "law of the land" at the time of the U.S. Constitution's Founding. Such work could inform, at least as a starting point, the question of how the phrases had evolved by 1876.

In the end, the purpose of my separate writing today is to encourage careful consideration of all the questions and scenarios that I have discussed and more. The stakes are too high for us to continue on the path of least resistance. We cannot build on foundations that are themselves merely assumptions.

CHAPTER X

RELIGION CLAUSES

The First Amendment to the United States Constitution says that "Congress shall make no law respecting an establishment of religion, or prohibiting the free exercise thereof." Relying on the Due Process Clause of the Fourteenth Amendment and the selective-incorporation doctrine, the United States Supreme Court has extended the restrictions of the Free Exercise and Establishment Clauses to the States. *See Cantwell v. Connecticut*, 310 U.S. 296 (1940) (free exercise clause); *Everson v. Bd. of Educ.*, 330 U.S. 1 (1947) (establishment clause).

Like the United States Constitution, most state constitutions contain religion clauses that prohibit governmental establishments of religion, *see* Jill Goldenziel, *Blaine's Name in Vain?: State Constitutions, School Choice, and Charitable Choice*, 83 Denv. U. L. Rev. 57, 63 (2005), and that provide protection for the free exercise of religious beliefs and practices, *see* Mechthild Fritz, *Religion in a Federal System: Diversity Versus Uniformity*, 38 Kan. L. Rev. 39, 49 (1989). Some of the state guarantees not only pre-date the Bill of Rights, but also were the models for the federal Religion Clauses. *See* Michael W. McConnell, *The Origins and Historical Understanding of Free Exercise of Religion*, 103 Harv. L. Rev. 1409, 1455–58 (1990). We will start with the state freedom of religion clauses, then turn to the state establishment clauses.

A. FREEDOM OF RELIGION

All fifty state constitutions contain provisions that safeguard the rights of their citizens to practice their faith.

Some state guarantees mirror the brief and general language of the national free exercise clause. *See, e.g.*, Mass. Const. amend. art. XLVI, § 1 ("No law shall be passed prohibiting the free exercise of religion."); Pa. Const. of 1776, art. II, *reprinted in* 2 *Federal and State Constitutions, Colonial Charters, and Other Organic Laws of the United States* 1328, 1450–51 (B. Poore ed., 2d ed. 1878) ("free exercise of religious worship"); Va. Decl. of Rights of 1776, § 16, *reprinted in* 2 *Federal and State Constitutions, Colonial Charters, and Other Organic Laws of the United States* 1908–09 ("all men are equally entitled to the free exercise of religion").

But most of the state guarantees are more specific (and more lengthy). The Ohio Constitution provides a good example:

> All men have a natural and indefeasible right to worship Almighty God according to the dictates of their own conscience. No person shall be compelled to attend, erect, or support any place of worship, or maintain any place of worship, against his consent; and no preference shall be given, by law, to any religious society; nor

shall any interference with the rights of conscience be permitted. No religious test shall be required, as a qualification for office, nor shall any person be incompetent to be a witness on account of his religious belief; but nothing herein shall be construed to dispense with oaths and affirmations. Religion, morality, and knowledge, however, being essential to good government, it shall be the duty of the general assembly to pass suitable laws to protect every religious denomination in the peaceable enjoyment of its own mode of public worship, and to encourage schools and the means of instruction.

Ohio Const. art. I, § 7. *See* Minn. Const. art. I, § 16; Neb. Const. art. I, § 4; Tex. Const. art. I, § 6; Ark. Const. art. II, § 24; N.Y. Const. art. I, § 3 ("The free exercise and enjoyment of religious profession and worship, without discrimination or preference, shall forever be allowed in this state"); Ill. Const. art. I, § 3; Va. Const. art. I, § 16 ("all men are equally entitled to the free exercise of religion"). For background on the development and history of state free exercise clauses, see Angela C. Carmella, *State Constitutional Protection of Religious Exercise: An Emerging Post-Smith Jurisprudence*, 1993 BYU L. Rev. 277, 293–305 (1993).

The law in this area has developed considerably in the last few decades—as the state and federal courts and legislatures have reacted to each other through various decisions and legislation. Of particular interest in both court systems has been the vexing problem of regulating religious practices. It is one thing to ensure that citizens may believe whatever they wish. It is quite another to allow them to practice their religion in whatever way they wish. That distinction is at play in the following cases, which present a classic story of federalism, one that starts with a decision by the United States Supreme Court, that leads to a response from Congress, that leads to a second Supreme Court decision, and that ends (for now) with responses from the state supreme courts and the state legislatures.

EMPLOYMENT DIVISION v. SMITH
494 U.S. 872 (1990)

SCALIA, J.

This case requires us to decide whether the Free Exercise Clause of the First Amendment permits the State of Oregon to include religiously inspired peyote use within the reach of its general criminal prohibition on use of that drug, and thus permits the State to deny unemployment benefits to persons dismissed from their jobs because of such religiously inspired use.

Respondents Alfred Smith and Galen Black were fired from their jobs with a private drug rehabilitation organization because they ingested peyote for sacramental purposes at a ceremony of the Native American Church, of which both are members. When respondents applied to petitioner Employment Division for unemployment compensation, they were determined to be ineligible for benefits because they had been discharged for work-related "misconduct." The Oregon Supreme Court held that respondents' religiously inspired use of peyote fell within the prohibition of the Oregon statute, which "makes no exception for the sacramental use" of the drug. It then considered whether that prohibition was valid under the Free Exercise Clause, and concluded that it was not.

The free exercise of religion means, first and foremost, the right to believe and profess whatever religious doctrine one desires. Thus, the First Amendment obviously excludes all "governmental regulation of religious *beliefs* as such." The government may not compel affirmation of religious belief, impose special disabilities on the basis of religious views, or lend its power to one or the other side in controversies over religious authority or dogma.

But the "exercise of religion" often involves not only belief and profession but the performance of (or abstention from) physical acts: assembling with others for a worship service, participating in sacramental use of bread and wine, proselytizing, abstaining from certain foods or certain modes of transportation. It would be true, we think that a State would be "prohibiting the free exercise of religion" if it sought to ban such acts or abstentions only when they are engaged in for religious reasons, or only because of the religious belief that they display. It would doubtless be unconstitutional, for example, to ban the casting of "statues that are to be used for worship purposes," or to prohibit bowing down before a golden calf.

Respondents in the present case, however, seek to carry the meaning of "prohibiting the free exercise of religion" one large step further. They contend that their religious motivation for using peyote places them beyond the reach of a criminal law that is not specifically directed at their religious practice, and that is concededly constitutional as applied to those who use the drug for other reasons. They assert, in other words, that "prohibiting the free exercise of religion" includes requiring any individual to observe a generally applicable law that requires (or forbids) the performance of an act that his religious belief forbids (or requires). We have never held that an individual's religious beliefs excuse him from compliance with an otherwise valid law prohibiting conduct that the State is free to regulate.

Our decisions have consistently held that the right of free exercise does not relieve an individual of the obligation to comply with a "valid and neutral law of general applicability on the ground that the law proscribes (or prescribes) conduct that his religion prescribes (or proscribes)."

There being no contention that Oregon's drug law represents an attempt to regulate religious beliefs, the communication of religious beliefs, or the raising of one's children in those beliefs, the rule to which we have adhered ever since *Reynolds* plainly controls. "Our cases do not at their farthest reach support the proposition that a stance of conscientious opposition relieves an objector from any colliding duty fixed by a democratic government."

Values that are protected against government interference through enshrinement in the Bill of Rights are not thereby banished from the political process. Just as a society that believes in the negative protection accorded to the press by the First Amendment is likely to enact laws that affirmatively foster the dissemination of the printed word, so also a society that believes in the negative protection accorded to religious belief can be expected to be solicitous of that value in its legislation as well. It is therefore not surprising that a number of States have made an exception to their drug laws for sacramental peyote use. But to say that a nondiscriminatory religious-practice exemption is permitted, or even that it is desirable, is not to say that it is constitutionally required, and that the appropriate occasions for its creation can be discerned by the courts. It may fairly be said that leaving accommodation to the political process will place at a relative disadvantage those religious practices that are not widely engaged in; but that unavoidable consequence of democratic government must be preferred to a system in which each conscience is a law unto itself or in which judges weigh the social importance of all laws against the centrality of all religious beliefs.

NOTES

1. *Smith* limited the reach of *Sherbert v. Verner*, 374 U.S. 398 (1963), which involved a free exercise claim by a man who refused to work on Saturdays due to his religious beliefs and who claimed that the State could not deny him unemployment compensation based on his religious practices. Whereas *Smith* applied rational basis review to a neutral law of general applicability and rejected the free exercise claim, *Sherbert* applied strict scrutiny (or something approximating strict scrutiny) to the State's unemployment compensation system and granted relief to the religious objector. *Id.* at 406. In *Church of the Lukumi Babalu Aye, Inc. v. Hialeah*, 508 U.S. 520 (1993), the Court followed the *Smith* test, but it applied strict scrutiny because the city had targeted the religious practices of a local religious group for specific regulation.

2. Three years after *Smith*, Congress enacted the Religious Freedom Restoration Act (RFRA). Invoking its powers under § 5 of the Fourteenth Amendment, Congress sought to require courts to apply strict scrutiny to claims that state or federal laws burdened the practices of sincere religious adherents. With RFRA, Congress sought to overrule *Smith* legislatively and, in the process, to extend strict scrutiny to all free exercise claims. Here is the Supreme Court's response.

CITY OF BOERNE v. FLORES
521 U.S. 507 (1997)

KENNEDY, J.

A decision by local zoning authorities to deny a church a building permit was challenged under the Religious Freedom Restoration Act of 1993. The case calls into question the authority of Congress to enact RFRA.

RFRA prohibits "government" from "substantially burdening" a person's exercise of religion even if the burden results from a rule of general applicability unless the government can demonstrate the burden "(1) is in furtherance of a compelling governmental interest; and (2) is the least restrictive means of furthering that compelling governmental interest."

Congress relied on its Fourteenth Amendment enforcement power in enacting the most far-reaching and substantial of RFRA's provisions, those which impose its requirements on the States. The Fourteenth Amendment provides, in relevant part:

> Section 5. The Congress shall have power to enforce, by appropriate legislation, the provisions of this article.

Congress' power under § 5 extends only to "enforcing" the provisions of the Fourteenth Amendment. The design of the Amendment and the text of § 5 are inconsistent with the suggestion that Congress has the power to decree the substance of the Fourteenth Amendment's restrictions on the States. Legislation which alters the meaning of the Free Exercise Clause cannot be said to be enforcing the Clause.

Respondent contends that RFRA is a proper exercise of Congress' remedial or preventive power. The Act, it is said, is a reasonable means of protecting the free exercise of religion as defined by *Smith*. It prevents and remedies laws which are enacted with the unconstitutional object of targeting religious beliefs and practices. To avoid the difficulty of proving such violations, it is said, Congress can simply invalidate any law which imposes a substantial burden on a religious practice unless it is justified by a compelling interest and is the least restrictive means of accomplishing that interest. If Congress can prohibit laws with discriminatory effects in order to prevent racial discrimination in violation of the Equal Protection Clause, then it can do the same, respondent argues, to promote religious liberty.

While preventive rules are sometimes appropriate remedial measures, there must be a congruence between the means used and the ends to be achieved. The appropriateness of remedial measures must be considered in light of the evil presented. Strong measures appropriate to address one harm may be an unwarranted response to another, lesser one.

Regardless of the state of the legislative record, RFRA cannot be considered remedial, preventive legislation, if those terms are to have any meaning. It appears, instead, to attempt a substantive change in constitutional protections. Preventive measures prohibiting certain types of laws may be appropriate when there is reason to believe that many of the laws affected by the congressional enactment have a significant likelihood of being unconstitutional. Remedial legislation under § 5 "should be adapted to the mischief and wrong which the Fourteenth Amendment was intended to provide against."

The stringent test RFRA demands of state laws reflects a lack of proportionality or congruence between the means adopted and the legitimate end to be achieved. If an objector can show a substantial burden on his free exercise, the State must demonstrate a compelling governmental interest and show that the law is the least restrictive means of furthering its interest. Claims that a law substantially burdens someone's exercise of religion will often be difficult to contest. Requiring a State to demonstrate a compelling interest and show that it has adopted the least restrictive means of achieving that interest is the most demanding test known to constitutional law. If "compelling interest really means what it says, many laws will not meet the test. The test would open the prospect of constitutionally required religious exemptions from civic obligations of almost every conceivable kind." Laws valid under *Smith* would fall under RFRA without regard to whether they had the object of stifling or punishing free exercise. We make these observations not to reargue the position of the majority in *Smith* but to illustrate the substantive alteration of its holding attempted by RFRA. This is a considerable congressional intrusion into the States' traditional prerogatives and general authority to regulate for the health and welfare of their citizens.

NOTES

1. Although *City of Boerne* invalidated RFRA as applied to the States and local governments, it did not invalidate the law as applied to the National Government. In the aftermath of *City of Boerne*, Congress returned to the drawing board and enacted the Religious Land Use and Institutionalized Persons Act (RLUIPA) of 2000, which applies to state and local governments. The new federal law, as its name suggests, applies only to land-use regulation and prison rules and regulations. RLUIPA, in contrast to RFRA, has withstood at least one constitutional challenge. *See Cutter v. Wilkinson*, 544 U.S. 709 (2005) (holding that RLUIPA does not violate the Establishment Clause).

2. In a federal system, decisions of the United States Supreme Court not only may provoke responses from Congress, but they also may prompt action by the States. The state courts and legislatures have responded to *Smith* and *City of Boerne* in a variety of ways. Some state courts have declined to follow *Smith* as a matter of state constitutional law. And several

state legislatures have enacted state-level RFRAs. The following cases explore these approaches.

HUMPHREY v. LANE
728 N.E.2d 1039 (Ohio 2000)

PFEIFER, J.

We hold that under Section 7, Article I of the Ohio Constitution, the standard for reviewing a generally applicable, religion-neutral state regulation that allegedly violates a person's right to free exercise of religion is whether the regulation serves a compelling state interest and is the least restrictive means of furthering that interest. We further hold that the prison-guard grooming policy in this case, while in furtherance of a compelling state interest, did not employ the least restrictive means of furthering that interest.

In employing our comparison to the Free Exercise Clause of the First Amendment, we are not doing a mere word count, but instead are looking for a qualitative difference. The Ohio Constitution does have an eleven-word phrase that distinguishes itself from the United States Constitution: "nor shall any interference with the rights of conscience be permitted." The United States Constitution states that Congress shall make no law "prohibiting the free exercise of religion." We find the phrase that brooks no "interference with the rights of conscience" to be broader than that which proscribes any law prohibiting free exercise of religion. The Ohio Constitution allows no law that even *interferes* with the rights of conscience. The federal Constitution concerns itself with laws that *prohibit* the free exercise of religion. By its nature the federal Constitution seems to target laws that specifically address the exercise of religion, *i.e.*, not those laws that tangentially affect religion. Ohio's ban on any interference makes even those tangential effects potentially unconstitutional.

The United States Supreme Court's interpretation of the federal Constitution makes it clear that "the right of free exercise does not relieve an individual of the obligation to comply with a valid and neutral law of general applicability on the ground that the law proscribes (or prescribes) conduct that his religion prescribes (or proscribes)." Under the standard enunciated by the court in *Smith*, the relevant issues are whether the regulation at issue is religion-neutral and whether it is generally applicable. If those elements are fulfilled, then the regulation does not violate the Free Exercise Clause.

We have made it clear that this court is not bound by federal court interpretations of the federal Constitution in interpreting our own Constitution. As this court held in *Arnold v. Cleveland* (Ohio 1993):

The Ohio Constitution is a document of independent force. In the areas of individual rights and civil liberties, the United States Constitution, where applicable to the states, provides a floor below which state court decisions may not fall. As long as state courts provide at least as much protection as the United States Supreme Court has provided in its interpretation of the federal Bill of Rights, state courts are unrestricted in according greater civil liberties and protections to individuals and groups.

As stated above, the Ohio Constitution's free exercise protection is broader, and we therefore vary from the federal test for religiously neutral, evenly applied government actions. We apply a different standard to a different constitutional protection. We adhere to the standard long held in Ohio regarding free exercise claims—that the state enactment must serve a compelling state interest and must be the least restrictive means of furthering that interest. That protection applies to direct and indirect encroachments upon religious freedom.

To state a prima facie free exercise claim, the plaintiff must show that his religious beliefs are truly held and that the governmental enactment has a coercive affect against him in the practice of his religion. There seems to be no dispute that Humphrey has successfully made those showings in this case. Forcing Humphrey to cut his hair would certainly infringe upon the free exercise of his religion.

Since Humphrey has made his prima facie case, the burden shifts to the state to prove that the regulation furthers a compelling state interest. Once that aspect has been satisfied, the state must prove that its regulation is the least restrictive means available of furthering that state interest.

We are satisfied that the state does have a compelling interest in establishing a uniform and grooming policy for its guards. Maintenance of a prison system is a central role of government, an area it is uniquely suited for. It is an undertaking essential to justice and to the safety of the citizenry, but by its nature is fraught with danger and thus must be tightly controlled. A prison is a dangerous, potentially explosive environment.

The state has sufficiently established that there is a compelling state interest in establishing uniform and grooming policies for prison workers. The state must further prove, however, that the policy is the least restrictive means of furthering that interest. We view the resolution of that issue to be a factual determination. The trial court found as a factual matter that the simple accommodation of allowing Humphrey to wear his hair pinned under his uniform cap was a less restrictive means of furthering Ohio's interest. The trial court saw Humphrey with his hair tucked beneath his cap and found that Humphrey presented the "professional and dignified image" required by the policy.

The trial judge also considered testimony concerning whether Humphrey's hair affected the attitudes of fellow guards, administrators, and inmates toward him, and viewed with his own eyes whether the accommodation was a practical one. The trial court found that a practical accommodation could be made. We defer to the trial court's factual finding.

Therefore, we hold that Ohio can further its compelling interest of a uniform grooming policy through a less restrictive means than the policy it currently employs. We accordingly reverse the judgment of the court of appeals and reinstate the trial court's declaratory judgment and injunction.

ATTORNEY GENERAL v. DESILETS
636 N.E.2d 233 (Mass. 1994)

WILKINS, J.

This case involves the tension between a statutory mandate that a landlord not discriminate against unmarried couples in renting accommodations and a landlord's sincerely held religious belief that he should not facilitate what he regards as sinful cohabitation.

The defendants have a policy of not leasing an apartment to any person who intends to engage in conduct that violates their religious principles. The defendants' sole reason for declining even to consider Lattanzi and Tarail as tenants was that religion-based policy. The defendants, who are Roman Catholics, believe that they should not facilitate sinful conduct, including fornication. Since developing the policy at least a decade earlier, the defendants have applied it ten or more times to deny tenancies to unmarried couples.

General Laws c. 151B, § 4(6) provided, in part, that it shall be an unlawful practice for the owner of a multiple dwelling "to refuse to rent or lease or otherwise to deny to or withhold from any person or group of persons such accommodations because of the race, religious creed, color, national origin, sex, age, ancestry or *marital status* of such person or persons." We shall conclude that the defendants violated the provisions of this statute and that, therefore, we must consider the defendants' argument that enforcement of the statute against them violates their rights under the State Constitution.

Despite the similarity of the Federal and State.[1] constitutional provisions, this court should reach its own conclusions on the scope of the protections of art. 46, § 1, and should not necessarily follow the reasoning adopted by the Supreme Court of the United States under the First Amendment. Indeed, after the release of our *Nissenbaum* opinion, the Supreme Court substantially altered its standard for determining whether

---

[1] Mass. Const. amend. art. 46, § 1, states: "No law shall be passed prohibiting the free exercise of religion."

conduct was protected under the free exercise of religion clause by its decision in *Employment Division v. Smith* (1990).

In interpreting art. 46, § 1, we prefer to adhere to the standards of earlier First Amendment jurisprudence, such as we applied in *Alberts v. Devine* (Mass. 1985) and *Attorney Gen. v. Bailey* (Mass. 1982). In each opinion, we used the balancing test that the Supreme Court had established under the free exercise of religion clause in *Wisconsin v. Yoder* (1972), *Sherbert v. Verner* (1963), and subsequent opinions. By applying the balancing test as we do, we extend protections to the defendants that are at least as great as those of the First Amendment. No further discussion of rights under the First Amendment is, therefore, necessary.

The next question is whether the prohibition against discrimination based on marital status substantially burdens the defendants' exercise of their religion. We first consider whether there is any burden at all on the defendants' free exercise of religion. We have said that the government's failure to provide a child with subsidized transportation to a private sectarian school does not burden the child's free exercise of religion. Here, the situation differs because the government has placed a burden on the defendants that makes their exercise of religion more difficult and more costly. The statute affirmatively obliges the defendants to enter into a contract contrary to their religious beliefs and provides significant sanctions for its violation. Moreover, both their nonconformity to the law and any related publicity may stigmatize the defendants in the eyes of many and thus burden the exercise of the defendants' religion.

The fact that the defendants' free exercise of religion claim arises in a commercial context, although relevant when engaging in a balancing of interests, does not mean that their constitutional rights are not substantially burdened. This is not a case in which a claimant is seeking a financial advantage by asserting religious beliefs.

We must, therefore, consider whether the record establishes that the Commonwealth has or does not have an important governmental interest that is sufficiently compelling that the granting of an exemption to people in the position of the defendants would unduly hinder that goal. At the least, the Commonwealth must demonstrate that it has a compelling interest in the elimination of discrimination in housing against an unmarried man and an unmarried woman who have a sexual relationship and wish to rent accommodations to which § 4(6) applies.

Without supporting facts in the record or in legislative findings, we are unwilling to conclude that simple enactment of the prohibition against discrimination based on marital status establishes that the State has such a substantial interest in eliminating that form of housing discrimination that, on a balancing test, the substantial burden on the defendants' free exercise of religion must be disregarded.

We reject any argument that a general rule must be applied because of problems in determining whether religious beliefs sincerely underlie a landlord's refusal to lease. The sincerity of such action assertedly founded on religious beliefs is open to challenge in a free exercise of religion case. We would, moreover, not readily subscribe to a rule that justified the denial of constitutional rights simply because the protection of those rights required special effort. For similar reasons, in the absence of proof, we would not find a compelling State interest in this case simply because other individuals might assert the right to be exempt from this or some other law on religious grounds and in doing so would make enforcement of that law difficult. Yet the practical problems of administering a law with the exemption that the defendants seek may be shown to be such as to make the operation of such an exemption impractical. Finally, the compulsion of the State's interest appears somewhat weakened because the statute permits discrimination by a religious organization in certain respects if to do so promotes the principles for which the organization was established.

We are not persuaded on the record that the Commonwealth's interests in the availability of rental housing for cohabiting couples must always prevail over the religion-based practices that people such as the defendants wish to pursue. On the other hand, we cannot say that it is certain that the Commonwealth could not prove in this case that it has some specific compelling interest that justifies overriding the defendants' interests.

The Commonwealth has the task of establishing that it has a compelling interest in eliminating housing discrimination against cohabiting couples that is strong enough to justify the burden placed on the defendants' exercise of their religion. A task of this sort has been carried out successfully in some cases and not in others.

The summary judgment record does not establish that there is no disputed material fact bearing on the compelling State interest question. In that circumstance summary judgment is inappropriate. There are factual circumstances that bear on the question, both as to the existence of a general State interest in the elimination of discrimination in housing based on marital status and as to the existence of a particularized State interest in the Turners Falls area. Uniformity of enforcement of the statute may be shown to be the least restrictive means for the practical and efficient operation of the antidiscrimination law. It should be remembered that the task is to balance the State's interests against the nature of the burden on the defendants and that we are concerned here with the business of leasing apartments, not with participation in a formal religious activity.

NOTES

1. In *Abdul-Alazim v. Superintendent, Massachusetts Correctional Institution, Cedar Junction*, 778 N.E.2d 946 (Mass. App. Ct. 2002), a

Massachusetts appeals court granted relief under *Desilets* to a claim filed by an inmate that prison officials had violated his state-law free exercise rights by prohibiting him from wearing a kufi, a prayer cap used by Muslims during religious worship. *Cf. Holt v. Hobbs*, 135 S. Ct. 853 (2015) (holding that prison-grooming policy violated inmate's free-exercise rights under RLUIPA).

2. In *Swanner v. Anchorage Equal Rights Commission*, 874 P.2d 274 (Alaska 1994), the court declined to follow the *Smith* test in rejecting a landlord's claim that he had a constitutional right to refuse to rent to unmarried, cohabitating persons of the opposite sex. In doing so, it reasoned as follows:

> Swanner is correct in asserting that a state court may provide greater protection to the free exercise of religion under the state constitution than is now provided under the United States Constitution. Thus, even though the Free Exercise Clause of the Alaska Constitution is identical to the Free Exercise Clause of the United States Constitution, we are not required to adopt and apply the *Smith* test to religious exemption cases involving the Alaska Constitution merely because the United States Supreme Court adopted that test to determine the applicability of religious exemptions under the United States Constitution. We will apply *Frank v. State*, 604 P.2d 1068 (Alaska 1979), to determine whether the anti-discrimination laws violate Swanner's right to free exercise under the Alaska Constitution.
>
> In *Frank v. State*, we adopted the *Sherbert* test to determine whether the Free Exercise Clause of the Alaska Constitution requires an exemption to a facially neutral law. We held that to invoke a religious exemption, three requirements must be met: (1) a religion is involved, (2) the conduct in question is religiously based, and (3) the claimant is sincere in his/her religious belief. Once these three requirements are met, "religiously impelled actions can be forbidden only where they pose some substantial threat to public safety, peace or order, or where there are competing governmental interests of the highest order and are not otherwise served."
>
> No one disputes that a religion is involved here (Christianity), or that Swanner is sincere in his religious belief that cohabitation is a sin and by renting to cohabitators, he is facilitating the sin. But Swanner made no showing of a religious belief which requires that he engage in the property-rental business.

BARR v. CITY OF SINTON
295 S.W.3d 287 (Tex. 2009)

HECHT, J.

The Texas Religious Freedom Restoration Act (TRFRA) provides that "a government agency may not substantially burden a person's free exercise of religion unless it demonstrates that the application of the burden to the person is in furtherance of a compelling governmental interest and is the least restrictive means of furthering that interest." TRFRA does not immunize religious conduct from government regulation; it requires the government to tread carefully and lightly when its actions substantially burden religious exercise.

In this case, a city resident, as part of a religious ministry, offered men recently released from prison free housing and religious instruction in two homes he owned. In response, the city passed a zoning ordinance that not only precluded the use of the homes for that purpose but effectively banned the ministry from the city. The trial court found that the city had not violated TRFRA, and the court of appeals affirmed. We reverse and remand to the trial court for further proceedings.

In 1998, Pastor Richard Wayne Barr began a religious halfway house ministry through Philemon Restoration Homes, Inc., a nonprofit corporation he directed. The purpose of the ministry was to offer housing, biblical instruction, and counseling to low-level offenders released from prison on probation or parole in transition back into the community. The guidelines emphasized to prospective residents that Philemon was "a biblical ministry, NOT a social service agency." Each morning began with group prayer and Bible study.

When Barr began his ministry, the City imposed no zoning or other restrictions on his use of the homes. In January 1999, Barr discussed his ministry with Sinton's mayor, city manager, and police chief, and a few weeks later he presented his ministry before the city council. In response to questions whether Philemon was in compliance with state law, Barr researched the matter and concluded that it was. In April, the city council held a public hearing at which a large number of people expressed both opposition to as well as support of Barr's ministry. A few days later, the city council passed Ordinance 1999-02, which added to the City Code a section that provided as follows:

> A correctional or rehabilitation facility may not be located in the City of Sinton within 1000 feet of a residential area, a primary or secondary school, property designated as a public park or public recreation area by any governmental authority, or a church, synagogue, or other place of worship.

As the city manager later confirmed, Ordinance 1999-02 targeted Barr and Philemon. The halfway houses they operated were unquestionably within 1,000 feet of a church; indeed, they were across the street from the Grace Fellowship Church, which was helping to support the ministry. But the ordinance was broader, and was intended to be. Because Sinton is small, it would be difficult for a halfway house to be located anywhere within the city limits.

Smith's construction of the Free Exercise Clause does not preclude a state from requiring strict scrutiny of infringements on religious freedom, either by statute or under the state constitution, and many states have done just that, Texas among them. The Texas Legislature enacted TRFRA in 1999, which like RFRA provides in part, that government "may not substantially burden a person's free exercise of religion unless it demonstrates that the application of the burden to the person is in furtherance of a compelling governmental interest; and is the least restrictive means of furthering that interest." The Act states that "the protection of religious freedom afforded by this chapter is in addition to the protections provided under federal law and the constitutions of this state and the United States."

Applying TRFRA to this case raises four questions, each succeeding question contingent on an affirmative answer to the one preceding:

- Does the City's Ordinance 1999-02 burden Barr's "free exercise of religion" as defined by TRFRA?
- Is the burden substantial?
- Does the ordinance further a compelling governmental interest?
- Is the ordinance the least restrictive means of furthering that interest?

A

The City argues that Barr's free exercise of religion is not involved because a halfway house need not be a religious operation. But the fact that a halfway house *can* be secular does not mean that it *cannot* be religious. TRFRA defines "free exercise of religion" as "an act or refusal to act that is substantially motivated by sincere religious belief", adding that "in determining whether an act or refusal to act is substantially motivated by sincere religious belief under this chapter, it is not necessary to determine that the act or refusal to act is motivated by a central part or central requirement of the person's sincere religious belief." Not only is such a determination unnecessary, it is impossible for the judiciary.

The trial court appears to have been troubled that an operation which can be and often is conducted for purely secular purposes could be entitled to increased protection from government regulation if conducted for religious reasons. But TRFRA guarantees such protection. Just as a Bible study group and a book club are not treated the same, neither are a halfway house operated for religious purposes and one that is not.

The City does not dispute that the purpose of Barr's ministry was to provide convicts a biblically supported transition to civic life. Applicants were required to sign a statement of faith, agree to abide by stated biblical principles, and commit as a group to daily prayer and Bible study. They were specifically told that Barr's halfway house was "a biblical ministry, NOT a social service agency." Barr considered the halfway house a religious ministry, and it appears to have been supported by his church. The record easily establishes that Barr's ministry was "substantially motivated by sincere religious belief" for purposes of the TRFRA.

B

To determine whether a person's free exercise of religion has been substantially burdened, some courts have focused on the burden on the person's religious beliefs rather than the burden on his conduct. Under what have been referred to as the compulsion and centrality tests, the issue is whether the person's conduct that is being burdened is compelled by or central to his religion. The problems with these approaches are the same as those in determining whether conduct is religious. It may require a court to do what it cannot do: assess the demands of religion on its adherents and the importance of particular conduct to the religion. And it is inconsistent with the statutory directive that religious conduct be determined without regard for whether the actor's motivation is "a central part or central requirement of the person's sincere religious belief." These problems are avoided if the focus is on the degree to which a person's religious conduct is curtailed and the resulting impact on his religious expression. The burden must be measured, of course, from the person's perspective, not from the government's. Thus, the United States Court of Appeals for the Fifth Circuit, after surveying decisions by other courts, recently held that under RLUIPA, "a government action or regulation creates a substantial burden on a religious exercise if it truly pressures the adherent to significantly modify his religious behavior and significantly violate his religious beliefs."

Ordinance 1999-02 prohibited Barr from operating his halfway house ministry in the two homes he owned adjacent to his supporting church, and the city manager testified that it was "a fair statement" that alternate locations were "probably minimal" and "possibly" "pretty close to nonexistent." The court of appeals stated that "there is nothing in the ordinance that precludes Barr from providing his religious ministry to parolees and probationers, from providing instruction, counsel, and helpful assistance in other facilities in Sinton, or from housing these persons outside the City and providing his religious ministry to them there." But there is no evidence of any alternate location in the City of Sinton where the ordinance would have allowed Barr's ministry to operate, or of possible locations outside the city. Moreover, while evidence of alternatives is certainly relevant to the issue whether zoning restrictions substantially burden free religious exercise, evidence of *some* possible alternative, irrespective of the difficulties presented, does not, standing alone, disprove substantial burden. In a related context, the Supreme Court has observed that "one is not to have the exercise of his liberty of expression in appropriate places abridged on the plea that it may be exercised in some other place." As a practical matter, the ordinance ended Barr's ministry, as the City Council surely knew it would. A burden on a person's religious exercise is not insubstantial simply because he could always choose to do something else.

C

"To say that a person's right to free exercise has been burdened, of course, does not mean that he has an absolute right to engage in the conduct." The government may regulate such conduct in furtherance of a compelling interest.

Although the government's interest in the public welfare in general, and in preserving a common character of land areas and use in particular, is certainly legitimate when properly motivated and appropriately directed, the assertion that zoning ordinances are per se superior to fundamental, constitutional rights, such as the free exercise of religion, must fairly be regarded as indefensible.

The Supreme Court held in *Smith*, not that the government's interest in neutral laws of general application is always compelling when compared to the people's interest in fundamental rights, but only that the United States Constitution does not require the two interests to be balanced every time they conflict. RFRA, RLUIPA, and TRFRA, as well as laws enacted in other states, now require that balance by statute when government action substantially burdens the free exercise of religion. The government's interest is compelling when the balance weighs in its favor—that is, when the government's interest justifies the substantial burden on religious exercise. Because religious exercise is a fundamental right, that justification can be found only in "interests of the highest order," to quote the Supreme Court in *Yoder*, and to quote *Sherbert*, only to avoid "the gravest abuses, endangering paramount interests."

The Sinton City Council's recitation in Ordinance 1999-02—that "the requirements of this section are reasonably necessary to preserve the public safety, morals, and general welfare"—is the kind of "broadly formulated interest" that does not satisfy the scrutiny mandated by TRFRA. Likewise, the trial court's brief finding—that "the ordinance was in furtherance of a compelling government interest"—falls short of the required scrutiny.

Although TRFRA places the burden of proving a substantial burden on the claimant, it places the burden of proving a compelling state interest on the government. The City argues that its compelling interest in Ordinance 1999-02 is established by statutes providing that correctional facility regulations presumptively meet strict scrutiny. As we have already explained, however, these statutes are inapplicable.

The City also asserts that Ordinance 1999-02 serves a compelling interest in advancing safety, preventing nuisance, and protecting children. But there is no evidence to support the City's assertion with respect to "the particular practice at issue"—Barr's ministry.

The City's failure to establish a compelling interest in this case in no way suggests that the government never has a compelling interest in zoning for religious use of property or in regulating halfway houses operated for religious purposes. TRFRA guarantees a process, not a result. The City's principal position in this case has been that it is exempt from TRFRA. We do not hold that the City could not have satisfied TRFRA; we hold only that it failed to do so.

D

Finally, TRFRA requires that even when the government acts in furtherance of a compelling interest, it must show that it used the least restrictive means of furthering that interest. The City has made no effort to show that it complied with this requirement. Ordinance 1999-02 is very broad. If, as the city manager testified, locations in the City of Sinton more than 1,000 feet from a residential area, school, park, recreational area, or church are "pretty close to nonexistent," the ordinance effectively prohibits any private "residential facility operated for the purpose of housing persons convicted of misdemeanors within one year after having been released from confinement in any penal institution" inside the city limits. Read literally, this would prohibit a Sinton resident from leasing a room to someone within a year of his having been jailed for twice driving with an invalid license. Such restrictions are certainly not the least restrictive means of insuring that religiously operated halfway houses do not jeopardize children's safety and residents' well being.

We conclude, based on the record before us, that Ordinance 1999-02, as applied to Barr's ministry, violates TRFRA.

CATHOLIC CHARITIES OF THE DIOCESE OF ALBANY v. SERIO
859 N.E.2d 459 (N.Y. 2006)

R.S. SMITH, J.

Plaintiffs challenge the validity of legislation requiring health insurance policies that provide coverage for prescription drugs to include coverage for contraception. Plaintiffs assert that the provisions they challenge violate their rights under the religion clauses of the federal and state constitutions. We hold that the legislation, as applied to these plaintiffs, is valid.

In 2002, the Legislature enacted what is known as the "Women's Health and Wellness Act" (WHWA), mandating expanded health insurance coverage for a variety of services needed by women, including mammography, cervical cytology and bone density screening. At issue here are provisions of the WHWA requiring that an employer health insurance contract "which provides coverage for prescription drugs shall include coverage for the cost of contraceptive drugs or devices."

At the heart of this case is the statute's exemption for "religious employers." Such an employer may request an insurance contract "without coverage for contraceptive methods that are contrary to the religious employer's religious tenets." Where a religious employer invokes the exemption, the insurer must offer coverage for contraception to individual employees, who may purchase it at their own expense "at the prevailing small group community rate."

Plaintiffs believe contraception to be sinful, and assert that the challenged provisions of the WHWA compel them to violate their religious tenets by financing conduct that they condemn. The sincerity of their beliefs, and the centrality of those beliefs to their faiths, are not in dispute.

Contending that they are constitutionally entitled to be exempt from the provisions of the WHWA providing for coverage of contraceptives, plaintiffs brought this action against the Superintendent of Insurance, seeking a declaration that these portions of the WHWA are invalid, and an injunction against their enforcement. The complaint asserts broadly that the challenged provisions are unconstitutional, but plaintiffs do not argue that they are unenforceable as to employers having no religious objections to contraception; in substance, plaintiffs challenge the legislation as applied to them.

Article I, § 3 of the New York Constitution provides:

> The free exercise and enjoyment of religious profession and worship, without discrimination or preference, shall forever be allowed in this state to all humankind; and no person shall be rendered incompetent to be a witness on account of his or her opinions on matters of religious belief; but the liberty of conscience hereby secured shall not be so construed as to excuse acts of licentiousness, or justify practices inconsistent with the peace or safety of this state.

In interpreting our Free Exercise Clause we have not applied, and we do not now adopt, the inflexible rule of *Smith* that no person may complain of a burden on religious exercise that is imposed by a generally applicable, neutral statute. Rather, we have held that when the State imposes "an incidental burden on the right to free exercise of religion" we must consider the interest advanced by the legislation that imposes the burden, and that "the respective interests must be balanced to determine whether the incidental burdening is justified." We have never discussed, however, how the balancing is to be performed. We now hold that substantial deference is due the Legislature, and that the party claiming an exemption bears the burden of showing that the challenged legislation, as applied to that party, is an unreasonable interference with religious freedom. This test, while more protective of religious exercise than the rule of *Smith*, is less so than the rule stated (though not always applied) in a number of other federal and state cases.

Since *Smith*, a number of state courts have interpreted their states' constitutions to call for the application of strict scrutiny. Often, however, the courts rejected claims to religious exemptions, and it is questionable whether the scrutiny applied by those courts is really as strict as their statement of the rule implies.

The apparent reluctance of some courts to pay more than lip service to "strict scrutiny" may be an implicit recognition of what we now explicitly decide: Strict scrutiny is not the right approach to constitutionally-based claims for religious exemptions. Where the State has not set out to burden religious exercise, but seeks only to advance, in a neutral way, a legitimate object of legislation, we do not read the New York Free Exercise Clause to require the State to demonstrate a "compelling" interest in response to every claim by a religious believer to an exemption from the law; such a rule of constitutional law would give too little respect to legislative prerogatives, and would create too great an obstacle to efficient government. Rather, the principle stated by the United States Supreme Court in *Smith*—that citizens are not excused by the Free Exercise Clause from complying with generally applicable and neutral laws, even ones offensive to their religious tenets—should be the usual, though not the invariable, rule. The burden of showing that an interference with religious practice is unreasonable, and therefore requires an exemption from the statute, must be on the person claiming the exemption.

The burden the WHWA places on plaintiffs' religious practices is a serious one, but the WHWA does not literally *compel* them to purchase contraceptive coverage for their employees, in violation of their religious beliefs; it only requires that policies that provide prescription drug coverage include coverage for contraceptives. Plaintiffs are not required by law to purchase prescription drug coverage at all. They assert, unquestionably in good faith, that they feel obliged to do so because, as religious institutions, they must provide just wages and benefits to their employees. But it is surely not impossible, though it may be expensive or difficult, to compensate employees adequately without including prescription drugs in their group health care policies.

It is also important, in our view, that many of plaintiffs' employees do not share their religious beliefs. (Most of the plaintiffs allege that they hire many people of other faiths; no plaintiff has presented evidence that it does not do so.) The employment relationship is a frequent subject of legislation, and when a religious organization chooses to hire nonbelievers it must, at least to some degree, be prepared to accept neutral regulations imposed to protect those employees' legitimate interests in doing what their own beliefs permit. This would be a more difficult case if plaintiffs had chosen to hire only people who share their belief in the sinfulness of contraception.

Finally, we must weigh against plaintiffs' interest in adhering to the tenets of their faith the State's substantial interest in fostering equality between the sexes, and in providing women with better health care. The

Legislature had extensive evidence before it that the absence of contraceptive coverage for many women was seriously interfering with both of these important goals. The Legislature decided that to grant the broad religious exemption that plaintiffs seek would leave too many women outside the statute, a decision entitled to deference from the courts. Of course, the Legislature might well have made another choice, but we cannot say the choice the Legislature made has been shown to be an unreasonable interference with plaintiffs' exercise of their religion. The Legislature's choice is therefore not unconstitutional.

NOTES

1. The U.S. Supreme Court faced a related issue under RFRA in *Burwell v. Hobby Lobby*, 134 S. Ct. 2751 (2014). At issue was the validity of a federal regulation promulgated under the Patient Protection and Affordable Care Act that required for-profit corporations to provide health insurance coverage for contraceptive methods. In invalidating the regulation, the Court reasoned that: (1) for-profit corporations are covered by RFRA's application to any "person"; (2) the contraceptives mandate substantially burdened the exercise of religion as applied to such corporations; and (3) the mandate failed RFRA's least-restrictive-means requirement.

2. In the more than three decades since *Smith*, at least three noteworthy things have happened in this area. A lot of the *federal* free-exercise enforcement actions has shifted to statutory cases under RFRA with respect to federal laws or under RLUIPA with respect to state land-use and prison-based laws. *See, e.g., Burwell v. Hobby Lobby*, 134 S. Ct. 2751 (2014) (RFRA); *Holt v. Hobbs*, 135 S. Ct. 853 (2015) (RLUIPA); *Gonzales v. O Centro Espirita Beneficente Uniao do Vegetal*, 546 U.S. 418 (2006) (RFRA). All manner of innovation has occurred at the *state* level, whether under their own constitutions or under state statutes modeled in part or in whole on RFRA. And through it all *Smith* continues to be subject to challenge. In *Fulton v. City of Philadelphia*, 141 S. Ct. 1868 (2021), the Court came close to overruling the decision. In a lengthy decision concurring in the judgment, Justice Alito, jointed by Justices Thomas and Gorsuch, explained why *Smith* should be overruled. In an opinion of her own, Justice Barrett, joined by Justice Kavanaugh in full and by Justice Breyer in part, acknowledged that "the textual and structural arguments against *Smith*" are "compelling." But at this point, she added, "a number of issues" needed to be worked through—including exactly what a post-*Smith* test would look like—before the decision should be overruled.

B. ESTABLISHMENT OF RELIGION

1. Background

Just as some state freedom of religion clauses mirror their federal counterpart, some state establishment clauses closely resemble the First Amendment of the United States Constitution. All told, eleven States have establishment clauses similar to the First Amendment. Jennifer Friesen, *State Constitutional Law: Litigating Individual Rights, Claims and Defenses* 4-84 (2006); *see, e.g.*, Cal. Const. art. I, § 4 ("The Legislature shall make no law respecting an establishment of religion."); Fla. Const. art. I, § 3 ("There shall be no law respecting the establishment of religion."); Haw. Const. art. I, § 4 ("No law shall be enacted respecting an establishment of religion."). Thirty-two States have no-preference clauses (two of which, Alabama and California, also have establishment clauses similar to the First Amendment). Friesen, *supra*, at 4-84; *see, e.g.*, N.J. Const. art. I, § 4 ("There shall be no establishment of one religious sect in preference to another."); Wis. Const. art. I, § 18 ("nor shall any preference be given to any religious establishments or modes of worship"). And nine States have neither an establishment nor a no-preference clause. Friesen, *supra*, at 4-84.

Unique to the state constitutions are clauses that limit using public funds to aid religious organizations. Thirty-four States have provisions to this effect. Friesen, *supra*, at 4-86. The history of these provisions varies among the States. New Jersey, for example, ratified its first no-aid clause in 1776. *See* N.J. Const. of 1776, art. XVIII. Other States adopted no-aid clauses in the next century. As the following excerpt explains, these nineteenth-century provisions, often called "Blaine Amendments," have a rich and controversial history.

Mark Edward DeForrest, *An Overview and Evaluation of State Blaine Amendments: Origins, Scope, and First Amendment Concerns*
26 Harv. J.L. & Pub. Pol'y 551 (2003)

The original Blaine Amendment was a proposed amendment to the federal Constitution. The amendment took its name from its sponsor and originator, Representative James Blaine of Maine, who introduced the amendment on December 14, 1875. The text of his proposed amendment reads as follows:

> No State shall make any law respecting an establishment of religion or prohibiting the free exercise thereof; and no money raised by taxation in any State for the support of public schools, or derived from any public fund therefore, nor any public lands devoted thereto, shall ever be under the control of any religious sect, nor shall any money so raised or lands so devoted be divided between religious sects or denominations.

The overarching purpose to the Blaine Amendment, as its plain text demonstrates, was to control the development of government involvement in religious issues at the state level in two critical ways. First, it would have applied the religion clauses of the First Amendment directly to the states. Prior to the development of the incorporation doctrine by the Supreme Court in the twentieth century, the provisions of the Bill of Rights (the first ten amendments to the United States Constitution) were not applied to the states by the courts. In Blaine's day, the states were yet to be restrained by the First Amendment; Blaine saw this as a deficiency and sought to remedy this situation by amending the Constitution to directly apply the religion clauses of the First Amendment to the states. The second effect of Blaine's amendment would have been to prohibit state governments from supporting private religious schools with funds from the public treasury.

The Blaine Amendment might have been expected to fade away into oblivion after its rejection by the Senate, but the opposite occurred. After its defeat on the national level, the Blaine Amendment took on new life in the states. Within a year of the defeat of Blaine's proposal, fourteen states had legislation on the books preventing state funds from being used in support of religious schools. By the 1890s, roughly thirty states would incorporate Blaine-style amendments into their constitutions. This trend continued into the 20th century; even as late as the 1950s, Alaska and Hawaii would incorporate Blaine-style language into their state charters.

Blaine Amendments are found in roughly thirty state constitutions. The language and scope of the state Blaine provisions vary widely, however. Some states adopted Blaine-like provisions prior to the formal proposal of the national Blaine Amendment. Other states, both in the 19th and 20th centuries, willingly adopted Blaine provisions after the national Blaine Amendment failed. Still other states had Blaine provisions forced upon them as a condition of entering the Union. It should therefore come as no surprise that the Blaine provisions in the states evidence a considerable diversity in language and scope.

The first group of state Blaine provisions to be examined are those that place the narrowest restrictions on state government actions to provide some indirect assistance or aid to private religious or sectarian education. Examples of these kinds of Blaine Amendments can be seen in both New Jersey and Massachusetts. For the most part, these Blaine provisions demonstrate two basic concerns. First, they seek to ensure that primary and secondary public education remains free of sectarian instruction. Second, they usually make certain that public educational funds will not be used to directly support private religious schools. Outside of these two concerns, however, the states with less restrictive Blaine provisions allow some very limited government assistance either with basic transportation or higher education.

While the states discussed in the previous paragraph have relatively liberal Blaine provisions in their state constitutions, other states have more stringent limitations on government aid to religious schools. While not as permissive as the less restrictive states and not as draconian as the most restrictive states, these states fall into a great middle ground regarding Blaine provisions. Most of these states' Blaine Amendments prohibit direct funding of religious institutions or schools, but leave open, at least within their constitutional texts, the question of whether or not indirect state funding, such as vouchers, are permissible. The language used in this intermediate tier of Blaine states varies considerably from state to state, as even brief examination of the state charters will demonstrate.

The Utah Constitution, which reflects church-state concerns unique to that state, contains two provisions dealing with public funding of religious education. The first, found at Article 1, Section 4 of the state charter, mandates that "no public money or property shall be appropriated for or applied to any religious worship, exercise or instruction, or for the support of any ecclesiastical establishment." The second Utah Blaine provision, found at Article 10, Section 9, forbids any direct aid to all religious schools: "neither the state of Utah nor its political subdivisions may make any appropriation for the direct support of any school or educational institution controlled by any religious organization." Other states have Blaine-style provisions of similar effect, although the wording is different. Delaware, which in 1897 included a Blaine provision in its state constitution, has an extensive section in its fundamental charter prohibiting direct aid: "No portion of any fund now existing, or which may hereafter be appropriated, or raised by tax, for educational purposes, shall be appropriated to, or used by, or in aid of any sectarian, church or denominational school."

Alabama, a state of the Old Confederacy, included a Blaine Amendment provision in its state constitution in 1901. This provision prohibits the use of state educational funds to support "any sectarian or denominational school." Kentucky includes a similar provision in its state constitution, but also includes additional language that prohibits the use of money from the state school fund for any purpose other than the "maintenance of the public schools."

The moderate Blaine language used by these states, while varied in expression, affirms the same fundamental principle: direct government aid for expressly sectarian education is prohibited, and for the most part, so is sectarian influence in public educational programs. The strength of this affirmation can be seen in the case of *Fiscal Court of Jefferson County v. Brady* (Ky. 1994). There, the Kentucky Supreme Court upheld a lower court ruling that struck down a state statute permitting county governments to establish programs to provide for the busing of students in religious or other private schools. Jefferson County had previously instituted a subsidy program that paid a direct sum to private schools to pay for the transportation of students. The private schools funded were overwhelmingly religious in character, and nearly half a million dollars was expended by the county through its subsidy program. The Kentucky Supreme Court found that the private schools involved in the subsidy program combined their own transportation funds with the county subsidy, providing the schools with control over government assets. The court noted specifically that the "financial aid is provided to the school rather than a transportation service to the child," and found that there was a constitutionally significant distinction between providing general transportation for all students and "providing direct payment to selected eligible schools."

The last group of state Blaine provisions to be examined uses language that places the broadest restrictions on government aid to religious schools and organizations. These Blaine provisions often go far beyond the prohibition of direct aid to schools by preventing indirect aid as well. In addition, many of the states include wording in their constitutions prohibiting aid not only to schools, but also to any religious or "sectarian" institution. Florida, for instance, combines a mandate that its state educational fund be used solely for "the support and maintenance of free public schools," with an absolute prohibition on the use of any state revenues "directly or indirectly in aid of any church, sect, or religious denomination or in aid of any sectarian institution." This sterner approach to direct or indirect government aid to religious schools or institutions is paralleled by several other states. Missouri's constitution prohibits the state from giving anything in aid to support:

> Any religious creed, church or sectarian purpose, or to help to support or sustain any private or public school, academy, seminary, college, university, or other institution of learning controlled by any religious creed, church or sectarian denomination whatever; nor shall any grant or donation of personal property or real estate ever be made by the state, or any county, city, town, or other municipal corporation, for any religious creed, church, or sectarian purpose whatever.

Like Florida, Missouri teams an extensive prohibition on government aid to religious bodies and religious schools with another constitutional provision that mandates that the state educational fund be used only for the establishment and maintenance of "free public schools."

While some state Blaine provisions only target education, some go much further. Oklahoma's constitution includes not only the familiar prohibition on support for sectarian educational institutions, but also includes a prohibition on any government aid in support of any "sectarian institution as such." The Indiana Constitution, in a one sentence article, prevents the state from allocating any funds from the treasury "for the benefit of any religious or theological institution." The Georgia State Constitution includes a similar article, expressly mandating that the state refrain from direct or indirect funding "of any sectarian institution." Colorado's state charter, ratified in the same year that the national Blaine

Amendment was voted on in the Senate, contains—along with the standard Blaine provisions prohibiting public funding of sectarian schools—a prohibition on state funding for any "charitable, industrial, educational or benevolent purposes" not controlled completely by the state, as well as any "denominational or sectarian institution or association." The Idaho Constitution, ratified in 1890 at the peak of the movement for inclusion of Blaine language in state constitutions, includes a lengthy article banning the allocation of "anything in aid" to religious schools or to religiously-affiliated "literary or scientific institutions," while at the same time containing a caveat allowing the state to provide some assistance to non-profit "health facilities" operated by religious groups. Nevada's constitution simply states that the state government cannot provide "funds of any kind or character" for sectarian purposes. The language of all of these provisions extends the standard Blaine provision's prohibition on direct aid to private sectarian schools to include any type of aid to virtually every sort of religiously-controlled institution.

The narrowly-defeated push for a national Blaine Amendment has had a wide-ranging effect on most state constitutions. States, willingly or by command of the federal government, incorporated Blaine provisions into their charters. This move to include Blaine provisions in state constitutions extended into the twentieth century. The overall effect of these Blaine-style provisions, by their express wording or through later judicial interpretations, was usually to preclude both the direct or indirect transfer of state funds to religious or sectarian schools and institutions. The motivation behind the Blaine Amendment was two-fold. First, there was a high degree of hostility towards the teaching and practice of the Roman Catholic Church, and correspondingly there existed a strong desire to ensure that Catholics would be precluded from using the resources of the government to support their parochial schools and other religious institutions. Second, there was an almost imperative desire on the part of the proponents of the Blaine Amendment to protect generic Protestant religiosity in the common schools and the public square. State courts in the twentieth century, with a few exceptions already discussed, rigorously enforced Blaine language to preclude direct, and in many cases indirect, aid and assistance to religious schools or those who wish to attend such schools.

State Blaine provisions do not exist in a constitutional vacuum, however. And while there is no question that states are free to decline to provide money or other forms of aid to private non-governmental entities across the board, there is a significant question as to whether or not the First Amendment allows states to preclude both direct and indirect funding to private religious institutions if those institutions are simply seeking equal access to state funding programs that are open to other private institutions that are of a non-religious character.

2. Cases

In the first case, the United States Supreme Court holds that the First Amendment's Free Exercise Clause prevented Missouri from relying on a Blaine provision in its state constitution to deny a church access to a grant program generally available to schools, daycare centers, and other non-profits. Since *Trinity Lutheran*, several state supreme courts have grappled with the scope of the U.S. Supreme Court's decision, addressing whether their States' constitutional provisions prohibiting state aid to churches violate the federal Free Exercise Clause. *See, e.g.*, *Freedom From Religion Found. v. Morris Cty. Bd. of Chosen Freeholders*, 181 A.3d 992 (N.J. 2018); *Caplan v. Town of Acton*, 92 N.E.3d 691 (Mass. 2018); *Taylor v. Town of Cabot*, 178 A.3d 313 (Vt. 2017). The New Jersey and Vermont decisions are excerpted below.

TRINITY LUTHERAN CHURCH OF COLUMBIA, INC. v. COMER
137 S. Ct. 2012 (2017)

ROBERTS, C.J.

The Missouri Department of Natural Resources offers state grants to help public and private schools, nonprofit daycare centers, and other nonprofit entities purchase rubber playground surfaces made from recycled tires. Trinity Lutheran Church applied for such a grant for its preschool and daycare center and would have received one, but for the fact that Trinity Lutheran is a church. The Department had a policy of categorically disqualifying churches and other religious organizations from receiving grants under its playground resurfacing program. The question presented is whether the Department's policy violated the rights of Trinity Lutheran under the Free Exercise Clause of the First Amendment.

Run by the State's Department of Natural Resources to reduce the number of used tires destined for landfills and dump sites, the program offers reimbursement grants to qualifying nonprofit organizations that purchase playground surfaces made from recycled tires. When the Center applied, the Department had a strict and express policy of denying grants to any applicant owned or controlled by a church, sect, or other religious entity. That policy, in the Department's view, was compelled by Article I, Section 7 of the Missouri Constitution, which provides:

> That no money shall ever be taken from the public treasury, directly or indirectly, in aid of any church, sect or denomination of religion, or in aid of any priest, preacher, minister or teacher thereof, as such; and that no preference shall be given to nor any discrimination made against any church, sect or creed of religion, or any form of religious faith or worship.

The Department ultimately awarded 14 grants as part of the 2012 program. Because the Center was operated by Trinity Lutheran Church, it did not receive a grant.

The First Amendment provides, in part, that "Congress shall make no law respecting an establishment of religion, or prohibiting the free exercise thereof." The parties agree that the Establishment Clause of that Amendment does not prevent Missouri from including Trinity Lutheran in the Scrap Tire Program. That does not, however, answer the question under the Free Exercise Clause, because we have recognized that there is "play in the joints" between what the Establishment Clause permits and the Free Exercise Clause compels.

The Department's policy expressly discriminates against otherwise eligible recipients by disqualifying them from a public benefit solely because of their religious character. Such a policy imposes a penalty on the free exercise of religion that triggers the most exacting scrutiny.

The Department's policy puts Trinity Lutheran to a choice: It may participate in an otherwise available benefit program or remain a religious institution. Of course, Trinity Lutheran is free to continue operating as a church, but that freedom comes at the cost of automatic and absolute exclusion from the benefits of a public program for which the Center is otherwise fully qualified.

The Department contends that merely declining to extend funds to Trinity Lutheran does not prohibit the Church from engaging in any religious conduct or otherwise exercising its religious rights. In this sense, says the Department, its policy is unlike the ordinances struck down in *Church of the Lukumi Babalu Aye, Inc. v. Hialeah* (1993), which outlawed rituals central to Santeria. Here the Department has simply declined to allocate to Trinity Lutheran a subsidy the State had no obligation to provide in the first place.

It is true the Department has not criminalized the way Trinity Lutheran worships or told the Church that it cannot subscribe to a certain view of the Gospel. But, as the Department itself acknowledges, the Free Exercise Clause protects against "indirect coercion or penalties on the free exercise of religion, not just outright prohibitions." As the Court put it more than 50 years ago, "it is too late in the day to doubt that the liberties of religion and expression may be infringed by the denial of or placing of conditions upon a benefit or privilege."

The Department attempts to get out from under the weight of our precedents by arguing that the free exercise question in this case is instead controlled by our decision in *Locke v. Davey* (2004). It is not. In *Locke*, Davey was selected for a scholarship but was denied the funds when he refused to certify that he would not use them toward a devotional degree.

He sued, arguing that the State's refusal to allow its scholarship money to go toward such degrees violated his free exercise rights.

This Court disagreed. Davey was not denied a scholarship because of who he was; he was denied a scholarship because of what he proposed to do—use the funds to prepare for the ministry. Here there is no question that Trinity Lutheran was denied a grant simply because of what it is—a church.

The State in this case expressly requires Trinity Lutheran to renounce its religious character in order to participate in an otherwise generally available public benefit program, for which it is fully qualified. Our cases make clear that such a condition imposes a penalty on the free exercise of religion that must be subjected to the "most rigorous" scrutiny.

Under that stringent standard, only a state interest "of the highest order" can justify the Department's discriminatory policy. Yet the Department offers nothing more than Missouri's policy preference for skating as far as possible from religious establishment concerns. In the face of the clear infringement on free exercise before us, that interest cannot qualify as compelling. As we said when considering Missouri's same policy preference on a prior occasion, "the state interest asserted here—in achieving greater separation of church and State than is already ensured under the Establishment Clause of the Federal Constitution—is limited by the Free Exercise Clause."

Nearly 200 years ago, a legislator urged the Maryland Assembly to adopt a bill that would end the State's disqualification of Jews from public office:

> If, on account of my religious faith, I am subjected to disqualifications, from which others are free, I cannot but consider myself a persecuted man. An odious exclusion from any of the benefits common to the rest of my fellow-citizens, is a persecution, differing only in degree, but of a nature equally unjustifiable with that, whose instruments are chains and torture.

The Missouri Department of Natural Resources has not subjected anyone to chains or torture on account of religion. And the result of the State's policy is nothing so dramatic as the denial of political office. The consequence is, in all likelihood, a few extra scraped knees. But the exclusion of Trinity Lutheran from a public benefit for which it is otherwise qualified, solely because it is a church, is odious to our Constitution all the same, and cannot stand.

FREEDOM FROM RELIGION FOUND. v. MORRIS CNTY. BD. OF CHOSEN FREEHOLDERS
181 A.3d 992 (N.J. 2018)

RABNER, C.J.

From 2012 to 2015, Morris County awarded $4.6 million in taxpayer funds to repair twelve churches, as part of a historic preservation program. This appeal raises two questions: whether the grant program violated the Religious Aid Clause of the New Jersey Constitution and, if so, whether the Religious Aid Clause conflicts with the Free Exercise Clause of the United States Constitution.

In 1992, the voters of Morris County approved a referendum to create a trust for open space and farmland preservation. Ten years later, the voters authorized the County Freeholder Board to permit historic preservation funding under the trust. At the time of the grants in question, the trust considered applications to stabilize, repair, rehabilitate, renovate, restore, improve, protect, or preserve historic properties. To be eligible for consideration, a property had to be located in Morris County and either be listed on the National or New Jersey Register of Historic Places or be eligible for listing by the State historic preservation office.

Only four kinds of entities could apply for grants: municipal governments within Morris County; Morris County government; charitable conservancies whose purpose includes historic preservation; and religious institutions. A review board evaluated applications and made recommendations to the Freeholder Board. The Freeholder Board approved final awards.

For religious institutions, grants could fund assessment reports, preparation of construction documents, construction projects for a building's exterior as well as its mechanical, electrical, and plumbing systems, and other items.

Certain conditions applied to grant recipients. Successful applicants that received construction grants of more than $50,000 cumulatively, over any number of funding cycles, had to execute a thirty-year easement agreement with the County. The "easement is a deed restriction that is used to assure long-term preservation of a historic property through proper maintenance and by limiting changes in use or appearance and preventing demolition of the property."

Grantees were also required to provide public access to properties that received grant funds. The County and the grant recipient were to "negotiate the days and hours that the property would be open to the public."

The New Jersey Constitution of 1947 includes the Religious Aid Clause. The clause states that no person shall "be obliged to pay tithes, taxes, or other rates for building or repairing any church or churches, place or places of worship, or for the maintenance of any minister or ministry, contrary to what he believes to be right or has deliberately and voluntarily engaged to perform."

The text of the Constitution has deep roots in our State's history. New Jersey's first Constitution, adopted on July 2, 1776, rejected the establishment of and compelled support for religion in two clauses. The first clause contains an express guarantee of the right to freedom from compelled support. The Religious Aid Clause in the 1776 Constitution provided as follows:

> That no Person within this Colony ever be obliged to pay Tithes, Taxes, or any other Rates, for the Purpose of building or repairing any Church or Churches, Place or Places of Worship, or for the Maintenance of any Minister or Ministry, contrary to what he believes to be right, or has deliberately or voluntarily engaged himself to perform.

The second provision contains language similar to the federal Establishment Clause.

The fact that New Jersey's first Constitution included a Religious Aid Clause is highly significant. First, it underscores the fundamental nature of the religious freedom clauses in our State's history. The 1776 Constitution is a brief document that outlines the organization of government and the powers of the executive, the legislative council, and the general assembly. The document guarantees only a few distinct rights: the right to vote; the right to religious freedom; the right of an accused to have counsel and call witnesses; and the right to trial by jury. Viewed in that context, it is telling that the founders devoted careful attention to religious liberty in the first Constitution.

Second, of the twelve states that adopted constitutions from 1776 to 1780, none included a compelled support clause as precise and clear as the Religious Aid Clause. North Carolina's first constitution, which took effect several months after New Jersey's, contained a provision most like the Religious Aid Clause. Even that relatively detailed clause, though, does not mention the "repair" of houses of worship or ban payment of "taxes." New Jersey's Religious Aid Clause thus stands out as particularly specific for its time.

Today, twenty-nine constitutions, including New Jersey's, have compelled support clauses. Ten other constitutions simply prohibit the use of public money in aid of religion. New Jersey's clause highlighted that New Jersey was at the forefront of a historic and substantial change, and signaled its longstanding and vigorous commitment to religious liberty and freedom from compelled support.

The Religious Aid Clause was left virtually untouched in the modern Constitution of 1947. The text of those provisions remains unchanged since 1947.

The above history makes clear that New Jersey's Religious Aid Clause can be traced to the establishment of an independent government in the State in the 1700s. The provision was not inspired by the "Blaine Amendment"; nor was it a response to anti-immigrant or anti-Catholic bias. As the United States Supreme Court has observed, Blaine Amendments have "a shameful pedigree that we do not hesitate to disavow." New Jersey's Religious Aid Clause long pre-dated the Blaine Amendments and reflected a concern for religious freedom, not discrimination or hostility toward a particular religion.

The First Amendment to the United States Constitution, of course, also protects religious freedom. The Free Exercise Clause provides that "Congress shall make no law prohibiting the free exercise" of religion. The Establishment Clause states that "Congress shall make no law respecting an establishment of religion."

The first step in our analysis is to determine whether the historic preservation grants awarded to repair twelve churches violated the Religious Aid Clause of the State Constitution. In light of the plain language of the clause, the question answers itself.

The clause does not prevent local or State authorities from providing taxpayer-funded police, fire, and emergency services to houses of worship. Nor does it preclude the provision of other services tied to general public safety. Instead, for more than 240 years, the Religious Aid Clause has banned the use of public funds to build or repair any place of worship.

Here, the County awarded $4.6 million to twelve churches to repair active houses of worship—from roofs to bell towers, from stained glass windows to ventilation systems. The use of public funds to pay for those repairs violated the plain language of the Religious Aid Clause. The clause does not ask about the governing body's intent—that is, whether the authorities meant to fund repairs to churches, to preserve history and promote tourism, or both. In fact, the change from the 1776 Constitution to the 1844 Constitution removed the bracketed phrase "no taxes for the purpose of building or repairing any church." Thus, for most of its existence, the Religious Aid Clause has banned public funding to repair a house of worship without regard to some other non-religious purpose. In short, there is no exception for historic preservation.

There is very little case law that construes the Religious Aid Clause, and no case is directly on point. Some cases have focused on the prohibition against "the maintenance of a minister or ministry," not the "repair" of "any church." Thus, nothing in the prior case law requires a departure from the plain language of the Religious Aid Clause. Nor do the other provisions about religion in the State Constitution.

We therefore find that the County's grants ran afoul of the State Constitution's Religious Aid Clause.

We turn now to a more challenging question: whether New Jersey's Religious Aid Clause is at odds with the Federal Constitution. If so, the clause cannot stand, notwithstanding its history. Based on our understanding of the current state of the law, including the United States Supreme Court's recent decision in *Trinity Lutheran*, we conclude that the Religious Aid Clause does not conflict with the Free Exercise Clause.

The question before the Supreme Court in *Trinity Lutheran* was whether the policy of the Missouri Department of Natural Resources "of categorically disqualifying churches and other religious organizations from receiving grants under its playground resurfacing program violated the rights of Trinity Lutheran Church under the Free Exercise Clause of the First Amendment."

The Court held that the Department's policy violated the Free Exercise Clause by "expressly denying a qualified religious entity a public benefit solely because of its religious character." By doing so, the Department forced an untenable choice: "participate in an otherwise available benefit program or remain a religious institution." The Court underscored that "the express discrimination against religious exercise here is not the denial of a grant, but rather the refusal to allow the Church—solely because it is a church—to compete with secular organizations for a grant."

The Court, however, did not opine on whether that key principle—that "a qualified religious entity" cannot be denied "a public benefit solely because of its religious character"—extends to religious uses of funding.

Trinity Lutheran's scope is important because the facts of this case extend well beyond playground resurfacing. Indeed, the public funds awarded in this case actually went toward "religious uses." It is clear from the stipulated facts in the record that the Churches all "have active congregations that regularly worship, or participate in other religious activities," and all hold "regular worship services in one or more of the structures that they have used, or will use," taxpayer-funded grants to repair. In addition to the stipulation, a number of the applications expressly stated that churches sought funding for repairs to continue to conduct worship services.

In our judgment, those grants constitute an impermissible religious use of public funds.

New Jersey's Religious Aid Clause and the grants awarded in this matter stand in stark contrast to the setting in *Trinity Lutheran*. As the history of the New Jersey Constitution reveals, the interest the Clause seeks to advance "is scarcely novel." The Religious Aid Clause reflects a substantial concern of the State's founders in 1776: to ensure that taxpayer funds would not be used to build or repair houses of worship, or to maintain any ministry.

New Jersey's antiestablishment interest in not using public funds to build or repair churches or maintain any ministry "lay at the historic core of the Religion Clauses. New Jersey's historic and substantial interest against the establishment of, and compelled support for, religion is indeed "of the highest order." The Religious Aid Clause was enacted before the Federal Constitution; it is not a Blaine Amendment. No history of discrimination taints the provision.

The holding of *Trinity Lutheran* does not encompass the direct use of taxpayer funds to repair churches and thereby sustain religious worship activities. We therefore find that the application of the Religious Aid Clause in this case does not violate the Free Exercise Clause.

TAYLOR v. TOWN OF CABOT
178 A.3d 313 (Vt. 2017)

ROBINSON, J.

This case involves a challenge under the Compelled Support Clause of the Vermont Constitution to the Town of Cabot's grant of federally derived but municipally managed funds for the purpose of repairs to a historic church. Plaintiffs challenged the Town of Cabot's award of a grant to fund repairs to the United Church of Cabot (UCC), and sought a preliminary injunction enjoining the grant.

Plaintiffs face strong headwinds in arguing that the Compelled Support Clause embodies a categorical prohibition against any public funding for physical repairs to a place of worship, and plaintiffs have not yet presented sufficient evidence to demonstrate a high likelihood of success on a narrower claim.

The Vermont Constitution protects against compelled support for religion. In particular, Chapter I, Article Three provides that "no person ought to, or of right can be compelled to attend any religious worship, or erect or support any place of worship, or maintain any minister, contrary to the dictates of conscience." Although Article Three promotes the same general goals as the First Amendment to the U.S. Constitution, this Court has recognized that the two provisions are textually distinct, and may lead to divergent outcomes in some cases.

The focus of the Compelled Support Clause is the support for "worship" itself. In *Chittenden Town School District v. Department of Education* (Vt. 1999), we considered whether a scheme that reimbursed tuition for sectarian schools from public monies ran afoul of the Compelled Support Clause. We explained that, "although the words might appear to be broader, Article 3 is not offended by mere compelled support for a place of worship unless the compelled support is for the worship itself." For the purposes of this case, the most critical lesson from *Chittenden Town School District* is that the fact that the recipient of government support is a religious organization is not itself determinative under the Compelled Support Clause; whether the funds are used to support religious worship is the critical question.

The Free Exercise Clause is a second critical touchstone impacting plaintiffs' likelihood of success on the merits. While public support to religious organizations potentially implicates the Compelled Support Clause of the Vermont Constitution, a refusal to afford religious organizations access to secular benefits generally available to like institutions on account of their religious affiliations may also trigger concerns under the Free Exercise Clause.

The U.S. Supreme Court recently reaffirmed this very point in *Trinity Lutheran*. Trinity Lutheran Church sought a grant to replace a large portion of the playground that served its preschool and daycare center. The program had a strict and express policy of denying grants to any applicant owned or controlled by a church, sect or other religious entity, and it rejected Trinity Lutheran's grant request on that basis. The Court explained, "the express discrimination against religious exercise here is not the denial of a grant, but rather the refusal to allow the Church—solely because it is a church—to compete with secular organizations for a grant."

The third foundation for our analysis—the record in this case—is not fully developed with respect to the anticipated and permitted use of the grant funds. The grant funds in this case were undisputedly allocated for the purpose of maintenance and repairs to a building that serves as a place of worship, is available for many nonsectarian community events and gatherings, and is an important and historic building in the town. The $10,000 grant amounts to a small portion of the total funds needed to repair the church. The warned question approved by the voters of the Town authorizes funding "for the purpose of repairing the steeple, stairwell and other interior sections in urgent need of repair at the United Church of Cabot." Although the parties relied on this warning as descriptive of the scope of the grant for the purpose of the preliminary injunction hearing, other uncontested documents in the record appear to significantly limit the scope of the grant.

Regarding the legal proposition, we are heavily influenced by the reasoning of the United States Court of Appeals for the Sixth Circuit in the case of *American Atheists, Inc. v. City of Detroit Downtown Development Authority* (6th Cir. 2009). In that case, the City of Detroit, in preparation for hosting a Super Bowl, created a program to refurbish the exteriors of downtown buildings and parking lots in a discrete section of downtown Detroit. Three churches within the designated district participated, and collectively received 6.4% of the $11.5 million allocated for completed and authorized projects. The question before the court was whether payments to the three churches pursuant to this program violated the Establishment Clause of the U.S. Constitution or the counterpart provision in the Michigan Constitution. *See* Mich. Const. art. I, § 4 ("No person shall be compelled to contribute to the erection or support of any place of religious worship.").

The Sixth Circuit emphasized several factors in concluding that the challenged grants were permissible. Detroit's "program allocated benefits in an evenhanded manner to a broad and diverse universe of beneficiaries." The program assessed a recipient's eligibility for benefits "in spite of, rather than because of, its religious character," and "made grants available to a wide spectrum of religious, nonreligious, and areligious groups." Nothing in the history or implementation of the program revealed any "overt or masked" purpose to advantage religious groups. Although the funds were used to upgrade some buildings in which religious worship took place, they were available to religious and secular entities alike based on criteria that have nothing to do with religion.

Although the *American Atheists* court analyzed the issue pursuant to the Establishment Clause of the First Amendment, many of its insights apply with respect to the Compelled Support Clause. Where funding is available on a neutral and nondiscriminatory basis to a broad and diverse group of potential recipients in order to promote a squarely secular goal of the broader community, there is no indication that the funds are intended to or do advantage religious organizations or activity, and the funds are used for structural repairs rather than, for example, erecting religious symbols, we cannot conclude that such funds support worship within the meaning of Article Three. To the extent that plaintiffs rely on the broad claim that spending any public money on repairs to any part of the UCC church building violates the Compelled Support Clause, they will face an uphill battle on the merits.

Plaintiffs' alternate path to success on the merits—establishing that this particular grant violates the Compelled Support Clause—is not well supported by the record as it currently exists. Plaintiffs may be able to establish that the grant program is not as neutral and broad-reaching as it appears, that the criteria for awarding the grants are so broad and vague that they cannot be described as neutral in the American Atheists sense, or that as designed or implemented it advantages the UCC as a religious organization; they have not done so on this record.

Likewise, plaintiffs may be able to establish that the award of the grant monies in this case crosses a line by funding religious worship. In their brief, they suggest that the approval by Town voters pursuant to the warned question is broad enough to allow the expenditure of public funds "on anything at all that needs repair, including purely religious parts of the building or religious artifacts." However, on this record the grant is limited to two particular purposes—painting three sides of the exterior of the church building and examining the window sills in the church. The cost of these two projects is only a small fraction of the overall cost of the renovation project, and the public funding will accordingly amount to only a small fraction of the overall cost of the UCC's broader renovation.

For the above reasons, we conclude on the basis of the current record that the plaintiffs' likelihood of success on the merits weighs against the issuance of a preliminary injunction.

NOTES

1. What is the scope of the U.S. Supreme Court's decision in *Trinity Lutheran*? What factors are relevant to determining whether a state constitutional provision prohibiting state aid to churches and other religious entities is consistent with the First Amendment? Does historic preservation make a difference? Does secular use of the space make a difference? And what of the history of a State's experiences before or after adopting a no-state-aid provision?

2. With the exception of the cases above, most modern disputes about the role of state Blaine Amendments have focused on governmental programs designed to provide parents (and students) choices outside of the public schools. The issue is whether the programs have the purpose or effect of providing aid to religious schools and other religious organizations on the one hand or of providing aid to the individuals who benefit from them on the other. We start by considering a decision of the United States Supreme Court, *Zelman v. Simmons-Harris*, 536 U.S. 639 (2002), which rejects a federal Establishment Clause challenge to a state voucher program. We then consider several state-court decisions, one that predates *Zelman* and several that follow it. The section concludes with a recent decision from the New Mexico Supreme Court that interprets the state's Blaine provision in light of the Supreme Court's decisions in *Trinity Lutheran* and *Masterpiece Cakeshop, Ltd. v. Colo. Civil Rights Comm'n*, 138 S. Ct. 1719 (2018).

ZELMAN v. SIMMONS-HARRIS
536 U.S. 639 (2002)

REHNQUIST, C.J.

The State of Ohio has established a pilot program designed to provide educational choices to families with children who reside in the Cleveland City School District. The question presented is whether this program offends the Establishment Clause of the United States Constitution. We hold that it does not.

There are more than 75,000 children enrolled in the Cleveland City School District. The majority of these children are from low-income and minority families. Few of these families enjoy the means to send their children to any school other than an inner-city public school.

The program provides two basic kinds of assistance to parents of children in a covered district. First, the program provides tuition aid for students in kindergarten through third grade, expanding each year through eighth grade, to attend a participating public or private school of their parent's choosing. Second, the program provides tutorial aid for students who choose to remain enrolled in public school.

The Establishment Clause of the First Amendment, applied to the States through the Fourteenth Amendment, prevents a State from enacting laws that have the "purpose" or "effect" of advancing or inhibiting religion. There is no dispute that the program challenged here was enacted for the valid secular purpose of providing educational assistance to poor children in a demonstrably failing public school system. Thus, the question presented is whether the Ohio program nonetheless has the forbidden "effect" of advancing or inhibiting religion.

To answer that question, our decisions have drawn a consistent distinction between government programs that provide aid directly to religious schools, and programs of true private choice, in which government aid reaches religious schools only as a result of the genuine and independent choices of private individuals. While our jurisprudence with respect to the constitutionality of direct aid programs has "changed significantly" over the past two decades, our jurisprudence with respect to true private choice programs has remained consistent and unbroken. Three times we have confronted Establishment Clause challenges to neutral government programs that provide aid directly to a broad class of individuals, who, in turn, direct the aid to religious schools or institutions of their own choosing. Three times we have rejected such challenges.

Mueller v. Allen (1983), *Witters v. Washington Department of Services for the Blind* (1986), and *Zobrest v. Catalina Foothills School District* (1993) make clear that where a government aid program is neutral with respect to religion, and provides assistance directly to a broad class of citizens who, in turn, direct government aid to religious schools wholly as a result of their own genuine and independent private choice, the program is not readily subject to challenge under the Establishment Clause. A program that shares these features permits government aid to reach religious institutions only by way of the deliberate choices of numerous individual recipients. The incidental advancement of a religious mission, or the perceived endorsement of a religious message, is reasonably attributable to the individual recipient, not to the government, whose role ends with the disbursement of benefits.

Respondents claim that even if we do not focus on the number of participating schools that are religious schools, we should attach constitutional significance to the fact that 96% of scholarship recipients have enrolled in religious schools. They claim that this alone proves parents lack genuine choice, even if no parent has ever said so. We need not consider this argument in detail, since it was flatly rejected in *Mueller*, where we found it irrelevant that 96% of parents taking deductions for tuition expenses paid tuition at religious schools. Indeed, we have recently found it irrelevant even to the constitutionality of a direct aid program that a vast majority of program benefits went to religious schools. The constitutionality of a neutral educational aid program simply does not turn on whether and why, in a particular area, at a particular time, most private schools are run by religious organizations, or most recipients choose to use the aid at a religious school.

In sum, the Ohio program is entirely neutral with respect to religion. It provides benefits directly to a wide spectrum of individuals, defined only by financial need and residence in a particular school district. It permits such individuals to exercise genuine choice among options public and private, secular and religious. The program is therefore a program of true private choice. In keeping with an unbroken line of decisions rejecting challenges to similar programs, we hold that the program does not offend the Establishment Clause.

JACKSON v. BENSON
578 N.W.2d 602 (Wis. 1998)

STEINMETZ, J.

We are once again asked to review the constitutionality of the Milwaukee Parental Choice Program. The Wisconsin legislature enacted the original Milwaukee Parental Choice Program (original MPCP) in 1989. The original MPCP permitted up to 1.5 percent of the student membership of the Milwaukee Public Schools (MPS) to attend at no cost to the student any private nonsectarian school located in the City of Milwaukee, subject to certain eligibility requirements. In 1995, the legislature amended the original MPCP. The legislature removed the limitation that participating private schools be "nonsectarian" and added an "opt-out" provision prohibiting a private school from requiring "a student attending the private school under this section to participate in any religious activity if the pupil's parent or guardian submits to the teacher or the private school's principal a written request that the pupil be exempt from such activities."

The next question presented in this case is whether the amended Milwaukee Parental Choice Program (amended MPCP), a school voucher program, violates art. I, § 18 of the Wisconsin Constitution. The Respondents argue, and the court of appeals concluded, that the amended

MPCP violates both the "benefits clause" and the "compelled support clause" of art. I, § 18. Upon review, we conclude that the amended MPCP violates neither provision.

The "benefits clause" of art. I, § 18 provides: "nor shall any money be drawn from the treasury for the benefit of religious societies, or religious or theological seminaries." This is Wisconsin's equivalent of the Establishment Clause of the First Amendment. This court has remarked that the language of art. I, § 18, while "more specific than the terser" clauses of the First Amendment, carries the same import; both provisions "are intended and operate to serve the same dual purpose of prohibiting the establishment of religion and protecting the free exercise of religion." Although art. I, § 18 is not subsumed by the First Amendment, we interpret and apply the benefits clause of art. I, § 18 in light of the United States Supreme Court cases interpreting the Establishment Clause of the First Amendment.

Unlike the court of appeals, which focused on whether sectarian private schools were "religious seminaries" under art. I, § 18, we focus our inquiry on whether the aid provided by the amended MPCP is "for the benefit of" such religious institutions. We have explained that the language "for the benefit of" in art. I, § 18 "is not to be read as requiring that some shadow of incidental benefit to a church-related institution brings a state grant or contract to purchase within the prohibition of the section." Furthermore, we have stated that the language of art. I, § 18 cannot be read as being "so prohibitive as not to encompass the primary-effect test." The crucial question, under art. I, § 18, as under the Establishment Clause, is "not whether some benefit accrues to a religious institution as a consequence of the legislative program, but whether its principal or primary effect advances religion."

We find the Supreme Court's primary effect test, focusing on the neutrality and indirection of state aid, is well reasoned and provides the appropriate line of demarcation for considering the constitutionality of neutral educational assistance programs such as the amended MPCP. Since the amended MPCP does not transgress the primary effect test employed in Establishment Clause jurisprudence, we also conclude that the statute is constitutionally inviolate under the benefits clause of art. I, § 18.

This conclusion is not inconsistent with Wisconsin tradition or with past precedent of this court. Wisconsin has traditionally accorded parents the primary role in decisions regarding the education and upbringing of their children. This court has embraced this principle for nearly a century, recognizing that: "parents as the natural guardians of their children are the persons under natural conditions having the most effective motives and inclinations and being in the best position and under the strongest obligations to give to such children proper nurture, education, and training."

In this context, this court has held that public funds may be placed at the disposal of third parties so long as the program on its face is neutral between sectarian and nonsectarian alternatives and the transmission of funds is guided by the independent decisions of third parties, and that public funds generally may be provided to sectarian educational institutions so long as steps are taken not to subsidize religious functions.

In *State ex rel. Weiss v. District Board* (Wis. 1890), this court held that reading of the King James version of the Bible by students attending public school violated the religious benefits clause of art. I, § 18. Although the court's reasoning in *Weiss* may have differed from ours, its holding is entirely consistent with the primary effects test the Supreme Court has developed and we apply today. Requiring public school students to read from the Bible is neither neutral nor indirect. The Edgerton schools reviewed in *Weiss* were directly supported by public funds, and the reading of the Bible was anything but religion-neutral. The program considered in *Weiss* is far different from the neutral and indirect aid provided under the amended MPCP. The holding in *Weiss*, therefore, does not control our inquiry in this case.

The Respondents additionally argue that the amended MPCP violates the "compelled support clause" of art. I, § 18. The compelled support clause provides "nor shall any person be compelled to attend, erect or support any place of worship, or to maintain any ministry without consent." The Respondents assert that since public funds eventually flow to religious institutions under the amended MPCP, taxpayers are compelled to support places of worship against their consent. This argument is identical to the Respondents' argument under the benefits clause. We will not interpret the compelled support clause as prohibiting the same acts as those prohibited by the benefits clause. Rather we look for an interpretation of these two related provisions that avoids such redundancy.

The amended MPCP does not require a single student to attend class at a sectarian private school. A qualifying student only attends a sectarian private school under the program if the student's parent so chooses. Nor does the amended MPCP force participation in religious activities. On the contrary, the program prohibits a sectarian private school from requiring students attending under the program to participate in religious activities offered at such school. The choice to participate in religious activities is also left to the students' parents. Since the amended MPCP neither compels students to attend sectarian private schools nor requires them to participate in religious activities, the program does not violate the compelled support clause of art. I, § 18.

NOTE

In *Jackson*, the Wisconsin Supreme Court anticipated the U.S. Supreme Court's decision in *Zelman*, both as a matter of federal and state constitutional law. More frequently, state-court individual rights decisions respond to United States Supreme Court decisions, either by following them in lockstep or by reacting against them. It is fair to ask whether constitutional law in general—state and federal—benefits from this top-down approach or whether we would benefit from a bottom-up approach in which the state courts initially wrestle with difficult constitutional issues before the Supreme Court announces the meaning of the relevant federal provision.

TAXPAYERS FOR PUB. EDUC. v. DOUGLAS CNTY. SCH. DIST.
351 P.3d 461 (Colo. 2015)

RICE, C.J.

Four years ago, the Douglas County School District implemented its Choice Scholarship Pilot Program (CPS), a grant mechanism that awarded taxpayer-funded scholarships to qualifying elementary, middle, and high school students. Those students could use their scholarships to help pay their tuition at partnering private schools, including religious schools.

The Colorado Constitution features broad, unequivocal language forbidding the State from using public money to fund religious schools. Specifically, article IX, section 7—entitled "Aid to private schools, churches, sectarian purpose, forbidden"—includes the following proscriptive language:

> Neither the general assembly, nor any county, city, town, township, school district or other public corporation, shall ever make any appropriation, or pay from any public fund or moneys whatever, anything in aid of any church or sectarian society, or for any sectarian purpose, or to help support or sustain any school, academy, seminary, college, university or other literary or scientific institution, controlled by any church or sectarian denomination whatsoever.

Although this provision uses the term "sectarian" rather than "religious," the two words are synonymous. That section 7 twice equates the term "sectarian" with the word "church" only reinforces this point. Therefore, this stark constitutional provision makes one thing clear: A school district may not aid religious schools.

Yet aiding religious schools is exactly what the CSP does. The CSP essentially functions as a recruitment program, teaming with various religious schools and encouraging students to attend those schools via the inducement of scholarships. To be sure, the CSP does not explicitly funnel money directly to religious schools, instead providing financial aid to students. But section 7's prohibitions are not limited to direct funding. Rather, section 7 bars school districts from "paying from any public fund or moneys *whatever*, *anything* in aid of any" religious institution, and from "helping *support or sustain* any school controlled by any church or sectarian denomination *whatsoever*" (emphasis added). Given that private religious schools rely on students' attendance (and their corresponding tuition payments) for their ongoing survival, the CSP's facilitation of such attendance necessarily constitutes aid to "support or sustain" those schools.

Respondents point out that the CSP does not *require* scholarship recipients to enroll in a religious school, nor does it force participating Private School Partners to be religious. Respondents thus suggest that the CSP features an element of private choice that severs the link between the District's aid to the student and the student's ultimate attendance at a (potentially) religious school. It is true that the CSP does not *only* partner with religious schools; several Private School Partners are non-religious. The fact remains, however, that the CSP awards public money to students who may then use that money to pay for a religious education. In so doing, the CSP aids religious institutions.

Respondents nevertheless contend that the plain language of section 7 is not plain at all, but that the term "sectarian" is actually code for "Catholic." In so doing, Respondents charge that section 7 is a so-called "Blaine Amendment" that is bigoted in origin. They thus encourage us to wade into the history of section 7's adoption and declare that the framers created section 7 in a vulgar display of anti-Catholic animus.

We need not perform such an exegesis to dispose of Respondents' argument. Instead, we need merely recall that "constitutional provisions must be declared and enforced as written" whenever their language is "plain" and their meaning is "clear." As discussed, the term "sectarian" plainly means "religious." Therefore, we will enforce section 7 as it is written.

Americans United for Separation of Church and State, Inc. v. State (Colo. 1982), by contrast revolved around the Colorado Student Incentive Grant Program, a scholarship for in-state college students. The grant program allowed eligible universities to recommend particular students deserving of scholarships to the Colorado Commission of Higher Education, which in turn administered the grants. The Commission awarded the grant money to the university, which then reduced the student's tuition by the amount of the grant. Although the grant program embraced most colleges and universities, it excluded institutions that were "pervasively sectarian," and it defined six eligibility criteria that schools needed to meet in order *not* to be branded pervasively sectarian.

The First Amendment to the United States Constitution provides in part that "Congress shall make no law respecting an establishment of religion, or prohibiting the free exercise thereof." Respondents contend that several federal cases interpreting the First Amendment constitute binding case law forbidding us from striking down the CSP. In particular, Respondents cite the U.S. Supreme Court's decision in *Zelman v. Simmons-Harris* (2002). Had Petitioners claimed that the CSP violated the Establishment Clause, *Zelman* might constitute persuasive authority. But they did not. Rather, Petitioners challenged the CSP under article IX, section 7 of the Colorado Constitution. By its terms, section 7 is far more restrictive than the Establishment Clause regarding governmental aid to religion, and the Supreme Court has recognized that state constitutions may draw a tighter net around the conferral of such aid. As such, *Zelman's* reasoning, rooted in the Establishment Clause, is irrelevant to the issue of whether the CSP violates section 7.

EID, J., concurring in part and dissenting in part.

Today, the plurality interprets article IX, section 7 as prohibiting the expenditure of any state funds that might incidentally or indirectly benefit a religious school. This breathtakingly broad interpretation would invalidate not only the CSP, but numerous other state programs that provide funds to students and their parents who in turn decide to use the funds to attend religious schools in Colorado. The plurality's interpretation barring indirect funding is so broad that it would invalidate the use of public funds to build roads, bridges, and sidewalks adjacent to such schools, as the schools, in the words of the plurality, "rely on" state-paid infrastructure to operate their institutions. Because I fundamentally disagree with the plurality's interpretation, I respectfully dissent from this part of its opinion on the following two grounds.

The plurality first takes a wrong turn in interpreting the language of section 7 as invalidating any government expenditure that indirectly benefits religious schools. That is not what the language of section 7 says.

Section 7 bars a government entity from "making any appropriation, or paying from any public fund or moneys whatever to help support or sustain any church or sectarian school whatsoever." This language bars the expenditure of public funds "to help support or sustain" certain schools. But here, the CSP funds are expended not "to help support or sustain" those schools, but rather to help the student recipients. The language does not suggest, as the plurality believes, that government funds that are directed to a student but happen to have an incidental beneficial effect on certain schools are also forbidden. The plurality stresses that the language prohibits a government entity from making such an expenditure "whatever" to certain schools "whatsoever." While these terms reinforce the prohibition on making certain expenditures, they do not modify or expand upon what kind of expenditures are prohibited—that is, expenditures "to support or sustain" a church or sectarian school. In other words, contrary to the plurality's reasoning, these words do not transform the prohibition on expenditures "to support or sustain" certain schools into a prohibition on any expenditures that have the incidental effect of benefiting certain schools.

We elucidated the distinction between direct and indirect assistance in *Americans United*, where we upheld a state grant program that disbursed state grant monies into the school accounts of student grant recipients who attended religious colleges. We concluded that the program's "primary effect" was not to advance religion because "the design of the statute was to benefit the student, not the institution."

The U.S. Supreme Court has recognized this same distinction in its Establishment Clause jurisprudence. In *Zelman*, for example, the Court upheld a program that gave tuition assistance to students from kindergarten to eighth grade in certain districts that could be used to attend any public or private school of their parents' choosing, including religious schools. The Court began by observing that the Establishment Clause prevents states from enacting laws that have the "purpose" or "effect" of advancing or inhibiting religion. There was no dispute that the program had a valid educational (and secular) purpose, and therefore the Court focused on whether it unconstitutionally advanced religion. The Court relied upon its "consistent and unbroken" line of precedent holding that aid programs generally do not impermissibly "advance religion" when "government aid reaches religious schools only as a result of the genuine and independent choices of private individuals."

Applying this principle to the case before it, the Court concluded that the program was one of "true private choice" and consistent with the Establishment Clause. Significantly, the Court recognized that there may be "incidental advancement of a religious mission" in these sorts of programs. However, such incidental advancement is "reasonably attributable to the individual recipient, not to the government, whose role ends with the disbursement of benefits." Moreover, the Court refused to attach constitutional significance to the fact that ninety-six percent of the aid recipients enrolled in religious schools. According to the Court, "the constitutionality of a neutral educational aid program simply does not turn on whether and why most recipients choose to use the aid at a religious school." The point is that aid recipients are the ones to make the choice.

The plurality rejects as "irrelevant" this wealth of Supreme Court precedent that reinforces our reasoning in *Americans United*, pointing out that it interprets the federal Establishment Clause, not section 7. But the plurality's approach is directly contrary to *Americans United*, where, as discussed above, we expressly relied upon our reasoning in considering the Establishment Clause claim in rejecting the section 7 claim. That the aid in question was expended to support students, not the institution, was a critical factor in both our Establishment Clause and section 7 inquiries.

More problematic is the plurality's conclusion that "by its terms, section 7 is far more restrictive than the Establishment Clause regarding governmental aid to religion." The plurality's mistake is to confuse specificity with restriction. Section 7 is certainly more specific than the Establishment Clause, in that it contains a specific prohibition against making public expenditures "to help support or sustain" certain schools. We made a similar point regarding the specificity of article II, section 4 of the Colorado Constitution—which recognizes the "free exercise and enjoyment of religious profession and worship," as well as that "no person shall be required to attend or support any ministry or place of worship"—in *Americans United*, observing that the state provisions are "considerably more specific than the Establishment Clause of the First Amendment." However, far from casting aside the federal counterpart and its accompanying jurisprudence, we declared that the state provisions should be read "to embody the same values of free exercise and government non-involvement secured by the religious clauses of the First Amendment." We reiterated that "although not necessarily determinative of state constitutional claims, First Amendment jurisprudence cannot be totally divorced from the resolution of these claims." Here, the Establishment Clause, as interpreted by the Supreme Court, ends up in the same place as the text of section 7—namely, prohibiting expenditures made to assist institutions, but not prohibiting expenditures made to support students.

A more fundamental problem with the plurality's opinion is that it holds that because section 7 is enforceable on its "plain language," it need not consider whether the provision is in fact enforceable due to possible anti-Catholic animus. As developed above, I believe the plurality is wrong on the plain language. But even if it were right, it would then be obligated to consider whether the language could be enforced to strike down the CSP. In this case, the plurality simply sticks its head in the sand and hopes that because it cannot see the allegations of anti-Catholic bias, no one else will.

The Supreme Court made this point clear in *Church of the Lukumi Babalu Aye, Inc. v. City of Hialeah* (1993), where it considered a challenge under the Free Exercise Clause to city ordinances that banned the ritual sacrifice of animals. The City argued that the ordinances were neutral on their face and therefore immune from constitutional scrutiny. The Court rejected this argument, holding instead that "facial neutrality is not determinative" of a Free Exercise claim. According to the Court, "the Free Exercise Clause extends beyond facial discrimination. The Clause protects against government hostility which is masked, as well as overt." The court concluded that "the record in this case compels the conclusion that suppression of the central element of the Santeria worship service was the object of the ordinances." Because the ordinances were not neutral, the

Court went on to consider whether they were narrowly tailored to advance a compelling state interest. The Court concluded that they were not.

Under *Lukumi*, the plurality cannot begin and end its analysis with the conclusion that the plain language of section 7 is not discriminatory. In fact, the very case upon which the plurality relies for the proposition that states "may draw a tighter net around the conferral of aid" to religion—*Locke v. Davey* (2004)—reinforces *Lukumi's* instruction that courts must look behind the text to discover any religious animus. In *Locke*, which involved a Washington state scholarship program that excluded students pursuing a degree in theology, the Court concluded that "far from evincing the hostility toward religion which was manifest in *Lukumi*, we believe that the Washington program goes a long way toward including religion in its benefits." The Court upheld the program against a free exercise challenge only after concluding that it could find nothing "that suggests animus toward religion." The relevant point here is not the Court's conclusion on the matter but that it performed the inquiry in the first place.

Moreover, in this instance, the text of section 7 is not as neutral as the plurality would have it. As noted above, the text bars expenditures "to help support or sustain any school" that is "controlled by any church or sectarian denomination whatsoever." The plurality equates the term "sectarian" with the term "religious," concluding that "the two words are synonymous." But even *Black's Law Dictionary*, upon which the plurality relies for its conclusion, does not equate the two terms, suggesting that sectarian relates to "*a particular* religious sect." In fact, in a 1927 case, this court upheld a school board rule requiring Bible reading in public schools against a section 7 challenge on the ground that such activity was not "sectarian"—that is, related to a particular sect. In sum, contrary to the plurality's interpretation, the term "sectarian" refers to a particular religious sect, not to religion generally.

In *Mitchell v. Helms* (2000), a plurality of the Court referred to the "shameful pedigree" of anti-sectarian sentiment in the 1870s. According to the plurality:

> Opposition to aid to "sectarian" schools acquired prominence in the 1870s with Congress' consideration (and near passage) of the Blaine Amendment, which would have amended the Constitution to bar any aid to sectarian institutions. Consideration of the amendment arose at a time of pervasive hostility to the Catholic Church and to Catholics in general, and it was an open secret that "sectarian" was code for "Catholic."

The plurality in this case "declines to ascribe to *Mitchell* the force of law" because it is a plurality opinion. But this passage from *Mitchell* is not relevant to this case because it has "the force of law," as the plurality implies; it is relevant for its description of historical context. And while Justice O'Connor, in her separate opinion concurring in the judgment joined by Justice Breyer, objected to the plurality's reasoning in *Mitchell*, she lodged no objection to the plurality's historical description. In fact, Justice Breyer, joined by Justices Stevens and Souter, recounted the same history in his dissent in *Zelman*. As Justice Breyer observed, anti-Catholic sentiment "played a significant role in creating a movement that sought to amend several state constitutions (often successfully), and to amend the United States Constitution (unsuccessfully) to make certain that government would not help pay for *sectarian (i.e., Catholic) schooling for children*."

In the end, the plurality's head-in-the-sand approach is a disservice to Colorado, as it allows allegations of anti-Catholic animus to linger unaddressed. The plurality should squarely address the issue of whether section 7 is enforceable, as this court has done with other provisions of the Colorado Constitution. Because the plurality fails to do so, and because it misinterprets the text of section 7 and ignores relevant Establishment Clause jurisprudence, I respectfully dissent from its opinion.

CAIN v. HORNE
202 P.3d 1178 (Ariz. 2009)

RYAN, J.

Article 2, Section 12, of the Arizona Constitution provides that "no public money shall be appropriated to any religious worship, exercise, or instruction, or to the support of any religious establishment." Article 9, Section 10, of the Arizona Constitution states that "no tax shall be laid or appropriation of public money made in aid of any church, or private or sectarian school, or any public service corporation." The issue before us is whether two state-funded programs violate these provisions of our constitution.

In 2006, the Legislature enacted two programs that, in part, appropriated state monies to allow students to attend a private school of their choice instead of the public school in the district in which they live.

The Arizona Scholarships for Pupils with Disabilities Program offers "pupils with disabilities the option of attending any public school of the pupil's choice or receiving a scholarship to any qualified school of the pupil's choice." Under this program, a public-school student with a disability may transfer to a private primary or secondary school, with the State paying a scholarship up to the amount of basic state aid the student would generate for a public school district. A parent of a disabled student may apply for a scholarship if the pupil attended a public school during the prior school year, the parent "is dissatisfied with the pupil's progress," and "the parent has obtained acceptance for admission of the pupil to a qualified school."

The Arizona Displaced Pupils Choice Grant Program allows the State to pay $5,000 or the cost of tuition and fees, whichever is less, for children in foster care to attend the private primary or secondary school of their choice. The program is limited to 500 pupils. A grant school is "a nongovernmental primary school or secondary school or a preschool that does not discriminate on the basis of race, color, handicap, familial status or national origin, that maintains one or more grade levels from kindergarten through grade twelve."

Sectarian and nonsectarian schools may participate in both programs; schools are not required to alter their "creed, practices or curriculum" in order to receive funding. Under both programs, (collectively "the voucher programs") parents or legal guardians select the private or sectarian school their child will attend. The State then disburses a check or warrant to the parent or guardian, who must "restrictively endorse" the instrument for payment to the selected school.

Horne and the intervenors argue that the Aid Clause should be interpreted just as the United States Supreme Court has interpreted the Establishment Clause of the United States Constitution, and that the parental choice involved in signing the state checks over to a private or sectarian school saves the voucher programs from unconstitutionality.

Contrary to Horne's assertion, *Kotterman v. Killian* (Ariz. 1999) and *Community Council v. Jordan* (Ariz. 1967) do not compel us to interpret the Aid Clause as a mirror image of the Religion Clause or to interpret the Aid Clause as no broader than the federal Establishment Clause. More importantly, both the text and purpose of the Aid Clause support the conclusion that the clause requires a construction independent from that of the Religion Clause.

First, the text of the Aid Clause encompasses more than does the Religion Clause. The Aid Clause prohibits the use of public funds not only to aid *private* or sectarian schools, but to aid public corporations as well. Thus, under the Aid Clause, a statute granting funds to aid a public service corporation engaged exclusively in secular activities might be prohibited; such a statute would pose no difficulties under the Religion Clause, nor could it be readily analyzed under the Supreme Court's Establishment Clause jurisprudence. Likewise, the Religion Clause would prohibit an appropriation to pay for religious instruction in a public school, but the Aid Clause says nothing about such an appropriation, as public schools are not among the forbidden recipients of appropriations under the Aid Clause.

Second, although the two clauses overlap to some extent, they serve different purposes. The Religion Clause appears in Article 2, entitled "Declaration of Rights," and reinforces other provisions in the constitution "dealing with the separation of church and state." The Aid Clause is found in Article 9, entitled "Public Debt, Revenue, and Taxation," and "unlike

Article 2, Section 12 prohibits public aid to private nonsectarian schools and to public service corporations." The Aid Clause is thus primarily designed to protect the public fisc and to protect public schools.

Both the Aid and Religion Clauses prohibit certain appropriations of public money. In *Kotterman*, this Court addressed whether tax credits for contributions to organizations providing scholarships to students attending non-governmental schools violated the two clauses. We held that neither provision precluded the Legislature from granting a tuition tax credit, because the tax credit was not an appropriation. Because the funds in *Kotterman* were credits against tax liability, not withdrawals from the state treasury, the funds were never in the state's treasury; therefore, the credits did not constitute an appropriation.

Unlike the funds in *Kotterman*, the funds at issue here are withdrawn from the public treasury and earmarked for an identified purpose. Horne and the intervenors do not dispute that the vouchers therefore constitute appropriations of public funds. But they argue that the funds do not aid the schools; rather they characterize the funds as aid to students under a "true beneficiary" theory.

Under the true beneficiary theory, individuals benefitted by a government program, rather than the institution receiving the public funds, are characterized as the true beneficiaries of the aid. For example, in *Jordan*, we held that using state funds to partially reimburse the Salvation Army's expenses in providing emergency aid to those in need did not violate the Aid Clause. *Jordan* thus stands for the proposition that an entity covered by the Aid Clause may contract with the State to provide non-religious services to members of the public when such an entity "merely acts as a conduit and receives no financial aid or support therefrom."

The voucher programs, however, vary significantly from the program at issue in *Jordan*. In contrast to the program in *Jordan*, the voucher programs do not provide reimbursement for contracted services. In fact, they are designed in such a way that the State does not purchase anything; rather it is the parent or the guardian who exercises sole discretion to contract with the qualified school.

The Aid Clause flatly prohibits "appropriation of public money in aid of any private or sectarian school." No one doubts that the clause prohibits a direct appropriation of public funds to such recipients. For all intents and purposes, the voucher programs do precisely what the Aid Clause prohibits. These programs transfer state funds directly from the state treasury to private schools. That the checks or warrants first pass through the hands of parents is immaterial; once a pupil has been accepted into a qualified school under either program, the parents or guardians have no choice; they must endorse the check or warrant to the qualified school.

In sum, the language and purpose of the Aid Clause do not permit the appropriations these voucher programs provide; to rule otherwise would allow appropriations that would amount to "aid of private or sectarian schools," and render the clause a nullity.

MEREDITH v. PENCE
984 N.E.2d 1213 (Ind. 2013)

DICKSON, C.J.

The plaintiffs challenge Indiana's statutory program for providing vouchers to eligible parents for their use in sending their children to private schools. Finding that the challengers have not satisfied the high burden required to invalidate a statute on constitutional grounds, we affirm the trial court's judgment upholding the constitutionality of the statutory voucher program.

To be eligible for the voucher program, a student must live in a "household with an annual income of not more than one hundred fifty percent (150%) of the amount required for the individual to qualify for the federal free or reduced price lunch program." The voucher amount is determined from statutorily defined criteria pegged to the federal free or reduced price lunch program with the maximum voucher being "ninety percent (90%) of the state tuition support amount," designated for the student in the public "school corporation in which the eligible individual has legal settlement."

The fact that a student's family might meet the statutory eligibility qualifications does not require them to participate in the voucher program and to select a program-eligible school. The parents of an eligible student are thus free to select any program-eligible school or none at all. The voucher program does not alter the makeup or availability of Indiana public or charter schools. In accepting program students, eligible schools are free to maintain and apply their preexisting admissions standards except that "an eligible school may not discriminate on the basis of race, color, or national origin." The program statute is silent with respect to religion, imposing no religious requirement or restriction upon student or school eligibility.

The plaintiffs assert that the school voucher program violates Article 1, Section 4, of the Indiana Constitution. Specifically, the plaintiffs argue that the voucher program is contrary to the decree that "no person shall be compelled to attend, erect, or support, any place of worship, or to maintain any ministry, against his consent." We have previously held that the religious liberty protections in the Indiana Constitution "were not intended merely to mirror the federal First Amendment." When Indiana's present constitution was adopted in 1851, the framers who drafted it and the voters who ratified it did not copy or paraphrase the 1791 language of the federal

First Amendment. Instead, they adopted seven separate and specific provisions, Sections 2 through 8 of Article 1, relating to religion.

For the most part, these separate provisions, including Section 4, were adapted from the 1816 Constitution. The text of Section 4 is "our primary source for discerning the common understanding of the framers and ratifiers." The plaintiffs' argument under Section 4 focuses on the framers' text declaring that "no person shall be compelled to *support*, any place of worship, or to maintain any ministry, against his consent." The word "support," the plaintiffs contend, "includes the compelled payment of taxes that are used for religious purposes," whether the tax is a specific directive (*e.g.*, forced contributions to a religious entity or a direct tax specifically earmarked for religious purposes), or general tax revenues used to "support" religious entities.

This argument improperly expands the language of Section 4 and conflates it with that of Section 6. The former explicitly prohibits a person from being "compelled to attend, erect, or support" a place of worship or a ministry against his consent. This clause is a restraint upon government compulsion of individuals to engage in religious practices absent their consent. To limit the government's taxing and spending related to religious matters, the framers crafted Section 6, which restrains government not as to its compulsion of individuals, but rather its expenditure of funds for certain prohibited purposes. ("No money shall be drawn from the treasury, for the benefit of any religious or theological institution.") The two clauses were drafted to specify separate and distinct objectives in their respective restraints upon government: Section 6 prohibiting expenditures to benefit religious or theological institutions, and Section 4 prohibiting compulsion of individuals related to attendance, erection, or support of places of worship or ministry. We view these language distinctions between Sections 4 and 6 to be purposeful. The religious liberty protections addressed by Section 4 prohibited government compulsion of individuals and was neither intended nor understood to limit government expenditures, which is addressed by Section 6.

The plaintiffs also assert that the school voucher program violates Article 1, Section 6, of the Indiana Constitution, which provides: "No money shall be drawn from the treasury, for the benefit of any religious or theological institution." In assessing whether the program violates this clause, two issues are potentially implicated: (A) whether the program involves government expenditures for benefits of the type prohibited by Section 6, and (B) whether the eligible schools at which the parents can use the vouchers are "religious or theological institutions" as envisioned by Section 6.

We first find it inconceivable that the framers and ratifiers intended to expansively prohibit any and all government expenditures from which a religious or theological institution derives a benefit—for example, fire and police protection, municipal water and sewage service, sidewalks and streets, and the like. Any benefit to religious or theological institutions in the above examples, though potentially substantial, is ancillary and indirect. We hold today that the proper test for examining whether a government expenditure violates Article 1, Section 6, is not whether a religious or theological institution substantially benefits from the expenditure, but whether the expenditure directly benefits such an institution. To hold otherwise would put at constitutional risk every government expenditure incidentally, albeit substantially, benefiting any religious or theological institution. Such interpretation would be inconsistent with our obligation to presume that legislative enactments are constitutional and, if possible, to construe statutes in a manner that renders them constitutional. Section 6 prohibits government expenditures that directly benefit any religious or theological institution. Ancillary indirect benefits to such institutions do not render improper those government expenditures that are otherwise permissible.

The plaintiffs assert that "the absence of any requirement that participating schools segregate the public funds they receive necessarily will directly fund the religious activities that take place in these schools," and that the voucher program "substantially" benefits these schools financially and by "promoting these schools' religious mission" by adding to their enrollment students who otherwise would not be able to afford the tuition. We disagree because the principal actors and direct beneficiaries under the voucher program are neither the State nor program-eligible schools, but lower-income Indiana families with school-age children.

We find that the only direct beneficiaries of the school voucher program are the participating parents and their children, and not religious schools. The program does not contravene Section 6 by impermissibly providing direct benefits to religious institutions.

In light of the prevailing social, cultural, and legal circumstances when Indiana's Constitution was enacted, we understand Section 6 as not intended to prohibit government support of primary and secondary education which at the time included a substantial religious component. This interpretation is consistent with the presumption of constitutionality which we apply when reviewing a claim of statutory unconstitutionality.

For these reasons, we hold that the phrase "religious or theological institutions" in Section 6 of the Indiana Constitution was not intended to, nor does it now, apply to preclude government expenditures for functions, programs, and institutions providing primary and secondary education. We affirm the grant of summary judgment to the defendants.

NOTES

1. For an example of a case in which the state supreme court held that the state and federal constitutions were coextensive, see *Anderson v. Town of Durham*, 895 A.2d 944 (Me. 2006), and for an example of a case in which the court held that they were not, see *Simmons-Harris v. Goff*, 711 N.E.2d 203 (Ohio 1999) ("There is no reason to conclude that the Religion Clauses of the Ohio Constitution are coextensive with those in the United States Constitution.").

2. For articles dealing with these issues in more depth, see Frank R. Kemerer, *The Constitutional Dimension of School Vouchers*, 3 Tex. F. on C.L. & C.R. 137 (1998); Joseph P. Viteritti, *Blaine's Wake: School Choice, The First Amendment, and State Constitutional Law*, 21 Harv. J.L. & Pub. Pol'y 657 (1998).

MOSES v. RUSZKOWSKI
458 P.3d 406 (N.M. 2018)

VIGIL, J.

In this opinion we reconsider the constitutionality of New Mexico's textbook loan program. In *Moses v. Skandera* (*Moses II*) (N.M. 2015), this Court considered whether using public funds to lend textbooks to private school students violated Article XII, Section 3 of the New Mexico Constitution, which precludes the use of public funds "for the support of any sectarian, denominational or private school, college or university." This Court held "that the plain meaning and history of Article XII, Section 3 forbids the provision of books for use by students attending private schools, whether such schools are secular or sectarian." The United States Supreme Court subsequently vacated this Court's judgment and remanded the case for further consideration in light of *Trinity Lutheran Church of Columbia, Inc. v. Comer* (2017).

The Instructional Material Law (IML) establishes an instructional material fund that is administered by the New Mexico Public Education Department. The Department uses the fund to purchase textbooks that are loaned free of charge to public and private school students enrolled in first through twelfth grades and in early childhood education programs. Although schools play a role in the implementation of the IML, they do so as agents for the benefit of their students. The Department allocates the money in the instructional material fund to schools based on the number of students enrolled.

"During the early nineteenth century, public education was provided in public schools known as common schools." These common schools were heavily influenced by non-denominational Protestantism. "By the middle of the nineteenth century," an "influx of Catholic immigrants created a demand for Catholic education, and consequently Catholics and other minority religionists challenged the Protestant influence in the common schools." Protestants responded by "calling for legislation prohibiting sectarian control over public schools and the diversion of public funds to religious institutions." At that time, "it was an open secret that sectarian was code for Catholic."

Although many states voluntarily chose to adopt state constitutional provisions prohibiting the use of public funds for religious schools based on the failed federal Blaine amendment, Congress forced New Mexico and other territories seeking admission to the union to adopt Blaine provisions as a condition of statehood. The Enabling Act required New Mexico to establish and maintain "a system of public schools free from sectarian control," and granted New Mexico "over thirteen million acres of federal land to be held in trust for the benefit of various public schools and other institutions."

In *Moses II*, this Court considered two interpretations of Article XII, Section 3: a permissive interpretation that would allow the state to lend textbooks to private school students under the IML, and a restrictive interpretation that would preclude such lending. Faced with two competing interpretations of Article XII, Section 3, this Court concluded that the more restrictive approach honored the intent behind the failed Blaine amendment and the mandate set forth in the Enabling Act to ensure that no public funds are used to support sectarian schools.

On remand we must consider whether this Court's interpretation of Article XII, Section 3 in *Moses II* conflicts with the First Amendment principles enunciated by the United States Supreme Court in *Trinity Lutheran*.

Under *Trinity Lutheran*, if a state permits private schools to participate in a generally available public benefit program, the state must provide the benefit to religious schools on equal terms. The Supreme Court also emphasized that a state's interest in maintaining church-state separation does not justify the withholding of generally available public benefits based on the religious status of the recipient.

Article XII, Section 3, as interpreted in *Moses II*, enunciates a facially neutral policy of prohibiting the expenditure of public funds to support private schools, both religious and secular. Article XII, Section 3 does not disqualify religious individuals or entities from receiving public benefits based solely on their religious status. Instead, it creates a distinction between public schools and private schools. The First Amendment requires government neutrality toward religious viewpoints; it does not require the state to treat public schools and private schools alike.

Although Article XII, Section 3 is facially neutral toward religion, the Free Exercise Clause may still be implicated if its adoption was motivated by religious animus. Evolving First Amendment jurisprudence suggests that courts should consider the historical and social context underlying a challenged government action to determine whether the action was neutral or motivated by hostility toward religion. *See Masterpiece Cakeshop, Ltd. v. Colo. Civil Rights Comm'n* (2018).

The federal Blaine amendment originated in anti-Catholic prejudice and Congress, through the Enabling Act, forced New Mexico to adopt a Blaine provision as a condition of statehood. This history casts constitutional doubt on the motive underlying Article XII, Section 3. We therefore consider whether the history or circumstances in New Mexico that led to the adoption of Article XII, Section 3 cured the provision's anti-Catholic origins.

New Mexico has a unique history and culture, and the public school debate within New Mexico took a different course than the debate at the national level. Formal schooling commenced in New Mexico with the arrival of the first Franciscan missionaries over four hundred years ago. During that time period, "New Mexico's remote location, its rugged landscape, and its struggling economy made a centralized system of schools no more than a far-off hope."

When New Mexico became a territory, the overwhelming majority of its population consisted of native-born New Mexicans. Catholic Church leaders established new parochial schools during the early territorial days, and the Church maintained control over education in New Mexico into the 1870s. Both New Mexico's public schools and its parochial schools employed members of the Catholic clergy as teachers and used textbooks published by a Catholic printing press.

Although native New Mexicans remained a majority, the number of Anglo-American Protestants in New Mexico increased significantly between 1850 and 1910. "Anglo-American transplants to New Mexico introduced a series of proposals for public education." These proposals met resistance because they "relied on the familiarly Protestant objection to sectarianism" and sought "to eliminate Catholic influence." "Between 1850 and 1891, New Mexico's government failed at multiple attempts to inaugurate a system of tax-supported schools." The ongoing debate over public education evidenced "mounting hostility between public education advocates and the Archdiocese of Santa Fe," and was one of the most pressing problems facing the territorial legislature.

Perceived problems with New Mexico's educational system and widespread illiteracy also posed obstacles to New Mexico becoming a state. Concerns about New Mexico's educational system were exacerbated by "strong prejudice toward its Spanish-speaking, Roman Catholic people." "Anglo-Protestant apprehension about Catholic influence motivated official scrutiny of the Church's role in schooling as soon as New Mexico became part of the United States." "By the last quarter of the century everyone understood that the territory's prospects for joining the Union depended upon the condition of its educational system. Above all, statehood would require schools free from Catholic influence."

In 1891, the territorial legislature passed "an act establishing common schools in the territory of New Mexico and creating the office of superintendent of public instruction." The 1891 act made school attendance compulsory and served as a precursor to the IML by authorizing free textbooks for a child whose "parent or guardian was not able by reason of poverty to buy books." In 1903, the 1891 act was amended to clarify that the textbooks were only loaned to the children and that ownership remained with the school districts.

When Congress passed the Enabling Act for New Mexico in 1910, New Mexico's centralized public school system had been in place for almost two decades. "New Mexico held a constitutional convention that same fall in Santa Fe, and nearly a third of the convention's one hundred elected delegates were native Spanish-speakers." The delegates drafted an array of constitutional provisions related to education. Consistent with the 1891 act, the New Mexico Constitution requires the state to establish and maintain a "uniform system of free public schools sufficient for the education of, and open to, all the children of school age in the state." The Constitution also includes explicit protections for the educational rights of New Mexico's Spanish-speaking citizens.

The constitutional delegation that incorporated explicit protections for Spanish-speaking students into the New Mexico Constitution also drafted Article XII, Section 3, which extended the Enabling Act's restrictions on public funding for sectarian schools to also include "private schools." We cannot ascertain what motivated the delegates to draft Article XII, Section 3. But under the circumstances, it appears that the drafters of Article XII, Section 3 intended to create a provision that would be acceptable to New Mexico voters while fulfilling the mandate set forth in the New Mexico Enabling Act. In the absence of sufficient proof that New Mexico adopted Article XII, Section 3 for a discriminatory purpose, we decline to impute an impermissible motive to the constitutional delegation and New Mexico voters, who approved the Constitution "by an overall majority of three to one."

Even though it appears that the people of New Mexico intended for Article XII, Section 3 to be a religiously neutral provision, the history of the federal Blaine amendment and the New Mexico Enabling Act lead us to conclude that anti-Catholic sentiment tainted its adoption. In *Moses II*, this Court looked to the history of the federal Blaine amendment and the

Enabling Act to conclude that Article XII, Section 3 was intended to preclude any whisper of support for private schools.

Prior to *Trinity Lutheran*, this Court's interpretation of Article XII, Section 3 in *Moses II* fell into the "play in the joints" between what the Establishment Clause permits and what the Free Exercise Clause requires. Following *Moses II*, the Supreme Court emphasized that the Free Exercise Clause is implicated by a law that "singles out the religious for disfavored treatment." The Supreme Court has since underscored in *Masterpiece Cakeshop* the state's constitutional duty to avert religious discrimination. Thus, we conclude that this Court's previous interpretation of Article XII, Section 3 in *Moses II* raises concerns under the Free Exercise Clause.

When interpreting the New Mexico Constitution, we avoid a construction that raises concerns under the federal constitution. When a state constitutional provision "is susceptible to two constructions, one supporting it and the other rendering it void," this Court "should adopt the construction which upholds its constitutionality."

To avoid constitutional concerns, we adopt a construction of Article XII, Section 3 that does not implicate the Free Exercise Clause under *Trinity Lutheran*. Like the 1891 act establishing New Mexico's public school system, the IML grants students access to appropriate textbooks regardless of their parents' financial resources, which helps students fulfill their duty to attend school. Any benefit to private schools is purely incidental and does not constitute "support" within the meaning of Article XII, Section 3. We hold that loaning secular textbooks to private school students under the IML does not violate Article XII, Section 3.

NAKAMURA, C.J., dissenting.

Moses II correctly concluded that the provision of school books under the IML to students who attend private schools—whether secular or religious—violates the plain language of Article XII, Section 3. Understanding what *Trinity Lutheran* does and does not do makes clear that this Court should not abandon this conclusion.

Trinity Lutheran holds that, "if a state awards grants, on religiously neutral criteria, to create safer playground surfaces, it cannot exclude an otherwise eligible playground simply because it is owned by a church." At the heart of the *Trinity Lutheran* Court's holding is the following thought: "If the state neutrally supports playground surfaces for religious and secular daycares alike, and for religious daycares of different faiths, it is supporting daycares, or just playgrounds, but not religion. Equal funding gives the religious daycares no advantage; funding only secular daycares would put religious daycares at a disadvantage." This thought is not a departure from settled First Amendment principles.

The "discrimination" we are faced with here is "public-private, not religious-secular." This difference is critical. Because of this difference, "motive" becomes essential. The question remand to this Court prompts is this: was Article XII, Section 3 "adopted because of a desire to prohibit funding for Catholic education?" "If Article XII, Section 3 was motivated by anti-Catholicism, it should be unconstitutional." Careful attention must be paid to the word "should" in the preceding sentence.

Trinity Lutheran does not resolve the question presented on remand. We can only make educated guesses about how the United States Supreme Court will resolve the issues reserved, and we will only know whether those guesses are correct when the Supreme Court takes up the "next round of cases." While we eagerly await future guidance, we must nevertheless answer the question before us: whether there is sufficient evidence that the motivations for the enactment of Article XII, Section 3 were discriminatory. I cannot conclude sufficient evidence exists.

"Proving the motivation behind official action is often a problematic undertaking." This is particularly true when the official action under review is the drafting of a constitutional provision that occurred a century ago. The problem is only further compounded when the provision under scrutiny is neutral and constitutional on its face.

The history the majority recounts suggests that a straight line of anti-Catholic bigotry runs from the motivations underlying the Blaine Amendment to Article XII, Section 3.

Any attempt at a summary of the many social forces at play in the lead-up to the creation of the Blaine Amendment is beyond the scope of this dissent. It suffices to state that there is reason to doubt the first link in the chain of inferences that must be accepted to conclude that Article XII, Section 3 was motivated by anti-Catholic animus (*i.e.*, that anti-Catholic animus was the sole force behind the Blaine Amendment). The next link— that between the Blaine Amendment and the Enabling Act—is equally susceptible to attack.

As *Moses II* observes, the drafters of our state constitution made a significant drafting decision when writing Article XII, Section 3. Unlike Section 8 of the Enabling Act which "precludes the use of public funds for the support of sectarian or denominational schools," Article XII, Section 3 restricts the use of public funds for "the much broader category of private schools." *Moses II* correctly notes that this drafting choice is self-evidently significant: The drafters of Article XII, Section 3 took affirmative measures to decouple the provision from the problematic language in the Enabling Act. Our understanding of the drafter's motives must incorporate these measures, which strongly suggest that their motives were not discriminatory but the opposite. The majority seems in agreement with this point.

The majority ultimately concludes that they cannot "impute an impermissible motive to the constitutional delegation," and doubt that it is possible to "ascertain what motivated the delegates to draft Article XII, Section 3." They do accept, however, that "the constitutional delegates agreed it was essential to guarantee the civil, religious, and political rights of the native New Mexicans," who were largely Catholic. It is difficult to see how the majority's conclusions and concessions do not end the inquiry in this case and dictate the outcome.

Respondents have not established that Article XII, Section 3 was the product of impermissible, discriminatory motives, and the majority appears to recognize this. All that has been established is that Article XII, Section 3 is guilty by association. But this is insufficient and does not amount to discriminatory intent or purpose as the United States Supreme Court has defined this concept.

Moses II's conclusion that the plain language of Article XII, Section 3 prohibits the state from loaning textbooks to children enrolled in private schools does not run afoul of the principles articulated in *Trinity Lutheran*. There is insufficient evidence Article XII, Section 3 stems from discriminatory motives. The majority disagrees and embraces a construction of Article XII, Section 3 that is inconsistent with the provision's plain language and permits the state to loan secular textbooks to private school students, including religious students. They do so to "avoid constitutional concerns," but these are concerns that do not exist.

NOTE

Nothing is static in this area. Since *Trinity Lutheran*, the U.S. Supreme Court has decided two more cases that seem to place greater limits on state efforts to enforce Blaine amendments and related limitations on providing state aid to religious entities. Both cases involve tuition vouchers that the States, Montana and Maine respectively, refused to allow students to use in faith-based schools. And in both cases, the Court refused to allow the States to enforce the restrictions. *See Espinoza v. Mont. Dep't of Revenue*, 140 S. Ct. 224 (2020); *Carson v. Makin*, 142 S. Ct. 1987 (2022).

CHAPTER XI

SCHOOL FUNDING CLAUSES

A. INTRODUCTION

In *Brown v. Board of Education*, the Supreme Court observed that "education is perhaps the most important function of state and local governments" before holding that access to public schools "must be made available to all on equal terms." 347 U.S. 483, 493 (1954). At the same time that *Brown* removed one impediment to equal educational opportunities, it left in place another: the disfiguring effects of wealth on the type of education that American children receive and the challenges that poverty poses for some public schools wishing to provide an education to their students "on equal terms" with the education offered by their wealthier counterparts.

In the late 1960s, while the federal courts faced lawsuits over the pace of desegregation under the "all deliberate speed" mandate of *Brown II*, *Brown v. Bd. of Educ.*, 349 U.S. 294, 301 (1955), and related lawsuits premised on removing the vestiges of segregation by requiring school districts to use busing to create racially balanced schools, a new form of institutional litigation related to public education emerged—one focused less on the racial makeup of primary and secondary schools and more on the disparities in the quality of education offered to students based on the property wealth of the school districts in which they lived. First in the California state courts, *see Serrano v. Priest*, 5 Cal.3d 584 (1971), and eventually in a federal-court lawsuit filed in Texas, *see Rodriguez v. San Antonio Indep. Sch. Dist.*, 337 F. Supp. 280 (W.D. Tex. 1971), litigants argued that their respective state systems of funding a public education were unconstitutional because they primarily relied on local funding and local control, which permitted wide disparities in the quality of the education that children within the State received based on little more than the property wealth of the school district in which their parents happened to live.

In *Serrano*, the California Supreme Court ruled in favor of the claimants. Relying on the State and Federal Constitutions, the Court made the following points: "the school financing system discriminates on the basis of the wealth of a district and its residents," 5 Cal.3d at 604; "the distinctive and priceless function of education in our society warrants, indeed compels, our treating it as a fundamental interest," *id.* at 608–09; the financing system is not necessary to accomplish a compelling state interest, *id.* at 614; and since the funding system "does not withstand strict scrutiny, it denies to the plaintiffs and others similarly situated the equal protection of the laws," *id.* at 614–15.

In *Rodriguez*, the claimants sought to extend *Serrano*'s federal equal-protection holding from California to Texas and eventually to all other States in the country. They premised their lawsuit on two theories of

595

unconstitutionality: that education is a fundamental right and that wealth is a suspect class. Both theories came to the same end, as each would have required Texas (and eventually each State) to satisfy the rigors of strict scrutiny in justifying its system of funding public schools—a test that would force a State to prove that it had done everything within its power to eliminate the marked disparities between the quality of a public education offered to children living in property-rich and property-poor school districts. A three-judge district court ruled for the plaintiffs. It invoked both grounds of unconstitutionality and held that the Equal Protection Clause guaranteed "fiscal neutrality" in Texas's creation and oversight of a school-funding system. 337 F. Supp. at 284, 286.

In a 5-4 decision, the United States Supreme Court reversed. 411 U.S. 1 (1973). In a decision written by Justice Powell, the Court rejected both claims of unconstitutionality. Education is not a fundamental right entitled to strict scrutiny, it held, because the Constitution nowhere mentions the topic, precluding fundamental-right status on that basis alone. *Id.* at 35. Nor, it added, do individuals have a fundamental right to a governmental benefit merely because that benefit is significant or even essential. Otherwise, a State's allocation of all manner of public benefits—access to housing, food, health care, to name a few—would face strict scrutiny. *Id.* at 37. In rejecting the contention that wealth was a suspect classification, Justice Powell noted that Texas guaranteed all children a free public education regardless of wealth. It thus had not denied its residents a public benefit on the basis of wealth, but had merely created a system that tolerated a relatively worse public benefit to be provided to some citizens on the basis of wealth. *Id.* at 38–39.

Justice Marshall wrote the principal dissent. As the lead advocate for the plaintiffs in *Brown*, he surely understood the stakes of the *Rodriguez* litigation, "including the possibility that the promises of *Brown* would never be fulfilled unless the courts not only eliminated de jure segregation by race but also curbed the effects of de facto segregation by wealth." Jeffrey S. Sutton, San Antonio Independent School District v. Rodriguez *and Its Aftermath*, 94 Va. L. Rev. 1963, 1970 (2008). He concluded that the plain connection between a meaningful education and other constitutional guarantees made it essential to subject discrimination against a "powerless class" over this public benefit to strict scrutiny. *Rodriguez*, 411 U.S. at 109 (Marshall, J., dissenting).

"For better, for worse, or for more of the same, the majority in *Rodriguez* tolerated the continuation of a funding system that allowed serious disparities in the quality of the education a child received based solely on the wealth of the community in which his parents happened to live or could afford to live. Yet even after the Court gave the States the green light to continue relying on that system, they eventually demanded change—in some instances because the political processes prompted it and in other instances because the state courts required it." Sutton, *Rodriguez and Its Aftermath*, 94 Va. L. Rev. at 1971. Thus, although the Supreme Court in *Rodriguez* rejected the California Supreme Court's *federal* equal-protection analysis in *Serrano*, it did not overrule—indeed, it had no power to overrule—*Serrano*'s *state* school-funding ruling or, for that matter, prevent other States from doing the same under their own constitutions.

This chapter focuses on the aftermath of *Rodriguez*. The state-court litigation that followed *Rodriguez* provides a rich example of the independence of state constitutions (and state legislatures) as a source for protecting rights that the Federal Constitution (and national legislature) have not protected. In the several decades since the United States Supreme Court's decision in *Rodriguez*, the vast majority of state supreme courts have considered similar claims under their state constitutions, and an increasing majority of them have ruled in favor of the plaintiffs. The purpose of this chapter is to explore the state courts' resolution of these claims—first by considering state constitutional decisions premised on equality theories of unconstitutionality, then by considering state decisions premised on adequacy theories of unconstitutionality, and finally by considering remedial issues that have arisen in the area.

B. EQUAL PROTECTION DECISIONS

The first wave of state-court decisions after *Rodriguez*, like the *Serrano* decision that preceded *Rodriguez*, principally addressed equal protection claims. As we saw in Chapter V, many state constitutions (but by no means all of them) contain equal protection clauses. In the immediate aftermath of *Rodriguez*, particularly from 1973 to 1989, many school-finance plaintiffs premised their claims for relief on the equal protection clause, or a comparable reading of another clause, found in the State's constitution. As in *Rodriguez*, the claimants focused on the gap in funding between rich and poor school districts and the challenges faced by property-poor districts in closing the gap. While some of these claims succeeded, most did not. *See, e.g., Dupree v. Alma Sch. Dist. No. 30*, 651 S.W.2d 90, 93 (Ark. 1983); *Horton v. Meskill*, 376 A.2d 359, 374 (Conn. 1977); *Pauley v. Kelly*, 255 S.E.2d 859, 878 (W. Va. 1979); *Washakie Cty. Sch. Dist. No. One v. Herschler*, 606 P.2d 310, 333–35 (Wyo. 1980); *see also* Molly S. McUsic, *The Future of* Brown v. Board of Education*: Economic Integration of the Public Schools*, 117 Harv. L. Rev. 1334, 1344 (2004) ("Prior to 1989, virtually every school finance case made its equity claim under a state constitution's equal protection clause."). By 1988, the State defendants had prevailed in 15 of the 22 cases in which an equal protection theory of invalidity had been raised. Michael A. Rebell, "Educational Adequacy, Democracy, and the Courts," *in* National Research Council, *Achieving High Educational Standards for All: Conference Summary* 218, 226–27, n.47 (Timothy Ready et al. eds. 2002). *See also* Sutton, *51 Imperfect Solutions:*

States and the Making of American Constitutional Law, Chapter 3 (Oxford 2018).

HORNBECK v. SOMERSET COUNTY BOARD OF EDUCATION
458 A.2d 758 (Md. 1983)

MURPHY, C.J.

This case involves a challenge to the constitutionality of Maryland statutes which govern the system of financing public elementary and secondary schools in the State's twenty-four school districts, *i.e.*, in the twenty-three counties of Maryland and in Baltimore City. The litigation focuses upon the existence of wide disparities in taxable wealth among the various school districts, and the effect of those differences upon the fiscal capacity of the poorer districts to provide their students with educational offerings and resources comparable to those of the more affluent school districts.

The plaintiffs maintain that the lower court correctly held that the Maryland system of public school finance violates the equal protection guarantee of Art. 24 of the Maryland Declaration of Rights. They contend, as the trial judge held, that the right to education, even if it is not fundamental under the federal constitution, is nevertheless of fundamental caliber under the state constitutional provision because, within the formulation of *Rodriguez*, the right is explicitly guaranteed by the state constitution. Plaintiffs seek to buttress their position by referring to the provisions of § 52 of Art. III of the Maryland Constitution which direct in paragraph (4)(f) that the state budget include an "estimate of all appropriations for the establishment and maintenance throughout the State of a thorough and efficient system of public schools in conformity with Article VIII of the Constitution and with the laws of the State." As paragraph (11) of § 52 directs the Governor to include such estimates for the public schools in the budget "without revision," and because paragraph (6) prohibits the General Assembly from amending the budget to affect the provisions made by the laws of the State for the public school system, the plaintiffs contend that public education is of such high status as to constitute a fundamental right in Maryland. Accordingly, the plaintiffs maintain that the lower court was right in concluding that the State's system of public school financing must be reviewed under the "strict scrutiny" standard, thereby requiring that the State demonstrate that the system promotes a compelling governmental interest—a test with which the Maryland system cannot comply.

While we have not considered the applicability of the *Rodriguez* test in determining whether a right is fundamental for purposes of equal protection review under Art. 24 of the Declaration of Rights, a number of states have considered, and rejected, that test in considering whether education is a fundamental right under state constitutional provisions similar to Art. VIII of the Maryland Constitution. These cases point out that state constitutions, unlike the federal constitution, are not of limited or delegated powers and are not restricted to provisions of fundamental import; consequently, whether a right is fundamental should not be predicated on its explicit or implicit inclusion in a state constitution.

These cases also point out that other public services, such as police, fire, welfare, health care, and other social services, which benefit the entire population, are equally as important as education, even though they may not be mentioned in the state constitution. The observation has been made by one court that in terms of "fundamentality" there is little by way of essential difference between any of these vital areas of state concern, so that to apply a strict scrutiny analysis to legislation dealing with any of these "rights" is "to render automatically suspect every statutory classification made by state legislatures in dealing with matters which today occupy a substantial portion of their time and attention." In this regard, it must be noted that many, if not all, of these rights could, within the *Rodriguez* formulation of fundamental rights, be deemed implicitly guaranteed in most state constitutions, thereby requiring application of the strict scrutiny test—a result which the defendants say is certain to wreak havoc with the ability of state legislatures to deal effectively with such critical governmental services. To conclude that education is a right so fundamental as to require strict scrutiny analysis would, the defendants say, likely render unconstitutional a substantial portion of the statutes, bylaws and practices that regulate education in Maryland. The defendants advance the further suggestion that if there must be, as the trial judge held, a compelling State interest that would justify deviation from mathematically exact dollar per pupil equality among all of the school districts, intradistrict disparities between areas, schools and even classes within schools in the same county could not be sustained. Similarly, if the right to education is fundamental, it is suggested that the State would be required to show a compelling interest for maintaining any differences among the State's school districts, even if the differences were not financial.

We recognize, as do all the school finance cases, the vital role public education plays in our society. And we share the view expressed in *Lujan v. Colorado State Board of Education* (Colo. 1982) that education "can be a major factor in an individual's chances for economic and social success as well as a unique influence on a child's development as a good citizen and on his future participation in political and community life." Nevertheless, we conclude that education is not a fundamental right for purposes of equal protection analysis under Art. 24 of the Declaration of Rights.

We decline to adopt the overly simplistic articulation of the fundamental rights test set forth in *Rodriguez*, *i.e.*, that the existence of a fundamental right is determined by whether it is explicitly or implicitly guaranteed in the constitution. Maryland's Constitution explicitly, not to mention implicitly, guarantees rights and interests which can in no way be considered "fundamental."

The directive contained in Article VIII of the Maryland Constitution for the establishment and maintenance of a thorough and efficient statewide system of free public schools is not alone sufficient to elevate education to fundamental status. Nor do the budgetary provisions of § 52 of Article III of the Constitution require that we declare that the right to education is fundamental. The right to an adequate education in Maryland is no more fundamental than the right to personal security, to fire protection, to welfare subsidies, to health care, or like vital governmental services; accordingly, strict scrutiny is not the proper standard of review of the Maryland system of financing its public schools.

Plaintiffs next argue that "heightened review" is the appropriate standard for determining the constitutionality of Maryland's system of public school finance under Art. 24 of the Declaration of Rights because the system affects important personal rights to education and significantly interferes with or denies the exercise of such rights. Under this standard, as another Court of Appeals of Maryland decision points out, a legislative classification must rest upon some ground of difference having a fair and substantial relationship to the object of the legislation. If this standard of review is applicable, it would, for reasons set forth hereinafter in considering the legislative purpose underlying the Maryland system of public school finance, satisfy the requirements of the "heightened review" test, *i.e.*, the means of financing the public school system do bear a fair and substantial relationship to the legitimate goal of providing an adequate education for all children, while at the same time maintaining the viability of local control. We hold, however, that the heightened review test is not applicable in this case because, as we have already observed, there has been no significant interference with, infringement upon, or deprivation of the underlying right to take advantage of a thorough and efficient education under Art. VIII of the Maryland Constitution.

HORTON v. MESKILL
376 A.2d 359 (Conn. 1977)

HOUSE, C.J.

As other courts have recognized, educational equalization cases are, "in significant aspects, sui generis" and not subject to analysis by accepted conventional tests or the application of mechanical standards. The wealth discrimination found among school districts differs materially from the usual equal protection case where a fairly defined indigent class suffers discrimination to its peculiar disadvantage. The discrimination is relative rather than absolute. Further, the children living in towns with relatively low assessable property values are afforded public education but, as the trial court found, the education they receive is to a substantial degree narrower and lower in quality than that which pupils receive in comparable towns with a larger tax base and greater ability to finance education. True, the state has mandated local provision for a basic educational program with a local option for a program of higher quality; but, as the trial court's finding indicates, that option, to a town which lacks the resources to implement the higher quality educational program which it desires, and which is available to property-richer towns, is highly illusory. As Mr. Justice Marshall put it in his dissent in *Rodriguez*: "This Court has never suggested that because some adequate level of benefits is provided to all, discrimination in the provision of services is therefore constitutionally excusable. The Equal Protection Clause is not addressed to the minimal sufficiency but rather to the unjustifiable inequalities of state action. It mandates nothing less than that all persons similarly circumstanced shall be treated alike." With justification, the trial court found merit to the complaints of the plaintiffs about "the sheer irrationality" of the state's system of financing education in the state on the basis of property values, noting that their argument "would be similar and no less tenable should the state make educational expenditures dependent upon some other irrelevant factor, such as the number of telephone poles in the district."

We find our thinking to be substantially in accord with the decisions of the New Jersey Supreme Court in *Robinson v. Cahill* (N.J. 1973) and the California Supreme Court in *Serrano v. Priest* (Cal. 1976) (*Serrano II*), and whether we apply the "fundamentality" test adopted by *Rodriguez* or the pre-*Rodriguez* test under our state constitution (as the California Supreme Court did in *Serrano II*) or the "arbitrary" test applied by the New Jersey Supreme Court in *Robinson v. Cahill*, we must conclude that in Connecticut the right to education is so basic and fundamental that any infringement of that right must be strictly scrutinized.

"Connecticut has for centuries recognized it as her right and duty to provide for the proper education of the young." Education is so important that the state has made it compulsory through a requirement of attendance. The General Assembly has by word, if not by deed, recognized that it is the concern of the state that "each child shall have equal opportunity to receive a suitable program of educational experiences." Indeed the concept of equality is expressly embodied in the constitutional provision for distribution of the school fund in that the fund "shall be inviolably appropriated to the support and encouragement of the public schools throughout the state, and for the equal benefit of all the people thereof."

The present-day problem arises from the circumstance that over the years there has arisen a great disparity in the ability of local communities to finance local education, which has given rise to a consequent significant disparity in the quality of education available to the youth of the state. It was well stated in the memorandum of decision of the trial court, which noted that the

> present method of financing education in the state is the result of legislation in which the state delegates to municipalities of disparate financial capability the state's duty of raising funds for operating public schools within that municipality. That legislation gives no consideration to the financial capability of the municipality to raise funds sufficient to discharge another duty delegated to the municipality by the state, that of educating the children within that municipality. The evidence in this case is that, as a result of this duty-delegating to Canton without regard to Canton's financial capabilities, pupils in Canton receive an education that is in a substantial degree lower in both breadth and quality than that received by pupils in municipalities with a greater financial capability, even though there is no difference between the constitutional duty of the state to the children in Canton and the constitutional duty of the state to the children in other towns.

We conclude that without doubt the trial court correctly held that, in Connecticut, elementary and secondary education is a fundamental right, that pupils in the public schools are entitled to the equal enjoyment of that right, and that the state system of financing public elementary and secondary education as it presently exists and operates cannot pass the test of "strict judicial scrutiny" as to its constitutionality. These were the basic legal conclusions reached by the court.

While the development of an appropriate legislative plan is not without its complexities, the problem is not insoluble. Nor do we share the alarm expressed in the dissenting opinion at what it concludes are "the implications of the decision" as requiring total state financing of education, loss of local administrative control over educational decisions, and the requirement that education in all towns "be brought up to the Darien standard," which, if it occurred, the trial court found would require an increase of $313,000,000 over the amounts being currently expended. To the contrary, as we have noted, the trial court expressly found that none of these consequences would of necessity follow the adoption by the state of a financing program designed to achieve a substantial degree of equality of educational opportunity and permit all towns to exercise a meaningful choice as to educational services to be offered to students, that the property tax is still a viable means of producing income for education, and that there is no reason why local control needs to be diminished in any degree merely because some system other than the one presently in effect is adopted. We find no reason to reject the validity of these findings. Obviously, absolute equality or precisely equal advantages are not required and cannot be attained except in the most relative sense. Logically, the state may recognize differences in educational costs based on relevant economic and educational factors and on course offerings of special interest in diverse communities. None of the basic alternative plans to equalize the ability of various towns to finance education requires that all towns spend the same amount for the education of each pupil. The very uncertainty of the extent of the nexus between dollar input and quality of educational opportunity requires allowance for variances as do individual and group disadvantages and local conditions.

VINCENT v. VOIGHT
614 N.W.2d 388 (Wis. 2000)

CROOKS, J.

A majority of this court holds that Wisconsin students have a fundamental right to an equal opportunity for a sound basic education. An equal opportunity for a sound basic education is one that will equip students for their roles as citizens and enable them to succeed economically and personally. The legislature has articulated a standard for equal opportunity for a sound basic education in Wis. Stat. §§ 118.30(lg)(a) and 121.02(L) (1997–98) as the opportunity for students to be proficient in mathematics, science, reading and writing, geography, and history, and to receive instruction in the arts and music, vocational training, social sciences, health, physical education, and foreign language, in accordance with their age and aptitude. An equal opportunity for a sound basic education acknowledges that students and districts are not fungible and takes into account districts with disproportionate numbers of disabled students, economically disadvantaged students, and students with limited English language skills. So long as the legislature is providing sufficient resources so that school districts offer students the equal opportunity for a sound basic education as required by the constitution, the state school finance system will pass constitutional muster.

We conclude that the school finance system articulated in Wis. Stat. ch. 121 is constitutional under both art. X, § 3 and art. I, § 1 of the Wisconsin Constitution. The Petitioners have not shown beyond a reasonable doubt that the current school financing system violates either art. X, § 3, or art. I, § 1, and therefore, they have not made out a prima facie case in support of their motion for summary judgment.

ABRAHAMSON, C.J., concurring in part and dissenting in part.

The framers of the Wisconsin Constitution recognized the importance of education when they created article X governing the establishment and funding of public schools. Creating a system of free and uniform public schools was considered to be among the most essential of the framers' tasks. Throughout the 1846 and 1848 conventions, the framers expressed the desire that all of Wisconsin's students, rich and poor, would be educated together in the public schools. For example, the requirement in article X, § 4 that localities contribute to school funding was included "directly for the advantage of the poor," because it increased the commitment to local schools. Without local support "the common schools languished, and select schools rose on their ruins."

Article X, read as a whole, demonstrates that the framers intended to require the legislature to create and finance a school system that is equitable and uniform in character throughout the state and that provides equal educational opportunity for all students.

The constitution "virtually declares that public education is a state power and function, based upon the well-established principle that the whole state is interested in the education of the children of the state and that this function must be exercised by the people as a whole." The framers believed that the creation of free and uniform public schools was "the only system on which we could depend for the preservation of our liberties." The legislature has recognized that "education is a state function" and that "the state must guarantee that a basic educational opportunity be available to each pupil."

The framers of the Wisconsin Constitution did not intend the school districts' boundaries to be uniform and therefore could not have envisioned the school districts' taxing and spending capacity to be uniform, since taxing and spending ability and school district boundaries are related. But the state school finance system must provide districts and schools with the funding needed to meet the constitutional mandate. The record, which is undisputed, shows that school districts vary widely in the amount spent per student (ranging from $13,534 to $5,301), in the ability to raise dollars for every mill levied, and in the actual levy rates.

The plaintiff-intervenors, the Wisconsin Education Association Council and a number of teachers and school administrators from school districts across the state, assert that the state school finance system is unconstitutional because it does not allow districts with significant numbers of high-needs students to offer these students an adequate educational opportunity. High-needs students include disabled children, economically disadvantaged children and children with limited skills in the English language. The State's brief concedes, as it must, that it probably costs more per child to educate high-needs students.

A non-uniform education can result from treating similarly situated students and school districts differently, but it can also result from treating differently situated students and school districts in the same way. Consequently, to ensure that all students have an opportunity for a sound basic education, school districts with a disproportionate number of high-needs students must be provided with extra financial resources to meet the standard that is constitutionally required.

Because the state school finance system fails to address the costs of educating high-needs students, the plaintiff-intervenors argue that schools or school districts with a disproportionate number of such students are not able to provide anywhere near the educational opportunities of other schools or school districts. While the state school finance system especially fails property-poor school districts with disproportionate numbers of high-needs students, the plaintiff-intervenors assert that even property-rich school districts that have disproportionate numbers of high-needs students, such as Madison, are unable to offer educational opportunities that are uniform with the rest of the state. School districts with large numbers of high-needs students may have to divert funds to pay for the higher costs associated with the high-needs students, leaving the other students at a disadvantage.

Although I realize that equal dollars do not necessarily translate to equal educational opportunity, it is clear that substantial funding differences may significantly affect students' opportunities to learn. Money is not the only variable affecting educational opportunity, but it is one that the legislature can equalize.

Both the circuit court and court of appeals acknowledged that they were unable to adequately adjudicate this case because of the lack of a developed standard from this court regarding the requirements of article X, § 3. I would remand the cause to the circuit court for further proceedings in light of the standard the majority opinion sets forth in the present case to determine whether the defendants have met their constitutional obligation.

SYKES, J., concurring in part and dissenting in part.

I agree with the majority's conclusion that the state school finance system is not unconstitutional under Wis. Const. art. X, § 3, the uniformity clause of the education article, or Wis. Const. art. I, § 1, the Equal Protection Clause. Therefore, I join some of the majority opinion, as well as the decision to affirm. However, I cannot agree with other parts of the majority opinion, which announce an expansive new state constitutional right under art. X, § 3 to "an equal opportunity for a sound basic education," defined as an education "that will equip students for their roles as citizens and enable them to succeed economically and personally."

The petitioners allege that the current school finance formula violates the uniformity clause of the education article as well as the Equal Protection Clause of the Wisconsin Constitution by creating or failing to redress alleged educational disparities in so-called "property-poor" districts, districts with many high-needs children, and districts where charter schools and the school choice program decrease the enrollment in the public schools.

Any definition of education or standard for educational adequacy is inherently a political and policy question, not a justiciable one. The people of this state—through their elected representatives in the legislature, the governor's office, and local school boards—decide what their schools will teach and how much education is adequate or desirable for their children. What constitutes an "adequate" or "sound" or even "basic" education is most emphatically not a question of constitutional law for this or any other court.

There is certainly nothing in the text of art. X, § 3 to support such a conclusion. Wisconsin Const. art. X, § 3 provides:

> The legislature shall provide by law for the establishment of district schools, which shall be as nearly uniform as practicable; and such schools shall be free and without charge for tuition to all children between the ages of 4 and 20 years.

The newly-minted constitutional right is as follows: "Wisconsin students have a fundamental right to an equal opportunity for a sound basic education. An equal opportunity for a sound basic education is one that will equip students for their roles as citizens and enable them to succeed economically and personally." The new right to education includes "the opportunity for students to be proficient in mathematics, science, reading and writing, geography, and history, and for them to receive instruction in the arts and music, vocational training, social sciences, health, physical education, and foreign language, in accordance with their age and aptitude." There is more: "An equal opportunity for a sound basic education acknowledges that students and districts are not fungible and takes into account districts with disproportionate numbers of disabled students, economically disadvantaged students, and students with limited English language skills." And the legislature must henceforward provide "sufficient resources" to meet the new standard; otherwise, it will be in violation of art. X, § 3.

The problem with all of this is that there is no support for it anywhere in the text of the Wisconsin Constitution. It is entirely the product of judicial invention, despite efforts to tie some parts of the standard to particular statutory enactments. This may be fine education policy, and as a parent and a citizen I certainly support the educational aspirations and goals expressed by the new standard, as well as the requirement that schools include instruction in the specified curricular subject areas. But as a judge, I am compelled to say as forcefully as I can that the court's exercise in education-clause standard-writing has nothing whatsoever to do with constitutional law.

My conclusion is based upon the text of art. X, § 3, the obvious lack of judicially discoverable or manageable standards for educational adequacy, and the impossibility of deciding the issue without undertaking an initial, clearly nonjudicial policy determination.

NOTE

Whether before 1989 or after, claimants who prevailed on state-law equal protection grounds were the exception that proved the proverbial rule. Most of these claims failed. One problem with this theory of unconstitutionality, as with many federal and state equal protection claims, is the all-or-nothing nature of tiers of review. For many state courts, applying strict or intermediate review to all manner of educational policy decisions—including what subjects are offered, when classes are taught, and what sports teams are available—was a bridge too far, establishing a level of scrutiny that was too difficult for States and local governments to satisfy. Yet at the same time, applying rational basis review created a level of scrutiny that was too easy for States to meet. Another problem, one to which we will return at the end of this chapter, concerned the remedy. Even when the claimants managed to win under this theory, the courts struggled to identify meaningful and realistic remedies for closing the equity gap. Some remedies effectively required a statewide school-funding system that precluded local school districts from supplementing state aid. Others created a system that came to the same result—one that set a floor and a ceiling on educational spending. Still another obstacle to litigation success in these cases is that state legislatures after *Rodriguez* increasingly removed the most problematic disparity-causing features of their systems for funding public schools. In particular, they adopted school-funding equalization formulas that, to one degree or another, ameliorated but did not eliminate funding disparities.

C. ADEQUACY DECISIONS

The obstacles facing these equal protection challenges prompted a second wave of state-court lawsuits. From 1989 to the present, claimants in this area frequently have seized on a different theory of unconstitutionality. Instead of focusing on equal protection and equity problems, as the claimants in *Rodriguez*, *Serrano*, and the above cases did, these plaintiffs relied on unique state constitutional provisions that have no counterpart in the Federal Constitution. Many States, for example, have provisions in their constitutions requiring the legislature to create a "thorough and efficient system of common schools." While some of the equity decisions looked to these provisions in deciding whether the State recognized a fundamental right to education, they generally did not use the provisions to assess the adequacy of the state system. Relying on these provisions, recent school-funding claimants have placed less emphasis on the equity gap between property-poor and property-wealthy school districts, targeting instead the States' methods for determining the *adequacy* of the education they were guaranteeing to all children and families within their jurisdiction. At the core of these lawsuits is the contention that a State's legislative commitment to equalize educational opportunities by guaranteeing to fund a base level of education, no matter how little revenue a local school district can raise on its own, came to little if the state-guaranteed funding level was too low. The objective of these lawsuits, then, was to rationalize and eventually to increase the state spending floor. In contrast to the first wave of litigation in this area, plaintiffs have won at least once in nearly two-thirds of these lawsuits after 1989. As the following cases illustrate, the principal debate in this litigation turns on whether the States' education clauses amount to mere delegations of authority to the state legislatures or whether they also contain judicially enforceable limits on that authority. The first of the cases comes from Texas, the same State that prevailed in the U.S. Supreme Court in *Rodriquez*.

EDGEWOOD INDEPENDENT SCHOOL DISTRICT v. KIRBY
777 S.W.2d 391 (Tex. 1989)

MAUZY, J.

There are approximately three million public school children in Texas. The legislature finances the education of these children through a combination of revenues supplied by the state itself and revenues supplied by local school districts, which are governmental subdivisions of the state. Of total education costs, the state provides about 42%, school districts provide about 50%, and the remainder comes from various other sources including federal funds. School districts derive revenues from local ad valorem property taxes, and the state raises funds from a variety of sources, including the sales tax and various severance and excise taxes.

There are glaring disparities in the abilities of the various school districts to raise revenues from property taxes because taxable property wealth varies greatly from district to district. The wealthiest district has over $14,000,000 of property wealth per student, while the poorest has approximately $20,000; this disparity reflects a 700 to 1 ratio. The 300,000 students in the lowest-wealth schools have less than 3% of the state's property wealth to support their education while the 300,000 students in the highest-wealth schools have over 25% of the state's property wealth; thus the 300,000 students in the wealthiest districts have more than eight times the property value to support their education as the 300,000 students in the poorest districts. The average property wealth in the 100 wealthiest districts is more than twenty times greater than the average property wealth in the 100 poorest districts. Edgewood I.S.D. has $38,854 in property wealth per student; Alamo Heights I.S.D., in the same county, has $570,109 in property wealth per student.

The state has tried for many years to lessen the disparities through various efforts to supplement the poorer districts. Through the Foundation School Program, the state currently attempts to ensure that each district has sufficient funds to provide its students with at least a basic education. Under this program, state aid is distributed to the various districts according to a complex formula such that property-poor districts receive more state aid than do property-rich districts. However, the Foundation School Program does not cover even the cost of meeting the state-mandated minimum requirements. Most importantly, there are no Foundation School Program allotments for school facilities or for debt service. The basic allotment and the transportation allotment understate actual costs, and the career ladder salary supplement for teachers is underfunded. For these reasons and more, almost all school districts spend additional local funds. Low-wealth districts use a significantly greater proportion of their local funds to pay the debt service on construction bonds while high-wealth districts are able to use their funds to pay for a wide array of enrichment programs.

Because of the disparities in district property wealth, spending per student varies widely, ranging from $2,112 to $19,333. Under the existing system, an average of $2,000 more per year is spent on each of the 150,000 students in the wealthiest districts than is spent on the 150,000 students in the poorest districts.

The lower expenditures in the property-poor districts are not the result of lack of tax effort. Generally, the property-rich districts can tax low and spend high while the property-poor districts must tax high merely to spend low.

Property-poor districts are trapped in a cycle of poverty from which there is no opportunity to free themselves. Because of their inadequate tax base, they must tax at significantly higher rates in order to meet minimum requirements for accreditation; yet their educational programs are typically inferior. The location of new industry and development is strongly influenced by tax rates and the quality of local schools. Thus, the property-poor districts with their high tax rates and inferior schools are unable to attract new industry or development and so have little opportunity to improve their tax base.

The amount of money spent on a student's education has a real and meaningful impact on the educational opportunity offered that student. High-wealth districts are able to provide for their students broader educational experiences including more extensive curricula, more up-to-date technological equipment, better libraries and library personnel, teacher aides, counseling services, lower student-teacher ratios, better facilities, parental involvement programs, and drop-out prevention programs. They are also better able to attract and retain experienced teachers and administrators.

Article VII, section 1 of the Texas Constitution provides:

> A general diffusion of knowledge being essential to the preservation of the liberties and rights of the people, it shall be the duty of the Legislature of the State to establish and make suitable provision for the support and maintenance of an efficient system of public free schools.

This is not an area in which the Constitution vests exclusive discretion in the legislature; rather the language of article VII, section 1 imposes on the legislature an affirmative duty to establish and provide for the public free schools. This duty is not committed unconditionally to the legislature's discretion, but instead is accompanied by standards. By express constitutional mandate, the legislature must make "suitable" provision for an "efficient" system for the "essential" purpose of a "general diffusion of knowledge." While these are admittedly not precise terms, they do provide a standard by which this court must, when called upon to do so, measure the constitutionality of the legislature's actions.

There is no reason to think that "efficient" meant anything different in 1875 from what it now means. "Efficient" conveys the meaning of effective or productive of results and connotes the use of resources so as to produce results with little waste; this meaning does not appear to have changed over time.

If our state's population had grown at the same rate in each district and if the taxable wealth in each district had also grown at the same rate, efficiency could probably have been maintained within the structure of the present system. That did not happen. Wealth, in its many forms, has not appeared with geographic symmetry. The economic development of the state has not been uniform. Some cities have grown dramatically, while their sister communities have remained static or have shrunk. Formulas that once fit have been knocked askew. Although local conditions vary, the constitutionally imposed state responsibility for an efficient education system is the same for all citizens regardless of where they live.

We conclude that, in mandating "efficiency," the constitutional framers and ratifiers did not intend a system with such vast disparities as now exist. Instead, they stated clearly that the purpose of an efficient system was to provide for a "*general* diffusion of knowledge." The present system, by contrast, provides not for a diffusion that is general, but for one that is limited and unbalanced. The resultant inequalities are thus directly contrary to the constitutional vision of efficiency.

The legislature's recent efforts have focused primarily on increasing the state's contributions. More money allocated under the present system would reduce some of the existing disparities between districts but would at best only postpone the reform that is necessary to make the system efficient. A band-aid will not suffice; the system itself must be changed.

We hold that the state's school financing system is neither financially efficient nor efficient in the sense of providing for a "general diffusion of knowledge" statewide, and therefore that it violates article VII, section 1 of the Texas Constitution. Efficiency does not require a per capita distribution, but it also does not allow concentrations of resources in property-rich school districts that are taxing low when property-poor districts that are taxing high cannot generate sufficient revenues to meet even minimum standards. There must be a direct and close correlation between a district's tax effort and the educational resources available to it; in other words, districts must have substantially equal access to similar revenues per pupil at similar levels of tax effort. Children who live in poor districts and children who live in rich districts must be afforded a substantially equal opportunity to have access to educational funds. Certainly, this much is required if the state is to educate its populace efficiently and provide for a general diffusion of knowledge statewide.

Although we have ruled the school financing system to be unconstitutional, we do not now instruct the legislature as to the specifics of the legislation it should enact; nor do we order it to raise taxes. The legislature has primary responsibility to decide how best to achieve an efficient system. We decide only the nature of the constitutional mandate and whether that mandate has been met. Because we hold that the mandate of efficiency has not been met, we reverse the judgment of the court of appeals. The legislature is duty-bound to provide for an efficient system of education, and only if the legislature fulfills that duty can we launch this great state into a strong economic future with educational opportunity for all.

DeROLPH v. STATE
677 N.E.2d 733 (Ohio 1997)

SWEENEY, J.

Section 2, Article VI of the Ohio Constitution requires the *state* to provide and fund a system of public education and includes an explicit directive to the General Assembly:

> The general assembly shall make such provisions, by taxation, or otherwise, as, with the income arising from the school trust fund, will secure a thorough and efficient system of common schools throughout the State.

The delegates to the 1850–1851 Constitutional Convention recognized that it was the *state's* duty to both present and future generations of Ohioans to establish a framework for a "full, complete and efficient system of public education." Thus, throughout their discussions, the delegates stressed the importance of education and reaffirmed the policy that education shall be afforded to every child in the state regardless of race or economic standing. Furthermore, the delegates were concerned that the education to be provided to our youth not be mediocre but be as perfect as could humanly be devised. These debates reveal the delegates' strong belief that it is the *state's* obligation, through the General Assembly, to provide for the full education of all children within the state.

In addition to deteriorating buildings and related conditions, it is clear from the record that many of the school districts throughout the state cannot provide the basic resources necessary to educate our youth. For instance, many of the appellant school districts have insufficient funds to purchase textbooks and must rely on old, outdated books. For some classes, there were no textbooks at all.

Additionally, many districts lack sufficient funds to comply with the state law requiring a district-wide average of no more than twenty-five students for each classroom teacher. Indeed, some schools have more than thirty students per classroom teacher, with one school having as many as thirty-nine students in one sixth grade class. As the testimony of educators established, it is virtually impossible for students to receive an adequate education with a student-teacher ratio of this magnitude.

All the facts documented in the record lead to one inescapable conclusion—Ohio's elementary and secondary public schools are neither thorough nor efficient. The operation of the appellant school districts conflicts with the historical notion that the education of our youth is of utmost concern and that Ohio children should be educated adequately so that they are able to participate fully in society. Our state Constitution was drafted with the importance of education in mind. In contrast, education under the legislation being reviewed ranks miserably low in the state's priorities. Consequently, the present school financing system contravenes the clear wording of our Constitution and the framers' intent.

Furthermore, rather than following the constitutional dictate that it is the *state's* obligation to fund education (as this opinion has repeatedly underscored), the legislature has thrust the majority of responsibility upon local school districts. This, too, is contrary to the clear wording of our Constitution. The responsibility for maintaining a thorough and efficient school system falls upon the state. When a district falls short of the constitutional requirement that the system be thorough and efficient, it is the state's obligation to rectify it

We also reject the notion that the wide disparities in educational opportunity are caused by the poorer school districts' failure to pass levies. The evidence reveals that the wide disparities are caused by the funding system's overreliance on the tax base of individual school districts. What this means is that the poor districts simply cannot raise as much money even with identical tax effort.

We recognize that disparities between school districts will always exist. By our decision today, we are not stating that a new financing system must provide equal educational opportunities for all. In a Utopian society, this lofty goal would be realized. We, however, appreciate the limitations imposed upon us. Nor do we advocate a "Robin Hood" approach to school financing reform. We are not suggesting that funds be diverted from wealthy districts and given to the less fortunate. There is no "leveling down" component in our decision today.

Moreover, in no way should our decision be construed as imposing spending ceilings on more affluent school districts. School districts are still free to augment their programs if they choose to do so. However, it is futile to lay the entire blame for the inadequacies of the present system on the taxpayers and the local boards of education. Although some districts have the luxury of deciding where to allocate extra dollars, many others have the burden of deciding which educational programs to cut or what financial institution to contact to obtain yet another emergency loan. Our state Constitution makes the state responsible for educating our youth. Thus, the state should not shirk its obligation by espousing cliches about "local control."

We recognize that money alone is not the panacea that will transform Ohio's school system into a model of excellence. Although a student's success depends upon numerous factors besides money, we must ensure that there is enough money that students have the chance to succeed because of the educational opportunity provided, not in spite of it. Such an opportunity requires, at the very least, that all of Ohio's children attend schools which are safe and conducive to learning. At the present, Ohio does not provide many of its students with even the most basic of educational needs.

MOYER, C.J., dissenting.

Only infrequently are the members of this court required to balance our appreciation for the principle of separation of powers among the three branches of government against our desire to use the considerable powers of this court to mandate action to improve the imperfect. The issue in this very important case is not whether education in Ohio should be better. All seven members of this court would agree that in an ideal school setting, all children would be taught in well-maintained school buildings by teachers with high salaries and would read from the latest-edition school books. Rather, the question presented is whether specific financing statutes adopted by the Ohio General Assembly violate the words and intent of the Ohio Constitution. By its words, the Constitution requires the General Assembly to "make such provisions, by taxation or otherwise, as will secure a thorough and efficient system of common schools throughout the state." We find that the statutes withstand plaintiffs' constitutional challenge because, rather than abdicating its duty, the General Assembly has made provisions by the challenged statutes for funding a system of schools with minimum standards throughout the state. The issues of the level and method of funding, and thereby the quality of the system, are committed by the Constitution to the collective will of the people through the legislative branch.

One cannot disagree with the aspirations of the majority to provide a school system that enables children to "participate fully in society," that provides "high quality educational opportunities," and that "allows its citizens to fully develop their human potential." However, the majority relies upon the phrase "thorough and efficient" to declare Ohio's education financing system unconstitutional despite the fact that our Constitution commits the responsibility for ascribing meaning to the phrase "thorough and efficient" to the General Assembly and not to this court. The majority of this court, moreover, apparently interprets the Constitution as requiring that all schools be of the same undefined level of high quality without relying on any supporting text of the Constitution, and equates imperfect schools with an unconstitutional system of funding. We disagree with these conclusions.

We conclude that the question of what level of funding satisfies the constitutional standard of a "thorough and efficient" system of education is a question of quality that revolves around policy choices and value judgments constitutionally committed to the General Assembly. We conclude that defining a "thorough and efficient" system of education financing is a nonjusticiable question.

Such restraint should be exercised only after the court has decided a threshold justiciable issue, that is, whether the General Assembly has made provision by taxation or otherwise to secure a thorough and efficient system of schools. In view of the clear intention of the delegates to the Constitutional Convention of 1851, the words of the Constitution, and the agreement among the parties to this case that all plaintiff school districts have met the minimum standards set by the State Department of Education, we conclude that the justiciable question has been answered in favor of the defendants.

Although we may personally favor it, it is not this court's place to order the General Assembly to give education "high priority" in its budget allocations, any more than it is our place to set policy or prioritize the allocation of funds to other state programs. Members of the legislative branch represent the collective will of the citizens of Ohio, and the manner in which public schools are funded in this state is a fundamental policy decision that is within the power of its citizens to change. Under our system of government, decisions such as imposing new taxes, allocating public revenues to competing uses, and formulating educational standards are not within the judiciary's authority.

In that determinations of educational funding adequacy and quality are inherently fluid, we believe that the majority's well-intentioned willingness to enter this fray today will only necessitate more comprehensive judicial involvement tomorrow as educational theories and goals evolve, conditions throughout the state change, and the General Assembly responds. The experiences of other states provide ample proof of the troubled history of litigation that ensues when the judiciary deems itself to be the ultimate authority in setting educational funding mechanisms and standards. Many cases from other states confirm the grim reality of a state supreme court involving itself in setting minimum educational standards, which has resulted in years of protracted litigation, ultimately placing the courts in the position of determining state taxation methods, budgetary priorities, and educational policy.

Plaintiffs stipulated in the trial court that they were all in compliance with state minimum standards on their most recent scheduled evaluations.

In that "an Ohio Administrative Code section is a further arm, extension, or explanation of statutory intent implementing a statute passed by the General Assembly," it follows that those plaintiff schools met the standard of adequacy established by the General Assembly at that time. Plaintiffs did not prove that compliance with the minimum standards then in effect was insufficient to provide an adequate education. Plaintiffs did not attempt to prove that any graduate of any of the plaintiff school districts had been refused entrance to college because his or her diploma was unacceptable. No Ohio school was shown to have been denied accreditation. Plaintiffs did not prove that any Ohio child was without a school to attend.

In the absence of proof of a constitutional violation, the fact that hard problems require hard solutions does not justify judicial second-guessing of the educational funding system established by the General Assembly. Regardless of the appeal of plaintiffs' policy arguments before this court, their arguments are simply addressed to the wrong branch of government. Those who believe that the Education Clause should be changed have procedures available to them by which the Constitution can be amended.

Our dissent should not be viewed as an endorsement of the status quo. However, in the absence of a showing that the statutes in question violate the Constitution, responsibility for correcting the funding of Ohio's educational system does not rest with this court.

DeROLPH v. STATE
754 N.E.2d 1184 (Ohio 2001)

MOYER, C.J.

Since it was first docketed in this court in 1995, this dispute has produced from this court no fewer than three signed majority opinions, a *per curiam* opinion, eleven separate concurrences and dissents, and a number of rulings on motions filed by plaintiffs and defendants. Every justice of the court has expressed her and his views regarding the constitutional issue that once again is presented for our disposition nearly six years after the court exercised its discretionary jurisdiction to review the merits. The written opinions of the justices reflect deeply held beliefs regarding the responsibility of the court as an institution and the principles that define the framework by which each justice decides issues brought to the court. The informal and formal discussions among the justices regarding the jurisdictional and merit issues have been of an intensity and duration unmatched by any other case.

The range of the opinions that reflect the decisional process is broad. Despite our differences, however, we all agree upon the fundamental importance of education to the children and citizens of this state. Educated, informed citizens sustain the vitality of our democratic institutions. We agree regarding the goals of public education; we have vigorously disagreed with respect to whether the legislature or the judiciary has the ultimate authority to determine if the goals have been achieved.

The current plan for funding public primary and secondary education adopted by the General Assembly and signed by the Governor is probably not the plan that any one of us would have created were it our responsibility to do so. But that is not our burden, and it is not the test we apply in this decision. None of us is completely comfortable with the decision we announce in this opinion. But we have responded to a duty that is intrinsic to our position as justices on the highest court of the state. Drawing upon our own instincts and the wisdom of Thomas Jefferson, we have reached the point where, while continuing to hold our previously expressed opinions, the greater good requires us to recognize "the necessity of sacrificing our opinions sometimes to the opinions of others for the sake of harmony."

A climate of legal, financial, and political uncertainty concerning Ohio's school-funding system has prevailed at least since this court accepted jurisdiction of the case. We have concluded that no one is served by continued uncertainty and fractious debate. In that spirit, we have created the consensus that we should terminate the role of this court in the dispute.

Despite the extensive efforts of the defendants to produce a plan that meets the requirements announced by this court, changes to the formula are required to make the new plan constitutional:

Base Cost Formula: H.B. 94 recalculates the cost of providing an adequate education to be $4,814 per student in fiscal year 2002. The base cost formula uses one hundred twenty-seven model school districts as a basis for determining base cost support. That number of school districts is achieved by screening out districts in the top and bottom five percent of all Ohio districts based on income and property wealth from the state's pool of the one hundred seventy top-performing districts. Also included within this number are several districts that did not meet twenty of twenty-seven performance standards, but were included regardless because of a rounding procedure included within H.B. 94. R.C. 3317.012(B)(1), last paragraph. As the plaintiffs note, rounding and wealth screens include districts that should not be considered in the base cost formula and exclude districts that should be considered. Plaintiffs' arguments and our review of the record convince us that the formula must be modified to include the top five percent districts and the lower five percent districts, and by considering only those districts that *actually* meet twenty of twenty-seven performance standards without rounding. We make no determination regarding the time in which the state must calculate and implement actual changes in the amount of funds distributed to each district pursuant to today's order, but the new calculations must be applied retroactive to July 1, 2001, and to the subsequent years designated in R.C. 3317.012. Moreover, in determining future biennial budgets through fiscal year 2007, the rate of millage charged off as the local share of base cost funding under divisions (A)(1) and (2) of R.C. 3317.022 may not be changed from twenty-three mills, irrespective of the language of R.C. 3317.012(D)(4) suggesting such a methodology.

The H.B. 94 model calculates its base cost amount using spending data for FY96, adjusted for inflation, or actual FY99 expenditure data, whichever is lower. The state uses the lower of the two figures to compensate for what it terms an "echo effect," or to adjust for districts that spent more than what was actually needed at the base level, due to line-item expenditures, other state funding outside of the foundation formula, and local enhancement revenues. The model districts subject to lowering of their base cost are those that the state determined to be model districts in 1996. As the plaintiffs' experts observed, there has been insufficient evidence presented by the state to justify lowering the base cost amount to adjust for this supposed echo effect. Accordingly, we are persuaded by the plaintiffs that choosing the lower of FY96 expenditures or FY99 actual expenditures is unsupported by the evidence and should not be used to lower the base cost amount figure.

Parity Aid: The parity aid program is a salutary attempt to provide poorer districts with funds similar to those available to wealthier districts that are used to substantially enhance the educational experience of each student. The plan as adopted would fully fund the parity aid program by fiscal year 2006. We have concluded that the parity aid program must be fully funded no later than the beginning of fiscal year 2004.

To summarize, we observe that the state has chosen to retain a foundation program of funding primary and secondary public education. We find that, having so elected, it must, in order to meet the requirements of *DeRolph I* and *DeRolph II*, formulate the base cost of providing an adequate education by using all school districts meeting twenty of twenty-seven performance standards as set forth by the General Assembly in R.C. 3317.012(B)(1)(a) through (aa), without adjustments to exclude districts based on wealth screens, without rounding adjustments to include additional lower-spending districts, and without use of the "echo effect" adjustment, beginning effective July 1, 2001. In addition, the parity aid program established by the General Assembly must be fully funded no later than July 1, 2003.

With full implementation of these modifications to the funding plan adopted by the General Assembly the plan will meet the test for constitutionality created in *DeRolph I* and *DeRolph II*. While the changes will have a fiscal impact, they will not require structural changes to the school foundation program set forth in R.C. Chapter 3317.

One final observation is in order. Historically, the construction and maintenance of school facilities have been considered the responsibility of local school districts. By 1989, the General Assembly had begun addressing school facilities needs and committing funds to construction and repair of school buildings. We have described previously the substantial commitment of the state to the availability of adequate school buildings for every student enrolled in public education. However, the unmet needs are enormous and the time in which it is feasible to meet them is lengthy. We urge the General Assembly to review and consider alternative means of funding school buildings and related facilities.

The state is hereby ordered to implement the changes described above. Because we have no reason to doubt defendants' good faith, we have concluded that there is no reason to retain jurisdiction of the matter before us. If the order receives less than full compliance, interested parties have remedies available to them.

NOTE

Reasonable as this compromise might have seemed, *DeRolph III* did not end the litigation. The State moved for reconsideration of *DeRolph III*, prompting the Court to order the parties to report to a special commissioner to try to settle the case. *DeRolph v. State*, 758 N.E.2d 1113 (Ohio 2001). That did not work either. In response, the Court vacated *DeRolph III* and ordered "a complete systematic overhaul" of the school-funding system. *DeRolph v. State*, 780 N.E.2d 529 (Ohio 2002). After the case was remanded to the trial court and after the trial court tried to enforce the most recent decision, the State successfully filed an original writ of prohibition in the Ohio Supreme Court, prohibiting the trial court from exercising jurisdiction over the case. *State v. Lewis*, 789 N.E.2d 195 (Ohio 2003). As the Court put it, "The duty now lies with the General Assembly to remedy an educational system that has been found by the majority in *DeRolph IV* to still be unconstitutional." *Id*. at 202. In the years since, the Ohio legislature has made changes to its school-funding system, which some claim do not satisfy the requirements of *DeRolph IV* but which no one has challenged in state court.

COLUMBIA FALLS ELEMENTARY SCH. DIST. NO. 6 v. STATE
109 P.3d 257 (Mont. 2005)

LEAPHART, J.

The State appeals from the District Court's order determining that the State of Montana's public school system violates Article X, Section 1(3), of the Montana Constitution.

Article X, Section 1(3), of the Montana Constitution mandates that "the legislature shall provide a basic system of free quality public elementary and secondary schools. It shall fund and distribute in an equitable manner to the school districts the state's share of the cost of the basic elementary and secondary school system." As we stated, the Legislature has made an initial policy determination regarding this language. It has created a public school system and a method of funding the system. Although Article X, Section 1(3), is textually committed to the Legislature in the first instance, once the Legislature acts we are not barred from reaching the question of whether the Legislature has fulfilled its constitutional obligation to "provide a basic system of free quality public elementary and secondary schools."

This funding system is not correlated with any understanding of what constitutes a "quality" education. The evidence for this is two-fold. First, as the State admitted at oral argument, in passing HB 667, the Legislature did not undertake a study of what the Public Schools Clause demands of it. That is, it did not seek to define "quality." As stated above, since the Legislature has not defined "quality" as that term is used in Article X, Section 1(3), we cannot conclude that the current funding system was designed to provide a quality education. Second, as found by the District Court, the Legislature, in creating the spending formula of HB 667, did not link the formula to any factors that might constitute a "quality" education.

The District Court found that the "major problems" with HB 667 were: it provided no mechanism to deal with inflation; it did not base its numbers on costs such as teacher pay, meeting accreditation standards, fixed costs, or costs of special education; increases in allowable spending were not tied to costs of increased accreditation standards or content and performance standards; relevant data was already two years old when the bill was passed; and no study was undertaken to justify the disparity in certain state-provided dollars dispensed to high schools as compared to elementary schools. From these credible findings we must conclude that the Legislature did not endeavor to create a school funding system with quality in mind. Unless funding relates to needs such as academic standards, teacher pay, fixed costs, costs of special education, and performance standards, then the funding is not related to the cornerstones of a quality education.

The above analysis is essentially prospective in nature—that is, it states what the Constitution demands of the Legislature and what the Legislature must do to fashion a constitutional education system. Nonetheless, in order to address the Coalition's claims we have to address the *educational product* that the present school system provides, not just the *manner* in which the Legislature funds that school system. Even given the absence of a definition of "quality" education, the District Court's findings demonstrate that whatever legitimate definition of quality that the Legislature may devise, the educational product of the present school system is constitutionally deficient and that the Legislature currently fails to adequately fund Montana's public school system.

The evidence that the current system is constitutionally deficient includes the following unchallenged findings made by the District Court:

school districts increasingly budgeting at or near their maximum budget authority; growing accreditation problems; many qualified educators leaving the state to take advantage of higher salaries and benefits offered elsewhere; the cutting of programs; the deterioration of school buildings and inadequate funds for building repair and for new construction; and increased competition for general fund dollars between special and general education.

The State counters by arguing that the District Court should have considered output measures, such as test scores, in determining whether the current system is constitutional, and that under such measures Montana compares very favorably with other states. Indeed, Montana's students often do perform quite well on standardized achievement tests. However, current test scores do not tell the whole story. First of all, a "system" of education includes more than high achievement on standardized tests. We have noted elsewhere, for example, that school districts have an interest in integrating their academic programs with extracurricular activities. Secondly, it may be that test scores are not attributable to the current educational system. The voluminous evidence presented at trial established that although Montana's students are testing well when compared with students in similar states, there are serious concerns as to whether this level of achievement will continue. With the District Court's findings of fact in mind, it may be that the achievement registered by Montana's students is not *because* of the current educational system.

Therefore, because the Legislature has not defined what "quality" means we cannot conclude that the current system is designed to provide a "quality" education. Article X, Section 1(3), explicitly requires the Legislature to fund a "quality" educational system. Therefore we defer to the Legislature to provide a threshold definition of what the Public Schools Clause requires. We also conclude, however, that given the unchallenged findings made by the District Court, whatever definition the Legislature devises, the current funding system is not grounded in principles of quality, and cannot be deemed constitutionally sufficient.

ABBOTT v. BURKE
971 A.2d 989 (N.J. 2009)

LaVECCHIA, J.

One of the fundamental responsibilities of the State is to provide a public education for its children. The New Jersey Constitution requires that

> the Legislature shall provide for the maintenance and support of a thorough and efficient system of free public schools for the instruction of all the children in the State between the ages of five and eighteen years.

Today we are almost a decade into the twenty-first century, and nearly twenty years have passed since this Court found that the State's system of support for public education was inadequate as applied to pupils in poorer urban districts. Finding that more severely disadvantaged pupils require more resources for their education, the Court held that the State must develop a funding formula that would provide all children, including disadvantaged children in poorer urban districts, with an equal educational opportunity as measured by the Constitution's thorough and efficient clause. A later decision added that the funding needed to be coupled to a set of educational program standards.

Today's decision marks the twentieth opinion or order issued in the course of the *Abbott* litigation. In the interim, much has changed. There have been significant demographic changes among school districts in terms of the distribution of at-risk pupils and changes in the level of State-provided education funding. The State now maintains that it has heeded our call to create a funding formula based on curriculum content standards and to demonstrate that the formula addresses the needs of disadvantaged students everywhere, thereby achieving constitutional compliance. Therefore, once again we assess the constitutionality of a State school funding system.

This matter is before us on the State's Motion for Review of the Constitutionality of the School Funding Reform Act of 2008 (SFRA). The State's motion seeks a declaration that SFRA's funding formula satisfies the requirements of the thorough and efficient education clause of the New Jersey Constitution and that, therefore, the State is released from the Court's prior remedial orders concerning education funding for students in *Abbott* districts. Specifically, the State asks for elimination of the requirements that *Abbott* districts be provided parity aid and supplemental funding.

We have reviewed the record, the Special Master's findings and recommendations, and the arguments of the parties. We conclude that SFRA is constitutional, to the extent that this record permitted its review. We therefore hold that SFRA's funding formula may be applied in *Abbott* districts, with the following caveats. Our finding of constitutionality is premised on the expectation that the State will continue to provide school funding aid during this and the next two years at the levels required by SFRA's formula each year. Our holding further depends on the mandated review of the formula's weights and other operative parts after three years of implementation.

Our approval of SFRA under the State Constitution relies, as it must, on the information currently available. But a state funding formula's constitutionality is not an occurrence at a moment in time; it is a continuing obligation. Today's holding issues in the good faith anticipation of a continued commitment by the Legislature and Executive to address whatever adjustments are necessary to keep SFRA operating at its optimal level. The three year look-back, and the State's adjustments based on that review, will provide more information about the efficacy of this funding formula. There should be no doubt that we would require remediation of any deficiencies of a constitutional dimension, if such problems do emerge.

With that understanding, SFRA may be implemented as it was designed, as a state-wide unitary system of education funding. The State shall not be required to continue separate funding streams mandated under past remedial orders. During the two-year period until the look-back review occurs, we cannot ignore, as a practical matter, the substantial amount of additional funds that will be available from non-SFRA sources for pupils in *Abbott* districts. The availability of those funds further cushions the transition to SFRA's funding scheme. In sum, although no prediction is without some uncertainty, the record before us convincingly demonstrates that SFRA is designed to provide school districts in this state, including the *Abbott* school districts, with adequate resources to provide the necessary educational programs consistent with state standards.

For several decades, this Court has superintended the ongoing litigation that carries the name *Abbott v. Burke*. The Court's one goal has been to ensure that the constitutional guarantee of a thorough and efficient system of public education becomes a reality for those students who live in municipalities where there are concentrations of poverty and crime. Every child should have the opportunity for an unhindered start in life—an opportunity to become a productive and contributing citizen to our society.

The legislative and executive branches of government have enacted a funding formula that is designed to achieve a thorough and efficient education for every child, regardless of where he or she lives. On the basis of the record before us, we conclude that SFRA is a constitutionally adequate scheme. There is no absolute guarantee that SFRA will achieve the results desired by all. The political branches of government, however, are entitled to take reasoned steps, even if the outcome cannot be assured, to address the pressing social, economic, and educational challenges confronting our state. They should not be locked in a constitutional straitjacket. SFRA deserves the chance to prove in practice that, as designed, it satisfies the requirements of our constitution.

The State's motion, seeking declarations that SFRA satisfies the requirements of the thorough and efficient clause of Article VIII, section 4, paragraph 1 of the New Jersey Constitution and that the funding formula may be implemented in the *Abbott* districts, and further seeking an order relieving the State from this Court's prior remedial orders concerning funding to the *Abbott* districts, is granted. Plaintiffs' cross-motion seeking an order preserving and continuing the status quo concerning enforcement of this Court's prior remedial orders addressing funding to *Abbott* districts is denied.

NOTES

1. The *Abbott* litigation lived on in *Abbott v. Burke*, 20 A.3d 1018 (N.J. 2011), and later motions before the New Jersey Supreme Court. The most recent decision is known as *Abbott XXI*.

2. The "thorough and efficient" clauses and similar guarantees placed in most state constitutions point to a conceptual difference between the state constitutions and their federal counterpart. As Emily Zackin helpfully explains in *Looking for Rights in All the Wrong Places: Why State Constitutions Contain America's Positive Rights* (Princeton 2013), the States, in contrast to the Federal Government, have a long tradition of placing "positive"—or affirmative—obligations on state and local governments in their constitutions, as opposed to merely "negative" restrictions on government. In support of her thesis, she refers to the state constitutional guarantees dealing with the promise of an adequate system of public schools, the rights of employees, and the guarantee of a safe and healthy environment. *See also* Jeffrey S. Sutton, *Courts as Change Agents: Do We Want More—Or Less?* 127 Harv. L. Rev. 1419 (2014) (reviewing Zackin's book).

CITIZENS FOR STRONG SCHOOLS, INC. v. FLORIDA STATE BOARD OF EDUCATION
262 So.3d 127 (Fla. 2019)

PER CURIAM

This case involves a nearly ten-year attempt by Petitioners to have the State of Florida's K-12 public education system declared unconstitutional due to the State's alleged failure to comply with article IX, section 1(a) of the Florida Constitution, which provides in relevant part as follows:

> The education of children is a fundamental value of the people of the State of Florida. It is, therefore, a paramount duty of the state to make adequate provision for the education of all children residing within its borders. Adequate provision shall be made by law for a uniform, efficient, safe, secure, and high quality system of free public schools that allows students to obtain a high quality education.

Specifically, Petitioners seek a declaration that the State is breaching its "paramount duty to make adequate provision for a uniform, efficient, safe, secure, and high quality system of free public schools that allows students to obtain a high quality education." And Petitioners request the courts to order the State "to establish a remedial plan that includes necessary studies to determine what resources and standards are necessary to provide a high quality education to Florida students."

The language in article IX, section 1(a) regarding "fundamental value," "paramount duty of the state," and "efficient, safe, secure, and high quality system of free public schools that allows students to obtain a high quality education" was added in 1998, after the changes were proposed by the

Constitution Revision Commission and approved by the voters. Prior to 1998, article IX, section 1 provided in relevant part as follows:

> Adequate provision shall be made by law for a uniform system of free public schools.

The 1998 amendments were, in part, a response to *Coalition for Adequacy & Fairness in School Funding, Inc. v. Chiles* (1996), in which this Court upheld the trial court's dismissal with prejudice of a complaint that "asked the trial court to declare that an adequate education is a fundamental right and that the State has failed to provide its students that fundamental right by failing to allocate adequate resources for a uniform system of free public schools." The allegations in *Coalition*—made in the context of "a blanket assertion that the entire system is constitutionally inadequate"—focused on purported inadequacies in funding and disparities relating to certain subgroups of students, including "economically deprived students," disabled students, and "students in property-poor counties." This Court upheld the dismissal because the appellants made "an insufficient showing to justify judicial intrusion" into the Legislature's powers and responsibilities.

We conclude that our precedent in *Coalition* defeats Petitioners' claim because they—like the appellants in *Coalition*—fail to present any manageable standard by which to avoid judicial intrusion into the powers of the other branches of government.

This case began in November 2009—in the wake of the Great Recession—when certain public school students, parents, and citizen organizations filed suit against the State Board of Education, the President of the Florida Senate, the Speaker of the Florida House of Representatives, and the Florida Commissioner of Education seeking a declaration that the State is breaching its paramount duty under article IX, section 1(a). Or, as the First District later described it, Petitioners' claim is "that the State's entire K-12 public education system—which includes 67 school districts, approximately 2.7 million students, 170,000 teachers, 150,000 staff members, and 4,000 schools—is in violation of the Florida Constitution."

This Court is being asked to determine whether in this case we have been presented with a manageable standard for assessing—in the context of a blanket challenge to the constitutionality of the K-12 education system—whether the State has made "adequate provision" for an "efficient" and "high quality" system of education "that allows students to obtain a high quality education" under article IX, section 1(a) of the Florida Constitution. The trial court and the First District both held in the negative, relying on the reasoning in *Coalition*.

We agree with the lower courts that Petitioners' blanket challenge does not survive the reasoning in *Coalition*, notwithstanding the 1998 amendments to article IX, section 1(a). This case turns in part on

Petitioners' failure to present the courts with any roadmap by which to avoid intruding into the powers of the other branches of government.

At the outset, we strongly reject any suggestion in the dissenting opinions that those of us agreeing to approve the result reached by the First District are shirking a constitutional duty or somehow care less than the dissenting justices about the education of Florida's children. Indeed, the refusal to recognize both the blanket nature of Petitioners' challenge and that this case amounts to a request for the courts to determine the appropriate amount of education funding explains in large part the asserted struggle to understand the "judicial universe" in which this case is being decided.

This suit began nearly a decade ago in what largely resembled a funding challenge to the "2009 Appropriations Act." Since then, not only has that appropriations act come and gone, but so too have many subsequent appropriations acts. Moreover, in that same time span, the Legislature has revised—on more than one occasion—the standards and assessments complained of by Petitioners. And the trial court explained how the State's process for developing, administering, scoring, and reporting is "an inclusive process involving Florida educators all along the way." The point being, the education system—and education policy itself—does not remain static and is instead continually being shaped by various interested parties. Thus, Petitioners' challenge is fundamentally different than a challenge to a specific program or a specific funding issue. In effect, Petitioners ask this Court to declare the current educational system unconstitutional based on years-old evidence.

In *Coalition*, this Court upheld a dismissal with prejudice of a blanket challenge to the "adequacy" of the entire K-12 system—a challenge that bears a close resemblance to the challenge here. This Court rejected the challenge in part because the phrase "adequate provision" did not have "straightforward content." In doing so, this Court explained that previous cases attempting to interpret the education article all involved some "specific" challenge. This Court thus balked at the possibility of intruding into the powers of the other branches, including possibly being expected "to evaluate, and either affirm or set aside, future appropriations decisions." However, this Court refused to say "never." Rather, the case turned on the challengers' "failure to demonstrate an appropriate standard that would not present a substantial risk of judicial intrusion."

The 1998 amendments to article IX, section 1 undoubtedly heightened the Legislature's mandate to "a paramount duty." But the fact that the Legislature's duty to make "adequate provision" was heightened does not in and of itself provide the courts with "an appropriate standard for determining adequacy." Rather, the primary issue here is whether the term "high quality" provides such a standard.

Looking to the language of article IX, section 1(a), we conclude that the term "high quality" in and of itself does not have "straightforward content," at least in the context of a blanket challenge to the adequacy of the entire K-12 system. Indeed, "high quality" can reasonably be viewed as "puffing." It is thus hardly surprising that article IX, section 1(a) was subsequently amended in 2002 to constitutionalize a *specific statewide policy*—a classroom-size policy—along with a funding directive to "assure that children attending public schools obtain a high quality education."

Petitioners' argument largely is that the constitutional test "for measuring whether the State is providing an opportunity for a high quality education" should be based solely on the assessment results that measure whether students have learned the core content standards established by the Legislature. In other words, Petitioners do not ask this Court to define "high quality." Rather, they assert that the Legislature itself has already defined "high quality" and how to measure it. They thus allege that the educational system is constitutionally inadequate because the "assessment results show low achievement and wide disparities," particularly "for children experiencing poverty or attending school in poorer school districts."

Petitioners essentially ask this Court to constitutionalize the Legislature's own standards, which, in part, serve as goals. We reject that argument. In effect, Petitioners' argument is that a "high quality" system is whatever the Legislature says it is, so long as some acceptable—yet unknown—percentage of all subgroups of students achieve a satisfactory level of "3" on the assessment. Nothing in the language of article IX, section 1(a) supports Petitioners' argument. Nor does this Court's case law. Moreover, as amicus Foundation for Excellence in Education logically points out, "adopting State standards as constitutional minima would have the perverse effect of encouraging the *weakening* of curriculum standards in order to achieve higher passage rates and to satisfy court-imposed requirements."

Not only do Petitioners conflate constitutional requirements with legislative standards, they also ignore—as do the dissenters—that in the years since this suit was first filed, the Legislature has revised the complained-of standards and assessments on more than one occasion. Moreover, Petitioners' argument flies in the face of the trial court's detailed findings, none of which Petitioners challenge for lacking a basis in the record. As just a few examples, the trial court found that: "Florida has been a national leader in education reform"; Florida *intentionally* adopted rigorous standards and set cut scores at a level that places the majority of students below the satisfactory level; scoring a "Level 1 or 2" on the assessment "is not an indication that a student can't read or is illiterate"; the State's "high performance standards have led to improvement over time"; and Florida "has outpaced the nation in closing" achievement and performance gaps that "exist throughout the country."

While Petitioners' proposed standard is problematic in and of itself, Petitioners' own pleadings expose the flaws in their arguments and highlight why *Coalition* requires that we approve the result reached by the First District. Indeed, what Petitioners seek is for the courts to order Respondents "to establish a remedial plan that includes *necessary studies to determine what resources and standards are necessary* to provide a high quality education to Florida students." In other words, Petitioners do not know what a "high quality system" looks like, how it can be achieved, or what resources and standards are necessary. Instead, they—and presumably the courts—will know an "efficient" and "high quality" system, as well as an "adequate" level of overall funding, when they see a study that shows what it is. Petitioners invite this Court to not only intrude into the Legislature's appropriations power, but to inject itself into education policy making and oversight. We decline the invitation for the courts to overstep their bounds.

NOTES

1. For cases in which the courts determined that educational-adequacy claims were non-justiciable, see *Okla. Educ. Ass'n v. State*, 158 P.3d 1058 (Okla. 2007); *Neb. Coal. for Educ. Equity & Adequacy v. Heineman*, 731 N.W.2d 164 (Neb. 2007); *Ex parte James*, 836 So.2d 813 (Ala. 2002); *Lewis E. v. Spagnolo*, 710 N.E.2d 798 (Ill. 1999); *Coal. for Adequacy & Fairness in Sch. Funding, Inc. v. Chiles*, 680 So.2d 400 (Fla. 1996).

2. For cases in which the courts determined that the claims were justiciable, see *William Penn Sch. Dist. v. Pa. Dep't Educ.*, 170 A.3d 414 (Pa. 2017); *Abbeville Cty. Sch. Dist. v. South Carolina*, 767 S.E.2d 157 (S.C. 2014); *Gannon v. Kansas*, 319 P.3d 1196 (Kan. 2014); *Brigham v. State*, 889 A.2d 715 (Vt. 2005); *Lake View Sch. Dist. No. 25 v. Huckabee*, 220 S.W.3d 645 (Ark. 2005); *DeRolph v. State*, 677 N.E.2d 733 (Ohio 1997); *Leandro v. State*, 488 S.E.2d 249 (N.C. 1997); *Idaho Schs. for Equal Educ. Opportunity, Inc. v. Evans*, 850 P.2d 724 (Idaho 1993).

3. On the merits, state supreme courts continue to reach divergent results. Some courts have invalidated school-funding systems in recent years. *See, e.g., Abbeville Cty. Sch. Dist. v. South Carolina*, 767 S.E.2d 157 (S.C. 2014); *Gannon v. Kansas*, 319 P.3d 1196 (Kan. 2014). Others have rejected such challenges. *See, e.g., Conn. Coal. for Justice in Educ. Funding, Inc. v. Rell*, 176 A.3d 28 (Conn. 2018); *Lobato v. Colorado*, 304 P.3d 1132 (Colo. 2013); *Davis v. South Dakota*, 804 N.W.2d 618 (S.D. 2011).

D. SCHOOL UNIFORMITY CLAUSES

In addition to containing "thorough and efficient" clauses, some state constitutions contain school "uniformity" clauses. The Florida Constitution, for example, provides: "Adequate provision shall be made by law for a *uniform*, efficient, safe, secure, and high quality system of free public schools." Fla. Const. art. IX, § 1(a) (emphasis added). This next case illustrates how school-uniformity clauses can limit legislative initiatives in the education arena—in this instance, by invalidating a Florida school voucher program.

BUSH v. HOLMES
919 So.2d 392 (Fla. 2006)

PARIENTE, C.J.

Under the Opportunity Scholarship Program (OSP), a student from a public school that fails to meet certain minimum state standards has two options. The first is to move to another public school with a satisfactory record under the state standards. The second option is to receive funds from the public treasury, which would otherwise have gone to the student's school district, to pay the student's tuition at a private school. The narrow question we address is whether the second option violates a part of the Florida Constitution requiring the state to both provide for "the education of all children residing within its borders" and provide "by law for a uniform, efficient, safe, secure, and high quality system of free public schools that allows students to obtain a high quality education."

As a general rule, courts may not reweigh the competing policy concerns underlying a legislative enactment. The arguments of public policy supporting both sides in this dispute have obvious merit, and the Legislature with the Governor's assent has resolved the ensuing debate in favor of the proponents of the program. In most cases, that would be the end of the matter. However, as is equally self-evident, the usual deference given to the Legislature's resolution of public policy issues is at all times circumscribed by the Constitution. Acting within its constitutional limits, the Legislature's power to resolve issues of civic debate receives great deference. Beyond those limits, the Constitution must prevail over any enactment contrary to it.

Our inquiry begins with the plain language of the second and third sentences of article IX, section 1(a) of the Constitution. The relevant words are these: "It is a paramount duty of the state to make adequate provision for the education of all children residing within its borders." Using the same term, "adequate provision," article IX, section 1(a) further states: "Adequate provision shall be made by law for a uniform, efficient, safe, secure, and high quality system of free public schools." For reasons expressed more fully below, we find that the OSP violates this language. It diverts public dollars into separate private systems parallel to and in competition with the free public schools that are the sole means set out in the Constitution for the state to provide for the education of Florida's children. This diversion not only reduces money available to the free schools, but also funds private schools that are not "uniform" when compared with each other or the public system. Many standards imposed by law on the public schools are inapplicable to the private schools receiving public monies. In sum, through the OSP, the state is fostering plural, nonuniform systems of education in direct violation of the constitutional mandate for a uniform system of free public schools.

In 1998, in response in part to another Florida Supreme Court case, the Constitutional Revision Commission proposed and the citizens of this state approved an amendment to article IX, section 1 to make clear that education is a "fundamental value" and "a paramount duty of the state," and to provide standards by which to measure the adequacy of the public school education provided by the state:

> *The education of children is a fundamental value of the people of the State of Florida*. It is, therefore, *a paramount duty of the state to make adequate provision for the education of all children residing within its borders*. Adequate provision shall be made by law for a *uniform, efficient, safe, secure, and high quality* system of free public schools that allows students to obtain a high quality education and for the establishment, maintenance, and operation of institutions of higher learning and other public education programs that the needs of the people may require.

The provision (1) declares that the "education of children is a fundamental value of the people of the State of Florida," (2) sets forth an education mandate that provides that it is "a paramount duty of the state to make adequate provision for the education of all children residing within its borders," and (3) sets forth *how* the state is to carry out this education mandate, specifically, that "*adequate* provision shall be made by law for a *uniform*, efficient, safe, secure, and *high quality system of free public schools*."

Article IX, section 1(a) is a limitation on the Legislature's power because it provides both a mandate to provide for children's education and a restriction on the execution of that mandate.

The second sentence of article IX, section 1(a) provides that it is the "paramount duty of the state to make adequate provision for the education of all children residing within its borders." The third sentence of article IX, section 1(a) provides a restriction on the exercise of this mandate by specifying that the adequate provision required in the second sentence "shall be made by law for a uniform, efficient, safe, secure and high quality system of *free public schools*." The OSP violates this provision by devoting the state's resources to the education of children within our state through means other than a system of free public schools.

The Constitution prohibits the state from using public monies to fund a private alternative to the public school system, which is what the OSP does. Specifically, the OSP transfers tax money earmarked for public education to private schools that provide the same service—basic primary education. Thus, contrary to the defendants' arguments, the OSP does not supplement the public education system. Instead, the OSP diverts funds that would otherwise be provided to the system of free public schools that is the exclusive means set out in the Constitution for the Legislature to make adequate provision for the education of children.

Although opportunity scholarships are not now widely in use, if the dissent is correct as to their constitutionality, the potential scale of programs of this nature is unlimited. Under the dissent's view of the Legislature's authority in this area, the state could fund a private school system of indefinite size and scope as long as the state also continued to fund the public schools at a level that kept them "uniform, efficient, safe, secure, and high quality." However, because voucher payments reduce funding for the public education system, the OSP by its very nature undermines the system of "high quality" free public schools that are the sole authorized means of fulfilling the constitutional mandate to provide for the education of all children residing in Florida. The systematic diversion of public funds to private schools on either a small or large scale is incompatible with article IX, section 1(a).

In addition to specifying that a system of free public schools is the means for complying with the mandate to provide for the education of Florida's children, article IX, section 1(a) also requires that this system be "uniform." The OSP makes no provision to ensure that the private school alternative to the public school system meets the criterion of uniformity. In fact, in a provision directing the Department of Education to establish and maintain a database of private schools, the Legislature expressly states that it does not intend "to regulate, control, approve, or accredit private educational institutions." This lack of oversight is also evident in section 1001.21, which creates the Office of Private Schools and Home Education Programs within the Department of Education but provides that this office "has no authority over the institutions or students served."

Further, although the parent of a student participating in the OSP must ensure that the student "takes all statewide assessments" required of a public school student, the private school's curriculum and teachers are not subject to the same standards as those in force in public schools. For example, only teachers possessing bachelor's degrees are eligible to teach at public schools, but private schools may hire teachers without bachelor's degrees if they have "at least 3 years of teaching experience in public or private schools, or have special skills, knowledge, or expertise that qualifies them to provide instruction in subjects taught."

In addition, public school teachers must be certified by the state. To obtain this certification, teachers must meet certain requirements that include having "attained at least a 2.5 overall grade point average on a 4.0 scale in the applicant's major field of study" and having demonstrated a mastery of general knowledge, subject area knowledge, and professional preparation and education competence.

Public teacher certification also requires the applicant to submit to a background screening. Indeed, all school district personnel hired to fill positions that require direct contact with students must undergo a background check. This screening is not required of private school employees.

Regarding curriculum, public education instruction is based on the "Sunshine State Standards" that have been "adopted by the State Board of Education and delineate the academic achievement of students, for which the state will hold schools accountable." Public schools are required to teach all basic subjects as well as a number of other diverse subjects, among them the contents of the Declaration of Independence, the essentials of the United States Constitution, the elements of civil government, Florida state history, African-American history, the history of the Holocaust, and the study of Hispanic and women's contributions to the United States. Eligible private schools are not required to teach any of these subjects.

In addition to being "academically accountable to the parent," a private school participating in the OSP is subject only "to the curriculum criteria adopted by an appropriate nonpublic school accrediting body." There are numerous nonpublic school accrediting bodies that have "widely variant quality standards and program requirements." Thus, curriculum standards of eligible private schools may vary greatly depending on the accrediting body, and these standards may not be equivalent to those required for Florida public schools.

In all these respects, the alternative system of private schools funded by the OSP cannot be deemed uniform in accordance with the mandate in article IX, section 1(a).

Reinforcing our determination that the state's use of public funds to support an alternative system of education is in violation of article IX, section 1(a) is the limitation of the use of monies from the State School Fund set forth in article IX, section 6. That provision states that income and interest from the State School Fund may be appropriated "only to the support and maintenance of free public schools."

In sum, article IX, section 1(a) provides for the manner in which the state is to fulfill its mandate to make adequate provision for the education of Florida's children—through a system of public education. The OSP contravenes this constitutional provision because it allows some children to receive a publicly funded education through an alternative system of private schools that are not subject to the uniformity requirements of the public school system. The diversion of money not only reduces public funds for a public education but also uses public funds to provide an alternative education in private schools that are not subject to the "uniformity" requirements for public schools. Thus, in two significant respects, the OSP violates the mandate set forth in article IX, section 1(a).

We do not question the basic right of parents to educate their children as they see fit. We recognize that the proponents of vouchers have a strongly held view that students should have choices. Our decision does not deny parents recourse to either public or private school alternatives to a failing school. Only when the private school option depends upon public funding is choice limited. This limit is necessitated by the constitutional mandate in article IX, section 1(a), which sets out the state's responsibilities in a manner that does not allow the use of state monies to fund a private school education. As we recently explained, "what is in the Constitution always must prevail over emotion. Our oaths as judges require that this principle is our polestar, and it alone."

E. TEACHER TENURE

In the past few years, challenges to teacher tenure rules have cropped up in state courts premised on alleged violations of both state equal-protection and adequate-education provisions. *See Forslund v. Minnesota*, 924 N.W.2d 25 (Minn. Ct. App. 2019) (dismissing parents' equal protection and adequacy claims); *Davids v. New York*, 74 N.Y.S.3d 228 (N.Y. App. Div. 2018) (holding that plaintiffs sufficiently alleged a violation of the right to "a sound basic education" under the New York Constitution); *Vergara v. California*, 209 Cal. Rptr. 3d 532 (Cal. Ct. App. 2016), *pet. for review denied*, 209 Cal. Rptr. 3d 558, 558–70 (Cal. 2016) (holding that California's teacher tenure statutes did not, on their face, violate equal protection). These lawsuits present novel and challenging questions. The excerpts below are taken from Justice Liu and Justice Cuéllar's statements dissenting from the California Supreme Court's denial of the *Vergara* plaintiffs' petition for review.

VERGARA v. CALIFORNIA
209 Cal. Rptr. 3d 558 (2016)

Dissenting Statement, LIU, J.

This case concerns the constitutionality of California's statutes on teacher tenure, retention, and dismissal. The plaintiffs are nine schoolchildren—Beatriz Vergara, Elizabeth Vergara, Clara Grace Campbell, Brandon Debose, Jr., Kate Elliott, Herschel Liss, Julia Macias, Daniella Martinez, and Raylene Monterroza—who attend California public schools. They allege that these statutes lead to the hiring and retention of what they call "grossly ineffective teachers" (*i.e.*, teachers in the bottom 5 percent of competence) and that being assigned to a grossly ineffective teacher causes significant educational harm. Plaintiffs further allege that they have suffered or are at risk of suffering these harms and that the harms fall disproportionately on minority and low-income students. After hearing eight weeks of evidence, the trial court ruled that the challenged statutes violate the equal protection clause of the California Constitution (Cal. Const. art. I, § 7, subd. (a)), noting that the evidence of detrimental effects that grossly ineffective teachers have on their students "is compelling" and "shocks the conscience." The Court of Appeal reversed, holding that plaintiffs failed to establish a viable equal protection claim.

There is considerable evidence in the record to support the trial court's conclusion that the hiring and retention of a substantial number of grossly ineffective teachers in California public schools have an appreciable impact on students' fundamental right to education. The trial court credited "a massive study" by Stanford economist Raj Chetty finding that "a single year in a classroom with a grossly ineffective teacher costs students $1.4 million in lifetime earnings per classroom." The trial court also cited a four-year study by Harvard economist and education professor Thomas Kane finding that "students in the Los Angeles Unified School District who are taught by a teacher in the bottom 5% of competence lose 9.54 months of learning in a single year compared to students with average teachers." Moreover, the trial court found "no dispute that there are a significant number of grossly ineffective teachers currently active in California classrooms" and cited testimony of the state's own expert estimating that 1 to 3 percent of California teachers are grossly ineffective, which translates to 2,750 to 8,250 teachers statewide.

The trial court also found that the challenged statutes substantially contribute to the hiring and retention of grossly ineffective teachers. The evidence is particularly suggestive with respect to the Dismissal Statutes. These statutes provide extensive procedural protections to teachers subject to dismissal for poor performance. At the time of trial, the laws required a district to first give a teacher a written statement of specific instances of unsatisfactory behavior, allow the teacher 90 days to improve, and then provide a written statement of charges and intent to dismiss. The teacher then had 30 days to request a hearing, which had to begin within 60 days of the request. The hearing was conducted by a three-member panel comprised of an administrative law judge, one teacher selected by the district, and one teacher selected by the teacher subject to the hearing. The panel had to issue a written decision, and the decision was subject to judicial review. If the district lost, it had to pay the hearing expenses and the teacher's attorney's fee. If the district won, the parties split the hearing expenses and paid their own attorney's fees.

The trial court found that "it could take anywhere from two to almost ten years and cost $50,000 to $450,000 or more to bring these cases to conclusion under the Dismissal Statutes, and that given these facts, grossly ineffective teachers are being left in the classroom because school officials do not wish to go through the time and expense to investigate and prosecute these cases." The trial court did not dispute that providing teachers with due process before dismissal was a legitimate and even compelling interest. But it concluded that this interest could be pursued without what it called the "*über* due process" that leads to retention of grossly ineffective teachers. The trial court observed that classified (*i.e.*, nonteacher) school employees, who are afforded due process rights to notice and a hearing, "had their discipline cases resolved with much less time and expense than those of teachers."

The trial court also concluded that other features of the challenged statutes contribute to the hiring and retention of grossly ineffective teachers. California is one of only five states with a two-year probation period before tenure, in contrast to three or more years in other states. The trial court cited "extensive evidence presented, including some from the defense," that two years "does not provide nearly enough time for an informed decision to be made regarding the decision of tenure (critical for both students and teachers)." Further, California is one of only 10 states that use seniority as the *sole* factor or as a factor that *must* be considered in laying off teachers. The trial court noted that many other states either treat seniority as one factor that may be considered or leave layoff criteria to the district's discretion. The trial court's findings do not suggest that teacher tenure invariably burdens students' fundamental right to education; instead, they suggest that California's particular scheme does.

Plaintiffs have styled this claim as an equal protection challenge, perhaps because this approach is supported by *Butt v. State of California* (Cal. 1992) and other cases that have applied strict scrutiny to equal protection claims alleging harms to fundamental rights. But this lawsuit at bottom states a claim that the teacher tenure and Dismissal Statutes, to the extent they lead to the hiring and retention of grossly ineffective teachers, violate students' fundamental right to education. Plaintiffs locate the source of that right in sections 1 and 5 of article IX of the California Constitution. These are the same provisions at issue in *Campaign for Quality Education v. State of California* (Cal. 2016), an education adequacy case in which this court also denies review today. The two cases involve different yet complementary claims concerning the importance of resources and reform to improving the education system. Both cases ultimately present the same basic issue: whether the education clauses of our state Constitution guarantee a minimum level of quality below which our public schools cannot be permitted to fall. This issue is surely one of the most consequential to the future of California.

Despite the gravity of the trial court's findings, despite the apparent error in the Court of Appeal's equal protection analysis, and despite the undeniable statewide importance of the issues presented, the court decides that the serious claims raised by Beatriz Vergara and her eight student peers do not warrant our review. I disagree. As the state's highest court, we owe the plaintiffs in this case, as well as schoolchildren throughout California, our transparent and reasoned judgment on whether the challenged statutes deprive a significant subset of students of their fundamental right to education and violate the constitutional guarantee of equal protection of the laws.

Dissenting Statement, CUELLAR, J.

We treat certain rights as fundamental under the California Constitution—the right to vote, for example, or to marry, to access our courts, to an expectation of privacy, and to an education—because they are foundational to how we choose to define our personal and civic lives. But it would border on madness to think that because these rights are fundamental, we can routinely expect perfection when the state protects—or through its activities, vindicates—these rights. The nature of any person's actual relationship to his or her fundamental rights is as much affected by ordinary governance—polling place and school locations, routine agency practices, long-past histories, and unexpected emergencies—as it is by a shared aspiration articulated in constitutional text or a judicial opinion that government honor such rights. Yet these realities make it even more important to distinguish routine shortcomings of implementation, or instances where government legitimately chooses to harmonize competing goals in a given way, from the infringement of a fundamental right by the imposition of an appreciable burden thereon.

The trial court found that such a burden was shown to exist in this case. The evidence, according to the trial court, established that the quality of education received by California's millions of schoolchildren depends substantially on the quality of instruction. The evidence further established that the existence of a substantial number of grossly ineffective teachers in the California school system—about 1 to 3 percent statewide, or 2,750 to 8,250 teachers—"has a direct, real, appreciable, and negative impact on a significant number of California students." Yet teacher dismissals "could take anywhere from two to almost ten years and cost $50,000 to $450,000 or more to bring these cases to conclusion under the Dismissal Statutes, and that given these facts, grossly ineffective teachers are being left in the classroom because school officials do not wish to go through the time and expense to investigate and prosecute these cases." There was also evidence, which the trial court credited, showing that two years is too short a time to properly evaluate teacher competence, and that California is one of only 10 states that use seniority as the sole factor in determining whether to lay off teachers. The Court of Appeal never disputed these findings.

These findings instead failed to justify a remedy, according to the Court of Appeal, because there was no identifiable group explicitly targeted or uniquely burdened by the statutes. This conclusion is, at best, in stark tension with settled law. We have long recognized that equal protection challenges may be brought "whenever the disfavored class is suspect *or* the disparate treatment has a real and appreciable impact on a fundamental right or interest." Strict scrutiny applies to both types of equal protection claims.

We can understand plaintiffs' claims here as involving equal protection grounded in a fundamental interest, or as ultimately predicated more directly on the argument that a fundamental interest has been unduly burdened. Under either conception, the Court of Appeal failed to appreciate the distinction we have drawn between claims involving a fundamental interest and those centered on a suspect class. To state a fundamental interest claim sounding in equal protection, the alleged disparate treatment need not be focused on a suspect class. When a fundamental interest is at stake, the sole preliminary inquiry is whether the challenged law has a real and appreciable impact on the exercise of that interest. If it does, the law will be invalidated unless the state can show it is necessary to achieve a compelling governmental interest. It is no answer under any standard of review—much less strict scrutiny—that violations of a fundamental right will be tolerated so long as they are felt at random.

And even if the law were more opaque, my doubts are grave about whether one could articulate a reasonable understanding of fundamental rights under the California Constitution that would countenance the imposition of material burdens on those rights without strict scrutiny or even the opportunity for judicial review under any standard, so long as those burdens were imposed largely at random. Invidious classifications deserve strict scrutiny even where fundamental rights are not at issue, while ordinary instances of treatment that could arguably be described as unequal do not merit particularly searching scrutiny where they do not involve fundamental rights. Where fundamental rights are at issue, however, we have never held that an equal protection challenge may proceed without the searching scrutiny that fundamental rights merit. We shouldn't start now simply because those rights may have been burdened arbitrarily. True: Arbitrary selection has at times been considered a means of rendering a governmental decision legitimate. But where an appreciable burden results—thereby infringing a fundamental right—arbitrariness seems a poor foundation on which to buttress the argument that the resulting situation is one that should not substantially concern us.

Just as the arbitrariness of the alleged injury is no cause to deny review, neither is the nature of the fundamental right so injured. That education is the right at issue has posed no insurmountable bar in the past. Why should we treat differently the material interference with a fundamental right arising from the challenged statutes—interference the trial court found to exist, and the Court of Appeal did not dispute—from the disruption occasioned by a shorter school year, or the drastic inequities in funding that undermine equal access to an education? The harmful consequences to a child's education caused by grossly ineffective teachers—the evidence for which the trial court found compelling—are no less grave than those resulting from a shortened period of instruction or financial shortfalls.

In considering this case, we must respect the role of the representative branches of government and the public itself in shaping education policy. But our responsibility to honor the court's proper constitutional role makes it as important for us to review a case that merits our attention as it is for us to avoid a dispute beyond the court's purview. This case is the former. It squarely presents significant questions of state constitutional jurisprudence that our court, rather than the Legislature or the executive branch, is best suited to address. Moreover, even in a world where we clarify our fundamental rights jurisprudence as this case requires—and address concerns associated with the Court of Appeal's decision—considerable room would remain for the legislative and executive branches to decide how best to address the important balance between honoring the fundamental right to education and addressing other goals, such as retaining protections for public employees from arbitrary dismissal.

F. REMEDY

One of the most vexing issues for courts that grant constitutional relief in this area is the question of remedy. It is one thing for a court to recognize an enforceable state constitutional right in this area and even to say that a current school funding system is inadequate. It is quite another to identify what the legislature must do to make its funding system constitutional (and to enforce that order). Claimants frequently seek structural changes to the system and usually demand increased state funding in doing so. The courts have struggled to identify a rationale for deciding how much guaranteed state funding suffices—with some focusing on the cost of certain educational "inputs," some focusing on the costs of certain educational "outputs," and some looking to both.

HOKE COUNTY BOARD OF EDUCATION v. STATE
599 S.E.2d 365 (N.C. 2004)

ORR, J.

The Court now turns its attention to the substantive issues brought forward on appeal by the State. In its first question presented to this Court, the State contends that the trial court erred by applying the wrong standards for determining: (1) when a student has obtained a sound basic education; (2) causation (for a student's failure to obtain a sound basic education); and (3) the State's liability (for a student's failure to obtain a sound basic education). In further support of its initial argument, the State proffers three subarguments, which allege and target specific evidentiary lapses and flaws in the trial court's reasoning. In its argument labeled I(A), the State contends that the trial court erred by using standardized test scores as "the exclusive measure" of whether students were obtaining a sound basic education. In argument I(B), the State argues that the trial court erred by concluding that a denial of the right to a sound basic education could be inferred from the number of socio-economically disadvantaged ("at-risk") students scoring below Level III proficiency on standardized tests. And in argument I(C), the State contends that the trial court erred when it held the State responsible for administrative decisions made by local school boards.

In *Leandro v. State* (N.C. 1997), this Court decreed that the children of the state enjoy the right to avail themselves of the opportunity for a sound basic education. Ultimately, the Court defined a sound basic education as one that provides students with at least: (1) sufficient knowledge of fundamental mathematics and physical science to enable the student to function in a complex and rapidly changing society; (2) sufficient fundamental knowledge of geography, history, and basic economic and political systems to enable the student to make informed choices with regard to issues that affect the student personally or affect the student's community, state, and nation; (3) sufficient academic and vocational skills to enable the student to successfully engage in post-secondary education or vocational training; and (4) sufficient academic and vocational skills to enable the student to compete on an equal basis with others in formal education or gainful employment in contemporary society.

After declaring a child's constitutional right to the opportunity to receive a sound basic education and defining the elements of such an education, the Court concluded that some of the allegations in plaintiffs' complaint stated claims upon which relief may be granted and ordered the case remanded to the trial court to permit plaintiffs to proceed on such claims.

At trial, plaintiffs presented evidence that, in accordance with *Leandro*, can be categorized as follows: (1) comparative standardized test score data; (2) student graduation rates, employment potential, post-secondary education success (and/or lack thereof); (3) deficiencies pertaining to the educational offerings in Hoke County schools; and (4) deficiencies pertaining to the educational administration of Hoke County schools. The first two evidentiary categories fall under the umbrella of "outputs," a term used by educators that, in sum, measures student performance. The remaining two evidentiary categories fall under the umbrella of "inputs," a term used by educators that, in sum, describes what the State and local boards provide to students attending public schools. We examine each evidentiary category in turn.

In its brief, the State contends, at great length, that the trial court erred by using test scores "as the exclusive measure of a constitutionally adequate education." However, as we proceed in our analysis, the Court notes that the record reflects that the trial court considered "output" evidence beyond the realm of test scores, and that evidence such as graduation rates, dropout rates, post-secondary education performance, employment rates and prospects, comports with both this Court's definition of a sound basic education *and* the factors we provided the trial court to consider upon remand. Thus, we reject the State's contention that the trial court used test scores as the "exclusive measure" of a sound basic education.

In continuing our examination of the trial court's order, we move next to the trial court's conclusion that additional "output" evidence—*e.g.*, graduation rates, dropout rates, employment potential, and post-secondary education readiness—further demonstrates that an unacceptably high number of Hoke County students are failing to obtain a sound basic education. In considering evidence concerning dropout and graduation rates, the trial court found that in the mid-1990s only 41% of Hoke County freshmen went on to graduate—a retention rate that was 19% lower than the state average and was the worst retention rate in the state's 100 counties. The trial court went on to conclude that the evidence showed that the primary reason Hoke County's dropout rate was so high was that a great number of Hoke students are "not well prepared for high school" and that "students who do not do well in the early grades are more likely than other students to later drop out of school."

As for the effect of such a high dropout rate, the trial court concluded that the failure of large percentages of Hoke County students to complete high school "not only results in those children who leave having failed to obtain a sound basic education" but is also evidence "of a systematic weakness in meeting the needs of many of Hoke County's students."

As for those students who did graduate, the trial court's assessment was no less bleak. After considering evidence concerning the employment potential and post-secondary education potential for Hoke County graduates, the trial court concluded that many among the graduates had not obtained a sound basic education in that the evidence showed "they are poorly prepared to compete on an equal basis in gainful employment and further formal education in today's contemporary society." In support of its conclusion, the trial court cited numerous examples of Hoke County graduates who pursued employment or who pursued further education at the college level.

In the realm of "outputs" evidence, we hold that the trial court properly concluded that the evidence demonstrates that over the past decade, an inordinate number of Hoke County students have consistently failed to match the academic performance of their statewide public school counterparts and that such failure, measured by their performance while attending Hoke County schools, their dropout rates, their graduation rates, their need for remedial help, their inability to compete in the job markets, and their inability to compete in collegiate ranks, constitute a clear showing that they have failed to obtain a *Leandro*-comporting education. As a consequence of so holding, we turn our attention to "inputs" evidence— evidence concerning what the State and its agents have provided for the education of Hoke County students—in an effort to determine the following two contingencies: (1) Does the evidence support the trial court's conclusion that the State's action and/or inaction has caused Hoke County students not to obtain a sound basic education and, if so; (2) Does such action and/or inaction by the State constitute a failure to meet its constitutional obligation to provide Hoke County students with the opportunity to obtain a sound basic education, as defined in *Leandro*?

It is one thing for plaintiffs to demonstrate that a large number of Hoke County students are failing to obtain a sound, basic public education. It is quite another for plaintiffs to show that such a failure is primarily the result of action and/or inaction of the State, which argues in this appeal that the trial court erred by concluding that a combination of State action and inaction resulted in the systematic poor performance of Hoke County students and graduates.

In defense of its educational offerings in Hoke County at trial, the State attempted to show that its combination of "inputs"—*i.e.*, expenditures, programs, teachers, administrators, etc.—added up to be an aggregate that met or exceeded this Court's definition of providing students with an opportunity for a sound basic education. In addition, both at trial and in this appeal, the State contended that the evidence showed the following: (1) that the educational offerings it provides in Hoke County have improved significantly since the mid-nineties; (2) that such improvements are part and parcel of the State's own recognition of ongoing problems and the need to address them; (3) that if a cognizable group of students within Hoke County are failing to obtain a sound basic education, it is due to factors other than the educational offerings provided by the State; and (4) that many of the deficiencies that may exist in the educational offerings of Hoke County are due to the administrative shortcomings of the semi-autonomous local school boards.

Plaintiffs, on the other hand, contend that the evidence at trial clearly showed that the State had consistently failed to provide Hoke County schools with the resources needed to provide students with the opportunity to obtain a sound basic education. In addition, plaintiffs argue that the evidence shows that Hoke County students have consistently failed to match the achievements of their statewide counterparts because the State has failed to: (1) provide adequate teachers and/or administrators; (2) provide the funding necessary to offer each student the opportunity to obtain a sound basic education; (3) recognize the failings of Hoke County students as a whole; and (4) implement alternative educational offerings that have and/or would address and correct the problems that have placed and/or place Hoke County students *at risk* of academic failure.

Although the trial court explained that it was leaving the "nuts and bolts" of the educational resources assessment in Hoke County to the other branches of government, it ultimately provided general guidelines for a *Leandro*-compliant resource allocation system, including the requirements: (1) that "every classroom be staffed with a competent, certified, well-trained teacher"; (2) "that every school be led by a well-trained competent principal"; and (3) "that every school be provided, in the most cost effective manner, the resources necessary to support the effective instructional program within that school so that the educational needs of all children, including at-risk children, to have the equal opportunity to obtain a sound basic education, can be met." Finally, the trial court ordered the State to keep the court advised of its remedial actions through written reports filed with the trial court every ninety days.

In our view, the trial court conducted an appropriate and informative path of inquiry concerning the issue at hand. After determining that the evidence clearly showed that Hoke County students were failing, at an alarming rate, to obtain a sound basic education, the trial court in turn determined that the evidence presented also demonstrated that a combination of State action and inaction contributed significantly to the students' failings. Then, after concluding that the State's overall funding and resource provisions scheme was adequate on a statewide basis, the trial court determined that the evidence showed that the State's method of funding and providing for individual school districts such as Hoke County was such that it did not comply with *Leandro*'s mandate of ensuring that all children of the state be provided with the opportunity for a sound basic education. In particular, the trial court concluded the State's failing was essentially twofold in that the State: (1) failed to identify the inordinate number of "at-risk" students and provide a means for such students to avail themselves of the opportunity for a sound basic education; and (2) failed to oversee how educational funding and resources were being used and implemented in Hoke County schools.

In short, the trial court: (1) informed the State what was wrong with Hoke County schools; (2) directed the State to reassess its educational priorities for Hoke County; and (3) ordered the State to correct any and all education-related deficiencies that contribute to a student's inability to take advantage of his right to the opportunity to obtain a sound basic education. However, we note that the trial court also demonstrated admirable restraint by refusing to dictate how existing problems should be approached and resolved. Recognizing that education concerns were the shared province of the legislative and executive branches, the trial court instead afforded the two branches an unimpeded chance, "initially at least," to correct constitutional deficiencies revealed at trial. In our view, the trial court's approach to the issue was sound and its order reflects both findings of fact that were supported by the evidence and conclusions that were supported by ample and adequate findings of fact. As a consequence, we affirm those portions of the trial court's order that conclude that there has been a clear showing of a denial of the established right of Hoke County students to gain their opportunity for a sound basic education and those portions of the order that require the State to assess its education-related allocations to the county's schools so as to correct any deficiencies that presently prevent the county from offering its students the opportunity to obtain a *Leandro-*conforming education.

CLAREMONT SCHOOL DISTRICT v. GOVERNOR
794 A.2d 744 (N.H. 2002)

DUGGAN, J.

The issues before this court are: (1) whether the State's obligation to provide a constitutionally adequate public education requires it to include standards of accountability in the educational system; and, if so, (2) whether existing statutes, regulations, and/or rules satisfy this obligation. We hold that accountability is an essential component of the State's duty and that the existing statutory scheme has deficiencies that are inconsistent with the State's duty to provide a constitutionally adequate education.

This litigation began in 1992 when the Claremont School District, along with four other "property poor" school districts, five school children and five taxpayers, filed a petition for declaratory relief in superior court alleging that the system by which the State financed education violated the New Hampshire Constitution. The trial court dismissed the lawsuit, ruling that the New Hampshire Constitution "imposes no qualitative standard of education which must be met" and "imposes no quantifiable financial duty regarding education." The plaintiffs appealed. After examining the meaning of the words used in the Encouragement of Literature Clause at the time the State Constitution was adopted in 1784, historical evidence of the significance of education to the constitutional framers, and the interpretation given almost identical language in the Massachusetts Constitution by that State's highest court, this court concluded that Part II, Article 83 requires the State to "provide a constitutionally adequate education to every educable child in the public schools in New Hampshire and to guarantee adequate funding."

In *Claremont I*, we observed that the New Hampshire Constitution "expressly recognizes education as a cornerstone of our democratic system" and the Encouragement of Literature Clause "expressly recognizes that a free government is dependent for its survival on citizens who are able to participate intelligently in the political, economic, and social functions of our system." "Given the complexities of our society today, the State's constitutional duty extends beyond mere reading, writing, and arithmetic. It also includes broad educational opportunities needed in today's society to prepare citizens for their role as participants and as potential competitors in today's marketplace of ideas."

This court specifically acknowledged that the task of defining the parameters of the education mandated by the constitution is in the first instance for the legislature and the Governor. That task includes the "responsibility to define the specifics of, and the appropriate means to provide through public education the knowledge and learning essential to the preservation of a free government."

Regarding educational adequacy, the opinion underscored that

> mere competence in the basics—reading, writing, and arithmetic—is insufficient in the waning days of the twentieth century to insure that this State's public school students are fully integrated into the world around them. A broad exposure to the social, economic, scientific, technological, and political realities of today's society is essential for our students to compete, contribute, and flourish in the twenty-first century.

Claremont II also set forth "seven criteria establishing general, aspirational guidelines for defining educational adequacy." This court deferred, however, in the first instance to the other branches of government to "promptly develop and adopt specific criteria implementing these guidelines."

After considering the pleadings and oral argument, this court decided to exercise its jurisdiction to resolve two specific legal questions:

> (1) Whether the State's obligation to provide a constitutionally adequate public education under part II, article 83 of the New Hampshire Constitution requires the State to include standards of accountability in New Hampshire statutes, regulations and/or rules; and if so
>
> (2) Whether existing statutes, regulations and/or rules satisfy this obligation.

Accountability is more than merely creating a system to deliver an adequate education. *Claremont I* did not simply hold that the State should deliver a constitutionally adequate education, but in fact held that it is the State's duty under the New Hampshire Constitution to do so. Accountability means that the State must provide a definition of a constitutionally adequate education, the definition must have standards, and the standards must be subject to meaningful application so that it is possible to determine whether, in delegating its obligation to provide a constitutionally adequate education, the State has fulfilled its duty. If the State cannot be held accountable for fulfilling its duty, the duty creates no obligation and is no longer a duty. We therefore conclude that the State's duty to provide a constitutionally adequate education includes accountability.

Having determined that standards of accountability are an essential component of the State's duty to provide a constitutionally adequate education, we must now determine whether the existing statutes, regulations and rules satisfy this obligation. The State argues that these existing laws, which include the definition of an adequate education in RSA 193-E:2; the

State's minimum standards for education set forth in the department of education rules; and the New Hampshire Education Improvement and Assessment Program (NHEIAP), together provide sufficient standards of accountability. According to the State, "it has given detailed curriculum instruction to schools and school boards, created a test to measure student performance, empowered State agencies to review and improve school performance, and enacted literally thousands of pages of other statutes, regulations, and rules to deliver an adequate education."

RSA 193-E:2 sets forth the criteria for an adequate education as follows:

I. Skill in reading, writing, and speaking English to enable them to communicate effectively and think creatively and critically.

II. Skill in mathematics and familiarity with methods of science to enable them to analyze information, solve problems, and make rational decisions.

III. Knowledge of the biological, physical, and earth sciences to enable them to understand and appreciate the world around them.

IV. Knowledge of civics and government, economics, geography, and history to enable them to participate in the democratic process and to make informed choices as responsible citizens.

V. Grounding in the arts, languages, and literature to enable them to appreciate our cultural heritage and develop lifelong interests and involvement in these areas.

VI. Sound wellness and environmental practices to enable them to enhance their own well-being, as well as that of others.

VII. Skills for lifelong learning, including interpersonal and technological skills, to enable them to learn, work, and participate effectively in a changing society.

The State contends that a wide range of satisfactory methods can produce an effective system to deliver what it has defined as an adequate education. The State also asserts that it may choose from a wide array of tools to ensure that school districts are implementing the standards it sets out for the system it chooses. We agree that "there are many different ways that the Legislature could fashion an educational system while still meeting the mandates of the Constitution." The system the State currently has in place appears to use both standards based on what school districts provide (input-based standards) and results that school districts achieve (output-based standards). While minimum standards for school approval set forth what the schools, at the very least, must provide to students, NHEIAP uses curriculum frameworks and mandatory tests to assess what the school districts have achieved.

The State argues that, as a central part of the system to deliver a constitutionally adequate education, it "dictates certain school approval standards that schools and school districts must meet. These input based standards are enforceable by the State and extend to virtually every aspect of education, from class size to teacher training to detailed curriculum requirements."

The board of education is required by statute to adopt rules relative to "minimum curriculum and educational standards for all grades of the public schools." These rules are commonly referred to as the State's "minimum standards" or "school approval standards." The minimum standards contain a number of requirements imposed by the State on local school districts so that schools may be approved by the State. For example, the minimum standards set forth the number of days in a standard school year, staff qualifications, maximum class sizes, heating and ventilation requirements, the minimum number of credits required to be offered in certain courses, and the areas of specific substantive materials which must be taught.

The education that the individual schools provide is measured against these standards for approval. If a school does not meet these standards, it can lose its approval. There are four categories of approval: approved with distinction, approved, conditionally approved from one to three years, and unapproved. If a school is unapproved, the department of education is required to work with the local school board to "correct all deficiencies until such time as an unapproved school meets all applicable standards and is designated as an approved school." The purpose of these rules is to hold school districts accountable for providing an adequate education.

Excused noncompliance with the minimum standards for financial reasons alone directly conflicts with the constitutional command that the State must guarantee sufficient funding to ensure that school districts can provide a constitutionally adequate education. As we have repeatedly held, it is the State's duty to guarantee the funding necessary to provide a constitutionally adequate education to every educable child in the public schools in the State.

The responsibility for ensuring the provision of an adequate public education and an adequate level of resources for all students in New Hampshire lies with the State. While local governments may be required, in part, to support public schools, it is the responsibility of the State to take such steps as may be required in each instance effectively to devise a plan and sources of funds sufficient to meet the constitutional mandate.

As noted above, the State may not take the position that the minimum standards form an essential component of the delivery of a constitutionally adequate education and yet allow for the financial constraints of a school or school district to excuse compliance with those very standards. We hold, therefore, that to the extent the minimum standards for school approval excuse compliance solely based on financial conditions, it is facially insufficient because it is in clear conflict with the State's duty to provide a constitutionally adequate education.

NHEIAP, RSA chapter 193-C, is characterized by the State as "another important element of the State's system for delivering the opportunity for an adequate education." The goals of the program are to define what students should know and be able to do, develop and implement methods for assessing that learning and its application, report assessment results to all citizens of New Hampshire, help to provide accountability at all levels, and use the results, at both the State and local levels, to improve instruction and advance student learning. The department of education pamphlet describes NHEIAP as the "cornerstone of the state's initiatives to continuously improve education for all students."

The responsibility for administering NHEIAP lies with the department of education. The commissioner of education is charged with "developing and implementing this program in conjunction with the state board of education and the legislative oversight committee." In fulfilling its duty pursuant to the statutory framework that makes up NHEIAP, the department of education is directed to develop a program that consists of three interlocking components. The first component is a set of educational standards, RSA 193-C:3, III(a), which the department of education has developed and implemented through curriculum frameworks. The second component is a statewide assessment program, which "shall be a valid and appropriate representation of the standards the students are expected to achieve." The final component is the "local education improvement and assessment plan which builds upon and complements the goals established for NHEIAP."

Under RSA 193-C:9, I, however, no school district is required to respond to the assessment results; rather "each school district in New Hampshire is *encouraged* to develop a local education improvement and assessment plan." This means that even if the assessment results show that all the students in a school are at novice level, neither the school district nor the department of education is required to do anything. Whether an individual school district is providing a constitutionally adequate education or not, it is merely encouraged to develop a local educational improvement plan, and if it opts to do so, the department of education is available to assist. Nothing more is required.

An output-based accountability system that merely encourages local school districts to meet educational standards does not fulfill the State's constitutional duty under Part II, Article 83. While the State may delegate its duty to provide a constitutionally adequate education, the State may not abdicate its duty in the process. The purpose of meaningful accountability is to ensure that those entrusted with the duty of delivering a constitutionally adequate education are fulfilling that duty. When the State chooses to use an output-based tool to measure whether school districts are providing a constitutionally adequate education, that tool must be meaningfully applied. The department of education cannot meaningfully apply the educational standards and assessment tests set out in RSA chapter 193-C when it cannot hold school districts accountable, but instead is limited to using the results to encourage school districts to develop a local education improvement and assessment plan. To the extent the State relies on RSA chapter 193-C to provide for accountability, it must do more than merely encourage school districts to meet the educational standards that are designed to indicate whether students are receiving a constitutionally adequate education.

The State suggests that "a student who receives an education of the quality described in RSA 193-E:2 and who acquires all of the various skills and types of knowledge expressed there would be well prepared as a citizen to participate in society." While we have no basis to disagree with this statement, the State has not provided a sufficient mechanism to require that school districts actually achieve this goal. We hold that because of deficiencies in the system as set out in this opinion, the State has not met its constitutional obligation to develop a system to ensure the delivery of a constitutionally adequate education.

As the State recognizes, "there are many different ways that the Legislature could fashion an educational system while still meeting the mandates of the Constitution." The development of meaningful standards of accountability is a task for which the legislative branch is uniquely suited. The policy choices to be made are complex, as there are several ways to address this issue. It is for the Governor and the legislature to choose how to measure or evaluate whether a constitutionally adequate education is being provided and what action to take if a school is determined to be deficient. The State's brief describes some of the issues involved:

> Formulating a system for delivery might require policy choices regarding what sort of standards should exist for teachers, students, schools, and school districts. For example, a delivery system might consist of detailed curriculum rules for each grade and subject area establishing the required substance of each lesson that students must be taught. Other delivery systems might make use of any number of other standards such as class size, graduation rate, college acceptance rate, test scores, or teacher qualifications.
>
> Devising a system to deliver educational services could also require decisions regarding how to implement the standards that are selected. If a school or school district is not meeting applicable standards, what will be the consequence? A system could rely on the Governor to ensure that local school districts are meeting statutory obligations through her power to enforce constitutional and statutory obligations. A different system might enforce standards by rewarding successful schools with increased funding. Alternatively, the system might impose penalties for not meeting standards, such as removing the principal, sending in a team of administrators to take control of the school, or any number of other consequences.

We agree with the State's contention that it may implement a variety of systems. However, when the State chooses a particular method to determine whether those it entrusts with the task are in fact providing a constitutionally adequate education, the State must include meaningful accountability to ensure that the State is fulfilling its constitutional duty.

We conclude that the State "needs to do more work" to fulfill its duty to provide a constitutionally adequate education and incorporate meaningful accountability in the education system. In light of the procedural history of this litigation, including efforts by the executive and legislative branches and their previous statements on this issue, and the application of settled law, this conclusion should be neither surprising nor unanticipated.

We remain mindful that "while the judiciary has the duty to construe and interpret the word 'education' by providing broad constitutional guidelines, the Legislature is obligated to give specific substantive content to the word and to the program it deems necessary to provide that education within the broad guidelines." We recognize that we are not appointed to establish educational policy and have not done so today.

NEELEY v. WEST ORANGE-COVE CONSOL. INDEP. SCH. DIST.
176 S.W.3d 746 (Tex. 2005)

HECHT, J.

Under article VII, section 1 of the Constitution of 1876, the accomplishment of "a general diffusion of knowledge" is the standard by which the adequacy of the public education system is to be judged. To achieve such a system, the Legislature has chosen to use local school districts. Borrowing from two statutory pronouncements, the district court concluded:

> To fulfill the constitutional obligation to provide a general diffusion of knowledge, districts must provide "*all Texas children access* to a quality education that enables them to achieve their potential and fully participate now and in the future in the social, economic, and educational opportunities of our state and nation." Districts satisfy this constitutional obligation when they provide all of their students with a *meaningful opportunity* to acquire the essential knowledge and skills reflected in curriculum requirements such that upon graduation, students are prepared to "continue to learn in postsecondary educational, training, or employment settings."

We agree, with one caveat. The public education system need not operate perfectly; it is adequate if districts are *reasonably* able to provide their students the access and opportunity the district court described.

The system the Legislature has devised prescribes an education curriculum, and by means of accreditation standards, holds schools and districts accountable for teaching it. Schools and districts rated "academically acceptable" provide what we have referred to as an accredited education, and we have presumed, simply in deference to the Legislature, that such an education achieves a general diffusion of knowledge. The district court found that the plaintiffs and intervenors have rebutted this presumption. The court's principal reasons, set out in detailed findings and conclusions, may be summarized as follows:

- TAKS tests (and other such tests) cover only a small part of the prescribed curriculum;
- the cut scores and passing rates for TAKS tests (or other such tests) are too low and are set, not to reliably measure achievement, but to ensure a low rate of failure;

- completion and dropout rates are understated and unreliable, in fact fewer than 75% of all students and 70% of minority students complete high school, and this high attrition, worse in larger districts, is unacceptable;
- other important factors in determining whether a general diffusion of knowledge has been achieved, like college preparedness of graduates, for example, are not considered in rating schools and districts "academically acceptable" and reflect unfavorably on the system;
- the requirements for an "academically acceptable" rating are set to assure, not that there will be a general diffusion of knowledge, but that almost every district will meet them;
- the prescribed curriculum and TAKS testing have been made more demanding while funding to satisfy statutory requirements has not kept pace, producing budget pressures that have resulted in—
- a shortage of qualified teachers, an increase in teachers having to teach outside their fields, and high attrition and turnover rates;
- difficulty in providing special programs and remediation for students at risk of not completing their education;
- there has also been a lack of funding to meet increased federal requirements, like the No Child Left Behind Act;
- the changing demographics of the student population—with a majority being economically disadvantaged, 15% having limited proficiency in English, and both groups continuing to grow—have increased education costs while funding has lagged;
- the I/R econometric study correctly shows that the cost of an accredited education exceeds available per-student revenue.

The State defendants contend that the district court focused too much on "inputs" to the public education system—that is, available resources. They argue that whether a general diffusion of knowledge has been accomplished depends entirely on "outputs"—the results of the educational process measured in student achievement. We agree that the constitutional standard is plainly result-oriented. It creates no duty to fund public education at any level other than what is required to achieve a general diffusion of knowledge. While the end-product of public education is related to the resources available for its use, the relationship is neither simple nor direct; public education can and often does improve with greater resources, just as it struggles when resources are withheld, but more money does not guarantee better schools or more educated students. To determine whether the system as a whole is providing for a general diffusion of knowledge, it is useful to consider how funding levels and mechanisms relate to better-educated students. This, we think, is all the district court did.

In the extensive record before us, there is much evidence, which the district court credited, that many schools and districts are struggling to teach an increasingly demanding curriculum to a population with a growing number of disadvantaged students, yet without additional funding needed to meet these challenges. There are wide gaps in performance among student groups differentiated by race, proficiency in English, and economic advantage. Non-completion and dropout rates are high, and the loss of students who are struggling may make performance measures applied to those who continue appear better than they should. The rate of students meeting college preparedness standards is very low. There is also evidence of high attrition and turnover among teachers statewide, due to increasing demands and stagnant compensation. But the undisputed evidence is that standardized test scores have steadily improved over time, even while tests and curriculum have been made more difficult. By all admission, NAEP scores, which the district court did not mention, show that public education in Texas has improved relative to the other states. Having carefully reviewed the evidence and the district court's findings, we cannot conclude that the Legislature has acted arbitrarily in structuring and funding the public education system so that school districts are not reasonably able to afford all students the access to education and the educational opportunity to accomplish a general diffusion of knowledge.

NOTE

For more cases dealing with these difficult remedial issues, see *Abbeville Cty. Sch. Dist. v. South Carolina*, 767 S.E.2d 157 (S.C. 2014); *Gannon v. Kansas*, 319 P.3d 1196 (Kan. 2014); *Campbell Cty. Sch. Dist. v. State*, 181 P.3d 43 (Wyo. 2008); *Paynter v. State*, 797 N.E.2d 1225 (N.Y. 2003).

Chapter XII

CIVIL REMEDIES: THE RIGHT TO A REMEDY AND OPEN COURTS; THE RIGHT TO A JURY TRIAL; SEPARATION OF POWERS; OTHER POSSIBLE CLAIMS

A. INTRODUCTION AND HISTORICAL BACKGROUND: RIGHT TO A REMEDY AND OPEN COURTS CLAUSES

State constitutions protect a variety of rights. A guarantee that most state constitutions include but that the federal constitution does not is a "right to a remedy" clause or what is sometimes referred to as an "open courts" clause. These provisions give citizens the right to pursue legal remedies for deprivations of their interests, usually in terms indicating a right to a "remedy by due course of law" or that the courts of the state "shall be open." These provisions often also include language guaranteeing that justice shall be "without denial," "prompt," or "without delay."

The right to a remedy and open courts provisions may limit a State's authority to withdraw or modify existing legal remedies. A frequent area of litigation under these provisions is tort reform, with plaintiffs arguing that damages caps, statutes of repose, worker's compensation systems, and other limitations on various tort actions (*e.g.* in the malpractice or governmental immunity contexts) violate these state constitutional provisions. There is an abundance of fascinating and challenging state cases interpreting these constitutional provisions, with courts applying various levels of scrutiny and a variety of tests—and a corresponding mix of outcomes.

The language behind these clauses has a long history. It predates the U.S. Constitution by centuries, with roots in the English Magna Carta. Even though the right to a remedy is enshrined only in the State constitutions (and not the federal constitution), Chief Justice John Marshall recognized the principle's worthy pedigree. In *Marbury v. Madison*, he quoted Blackstone's *Commentaries* for the proposition that "it is a general and indisputable rule, that where there is a legal right there is also a legal remedy by suit or action at law, whenever that right is invaded."

Many state constitutions also provide that the "right of trial by jury shall remain inviolate," or words to similar effect. Some state supreme courts have interpreted these provisions to limit legislative authority to enact tort reform such as statutory caps on damages. And in a more general sense, claims have been made that legislative efforts to enact tort reform may cross separation of powers lines by intruding upon judicial prerogatives. This chapter explores all of these issues as well as the question whether state constitutional provisions may themselves create "implied rights of actions" that entitle persons aggrieved by constitutional violations to bring a lawsuit to enforce their rights—often called *Bivens* actions under federal law.

Shannon M. Roesler, *The Kansas Remedy by Due Course of Law Provision: Defining a Right to a Remedy*
47 Kan. L. Rev. 655 (1999)

The state constitutions of thirty-nine states contain "remedy by due course of law" provisions. Historically, these provisions were intended as constitutional safeguards of an individual's right to a legal remedy. More than state equivalents of the federal Due Process Clause, these remedy provisions have resulted in a myriad of interpretations by state courts. Plaintiffs generally use state remedy provisions to challenge statutes restricting or eliminating previously established causes of action. In the last few decades, for example, injured parties have used state remedy provisions to challenge tort reform legislation, such as workers' compensation acts and statutory caps on medical malpractice damages.

Most states with remedy provisions adopted the provision from earlier state constitutions. In constructing the first state constitutions, the colonial and early American writers looked to English law and history, adopting Sir Edward Coke's interpretation of language in the Magna Carta. Like Coke, they sought to protect the judiciary from corruption and to ensure its independence.

The history of the remedy provision begins with King John in the thirteenth century. King John's courts administered justice for a fee; those seeking access to the courts had to purchase writs, and the more costly writs guaranteed speedier and more successful claims. In response to the Crown's corrupting influence, Chapter 40 of the Magna Carta was written to restore the integrity of the courts by specifically prohibiting the selling of writs: "to no one will we sell, to no one will we refuse or delay, right or justice."

Because the Magna Carta's purpose was to protect the courts from the Crown's corruption, it provided compelling authority for Sir Edward Coke as he battled King James and argued for the supremacy of the common law in the seventeenth century. As an absolutist monarch, King James exercised power over the courts, arguing judges were merely servants of the Crown. Coke not only argued that the judiciary was independent from the Crown, but also that the King was subject to the common law. In his crusade to justify the judiciary's independence, Coke wrote the Second Institute; the remedy provision first appears in this context as part of Coke's interpretation of the language in Chapter 40 of the Magna Carta.

Coke expounded on the language in the Magna Carta to fashion a remedy guarantee: "Every subject of this Realm, for injury done to him may take his remedy by the course of the Law, and have justice and right for injury done him, freely without sale, fully without any denial, and speedily without delay." Although commentators have criticized Coke for misreading the Magna Carta, his intent in fashioning the provision, not his accuracy in translation, sheds light on the remedy provision and its historical development. Like the authors of the Magna Carta, he struggled to protect the English court from outside corruption and influence, thereby safeguarding its independence; he did not, however, seek to guarantee the creation of remedies for every injury. The remedy provision was not created, therefore, to address the relationship between the judiciary and the legislature, although this is its context today.

When the remedy provision appeared in the Delaware Declaration of Rights, Coke's interpretation of Chapter 40 of the Magna Carta was the only textual authority for an independent judiciary. Although the English judiciary's independence was finally recognized in 1701, the colonial courts remained subject to the corrupt devices of the Crown. Thus, shortly before the American Revolution, grievances similar to those of Coke motivated colonists to seek language that would guarantee the integrity of the courts. Not surprisingly, five early bills of rights contain remedy provisions derived from Coke's Second Institute. Moreover, though the federal Bill of Rights does not contain a remedy provision, at least two states, Virginia and North Carolina, argued for the inclusion of remedy language.

The modern context of the remedy provision bears little resemblance to the provision's origins. Litigation involving the remedy provision often surfaces in response to fairly recent areas of law, such as workers' compensation, medical malpractice, and statutes of repose. Though the cases contain similar subject matter from state to state, interpretation of the remedy provision continues to be an area of rich diversity in state constitutional law.

Commentators have categorized the different state interpretations according to various schemes. Often classification schemes draw upon federal equal protection, distinguishing different courts' approaches by varying degrees of judicial scrutiny and by using federal language, such as "fundamental rights." One commentator has divided the varied approaches into two large groups: one group consists of judicially created bright line, or per se, rules while the other group contains ad hoc balancing tests that focus on the particular costs and benefits of a challenged statute.

KENTUCKY v. CLAYCOMB
566 S.W.3d 202 (Ky. 2018)

MINTON, C.J.

Of all the rights guaranteed by state constitutions but absent from the federal Bill of Rights, the guarantee of a right of access to the courts to obtain a remedy for injury is possibly the most important. Kentucky's version of this guarantee, referred to in our jurisprudence as the open-courts provision, appears in the Bill of Rights, Section 14, of the Kentucky Constitution, which states: "All courts shall be open, and every person for an injury done him in his lands, goods, person or reputation, shall have remedy by due course of law, and right and justice administered without sale, denial or delay."

The Kentucky General Assembly in its 2017 regular session enacted Kentucky Revised Statutes Chapter 216C, the Medical Review Panel Act, establishing a mandatory process to delay certain medical-malpractice claimants' ability to access immediately the courts of the Commonwealth by creating medical-review panels and requiring a panel's opinion about the merits of the claimant's proposed complaint against health-care providers before the claimant may file suit. We hold that because the Act delays access to the courts of the Commonwealth for the adjudication of common-law claims, it violates the Kentucky Constitution.

The medical review panel must first review any malpractice or malpractice-related claim filed on or after June 29, 2017, against any individual or entity bearing some sort of relationship to the health care profession and industry, "other than claims validly agreed for submission to a binding arbitration procedure," before that claim is subject to adjudication. The panel does not engage in any adjudication of a claimant's claim. Rather, the entire purpose and function of the panel is to generate an opinion about the merits of the claim, an opinion that may or may not have any evidentiary usefulness in a court of law.

For more than two and a quarter centuries, the language of Section 14 has appeared verbatim in all four of Kentucky's constitutions, first as Article XII, § 13 of the original one in 1792. But as the former Dean of the University of Kentucky College of Law, the late Thomas R. Lewis, notes in his scholarly analysis, the remedy guarantee provided for in Section 14 is an ancient right dating from Magna Carta in 1215.

Tracing the pedigree of Section 14 to Magna Carta brings up a fundamental question with which Kentucky's highest court has famously struggled since the antebellum years of the Commonwealth: Is Section 14 a limitation on *all* departments of state government interfering with its guarantees, or *just the judiciary?*

Dean Lewis's ultimate conclusion about the reach of Section 14, as confirmed by his study of the historic explication of the right by Sir William Blackstone, is: "That common law courts resolve disputes, creating precedents, and thus law, in the absence of governing legislation *but subject to modification by the people through their elected representatives.*" In other words, Blackstone and Dean Lewis would likely argue, as has the Commonwealth in this case, that the constraints on government reflected in Section 14 do not apply to the popularly elected legislature.

Almost 200 years ago, this Commonwealth's highest court "found that access to courts was clearly indicative of the duty which the functionaries of the government owe to the citizens and that if it shall occur that the right of the citizen has been invaded contrary to the constitution, it is the duty of the judiciary to shield him from oppression." In "*Blair v. Williams* (Ky. 1823) and *Lapsley v. Brashears* (Ky. 1823), Kentucky's highest court held unconstitutional an act of the legislature permitting a stay of two years on the debtor giving bond and security unless the creditor endorsed on his execution a willingness to accept notes on the Bank of Kentucky or the Bank of the Commonwealth of Kentucky." Those decisions "nearly destroyed this court." "The Judges were charged with arrogating supremacy over the popular will—their authority to declare void any act of the Legislature was denied, and they were denounced by the organs and stump orators of the dominant relief party as usurpers and self-made kings."

Some years later, after the "hard money" fight had subsided, the court in *Johnson v. Higgins* (Ky. 1861) and *Barkley v. Glover* (Ky. 1862) "held that Section 14 of the Kentucky Constitution was a limitation on the judicial branch of the government and not a limitation on the legislative branch, and that it prohibited the courts from arbitrarily delaying or denying to its citizens the administration of justice, but constituted no limitation upon the legislature in formulating procedural methods to be used by the courts."

This rule changed with the decision in *Ludwig v. Johnson* (Ky. 1932), the seminal case establishing the open-courts and jural rights doctrines in Kentucky jurisprudence. Our predecessors on the Commonwealth's highest court recognized in *Ludwig* that when Section 14 is read in conjunction with Section 26, the Bill of Rights of the Kentucky Constitution establishes "a limitation on the power of the legislature to enact laws which are in contravention of the plain provisions of Section 14." This conclusion led our predecessors in *Commonwealth ex rel. Tinder v. Werner* (Ky. 1955) to the ultimate conclusion "that section 14, when construed in the light of section 26, prohibits the legislature from invading the province of the judiciary and that the prohibition of section 14 applies to the legislative branch of the government as well as to the judicial." This Court has never retreated from that position, and we find no reason to do so today.

Sir Edward Coke and Blackstone, two of England's most preeminent legal scholars, undeniably viewed the ancient guarantees now reflected in the language of Section 14 of Kentucky's Constitution as checks on royal abuse, not on parliamentary excesses. With all due respect to the conclusion reached by Dean Lewis, who would exempt the modern legislative branch from the constraints of Section 14, that conclusion overlooks a fundamental difference between English and American jurisprudence:

> Unlike Coke and Blackstone, the rebellious American colonists saw both the Crown *and Parliament* as oppressors. Parliamentary initiatives during the 1760s and 1770s convinced the colonists that the informal constitution securing English rights against royal infringement *was inadequate to protect against all forms of government oppression.* When independence was declared, some of the new American states began adopting formal written constitutions to structure their new

governments and to help secure their most fundamental rights. As Gordon Wood notes, they recognized that laws protecting their basic freedoms must be of "a nature more sacred than those which established a turnpike road."

Furthermore, "in contrast to England, early state constitutions transformed the right from a restriction on monarchical power to a positive obligation to provide access to an independent judiciary for vindication of rights, *particularly against overreaching legislatures.*"

Although much of our law is rooted in English law, we cannot ignore the fundamental distinctions that developed in America. The framers of written constitutions for the new American states were clearly wary of the power of *all* branches of government. "Many framers of the original state constitutions in colonial America adopted Section 14's guarantees as their own, recognizing it as a constraint on both judicial and legislative power."

To characterize certain sections of the Kentucky Bill of Rights as applying only to the judicial department of the Commonwealth is to ignore the common understanding of the original framers and the original meaning of the words they employed—*all* branches of government can oppress the people and such oppression must be guarded against. So the framers of Kentucky's First Constitution included Section 28 in the Kentucky Bill of Rights: "To guard against transgressions of the high powers which we have delegated, WE DECLARE, that everything in this article is excepted out of the general powers of government, and shall forever remain inviolate; and that all laws contrary thereto, or contrary to this Constitution, shall be void." This is the same provision, now Section 26, that this Court in *Ludwig* identified as making clear that Section 14 applies to *all* branches of government.

Based upon the plain text of Section 14, its history, and our long-standing precedent interpreting its reach, we hold that Section 14 acts as a restraint on the power of all departments of state government. It is a right "of the people," and the people deserve to be protected against all departments of government infringing on their right to seek immediate redress for common-law personal-injury claims.

We have held that Section 14 protects "the right of every individual in society to access a system of justice to redress wrongs," and such protection "is basic and fundamental to our common law heritage." The right to a remedy protected in Section 14 applies to actions for death and personal injuries, among other types of actions. And medical-malpractice claims fall under this category of claims.

Blackstone described the right to a remedy as "one of the five subordinate rights through which people vindicated their absolute rights, and it encompassed both the substance of the law and the procedures through which courts applied that law." Once a person was injured, the right to an "adequate remedy" immediately attached, though judicial process might be necessary to ascertain the exact parameters of that right. "The right to a remedy dictated that common-law courts exercise general jurisdiction, being open for all cases involving injury to individual rights, for it is a settled and invariable principle that every right when withheld must have a remedy, and every injury its proper redress."

Coke and Blackstone observed that included among the rights protected by the remedies guarantee are "the rights of subjects in their private relations with one another," which includes the "absolute right of personal security." In order to protect against violations of such rights, Coke and Blackstone identified the necessary remedy that immediately attaches upon injury done to a person: "Every subject of this realm, for injury done to him in goods, lands, or person, by any other subject may take his remedy by the course of the law, and have justice, and right for the injury done to him *speedily without delay.*" Indeed, "the placement of access to courts provisions in states' bills of rights suggests that the drafters of state constitutions did not view the right as merely an operational detail of the courts but rather as an individualized, particularized and positive right."

The General Assembly, through Chapter 216C, has created a mandatory delay affecting the ability of all medical-malpractice claimants to seek *any* redress, unless all parties either "validly agree to a binding arbitration procedure" or agree to bypass the medical review panel process. Chapter 216C takes away the ability of medical-malpractice claimants to seek immediate redress in the forum of the claimant's choosing. Chapter 216C contravenes one of the main purposes of Section 14—to prohibit legislatively created delays in the ability of a claimant to seek immediate redress in the courts of the Commonwealth for common-law personal injury.

Forcing a medical-malpractice claimant seeking immediate redress for an alleged common-law personal-injury to be at the mercy of the other parties involved when attempting to bypass the panel process cannot satisfy Section 14's mandate that "all courts be open" and every Kentuckian "shall have remedy by due course of law, and right and justice administered without delay." Admittedly, delays are inherent in every adjudicatory proceeding. What makes the delay imposed by Chapter 216C unconstitutional is the General Assembly's *usurpation* of a claimant's freedom to access the adjudicatory method of his or her choosing at the time of his or her choosing. This is an untenable restriction on the exercise of the individual's right to receive "remedy by due course of law, and right and justice administered without delay" from an "open" court system.

Chapter 216C is an unacceptable deviation from the "the right of every individual in society to access a system of justice to redress wrongs." Instead of affording claimants the ability to choose the process of redress they wish at the time they wish to exercise it, Chapter 216C forecloses all immediate access to any system of justice unless the other side agrees. Access to the adjudicatory method of their choice for *immediate* redress of common-law personal-injury claims is a constitutional right that all claimants have, unless they choose to give it up; the government cannot take away that right.

We do note, however, that proceeding through an alternative means of adjudication of a claim is not per se unconstitutional under Section 14. Whether through arbitration, mediation, administrative proceedings, or some other form of dispute-resolution process, if a claimant (1) has voluntarily agreed to seek redress of their common-law claims through that process and (2) has meaningfully waived access to the courts, then proceeding through a dispute-resolution process outside the court system that resulted in a delayed adjudication of a claim would, nevertheless, seem to pass constitutional muster under Section 14. But under Chapter 216C, common-law personal-injury claimants have no ability to seek *any immediate redress from the adjudicatory forum of their choosing* unless all parties agree to bypass the panel process. Under these circumstances, with their backs against the wall, claimants choosing to arbitrate cannot be said to have meaningfully waived their right to immediate access to the courts.

We must also point out that the remedy guarantee of Section 14 applies only to claims, "for an injury done to a claimant in his lands, goods, person or reputation." And the protections of Section 14 apply only to *claims originating out of the common law.* If the legislature affords a right to claimants outside the common law, a delay in adjudication of that claim is not per se unconstitutional under Section 14. Section 14 only prevents the legislature from encroaching upon the realm of the judiciary, the creator of the common law, by imposing mandatory delays in the adjudication of common-law claims grounded in claims "for an injury done to the claimant in his lands, goods, person or reputation." Here, medical-malpractice claims, a subset of personal-injury and wrongful-death claims, have been a recognized part of the common law for centuries, and as such, the legislature cannot delay claimants from seeking immediate redress of such claims through the courts.

Lastly, there is no support, either from the text of Section 14, or from case law interpreting that provision, to interpose a "reasonableness" evaluation of the delay to determine if a delay can, in some circumstances, be constitutionally tolerable. "Where a constitutional provision is free from all ambiguity there is no room for interpretation or addition. It must be accepted by the courts as it reads." "The basic rule is to interpret a constitutional provision according to what was said and not what might have been said." "Neither legislatures nor courts have the right to add to or take from the simple words and meaning of the constitution." Finally, "It is hornbook law that in interpreting Constitutions the words employed therein should be given the meaning and significance that they possessed at the time they were employed, and the one that the delegates of the convention that framed the instrument, and the people who voted their approval of it, intended to express and impart." Section 14, originally written and adopted in 1792, does not proscribe the creation of "undue" or "unreasonable" delay on a Kentuckian's access to due course of law; Section 14 plainly proscribes delay.

We must acknowledge that the majority of our sister courts have upheld the constitutionality of statutes establishing medical review panels. But a minority of our sister courts have struck down the entirety or some provisions of medical review panel acts based on the same open-courts doctrine we apply to strike down Chapter 216C here. And a review of the laws of the 17 states and U.S. territories currently having medical review panels further reveals support for our holding.

The entirety of Chapter 216C violates Section 14, and there is "no set of circumstances under which the Act would be valid." Therefore, we must declare the entire Act void as unconstitutional.

B. CASES DEFINING THE RIGHT TO A REMEDY/OPEN COURTS

MELLO v. BIG Y FOODS, INC.
826 A.2d 1117 (Conn. 2003)

BORDEN, J.

The two issues in this reservation are, first, whether the plaintiff's claim for permanent and significant scarring on her foot and ankle is barred by the exclusive remedy provision of the Workers' Compensation Act, and second, if so, whether that bar violates article first, § 10, of the constitution of Connecticut. We answer the first question in the affirmative and the second question in the negative.

The parties stipulated to the following facts. The plaintiff was employed by the defendant. On July 3, 1998, during the course of and in the scope of her employment, the plaintiff sustained a compensable burn injury to her right foot and ankle, which later resulted in permanent and significant scarring. The plaintiff filed a claim pursuant to chapter 568 of the General Statutes seeking workers' compensation benefits, including a claim for benefits for permanent and significant scarring. The defendant accepted the compensability of the plaintiff's underlying injury to her foot by way of voluntary agreement, and paid for medical treatment and indemnity benefits for missed work, and for a 3 percent permanent disability to her right foot. The defendant denied compensability, however, for the scarring to the plaintiff's foot and ankle. Thereafter, the commissioner found that there was no scarring to the plaintiff's face, head or neck, and that the scarring to her foot and ankle did not interfere with her ability to obtain or continue work.

Accordingly, the commissioner denied the plaintiff's claim for scarring to her foot and ankle.

We begin by addressing the first reserved question: whether the plaintiff's claim is barred by the exclusivity provision of the act. We conclude that the plaintiff's claim that her scarring should be actionable against her employer outside the workers' compensation system is inconsistent with the act. In place of the trade-offs provided by the act would be a situation in which employees could seek compensation for those aspects of their compensable injuries that are specifically enumerated in the act, while seeking damages in tort against their employers for those aspects of their injuries not specifically enumerated. Such a result would, in many cases, including the present action, expose employers to liability under both the act and the common law. The costs and the lack of predictability that would result from such a rule would be unreasonable in light of the legislature's endeavor to reduce the costs of the system and in light of the public policy behind the act, which seeks to afford remedies quickly and efficiently to injured employees.

Having answered the first question in the affirmative, we now turn to the second question: whether the exclusivity provision, as applied to the facts of this case, violates article first, § 10, of the constitution of Connecticut. Is the act's exclusivity provision unconstitutional, as applied to the facts of this case, because it precludes the plaintiff from exercising her preexisting common-law right to bring an action in negligence seeking damages for her scarring? We conclude that it is not.

Article first, § 10, of the constitution of Connecticut provides that "all courts shall be open, and every person, for an injury done to him in his person, property or reputation, shall have remedy by due course of law, and right and justice administered without sale, denial or delay." "This provision appears in the constitution of 1818 and in its several revisions and reenactments, and has been referred to as the right to redress." It is settled law that this provision restricts the power of the legislature to abolish a legal right existing at common law prior to 1818 without also establishing a "reasonable alternative to the enforcement of that right." In order to be reasonable, however, an alternative need not be the *exact* equivalent of the abolished common-law right or its remedy. "Thus for each remedy or item of damage existing under the prior fault system, it is not required that that item be duplicated under the alternative act but that the bulk of remedies under the act be of such significance that a court is justified in viewing this legislation on the whole as a substitute, the benefits from which are sufficient to tolerate the removal of the prior cause of action." In other words, in determining whether an alternative is reasonable, a court need only consider the aggregated benefits of the legislative alternative and assess whether those aggregated benefits reasonably approximate the rights formerly available under the common law.

We have concluded that the act is a reasonable alternative to claims in tort for damages that existed at common law as actions for trespass on the case. In *Daily v. New Britain Machine Co.* (Conn. 1986), the plaintiff claimed that the injury to his hand, sustained during routine maintenance of a precision machine, was actionable under a product liability theory, despite the fact that he had been receiving benefits under the act. We disagreed and concluded that through "the aggregate benefits associated with the workers' compensation laws the legislature provided a reasonable alternative to workers having product liability claims and that it did not enact legislation violative of article first, § 10, of the Connecticut constitution."

We conclude that the act's rights and remedies provide a reasonable alternative to the plaintiff's common-law right to bring a negligence action for damages resulting from her scarring. The plaintiff has been compensated, through the act, for all compensable losses associated with the injury she sustained to her foot. This compensation included medical costs, lost wages and a permanent disability payment of 3 percent. Under the terms of the act, the plaintiff received these benefits without the delay of filing an action and the burden of proving negligence. This is the exchange offered by the act; workers forego certain damages and remedies available to them under common law, but they gain a predictable, reliable, speedy and inexpensive means of obtaining compensation. The rights and remedies available under a legislative "reasonable alternative" need not equate, in every respect and detail, the superseded common-law rights and remedies. The aggregated benefits need only reasonably approximate the former right.

YANAKOS v. UNIVERSITY OF PITTSBURGH MEDICAL CENTER, ET AL.
218 A.3d 1214 (Pa. 2019)

MUNDY, J.

We consider whether the seven-year statute of repose in Section 1303.513(a) of the Medical Care Availability and Reduction of Error Act (MCARE Act) comports with Article I, Section 11 of the Pennsylvania Constitution, which guarantees "all courts shall be open; and every man for an injury done him in his lands, goods, person or reputation shall have remedy by due course of law." Pa. Const. art. I, § 11. Because we conclude the seven-year statute of repose is not substantially related to an important government interest, we reverse the Superior Court's order affirming the trial court's grant of judgment on the pleadings and remand for further proceedings.

Susan Yanakos suffers from a genetic condition called Alpha-1 Antitrypsin Deficiency (AATD). Patients with AATD do not produce enough Alpha-1 Antitrypsin, a protein synthesized in the liver that plays an important role in protecting the lungs from damage. In the summer of 2003, one of Susan's physicians, Dr. Amadeo Marcos, advised her that she needed a liver transplant due to the progression of her AATD. Because Susan was not a candidate for a cadaver liver, her son Christopher volunteered to donate a lobe of his liver to his mother.

Christopher underwent an extensive medical evaluation to determine whether he was a suitable liver donor. As part of that process, and at Dr. Marcos's request, Dr. Thomas Shaw-Stiffel evaluated Christopher. Christopher advised Dr. Shaw-Stiffel that several of his family members suffered from AATD, but that he was unsure whether he did as well. Dr. Shaw-Stiffel ordered additional laboratory tests for Christopher, but never informed him of the results, which allegedly showed that Christopher had AATD and was not a candidate for liver donation. One month after Christopher's consultation with Dr. Shaw-Stiffel, in September 2003, Dr. Marcos went forward with the operation, removing a portion of Christopher's liver and transplanting it into Susan.

More than twelve years later, Christopher, Susan, and Susan's husband, William Yanakos sued UPMC, University of Pittsburgh Physicians, Dr. Marcos, and Dr. Shaw-Stiffel. In their complaint, the Yanakoses raised claims for battery/lack of informed consent, medical malpractice, and loss of consortium. The Yanakoses alleged that they did not discover Appellees' negligence until eleven years after the transplant surgery, when additional testing revealed that Susan still had AATD, which the transplant should have eliminated.

The Pennsylvania Constitution provides our citizens with a right to a remedy in Article I, Section 11, which states: "All courts shall be open; and every man for an injury done him in his lands, goods, person or reputation shall have remedy by due course of law, and right and justice administered without sale, denial or delay. Suits may be brought against the Commonwealth in such manner, in such courts and in such cases as the Legislature may by law direct."

In the past, this Court has recognized that Article 1, Section 11 "provided that where a legal injury is sustained, there shall and will always be access to the courts of this Commonwealth." Although the Federal constitution does not contain an analogous protection, the majority of state constitutions include a similar provision. *See* David Schuman, *The Right to a Remedy*, 65 Temp. L. Rev. 1197, 1201 (1992) (noting "the citizens of thirty-nine states can claim a constitutional 'right to a remedy.'").

Historically, this Court and other state courts have traced the foundation of the "right to a remedy" to the Magna Carta. The Remedies Clause was added to the Pennsylvania Constitution in 1790. In recognizing that Article I, Section 11 protects a citizen's right to a remedy, this Court has interpreted it as an "imperative limitation on legislative authority, and imperative imposition of judicial duty." Notwithstanding this interpretation, however, in more recent opinions, we have recognized the inherent legislative prerogative of guiding the formation of the law. Indeed, in upholding a statute of repose that limited the liability of individuals performing building repairs, we noted the balance between the legislature guiding the law and the courts in interpreting it: "This Court would encroach upon the Legislature's ability to guide the development of the law if we invalidated legislation simply because the rule enacted by the Legislature rejects some cause of action currently preferred by the courts. Such a result would offend our notion of the checks and balances between the various branches of government, and of the flexibility required for the healthy growth of the law."

In crafting the jurisprudence surrounding the remedies clause in this way, we diverged from a quid pro quo analysis of the remedies clause, where "we originally required the legislature to provide a substitute remedy anytime it eliminated a remedy." This line of cases represented a shift away from treating the constitutional protections inherent in the remedies clause as a fundamental right. Because this Court has "curtailed the reach of the remedies clause" in the past, it follows that the right to a remedy is not a fundamental right. Nonetheless, based on the right's explicit inclusion in our constitution, coupled with its historical significance, the right to a remedy is an important right.

Because the MCARE Act curtails the important constitutional right to a remedy, we must apply intermediate scrutiny to determine whether the MCARE statute of repose is substantially related to achieving an important government interest. Statutes which infringe on the right to a remedy—and other important rights—are subject to a heightened level of scrutiny. Under intermediate scrutiny, the proponent of the statute "bears the burden of proof on the appropriateness of the means it employs to further its interest."

That this Court has identified the Article I, Section 11 right as important and applied intermediate scrutiny in evaluating challenges implicating that right belies the dissenting opinion's position that intermediate scrutiny is "manifestly incompatible with our existing Remedies Clause jurisprudence." Further, the dissent's recognition that the 1790 Constitution was a response to unchecked legislative power is in tension with its adoption of a "heightened scrutiny" test that is deferential to legislative enactments. The dissent's "heightened scrutiny" is a hybrid test that subjects the legislature's goal to higher scrutiny ("response to a clear social or economic need") but does not similarly subject the legislature's means to any additional scrutiny ("a rational and non-arbitrary connection to that need").

Under this "heightened scrutiny," as long as the legislature seeks to ameliorate a clear social or economic need, the means it selects, i.e. the legislation, are reviewed under a rational basis standard to determine if they are rational and non-arbitrary. Pennsylvania courts have never utilized such a test in connection with the Remedies Clause or otherwise. Further, we reject this test because it does not adequately safeguard the important right to a remedy.

Applying intermediate scrutiny, we conclude the governmental interest in controlling the rising costs of medical malpractice insurance premiums and of medical care is important. However, the MCARE Act's statute of repose as enacted is not substantially related to achieving those goals. Generally, statutes of repose are intended to provide actuarial certainty to insurers in calculating insurance premium rates. Theoretically, by cutting off a defendant's liability after a given number of years, statutes of repose lead to more certain liability and thus provide greater actuarial precision in setting insurance rates. More certain liability and stabilized insurance rates in turn facilitate efficient business planning and ultimately benefit businessmen, professionals, consumers, and the economy.

The effect of the seven-year repose period for most medical malpractice actions is to limit the "discovery rule" to seven years. In most cases, if a malpractice victim discovers the injury and its cause within seven years, the victim may bring a timely lawsuit; however, after seven years, the statute of repose bars the action. Additionally, foreign objects cases are exempt from the statute, and minors can file a lawsuit either seven years from the date of injury or until their twentieth birthday, whichever is later. Thus, the statute of repose prevents most medical malpractice victims, except foreign objects plaintiffs and certain minors, from exercising the constitutional right to a remedy after seven years.

In order for this statutory scheme to pass intermediate scrutiny, it must be substantially or closely related to an important government interest. As noted, the goal of the statute of repose was to control medical malpractice premium rates by providing actuarial certainty. Accordingly, the question is whether the seven-year statute of repose is substantially related to controlling the cost of medical malpractice premium rates. In this case, there was no evidence to show the initially proposed four-year statute of repose would provide actuarial certainty, except that it "seemed like a reasonable resolution" to "provide some stability and predictability" to insurers. Moreover, there is no evidence in the legislative history as to how the General Assembly arrived at a seven-year statute of repose with exceptions for foreign objects cases and minors. The legislature did not cite any statistics on the number of medical malpractice actions that are commenced after seven years of the occurrence giving rise to the action. There is no indication that such a time period, as opposed to a longer or shorter period, will have any effect on malpractice insurance costs.

Likewise, the parties in their current briefing failed to suggest the seven-year repose period has any substantial relationship to the legislative goal of controlling malpractice insurance costs. Appellees narrowly focus on the foreign objects exception, arguing that exception is substantially related to an important government interest. However, the proper focus is on the manner in which the statute of repose infringes on the Article I, Section 11 right to a remedy: the statute permits malpractice victims who discover their injury and its cause within seven years, foreign objects plaintiffs, and minors to exercise their constitutional right to a remedy; on the other hand, the statute deprives malpractice victims who do not discover their injury or its cause within seven years of their right to a remedy. Appellees have not demonstrated that this seven-year period is substantially related to the goal of controlling insurance premiums.

Additionally, the statute of repose as enacted does not offer insurers a definite period after which there will be no liability because it exempts foreign objects cases and minors, so insurers still have to account for those unpredictable "long-tail" cases in calculating malpractice insurance premiums. Therefore, the seven-year statute of repose, with exceptions for foreign objects cases and minors, is not substantially related to controlling the cost of malpractice insurance rates by providing actuarial predictability to insurers. Accordingly, we conclude the MCARE Act's statute of repose is unconstitutional.

DONOHUE, J., concurring and dissenting.

I concur in the result reached by Justice Mundy in the lead Opinion. I respectfully dissent, however, from the lead Opinion's conclusion that the right to a remedy guaranteed by Article I, Section 11 of the Pennsylvania Constitution is not a fundamental right mandating the application of strict scrutiny.

I agree with the lead Opinion that the legislative branch plays a role in guiding the development of the law. However, for the reasons discussed in this opinion and contrary to the lead Opinion, I cannot agree with any effort to demote, for the first time, our inviolate Article I, section 11 rights to mere "important" status.

Rather, I would begin with the basic acknowledgment that the right to a remedy in Article I, Section 11 is a fundamental right which can only be infringed when there is a showing of a compelling state interest and that the means chosen to advance it are narrowly tailored to achieve the end. Applying that test, in my view, the statute of repose in the MCARE Act violates Article I, Section 11 of the Constitution. The test the lead Opinion adopts limits the transgressions of the General Assembly to those instances where the Commonwealth cannot show that legislation is "substantially related" to achieving some important governmental interest. While I agree with the lead Opinion that the MCARE Act's statute of repose does not even meet this low threshold, in the larger picture I fear that the undemanding test the lead Opinion adopts today places an illusory limit on the General Assembly's prerogative to infringe on the right to a remedy enshrined in Article I and instead ties this Court's hands in fulfilling our obligation to scrupulously protect the right to a remedy afforded in Article I, Section 11.

WECHT, J., dissenting.

A majority of the Court concludes that the General Assembly's application of a seven-year statute of repose to most medical professional liability claims violates Article I, Section 11 of the Pennsylvania Constitution, which provides that every person who suffers an injury "shall have remedy by due course of law." I am unable to agree. Both the lead Opinion and the Concurring and Dissenting Opinion flout the General Assembly's policymaking authority by constitutionalizing and imposing a standard that neither the text nor the history of our Constitution supports. Because existing jurisprudence supplies a different standard, and because it is not this Court's role to upend duly enacted legislation simply because we might sometimes deem it imperfect or unwise, I must respectfully dissent.

At issue is the right to a "remedy by due course of law." This wording is found in the constitutions of at least thirty-nine states, but has no counterpart in the federal constitution. Such provisions, commonly referred to as remedies clauses, derive from Magna Carta and Sir Edward Coke's seventeenth century commentary on the Great Charter, which influenced the drafters of many early American state constitutions. Some state supreme courts have concluded that various statutes of limitations and statutes of repose violate their constitutions' Remedies Clauses. Yet considerable disagreement persists among state courts over the correct interpretation of Open Courts provisions and Remedies Clauses. For every decision striking down a statutory restriction on a common law cause of action, one could find another decision (likely in a state with an identical Open Courts provision) upholding a similar restriction. *See* Thomas R. Phillips, *The Constitutional Right to A Remedy*, 78 N.Y.U. L. Rev. 1309, 1314-15 (2003).

To complicate matters further, the ordinary challenges of constitutional interpretation are magnified because the historical record does not reveal what led the framers of early state constitutions to embrace Open Courts provisions. Those few documents that survive from Pennsylvania's 1790 constitutional convention do not describe any debates about the Open Courts provision generally, nor the Remedies Clause specifically. So it is not clear what the drafters meant when they guaranteed a remedy "by due course of law" for every injury. Perhaps they understood "due course of law" to mean "the law of the land," in which case Article I, Section 11 merely guarantees a right to "whatever remedy the law allows." Or maybe the drafters intended to constitutionalize then-existing common law remedies, thus shielding those remedies from legislative modification or abolition absent a constitutional amendment. We don't know.

Faced with this lack of authoritative guidance, Pennsylvania courts—along with many other state courts—have struggled for well over a century to define what, if any, limits the Remedies Clause imposes on the legislature's authority to modify or abolish common law causes of action. Indeed, significant disagreement persists among judges and scholars as to whether the "by due course of law" language found in most Open Courts provisions presupposes that the legislature has the authority to decide what "course of law" is "due" in any given circumstance. Some have questioned why the promise of a remedy for every "injury" necessarily should preclude the legislature from defining what constitutes a "legal injury" in the first instance.

Though these substantial difficulties have resulted in divergent interpretations among and between different courts, the lead Opinion barely mentions them. Instead, the lead Opinion simply takes for granted that intermediate scrutiny "must apply" given the right to a remedy's "historical significance" and its "explicit inclusion in our constitution." The matter is not so simple. Although the framers' intent in drafting Pennsylvania's original Open Courts provision is somewhat opaque, the circumstances that precipitated the 1790 constitutional convention are well understood. When Pennsylvania's first Constitution was ratified in 1776, "the legislative branch was seen as the people's servant and salvation," while "the executive branch was distrusted." The Pennsylvania Constitution of 1776 reflected this underlying political philosophy. It created a "unitary government in which legislative power, and supervisory power over both the executive and the judiciary, were concentrated in a single annually elected Assembly."

In the ensuing decades, the citizens of Pennsylvania "became disillusioned with legislative supremacy" following many well-documented abuses of that power. Throughout this era, the legislature all too often exceeded its constitutional authority, obstructed legitimate exercises of executive power, ignored judicial decisions, and disregarded individual liberties. "By the mid-1780s, there was general agreement that 'many of the existing ills could be traced to an impotent judiciary,'" and that Pennsylvania's constitutional system lacked essential safeguards on unchecked legislative power.

In 1789, a substantial majority of the legislature agreed that revisions to the Pennsylvania Constitution were necessary. The product of the ensuing convention—the Constitution of 1790—reflected a dramatic shift in the structure of our state government. Unlike its predecessor, this new Constitution vested executive power in a unitary executive with veto and appointment powers, created a bicameral legislature consisting of a house and senate, provided for an independent judiciary, and explicitly prohibited the legislature from infringing upon any of the individual rights enumerated in the Declaration of Rights.

Given this historical context surrounding the introduction of the Remedies Clause in the Constitution of 1790, Article I, Section 11 should be understood to impose some outer limit on the General Assembly's power to enact legislation that curtails or eliminates a common law cause of action. Together with the history of the Remedies Clause and this Court's precedent, the text and structure of the Constitution also support the conclusion that laws infringing the right to a remedy should be subject to some form of heightened judicial scrutiny. The preamble to Article I of the Constitution makes clear that the rights enumerated in the Declaration of Rights are "essential principles of liberty and free government" and must be protected from legislative encroachment. Similarly, Article I, Section 25 reveals the framers' intent to prohibit all branches of government—including the legislature—from interfering with the exercise of the rights enumerated in the Declaration of Rights.

For all of these reasons, I am willing to accept that laws which modify traditional common law remedies should be subject to some form of heightened judicial scrutiny. I disagree, however, with the lead Opinion's conclusion that intermediate scrutiny should apply. As this Court has cautioned in prior cases, "societal conditions occasionally require the law to change in a way that denies a plaintiff a cause of action available in an earlier day." While it is not often that the legislature decides that a common law theory of recovery has outlived its useful life, neither is it unprecedented. This Court itself has not hesitated to abrogate common law anachronisms. Consider, for example, the tort of criminal conversation—an action that could be brought against a third party who "engaged in at least a single act of sexual intercourse" with the plaintiff's spouse.

These concerns evince the principle that a legislature, like a court, may from time to time recognize that life and experience have consigned a common law rule to obsolescence, leaving that rule subject both to judicial modification and to statutory revision. Our own expressions throughout our Article I, Section 11 case law have, for at least a century, harmonized consistently with this perspective. It follows that the intermediate scrutiny standard fails to afford the legislature sufficient latitude to modify traditional common law remedies. In other words, today's decision impedes and flouts the General Assembly's policymaking authority, thus countenancing the "stagnation of the law in the face of changing societal conditions" that this Court has warned our Constitution does not mandate.

In sum, I would hold that statutes which modify or abolish common law causes of action violate Article I, Section 11 of the Pennsylvania Constitution unless the challenged legislation is supported by a clear social or economic need for reform. If a law is not supported by such a need, or if the means chosen to address the social or economic problem are arbitrary or irrational, then the law is unconstitutional. The MCARE Act's statute of repose satisfies this benchmark.

McINTOSH v. MELROE CO.
729 N.E.2d 972 (Ind. 2000)

BOEHM, J.

This case deals with the validity of the provision in the Product Liability Act that bars product liability claims for injuries sustained more than ten years after the product is delivered to its "initial user or consumer." The plaintiffs argue that this provision violates their constitutional right under Article I, Section 12 of the Indiana Constitution to a remedy by due course of law.

On June 9, 1993, James McIntosh was injured in an accident involving a Clark Bobcat skid steer loader manufactured by Melroe. McIntosh and his wife filed suit alleging that his injuries and her resulting loss of companionship were caused by a defect in the loader. Melroe responded with a motion for summary judgment based on the ten-year statute of repose. That section provides that "a product liability action must be commenced within ten years after the delivery of the product to the initial user or consumer." Melroe designated evidence establishing that the loader had been delivered to its initial user on September 9, 1980, almost thirteen years before the accident. The McIntoshes replied that the statute of repose violated their rights under Article I, Sections 12 of the Indiana Constitution.

Article I, Section 12 of the Indiana Constitution provides, in relevant part: "All courts shall be open; and every person, for injury done to him in his person, property, or reputation, shall have remedy by due course of law." We agree with the dissent that the various frequently invoked constitutional talismans—constitutional text, history of the times, intent of the framers, etc.—are proper keys to the interpretation of Article I, Section 12. But apart from the text itself, precedents of this Court, and precedents from other states with similar provisions, we find no relevant guideposts on this point. In particular, there appears to be no unique Indiana history surrounding the adoption of this Clause in 1816 or its redrafting in 1851.

The McIntoshes argue that they have a constitutional right to a remedy for their injuries because the framers of the 1851 Constitution "decided not to give the General Assembly broad powers to abolish the common law." From this they suggest that they have a protectable constitutional right to the remedy provided by the common law for product liability injuries. This amounts to a claim that common law remedies may not be abolished. It is fundamentally a claim that these remedies constitute a protected species similar to the rights thought embedded in the constitution by substantive due process. This Court has long recognized the ability of the General Assembly to modify or abrogate the common law. "Indiana courts have uniformly held that in cases involving injury to person or property, Article I, § 12 does not prevent the legislature from modifying or restricting common law rights and remedies." In sum, the courts of this State, like those of most others, "generally agree that the constitutional assurance of a remedy for injury does not create any new substantive rights to recover for particular harms. Rather, the clause promises that, for injuries recognized elsewhere in the law, the courts will be open for meaningful redress."

Although there is a significant split in other states as to whether provisions similar to our "remedy by due course" provision permit the legislature to impose a statute of repose in product liability cases, we agree with the Supreme Court of Oregon that "the legislature has the authority to determine what constitutes a legally cognizable injury." Indeed, we believe that there is a very powerful reason that the General Assembly must have the authority to determine what injuries are legally cognizable, *i.e.*, which injuries are wrongs for which there is a legal remedy. A contrary view implies a static common law that is inconsistent with the evolution of legal doctrine before and after 1851. Perhaps equally important, if we are to find some remedies chiseled in constitutional stone, we wander into the area of "scarce and open-ended" guideposts for identifying which remedies are of constitutional dimension, and which are not.

We have long held that the General Assembly has the authority to modify the common law and that there is no "fundamental right" to bring a particular cause of action to remedy an asserted wrong. Rather, because individuals have "no vested or property right in any rule of common law," the General Assembly can make substantial changes to the existing law without infringing on citizen rights. Because no citizen has a protectable interest in the state of product liability law as it existed before the Product Liability Act, the General Assembly's abrogation of the common law of product liability through the statute of repose does not run afoul of the "substantive" due course of law provision of Article I, Section 12.

In this case, the General Assembly has determined that injuries occurring ten years after the product was delivered to a user are not legally cognizable claims for relief. Accordingly, the McIntoshes are not entitled to a "remedy" under Section 12. Thus, the statute of repose "does not bar a cause of action; its effect, rather, is to prevent what might otherwise be a cause of action from ever arising. The injured party literally has *no* cause of action. The harm that has been done is *damnum absque injuria*—a wrong for which the law affords no redress."

Although the state constitution requires courts to be open to provide remedy by due course of law, legislation by rational classification to abolish a remedy is consonant with due course of law. If the law provides no remedy, Section 12 does not require one.

Finally, the dissent concludes that Article I, Section 12 guarantees to each citizen "a substantive right to remedy for injuries suffered." We think this confuses "injury" with "wrong." There is not and never has been a right to redress for every injury, as victims of natural disasters or faultless accidents can attest. Nor is there any constitutional right to any particular remedy. Indeed, as we have pointed out, some forms of "wrong" recognized at common law have long since been abolished by the legislature without conflict with the Indiana Constitution. Ironically, the wrong the dissent contends in this case to be preserved by the constitution against legislative interference, strict liability for product flaws, did not exist in 1851; it was adopted as part of the Product Liability Act in 1978. It is true, as the dissent notes, that the concept of strict liability did not originate with the Product Liability Act. Although strict liability did not exist in 1851, by the 1970s, it had become a recognized theory of recovery.

Although we reject the McIntoshes' challenge, the legislature's authority is not without limits. Section 12 requires that legislation that deprives a person of a complete tort remedy must be a rational means to achieve a legitimate legislative goal. We also have held that, as applied to the individual case, the limitation must not be an unreasonable impediment to the exercise of an otherwise valid claim.

The Product Liability Act meets both tests. The statute of repose represents a determination by the General Assembly that an injury occurring ten years after the product has been in use is not a legally cognizable "injury" that is to be remedied by the courts. This decision was based on its apparent conclusion that after a decade of use, product failures are "due to reasons not fairly laid at the manufacturer's door." The statute also serves the public policy concerns of reliability and availability of evidence after long periods of time, and the ability of manufacturers to plan their affairs without the potential for unknown liability. It provides certainty and finality with a bright line bar to liability ten years after a product's first use. It is also rationally related to the General Assembly's reasonable determination that, in the vast majority of cases, failure of products over ten years old is due to wear and tear or other causes not the fault of the manufacturer.

In sum, the McIntoshes do not have a vested interest in the state of the common law as it existed before the Product Liability Act was passed. The General Assembly has made the permissible legislative choice to limit product liability actions to the first ten years of a product's use. Accordingly, the McIntoshes' injuries, which occurred after the ten-year statute of repose ended, were not legally cognizable injuries for which a remedy exists.

DICKSON, J., dissenting.

This case presented us with an opportunity to restore to Indiana's jurisprudence important principles of our state constitution. By doing so, we could have vividly exemplified the Rule of Law notwithstanding the allure of pragmatic commercial interests. We should hold that the ten-year statute of repose provision in the Indiana Products Liability Act violates the Right to Remedy Clause of the Indiana Constitution.

Within the Bill of Rights of the Indiana Constitution, Section 12 provides in relevant part: "All courts shall be open; and every person, for injury done to him in his person, property, or reputation, shall have remedy by due course of law." The majority today holds that the statute of repose in the Indiana Products Liability Act, which denies a remedy to citizens injured by defective products that happen to be more than ten years old, does not violate this provision. Noting prior cases that have considered the Due Course of Law Clause of the Indiana Constitution analogous to the Due Process Clause of the U.S. Constitution, the majority correctly acknowledges that the two provisions are not synonymous, but nevertheless finds the statute of repose provision proper because it concludes that there is no constitutional right to remedy in Indiana. I disagree.

Thirty-seven other state constitutions also include a "remedies" provision. These provisions trace their roots to chapter 40 of the Magna Carta: "To no one will we sell, to no one will we deny, or delay right or justice." It is this assurance of access to justice that is embodied in our Right to Remedy Clause.

Applying our well-established methodology of constitutional interpretation, I conclude that Section 12 provides separate and distinct protections and is not coextensive with federal due process jurisprudence. I am also convinced that Section 12 ensures not only that procedures must comply with due course of law, but further that both the text and the history provide strong support for understanding Section 12 of Indiana's Bill of Rights to provide a substantive right to remedy for injuries suffered.

The legislature has the authority to modify or abrogate common law rights as long as such change does not interfere with constitutional rights. Although constitutional rights may be subjected to legislative restraints and burdens necessitated by the State's exercise of its police power to promote the peace, safety, and well-being of the public, this police power is not unlimited: "There is within each provision of our Bill of Rights a cluster of essential values which the legislature may qualify but not alienate." "A right is impermissibly alienated when the State materially burdens one of the core values which it embodies." The right to remedy for injury is such a core value.

While legislative qualifications of this right may be enacted under the police power, the total abrogation of an injured person's right to remedy is an unacceptable burden. The statute of repose provision in the Products Liability Act is no mere qualification. It does not merely limit the time within which to assert a remedy, nor does it merely modify the procedure for enforcing the remedy. Nor is it a narrow, limited immunity necessitated by police power. On the contrary, the repose provision completely bars the courthouse doors to all persons injured by products over ten years old, even for claims alleging negligence, and even where the products were designed and purchased with the expectation of decades of continued use. Although this provision denies all Indiana citizens access to justice ensured by the Right to Remedy Clause, it is especially pernicious to those economically disadvantaged citizens who must rely on used products rather than new ones.

NOTES

1. What level of scrutiny do the courts apply when evaluating claims that a statutory enactment has violated the right to a remedy or open courts provisions? Does the standard resemble any standard applied in other state or federal contexts, e.g., in federal equal protection or due process analysis? What standard of review, if any, should they apply?

2. Is the "right to a remedy by due course of law" a procedural guarantee? A substantive protection? Or both?

LANEY v. FAIRVIEW CITY
57 P.3d 1007 (Utah 2002)

DURHAM, C.J.

This case addresses whether Utah Code Ann. § 63-30-2(4)(a) violates the "open courts" clause, of the Utah Constitution. The district court held that Fairview City is immune from suit for its alleged negligence under the Utah Governmental Immunity Act. We hold that the 1987 amendment, declaring all acts of municipalities to be governmental functions, is unconstitutional as applied to municipalities operating electrical power systems.

On September 16, 1991, John Laney was electrocuted and killed while moving irrigation pipe. The thirty-foot aluminum water irrigation pipe that Laney was carrying came into contact with, or within arcing distance of, high voltage power lines. The power lines were owned by the City.

Laney's wife and children brought a wrongful death action against the City claiming that the City was negligent for failing to maintain the power lines in a safe condition. The Laneys complain that the power lines did not meet minimum safety standards because they were too low to the ground. They also allege that the lines were unsafe because they were not insulated and did not contain warnings.

The City moved for summary judgment asserting that the decision whether or not to improve the power lines was a discretionary function entitled to immunity under Utah Code Ann. § 63-30-10(1). Discretionary function immunity is an exception to a waiver of sovereign immunity within the Utah Governmental Immunity Act. The Utah Governmental Immunity Act declares that all governmental entities are immune from suit for any injury which results from the exercise of a "governmental function." The term governmental function is broadly defined in section 63-30-2(4)(a), and by virtue of that broad definition, the statute cloaks governmental entities with immunity for a wide range of activities. However, Utah Code Ann. § 63-30-10 waives sovereign immunity "for injury proximately caused by a negligent act or omission." Then, subsection (1) creates an exception to this waiver for negligence and immunizes governmental entities for "the exercise or performance or the failure to exercise or perform a discretionary function."

Because we find that the City's maintenance of the power lines constitutes a discretionary function within the meaning of the Governmental Immunity Act, we must address the plaintiffs' constitutional challenge. Article I, section 11 of the Utah Constitution provides:

> All courts shall be open, and every person, for an injury done to him in his person, property, or reputation, shall have remedy by due course of law, which shall be administered without denial or unnecessary delay; and no person shall be barred from prosecuting or defending before any tribunal in this state, by himself or counsel any civil cause to which he is a party.

Although some states with open courts provisions have construed them to guarantee only procedural rights and court access, such a construction has never been accepted in Utah. Article I, section 11's constitutional guarantee has been interpreted to protect substantive rights to remedies throughout our state's history. The open courts provision was adopted, as part of the original Constitution itself, at the end of the nineteenth century, during a period when abuse had generated concern and distrust of the legislative branch in numerous states. That abuse included misuse of political influence by railroads and other corporate interests, who convinced state legislators to favor private interests through legislative enactments insulating them from the general laws.

Focusing entirely on the "procedural" content of the language found in section 11, as the State does, is misleading. Constitutional language must be viewed in context, meaning that its history and purpose must be considered in determining its meaning. The language that a remedy shall be had by "due course of law" describes the law by which the remedy is secured, as well as the procedural guarantees also protected by this section. Article I, section 7 already contains a due process provision guaranteeing procedural rights. Thus, if the State's reading of section 11 is correct, section 11 is redundant and mere surplusage—it has no constitutional role or function that is not already performed by section 7. That view has never been embraced by any Utah decision.

We now turn to the analysis of the constitutionality of subsection 63-30-2(4)(a) using the test set forth in *Berry*. A legislative enactment that does not eliminate a remedy is not unconstitutional under the open courts provision. Therefore, we must first determine whether a cause of action has been abrogated by the legislative enactment. If no remedy was eliminated, there is no need to proceed with the *Berry* test.

Plaintiffs assert that the 1987 amendment abrogated a remedy because the law in effect prior to the amendment provided individuals negligently injured by municipality-operated power lines with a cause of action against the municipality. Prior to the amendment, the scope of sovereign immunity depended on whether the governmental activity complained of was found to be a "governmental function" or a "proprietary function." Only those activities determined to be governmental functions were afforded immunity. The Act did not define what constituted a governmental function, therefore this court established a standard whereby a function could be considered a governmental function. This definition of governmental function was used to determine whether an activity was covered by the Act until the legislature redefined the term in 1987.

Plaintiffs argue that the City's operation and maintenance of a municipal electrical power system would not have been a governmental function under this Court's standard because maintaining power lines is not "of such a unique nature that it can only be performed by a governmental agency or that is essential to the core of governmental immunity." We agree.

Prior to the 1987 amendment, the operation of an electrical power system was considered a proprietary function, which was not entitled to immunity under the Act. Under the 1987 amendment, however, a claim against a municipality for negligent maintenance of power lines can be barred by the scope of immunity protection afforded the City. Although the Act waives immunity for governmental functions if there is negligence involved, a plaintiff suing a municipality is now subject to the exceptions to the waiver of immunity. By defining a governmental function as *any* act of a governmental entity, whether or not the activity is characterized as governmental or proprietary, the 1987 amendment effectively grants immunity protection for some activities that formerly were not entitled to immunity. Therefore, we find that the 1987 amendment partially abrogated a remedy for a municipality's negligence. Because a remedy has been abrogated, we proceed with the *Berry* test to determine the constitutionality of the amendment under the open courts provision.

Under the first prong of the *Berry* analysis, when a remedy has been abrogated, this court determines whether the legislature has provided a "reasonable alternative remedy 'by due course of law' for vindication of a plaintiff's constitutional interest." In *Berry*, we held that the substitute benefit "must be substantially equal in value or other benefit to the remedy abrogated in providing essentially comparable substantive protection to one's person, property, or reputation, although the form of the substitute remedy may be different." In the instant case, we find no indication that the legislature provided any substitute remedy, nor does the State make this argument. Therefore, we must turn to the second prong of the *Berry* test.

The State contends that even if a remedy was abrogated, the amendment is constitutional under the second prong of the *Berry* test, which provides that where no alternative remedy has been provided, "abrogation of the remedy or cause of action may be justified only if there is a clear social or economic evil to be eliminated and the elimination of an existing legal remedy is not an arbitrary or unreasonable means for achieving the objective."

Cases involving statutes of limitation and statutes of repose have come before this court with mixed results. In an early case, we held that article I, section 11, did not preclude the legislature from prescribing a one-year statute of limitations for the time within which to assail the regularity or organization of an irrigation district. In three cases, statutes of repose were struck down because they barred actions without regard to the occurrence of an injury and did not provide a reasonable amount of time to file a lawsuit. No effective and reasonable alternative was provided, and the abrogation of the remedy was held to be arbitrary and unreasonable.

In the only case that we have found which did *not* involve an act of the legislature, this court abolished the common law tort of criminal conversation and justified its abolition under the open courts provision on the ground that the cause of action was "unfair and bad policy," "served" no useful purpose, was subject to abuse, and protected interests that were already adequately served by the tort of alienation of affections.

Recently, in *Day v. State* (Utah 1999), we relied on the open courts provision to strike down a statute granting immunity for negligent operation of an emergency vehicle in circumstances where immunity had not previously existed. We declared the statute unconstitutional because the legislature was not acting to obviate a "clear social evil" in this state. The sponsor of the legislation had explained that the statute was necessary because of a rash of frivolous lawsuits, "especially in California." We noted that on its face, the sponsor's statement did not identify any social, economic, or any other evil in Utah.

With that backdrop, we turn to the instant case. The 1987 amendment eliminates the appellants' right to sue for Mr. Laney's wrongful death. The statutory amendment thus sharply limited instances where municipalities operating a power system could be held liable for their negligence.

The 1987 amendment was proposed in the "hope that passage of these bills will make it easier or cheaper for a government entity to obtain liability insurance." Thus the legislative objective appears to have been to make liability insurance more affordable for government entities by reducing liability risks. While that objective is worthy, the legislature swept too broadly when it severely curtailed negligence actions against municipalities operating power systems. The legislative concern about increased damage awards against governmental entities is stated in very general terms; no specifics are given. We do not know whether any municipality in this state operating an electrical system has sustained a large damage award. We do know that only a small fraction operate municipal power systems. The legislative findings do not show that large damage awards have been made against municipalities in connection with their operation of an electrical power system, or that its operation has been affected in any way by potential liability.

Equally disturbing is the broad sweep that the legislature took to meet its objective. In the instant case, the legislature has defined *all* activities of municipalities as governmental action, regardless of their nature. In its sweep, the operation of both a sewer system and a golf course is governmental, along with the operation of a municipal electrical power system, even though the potential for negligently causing death by the municipality is vastly greater in the latter activity.

If large verdicts are vexatious to cities, a reasonable approach might be to create very limited immunities to address specific problems, or to place "caps" on the amount of damages, as the legislature has done elsewhere in the Governmental Immunity Act. This court has, for example, upheld statutory caps on judgments for damages for personal injury against a governmental entity.

We therefore hold that the 1987 amendment is unconstitutional as it applies to municipalities operating electrical power systems. No clear social or economic evil has been specifically identified, and the broad sweep of the amendment is arbitrary and unreasonable when applied to the operation of a municipal electrical power system, where a high duty of care is imposed. We express no opinion on the constitutionality of the amendment as applied to other municipal activities since a lower standard of care may apply and different considerations may be relevant.

WILKINS, J., concurring in part and dissenting in part.

In my opinion, section 63-30-2(4)(a) of the Utah Governmental Immunity Act, does not violate article I, section 11 of the Utah Constitution, the Open Courts Clause. In my view, the Legislature acted within its constitutional authority in setting forth the current scheme of sovereign immunity in Utah. Under the statute, Fairview City should be entitled to immunity for its omissions, to not raise the height of, insulate, or provide further warnings on its power lines, a discretionary function within the discretionary function exception of the Utah Governmental Immunity Act.

In my view, the *Berry* test permits a majority of this court to substitute its judgment of what constitutes good public policy for the judgment of the legislature, the branch of government that is not only best suited to determine and implement public policy under our system of government, but is constitutionally obligated to do so. I am of the opinion that whether a substitute remedy is of "substantially equal value or other benefit to the remedy abrogated," and whether there is a clear social or economic evil to be eliminated, are two questions that should be answered by the legislature, not this court, and that we overstep our bounds in so doing. I agree that the Open Courts Clause limits legislative authority. Numerous constitutional provisions prevent the legislative branch from eliminating constitutional or inalienable rights. I do not think, however, that the Open Courts Clause guarantees one the right to a judicial remedy for every injury done to one's person, property, or reputation.

The first *Berry* assumption with which I disagree is the assumption that those who suffer because of legislation preventing recovery for personal injury are individuals who are somehow part of a minority that is not represented or underrepresented in the political process. Individuals who suffer injury to their person, property, or reputation are not a discreet and insular minority. All persons, regardless of ethnic background, economic background, gender, religious persuasion, or other affiliations, may suffer injury. Viewing an injured individual or group retrospectively, after they have suffered injury, they may very well be unable to rally the political process. Prospectively, however, all of us as citizens, regardless of status, are subject to legislation limiting our ability to recover for personal injury. No group is singled out by legislation that limits the ability to recover for personal injuries. All citizens face the possibility of personal injury, even those who are generally visible in society that belong to what we may think are privileged, identifiable groups. Those thwarted by the Utah Governmental Immunity Act, those who have suffered personal injuries at the hands of the government, may be any of us; they do not comprise a distinct and insular group whose voice may not be heard through the political process.

Second, *Berry* assumes that the Open Courts Clause contains language which should be interpreted to protect against majoritarian abuse. I disagree. Other provisions in our constitution are more suited to protecting against majoritarian abuse. They contain language which more specifically implies protection for political minorities, and these provisions have also been interpreted to protect groups and individuals that are isolated from the political process. The language of the Open Courts Clause is ill-suited to protect against majoritarian abuse.

The real danger presented by the *Berry* test is that of majoritarian abuse by the members of this court. The risk, in my mind, lies in requiring that new legislation satisfy the policy predilections of a majority of the members of this court by providing, in the eyes of this court, an adequate alternative remedy; or by eliminating what is viewed as a clear social or economic evil by this court. The constitution vests power in the legislature to implement, as law, the will of the majority of the citizens of this State.

Third, the *Berry* interpretation assumes that each individual who suffers an injury to his or her person, property, or reputation, is constitutionally entitled to a remedy. The idea that a remedy can be fashioned for every injury is optimistic and well-intentioned, but, as a practical matter, impossible. The law cannot, and therefore does not, guarantee a remedy for every injury.

Individuals who have been injured in their persons, property, or reputation, are entitled to a remedy only when the law, statutory or common, recognizes an injury and permits a remedy. The Open Courts Clause should not be interpreted to provide a right to a remedy. It should be interpreted to guarantee *access* to seek a judicial determination as to whether the law grants a remedy for the injury suffered. The courts, through the common law, may create remedies when public policy dictates that certain interests are worthy of protection and the legislature has not spoken. Likewise, the legislature creates remedies when it determines, as a matter of public policy, that certain interests are worthy of protection. If the law provides for a remedy, then the Open Courts Clause guarantees the right to seek that permitted remedy through the courts.

The *Berry* test places this court in the position of sitting as a second legislature, re-weighing the social or economic policy, instead of analyzing, as other methods of constitutional analysis do, whether the law is rationally related to its avowed purpose. Substitution of the policy of three or more judges for the policy of the legislature, absent specific constitutional authority, is contrary to our system of government.

TINDLEY v. SALT LAKE CITY SCHOOL DISTRICT
116 P.3d 295 (Utah 2005)

PARRISH, J.

This appeal concerns the constitutionality of section 63–30–34 of the Utah Governmental Immunity Act, which limits the damages recoverable in actions against the state or its political subdivisions. Plaintiffs brought this action against the Salt Lake City School District, asserting that the limitation violates both the Utah and the United States Constitutions. The District successfully moved for summary judgment. Plaintiffs appealed. We affirm.

David Smith was employed by the District as a teacher and debate team coach at Highland High School in Salt Lake City, Utah. Smith selected eight students, including Erin Anderson, Matt Ehrman, Brian and Jeff Horman, and Eric Sabodski, to compete in a debate tournament at the University of Southern California. The tournament began on a Friday and concluded the following Sunday. Each student competing in the tournament paid a portion of the costs to attend, with the remaining costs paid by funds raised through the high school debate club.

Intending to drive the team to USC, Smith reserved a fifteen-passenger van from a rental agency. When Smith arrived at the rental agency, however, he learned that the van he had reserved was unavailable. Consequently, Smith rented two minivans to transport the students to the competition. District employee and assistant debate team coach Christian Bradley drove one of the vans, while Smith drove the other.

The debate team arrived at USC and participated in both the preliminary and the elimination rounds of the competition. Following the elimination rounds on Sunday afternoon, the team began the return trip to Salt Lake City. Bradley left at approximately 1:00 p.m., driving one of the rented minivans, with Eric, Jeff, Erin, Brian, and Matt as passengers. Smith followed shortly thereafter with the remaining students. Late that evening, while traveling through Millard County, Utah, Bradley lost control of the minivan due to his own negligence. The vehicle flipped several times, ejecting Eric, Jeff, and Erin.

Eric and Jeff were killed in the accident, and the remaining three students were seriously injured. Erin sustained numerous injuries, including a severe traumatic brain injury. Brian's injuries included crushed vertebrae and a fractured hand and foot, and Matt suffered an injury to his knee, as well as multiple contusions and abrasions. It is uncontested that plaintiffs' aggregate damages exceeded $500,000.

Recognizing its liability for Bradley's negligence, the District and its insurer, the Utah State Division of Risk Management, entered into a settlement agreement with plaintiffs Erin, Brian, Matt, and the parents and estates of Eric and Jeff. Under the settlement agreement, the District agreed to pay plaintiffs collectively $500,000, the maximum amount then recoverable under the Utah Governmental Immunity Act. In exchange, plaintiffs agreed to relinquish their rights to pursue any claims against the District or its employees, but reserved the right to challenge the constitutionality of the damage cap imposed by the Governmental Immunity Act.

In accordance with the settlement agreement, plaintiffs filed suit in district court, alleging that the cap violates several provisions of the Utah Constitution, including the open courts clause, as well as the provisions guaranteeing due process, uniform operation of laws, and the right to recover damages for injuries resulting in death.

Historically, the ability to sue the State of Utah or one of its political subdivisions rested on a determination of whether the governmental entity was protected by the common law doctrine of sovereign immunity. That changed in 1965, when the Utah Legislature enacted the Utah Governmental Immunity Act, which barred all causes of action against the state and its political subdivisions unless expressly authorized by statute. Specifically, the Act provided that "all governmental entities," including school districts, "are immune from suit for any injury which results from the exercise of a governmental function." Despite its broad grant of immunity, the Act expressly waived immunity for "injury proximately caused by a negligent act or omission of an employee committed within the scope of employment." Judgments obtained pursuant to this waiver, however, were limited. The Act provided that

> If a judgment for damages for personal injury against a governmental entity, or an employee whom a governmental entity has a duty to indemnify, exceeds $250,000 for one person in any one occurrence, or $500,000 for two or more persons in any one occurrence, the court shall reduce the judgment to that amount.

We first address plaintiffs' claim that the cap violates the open courts clause found in article I, section 11 of the Utah Constitution. The open courts clause is not merely a procedural protection. Rather, this court has held that the open courts clause provides citizens of Utah the "right to a remedy for an injury." In *Laney v. Fairview City* (Utah 2002), we declared that "the plain meaning of the open courts clause imposes some *substantive* limitation on the legislature's ability to abolish judicial remedies in a capricious fashion." In other words, the open courts clause provides more than procedural protections; it also secures substantive rights, thereby restricting the legislature's ability to abrogate remedies provided by law.

Although the open courts clause protects both substantive and procedural rights, the clause is not an absolute guarantee of all substantive rights. Rather, it applies only to legislation which "abrogates a cause of action existing at the time of its enactment." The legislature thus remains free to abrogate or limit claims that could not have been brought under then-existing law. Claims barred by the doctrine of governmental immunity are an example of this principle.

In addition, the mere fact that legislation abrogates an existing legal remedy does not render it impermissible under the open courts clause. Such legislation is acceptable under *Berry* so long as it either "provides an injured person an effective and reasonable alternative remedy" or seeks to eliminate "a clear social or economic evil." With respect to the second alternative, "the abrogation of an existing legal remedy cannot be an arbitrary or unreasonable means for achieving the objective."

The District argues that the doctrine of sovereign immunity rendered it immune from suit prior to the passage of the Act. Accordingly, it reasons that the Act could not have abrogated any "existing remedy" in violation of the open courts clause. Plaintiffs urge us to reject this conclusion for two reasons. First, plaintiffs argue that the doctrine of sovereign immunity was not part of Utah law at the time the Utah Constitution was adopted. Second, even assuming that sovereign immunity was part of Utah law, they assert that it protected governmental entities only when those entities were performing activities constituting a governmental function, and that transporting students to an out-of-state, extracurricular debate tournament does not qualify as such. We decline plaintiffs' invitation to revisit the historical evolution of sovereign immunity under Utah law because we conclude that the District would have been entitled to immunity for its activity in this case prior to the adoption of the Act.

Here, we are unwilling to conclude that a school's operation of an extracurricular student debate team, including its transport of the team to and from out-of-state competitions, falls outside the realm of a school district's core activities. Such an activity clearly benefits student education and is unlikely to be available to public school students if not offered through their schools. Moreover, imposing tort liability on a school district for the operation of such activities is more likely to deter schools from offering them than to promote public safety. We note that other jurisdictions have consistently held that similar extracurricular activities fall within the scope of a public school's traditional governmental immunity.

We conclude that school districts have always enjoyed governmental immunity for the operation of such programs as the one at issue. Thus, the Act did not in any way limit or abrogate a right to recover from the District.

NOTES

1. Are right to a remedy/open courts provisions substantive, procedural, or both? What does "substantive" and "procedural" mean in this context?

2. How difficult is it for the courts to give content and meaning to right to a remedy/open courts provisions without usurping the legislative function? Are the separation of powers considerations in this context similar to or different from such concerns generally?

3. Does it matter to the courts whether a challenged limitation affects only a common law claim? A statutory claim? Is there justification for treating statutory and common law claims differently?

4. Right to a remedy/open courts provisions have been litigated in a variety of contexts, as the cases illustrate. Should all contexts be treated the same for constitutional purposes? Or are there reasons to evaluate damages caps, repose periods, defenses, workers' compensation, or procedural limitations differently? Note that such cases might also arise in the criminal context. *See, e.g., Dorsey v. State*, 716 A.2d 807 (Del. 2000) (declaring a state

constitutional right to a suppression of evidence remedy in the context of an unconstitutional search).

5. How do the standards the state courts use in evaluating right to a remedy/open courts provisions compare to federal due process and equal protection standards? Are they the same, similar, or distinctly different? Do right to a remedy provisions serve the same purposes as the Fourteenth Amendment's Due Process and Equal Protection Clauses?

6. For additional reading on state constitutional right to remedy/open courts provisions, see David Schuman, *The Right To A Remedy*, 65 Temple L. Rev. 1197 (1992); Jonathan M. Hoffman, *Questions Before Answers: The Ongoing Search to Understand the Origins of the Open Courts Clause*, 32 Rutgers L.J. 1005 (2001). *See also* John C.P. Goldberg, *The Constitutional Status of Tort Law: Due Process and the Right to a Law for the Redress of Wrongs*, 115 Yale L.J. 524 (2005).

C. JURY TRIAL RIGHTS (AND OTHER POTENTIAL CHALLENGES) UNDER STATE CONSTITUTIONS—ARE STATUTORY DAMAGES CAPS CONSTITUTIONAL?

States must provide juries in serious criminal cases as a matter of federal constitutional law, *Duncan v. Louisiana* (1968), and those juries must render unanimous verdicts, *Ramos v. Louisiana* (2020), because the U.S. Supreme Court has deemed those features of criminal procedure to be fundamental to the "due process" required under the Fourteenth Amendment. But the Court has never held the Seventh Amendment's right to a jury trial in civil cases involving more than $20 to apply to the States. *See Minneapolis & St. Louis R.R. Co. v. Bombolis*, 241 U.S. 211 (1916).

Nonetheless, many state constitutions provide explicit and strong protection for jury trial rights in civil cases. A common formulation in numerous state constitutions is along the lines of "The right of trial by jury shall be inviolate." *E.g.*, Kan. Const. Bill of Rights § 5. These provisions have become important when state legislatures engage in "tort reform" efforts and seek to limit remedies available to plaintiffs, for example by capping non-economic or punitive damages. The next cases illustrate how state supreme courts have divided over state constitutional challenges to such legislation.

HILBURN v. ENERPIPE LTD.
442 P.3d 509 (Kan. 2019)

BEIER, J.

This case requires us once again to examine the constitutionality of K.S.A. 60-19a02, which caps jury awards for noneconomic damages in personal injury actions. Plaintiff Diana K. Hilburn argues that the application of K.S.A. 60-19a02 to reduce her jury award of $ 335,000 to a judgment of $ 283,490.86 violated her rights under section 5 and section 18 of the Kansas Constitution Bill of Rights.

Hilburn was injured in November 2010 when the car in which she was riding was rear-ended by a semi-truck. Hilburn sued the truck's owner, Enerpipe Ltd., alleging that the truck driver's negligence caused the collision and that Enerpipe was vicariously liable for its driver's actions. In its answer to Hilburn's Petition, Enerpipe admitted the driver's negligence and conceded its vicarious liability. The case proceeded to a trial on damages, after which a jury awarded Hilburn $335,000 in damages comprising $ 33,490.86 for medical expenses and $301,509.14 for noneconomic losses. Defense counsel prepared an entry of judgment against Enerpipe for $ 283,490.86 because, "pursuant to K.S.A. 60-19a02(d), judgment must be entered in the amount of $ 250,000 for all of Diana K. Hilburn's noneconomic loss." Hilburn objected on the ground that K.S.A. 60-19a02 is unconstitutional. She alleged violations of sections 1, 5, and 18 of the Kansas Constitution Bill of Rights.

Section 5 of the Kansas Constitution Bill of Rights states that "the right of trial by jury shall be inviolate." We have little difficulty deciding that the right protected by section 5 is a "fundamental interest" expressly protected by the Kansas Constitution Bill of Rights. As such, we will not apply a presumption of constitutionality to challenges brought under section 5.

"Section 5 preserves the jury trial right as it historically existed at common law when our state's constitution came into existence." We have consistently held that the determination of noneconomic damages was a fundamental part of a jury trial at common law and protected by section 5. The noneconomic damages cap in K.S.A. 60-19a02 clearly implicates section 5's "inviolate" jury trial right, as that right has historically been understood. The next question is whether it impairs that right by interfering with the jury's fundamental function.

"The individual right to trial by jury cannot remain inviolate when an injured party is deprived of the jury's constitutionally assigned role of determining damages according to the particular facts of the case. Giving the jury a practically meaningless opportunity to assess damages simply "pays lip service to the form of the jury but robs it of its function." Despite this infringement of section 5's jury trial right by K.S.A. 60-19a02, a majority of this court held in *Miller* that any impairment was permissible as long as the two-part due process-based quid pro quo test applicable in section 18 analysis was satisfied. But the overlay of the quid pro quo test "transforms what the people made inviolate into something violable at will." The court's previous decision to apply the quid pro quo test to section 5 "overlooked long-standing limitations on the legislature's power to modify the common law; overestimated the persuasive force of prior Kansas cases; and shortcut the necessary cost-benefit evaluation" when examining whether to keep or jettison originally erroneous precedent.

Looking beyond our state borders, we note that, at the time *Miller* was decided, 19 states had addressed whether damages caps violated their state's constitutional jury protections, and not one had employed the quid pro quo test in its analysis. On this point of law, Kansas has stood strangely alone. For all of the reasons outlined above, we abandon the quid pro quo test for analyzing whether the noneconomic damages cap is unconstitutional under section 5 of the Kansas Constitution Bill of Rights.

Because the *Miller* majority concluded that K.S.A. 60-19a02 satisfied the quid pro quo test, it did not need to engage in an exhaustive discussion of the more basic question of whether the damages cap infringes on section 5's right to trial by jury. It merely conceded quickly that the cap "encroaches" upon the jury trial right and moved to the quid pro quo analysis to excuse what would otherwise have been a fatal constitutional violation. As discussed in the concurring and dissenting opinion in *Miller*, the "encroachment" conclusion is logically and legally indistinguishable from a conclusion that the cap impairs the jury trial right of section 5 and is thus unconstitutional, and it should have ended the matter. It still should and does.

The decisions from 14 of our sister states that have upheld damages caps under attack for violating constitutional jury trial protections do not persuade us. First, only 8 of the 14 interpreted and applied constitutional provisions including language similar to that of our section 5's "inviolate." These eight decisions compose a small majority when compared to those of the highest courts of five states that have struck down damages caps as unconstitutional under constitutional provisions that make the jury trial right "inviolate." Second, we cannot square a right specially designated by the people as "inviolate" with the practical effect of the damages cap: substituting juries' factual determinations of actual damages with an across-the-board legislative determination of the maximum conceivable amount of actual damages. Although, as a purely technical, theoretical matter, we agree that the mere application of an existing damages cap to reduce a jury's award is a matter of law, this statement begs the question at the heart of this case: To whom have the people of Kansas assigned the determination of the amount of the award? Unless an injured party has decided to waive his or her right under section 5, the answer is "the jury."

Regardless of whether an existing damages cap is technically or theoretically applied as a matter of law, the cap's effect is to disturb the jury's finding of fact on the amount of the award. Allowing this substitutes the Legislature's nonspecific judgment for the jury's specific judgment. The people deprived the Legislature of that power when they made the right to trial by jury inviolate. Thus we hold that the cap on damages imposed by

K.S.A. 60-19a02 is facially unconstitutional because it violates section 5 of the Kansas Constitution.

McCLAY v. AIRPORT MANAGEMENT SERVICES, LLC
596 S.W.3d 686 (Tenn. 2020)

BIVINS, C.J.

We accepted certification of the following questions of law from the United States District Court for the Middle District of Tennessee regarding the constitutionality of Tennessee's statutory cap on noneconomic damages, codified at Tennessee Code Annotated section 29-39-102: "(1) Does the noneconomic damages cap in civil cases imposed by Tenn. Code Ann. § 29-39-102 violate a plaintiff's right to a trial by jury, as guaranteed in Article I, section 6, of the Tennessee Constitution?; and (2) Does the noneconomic damages cap in civil cases imposed by Tenn. Code Ann. § 29-39-102 violate Tennessee's constitutional doctrine of separation of powers between the legislative branch and the judicial branch? Upon review, we answer each of the District Court's questions in the negative.

The certified questions of law at issue in this appeal arise from a personal injury action brought in the United States District Court for the Middle District of Tennessee. Plaintiff Jodi McClay filed suit against Defendant Airport Management Services, seeking damages for injuries she sustained in a store at the Nashville International Airport in August 2016. A jury returned a verdict for Plaintiff in the amount of $444,500 for future medical expenses and $930,000 for noneconomic damages, including pain and suffering, permanent injury, and loss of enjoyment of life. The District Court entered judgment against Defendant in accordance with the verdict. Defendant then moved to apply the statutory cap on noneconomic damages in Tennessee Code Annotated section 29-39-102, which generally limits noneconomic damages in civil liability actions to $750,000. Plaintiff responded to Defendant's motion by arguing the statutory cap on noneconomic damages is unconstitutional. The District Court then certified these questions of law.

Tennessee Supreme Court Rule 23 provides that this Court "may, at its discretion, answer questions of law certified to it by a District Court of the United States in Tennessee" if the questions of state law are "determinative of the cause" and "there is no controlling precedent in the decisions of the Supreme Court of Tennessee." Tenn. Sup. Ct. R. 23, § 1. "Rather than requiring a federal court to make the law of this State or to abstain from deciding the case until the state courts resolve the point of law, answering certified questions from federal courts promotes judicial efficiency and comity and protects this State's sovereignty." *Yardley v. Hosp. Housekeeping Sys.* (Tenn. 2015).

The General Assembly enacted the statutory cap on noneconomic damages as part of the Tennessee Civil Justice Act of 2011. Specifically, Tennessee Code Annotated section 29-39-102(a)(2) provides that, in a civil action, awards may include "compensation for any noneconomic damages suffered by each injured plaintiff not to exceed seven hundred fifty thousand dollars ($750,000) for all injuries and occurrences that were or could have been asserted, regardless of whether the action is based on a single act or omission or a series of acts or omissions that allegedly caused the injuries or death."

The cap is increased to $1,000,000 for certain "catastrophic loss or injury." The statute also exempts certain kinds of cases from the cap, such as those in which the defendant had a specific intent to inflict serious physical injury, the defendant was intoxicated, or the defendant committed a felony in causing the injury. None of those exemptions is at issue in this case. Plaintiff argues that, under the Tennessee Constitution, the statutory cap violates the right to trial by jury, the doctrine of separation of powers, and discriminates disproportionately against women in violation of equal protection guarantees.

The right to a jury trial in Tennessee is expressly guaranteed by Article 1, Section 6, of the Tennessee Constitution, which mandates that "the right of trial by jury shall remain inviolate." We have explained that this provision guarantees the right to trial by jury as it existed at common law under the laws and constitution of North Carolina at the time of the adoption of the Tennessee Constitution of 1796. We further have held that "the right to a jury trial envisions that all contested factual issues will be decided by jurors who are unbiased and impartial." We also have long-recognized that the ascertainment of damages is a question of fact for the jury. We assume for purposes of this opinion that noneconomic damages were available at the time of the adoption of the Tennessee Constitution. Thus, we also assume that a plaintiff has the right to an unbiased and impartial jury to decide, as a question of fact, the amount of any noneconomic damages sustained by the plaintiff.

As an initial matter, we recognize that it is within our General Assembly's authority to legislatively alter the common law. Indeed, there are numerous examples of the General Assembly altering common law causes of action and available remedies. For example, in *Lavin v. Jordon* (Tenn. 2000), we held that the common law tort of negligent control and supervision of a child had been superseded by statute when the damage caused by the child was intentional or malicious. The General Assembly also has expressly abrogated common law causes of action, including alienation of affections, seduction, and criminal conversation. This Court has recognized that the abrogation of those causes of action was within the General Assembly's authority and represented the legislative expression of the public policy of the state. Here, one could view the statutory cap on noneconomic damages as a limitation on the available remedy for certain causes of action, or as an abrogation of causes of action for claims exceeding the statutory limit. Under either view, the General Assembly was within its legislative authority to alter the common law by enacting the statutory cap on noneconomic damages. Of course, the General Assembly may only exercise its authority to alter the common law within constitutional limits.

The right to a jury trial mandates that all contested factual issues be decided by an unbiased and impartial jury. However, the right to a jury trial under the Tennessee Constitution does not entitle a plaintiff to any particular cause of action or any particular remedy. Instead, what causes of action a plaintiff may bring, or what remedies a plaintiff may seek, are matters of law subject to determination by the legislature. Under Tennessee Code Annotated section 29-39-102(g), the statutory cap on noneconomic damages is not disclosed to the jury, but is instead applied by the trial court to any award of noneconomic damages. Thus, a jury determines, as a question of fact, the amount of any noneconomic damages sustained by a plaintiff. The trial judge then applies, as a matter of law determined by the legislature, the statutory cap on noneconomic damages in entering the final judgment. This application of law by the trial judge does not violate the plaintiff's right to have a jury determine the underlying facts of the case. In reaching this conclusion, we find persuasive the reasoning from many of our sister states that have similarly concluded a variety of statutory caps on damages do not violate a plaintiff's right to trial by jury. We hold that the statutory cap on noneconomic damages in Tennessee Code Annotated section 29-39-102 does not violate the right to trial by jury under the Tennessee Constitution.

Plaintiff also argues that the statutory cap violates the separation of powers provisions of the Tennessee Constitution. Article II, section 1 of the Tennessee Constitution provides that "the powers of the Government shall be divided into three distinct departments: the Legislative, Executive, and Judicial." Section 2 of the same Article provides that "no person or persons belonging to one of these departments shall exercise any of the powers properly belonging to either of the others, except in the cases herein directed or permitted." "In general, the 'legislative power' is the authority to make, order, and repeal law; the 'executive power' is the authority to administer and enforce the law; and the 'judicial power' is the authority to interpret and apply law." We have recognized, however, that "while the three branches of government are independent and co-equal, they are to a degree interdependent as well, with the functions of one branch often overlapping that of another."

We have further explained that this Court alone "has the inherent power to promulgate rules governing the practice and procedure of the courts of this state," which "cannot be constitutionally exercised by any other branch of government." Thus, this Court previously has held that the General Assembly oversteps constitutional boundaries in violation of the separation of powers when it exercises its legislative power in a way that directly contradicts existing procedural rules of the courts. However, the separation of powers doctrine in our constitution does not prevent the Generally Assembly from enacting substantive law.

The statutory cap on noneconomic damages is a substantive change in the law that was within the General Assembly's legislative authority to enact. The statutory cap does not interfere with the judicial power of the courts to interpret and apply law. To the contrary, courts exercise their judicial authority, and fulfill their constitutional responsibilities, by applying the statutory cap on noneconomic damages to the cases before them. The statutory cap on noneconomic damages in Tennessee Code Annotated section 29-39-102 does not violate the separation of powers doctrine under the Tennessee Constitution.

CLARK, J., dissenting.

I would hold that Tennessee Code Annotated section 29-39-102(e) (2012) violates article I, section 6 of the Tennessee Constitution by usurping the jury's essential and constitutionally protected fact-finding function.

Every version of the Tennessee Constitution dating back to the attainment of statehood in 1796 has declared "[t]hat the right of trial by jury shall remain inviolate." The contours of this right thus "have remained unchanged" for the past 223 years. This constitutional guarantee preserves "the right of trial by jury as it existed at common law and was in force and use under the laws and Constitution of North Carolina at the time of the formation and adoption" of the Tennessee Constitution of 1796. As for claims that would have been tried to a jury at common law, this constitutional guarantee ensures that the right of trial by jury "shall remain inviolate." Article I, section 6 therefore preserves the essential functions of the jury. One of those essential functions "is that all contested factual issues be determined by an unbiased, impartial jury." This constitutionally guaranteed fact-finding function encompasses the jury's determination of the type and amount of damages.

Article I, section 6 squarely places the determination of damages "within the strict province of the jury." Indeed, the jury's constitutionally protected function of determining damages is so well established that, "to avoid contravention of the right to jury trial clauses of the federal and state constitutions, the trial court must obtain the consent of the party against whom an additur or remittitur is to be entered; if that party does not consent, the trial court must order a new trial."

Tennessee Code Annotated section 29-39-102(e) usurps and replaces the jury's constitutionally protected function of determining damages with an arbitrary ceiling on damages mostly unrelated to the specific facts and circumstances of each litigant's claim. The effect of Tennessee Code Annotated section 29-39-102(e) is a mandatory remittitur that would otherwise be unenforceable unless a trial court first determined that the evidence in a particular case preponderated against the jury's determination of damages and the plaintiff then consented to the remittitur. By usurping the jury's constitutionally protected function of determining damages and rendering the jury's factual findings meaningless, Tennessee Code Annotated section 29-39-102(e) clearly contravenes article I, section 6.

In so concluding, I adopt the reasoning of the high courts of Alabama, Georgia, Kansas, Missouri, and Washington, which have eloquently explained how statutes capping damages in their own jurisdictions violate their own state constitutional provisions preserving "inviolate" the right to trial by jury. As the Alabama Supreme Court explained, "because the statute caps the jury's verdict automatically and absolutely, the jury's function, to the extent the verdict exceeds the damages ceiling, assumes less than an advisory status." The Missouri Supreme Court pointed out that a statute imposing an arbitrary limit on damages "directly curtails the individual right to one of the most significant constitutional roles performed by the jury—the determination of damages." The Georgia Supreme Court reasoned that, by requiring courts "to reduce a noneconomic damages award determined by a jury that exceeds the statutory limit," a statute capping damages "clearly nullifies the jury's findings of fact regarding damages and thereby undermines the jury's basic function." Like the Kansas Supreme Court, I "simply cannot square a right specially designated by the people as 'inviolate' with the practical effect of the damages cap: substituting juries' factual determinations of actual damages with an across-the-board legislative determination of the maximum conceivable amount of actual damages." Finally, as the Washington Supreme Court noted, a statute capping damages "directly changes the outcome of a jury determination" by altering a jury's factual finding "to conform to a predetermined formula," and thereby "robs the jury of its function."

LEE, J., dissenting.

Section 29-39-102 improperly "amends" Article I, section 6 of the Tennessee Constitution to diminish the right to trial by jury. Now section 6 might as well read: "the right of trial by jury shall remain inviolate—as long as the jury, which has considered all the evidence and followed the law, awards an injured party less than $750,000 in noneconomic damages (or less than $1,000,000 when the injuries are catastrophic)." Under this legislative "amendment" to the Constitution, a jury's verdict for noneconomic damages is meaningless when the verdict exceeds the damages cap. The cap on damages is one-size-fits-all and fails to consider the extent of a party's noneconomic losses. And the injured party has to accept the reduced award of damages. Thus, the damages cap statute unconstitutionally takes away a citizen's right to trial by jury on noneconomic damages. The jury's role in a civil jury trial becomes a mere procedural formality.

Noneconomic damages include compensation for physical and emotional pain; suffering; inconvenience; disfigurement; mental anguish; emotional distress; loss of enjoyment of normal activities, benefits, and pleasures of life; and loss of physical health, well-being, or bodily functions. Noneconomic damages are necessarily subjective and not as easily determined as economic damages, which include medical bills and lost wages. That is why we have long considered noneconomic damages to be especially within the province of the jury.

This Court has explained that "a jury has wide latitude in assessing non-economic damages. We trust jurors to use their personal experiences and sensibilities to value the intangible harms such as pain, suffering, and the inability to engage in normal activities." "It is not our role to second-guess the jury and to substitute our judgment." It is the jury's role to observe the witnesses and examine the evidence to make these intangible findings—how much pain and suffering the injured person has endured, how much the quality of that person's life has been diminished, how great is the severity and permanency of the injuries—that is, what the plaintiff has lost. Thus, the constitutional right to a jury trial requires that the "community" decide the subjective element of noneconomic damages. By enacting the statutory caps, the legislature has impermissibly substituted its judgment for the jury's assessment of noneconomic damages, without regard for the value a jury might place on those intangible losses.

In deference to a jury's decision, this Court's past rulings recognized that a jury's verdict should be affirmed when any material evidence supported the verdict because "if it were otherwise, the parties would be deprived of their constitutional right to trial by jury." The appellate court's role is "only to determine whether there was any substantial evidence to support the verdict; and it must be governed by the rule, safeguarding the constitutional right of trial by jury, which requires us to take the strongest legitimate view of all the evidence to uphold the verdict."

The majority suggests that the General Assembly simply exercised its power to alter the common law by enacting the statutory cap. But the damages cap statute did not change the common law negligence cause of action. As long as the negligence cause of action is available, parties injured because of the carelessness of others have the constitutional right to have a jury decide the amount of fair and adequate compensation. The right to a jury trial is a constitutional right that cannot be eliminated by the enactment of a statute.

The majority also notes that the General Assembly has the authority to eliminate causes of action that existed under common law, pointing out statutes abolishing the torts of alienation of affection, seduction, and criminal conversation. That's true. Once a common law tort is abolished, the right to a jury trial for that cause of action ends. But here, the injured party's claim was based on negligence, and the legislature has not abolished negligence as a cause of action. Thus, the right to trial by jury in a negligence cause of action remains (or should remain) inviolate.

The majority's second justification for upholding the statutory caps is that the jury still determines the amount of any noneconomic damages sustained by an injured party, and it is only after the jury returns its verdict that the trial court applies the cap and cuts the award. This is smoke and mirrors. A jury's award of damages that exceeds the damages cap is ignored; the jury might as well have not deliberated and made its award.

D. IS THERE AN AFFIRMATIVE RIGHT TO A STATE REMEDY?

The Federal Constitution has no "right to a remedy" or "open courts" provision. Going back to Chief Justice Marshall's decision in *Marbury v. Madison*, however, there has been judicial recognition that for a violation of a right there generally should be a legal remedy. The Supreme Court has wrestled with recognizing an "implied" remedy for violation of individual federal constitutional rights in the *Bivens* line of cases addressed in the next case. Recognize that the open courts/right to a remedy provisions in state constitutions are interpreted as a potential limitation on legislative alteration or elimination of common law remedies, while the next case considers whether a state constitutional protection itself provides an affirmative remedy for a constitutional violation. And notice that there is a split in the state courts on the question, perhaps a somewhat quieter and longer unfolding version of the *Kelo* story we saw in the Property chapter: the U.S. Supreme Court initially recognized implied constitutional rights of action under the Fourth and Eighth Amendments, but for over forty years now has declined to do so. But during that time a number of state supreme courts have recognized implied rights of action for violation of analogous state constitutional provisions.

FIELDS v. MELLINGER
851 S.E.2d 789 (W. Va. 2020)

JENKINS, J.

The United States District Court for the Southern District of West Virginia presents the following certified question for resolution by this Court: "Does West Virginia recognize a private right of action for monetary damages for violations of Article III, Section 6 of the West Virginia Constitution?" We conclude that there is no private right of action for monetary damages for a violation of Article III, Section 6 of the West Virginia Constitution.

Under Article III, Section 6 of the West Virginia Constitution, "the rights of the citizens to be secure in their houses, persons, papers and effects, against unreasonable searches and seizures, shall not be violated. No warrant shall issue except upon probable cause, supported by oath or affirmation, particularly describing the place to be searched, or the person or thing to be seized." Mr. Fields seeks monetary compensation under this provision for personal injuries allegedly resulting from the use of excessive force by officers of the Sheriff's Department. Patently absent from this provision is any allowance for a private right of action for monetary damages. Thus, we must determine whether a private right of action corresponds with the intent of the drafters and the electorate of our constitution.

Mr. Fields observes that, in two other contexts, this Court has acknowledged a private cause of action for damages arising from a constitutional violation. He first cites this Court's opinion in *Fox v. Baltimore & Ohio R.R. Co.*, 12 S.E. 757 (W. Va. 1890). But it and other cases involved claims under the takings clause. Notably, unlike Article III, Section 6, which is at issue herein, Article III, Section 9, which the Court addressed in its prior holdings, guarantees "just compensation": "Private property shall not be damaged or taken for public use without just compensation; nor shall the same be taken by any company incorporated for the purpose of internal improvement until just compensation shall have been paid or secured to be paid to the owners; and, when private property shall be taken or damaged for public use or for the use of such corporations, the compensation to the owner shall be ascertained in such manner as may be prescribed by general law."

Mr. Fields additionally points to a second occasion when this Court acknowledged a private cause of action for a constitutional violation. *See Hutchison v. City of Huntington*, 479 S.E.2d 649 (1996). *Hutchison* addressed a violation of the Due Process Clause of Article III, Section 10 of the West Virginia Constitution, and held: "Unless barred by one of the recognized statutory, constitutional or common law immunities, a private cause of action exists where a municipality or local governmental unit causes injury by denying that person rights that are protected by the Due Process Clause embodied within Article 3, § 10 of the West Virginia Constitution.

In reaching this conclusion, the *Hutchison* Court provided no analysis; instead, the Court merely observed that "there is no dispute among the parties that a private cause of action exists where state government, or its entities, cause injury to a citizen by denying due process. To suggest otherwise would make our constitutional guarantees of due process an empty illusion." The Court then found the plaintiff's constitutional claim was barred by statutory immunity. Thus, we find little guidance from the *Hutchison* opinion to aid us in analyzing the certified question.

Having found no grounds to find the drafters and the electorate intended to create a cause of action for monetary damages for a violation of Article III, Section 6, from existing West Virginia precedent, we next consider how other courts have addressed this issue.

The leading case by the United States Supreme Court that recognized a constitutional tort is *Bivens v. Six Unknown Named Agents of Federal Bureau of Narcotics*, 403 U.S. 388 (1971). The Court recognized that a violation of the Fourth Amendment to the United States Constitution "by a federal agent acting under color of his authority gives rise to a cause of action for damages consequent upon his unconstitutional conduct." The Court made this finding despite the fact that "the Fourth Amendment does not in so many words provide for its enforcement by an award of money damages for the consequences of its violation." In analyzing whether to adopt an implied cause of action, the Court acknowledged the well-settled principle that, "where legal rights have been invaded, and a federal statute provides for a general right to sue for such invasion, federal courts may use any available remedy to make good the wrong done." However, even in the absence of a federal statute that provided a general right to sue under the circumstances presented in *Bivens*, the Court found that the case "involved no special factors counseling hesitation in the absence of affirmative action by Congress." Also significant to the decision in *Bivens* was the lack of any alternate remedy for the plaintiff.

In the time since the *Bivens* decision was handed down, however, the Court has been reluctant to extend its holding. Indeed, the Court has refused to do so for the past 30 years.

Relying on the Supreme Court's change in approach to recognizing an implied cause of action for monetary damages based upon a constitutional violation, numerous state courts have declined to adopt such a cause of action. And, even though state courts have utilized somewhat varying approaches to address this issue, the existence of alternative remedies frequently is the deciding factor. *See, e.g., State, Dep't of Corr. v. Heisey* (Alaska 2012) (commenting that "the availability of an alternative remedy is dispositive on the issue of a *Bivens*-type remedy"); *Bd. of Cty. Comm'rs of Douglas Cty. v. Sundheim* (Colo. 1996) ("While it may be appropriate to recognize an implied state constitutional cause of action when there is no other adequate remedy, we agree that where other adequate remedies exist, no implied remedy is necessary."); *Kelley Prop. Dev., Inc. v. Town of Lebanon* (Conn. 1993) (observing that "the several sister jurisdictions that have addressed the issue of whether to recognize a state *Bivens* action have pursued varying methods of analysis, with varying results. In a significant number of cases, however, the focus has been on the presence or absence of an existing alternative remedy, either by way of statute or under the common law, to provide some measure of relief for the injured party."); *St. Luke Hosp., Inc. v. Straub* (Ky. 2011) (declining to provide money damages for due process violations under state constitution because "adequate alternative remedies exist, as evidenced by the fact that Straub's complaint alleged four alternative theories of recovery against all the defendants"); *Provens v. Stark Cty. Bd. of Mental Retardation & Dev. Disabilities* (Ohio 1992) (holding that "public employees do not have a private cause of civil action against their employer to redress alleged violations by their employer of policies embodied in the Ohio Constitution when it is determined that there are other reasonably satisfactory remedies provided by statutory enactment and administrative process").

Clearly, reasonable alternative remedies are available for a violation of Article III, Section 6 of the West Virginia Constitution. This is evidenced in the instant matter by the fact that Mr. Fields has asserted state law claims for negligence in the hiring, retention, and/or supervision of employees; battery; and outrageous conduct/intentional infliction of mental, physical, and emotional distress.

Based upon the foregoing discussion, and because alternate remedies are available for a violation of Article III, Section 6 of the West Virginia Constitution, we now hold that West Virginia does not recognize a private right of action for monetary damages for a violation of Article III, Section 6.

WORKMAN, J., dissenting.

I fundamentally disagree with the majority's refusal to recognize a private cause of action for damages under article III, section 6 of the West Virginia Constitution. This Court long ago recognized that our "constitution is the fundamental law by which all people of the state are governed. It is the very genesis of government. Unlike ordinary legislation, a constitution is enacted by the people themselves in their sovereign capacity and is therefore the paramount law." Thus, as a means of upholding the West Virginia Constitution, this Court has long held that various private causes of action exist under article III of the West Virginia Constitution beginning with a private cause of action for the state's taking of private property without just compensation. *See Syl. Pt. 1, Fox v. Baltimore & O. R. Co.* (1890). Next, in *Harrah v. Leverette* (1980), the Court recognized a cause of action for violating article III, section 5 of the West Virginia Constitution, stating that "a person brutalized by state agents while in jail or prison" may be entitled to "a civil action in tort," because "Article III, §5 of the West Virginia Constitution prohibits cruel and unusual punishment." In so doing, we clearly and unequivocally announced that this Court "is dedicated to the preservation of the rights vested in every person by our constitution and the federal constitution. Any attempt by the government to abridge those rights is anathema to us; repeated infractions, despite clear proscriptions by this Court and federal courts, are unforgivable."

In the instant case, this Court should easily have recognized a private cause of action for the alleged violation of article III, section 6 based upon our precedents. This extension of our law would have been incremental, logical, and predictable, and would have given the citizens of our State a means of protecting the rights afforded to them by the West Virginia Constitution.

Looking beyond this Court's precedents, an examination of federal and state law in other jurisdictions lends further support for recognizing a private constitutional cause of action; quite frankly, the idea that such a cause of action may be necessary to vindicate a violation of a person's constitutional rights by a public servant is not novel. Going back to *Marbury v. Madison* (1803), there has been widespread recognition that "the very essence of civil liberty certainly consists in the right of every individual to claim the protection of the laws, whenever he receives an injury." Almost fifty years ago, in *Bivens v. Six Unknown Named Agents of Federal Bureau of Narcotics*, 403 U.S. 388 (1971), the United States Supreme Court first recognized a direct cause of action for damages under the Fourth Amendment to the United States Constitution. In reversing the dismissal of the petitioner's complaint for failure to state a cause of action, the Supreme Court rejected the respondents' contention that because he had state tort remedies available, *i.e.*, trespass and invasion of privacy, there was no need to recognize a federal cause of action to vindicate his constitutional rights.

Thus, this Court should have easily recognized a private cause of action under our State Constitution for a violation of article III, section 6, following the analysis of the Supreme Court in *Bivens*. Persuasive authority for such a cause of action does not end with *Bivens*, however, because other state supreme courts have similarly recognized this type of remedy for search and seizure violations. For example, in *Brown v. State* (1996), the Court of Appeals of New York found that a cause of action existed for alleged violations of the equal protection and search and seizure provisions of the New York Constitution. The plaintiffs were a class of "nonwhite males" who were stopped and questioned by police officers in Oneonta, New York, over a five-day period in 1992, while the officers investigated an attack of a seventy-seven-year-old white woman. The victim described her assailant as a black male. Because authorities were unable to identify a suspect based upon such cursory information, they first obtained a computer-generated list of all African American men attending the nearby State University and began systematically questioning each individual on the list. When these efforts failed to identify a suspect, law enforcement officers began a five-day "street sweep" in which every "nonwhite male" found in the city was stopped and interrogated. No one was arrested for the crime.

In concluding that such conduct on the part of law enforcement gave rise to a private cause of action, the New York high court reasoned, in part: "Claimants alleged that the defendant's officers and employees deprived them of the right to be free from unlawful police conduct violating the Search and Seizure Clause and that they were treated discriminatorily in violation of the State Equal Protection Clause. The harm they assert was visited on them was well within the contemplation of the framers when these provisions were enacted for fewer matters have caused greater concern throughout history than intrusions on personal liberty arising from the abuse of police power. A damage remedy in favor of those harmed by police abuses is appropriate and in furtherance of the purpose underlying the sections."

Likewise, in *Dorwart v. Caraway* (2002), the Supreme Court of Montana recognized a private cause of action for violations of the Montana Constitution. In *Dorwart*, the plaintiffs alleged that two deputy sheriffs unlawfully entered a home where they conducted a warrantless, unlawful and unreasonable search and seizure of the property, trespassed, invaded plaintiffs' privacy, and wrongfully converted certain items of their property, all in violation of Montana's constitutional provisions concerning right to privacy, right to be free from unreasonable searches and seizure, and right to due process of law. The court recognized that "by 1998, twenty-one states had recognized an implied cause of action for state constitutional violations."

More recently, in *Zullo v. State* (2019), the Supreme Court of Vermont recognized, as a matter of first impression, that a direct private cause of action for money damages exists for violations of Vermont's constitutional search and seizure provision. The plaintiff alleged that a state trooper had violated his constitutional rights by stopping him without reasonable suspicion of any traffic violation, causing him to exit his vehicle without any reasonable suspicion of danger or the commission of a crime, seizing his car without probable cause, and searching his car without probable cause. The Vermont high court undertook an analysis of whether the constitutional provision at issue was self-executing, meaning that the right did not "need further legislative action to become operative," and whether an alternative remedy was already available to address the injuries caused by the violation of constitutional rights. The court first found that the constitutional provision prohibiting unwarranted searches and seizures was self-executing, and also concluded that "the standard remedy for a violation in a criminal context—the exclusionary rule—provides no relief to the instant plaintiff, who was not charged with a crime." The court further rejected the State's argument that other alternative remedies, including an action against the officer pursuant to 42 U.S.C. § 1983, injunctive relief, or administrative relief, provided "meaningful redress to plaintiff for the constitutional transgression he alleges." Instead, the *Zullo* court concluded that "none of the alternative remedies proffered by the State can substitute as a viable remedy for someone subjected to an allegedly unconstitutional search or seizure, most particularly in a case like this where plaintiff was not charged with a crime. In addition to providing a compensatory remedy for particular individuals whose constitutional rights have been violated by state officials, the adjudication of constitutional torts has played a critical role in establishing specific constitutional limits on governmental power in a way that could not be provided by injunctive relief or common law actions."

In summary, the majority, relying upon this Court's precedent, as well as legal authority from the United States Supreme Court and many other state courts, should have recognized a private cause of action for damages to redress a violation of West Virginia Constitution article III, section 6. This type of action is necessary to enforce West Virginia's citizens' constitutional rights and to ensure the government's responsibility to provide and to protect those rights from governmental wrongdoing or deprivation.

NOTES

1. Could the plaintiff have argued that a state constitutional "right to a remedy" provision supported his claim for damages as a remedy for a constitutional violation? Why or why not? How would you evaluate such an argument if you were the judge?

2. Should state courts look to analogous federal doctrines when interpreting state constitutions, as the court does in this case when it relies on the federal *Bivens* line of cases? Are there reasons why the U.S. Constitution and state constitutions might be (or even should be) interpreted differently in this regard?

3. Do you see a separation of powers argument lurking in this case? One could ask the question *which branch* of state government—the courts or the state legislature—should determine what remedies, if any, are to be available for violations of State-created legal rights and interests? That proposition has been raised and discussed explicitly in the federal *Bivens* cases, with the U.S. Supreme Court and individual Justices often arguing that the creation of any federal remedy for violations of federal rights should be left to Congress to determine rather than for the Court to create. As the majority opinion notes, the U.S. Supreme Court has come down strongly against any judicial expansion of the *Bivens* implied remedies in recent decades. *See Ziglar v. Abbasi* (2017).

4. It is fair to say that both federal and state courts have been wary of litigants' efforts to characterize their constitutional claims as generic "due process" violations when they seem to fit under more specific constitutional provisions. For example, when a case involves alleged excessive force by police officers, courts treat the claims as a Fourth Amendment claim, *see Graham v. Connor*, 490 U.S. 386 (1989), or the analogous state constitutional claim, *Stepp v. Cottrell on behalf of Estate of Cottrell* (W.Va.), rather than engaging in a more open-ended due process analysis. *See also Albright v. Oliver*, 510 U.S. 266 (1994) (using Fourth Amendment to analyze charging decisions under probable cause standard rather than due process principles).

Chapter XIII

OTHER STATE INDIVIDUAL RIGHTS

A. PRIVACY

The right of privacy is a broad concept, used to refer to a variety of claims or entitlements. Professor Friesen notes that:

> The right of privacy under state constitutions potentially embraces at least three distinct types of interests: (1) the right to be free of unreasonable government (or, sometimes, private) surveillance; (2) the right to prevent the accumulation or dissemination of certain kinds of information (sometimes called "informational" privacy); and (3) the right to make important choices about personal or family life free of state coercion (sometimes called "autonomy" rights).

Jennifer Friesen, *State Constitutional Law: Litigating Individual Rights, Claims and Defenses* § 2.01 (4th ed. 2006).

The right of an individual to make personal decisions free from government control is covered earlier in the textbook. The focus here is on the right to be free from unreasonable governmental interference with one's private affairs.

While the United States Constitution does not contain an express right of privacy, there is an explicit enumerated right to privacy in the state constitutions of Alaska, Arizona, California, Florida, Hawaii, Illinois, Louisiana, Montana, New Hampshire, South Carolina, and Washington. Alaska Const. art. I, § 22; Ariz. Const. art. II, § 8; Cal. Const. art. I, § 1; Fla. Const. art. I, § 23; Haw. Const. art. I, § 6; Ill. Const. art. I, § 6; La. Const. art. I, § 5; Mont. Const. art. II, § 10; N.H. Const. art. 2-b; S.C. Const. art. I, § 10; and Wash. Const. art. I, § 7. The privacy provision in the Florida Constitution states:

> Every natural person has the right to be let alone and free from governmental intrusion into the person's private life except as otherwise provided herein. This section shall not be construed to limit the public's right of access to public records and meetings as provided by law.

Fla. Const. art I, § 23. Six other state constitutions, although not having a separate right to privacy, protect forms of privacy through the "search and seizure" section of the state constitution.

YORK v. WAHKIAKUM SCHOOL DISTRICT NO. 200
178 P.3d 995 (Wash. 2008)

SANDERS, J.

The question before us is whether random and suspicionless drug testing of student athletes violates article I, section 7 of the Washington State Constitution.

The Wahkiakum School District randomly drug tests all student athletes under the authority of Wahkiakum School Board Policy No. 3515. Aaron and Abraham York and Tristan Schneider played sports for Wahkiakum High School, agreed to the policy, and were tested. Their parents sued the school district alleging its drug testing policy violated article I, section 7 of the Washington State Constitution.

Wahkiakum requires its student athletes to refrain from using or possessing alcohol or illegal drugs. Beginning in 1994, the school district implemented myriad ways to combat drug and alcohol use among the student population. Nevertheless, drug and alcohol problems persisted. Acting independently of the school district, the Wahkiakum Community Network began surveying district students. From these surveys, the community network ranked teen substance abuse as the number one problem in Wahkiakum County. As reiterated by the trial court, the community network's surveys showed that in 1998, 40 percent of sophomores reported previously using illegal drugs and 19 percent of sophomores reported illegal drug use within the previous 30 days, while 42 percent of seniors reported previously using illegal drugs and 12.5 percent reported illegal drug use within the previous 30 days. In 2000, 50 percent of student athletes self-identified as drug and/or alcohol users.

As a result, the school district decided to implement random drug testing where all students may be tested initially and then subjected to random drug testing during the remainder of the season. The school district formed the Drug and Alcohol Advisory Committee to help deal with the student substance abuse problems.

As part of the policy, all student athletes must agree to be randomly drug tested as a condition of playing extracurricular sports. The drug testing is done by urinalysis, with the student in an enclosed bathroom stall and a health department employee outside. The sample is then mailed to Comprehensive Toxicology Services in Tacoma, Washington. If the results indicate illegal drug use, then the student is suspended from extracurricular athletic activities; the length of suspension depends on the number of infractions and whether the student tested positive for illegal drugs or alcohol. Also, the school district provides students with drug and alcohol counseling resources. The results are not sent to local law enforcement or included in the student's academic record. And the student is not suspended from school, only extracurricular sports.

The question before us is narrow: Whether Wahkiakum School District's blanket policy requiring student athletes to submit to random drug testing is constitutional. The United States Supreme Court has held such activity does not violate the Fourth Amendment to the federal constitution. But we have never decided whether a suspicionless, random drug search of student athletes violates article I, section 7 of our state constitution.

Therefore, we must decide whether our state constitution follows the federal standard or provides more protection to students in the state of Washington.

The school district argues we should follow federal cases and allow suspicionless, random drug testing of its student athletes. Two federal cases are apposite to our consideration. These cases, while helpful, do not control how we interpret our state constitution. There are stark differences in the language of the two constitutional protections; unlike the Fourth Amendment, article I, section 7 is not based on a reasonableness standard.

The United States Supreme Court has held public school searches presented a "special need," which allowed a departure from the warrant and probable cause requirements. *New Jersey v. T.L.O.* (1985). The *T.L.O.* Court held school teachers and administrators could search students without a warrant if: (1) there existed "reasonable grounds for suspecting that the search will turn up evidence that the student has violated or is violating either the law or the rules of the school," and (2) the search is "not excessively intrusive in light of the age and sex of the student and the nature of the infraction."

Next, in *Vernonia School District 47J v. Acton* (1995), another U.S. Supreme Court case, a public school district implemented a random drug testing of school athletes, similar to the one at issue here. Each student athlete was tested at the beginning of the season and then each week 10 percent were randomly selected for testing. Most critics of *Acton* are not persuaded the majority's analysis justifies a suspicionless search of the student athletes. But the *Acton* majority claimed individualized suspicion would unduly interfere with the government's goals and might actually make the situation worse. Its reasoning was based primarily on three rationales: (1) individualized suspicion would "transform the process into a badge of shame," where teachers could claim any troublesome student was abusing drugs; (2) teachers and student officials are neither trained nor equipped to spot drug use; and (3) individualized suspicion creates an unnecessary loss of resources in defending claims and lawsuits against arbitrary imposition, when students and parents will inevitably challenge whether reasonable suspicion did indeed exist.

But these arguments were unpersuasive several years earlier when the Court applied an individualized suspicion standard to public schools in *T.L.O.* The *Acton* majority never adequately explained why individual suspicion was needed in *T.L.O.* but not in *Acton*. Justice O'Connor spent much of her dissent taking issue with this standard:

> Nowhere is it *less* clear that an individualized suspicion requirement would be ineffectual than in the school context. In most schools, the entire pool of potential search targets—students—is under constant supervision by teachers and administrators and coaches, be it in classrooms, hallways, or locker rooms.
>
> The great irony of this case is that most (though not all) of the evidence the District introduced to justify its suspicionless drug testing program consisted of first- or

second-hand stories of particular, identifiable students acting in ways that plainly gave rise to reasonable suspicion of in-school drug use—and thus that would have justified a drug-related search under our *T.L.O.* decision.

The Wahkiakum School District modeled its policy after the one used by the Vernonia School District. But simply passing muster under the federal constitution does not ensure the survival of the school district's policy under our state constitution. The Fourth Amendment provides for "the right of the people to be secure in their persons, houses, papers, and effects, against unreasonable searches and seizures." Therefore, a Fourth Amendment analysis hinges on whether a warrantless search is reasonable, and it is possible in some circumstances for a search to be reasonable without a warrant. But our state constitutional analysis hinges on whether a search has "authority of law"—in other words, a warrant.

Our state constitution provides: "No person shall be disturbed in his private affairs, or his home invaded, without authority of law." Wash. Const. art. I, § 7. It is well established that in some areas, article I, section 7 provides greater protection than its federal counterpart—the Fourth Amendment. When determining whether article I, section 7 provides greater protection in a particular context, we focus on whether the unique characteristics of the constitutional provision and its prior interpretations compel a particular result. We look to the constitutional text, historical treatment of the interest at stake, relevant case law and statutes, and the current implications of recognizing or not recognizing an interest.

This requires a two-part analysis. First, we must determine whether the state action constitutes a disturbance of one's private affairs. Here that means asking whether requiring a student athlete to provide a urine sample intrudes upon the student's private affairs. Second, if a privacy interest has been disturbed, the second step in our analysis asks whether authority of law justifies the intrusion. The "authority of law" required by article I, section 7 is satisfied by a valid warrant, limited to a few jealously guarded exceptions. Because the Wahkiakum School District had no warrant, if we reach the second prong of the analysis we must decide whether the school district's activity fits within an exception to the warrant requirement. Relying on federal law, the school district claims there is a "special needs" exception to the warrant requirement that we should adopt. The York and Schneider parents point out we have not adopted such an exception and urge us not to do so here.

When inquiring about private affairs, we look to "those privacy interests which citizens of this state have held, and should be entitled to hold, safe from governmental trespass absent a warrant." This is an objective analysis.

The private affair we are concerned with today is the State's interference in a student athlete's bodily functions. Specifically, does it intrude upon a privacy interest to require a student athlete to go into a bathroom stall and provide a urine sample, even against that student's protest? Federal courts and our court both agree the answer is an unqualified yes, such action intrudes into one's reasonable expectation of privacy. Indeed, we offer heightened protection for bodily functions compared to the federal courts.

We have long held a warrantless search is *per se* unreasonable, unless it fits within one of the "jealously and carefully drawn exceptions." These exceptions include exigent circumstances, consent, searches incident to a valid arrest, inventory searches, the plain view doctrine, and *Terry* investigative stops. Any exceptions to the warrant requirement must be rooted in the common law. And it is always the government's burden to show its random drug testing fits within one of these narrow exceptions. Today the school district asks us to accept an analog to the federal special needs doctrine to justify its drug testing policy. The York and Schneider parents point out we have never formally adopted a special needs exception and therefore claim no exception to the warrant requirement exists here.

Before addressing whether we have adopted or will adopt such a special needs exception, it is helpful to briefly examine the federal exception to understand both its requirements and its breadth. The United States Supreme Court has held there are certain circumstances when a search or seizure is directed toward "special needs, beyond the normal need for law enforcement" and "the warrant and probable-cause requirement are impracticable." For there to be a special need, not only must there be some interest beyond normal law enforcement but also any evidence garnered from the search or seizure should not be expected to be used in any criminal prosecution against the target of the search or seizure. The Court has applied such reasoning to administrative searches, border patrols, and prisoners and probationers.

The United States Supreme Court has also held drug testing presents a special need and may be done under certain circumstances without a warrant or individualized suspicion. In *Skinner v. Railway Labor Executives' Assoc.* (1989), the Court upheld warrantless and suspicionless blood and urine testing of railroad employees following major train accidents. The Court applied similar reasoning in *National Treasury Employees Union v. Von Raab* (1989), when it held immigration officials may be subjected to random drug testing.

We have never adopted a special needs exception but have looked to federal special needs cases when dealing with similar issues. In cases concerning administrative searches, border patrols, and prisoners and probationers, our courts have departed from the warrant requirement in similar, but not always identical, ways.

We cannot countenance random searches of public school student athletes with our article I, section 7 jurisprudence. As stated earlier, we require a warrant except for rare occasions, which we jealously and narrowly guard. We decline to adopt a doctrine similar to the federal special needs exception in the context of randomly drug testing student athletes. In sum, no argument has been presented that would bring the random drug testing within any reasonable interpretation of the constitutionally required "authority of law."

Accordingly, we hold the school district's policy 3515 is unconstitutional and violates student athletes' rights secured by article I, section 7.

NOTE

The "special needs" rationale was adopted by the Supreme Court of New Jersey and led it to hold that the search and seizure protection in the state constitution did not prohibit a drug testing program in a public high school. The school's policy provided for the random, suspicionless drug and alcohol testing of all students who engaged in an extracurricular activity or who possessed a parking permit. *Joye v. Hunterdon Cent. Reg'l High Sch. Bd. of Educ.*, 826 A.2d 624 (N.J. 2003).

B. FREE SPEECH AND EXPRESSION

Although the texts of state constitutions regarding freedom of speech often are quite similar to each other, they are usually different from the language in the First Amendment. The origins of the provisions in state constitutions can be traced to William Blackstone's Commentaries:

> Every freeman has an undoubted right to lay what sentiments he pleases before his public; to forbid this, is to destroy the freedom of the press: but if he publishes what is improper, mischievous, or illegal, he must take the consequences of his own temerity. 4 William Blackstone, *Commentaries* 152.

The first time that Blackstone's "abuse" qualification appeared in an American Constitution was the text of the Pennsylvania Constitution of 1790:

> The free communication of thoughts and opinions is one of the invaluable rights of man; and every citizen may freely speak, write, and print on any subject, being responsible for the abuse of that liberty. Pa. Const. of 1790, art. IX, § 7.

Today, protections for speech, expression and the press are found in all state constitutions. The provision in the New York Constitution is typical:

> Every citizen may freely speak, write and publish his or her sentiments on all subjects, being responsible for the abuse of that right; and no law shall be passed to restrain or abridge the liberty of speech or of the press. N.Y. Const. art. I, § 8.

The free speech provisions in state constitutions generally have two components. The first part describes the protected right and the responsibility for the abuse of those rights. The second part prohibits laws that abridge the protected rights.

FASHION VALLEY MALL v. NLRB
172 P.3d 742 (Cal. 2007)

MORENO, J.

We granted the request of the United States Court of Appeals for the District of Columbia Circuit to decide whether, under California law, a shopping mall may enforce a rule prohibiting persons from urging customers to boycott a store in the mall. For the reasons that follow, we hold that the right to free speech granted by article I, section 2 of the California Constitution includes the right to urge customers in a shopping mall to boycott one of the stores in the mall.

On October 4, 1998, thirty to forty Union members had distributed leaflets to customers entering and leaving the Robinsons-May store at the Mall. The leaflets stated that Robinsons-May advertises in the Union-Tribune, described several ways that the newspaper allegedly treated its employees unfairly, and urged customers who believed "that employers should treat employees fairly" to call the newspaper's "CEO," listing his name and telephone number. The administrative law judge concluded: "From all indications, the leafleters conducted their activity in a courteous and peaceful manner without a disruption of any kind and without hindrance to customers entering or leaving" the store.

Within fifteen or twenty minutes, Mall officials "arrived on the scene to stop the leafleting," notifying the Union members that they were trespassing because they had not obtained a permit from the Mall "to engage in expressive activity," and warning them that they "would be subject to civil litigation and/or arrest if they did not leave." A police officer appeared and, following a brief argument, the Union members moved to public property near the entrance to the Mall and continued distributing leaflets briefly before leaving the area.

The Mall has adopted rules requiring persons who desire to engage in expressive activity at the Mall to apply for a permit five business days in advance. The applicant "must agree to abide by" the Mall's rules, including rule 5.6.2, which prohibits "impeding, competing or interfering with the business of one or more of the stores or merchants in the shopping center by: urging, or encouraging in any manner, customers not to purchase the merchandise or services offered by any one or more of the stores or merchants in the shopping center."

The administrative law judge found that the Union "was attempting to engage in a lawful consumer boycott of Robinsons-May because Robinsons-May advertised in the Union-Tribune newspaper" and further found "that it would have been utterly futile for the Union to have followed the Mall's enormously burdensome application-permit process because its rules contained express provisions barring the very kind of lawful conduct the Union sought to undertake at the Mall." The administrative law judge thus ordered the Mall to cease and desist prohibiting access to the Union's "leafleters for the purpose of engaging in peaceful consumer boycott handbilling."

Article I, section 2, subdivision (a) of the California Constitution declares: "Every person may freely speak, write and publish his or her sentiments on all subjects, being responsible for the abuse of this right. A law may not restrain or abridge liberty of speech or press." Nearly 30 years ago, in *Robins v. PruneYard Shopping Center* (Cal. 1979), we held that this provision of our state Constitution grants broader rights to free expression than does the First Amendment to the United States Constitution by holding that a shopping mall is a public forum in which persons may exercise their right to free speech under the California Constitution. We stated that a shopping center "to which the public is invited can provide an essential and invaluable forum for exercising free speech rights." We noted that in many cities the public areas of the shopping mall are replacing the streets and sidewalks of the central business district which "have immemorially been held in trust for the use of the public and, time out of mind, have been used for purposes of assembly, communicating thoughts between citizens, and discussing public questions." Because of the "growing importance of the shopping center, to prohibit expressive activity in the centers would impinge on constitutional rights beyond speech rights," particularly the right to petition for redress of grievances. Accordingly, we held that the California Constitution "protects speech and petitioning, reasonably exercised, in shopping centers even when the centers are privately owned." We added the caveat in *PruneYard* that "by no means do we imply that those who wish to disseminate ideas have free rein," noting our previous "endorsement of time, place, and manner rules."

The Mall in the present case generally allows expressive activity, as mandated by the California Constitution, but requires persons wishing to engage in free speech in the Mall to obtain a permit. Under rule 5.6.2, the Mall will not issue a permit to engage in expressive activity unless the applicant promises to refrain from conduct "urging, or encouraging in any manner, customers not to purchase the merchandise or services offered by any one or more of the stores or merchants in the shopping center." We must determine, therefore, whether a shopping center violates California law by banning from its premises speech urging the public to boycott one or more of the shopping center's businesses.

The idea that private property can constitute a public forum for free speech if it is open to the public in a manner similar to that of public streets and sidewalks long predates our decision in *PruneYard*. The United States Supreme Court recognized more than half a century ago that the right to free speech guaranteed by the First Amendment to the United States Constitution can apply even on privately owned land. In *Marsh v. Alabama*

(1946), the high court held that a Jehovah's Witness had the right to distribute religious literature on the sidewalk near the post office of a town owned by the Gulf Shipbuilding Corp., because the town had

> all the characteristics of any other American town. In short, the town and its shopping district are accessible to and freely used by the public in general, and there is nothing to distinguish them from any other town and shopping center except the fact that the title to the property belongs to a private corporation.

The high court stated: "The more an owner, for his advantage, opens up his property for use by the public in general, the more do his rights become circumscribed by the statutory and constitutional rights of those who use it."

Our decision that the California Constitution protects the right to free speech in a shopping mall, even though the federal Constitution does not, stems from the differences between the First Amendment to the federal Constitution and article I, section 2 of the California Constitution. We observed in *Gerawan Farming, Inc. v. Lyons* (Cal. 2000), that the free speech clause in article I of the California Constitution differs from its counterpart in the federal Constitution both in its language and its scope:

> It is beyond peradventure that article I's free speech clause enjoys existence and force independent of the First Amendment's. In section 24, article I states, in these very terms, that "rights guaranteed by the California Constitution are not dependent on those guaranteed by the United States Constitution." This statement extends to all such rights, including article I's right to freedom of speech. For the California Constitution is now, and has always been, a "document of independent force and effect particularly in the area of individual liberties."
>
> As a general rule, article I's free speech clause and its right to freedom of speech are not only as broad and as great as the First Amendment's, they are even "broader" and "greater."

In *PruneYard*, high school students in the mall were prohibited from soliciting support for their opposition to a United Nations resolution against Zionism. We held that the mall could not prohibit the students' efforts despite the fact that this free speech activity was unrelated to the business of the center. In so holding, we relied upon our earlier decision in *Schwartz-Torrance*, which, we noted, "held that a labor union has the right to picket a bakery located in a shopping center." We cautioned, however, that we did not "imply that those who wish to disseminate ideas have free rein," noting our previous "endorsement of time, place, and manner rules." We also repeated Justice Mosk's observation in his dissent in *Diamond II* that compelling a shopping center to permit "a handful of additional orderly persons soliciting signatures and distributing handbills in connection therewith, under reasonable regulations adopted by defendant to assure that these activities do not interfere with normal business operations, would not markedly dilute defendant's property rights."

The Mall argues that its rule banning speech that advocates a boycott is a "reasonable regulation" designed to assure that free expression activities "do not interfere with normal business operations" within the meaning of our decision in *PruneYard*. According to the Mall, it "has the right to prohibit speech that interferes with the intended purpose of the Mall," which is to promote "the sale of merchandise and services to the shopping public." We disagree.

It has been the law since we decided *Schwartz-Torrance* in 1964, and remains the law, that a privately owned shopping center must permit peaceful picketing of businesses in shopping centers, even though such picketing may harm the shopping center's business interests. Our decision in *Diamond* recognized that citizens have a strengthened interest, not a diminished interest, in speech that presents a grievance against a particular business in a privately owned shopping center, including speech that advocates a boycott.

The level of scrutiny with which we review a restriction of free speech activity depends upon whether it is a content-neutral regulation of the time, place, or manner of speech or restricts speech based upon its content. A content-neutral regulation of the time, place, or manner of speech is subjected to intermediate scrutiny to determine if it is "(i) narrowly tailored, (ii) serves a significant government interest, and (iii) leaves open ample alternative avenues of communication." A content-based restriction is subjected to strict scrutiny. "Decisions applying the liberty of speech clause of the California Constitution, like those applying the First Amendment, long have recognized that in order to qualify for intermediate scrutiny (*i.e.*, time, place, and manner) review, a regulation must be content neutral, and that if a regulation is content based, it is subject to the more stringent strict scrutiny standard."

Prohibiting speech that advocates a boycott is not a time, place, or manner restriction because it is not content neutral. The Mall's rule prohibiting persons from urging a boycott is improper because it does not regulate the time, place, or manner of speech, but rather bans speech urging a boycott because of its content. Restrictions upon speech "that by their terms distinguish favored speech from disfavored speech on the basis of the ideas or views expressed are content based."

The Mall argues that its rule prohibiting speech that urges a boycott is "a content-neutral restriction under California law because it applies to any and all requests for a consumer boycott of the Mall's merchants regardless of the subject matter or viewpoint of the speaker advocating the boycott." The Mall is mistaken. The Mall's rule prohibiting all boycotts may be viewpoint neutral, because it treats all requests for a boycott the same way, but it is not content neutral, because it prohibits speech that urges a boycott while permitting speech that does not.

The rule at issue here prohibiting speech that advocates a boycott cannot similarly be justified by legitimate concerns that are unrelated to content.

Peacefully urging a boycott in a mall does not by its nature cause congestion, nor does it promote fraud or duress. "The boycott is a form of speech or conduct that is ordinarily entitled to protection under the First and Fourteenth Amendments." Our California Constitution provides greater, not lesser, protection for this traditional form of free speech. Unlike the ordinance in *Alliance*, the Mall's rule in the instant case is not concerned with the inherently intrusive nature of such speech, but rather with the impact such speech may have on its listeners. "Handbills depend entirely on the persuasive force of the idea. The loss of customers because they read a handbill urging them not to patronize a business is the result of mere persuasion." The Mall is concerned that the speech may be effective and persuade customers not to patronize a store. But "listeners' reaction to speech is not a content-neutral basis for regulation." The Mall seeks to prohibit speech advocating a boycott solely because it disagrees with the message of such speech, which might persuade some potential customers not to patronize the stores in the Mall.

The Mall's rule prohibiting speech that advocates a boycott cannot withstand strict scrutiny. The Mall's purpose to maximize the profits of its merchants is not compelling compared to the Union's right to free expression. Urging customers to boycott a store lies at the core of the right to free speech. "The safeguarding of these rights to the ends that men may speak as they think on matters vital to them and that falsehoods may be exposed through the processes of education and discussion is essential to free government. Those who won our independence had confidence in the power of free and fearless reasoning and communication of ideas to discover and spread political and economic truth." The fact that speech may be convincing is not a proper basis for prohibiting it. The right to free speech "extends to more than abstract discussion, unrelated to action." The First Amendment is a charter for government, not for an institution of learning. "Free trade in ideas" means free trade in the opportunity to persuade to action, not merely to describe facts. The Mall cites no authority, and we are aware of none, that holds that a store has a compelling interest in prohibiting this traditional form of free speech.

A shopping mall is a public forum in which persons may reasonably exercise their right to free speech guaranteed by article I, section 2 of the California Constitution. Shopping malls may enact and enforce reasonable regulations of the time, place and manner of such free expression to assure that these activities do not interfere with the normal business operations of the mall, but they may not prohibit certain types of speech based upon its content, such as prohibiting speech that urges a boycott of one or more of the stores in the mall.

NOTE

The United States Supreme Court decided one of the seminal cases involving state constitutional rights in *PruneYard Shopping Center v. Robins*, 447 U.S. 74 (1980). The issue before it was framed as "whether state constitutional provisions, which permit individuals to exercise free speech and petition rights on the property of a privately owned shopping center to which the public is invited, violate the shopping center owner's property rights under the Fifth and Fourteenth Amendments or his free speech rights under the First and Fourteenth Amendments." The California Supreme Court held that article 1, sections 2 and 3 of the California Constitution "protects speech and petitioning, reasonably exercised, in shopping centers even when the centers are privately owned" and have a policy not to permit *any* publicly expressive activity, that is strictly enforced in a non-discriminatory fashion. *Robins v. PruneYard Shopping Ctr.*, 592 P.2d 341, 347 (Cal. 1979).

In *Lloyd Corp. v. Tanner*, 407 U.S. 551 (1972), the United States Supreme Court had considered a similar issue in the context of First Amendment rights. In *Lloyd*, the court held that when a shopping center owner opens its private property to the public for the purpose of shopping, the First Amendment of the United States Constitution does not create individual rights in expression beyond those already existing under applicable law. In *PruneYard*, the court's holding in *Lloyd* was distinguished on the basis that it did "not *ex proprio vigore* limit the authority of the State to exercise its police power or its sovereign right to adopt in its own Constitution individual liberties more expansive than those conferred by the Federal Constitution."

The United States Supreme Court then pointed out that in *Lloyd*, unlike the situation presented in *PruneYard*, "there was no state constitutional or statutory provision that had been construed to create rights to the use of private property by strangers, comparable to those found to exist by the California Supreme Court." The Supreme Court then addressed the argument that the rights conferred by the California Constitution, if exercised at the private shopping center, would constitute a taking of property without just compensation in violation of the Fifth and Fourteenth Amendments:

> It is true that one of the essential sticks in the bundle of property rights is the right to exclude others. And here there has literally been a "taking" of that right to the extent that the California Supreme Court has interpreted the State Constitution to entitle its citizens to exercise free expression and petition rights on shopping center property. But it is well established that "not every destruction or injury to property by governmental action has been held to be a taking in the constitutional sense."
>
> Here the requirement that appellants permit appellees to exercise state-protected rights of free expression and petition on shopping center property clearly does not

amount to an unconstitutional infringement of appellants' property rights under the Taking Clause. There is nothing to suggest that preventing appellants from prohibiting this sort of activity will unreasonably impair the value or use of their property as a shopping center. The PruneYard is a large commercial complex that covers several city blocks, contains numerous separate business establishments, and is open to the public at large. The decision of the California Supreme Court makes it clear that PruneYard may restrict expressive activity by adopting time, place, and manner regulations that will minimize any interference with its commercial functions. Appellees were orderly, and they limited their activity to the common areas of the shopping center. In these circumstances, the fact that they may have "physically invaded" appellants' property cannot be viewed as determinative.

Accordingly, the unique right of petition afforded by the California Constitution prevailed in *PruneYard* even though the assertion of a First Amendment right had not succeeded in *Lloyd*, despite an almost identical factual context.

The United States Constitution does not confer a general right to free speech in a privately owned shopping center. Most state constitutions have been construed the same way. The state constitutions of California, Oregon, Massachusetts, New Jersey and Colorado have been interpreted to confer certain rights of expression at privately owned shopping centers.

STATE v. STUMMER
194 P.3d 1043 (Ariz. 2008)

BERCH, V.C.J.

Petitioners Hubert August Stummer and Dennis Allen Lumm were charged with violating section 13-1422 of the Arizona Revised Statutes, which forbids adult bookstores from remaining open during certain early morning hours. We have been asked to determine whether the hours of operation provision violates the free speech provision of the Arizona Constitution.

Petitioners operate adult-oriented businesses in Phoenix that sell sexually explicit books and magazines. They were charged with violating section 13-1422(A), which requires adult bookstores to close for fifty-three hours each week: from 1 a.m. to 8 a.m., Monday through Saturday, and from 1 a.m. to noon on Sunday.

Petitioners moved to dismiss the charges, citing our decision in *Empress Adult Video & Bookstore v. City of Tucson* (Ariz. 2002), which held the hours of operation provision in section 13-1422(A) unconstitutional. Bound by *Empress*, the superior court granted the motion. The State appealed, arguing that *Empress* was wrongly decided.

The Arizona Legislature enacted section 13-1422 in response to complaints from citizens and local businesses that "adult" businesses were causing negative effects, including increased prostitution and sexually oriented litter, in the surrounding communities. These negative effects were alleged to be more prevalent during the early morning hours and the proponents therefore urged the legislature to restrict the operating hours of these businesses to reduce the problems.

The issue presented in this case is not whether section 13-1422 violates the First Amendment to the United States Constitution, but rather whether it passes muster under article 2, section 6 of the Arizona Constitution. Both the First Amendment and article 2, section 6, protect speech from abridgment by the government. The First Amendment does so by restraining government interference with speech rights. It provides that "Congress shall make no law abridging the freedom of speech, or of the press." U.S. Const. amend. I. Arizona's free speech provision, in contrast, guarantees each individual's right to speak freely. It states that "every person may freely speak, write, and publish on all subjects, being responsible for the abuse of that right." Ariz. Const. art. II, § 6.

The encompassing text of article 2, section 6 indicates the Arizona framers' intent to rigorously protect freedom of speech. In addressing censorship, we have said that the words of Arizona's free speech provision "are too plain for equivocation. The right of every person to freely speak, write and publish may not be limited."

Arizona courts have had few opportunities to develop Arizona's free speech jurisprudence. With regard to unprotected speech, Arizona courts construing article 2, section 6 have followed federal interpretations of the United States Constitution. For example, in being "responsible for the abuse" of the right to speak, write, and publish on "all subjects," one may be held liable for defamation, notwithstanding the right to "freely speak."

We have also stated that article 2, section 6 has "greater scope than the First Amendment." This is not a case, however, in which we need to determine the boundaries of Arizona's free speech provision. The State does not argue that the books and magazines in Petitioners' bookstores are obscene. Thus in selling those materials, Petitioners are engaging in protected speech under article 2, section 6. We need only decide whether and to what extent the State may curtail this protected speech in order to reduce secondary effects.

Our opinion in *Mountain States Telephone & Telegraph Co. v. Arizona Corporation Commission* (Ariz. 1989), is the starting point for our analysis of this issue. That case involved the regulation of "ScoopLines": pay-per-call telephone numbers that provided customers with messages on a variety of topics, such as sports and weather. In response to consumer complaints, the Arizona Corporation Commission ordered Mountain States to block ScoopLines and "to propose a presubscription plan for the Commission's approval." Mountain States sought relief from this Court, arguing that the Commission's order violated article 2, section 6.

There, as here, the government argued that the regulation was intended to accomplish a goal unrelated to the suppression of protected speech and that any effect on speech rights was "incidental and permissible." Although we concluded that the Commission could impose content-neutral "time, place, and manner" regulations, we cautioned that, "given Arizona's constitutional protections, when dealing with regulations that affect speech, the government must regulate with narrow specificity so as to affect as little as possible the ability of the sender and receiver to communicate."

In *Empress*, the court of appeals interpreted *Mountain States'* "narrow specificity" language as requiring that the regulation "affect *as little as possible* the ability of the sender and receiver to communicate." The court of appeals thus effectively adopted a "least restrictive means" standard. Applying this standard, the court concluded that section 13-1422 violated the Arizona Constitution because closing adult businesses for at least seven hours a day was not the least restrictive means of addressing the secondary effects of adult businesses.

The booksellers here urge that we adopt the *Empress* standard. We conclude, however, that such a standard is not appropriate for judging the constitutionality of secondary effects regulations. When a regulation is content based, but directed at addressing the secondary effects of speech, the legislative choice is entitled to more deference than the strict scrutiny test permits. The government may have a substantial interest in addressing certain secondary effects of speech, and applying strict scrutiny may effectively preclude regulations designed to prohibit such effects.

The State urges us instead to apply the federal intermediate scrutiny standard articulated by the Supreme Court in *City of Renton v. Playtime Theatres* (1986) and *City of Los Angeles v. Alameda Books* (2002), as did the Ninth Circuit in *Center for Fair Public Policy v. Maricopa County* (9th Cir. 2003) and the court of appeals panel in this case. We decline to strictly apply the federal test because it is inconsistent with the broad protection of speech afforded by the Arizona Constitution. Because Arizona's speech provision safeguards the right to speak freely on all topics, our test must more closely scrutinize laws that single out speech for regulation based on its disfavored content. We thus turn to the question of the appropriate test for determining the constitutionality, under article 2, section 6, of secondary effects regulations.

The appropriate test for measuring the constitutionality of content-based secondary effects regulations must vindicate the constitutional right to free speech, yet accommodate the government's interest in protecting the public health, safety, and welfare. The test has two phases. First, to qualify for intermediate scrutiny, the State must demonstrate that a content-based regulation is directed at ameliorating secondary effects, not at suppressing protected speech. Second, to survive intermediate scrutiny, the State must show that, in addressing the secondary effects, the regulation does not sweep too broadly.

In the first phase, the challenger must demonstrate that the challenged provision interferes with the right to freely speak, write, or publish. Once the challenger has shown that a content-based or content-correlated regulation affects free expression, the State bears the burden of demonstrating that the enacting body had a reasonable basis for believing that the speech singled out for regulation created secondary effects different from or greater than the effects of speech generally, and that the challenged regulation was designed to suppress those secondary effects, not to suppress the speech itself.

The State may carry that burden by demonstrating to the court that, on the basis of the evidence before it, the enacting body might reasonably believe that the regulated speech created negative secondary effects greater than those created by speech generally and that the regulation would address those effects. If the State meets this burden of showing that the legislative body enacted the challenged regulation to respond to secondary effects rather than disfavored speech, we will address the challenged regulation under a form of intermediate scrutiny.

In the second phase of the inquiry for determining the constitutionality of a content-based secondary effects regulation, the court must examine whether the regulation protects substantial government interests and whether it significantly reduces secondary effects without unduly interfering with protected speech. The deference afforded at the first phase, in which the court determines whether intermediate scrutiny applies, does not extend to the second phase, in which the court assesses the effects of the challenged law. For the regulation to survive, its proponent must show that the government has a substantial interest, that the regulation significantly furthers that interest, and that the challenged regulation does not unduly burden speech. To establish or disprove these prongs, the challenger and the proponent of the regulation may bring forth pre- and post-enactment evidence.

In applying the phase-two test, the court must first assess the importance of the government's asserted interest. Regulations designed to reduce crime, protect children, or safeguard constitutional rights, for example, may justify some infringement on speech rights. Lesser concerns, such as the abatement of mere litter or governmental convenience, will not justify suppression of speech.

If the government advances a substantial interest, the court must then determine whether the regulation significantly furthers that interest. A court may find this prong satisfied if the regulation substantially reduces or has a significant ameliorative impact on secondary effects. In this analysis, the court must consider the likelihood that the regulation will achieve its intended result. For example, the court may consider how much sex-related crime occurs during the hours of forced closure. The answer to this inquiry may elucidate whether the regulation is designed to significantly reduce such negative secondary effects and thus whether it may achieve its intended result.

Finally, the third prong—whether the regulation unduly burdens speech—may be satisfied by establishing that the government's substantial interest would be less effectively achieved without the regulation and ample alternative means of communication exist. Although the test does not require the least restrictive means possible, the proponent must show a close fit or nexus between the ends sought and the means employed for achieving those ends.

In analyzing the facts of this case under the first phase of Arizona's secondary effects test, we conclude that the Petitioners have established that their protected speech is burdened by a content-based regulation. The State, in turn, has met its burden of demonstrating that the hours provision of section 13-1422 was designed to curb the secondary effects of speech, not to prohibit the speech itself. The State adduced evidence that the legislature reasonably believed that adult businesses encourage criminal activity and sexually oriented litter, that these effects were worse in the nighttime hours, and that the statute at issue would ameliorate those effects. We therefore turn to the second phase of the inquiry, application of the three-part test: whether the government's interests are substantial, whether the regulation significantly furthers those interests, and whether the regulation unduly burdens speech.

In the second phase, the court must first assess the significance of the government's interests. The existence of mere litter is not by itself sufficiently important to permit a substantial restriction on speech. As we stated in *New Times, Inc. v. Arizona Board of Regents* (Ariz. 1974), "minor matters of public inconvenience or annoyance cannot be transformed into substantive evils of sufficient weight to warrant the curtailment of liberty of expression." Combating criminal activity such as prostitution and public indecency, however, is a substantial governmental interest. We therefore move to the second and third prongs of the phase-two analysis.

As to the second prong, whether the statute significantly furthers the government's interest, the record is devoid of evidence that secondary effects are greater during the hours of forced closure. The record reflects only two pieces of evidence on this point. One was the testimony of a representative of the City of Phoenix who testified that the city could *not* show a relationship between the hours of operation and the incidence of crime. The other was a study from Glendale, Colorado, finding that *fewer* police calls or incidents arose from a particular adult business during the late night hours than during other times. Neither piece of evidence supports the assertion that the effects are greater during the hours of forced closure. Without such a showing, the State may have difficulty establishing that closure is an appropriate remedy—that is, that this statute significantly furthers the government's interest in reducing secondary effects. The government must establish that, during their early morning operation, adult bookstores disproportionately cause negative secondary effects and that these negative effects are or will be significantly lessened by closure during those hours.

Finally, regarding the third prong, the State has not shown that any substantial interests would be achieved less effectively without the bookstores' closure for fifty-three hours each week. The record also does not contain evidence regarding the availability of alternative channels of communication during the hours of closure.

In short, because this case was decided on a motion to dismiss, the record contains no evidence of the significance of the infringement on speech, the effectiveness of the statute in reducing negative secondary effects, the nexus between the ends sought and the means employed, or the availability of alternative measures.

Because no court below has had the opportunity to apply the test we formulate today for evaluating the constitutionality of content-based secondary effects regulations, we conclude that all parties should have the opportunity to present additional evidence supporting their positions, and the trial court should have the opportunity to apply the test for constitutionality detailed above. We therefore remand this case to the superior court for further proceedings consistent with this opinion.

NOTES

1. The federal secondary effects standards have been adopted in construing the constitutions of some states. *See People v. Superior Court*, 774 P.2d 769 (Cal. 1989); *DiRaimo v. City of Providence*, 714 A.2d 554 (R.I. 1998).

2. The Tennessee Supreme Court held that a state obscenity statute, based upon the *Miller* test, did not violate the state constitution's guarantee in article I, section 19 of free communication of thoughts and opinions. *Tennessee v. Marshall*, 859 S.W.2d 289 (Tenn. 1993). The States of Maryland, Minnesota, Ohio, Texas and Washington have followed the First Amendment jurisprudence on obscenity even when there have been differences in the text of their respective state constitutions.

C. CIVIL JURY TRIAL

Although the Sixth Amendment right to trial by jury in a criminal proceeding has been made binding upon the States by virtue of the Fourteenth Amendment, *Duncan v. Louisiana*, 391 U.S. 145, 156 (1968), the United States Supreme Court has thus far declined to hold that the

Seventh Amendment right to trial by jury in a civil proceeding is binding upon the States. *See Minneapolis & St. Louis R.R. Co. v. Bombolis*, 241 U.S. 211 (1916). Accordingly, the right to a jury trial in civil proceedings has always been and remains exclusively protected by provisions in the state constitutions. Louisiana is the only State without a civil jury clause.

SOFIE v. FIBREBOARD CORP.
771 P.2d 711 (Wash. 1989)

UTTER, J.

Austin and Marcia Sofie challenge the constitutionality of section 4.56.250 of the Washington Code. This statute, part of the 1986 tort reform act, places a limit on the noneconomic damages recoverable by a personal injury or wrongful death plaintiff. The Sofies brought a direct appeal to this court after the trial judge in their tort action, under the direction of the statute, reduced the jury's award of noneconomic damages.

The Washington Legislature passed section 4.56.250 in 1986 partly as a response to rising insurance premiums for liability coverage. The damages limit that the statute creates operates on a formula based upon the age of the plaintiff. As a result, the older a plaintiff is, the less he or she will be able to recover in noneconomic damages. The trial judge applies the limit to the damages found by the trier of fact. If the case is tried before a jury, the jury determines the amount of noneconomic damages without knowledge of the limit. The jury goes about its normal business and the judge reduces, according to the statute's formula and without notifying the jury, any damage verdicts that exceed the limit.

In September 1987, the Sofies sued Fibreboard Corp. and other asbestos manufacturers for the harm caused to Mr. Sofie by their asbestos products. Mr. Sofie, then aged 67, was suffering from a form of lung cancer—mesothelioma—caused by exposure to asbestos during his career as a pipefitter. At trial, Mr. Sofie's attorneys presented evidence of the extreme pain he experienced as a result of the disease. The testimony indicated that Mr. Sofie spent what remained of his life waiting for the next "morphine cocktail," for the next hot bath, for anything that would lessen his consuming physical agony.

At the end of the trial, the jury found the defendants at fault for Mr. Sofie's disease. They returned a verdict of $1,345,833 in favor of the Sofies. Of this amount, $1,154,592 went to compensate noneconomic damages: $477,200 for Mr. Sofie's pain and suffering and $677,392 for Mrs. Sofie's loss of consortium. While the trial judge specifically found the jury's finding of damages reasonable, he indicated he was compelled under the damages limit to reduce the noneconomic portion of the verdict to $125,136.45, resulting in a total judgment of $316,377.45.

The dispositive issue of this case is the right to a jury trial. This court has long approached the review of legislative enactments with great care. The wisdom of legislation is not justiciable; our only power is to determine the legislation's constitutional validity. In matters of economic legislation, we follow the rule giving every reasonable presumption in favor of the constitutionality of the law or ordinance. We employ this caution to avoid substituting our judgment for the judgment of the Legislature.

Other courts, faced with unconstitutional tort damage limits, have adhered to similar principles when reviewing those legislative actions. The Kansas Supreme Court put it well:

> This court is by the Constitution not made the critic of the legislature, but rather, the guardian of the Constitution. The constitutionality of a statute is presumed, and all doubts must be resolved in favor of its validity. Before a statute may be stricken down, it must clearly appear the statute violates the Constitution. Moreover, it is the court's duty to uphold the statute under attack, if possible, rather than defeat it, and if there is any reasonable way to construe the statute as constitutionally valid, that should be done.

To determine the extent of the right to trial by jury as it applies here, we must first identify the source of the constitutional protection. The seventh amendment to the United States Constitution does not apply through the Fourteenth Amendment to the states in civil trials. The right to jury trial in civil proceedings is protected solely by the Washington Constitution in article 1, section 21. Therefore, the relevant analysis must follow state doctrine; our result is based entirely on adequate and independent state grounds.

Article 1, section 21 states:

> The right of trial by jury shall remain inviolate, but the legislature may provide for a jury of any number less than twelve in courts not of record, and for a verdict by nine or more jurors in civil cases in any court of record, and for waiving of the jury in civil cases where the consent of the parties interested is given thereto.

Our basic rule in interpreting article 1, section 21 is to look to the right as it existed at the time of the constitution's adoption in 1889. We have used this historical standard to determine the scope of the right as well as the causes of action to which it applies. These two issues, scope and the applicable causes of action, merit separate discussion.

State ex rel. Mullen v. Doherty (Wash. 1897), being close in time to 1889, provides some contemporary insight on the scope issue. In *Mullen*, we cited section 248 of the Code of 1881, in force at the time of the constitution's passage, to determine the jury's role in the constitutional scheme: "either party shall have the right in an action at law, upon an issue of fact, to demand a trial by jury." Subsequent cases underscore the jury's fact finding province as the essence of the right's scope.

At issue in the present case is whether the measure of damages is a question of fact within the jury's province. Our past decisions show that it is indeed. The constitutional nature of the jury's damage-finding function is underscored by *Baker v. Prewitt* (Wash. 1888). In that case, the territorial Supreme Court stated:

> Sections 204 and 289 of the territorial Code seem to require that in all actions for the assessment of damages the intervention of a jury must be had, save where a long account may authorize a referee, etc. This statute is mandatory, and we are satisfied that where the amount of damages is not fixed, agreed upon, or in some way liquidated, a jury must be called, unless expressly waived.

If our state constitution is to protect as inviolate the right to a jury trial at least to the extent as it existed in 1889, then *Baker*'s holding provides clear evidence that the jury's fact-finding function included the determination of damages. This evidence can only lead to the conclusion that our constitution, in article 1, section 21, protects the jury's role to determine damages.

The present case is not the first time we have recognized the constitutional nature of the jury's damage-determining role. In *James v. Robeck* (Wash. 1971), we stated: "To the jury is consigned under the constitution the ultimate power to weigh the evidence and determine the facts—and the amount of damages in a particular case is an ultimate fact."

The jury's role in determining noneconomic damages is perhaps even more essential. In *Bingaman v. Grays Harbor Cmty. Hosp.* (Wash. 1985), the husband of a woman who died painfully 35 hours after giving birth, the result of medical malpractice, brought a wrongful death and survival action. The only issue before this court was whether the trial judge had properly reduced the jury's damage verdict of $412,000 for the woman's pain and suffering. In resolving the issue in the plaintiff's favor, we stated: "The determination of the amount of damages, *particularly in actions of this nature*, is primarily and peculiarly within the province of the jury, under proper instructions."

United States Supreme Court jurisprudence on the Seventh Amendment's scope in federal civil trials, while not binding on the states, also provides some insight. In *Dimick v. Schiedt* (1935), the Court used historical analysis to determine whether the Seventh Amendment allowed additur. Citing cases and treatises dating from the time of the amendment's adoption, the Court found that determining damages, as an issue of fact, was very much within the jury's province and therefore protected by the Seventh Amendment. The Court also indicated that a judge should give more deference to a jury's verdict when the damages at issue concern a noneconomic loss. The Court quoted the English case of *Beardmore v. Carrington* (1764):

> There is great difference between cases of damages which may be certainly seen, and such as are ideal, as between assumpsit, trespass for goods where the sum and value may be measured, and actions of imprisonment, malicious prosecution,

slander and other personal torts, where the damages are a matter of opinion, speculation, ideal.

The Court clarified the implications of the difference between these two classes of actions by quoting from Mayne's Treatise on Damages, at 571: "in cases where the amount of damages was uncertain their assessment was a matter so peculiarly within the province of the jury that the Court should not alter it."

A method of historical analysis used by the United States Supreme Court in *Tull v. United States* (1987) provides further insight. The *Tull* Court looked for proceedings analogous to the enforcement action under the federal clean water act which were contemporary with the Seventh Amendment's adoption. Finding that the common law proceeding of debt, in which the litigants had a right to a jury, was analogous to the clean water act enforcement action, the Court applied the Seventh Amendment right to the modern action. Without stretching the analogy as far as the Supreme Court did, it is logical to apply the more recent tort theories by analogy to the common law tort actions that existed in 1889. We note again that we reach our result today on adequate and independent state grounds. The holding in *Tull*, like all United States Supreme Court precedent in the civil trial area of the Seventh Amendment, is not binding on the states and merely serves as an example to us. It does not compel the result we reach.

Ultimately, there is not even an issue whether the right to a jury attaches to the Sofies' case. While they asserted "newer" tort theories in their complaint, the heart of the appellants' cause of action centered on negligence and willful or wanton misconduct resulting in personal injury. These basic tort theories are the same as those that existed at common law in 1889. Subsequent cases and statutes have recognized newer theories of recovery within the framework of these basic tort actions, but the basic cause of action remains the same. Therefore, the right to trial by jury—with its scope as defined by historical analysis—remains attached here.

The potential impact of the constitution's language was not lost on the Legislature. During the floor debates on the Tort Reform Act, the legislators were warned of the possible constitutional problems with their new legislation. Senator Talmadge stated:

> The Constitution of this state in Article I, Section 21, talks about the right to trial by jury being inviolate, not being something that we can invade as members of the Legislature, and when you start to put limitations on what juries can do, you have, in fact, invaded the province of the jury and have not preserved the right to a trial by jury inviolate.

It is highly persuasive that in Kansas, Texas, Ohio, and Florida, states that have found the damages limit unconstitutional, the operative language of the right to jury trial provisions in those states' constitutions is nearly identical to our own. *See* Kan. Const. Bill of Rights § 5 ("The right of trial by jury shall be inviolate"); Tex. Const. art. I, § 15 ("The right of trial by jury shall remain inviolate"); Ohio Const. art. I, § 5 ("The right of trial by jury shall be inviolate"); Fla. Const. art. I § 22 ("The right of trial by jury shall be secure to all and remain inviolate").

The weight of authority from other states, both numerically and persuasively, supports the conclusion that Washington's damages limit violates the right to trial by jury.

NOTE

The following States have held that caps on noneconomic damages violate the right to a jury trial: Alabama, Georgia, Missouri, South Dakota, Washington and Kansas. *See, e.g., Hilburn v. Enerpipe Ltd.*, 442 P.3d 509 (Kan. 2019) (holding that the statutory cap on jury awards for noneconomic damages in personal injury actions violated the constitutional guarantee of the right of trial by jury).

McCOOL v. GEHRET
657 A.2d 269 (Del. 1995)

HOLLAND, J.

The plaintiffs-appellants, Paul and Tammera McCool alleged medical negligence by the defendant-appellee, John Gehret, M.D., and certain other health care providers. The complaint was amended to allege tortious interference by Dr. Gehret with the plaintiffs' medical expert witness, Robert Dein, M.D. Over the plaintiffs' objection, the Superior Court granted Dr. Gehret's motion to sever the trial of the McCools' claim for medical malpractice from the trial of their claim for tortious interference.

A jury trial was held on the medical malpractice claim only, beginning on January 18, 1994. The jury returned a verdict in favor of Dr. Gehret on January 26, 1994. On February 3, 1994, the plaintiffs filed a motion for a mistrial or, in the alternative, a new trial.

On April 20, 1994, a one-day bench trial was held regarding the tortious interference claim. This bench trial was held before a different Superior Court judge than the one who had presided at the malpractice trial.

The McCools contend that forcing them to proceed with a bench trial on their tortious interference claim, despite their objection, violated their Delaware Constitutional right to have a trial by jury in that civil proceeding. The historical origins of the right to trial by jury, which is provided for in the Delaware Constitution, was reviewed by this Court in *Claudio v. State* (Del. 1991). In *Claudio*, this Court noted that when Delaware adopted its Constitution in 1792, notwithstanding the ratification of the first ten amendments or federal Bill of Rights in 1791, it did not create "a mirror image of the United States Constitution" with regard to trial by jury.

When the Delaware Constitution of 1792 was adopted, the right to trial by jury set forth in the federal Bill of Rights as the Sixth and Seventh Amendments to the United States Constitution was only a protection against action by the federal government. Following the adoption of the Fourteenth Amendment to the United States Constitution, the Sixth Amendment right to trial by jury in *criminal* proceedings has been deemed to have been incorporated by the Due Process clause and now also provides protection against state action. Nevertheless, the United States Supreme Court has not held that the Seventh Amendment's guarantee of jury trials in *civil* proceedings was made applicable to the states by the incorporation doctrine with the adoption of the Fourteenth Amendment to the United States Constitution.

Accordingly, the right to a jury trial in civil proceedings has always been and remains exclusively protected by provisions in the Delaware Constitution. Delaware adopted its first Constitution in 1776, which provided, in pertinent part:

> The common law of England, as well as so much of the statute law as have been heretofore adopted in practice in this state, shall remain in force, unless they shall be altered by a future law of the Legislature; such parts only excepted as are repugnant to the rights and privileges contained in this constitution and the declaration of rights agreed to by this convention.

Delaware also adopted its own *Declaration of Rights* in 1776, which guaranteed the right to trial by jury to all citizens of the State of Delaware and included a statement "that trial by jury of facts where they arise is one of the greatest securities of the lives, liberties and estates of the people."

When Delaware adopted its next Constitution in 1792, its citizens were guaranteed the right to trial by jury "as heretofore." Consequently, since its inception in 1776, the Delaware Constitution has afforded its citizens the right to trial by jury in both criminal and civil proceedings. In doing so, the Delaware Constitution has expressly preserved all of the fundamental features of the jury system as they existed at common law.

A *sine qua non* of that common law jurisprudence is the principle that either party shall have the right to demand a jury trial upon an issue of fact in an action at law. As previously noted, the 1776 Delaware *Declaration of Rights*, which was preserved by the "heretofore" text in the 1792 Constitution, referred to the right to trial by jury regarding factual issues as "one of the greatest securities of the lives, liberties and estates of the people." Similarly, in a letter to Pierre S. DuPont, Thomas Jefferson described the fact finding function of jurors as:

> the very essence of a Republic. We of the United States think experience has proved it safer for the mass of individuals composing the society to reserve to themselves personally the exercise of all rightful powers to which they are competent.

Hence, with us, the people being competent to judge of the facts occurring in ordinary life, have retained the functions of judges of facts under the name of jurors.

I believe that action by the citizens, in person in affairs within their reach and competence, and in all others by representatives chosen immediately and removable by themselves, constitutes the essence of a Republic.

In 1855, the Delaware General Assembly enacted a statute that purportedly allowed judges to decide issues of fact without a jury in actions at law, with the agreement of all the parties. Nevertheless, because the Delaware Constitution preserved the right to trial by jury as "heretofore," Delaware judges took the position that, absent constitutional amendment, the General Assembly could not alter the right by statute. Therefore, notwithstanding the enactment of the 1855 statute by the General Assembly, Delaware judges remained reluctant to decide issues of fact in an action at law because they concluded that the Delaware Constitution required a jury to decide such questions.

When the present Delaware Constitution was rewritten in 1897, the General Assembly included several significant provisions regarding the right to trial by jury. Article I of the 1897 Delaware Constitution was denominated for the first time as the "Bill of Rights." Section 4 of that article provided for the right to trial by jury as "heretofore." Article IV, section 19 was a new addition in the 1897 Constitution and provided: "Judges shall not charge juries with respect to matters of fact, but may state the questions of fact in issue and declare the law." The reason given during the Constitutional debates for the adoption of section 19 was to ensure "that Judges shall confine themselves to their business, which is to adjudge the law and leave juries to determine the facts."

In *Storey v. Camper* (Del. 1979), this Court characterized section 19 as perpetuating Delaware's commitment to trial by jury in civil actions at law with regard to issues of fact. In examining when a trial judge may set aside a jury verdict, this Court described Delaware's long history of commitment to trial by jury. We explained that section 19 reaffirmed Delaware's commitment to the common law principles regarding trial by jury:

> In the policy of the law of this state, declared by the courts in numberless decisions, the jury is the sole judge of the facts of a case, and so jealous is the law of this policy that by express provision of the Constitution the court is forbidden to touch upon the facts of the case in its charge to the jury.

In 1897, another new section was added to article IV of Delaware's Constitution. Article IV, section 20 provides that, "in civil causes where matters of fact are at issue, if the parties agree, such matters of fact shall be tried by the court, and judgment rendered upon their decision thereon as upon a verdict by a jury." According to the Constitutional debates, the purpose of the new section was to address the concerns of Delaware's jurists about the constitutionality of the 1855 statutory authorization for litigants to waive a trial by jury in an action at law on an issue of fact.

In this case the McCools specifically demanded a jury trial on their medical malpractice claim and their tortious interference claim. When the jury that heard their medical malpractice claim was discharged, the McCools agreed to waive their right to a jury trial regarding their tortious interference claim only because the original trial judge offered to decide the remaining claim as a bench trial. The record contains the following statement by the McCools' attorney to the second trial judge:

> For practical reasons, the medical malpractice trial went a bit longer than we expected. Because of the two-week period of the jury panel, the original trial judge explained to us that it did not appear we would be able to get the same jury.
>
> Discussing this in chambers as well as I think in the courtroom, the original trial judge proposed to personally hear this count as a bench trial, the benefit being, again, that even though we don't have the jury, at least we have a judge who did have the benefit of hearing all the testimony.

When the original trial judge subsequently declined to hear the tortious interference claim, the McCools objected to proceeding with a bench trial before another judge. Their attorney advised the second judge:

> Based on our understanding that the matter would be heard on the bench trial before the original trial judge, my clients and I agreed to have it heard that way rather than by jury trial. I just want to go on record that is their position. They still are opposed to the assignment of your honor.

Although a party has no right to insist on a bench trial before a particular judge, the record reflects that the McCools' waiver of their right to a jury trial was, in fact, permitted to be premised upon such a condition. The McCools only waived their right to a jury trial on the condition that the bench trial would be held before the original judge who had heard the medical malpractice claim and was familiar with much of the evidence relevant to the tortious interference claim. When the original trial judge, who had induced the McCools to waive their right to a jury trial, refused to hear their tortious interference claim, the condition upon which the McCools' waiver had been predicated ceased to exist.

This Court has recognized that the right to a trial by jury, as guaranteed by the Delaware Constitution, may be relinquished pursuant to a valid waiver. Under the circumstances presented in this case, however, the McCools could not be forced to proceed with a bench trial before a second judge, in the absence of an unconditional waiver of their fundamental right to a trial by jury. Consequently, the bench trial of the tortious interference claim that proceeded, without the McCools' express and unconditional waiver of a jury trial, violated article IV, section 20 and article I, section 4 of the Delaware Constitution.

NOTES

1. In civil cases, the Kentucky Constitution has been construed as recognizing exceptions to the right to a jury trial, including causes of action at common law that would have been regarded as equitable.

2. The Pennsylvania Constitution was amended to provide that a verdict may be rendered by not less than five-sixths of the jury in any civil case. Subject to that amendment, however, the right to trial by jury remained "as heretofore" and "inviolate." Pa. Const. art. I, § 6. In a civil case, twelve jurors retired to deliberate but one juror did not complete the deliberations. After the plaintiff-appellant's motion for a mistrial was denied, the eleven remaining jurors returned a unanimous verdict. The Pennsylvania Supreme Court reversed and held that the parties were entitled to a verdict of twelve jurors, notwithstanding the fact that the unanimous verdict of eleven jurors was greater than five-sixths of twelve. *See Blum v. Merrell Dow Pharmaceuticals, Inc.*, 626 A.2d 537 (Pa. 1993).

D. RIGHT TO BEAR ARMS

ROCKY MOUNTAIN GUN OWNERS v. POLIS
467 P.3d 314 (Colo. 2020)

MARQUEZ, J.

In recent decades, Colorado has been the setting of two of the nation's most notorious mass shootings: Columbine High School in 1999 and the Aurora movie theater in 2012. In both attacks, the shooters used large-capacity ammunition magazines. Collectively, the shooters killed over two dozen people and wounded scores more.

In response to these shootings, the Colorado General Assembly passed House Bill 13-1224 ("HB 1224"), which limits the capacity of magazines acquired after July 1, 2013. Relevant here, HB 1224 generally prohibits the sale, transfer, or possession of any "large-capacity magazine" (LCM), defined to include "a fixed or detachable magazine, box, drum, feed strip, or similar device capable of accepting, or that is designed to be readily converted to accept, more than fifteen rounds of ammunition."

Rocky Mountain Gun Owners, the National Association for Gun Rights, and John A. Sternberg challenge this law as an infringement on the right to bear arms—not under the Second Amendment to the U.S. Constitution, but under article II, section 13 of the Colorado Constitution. Plaintiffs construe HB 1224's definition of "large-capacity magazine" to encompass all magazines with removable base pads because such magazines can be "readily converted to accept more than fifteen rounds of ammunition." They argue that HB 1224 therefore operates to ban practically all detachable magazines, violating Coloradans' state constitutional right to bear arms in defense of home, person, and property.

We disagree. We conclude that Plaintiffs' interpretation of the definition of "large-capacity magazine" is inconsistent with the provision's plain text because it ignores the narrowing language, "designed to be readily converted to accept more than fifteen rounds of ammunition." Relying on our longstanding test under *Robertson v. City & County of Denver* (Colo. 1994) for examining challenges brought under article II, section 13, we hold that Plaintiffs failed to prove beyond a reasonable doubt that HB 1224 violates the state constitutional right to bear arms.

Plaintiffs argue that article II, section 13 of the Colorado Constitution should be interpreted in terms of its own text and history and that the right it guards is broader than the one encompassed by the Second Amendment to the U.S. Constitution. Plaintiffs further contend that because *McDonald v. Chicago* (2010) deemed the Second Amendment right fundamental, we must abandon *Robertson* (and, they suggest, adopt a "common lawful use" test purportedly derived from *District of Columbia v. Heller* (2008) in its place). In other words, Plaintiffs argue that, though we are free to interpret Colorado's constitution to be more protective of the right to bear arms than the Second Amendment, the U.S. Supreme Court's interpretation of the federal provision sets the constitutional "floor" for our interpretation of article II, section 13.

We agree with Plaintiffs' starting premise that article II, section 13 has a text and constitutional tradition distinct from the Second Amendment's. But precisely for this reason, we reject Plaintiffs' contention that our state constitutional provision must be interpreted in lockstep with its federal counterpart. The U.S. Supreme Court has long recognized that state courts are free to interpret their own state constitutions as they wish.

To be sure, the U.S. Constitution sets a federal floor of protection available to those who allege state infringement of their individual liberties. As such, Plaintiffs were entitled to invoke the protection afforded by the Second Amendment. But they chose not to. Instead, they proceeded under article II, section 13, the distinctive text of a separate sovereign, with meaning independent of the federal provision. *See* Sutton, *51 Imperfect Solutions: States and the Making of American Constitutional Law* 174 (2018) ("There is no reason to think, as an interpretive matter, that constitutional guarantees of independent sovereigns, even guarantees with the same or similar words, must be construed in the same way."). Accordingly, because *Heller* and *McDonald* construe the U.S. Constitution and not our differently worded state constitutional provision, they do not control the analysis in this case.

Of course, that our test under article II, section 13 may be different does not mean it is less protective of the state constitutional right. In any case, our independent interpretation of Colorado's constitutional provision does not somehow lower the federal constitutional floor. When interpreting our own constitution, we do not stand on the federal floor; we are in our own house.

We acknowledge that in some contexts, we have borrowed from federal analysis of the U.S. Constitution in construing our own constitutional text, particularly where a party has asserted dual constitutional claims under both a federal provision and its Colorado counterpart. We have leaned on federal analysis primarily where the text of the two provisions is identical or substantially similar. That said, even parallel text does not mandate parallel interpretation.

We have also tended to follow federal jurisprudence where, based on our independent analysis, we find the U.S. Supreme Court's reasoning to be sound, and where no party has argued that the Colorado provision calls for a distinct analysis.

None of these considerations is present here. First, as masters of their complaint, Plaintiffs did not bring dual constitutional claims but instead elected to challenge HB 1224 solely under the Colorado Constitution. Had Plaintiffs wished to have their allegations judged under *Heller* or *McDonald*, they could have raised a claim under the Second Amendment. But they chose to challenge HB 1224 solely on state constitutional grounds. Having done so, Plaintiffs cannot now insist that federal constitutional law controls the analysis of their case.

Second, article II, section 13 does not mirror the language of the Second Amendment. The Second Amendment provides, "a well regulated Militia, being necessary to the security of a free State, the right of the people to keep and bear Arms, shall not be infringed." The text of article II, section 13 differs in several respects:

> The right of no person to keep and bear arms in defense of his home, person and property, or in aid of the civil power when thereto legally summoned, shall be called in question; but nothing herein contained shall be construed to justify the practice of carrying concealed weapons.

Of particular relevance here, article II, section 13 confers a limited, individual right to bear arms "in defense of home, person and property."

Reflecting the significant textual differences between the two provisions, our precedent construing article II, section 13 long ago charted a different course from case law interpreting the Second Amendment.

In *People v. Nakamura* (Colo. 1936) we construed article II, section 13 to provide a "personal right to bear arms in defense of home, person, and property" rather than merely "one of collective enjoyment for common defense." At that time, consensus reflected a different view regarding the scope and meaning of the Second Amendment.

We also held in *Nakamura* that the right to bear arms in self-defense under article II, section 13 extended to "unnaturalized foreign-born residents," a question still the subject of debate in the federal arena today.

And our early decisions examining the felon-in-possession statute against article II, section 13 clearly proceeded from the premise that our constitutional provision protects persons convicted of felonies, a conclusion that stands in contrast to some federal courts' pronouncements regarding the Second Amendment.

The point is that we have consistently determined the scope of our provision based on an independent analysis of the Colorado Constitution, rather than by reference to the meaning of its federal counterpart. Not a single one of our opinions construing article II, section 13 looked to interpretations of the Second Amendment right. Certainly our reasoning in these cases has never suggested that our interpretation of article II, section 13 must lock in on the moving target of federal jurisprudence.

Like the present case, *Robertson* involved a constitutional challenge brought solely under article II, section 13 of the Colorado Constitution. As previously noted, *Robertson* concerned a Denver ordinance banning the manufacture, sale, or possession of assault weapons. Reviewing our case law construing the provision, we observed that we had "never found it necessary to decide the status accorded the article II, section 13 right." Instead, we had "consistently concluded that the state may regulate the exercise of that right under its inherent police power so long as the exercise of that power is reasonable." We therefore held conclusively in *Robertson* that it was unnecessary to reach whether the right is fundamental:

> When confronted with a challenge to the validity of a statute or ordinance regulating the exercise of the right to bear arms guaranteed under article II, section 13 of the Colorado Constitution, a reviewing court need not determine the status of that right. Rather, the question in each case is whether the law at issue constitutes a reasonable exercise of the state's police power.

Given these clear pronouncements, we now expressly disapprove of the conclusion that in *Robertson* we "implicitly found that the right to bear arms is not a fundamental right." Rather, we effectively rejected the importation of federal tiers of scrutiny into our article II, section 13 jurisprudence. As *Rocky Mountain Gun Owners v. Hickenlooper* (Colo. 2016) correctly understood, we reasoned that whether the right under article II, section 13 is fundamental or not, a restriction on that right is nonetheless subject to review under a reasonable exercise of police power test.

We take this opportunity to clarify the distinction between the reasonable exercise test and rational basis review. In *Town of Dillon v. Yacht Club Condominiums Home Owners Ass'n* (Colo. 2014), we explained that the police power "is an inherent attribute of sovereignty with which the state is endowed for the protection and general welfare of its citizens." We held that the police power, though broad, is "limited by due process," such that legislation or regulation based on the exercise of the state's police power must "bear a rational relationship to a legitimate government interest." Under the approach we took there, which we described as essentially rational basis review, "it is entirely irrelevant for constitutional purposes whether the conceived reason for the challenged legislation actually motivated the legislature." In other words, the rational basis test ensures rational government enactments.

But the due process limitation is independent from the separate and distinct constraint located in article II, section 13 of the Colorado Constitution and guarded by what we have referred to in shorthand as our "reasonable exercise" test. True, the reasonable exercise test demands that government enactments implicating the article II, section 13 right have a legitimate government end within the police power, such as promoting the public health, safety, or welfare. And as its name suggests, it requires a "reasonable" fit between purpose and means. But in the article II, section 13 context, the ultimate function of the reasonable exercise test is to effectuate the substantive constraints imposed by article II, section 13 on otherwise rational government regulation.

Reflecting that function, the article II, section 13 reasonable exercise test—unlike ordinary rational basis review—demands not just a conceivable legitimate purpose but an actual one. And, importantly, it does not tolerate government enactments that have either a purpose or effect of rendering the right to bear arms in self-defense a nullity. In short, the reasonable exercise test permits restrictions that may burden the right to bear arms but that still leave open ample means to exercise the core of that right; on the other hand, the test forbids restrictions that are so arbitrary or onerous as to amount to a denial of the right.

Having clarified the appropriate standard, we now turn to the merits of their claim. We conclude that HB 1224 constitutes a reasonable exercise of the police power and does not work a nullity of the right to bear arms in defense of home, person, or property under article II, section 13.

We credit the trial court's finding that the purpose of HB 1224 was to "reduce the number of people who are killed or shot in mass shootings." The court's finding is amply supported by the record and we affirm both lower courts' conclusions that this discrete purpose of the legislation lies well within the state's police power. Indeed, it can hardly be argued that seeking to reduce the lethality of mass shootings and to contain their rippling, traumatic effects does not relate to the public health, safety, or welfare.

We further agree with the court of appeals that the prohibition on LCMs is reasonably related to that legitimate—and increasingly critical—state interest. Evidence at trial established that the use of LCMs in mass shootings increases the number of victims shot and the fatality rate of struck victims. It also established that LCMs were used in some of the most horrific shootings in recent memory. These statistics have been deeply felt in Colorado, where LCMs played a lethal role in the Columbine and Aurora massacres. Finally, the record supports the trial court's finding that the pause created by the need to reload or replace a magazine creates an opportunity for potential victims to take life-saving measures. In short, the evidence overwhelmingly demonstrated the reasonableness of the General Assembly's choice to set a limit on the number of rounds that can be fired before a shooter needs to reload.

The gravamen of Plaintiffs' claim that HB 1224 violates the state constitutional right to bear arms rests on their interpretation of the phrase "designed to be readily converted to accept." In their view, this language in the statutory definition of an LCM encompasses any magazine with a design that makes it capable of being "readily converted to accept" more than fifteen rounds. Because magazines with removable base pads can be readily converted to accept more than fifteen rounds, Plaintiffs argue that such magazines fall under the statutory definition. And because 90% of detachable magazines contain removable base pads, Plaintiffs maintain that HB 1224 therefore bans the overwhelming majority of magazines, thus denying their right to bear arms under article II, section 13.

We hold that HB 1224 is a reasonable exercise of the police power that has neither the purpose nor effect of nullifying the right to bear arms in self-defense encompassed by article II, section 13 of the Colorado Constitution.

JANE DOE v. WILMINGTON HOUSING AUTHORITY
88 A.3d 654 (Del. 2014)

RIDGELY, J.

In this certified question proceeding, we address whether lease provisions for apartments of a Delaware public housing authority that restrict when residents, their household members, and their guests may carry and possess firearms in the common areas violate the right to keep and bear arms guaranteed by Article I, Section 20 of the Delaware Constitution. We accepted two questions of state law from the United States Court of Appeals for the Third Circuit. Pending before the Third Circuit is an appeal from a judgment of the United States District Court for the District of Delaware in *Doe. v. Wilmington Housing Authority*. The District Court found no violation of the Second Amendment or the Delaware Constitution. The certified questions are:

> 1. Whether, under Article I, § 20 of the Delaware Constitution, a public housing agency such as the WHA may adopt a policy prohibiting its residents, household members, and guests from displaying or carrying a firearm or other weapon in a common area, except when the firearm or other weapon is being transported to or from a resident's housing unit or is being used in self-defense.
>
> 2. Whether, under Article I, § 20 of the Delaware Constitution, a public housing agency such as the WHA may require its residents, household members, and guests to have available for inspection a copy of any permit, license, or other documentation required by state, local, or federal law for the ownership,

possession, or transportation of any firearm or other weapon, including a license to carry a concealed weapon, as required by Del. Code Ann. tit. 11, § 1441, on request, when there is reasonable cause to believe that the law or policies have been violated.

We answer both certified questions in the negative.

Appellants Jane Doe and Charles Boone filed suit in the Delaware Court of Chancery against the Wilmington Housing Authority (WHA), a nonprofit agency of the State of Delaware that provides housing to low-income individuals and families, and against WHA's Executive Director, Frederick Purnell. Jane Doe lived in the Park View, a privately owned housing facility managed by the WHA. Doe's lease required her to follow the "House Rules." The original version of House Rule 24, in effect when the suit was filed, stated, "Tenant is not permitted to display or use any firearms, BB guns, pellet guns, slingshots, or other weapons on the premises." Charles Boone lived in the Southbridge Apartments, a public housing facility owned and operated by the WHA. Boone's lease stated that residents are "not to display, use, or possess any firearms, (operable or inoperable) or other dangerous instruments or deadly weapons as defined by the laws of the State of Delaware anywhere on the property of the Authority." Residents were subject to eviction if they, their household members, or their guests violated the lease provisions and rules.

Doe and Boone alleged that the restrictions on gun use and possession violated their right to bear arms as provided in the Second Amendment to the United States Constitution and in Article I, Section 20 of the Delaware Constitution. They also alleged that the WHA firearms rules and policies were preempted by Delaware law and that the WHA exceeded its statutory authority by enacting them.

The defendants removed the case to the United States District Court for the District of Delaware on June 1, 2010. On June 28, 2010, the Supreme Court of the United States decided *McDonald v. City of Chicago*, holding that the Second Amendment applies to the states through the Due Process Clause of the Fourteenth Amendment. The defendants informed the District Court that they were reevaluating the constitutionality of the WHA firearm rules and policies in light of *McDonald*.

On October 25, 2010, the WHA adopted a new firearms policy for its public housing units, including Southbridge. The Revised Policy provides, in full:

Lease Modification (Replaces Lease Part I § DC.P.):

WHA recognizes the importance of protecting its residents' health, welfare, and safety, while simultaneously protecting the rights of its residents to keep and bear arms as established by the federal and state constitutions. WHA therefore adopts the following Firearms and Weapons Policy. Residents, members of a resident's household, and guests:

1. Shall comply with all local, state, and federal legal requirements applicable to the ownership, possession, transportation, and use of firearms or other weapons. The term "firearm" includes any weapon from which a shot, projectile or other object may be discharged by force of combustion, explosive, gas and/or mechanical means, whether operable or inoperable, loaded or unloaded, and any weapon or destructive device as defined by law.

2. Shall not discharge or use any firearm or other weapons on WHA property except when done in self-defense.

3. Shall not display or carry a firearm or other weapon in any common area, except where the firearm or other weapon is being transported to or from the resident's unit, or is being used in self-defense.

4. Shall have available for inspection a copy of any permit, license, or other documentation required by state, local, or federal law for the ownership, possession, or transportation of any firearm or other weapon, including a license to carry a concealed weapon as required by 11 Del C. § 1441, upon request, when there is reasonable cause to believe that the law or this Policy has been violated.

5. Shall exercise reasonable care in the storage of loaded or unloaded firearms and ammunition, or other weapons.

6. Shall not allow a minor under 16 years of age to have possession of a firearm, B.B. gun, air gun, or spear gun unless under the direct supervision of an adult.

7. Shall not give or otherwise transfer to a minor under 18 years of age a firearm or ammunition for a firearm, unless the person is that child's parent or guardian, or unless the person first receives the permission of the minor's parent or guardian.

Violation of this Policy by any resident or member of the resident's household shall be grounds for immediate Lease termination and eviction. In addition, a resident or member of the resident's household who knowingly permits a guest to violate this Policy shall be subject to immediate Lease termination and eviction.

Residents filed an amended complaint challenging only paragraph 3, the Common Area Provision, and paragraph 4, the Reasonable Cause Provision, of the Revised Policy.

We begin by noting that the Declaration of Rights in the Delaware Constitution has not always been interpreted identically to the counterpart provisions in the federal Bill of Rights. As we have previously explained:

> The Declaration of Rights in the Delaware Constitution is not a mirror image of the federal Bill of Rights. Consequently, Delaware judges cannot faithfully discharge the responsibilities of their office by simply holding that the Declaration of Rights in Article I of the Delaware Constitution is necessarily in "lock step" with the United States Supreme Court's construction of the federal Bill of Rights.

To determine whether a state constitutional provision is substantively identical to an analogous provision of United States Constitution, this Court considers the list of nonexclusive factors originally articulated in the concurring opinion of Justice Handler of the New Jersey Supreme Court in *State v. Hunt* (N.J. 1982). The *Hunt* factors provide a framework to determine whether a state constitutional provision affords an independent basis to reach a different result than what could be obtained under federal law. The seven factors include:

(1) Textual Language—A state constitution's language may itself provide a basis for reaching a result different from that which could be obtained under federal law. Textual language can be relevant in either of two contexts. First, distinctive provisions of our State charter may recognize rights not identified in the federal constitution. Second, the phrasing of a particular provision in our charter may be so significantly different from the language used to address the same subject in the federal Constitution that we can feel free to interpret our provision on an independent basis.

(2) Legislative History—Whether or not the textual language of a given provision is different from that found in the federal Constitution, legislative history may reveal an intention that will support reading the provision independently of federal law.

(3) Preexisting State Law—Previously established bodies of state law may also suggest distinctive state constitutional rights. State law is often responsive to concerns long before they are addressed by constitutional claims. Such preexisting law can help to define the scope of the constitutional right later established.

(4) Structural Differences—Differences in structure between the federal and state constitutions might also provide a basis for rejecting the constraints of federal doctrine at the state level. The United States Constitution is a grant of enumerated powers to the federal government. Our State Constitution, on the other hand, serves only to limit the sovereign power which inheres directly in the people and indirectly in their elected representatives. Hence, the explicit affirmation of fundamental rights in our Constitution can be seen as a guarantee of those rights and not as a restriction upon them.

(5) Matters of Particular State Interest or Local Concern—A state constitution may also be employed to address matters of peculiar state interest or local concern. When particular questions are local in character and do not appear to require a uniform national policy, they are ripe for decision under state law. Moreover, some matters are uniquely appropriate for independent state action.

(6) State Traditions—A state's history and traditions may also provide a basis for the independent application of its constitution.

(7) Public Attitudes—Distinctive attitudes of a state's citizenry may also furnish grounds to expand constitutional rights under state charters. While we have never cited this criterion in our decisions, courts in other jurisdictions have pointed to public attitudes as a relevant factor in their deliberations.

"These enumerated criteria, which are synthesized from a burgeoning body of authority, are essentially illustrative, rather than exhaustive." But those criteria do "share a common thread—that distinctive and identifiable attributes of a state government, its laws and its people justify recourse to the state constitution as an independent source for recognizing and protecting individual rights."

This case concerns the right to keep and bear arms under Article I, Section 20 of the Delaware Constitution. Although Section 20 was not enacted until 1987, Delaware has a long history, dating back to the Revolution, of allowing responsible citizens to lawfully carry and use firearms in our state. The parties agree, as does this Court, that Delaware is an "open carry" state. Like the citizens of our sister states at the founding, Delaware citizens understood that the "right of self-preservation" permitted a citizen to "repel force by force" when "the intervention of society in his behalf, may be too late to prevent an injury." An individual's right to bear arms was "understood to be an individual right protecting against both public and private violence." The right to keep and bear arms was also understood to exist for membership in the militia and for hunting.

In 1791, Delaware delegates to the state constitutional convention were unable to agree on the specific language that would codify in our Declaration of Rights the right to keep and bear arms in Delaware. After several attempts, the effort was abandoned. Concerns over groups of armed men stood in the way of an agreement even though there was an apparent consensus among the delegates on an individual's right to bear arms in self-defense.

Not until almost 200 years later did the Delaware General Assembly agree on the language to be used. Article I, Section 20 provides: "A person has the right to keep and bear arms for the defense of self, family, home and State, and for hunting and recreational use." The General Assembly's stated purpose in enacting the constitutional amendment was to "explicitly protect the traditional right to keep and bear arms," which it defined in the text of the amendment. By including the right to keep and bear arms in the Delaware Constitution, the General Assembly has recognized this right as fundamental.

This Court has previously addressed the application of Article I, Section 20 of the Delaware Constitution on four occasions. In *Short v. State* (Del. 1991), we held that 11 Del. C. § 1448, which prohibits felons from possessing a deadly weapon, does not violate Section 20. In *Smith v. State* (Del. 2005), we held that Section 20, when enacted, did not alter the then-existing law pertaining to the crime of carrying a concealed deadly weapon without a license and the statutory privilege to carry a concealed deadly weapon with a license. In *Dickerson v. State* (Del. 2009), we affirmed a conviction for carrying a concealed weapon without a license outside of the home. And most recently in *Griffin v. State* (Del. 2011), we considered an as-applied challenge to a conviction for carrying a concealed deadly weapon without a license in the home. In *Griffin*, we explained that although the right to bear arms "is not absolute," "Griffin's constitutional right to bear arms authorized his carrying a concealed knife in his home." That did not end the inquiry, because after the police arrived "the balance between Griffin's interest in carrying a concealed weapon in his home and the State's interest in public safety shifted in favor of the State."

In all of these cases but one, no federal Second Amendment jurisprudence was cited. Although both Section 20 and the Second Amendment share a similar historical context that informs our analysis, the interpretation of Section 20 is not dependent upon federal interpretations of the Second Amendment. The text of Section 20, enacted in 1987, and the Second Amendment, effective beginning in 1791, is not the same. On its face, the Delaware provision is intentionally broader than the Second Amendment and protects the right to bear arms outside the home, including for hunting and recreation. Section 20 specifically provides for the defense of self and family *in addition to* the home. Accordingly, our interpretation of Section 20 is not constrained by the federal precedent relied upon by the WHA, which explains that at the core of the Second Amendment is the right of law abiding, responsible citizens to use arms in defense of "hearth and home." We agree with Residents that Article I, Section 20 is not a mirror image of the Second Amendment and that the scope of the protections it provides are not limited to the home.

Our conclusion that the interpretation of Article I, Section 20 is a source, independent from the Second Amendment, for recognizing and protecting individual rights, is supported by the *Hunt* factors. The distinctive language of Section 20 and the legislative history demonstrates the General Assembly's intent to provide a right to keep and bear arms independent of the federal right. Moreover, public attitudes, as reflected in the laws passed by the General Assembly, and Delaware's long tradition of allowing responsible, law-abiding citizens to keep and bear arms outside of the home, favor recognizing an independent right under the Delaware Constitution. Two *Hunt* factors—the structural differences in constitutional provisions and matters of particular state interest—do not require that Section 20 be interpreted coextensively with the Second Amendment.

Where government action infringes a fundamental right, Delaware courts will apply a heightened scrutiny analysis. The parties have not argued otherwise here. Where heightened scrutiny applies, the State has the burden of showing that the state action is constitutional. Here, the parties differ on the appropriate heightened scrutiny analysis. Residents argue for strict scrutiny and the WHA argues for intermediate scrutiny. For the reasons which follow, we conclude that intermediate scrutiny is the proper level of constitutional review.

"A governmental action survives strict scrutiny only where the state demonstrates that the test is narrowly tailored to advance a compelling government interest." "Strict scrutiny is a tool to determine whether there is a cost-benefit justification for governmental action that burdens interests for which the Constitution demands unusually high protection." In contrast, intermediate scrutiny requires more than a rational basis for the action, but less than strict scrutiny. Intermediate scrutiny seeks to balance potential burdens on fundamental rights against the valid interests of government. To survive intermediate scrutiny, governmental action must "serve important governmental objectives and must be substantially related to the achievement of those objectives." The governmental action cannot burden the right more than is reasonably necessary to ensure that the asserted governmental objective is met.

Although the right to bear arms under the Delaware Declaration of Rights is a fundamental right, we have already held that it is not absolute. The General Assembly that enacted Article I, Section 20 left in place a series of statutes affecting the right to keep and bear arms in Delaware. Our prior cases so recognized and found no legislative intent (for example) to invalidate laws prohibiting felons from possessing deadly weapons or prohibiting (with certain exceptions) the carrying of a concealed deadly weapon outside the home without a license. The General Assembly's careful and nuanced approach supports an intermediate scrutiny analysis that allows a court to consider public safety and other important governmental interests.

It is undisputed that Residents are subject to eviction under the WHA lease provision and rules if they, their household members, or their guests violate the Common Area Provision that restricts the possession of firearms in the common areas of the WHA properties where the Residents and their household members live. That restriction infringes the fundamental right of responsible, law-abiding citizens to keep and bear arms for the defense of self, family, and home. WHA therefore has the burden to demonstrate that its governmental action passes intermediate scrutiny.

To satisfy its burden, WHA argues that it has an important governmental interest in protecting the health, welfare, and safety of all WHA residents, staff, and guests who enter onto WHA property. WHA argues that an accidental discharge of a firearm may have serious fatal consequences and that dangers inherent in the increased presence of firearms. But these same concerns would also apply to the area within any apartment—interior locations where the WHA concedes it cannot restrict the possession of firearms for self-defense. The Revised Policy does more than proscribe the unsafe *use* of a firearm. It also prohibits *possession* in the public housing common areas except where the firearm is being transported to or from an apartment. In this context, WHA must show more than a general safety concern and it has not done so.

In *Griffin v. State* we explained that an individual's interest in the right to keep and bear arms is strongest when "the weapon is in one's home or business and is being used for security." Residents have a possessory interest in both their apartments and the common areas. And although Residents cannot exclude other residents or the public from the common areas, their need for security in those areas is just as high for purposes of Section 20 as it would be inside their apartment or business. The common areas are effectively part of the residences. The laundry rooms and TV rooms are similar to those typically found in private residences; and the

Residents, their families, and their guests will occupy them as part of their living space.

With the Common Area Provision in force under penalty of eviction, reasonable, law-abiding adults become disarmed and unable to repel an intruder by force in any common living areas when the intervention of society on their behalf may be too late to prevent an injury. Even active and retired police officers who are residents, household members, or guests are disarmed by the Common Area Provision. They are restricted in possessing firearms in the public housing common areas of the apartment buildings despite their exemption by the General Assembly from concealed-carry license requirements.

Nor is the Common Area Provision sustainable under intermediate scrutiny because the WHA owns the property and is a landlord. WHA contends that it is acting as a landlord and not as a sovereign. We recognize that where the government is a proprietor or employer, it has a legitimate interest in controlling unsafe or disruptive behavior on its property. But WHA has conceded that after *McDonald*, as a landlord it may not adopt a total ban of firearms. Thus, occupying the status of government landlord, alone and without more, does not control. How the property is used must also be considered. Public housing is "a home as well as a government building." The WHA is different from other public agencies in that it essentially replicates for low-income families services similar to those provided by a private landlord. The individual's need for defense of self, family, and home in an apartment building is the same whether the property is owned privately or by the government.

Unlike a state office building, courthouse, school, college, or university, the services provided by the WHA in the common areas are not the services typically provided to the public on government property. They are limited to supplying adequate housing for low-income families and individuals and to maintaining the grounds and buildings for the residents. Some regulation of possessing firearms on WHA property could pass intermediate scrutiny, for example prohibiting possession in offices where state employees work and state business is being done. Here, however, the restrictions of the Common Area Provision are overbroad and burden the right to bear arms more than is reasonably necessary. Indeed, the Common Area Provision severely burdens the right by functionally disallowing armed self-defense in areas that Residents, their families, and guests may occupy as part of their living space.

The record before us shows that the Revised Policy was adopted by the WHA during the litigation before the District Court and after the United States Supreme Court decision in *McDonald v. City of Chicago*. The WHA "suspended, reviewed, and replaced" its original policies banning all firearms on its property pursuant to "the HUD-mandated procedure for doing so in view of the Supreme Court's holding in *McDonald*." The Reasonable Cause Provision of the Revised Policy requires the production upon request by a resident, household member, or guest of

> a copy of any permit, license, or other documentation required by state, local, or federal law for the ownership, possession, or transportation of any firearm or other weapon, including a license to carry a concealed weapon as required by 11 Del. C. § 1441, upon request, when there is reasonable cause to believe that the law *or this Policy* has been violated.

By it terms, the Reasonable Cause Provision exists, as least in part, to enforce compliance with the Common Area Provision, which we have found to be overbroad and unconstitutional.

Where a statute, regulation, or state action faces a constitutional challenge, "a Court may preserve its valid portions if the offending language can lawfully be severed." But where it is evident that the remaining provisions would not have been enacted without the unconstitutional provision, a court should invalidate the entire provision. The Reasonable Cause Provision was enacted, together with the Common Area Provision, by the WHA in response to *McDonald*. Because the unconstitutional Common Area Provision is not severable as a matter of Delaware law, the Reasonable Cause Provision which enforces it is unconstitutional and overbroad as well. For that reason, we answer the second certified question in the negative.

STATE v. MISCH
256 A.3d 519 (Vt. 2021)

PER CURIAM

This case requires us to decide whether Vermont's ban on large-capacity magazines violates the right to bear arms under Chapter I, Article 16 of the Vermont Constitution. We conclude that the magazine ban is a reasonable regulation of the right of the people to bear arms for self-defense, and therefore affirm the trial court's denial of defendant's motion to dismiss the charges against him.

Defendant was charged with two counts of unlawfully possessing a large-capacity magazine. Section 4021 states, "a person shall not manufacture, possess, transfer, offer for sale, purchase, receive or import into this State a large capacity ammunition feeding device," defined as:

> a magazine, belt, drum, feed strip, or similar device that has a capacity of, or that can be readily restored or converted to accept more than 10 rounds of ammunition for a long gun; or more than 15 rounds of ammunition for a hand gun.

Defendant allegedly traveled to a New Hampshire retailer, purchased two thirty-round magazines for a rifle, and transported them back into Vermont. Defendant moved to dismiss the charges on the grounds that the statute unconstitutionally impinges on the right to bear arms in Article 16.

The full text of Article 16 provides:

> That the people have a right to bear arms for the defense of themselves and the State—and as standing armies in time of peace are dangerous to liberty, they ought not to be kept up; and that the military should be kept under strict subordination to and governed by the civil power.

"We approach interpretation of the Vermont Constitution differently than we do the interpretation of statutes." We have often relied on historical context to "illuminate the meaning" of a constitutional provision. Historical context is "one of our most useful tools to determine the meaning of a constitutional provision," because the plain meaning of the right to bear arms as commonly understood today does not necessarily align with its plain meaning when it was written in 1777.

The historical context here is significant. Although the historical record contains scant evidence of public debate concerning the right of individuals to keep or carry weapons for nonmilitia purposes, the status and control of state militias and the desirability of a standing national army were hotly debated throughout the states during the era when Vermont's founders adopted the first Vermont Constitution. The Virginia Declaration of Rights, which was the oldest and most influential declaration of rights, stated that "a well-regulated Militia, composed of the body of the people, trained to arms, is the proper, natural and safe defence of a free State." It did not reference a specific right to "bear arms." The Pennsylvania Constitution was influenced by the Virginia Constitution, and was the first to affirmatively declare a right to "bear arms" tied to "defense of themselves" in the context of a comparable provision. Most of the remaining state constitutions drew from one or both of these constitutions; only four of the state constitutions adopted prior to the federal constitution included a right to "bear arms," and only two, including Vermont's, included a reference to "defense for themselves." The Vermont Declaration of Rights incorporates the language from the Pennsylvania Constitution verbatim.

The debate underlying these various provisions, including the Second Amendment to the United States Constitution, arose from a "fear of standing armies in the hands of a powerful central government" that had "instilled in Americans a belief that a militia was the proper form of defense." The goal animating these various provisions was to protect the ability of states to maintain effective state-regulated militias.

The phrase "bear arms for the defense of the State" by itself most likely meant, in the eighteenth century, to bear arms for the purpose of serving in a state militia. To the extent the right to bear arms is borne of and shaped by the purpose of ensuring a ready force to serve in the state militia, it does not apply in the modern context.

Our understanding of the meaning of the constitutional right to "bear arms" in 2021 is necessarily informed by an understanding of the meaning of that term when Vermont's founders established the constitutional right, as reflected in general linguistic usage in the founding era as well as the specific terminology in the Vermont Constitution. In recent years, Brigham Young University has released two databases—the Corpus of Founding Era American English, which contains over 120,000 texts, including legal writings, books, pamphlets, letters, and other documents dated between 1760 and 1799, and the Corpus of Early Modern English, which contains over 40,000 texts, including those published in England as well as the United States. Coupled with "for the defense of the State," and in light of the history set forth above, the phrase relates to a right to bear arms as a necessary condition to service in a State militia.

This understanding is consistent with the context and use of "bear arms" and "bearing arms" in the Vermont Constitution. The phrase "bear arms" in the first clause of Article 16 refers at least in part to the "defense of the State," and the latter two clauses of Article 16 clearly relate to the roles and power of the standing army and military. In this context, it makes sense to read "bear arms" as being connected to militia service. And Chapter I, Article 9, the other constitutional provision containing the phrase "bearing arms," uses the term to refer to the duty to bear arms in militia service. Article 9 contains a conscientious-objector clause: no person "who is conscientiously scrupulous of bearing arms" can "be justly compelled thereto." Use of the phrase "bearing arms" in Article 9 to mean military service reinforces an inference that in Article 16 the phrase "bear arms" means to carry weapons in a military context. Based on the language of the Constitution and its historical context, the right to "bear arms for the defense of the State" in Article 16 was most likely a right to bear arms for the purpose of service in the state militia.

To the extent that a right to "bear arms" is tied to the purpose of preserving a state militia force, there is no modern predicate to application of the right. During the framers' era, while the militia was made up of civilians, not professionals, it was an organized body, functioning both as part of the government and as an independent force to protect the community. The Vermont militia, which was regulated by statute and in which every eligible and nonexempt man was enrolled, was first and foremost a domestic defense force. "The essential duty of the militia was to be ready to respond, to be called out on a Colonel's orders, upon any alarm, invasion, or notice of the appearance of an enemy, either by water or land."

A state militia no longer exists. By 1840, the Vermont militia's "glory days were over," and in 1941, "when a revised chapter on the National Guard was enacted, the practice of requiring universal manhood military service finally ended for good in Vermont." The core function of the militia is now entrusted to the National Guard, which serves dual functions as "the militia of the states and a permanent reserve component of the U.S. Army."

Although the National Guard is the closest living descendant of the colonial-era militias, it is a distant cousin at best because the federal government controls its weapons and supplies. Moreover, because the government now supplies weapons to members of the National Guard, regulations on firearms do not threaten the effectiveness of the militia.

But Article 16 goes further by expressly stating that "the people" have a right to "bear arms for the defense of themselves and the State." The inclusion of language indicating that the "people" have a right to bear arms "for the defense of themselves and the State" introduces the possibility that the founders intended to establish a broader right to "bear arms" in individual self-defense, unmoored from potential militia service. The language of Article 16 is not inconsistent with the conclusion that the right to bear arms extends beyond potential militia service to individual self-defense.

The language of Article 16 describes a right of "the people" to bear arms for the purpose of defending not only the State, but also "themselves." Although the reference to "defense of themselves" lends support to the view that Article 16 establishes a right to bear arms to protect individual interests, the meaning of the text in historical context is equivocal. The association of the right with "the people," rather than persons, distinguishes it from many, though not all, rights enumerated in the Vermont Constitution that protect individual liberty or action disconnected from the body politic. The Constitution recognizes that all "persons" are born equally free and independent, and have inherent, unalienable rights; requires compensation when any "person's" property is taken for public use; recognizes freedom of religion for all "persons"; indicates that every "person" ought to have a remedy at law for injuries or wrongs.

In contrast, the Vermont Constitution generally refers to "the people" when recognizing rights associated with the body politic, to be exercised collectively. For example, the rights of governing and regulating the internal police is assigned to "the people"; government is accountable to "the people"; free debate and deliberation in the Legislature is essential to the rights of "the people"; adherence to "justice, moderation, temperance, industry, and frugality" are necessary to preserve the blessings of liberty, and "the people" in directing their legislators and magistrates ought to pay particular attention to these principles.

Some Articles include both terms, depending on whether the specific context implicates an individual or collective right or action. Considering the Declaration of Rights in the Vermont Constitution as a whole, the description of the right to bear arms in Article 16 as belonging to "the people" places it in the category of rights generally associated with and exercised by the body politic as contrasted with rights conferred on and exercised by an individual.

In sum, the text of Article 16, as written in the eighteenth century, was likely designed to protect the right of the people to bear arms for the purpose of constituting and serving in the state militia—a purpose that renders the right essentially obsolete in modern times. However, this interpretation does not foreclose the possibility that the provision can and should be understood to protect the right of individuals to own firearms for individual self-defense, independent of service in a state militia. To help further elucidate the meaning of the constitutional provision, we turn to our case law interpreting Article 16.

In this Court's history, we have relied on Article 16 only twice: in *State v. Rosenthal* (Vt. 1903) and *State v. Duranleau* (Vt. 1969). Neither case includes a detailed analysis of Article 16. However, both cases offer important insight into how we have historically understood that right: first, we have assumed that Article 16 protects an individual right to bear arms outside of the context of actual or potential militia service, and second, we have assumed that the right is subject to regulation by the Legislature.

Case law from our sister states, while not binding on us as we interpret the Vermont Constitution, supports the conclusion that the scope of the right to bear arms in Article 16 includes an individual right to possess arms for the purpose of self-defense. Courts in most states with constitutional provisions relating to a right to "bear arms," whether they have constitutional provisions very similar to Article 16 or substantially different, have concluded that their constitutions protect an individual right to bear arms for self-defense.

Courts in states with constitutional provisions substantially identical to Vermont's in referencing a right of "the people" to bear arms for "the defense of themselves and the State" have consistently construed these provisions to protect an individual right to bear arms for self-defense. Considering the scope of its constitutional provision declaring that "the people shall have the right to bear arms for the defence of themselves, and the State," the Oregon Supreme Court reviewed the historical genesis of this language and concluded that the constitutional provision includes, among other things, an individual's right to bear arms "for defense of person and property."

Similarly, prior to its revision in 1968, the Florida Constitution provided, "The right of the people to bear arms in defence of themselves and the lawful authority of the State, shall not be infringed, but the Legislature may prescribe the manner in which they may be borne." Construing this language, the Florida Supreme Court wrote, "Doubtless the guarantee was intended to secure to the people the right to carry weapons for their protection while the proviso was designed to protect the people also—from the bearing of weapons by the unskilled, the irresponsible, and the lawless."

Moreover, courts in some states with constitutional provisions relating to the right to bear arms that do not include any reference to defense of "themselves," have concluded that their constitutions protect a right to bear arms for individual self-defense.

Collectively, these decisions reflect a widespread, though not universal, contemporary understanding that bearing arms for self-defense, albeit subject to restrictions, is among the individual rights separately protected by many state constitutions, including those with language similar to Vermont's.

Our conclusion that the right to bear arms for individual self-defense is subject to limitations and regulation is consistent with Vermont's history of public-safety regulations of both the militia and individual gun ownership. Article 16 itself admonishes that "the military should be kept under strict subordination to and governed by the civil power."

We conclude that Article 16 protects a right to possess firearms for self-defense. As understood in modern times, this right is tied to the defense of self, family, and home, and is not tied to prospective military use in the context of a state militia. Its scope is accordingly limited.

This interpretation is the best available way to harmonize and honor the core principles of security and self-protection implicit in the right, the individual right to carry guns as implicitly recognized in our case law, and modern persuasive analysis from sister states. These considerations, as well as the historical regulation of the right in Vermont, also support our conclusion that the right to bear arms is subject to reasonable regulation pursuant to the State's police power. Whereas we have previously relied on stated or unstated assumptions that the individual right to bear arms in self-defense exists but is not unlimited, we now expressly hold as much. And while defendant argues that we should presume a restriction on the right to bear arms is unconstitutional, our case law supports the opposite presumption: we presume the reasonableness and constitutionality of an act of the Legislature, including those that restrict the right to bear arms.

Under the reasonable-regulation balancing test we now adopt, the right to bear arms in self-defense may be "regulated but not prohibited." This means that the government may regulate firearms as long as any enactment is a reasonable exercise of police power and there is a reasonable fit between the purpose and means of regulation. Regulation of firearms is not reasonable if it renders Article 16 a nullity. In applying this test to restrictions on specific firearms, ammunition, or accessories, courts may consider, among other factors, "characteristics of the particular weapon restricted," the "typical use for the proscribed weapons," and the "number and nature of the weapons subjected to the ban compared with the number and nature of the weapons that remain available for the vindication of the right."

This test is not the same as rational-basis review under the U.S. Constitution. Article 16 "stands as an independent, substantive limitation on otherwise rational government action." The reasonable-regulation test "requires an actual, not just conceivable, legitimate purpose related to health, safety, and welfare." Although our inquiry looks to an actual balance of interests, rather than merely a conceivable one, it does not override our general deference to the Legislature on matters within its authority. The question for courts is not whether we would strike the same balance as the Legislature, but is whether the Legislature's choices are anchored to a real, as opposed to hypothetical, foundation. And even regulations that would otherwise satisfy that standard may still be unconstitutional if ultimately they render the right at stake a nullity.

Applying the reasonable-regulation test to the large-capacity magazine ban, we conclude that the statute does not violate the right to bear arms. The available evidence supports the Legislature's conclusion that a large-capacity magazine ban does not significantly impair the right to bear arms for self-defense. It does not prevent Vermonters from buying or using the gun of their choice—it restricts only the capacity to shoot more than ten or fifteen rounds at a time, and thus places minimal restriction on their ability to bear arms in self-defense. Additionally, in contrast to their ubiquity among mass shootings, large-capacity magazines appear to be rarely used for self-defense purposes. Therefore, the large-capacity magazine ban does not render Article 16 a nullity.

Section 4021 restricts only magazine capacity. It does not purport to restrict the use of firearms that accept large-capacity magazines. The Legislature has chosen not to restrict individuals' choice of firearms for self-defense or other purposes, but instead has sought to curb the potential of those weapons to inflict large-scale harm. It has done this by "setting a limit on the number of rounds that can be fired before a shooter needs to reload."

We find no constitutional infirmity in § 4021 on the grounds defendant advances, and affirm the trial court's denial of defendant's motion to dismiss.

NOTES

1. The Second Amendment to the United States Constitution reads: "A well regulated militia being necessary to the security of a free State, the right of the people to keep and bear arms shall not be infringed." U.S. Const. amend. II. The United States Supreme Court construed that language in *District of Columbia v. Heller*, 554 U.S. 570 (2008), holding that the amendment protects an *individual* right to bear arms.

2. In *Heller*, the Supreme Court declared that felon-in-possession statutes are permitted by the United States Constitution. In *Britt v. State*, 681 S.E.2d 320 (N.C. 2009), however, the North Carolina Supreme Court held that its

state constitutional right to bear arms precluded the State from imposing a ban on a non-violent felon possessing a firearm. Thus, the North Carolina Constitution provides greater protection than the Second Amendment.

3. The constitutions of forty-four States contain a provision that protects the right to bear arms. The texts of those state constitutional guarantees are often different from the Second Amendment. For example, the New Hampshire Constitution provides: "All persons have the right to keep and bear arms in defense of themselves, their families, their property and the state." N.H. Const. pt. 1, art. 2-a. Michigan's constitution states that "every person has a right to keep and bear arms for the defense of himself and the state." Mich. Const. art. I, § 6. Oklahoma's constitution holds that "the right of a citizen to keep and bear arms in defense of his home, person, or property, or in aid of the civil power, when thereunto legally summoned, shall never be prohibited." Okla. Const. art. II, § 26.

4. Two States (Alaska and Utah) suggest the existence of an *individual* right to keep and bear arms in the text of their constitutions. Alaska's constitution states that "the individual right to keep and bear arms shall not be denied or infringed by the State or a political subdivision of the State." Alaska Const. art. II, § 19; *see also* Utah Const. art. I, § 6 ("The individual right of the people to keep and bear arms for security and defense of self, family, others, property, or the state, as well as for other lawful purposes shall not be infringed; but nothing herein shall prevent the Legislature from defining the lawful use of arms.")

5. Three other States (Illinois, Arizona, and Washington) recognize that the right belongs to an "individual citizen." Ariz. Const. art. II, § 26 ("The right of the individual citizen to bear arms in defense of himself or the state shall not be impaired, but nothing in this section shall be construed as authorizing individuals or corporations to organize, maintain, or employ an armed body of men."); Ill. Const. art. I, § 22 ("Subject only to the police power, the right of the individual citizen to keep and bear arms shall not be infringed."); Wash. Const. art. I, § 24 ("The right of the individual citizen to bear arms in defense of himself, or the state, shall not be impaired, but nothing in this section shall be construed as authorizing individuals or corporations to organize, maintain or employ an armed body of men.").

6. Five States contain a general grant of the right to keep and bear arms. Some were unqualified, such as Rhode Island's constitution, which provides that "the right of the people to keep and bear arms shall not be infringed." R.I. Const. art. I, § 22. Other state constitutions contain limitations on the right to keep and bear arms, such as Idaho's constitution, which states that:

> The people have the right to keep and bear arms, which right shall not be abridged; but this provision shall not prevent the passage of laws to govern the carrying of weapons concealed on the person nor prevent passage of legislation providing

minimum sentences for crimes committed while in possession of a firearm, nor prevent the passage of legislation providing penalties for the possession of firearms by a convicted felon, nor prevent the passage of any legislation punishing the use of a firearm. No law shall impose licensure, registration or special taxation on the ownership or possession of firearms or ammunition. Nor shall any law permit the confiscation of firearms, except those actually used in the commission of a felony.

Idaho Const. art. I, § 11.

7. Louisiana's constitution provides a strict scrutiny clause, stating that "the right of each citizen to keep and bear arms is fundamental and shall not be infringed. Any restriction on this right shall be subject to strict scrutiny." La. Const. art. I, § 11. This is the most stringent standard of judicial review.

8. The States without a constitutional provision that protects the right to keep and bear arms are California, Iowa, Maryland, Minnesota, New Jersey, and New York.

E. ENVIRONMENTAL RIGHTS

PENNSYLVANIA ENVIRONMENTAL DEFENSE FOUND. v. COMMONWEALTH
161 A.3d 911 (Pa. 2017)

DONOHUE, J.

In 1971, by a margin of nearly four to one, the people of Pennsylvania ratified a proposed amendment to the Pennsylvania Constitution's Declaration of Rights, formally and forcefully recognizing their environmental rights as commensurate with their most sacred political and individual rights. Article I, Section 27 of the Pennsylvania Constitution provides:

> The people have a right to clean air, pure water, and to the preservation of the natural, scenic, historic and esthetic values of the environment. Pennsylvania's public natural resources are the common property of all the people, including generations yet to come. As trustee of these resources, the Commonwealth shall conserve and maintain them for the benefit of all the people.

In this case, we examine the contours of the Environmental Rights Amendment in light of a declaratory judgment action brought by the Pennsylvania Environmental Defense Foundation, an environmental advocacy entity, challenging the constitutionality of statutory enactments relating to funds generated from the leasing of state forest and park lands for oil and gas exploration and extraction. Because state parks and forests, including the oil and gas minerals therein, are part of the corpus of Pennsylvania's environmental public trust, we hold that the Commonwealth, as trustee, must manage them according to the plain language of Section 27, which imposes fiduciary duties consistent with Pennsylvania trust law. We further find that the constitutional language controls how the Commonwealth may dispose of any proceeds generated from the sale of its public natural resources.

Section 27 contains an express statement of the rights of the people and the obligations of the Commonwealth with respect to the conservation and maintenance of our public natural resources. In *Robinson Township v. Commonwealth* (Pa. 2013), a plurality of this Court carefully reviewed the reasons why the Environmental Rights Amendment was necessary, the history of its enactment and ratification, and the mischief to be remedied and the object to be attained. At the outset of this opinion, we reiterate this historical background, which serves as an important reminder as we address the issues presented in the present case:

> It is not a historical accident that the Pennsylvania Constitution now places citizens' environmental rights on par with their political rights. Approximately three and a half centuries ago, white pine, Eastern hemlock, and mixed hardwood forests covered about 90 percent of the Commonwealth's surface of over 20 million acres. Two centuries later, the state experienced a lumber harvesting industry boom that, by 1920, had left much of Pennsylvania barren. Regeneration of our forests (less the diversity of species) has taken decades.
>
> Similarly, by 1890, "game" wildlife had dwindled "as a result of deforestation, pollution and unregulated hunting and trapping." In 1895, the General Assembly created the Pennsylvania Game Commission and, two years later, adopted a package of new game laws to protect endangered populations of deer, elk, waterfowl, and other game birds. Over the following decades, the Game Commission sought to restore populations of wildlife, by managing and restocking species endangered or extinct in Pennsylvania, establishing game preserves in state forests, and purchasing state game lands. Sustained efforts of the Game Commission over more than a century returned a bounty of wildlife to the Commonwealth.
>
> From the middle of the nineteenth well into the twentieth century, the coal industry and the steel industry it powered were the keystone of Pennsylvania's increasingly industrialized economy. "When coal was a reigning monarch," the industry operated "virtually unrestricted" by either the state or federal government. The result, in the opinion of many, was devastating to the natural environment of the coal-rich regions of the Commonwealth, with long-lasting effects on human health and safety, and on the esthetic beauty of nature.
>
> The drafters of the Environmental Rights Amendment recognized and acknowledged the shocks to our environment and quality of life. With these events in the recent collective memory of the General Assembly, the proposed Environmental Rights Amendment received the unanimous assent of both chambers.
>
> The decision to affirm the people's environmental rights in a Declaration or Bill of Rights, alongside political rights, is relatively rare in American constitutional law. In addition to Pennsylvania, Montana and Rhode Island are the only other states of the Union to do so.
>
> That Pennsylvania deliberately chose a course different from virtually all of its sister states speaks to the Commonwealth's experience of having the benefit of vast natural resources whose virtually unrestrained exploitation, while initially a boon to investors, industry, and citizens, led to destructive and lasting consequences not only for the environment but also for the citizens' quality of

life. The drafters and the citizens of the Commonwealth who ratified the Environmental Rights Amendment, aware of this history, articulated the people's rights and the government's duties to the people in broad and flexible terms that would permit not only reactive but also anticipatory protection of the environment for the benefit of current and future generations. Moreover, public trustee duties were delegated concomitantly to all branches and levels of government in recognition that the quality of the environment is a task with both local and statewide implications, and to ensure that all government neither infringed upon the people's rights nor failed to act for the benefit of the people in this area crucial to the well-being of all Pennsylvanians.

We entertained oral argument in this case to examine the following two overarching issues:

1. The proper standards for judicial review of government actions and legislation challenged under the Environmental Rights Amendment, Article I, Section 27 of the Pennsylvania Constitution;

2. Constitutionality under Article I, Section 27, of Section 1602–E and 1603–E of the Fiscal Code and the General Assembly's transfers/appropriations from the Lease Fund.

To start, the General Assembly derives its power from Article III of the Pennsylvania Constitution which grants broad and flexible police powers to enact laws for the purposes of promoting public health, safety, morals, and the general welfare. These powers, however, are expressly limited by fundamental rights reserved to the people in Article I of our Constitution. Specifically, Section 1 affirms, among other things, that all citizens "have certain inherent and indefeasible rights. As forcefully pronounced in Section 25, the rights contained in Article I are "excepted out of the general powers of government and shall forever remain inviolate."

Among the "inherent and indefeasible" rights in Article I of the Pennsylvania Constitution are the rights set forth in the Environmental Rights Amendment.

This constitutional provision grants two separate rights to the people of this Commonwealth. The first right is contained in the first sentence, which is a prohibitory clause declaring the right of citizens to clean air and pure water, and to the preservation of natural, scenic, historic and esthetic values of the environment. This clause places a limitation on the state's power to act contrary to this right, and while the subject of this right may be amenable to regulation, any laws that unreasonably impair the right are unconstitutional. The second right reserved by Section 27, set forth in its second sentence, is the common ownership by the people, including future generations, of Pennsylvania's public natural resources. The "public natural resources" referenced in this second sentence include the state forest and park lands leased for oil and gas exploration and, of particular relevance in this case, the oil and gas themselves. The provision was initially drafted as "Pennsylvania's natural resources, including the air, waters, fish, wildlife, and the public lands and property of the Commonwealth," but was revised to remove the enumerated list and thereby discourage courts from limiting the scope of natural resources covered.

The third clause of Section 27 establishes a public trust, pursuant to which the natural resources are the corpus of the trust, the Commonwealth is the trustee, and the people are the named beneficiaries. The terms "trust" and "trustee" carry their legal implications under Pennsylvania law at the time the amendment was adopted. Notably, the Commonwealth's role was plainly intended to be that of a "trustee," as opposed to "proprietor." As a trustee, the Commonwealth must deal "with its citizens as a fiduciary, measuring its successes by the benefits it bestows upon all its citizens in their utilization of natural resources under law." Under Section 27, the Commonwealth may not act as a mere proprietor, pursuant to which it "deals at arms' length with its citizens, measuring its gains by the balance sheet profits and appreciation it realizes from its resources operations."

The *Robinson Township* plurality aptly described the Commonwealth's duties as the trustee of the environmental trust created by the people of Pennsylvania as follows:

> As trustee, the Commonwealth is a fiduciary obligated to comply with the terms of the trust and with standards governing a fiduciary's conduct. The explicit terms of the trust require the government to "conserve and maintain" the corpus of the trust. The plain meaning of the terms conserve and maintain implicates a duty to prevent and remedy the degradation, diminution, or depletion of our public natural resources. As a fiduciary, the Commonwealth has a duty to act toward the corpus of the trust—the public natural resources—with prudence, loyalty, and impartiality.

Pennsylvania's environmental trust thus imposes two basic duties on the Commonwealth as the trustee. First, the Commonwealth has a duty to prohibit the degradation, diminution, and depletion of our public natural resources, whether these harms might result from direct state action or from the actions of private parties. Second, the Commonwealth must act affirmatively via legislative action to protect the environment. Although a trustee is empowered to exercise discretion with respect to the proper treatment of the corpus of the trust, that discretion is limited by the purpose of the trust and the trustee's fiduciary duties, and does not equate "to mere subjective judgment." The trustee may use the assets of the trust "only for purposes authorized by the trust or necessary for the preservation of the trust; other uses are beyond the scope of the discretion conferred, even where the trustee claims to be acting solely to advance other discrete interests of the beneficiaries."

The Commonwealth argues that the revenue obtained from the disposition of trust assets need not be returned to the corpus of the trust or otherwise dedicated to trust purposes, for two reasons. First, the Commonwealth contends that the Environmental Rights Amendment is "silent" as to the use of proceeds from the sale of natural resources, and "addresses neither the appropriations process nor funding for conservation purposes." This is plainly inaccurate, as Section 27 expressly creates a trust, and pursuant to Pennsylvania law in effect at the time of enactment, proceeds from the sale of trust assets are part of the corpus of the trust. The unavoidable result is that proceeds from the sale of oil and gas from Section 27's public trust remain in the corpus of the trust.

Second, the Commonwealth insists that the concluding phrase of Section 27, "for the benefit of all the people," confers discretion upon the General Assembly to direct the proceeds from oil and gas development toward any uses that benefit all the people of the Commonwealth, even if those uses do nothing to "conserve and maintain" our public natural resources. We are wholly unconvinced. The phrase "for the benefit of all of the people" may not be read in isolation and does not confer upon the Commonwealth a right to spend proceeds on general budgetary items. The Commonwealth's fiduciary duty to "conserve and maintain" our public natural resources is a duty owed to the beneficiaries of the public trust, namely "the people, including generations yet to come," as set forth in the second sentence of Section 27. The "people," in turn, are those endowed with "a right to clean air, pure water, and to the preservation of the natural, scenic, historic and esthetic values of the environment," as set forth in the first sentence of Section 27.

Accordingly, the Environmental Rights Amendment mandates that the Commonwealth, as a trustee, "conserve and maintain" our public natural resources in furtherance of the people's specifically enumerated rights. Thus, understood in context of the entire amendment, the phrase "for the benefit of all the people" is unambiguous and clearly indicates that assets of the trust are to be used for conservation and maintenance purposes. Only within those parameters, clearly set forth in the text of Section 27, does the General Assembly, or any other Commonwealth entity, have discretion to determine the public benefit to which trust proceeds—generated from the sale of trust assets—are directed.

By arguing that proceeds obtained from the sale of our natural resources are not part of the corpus of the trust, the Commonwealth improperly conceives of itself as a mere proprietor of those public natural resources, rather than as a trustee. In the Commonwealth's view, it may dispose of our public natural resources as it so chooses and for any purpose it so conceives, so long as such disposition broadly benefits the public (apparently without regard to "generations yet to come"). As such, it urges us to substantially diminish its fiduciary obligation to prevent and remedy the degradation of our natural resources. We decline to do so.

We hold, therefore, that sections 1602–E and 1603–E, relating to royalties, are facially unconstitutional. They plainly ignore the Commonwealth's constitutionally imposed fiduciary duty to manage the corpus of the environmental public trust for the benefit of the people to accomplish its purpose—conserving and maintaining the corpus by, inter alia, preventing and remedying the degradation, diminution and depletion of our public natural resources. Without any question, these legislative enactments permit the trustee to use trust assets for non-trust purposes, a clear violation of the most basic of a trustee's fiduciary obligations.

To the extent the remainder of the Fiscal Code amendments transfer proceeds from the sale of trust assets to the General Fund, they are likewise constitutionally infirm.

The Commonwealth (including the Governor and General Assembly) may not approach our public natural resources as a proprietor, and instead must at all times fulfill its role as a trustee. Because the legislative enactments at issue here do not reflect that the Commonwealth complied with its constitutional duties, the order of the Commonwealth Court with respect to the constitutionality of 1602–E and 1603–E is reversed, and the order is otherwise vacated in all respects.

NOTES

1. The United States Constitution contains no reference to environmental concerns or protections. However, forty-six States have added environment-related provisions to their constitutions. These provisions vary in many respects and range from resource conservation to individual rights to a healthy environment.

2. The constitutions of five States, Hawaii, Illinois, Massachusetts, Montana and Pennsylvania, embody a right to a "quality" environment. What constitutes a "quality" environment differs between the States. For example, Hawaii and Montana protect the right to a "clean and healthful environment" while Illinois guarantees a right to a "healthful environment." Haw. Const. art. XI, § 9; Mont. Const. art. II, § 3; Ill. Const. art. XI, § 2.

3. Environmental protection is not a new constitutional concept. Rhode Island began the trend in 1842 by protecting "all the rights of fishery, and the privileges of the shore." R.I. Const. of 1842, art. I, § 17.

4. Many of the environmental provisions are not self-executing, meaning the provision requires legislative implementation. Michigan's environmental provision states: "the legislature shall provide for the protection of the air, water and other natural resources of the state from pollution, impairment and destruction." Mich. Const. art. IV, § 52. While most of the state constitutions are silent or ambiguous regarding the requirement of legislative implementation, the environmental rights provisions embodied in the Constitutions of Hawaii and Illinois expressly indicate the rights are self-executing and do not require legislative action.

5. Montana applies a strict scrutiny standard to state laws challenged under article II, section 3 of the state constitution, given that the right to a clean

and healthful environment has been declared a fundamental right. *Mont. Env't Info. Ctr. v. Dep't of Env't Quality*, 988 P.2d 1236 (Mont. 1999).

6. Most constitutional provisions involving a right to a healthful environment do not extend the protections to endangered species, but rather limit the application to the health of individuals. The Supreme Court of Illinois considered this issue in *Glisson v. City of Marion* in which the plaintiff claimed the city's plan to dam a creek would compromise the habitat of two endangered species, resulting in a violation of article XI, section 2 of the Illinois Constitution. 720 N.E.2d 1034, 1039 (Ill. 1999). The court rejected the plaintiff's argument and explained that "the primary concern of the drafters of the constitutional provision was the effect of pollution on the environment and human health." *Id.* at 1042. Using a historical analysis, the court declined to interpret "healthful environment" to include the protection of endangered and threatened species. *Id.*

7. The States without constitutional provisions addressing natural resources or the environment are Connecticut, Delaware, Georgia and Maryland.

F. CRIME VICTIMS' RIGHTS

STATE v. STROM
921 N.W.2d 660 (N.D. 2019)

TUFTE, J.

Melinda Strom appeals from an amended criminal judgment and order for restitution. Strom argues the district court abused its discretion in awarding restitution because it did not consider her ability to pay as required by N.D.C.C. § 12.1-32-08(1). We declare the statute unconstitutional in part and affirm the restitution order and judgment.

Strom pled guilty to misapplication of entrusted property in excess of $50,000. Strom was sentenced to five years, all suspended for three years of supervised probation. A restitution hearing was held on April 9, 2018. The district court concluded that article I, § 25(1)(n) of the North Dakota Constitution, which was adopted in the 2016 election, overrides the requirement under N.D.C.C. § 12.1-32-08(1) to take into account the ability of the defendant to pay monetary reparations in setting the total amount of restitution. The district court issued the restitution order requiring Strom to make restitution in the amount of $690,910.67.

Both Strom and the State frame the issue on appeal as whether article I, § 25(1)(n) of the North Dakota Constitution overrides prior law requiring the district court to consider a defendant's ability to pay when determining restitution. Strom argues the district court abused its discretion by ordering restitution without considering her ability to pay because she contends the constitution and statute can be reconciled. At oral argument the State argued the two provisions are in conflict and thus the statute is unconstitutional.

Section 12.1-32-08(1), N.D.C.C., lists three factors the court must consider when ordering restitution. At issue here, "the court shall take into account: (b) the *ability of the defendant* to restore the fruits of the criminal action or *to pay monetary reparations*." The statute continues, "the court shall fix the amount of restitution or reparation, which *may not exceed an amount the defendant can or will be able to pay*, and shall fix the manner of performance of any condition or conditions of probation established pursuant to this subsection."

In addition to the statutory requirements, we must consider how article I, § 25(1)(n) of the North Dakota Constitution applies here. A crime victim has the "right to full and timely restitution in every case and from each offender for all losses suffered by the victim as a result of the criminal or delinquent conduct." We have not previously decided whether article I, § 25(1)(n) abrogates the required consideration of the defendant's ability to pay restitution under factor (b) of N.D.C.C. § 12.1-32-08(1).

When interpreting a constitutional provision, "we apply general principles of statutory construction. In construing statutory and constitutional provisions, we will attempt to give meaning to every word, phrase, and sentence, and, if necessary, we will attempt to reconcile and harmonize potentially conflicting provisions." Absent an applicable definition, words enacted in statutes carry the plain, ordinary, and commonly understood meaning as of the time of enactment.

Article I, § 25(1)(n) clearly states the compensation amount to which a victim of a crime is constitutionally entitled. Section 25(1)(n) provides a victim the "right to full and timely restitution in every case and from each offender for all losses suffered by the victim as a result of the criminal or delinquent conduct." The words enacted to describe the restitution amount, "full" and "all losses," leave no room for implication that the commonly understood meaning would permit any reduction of the restitution amount in consideration of the defendant's ability to pay. The plain meaning of "restitution" is an amount calculated to make the victim whole. The addition of the modifier "*full* restitution" underscores the point that the amount must make the victim whole by restoring the victim to his position prior to the offense. To award less than the amount required to make the victim whole would not be "full" restitution. The further addition of "*all* losses" suggests a belt-and-suspenders approach in drafting this provision: no reasonable member of the public could overlook the double emphasis that restitution is not to be reduced. If the word "restitution" within the constitutional amendment were construed to be the same as the amount determined under N.D.C.C. § 12.1-32-08(1), thus "allowing for the amount of constitutionally mandated restitution to be reduced by the defendant's ability to pay," it would render the words "full" and "all losses" meaningless.

Where the constitutional provision was adopted after a conflicting statute, we cannot logically declare it void "as if it never were enacted." The statute at issue here was constitutional when enacted; thus the facial challenge here does not turn on whether the Legislative Assembly exceeded its constitutional authority in enacting a law not permitted by the constitution. The test where a statute predates a conflicting constitutional provision is whether the statute could have been passed after the new constitutional provision took effect. If not, repeal of the statute is implicit in adoption of the new constitutional provision. Here, we resolve the irreconcilable conflict between the constitutional amendment and the statute by interpreting N.D. Const. art. I, § 25(1)(n) as implicitly repealing the conflicting portion of N.D.C.C. § 12.1-32-08(1).

To clearly state the scope of this decision, it is necessary to articulate what we do not decide here. In this matter, we examine only an award of restitution and not a contempt hearing or probation revocation for non-payment, and thus we limit consideration of ability to pay only in the context of setting the total amount of restitution. We do not completely preclude consideration of ability to pay. There may be times when such consideration may be appropriate, *i.e.*, when determining the time or manner of payment or whether a defendant's failure to pay is willful.

In short, a district court may not consider a defendant's ability to pay in determining the amount of restitution awarded to a victim.

We conclude the district court did not abuse its discretion in fixing the amount of restitution without regard to the defendant's ability to pay. We affirm the amended criminal judgment and the order for restitution in the amount of $690,910.67.

STATE v. DAMATO-KUSHEL
173 A.3d 357 (Conn. 2017)

PALMER, J.

The victim claims that the trial court improperly precluded him, either personally or through his attorney, from attending plea negotiations and other discussions involving the court, the state's attorney and defense counsel during in-chambers, pretrial disposition conferences in the criminal prosecution of Kyle Damato-Kushel. In that criminal case, Damato-Kushel is charged with various offenses arising out of her alleged sexual misconduct involving the victim commencing when Damato-Kushel was a teacher's aide in the school system of the town of Stratford and when the victim was a fourteen-year-old student attending a school in that town. The victim claims that the trial court's ruling barring his attendance at the pretrial disposition conferences violated his right as a victim "to attend the trial and all other court proceedings the accused has the right to attend" under article first, § 8, of the Connecticut constitution, as amended by articles seventeen and twenty-nine of the amendments. Damato-Kushel and the Superior Court, judicial district of Fairfield, maintain that the trial court correctly determined that such conferences, when they are conducted in chambers and off the record, do not constitute "court proceedings the accused has the right to attend" within the meaning of amendment XXIX (b)(5) and, therefore, that the court properly precluded the victim from attending them. We agree.

The following facts and procedural history are undisputed. On the basis of allegations lodged by the victim, Damato-Kushel was arrested and charged with sexual assault in the second degree, risk of injury to a child, sexual assault in the fourth degree, and tampering with a witness. Shortly thereafter, Attorney James Clark of the Victim Rights Center of Connecticut, Inc., filed an appearance in the criminal case on behalf of the victim.

At Damato-Kushel's arraignment, her counsel noted that Clark had filed an appearance in the case and advised the court that he objected to Clark's presence at any pretrial disposition conferences held in chambers. The court sustained the objection, explaining that amendment XXIX (b)(5) allows a victim to attend only those court proceedings that the defendant has a right to attend, and concluding that, because a defendant has no right to attend in-chambers, "judicial pretrial" conferences—generally, only his or her attorney attends such conferences—a victim also has no right to attend those conferences.

Thereafter, the victim filed a motion for reconsideration, claiming that, contrary to the determination of the trial court, a victim does have a right to attend pretrial disposition conferences because, under Practice Book § 39-13, the defendant is required to appear at such conferences. In the alternative, he maintained that, because counsel for a defendant attends a disposition conference solely as a representative of the defendant, the presence of such counsel at the conference is legally indistinguishable from the presence of the defendant, and, therefore, the fact that only counsel attends the conference is not a basis for denying the victim the right to do so. In response, Damato-Kushel argued that, contrary to the contentions of the victim, a defendant has no right to attend in-chambers discussions between the presiding judge and the parties' attorneys and that permitting victims' attorneys to be present during such discussions would have an adverse chilling effect on pretrial plea negotiations.

The trial court subsequently granted the victim's motion for reconsideration but denied the relief requested therein. In so ruling, the court acknowledged that a victim's right to attend court proceedings is "in parity with that of the defendant" but observed that Practice Book § 44-7 lists only five instances in which a defendant has the right to be present, none of which involves in-chambers, pretrial conferences. In light of the nature of the proceedings enumerated in § 44-7, the court concluded that the term "court proceedings" under amendment XXIX (b)(5) was most reasonably interpreted to mean "proceedings on the record in open court." The court also agreed with Damato-Kushel that the presence of the victim or his representative would undermine the ability of the parties to discuss the case openly and frankly, and observed that, because the victim's rights amendment obligates the state to keep the victim informed about the progress of the case and any potential disposition that may be the product of plea negotiations, excluding the victim from in-chambers conferences would not impair the victim's ability to express his views on any potential plea agreement resulting from those discussions.

Damato-Kushel and the Superior Court also assert that the victim is not aggrieved by the trial court's ruling preventing his attendance at pretrial disposition conferences because the trial court never determined, "even preliminarily," that the victim was, in fact, a "victim" for purposes of the victim's rights amendment, and, therefore, the victim never had any constitutional rights that might be "injuriously affected" by the actions of the trial court. We disagree with this contention.

As the victim observes, the issuance of an arrest warrant requires a finding of probable cause that a crime was committed by a particular defendant. It is undisputed, moreover, that, in the present case, the arrest warrant application clearly alleged that Damato-Kushel's criminal misconduct was perpetrated against the victim specifically. In such circumstances, we agree with the victim that the arrest warrant constitutes a sufficient determination of his status as a victim to trigger the rights afforded by amendment XXIX(b) of the Connecticut constitution. Furthermore, we see no inconsistency between this conclusion and our unwillingness to condone the use of the term "victim" during certain trial proceedings before a jury prior to conviction because, in those circumstances, the jury must decide whether the complainant was, in fact, the victim of a crime perpetrated by the defendant.

We turn now to the merits of the victim's claims. Amendment XXIX(b) of the Connecticut constitution provides in relevant part that, "in all criminal prosecutions, a victim shall have the right to attend the trial and all other court proceedings the accused has the right to attend, unless such person is to testify and the court determines that such person's testimony would be materially affected if such person hears other testimony." With respect to the contention of Damato-Kushel and the Superior Court that the victim has no right to attend the pretrial conferences at issue because they are not "court proceedings," as that term is used in amendment XXIX(b)(5), the term appears twice in the victim's rights amendment but the term is not defined in the state constitution, in our statutes, or in any case of this court or the Appellate Court. At the time of the amendment, however, Black's Law Dictionary defined "proceeding" as, inter alia, "an act that is done by the authority or direction of the court, agency, or tribunal, express or implied" and noted that it "may be used to describe any act done by authority of a court of law." The modifier "court" therefore might reasonably distinguish proceedings undertaken pursuant to the authority of a court of law, such as disposition conferences, from those undertaken by an agency or other tribunal. On the other hand, "court proceedings" also may reasonably be construed to limit the "acts done by authority of a court of law" to those taking place within the physical bounds of a courtroom, as opposed to those acts, like the execution of a bench warrant, undertaken elsewhere.

The text of amendment XXIX(b) makes clear that a victim's right to attend such conferences is wholly contingent on the defendant's right of attendance. This court has previously determined, however, in *State v. Lopez* (Conn. 1985), that a defendant possesses no such right under our rules of practice. In that case, the defendant, Jose Lopez, claimed that the trial court improperly had excluded him from "a secret pretrial conference between the court, the state's attorney, and defense counsel," in which plea negotiations were conducted. We rejected Lopez' claim, explaining that, "although there may have been a disposition conference from which Lopez was excluded, under our established rules of practice neither Lopez nor the public is entitled to attend such a proceeding. In fact, under Practice Book §§ 39-1 and 39-2, the state is not permitted to engage in plea negotiations directly with a defendant who is represented by counsel, except with defense counsel's permission. Furthermore, Practice Book § 44-7 does not include the disposition conference or plea negotiations among the specifically enumerated situations in which a criminal defendant has the right to be present." Thus, *Lopez*—and, indeed, Practice Book § 44-7 itself—leaves no doubt that a defendant has no right to attend a disposition conference under our rules of practice. Moreover, the victim makes no claim that he has a statutory or constitutional right independent of the victim's rights amendment to attend such a conference.

By contrast, a victim's right to participate meaningfully in the plea bargaining process is safeguarded by other provisions of the victim's rights amendment—in particular, "the right to communicate with the prosecution" under amendment XXIX(b)(6), "the right to make a statement to the court" regarding any plea agreement prior to its acceptance under amendment XXIX(b)(7), and the broader, more encompassing right under amendment XXIX(b) "to be treated with fairness and respect throughout the criminal justice process." To the extent that the victim suggests that state's attorneys cannot be relied on to adequately communicate the information necessary for a victim to comment on the appropriateness of any plea bargain, we reject that assertion. We have every reason to believe that state's attorneys will fully discharge their constitutional, statutory, and professional responsibilities to victims.

We therefore conclude that in-chambers, off-the-record disposition conferences between the prosecuting attorney, defense counsel, and the presiding judge are not "court proceedings the accused has the right to attend" under amendment XXIX(b)(5). Consequently, neither the victim nor his authorized representative has a right to attend them.

NOTES

1. In 1982, California was the first State to pass a victims' rights amendment to its constitution. *See* Timothy A. Razel, Note, *Dying to Get Away with It: How the Abatement Doctrine Thwarts Justice—And What Should be Done Instead*, 75 Fordham L. Rev. 2193, 2207 (2007); *see also* Alice Kosklea, Comment, *Victim's Rights Amendments: An Irresistible Political Force Transforms the Criminal Justice System*, 34 Idaho L. Rev. 157, 165 (1997). The provision, approved by the California electorate, gave victims the right to "restitution, safe schools, consideration of public safety when setting bail, and an unrestricted admissibility of prior felony convictions," as well as "the absolute right to appear at sentencing and parole proceedings." Cal. Const. art. I, § 28. Florida and Michigan followed with voter-approved amendments in 1988. That same year, the States of Arizona and Washington attempted, but failed, to pass victims' rights amendments to their constitutions. Washington and Texas passed victims' rights amendments in 1990. By 1996, twenty-eight States had victims' rights constitutional amendments. Today, thirty-five States have victims' rights constitutional amendments.

2. The victims' rights amendments vary by State, but all seek to achieve one or more of the following objectives: (1) make the victim whole economically; (2) develop administrative sensitivity to the distress of the victim; (3) respect the victim's privacy; (4) provide protection against potential victim intimidation; (5) reduce the burdens on victims willing to assist with the prosecution of the defendant; (6) increase victim participation in the prosecution beyond simply appearing as a witness. *See* Jay M. Zitter, Annotation, *Validity, Construction, and Application of State Constitutional or Statutory Victims' Bill of Rights*, 91 A.L.R.5th 343 § 2[a] (2008); LaFave et al., 1 Criminal Procedure § 1.4(k) (2d ed. 2004).

3. Although Montana does not have a victims' rights amendment, in 1998, the voters approved a constitutional amendment that expanded the purpose of the criminal justice system to include restitution to crime victims. Mont. Const. art. II, § 28(1) ("Laws for the punishment of crime shall be founded

on the principles of prevention, reformation, public safety, and restitution for victims.").

4. A victims' right that has been the subject of case law in various States is the right to be present at trial. *See, e.g.*, Ariz. Const. art. II, § 2.1(A)(3) (giving victims of crimes the right "to be present at all criminal proceedings where the defendant has the right to be present"); Utah Const. art. I, § 28 (stating that the victim has the right "to be present at important criminal justice hearings related to the victim"). The victim's presence at trial has been argued to be prejudicial to the defendant because the victim hears the testimony of the other witnesses before testifying against the defendant. *See Gore v. State*, 599 So.2d 978 (Fla. 1992) (holding that the trial court's excusal of the murder victim's stepmother from the rule of witness sequestration because she was a relative of the victim and had the right to be present in the courtroom during trial did not prejudice the defendant). Some constitutional provisions try to balance the rights of the victim with the rights of the defendant by permitting the victim to be present at trial only where it does not interfere with the defendant's rights. Fla. Const. art. I, § 16(b) (giving victims of crimes "the right to be present at all crucial states of criminal proceedings, to the extent that these rights do not interfere with the constitutional rights of the accused").

5. The Marsy's Law concept for state constitutional protections of victims' rights began in California in 1983 after Marsalee "Marsy" Nicholas was murdered. The Nicholas family sought to amend the California Constitution after the killer was released on bail without a warning to them. The measure passed in California in 2008. Since then, ten other States have amended their constitution to include a Marsy Law. Those States are Illinois, South Dakota, North Dakota, Florida, Georgia, Kentucky, Oklahoma, Nevada, Ohio and North Carolina. The Montana Marsy Law was invalidated on the basis that it violated the state constitution's separate vote requirement for enacting a citizen-initiated amendment. The Marsy's Law amendments vary from State to State, but all make it a constitutional right for people directly harmed by a crime to request and receive notification when an alleged perpetrator is released from jail or prison. They also provide for a right to be informed of and attend public proceedings involving the criminal; and to be heard in any sentencing, release and plea proceeding.

G. RIGHT TO HUNT AND FISH

CABOT v. THOMAS
514 A.2d 1034 (Vt. 1986)

ALLEN, J.

The material facts in this case are undisputed. Plaintiffs and their immediate predecessors in title have owned a tract of marshland of approximately 360 acres near West Swanton, Vermont since 1933.

Charcoal Creek borders the western portion of their marsh. The creek, so-called, is actually an inlet from Lake Champlain. At its source, the creek connects through a narrow opening to the lake. It ultimately arrives at a dead end in a wooded area.

Although the level of Charcoal Creek is subject to periodic fluctuations, the parties agree it has a definite low water line along plaintiffs' marsh at 93.055 feet above mean sea level. At this low water line the marsh owners have since 1949 posted signs proclaiming: "No Hunting, Shooting, or Trapping."

On October 3, 1979, the water level was 95.36 feet above sea level. Thus, it rose well above the low water line and covered a portion of plaintiffs' land beyond the signs. An area of the marsh designated Jake Nokes Slough was inundated at that time. During drier seasons this slough was soft mud and bog and was separated from Charcoal Creek by a ridge of land.

Defendants entered Jake Nokes Slough from Lake Champlain by way of Charcoal Creek in a sixteen-foot flat bottom boat on October 3, 1979. They were aware of the plaintiffs' signs and of having passed beyond the signs, as they had done previously. Intending to hunt ducks, defendants stopped their boat in a weed bed two hundred yards to the inland side of the signs. The bottom of the boat rested in the mud at a point where the water was approximately five or six inches deep.

A police officer told the defendants they were hunting on private posted land. When they announced their intent to continue hunting there, the officer cited them for criminal trespass and poaching. Based on these facts, plaintiffs then sought and received the injunction which is the subject of this appeal.

As a definite low water line exists along Charcoal Creek, plaintiffs' ownership extends to that line. Defendants contend, however, that notwithstanding private ownership of the underlying lands, the public enjoys the right to hunt from boats on the waters overlying plaintiffs' marsh to the ordinary high water line.

Essentially, defendants argue that the public has a navigational easement across the waters overlying plaintiffs' land between the ordinary low and high water lines, and that this easement permits recreational uses as well. Among the recreational uses the public enjoys as of right, according to defendants, are hunting and fowling.

Marshland adjoining Charcoal Creek has been the locus of trespass actions between landowners and hunters since before the turn of the century. Hunters and marsh owners have pressed their respective claims of right with remarkable persistence.

In the late 1890s, W.G. Payne, an earlier landowner along this same creek, commenced a trespass action against Watson Gould, a hunter. Eventually, in *Payne v. Gould* (Vt. 1902), the hunter prevailed because the owner had not sufficiently enclosed his land. This Court concluded that Gould was simply exercising his state constitutional right to hunt on "lands not enclosed."

Subsequent landowners, including the immediate predecessor in title of plaintiffs Cabot, sought court sanction of their destruction of a hunting guide's duck blinds which they alleged were situated in their marsh. Although the case came before this Court on a collateral matter, the primary focus of the underlying dispute was the western boundary of the privately owned marshland along Charcoal Creek. At that time, the Court indicated in dictum that establishing the westerly boundary would determine if the duck blinds in question could properly have been maintained where they had been placed. In 1949, a Franklin County court determined that the marsh's western boundary was the low water line along the creek at 93.055 feet above mean sea level. The owners of the marsh thereafter moved their signs to that line and have maintained them there ever since

Recent duck hunters have been more inventive: they assert a public right of recreational use, including hunting, on the waters of Lake Champlain and its inlet creeks all the way to the normal high water line without regard to the ownership of the underlying land.

The questions raised in this case and in prior Charcoal Creek controversies lie at the crosscurrents of two important concerns: the individual's desire for private enjoyment of privately owned land and the public's wish for sporting access to the forests, fields, and waterways of this state. These are concerns that have long been in conflict.

In the colonial period, residents of the New Hampshire grants (what was later to be Vermont) were well aware of the history of abuses that had occurred in England under authority of fish and game laws:

> They were then smarting under the oppression and inequalities of the English system under which individual development among the common people was impeded and often prevented, and the rights and enjoyments of the many were subjected to the pleasure of a favored few. Among the instrumentalities used to bring about this undesirable condition of life, were the iniquitous fish and game laws of England, enacted by the ruling class for their own enjoyment, and which led to a system under which the catching of a fish or the killing of a rabbit was deemed of more consequence than the happiness, liberty or life of a human being.

One response to the sometimes conflicting concerns of the individual and the larger group of society was Chapter II, Section 39 of the Vermont Constitution of 1777. Now found at Chapter II, Section 67, this provision guarantees to the public the "liberty," subject to legislative regulation, to hunt and fish in certain places:

> The inhabitants of this State shall have liberty in seasonable times, to hunt and fowl on the lands they hold, and on other lands not enclosed, and in like manner to fish in all boatable and other waters (not private property) under proper regulations, to be made and provided by the General Assembly.

Section 67 is an accommodation of goals. It offers a general delineation of not only the respective rights of landowners and sportsmen but also the authority of government to regulate those rights in the context of hunting and fishing.

Understanding Section 67 requires a knowledge of the common law which it altered. English law, as we received it, treated hunting on privately owned land as a personal privilege of the landowner.

Waterways overlying private property were not in every instance entirely private, however. Tidal waters could not be privately owned. Although an individual could own inland lakes and rivers, the public could use them for navigational purposes if the waterways were susceptible to use for commercial passage and transportation. Thus, the common law recognized a "public easement" for navigation on such waters.

This public right of passage did not initially include a right to fish or hunt on nontidal waterways. The right of fishery was personal to the owner of the underlying land. Also personal to the landowner was the right to hunt and fowl on those overlying waters.

Chapter II, Section 67 extended rights to citizens which the common law had not recognized. It recognized rights to hunt and fish, given certain circumstances, in what had previously been the landowner's private domain.

In *New England Trout & Salmon Club v. Mather* (Vt. 1896) this Court, focusing on the right to fish, reasoned that the constitutional provision at issue does more than just recognize a right to fish in boatable waters under appropriate legislative regulation; it also

> affords the test by which to determine over what waters the State has jurisdiction de jure thus: "And in like manner to fish in all boatable and other waters (not private property) under proper regulations to be hereafter made and provided by the General Assembly." Thus was jurisdiction expressly reserved to the State over boatable waters and waters not private property. Hence, unless the waters in question are boatable, they are not public, but private, and the State has no jurisdiction over them.

By imposing the boatability requirement, Section 67 also limits the State's authority to enforce and regulate an easement across waters overlying an individual's private land. In this way, Section 67 incorporates protections for landowners as well as for those who fish.

Mather's reasoning in the context of fishing applies equally to Section 67's hunting provision. By virtue of Section 67, the State has authority to permit and regulate public hunting on private property, but only when that land is not enclosed.

If landowners fail to take adequate measures to enclose their lands, then individuals who hunt there without first seeking permission would not normally be trespassers. We believe that the presence of water, whether boatable or nonboatable, is irrelevant for purposes of Section 67's right to hunt on nonenclosed, privately owned land. By attaching "boatable waters" and "lands not enclosed" limitations on the respective rights of fishing and hunting, the Vermont Constitution has designated those points beyond which private property becomes inviolate for fishing and hunting purposes—nonboatability for the former and enclosure for the latter.

Defendants correctly state that most states now interpret their common law to extend the navigational easement to include most water-related recreational activities, including hunting from boats. As noted previously, this was not always so. Moreover, those states do not have provisions like Chapter II, Section 67 of the Vermont Constitution to limit the evolution of their common law.

Nothing in Section 67 suggests that its framers intended that boatability would be the standard for hunting either from boats or while standing in water. Indeed, since the provision uses a single standard for "hunting and fowling," applying a separate standard for hunting waterfowl would comport neither with common logic nor with normal use of language. Accordingly, we conclude that the appropriate inquiry in the present case is whether the private lands were enclosed. Such a disparate treatment of hunters and fishers is rational since hunting is normally more dangerous to and intrusive of the landowner's interests.

Defendants do not dispute that the boundary along Charcoal Creek was sufficiently marked to be enclosed according to the terms of Chapter II, Section 67. In view of defendants' stated intent to continue hunting in plaintiffs' marsh, the superior court did not err when it "enjoined defendants from hunting, shooting, or trapping upon the lands of the plaintiffs."

The court did not stop there, however. It also enjoined "entering upon the lands of plaintiffs, by boat or otherwise, at any point behind their boundary line or as marked by plaintiffs' posters." We cannot find support in the court's findings for such a broad injunction. This portion of the court's order plainly implicates the boatability aspects of the common law's navigational easement and Section 67's guarantee to those who fish. The sole basis for this part of the superior court's injunction appears to be the nonboatability of the water at that point where defendants' boat was resting in the mud on October 3, 1979. Water level on a single day will not normally support a finding of boatability or nonboatability for a body of water subject to seasonal fluctuations. Nor, logically, can an injunction affecting a large area rest on a finding merely that a single point in that area is nonboatable.

We accordingly affirm the superior court's injunction order as it pertains to hunting, shooting, or trapping, and we strike that portion of the order which prohibits entering by boat upon the waters overlying plaintiffs' land.

NOTE

Twenty-two States guarantee the right to hunt and fish in their constitutions. Vermont's provision dates back to 1777. The rest of these constitutional provisions—in Alabama, Arkansas, Georgia, Idaho, Indiana, Kansas, Kentucky, Louisiana, Minnesota, Mississippi, Montana, Nebraska, North Dakota, North Carolina, Oklahoma, South Carolina, Tennessee, Texas, Virginia, Wisconsin and Wyoming—have passed since 1996. The constitutions of California and Rhode Island guarantee the right to fish, but not to hunt.

H. NATURAL OR INALIENABLE RIGHTS

Thirty-nine state constitutions include Lockean rights clauses that refer to a contractarian understanding of fundamental rights that exist in natural law form, prior to the creation of the state. Arkansas's constitution contains a common formulation:

> All men are created equally free and independent, and have certain inherent and inalienable rights; amongst which are those of enjoying and defending life and liberty; of acquiring, possessing and protecting property, and reputation; and of pursuing their own happiness. To secure these rights governments are instituted among men, deriving their just powers from the consent of the governed.

Ark. Const. art. II, § 2.

Massachusetts's constitution contains another common format:

> All people are born free and equal and have certain natural, essential and unalienable rights; among which may be reckoned the right of enjoying and defending their lives and liberties; that of acquiring, possessing and protecting property; in fine, that of seeking and obtaining their safety and happiness. Equality under the law shall not be denied or abridged because of sex, race, color, creed or national origin.

Mass. Const. amend. art. CVI.

I. UNENUMERATED RIGHTS

Thirty-three state constitutions have provisions that are analogous to the Ninth Amendment in the Federal Constitution. These provisions declare that the enumeration of rights in state constitutions should not be construed to impair or deny other rights retained by the people. Utah's constitution contains a formulation that is almost identical to the Federal Constitution, and provides that "this enumeration of rights shall not be construed to impair or deny others retained by the people." Utah Const. art. I, § 25.

CHAPTER XIV

LEGISLATIVE PROCESS PROVISIONS WITH NO FEDERAL COUNTERPARTS

A. INTRODUCTION

Many state constitutional provisions, as we have seen, have no counterparts in the Federal Constitution. While the Federal Constitution does not mention education, all state constitutions contain education articles that guarantee the right to a free public education. And while the Federal Constitution does not contain provisions guaranteeing a right to a remedy or open courts, many state constitutions contain explicit guarantees in this area. On top of these examples, mentioned in earlier chapters, a growing number of state constitutions contain provisions directing the legislature to protect the environment or guaranteeing public rights to a clean and healthy environment. *See* Barton H. Thompson, Jr., "The Environment and Natural Resources," *in State Constitutions in the 21st Century* (G. Alan Tarr & Robert E. Williams eds. 2006). Some state constitutions also guarantee individuals the right to enjoy the fruits of their own labor. See *Tully v. City of Wilmington* in Chapter IV, sect. F. The New Jersey Constitution, for example, guarantees employees in the private sector the right to "organize and bargain collectively." N.J. Const. art. I, § 19. A few state constitutions include provisions mandating aid for the needy. The Montana Constitution, for instance, states: "The legislature shall provide such economic assistance and social and rehabilitative services as may be necessary for those inhabitants who, by reason of age, infirmities, or misfortune may have need for the aid of society." Montana Const. art. XII, § 3(3). Other state constitutions have uncommon provisions, such as article XII, § 13 of the Ohio Constitution, which bars the taxation of food sold for human consumption, or article VIII, § 15 of the Alaska Constitution, which forbids the creation of any "exclusive right or special privilege of fishery" within Alaskan waters.

In this Chapter, we focus on another distinct state guarantee—state constitutional provisions that place process limits on legislative authority. Two main areas will be covered: (1) single subject and clear title requirements, and (2) public use requirements.

As their name suggests, single subject rules require that each bill considered by the legislature address just one subject. Clear title rules require that the subject of each bill be clearly expressed in its title. These types of provisions first began to appear around the end of the eighteenth century to counteract corruption and undue influence of special interest groups in state legislatures. *See* Millard H. Ruud, *No Law Shall Embrace More than One Subject*, 42 Minn. L. Rev. 389, 414–52 (1958). Today, they are included in the vast majority of state constitutions as a means to bring transparency, order, and fairness to the legislative process. As of 2017, forty-three states have single-subject requirements, and forty states have clear-title requirements. Sutton, *Who Decides? States as Laboratories of Constitutional Experimentation*, 242 (Oxford 2021)

Most state constitutions also include provisions requiring that public funds be spent only for public purposes. The Illinois Constitution, for example, states that "Public funds, property or credit shall be used only for public purposes." Ill. Const. art. VIII, § 1. A public policy requirement also may be found underlying state constitutional provisions that prohibit the granting of special privileges or immunities. By banning special entitlements, state constitutions imply that legislation must be for the benefit of the public. *See* Jeffrey M. Shaman, *Equality and Liberty in the Golden Age of State Constitutional Law* 28–33 (2008). In other States, notwithstanding the absence of an express constitutional mandate, the courts have read a "public purpose doctrine" into their state constitutions. In Wisconsin, for instance, the public purpose doctrine is a well-established constitutional principle, even though it is not recited in any specific clause of the state constitution. *State ex rel. Warren v. Nusbaum*, 208 N.W.2d 780, 795 (Wis. 1973). Whether explicit or implicit, the tenet that state legislatures and governors spend public funds only for public purposes is an important requirement of state constitutional law. *See generally* Sutton, *Who Decides?* Chapter 7 (covering state constitutional single subject, clear title, and public use requirements).

B. SINGLE SUBJECT AND CLEAR TITLE RULES

Martha J. Dragich, *State Constitutional Restriction on Legislative Procedure: Rethinking the Analysis of Original Purpose, Single Subject, and Clear Title Challenges*
38 Harv. J. Legis. 103 (2001)

State constitutions contain a variety of provisions governing legislative procedures. Unlike substantive limits, procedural restrictions regulate only the process by which legislation is enacted. Common examples are original purpose, single subject, and clear title restrictions. Original purpose clauses prohibit the amendment of a bill so "as to change its original purpose." Single subject rules limit each bill to one subject. Clear title rules require that the subject of the bill be clearly expressed in the bill's title. These provisions are designed to eradicate perceived abuses in the legislative process, such as hasty, corrupt, or private interest legislation. They are intended to promote open, orderly, and deliberative legislative processes, and can be found in almost all state constitutions.

The genesis of state constitutional restrictions on legislative procedure has been recounted elsewhere. The clear title rule, for example, was first adopted in 1798 in Georgia and the single subject rule first appeared in 1818 in Illinois. Most other states followed suit in the mid-nineteenth century. Constitutional restrictions on legislative procedure have survived and have been re-adopted in modern constitutions despite criticism that they allow the invalidation of legislation on "technical" grounds.

State constitutional restrictions on legislative procedure, unlike legislative rules adopted by the two houses of Congress, provide an avenue for challenging statutes, and such litigation is fairly common. The large number of procedural challenge cases seems surprising since State courts consistently proclaim that statutes are presumed constitutional. The Missouri Supreme Court, for example, has long insisted that "the use of these procedural limitations to attack the constitutionality of statutes is not favored. A statute has a presumption of constitutionality. We interpret procedural limitations liberally and will uphold the constitutionality of a statute against such an attack unless the act *clearly and undoubtedly* violates the constitutional limitation. The burden of establishing a statute's unconstitutionality rests upon the party questioning it."

Other states likewise favor a liberal construction of procedural restrictions. Courts have used a variety of phrases to express the high standard to be applied in these cases, stating that statutes will be held unconstitutional, for example, only if "clearly, plainly and palpably so," only if shown "beyond a reasonable doubt" to violate the constitution, or only in case of a "manifestly gross and fraudulent violation." As a result of these high standards, state courts uphold legislation against procedural challenges "more often than not." The Minnesota Supreme Court observed that from the late 1970s until 2000, it had decided five single subject/clear title cases, upholding the statute in every case. In 1984, a Missouri judge indicated that the Missouri Supreme Court had not sustained a procedural challenge in twenty years.

Why, then, do litigants continue to raise original purpose, single subject, and clear title claims? One explanation of this behavior is that "such challenges are easy to make because all that is necessary is reference to the face of the statute." Another explanation is that each of these cases, depending as it does on the specific text of a particular enactment, is sui generis. As such, there is always a chance that a court will sustain a challenge to one piece of legislation even though it has rejected challenges to many other statutes. A more cynical explanation is that procedural challenges offer litigants one last chance to attack legislation they were unable to defeat during the legislative process.

Whatever their motivations, these claims have begun to pay off. The Minnesota Supreme Court, for example, "sounded an alarm that it would not hesitate to strike down" legislation violating single subject and clear title provisions. The Missouri Supreme Court has heard ten procedural challenge cases since 1994, finding violations in five of them. The Illinois Supreme Court sustained only one single subject challenge from 1970 to 1996, but it has sustained four challenges since 1997.

An Illinois decision led to a nationally publicized furor in the Illinois legislature. In *People v. Cervantes* (Ill. 1999), the Illinois Supreme Court struck down the Safe Neighborhoods Law for violation of the single subject restriction. The law had been in effect nearly five years at the time of the decision. The scope of the Illinois court's ruling—striking down the entire enactment—is important. The court found that the Safe Neighborhoods Law was intended to address neighborhood safety problems relating to "gangs, drugs, and guns." Two portions of the law were found to constitute separate subjects: provisions amending the WIC (Women, Infants, and Children nutrition program) Vendor Management Act, and provisions relating to the licensing of secure residential youth care facilities. The Illinois Supreme Court discerned "no natural and logical connection" between these provisions and neighborhood safety. The portion of the Safe Neighborhoods Law challenged in *Cervantes* related not to the WIC vendor management program or the licensing of residential youth care facilities, but to weapons. Because the entire act was ruled unconstitutional, however, the defendant's gunrunning charge was dismissed. In fact, prosecutors were "forced to dismiss" firearms charges against numerous defendants. Five years after initial passage of the Safe Neighborhoods Law, the Illinois legislature found itself sharply divided on the merits of reenacting the gun control provisions. The measure has not been reenacted even though the Governor called a special session of the legislature for that purpose.

The Safe Neighborhoods Law exemplifies one consistent thread among recent procedural challenge cases: major changes were introduced into the challenged bills very late in the legislative process. This type of legislative procedure runs directly counter to the open, rational, and deliberative model the constitutional restrictions contemplate. Bills enacted in a hasty, apparently deceptive, or ill-considered process thus seem to invite procedural challenges. To return to *Cervantes*, the original Senate bill, relating to community service sentencing, was amended in the House so as to replace its entire contents with new provisions, now described as the "Safe Neighborhoods Law." The Senate refused to concur with the House amendment. A conference committee was formed, and that body deleted the entire House amendment and substituted another entirely new bill, 157 pages long and containing three components. That version then passed the Senate and the House and was signed by the governor. Similarly, in a Missouri case, *St. Louis Health Care Network v. State* (Mo. 1998), a substitute bill was offered on the last day of the legislative session for a bill originally relating to the Missouri Family Trust. The substitute bill contained provisions relating to nonprofit corporations, charitable gift annuities, and same-sex marriages. In both cases, the timing and scope of the changes raised suspicion.

A court's description of the legislative procedure leading to passage of the bill at issue sometimes indicates that the court's willingness to overturn the law is based on a suspicion that the process was tainted. For example, the Maryland Court of Appeals described the "transmogrification" of a one-page bill concerning a specific tax into "lengthy emergency legislation" extending to government ethics and county taxing authority. Similarly, the Supreme Court of Appeals of West Virginia explained how a bill on thoroughbred racing became "an omnibus bill which encompassed authorization for all agency rules considered that year."

1. Original Purpose

Missouri's original purpose provision is typical. It reads in pertinent part:

> No law shall be passed except by bill, and *no bill shall be so amended in its passage through either house as to change its original purpose*. Bills may originate in either house and may be amended or rejected by the other. Every bill shall be read by title on three different days in each house.

By its text, section 21 not only establishes the original purpose rule, but also implies a limitation of the rule and hints at the rule's underlying rationale. The text makes clear that the original purpose rule does not prohibit amendments to a bill during the course of its consideration and passage. In fact, it explicitly permits either house to amend bills originating in the other house. The Missouri Supreme Court has indicated that "Article III, § 21 was not designed to inhibit the normal legislative processes, in which bills are combined and additions necessary to comply with the legislative intent are made." At least one other state agrees that the original purpose rule should not be applied in such a way as to "unduly hamper the legislature."

In essence, the original purpose rule is "designed to prevent the enactment of statutes in terms so blind that legislators themselves would fail to become apprised of the changes in the laws." The final sentence of section 21 supports this rationale. It provides for the reading by title of each bill on three different days in each house. The rule protects the legislative process by allowing bills to be read and monitored by title alone. That is, a legislator is entitled to read bills as originally introduced and to decide, on that basis, how extensively to monitor each bill's progress. Legislators are assured that the purpose of a bill will not have changed dramatically following its introduction. This same reasoning serves to provide adequate notice to members of the public who wish to monitor pending legislation.

The original purpose rule also reinforces the deadline for introduction of new bills by preventing legislators from disguising new bills as amendments to existing bills. Accordingly, the original purpose rule is concerned with *changes* in content of the bill. By aiding legislators in monitoring hundreds of bills introduced in each legislative session, the original purpose rule helps legislators to represent the desires of their constituents.

Though only a few of the recent cases involve original purpose claims, the outcomes are instructive. In *Barclay v. Melton* (Ark. 1999), a bill that "had as its sole purpose the creation of a tax credit for dependents" was amended by deleting all of the provisions contained in the introduced version and replacing them with new contents. As passed, the bill "assessed a tax surcharge against residents of certain school districts." The Arkansas Supreme Court concluded that the change from a tax credit to a tax surcharge was a change in the bill's original purpose.

Changes less extreme than this about-face seem not to trigger invalidation on original purpose grounds. *Advisory Opinion No. 331* (Ala. 1991) appears to be unusual in this regard. There, the Alabama Supreme Court ruled that a bill whose original purpose was "to make appropriations for the ordinary expenses of the government" was unconstitutionally altered so as to change its original purpose when provisions limiting the powers of government officials to make necessary expenditures were added. According to the court, the purpose of the bill changed "from one of making general appropriations to one of repealing and changing other provisions of law." This bill represents a more subtle change. As finally passed, it contained two contradictory elements: provisions authorizing expenditures and provisions limiting the same expenditures. This case adds credence to the notion that a change in direction is fundamental in establishing an original purpose violation.

2. Single Subject and Clear Title

In most states, the single subject and clear title rules are combined in one section of the constitution. The combined rule is commonly phrased: "no bill shall contain more than *one subject*, which shall be *clearly expressed* in its title." In some states, a bill must embrace "one subject, and matters properly connected therewith." Exceptions are commonly made for certain types of bills, such as "general appropriation bills, which may embrace the various subjects and accounts for which moneys are appropriated," and bills revising or codifying the law. It is well-established that even when combined, the single subject/clear title provision sets forth two independent requirements—that a bill have only one subject, and that the bill's title clearly express that subject. The common phrasing of the rule suggests that clear title analysis cannot proceed until the subject of the bill has been determined and found to be "single."

a. Single Subject

Two reasons are thought to support the single subject requirement: the prevention of logrolling and the preservation of a meaningful role for the governor. Simply stated, the single subject rule exists "to secure to every distinct measure of legislation a separate consideration and decision, dependent solely upon its individual merits." One leading commentator observed, "limiting each bill to a single subject" allows legislators to "better grasp and more intelligently discuss" the issues presented by each bill. Without the rule, the danger is that "several minorities may combine their several proposals as different provisions of a single bill and thus consolidate their votes so that a majority is obtained for the omnibus bill where perhaps no single proposal could have obtained majority approval separately."

Furthermore, the single subject rule protects the governor's veto prerogative by "preventing the legislature from forcing the governor into a take-it-or-leave-it choice when a bill addresses one subject in an odious manner and another subject in a way the governor finds meritorious." The rule is "intended to prohibit anti-majoritarian tactics." In a word, the single subject rule protects the *decision* of the legislators and governor on each individual legislative proposal.

Hammerschmidt v. Boone County (Mo. 1994) is a classic case of a single subject violation. Two very narrow bills relating to the conduct of elections were combined, and thereafter provisions relating to the form of county governance were added. There was no "rational unity" between the provisions relating to election procedures and those relating to county governance, and no reason except "tactical convenience" for combining them in a single bill. Election procedures and county governance cannot be reconciled as parts of any single subject. No title could be written to express a single subject incorporating both of these elements.

Another good example is *People v. Cervantes* (Ill. 1999), an Illinois case. A bill originally relating to community service sentencing was amended several times during the course of its consideration. As passed, the bill expanded the offenses for which a minor can be tried as an adult, permitted longer sentences for felonies committed in furtherance of the activities of a gang, amended sentences for driving while intoxicated, adjusted sentences for drug offenses, and amended various other sentencing provisions. All of these provisions were found to be related to the amended bill's subject matter, neighborhood safety. Portions of the bill relating to the licensing of youth correctional facilities and welfare program vendor fraud, however, were held to relate to other subjects unconnected with neighborhood safety.

b. Clear Title

Two distinct purposes support the clear title requirement. Most importantly, the requirement "is designed to assure that the people are fairly apprised of the subjects of legislation that are being considered in order that they have an opportunity of being heard thereon." Secondarily, by requiring the title to express the whole subject of the bill, the rule "defeats surprise within the legislative process" and prohibits a legislator from "surreptitiously inserting unrelated amendments into the body of a pending bill." These two purposes reflect a widespread concern with special interest legislation in the nineteenth century. The clear title rule, properly understood, safeguards openness and honesty in the legislative process and facilitates public participation.

There are two common variations of clear title violations: overly broad, "amorphous" titles and under-inclusive titles. *St. Louis Health Care Network v. State* is a paradigmatic case of an amorphous title so broad that it gave no notice of the contents of the bill. This Article classifies *St. Louis Health Care Network* as a clear title case rather than a single subject case precisely because the title is so vague that one cannot discern from it what the bill itself provides. Clear title is properly the basis on which this case was resolved.

National Solid Waste Management Association v. Director, Department of Natural Resources (Mo. 1998) is a paradigmatic case of an under-inclusive title. The title—"relating to solid waste management"—accurately described the subject of most of the bill's provisions, but failed to give any hint of its application to hazardous waste. As a result, the title failed to provide notice of a portion of the bill's subject. The court assumed that the bill's two aspects, solid waste and hazardous waste, could be reconciled as part of a broader subject, but because the title failed to express the full extent of the bill's subject, the court invalidated the law.

The preceding analysis demonstrates that the original purpose, single subject, and clear title provisions, though related, are distinct. The original purpose requirement allows legislators to monitor vast numbers of bills by reference to their titles, confident that each bill's original purpose will remain reasonably constant throughout the process of consideration. It also secures adequate time for the consideration of each proposal by preventing late amendments that drastically alter the bill. The single subject rule assures that legislators and the governor can make a choice based upon the merits of legislation on each subject by preventing them from having to swallow unrelated bitter provisions with the sweet. Finally, the clear title rule protects the right of the public to know the subjects of legislation being considered and to voice opinions on measures of concern to them, and protects against fraudulent or surreptitious legislation.

GREGORY v. SHURTLEFF
299 P.3d 1098 (Utah 2013)

DURHAM, J.

Appellants argue that the Bill treats too many separate aspects of the public education system to pass muster under the single-subject rule. In their complaint, Appellants supported this claim by extensive reference to the legislative history of the items contained in the Bill. They point out that, when introduced as separate items, some had failed on a floor vote, some passed in one chamber but were held in committee in the other, and some were never submitted for even committee consideration as individual items. They further assert that popular bills were "used as hostages to extort or compel enactment of the less popular bills."

Almost a century ago, this court opined that while the single-subject rule is mandatory and binding alike upon the courts and the Legislature, yet it should be liberally construed in favor of upholding a law, and should be so applied as to effectuate its purpose in preventing the combination of incongruous subjects neither of which could be passed when standing alone. A too strict application of the provision might, however, result in hampering wholesome legislation upon any comprehensive subject rather than in preventing evils. Furthermore, while bills must address a single subject, "there is no constitutional restriction as to the *scope or magnitude* of the single subject of a legislative act." "A liberal view should be taken of both the act and the constitutional provisions so as not to hamper the law making power, but to permit the adoption of comprehensive measures covering a whole subject."

Examined on its face, under this liberal standard the Bill does not violate the single-subject rule. All its provisions deal with public education. It is easy to imagine a law that all would agree violates the single-subject rule. For instance, a bill dealing with pet licenses, mining regulation and beekeeping could not be plausibly argued to fit under any all-encompassing rubric less general than "legislation," or at the most specific "safety" (assuming that the pet licensing regime had that as its purpose). Similarly, one can imagine items of legislation so targeted that no plausible argument could be made that they violate the single-subject rule. Most actual legislation, of course, falls somewhere in between, and while the single-subject rule is mandatory and must be policed by this court, under our tradition of liberal construction a bill addressing even a relatively large number of educational programs does not violate that rule.

In addition to their general argument that the Bill contains too many disparate subjects, Appellants argue that it violates the single-subject rule for two specific reasons. First, they argue that it combines substantive law and appropriations measures, and that such a combination is a per se violation of the rule. Second, they include in their complaint a detailed legislative history of the components of the Bill, and argue that the fact that some of these components were rejected by the legislature as individual bills, while others passed committee or a floor vote in one house but were then held and combined with the rest of the Bill's components, demonstrates that the Bill constitutes impermissible "bundling" and "log-rolling" in violation of the spirit of the single-subject rule.

Appellants urge us to adopt what they represent as the rule of *Washington State Legislature v. State* (Wash. 1999): a bright-line test holding that the combination in one bill of substantive and appropriations measures violates the single-subject rule. But it is not clear to us that *Washington State Legislature* establishes any such bright-line test. We are unpersuaded by the other cases cited by Appellants in their urging us to establish a rule that the combination of substantive and appropriations measures always violates the single-subject rule. We therefore decline to adopt such a rule. As explained above, the Bill on its face treats a single, albeit broad, subject: education. The presence in the Bill of funding measures directed towards education programs does not render it unconstitutional. We are left, then, with Appellants' remaining argument on this point: that the legislative history of the items in the Bill reveal that it is the product of impermissible "log-rolling." and that it therefore violates the single-subject rule.

In Appellants' description, the Bill is the sum of 14 bills, all of which started as single subject measures. All initially were introduced, reviewed, considered, and debated as separate, stand-alone legislation. Two of these bills were defeated by majority vote in the House. Two others lacked sufficient merit to survive committee hearings. These failed bills were revived and, through bundling were allowed to ride "piggy-back" on popular legislation and money measures to enactment at the eleventh hour of the 2008 general session.

For three reasons, however, we conclude that these facts—even taken at face value, as we do when reviewing the grant of a motion to dismiss—do not state a claim that the Bill violates the single-subject rule.

First, the text of Article VI, Section 22 speaks to the contents and title of the Bill itself; it makes no reference to legislative motive. We have determined that the Bill itself, in treating multiple programs related to education, handles a "single subject"; we further determine that an itemized list of those programs is a clear expression of the Bill's content, which is what the clear-title rule requires. It is true that in *Salt Lake City v. Wilson* (Utah 1915) we identified the "purpose" of the single-subject rule as "preventing the combination of *incongruous subjects* neither of which could be passed when standing alone." But in light of our tradition of liberally construing the single-subject rule, we have already concluded that the subjects in the Bill are *not* incongruous in the constitutional sense. Therefore, even taking at face value Appellants' assertions that portions of the Bill "could not be passed when standing alone," *Wilson* neither requires nor empowers us to find them unconstitutional solely on that basis if we have not determined that they are "incongruous." While the prevention of "log-rolling" may be a *purpose* of the single-subject rule, the *text* of that rule requires us to focus on a bill's contents, rather than conducting a review of a law's "backstory" as revealed in legislative history.

Second, Appellants have not identified—and we have not independently found—any prior opinion of this court that analyzes a single-subject claim by reference to the legislative history of the bill at issue. Appellants cite *McGuire v. University of Utah Medical Center* (Utah 1979) and *Jensen v. Matheson* (Utah 1978), for the proposition that this court has previously examined legislative journals in its Article VI, Section 22 jurisprudence. This is true, but those cases dealt with other provisions of the section: respectively, the clear-title rule and a voting/recordation provision. These cases do not establish the propriety of undertaking an extensive search of legislative history in the application of the single-subject rule, and we are not persuaded that we should depart from an examination of the Bill on its face, at least absent any ambiguity or other interpretive problems revealed by such a facial examination. To do so would put us in the position of examining the motives and strategies of the Legislature, rather than its acts.

Finally, where a bill has not been shown to violate the single-subject rule, separation-of-powers considerations make us hesitate to inquire into the internal process that led to the bill's passage. Sometimes we are required to, as it were, "pierce the veil" of the legislative text—for instance, when a facially neutral bill is alleged to have some impermissible invidious motive. And allegations of outright illegality, in the form of bribery or the like, have their remedy elsewhere in the law. But the line between forbidden "log-rolling" and mere "horse-trading" may be a fine one, and we are not confident in our ability—or even our constitutional power—to police it in the manner which Appellants ask of us.

The Bill was entitled "MINIMUM SCHOOL PROGRAM BUDGET AMENDMENTS." Under this title came a caption identifying the session in which the Bill was submitted and its chief sponsor and sponsor in the House. Under this caption came a double line, then the following: "LONG TITLE. General Description: This bill provides funding for the Minimum School Program and other education programs. Highlighted Provisions: This bill:" followed by a bullet-pointed list of short descriptions of the various components of the bill. Appellants argue that the Bill violates the clear-title rule for two reasons. First, they argue that the "short title" is under-inclusive and misleading. Second, they argue that the "long title" does not cure the constitutional defect.

This court considered the clear-title rule in Utah's first year of statehood. *Ritchie v. Richards* (Utah 1896). There, we held that a bill entitled "An act relating to and making sundry provisions concerning *elections*," could not constitutionally contain a provision governing the *appointment* of persons to vacated positions. "This section," we determined, "does not relate to elections, nor does it concern elections. Therefore the title does not embrace it." A more recent opinion saw the purpose of the clear-title rule as ensuring that "the legislators will be advised of the subject and purpose of the act in order that there be no misunderstanding, omitting, nor burying or obscuring of what is being proposed."

Here, the bill's "long title" informs the reader that "this bill provides funding for the Minimum School Program and other education programs," proceeding to give a full list of those programs in bullet-point format. This is constitutionally sufficient—*if* the "long title" can be considered part of the "title" which the constitution says must clearly express the bill's "subject."

Appellants insist it cannot be so considered. First, they observe that Article VI, Section 22 speaks of the bill's "title" in the singular. Second, they argue that our case law has treated additional or supplementary titles of laws as unnecessary surplusage. Third, they argue that the clear-title rule is intended to benefit the public and that the public is less likely than the legislators to notice the presence of such additional titles.

Appellees and Amicus counter that a "long title" is an acceptable manner of observing the constitutional clear-title rule, and that in this case the Bill's "long title," as the constitution requires, clearly expresses the Bill's subject. We agree that the "long title" of this Bill is its title for purposes of Article VI, Section 22 and that it clearly expresses the Bill's subject. The Bill therefore does not violate the clear-title rule.

First, the fact that Article VI, Section 22 speaks of a bill's "title" in the singular is not dispositive. The Bill before us *has* a singular title. That title, it is true, is divided into a five-word header ("MINIMUM SCHOOL PROGRAM BUDGET AMENDMENTS") and a longer title, which is in turn divided into a "General Description" and a list of "Highlighted Provisions." But the text of Section 22 does not indicate how long or detailed a bill's "title" must be, or whether it may be divided into sub-parts. As we have interpreted and applied it above, the single-subject rule permits one bill to treat multiple aspects of the public education system. Accordingly, a title such as the one this Bill has is arguably the fairest way of putting legislators and citizens on notice of what the Bill contains. If the Bill's contents are constitutional in scope—and we have determined that they are—then an itemized description of them is a constitutionally acceptable way to clearly express those contents.

Appellants cite *State v. Edwards* (Utah 1908) in support of their argument that "the use of a second title may be constitutionally improper." The case is inapposite. In *Edwards*, we determined that certain "extraneous matter added to what constitutes the actual title is *harmless* and wholly unnecessary, and the elimination of this surplus matter is required of us in order to preserve" an otherwise constitutional law. But here we have, if anything, the opposite situation. By itself, "MINIMUM SCHOOL PROGRAM BUDGET AMENDMENTS" might well be unconstitutionally under-inclusive. The "long title," with its list of programs contained in the Bill, removes the cloud over the Bill's constitutionality.

Third and finally, we disagree that the "long title" is of use only to legislators. It is not written in technical or misleading language. It puts anyone reading it, whether they be a member of the legislature or of the general public, on notice of the Bill's contents. For all these reasons, we determine that the full title of the Bill comports with the constitutional requirement that it "clearly express" the subject of the Bill.

KOUSSA v. ATTORNEY GENERAL
188 N.E.3d 510 (Mass. 2022)

KAFKER, J.

The plaintiffs, twelve voters registered in Massachusetts, challenge the Attorney General's certifications of two initiative petitions, each proposing "A Law Defining and Regulating the Contract-Based Relationship Between Network Companies and App-Based Drivers." The plaintiffs contend that these petitions violate the requirement under art. 48 of the Amendments to the Massachusetts Constitution that initiative petitions must contain only related or mutually dependent subjects. The plaintiffs also object to the Attorney General's summaries of the proposed laws, arguing that they are not "fair" for purposes of art. 48 because the summaries do not adequately explain how the petitions, if approved by the voters, would change existing law.

The laws proposed by the petitions each contain a provision that would classify any covered app-based driver as "an independent contractor and not an employee or agent" of a network company "for all purposes with respect to his or her relationship with the network company," "notwithstanding any other law to the contrary" (first classification provision)—that is, regardless of the classification of app-based drivers under existing law. The proposed laws also specify a minimum level of compensation that network companies must pay to app-based drivers, calculated based on the total amount of a driver's "engaged time" or time spent fulfilling delivery or transportation requests. The proposed laws further specify various benefits that network companies must provide or make available to app-based drivers, including a health care stipend for drivers who meet a certain minimum of average engaged time per week, earned paid sick time, contributions to drivers' coverage under the paid family and medical leave program, and occupational accident insurance covering drivers' medical expenses, disability payments, and death benefits. The proposed laws would also provide app-based drivers with some form of protection against invidious discrimination by prohibiting network companies from refusing to contract with or terminating the contract of a driver based on certain protected characteristics.

Under art. 48, a measure proposed by an initiative petition must "contain only subjects which are related or which are mutually dependent." This related subjects requirement arises from a recognition that "a voter, unlike a legislator, has no opportunity to modify, amend, or negotiate the sections of a law proposed by popular initiative."

We have interpreted the related subjects requirement to allow for an initiative petition to include multiple subjects, "provided that the joined subjects have a common purpose to which each element is germane." But recognizing that "at some high level of abstraction, any two laws may be said to share a common purpose," we have looked to two further factors to determine whether the different subjects in a petition are sufficiently tied to a common policy scheme, taking care not to define the required degree of relatedness "so broadly that it allows the inclusion in a single petition of two or more subjects that have only a marginal relationship to one another." First, we ask whether "the similarities of an initiative's provisions dominate what each segment provides separately so that the petition is sufficiently coherent to be voted on 'yes' or 'no' by the voters." Second, we consider whether "the initiative petition expresses an operational relatedness among its substantive parts that would permit a reasonable voter to affirm or reject the entire petition as a unified statement of public policy." Determining whether a petition's provisions come together to present voters with a sufficiently coherent or unified policy proposal is the "crux of the relatedness controversy."

We conclude that the initiative petitions at issue each encompass at least two distinct public policy decisions. Most of the petitions' provisions are devoted to defining a new contract-based relationship between network companies and app-based drivers, including an associated wage and benefit scheme that the companies will provide to the drivers. In accomplishing this purpose, the petitions define the drivers as independent contractors, regardless of whether they would have been so classified under existing law, and provide drivers with the specified wage and benefit scheme, regardless of what they would have been entitled to receive in wages and benefits under existing law.

However, in vaguely worded provisions placed in a separate section near the end of the laws they propose, the petitions move beyond defining the relationship between app-based drivers and network companies and the associated statutory wages and benefits. These provisions extend the classification of app-based drivers as independent contractors rather than employees or agents to potential lawsuits involving third parties, including apparently the victims of torts committed by app-based drivers, such as those assaulted by drivers or injured in traffic accidents. These provisions would thus have the apparent effect that in any actions seeking relief for torts committed by app-based drivers, the drivers are to be deemed independent contractors and not employees or agents, regardless of how they would have been classified under existing law. This would narrow the tort liability of network companies for drivers' misconduct or negligence, whether on a negligent hiring or retention theory or on a respondeat superior theory.

The petitions thus violate the related subjects requirement because they present voters with two substantively distinct policy decisions: one confined for the most part to the contract-based and voluntary relationship between app-based drivers and network companies; the other—couched in confusingly vague and open-ended provisions—apparently seeking to limit the network companies' liability to third parties injured by app-based drivers' tortious conduct.

We therefore conclude that, by including the vaguely worded classification provisions and burden-of-proof provision, the petitions go well beyond the contract-based relationship between network companies and app-based drivers, and the compensation and benefits associated therewith. Instead, they mandate that app-based drivers may not be deemed agents or employees of network companies either directly or indirectly, that is, in lawsuits brought by third parties. In so doing, they apparently redefine the scope of tort recovery for third parties, including those who may have been injured in traffic accidents caused by the negligence of app-based drivers, or even sexually assaulted by them.

We conclude that limiting the scope of third parties' tort recovery for injuries caused by app-based drivers is a substantively distinct policy issue from defining the wage and benefit structure of those drivers. Voters may support one and not the other. They may, for example, strongly approve of better wages and benefits for drivers struggling to make ends meet in the gig economy, but at the same time strongly oppose limiting their own rights to recover money damages from network companies if the tortious actions of drivers who provide services through those companies' platforms cause them injury.

The defendants and the interveners argue nonetheless that the petitions' effect on third parties' scope of tort recovery is simply a downstream consequence of the petitions' purpose of defining the contract-based relationship between app-based drivers and network companies and the associated classification of drivers as independent contractors. To be sure, we have previously held that even if an initiative petition would have "consequences under an assortment of other statutes," that alone does not make the provision fail the related subjects inquiry, provided that these consequences are "logically related to the petition's aim."

Here, by contrast, we are not just dealing with downstream consequences. The initiative petitions provide instructions and directions on how courts should interpret and apply the provisions of the laws they propose, notwithstanding any other laws to the contrary. By instructing or directing that covered app-based drivers are to be deemed independent contractors and not agents or employees, regardless of how they would otherwise be classified under existing agency or tort law, the petitions move well beyond the consequences of establishing a scheme of wages and benefits for app-based drivers as independent contractors. An express instruction or directive in an initiative petition is different from a consequential effect.

Finally, we emphasize that the petitions' redefining of the network companies' third-party liability in murky language, and their burying of these provisions in the final substantive section of the proposed laws, raise particular concerns from the perspective of art. 48. As explained, we are conscious that a "recurring topic of concern" among the framers of art. 48 was "the possibility that well-financed special interests would exploit the initiative process to their own ends by packaging proposed laws in a way that would confuse the voter," in particular by prominently placing "alluring provisions" in the front of the petition while "burying more controversial proposals farther down." Indeed, the delegates to the constitutional convention expressed a more general concern that the initiative process might be abused by presenting voters with confusingly and misleadingly formulated petitions.

Petitions that bury separate policy decisions in obscure language heighten concerns that voters will be confused, misled, and deprived of a meaningful choice—the very concerns that underlie art. 48's related subjects requirement. Voters are not only unable to separate one policy decision from another; they may not even be aware they are making the second, unrelated policy decision. When even lawyers and judges cannot be sure of the meaning of the contested provisions, it would be unfaithful to art. 48's design to allow the petition to be presented to the voters, with all the attendant risks that voters will be confused and misled.

BURNS v. CLINE
382 P.3d 1048 (Okla. 2016)

WATT, J.

The issue before this Court concerns the constitutionality of SB 642, passed by the Legislature and signed into law by the Governor on June 4, 2015. This legislation includes one section modifying an existing statute relating to abortions, and enacts three unrelated new sections in this same title. We reverse the district court's findings and hold the statute unconstitutional as it violates the single subject rule set forth in Okla. Const. art. 5, § 57.

Art. 5, § 57 of the Oklahoma Constitution provides: "Every act of the Legislature shall embrace but one subject, which shall be clearly expressed in its title." This clause is commonly referred to as the "single subject rule." The purpose of this constitutional provision is not to impede legislation. Rather it is to insure transparency in the legislative process. The single subject rule is to prevent the Legislature from making a bill "veto proof" by appending unpopular legislation within popular bills. The recognition of this doctrine extends back to statehood. This constitutional provision acts as a safeguard against enacting legislation which, if introduced as a single bill, could never command the approval of a majority of the legislature.

Defendants advance two theories in support of their argument that SB 642 is constitutional. First, defendants attempt to argue that this legislation does not violate the single subject rule because it is germane, relative and cognate to one subject, the protection of women's reproductive health. Defendants next contend that SB 642 is simply *comprehensive* legislation, and that this Court has found that comprehensive legislation does not necessarily violate Okla. Const. art. 5, § 57. Upon careful review of Oklahoma jurisprudence, we find defendants' arguments are not in accord with our prior decisions on the single subject rule.

Defendants posit that SB 642 is constitutional under the single subject rule, because all sections in this legislation relate to protecting the reproductive health of women. To reinforce this point, the State argues that all four sections in SB 642 simply create enforcement mechanisms and put "teeth into existing laws designed to protect women's reproductive health."

The sections of SB 642 contain the following provisions:

(a) Section 1, amends 63 O.S. 2011 § 1-740.4b, adding powers to the Attorney General (A.G.) or the District Attorney (D.A.) to enjoin certain conduct relating to requisite consents for minors seeking abortions;

(b) Section 2, adds a new section of law, authorizing the Oklahoma Bureau of Investigations (OSBI) to create a new forensic protocol or statutory rape investigations;

(c) Section 3, adds a new section of law creating a new licensing and inspection scheme for abortion facilities, directing the Oklahoma State Department of Health (OSDH) to develop requisite regulatory protocols;

(d) Section 4, adds a new broad-sweeping section, imposing felony penalties as well as civil penalties up to One Hundred Thousand Dollars for a violation of any existing regulation relating to abortion statutes contained in 63 O.S. 2011 §§ 1-737.7 to 1-737.16.

We have consistently found legislation is related to one subject when the provisions are "germane, relative, and cognate to a readily apparent common theme and purpose." However, it is not enough for defendants to simply articulate some rational connection between similar or related provisions. Instead, our focus is "whether it appears that either the proposal is misleading or provisions in the proposal are so unrelated that many of those voting on the law would be faced with an unpalatable all-or-nothing choice."

Section 1 amends 63 O.S. 2011 § 1-740.4b, dealing with the consent required for an abortion to be performed on a minor and delineating civil and criminal penalties for any violation. The amendment creates a new class of people subject to this prohibition and adds new authority to both the A.G. and D.A. Sections 2 and 3 both place new duties and directives on OSBI and OSDH respectively. Section 4 is a very broad sweeping provision that provides for substantial civil as well as criminal penalties for any violation of any statute contained in 63 O.S. 2011 §§ 1-737.7 to 1-737.16.

We reject defendants' arguments and find this legislation violates the single subject rule as each of these sections is so unrelated and misleading that a legislator voting on this matter could have been left with an unpalatable all-or-nothing choice. The heart of the single subject rule is to insure constitutional protection that each piece of legislation enacted is worthy of the approval of the voter and to prevent the enactment of unpopular provisions by logrolling or attaching it to a favorable bill. We also find this legislation violates the single subject rule under *Fent v. State ex rel. Oklahoma Capitol Improvement Authority* (Okla. 2009), as it delegates authority to three different state agencies.

Although we have already concluded that this legislation fails for violating the single subject rule, we will briefly address defendants' second contention. Defendants assert that SB 642 is simply comprehensive legislation, and that this Court has found that comprehensive legislation does not necessarily violate Okla. Const. art. 5, § 57. *Coates v. Fallin*, (Okla. 2013), does not stand for the proposition proffered by defendants, that comprehensive legislation does not violate the single subject rule. Whether or not legislation is comprehensive is not the determinative factor for constitutional challenge under art. 5, § 57. We reject defendants' argument on this point.

The legislation before us is indistinguishable from legislation we determined violated the single subject rule in *Nova Health Systems v. Edmondson* (Okla. 2010). In Nova Health, we examined the "Freedom of Conscience Act" and its multiple sections. Most sections in the Freedom of Conscience Act contained some reference to abortion procedures. However, a common connection or theme is not sufficient to satisfy the single subject rule where the legislation is potentially misleading or leaves the Legislature with an all-or-nothing choice.

We find that each of the four sections of SB 642, lack a common purpose and are not germane, relative and cognate. Although each section relates in some way to abortion, the broad sweep of each section does not cure the single subject defects in this bill. Although defendants urge that SB 642 does not constitute logrolling, we find the provisions are so unrelated that those voting on this bill were faced with a constitutionally prohibited all-or-nothing choice to ensure the passage of favorable legislation.

We conclude that SB 642 contains different and unrelated purposes contrary to the single subject requirement of Okla. Const. art. 5, § 57. Although we understand the power of the Legislature in enacting new laws, we are bound to uphold our Constitution. SB 642 is unconstitutional and void.

NOTE

The Supreme Court of Arizona has long recognized that the single subject rule of the state constitution applies only to acts of the legislature and not to initiative measures proposed and enacted by the electorate. *See Citizens Ariz. Chamber of Commerce & Indus., et al. v. Kiley*, 399 P.3d 80 (Ariz. 2017) (holding that the single subject rule did not apply to a voter-approved measure raising the minimum wage). But the Court has taken the position that the single subject rule does apply to referenda proposed by the legislature and submitted to the electorate for enactment. *See Hoffman v. Regan*, 429 P.3d 70 (Ariz. 2018) (applying single subject rule to legislative measure referred to the people for approval).

TURNBULL v. FINK
668 A.2d 1370 (Del. 1995)

HARTNETT, J.

In this Court, Appellants raise for the first time a claim that Section 68 of the 1989 Bond Act, which enacted 2 Del. C. § 1329, is unconstitutional. Specifically, they assert that the Act violated Article II, Section 16 of the Delaware Constitution because it contained more than one subject and that the subject "waiver of sovereign immunity" was not set forth in the title to the bill. The text of Article II § 16 of the Delaware Constitution precludes Appellant's argument. It states: "No bill or joint resolution, except bills appropriating money for public purposes, shall embrace more than one subject, which shall be expressed in its title." Delaware courts have consistently followed the "plain meaning rule" for construction of statutes or the Delaware Constitution. One formulation used by this Court in stating the "plain meaning rule" is: "In the absence of any ambiguity, the language of the statute must be regarded as conclusive of the General Assembly's intent. The judicial role is then limited to an application of the literal meaning of the words."

As noted by Millard H. Ruud in his article *No Law Shall Embrace More than One Subject*, the text of the Delaware Constitution is more permissive than any other state constitution because it provides that a bill of the Delaware General Assembly which appropriates money for public purposes is free of the restraint that it be limited to one subject. As Professor Ruud points out, in 1958 18 states had adopted constitutional provisions specifically dealing with the limitation of contents of bills making appropriations—both general appropriations bills and other appropriation bills. The Constitutions of seven of those 18 states (including Pennsylvania) expressly excepted only general appropriation bills from the one subject restriction. There are only four states, including Delaware, in which a "one subject" limitation provision in the State's Constitution is exempted as to all appropriation bills. Of these four states only the Delaware Constitution provides that any bill appropriating money for public purposes is excepted from the one-subject and title requirements.

The 1989 Bond Act is clearly a bill appropriating money for public purposes and its provision relating to the waiver of sovereign immunity in Section 68 relates to the insurance authorized to be purchased in the Act. The 1989 Bond Act is similar to the Annual Budget Act and differs only as to the number of appropriations and its source of funds. The 1989 Bond Act makes over 130 separate appropriations and the money appropriated has several sources including the General Fund, general obligation bonds, revenue bonds, funds made available from the repeal of prior appropriations not yet expended, and certain special funds. As a bill appropriating money for public purposes, the 1989 Bond Act clearly falls within the exception in Article II, § 16 of Delaware Constitution. No other provision in the Delaware Constitution requires a one-subject limitation or a requirement for a title for a bill appropriating money for public purposes. There is, therefore, no requirement in the Delaware Constitution that the 1989 Bond Act be limited to one subject that is expressed in its title. The framers of the Delaware Constitution undoubtedly recognized, even in 1897, the difficulties in limiting an appropriation bill to one subject or setting forth its provisions in a title.

Appellants do not assert that they have been misled or prejudiced by any deficiencies in the 1989 Bond Act. To the contrary, they are benefitted by the enactment of Section 68 that enacted 2 Del. C. § 1329 because it waives the constitutional doctrine of sovereign immunity, up to $300,000 per occurrence, if DART has in place the insurance coverage authorized to be purchased by the Act. Without Section 68, Appellants would not have the benefit of this waiver.

HOLLAND, J., dissenting.

The two general provisions in Article II, § 16 of the Delaware Constitution, that a bill contain only one subject and that the title of the bill express its subject, are distinct requirements. Nevertheless, these two requirements are often combined in a single provision, such as Article II, § 16 of the Delaware Constitution, to achieve a common purpose.

The potential problem caused by an omnibus bill, which includes unrelated provisions on heterogeneous matters, is an uninformed legislative vote. This was recognized by the Romans. In 98 B.C., the Lex Caecilia Didia was enacted to prohibit the adoption of laws which contained unrelated provisions—the lex satura. The omnibus bill continued to be a cause for concern in colonial America prior to the Revolutionary War. Consequently, the constitution of nearly every state now contains a general requirement that legislation be limited to a single subject.

The other general requirement in Article II, § 16, that the subject matter of a bill be expressed in its title, originated with the Georgia Constitution of 1798. In 1795, the Georgia legislature passed the Yazoo Act, which made grants to private persons that were not reflected in the statute's title. The Georgia Constitution was amended in 1798. The constitution of almost every state now requires that the title of a bill adequately express its subject matter. These provisions are also intended to insure informed legislative action, as the 1897 debates on the Delaware Constitution reflect:

> Oftentimes bills have been introduced in the Legislature with very harmless titles, but amendments have been added to those bills and when they have passed both Houses, they are entirely different from what they were originally.

Consistent with the foregoing historical background, this Court has recognized that the two general requirements of Article II, § 16 were included in the Delaware Constitution of 1897 in order to "prevent deception of the general public and the members of the General Assembly by titles to bills which give no adequate information of the subject matter of the bills." The single-subject and title provisions in Article II, § 16 are intended to assure sufficient notice that "legislation, the content of which was inadequately brought to the public attention, or so-called sleeper legislation" does not slip through the General Assembly. If a bill contains multiple subjects or the title of the bill is such that it would "trap the unwary into inaction," it must be struck down as a violation of this section of the Delaware Constitution.

Nevertheless, appropriation bills have traditionally been conditionally exempted from both of the general requirements, the single-subject and the title provisions, in state constitutions. In view of the historical fear of omnibus legislation, which led to the constitutional proscriptions against bills with multiple subjects or nondescript titles, however, the exceptions for appropriation bills are always narrow. The condition for exemption is usually a limitation that the provisions in an appropriation bill relate only to appropriations.

While appropriation bills must contain no other substantive provisions than appropriations matters, this does not mean that an appropriation bill must merely be a list of monetary appropriations and respective recipients. Rather, appropriation bills may contain substantive language which relates to the specific appropriations in the appropriation bill. Such language may be found to be "conditional" or "incidental" to an appropriation and, therefore, properly included in an appropriation bill. Factors which indicate that language in an appropriation bill is not merely "conditional" or "incidental," but rather is improperly substantive are: first, the provision is not germane to any appropriation in the appropriation bill; second, the provision amends or repeals an already existing law; and third, the provision is permanent in nature, extending beyond the life of the appropriation act. If an appropriation act contains substantive, non-financial legislation, it then becomes precisely the kind of omnibus bill the single-subject and title rules were meant to prohibit. Accordingly, an appropriation act is an improper place for an enactment of matters unrelated to appropriations. Otherwise, the purpose behind the single-subject and title rules would be meaningless, since they could be circumvented simply by putting a substantive change into legislation otherwise primarily devoted to appropriations.

The narrow exemption for appropriation bills in Article II, § 16 is similar to the limited authorization for the gubernatorial line-item veto in Article III, § 18. In construing the latter provision, this Court has recognized the distinction between bills which have the fundamental purpose of appropriating money for public purposes, and bills which are fundamentally substantive in nature, but which also include an appropriation relating to the substantive issues. As to the former type of bill, the Governor has line-item veto power, but as to the latter, the Governor may only approve or veto the bill in its entirety.

The provisions in Article II, § 16 and Article III, § 18 of the Delaware Constitution, when viewed in historical context and read in para materia, reflect that to be an appropriation bill the provisions in the legislation must all relate to appropriations. The purpose of exempting appropriation bills from the single-subject and title rules of Article II, § 16 was to allow appropriation bills to designate money for more than one purpose without running afoul of the constitutional mandate that a bill embrace only the one subject expressed in its title. The exception for appropriation bills in Article II, § 16 was not intended to allow substantive provisions other than money appropriations to be included in appropriation bills.

Although Article II, § 16 of the Delaware Constitution specifically excludes appropriation bills from its purview, Section 68 of the 1989 Bond Act does not fall within that exclusion. The Constitutional Debates of 1897 reflect that the purpose of excluding appropriation bills from this section was to allow the legislature to make appropriations for many different purposes at once. Those debates also reflect the drafters of Article II, § 16 did not intend to permit the passage of "sleeper" legislation by including substantive non-monetary enactments in an appropriation bill.

Section 68 of the 1989 Bond Act, through which 2 Del. C. § 1329 was enacted, is the type of legislation that was intended to be prevented by Article II, § 16 of the Delaware Constitution. Section 68 of the 1989 Bond Act amends Title 2 of the Delaware Code to waive the State's sovereign immunity for DART operations that are covered by commercial insurance and to impose a liability cap of $300,000. This is a substantive enactment of a permanent nature, which is improper in a bill otherwise completely devoted to "appropriating money for public purposes. There is also no indication in the title of the 1989 Bond Act that any change was to be made in the substantive law relating to sovereign immunity. Consequently, as a substantive change to the law of sovereign immunity, which was part of an appropriation bill, Section 68 violated Article II, § 16 of the Delaware Constitution.

What are the ramifications of concluding that Section 68 of the 1989 Bond Act is unconstitutional? The other sections of the 1989 Bond Act are unaffected because of the severability provision in Section 73:

> If any section, part, phrase, or provision of this Act or the application thereof be held invalid by any court of competent jurisdiction, such judgment shall be confined in its operation to the section, part, phrase, provision, or application directly involved in the controversy in which such judgment shall have been rendered and shall not affect or impair the validity of the remainder of this Act or the application thereof.

Therefore, although Section 68 is unconstitutional, it does not invalidate the remaining provisions of the 1989 Bond Act.

NOTE

When courts identify a single subject or clear title violation, they must consider the vexing question of remedy. Should the violation be remedied by severing the offending provisions and allowing the remainder of the statute to stand, or should the entire statute be treated as unenforceable? Some state constitutional provisions provide an answer to this question themselves by opting for severability. The constitutions of Iowa and Oregon, for example, say that "If any subject shall be embraced in an act which shall not be expressed in the title, such act shall be void only as to so much thereof as shall not be expressed in the title." Iowa Const. art. III, § 29; Or. Const. art. IV, §20. In other States where constitutional provisions do not specify a remedy, some courts, as a matter of statutory interpretation, have followed a general preference for severability rather than refusing to enforce an entire statute. In *Hammerschmidt v. Boon County*, 877 S.W.2d

98 (Mo. 1994), the Supreme Court of Missouri set forth the following criteria for severability:

> Under the usual circumstances, this Court bears an obligation to sever unconstitutional provisions of a statute unless the valid provisions of the statute are so essentially and inseparably connected with, and so dependent upon, the void provision that it cannot be presumed the legislature would have enacted the valid provisions without the void one; or unless the court finds that the valid provisions, standing alone, are incomplete and are incapable of being executed in accordance with the legislative intent.
>
> Where, as here, the procedure by which the legislature enacted a bill violates the Constitution, severance is a more difficult issue. When the Court concludes that a bill contains more than one subject, the entire bill is unconstitutional unless the Court is convinced beyond reasonable doubt that one of the bill's multiple subjects is its original, controlling purpose and that the other subject is not. In reaching this determination, the Court will consider whether the additional subject is essential to the efficacy of the bill, whether it is a provision without which the bill would be incomplete and unworkable, and whether the provision is one without which the legislators would not have adopted the bill.
>
> Where the Court is convinced that the bill contains a "single central remaining purpose," we will sever that portion of the bill containing the additional subject(s) and permit the bill to stand with its primary, core subject intact. In determining the original, controlling purpose of the bill for purposes of determining severance issues, a title that "clearly" expresses the bill's single subject is exceedingly important.

The Supreme Court of Pennsylvania has pointed out that there are significant policy justifications militating against severance in cases where logrolling may have occurred. *Pennsylvanians Against Gambling Expansion Fund, Inc. v. Commonwealth*, 877 A.2d 383, 403 (Pa. 2005). The practice of logrolling—combining unrelated subjects in one bill in order to obtain majority approval of the entire bill—does not comport with the fair and deliberative process anticipated by single subject and clear title provisions. Where logrolling occurs, the entire law in question may be tainted, and arguably should be struck down in its entirety.

Refusing to enforce an act in its entirety is stiff medicine, a remedy most state courts have been reluctant to require. In that regard, re-consider the discussion of *People v. Cervantes* in the excerpt from Professor Dragich's article at the beginning of this section.

C. PUBLIC PURPOSE REQUIREMENTS

MAREADY v. CITY OF WINSTON-SALEM
467 S.E.2d 615 (N.C. 1996)

WHICHARD, J.

Plaintiff-appellant, William F. Maready, instituted this action against the City of Winston-Salem, its Board of Aldermen, Forsyth County, its Board of Commissioners, and Winston-Salem Business, Inc. Plaintiff contends that N.C.G.S. § 158-7.1, which authorizes local governments to make economic development incentive grants to private corporations, is unconstitutional because it violates the public purpose clause of the North Carolina Constitution and because it is impermissibly vague, ambiguous, and without reasonably objective standards.

This action challenges twenty-four economic development incentive projects entered into by the City or County pursuant to N.C.G.S. § 158-7.1. The projected investment by the City and County in these projects totals approximately $13,200,000. The primary source of these funds has been taxes levied by the City and County on property owners in Winston-Salem and Forsyth County. City and County officials estimate an increase in the local tax base of $238,593,000 and a projected creation of over 5,500 new jobs as a result of these economic development incentive programs. They expect to recoup the full amount of their investment within three to seven years. The source of the return will be revenues generated by the additional property taxes paid by participating corporations. To date, all but one project has met or exceeded its goal.

The typical procedures the City and County observe in deciding to make an economic development incentive expenditure are as follows: A determination is made that participation by local government is necessary to cause a project to go forward in the community. Officials then apply a formula set out in written guidelines to determine the maximum amount of assistance that can be given to the receiving corporation. The amounts actually committed are usually much less than the maximum. The expenditures are in the form of reimbursement to the recipient for purposes such as on-the-job training, site preparation, facility upgrading, and parking. If a proposal satisfies the guidelines as well as community needs, it is submitted to the appropriate governing body for final approval at a regularly scheduled public meeting. If a project is formally approved, it is administered pursuant to a written contract and to the applicable provisions and limitations of N.C.G.S. § 158-7.1.

Article V, Section 2(1) of the North Carolina Constitution provides that "the power of taxation shall be exercised in a just and equitable manner, for public purposes only." In *Mitchell v. North Carolina Indus. Dev. Fin. Auth.* (N.C. 1968), Justice (later Chief Justice) Sharp, writing for a majority of this Court, stated:

> The power to appropriate money from the public treasury is no greater than the power to levy the tax which put the money in the treasury. Both powers are subject to the constitutional proscription that tax revenues may not be used for private individuals or corporations, no matter how benevolent.

In determining whether legislation serves a public purpose, the presumption favors constitutionality. Reasonable doubt must be resolved in favor of the validity of the act. The Constitution restricts powers, and powers not surrendered inhere in the people to be exercised through their representatives in the General Assembly; therefore, so long as an act is not forbidden, its wisdom and expediency are for legislative, not judicial, decision.

In exercising the State's police power, the General Assembly may legislate for the protection of the general health, safety, and welfare of the people. It may "experiment with new modes of dealing with old evils, except as prevented by the Constitution." The initial responsibility for determining what constitutes a public purpose rests with the legislature, and its determinations are entitled to great weight.

The enactment of N.C.G.S. § 158-7.1 leaves no doubt that the General Assembly considers expenditures of public funds for the promotion of local economic development to serve a public purpose. When making amendments to chapter 158 and adding other provisions designed to promote economic development, the General Assembly mandated: "This act, being necessary for the prosperity and welfare of the State and its inhabitants, shall be liberally construed to effect these purposes." The General Assembly has further demonstrated its commitment to economic development by enacting several other statutes that permit local governments to appropriate and spend public funds for such purposes. These enactments clearly indicate that N.C.G.S. § 158-7.1 is part of a comprehensive scheme of legislation dealing with economic development whereby the General Assembly is attempting to authorize exercise of the power of taxation for the perceived public purpose of promoting the general economic welfare of the citizens of North Carolina.

While legislative declarations such as these are accorded great weight, ultimate responsibility for the public purpose determination rests with this Court. If an enactment is for a private purpose and therefore inconsistent with the fundamental law, it cannot be saved by legislative declarations to the contrary. It is the duty of this Court to ascertain and declare the intent of the framers of the Constitution and to reject any act in conflict therewith.

This Court has addressed what constitutes a public purpose on numerous occasions. It has not specifically defined "public purpose," however; rather, it has expressly declined to "confine public purpose by judicial definition, leaving each case to be determined by its own peculiar circumstances as from time to time it arises." As summarized by Justice Sharp in *Mitchell*:

> A slide-rule definition to determine public purpose for all time cannot be formulated; the concept expands with the population, economy, scientific knowledge, and changing conditions. As people are brought closer together in congested areas, the public welfare requires governmental operation of facilities which were once considered exclusively private enterprises, and necessitates the expenditure of tax funds for purposes which, in an earlier day, were not classified as public. Often public and private interests are so co-mingled that it is difficult to determine which predominates. It is clear, however, that for a use to be public

its benefits must be in common and not for particular persons, interests, or estates; the ultimate net gain or advantage must be the public's as contradistinguished from that of an individual or private entity.

Plaintiff also argues, and the trial court apparently agreed, that this question falls squarely within the purview of *Mitchell*. There we held unconstitutional the Industrial Facilities Financing Act, a statute that authorized issuance of industrial revenue bonds to finance the construction and equipping of facilities for private corporations. The suit was filed as a test case, before any bonds were issued, to enjoin the appropriation of $37,000 from the State Contingency and Emergency Fund for the purpose of enabling the Authority to organize and begin operations. We find *Mitchell* distinguishable.

One of the bases for the *Mitchell* decision was that the General Assembly had unenthusiastically passed the enacting legislation, declaring it to be bad policy. The opinion stated:

> At the time the General Assembly passed the Act, it declared in Resolution No. 52 that it considered the Act bad public policy. It explained that it felt compelled to authorize industrial revenue bonds in order to compete for industry with neighboring states which use them. As proof of its reluctance to join the industry-subsidizing group of states, the General Assembly requested the President and the other forty-nine states to petition Congress to make the interest on all such bonds thereafter issued subject to all applicable income-tax laws.

The resolution recited that the General Assembly passed the act reluctantly, with reservations, and as a defensive measure. The Assembly's obvious apprehension over using public funds to benefit private entities in this manner clearly served to undermine the Court's confidence in the constitutionality of the legislation. The converse is true here in that the Assembly has unequivocally embraced expenditures of public funds for the promotion of local economic development as advancing a public purpose.

Further, and more importantly, the holding in *Mitchell* clearly indicates that the Court considered private industry to be the primary benefactor of the legislation and considered any benefit to the public purely incidental. Notwithstanding its recognition that any lawful business in a community promotes the public good, the Court held that the "Authority's primary function, to acquire sites and to construct and equip facilities for private industry, is not for a public use or purpose." The Court rightly concluded that direct state aid to a private enterprise, with only limited benefit accruing to the public, contravenes fundamental constitutional precepts. Thus, the Court implicitly rejected the act because its primary object was private gain and its nature and purpose did not tend to yield public benefit.

This Court most recently addressed the public purpose question in *Madison Cablevision v. City of Morganton* (N.C. 1998), where it unanimously held that N.C.G.S. § 160A, art. 16, part 1, which authorizes cities to finance, acquire, construct, own, and operate cablevision systems, does not violate the public purpose clause of Article V, Section 2(1). The Court stated that "two guiding principles have been established for determining that a particular undertaking by a municipality is for a public purpose: (1) it involves a reasonable connection with the convenience and necessity of the particular municipality; and (2) the activity benefits the public generally, as opposed to special interests or persons." Application of these principles here mandates the conclusion that N.C.G.S. § 158-7.1 furthers a public purpose and hence is constitutional.

As to the first prong, whether an activity is within the appropriate scope of governmental involvement and is reasonably related to communal needs may be evaluated by determining how similar the activity is to others which this Court has held to be within the permissible realm of governmental action. We conclude that the activities N.C.G.S. § 158-7.1 authorizes are in keeping with those accepted as within the scope of permissible governmental action.

Economic development has long been recognized as a proper governmental function. In *Wood v. Commissioner of Oxford* (N.C. 1887), this Court upheld the statutory, voter-approved borrowing of money for the purchase of railroad capital stock and donations by towns located along a privately owned, for-profit railroad.

Further, the activities that N.C.G.S. § 158-7.1 authorizes invoke traditional governmental powers and authorities in the service of economic development. For example, subsections 158-7.1(b)(5) and (6) authorize economic development expenditures in connection with local government operation of water, sewer, and other utility systems, matters long considered a proper role of government. Likewise, the power under (b)(1) to acquire land for an industrial park, develop it for its intended use, and then convey it is analogous to the powers granted by the Urban Redevelopment Law, which this Court has consistently upheld as meeting the public purpose test. Urban redevelopment commissions have power to acquire property, clear slums, and sell the property to private developers. In that instance, as here, a private party ultimately acquires the property and conducts activities which, while providing incidental private benefit, serve a primary public goal.

As to the second prong of the *Madison Cablevision* inquiry, under the expanded understanding of public purpose, even the most innovative activities N.C.G.S. § 158-7.1 permits are constitutional so long as they primarily benefit the public and not a private party. "It is not necessary, in order that a use may be regarded as public, that it should be for the use and benefit of every citizen in the community." Moreover, an expenditure does not lose its public purpose merely because it involves a private actor. Generally, if an act will promote the welfare of a state or a local government and its citizens, it is for a public purpose.

Viewed in this light, section 158-7.1 clearly serves a public purpose. Its self-proclaimed end is to "increase the population, taxable property, agricultural industries and business prospects of any city or county." However, it is the natural consequences flowing therefrom that ensure a net public benefit. The expenditures this statute authorizes should create a more stable local economy by providing displaced workers with continuing employment opportunities, attracting better paying and more highly skilled jobs, enlarging the tax base, and diversifying the economy. Careful planning pursuant to the statute should enable optimization of natural resources while concurrently preserving the local infrastructure. The strict procedural requirements the statute imposes provide safeguards that should suffice to prevent abuse.

The public advantages are not indirect, remote, or incidental; rather, they are directly aimed at furthering the general economic welfare of the people of the communities affected. While private actors will necessarily benefit from the expenditures authorized, such benefit is merely incidental. It results from the local government's efforts to better serve the interests of its people. Each community has a distinct ambience, unique assets, and special needs best ascertained at the local level. Section 158-7.1 enables each to formulate its own definition of economic success and to draft a developmental plan leading to that goal. This aim is no less legitimate and no less for a public purpose than projects this Court has approved in the past.

Finally, while this Court does not pass upon the wisdom or propriety of legislation in determining the primary motivation behind a statute, it may consider the circumstances surrounding its enactment. In that regard, a Legislative Research Commission committee made a report to the 1989 General Assembly, warning that:

> The traditional foundations of North Carolina's economy—agriculture and manufacturing—are in decline. And, the traditional economic development tool—industrial recruitment—has proven inadequate for many of North Carolina's communities. Low wages and low taxes are no longer sufficient incentives to entice new industry to our State, especially to our most remote, most distressed areas.

In the economic climate thus depicted, the pressure to induce responsible corporate citizens to relocate to or expand in North Carolina is not internal only, but results from the actions of other states as well. To date, courts in forty-six states have upheld the constitutionality of governmental expenditures and related assistance for economic development incentives. Thus, by virtue of the trial court's ruling, North Carolina currently stands alone in so holding. Considered in this light, it would be unrealistic to assume that the State will not suffer economically in the future if the incentive programs created pursuant to N.C.G.S. § 158-7.1 are discontinued.

ORR, J., dissenting.

At issue in this case is the City of Winston-Salem and Forsyth County's authorization, pursuant to N.C.G.S. § 158-7.1, to expend public funds directly to, and for the benefit of, selected private businesses as an inducement to these businesses to either expand or locate in the community. The majority opinion sanctions this practice on the theory that since jobs were created and the tax base increased by virtue of the inducements, the expenditures, totaling $13.2 million for the twenty-four challenged projects, were for a public purpose as required by Article V, Section 2 of the North Carolina Constitution. As a result, it appears to me that little remains of the public purpose constitutional restraint on governmental power to spend tax revenues collected from the public. Because I believe that the majority's holding in this case is (1) based on a theory unsupported by the evidence, and (2) contrary to established precedent interpreting the intent of the North Carolina Constitution, I respectfully dissent.

The logic upon which the majority opinion rests its conclusion that the expenditure of these funds was for a public purpose can be stated as follows: The creation of new jobs and an increase in the tax base ipso facto benefits the general public. Therefore, local government expenditure of tax dollars to a private business for its private benefit in order to induce the business to either expand or locate in the community is for a public purpose if it creates new jobs and increases the tax base.

The fallacy of this reasoning begins with the assumption that new jobs and a higher tax base automatically result in significant benefit to the public. No evidence was presented that incentives paid or committed by the City and County improved the unemployment rate or that they otherwise resulted in meaningful economic enhancement. No evidence was presented that the incentive grants made by the City and County reduced the net cost of government or resulted in a reduction in the amount or rate of property taxes paid by, or the level of services rendered to, the citizens of Winston-Salem and/or Forsyth County.

In examining the stated purposes of the grants, it is obvious that the $13.2 million was authorized for the specific benefit of the companies in question. The money expended was directly for the use of these private companies to pay for such activities as on-the-job training for employees, road construction, site improvements, financing of land purchases, upfitting of the facilities, and even spousal relocation assistance. In weighing these direct "private benefits" paid for by the taxpayers against the limited "public benefits," only one conclusion can be reached—that the trial court correctly held that the expenditures in question were not for a public purpose. The opposite conclusion reached by the majority can be reached only by ignoring the weight of the private benefits and relying instead on the assumption that simply creating new jobs and increasing the tax base is a public purpose that justifies the payment of tax dollars to the private sector. As previously noted, there is simply no evidence to support such a conclusion, and the majority's position must fail.

The majority also relies on a "changing times" theory to ignore the law as set forth in *Mitchell* and *Stanley*. While economic times have changed and will continue to change, the philosophy that constitutional interpretation and application are subject to the whims of "everybody's doing it" cannot be sustained.

Finally, many of the arguments presented to this Court rest on public policy. Advocates for these business incentives contend that without them, North Carolina will be at a significant competitive disadvantage in keeping and recruiting private industry. They further contend that the economic well-being of our state and its citizens is dependent on the continued utilization of this practice. These arguments are compelling, and even plaintiff admits that a public purpose is served by general economic development and recruitment of industry. However, plaintiff and those supporting his point of view argue that direct grants to specific, selected businesses go beyond the acceptable bounds of public purpose expenditures for economic development. Instead, they say that this is selected corporate welfare to some of the largest and most prosperous companies in our State and in the country. Moreover, these opponents contend that the grants are not equitably applied because they generally favor the larger companies and projects and, in this case, under the County's Economic Incentives Program Guidelines, completely eliminate retail operations from being considered. In challenging the actual public benefit, a question also is raised about the economic loss and devastation to smaller North Carolina communities that lose valued industry to larger, wealthier areas. For example, the move of Southern National Bank headquarters from Lumberton to Winston-Salem undoubtedly adversely affected Lumberton.

Also troubling is the question of limits under the majority's theory. If it is an acceptable public purpose to spend tax dollars specifically for relocation expenses to benefit the spouses of corporate executives moving to the community in finding new jobs or for parking decks that benefit only the employees of the favored company, then what can a government not do if the end result will entice a company to produce new jobs and raise the tax base? If a potential corporate entity is considering a move to Winston-Salem but will only come if country club memberships are provided for its executives, do we sanction the use of tax revenue to facilitate the move? I would hope not, but under the holding of the majority opinion, I see no grounds for challenging such an expenditure provided that, as a result of such a grant, the company promises to create new jobs, and an increased tax base is projected.

HOPPER v. CITY OF MADISON
256 N.W.2d 139 (Wis. 1977)

HANLEY, J.

Three issues are presented on appeal:

1. Does the appropriation for services to be provided by the Madison Tenant Union constitute the expenditure of public funds for other than a public purpose?

2. Does the appropriation for services to be provided by the Spanish-American Organization constitute the expenditure of public funds for other than a public purpose?

3. Does the appropriation to the public health department for a day care program constitute the expenditure of public funds for other than a public purpose?

Although not established by any specific clause in the state constitution, the public purpose doctrine is a well-established constitutional tenet. "Public funds may be expended for only public purposes. An expenditure of public funds for other than a public purpose would be abhorrent to the constitution of Wisconsin." This rule applies to the expenditure of public funds by municipalities.

What constitutes public purpose is in the first instance a question for the legislature to determine and its opinion should be given great weight. This court, however, is not bound by the legislature's enactment or declarations regarding its purpose, for it is the court's constitutional burden to examine the challenged legislation and assess its realistic operation.

The court is not concerned with the wisdom, merits or practicability of the legislature's enactment, but only with its validity in light of specific constitutional principles. It is constitutionally sufficient if any public purpose can be conceived which might reasonably be deemed to justify or serve as a basis for the expenditure. "A court can conclude that no public purpose exists only if it is 'clear and palpable' that there can be no benefit to the public."

To sustain a public purpose, the benefit to the public must be direct and not merely indirect or remote. However, the fact that the appropriation is made to a private agency does not render it unconstitutional. If an appropriation is designed in its principal parts to promote a public purpose so that its accomplishment is a reasonable probability, private benefits which are necessary and reasonable to the main purpose are permissible.

The city council appropriated $10,000 to the budget of the City Planning Department to be granted to MTU in exchange for services to be performed pursuant to the terms of a written agreement between the city and MTU. Under this contract, MTU is obligated to "perform services for the City as outlined in the attached Human Resources Funding Application Form and any amendments thereto." MTU's application form describes the service to be provided generally as an information and grievance service for tenants, designed to inform tenants of their rights and assist them with problems in the landlord-tenant relationship. This service will be provided by grievance workers who will answer telephone inquiries and meet with individual tenants. These workers will be familiar with the applicable statutory law and the entire situation of tenants in Madison.

The appellant also contends this appropriation lacks a public purpose generally. In support of this position, the appellant argues that only that part of the city comprised of tenants could benefit from the services purchased from MTU. Although the number of beneficiaries is a pertinent factor in determining whether an appropriation has a public purpose, this court has stated many times "the fact the appropriation may benefit certain individuals or one particular class of people, more immediately than other individuals or classes does not necessarily deprive the appropriation of its public purpose."

The appellant also makes the argument that the trial court, in concluding the MTU appropriation was for a public purpose, only considered the grievance operation in the most favorable light and failed to consider what MTU would in fact do with the appropriation. The appellant claims evidence of certain MTU activities demonstrates that MTU is not concerned with promoting peaceful and equitable landlord-tenant relations, the adherence to local and state laws controlling these relations, or understanding by tenants of the rights and problems of landlords. The evidence referred to, appellant claims, shows that MTU's only interest is in furthering tenants' rights against those of landlords in any possible manner, including the promotion of rent strikes, picketing, boycotts, and blacklisting of selected landlords. Appellant argues that there is no reason to believe that the Tenant Union would act any differently in the future, simply because it is being subsidized by the city, than it has in the past.

However, the appropriated funds may be used only as provided in the contract between the city and MTU. This contract does not include any of the above-mentioned activities.

The record shows that of all housing units in the city, 49.3 percent are occupied by tenants. MTU's application for funding states that MTU receives approximately 75 telephone calls concerning landlord-tenant problems each week. A community with such a significant tenant segment has an interest in equitable landlord-tenant relations. These relations are a matter of public welfare. The expenditure for informational and grievance services for tenants who lack the expertise held by landlords in landlord-tenant law promotes such equitable relations. This program will also promote adherence to local and state laws governing landlord-tenant relations. Upon this record, it is not clear and palpable that there can be no benefit to the public by this expenditure. It has not been established beyond a reasonable doubt that no public purpose can be conceived which might reasonably justify this expenditure. It is not, therefore, unconstitutional.

The city appropriated $14,000 to SAO for its program, a bilingual multi-service center. SAO's application, which outlines the services purchased under SAO's contract with the city, states that SAO will provide:

(1) bi-lingual outreach and referral services to Spanish-speaking residents of Madison and Spanish-speaking migratory farm workers;

(2) employment and educational counseling for migrant workers in the transitional process of resettlement;

(3) in cooperation with the Area Technical College, courses in adult basic education and English as a second language;

(4) temporary accommodations for migrant families in the process of resettlement and assistance in locating adequate permanent housing; and

(5) in cooperation with the Wisconsin State Employment Service, bi-lingual job counseling, development and placement services to Spanish-speaking residents.

The appellant further claims that the SAO expenditure generally lacks a public purpose because only a small number of persons will benefit and because some of the persons served will be migrant workers who are not residents of the city. As stated above in respect to the MTU appropriation, the fact a certain group of persons are the immediate beneficiaries of the appropriation does not necessarily deprive the appropriation of its public purpose.

In its application for funding, SAO stated:

The 1970 U.S. Census indicates that there are over 2,200 residents in Dane County whose principal language is Spanish. The area Spanish-speaking community is one of the fastest growing sub-communities in the State of Wisconsin and in Madison. With the gradual decline of the migrant labor market, many former migrant families, a majority of who are Chicano, have chosen to resettle in Wisconsin. Although the greater share of resettlement has taken place in the State's south-eastern counties, Madison continues to receive an additional 10 to 20 families each year. 1973-74 public school enrollment data shows that the Spanish-speaking community of Madison is the 5th largest in the State. In addition, nearby food processing plants annually attract several hundred Spanish-speaking migratory workers who travel through Madison on their way to other jobs or in the resettlement process.

The services to be provided under the contract between SAO and the city seek to assist these persons in solving their various problems caused in large part by their language barrier. A community center which provides such assistance serves a public purpose. In the absence of such services, the public may be harmed by the recognized social consequences of poverty and illiteracy. It is a reasonable conclusion that these services will enable Spanish-speaking persons to contribute economically and culturally to the community. These matters are within the objective of the public welfare, the promotion of which will benefit the community as a whole.

In regard to the services provided by SAO to persons in the migrant stream, the citizenry receives the benefit of satisfaction from fulfilling a perceived moral duty by providing temporary assistance to these shelterless, needy persons. Such temporary accommodations also avoid the problem of these persons having nowhere but the streets to go. These benefits are certainly not as significant as those received by the public when the persons receiving the service are residents of the city, and it would be difficult to find a constitutionally sufficient public purpose served by an expenditure for service only for migrants. However, in this case, services provided to migrant workers are only a portion, the record shows, of all the services to be provided by SAO under its program. The SAO program, as a whole, promotes a public purpose, and therefore the expenditure to purchase services provided by that program is constitutional.

The city appropriated a total of $198,000 to the budget of the City Department of Public Health for various day care services. $117,000 of this money was designated as tuition aids to be distributed based upon standards of family need. These standards had not been established by the city council at the time of the commencement of the action, and the trial court therefore granted summary judgment to the defendant in respect to this portion of the appropriation for the reason that it could not be determined what persons would be served by the funds. The appellant does not challenge the trial court's decision in respect to this $117,000 appropriation for a day care tuition aids program.

The appellant does claim, however, that the trial court erred in not finding the appropriation of the remaining approximately $81,000 to be for other than a public purpose. Generally stated, these funds are to be allocated for two operations: (1) administration of the city's day care program, which includes salaries and benefits for city employees overseeing the program, and (2) direct aid to day care centers to improve their quality.

The appellant's major challenge to this expenditure for day care is that it lacks a public purpose because it is not to be limited for the benefit of poor and needy families, and therefore will aid families who do not need assistance.

The city's expenditure to ensure the availability of quality day care benefits the community as a whole. The record reasonably supports the conclusion that there is a need for improved day care service. The report of the City Committee on Day Care shows that in the city over 35 percent of women with children under the age of six are in the labor force. The report further states that less than half the children under the age of six who require out of home care may be accommodated in the presently available facilities. The vast majority of children in grades kindergarten through fifth who need extended care are not provided for. The two aspects of the day care program which are challenged here are to a great degree intertwined with the tuition aids program, which provides relief to poor and needy families, enabling the parents to work and contribute economically to the city.

It may not be seriously questioned that the care and supervision of the city's children is a matter of public health and welfare. It is reasonable to conclude that the city's program to improve and make more available day care service promotes these objectives. The appellant's claim that present day care facilities are adequate goes to the wisdom of the legislation, not whether it serves a public purpose.

We conclude that the challenged appropriations were not made contrary to the law. They constituted expenditure of funds for public purposes by promoting the health and general welfare of the public.

TOWN OF BELOIT v. COUNTY OF ROCK
657 N.W.2d 344 (Wis. 2003)

CROOKS, J.

Belle Zyla, Marvin Prothero, and the Green-Rock Audubon Society petitioned for review of a court of appeals decision, which reversed and remanded the decision of the Circuit Court for Rock County, William D. Johnston, Circuit Court Judge. The court of appeals held that the Town of Beloit has the statutory authority to spend public tax monies to develop and sell property in the Heron Bay subdivision, and that the town's goals in developing the subdivision constitute legitimate and valid public purposes.

We affirm the court of appeals decision. In *Libertarian Party of Wisconsin v. State* (Wis. 1996), this court held that creating jobs and enhancing the tax base were legitimate and valid reasons, along with others, for finding a legislative public purpose in the expenditure of public funds to build the Milwaukee Brewers' Miller Park. Accordingly, we hold that the combination of the town's enunciated goals of creating jobs, promoting orderly growth, increasing the tax base, and preserving and conserving an environmentally sensitive area for the benefit of the citizens of the town is a legitimate and valid public purpose under Wisconsin statutes, case law, and the United States and Wisconsin Constitutions.

This case involves a question of whether the Town of Beloit violated the public purpose doctrine. Although there is no specific clause in the Wisconsin Constitution establishing the public purpose doctrine, this court has recognized that the doctrine is firmly accepted as a basic constitutional tenet of the Wisconsin Constitution and the United States Constitution, mandating that public appropriations may not be used for other than public purposes. Courts are to give great weight and afford very wide discretion to legislative declarations of public purpose, but are not bound by such legislative expressions. It is the duty of this court to determine whether a public purpose can be conceived, which might reasonably be deemed to justify the basis of the duty. Under the public purpose doctrine, "we are not concerned with the wisdom, merits or practicability of the legislature's enactment. Rather we are to determine whether a public purpose can be conceived which might reasonably be deemed to justify or serve as a basis for the expenditure."

Consequently, a conclusion that no public purpose exists can be determined only if it is "clear and palpable" that there can be no benefit to the public. In *State ex rel. Warren v. Reuter* (Wis. 1969), this court described the public purpose concept as fluid:

> The concept of public purpose is a fluid one and varies from time to time, from age to age, as the government and its people change. Essentially, public purpose depends on what the people expect and want their government to do for the society as a whole and in this growth of expectation, that which often starts as hope ends in entitlement.

Although courts are not bound by legislative expressions of public purposes, they nevertheless have a constitutional burden to examine legislative actions for the existence of a public purpose pursuant to the Wisconsin Constitution. However, the court's duties are limited to determining whether the legislation contravenes the provisions of the constitution. The presumption of constitutionality is applicable in making such a determination. As such, courts are to give great weight to the opinion of the legislative body, and "if any public purpose can be conceived which might rationally justify the expenditure, the constitutional test is satisfied." Consequently, a court will conclude that there is no public purpose only if it is "clear and palpable that there can be no benefit to the public."

Because of the accepted view that local governments are often in the best position to determine the needs of the public in that locality, Wisconsin municipalities have traditionally been given wide discretion to determine whether a public expenditure is warranted due to public necessity, convenience, or welfare. As such, the public purpose doctrine has been broadly interpreted.

A review of Wisconsin case law illustrates that the trend of Wisconsin courts is to extend the concept of public purpose. In *State ex rel. Bowman v. Barczak* (Wis. 1967), the industrial development through the creation of separate county agencies and bond issues, pursuant to Wis. Stat. § 59.071, was determined to be a valid constitutional enactment as it related to a declaration of public purpose. In *West Allis v. Milwaukee County* (Wis. 1968), construction of incinerators and waste disposal facilities was considered a public purpose. In addition, financial aid to the Marquette School of Medicine (now the Medical College of Wisconsin), a private nonprofit corporation, was upheld on the premise that public health is a public purpose. This court upheld the industrial bonding law under § 66.521, as a public purpose, because the protection of the economic interests of the general public fell within the scope of promotion of the general welfare. Similarly, the elimination of unsafe, unsanitary and overcrowded housing was found to promote the overall public purpose of providing stable residences for those of lower income.

A few years later, this court upheld the creation and operation of the Wisconsin solid waste recycling authority, in part because "recycling can be defined as a means of garbage collection, and, as such, has been denominated as clearly a matter justifying expenditure of public funds."

Wisconsin courts have continued the liberal application of the public purpose doctrine. In 2001, the court of appeals held that the construction of a parking lot to promote rehabilitation of the downtown area was held to be a public purpose. In a similar vein, a city's expenditure of funds to increase the tax base and generally enhance the economic climate of the community was held to satisfy the public purpose doctrine.

Most significantly, this court was recently presented with the question of whether the expenditure of public funds for the construction of the new Milwaukee Brewers' Miller Park satisfied the public purpose doctrine. The purported goals of creating jobs and enhancing the tax base were held to be valid reasons, along with other reasons, by this court. In our analysis, we recognized that enhancing the tax base and creation of new jobs are legitimate and valid public purposes, and held that:

> The purpose of the Stadium Act is to promote the welfare and prosperity of this state by maintaining and increasing the career and job opportunities of its citizens and by protecting and enhancing the tax base on which state and local governments depend upon. It is clear that the community as a whole will benefit from the expenditures of these public funds. Creation of new jobs is of vital importance to the State of Wisconsin and economic development is a proper function of our government.

Accordingly, the goal of increasing the tax base, as well as creation of new jobs, has been recognized by this court, and other Wisconsin courts to be a legitimate and valid public purpose justifying the expenditure of public funds.

The record is replete with references to the underlying reasons for the town's decision to develop the Heron Bay Subdivision. In particular, the town was motivated to develop the land by its desire to create jobs, expand the tax base and create an orderly growth of single family housing for the benefit of members of the community.

The town was also concerned with the environmental impact that a subdivision would have in this ecologically sensitive area. As a result of that concern, the town ultimately determined that it was its duty to ensure that an ecologically fragile area was properly developed and that the best way to accomplish this goal was to carry out the development itself.

Thus, contrary to the Intervenors' argument, the record clearly indicates that the town acted on behalf of the public welfare. Finally, as noted by the town, any profit realized from the sale of the subdivision would in fact benefit the Town of Beloit in that the profit would go into the Town Treasury and ultimately benefit all of the citizens of the town by way of decreased taxes and reduced debt.

In summary this court has recognized, pursuant to our decision in *Libertarian Party*, that purposes for legislative action such as increasing the tax base and creation of new jobs, along with other reasons, are legitimate public purposes justifying the expenditure of public funds. This court holds that the combination of goals here of creating jobs, promoting orderly growth, enhancing the tax base, and preserving and conserving environmentally sensitive lands is a legitimate and valid public purpose justifying the expenditure of public funds by the Town of Beloit. Accordingly, we affirm the court of appeals decision.

ABRAHAMSON, C.J., dissenting.

I would affirm the order of the circuit court granting summary judgment to the intervenors on the ground that the town's proposed expenditure for the development of the subdivision did not serve a public purpose.

An expenditure is for a public purpose if it provides a direct advantage or benefit to the public at large. It is not for a public purpose if the advantage to the public is indirect, remote, or uncertain. The constitutional public purpose test is satisfied when the purposes expressed by the legislative body or "conceived" by the court rationally justify the expenditure. In determining whether a public purpose exists the judiciary accords the legislative branch deference and thus plays a limited role. Nevertheless, the court does not merely rubber-stamp government expenditures. The state and federal constitutions demand that courts perform their independent function to assess the realistic operation of the law to protect the public. A court "is not bound by the legislature's enactment or declarations regarding its purpose, for it is the court's constitutional burden to examine the challenged legislation and assess its realistic operation."

The combination of goals enunciated by the majority opinion as constituting a legitimate and valid public purpose for the Town of Beloit's expenditures properly includes a list of benefits that might conceivably, in some circumstances, provide a direct benefit to taxpayers and thereby satisfy the public purpose doctrine. An expenditure of funds that is legitimately designed to create jobs, promote orderly growth, increase the tax base, and preserve an environmentally sensitive area is made for a public purpose.

I dissent in this case, however, to express my conviction that some of the goals on which the majority opinion rests its conclusion are merely assertions unsupported by the facts of this case while others are admittedly hoped for but distant outcomes, not justifications. The public purpose doctrine becomes a charade if a town may justify expenditures by merely offering enough of the proper buzzwords, "job creation," "orderly growth," "increasing the tax base," and "environment concerns," without any facts to back up the assertions. Moreover, judicial review cannot begin and end simply with the recitation of those buzzwords, without any analysis.

I dissent because I conclude on the basis of this record that it is clear beyond a reasonable doubt that the taxpayers of the Town of Beloit will be paying taxes to support the sale of lots for the future construction of private housing from which any benefit to the taxpayers is indirect, remote, and uncertain.

This case is before the court on summary judgment and so our analysis is based upon stipulated facts and affidavits. The parties' stipulation regarding the public purpose states only that the development is based on a policy decision that the town will be able to sell the lots to private individuals, realize a profit, expand the town's tax base, and open up the northwest side of the town in an orderly planned manner. The affidavits do not discuss any particular public purpose except in passing and in conclusory terms. Indeed, analysis of the record exposes the town's asserted justifications and those conceived of by the majority of this court as nothing more than a recitation of buzzwords.

I begin by looking at the four justifications upon which the majority opinion rests its holding: job creation, expanding the tax base, promoting orderly growth, and environmental conservation.

The majority opinion lists job creation as an express goal of the town's expenditure in this case, despite the fact that the town did not articulate that benefit as a goal in its stipulation, brief, or oral argument. Indeed, there is no evidence in the record that the Town of Beloit ever intended the expenditure of monies to develop and sell property in the Heron Bay subdivision to create jobs, let alone that the expenditure would in fact create jobs.

The majority opinion includes this noble public goal based solely upon a single affidavit from the town's attorney, asserting in broad terms, not necessarily related to this subdivision development, that "the Town of Beloit has a history of leading development for the benefit of its citizens. The purpose of development has been to develop jobs, a greater tax base for the community and places for citizens to live."

No evidence appears in the record of the types of jobs that would be created in this case, who would receive those jobs, or how long those jobs would last. The only jobs immediately on the horizon may be jobs related to development of the subdivision. If homes are constructed in the future, one-time construction jobs might be made available in the community. A public purpose cannot rest on conjecture alone.

The court's emphasis on the public purpose of preservation of an environmentally sensitive strip of land along the Rock River also amounts to reliance on buzzwords. In any event, it is unclear why any expenditure of funds for subdivision improvement is necessary for environmental protection of land the town owns along the river. The monies expended go to the development of the sites, not the creation or enforcement of any environmental easement or covenant. According to the parties' stipulation, the public can access these lands for recreation and enjoyment at the present time. To conclude that the town is justified in expending funds for sewer, water, roads, gas, electricity, storm sewer management and any other appurtenances necessary for development of the subdivision for sale for homes because the public would benefit from no development on a particular strip of town-owned land is doublespeak.

The two other goals in the combination of objectives the majority opinion says supports the expenditures for a public purpose are the promotion of orderly growth and increasing the tax base. The town, however, makes no showing of the relationship of the subdivision to orderly growth. Orderly growth is accomplished by a master plan, zoning codes, and regulation of private land developers. The Town of Beloit has such a master plan in place. How the town is promoting orderly growth by development of the subdivision is therefore unclear. The majority opinion appears to have accepted the town's mere suggestion of promoting orderly growth. It certainly cannot base its conclusion on facts because the record is devoid of any such facts.

The final objective of the expenditures is to increase the tax base. The tax base will increase if the lots are sold and houses are constructed. Yet the stipulation states that the "Town has not sold any portion of the Heron Bay Lands as of this date. The Town has no guarantee that anyone will purchase any of the future residential lots."

The majority opinion's combination of goals justifying the expenditures in this case thus boils down to this: the expenditure serves an acceptable public purpose because the town's tax base might be enhanced. I disagree with this position. An enhanced tax base from the sale of land and the construction of homes is an indirect, remote, and uncertain benefit of the expenditure in the present case and is not a sufficient public purpose to justify the town's running a for-profit real estate development business and engaging in the non-traditional enterprise of building residential home sites.

CHAPTER XV

ORGANIZATION OF STATE GOVERNMENTS

A. INTRODUCTION

The Supreme Court of the United States has made clear on several occasions that the U.S. Constitution has nothing to say about the structure and organization of state governments. *See, e.g., Sweezy v. New Hampshire*, 354 U.S. 234, 255 (1957) ("This Court has held that the concept of separation of powers embodied in the United States Constitution is not mandatory in state governments."); *Highland Farms Dairy v. Agnew*, 300 U.S. 608, 612 (1937) ("How power shall be distributed by a state among its governmental organs is commonly, if not always, a question for the state itself."). The federal constitution thus does not compel States to allocate certain powers to particular branches of government or indeed even to have the traditional three federal branches. As a result, although most state government systems bear significant similarities to the federal government's structure and organization, there also are significant and interesting differences between the organization of the state governments and the federal system. This chapter explores some of those differences.

B. LEGISLATIVE POWER

1. Introduction

State legislative organization generally is defined at some length in state constitutions. All States but Nebraska have a bicameral legislature, not unlike the federal Congress, though the state legislatures vary in their specifics. Generally, state legislatures have responsibility for all lawmaking and exercise traditional police powers, meaning that their actions are limited only by political will and constitutional constraints such as may be found in the federal or relevant state constitution. Thus, state legislatures can and do legislate on a wide array of topics and subject matters, including taxation and spending, criminal law, domestic relations, education, and infrastructure.

This section considers one potentially significant way in which the States and local governments may differ from the federal Congress—the imposition of term limits. And it also examines some unique state constitutional legislative processes.

2. Term Limits for State and Local Officials

The Supreme Court of the United States held in *U.S. Term Limits, Inc. v. Thornton*, 514 U.S. 779 (1995), excerpted in Chapter III, that the States may not impose term limits on their members of Congress, because the Qualifications Clauses in the federal constitution provide the exclusive credentials for determining those qualified to sit in Congress. Thus, there are no enforceable state term limits for U.S. Senators and members of the U.S. House of Representatives.

But there is no federal constraint on the imposition of term limits on members of state legislatures, state executive officials such as governors and attorneys general, local government bodies, or even potentially state judges. Thus, the States have been a fertile source of trial and error when it comes to the adoption and constitutionality of measures limiting the terms of various state and local government officials. Several States have adopted such limits and in many cases, though not all of them, term limits have withstood challenges under state constitutions.

HOERGER v. SPOTA
997 N.E.2d 1229 (N.Y. 2013)

PER CURIAM

At issue in this appeal is the validity of Suffolk County's term limit law pertaining to the office of district attorney. Petitioners allege that, as a consequence of such local law, respondent District Attorney Thomas J. Spota III is ineligible to hold the office he seeks. We conclude that the County is without the power to regulate the number of terms the district attorney may serve, and therefore we affirm the order finding the designating petitions valid.

The Suffolk County Legislature imposed term limits on county officials, including the district attorney. After approval by public referendum, the measure was added to the Suffolk County Charter, which specifies that "no person shall serve as District Attorney for more than 12 consecutive years." Respondent, who was elected district attorney in 2001, will have served three full four-year terms (or 12 consecutive years) as of December 31, 2013. Spota, however, has been designated as a candidate in the upcoming primary election for the Democratic, Republican, Independence and Conservative Parties.

Petitioner Raymond G. Perini is a candidate for district attorney in the Republican Party primary. Petitioners-objectors are registered voters who filed objections to respondent's designating petitions with the Suffolk County Board of Elections. They commenced this special proceeding seeking to invalidate the designating petitions.

The State Constitution requires that "in each county a district attorney shall be chosen by the electors once in every three or four years as the legislature shall direct." For counties outside of New York City, the state legislature has determined that the term of office shall be four years. In addition, a district attorney is subject to removal from office, not by county officials, but by the Governor. The Governor is likewise vested with the authority to fill a vacancy existing in that office.

We have therefore recognized that "a district attorney is a constitutional officer chosen by the electors of a county." In other words, although the district attorney may be an officer serving a county, the office and its holder clearly implicate state concerns. For example, there is a strong state interest in establishing adequate salaries for district attorneys, as the representatives of the People of the State of New York responsible for enforcing the Penal Law at the local level.

Existing law further illustrates the necessity of statewide uniformity of qualifications for district attorneys. An individual must be at least 18 years old, a resident of the county and a citizen of the United States. We have also mandated that a district attorney must be an attorney admitted to practice in order to properly fulfill the duties of the office and that a county may not alter that prerequisite even in the face of major practical obstacles. The office of district attorney is plainly subject to comprehensive regulation by state law, leaving the counties without authority to legislate in that respect. In this light, we view the limitation on the length of time a district attorney can hold office to be an improper imposition of an additional qualification for the position.

Permitting county legislators to impose term limits on the office of district attorney would have the potential to impair the independence of that office because it would empower a local legislative body to effectively end the tenure of an incumbent district attorney whose investigatory or prosecutorial actions were unpopular or contrary to the interests of county legislators. The State has a fundamental and overriding interest in ensuring the integrity and independence of the office of district attorney.

SMITH, J., dissenting.

I dissent, because I see nothing in the State Constitution or any state statute that prevents Suffolk County from imposing a limit on the number of consecutive years that a district attorney may serve. On the contrary, article IX, § 2(c)(ii)(1) of the Constitution and Municipal Home Rule Law § 10(1)(ii)(a)(1) empower local governments to adopt local laws relating to the "qualifications" and "terms of office" of their "officers and employees," in the absence of inconsistent state legislation, and no state legislation that is inconsistent with Suffolk County Local Law No. 27-1993 exists.

It is irrelevant that, as the majority notes, a district attorney is "a constitutional officer" as well as a county officer and that the office of district attorney is a subject of statewide concern. These premises lead, at most, to the conclusion that the State has the power to prohibit the limitation of district attorneys' terms—a proposition petitioners do not contest. The issue is whether the State has exercised that power; the majority cites no statute in which it has done so. Nor can it fairly be said that there is a "*necessity* of statewide uniformity" on this issue. No calamity will occur if some counties have term limits for district attorneys and others do not. Perhaps statewide uniformity is desirable, but that is for the state legislature, not this Court, to decide.

TELLI v. BROWARD COUNTY
94 So.3d 504 (Fla. 2012)

PER CURIAM

In 2000, Broward County voters approved an amendment to the Broward County charter providing for term limits on county commissioners. The charter, as amended, limited county commissioners to no more than three consecutive four-year terms.

In February 2010, William Telli filed a complaint against Broward County for declaratory relief, arguing that the term limits were unconstitutional under the Florida Constitution.

Provisions throughout the Florida Constitution impose or specifically delegate imposition of "qualifications" for specific offices. But in *Cook v. City of Jacksonville* (Fla. 2002), this Court held that term limit provisions imposed disqualifications from office, and that article VI, section 4, of the Florida Constitution "provides the exclusive roster of those disqualifications which may be permissibly imposed." Article VI, section 4(b), provides that

> no person may appear on the ballot for re-election to any of the following offices:
>
> (1) Florida representative,
>
> (2) Florida senator,
>
> (3) Florida Lieutenant governor, or
>
> (4) any office of the Florida cabinet,
>
> if, by the end of the current term of office, the person will have served in that office for eight consecutive years.

At the time article VI was amended to include section 4(b), separate constitutional provisions already imposed term limits on the governor and age limits on justices and judges.

In *Cook*, this Court reviewed two consolidated cases in which county charters were amended to impose term limits on, among other officers, those county officers listed in article VIII, section 1(d), of the Florida

Constitution: sheriff, tax collector, property appraiser, supervisor of elections, and clerk of the circuit court. This Court in *Cook* concluded that the county charter-imposed term limits on those offices were unconstitutional:

> Clearly, by virtue of article VI, section 4(b), the Florida Constitution contemplates that term limits may be permissibly imposed upon certain offices authorized by the constitution. By the constitution identifying the offices to which a term limit disqualification applies, we find that it necessarily follows that the constitutionally authorized offices not included in article VI, section 4(b), may not have a term limit disqualification imposed.

This Court further noted in *Cook* that "the broad authority granted to charter counties" does not include the authority to impose additional "disqualifications which pertain to these offices authorized by the constitution."

Justice Anstead dissented. He analyzed the broad home rule authority granted to counties under the Florida Constitution:

> This broad language was obviously intended to allow charter counties wide latitude in enacting regulations governing the selection and duties of county officers. The term limit provisions in the charters in these cases are not inconsistent with any provision of general law relating to elected county officers. Given this grant of broad authority and consistency with general law, I can find no legal justification for concluding that charter counties should not be allowed to ask their citizens to vote on eligibility requirements of local elected officials, including term limits, since they could abolish the offices completely or decide to select the officers in any manner of their choosing.

Justice Anstead also disagreed with the majority's position that article VI, section 4(b), Florida Constitution, listing the state elected offices with mandatory term limits, somehow excluded charter counties from imposing term limits. He pointed out that there was "no wording in article VI, section 4(b) (or anywhere else in the Florida Constitution or the Florida Statutes) that indicates that the named officers in article VI, section 4(b) are subject to term limits *to the exclusion of all other government officers, state or local*, in the State of Florida." The "disqualification" distinction was not persuasive to him because regardless of whether it is called a "qualification" or "disqualification," it determines whether someone will hold office. "The reference to term limits as a disqualification cannot logically be stretched to mean that the absence of a reference to county offices in article VI, section 4(b) *precludes* term limits from being enacted at the county level."

The implied prohibition in *Cook* against term limits for county officers and county commissioners from the lack of inclusion in article VI, section 4, of the Florida Constitution, overly restricts the authority of counties pursuant to their home rule powers under the Florida Constitution. Because we now agree with Justice Anstead's dissenting opinion, and recede from *Cook*, we need not reach the issue of whether the office of county commissioner is one of those constitutional offices to which *Cook* applies.

In this case, the prior opinion in *Cook* undermines the ability of counties to govern themselves as that broad authority has been granted to them by home rule power through the Florida Constitution. Interpreting Florida's Constitution to find implied restrictions on powers otherwise authorized is unsound in principle.

Receding from the *Cook* decision will promote stability in the law by allowing the counties to govern themselves, including by imposing term limits on their officials, in accordance with their home rule authority. Because the qualifying deadlines have not occurred, there are no reliance issues implicated by this ruling.

Therefore, we hold that the term limits provided in Broward County's charter do not violate the Florida Constitution.

KEMP ET AL. v. GONZALEZ ET AL.
849 S.E.2d 667 (Ga. 2020)

MELTON, C.J.

This election case comes before us based on the following certified question submitted to this Court by the United States Court of Appeals for the Eleventh Circuit: Does OCGA § 45-5-3.2 conflict with Georgia Constitution Article VI, Section VIII, Paragraph I (a) (or any other provision) of the Georgia Constitution?

For the reasons that follow, we conclude that the answer to the question is "yes" to the extent that OCGA § 45-5-3.2 authorizes a district attorney appointed by the Governor to serve beyond the remainder of the unexpired four-year term of the prior district attorney without an election as required by Article VI, Section VIII, Paragraph I (a) of the Georgia Constitution of 1983 ("Paragraph I (a)").

The facts are not in dispute. On March 6, 2020, Deborah Gonzalez attempted to qualify for the November 3, 2020 general election for the office of district attorney for the Western Judicial Circuit after Ken Mauldin resigned from the office effective February 29. The Georgia Secretary of State determined that Gonzalez could not qualify for the November 2020 election for district attorney because, under OCGA § 45-5-3.2 (a), there would not be an election for that position until November 2022— the state-wide general election immediately prior to the expiration of the Governor's future appointee's term. Though the vacancy began more than six months before the scheduled November 2020 election, the Governor did not make an appointment in time to maintain that scheduled election pursuant to the provisions of the statute.

Our analysis begins with the text of Paragraph I (a), which states:

> There shall be a district attorney for each judicial circuit, who shall be elected circuit-wide for a term of four years. The successors of present and subsequent

incumbents shall be elected by the electors of their respective circuits at the general election held immediately preceding the expiration of their respective terms. District attorneys shall serve until their successors are duly elected and qualified. Vacancies shall be filled by appointment of the Governor.

Notably, this text closely resembles constitutional language that set the term of office for elected superior court judges under the 1877 Constitution (as amended in 1898), which this Court interpreted in *Hooper v. Almand*, 25 S.E.2d 778 (1943). In *Hooper*, an incumbent judge died shortly before the end of his four-year term, and this Court determined that a judge appointed to fill the vacancy could not serve for longer than the unexpired term of the deceased judge without an election for a successor taking place.

The same pertinent constitutional language also existed at that time with respect to the selection of solicitors general, whose duties later became those of district attorneys. *See Copland v. Wohlwender*, 30 S.E.2d 462 (1944). Both *Hooper* and *Copland* determined that when this language is used in our Constitution, the timing of the election for a successor to an office is tied to the specific term for the office as measured by the Constitution. And, although the constitutional language analyzed in *Hooper* setting the terms for *judges* appointed to elective offices was materially changed in the 1983 Constitution, the constitutional language applicable to the terms of district attorneys under the 1983 Constitution is consistent with the language of prior versions of the Georgia Constitution that set fixed terms of office for elected judges and solicitors general. Thus, *Hooper* and *Copland* are controlling in this case.

The final sentence of Paragraph I (a) says simply, "Vacancies shall be filled by appointment of the Governor." It does not say that appointments to fill vacancies do anything to change the existing, fixed, four-year term of office held by the district attorney who vacated the office before the end of that term. We therefore do not construe this language to change the fixed four-year term for district attorneys as established in the other three sentences of Paragraph I (a).

Accordingly, when the Governor's appointee fills a vacancy in an office of district attorney, he or she steps only into the remainder of the unexpired fixed four-year term for the office. Because the four-year term runs with the office, and not the individual in the office, the appointee would not begin a new term by being appointed, but would serve out the remainder of the existing term as the new "incumbent" until his or her successor (who could be the incumbent) is *elected* at the general election immediately preceding the expiration of that existing term.

In this case, there is no language in the constitutional provision relating to the terms for district attorneys that would allow for appointed district attorneys to serve beyond the remainder of the unexpired terms of their predecessors, and we cannot rewrite the Constitution to insert such language.

Because Paragraph I (a) fixes a four-year term for district attorneys that a vacancy appointee simply steps into until a successor can be duly elected in the general election before that term expires, OCGA § 45-5-3.2 (a) cannot operate to change the length of that fixed term. To the extent that OCGA § 45-5-3.2 provides otherwise, it is violative of the Georgia Constitution and may not be enforced.

NOTES

1. For other examples of litigation over term limits provisions, see *Massey v. Secretary of State*, 579 N.W.2d 862 (Mich. 1998) (upholding Michigan term limits); *Bailey v. County of Shelby*, 188 S.W.3d 539 (Tenn. 2006) (upholding term limits imposed on county officials); *Child v. Lomax*, 188 P.3d 1103 (Nev. 2008) (holding that a candidate's term of office that began before the term-limit amendment's effective date does not count towards the term limit).

2. Should it matter how the term limits are imposed? In some States, they have been imposed by constitutional amendment, whether by popular initiative or otherwise, while in others it has been done by statute.

3. Do term limits make more sense for certain officials but perhaps not others? For example, are the arguments for or against term limits stronger depending on whether the officials are state legislators, state-wide executive officers such as the governor, attorney general, or secretary of state, or local officials such as county or city commissioners, or even local mayors?

4. Should some officials be "off limits" in this context? What about state judges? Colorado had a vigorous public debate several years ago and defeated a proposal to limit the terms of state judges.

3. Legislative Processes and Procedures

OPINION OF THE JUSTICES
247 A.3d 831 (N.H. 2020)

PER CURIAM

On September 17, 2020, the clerk of the New Hampshire House of Representatives notified the associate justices of the supreme court that a "request for an opinion of the justices pursuant to Part II, Article 74 of the New Hampshire Constitution was adopted by the House of Representatives on September 16, 2020" upon the following question of law: "Would holding a session of the New Hampshire House of Representatives remotely, either wholly or in part, whereby a quorum could be determined electronically, violate Part II, Article 20 of the New Hampshire Constitution?"

To the Honorable House:

Having considered the oral and written submissions we received, the following response is respectfully returned:

> The House has asked a single question: whether holding a House session remotely, either wholly or in part, whereby a quorum could be determined electronically, would violate Part II, Article 20 of the New Hampshire Constitution. We answer this question in the negative.

Before explaining our answer, we address two preliminary issues. First, we observe that our advisory duty under Part II, Article 74 does not ordinarily require us "to furnish an opinion when the question submitted is not pending and awaiting action in the body propounding the inquiry." "It is our conviction, however, that the reasons which require adherence to this rule do not exist in the present instance." Here, an "unforeseeable emergency" caused by the COVID-19 pandemic resulted in the House conducting business remotely.

Moreover, the question propounded in this matter "relates to the constitutional authority of the House itself," and, thus, "may be of use to the present Legislature in the performance of its official duty." In answering the House's question, "we do not intend to depart from the settled interpretation of the Constitution or to set a precedent for future advisory opinions."

Second, we note that two private individuals ask us to consider whether holding House sessions remotely, either wholly or in part, whereby a quorum could be determined electronically, would violate Part I, Articles 8 and 31 and Part II, Articles 3, 8, and 21 of the State Constitution. We decline to answer their question for the following reasons.

As we have often noted, Part II, Article 74 "empowers the justices of the supreme court to render advisory opinions, outside the context of concrete, fully-developed factual situations and without the benefit of adversary legal presentations, only in carefully circumscribed situations." "The bodies authorized to obtain advisory opinions are limited by Part II, Article 74 to the branches of the Legislature and the Governor and Council." Part II, Article 74 does not authorize the justices to render advisory opinions to private individuals. Nor does "the constitutional duty of the justices of the supreme court to give advisory opinions include answering legal questions that require resolving questions of fact."

Moreover, it is not "within our province to speculate upon whether other constitutional issues might be raised." Nonetheless, we observe that, although the attorney arguing in support of an affirmative answer to the question presented expressed concern that remote House sessions diminish public access to legislative proceedings, attorneys arguing in support of a negative answer to the question countered that remote House sessions may actually enhance such access.

We turn now to the question the House has asked us to answer. Part II, Article 20 of the New Hampshire Constitution provides: "A majority of the members of the house of representatives shall be a quorum for doing business: But when less than two-thirds of the representatives elected shall be present, the assent of two-thirds of those members shall be necessary to render their acts and proceedings valid."

The language of Part II, Article 20 has been a part of the New Hampshire Constitution since 1784. The permanent constitution ultimately approved by the citizenry, which became effective in 1784, did not limit the number of the members of the house of representatives, and included the quorum clause as it exists today.

The language of the first clause of Part II, Article 20 ("A majority of the members of the house of representatives shall be a quorum for doing business") is nearly identical to that found in the Federal Quorum Clause. The Federal Quorum Clause provides:

> Each house shall be the judge of the elections, returns and qualifications of its own members, and *a majority of each shall constitute a quorum to do business*; but a smaller number may adjourn from day to day, and may be authorized to compel the attendance of absent members, in such manner and under such penalties as each house may provide.

U.S. CONST. art. I, § 5, cl. 1. Because of the similarity in language, we find the history of the Federal Quorum Clause, adopted in 1787, after the first permanent New Hampshire Constitution was adopted, instructive.

The language of the Federal Quorum Clause, Article 1, Section 5, Clause 1 of the Federal Constitution, was settled in September 1787. "By the time of the 1787 Convention, the legislative bodies of the thirteen states generally operated under majority quorum requirements." When the Committee of Detail reported back to the Convention on August 6th with a draft based on the Convention's earlier debates, it included a section in Article VI establishing that a majority of members of each House constituted a quorum to do business." "The Convention had not debated the issue before this time, so it appears that the members of the Committee of Detail, as they did in other sections, took this language from contemporary state constitutions."

> Justices of this court have explained with respect to Part II, Article 20:
>
> > The State Constitution provides that neither the house of representatives, nor the senate may act in the absence of a specified quorum. Left unstated, yet implicit in this constitutional scheme, is the requirement that the legislative authority of the government may be exercised only by a quorum of the two bodies of the General Court. Although the legislature may delegate a portion of the legislative authority to an administrative agency which is not subject to this requirement, it may not delegate its lawmaking authority to a smaller legislative body and

thereby evade the requirement for action by a majority of a quorum of both legislative bodies.

Opinion of the Justices, 431 A.2d 783 (1981).

The evident principal aim of the majority quorum requirement in the first clause of Part II, Article 20, and the two-thirds quorum requirement in the second clause, "is to ensure that a certain number of members are present" before the House "can transact business." Within the meaning of Part II, Article 20, "present" means "not absent; being face to face; being at hand." 2 Samuel Johnson, *A Dictionary of the English Language.* As a practical matter in the eighteenth century, physical presence was required for there to be a quorum, and because of distance and travel, it could take time for a quorum to be present.

"We may assume" that the framers of the State Constitution, in adopting Part II, Article 20, "did not have specifically in mind" virtual presence "any more than the framers of the Federal Constitution contemplated the application of the commerce clause to interstate telephone, telegraph and wireless communication, which are concededly within it."

"But in determining whether a provision of the Constitution applies to a new subject matter, it is of little significance that it is one with which the framers were not familiar." As long as the requisite number of representatives is "present," either in person or virtually, meaning that the requisite number is "at hand" and "not absent," Part II, Article 20 is satisfied. Moreover, the State Constitution, like the Federal Constitution, "prescribes no method" for determining whether a quorum is present. The State Constitution, like the Federal Constitution, commits to each house of the legislature the authority to adopt its own rules of proceedings.

We conclude that holding a House session remotely, either wholly or in part, whereby a quorum could be determined electronically, would not violate Part II, Article 20 of the New Hampshire Constitution.

MARKWELL v. COOKE
482 P.3d 422 (Colo. 2021)

SAMOUR, J.

The constitutional axis on which this case revolves is the reading requirement in article V, section 22: "Every bill shall be read by title when introduced, and at length on two different days in each house; provided, however, any reading at length may be dispensed with upon unanimous consent of the members present." Colo. Const. art. V, § 22. The question before us is whether uploading a bill to multiple computers and using automated software to simultaneously give voice to different portions of the bill at a speed of about 650 words per minute complies with the reading requirement in article V, section 22. We think not.

There are unquestionably different ways by which the legislature may comply with the reading requirement. But the cacophony generated by the computers here isn't one of them. While we have no business dictating the specifics of *how* the legislature might comply with the reading requirement, it *is* our prerogative and responsibility to declare that the legislature *did not* comply with that requirement.

We therefore agree with the district court's determination that the unintelligible sounds produced by the computers did not fulfill the reading requirement. But we affirm in part and reverse in part because we conclude that it was not within the district court's domain to dictate the *form or manner* by which the legislature may comply with the reading requirement.

In late February 2019, House Bill 19-1172 ("HB 1172")—a 2,023-page recodification of Title 12 of the Colorado Revised Statutes ("Professions and Occupations")—passed the Colorado House of Representatives. It was then introduced in the Colorado Senate and assigned to the Senate Committee on the Judiciary. On March 4, 2019, after receiving unanimous approval in that committee, the bill was referred for consideration by the full Senate.

The events that sparked this litigation occurred on March 11, 2019, when the bill was introduced in the Senate for its second reading. That morning, a member of the Senate asked for unanimous consent to waive the reading of the bill at length. Pursuant to article V, section 22 of the Colorado Constitution, Senator John B. Cooke requested that the bill be read at length. Because there wasn't unanimous consent to dispense with an at-length reading of the bill, article V, section 22 required that the bill be read in full. A pair of Senate staffers duly began reading the bill aloud, taking turns reading at a quick, but intelligible pace. This continued until the staffers were instructed to stop, approximately three and a half hours after they began reading the bill.

The Senate Secretary, Cindi Markwell, then directed Senate staff to upload HB 1172 to multiple computers and to use automated software to recite different portions of the bill simultaneously at the maximum rate of about 650 words per minute. It is undisputed that four to six computers were then simultaneously used, each for a different part of the bill, and they created a babel of sounds.

Through their staff, Senators Cooke and Robert S. Gardner objected to this procedure and asked the Senate Secretary to slow down the computers. The Senate Secretary declined to change course, however. Then, at 3:15 p.m., Senate Minority Leader Chris Holbert asked the Senate President, Leroy M. Garcia, Jr., to slow down the computers. But, like the Senate Secretary, the Senate President refused to do so. Thus, between four and six computers continued to churn out unintelligible sounds for approximately four hours until the process completed shortly after 5 p.m.

The next morning, Senators Cooke, Gardner, and Holbert filed a verified complaint for injunctive relief and declaratory judgment against Senate President Garcia and Senate Secretary Markwell in Denver District Court. Almost immediately, the court granted a temporary restraining order preventing petitioners from: (1) "refusing to read legislation"—including HB 1172—"in an intelligible fashion" without unanimous consent to dispense with the reading requirement, and (2) passing HB 1172 in violation of article V, section 22 "by failing to read the bill out loud on two consecutive days."

Since we have concluded that this case is justiciable, we proceed to settle the parties' disagreement. Before getting ahead of ourselves, though, we pause to underscore the constricted scope of the question we resolve today: Did the unintelligible sounds generated by the computers on the Senate floor on March 11, 2019, satisfy the reading requirement in article V, section 22? Although we answer the question in the negative, we abstain from specifying the form or manner by which the legislature may comply with the reading requirement. Where, as here, a "constitutional requirement can be complied with in a number of ways," our task is limited: We simply "determine whether the method actually chosen is in conformity,"—no more, no less. Thus, while it falls to us to discern whether the unintelligible computer sounds complied with the reading requirement, the possible forms or manners of compliance fall within "the sole province of the Legislature."

Recall that the reading requirement provides in pertinent part: "Every bill shall be *read* by title when introduced, and at length on two different days in each house." Colo. Const. art. V, § 22. The constitution does not define the word "read." What, then, is its ordinary and popular meaning?

Predictably, the parties come to loggerheads over the answer to this question, each side advocating for the dictionary definitions most compatible with its respective position. But we need not decide which definition reigns supreme. It suffices to declare that the unintelligible computer sounds did not conform with *any* of the proffered definitions or the definitions that we have independently consulted.

An 1866 edition of Webster's Dictionary (roughly contemporaneous with the 1876 adoption of the Colorado Constitution and the reading requirement) defined "read" to mean: "to utter or pronounce written or printed words, letters or characters *in the proper order*; to repeat the names or *utter the sounds customarily annexed to words*, letters or characters." *Read*, A Dictionary of the English Language 818 (10th ed. 1866) [https://perma.cc/BEZ8-CW9J]. We deem it significant that under this definition, which petitioners fully embrace in their reply brief, the unintelligible sounds produced by the computers clearly did not constitute a "reading" of HB 1172. The words of the bill were certainly not uttered or pronounced in their proper order. Nor were the sounds that customarily accompany those words ever uttered. Instead, the computers combined to create a noisy mishmash. The indiscernible sounds generated by the computers could not have been confused with the sounds that customarily accompany the words of HB 1172.

An 1890s Webster's Dictionary is equally unavailing for petitioners. That dictionary defined "read" to mean, among other things: (1) "to interpret; to explain"; (2) "to tell; to declare; to recite"; (3) "to go over, as characters or words, and utter aloud, or to recite to one's self inaudibly; to take in the sense of, as of language, by interpreting the characters with which it is expressed; to peruse"; (4) "to know fully; to comprehend"; and (5) "to discover or understand by characters, marks, features, etc.; to learn by observation." *Read*, Webster's International Dictionary 1194 (1890). The unintelligible computer sounds fit within none of these definitions. There was no way to interpret, explain, know fully, comprehend, learn, discover, or understand the text of HB 1172 by listening to the noise made by the computers. And that noise could not have been fairly characterized as telling, declaring, reciting, perusing, going over words and reciting, or "taking in the sense of language." *Id.* What the computers produced was pure dissonance.

Current dictionaries define "read" along similar lines and reveal that the meaning of the word has not changed substantially since article V, section 22 was adopted in 1876.

These and other definitions demand the same conclusion: Whatever the legitimate contours of the reading requirement, the unintelligible sounds from the computers do not fall within them. Put differently, while there are no doubt different ways to describe the noise made by the computers, "reading" isn't one of them.

Significantly, today's decision aligns with the animating purpose behind the reading requirement. This is a strong bang to the gong that signals that petitioners' interpretation of the reading requirement is untenable. As we mentioned, the cardinal rule of constitutional interpretation calls on us to give life to the intent of the framers and the people of the State of Colorado. We underscore that the objective of the reading requirement is "to afford protection from hasty legislation," which, in turn, helps preserve the integrity of the bill-enactment process. Our review of the inscrutable computer sounds leads us to proclaim without hesitation that they can in no way be reasonably viewed as consistent with the reading requirement's objective. To the contrary, accepting the jumbled computer sounds as "reading" under article V, section 22 would directly undermine the purpose of the reading requirement.

MÁRQUEZ, J., dissenting.

The majority concludes that the computerized recitation of House Bill 1172 on March 11, 2019, was not really a "reading" of the bill—at least for purposes of article V, section 22. But it does not explain why this is so, reasoning that its only task is to determine *whether* the reading requirement was met, "no more, no less." One is thus left to wonder what article V, section 22 in fact requires. Must the words of a bill be "pronounced in their proper order?" Must listeners be able to "know fully, comprehend, learn, discover, or understand the text" of the bill being read? Must the reading be done in a manner consistent with what the majority identifies as the "animating purpose" of the reading requirement? The majority hints at all these possibilities but does not clearly say which, if any, are constitutional requirements.

In my view, the plain language of article V, section 22 simply requires that bills be "read," or uttered aloud. Nothing more. The provision does not, for example, demand that the bill be read "by a human voice" or "slowly enough to be intelligible," or that the sections of the bill be read "in sequence" or even at a particular decibel level. Not only is this interpretation consistent with the plain language of the provision, but it also conforms with the history and purpose of the reading requirement and accords proper deference to actual legislative practice. Here, because the entirety of HB 1172 was, in fact, read aloud, article V, section 22 was satisfied.

In sum, today's decision is neither demanded by the constitution nor appropriate under separation of powers principles or this court's traditional deference to the legislature's interpretations of provisions that govern their internal processes. Moreover, I fear that, in addition to offering no guidance on what article V, section 22 requires, the majority's ruling today also calls into question the constitutional validity of previous legislation enacted following readings similar to HB 1172.

Article V, section 22 of our state constitution requires that "every bill shall be read by title when introduced, and at length on two different days in each house; provided, however, any reading at length may be dispensed with upon unanimous consent of the members present." Nothing in the plain language of this provision requires the legislature to read bills in a particular way; the bills simply must be "read."

The word "read" is a term of "extensive and various application." The 1866 Edition of Webster's Dictionary, cited by the majority, alone contains more than a dozen definitions of the term. Some of these definitions are relevant while some—"to suppose; to guess," for example—are not.

Most dictionaries contemporaneous to the 1876 ratification of our state constitution define the term "read" to mean, at least in part, something along the lines of "to speak it aloud." Given the uniformity of these definitions, "it cannot be maintained that the verb to read, in all its moods and tenses, when applied to bills for acts pending before legislative bodies, has acquired a purely technical signification which absolutely excludes its ordinary meaning." Put simply, the term "read" as it is used in article V, section 22 means nothing more than the ordinary act of uttering words aloud.

The 1866 Webster's Dictionary cited by the majority is the only roughly contemporaneous dictionary I found that adds the proviso "in the proper order." And, as the majority notes, that language was later dropped from the 1890 edition of the same dictionary. Modern dictionaries similarly decline to adopt a definition of "read" that depends on pronouncing words in a particular sequence.

Accordingly, I conclude that the plain language of article V, section 22 is unambiguous and requires only that every word of the bill at issue be uttered aloud. Because every word of HB 1172 was, in fact, recited aloud, the reading requirement in article V, section 22 was met.

HOOD, J., dissenting.

I agree with Justice Márquez's dissent, but I write separately to make three additional points. First, although this court has repeatedly paid lip service to *Baker v. Carr*, 369 U.S. 186 (1962), that case does not control political question analysis under the Colorado Constitution. Second, to the extent that the word "read" is ambiguous, the majority fails to implement Colorado's homegrown separation-of-powers jurisprudence by showing insufficient deference to the Senate's interpretation of a constitutional provision governing the internal affairs of the legislative branch. Third, I agree with the majority that courts cannot restrain the General Assembly from passing a bill absent extraordinary circumstances, but I would reach the issue of whether a pre-enactment injunction was justified here. It was not.

Overall, my concern is this: The majority lauds the separation-of-powers doctrine but minimizes it in practice by authorizing courts to decide all cases involving constitutional interpretation *and* to review the General Assembly's implementation of constitutional procedures de novo. Separation of powers demands more than the majority's rule that courts can't tell the legislative branch what *to* do but can tell it what *not* to do.

C. EXECUTIVE POWER

1. The Selection and Organization of the Executive

The federal constitution deposits all executive authority in the President of the United States. As a result, the President nominates his cabinet members, including the Attorney General, the Secretary of State, and the Secretary of the Treasury. In a real sense, this is a "unitary" executive model, because the President retains control over the important executive branch officials. As one legal scholar observed, "many states have diverged from the federal model by having other elected statewide officials, particularly an independently elected state attorney general. Which model is better: the federal or the state? Is a unitary executive optimal in a democracy like ours, or would an unbundled plural executive be better?" Steven G. Calabresi, *The Fatally Flawed Theory of the Unbundled Executive*, 93 Minn. L. Rev. 1696, 1697 (2009).

Thus, although the executive power in the States is often the same or similar to the power exercised in the federal system, it is frequently exercised by multiple state officials all of whom are elected, with the result that such officials are not necessarily beholden to the Governor or subject to the Governor's control and supervision. Indeed, it is quite common for a State to elect its Attorney General, its Secretary of State, and its Treasurer. Such a system obviously can at times lead to conflict between the Governor and these officials. Further complicating the situation, in many States these elected executive officials may to some extent be subject to the will and supervision of the legislature, rather than the Governor, and in some cases may, by statute or constitution, supersede the Governor's power over a particular matter.

For example, in some States, the Attorney General may be required to take particular legal action at the direction of the Legislature. Indeed, a legislature may even direct the Attorney General to sue the Governor. *See, e.g., State of Kansas ex rel. Stephan v. Finney*, 836 P.2d 1169 (Kan. 1992) (Attorney General sued the Governor at the legislature's direction in a mandamus action seeking a determination whether the Governor had the constitutional authority to enter into a binding gaming compact with an Indian tribe without approval of the legislature).

In many States that elect their Attorneys General, the Attorney General alone has the constitutional authority to represent the State in court proceedings. A Governor thus may need or retain separate counsel to assert his or her position in a particular matter in the event that position conflicts with the Attorney General's.

Many States do not follow the federal constitution's distinctions between "principal" and "inferior" executive officers, and as a result many executive officials who would be appointed by the President in the federal system are not appointed by the Governor or are elected instead. Likewise, many state appointments, *e.g.*, to the state supreme court, are not subject to a legislative confirmation process, as would be the case in the federal system, which requires Senate confirmation of all Article III judges.

The issues here are numerous and sometimes complex, and the differences among States are significant. The purpose of this section is only to highlight the fact that the executive powers may be exercised by different officials in the States than would be the case in the federal system, setting up conflicts unknown at the federal level.

PERDUE v. BAKER
586 S.E.2d 606 (Ga. 2003)

FLETCHER, C.J.

Governor Sonny Perdue filed a petition for writ of mandamus seeking to compel Attorney General Thurbert Baker to dismiss an appeal filed on behalf of the State of Georgia in a case involving legislative reapportionment under the Voting Rights Act. The trial court denied the Governor's petition, ruling that the Attorney General had exclusive authority to decide whether to continue the State's efforts to enforce a law enacted by the General Assembly and signed by the Governor. The issue presented here is whether the Attorney General has the authority under state law to appeal a court decision invalidating a state redistricting statute despite the Governor's order to dismiss the appeal. Because there is constitutional authority for the General Assembly to vest the Attorney General with specific duties and a state statute vested the Attorney General with the authority to litigate in the voting rights action, we hold that the Attorney General had the power to seek a final determination on the validity of the State Senate redistricting statute under the federal Voting Rights Act.

Following the 2000 decennial census, the General Assembly enacted a bill that reapportioned State Senate districts and Governor Roy Barnes signed the bill into law. The State then filed a civil action in the United States District Court for the District of Columbia seeking preclearance of the Senate redistricting plan under Section 5 of the Voting Rights Act, a prerequisite to enforcing the law. The State sought a declaratory judgment that the plan did not have the purpose or effect of "denying or abridging the right to vote on account of race or color or membership in a language minority group." Denying the State's request for a declaratory judgment, the district court held that the State failed to meet its burden of proof under Section 5 that the State Senate redistricting plan did not have a retrogressive effect on the voting strength of African-American voters in Georgia. It denied preclearance.

The General Assembly enacted a revised Senate redistricting plan and the State submitted the new plan to the district court for preclearance. In June 2002, the three-judge district court approved the revised Senate redistricting plan. Act 444 expressly provides that its senatorial districts are contingent and shall take effect only if the original Senate redistricting plan cannot lawfully be implemented under the federal Voting Rights Act. To obtain a final determination, the Attorney General filed a direct appeal in July 2002 to the United States Supreme Court challenging the federal district court's order rejecting the original Senate redistricting plan. The Supreme Court granted review in January 2003.

Ten days later, soon after being installed into office, Governor Perdue requested that Attorney General Baker dismiss the appeal. The Governor contended that the Georgia Constitution vests his office with the chief executive powers to dismiss an appeal pending in the U.S. Supreme Court when the State of Georgia is the sole-named appellant. The Attorney General disagreed, citing constitutional provisions that vest his office with exclusive authority in all legal matters related to the executive branch in state government. Faced with this refusal, the Governor sought a writ of mandamus to require the Attorney General to dismiss the pending appeal in the Supreme Court.

Both the Governor and Attorney General are elected constitutional officers in the executive branch of state government, which is responsible for enforcing state statutes. The Georgia Constitution provides that the Governor is vested with the chief executive powers. Among those powers is the responsibility to see that the laws are faithfully executed. Other executive officers, including the Attorney General, are vested with the powers prescribed by the constitution and by law. The constitution states that the Attorney General "shall act as the legal advisor of the executive department, shall represent the state in the Supreme Court in all capital felonies and in all civil and criminal cases in any court when required by the Governor, and shall perform such other duties as shall be required by law."

Within the executive branch, both the Governor and Attorney General have statutory authority to direct litigation on behalf of the State of Georgia. Under the State Government Reorganization Act of 1931, which established the Department of Law, the Governor "shall have power to direct the Department of Law, through the Attorney General as head thereof, to institute and prosecute in the name of the State such matters, proceedings, and litigations as he shall deem to be in the best interest of the people of the State." The Governor also has the power to provide for the defense of any action in which the State has an interest.

OCGA § 45-15-3 sets out the Attorney General's general responsibilities. It repeats his constitutional duties to serve as the executive branch's legal adviser, represent the State in all capital felony appeals, and represent the State in all civil and criminal actions when required by the Governor; it further provides that the Attorney General may give written legal opinions to state departments on request and prepare all state contracts when advisable. Subsection (6) gives the Attorney General independent authority to represent the State in any civil action without the Governor's request: "It is the duty of the Attorney General to represent the state in all civil actions tried in any court." The final subsection is a catch-all phrase similar to the language in the constitution, giving the Attorney General authority to perform "other services as shall be required of him by law."

Construed together, these constitutional provisions and statutes do not vest either officer with the exclusive power to control legal proceedings involving the State of Georgia. Instead, these provisions suggest that the Governor and Attorney General have concurrent powers over litigation in which the State is a party. Both executive officers are empowered to make certain that state laws are faithfully enforced; both may decide to initiate legal proceedings to protect the State's interests; both may ensure that the State's interests are defended in legal actions; and both may institute investigations of wrongdoing by state agencies and officials. Thus, they share the responsibility to guarantee that the State vigorously asserts and defends its interests in legal proceedings.

As a result, we reject the broader claim by each officer that he has the ultimate authority to decide what is in the best interest of the people of the State in every lawsuit involving the State of Georgia. By giving both the Governor and Attorney General the responsibility for enforcing state law, the drafters of our constitutions and the General Assembly have made it less likely that the State will fail to forcefully prosecute or defend its interests in a court of law or other legal proceeding. This overlapping responsibility is also consistent with the existing practice in state government. Most important, it provides a system of checks and balances within the executive branch so that no single official has unrestrained power to decide what laws to enforce and when to enforce them.

The State of Georgia is not one branch of government, one office, or one officer. The State's authority resides with the people who elect many officers with different responsibilities under valid law.

Our conclusion that both officers have the duty to enforce state laws is consistent with the language and legislative history of article V of the 1983 Georgia Constitution. The first paragraph on the Governor's duties and powers in the Executive Article states the following: "The chief executive powers shall be vested in the Governor. The other executive officers shall have such powers as may be prescribed by this Constitution and by law."

To support his claim that "the Governor, and the Governor alone," is authorized to make decisions related to litigation filed in the State's name, the Governor relies on the constitutional provision describing the Attorney General's duties and a statute. The 1983 Constitution, like all the constitutions since 1868, provides that the Attorney General "shall represent the state in all civil and criminal cases in any court when required by the Governor." In addition, OCGA § 45-15-35 vests the Governor with the power to direct the Department of Law to institute and prosecute litigation in the name of the State. The Governor contends that this language means the Attorney General must follow his orders to dismiss or withdraw an appeal in any case regardless of the circumstances.

Contrary to the Governor's contention, we do not read these constitutional or statutory provisions as denying power to the Attorney General in representing the State, but instead interpret them as granting additional power to the Governor. As a result, we decline to address the Governor's contention, adopted by the dissent, that his express right to initiate litigation always includes the implicit right to end any lawsuit. Rather, the dispositive issue is whether any laws of this State grant the Attorney General independent authority to continue the litigation in this case. To decide whether the Governor's powers as chief executive include the absolute right to direct the Attorney General to dismiss the State's appeal, we look to the powers and duties of the Attorney General as prescribed under the Georgia Constitution and statutory law.

The Attorney General is a state executive officer elected at the same time and holding office for the same term as the Governor. As an elected state constitutional officer, the Attorney General has the powers prescribed to him by the 1983 Constitution, statutes, and case law. The General Assembly has given the Attorney General specific authority to act independently on behalf of the State in a variety of civil and criminal cases. For example, the code chapter on the Attorney General empowers that officer to represent the State in all civil actions in any court, and represent the State before the United States Supreme Court.

Act 444 was enacted after the federal district court had denied preclearance to the original Senate redistricting plan, but before the State filed an appeal of that decision to the U.S. Supreme Court. By its terms, Act 444 expresses the legislature's intent that the original redistricting plan for the State Senate should be followed if allowed by federal law. Section 1(d) states that the original plan's provisions are "suspended" until the State can obtain a final determination on the legality of the original plan under the federal Voting Rights Act. At the time the General Assembly enacted Act 444, the first step in the process for the State to obtain a "final determination" on its ability to enforce the reapportionment plan under the federal Voting Rights Act was to file a direct appeal with the Supreme Court seeking to reverse the district court's opinion.

As the State's chief legal officer, the Attorney General is the official charged with representing the State in reapportionment cases. Before any change affecting voting qualifications, standards, practices, and procedures may take effect, the State must obtain preclearance of the change under Section 5 of the Voting Rights Act. If preclearance is declined by the district court, the State's only remedy is to file a direct appeal to the United States Supreme Court. OCGA § 45-15-9 provides that the Attorney General "shall represent the State in all actions before the Supreme Court."

Accordingly, after the three-judge court denied preclearance, the Attorney General appealed to the Supreme Court. By appealing, the Attorney General was fulfilling his general duty as chief legal officer to execute state law and his specific duty to defend the reapportionment law as enacted by the General Assembly.

We next consider whether Act 444 violates the doctrine of separation of powers by directing that it takes effect only after a final determination is made regarding the enforceability of the provisions of earlier redistricting plan under the Voting Rights Act. Because Act 444 does not impermissibly encroach on the power of the executive branch to control litigation, but instead is a proper assertion of legislative power to determine reapportionment, we conclude that it does not violate separation of powers.

The core legislative function is the establishment of public policy through the enactment of laws. Thus, the expressed intent of the legislative body to prefer one reapportionment scheme over another is plainly proper and within the sphere of legislative power. Nothing prevents the legislature from expressing this intent through a fallback or contingency provision.

On the other hand, the executive branch generally has the power and authority to control litigation as part of its power to execute the laws, and a law that removes from the executive branch sufficient control of litigation may well violate separation of powers. However, the executive branch does not have the authority to decline to execute a law under the guise of executing the laws. What the executive branch cannot do directly, it cannot do indirectly. Thus, even though the executive branch generally has the power and authority to control litigation, it cannot exercise this power in order to prevent the execution of a law.

Balancing these principles in light of this case, we conclude that the legislature may require an appeal to the U.S. Supreme Court so that the legislature's preferred reapportionment scheme be implemented. The intrusion by the legislature into the executive branch function of control of litigation is justified by the limited nature of the encroachment—pursuit of one case—and by the subject matter of the litigation—legislative reapportionment.

The Constitution mandates that the Attorney General perform "such other duties as shall be required by law." Act 444 suspends the operation of the new redistricting provisions "pending a final determination of their enforceability under the federal Voting Rights Act of 1965," which requires federal court resolution. Accordingly, when the Attorney General declined to dismiss the appeal, he was fulfilling a duty required by Act 444. Because the Attorney General was acting consistently with his constitutional and statutory duties, we conclude that the Governor does not have a clear legal right to compel the Attorney General to dismiss the appeal or case from the courts. Therefore, the Governor is not entitled to the writ of mandamus.

NOTE

Because many state governments are organized differently from the federal government (*e.g.*, no unitary Executive Branch), it is not uncommon to see disputes over "who" actually represents the interests of "the State" in litigation. Two recent U.S. Supreme Court decisions, both based on federal law, illustrate the challenge.

In *Cameron v. EMW Women's Surgical Ctr.*, 142 S. Ct. 1002 (2022), Kentucky enacted a restrictive abortion law regulating the procedure commonly known as "dilation and evacuation." When the law was challenged in federal court, the Kentucky Attorney General represented the Secretary for Health and Family Services. The litigation proceeded but, after a loss in the U.S. Court of Appeals for the Sixth Circuit, the Secretary indicated he no longer wanted to pursue the litigation.

The Kentucky Attorney General asked to intervene in the case to seek rehearing en banc and to file a possible petition for a writ of certiorari in the U.S. Supreme Court. The Sixth Circuit denied the Kentucky AG's attempt to intervene, but the U.S. Supreme Court reversed. The Court pointed out that the Kentucky AG moved to intervene as soon as he learned the Secretary no longer wanted to defend the suit, that important state sovereign interests were at stake, and that there was no realistic prejudice to the plaintiffs.

In *Berger v. North Carolina State Conference of the NAACP*, 142 S.Ct. 2191 (2022), the North Carolina Legislature enacted a voter identification law that was challenged in federal court. The Secretary of State, the official charged with running elections in North Carolina and represented by the Attorney General of North Carolina, defended the lawsuit and obtained initial favorable judicial rulings. But the Speaker of the House of Representatives and the President of the Senate sought to intervene, arguing that the Attorney General and Secretary did not share their political views or interests in the litigation, and thus might not defend the law with the same vigor their own lawyers would.

In an 8-1 decision, the U.S. Supreme Court held that the legislative leaders were entitled to intervene in the lawsuit as a matter of federal law under the Federal Rules of Civil Procedure.

These sorts of cases raise questions about "who" represents the interests of "the State" in litigation over state laws. And who will be given a voice in the court systems to express views and advocate positions? Many state court cases address the same problem under state law.

STATE v. STEPHENS
2021 WL 5917198 (Tex. Crim. App. 2021)

McCLURE, J.

Zena Collins Stephens appeals both the court of appeals' denial of a pretrial writ of habeas corpus and its reversal of the district court's decision to quash Count I of the indictment. She presents the following question: May the Texas Legislature delegate to the Attorney General, a member of the executive department, the prosecution of election-law violations in district and inferior courts? No. Because Texas Election Code section 273.021 delegates to the Attorney General a power more properly assigned to the judicial department, we conclude that the statute is unconstitutional.

Zena Collins Stephens was elected to the position of sheriff of Jefferson County in 2016. While investigating someone else, the FBI uncovered information regarding potential campaign-finance violations concerning Stephens. The FBI then turned this information over to the Texas Rangers. The Rangers' investigation concluded that Stephens received individual cash campaign contributions in excess of $100. The Rangers presented their findings to the Jefferson County District Attorney, who declined to prosecute, referring the Rangers to the Attorney General. The Rangers presented the results of their investigation to the Attorney General, who presented the case to the grand jury in Chambers County, a county adjoining Jefferson County. The Attorney General relied on Texas Election Code section 273.021 to prosecute a criminal offense "prescribed by the election laws of this state."

In *Saldano v. State*, 70 S.W.3d 873 (Tex. Crim. App. 2002), this Court reviewed the history of the powers of the Attorney General and noted that "the office of the Attorney General of Texas has never had authority to institute a criminal prosecution. Before 1876 it had constitutional authority to represent the State in appeals of criminal cases, and it had statutory authority to do so until 1923." The 1876 Texas Constitution completely eliminated the specific constitutional authority of the Attorney General to represent the State in appeals of criminal cases in a deliberate response to the "despotic control of the reconstruction governor." Since then, it has had no authority to represent the State in a criminal case in any court, except when a county or district attorney requests it to assist.

The Constitution of 1876, which our state still operates under, expressly divides the powers of government into three distinct departments—legislative, executive, and judicial—and prohibits the exercise of any power "properly attached to either of the others," unless that power is grounded in a constitutional provision. Tex. Const. art. II, § 1. "This separation of powers provision reflects a belief on the part of those who drafted and adopted our state constitution that one of the greatest threats to liberty is the accumulation of excessive power in a single branch of government." *Armadillo Bail Bonds v. State*, 802 S.W.2d 237, 239 (Tex. Crim. App. 1990). It has the incidental effect of "promoting effective government by assigning functions to the branches that are best suited to discharge them."

The Texas Constitution contains this explicit separation of powers provision unlike the federal Constitution which contains no express separation of powers provision. Instead, separation of powers is implied through the federal constitution's structure, dividing government into three branches, and through vesting into each branch its particular power, legislative, executive, or judicial. We have previously held that this textual difference between the United States and Texas constitutions suggests that Texas would "more aggressively enforce separation of powers between its governmental branches than would the federal government."

The Texas Constitution provides that the office of the Attorney General is in the executive branch. The constitutional duties of the office are as follows:

> The Attorney General shall represent the State in all suits and pleas in the Supreme Court of the State in which the State may be a party, and shall especially inquire into the charter rights of all private corporations, and from time to time, in the name of the State, take such action in the courts as may be proper and necessary to prevent any private corporation from exercising any power or demanding or collecting any species of taxes, tolls, freight or wharfage not authorized by law. He shall, whenever sufficient cause exists, seek a judicial forfeiture of such charters, unless otherwise expressly directed by law, and give legal advice in writing to the Governor and other executive officers, when requested by them, and perform such other duties as may be required by law.

Tex. Const. art. IV, § 22.

The offices of county and district attorney, on the other hand, are in the judicial branch of government. Tex. Const. art. V, § 21. The constitutional duties of the county and district attorneys are as follows:

> The County Attorneys shall represent the State in all cases in the District and inferior courts in their respective counties; but if any county shall be included in a district in which there shall be a District Attorney, the respective duties of District Attorneys and County Attorneys shall in such counties be regulated by the Legislature."

Tex. Const. art. V, § 21.

Although the duties of the county and district attorney are not enumerated in article V, section 21, our courts have long recognized that, along with various civil duties, their primary function is "to prosecute the pleas of the state in criminal cases." *Meshell v. State*, 739 S.W.2d 246, 254 (Tex. Crim. App. 1987); *see also Saldano*, 70 S.W.3d at 877 (holding that the express provision conferring on the county and district attorneys the authority to represent the State in "the District and inferior courts," Tex. Const. art. V, § 21, mandates a vertical separation of powers between the Attorney General and the district attorneys in matters of criminal prosecution).

Relying on this history, Stephens claims that the Attorney General's authority to prosecute an election law offense under Texas Election Code section 273.021 is unconstitutional because the Texas Constitution prohibits the legislature from granting independent criminal prosecution power to the Attorney General in district and inferior courts.

The Attorney General argues that the Texas Constitution provides legislative authority to empower the Attorney General with "other duties" and that the Legislature, by enacting Election Code section 273.021, has conferred upon the Attorney General the authority to prosecute this case.

Section 273.021 of the Texas Election Code was enacted in 1985 and is titled "Prosecution by Attorney General Authorized." The statute, in its entirety is as follows:

> (a) The attorney general may prosecute a criminal offense prescribed by the election laws of this state.
>
> (b) The attorney general may appear before a grand jury in connection with an offense the attorney general is authorized to prosecute under Subsection (a).
>
> (c) The authority to prosecute prescribed by this subchapter does not affect the authority derived from other law to prosecute the same offenses.

Tex. Elec. Code § 273.021.

The court below, in agreement with the Attorney General, concluded that, by enacting section 273.021, the Legislature properly authorized the Attorney General, a member of the executive department, to represent the State in district and inferior courts to prosecute election-law violations. Against this, Stephens argues that the lower court broadened the Attorney General's power in a manner violative of the separation of powers requirement in the Texas Constitution. We agree with Stephens.

As applied to this case, the Texas Constitution contains no provision that expressly permits the Attorney General to prosecute election law violations in district courts. However, the court of appeals interprets the constitutional clause "perform such other duties as may be required by law," Tex. Const. art. IV, § 22, to provide the requisite express permission for statewide prosecutorial power.

The enumerated duties of the Attorney General, as specified by the Constitution, are limited to inquiring into charter rights of private corporations, suing in state court to prevent private corporations from exercising powers not authorized by law, seeking judicial forfeiture of charters, and providing legal advice to the governor and other executive officers. Notably absent from these enumerations is a specific grant of authority to the Attorney General concerning the prosecution of criminal proceedings. Undeterred by this omission, the court of appeals applied an expansive interpretation of the *ejusdem generis* doctrine, holding that, because the Attorney General may act on behalf of the State against corporations, and because corporations, like elections and elected officials, are wholly creatures of state actions, it follows that the Attorney General has authority to prosecute election law violations.

This is a misapplication of the *ejusdem generis* doctrine. The court of appeals disregarded the doctrine's fundamental point: that "the principle of ejusdem generis warns against the *expansive interpretation* of broad language that immediately follows narrow and specific terms, and counsels us to construe the broad in light of the *narrow.*" *Marks v. St. Luke's Episcopal Hosp.*, 319 S.W.3d 658, 663 (Tex. 2010); *see also* Antonin Scalia & Bryan A. Garner, *Reading Law: The Interpretation of Legal Texts* (2012) ("Where general words follow an enumeration of two or more things, they apply only to persons or things of the same general kind or class specifically mentioned."). Representing the state in a criminal prosecution for election law violations is not of the same character as representing the state in suits to prevent corporations from exercising authority not authorized by law.

To elucidate the absurd results that such an interpretation of "other duties" would render, Stephens notes that the Constitution also permits the Legislature:

- to assign the secretary of state and the Texas Water Development Board "other duties," Tex. Const. art. III § 49-c & *id.* art. IV § 21;
- to assign notaries public "such duties as may be prescribed by law," *id.* art. IV § 26; and,
- to assign duties to county clerks and sheriffs, *id.* art. V, §§ 20 & 23.

If we were to adopt the reasoning of the court below, then the Legislature could grant the Water Development Board with prosecutorial authority. Perhaps this example is extreme, but it certainly emphasizes how relying on "other duties" would render meaningless the separation of powers. Since the "other duties" clause says nothing about the governmental branch from which those duties may derive, this silence must be interpreted to mean that the Attorney General's "other duties" must be executive branch duties.

The Attorney General relies on the Texas Supreme Court's opinion in *Brady v. Brooks*, 89 S.W. 1052 (1905), to support his argument that the constitutional grant of authority to district and county attorneys does not prevent the legislature from empowering the Attorney General to represent the State in district court. In *Brady,* the Attorney General, under the authority of two separate legislative acts brought suit in district court to recover taxes, penalties, and forfeitures from a railroad company and an oil and fuel company. The county and district attorneys filed motions to be permitted to bring the suits without the participation of the Attorney General. The Supreme Court of Texas ultimately refused the county and district attorneys' writs. It held that that article V, section 21 of the Texas Constitution does not preclude the Legislature, pursuant to the authority of the attorney general to "perform such other duties as may be required by law," from empowering the attorney general to represent the State in district court.

We find *Brady* distinguishable from the facts of the instant case for three reasons. First, *Brady* involved a civil matter, namely, suits to recover tax money. That dispute was of the same class and character as the cases that fall within the express constitutional authority of the attorney general to sue corporations. The present case involves the criminal prosecution of an individual.

Second, *Brady* appears to misstate the standard of review as to when one branch of government may exercise powers of another branch. In *Brady*, the Texas Supreme Court held that the "other duties" clause does not encompass every duty, no matter where it lies in the Texas Constitution, but instead, opined that the line is crossed if the Legislature "took away from the county attorneys as much of their duties as to practically destroy their office." This is an incorrect standard to apply when analyzing a separation of powers violation. The standard for whether this is a violation of the separation of powers is not whether a legislative grant of authority to the attorney general would "destroy" the county or district attorney's office. Instead, the Constitution provides that an official of one branch of government may only exercise functions of another branch if "expressly permitted" by the Constitution itself. The explicit separation of powers provision does not say that another branch can abridge a duty from another branch so long as he does not "destroy" that branch.

Third, the *Brady* Court erroneously held that the "other duties" clause somehow authorizes the Legislature to extend the constitutionally granted duties of the judicial branch to the AG in the executive branch. As discussed above, article V, section 21 of the Texas Constitution provides that county and district attorneys are judicial officers who "shall" represent the state in "all cases" in the district courts. Likewise, article IV, section 22 of the Texas Constitution provides that the attorney general is an executive officer with certain enumerated duties and to whom the legislature may assign "other duties." However, the "other duties" clause does not permit the Legislature to assign to the attorney general any duty without regard to the branch of government to which it attaches. Simply put, the "other duties" clause may not transform the judicial duty of prosecutorial power into an executive duty. Such an interpretation would exempt the attorney general from the explicit separation-of-powers limitation.

We hold that the grant of prosecutorial authority in section 273.021 of the Texas Election Code violates article II, section 1 of the Texas Constitution, the Separation of Powers Clause.

YEARY, J., dissenting.

The separation of powers provision of the Texas Constitution has remained essentially unchanged since 1845. The major change that occurred within the 1845 version was its "recognition that the doctrine of separation, however rigid in principle, was subject to exceptions expressly provided in the constitution." George D. Braden, et al., 1 The Constitution of the State of Texas: An Annotated and Comparative Analysis, at 89 (1977). Article II, Section 1 of the Texas Constitution divides the government of the state into "three distinct departments": the "Legislative," the "Executive," and the "Judicial." Tex. Const. art. II, § 1. It then explicitly declares that "no person, or collection of persons, being of one of these departments, shall exercise any power properly attached to either of the others, *except in the instances herein expressly permitted.*" Id.

The Texas Constitution establishes the offices of County and District Attorneys under the "Judicial" department of government, and it provides that those officers "shall represent the State in all cases in the District and inferior courts in their respective counties." Tex. Const. art. V, § 21. The Attorney General is a "person" established within the "Executive" department. Notwithstanding this arrangement, Section 273.021(a) of the Election Code, which was first enacted in 1985, expressly provides that "the Attorney General may prosecute a criminal offense prescribed by the election laws of this state." Subsection (b) of this provision likewise authorizes the AG to appear before a grand jury in connection with prosecuting such offenses, and Subsection (c) provides that the AG's authority in these regards is not exclusive; that is to say, it "does not affect the authority derived from other law to prosecute the same offenses."

The question in this case, then, is whether the Constitution has elsewhere "expressly permitted" the AG to "exercise" a power more "properly attached" to local prosecuting authorities. Absent some "express" language in the Texas Constitution—beyond Article II, Section 1—that "permits" the Legislature to authorize the AG to exercise a power otherwise assigned to officers established within the Judicial department, it would seem that Section 273.021 of the Election Code might violate separation of powers.

But there *is* such express language. It appears in the very provision that pertains to the office of the AG, Article IV, Section 22 of the Texas Constitution. Among the "duties" specifically set out in this provision is a catch-all: "and perform such other duties as may be required by law."

It was long ago held, in *Brady v. Brooks*, that this catch-all provision authorizes the "Legislative" department to pass statutes authorizing even *exclusive* authority in the AG to initiate civil lawsuits on behalf of the State in certain kinds of cases, notwithstanding what would otherwise constitute an unconstitutional encroachment upon a "power" otherwise residing in the "Judicial" department. When I examine these cases, they persuade me that Section 273.021(a) does not violate the principle of separation of powers embodied in Article II, Section 1, of our state constitution.

DUNLEAVY v. THE ALASKA LEGISLATIVE COUNCIL
498 P.3d 608 (Alaska 2021)

MAASSEN, J.

Under the Alaska Constitution, many executive positions subject to appointment by the governor—including agency heads and members of boards and commissions—require legislative confirmation. This case concerns the effect of the Alaska Legislature's failure to exercise its confirmation power during the disruptions in regular government activity due to the COVID-19 pandemic. The legislature relies on a preexisting statute and a 2020 modification of it to assert that its failure to act is the same as a denial of confirmation for all those appointees, with the consequence that they could not continue to serve as recess appointments. The governor argues that his appointees remain in office and continue to serve until the legislature votes on their confirmation, one way or the other, in joint session. The superior court granted summary judgment to the legislature, and the governor appealed.

In April 2021 we considered the appeal on an expedited basis and reversed the superior court's judgment in a brief order. We concluded that the laws defining legislative inaction as tantamount to rejection violate article III, sections 25 and 26 of the Alaska Constitution, which require that the legislature consider a governor's appointees in joint session. This opinion explains our reasoning.

The Alaska Constitution directs that "all executive and administrative offices, departments, and agencies of the state government and their respective functions, powers, and duties shall be allocated by law among and within not more than twenty principal departments, so as to group them as far as practicable according to major purposes." Each of these "principal departments" is headed by either "a single executive" or "a board or commission." The appointment process is the same in each case. Under article III, section 25, an individual named to head a principal department as "a single executive" "shall be appointed by the governor, subject to confirmation by a majority of the members of the legislature in joint session." And under article III, section 26, "when a board or commission is the head of a principal department or a regulatory or quasi-judicial agency, its members shall be appointed by the governor, subject to confirmation by a majority of the members of the legislature in joint session."

The legislature has further defined by statute the process for confirming these appointees. Alaska Statute 39.05.080(3) provides, among other things, that a "person whose name is refused for appointment by the legislature" may not hold an interim appointment while the legislature is in recess. The statute also provides that the effect of legislative inaction in the confirmation context is "tantamount to a declination of confirmation." The central legal question in this case is whether this latter provision violates article III, sections 25 and 26 of the Alaska Constitution.

In 2020, during the Second Regular Session of the Thirty-First Alaska State Legislature, Governor Mike Dunleavy presented over 90 appointees to the legislature for confirmation. Soon after, the global COVID-19 pandemic disrupted the normal functioning of government. In March 2020 the governor declared a public health emergency.

Later in the month the legislature, uncertain about when the pandemic would allow it to physically meet, passed legislation effectively extending the deadline for confirmation of the governor's appointees beyond the end of the regular session. House Bill 309 allowed the Second Session of the Thirty-First Alaska State Legislature to act on appointments "at any time." It overrode the prior statutory deadline by making the failure to act on confirmations by the end of the legislative session "*not* tantamount to a declination of confirmation" until the earlier of January 18, 2021, or 30 days after either the expiration of the governor's March public health emergency order or a proclamation that the emergency no longer existed. Senate Bill 241 extended the governor's declaration of a public health emergency to November 15, 2020. The legislature then went into extended recess, having confirmed no appointees.

The governor's public health emergency declaration expired on November 15. Under H.B. 309, the legislature's failure to act on the governor's nominations became "tantamount to a declination of confirmation" on December 15. The next day the governor asserted in letters to the senate president and the speaker of the house that his appointees would "continue to serve under valid appointments" and that he was "exercising his constitutional authority under the Alaska Constitution, article III, Section 27"—the recess appointment clause—"to continue their appointments."

In December 2020 the Legislative Council filed a complaint against the governor in superior court. The Legislative Council requested a declaration that the governor had violated statutory provisions and article III, sections 25 and 26 of the Alaska Constitution in his attempt to continue the appointments beyond the deadlines provided by law. The governor argued that the laws the Legislative Council claimed he violated themselves violated article III, sections 25 and 26, that his appointees were never lawfully rejected and, in the alternative, that he had validly exercised his recess appointment power to reappoint them.

The superior court granted the Legislative Council's motion, deciding that the disputed statutes were constitutional, the appointees had therefore been effectively rejected by the legislature, and they were ineligible for recess appointment. The governor appealed to this court. We conclude that the statutes limiting the Governor's appointment powers violate the Alaska Constitution, article III, sections 25 and 26.

The first challenged law on this appeal is the last sentence of AS 39.05.080(3), which reads: "Failure of the legislature to act to confirm or decline to confirm an appointment during the regular session in which the appointment was presented is tantamount to a declination of confirmation on the day the regular session adjourns." The second challenged law is the legislature's attempt to adapt this statutory mandate to the circumstances of the COVID-19 pandemic, providing in H.B. 309 that the legislature's failure "to confirm or decline to confirm an appointment presented by the governor during the Second Regular Session of the Thirty-First Alaska State Legislature" is not "tantamount to a declination of confirmation" until later dates as dictated by the public health emergency.

The starting point for our analysis of a constitutional question not directly controlled by precedent is the plain text of the constitutional provision, as clarified by its drafting history. Applying these rules we conclude that the Constitution's plain text, as supported by its drafting history, requires a joint session vote to either confirm or reject a governor's appointees. Alaska Statute 39.05.080(3) and H.B. 309, by defining legislative inaction to mean a denial of confirmation, nullify the requirement of a joint session vote. We therefore conclude that AS 39.05.080(3) and H.B. 309's "tantamount to a declination" provisions are unconstitutional.

The governor relies on the plain language of sections 25 and 26 for his argument that appointees continue to serve until the legislature affirmatively votes to reject their appointments. He points to the phrase "subject to confirmation by a majority of the members of the legislature in joint session" and argues that the delegates "intended that confirmation would turn on a joint session majority vote." He argues that "confirmation and declination are simply two sides of the same coin"; both are results of a process that can "necessarily only be effectuated by a vote."

We agree with the governor's analysis. Both of the Constitution's confirmation provisions, article III, sections 25 and 26, declare that appointments are "subject to confirmation *by a majority of the members of the legislature in joint session.*" The provisions' text dictates the manner in which confirmation must be done: by majority vote in joint session.

The Legislative Council argues that article III's plain language requires a joint session vote only for confirmation, not declination. But we believe this to be an oversimplification of the Constitution's text. Confirmation may be defined as the successful result of a confirmation vote—an interpretation the Legislative Council appears to advance—but it may also be defined as the process by which an appointee is determined to be either confirmed *or* rejected. Confirmation as a process is a check on a governor's appointment power. Because the Constitution describes the governor's appointment powers as "subject to" confirmation, it is clear to us that "confirmation" in this sense is the check, or the process of confirmation, rather than the result of that process. And the Constitution mandates that this process—whether it results in confirmation or rejection—be done by joint session vote.

The Legislative Council argues that the statutes merely establish procedures for rejection and therefore do not conflict with the Constitution's plain language. But although the legislature may set out its own procedure when the Constitution is silent on process, the Constitution is not silent here: the phrase "confirmation by a majority of the members of the legislature in joint session" is descriptive enough for us to consider it a mandate. As we stated in *Bradner v. Hammond*, "sections 25 and 26 of article III describe the outer limits of the legislature's confirmation authority." Allowing inaction to substitute for a joint session vote pushes beyond those "outer limits."

The Legislative Council also argues that the governor's position requires adding language to the Constitution, because under his reading appointments are "subject to confirmation *or declination*" by a majority of the members of the legislature in joint session. The Legislative Council argues that adding these words to article III, sections 25 and 26, "would require a complete restructuring of the established procedure for legislative confirmation and upset the system of checks and balances that has been in existence since before statehood." The Legislative Council is correct in that requiring joint session action to reject an appointee means that appointments continue indefinitely unless and until the legislature acts to decline them. But this is not inconsistent with our prior case law or other constitutional provisions. Nor does it require adding a term to the Constitution as long as we recognize that confirmation is the process by which an appointment may be either confirmed or rejected—the procedural check on the governor's appointment power.

In sum, because the rejection-by-inaction language of AS 39.05.080(3) and H.B. 309 conflicts with the Constitution's joint session requirement, those provisions of the laws are unconstitutional.

2. The "Line Item" Veto Power

In *Clinton v. City of New York*, 524 U.S. 417 (1998), the Supreme Court of the United States struck down an Act of Congress that had been described as giving the President a "line item" veto power, in other words giving the President power to strike or cancel individual items within a bill presented for his signature. Article I, § 7 of the U.S. Constitution provides no such power to the President explicitly, but instead declares in the Presentment Clause as follows: "Every Bill which shall have passed the House of Representatives and the Senate, shall, before it becomes a Law, be presented to the President of the United States; If he approve he shall sign it, but if not he shall return it, with his Objections." The Supreme Court held that the law purporting to give the President the power to strike particular items from a bill while permitting the remainder of the bill to become law violated the Presentment Clause.

Line-item veto powers did not appear in the early state constitutions but instead appeared much later, notably for the first time in the Confederacy's constitution during the Civil War. Well over 40 States now give their Governors such authority. The line-item veto provisions vary in their nature and scope, with most limited to appropriations measures and some applicable to any legislation. Further, the States' line-item veto measures have proven a frequent source of litigation between Governors and legislatures, which often have been granted standing by state courts to challenge gubernatorial exercises of the power.

The following cases offer three examples of state court litigation over a Governor's exercise of the line-item veto power. Carefully note the contexts in which the disputes arise and the parties.

ST. JOHN'S WELL CHILD & FAMILY CTR. v. SCHWARZENEGGER
239 P.3d 651 (Cal. 2010)

GEORGE, C.J.

We grant review to address the propriety of the Governor's use of the so-called "line-item veto" under the asserted authority of article IV, section 10, subdivision (e) of the California Constitution, to further reduce funding that already had been reduced by the Legislature in its midyear adjustments to the Budget Act of 2009.

In the context of the constitutionally prescribed budget process, the power to *appropriate* public funds belongs exclusively to the Legislature. With respect to a bill containing appropriations, the Governor has three options: (1) to sign the bill, (2) to veto the measure in its entirety, or (3) to *"reduce or eliminate one or more items of appropriation."* The question posed by this case is whether the Governor exceeded his limited powers under article IV, section 10(e), by using his line-item authority to further reduce funding levels set forth in midyear reductions that the Legislature had made to the Budget Act of 2009, thereby imposing a reduction of appropriated sums greater than the reduction made by the Legislature.

On February 20, 2009, the Governor signed into law the 2009 Budget Act, which set forth various appropriations of state funds for the 2009–2010 fiscal year. Thereafter, California's economy worsened; the revenue assumptions upon which the 2009 Budget Act was based proved to be far too optimistic, and the state's overall cash-flow positions continued to deteriorate. The Governor, pursuant to California Constitution, article IV, section 10, subdivision (f) proclaimed a fiscal crisis, and the Legislature assembled in special session to address the fiscal emergency. Following months of negotiations, the Legislature passed Assembly Bill 4X 1 on July 23, 2009.

On July 28, 2009, the Governor exercised his line-item authority to reduce or eliminate several items contained in Assembly Bill 4X 1, and then signed the measure into law. The Governor eliminated numerous separate line items contained in various sections of Assembly Bill 4X 1. The effect of these reductions was to further decrease the total amount appropriated in the 2009 Budget Act by more than $488 million. Many of the items reduced by the Governor already had been reduced by the Legislature in Assembly Bill 4X 1 from the amounts appropriated in the 2009 Budget Act.

Neither the so-called "item veto," nor the "line-item veto" allowing the Governor to eliminate or reduce items of appropriation, confers the power to selectively veto *general* legislation. The Governor has no authority to veto part of a bill that is not an "item of appropriation." "Article III, section 3 provides that one branch of government may not exercise the powers granted to another except as permitted by this Constitution. Case law, commentators, and historians have long recognized that in exercising the veto the Governor acts in a legislative capacity. It follows that in exercising the power of the veto the Governor may act only as permitted by the Constitution. That authority is to veto a bill or to reduce or eliminate one or more items of appropriation."

The dispositive issue, then, is whether the funding in question—specified in the seven sections of Assembly Bill 4X 1 that the Governor further reduced—encompassed "items of appropriation" as to which the Governor could exercise his line-item authority.

Petitioners and interveners contend that, because the items at issue in Assembly Bill 4X 1 *reduced* the amounts previously appropriated in the 2009 Budget Act, these items were not "appropriations." They maintain that a "reduction" cannot be an "appropriation," and observe that there are no instances in which a California governor previously has exercised line-item authority in this manner.

Petitioners, interveners, and their amici curiae insist that only an *increase* in spending authority can constitute an appropriation. They further argue that because the 2009 Budget Act *already* had set aside sums of money to be paid by the treasury for specific purposes, those items and sections of Assembly Bill 4X 1 that proposed only reductions to existing, previously enacted appropriations did not satisfy the requirement of money set aside for a particular purpose. The argument, in other words, is that a reduction in a set-aside cannot itself be considered a set-aside or an appropriation. We disagree.

The cases do not require, as petitioners and interveners suggest, that *solely* items that add amounts to funds already provided can constitute "items of appropriation." Whether spending authority is increased or decreased, it still fundamentally remains spending authority. Although described as reductions in specified items and sections, each of the provisions at issue in Assembly Bill 4X 1 nevertheless directs the "specific setting aside of an amount, not exceeding a definite fixed sum, for the payment of certain particular claims or demands." The items in Assembly Bill 4X 1 that were eliminated or further reduced by the Governor's exercise of line-item authority *capped* the spending authority at an amount less than that set forth in the 2009 Budget Act.

There is no substantive difference between a Governor's reduction of an item of appropriation in the original 2009 Budget Act, to which interveners and petitioners raise no objection, and a Governor's reduction of that same item in a subsequent amendment to the 2009 Budget Act—that is, Assembly Bill 4X 1. Both actions involve changes in authorized spending.

Interveners insist in their reply brief that the Governor was entitled, in essence, to only one bite at the budget apple. They concede that although he "had the authority to reduce or eliminate each of the items of appropriation at issue here when they were first passed in February, 2009," he nevertheless did not possess that same authority a few months later with regard to "the legislative reductions made in July." We discern no reason why the Governor should have the power to reduce items of appropriation when first enacted, and yet not retain that same power when the Legislature, in response to changed circumstances, sees fit to amend those same appropriations.

The determination whether the items in Assembly Bill 4X 1 at issue constitute appropriations cannot be made by characterizing the Governor's use of line-item authority as "increasing" the Legislature's reductions and then categorizing that act as impermissibly affirmative or "creative." Treating the exercise of line-item authority as an *increase in the reduction*, rather than as a *decrease in the appropriation* is as arbitrary as differentiating between the description of a glass of water as half full and a description of the same vessel as half empty.

Interveners' separation-of-powers argument thus begs the question. True, the Governor's challenged acts were legislative in nature and, "as an executive officer, the Governor is forbidden to exercise any legislative power or function *except as the Constitution expressly provides*." Thus, the question before us is not whether the gubernatorial act at issue was legislative in nature, but whether it was constitutionally authorized. As we earlier explained, the act undertaken by the Governor was authorized by the opening sentence of article IV, section 10(e) of our Constitution.

JACKSON v. SANFORD
731 S.E.2d 722 (S.C. 2011)

KITTREDGE, J.

The annual appropriations bill for fiscal year 2010–2011 allocated $248,882,042 to the State Budget and Control Board, $25,234,009 of which was to be drawn from the General Fund. Some of the Board's expenditures were to be financed entirely from the General Fund, while other expenditures were financed using other sources or a combination of sources. The bill set aside the amounts to be drawn from the General Fund in a separate column. In another column, the bill listed the total appropriation for each expenditure, reflecting both General Funds and funds from other sources. The bill did not include separate columns delineating the amounts to be drawn from each of the other sources.

In his Veto 52, Governor Sanford purported to veto the entire amount of General Funds appropriated to the Board. In his accompanying veto message, Governor Sanford stated the Board had "over $1 billion in carry-forward funds" and could use "available funds and cost-cutting measures" to "sustain the agency over the next fiscal year."

Article IV, section 21 of the South Carolina Constitution provides in relevant part:

> Every bill or joint resolution which shall have passed the General Assembly shall, before it becomes a law, be presented to the Governor, and if he approves he shall sign it; if not, he shall return it, with his objections, to the house in which it originated, which shall enter the objections at large on its Journal and proceed to reconsider it.
>
> Bills appropriating money out of the Treasury shall specify the objects and purposes for which the same are made, and appropriate to them respectively their several amounts in distinct items and sections. If the Governor shall not approve any one or more of the items or sections contained in any bill appropriating money, but shall approve of the residue thereof, it shall become a law as to the residue in like manner as if he had signed it. The Governor shall then return the bill with his objections to the items or sections of the same not approved by him to the house in which the bill originated, which house shall enter the objections at large upon its Journal and proceed to reconsider so much of the bill as is not approved by the Governor.

The veto power is "a negative power to void a distinct item." In *Drummond v. Beasley* (S.C. 1998), we explained that the Governor may not "modify legislation rather than nullify legislation" by removing conditions and restrictions on expenditures while leaving the expenditures themselves intact.

The dispositive question before the Court may be framed in one of two ways, either of which compels a finding of an unconstitutional veto. First, a Governor is constitutionally permitted to veto an item in its entirety, but not partially. Stated differently, we must determine whether Veto 52 was a nullification of legislation or a modification of legislation. Putting these concepts together, the rule of law is that a veto of an item in its entirety is a nullification, while a veto of only part of an item is a modification. If a nullification, Veto 52 is constitutional; if a modification, Veto 52 is unconstitutional.

We begin with defining an "item" for constitutional purposes. Our constitution uses the term "item" to embrace a specified sum of money together with the "object and purpose" for which the appropriation is made.

We disagree with Governor Sanford that the column designating the amount of General Funds to be expended was a standalone "item" that could be vetoed without vetoing the objects and purposes to which those General Funds were devoted. The Governor vetoed one source of appropriated funds while leaving the remainder of the total appropriation, and the specified "objects and purposes" of the appropriation, intact.

The Governor attempted to veto funds arising from a particular source, but he did not veto the purpose to which those funds were allocated. The net result, then, was that the total appropriation for each of the Board's programs, positions, and expenses was reduced by the amount the General Assembly had designated to be drawn from the General Fund, but the programs, positions, and expenses themselves were not eliminated. This was an improper modification of legislation.

The Governor seeks refuge in the contention that Veto 52 is consistent with the historical practice of South Carolina Governors. Because other Governors have exercised their veto authority in a similar manner, the argument goes, the Court should defer to the historical practice. The Governor's position has ostensible merit, for "long established practice has great weight in interpreting constitutional provisions relative to executive veto power." However, we are not persuaded that the practice of vetoing only one of several sources of funds without vetoing the corresponding objects and purposes is as well rooted in our history as the Governor suggests. Thus, we are not convinced that the interpretation advanced by the Governor is as "long established" as he contends.

We find the Governor's veto of only the General Fund portion of the appropriation to the Budget and Control Board was unconstitutional because it exceeded the authority granted to him by article IV, section 21 of the South Carolina Constitution. The Governor is empowered to veto "items," which comprise both the designated funds and the objects and purposes for which the appropriation is intended. By vetoing only one of several sources of funds, the Governor vetoed only part of an item, rendering the veto unconstitutional. Having declared Veto 52 unconstitutional, we hold the General Assembly's appropriation of General Funds to the Budget and Control Board is effective and has the force of law.

HOMAN v. BRANSTAD
812 N.W.2d 623 (Iowa 2012)

WATERMAN, J.

This appeal requires our court to resolve another dispute between the executive and legislative branches of our state government over the scope of the Governor's item veto power. On July 27, 2011, Governor Terry E. Branstad item vetoed several provisions in Senate File 517, an appropriations bill passed in the final days of the Eighty-fourth General Assembly. Primarily at issue is $8.66 million the legislature appropriated in section 15(3) for the operation of Iowa Workforce Development (IWD) field offices. The Governor, without vetoing that appropriation, item vetoed section 15(3)(c), prohibiting the closure of field offices, and section 15(5), defining "field office" to require the presence of a staff person. His accompanying item-veto message noted his purpose was to provide "enhanced benefits through maximum efficiencies" by replacing staffed field offices with numerous additional "virtual access point computer workstations" for the delivery of employment services to Iowans throughout our state. The Governor also item vetoed section 20, which restricts IWD from spending any appropriated funds on the National Career Readiness Certificate Program, without item vetoing any of the several appropriations to IWD in Senate File 517. And, the Governor item vetoed similar provisions in the bill for the following fiscal year.

This is not an easy case. The legislature failed to use language in section 15(3) expressly conditioning the $8.66 million appropriation on the restrictions against closing staffed field offices. Nonetheless, we conclude the definition of "field office" in section 15(5) qualifies or restricts the $8.66 million appropriation in section 15(3)(b) "for the operation of field offices." Accordingly, the Governor could not veto section 15(5) without vetoing the accompanying appropriation in section 15(3). We further conclude the Governor impermissibly item vetoed the restriction in section 20 on use of IWD appropriations for the national certificate program.

Simply stated, the legislature appropriated funds to IWD with strings attached, and our constitution does not permit the Governor to cut the strings and spend the money differently.

The Governor's item-veto power is set forth in article III, section 16 of the Iowa Constitution, which provides in pertinent part:

> *The governor may approve appropriation bills in whole or in part, and may disapprove any item of an appropriation bill;* and the part approved shall become a law. Any rejected item of an appropriation bill may be enacted into law notwithstanding the governor's objections, in the same manner as provided for other bills.

"The purpose of the item veto provision of our constitution is to give the governor a larger role in the state budgetary process." In *Rants v. Vilsack* (Iowa 2004), we further observed "the item veto power developed to control logrolling, or the legislators' practice of combining in a single bill provisions supported by various minorities in order to create a legislative majority." "The item veto power grants the governor a limited legislative function in relation to appropriation bills." "Whatever the veto's successes in dealing with budget problems, by empowering the executive to veto a part of a bill, the item veto opens up a set of knotty legal and conceptual difficulties."

Defining the scope of an "item" subject to veto has proven difficult. By its terms, article III, section 16 permits the Governor to "disapprove any item of an appropriation bill." In *Welden v. Ray* (Iowa 1975), however, we held "that if the Governor desires to veto a legislatively-imposed qualification upon an appropriation, he must veto the accompanying appropriation as well." We have used the terms "proviso," "restriction," "qualification," "limitation," and "condition" interchangeably to "denote a provision in a bill that limits the use to which an appropriation may be put." The point is this: when the legislature makes a specific appropriation for a specific purpose, the Governor can veto the appropriation as an item, but cannot veto the purpose and use the appropriation for a different purpose.

Section 15(5) defines "field office" as requiring the physical presence of an employee at each field office. This definition applies throughout section 15 and, thus, controls the meaning of "field office" in section 15(3)(b), which appropriates $8.66 million "for the operation of field offices." The legislature textually linked section 15(5) to the appropriation in section 15(3). Reading the provisions together, as the legislature directed, makes clear that each "field office" funded in section 15(3)(b) is to be staffed with an IWD employee. That is, a location with a computer workstation but no employee physically present is not a "field office" within the meaning of the appropriation provision.

To allow the Governor to veto the definition in section 15(5) without vetoing the accompanying appropriation in section 15(3)(b) would impermissibly "distort legislative intent" or "divert money appropriated by the legislature for one purpose so that it may be used for another." Specifically, the Governor would be disregarding the express legislative direction requiring staffed field offices and diverting the money appropriated for a different purpose—unmanned computer kiosks. We conclude section 15(5) is impervious to an item veto without a veto of section 15(3).

We now turn to Governor Branstad's item veto of section 20, which states: "The department of workforce development shall not use any of the moneys appropriated in this division of this Act for purposes of the national career readiness certificate program."

We have cautioned the legislature cannot tie unrelated provisions in a bill together to frustrate the Governor's item-veto power. But the fact IWD received appropriations through four different provisions of Senate File 517, specifically sections 15, 17, 18, and 19, does not make the express restriction on use of the money in section 20 overly broad or a rider subject to item veto. A "rider" is "an unrelated substantive piece of legislation incorporated in the appropriation bill." Section 20 is not "unrelated" to the IWD appropriations. To the contrary, section 20 explicitly restricts the use of IWD's appropriations, and that is all it does.

"Inherent in the power to appropriate is the power to specify how the money shall be spent." We have held provisions restricting executive branch agencies from spending appropriated money for nonspecified purposes are conditions not subject to independent veto. Section 20 precludes IWD from spending any of its appropriations on the national certificate program. Without this restriction, IWD could transfer funds appropriated for another purpose to the program.

We hold the Governor's item veto of section 20 was unconstitutional.

We now turn to the remedy required by our holdings that the Governor's item vetoes of section 15(5) and section 20 were unconstitutional. The district court granted the remedy sought by plaintiffs in their petition and declared that "Senate File 517 became law as if the Governor had not exercised the item vetoes which were herein determined to be void." Governor Branstad argues on appeal the proper remedy for an invalid veto of a condition on an appropriation is to invalidate the entire item containing the appropriation. The Governor is correct on this point.

Our constitution provides the Governor "may approve appropriation bills in whole or in part, and may disapprove any item of an appropriation bill; and the part approved shall become law." Because the Governor may approve or disapprove any *item* in an appropriation bill, an ineffective item veto is not fatal to the entire bill, but only to the affected items.

We hold that, when the Governor impermissibly item vetoes a condition on an appropriation during the pocket veto period, the appropriation item fails to become law. This result is mandated by our constitutional requirement that enactments do not become law without the approval of both elected branches except when a legislative supermajority overrides a veto. Here, the Governor did not approve the IWD appropriations with the conditions. Yet, the legislature did not pass the appropriations without the conditions. Thus, the IWD appropriations without the conditions could not become law because the approval of both elected branches was lacking.

NOTES

1. Is the question whether the Governor has properly exercised a line-item veto a "legal" rather than "political" question? Can you articulate the arguments for and against the courts' involvement?

2. Who should have "standing" to challenge a Governor's line-item veto? The Legislature? Individual legislators? Citizens or entities actually affected by the veto, such as those who would have received state funds but for the Governor's veto?

3. How difficult is it to define what constitutes an "appropriation" for line-item veto purposes? What if the Governor vetoes a particular tax deduction or exemption provisions in a major tax system overhaul bill? Or vetoes a provision eliminating mandatory retirement for judges at age 70 (on the ground that the provision will permit judges to serve longer and accrue larger retirement benefits that the State will be obligated to pay)? Or vetoes a provision requiring local sheriffs' departments to conduct background checks on all firearms purchases in their counties (on the ground that such a requirement will require more state funding for sheriffs)?

4. For additional commentary on this topic, see Winston David Holliday, Jr., *Tipping the Balance of Power: A Critical Survey of the Gubernatorial Line Item Veto*, 50 S.C. L. Rev. 503 (1999) (discussing South Carolina's experience and comparing it with Iowa, Wisconsin, and Virginia); Richard Briffault, *The Item Veto in State Courts*, 66 Temple L. Rev. 1171 (1993).

D. JUDICIAL POWER

This section considers three important differences between the federal and state judicial branches: (1) the selection of judges (most state court judges are elected or appointed using "merit" nominating commission); (2) state constitutional "justiciability" principles which may vary significantly from federal Article III rules; (3) the authority of federal judges to certify questions of state law to the state supreme courts; and (4) state limitations on judicial tenure or service.

1. The Selection of Judges

One of the key distinctions between the federal and state judiciaries is their manner of selection and tenure of service. Under the United States Constitution, the President nominates federal judges, and the Senate confirms them. Once confirmed, federal judges serve for life or, as Article III puts it, during "good behavior." As the excerpt from the following article shows, that is a far cry from the way most States choose their judges.

Judith L. Maute, *Selecting Justice in State Courts: The Ballot Box or the Backroom?*
41 S. Tex. L. Rev. 1197 (2000)

Currently, there are four basic systems of judicial selection in the United States. Judges are chosen through either partisan or nonpartisan elections in twenty-one states; eleven additional states use elections for some judgeships, usually the lower courts. What has become known as merit selection is the sole selection method in fourteen states. Seven jurisdictions use a combination of merit and election methods with the remaining states using a combination of merit and appointive systems. At present, twenty-two states use merit selection for at least their highest appeals courts. This figure can be misleading. Approximately eighty-seven percent of all state court judges are selected or retained on the basis of popular elections, although about eighty percent of all judicial offices are initially filled by appointment to complete unexpired terms.

A. Appointment

The oldest method of judicial selection in the United States is appointment. In the original thirteen states, to avoid giving exclusive power to one individual, the legislature, or the governor with legislative approval, appointed judges. Today, most states use various combinations of the appointive system. California judges, except for superior court judges, are appointed by the governor, and must then be approved by a commission on judicial appointments. New Hampshire uses an elected executive council to approve appointments by the governor. In New York, only court of appeals judges are appointed by the governor with the consent of the senate, while the remaining judges are chosen in partisan elections. Most states fill interim vacancies by gubernatorial appointment.

B. Partisan Elections

Partisan election of judges began after Andrew Jackson's populist presidency. Some authorities believe the move to elections was a response to widespread dissatisfaction with the perceived elitism of judges. Proponents maintain that judicial elections assure accountability to the people and are the only reliable method for removing judges whose decisions are unacceptable to the populace. Voters may have little information on the individual judicial candidates. Partisan elections can cue voters on a candidate's ideology through the identification of political affiliation. The political party of the judicial candidate can be used for screening purposes. "Although it has been proven otherwise in some cases, it was thought that with the party footing the bill for and controlling recruitment, special interests would be kept at arm's length from the process."

Some voters favor judicial elections because it gives them a choice between parties and a voice in the system. There is a greater electoral turnout when voters have more information on which to make a decision, such as political party cues. One unfortunate method of increasing voter participation is the heightened negativity of judicial campaigns. Wisconsin Supreme Court Justice Shirley Abrahamson faced blistering campaign attacks by opponent Sharren Rose in the 1999 race. Critics of partisan judicial elections claim that increased costs of campaigning and problematic funding sources create an image of justice going to the highest bidder. Special interest groups try to help elect judges favorable to their cause by pouring money into those judges' campaign coffers. Six candidates spent almost six million dollars in 1990 Texas judicial campaigns. Abrahamson and Rose spent over one million dollars on their campaigns.

Another cost of judicial elections is time spent campaigning for office instead of fulfilling the judge's duties. Successful lawyers may be reluctant to run for office, investing their reputation, time, money and effort seeking a job that is neither guaranteed nor highly paid. Additionally, having to answer to political parties and vocal contributors can deter qualified individuals from running for a judicial position.

It is debatable whether partisan elections in fact make judges accountable to the public. Most judges are initially appointed to fulfill vacant positions by the state governor, and run unopposed in the next periodic election. This scenario effectively removes the voter from the equation. Even when there is opposition in a judicial race, voter turnout is typically low. Unless the judicial election takes place during the general election and has become a hotly contested race, most voters either do not vote for the judicial offices or vote with little information, evidenced by the fact that they cannot remember who they voted for immediately afterwards.

C. *Nonpartisan Elections*

Thirteen states use nonpartisan elections for judicial offices, and seven additional states use it only for selected judicial offices. Ohio is unique in that it nominates judicial candidates in partisan primaries and then places them on a nonpartisan ballot for the general election. Supporters claim that nonpartisan elections remove the problem of politics entailed by partisan elections while keeping accountability to the voters. Adopted in response to the problem of judges controlled by party politics, nonpartisan elections were intended to involve voters in the process and exclude politics and special interests.

"Most commentators contend that, far from being an improvement upon partisan elections, nonpartisan elections are an inferior alternative to partisan elections because they possess all of the vices of partisan elections and none of the virtues." Voters lose their main cue for information on who to vote for and, lacking more relevant information on individual candidates, rely on other factors such as ballot position or name recognition. Candidates who served in prior political offices as prosecutor, legislator or county commissioner, have greater name recognition which helps them in later campaigns for judicial office. Voter apathy may be greater in nonpartisan elections, with lower turn-outs and voter roll-off (not voting in certain races), so that the judicial incumbents usually win. To counter this information problem, some jurisdictions print and distribute voter pamphlets, which greatly increases the election costs. Nonpartisan elections are becoming increasingly expensive and involve many of the same problems with campaign contributions as partisan elections. The most obvious example is the highly politicized, nasty and expensive battle between Ohio Supreme Court incumbent Justice Alice Robie Resnick, a Democrat, and her Republican challenger District Court of Appeals Judge Terrence O'Donnell. Business and insurance groups, with generous backing from the Chamber of Commerce, targeted Resnick for defeat because of her votes in two controversial cases. While ultimately unsuccessful, the bruising fight has prompted state leaders to reconsider selection methods.

D. Merit Selection

Albert Kales, a Northwestern University law professor, first called for merit selection of judges in 1914 when the American Judicature Society was founded.

> Kales' plan called for (1) the nomination of judicial candidates based solely on merit by a commission of presiding judges, (2) the selection of judges from this list of nominees by an elected chief justice, and (3) retention elections conducted on a noncompetitive basis. In 1926, British political scientist Harold Laski suggested that the Kales plan be modified in certain respects. Laski recommended that the Governor rather than the chief justice appoint judges and that the advisory committee consist of a judge or judges from the state supreme court, the attorney general, and the president of the state bar association.

California was the first state to adopt a type of merit plan for its supreme court and intermediate courts; it is still in use today. The governor makes nominations to fill vacant positions which must be approved by a commission including the chief justice, a present justice of the court of appeals and the attorney general. After confirmation, the judges must stand for retention at regular intervals. California is also noteworthy for having been the first state in which hotly contested retention elections resulted in the ouster of judges because of their unpopular decisions.

The most widely known merit selection plan, the "Missouri Plan," was first adopted in 1940. A judicial nominating committee makes recommendations to the governor who then chooses one of the nominees to fill a vacancy. Like many other states, Missouri now uses a "modified" merit system, in which appellate and metropolitan trial courts use a merit appointment process, but elections select the trial bench in rural areas. The judge must thereafter stand for retention at regular intervals. Missouri continues to use this system for its supreme court, courts of appeals and its trial courts in large metropolitan areas such as Kansas City and St. Louis.

Three separate nominating commissions are used in Missouri: one for the appellate courts, and one each for Jackson county and St. Louis county circuit courts. Although repeal measures have been regularly introduced, the plan has yet to be revoked. All other state judges are selected in partisan elections.

Alaska was the first state to enact a merit plan for all state judges, in 1959. Rhode Island is the latest state to change to the merit plan for its trial judges in 1994. Delaware, Hawaii, Massachusetts, and Nebraska are the only other states which use merit selection for all judicial appointments.

Judicial nomination committees are composed of lawyers and laypersons. Some jurisdictions require the nominating commission be divided between political parties. Arizona dictates that the names submitted to the governor must be balanced based on political parties. According to Sheldon and Maule, the nomination committee lessens the political pressure on the appointing authority, usually the governor, so that the most qualified persons are submitted as finalists.

Merit selection proponents maintain that it: 1) removes politics from the selection process as much as possible, especially when there are effective controls for politics in the selection of nomination committee members; 2) removes the need to campaign for office and raise contributions; 3) results in more qualified applicants and selections; 4) removes the issue of voter apathy and the problem with ethical restrictions on judicial campaign speech; 5) allows accountability to voters by using retention elections to remove bad judges; and 6) increases minority representation on the bench. They contend it is the best method to reduce the influence of politics in judicial selection.

Opponents disagree with most of these assertions. They contend merit selection is elitist and merely moves the politics outside the light of the electoral system and into the backroom, allowing for private decisionmaking by politically-appointed nomination committees. They assert that retention elections are undemocratic, misleading to voters, and allow little meaningful choice. Campaign contributions must still be addressed if a judge up for retention is targeted by a special interest group based on an unpopular decision. A courageous judge may have a difficult time defending her record against an anonymously funded soft money campaign. In contested judicial elections, at least the voters are presented with a known alternative to the incumbent, enabling them to vote in a more meaningful way.

E. *Hybrid Selection*

Eight states use some combination of merit selection, appointment, or elections to fill their judicial positions. In South Carolina, for instance, a merit commission nominates candidates, but the judge is elected by the legislature. The legislature also elects the judges in Virginia. In Maine, judges are confirmed by the Senate after being appointed by the governor. In New Hampshire, judges are appointed by the governor, then confirmed by an elected five member executive council. Floridians recently amended their constitution to provide for counties to vote on whether to "opt-in" to selecting trial court judges through the merit system.

NOTES

1. Some see the election of judges to a term of years as a threat to judicial independence. How can popularly elected judges, who often must raise considerable campaign funds to win elections, maintain the independence of mind to rule fairly on the issues that come before them? And even when that is not a problem, how can majoritarian-elected judges be entrusted to enforce the counter-majoritarian guarantees of the state constitution? *See* Sandra Day O'Connor, *The Threat to Judicial Independence*, The Wall Street Journal, Sept. 27, 2006, at A18; Sandra Day O'Connor, *Judicial Independence and Civics Education*, Utah Bar Journal, Sept./Oct. 2009, at 10. Others see the election of judges in Jacksonian terms—as the only way to place a check on the judiciary, particularly at a time when so many of the most important issues of the day are coming before the courts.

2. State judicial elections may implicate questions of *federal* constitutional law. For example, the free-speech guarantees of the First Amendment place some restrictions on the ability of state judicial ethics codes to restrict what candidates may say in running for judicial office. *See, e.g., Republican Party of Minn. v. White*, 536 U.S. 765 (2002) (holding that the First Amendment does not permit the Minnesota Supreme Court to prohibit candidates for judicial election from announcing their views on disputed legal and political issues). *But see Williams-Yulee v. Fla. Bar*, 575 U.S. 433 (2015) (holding that a State bar can prohibit candidates for judicial office from personally soliciting campaign funds). The due process guarantee of the Fourteenth Amendment requires judges to recuse themselves in some settings, most notably when they have directly or indirectly received considerable campaign funds from a party to a case before the judge. *See Caperton v. A.T. Massey Coal Co.*, 556 U.S. 868 (2009).

3. In recent years there has been political pushback at times regarding the Missouri Plan and judicial nominating commissions. In Kansas, a suit was brought to declare the Kansas Judicial Nominating Commission (in place since the late 1950s) unconstitutional as a matter of federal law:

> A group of Kansas voters, none of them lawyers, sued the attorney members of the Supreme Court Nominating Commission (Commission) and the Clerk of the Appellate Courts requesting a temporary restraining order and preliminary injunction to prevent any vacancies from being filled while this lawsuit is pending. The Commission is composed of five attorneys elected by attorneys and four non-attorneys appointed by the Governor. *Appellant voters claim the selection of the Commission's attorney members violates the one person, one vote principle of the Equal Protection Clause because the franchise is closed to all but attorneys.*

Dool v. Burke, 497 F. App'x 782, 783–84 (10th Cir. 2012) (emphasis added). The District Court rejected the constitutional challenge and a panel of the Tenth Circuit affirmed by a 2-1 decision, with three separate opinions.

One Tenth Circuit judge concluded as follows:

> Kansas designed the Commission to favor lawyers in order to limit the influence of politics on the nomination process and ensure the quality of its judicial nominees. Preserving the quality and independence of the judiciary is a legitimate government interest, and having attorneys elect a majority of the Commission's members is a rational way to accomplish that goal. Attorneys are better equipped than non-attorneys to evaluate the temperament and legal acumen of judicial candidates and more likely to base their votes on factors other than party affiliation. This is owing in part to their training, which enables informed judgments about a candidate's experience—his credentials, his area of expertise, his body of work—and the extent to which it strengthens or weakens his candidacy. Another part is propinquity—typical of many tightly knit legal communities like the Kansas bar, attorney members of the Commission will often be personally familiar with a candidate, whether by virtue of having worked with her (or appeared before her), or else because they know someone who has.

Id. at 792 (O'Brien, J.).

A second judge agreed the Kansas system was constitutional, but for different reasons:

> I would affirm on the same grounds as *Carlson v. Wiggins*, 675 F.3d 1134 (8th Cir. 2012), which rejected a similar challenge to Iowa's merit judicial selection system. The Eighth Circuit determined that Iowa's limitation on voting for attorney members of its nominating commission to Iowa lawyers was entitled to rational basis review because the commission performs a limited purpose, affects attorneys more than others, and therefore meets the Supreme Court's *Salyer/Ball* standard. *See Ball v. James*, 451 U.S. 355, 370–71 (1981); *Salyer Land Co. v. Tulare Lake Basin Water Storage Dist.*, 410 U.S. 719, 728 (1973).
>
> Judge O'Brien's opinion concludes that the election of attorney members to the Kansas Supreme Court Nominating Commission ("Commission") does not fit in the line of strict scrutiny cases that flow from *Kramer v. Union Free School District No. 15*, 395 U.S. 621 (1969). It also maintains that the franchise restriction does not fit comfortably within the *Salyer/Ball* exception to *Kramer*. Thus, because the Commission does not perform general government functions, the restriction on who may vote for attorney members of the Commission should not require strict scrutiny.
>
> I agree strict scrutiny does not apply, but would rely on the *Salyer/Ball* exception to reach this conclusion.

Id. at 792-793 (Matheson, J.)

A third judge on the panel dissented, arguing:

> The end objective of the process at issue is the selection of judges whose impact is fundamentally general. The impact of this process on the employment of lawyers is of little consequence when measured against its impact on litigants and the rules governing social behavior.
>
> In *Salyer* and *Ball*, the end impact was on discrete groups. That is, the election in those cases directly determined the governing officers for a water district that

"disproportionately affected landowners." The general public was only nominally impacted.

Here, by contrast, the election at issue is for a majority of the members of the nominating commission which limits the governor as judicial-appointing authority to one of three candidates. The selection of judicial candidates is quintessentially governmental in nature, and a judicial nominating commission "bears no resemblance at all to the nominally public business enterprises at issue in *Ball*." Nelson Lund, *May Lawyers Be Given the Power To Elect Those who Choose Our Judges? "Merit Selection" and Constitutional Law,* 34 Harv. J.L. & Pub. Pol'y 1043, 1053 (2011).

Nor does the governor's final say in the appointment process insulate the nominating commission election from constitutional concerns. The nominating commission does not simply screen and recommend candidates in an advisory fashion—it presents three possible candidates to the governor, one of whom he must select even if he finds all three unacceptable. This process is subject to manipulation, as the commission can effectively choose its own candidate by nominating only one acceptable choice along with two individuals it knows the governor will not select. Moreover, there is not even the saving grace of confirmation of the appointment choice by the legislature (a representative elected body).

Id. at 794-95 (McKay, J.)

BROWN v. GIANFORTE
488 P.3d 548 (Mont. 2021)

SHEA, J.

In this original proceeding, Petitioners challenge the constitutionality of Senate Bill 140, a bill passed by the 2021 Montana Legislature and signed into law by the Governor. SB 140 abolishes Montana's Judicial Nomination Commission and the process that had previously been in place to screen applicants for vacancies on the Supreme Court and the District Courts and replaced it with a process by which any person who otherwise satisfies the eligibility requirements for a Supreme Court Justice or District Court Judge can be considered for appointment by the Governor provided they obtain letters of support from three Montana adults.

We address the following issues:

Issue One: Do the Petitioners have standing to challenge the constitutionality of SB 140?

Issue Two: Whether urgency or emergency factors justify an original proceeding in this Court pursuant to M. R. App. P. 14(4)?

Issue Three: Does SB 140 violate Article VII, Section 8(2) of the Montana Constitution?

We conclude the Petitioners have standing to challenge the constitutionality of SB 140, and that SB 140 does not violate Article VII, Section 8(2) of the Montana Constitution.

The original Montana Constitution of 1889 provided that in case of a vacancy on the Supreme Court, or any of the District Courts, the vacancy "shall be filled by appointment, by the governor of the State." Mont. Const. art. VIII, § 34. This procedure was changed by ratification of the 1972 Constitution, which provided that in case of judicial vacancies, the Governor would appoint a replacement from nominees selected in a manner provided by law. Mont. Const. art. VII, § 8.

Pursuant to the newly ratified Constitution, the 1973 Legislature passed Senate Bill 28, which was codified at § 3-1-1001, MCA, and provided for the creation of a "Judicial Nomination Commission." The Commission was composed of seven members, appointed to staggered four-year terms: four lay members were appointed by the Governor, two attorney members were appointed by the Supreme Court, and the final member was a sitting district court judge. The procedure enacted by SB 28 provided that when there was a judicial vacancy, any individual who satisfied the constitutional requirements to serve as a Supreme Court Justice or District Court Judge could submit an application to the Commission for that position. After a public comment period, the Commission would then screen the applicants and forward a list of three to five nominees from which the Governor could appoint a replacement to fill the vacancy. The appointee would then stand for election at the next election and, if elected, for all subsequent elections in the regular course. Depending on the timing of the appointment, the appointee may also be subject to Senate confirmation.

The commission system enacted in 1973 remained the procedure for filling judicial vacancies until this year, when the 2021 Legislature passed SB 140. SB 140 abolished the Judicial Nomination Commission and replaced it with a procedure by which any individual who otherwise satisfies the constitutional requirements to serve as a Supreme Court Justice or District Court Judge may apply directly to the Governor. After a public comment period, the Governor may appoint any applicant who has received a letter of support from at least three Montana adults. The appointee would then stand for election at the next election and, if elected, for all subsequent elections in the regular course and, depending on the timing of the appointment, the appointee may also be subject to Senate confirmation.

The constitutional provision at the heart of this dispute provides in relevant part: "For any vacancy in the office of supreme court justice or district court judge, the governor shall appoint a replacement from nominees selected in the manner provided by law." Petitioners contend that SB 140 violates Article VII, Section 8(2) to the extent that it abolished the Judicial Nomination Commission and replaced it with a different procedure by which judicial nominees may be selected. Petitioners point to the 1972 Constitutional Convention transcripts as evidence that the delegates intended to require a commission-type of selection process. While we also deem it appropriate in this case to consider the Constitutional Convention transcripts to determine the Framers' intent, our consideration does not lead us to the same conclusion as Petitioners—that the commission process was the *only* agreed-upon method by which judicial nominees could be selected.

The Convention transcripts reveal drastically divergent views as to how judicial vacancies should be filled. While some delegates envisioned a commission process that would supply a limited number of names from which the Governor's appointment must be made, others advocated for a system that would vest even greater discretion in the Governor in making appointments than that which was prescribed by the 1889 Constitution.

Most notable of those who would vest essentially unfettered power in the Governor to make judicial appointments was Delegate Joyce. Joyce introduced an amendment that not only would have retained the direct appointment system of the 1889 Constitution but would have eliminated the requirement that the Governor's appointee be confirmed by the senate.

Delegate Joyce's motion that would have retained the direct appointment process and eliminated the senate confirmation requirement was defeated by a vote of 69 to 26. It illustrates, though, that contrary to Petitioners' contention that "all delegates envisioned a judicial nomination commission/committee," this was far from the case. In fact, among the delegates who voted for Delegate Joyce's proposal, some questioned whether a nominating commission could be fair and independent.

To be sure, there were proponents of a commission system as well. Notable among the committee/commission proponents was Delegate Berg. Delegate Berg advocated for what he referred to as a "blue-ribbon system," in which a committee or commission would submit a limited number of nominees to the Governor.

What emerged from these diametrically opposed proposals was a compromise, proposed by Delegate Melvin, that neither required the creation of a commission/committee, nor precluded it. The Melvin amendment passed unanimously, and is what ultimately became Article VII, Section 8(2).

Petitioners argue that "although the Constitution left the details to the Legislature, the transcripts leave no doubt that the framers envisioned a separate commission to evaluate and nominate the nominees." In this case, however, the devil is in the details. Petitioners rely on statements by individual delegates—some of which are statements *criticizing* the idea of a nominating commission—and make the unsupported leap that it was clear that all delegates understood that the proposal envisioned a separate commission/committee to be established to select a list of nominees. And yet neither the words "commission" nor "committee" appear anywhere in Article VII, Section 8(2).

Both the language of Article VII, Section 8(2), and the circumstances and objectives evinced from the Constitutional Convention debates, make clear that while some individual delegates supported a committee or commission to screen candidates for a judicial vacancy, others voiced distrust in such a commission and supported a process that would have vested virtually unfettered discretion in the Governor. As is the nature of compromise, the result was a system that was not entirely what either side wanted—a process that neither mandated a commission/committee, nor precluded it, but rather delegated the process for selecting nominees to the Legislature in broad language that the selection of nominees be "in the manner provided by law."

Although the Constitution delegates the process for selecting judicial nominees to the Legislature, the process itself is not without constitutional bounds. The delegates may have disagreed as to what would be the best process for making judicial appointments, but the clear constitutional intent of Article VII, Section 8(2) was a process that would result in the appointment of good judges. As summed up by Delegate Garlington: "There is clear agreement on the part of all that we do need good judges. The question is how to recruit them."

"We have long held that we must determine constitutional intent not only from the plain meaning of the language used, but also in light of the historical and surrounding circumstances under which the Framers drafted the Constitution, the nature of the subject matter they faced, and the objective they sought to achieve." The manifest constitutional objective of Article VII, Section 8(2) was the appointment of good judges. The fact that the process does not require a commission to achieve that objective does not mean that any process will be constitutionally sound. We therefore must still consider whether SB 140 achieves the constitutional objective the Framers sought to achieve by the enactment of Article VII, Section 8(2).

Although there are some key differences between SB 140 and the commission process it replaces, many aspects of the SB 140 process are not appreciably different. Both processes require applicants to be lawyers in good standing who satisfy the qualifications set forth by law for holding judicial office; both processes provide for a period of time for the submission of applications, followed by a public comment period of at least 30 days; both processes allow the Governor no more than 30 days to make the appointment, after which time the appointment shall be made by the Chief Justice; finally, both processes require Senate confirmation for all interim appointments and election for the remainder of the term.

Where the respective processes diverge is the "selection" process by which an "applicant" for a judicial vacancy becomes a "nominee" who the Governor may consider for appointment to the position. The commission process provided that after screening the applicants for the position, the Commission was required to submit to the governor a list of "not less than three or more than five nominees for appointment to the vacant position."

The list of nominees must be accompanied by a written report indicating the vote on each nominee, the content of the application submitted by each nominee, letters and public comments received regarding each nominee, and the Commission's reasons for recommending each nominee for appointment. The report must give specific reasons for recommending each nominee.

In contrast to the commission process, the selection process of SB 140 requires that an applicant "receives a letter of support from at least three adult Montana residents by the close of the public comment period," to be considered a nominee eligible for appointment by the Governor. Petitioners describe this process as "a crude attempt" to replace the commission process that provided "a list of nominees carefully vetted by an independent source." At the end of the day, however, it is not the task of this Court to assess the relative "crudeness" of the process; it is to assess the constitutionality of the process within the requirements of Article VII, Section 8(2).

Petitioners equate the absence of a commission to screen the candidates with the lack of a vetting process. But this argument ignores the very public vetting to which all applicants for a judicial vacancy are subjected during the public comment period. Indeed, it could be argued that SB 140 meets the Convention delegates' concern about selecting "good judges" by incorporating at least part of Delegate Joyce's objective—allowing the Governor to make a direct appointment after providing reasonable notice "to see if there wouldn't be a great hullabaloo go up around the state." As any individual who might consider applying for a judicial appointment is no doubt aware, the internet is a hullabaloo-friendly place. Thus, it can hardly be said that the lack of a nominating commission means that applicants for judicial vacancies will not be subject to a vetting process.

As for the requirement that an applicant receive a letter of support from three adult Montana residents in order to be considered a "nominee" eligible for appointment to the bench, Petitioners argue that this is nothing more than "equating an applicant with the term nominee and does not salvage constitutionality." Although it could be argued this lowers the bar for an applicant to be considered by the Governor, under the commission process, an applicant could be forwarded for the Governor's consideration with *no* public support.

Our opinion is not intended to impugn the hard work and dedicated service that Commission members have put in over the past forty-eight years. The Judicial Nomination Commission has been in place since 1973. During this time, its members have included appointees from all over the State, who have been appointed by governors of both parties and this Court, as well as selected by the district court judges from across the State, seeking to honor the constitutional objective of recruiting good judges to serve the citizens of Montana. During the debate over SB 140, some contended that the Commission should continue unaltered, some contended that it should be modified, and some contended that it should be abolished. In the final analysis, however, it is not this Court's function to determine which process is the better for making judicial appointments—it is to determine whether the process the Legislature chose complies with the Montana Constitution. We conclude that it does.

McKINNON, J., dissenting.

Before addressing the construction of the constitutional provision at issue and the particulars of the Framers' intent, some preliminary observations for purposes of context are warranted. Article VII, Section 8(2) must be considered in its entirety and consistent with the intent of the Framers. While "in the manner provided by law" gives the Legislature discretion to develop a selection process for interim vacancies, that discretion must be exercised consistent with the constitutional provision as a whole, and with the intent of the Framers to provide a merit selection process for interim vacancies. The merit selection process unanimously agreed upon for interim vacancies was part of a larger conversation amongst the Framers about whether, in general, judges should be elected—the prevailing and majority proposal—or selected based upon merit—the minority proposal known as the "Missouri Plan." While proponents of the merit process lost the war respecting judicial selection as a whole, they won the battle for interim vacancies.

However, it is important to place the Framers' debate in proper context. Because of Montana's biennial election cycle, it was *impossible* to fill an interim vacancy by election, the preferred method. As the Framers were united in their position that placing power in the governor to make judicial appointments posed a threat to the independence of Montana's judiciary, a selection process based on merit, the only reasonable type of vetting process, was the best solution short of an election. As they developed the judiciary article, the Framers repeatedly referred to Montana's history of big business, political corruption, outside influences, and control of Montana's courts by the executive branch. They were united in their conviction that the judiciary must be independent and protected from executive overreach.

While the Framers unanimously agreed that a merit selection process was preferable to direct gubernatorial appointments, they likewise understood that commissions were also subject to political influences. While leaving employment of the merit selection process in the Legislature's hands, the Framers' intent was clear that the nominees from whom the governor could appoint would be vetted based on merit—the only way to protect against a direct gubernatorial appointment. Unfortunately, fifty years after the 1972 Constitutional Convention, this Court reaches a conclusion contrary to the Framers' intent and which enables what the Framers clearly sought to prevent—a direct gubernatorial appointment. SB 140 is not a merit based nomination process and does nothing to prevent direct appointments by the governor—and the Court should call it for what it is. It quite simply allows the governor to make a direct appointment from self-nominated applicants.

At the 1972 Constitutional Convention, the Framers debated whether Montana judges should be popularly elected or selected under a merit based process known as the Missouri Plan. The majority proposal, which supported election of judges, provided that interim vacancies of the Supreme Court would be filled by the governor and district court vacancies would be filled by the county commissioners within the judicial district. However, the minority was dissatisfied by the unlimited gubernatorial appointive power of judges and proposed limiting the governor's power to appointing from nominees selected by a committee, created by and dependent upon the Legislature. It was believed such a system would afford an effective check and balance. The minority plan also envisioned creating a vetting committee. "The object here was to insure as nearly as possible that this committee will not be dominated by one party to the other. Likewise, we were concerned about this committee being dominated by some vested interest."

In the end, the Framers unanimously agreed to change the 1889 Constitution and limit the governor's appointment power by requiring the governor to appoint "from" "nominees" who were "selected." The Framers, however, left the details of the nomination selection process to the Legislature, expressing concern that there needed to be flexibility to address changing circumstances. There was still distrust among some of the Framers that partisan interests would control a committee or commission. However, there is little doubt that all delegates understood that the proposal for selection of interim judges envisioned a commission or committee which would "select" and "nominate" individuals to be considered by the governor for appointment.

The result of the 1972 Constitutional Convention was a revised judiciary article that continued to provide for the election of judges as in the 1889 Constitution, but rejected the 1889 Constitution's provision allowing for the governor to make direct appointments for interim vacancies. Although the process for selecting nominees was not written into the 1972 Constitution and was left to the discretion of the Legislature, there is little doubt that the intent of the Framers was to eliminate the direct appointment power of the governor and provide a selection process based upon merit. In 1973, the Legislature responded and created the Judicial Nomination Commission and established a nonpartisan process to select nominees from which the governor could make an appointment. "Not satisfied with the current process of unlimited gubernatorial appointive power of judges," those who favored the minority report suggested a committee that was "bi-partisan in nature." Still there was concern about the governor having the power to appoint a majority of the nominating commission.

The Court equates the public comment period of SB 140 to a vetting process which presumably will expose unqualified candidates. However, while public comment satisfies Montana's constitutional right to know and participate in government, I fail to see how either a public comment period or three letters of reference are a screening process, as contemplated by the Framers, to obtain qualified judicial nominees for appointment by the governor. More importantly, the ability of the public to comment on an applicant does not convert SB 140 into a screening process based on merit and does little to advance the Framers' intent to change the 1889 Constitution and limit the governor's appointment power to appoint "from" "nominees" who are "selected."

In my opinion, by giving the governor plenary power to select judges, SB 140 poses precisely the threat to the independence of Montana's judiciary that Montana has historically been burdened with and that the 1972 Framers sought to prevent. This Court's failure to call SB 140 for what it is gives a green light to a partisan branch of government to select judges who are charged with the responsibility of providing a check on that power. While perhaps this design exists in other states and federally, the 1972 Framers did not want it to exist in Montana. Obviously, this Court will have to consider the constitutionality of statutes enacted by the Legislature and signed into law by the governor. Principals of separation of power and our constitutional design provide that the necessary check on partisan power and overreach is through an independent and nonpartisan judiciary.

The Court's decision today weakens that balance. There is little question in my mind that the Framers, burdened with a history of political corruption and overreach and committed to a qualified and independent judiciary, were united in their conviction that the governor should no longer have plenary authority to make a direct appointment, as in the 1889 Constitution. Foremost on the Framers' minds was an independent judiciary and ensuring that power was not disproportionately placed in one branch of government. In my opinion, SB 140 is inconsistent with the plain language of Article VII, Section 8, and what was at the core of the Framers' convictions—to preserve the integrity and independence of Montana's judiciary in light of our significant history of political corruption and overreach into the courts.

2. Justiciability in State Courts

a. Standing

GREGORY v. SHURTLEFF
299 P.3d 1098 (Utah 2013)

DURHAM, J.

In March 2008, the legislature enacted Senate Bill 2. The Bill contained some fourteen items relating to education, establishing new programs and amending existing programs; it also contained funding provisions for some programs.

Appellants are a group of current and former legislators, other elected and unelected government officials, and self-described "good citizens." They include current and former members of the Utah State Board of Education. However, they appear in their individual capacities, and the Board itself is not a party to this litigation.

Since standing is a jurisdictional requirement, we first must determine whether Appellants have standing to bring any of their claims.

"Unlike the federal system, the judicial power of the state of Utah is not constitutionally restricted by the language of Article III of the United States Constitution requiring cases and controversies, since no similar requirement exists in the Utah Constitution." While it is "the usual rule that one must be personally adversely affected before he has standing to prosecute an action, it is also true this Court may grant standing where matters of great public interest and societal impact are concerned."

In a recent case, we summarized this alternative basis for standing as follows: "The statutory and the traditional common law tests are not the only avenues to gain standing; Utah law also allows parties to gain standing if they can show that they are *an appropriate party* raising issues of significant public importance."

Our public-interest standing doctrine is not unusual in state jurisprudence. Numerous other states, mindful that their constitutions do not impose the same restrictions on their judicial power that the federal constitution imposes on federal courts, have similarly established (under various names) a doctrine of public-interest standing.

Appellants do not meet the traditional requirements for standing on any of their four claims. We therefore consider whether they meet the requirements for public-interest standing. First, we examine their Article VI Claims, and determine that they do meet those requirements.

Article VI, Section 22 of the Utah Constitution provides: "Except general appropriation bills and bills for the codification and general revision of laws, no bill shall be passed containing more than one subject, which shall be clearly expressed in its title." These provisions, we have observed, "reflect an intent to limit legislative power and prevent special interest abuse" and are "clearly motivated by a wariness of unlimited legislative power."

The restrictions placed on legislative activity by Article VI, Section 22 of the Utah Constitution are part of the fundamental structure of legislative power articulated in our constitution. They are accordingly of sufficient importance and general interest that claims of their violation may be brought even by plaintiffs who lack standing under the traditional criteria. Not every constitutional provision, to be sure, is of such importance that a claim of its violation will necessarily rise to the level of "significant public importance" required for public-interest standing. But today we hold that the single-subject and clear-title rules of Article VI, Section 22 do.

The importance of the issue by itself is not enough to give parties public-interest standing. One must also be "an appropriate party." "An appropriate party has the interest necessary to effectively assist the court in developing and reviewing all relevant legal and factual questions." To demonstrate that it is an "appropriate party," a plaintiff must further show that "the issues are unlikely to be raised if the party is denied standing."

First, Appellants are "appropriate parties" with "the interest necessary to effectively assist the court in developing and reviewing all relevant legal and factual questions" with respect to the Article VI Claims. The "appropriateness" of a party under the public-interest standing doctrine is a question of *competency*. In *Utah Chapter of the Sierra Club v. Utah Air Quality Board* (Utah 2016), we determined that the Club "would have standing under the alternative public-interest test" due to its policy concerns and status as an "entity focused on protecting the environment." The coalition of Appellants in the instant case is not as well-established or long-standing as the Sierra Club, but it similarly has policy concerns and has come together to "focus on" the instant constitutional challenge. Further, Appellants have shown themselves able to "effectively assist the court" in its consideration of the Article VI Claims. Appellants have done an admirable job of briefing the facts and controlling law.

Second, *Sierra Club* requires that "the issues be unlikely to be raised if the party is denied standing." We can certainly construct hypothetical plaintiffs who might be seen to have traditional standing to bring at least some of Appellant's claims. For instance, a teacher whose colleagues' salaries were raised under the Teacher Salary Supplement Program, but whose own salary was left unchanged, might invoke direct economic interests. Similarly, we can imagine a suit brought by a textbook publisher whose materials were rejected pursuant to the Textbook Approval Program. But our inquiry is not whether some hypothetical plaintiff can be imagined; it is whether "the issues are *unlikely* to be raised if the party is denied public-interest standing." Here, where the Board itself is silent and no other plaintiff has emerged in the years since the Bill's passage, we think that is indeed unlikely.

One more feature of our prior statements on public-interest standing deserves mention. In *Sierra Club*, we observed that a court's recognition that a party has public-interest standing

> requires the court to determine not only that the issues are of a sufficient weight but also that they are not more appropriately addressed by another branch of government pursuant to the political process. The *more generalized* the issues, the more likely they ought to be resolved in the legislative or executive branches.

In other words, public-interest standing should not be used by courts to engage in review of nonjusticiable political questions. Here, Appellants' claims do not raise that type of question. Rather, they seek to enforce an explicit and mandatory constitutional provision dealing primarily with questions of form and process.

LEE, J., concurring in part and dissenting in part.

In the past several decades, this court's standing jurisprudence has strayed further and further from its traditional mooring in the judicial power clause of the Utah Constitution. Thus, although we have long recognized a "traditional" conception of standing requiring individualized injuries sustaining private rights of action, our more recent decisions have exhibited increasing willingness to overlook that requirement under a "public interest" exception. That exception, as reconceived by the court today, stretches the principle of standing beyond recognition.

I respectfully dissent from the majority's invocation—and extension—of this "public interest" exception to the traditional requirement of standing. Its methodology is incompatible with the judicial power clause in Article VIII of the Utah Constitution. That clause limits our authority to the resolution of cases that fall within the traditional conception of the judicial power. In overriding these constraints, the majority robs the constitutional limits on our power of meaningful content. It does so to uphold standing for the Article VI claimants in this case on public interest grounds, thereby subjecting the standing inquiry to the arbitrary discretion of the court, under a standardless "test" that is little more than a post-hoc justification for a preferred result. Under this test, the standing question is left to a subjective, case-by-case assessment of a majority of the court as to whether the claims seem sufficiently "important" to merit review.

Instead of expanding the public interest exception, I would repudiate our prior dicta on this point and reject the exception altogether. And I would resolve the case under a traditional formulation of standing—one requiring an assertion of injury sustaining a private action. That formulation, in my view, requires dismissal of all of the claims at issue in this case, including the Article VI claims the majority reaches on public interest grounds.

Standing is not a judge-made principle of judicial restraint subject to common-law evolution over time. It is an essential element of the constitutional provisions defining and limiting the judicial power. Such an element requires careful definition, rooted in an interpretation of the binding text of our constitution. We assail the very principle of constitutionalism when we ignore that interpretive role and opt instead to invoke and refine standardless "exceptions" justifying (but failing to explain) our case-by-case preferences to exercise jurisdiction in some cases but not in others.

Thus, I cannot accept the "public interest" test invoked by the court. I would instead interpret Article VIII of our constitution to confine the authority of the Utah courts to hear cases filed by private plaintiffs only where they vindicate "private rights," as that term was historically understood at the time of the framing of the Utah Constitution. That standard requires dismissal of all claims in this case for lack of standing.

The exercise of unfettered discretion is troubling, especially on a matter constituting a limit on our power under the Utah Constitution. We ignore that responsibility when we treat the constitutional limits on our power as "mere matters of convenience or judicial discretion." And we undermine the fundamental notion of a written constitution when we adopt jurisdictional standards that show no fidelity to that document and seize unbridled "discretion to decide which cases should be spun out and which cut off based on some vague sense of fairness or importance of the issue."

For all these reasons, we should reinforce the constitutional basis for our traditional conception of standing and repudiate the public interest exception as incompatible with our constitutional tradition. And we should vacate and dismiss this case for lack of standing.

The bounds of our judicial power cannot accommodate the kind of expansion that "public right" standing for merely "competent" plaintiffs involves. We cannot properly allow less than directly interested parties to litigate before us. To do so risks unrestrained decision-making based on underdeveloped facts and law and ultimately against the will and rights of those directly harmed. It also risks invasion of the province of the legislature. Public dispute resolution is beyond our constitutional authority in a case filed by private plaintiffs.

BENSON v. McKEE
273 A.3d 121 (R.I. 2022)

GOLDBERG, J.

This case came before the Supreme Court on January 27, 2022, on appeal by the plaintiffs, Michael Benson; Nichole Leigh Rowley; Nichole Leigh Rowley, as parent and next friend of Baby Roe; Jane Doe; Jane Doe, as parent and next friend of Baby Mary Doe; and Catholics for Life, Inc., dba Servants of Christ for Life. The plaintiffs appeal from a Superior Court judgment following the grant of a motion to dismiss brought by the defendants—Daniel McKee, in his official capacity as Governor for the State of Rhode Island; Dominick J. Ruggerio, in his official capacity as President of the Rhode Island Senate; Joseph Shekarchi, in his official capacity as Speaker of the Rhode Island House of Representatives; Peter F. Neronha, in his official capacity as Attorney General for the State of Rhode Island; and Francis McCabe, in his official capacity as Clerk of the Rhode Island House of Representatives.

The case before us involves a monumentally controversial issue as reflected in a deep and enduring societal divide. This Court appreciates the sensitive nature of the controversy surrounding the issue of the right to abortion, and we acknowledge the genuine concerns of the parties and amici in this case.

In *Roe v. Wade*, 410 U.S. 113 (1973), the United States Supreme Court recognized that "the right of personal privacy includes the abortion decision" and declared that "the word person, as used in the Fourteenth Amendment, does not include the unborn." Following *Roe*, the United States District Court for the District of Rhode Island declared unconstitutional Rhode Island's criminal-abortion statute that prohibited abortions, except when necessary to preserve the life of the mother. *See Women of Rhode Island v. Israel*, No. 4605, slip op. at 3, 4 (D.R.I. Feb. 7, 1973).

Soon after, the Rhode Island General Assembly hastily enacted another criminal-abortion statute set forth in the same chapter and title as the first version, designated as §§ 11-3-1 through 11-3-3, maintaining the same language, but inserting new language in §§ 11-3-4 and 11-3-5 (the criminal-abortion statute). This version of § 11-3-4 declared that "human life commences at the instant of conception and that said human life is a person within the meaning of the fourteenth amendment of the constitution of the United States." The United States District Court again found these sections unconstitutional on their face, and the United States Court of Appeals for the First Circuit agreed with that decision. *See Doe v. Israel*, 482 F.2d 156, 159 (1st Cir. 1973).

Undaunted, in 1975 the Legislature enacted another abortion-related statute, G.L. 1956 § 11-23-5, (the quick child statute), criminalizing the willful killing of an unborn "quick child," defined as "an unborn child whose heart is beating, who is experiencing electronically-measurable brain waves, who is discernibly moving, and who is so far developed and matured as to be capable of surviving the trauma of birth with the aid of usual medical care and facilities available in this state." After a successful challenge in federal court in which the statute was declared unconstitutional, the case ultimately was dismissed on appeal in the circuit court due to lack of standing.

Similarly, in 1997 the General Assembly enacted a new statute to prohibit partial birth abortion. A year later, the United States District Court for the District of Rhode Island declared that statute unconstitutional, and the circuit court affirmed that decision. *See Rhode Island Medical Society v. Whitehouse*, 66 F. Supp. 2d 288, 294-95 (D.R.I. 1999), *aff'd*, 239 F.3d 104 (1st Cir. 2001).

In 2019 the General Assembly enacted the Reproductive Privacy Act (the RPA), effectively granting a right to abortion in line with *Roe*, and repealing certain statutes otherwise prohibiting abortion in this state that were flatly unconstitutional. The plaintiffs initiated this action in the Superior Court on June 19, 2019, seeking to halt the passage of the RPA.

The plaintiffs claim that they have sufficiently alleged standing at this stage of litigation. They also claim that the trial justice erroneously reached the merits of their claims when assessing standing. In the alternative, they contend that the General Assembly did not have the constitutional authority to enact the RPA after (1) the repeal of the continuing powers clause in article 6, section 10 of the Rhode Island Constitution, which, they argue, stripped the General Assembly of its plenary powers, and (2) based on the restrictive language concerning abortion set forth in article 1, section 2 of our constitution, which includes the state's constitutional guarantees of equal protection and due process, but provides that "nothing in this section shall be construed to grant or secure any right relating to abortion or the funding thereof."

The defendants argue that plaintiffs are without standing to bring these claims because they do not allege an injury-in-fact and have failed to present some legal hypothesis that would entitle them to real and articulable relief. The defendants claim that the General Assembly had the authority to enact the RPA because the repeal of the continuing powers clause in the state constitution is of no moment to the Legislature's authority to enact law. They also contend that a careful reading of article 1, section 2 clearly reveals that the restrictive sentence upon which plaintiffs rely does not restrain the General Assembly from enacting the RPA because that sentence is confined to article 1, section 2.

A party who lacks standing to pursue a cause of action cannot prevail under any conceivable set of facts. In order for a case to be justiciable, a party must have "standing to bring suit" and present "some legal hypothesis which will entitle the plaintiff to real and articulable relief." Simply put, a plaintiff must have suffered injury-in-fact to have standing to commence a suit. The plaintiff's injury must be "concrete and particularized, not conjectural or hypothetical."

The plaintiff must "demonstrate a personalized injury distinct from that of the community as a whole." Critically, "generalized claims alleging purely public harm are an insufficient basis for sustaining a private lawsuit."

The parties bringing the action "must demonstrate that they have a stake in the outcome that distinguishes their claims from the claims of the public at large." "Standing is generally limited to those plaintiffs asserting their own rights, not the rights of others."

"At the outset, when confronted with a declaratory judgment claim, the inquiry is whether the Superior Court has been presented with an actual case or controversy." "A declaratory-judgment action may not be used for the determination of abstract questions or the rendering of advisory opinions," "nor does it license litigants to fish in judicial ponds for legal advice."

The adult plaintiffs' claims may be summarized as alleged voter suppression and deprivation of the right to vote. Viewing the allegations in their pleadings in the light most favorable to the adult plaintiffs, we are of the opinion that they lack standing to bring this action under any conceivable set of facts. The adult plaintiffs merely assert that they had the right to vote against passage of the RPA and were deprived of that right. However, no member of the public—other than elected legislators—was afforded an opportunity to vote for or against its enactment. We know of no authority to suggest that a general election or referendum was mandated in this instance, nor do the adult plaintiffs provide us with any authority.

The adult plaintiffs do not assert a particular injury that distinguishes them from other voters, save for the purported deprivation of an opportunity to vote against passage of the RPA, which they suggest, with no citation to authority, required voter approval. The adult plaintiffs have not been treated or placed in a different position, because no other registered voters were afforded the right to vote on the passage of the RPA. At best, this is a generalized grievance shared with the public at large, because there was no general election or referendum where anyone cast a vote. Indeed, in their prayer for relief, plaintiffs requested "a declaration that Plaintiffs, and *all* the citizens of Rhode Island, have a right to vote, for or against, the establishment of a new fundamental right to abortion (and the funding thereof) in the State of Rhode Island." The adult plaintiffs therefore acknowledge that their claims are identical to those of the voting public. Accordingly, the trial justice correctly found that the adult plaintiffs lacked standing in this case.

The unborn plaintiffs essentially claim that (when this action commenced) they were "persons" under the declaratory judgment act because they fall within the language of § 11-3-4 of the criminal-abortion statute, declaring that "human life commences at the instant of conception and that said human life is a person." Additionally, Baby Mary Doe claims that she also falls within the definition of "quick child" under § 11-23-5(c). The unborn plaintiffs argue that, when the General Assembly in 2019 repealed these statutes, upon which statutes they base their standing, they were stripped of their legal rights and status and suffered harm. *See* P.L.

2019, ch. 27, §§ 2, 4 (repealing the criminal-abortion statute and the quick child statute). They are mistaken.

The United States Supreme Court in *Roe* held that "the word person, as used in the Fourteenth Amendment, does not include the unborn." This Court has acknowledged that "state constitutional and statutory law is subordinate to the United States Constitution." Accordingly, the unborn plaintiffs fail to assert a legally cognizable and protected interest as persons pursuant to these repealed statutes, which are contrary to the United States Constitution as construed by the United States Supreme Court.

Furthermore, with regard to the unborn plaintiffs' standing as a "person" under § 11-3-4, before the RPA was enacted, the entirety of the criminal-abortion statute—which, in part, prohibited the "procuring, counseling, or attempting miscarriage"—was declared unconstitutional under the United States Constitution by the United States District Court for the District of Rhode Island. Therefore, at the time the RPA was enacted, the unborn plaintiffs had no legal rights or status under chapter 3 of title 11. With respect to Baby Mary Doe's standing under the quick child statute—which criminalized the willful killing of an unborn "quick child"—this criminal statute did not afford private citizens any legal rights. Thus, this statute did not provide Baby Mary Doe with any "legally cognizable" claim.

Lastly, the unborn plaintiffs failed to allege any concrete and actual (or imminent) injury at the time they sought judicial relief. There was no suggestion in their pleadings that the unborn plaintiffs were in danger or somehow threatened as potential crime victims. In fact, each was born during the pendency of this case. Accordingly, we conclude that, because the unborn plaintiffs lacked standing, their claims were properly dismissed.

The corporate plaintiff, the SOCL, alleges claims that are derivative from those of the unborn plaintiffs, as well as its own injury to "its legal relations and status as advocates for the unborn." With respect to the derivative claims, because we have determined that the unborn plaintiffs lack standing, these derivative claims similarly fail. Turning to the SOCL's individual claim to its right to advocate for the unborn, this is a disqualifying abstract injury. The SOCL has failed to show that it has suffered any injury or is in imminent danger of harm. Without question, the SOCL may continue to advocate for the unborn, but not in the context of this case. Because plaintiffs have not provided any authority supporting their contentions, the SOCL is without standing in this action.

The plaintiffs claim that, even if they cannot establish an injury-in-fact, the substantial-public-interest exception operates to confer standing. We disagree. Although plaintiffs' contentions implicate an important question as they challenge the Legislature's authority to enact laws, their substantive claims with respect to the constitutionality of the RPA itself are not a matter of substantial public interest because this question has been answered by the United States Supreme Court.

b. Mootness

COUEY v. ATKINS
355 P.3d 866 (Or. 2015)

LANDAU, J.

ORS 250.048(9) provides that a person who is registered with the Secretary of State to collect initiative petition signatures for pay may not, "at the same time, obtain signatures on a petition or prospective petition for which the person is not being paid." Plaintiff initiated this action against the Secretary of State, challenging the constitutionality of that statute. At the time he initiated the action, he had registered to collect initiative petition signatures for pay and had been hired to do just that. At the same time, he wanted to collect signatures on other measures on a volunteer basis. He contended that ORS 250.048(9) violated his constitutional rights of freedom of expression and association.

During the pendency of the litigation, however, plaintiff stopped working as a paid signature collector, and his registration expired. The secretary moved for summary judgment on the ground that the action had become moot. Plaintiff opposed the motion, submitting an affidavit stating that he intended to work as a paid signature collector in the future and that he might be interested in collecting signatures on a volunteer basis on other measures at the same time. He also argued that, even if his action had become moot, the action nevertheless should proceed because it is "likely to evade judicial review in the future," and ORS 14.175 expressly authorizes courts to adjudicate such cases.

That statute provides:

> In any action in which a party alleges that an act, policy or practice of a public body is unconstitutional or is otherwise contrary to law, the party may continue to prosecute the action and the court may issue a judgment on the validity of the challenged act, policy or practice even though the specific act, policy or practice giving rise to the action no longer has a practical effect on the party if the court determines that:
>
> (1) The party had standing to commence the action;
>
> (2) The act challenged by the party is capable of repetition, or the policy or practice challenged by the party continues in effect; and
>
> (3) The challenged policy or practice, or similar acts, are likely to evade judicial review in the future."

Thus, ORS 14.175 provides that, if a judgment in a case "no longer has a practical effect on the party" who initiated it—that is, if a case has become moot—the court is nevertheless authorized to issue such a judgment if the party can meet each of the three stated requirements. In this case, the parties agree that plaintiff satisfied the first two requirements of the statute. They dispute whether he satisfied the third, that is, that the challenged policy or practice is "likely to evade judicial review in the future."

Plaintiff contends that ORS 14.175 requires only that it is "likely" that such challenges as the one that he has initiated will evade review in the future. Election law challenges, he contends, are not likely to be adjudicated to final judgment within the short, two-year election cycle that the law provides. Indeed, plaintiff notes that in this case, the time between the date the law went into effect and the end of the election cycle was even shorter: six months. Under the circumstances, it was extremely unlikely that his claim would not evade review. Plaintiff observes that ORS 14.175 adopts the "capable of repetition, yet evading review" exception to the rule against deciding moot cases, which federal courts have embraced for many years. Because of that borrowing, he argues, federal cases are especially relevant. And those federal cases make clear that election cases such as this one are precisely the sort of cases that come within the exception.

The Secretary of State insists that two years is adequate time to resolve claims such as plaintiff's. According to the secretary, plaintiffs advancing such claims may take advantage of statutory opportunities to request expedited consideration or certification directly to this court.

This time, we agree with plaintiff. Whether such challenges as plaintiff's are "likely to evade judicial review" is a question of statutory construction, which we examine by applying familiar principles. We review the text of the statute, in context, along with any relevant legislative history and settled rules of construction.

The settled case law concerning the capable of repetition exception persuades us that ORS 14.175 applies to election cases such as the one before us. We find no indication from the text of the statute or its history that the legislature intended to include a requirement that the plaintiffs in each case exhaust every possible avenue of expedition as a predicate to invoking the statutory exception to the rule against deciding moot cases.

That brings us to the "obvious question": whether the statute violates the Oregon Constitution because it runs afoul of this court's decision in *Yancy v. Shatzer* (Or. 2004), which held that the "judicial power" that the Oregon Constitution confers on the courts does not include the authority to decide moot cases and, in addition, does not include the authority to recognize any exceptions to that limitation, including an exception for controversies that are capable of repetition, yet evade review.

This court's decisions in *Yancy* and *Kellas v. Dept. of Corrections* (Or. 2006), have caused uncertainty about the extent to which the state constitution imposes justiciability limitations on the exercise of judicial power by the courts. The problem lies in the fact that *Yancy* and *Kellas* reflect two starkly different—and irreconcilable—views of the power conferred by Article VII (Amended), section 1.

In *Yancy*, the court addressed whether it should recognize an exception to the doctrine that the court lacks constitutional authority to decide moot cases. The court explained that such issues as standing, ripeness, and mootness are all aspects of justiciability—that is, the authority of the court to exercise "judicial power." The court noted that the relevant test of justiciability has always been whether "the court's decision in the matter will have some practical effect on the rights of the parties to the controversy."

Justice (now Chief Justice) Balmer specially concurred, explaining that the relevant history and prior case law reflect a prevailing view of "the contours of mootness as a *prudential*, rather than a constitutional, matter."

In *Kellas*, the court took a completely different approach to justiciability—one easier to reconcile with Justice Balmer's specially concurring opinion in *Yancy* than with the majority opinion in that case. At issue in *Kellas* was the constitutionality of a statute that conferred on "any person" standing to challenge the validity of administrative rules, regardless of whether those persons would be affected by those rules. The court cautioned against reading into the judicial power clause of Article VII (Amended), section 1, "constitutional barriers to litigation with no support in either the text or history of Oregon's charter of government." The court noted that the "cases" or "controversies" clause of Article III, section 2, of the United States Constitution had given rise to an extensive body of case law regarding the justiciability of disputes in federal court, which includes such matters as standing, mootness, and ripeness. But, the court observed, "The Oregon Constitution contains no cases or controversies provision." For that reason, the court concluded, "we cannot import federal law regarding justiciability into our analysis of the Oregon Constitution."

The fact of the matter is that none of the aspects of justiciability that the majority in *Yancy* listed—standing, mootness, or ripeness—finds the sort of direct textual support that *Kellas* suggests is required to support a "constitutional barrier to litigation." The two decisions cannot be reconciled.

We are left with essentially two competing conceptions of justiciability in our case law. On the one hand, we have *Yancy*, which viewed justiciability as a constitutional requirement inherent in the nature of "judicial power" conferred under Article VII (Amended), section 1, of the state constitution. On the other hand, we have *Kellas*, which concluded that nothing in the text or historical context of Article VII (Amended), section 1, suggests such limitations on the exercise of judicial power.

In light of our reexamination of the text, historical context, and case law relevant to the adoption of Article VII (Amended), section 1, we conclude that *Kellas* has the better of the argument, at least to the extent that courts are presented with "public actions" or cases involving matters of "public interest." *Kellas* correctly observed that nothing in the text imposes any limits on the exercise of "judicial power" under Article VII (Amended), section 1.

The same cannot be said of *Yancy*, which claimed support for its interpretation of "judicial power" in essentially three places. First, it relied on the several instances in which the justices of the United States Supreme Court declined to issue advisory opinions, in particular, *Hayburn's Case* (1792). But those instances concerned the exercise of judicial power under the federal constitution, which, as we have noted, is subject to limitations not present in Article VII (Amended), section 1.

Second, *Yancy* claimed support from more recent federal court case law. But, as we have noted, federal justiciability case law is not predicated on the meaning of "judicial power" *simpliciter*, but on the case-or-controversy *limitations* on the judicial power.

Third, *Yancy* claimed support from one early Oregon decision, *Burnett*. As *Yancy* characterized it, *Burnett* stands for the proposition that, to be a proper exercise of the judicial power, proper parties with a personal stake in the outcome must appear before the court. That, however, is not what *Burnett* stands for.

In short, *Yancy's* analysis is undercut by significant omissions and by misinterpretations of the historical evidence of what the framers likely would have understood of the "judicial power" conferred by the constitution. The decision must be disavowed in favor of *Kellas*.

Under *Kellas*, the legislature's authority to enact legislation is "plenary, subject only to limitations that arise either from the Oregon Constitution or from a source of supreme federal law." We are aware of no limitation on the legislature's authority to enact legislation authorizing litigants to maintain an action that, although otherwise moot, is capable of repetition, yet evading review. Such legislation purports to confer no more authority than what we have just concluded the courts possess under Article VII (Amended), section 1.

In re GUARDIANSHIP OF TSCHUMY
853 N.W.2d 728 (Minn. 2014)

GILDEA, C.J.

The question presented in this case is whether court approval is required before a guardian who has the power to consent to necessary medical treatment for a ward under Minn. Stat. § 524.5–313(c)(4)(i) (2012), may consent to remove the ward from life-sustaining treatment when all the interested parties agree that such removal is in the ward's best interests.

On April 23, 2012, Abbott Northwestern Hospital, filed a motion asking the Hennepin County District Court to amend the letters of general guardianship empowering Joseph Vogel to act on Jeffers Tschumy's behalf to "specifically authorize the guardian to request removal of life support systems." The district court held a hearing the next day. Vogel opposed the motion to amend the letters, arguing that he already had the authority to approve the removal of life support. The court appointed attorney Michael Biglow to represent Tschumy, investigate what Tschumy would want, and make a recommendation to the court.

In an order filed May 11, 2012, the district court authorized the guardian and the hospital to remove Tschumy's life support systems. The court held that the medical power granted to a guardian does not grant the guardian the unrestricted authority to direct the removal of life support but said it would explain that holding in a later order, so as not to postpone Tschumy's removal from life support. Tschumy was removed from life support, and he died soon thereafter. On May 17, 2012, the court discharged Vogel as Tschumy's guardian.

On October 18, 2012, the district court filed a second order, explaining why it concluded guardians do not have the power under Minn. law to direct the removal of life support without prior court approval.

Vogel appealed the order. The court of appeals asked the parties to file "informal memoranda" addressing three questions including whether the appeal was moot. After the parties filed their informal memoranda, the court found the case was not moot because it was "capable of repetition, yet evaded review" and involved an important public issue of statewide significance.

The parties do not contend that we lack jurisdiction. But the existence of a justiciable controversy is essential to our exercise of jurisdiction, so we can raise the issue on our own.

There are several interrelated, potential jurisdictional problems in this case. Tschumy has died, and no ruling we make will affect him. Vogel has been discharged as Tschumy's guardian, and similarly, no ruling we make will affect the scope of his guardianship over Tschumy.

We have not previously considered whether we should dismiss an appeal that arises in the unusual context presented here. Several states have addressed the mootness issue in this context, however, and almost all of them have concluded that even though the person on life support had died pending an appeal, the appellate court should still resolve issues over the authority to order the discontinuation of life-sustaining treatment.

Our precedent similarly permits us to exercise our discretion to consider a case that might be technically moot as an exception to our mootness doctrine. We have said that we have authority to decide cases that are technically moot when those cases are functionally justiciable and present important questions of statewide significance. Our mootness doctrine therefore is flexible and discretionary; it is not a mechanical rule that we invoke automatically. Our precedent illustrates our careful analysis of all aspects of the issues presented before we determine whether to dismiss the case or exercise our discretion to consider the appeal as an exception to the mootness doctrine.

The question of whether a guardian needs prior court approval to consent to the removal of life-sustaining treatment is functionally justiciable. The question was ably briefed and argued by the parties and the record contains the factual information necessary for a decision. In addition, there was thoughtful and informative amicus support for the position that each party advocated.

In addition, this case presents an important public issue of statewide significance. The impact of uncertainty on such an important question also counsels in favor of exercising our discretion to resolve this issue in this case. A decision from our court will help clarify for the guardians and their wards the scope of the guardians' authority to make one of life's most fundamental decisions.

Because this case is functionally justiciable and the issue presented is one of public importance and statewide significance that we should decide now, our precedent provides us with the authority to decide this case even though it is technically moot. The prudential considerations weigh heavily in favor of exercising jurisdiction in the unusual context presented here, given that it is our obligation to afford paramount consideration to the "welfare" of the ward. We therefore hold that we have jurisdiction and turn to the merits of the case.

STRAS, J., dissenting.

If the caption of this case accurately reflected the nature of this appeal, it would say *In re the Interpretation of Minn. Stat. § 524.5–313(c)(4)(i)*, rather than *In re the Guardianship of: Jeffers J. Tschumy, Ward*.

The reason is that this appeal has little to do with Jeffers Tschumy. When Tschumy was alive, Abbott Northwestern Hospital sought and obtained a court order to cease providing life-sustaining medical treatment to Tschumy, who died shortly thereafter. At that point, there was nothing left for the district court, or any other court, to decide in order to resolve the parties' dispute. It is now more than two years after the cessation of treatment and Tschumy's death, and the parties to the original dispute have received exactly the relief that they requested. Yet the parties still seek an answer to the question of whether a court order was required to remove life support, a controversial and difficult legal question that is purely academic at this point.

The parties' request strikes at the very heart of judicial power. For nearly 150 years, we have consistently declined to answer purely academic questions, no matter how interesting or important they are, because courts do "not issue advisory opinions or decide cases merely to make precedent." Yet despite our longstanding prohibition on advisory opinions, the plurality is ready and willing to answer the parties' question because, in its view, the case is functionally justiciable and the legal issue is sufficiently important.

It is still unclear why, or how, this case is before us, and on whose behalf the two parties are acting. For its part, the plurality asserts that the legal issue in this case is important and the case is functionally justiciable, so we should just go ahead and decide it. The problem is that this case has *all* of the hallmarks of a nonjusticiable controversy. The parties appealed from an advisory opinion of the district court, the same pot of money is paying for the legal fees incurred by both parties, and there is no way to order meaningful relief for anyone in this litigation regardless of the legal conclusion that we reach.

We are not a junior-varsity legislature. The parties ask us to decide a legal question that is completely disconnected from any case or controversy and to make a pure policy decision about how guardians *should* act in the future when making life-ending decisions for a ward. Instead of reiterating the longstanding principle that we do not decide cases merely to make precedent and recognizing that pure policy decisions are for the Legislature to make, the plurality would adopt what is, in essence, a different rule: we do not decide cases merely to make precedent, unless we say differently.

The controversy between *Tschumy and the Hospital*—neither of which has any interest in the proceedings before this court—was justiciable at its inception. When the district court authorized Tschumy's removal from life support in May 2012, however, the controversy ended and there was nothing left to decide.

The only person left unsatisfied by the district court's decision was Vogel. In his capacity as Tschumy's guardian, Vogel received exactly the relief he sought, and he has never contended otherwise. However, in his *personal* capacity as a professional guardian—entirely separate from his role in this particular case—Vogel would have preferred to win in a different way. Instead of obtaining court approval to withdraw treatment, Vogel wanted a court order saying that he already had the authority to direct the withdrawal of life support.

Vogel's position, which the plurality must necessarily view as sufficient to create a justiciable controversy, suffers from several problems. First, Vogel's standing in this litigation has always been derivative of Tschumy's interests, and he has thus lacked standing throughout the appellate process, both because neither Tschumy nor his estate has any further interest in the case, and because Vogel is no longer serving as Tschumy's guardian.

Second, even if Vogel could now assert a purely personal interest on appeal, "you cannot persist in suing after you've won." Once a litigant has obtained the relief that he or she requested below, the fact that the litigant wishes the court had said something different in its opinion does not provide a sufficient continuing interest for an appeal.

Third, the personal interest asserted by Vogel on appeal—that the district court adopted the wrong legal rule—is clearly insufficient in light of the fact that district court orders have no precedential value and govern *only* the rights of the parties to the litigation.

Fourth, it is questionable whether there are any adverse parties in this case at all. Vogel, ostensibly acting as Tschumy's guardian, is depleting the funds in Tschumy's estate in an effort to obtain a non-"awful precedent" from this court. But Tschumy's estate is also paying the legal fees incurred by the other side—represented by Biglow, the court-appointed attorney who ostensibly represents Tschumy in this appeal—to advocate against Vogel's position. Tschumy's estate cannot simultaneously have an interest in two totally opposite rules: on the one hand, a rule that a court order is not required to remove life support (advanced by Vogel), and on the other, a rule that a court order is required to remove life support (advanced by Biglow).

What is clear, therefore, is that Vogel and Biglow seek an advisory opinion—that is, they do not truly wish to resolve a current dispute, but instead seek our advice, as they sought the advice of the court of appeals, on an abstract legal question.

The requirement of a justiciable controversy is not an excuse for courts to decline to decide tough or important questions. Rather, it is a constitutional constraint on the authority of the judiciary. The Minnesota Constitution divides the powers of the government into three "distinct departments," and provides that "no person or persons belonging to or constituting one of these departments shall exercise any of the powers properly belonging to either of the others except in the instances expressly provided in this constitution." The judiciary is limited to "judicial acts." The resolution of an abstract legal question outside of the context of a justiciable controversy is not a "judicial act," it is a legislative act, and I cannot subscribe to the plurality's approach because it requires us to act as legislators, not as judges.

Not only does this case fail to satisfy our general definition of a justiciable controversy, which alone warrants dismissal, it is also moot. A case becomes moot when "the court is unable to grant effectual relief." The plurality concludes, and I agree, that this case is moot because we are unable to grant effective relief to anyone, much less Tschumy.

It is true, as the plurality notes, that courts in other jurisdictions have decided controversies that are similar to this one. But these foreign cases were all decided under different constitutions—some of which permit advisory opinions in certain circumstances—and in the face of different facts—none of which required an appellate court to review what was itself an advisory opinion.

The scope of a guardian's authority to make end-of-life decisions for a ward is, without question, an exceedingly important question. But it is a bedrock constitutional principle that Minnesota courts lack the authority to decide *any* legal question, even an exceedingly important one, when a justiciable controversy is missing, as it is here. In the absence of a justiciable controversy, it is the Legislature's job, not ours, to clarify the scope of a guardian's authority in making end-of-life decisions for a ward. For these reasons, I would vacate the decision of the court of appeals and remand with instructions to dismiss the appeal for lack of subject matter jurisdiction.

c. Political Questions

BERRY v. CRAWFORD
990 N.E.2d 410 (Ind. 2013)

DICKSON, C.J.

With this case we confront whether the judicial branch may, consistent with the Indiana Constitution, review actions of and intervene in the internal management of the legislative branch, specifically the decision of the House of Representatives to collect fines from House members who left the state to prevent the formation of a quorum. We hold that when, as here, the Indiana Constitution expressly assigns certain functions to the legislative branch without any contrary constitutional qualification or limitation, challenges to the exercise of such legislative powers are nonjusticiable and the doctrine of separation of powers precludes judicial consideration of the claims for relief.

During the 2011 legislative session, members of the Indiana House of Representatives Democratic Caucus left the House Chambers and the state to prevent the formation of a quorum in order to block a vote on impending legislation. Members of the House Republican Caucus imposed, by motion, fines on the absent legislators. The Speaker of the House then directed the Principal Clerk to submit payroll grids to the Auditor of State, withholding the fines from legislative pay. The plaintiffs, affected members of the House Democratic Caucus, brought suit in Marion Superior Court seeking to recover the withheld pay and enjoin future action to recover the fines.

During the 2012 legislative session, members of the House Democratic Caucus again absented themselves from the House Chambers in order to block a vote on impending legislation. House Republicans again passed motions to compel and fine the absent members. The trial court consolidated the trial on the merits with the previous hearing on the motion for preliminary injunction and entered final judgment for the plaintiffs. The court ordered return of the withheld amounts and issued a permanent injunction preventing future withholding, finding that the seizure of the members' pay in satisfaction of the legislative fines violated the Indiana Wage Payment Statutes.

In granting the defendants' motion to dismiss in part, the trial court found that it could not "interfere with the House's exclusive constitutional authority to compel attendance or determine a fine, even if it violates statutory law when doing so." We agree. For courts to get involved in such a legislative function would amount to the type of "constitutionally impermissible judicial interference with the internal operations of the legislative branch" which we have rejected in the past. Yet, in denying the motion with regard to review of the collection of the legislative fines, the trial court found that "the House's exclusive constitutional authority to compel attendance does not preclude Indiana courts from otherwise interpreting and enforcing applicable Indiana statutes—which is the courts' exclusive constitutional authority." Thus, the trial court concluded, it was not precluded from deciding plaintiffs' Indiana wage claims and Indiana constitutional claims relating to the collection of the fines. This is incorrect.

The defendants assert that "the Indiana Constitution commits legislative discipline exclusively to the respective houses of the General Assembly, and discipline of members is not subject to judicial review." In support, the defendants cite various provisions of Article 4 of the Indiana Constitution, which delineate the powers of the legislative department. Article 4, Section 10, states, in relevant part, "Each House, when assembled, shall choose its own officers; judge the elections, qualifications, and returns of its own members; determine its rules of proceeding, and sit upon its own adjournment." The defendants also rely on Article 4, Section 11:

> Two-thirds of each House shall constitute a quorum to do business; but a smaller number may meet, adjourn from day to day, and *compel the attendance of absent members*. A quorum being in attendance, if either House fail to effect an organization within the first five days thereafter, the members of the House so failing, shall be entitled to no compensation, from the end of the said five days until an organization shall have been effected.

Finally, the defendants cite Article 4, Section 14, relating to discipline of members: "Either House *may punish its members for disorderly behavior*, and may, with the concurrence of two-thirds, expel a member; but not a second time for the same cause." Therefore, the defendants argue, the trial court, in reviewing the plaintiffs' claims and entering final judgment for the plaintiffs, acted in violation of the principles of separation of powers decreed by the Indiana Constitution.

The separation of powers doctrine is embodied in Article 3, Section 1, of the Indiana Constitution, which states,

> The powers of the Government are divided into three separate departments; the Legislative, the Executive including the Administrative, and the Judicial: and no person, charged with official duties under one of these departments, shall exercise any of the functions of another, except as in this Constitution expressly provided.

Article 7, Section 1, of the Indiana Constitution vests the judicial power of the state in the courts. The circuit courts exercise jurisdiction "as may be prescribed by law," and the intermediate appellate courts and Supreme Court "shall exercise appellate jurisdiction" as specified by rules promulgated by the Supreme Court. Although jurisdiction is granted to the courts by the Constitution, such jurisdiction is neither absolute nor unlimited. Our cases have repeatedly held that prudential concerns may render a dispute nonjusticiable by the courts. The distinction between jurisdiction and justiciability is a fine one and has been confused in the past. It is necessary here to clearly explain this distinction. Jurisdiction is defined as "a court's power to decide a case or issue a decree." It is the power in the first instance for a court to exercise authority over and rule on a dispute. Justiciability, on the other hand, is "the quality or state of being appropriate or suitable for adjudication by a court." Accordingly, prudential concerns over the appropriateness of a case for adjudication may preclude the courts from deciding a dispute on the merits.

Traditionally, the justiciability discussion under Indiana law has focused on questions of standing and mootness. However, a separate justiciability concern arises when courts are asked to review internal matters of a coordinate branch of government. In such situations, although the courts have jurisdiction to review the case in the first instance, justiciability concerns stemming from Article 3, Section 1, caution the courts to intervene only where doing so would not upset the balance of the separation of powers. Thus, the decree issued by a court pursuant to its lawful *jurisdiction* may, on occasion, state that, for prudential reasons, the issues in the case at hand are *nonjusticiable*.

Article 4, Section 1, of the Indiana Constitution vests the legislative power in the General Assembly, consisting of the Senate and the House of Representatives. Article 4, Section 10, directs each house of the legislature to determine its own rules of proceeding. Here, the plaintiffs' fines were imposed pursuant to two House Rules: Rule 36, which requires members' attendance at legislative session, and Rule 4, which authorizes House leadership to enforce Rule 36 by compelling attendance of members. Much like the constitutional grant of jurisdiction to the General Assembly over "the elections, qualifications, and returns of its own members," the constitutional grant of jurisdiction to the legislature over its internal proceedings and the discipline of its members is exclusive. Sections 10, 11, and 14 of Article 4 represent an express constitutional commitment to the legislature. Absent any further express constitutional limitation or qualification on this grant of authority, the plaintiffs' claims are nonjusticiable.

Plaintiffs put forth two constitutional bases which they contend support their challenge to the imposition and collection of fines for their nonattendance: Article 4, Section 26, the right to protest, and Article 4, Section 29, the right to compensation for services. However, neither of these provisions provides an express constitutional limitation to the right of each house to determine its rules of proceedings, compel the attendance of absent members, and punish its members for disorderly conduct.

The plaintiffs in this case were disciplined for their nonattendance and resulting obstruction to the formation of a quorum necessary for conducting the regular business of the House of Representatives, a core legislative function. It is not within the constitutional authority of the courts to determine what constitutes proper discipline under Article 4, nor to limit the House of Representatives' enforcement of legislative discipline as it relates to this core legislative function. The issues are nonjusticiable, and, as a constitutional and prudential matter, it is improper for the judicial branch to entertain consideration of the plaintiffs' requests for relief.

This is not to say that any or all disputes within a political branch of government fall outside the purview of the judicial authority. If House leadership attempted to discipline members for actions that were outside the "core legislative function," the courts could more readily take action. If the method of legislative discipline took the form of criminally punishable action, the courts could certainly entertain criminal prosecution of the offenders. But the actions taken here were within the authority granted both in the Indiana Constitution and in the House Rules passed pursuant to constitutional authority. Thus, there is no constitutional basis on which the plaintiffs' claims are justiciable in Indiana courts.

RUCKER, J., dissenting.

As I understand the majority's position, this Court has the authority to decide the issue presented to us today, but for matters of "prudence" the Court declines to exercise that authority. And in determining whether prudence demands this Court should not intervene, the majority adopts a test that finds no support in our long-standing case authority. That is, an "*express* constitutional *limitation*" on an otherwise constitutionally sanctioned legislative act. In other words, according to the majority, so long as a particular constitutional provision permits the Legislature to take certain action, then the Court will not intervene unless *another* constitutional provision expressly limits the legislature from taking that action. Here, in my view, the Legislature appears to have been acting contrary to specific constitutional authority. And thus the issue before us does not support the "prudence" the majority invokes.

To begin, it is important to note this controversy is not about the ability of the Legislature to discipline its members, including the assessment of fines and penalties. Instead, what is at stake is the ability of the Legislature to collect the fines it imposed by withholding wages and the per diem payments of some of its members to which those members are entitled.

There is specific Indiana constitutional authority addressing legislative pay. Article 4, Section 29 declares: "The members of the General Assembly *shall receive for their services a compensation to be fixed by law;* but no increase of compensation shall take effect during the session at which such increase may be made." Under our longstanding and traditional approach in addressing issues of justiciability, the question before us is straightforward, namely: whether the majority caucus "on its face" was "acting contrary" to this constitutional authority. It appears plain to me—without engaging in excessive formalism—that by reducing the compensation to which the minority caucus members were entitled, the majority caucus at the very least was acting "on its face" contrary to Article 4, Section 29.

In the case before us the majority abandons this Court's own authority on the question of when an issue is or is not justiciable in favor of a test apparently endorsed in other jurisdictions. I make two observations. First, if the Article 4, Section 29 directive that legislative compensation "shall be fixed by law" does not in the majority's view provide an "express constitutional limitation" on the legislature's power to discipline its members by withholding compensation, I am hard pressed to discern what might so qualify. Second, the authority on which the majority relies actually supports the view that the issue before us passes the justiciability test.

In sum, I would hold that Indiana's Wage Payment Statute applies squarely to these facts. The House's constitutionally-granted Legislative discretion to punish its members does not include the discretion to reduce its members' compensation. Defendants' actions are in direct conflict with Article 4, Section 29 of the Indiana Constitution.

In re ABBOTT
628 S.W.3d 288 (Tex. 2021)

BLACKLOCK, J.

"Two-thirds of each House shall constitute a quorum to do business, but a smaller number may adjourn from day to day, and compel the attendance of absent members, in such manner and under such penalties as each House may provide." Tex. Const. art. III, § 10.

Plaintiffs in the underlying suit are members of the Texas House of Representatives who denied the House a quorum by fleeing the state on July 12, 2021. They broke quorum to prevent the legislature, in special session, from enacting voting legislation they oppose. They fled the state to escape the jurisdiction of the House, whose internal rules provide that absent members may be "arrested" and their attendance "secured and retained." On August 8, twenty-seven days after leaving the state and twenty-six days after the House first voted to invoke House Rule 5 to compel their attendance, Plaintiffs sued the Governor and the Speaker of the House in Travis County district court, seeking an injunction prohibiting their arrest.

The district court on August 8 granted an *ex parte* temporary restraining order prohibiting the defendants from compelling the plaintiffs' attendance by arrest or other confinement or restraint for the next fourteen days. One day later, the defendants sought emergency relief in this Court. They seek a writ of mandamus directing the district court to withdraw the TRO.

The question now before this Court is not whether it is a good idea for the Texas House of Representatives to arrest absent members to compel a quorum. Nor is the question whether the proposed voting legislation giving rise to this dispute is desirable. Those are political questions far outside the scope of the judicial function. The legal question before this Court is whether the Texas Constitution gives the House of Representatives the authority to physically compel the attendance of absent members. We conclude that it does, and direct the district court to withdraw the TRO.

After examining the text and history of article III, section 10, together with the relevant judicial precedent, we conclude that the disputed provision means just what it says. The Texas Constitution empowers the House to "compel the attendance of absent members" and authorizes the House to do so "in such manner and under such penalties as the House may provide." The text of article III, section 10 is clear, and the uniform understanding of the provision throughout our state's history—including around the time of its enactment—has been that it confers on the legislature the power to physically compel the attendance of absent members to achieve a quorum. Plaintiffs proffer a novel understanding of article III, section 10 under which the House's power to "compel the attendance of absent members" authorizes only persuasion and dialogue, rather than true compulsion. That is simply not what the constitution says. Adopting Plaintiffs' view of article III, section 10 would restructure the Texas Constitution's careful balance between the right of a legislative minority to resist legislation and the prerogative of the majority to conduct business. This we cannot do. Article III, section 10 is a foundational constitutional rule governing the law-making process in Texas. Neither the passage of time nor the passions of a hotly contested legislative dispute change what it means.

Article III, section 10 provides that two-thirds of the members of a legislative chamber "constitute a quorum to do business." It also authorizes "a smaller number"—less than two-thirds—to "compel the attendance of absent members, in such manner and under such penalties as each House may provide." Thus, in addition to setting the now-well-known quorum requirement at two-thirds, the constitution in its next breath gives the present members of each chamber a remedy against the absent members when a quorum is lacking. They may "compel the attendance of absent members" in order to achieve a quorum so that business may be done. Just as article III, section 10 enables "quorum-breaking" by a minority faction of the legislature, it likewise authorizes "quorum-forcing" by the remaining members.

Article III, section 10 imposes no restrictions on the means by which compulsion of the attendance of absent members may be achieved. Instead, it commits that question to the discretion of the chamber by authorizing the present members to "compel the attendance of absent members, *in such manner and under such penalties as each House may provide.*" The Texas House of Representatives has established the "manner" and "penalties" under which it will exercise its constitutional authority to compel the attendance of absent members by instituting House Rule 5, section 8. This internal House rule authorizes the physical "arrest" of absent members to compel their attendance: "All absentees for whom no sufficient excuse is made may, by order of a majority of those present, be sent for and arrested, wherever they may be found, by the sergeant-at-arms or an officer appointed by the sergeant-at-arms for that purpose, and their attendance shall be secured and retained." Tex. H.R. 4, Rule 5, § 8, 87th Leg., R.S., H.J. of Tex. 47, 93, *reprinted in Rules of the House*, Texas Legislative Manual 87 (2021).

Although this Court has never had occasion to address the matter, the prevailing historical understanding in Texas has been that physical restraint of absent members of the legislature to "compel their attendance" is a valid exercise of the quorum-forcing authority granted to each chamber by article III, section 10. Since the middle of the nineteenth century—around the time of article III, section 10's adoption at the advent of statehood in 1845—the rules of both chambers have provided for the physical compulsion of absent members to secure a quorum.

Our goal when interpreting the Texas Constitution is to give effect to the plain meaning of the text as it was understood by those who ratified it. The legislature's mid-nineteenth century view that article III, section 10 authorized it to take absent members "into custody" is therefore particularly compelling evidence of the original understanding of the provision.

The view that article III, section 10 gives the legislature the power to physically compel members' attendance is no mere artifact of history. Well-known modern commentaries on the Texas Constitution reinforce this longstanding interpretation. "The usual manner to secure a quorum when members absent themselves so as to prevent a quorum is to arrest the absentees and force them to attend the sessions of the house of which they are members." Tex. Const. art. III, § 10 interp. commentary. "Securing a quorum usually takes the form of sending out the sergeant-at-arms to bring in absent members, and the house rules make clear that he may arrest them for this purpose." George D. Braden et al., The Constitution of the State of Texas: An Annotated and Comparative Analysis 117 (1977). A further demonstration of this understanding is Plaintiffs' behavior. They assumed, as did previous generations of quorum-breaking legislators, that a successful break of quorum required their absence from the state because they were subject to arrest and compelled attendance if they remained within Texas.

That assumption was not mere speculation. The historical understanding of article III, section 10 flows naturally from the provision's uncomplicated text, which authorizes the present members to "compel the attendance of absent members" in the manner of the chamber's choosing. Plaintiffs do not explain—and we are unable to imagine—how the present members could truly *compel* the attendance of absent members without the power to physically restrain them. Plaintiffs suggest the House can compel a quorum by "making insistent requests and engaging in meaningful debate." Such "compulsive discourse," as they put it, is allowed, but "forcible arrest" is not. The constitution, however, does not authorize suggestion, persuasion, or even coercion to achieve a quorum. It authorizes *compulsion* of *attendance*. Attendance in the House chamber is a physical state of being. We are aware of no method of compelling an unwilling person to be physically in attendance at a particular place without the power of physical restraint. Although arrest of absent members may seem an extreme step to some observers, the fact remains that if the absent members are sufficiently motivated to resist, the quorum-forcing authority given by the constitution to the present members can only be effectuated by physical compulsion. Article III, section 10 has long been understood to contemplate the possibility that it may become necessary to use physical compulsion to force a quorum, and the provision's text fully supports that understanding.

In addition to vesting each chamber with the power to "compel the attendance of absent members," the constitutional text gives each chamber the authority to achieve this compulsion *"in such manner and under such penalties as each House may provide."* Article III, section 10 thereby leaves it to each chamber to decide for itself the "manner" by which it will compel attendance and the "penalties" it will impose in so doing. Thus, even if arrest were only one of many potential ways of compelling a quorum, the decision whether to employ arrest—or any other potential method of compelling attendance—is textually committed to the discretion of each legislative chamber, not to the courts.

None of Plaintiffs' other arguments successfully undermine the well-settled understanding of article III, section 10. Plaintiffs argue that the House cannot arrest them because the mechanism for doing so would not afford them all the statutory and constitutional protections governing civil or criminal arrests. In other words, Plaintiffs ask us to radically reinterpret article III, section 10 because the arrest power it has historically been understood to provide is not perfectly analogous to any of the more commonly exercised arrest powers with which modern courts and law enforcement are more familiar. Our task, however, is to determine the meaning of article III, section 10 within its historical context.

Article III of our constitution has become a lengthy document over the years. Its opening sections, however, date to the advent of Texas statehood or before. They establish the foundational pillars of the legislature's constitutional authority, of which section 10 is a structural component. Section 10 represents a conscious decision by those who framed our constitution to counter-balance the minority's quorum-breaking ability with a quorum-forcing authority vested in the present members. They patterned this quorum-forcing authority on the federal constitution, which has long been interpreted to authorize arrest and imprisonment to force a quorum. We are provided with no reason to doubt that the framers of our constitution understood article III, section 10 to operate just as it has been understood to operate in the many decades since its ratification—to authorize each chamber to compel the attendance of absent members, by physical compulsion if necessary. We decline Plaintiffs' invitation to undermine this foundational authority, which has long been embedded in the very structure of our government.

BURT v. SPEAKER OF THE HOUSE OF REPRESENTATIVES
243 A.3d 609 (N.H. 2020)

BASSETT, J.

The appellant, John Burt, a member of the New Hampshire House of Representatives, appeals an order of the Superior Court (*Kissinger*, J.) dismissing his complaint against Stephen Shurtleff, in his official capacity as the Speaker of the New Hampshire House of Representatives. In the complaint, the appellant, together with co-plaintiffs each a member of the New Hampshire House of Representatives, alleged that House Rule 63—which, with limited exceptions, prohibits the carrying or possession of any deadly weapon in Representatives Hall, as well as in the anterooms, cloakrooms, and House gallery—violates their fundamental rights under Part I, Article 2-a of the New Hampshire Constitution. The trial court dismissed the plaintiffs' complaint, concluding that, because the issue presents a nonjusticiable political question, the court lacked subject matter jurisdiction. We reverse and remand.

The pertinent facts are as follows. On January 2, 2019, the New Hampshire House of Representatives amended House Rule 63 to provide that "no person, including members of the House, except law enforcement officers while actively engaged in carrying out their duties as such, shall carry or have in possession any deadly weapon while in the House Chamber, anterooms, cloakrooms, or House gallery." Previously, House Rule 63 permitted members of the House, and others, to carry weapons in the House Chamber so long as the weapons were not displayed.

Plaintiffs filed a complaint in the superior court challenging the constitutionality of House Rule 63. They alleged the rule violates their fundamental rights under Part I, Article 2-a of the State Constitution, which provides that "all persons have the right to keep and bear arms in defense of themselves, their families, their property and the state." The Speaker moved to dismiss the complaint, arguing the complaint presented a nonjusticiable political question. The trial court agreed.

Whether a controversy is nonjusticiable presents "a question of law, which we review *de novo*." Here, the State Constitution demonstrably commits to the legislature the authority to enact its own internal rules of proceedings. Part II, Article 22 provides that the House of Representatives "shall choose their own speaker, appoint their own officers, and *settle the rules of proceedings in their own house*." However, "our conclusion that the constitution commits to the legislature such exclusive authority does not end the inquiry into justiciability." "While it is appropriate to give due deference to a co-equal branch of government as long as it is functioning within constitutional constraints, it would be a serious dereliction on our part to deliberately ignore a clear constitutional violation." *Baines v. N.H. Senate President*, 876 A.2d 768 (2005).

In *Baines*, we faced the question of whether a law passed by the legislature constituted a "money bill," and thus whether the constitution required that the bill originate in the House. Although we recognized that the authority to adopt internal procedural rules had been demonstrably committed to the legislature, we held that "the question of whether the procedures set forth in Part II, Articles 2, 20, 37 and 44 of the State Constitution were violated is justiciable." As the final arbiter of state constitutional disputes, we concluded that, "while we will not inquire into every allegation of procedural impropriety in the passage of legislation, when the question presented is whether or not a violation of a mandatory constitutional provision has occurred, it is not only appropriate to provide judicial intervention, we are mandated to do no less."

Similarly, in *Hughes*, we found that the legislature's internal rulemaking authority, although "continuous" and "absolute," remains subject to constitutional limitations. We observed that "courts generally consider that the legislature's adherence to the rules or statutes prescribing procedure is a matter entirely within legislative control and discretion, not subject to judicial review *unless* the legislative procedure is mandated by the constitution." Thus, although claims regarding the legislature's compliance with such rule-based or statutory procedures are not justiciable, "claims regarding compliance with mandatory constitutional provisions *are* justiciable." "It is our duty," we stated, "to interpret constitutional provisions and to determine whether the legislature has complied with them."

The legislature may not, even in the exercise of its "absolute" internal rulemaking authority, violate constitutional limitations. Indeed, "no branch of State government can lawfully perform any act which violates the State Constitution." Therefore, "any legislative act violating the constitution or infringing on its provisions must be void because the legislature, when it steps beyond its bounds, acts without authority." Because "it is the role of this court in our co-equal, tripartite form of government to interpret the Constitution," and "to determine whether the legislature has complied with its provisions," we conclude that the controversy as to whether House Rule 63 violates the appellant's fundamental right to keep and bear arms under Part I, Article 2-a of the State Constitution is justiciable, and that the trial court erred when it dismissed the complaint.

d. Advisory Opinions

The "case" and "controversy" requirement of Article III of the United States Constitution prohibits federal courts from issuing advisory opinions to the other branches of government. Many States take the same view under their state constitutions (even without a "case or controversy" requirement) but other States have different rules. Thus, some state constitutions permit their state supreme courts, in appropriate circumstances, to issue advisory opinions about the validity of existing laws or those under consideration. The following cases offer a small sample of the types of issues that may arise in this area.

STATE OF KANSAS ex rel. MORRISON v. SEBELIUS
179 P.3d 366 (Kan. 2008)

LUCKERT, J.

During the 2007 Kansas legislative session, the legislature passed and the governor signed an Act regulating the time and place of protests at funerals. In a section the parties refer to as the judicial trigger provision, the legislature provided that the funeral protest provisions of the new legislation would not become operative unless and until this court or a federal court determined the funeral protest provisions were constitutional. In another provision, referred to as the judicial review provision, the legislature directed the attorney general to file a lawsuit challenging the constitutionality of the funeral protest provisions.

This lawsuit is not the action suggested in those provisions, however. In this action, the attorney general challenges the constitutionality of the judicial trigger provision, arguing the legislature violated the separation of powers doctrine by directing the attorney general to file the lawsuit contemplated in the provision. This argument is constructed on two premises. First, according to the attorney general, the legislature usurped or intruded into executive and judicial powers by ordering the attorney general to file a lawsuit he believes would seek an unconstitutional remedy and, as a result, would lack merit. Second, the attorney general's conclusion regarding the merits of the suit is based upon an argument that the judicial trigger lawsuit would require a court to provide advice to the legislature as to whether the funeral protest provisions are constitutional and should become operative; he notes that courts do not have the judicial power to provide advisory opinions. If we agree with the attorney general on these points, he requests an order severing the judicial trigger provision from the Kansas Funeral Privacy Act.

In arguing a present controversy exists, the governor's argument is based, in part, upon section 6 of the Kansas Funeral Privacy Act, which provides the Act shall "take effect and be in force from and after its publication in the statute book."

The impact of this provision is diluted by the so-called judicial trigger, which makes some of the Act's provisions inoperative until the Kansas Supreme Court or a federal court "upholds the constitutionality thereof."

Section 3 of the Act states that, "in accordance with K.S.A. 75–702, the attorney general shall seek judicial determination of the constitutionality" of those inoperative provisions.

The combined effect is that the attorney general is under a current statutory obligation to challenge the constitutionality of the Kansas Funeral Privacy Act. This obligation creates a current controversy regarding whether the legislature's directive violates the separation of powers doctrine.

Regarding the essential nature of the power of the attorney general and of the legislature with respect to the attorney general, the Kansas Constitution designates the attorney general as an executive officer in Article 1, § 1. The Kansas Constitution does not define the attorney general's duties, however.

In defining the attorney general's duties, the legislature obligated the attorney general to "give his or her opinion in writing, without fee, upon all questions of law submitted to him or her by the legislature, or either branch thereof." This power is consistent with the long-held view that the giving of advisory opinions is an executive, not a judicial, power.

The legislature, like the governor, lacks constitutional authority to intrude into the attorney general's duties as an officer of the court. The legislature cannot override an attorney's ethical duties to not "bring or defend a proceeding, or assert or controvert an issue therein, unless there is a basis for doing so that is not frivolous, which includes a good faith argument for an extension, modification or reversal of existing law." Moreover, the attorney general is duty bound to uphold the constitution. Consequently, the legislature cannot direct the attorney general to file an action if the attorney general has a good faith belief that the action seeks an unconstitutional remedy.

The attorney general does not suggest this conclusion ends our analysis. Nor does he argue his conclusion regarding the merits of a judicial trigger action should not be tested. Indeed, the point of this action is to seek an adjudication that an action attacking the inoperative Kansas Funeral Privacy Act's funeral protest provisions would necessarily seek a remedy that is constitutionally prohibited—*i.e.*, an advisory opinion.

The issues presented in the judicial trigger suit contemplated by the Act would be hypothetical, essentially asking: If the provisions were being enforced, would they infringe on any constitutional right? The parties and the court would speculate on what rights an aggrieved party might assert as having been violated, and those issues would be considered in the abstract without actual facts to inform the court's analysis and resolution of the questions.

Each state is free to define the judicial powers of its courts. The Kansas Constitution's jurisdictional provisions do not vary from those in the United States Constitution as drastically as other states' constitutions. Several states have explicitly empowered state courts to give advisory opinions. Kansas is not one of those jurisdictions.

Nevertheless, Kansas courts have repeatedly recognized that the "judicial power" is the "power to hear, consider and determine controversies between rival litigants." In recognizing a constitutional case-or-controversy requirement, Kansas courts have relied solely on the separation of powers doctrine embodied in the Kansas constitutional framework.

Like federal decisions, this court's decisions note the policy considerations that underlie the requirement of justiciability and the prohibition against advisory opinions: controversies provide factual context, arguments are sharpened by adversarial positions, and judgments resolve disputes rather than provide mere legal advice. As in federal court, less rigorous requirements have been imposed in declaratory judgment cases; yet, actual cases and controversies are still required.

Thus, despite the differences between our Kansas Constitution and the Constitution of the United States, both limit the judicial power to actual cases and controversies. The judicial power granted by Article 3 of the Kansas Constitution does not include the power to give advisory opinions.

Where, as here, the lawsuit would request an opinion regarding the constitutionality of inoperative legislation, an additional separation of powers issue is presented: Does the judicial trigger provision abdicate legislative power by seeking advice regarding the constitutionality of inoperative legislation?

Power is shifted away from the legislature when the legislature does not reach its own independent conclusion, albeit preliminary, regarding the constitutionality of a statute. The giving of a judicial opinion regarding the constitutionality of pending legislation "violates the principle of separation of powers by facilitating abdication by the legislature of its duty to make a judgment on the constitutionality of a pending statute independent of that made by the justices."

The governor suggests a different situation is presented because the attorney general would not be seeking an opinion regarding pending legislation. Rather, the Kansas Funeral Privacy Act will not be further considered by the legislature; once this court renders a decision regarding the constitutionality of the substantive provisions of the Act, those provisions would become operative without further legislative action.

The attorney general disagrees, suggesting that because the substantive provisions are inoperative the legislature has requested advice on whether the provisions should become operative rather than making that decision as a legislative body.

We agree with the attorney general on this point. The Kansas Funeral Privacy Act provisions criminalizing funeral protests are not in effect.

Consequently, we conclude the judicial trigger provision seeks an unconstitutional remedy that would violate the separation of powers doctrine in two respects. First, a lawsuit filed pursuant to the provision would not present an actual case or controversy. It would seek an advisory opinion, and a court would not have the judicial power to grant the remedy. Second, the provision purports to make the Kansas Supreme Court an advisor to the legislature on whether the inoperative funeral protest provisions are facially constitutional and should be allowed to become operative.

Request for an OPINION OF THE JUSTICES
274 A.3d 269 (Del. 2022)

Opinion

Dear President Pro Tempore Sokola and Speaker of the House Schwartzkopf:

Senate Concurrent Resolution No. 63 requests the opinion of the Justices on the construction of Article III, Section 13 of the Delaware Constitution. The Supreme Court appointed amici counsel on January 26,

2022, to help answer the General Assembly's questions. We have their submissions in hand and thank the attorneys for their volunteer service to the Court and to the State. What follows are the questions and summary answers. We then explain our answers in more detail.

1. May "reasonable cause" under Section 13 include an indictment returned by a grand jury?

Reasonable cause for a bill of address to the Governor may include an indictment, but an indictment standing alone is not sufficient.

2. Does the authority under Section 13 to remove a public official implicitly include the authority to take a lesser action, such as suspension of that public official? If Section 13 does implicitly include the authority to take a lesser action, must the General Assembly address the Governor on the lesser action or can the Governor choose to take a lesser action than that addressed to the Governor?

The Governor's authority to remove a public official upon a bill of address does not include the authority to take a lesser action such as suspension.

3. Does the application of Section 13 require a hearing on the matter prior to a vote in either House to address the Governor to remove an officer?

A hearing is required prior to the vote on a bill of address.

a. If the application of Section 13 requires a hearing, must each House hold a hearing prior to its respective vote to address the Governor, or does a hearing in the first House satisfy the requirement?

A hearing in the first House or a joint hearing in both Houses satisfies the hearing requirement.

b. If the application of Section 13 requires a hearing in each House, would a joint hearing satisfy the requirement?

As noted in our response to Question 3(a), a hearing in the first House or a joint hearing satisfies the hearing requirement.

c. If the application of Section 13 requires a hearing, what are the elements that must be satisfied? For example, must the person against whom each House seeks to proceed be provided the opportunity to attend the hearing, to be represented at the hearing by counsel, to testify at the hearing, to call witnesses, or to introduce evidence at the hearing?

Both Houses would issue a joint notice ten days prior to the hearing. The individual must have a hearing, which preferably would include the right to attend, be represented by counsel, call witnesses, and introduce evidence. The other parameters of the hearing are within the discretion of the General Assembly.

4. Does Section 13 require a 10-day notice for only the first House to take action, or are separate notices required for each House? If Section 13

requires separate 10-day notices for each House's action, may those notices be issued concurrently, or must the second House issue its notice only after the first House has acted pursuant to its respective notice?

A Joint Resolution by both Houses is required at least ten days before the hearing in the first House or before a joint hearing.

5. Is there a mechanism for an appeal of the decision by the Governor to remove a public officer under Section 13?

There is no appeal from the Governor's decision. We do not express an opinion on whether judicial review is available through other avenues.

Section 13 of Article III of the Delaware Constitution provides as follows:

> The Governor may for any reasonable cause remove any officer, except the Lieutenant-Governor and members of the General Assembly, upon the address of two-thirds of all the members elected to each House of the General Assembly. Whenever the General Assembly shall so address the Governor, the cause of removal shall be entered on the journals of each House. The person against whom the General Assembly may be about to proceed shall receive notice thereof, accompanied with the cause alleged for his or her removal, at least ten days before the day on which either House of the General Assembly shall act thereon.

When a constitutional provision is unambiguous, we rely on its plain language. Section 13 is unambiguous in certain respects. Other than the Lieutenant Governor and members of the General Assembly, the Governor may—not must—remove any public officer for reasonable cause if the General Assembly presents a bill of address to the Governor, after a vote by two-thirds of each House. The individual to be removed must receive at least ten days' notice of the bill of address and the cause alleged for removal. What is missing from Section 13, however, and no doubt caused the General Assembly's request for an Opinion of the Justices, are details about how to undertake a bill of address, what constitutes reasonable cause, and the rights of the public officer involved.

When a constitutional provision is ambiguous, or its application uncertain, we examine other sections of the Constitution that give meaning to the provision under consideration. We also look to the Delaware Constitutional Debates of 1897 ("Delaware Debates") to see what the Framers intended. In the words of Justice William Spruance, who was intimately involved in drafting the Delaware Constitution: "In ascertaining the meaning of a remedial provision of a constitution or statute, where the language is not clear, it is often necessary to consider the mischiefs intended to be prevented." The Delaware Debates are especially relevant here because the Delaware Constitution of 1897 was not ratified by the public, but adopted by the same men who debated the provisions (the "Delaware Delegates").

Having identified textual ambiguities, we begin our construction of Article III, Section 13 by examining other provisions of the Delaware Constitution that shed light on how Section 13 was intended to operate. Using the Pennsylvania Constitution as a model, Spruance explained that the new Delaware Constitution would provide three methods for removal of officers:

> There are three ways of getting rid of an officer. One is, under these lines, on misbehavior in office, or any infamous crime, and the Governor shall remove that man, because it is his duty to do so. That means where he has been convicted on indictment of misbehavior in office or infamous crime. The next deals with removal on the address of the legislature; and then we have the third one, that of impeachment.

Article XV, Section 6 addresses removal from office by the Governor for criminal convictions:

> All public officers shall hold their offices on condition that they behave themselves well. The Governor shall remove from office any public officer convicted of misbehavior in office or of any infamous crime.

Thus, the Governor must remove a public officer when the officer is convicted of certain crimes. A public official can also be removed from office after impeachment proceedings in the House and a trial in the Senate:

> The Governor and all other civil officers under this State shall be liable to impeachment for treason, bribery, or any high crime or misdemeanor in office. Judgment in such cases shall not extend further than to removal from office, and disqualification to hold any office of honor, trust or profit, under this State; but the party convicted shall, nevertheless, be subject to indictment, trial, judgment and punishment according to law.

Section 13 does not mention conviction. It refers only to "reasonable cause" for removal. As our review of the Delaware and Pennsylvania debates shows, a bill of address—with its reasonable cause requirement—was intended to cast a wider net and covers misconduct by public officials that might lead to criminal charges but not necessarily end in a criminal conviction.

We turn to the Delaware Debates. The Delaware Delegates adopted the most recent Delaware Constitution on July 4, 1897.

William C. Spruance, a lawyer and delegate, introduced Article III, Section 13. He explained that he found the "provision in the Constitution of Pennsylvania and it is a good safe one." The Delaware Delegates first discussed requiring removal from office if an officer had been "convicted of misbehavior in office or of any infamous crime" and agreed that when an individual "has had his day in Court, and he has been indicted and he has been convicted," "he certainly ought to come out of office." The Governor was therefore required, under the new Constitution, to remove any officer who had been convicted.

After agreeing on the infamous crime provision, the Delaware Delegates considered removal by bill of address to the Governor. Spruance, the author of Section 13, explained that the Governor could not remove appointed officials without cause under the provision—a crucial difference from the Pennsylvania Constitution of 1874. He also stressed that the Delaware provision was "more carefully framed and safer" than its Pennsylvania counterpart because it required a vote of two-thirds of the General Assembly rather than just two-thirds of the Senate. He gave an example of conduct which would justify removal:

> And we have had an instance in the two late Honorable gentlemen who were on the Judiciary, and who had come to the condition of health and mind and body that they could not perform their functions, and unless they had resigned, there would have been no way of carrying on the business of the Courts except by their removal by the General Assembly.

The Delaware Delegates then extensively debated the notice requirement. Finally, Wilson T. Cavender spoke:

> The spirit of the language of this section, it seems to me, is very clear that this notice should be given in the shape of a joint resolution. It seems to me it would not be proper in any other shape.
>
> What is the General Assembly? The General Assembly is not the House, nor the Senate separately, but it is the Senate and House both, and a notice coming from the General Assembly would come in the shape of a joint resolution.

They also debated the nature of the hearing, and where it should take place. Saulsbury believed the language required a joint trial, but Spruance replied that he thought the provision required only ten days' notice before the hearing in the first House—and that the other House could then proceed to address the Governor without having its own, independent hearing.

The Delaware Delegates thought the number and structure of hearings would be a matter of preference for the legislature—each House of the General Assembly was entitled, but not required, to have its own proceeding. If the second House believed that the first hearing had shown reasonable cause, it was entitled to vote on the bill of address without a second hearing.

The nature of the hearing also came up in the Debates. At various times, the Delaware Delegates discussed allowing enough time for the individuals to provide a defense to the charges laid against them. One delegate referred to the hearing as a jury trial, distinguishing it from the process for impeachment. Again, the Delegates reached agreement: "A man is entitled, when he gets this notice, to a hearing, and in the question of introducing testimony, and the things that are to be brought in." It appears the Delegates intended the hearing to afford the individuals a full and fair presentation of the evidence against them and an opportunity to respond.

Having reviewed the debates surrounding the removal provisions, we answer the questions posed by the General Assembly.

Response to Question 1. Reasonable cause for a bill of address to the Governor may include an indictment, but an indictment standing alone is not sufficient.

When addressing removal, the Framers targeted three ways to remove a public official—certain criminal convictions, impeachment and conviction, and a bill of address. The first two means of removal from office concern only convictions. The third—the bill of address—was intended to cast a wider net and to capture criminal conduct that has not yet resulted in a conviction, general misbehavior in office, and incapacity of many kinds.

The Delaware Delegates remarked about the breadth of the reasons for removal: "there is another class of cases where there is no crime, but there is physical disability, or 1000 other things that might make it desirable that a man should be taken off the Bench or removed from any other office." Thus, reasonable cause can include an indictment. For instance, the public official might be indicted for a crime that makes it impossible for an officer to perform their duties. Nonetheless, as we explain later, before a bill of address, there must be a hearing and an opportunity for the accused public official to be heard on the grounds for removal. The legislative body must also make a specific finding of reasonable cause to support the removal. While the conduct underlying an indictment may ultimately support that finding, the mere fact of an indictment is not reasonable cause.

Response to Question 2. The Governor's authority to remove a public official upon a bill of address does not include the authority to take a lesser action such as suspension.

Section 13 states that the Governor may "remove any officer." It does not mention suspension. During the Delaware Debates, all discussion about Section 13 focused on removing an officer from office. The Delaware Delegates did not contemplate a lesser included remedy, such as the ability to suspend an officer.

Reading the removal provision to include lesser powers would also have significant policy implications. If the Governor could suspend or conditionally suspend public officers, this would create limbo in those offices, and a new level of power in the executive, one of supervisory authority. While the Constitution provides a method for replacement of officers when there is a vacancy in office, there is no provision for dealing with officers who have been suspended, and no potential check on any conditions the Governor could choose to adopt before the officers could be reinstated. Functionally, this would be a delegation of legislative power to the executive, and is not a reasonable reading of the provision.

Finally, we need not reach whether the General Assembly's bill of address to the Governor can recommend suspension rather than removal, as we find that the Governor cannot suspend public officials.

Response to Question 3. A hearing is required prior to the vote on a bill of address.

Section 13 states that "the person against whom the General Assembly may be about to proceed shall receive notice thereof" but does not address what it means to proceed against a public officer. We therefore turn to the Debates.

The delegates raised the need for a hearing prior to a vote on the charges. As the Framers anticipated, the notice requirement allows the individual time to provide a defense and to allow both Houses to consider the matter. The hearing serves as "a more speedy remedy" than impeachment, but not one "without due consideration" or the "check" of each House of the General Assembly. The "notice" of "charges" required at least 10 days for the accused to mount a defense. The Delaware Delegates also anticipated that the hearing would take place before any vote on the charges and the hearing could take several days.

While the Delaware Delegates were discussing the structure of the hearing and whether it needed to take place in each House of the General Assembly, Cooper asked, "legislative enactment would provide the formula, would it?" and Spruance replied, "I think so." We understand those remarks to mean that the General Assembly can decide how the hearing will proceed, other than the minimum requirement of the public officer's notice of the charges and the right to be heard.

Response to Question 3a. and b. A hearing in the first House or a joint hearing satisfies the hearing requirement.

While Section 13 addresses the notice requirement and refers to a proceeding, those references do not explain what the hearing requires, nor which House must conduct the hearing. The Delaware Debates offer guidance on the question. The Delaware Delegates were concerned about the notice and hearing requirement taking too long, and discussed the issues that would arise with two separate trials. The Delaware Delegates concluded that one hearing would be sufficient, or that the General Assembly could conduct a joint hearing.

It is acceptable to have one hearing—in either House of the General Assembly which has provided the ten-day notice—or a joint hearing before both Houses.

Response to Question 3c. Both Houses would issue a joint notice ten days prior to the hearing. The individual must have a hearing, which preferably would include the right to attend, be represented by counsel, call witnesses, and introduce evidence. The other parameters of the hearing are within the discretion of the General Assembly.

The Delaware Delegates described the opportunity to be heard as akin to a "jury trial." By this time, the role of the jury and structure of a jury trial were largely analogous to what we have today. Although the Delaware Debates do not provide a definitive answer to the question, given the reference to a trial, and a trial similar to one involving a jury, we believe the Delaware Delegates would have wanted to give the accused the procedural protections associated with a trial—the right to be represented by counsel, the right to offer evidence, and the right to call witnesses—as would be expected for an individual making their own "defense."

Response to Question 4. A Joint Resolution by both Houses is required at least ten days before the hearing in the first House or before a joint hearing.

As discussed above, this was a point that was heavily debated at the Delaware Constitutional Convention. The Delegates contemplated that the General Assembly would adopt a Joint Resolution at least ten days before the hearing date. Either House may hold a hearing after that 10-day period has elapsed, or the General Assembly may hold a joint hearing.

Response to Question 5. There is no appeal from the Governor's decision. We do not express an opinion on whether judicial review is available through other avenues.

Section 13 has no mechanism for a direct appeal of the Governor's decision to remove an official upon a bill of address. We were not asked to explore whether there are other avenues for relief through the courts.

3. Certified Questions

Although federal courts are courts of limited jurisdiction, they frequently entertain questions of state law under their diversity jurisdiction and pendent jurisdiction. When an outcome-dispositive state law question arises in a federal-court case, one or both litigants may ask the court to certify the question to the relevant state supreme court—so that the final dispositor of state law may resolve the question. The process is regulated by the state supreme courts, which generally retain authority to accept or reject the invitation. For like reasons, a federal court on its own initiative may seek to certify the question.

LEHMAN BROTHERS v. SCHEIN
416 U.S. 386 (1974)

DOUGLAS, J.

Plaintiffs claim that Chasen and the other defendant are liable on the theory that "inside" information of an officer or director of a corporation is an asset of the corporation which had been acquired by the insiders as fiduciaries of the company and misappropriated in violation of trust. The District Court in examining Florida law concluded that, although the highest court in Florida has not considered the question, several district courts of appeal indicate that a complaint which fails to allege both wrongful acts and damage to the corporation must be dismissed. As Chasen, the only fiduciary involved in the suits, never sold any of his holdings on the basis of inside information, the District Court accordingly dismissed the complaints.

The Court of Appeals by a divided vote reversed the District Court. While the Court of Appeals held that Florida law was controlling, it found none that was decisive. So it then turned to the law of other jurisdictions, particularly that of New York, to see if Florida "would probably" interpret *Diamond v. Oreamuno* (N.Y. 1969) to make it applicable here. The Court of Appeals concluded that the defendants had engaged with Chasen "to misuse corporate property," and that the theory of *Diamond* reaches that situation, "viewing the case as the Florida court would probably view it." There were emanations from other Florida decisions that made the majority on the Court of Appeals feel that Florida would follow that reading of *Diamond*. Such a construction of *Diamond*, the Court of Appeals said, would have "the prophylactic effect of providing a disincentive to insider trading." And so it would. Yet under the regime of *Erie R. Co. v. Tompkins* (1938), a State can make just the opposite her law, providing there is no overriding federal rule which pre-empts state law by reason of federal curbs on trading in the stream of commerce.

The dissenter on the Court of Appeals urged that that court certify the state-law question to the Florida Supreme Court as is provided in Fla. Stat. Ann. § 25.031 and its Appellate Rule 4.61. That path is open to this Court and to any court of appeals of the United States. We have, indeed, used it before, as have courts of appeals.

Here resort to it would seem particularly appropriate in view of the novelty of the question and the great unsettlement of Florida law, Florida being a distant State. When federal judges in New York attempt to predict uncertain Florida law, they act, as we have referred to ourselves on this Court in matters of state law, as "outsiders" lacking the common exposure to local law which comes from sitting in the jurisdiction.

The judgment of the Court of Appeals is vacated and the cases are remanded so that that court may reconsider whether the controlling issue of Florida law should be certified to the Florida Supreme Court pursuant to Rule 4.61 of the Florida Appellate Rules.

REHNQUIST, J., concurring.

I agree with the Court, but think it appropriate to emphasize the scope of the discretion of federal judges in deciding whether to use such certification procedures.

Petitioners here were defendants in the District Court. That court, applying applicable New York choice-of-law rules, decided that Florida law governs the case and, finding that the respondents' complaint requested relief which would extend the substantive law even beyond New York's apparently novel decision in *Diamond*, dismissed the complaint on the merits. The Court of Appeals agreed that Florida law applied, but held that Florida law would permit recovery on the claim stated by respondents. The opinion of the dissenting judge of the Court of Appeals, disagreeing with the majority's analysis of Florida law, added in a concluding paragraph that in light of the uncertainty of Florida law, the Florida certification procedure should have been utilized by the Court of Appeals. On rehearing, petitioners requested the Court of Appeals to utilize this procedure, but they concede that this is the first such request that they made. Thus petitioners seek to upset the result of more than two years of trial and appellate litigation on the basis of a point which they first presented to the Court of Appeals upon petition for rehearing.

The authority which Congress has granted this Court to review judgments of the courts of appeals undoubtedly vests us not only with the authority to correct errors of substantive law, but to prescribe the method by which those courts go about deciding the cases before them. But a sensible respect for the experience and competence of the various integral parts of the federal judicial system suggests that we go slowly in telling the courts of appeals or the district courts how to go about deciding cases where federal jurisdiction is based on diversity of citizenship, cases which they see and decide far more often than we do.

This Court has held that a federal court may not remit a diversity plaintiff to state courts merely because of the difficulty in ascertaining local law; it has also held that unusual circumstances may require a federal court having jurisdiction of an action to nonetheless abstain from deciding doubtful questions of state law. In each of these situations, our decisions have dealt with the issue of how to reconcile the exercise of the jurisdiction which Congress has conferred upon the federal courts with the important considerations of comity and cooperative federalism which are inherent in a federal system, both of which must be subject to a single national policy within the federal judiciary.

At the other end of the spectrum, however, I assume it would be unthinkable to any of the Members of this Court to prescribe the process by which a district court or a court of appeals should go about researching a point of state law which arises in a diversity case. Presumably the judges of the district courts and of the courts of appeals are at least as capable as we are in determining what the Florida courts have said about a particular question of Florida law.

State certification procedures are a very desirable means by which a federal court may ascertain an undecided point of state law, especially where, as is the case in Florida, the question can be certified directly to the court of last resort within the State. But in a purely diversity case such as this one, the use of such a procedure is more a question of the considerable discretion of the federal court in going about the decisionmaking process than it is a question of a choice trenching upon the fundamentals of our federal-state jurisprudence.

While certification may engender less delay and create fewer additional expenses for litigants than would abstention, it entails more delay and expense than would an ordinary decision of the state question on the merits by the federal court. The Supreme Court of Florida has promulgated an appellate rule, which provides that upon certification by a federal court to that court, the parties shall file briefs there according to a specified briefing schedule, that oral argument may be granted upon application, and that the parties shall pay the costs of the certification. Thus while the certification procedure is more likely to produce the correct determination of state law, additional time and money are required to achieve such a determination.

If a district court or court of appeals believes that it can resolve an issue of state law with available research materials already at hand, and makes the effort to do so, its determination should not be disturbed simply because the certification procedure existed but was not used. The question of whether certification on the facts of this case, particularly in view of the lateness of its suggestion by petitioners, would have advanced the goal of correctly disposing of this litigation on the state law issue is one which I would leave, and I understand that the Court would leave, to the sound judgment of the court making the initial choice. But since the Court has today for the first time expressed its view as to the use of certification procedures by the federal courts, I agree that it is appropriate to vacate the judgment of the Court of Appeals and remand the cases in order that the Court of Appeals may reconsider certification in light of the Court's opinion.

HALEY v. UNIVERSITY OF TENNESSEE-KNOXVILLE
188 S.W.3d 518 (Tenn. 2006)

ANDERSON, J.

In addition to the dispute that is the basis of the certified question, the parties have also raised the question of whether the Supreme Court has the authority to answer the certified question. We address that issue first.

Rule 23 of the Tennessee Rules of the Supreme Court provides:

> The Supreme Court may, at its discretion, answer questions of law certified to it by the Supreme Court of the United States, a Court of Appeals of the United States, a District Court of the United States in Tennessee, or a United States Bankruptcy Court in Tennessee. This rule may be invoked when the certifying court determines that, in a proceeding before it, there are questions of law of this state which will be determinative of the cause and as to which it appears to the certifying court there is no controlling precedent in the decisions of the Supreme Court of Tennessee.

This Court adopted Rule 23 in 1989 and has since accepted and answered numerous certified questions from the federal courts. In spite of the fact that the rule has been in place for seventeen years, the University of Tennessee (U.T.) argues that it is unconstitutional and that this Court lacks jurisdiction to decide the certified question. For the following reasons, we reject U.T.'s argument.

A certification procedure permits a state's highest court to accept and answer a question of state law certified to it by the federal court to assist the federal court in deciding a question of state law. A majority of states have in place a procedure similar to our Rule 23. As the United States Supreme Court recognized in *Erie Railroad Co. v. Tompkins* (1938), "except in matters governed by the Federal Constitution or by Acts of Congress, the law to be applied in any case in federal court is the law of the state." In cases where the "law of the state" is unclear, absent a certification procedure the federal court must either "(1) guess at the law and risk laying down a rule which may later prove to be out of harmony with state decisions or (2) abstain from deciding the case until the state courts pass upon the point of law involved." Certification procedures assist the federal courts in correctly disposing of state law issues without incurring the delay inherent in the abstention process. Certification thus "saves time, energy, and resources and helps build a cooperative judicial federalism."

More importantly, the certification procedure protects states' sovereignty. "To the extent that a federal court applies different legal rules than the state court would have, the state's sovereignty is diminished because the federal court has made state law." Such an impact on state sovereignty "is no small matter, especially since a federal court's error may perpetuate itself in state courts until the state's highest court corrects it."

Notwithstanding the strong policy arguments weighing in favor of a certification procedure, U.T. argues that because this Court's jurisdiction is limited by the Tennessee Constitution to appellate jurisdiction, the Court lacks jurisdiction to answer certified questions. Article VI, section 2 of the Tennessee Constitution provides that the jurisdiction of the Supreme Court "shall be appellate only, under such restrictions and regulations as may from time to time be prescribed by law; but it may possess such other jurisdiction as is now conferred by law on the present Supreme Court."

We have consistently held that Article VI, section 2's grant of power limits this Court to adjudicating appellate matters only. In construing the scope of our jurisdiction under Article VI, section 2, however, we have in the past been concerned exclusively with the Court's authority to adjudicate, that is, to finally settle, disputes before this Court. Because answering a certified question is not an adjudicative function, it is not an exercise of this Court's jurisdiction and is not prohibited by Article VI, section 2.

Our power to answer certified questions comes, then, not from the Tennessee Constitution's grant of jurisdiction. Rather, our power to answer certified questions is grounded in Article VI, section 1 of the Constitution. That section provides that "the judicial power of this State shall be vested in one Supreme Court and in such Circuit, Chancery and other inferior Courts as the Legislature shall from time to time, ordain and establish; in the Judges thereof, and in Justices of the Peace." As the head of the judiciary, this Court is "the repository of the inherent power of the judiciary in this State." As an exercise of that inherent power, it is within the realm of the Court's authority to answer questions certified to us by the federal courts.

We have stated that answering certified questions not only furthers judicial efficiency and comity, but also protects this state's sovereignty against encroachment from the federal courts. Answering certified questions thus protects the "dignity, independence and integrity" of not only this Court but of the state as a whole and is therefore within the inherent power of this Court. As a sovereign state, Tennessee has "the power to exercise and the responsibility to protect" the sovereignty granted to it by the United States Constitution.

We therefore hold that we may answer certified questions consistent with the inherent power of this Court and with our responsibility to protect the sovereignty of the state.

4. State Limitations on Judicial Tenure and Service

Federal Article III judges cannot be required by statute to retire at a particular age, nor can their tenure as a judge be limited, because Article III states they serve during "good behavior." This is understood as life tenure with impeachment the only mechanism for removal.

In *Gregory v. Ashcroft*, 501 U.S. 452 (1991), the United States Supreme Court held that a Missouri constitutional provision requiring judges to retire at age 70 did not violate either federal equal protection principles (applying rational basis review) or the federal Age Discrimination in Employment Act, which the Court interpreted not to apply to state judges.

So, the remaining question is whether other state constitutional provisions might preclude States from imposing mandatory retirement ages on their judges? The answer is probably no, as the next case illustrates.

CANTRELL v. STATE
2020 WL 4251393 (La. 2020)

PER CURIAM

The plaintiff judges in these consolidated cases are over age seventy, their terms expire on December 31, 2020, and they intend to qualify and run for re-election despite the mandatory retirement age imposed by La. Const.

Art. V, § 23(B), which states: "Except as otherwise provided in this Section, a judge *shall not* remain in office beyond his seventieth birthday. A judge who attains seventy years of age while serving a term of office shall be allowed to complete that term of office."

Judge Clark contends Art. V, § 23(B) is in conflict with three other provisions of the Louisiana Constitution: Art. I, § 3 ("No person shall be denied the equal protection of the laws."); Art. I, § 7 ("No law shall curtail or restrain the freedom of speech."); and Art. II, § 2 ("Except as otherwise provided by this constitution, no one of these branches, nor any person holding office in one of them, shall exercise power belonging to either of the others."). Judge Cantrell makes an equal protection argument and, in addition, claims the 2018 enactment of La. Const. Art. I, § 10.1, prohibiting certain convicted felons from seeking or holding public office, tacitly repeals Art. V, § 23(B), or otherwise renders it inactive. We find no merit in these assertions.

As we held in *Giepert v. Wingerter*, 531 So.2d 754, 755-56 (La. 1988), the validity of a constitutional mandatory retirement age for judges is not in doubt. Other state and federal courts considering this question have likewise upheld the validity of such provisions. Those who wish to change the mandatory retirement age provisions in Art. V, § 23(B) are provided an avenue for doing so by La. Const. Art. XIII, § 1 ("An amendment to this constitution may be proposed by joint resolution at any regular session of the legislature.").

Art. V, § 23(B), like other mandatory judicial-retirement provisions, "draws a line at a certain age which attempts to uphold the high competency for judicial posts and which fulfills a societal demand for the highest caliber of judges in the system." *Gregory v. Ashcroft*, 501 U.S. 452, 471 (1991). While it is based on a generalization about age and performance that is not true for many if not most judges, Art. V, § 23(B) nevertheless ensures increased opportunities for qualified persons to share in the judiciary through orderly retirements. Because this explanation is a rational basis for the disparate treatment of judges by age, Art. V, § 23(B) survives scrutiny under the Equal Protection Clause of the U.S. Constitution.

As the plaintiffs point out, Art. V, § 23(B) permits a judge "who attains seventy years of age while serving a term of office to complete that term of office." This admittedly undermines the premise that a judge over age seventy should no longer serve. Furthermore, depending on when a judge's birthday falls in his term, this provision permits some judges to serve years longer than a colleague who may only be weeks or days older. However, despite these inequities, the provision has a rational basis in a legitimate state interest: avoidance of the substantial expense of special elections and *pro tempore* judicial appointments that would otherwise be necessary every time a judge reaches age seventy. Supported by that rational basis, Art. V,

§ 23(B)'s concession allowing limited judicial service beyond age seventy does not violate the Equal Protection Clause.

When a judge nears the completion of his or her term, an election is scheduled to fill that position. It is essential, therefore, that whoever seeks judicial office be able to serve. The purpose of an election is to select someone who will serve in the office. If a person cannot serve, he or she cannot be a candidate for office. Pursuant to Art. V, § 23(B), a judge who attains age seventy during their term of office cannot be a candidate for judicial office because that judge cannot serve another term.

The plaintiffs seek to avoid the straightforward effect of Art. V, § 23(B) by pitting other state constitutional provisions against it. For example, they contend the provisions in La. Const. art. I, § 3 securing equal protection must defeat Art. V, § 23(B). Therefore, this is not a case where a statute enacted by the legislature or some action by a governmental agency bars these judges from serving another term of office. Instead, the plaintiffs argue that some of the provisions of the constitution must topple other provisions.

Longstanding principles defeat that line of argument. As this court has recognized, "constitutional provisions should be construed, where possible, to allow each provision to stand and be given effect." "If one constitutional provision addresses a subject in general terms, and another with the same subject in a more detailed way, the two should be harmonized if possible, but if there is any conflict, the latter will prevail." The provision addressing eligibility for retaining judicial office, Art. V, § 23(B), speaks directly to judicial retirement. Although this provision has been amended, judicial retirement was contemplated at the inception of our state constitution, just as was equal protection. Indeed, judicial retirement was a feature of the prior constitution and as previously noted, when the occasion allowed consideration of the interplay between the prior and current constitutions, this court observed: "The validity of some constitutional mandatory retirement age for judges is not in doubt."

The plaintiffs fail to demonstrate why judicial retirement cannot be given effect as the electorate intended, without running afoul of the equal protection provision or other provisions in the same constitution. In so concluding, we draw from the observations by judicial colleagues from another state, whose constitution similarly contained both an Article I declaration of rights with equal protection and another Article with a judicial retirement age. "Even if the challengers are correct in their assertion that implicit in the various provisions of Article I there is a prohibition against classifications predicated upon age, such a prohibition would only restrain governmental classifications, but would not prevent the people from using such classifications in structuring the government itself." *Gondelman v. Commonwealth*, 554 A.2d 896, 905 (Pa. 1989).

We hold that a person constitutionally barred from serving as a judge cannot be a candidate for judicial office. Art. V, § 23(B) mandates that "a judge shall not remain in office beyond his seventieth birthday." The reason to seek office is to "remain in office." While Art. V, § 23(B) allows a 70-year-old judge to serve out his or her term, it does not allow him or her, as the plaintiffs contend, to seek re-election for another term.

E. SEPARATION OF POWERS

STATE ex rel. JUSTICE v. KING
852 S.E.2d 292 (W. Va. 2020)

JENKINS, Acting C.J.

This Court is being asked to stop the Circuit Court of Kanawha County from enforcing a constitutional provision requiring the Governor of West Virginia to reside at the seat of government during his or her term of office. Upon his inauguration, Petitioner, James Conley Justice, II, Governor of the State of West Virginia ("Governor Justice"), took an oath, in which he explicitly swore to "support the constitution" and to "faithfully discharge the duties of the office of Governor of the State of West Virginia." One of those duties that Governor Justice swore to uphold—a constitutional provision located at Section 1 of Article VII of the West Virginia Constitution—is a duty to "reside at the seat of government" during his term of office. However, Respondent, G. Isaac Sponaugle, III alleges that Governor Justice is failing to uphold his constitutional duties because he refuses to comply with said provision.

Mr. Sponaugle filed a petition for writ of mandamus directing Governor Justice to reside in Charleston. In his petition, Mr. Sponaugle contended that Governor Justice has not spent more than a "handful of nights" at the Governor's Mansion or at any other residence located within the State's seat of government, *i.e.* Charleston, since becoming Governor of the State of West Virginia. According to Mr. Sponaugle, Governor Justice has made consistent and repeated public remarks that he has not, is not, and will not reside in Charleston. Moreover, Mr. Sponaugle claimed that Governor Justice's failure to reside in Charleston has negatively impacted the efficient operations of state government.

Governor Justice filed a motion to dismiss the petition for writ of mandamus and argued that (1) mandamus cannot be employed to prescribe the manner in which a government official shall act; (2) a writ prescribing the amount of time the governor must spend in Charleston is contrary to the political question doctrine and corresponding separation of powers principles; (3) mandamus is not available to compel a general course of conduct; and (4) other adequate and more appropriate remedies exist.

The circuit court denied Governor Justice's motion to dismiss holding that mandamus is available to compel Governor Justice to comply with the constitutional provision.

Governor Justice seeks a writ of prohibition to prevent the circuit court below from granting a writ of mandamus under two theories. First, Governor Justice contends that, under the political question doctrine and corresponding separation of powers principles, the circuit court does not have jurisdiction to issue a writ of mandamus compelling him to comply with the constitutional residency requirement. Second, Governor Justice contends that, even if the circuit court had jurisdiction, it still erred in denying his motion to dismiss Mr. Sponaugle's petition for writ of mandamus. In support, Governor Justice argues that mandamus is unavailable as a matter of law to compel residency at the seat of government because the duty to reside is a discretionary duty imposed upon the governor that cannot be controlled through mandamus.

In the present matter, the crux of this case turns on whether the circuit court has jurisdiction to issue a writ of mandamus and, if it does have jurisdiction, whether the circuit court has exceeded its legitimate powers in denying Governor Justice's motion to dismiss Mr. Sponaugle's petition for mandamus relief. In determining whether jurisdiction exists, we must first examine (1) whether the constitutional residency provision is a nondiscretionary or discretionary duty; and (2) whether mandamus is proper to enforce compliance with said duty.

Before reaching the circuit court's jurisdiction, we must consider the context in which the present proceeding arises. That is, in order to determine the circuit court's jurisdiction, we must first examine the constitutional provision giving rise to this controversy, *i.e.* the residency requirement set forth in Section 1 of Article VII of the West Virginia Constitution. Challenges to constitutional language are not foreign to this Court. As the highest court in the State, it is clear that we are vested with the authority to review and interpret provisions of our State Constitution when presented with such cases and controversies.

In the West Virginia Constitution of 1863, Article V was dedicated to setting the framework for the executive branch of government. In particular, the framers included a provision requiring the Governor—and other executive officers—to reside at the seat of government. Then, in 1872, a second constitutional convention convened, and a new constitution was ratified by a vote of the citizens. The residency requirement was carried over to the new constitution and was placed in a new article containing provisions about the executive branch. Section 1 of Article VII of the West Virginia Constitution of 1872—the same constitution that governs the State today—adopted the residency requirement in its current format. This language currently provides, in full:

The Executive department shall consist of a governor, secretary of state, auditor, treasurer, commissioner of agriculture and attorney general, who shall be ex officio reporter of the court of appeals. Their terms of office shall be four years, and shall commence on the first Monday after the second Wednesday of January next after their election. They *shall reside at the seat of government* during their terms of office, keep there the public records, books and papers pertaining to their respective offices, and shall perform such duties as may be prescribed by law.

W. Va. Const. art. VII, § 1 (amend. 1958).

We have stated that "the provisions of the Constitution, the organic and fundamental law of the land, stand upon a higher plane than statutes, and they will as a rule be held mandatory in prescribing the exact and exclusive methods of performing the acts permitted or required." Syl. pt. 2, *Simms v. Sawyers*, 101 S.E. 467 (1919). *See also Harbert v. Cty. Court*, 39 S.E.2d 177, 184 (1946) ("The Constitution of this State is the supreme law of West Virginia. The Constitution of West Virginia is binding upon all the departments of government of this State, all its officers, all its agencies, all its citizens and all persons whomsoever within its jurisdiction. The three branches of our government, the legislative, the executive, and the judiciary, alike derive their existence from it; and all of them must exercise their power and authority under the Constitution solely and strictly in accordance with the will of the sovereign, the people of West Virginia, as expressed in that basic law. It is the solemn duty of this Court, its creature, to obey and give full force and effect to all its terms and provisions.").

Having reaffirmed that this Court has the authority to review and interpret our State constitution, we now turn to the issue of jurisdiction.

This Court has long held that "a writ of mandamus will not issue unless three elements coexist – (1) a clear legal right in the petitioner to the relief sought; (2) a legal duty on the part of respondent to do the thing which the petitioner seeks to compel; and (3) the absence of another adequate remedy." In this case, in its order denying Governor Justice's motion to dismiss, the circuit court found the following: (1) Mr. Sponaugle was a private citizen and taxpayer of the State of West Virginia; (2) Mr. Sponaugle sufficiently pled and provided theories under which relief could be granted (*i.e.* the West Virginia Constitution and West Virginia Code impose a residency requirement on the governor and other elected officials); and (3) Mr. Sponaugle's alternative remedies—waiting for a future election or waiting for an impeachment procedure to take place—were not as equally convenient, beneficial, or effective as this mandamus action.

In framing the issue before us in this writ of prohibition, we must disentangle the terms mandatory and non-discretionary. At first, the terms appear synonymous; however, they have not been ascribed the same meaning under our mandamus jurisprudence concerning public officials. A duty is mandatory if the official has no discretion *not* to perform the duty, and here it is apparent that the language of the Constitution gives the Governor and other executive officers no leeway *not* to reside at the seat of government.

Under our Constitution and Code, the language plainly states that the Governor "shall" reside in Charleston. "It is well established that the word shall, in the absence of language in the statute showing a contrary intent on the part of the Legislature, should be afforded a mandatory connotation."

The constitutional and statutory language *sub judice* is plain, and undoubtedly sets forth a mandatory constitutional duty with which the Governor must comply during his or her term of office. In fact, this Court already has found that this constitutional provision in particular is a mandatory duty imposed upon the Governor:

> It was the Governor's duty to do so, in fidelity to his oath of office to support the constitution of the State; and the constitution of the State *unequivocally requires* that he *shall reside at the seat of government* during his term of office, and keep there the public records of his office, and commands him, as the chief executive officer, in whom is vested the chief executive power, to "take care that the laws be faithfully executed."

Slack v. Jacob, 8 W. Va. 612, 657 (1875).

The Governor does not dispute that he, and other executive officials enumerated in Section 1 of Article VII have a mandatory duty to reside at the seat of government. Rather, he contends that the term "reside" is subject to his own discretion. He argues that the judiciary, in employing mandamus, would require him to be physically present at the seat of government and that such directive would infringe on the separation of powers and violate the political question doctrine should it attempt to dictate his "residence." In other words, the Governor argues that "reside" is a discretionary duty and that he must be able to come and go as the duties of his office require without interference or regulation from the courts. And, that he is physically present in Charleston as often as he needs to be "as determined by the judgment, autonomy, and discretion inherent in his office." We agree that, if mandamus were to regulate the comings and goings of the Governor, such action would violate separation of powers principles. We disagree, however, that "residing" is a matter of discretion, and we also disagree that granting mandamus to enforce the Governor's mandatory duty to reside in Charleston would take the form of regulating the comings and goings of the Governor. In reaching this conclusion, we first examine Governor Justice's contention that "reside" is a discretionary duty.

Governor Justice argues that "reside" is a vague term that means different things in different contexts and that, therefore, the word is incapable of definition that is devoid of discretion because "to reside" is a course of conduct, not a discrete act. Stated differently, the Governor contends that the courts may not dictate that the Governor "reside" at the seat of government because the Governor must come and go as the demands of his office require in the exercise of his discretion.

While we recognize that the word "reside" does not necessarily have a precise definition, we find that the meaning and import of this word can be understood by examining the understanding of the citizens who ratified our Constitution. The word "reside" is a word that is frequently included in constitutions, statutes, and court rules; yet, the word is often left undefined. It is surmised that "reside" is usually left undefined because its legal meaning is no different than the meaning in everyday use.

However, to the extent the Governor argues that interpretation of "reside" is subject to his own discretion because it is *ambiguous*, as opposed to discretionary, we note at the outset that any *ambiguity* in the term "reside" as it is used in the Constitution is a matter for resolution and definition by this Court, not the executive branch. Our Constitution does not define the word "reside" in relation to this provision or elsewhere in the Constitution where the term or any derivative of it is employed. Accordingly, we turn to the context and purpose of Section 1 of Article VII of the West Virginia Constitution, and the prior versions from which it evolved, for guidance.

While there was no debate specifically relating to the requirement that the Governor reside at the seat of government, debates as to the appropriate salary provide clear insight into what the framers were requiring of the Governor in using the term reside. In support of an increased salary, Delegate Van Winkle discussed the additional financial obligations required of the Governor as opposed to other officers and stated "*he must remove to the seat of government and remain there permanently. He has got to provide his own house* and that of better quality than most of us have occasion to in our private houses. Strangers of distinction have to be entertained by the governor." *See February 4, 1862, Debates and Proceedings of the First Constitutional Convention of West Virginia*, West Virginia Division of Culture and History.

The constitutional provision that resulted from this debate directed the Governor to reside at the seat of government and approved a salary of two thousand dollars per year. *See* W. Va. Const. art. V, § 2 (1863). *See also id.* at art. IV, § 22 ("The seat of Government shall be at the City of Wheeling, until a permanent Seat of Government be established by law."). The approved constitution further contained a provision to divest the Governor of the authority of his office and to vest it in the President of the Senate should the Governor remove himself from the seat of government. *See* W. Va. Const. art. V, § 6 (1863). Suffice it to say it was so important to the framers that their State's chief executive reside at the seat of government, that not only did the Governor's salary incorporate funds to relocate to the seat of government and to purchase a residence at the seat of government, but the Governor would also be relieved of his duties if he removed himself from the seat of government.

In January of 1872, a new constitutional convention convened. The substantial constitutional revisions, which were ratified in April 1872, nonetheless maintained the requirement that the Governor "shall reside at the Seat of Government" during the term of office and additionally imposed the same residency requirement for other officers of the executive branch. But, it did not incorporate an automatic divestment of gubernatorial authority if the Governor removed himself from the seat of government. The 1872 Constitution also included the requirement that executive officers "keep there at the seat of government the public records, books and papers, pertaining to their respective offices."

History and the intent of the framers is afforded due consideration—and it should be noted that both this history and the logic that ensues from these debates dictate the same result. It is obvious that the framers of the 1863 Constitution, and later the 1872 Constitution, required the Governor and other executive officers to reside at the seat of government for a reason. At the time the 1872 Constitution was approved by the convention and ratified by the electorate, the state had not yet purchased a residence for the Governor at the seat of government, but Governors of the State were nonetheless required to house themselves as they had done under the 1863 Constitution. If the 1872 framers intended that location of the Governor's *office*, itself, at the seat of government was sufficient to meet the residency requirement, then it can be concluded that keeping the records of the office there accomplishes that purpose and the imposition of a duty on the Governor, himself, to *reside* at the seat of government would be superfluous. In other words, there is no need for *both* a provision requiring the office of the Governor to be at the seat of government *and* a provision requiring the Governor to reside at the seat of government if the two directives accomplish the same goal. The existence of these two distinct directives, then, makes it clear that residence at the seat of government was not intended to be in the name of the Governor's office only. Rather, the State's eventual purchase of an Executive Mansion for the Governor's dwelling evidences a distinct intent that the residency of the Governor, himself, at the seat of government also is required by our State Constitution.

Further, the text of the debates from the 1862 Constitutional Convention are clear that the delegates intended the Governor to *live* at the seat of government, not merely maintain an office there or have transitory presence. While we do not have the benefit of the 1872 debates, we are mindful that, at the time of ratification, transportation was limited and the technology that keeps us connected today in the twenty-first century was not available to the individuals leading our State in the late 1800s. Undoubtedly, the citizens who ratified our Constitution desired to have the leaders of our executive branch—including the Governor—live in a central location to provide for an efficient, present, and unified government. We recognize that such a provision might not be included if a new constitution were to be drafted in today's world, with today's conveniences, technology, and modes of transportation. But it is not for this Court to speculate what this provision means in the context of our current society.

Specifically, "residing" is not a matter of *discretion*, but rather one of *intent*—specifically, the intent to return to a certain place. As we previously have held when considering the meaning and effect of "residence," "the controlling factor is the intent, as evinced primarily by the acts, of the person whose residence is questioned. If an absence from a residence is intended to be temporary, it does not constitute an abandonment or forfeiture of the residence."

To the extent the Governor suggests "reside" in the context of this constitutional provision is incapable of a definition that does not seek to control his executive discretion, we disagree. We now hold that, for purposes of the residency provision located in Section 1 of Article VII of the West Virginia Constitution, "reside" means to live, primarily, at the seat of government and requires that the executive official's principal place of physical presence is the seat of government for the duration of his or her term of office. Residency, once established, is not lost through temporary absence. Rather, the controlling factor of residency is the intent to return to that principal place of physical presence.

We disagree that requiring officers of the executive branch to comply with their constitutional mandate to reside at the seat of government involves judicial regulation of their discretion in discharging the duties of their office such that mandamus, as a matter of law, would be improper under separation of powers principles. Accordingly, we hold that the duty of executive officers to reside at the seat of government, as required by Section 1 of Article VII of the West Virginia Constitution, is a mandatory, non-discretionary duty for which a writ of mandamus may lie to require compliance with that duty.

We acknowledge that the enforcement of a writ of mandamus against a governor is not commonplace. However, as evidenced above, the rarity of this legal action and the speculative nature of the enforcement of remedies that may result does not mean that courts should not—or are without authority to—issue writs of mandamus against public officials. The public has a reasonable expectation that its elected officials will uphold the duties of their offices/positions and follow the law, and writs of mandamus to compel compliance with these obligations will be issued when deemed necessary by the courts. Accordingly, given the high standard for the issuance of a writ of prohibition by this Court, Governor Justice has failed to meet his burden to show that the circuit court exceeded its legitimate powers. He has not shown that the circuit court clearly erred in denying his motion to dismiss the petition for writ of mandamus, and as such, the petition for writ of prohibition must be denied.

HUTCHISON, J., dissenting.

The majority opinion is a well-written exposition on the 1863 and 1872 Constitutional debates. The founders of West Virginia believed every governor "must remove to the seat of government" and "live at the capital so we may at least find him."

But the statements made in those debates must be taken with a grain of salt. In the same passages of the debates quoted by the majority opinion, the founders debated whether the governor should be furnished with "a horse and buggy." I doubt the founders conceived of the notion that a governor would someday be able to travel to all four corners of the state in a single day by car or plane. Except for the telegraph, the founders never suspected the governor would be able to speak at length with faraway "strangers parties, individuals, companies, associations or their officers" in the four corners of the globe and give them "information as to the geography or resources" of West Virginia using a cellphone or video conference technology.

Still, these are academic considerations. We can dicker all day about what the founders really meant in 1862 when discussing the governor's proper abode, or how the century-and-a-half old Constitution should be applied in the modern day. The majority opinion does a great job concluding that the word "reside" means "reside," and then dumps the case back on the circuit judge to figure out what "reside" *really* means on the facts of this case.

I dissent because, for all the sound and fury and righteous indignation embodied within the majority opinion, I cannot foresee a satisfactory end result forthcoming from the circuit court. The question I had running through my mind when I read the opinion is simple: How does this end?

The Constitution of this State declares that the "legislative, executive and judicial departments shall be separate and distinct." W. Va. Const. Art. V., § 1.

The separation of powers clause gives each branch of government the discretion to decide *how* to fulfill the obligations imposed by the Constitution:

> The separation of powers doctrine implies that each branch of government has inherent power to "keep its own house in order," absent a specific grant of power to another branch, such as the power to impeach. This theory recognizes that each branch of government must have sufficient power to carry out its assigned tasks and that these constitutionally assigned tasks will be performed properly within the governmental branch itself.

State v. Clark, 752 S.E.2d 907, 925 (2013).

Furthermore, no constitution is a living document. It is the people and their chosen representatives who breathe life into a constitution's words and give them effect. The separation of powers clause only works, and only protects our tripartite system of checks and balances, if every officer of every branch deliberately respects the right of the other branches to function freely.

Now, I say this knowing full well that Mr. Sponaugle's lawsuit against the governor is well-intentioned and is not some scheme aimed toward despotism. My problem with Mr. Sponaugle's lawsuit is that I cannot see how it ends or if it ends.

The majority opinion brushes off the Governor's argument that any remedy imposed by a circuit court would be impractical and unmanageable. In support of their opinion, the majority quotes an article from 1936 that says that simply because crafting a remedy may be difficult is no reason to not try and find a remedy. That *sounds* good, but this is not an academic question being debated in a classroom. I cannot foresee either a practical or constitutional manner in which the judge can bring this case to a conclusion. This is the heart of my disagreement with the majority opinion.

Judges have broad constitutional authority to order executive officials to carry out their mandatory duties. Of this, I am certain. But even the majority opinion concedes that the Governor has *discretion* to decide how to carry out a mandatory duty. Under the separation of powers doctrine, members of the executive branch have the power to keep their own house in order. So, in the end, if the circuit court says the Governor must reside in Charleston, what force and effect would that order have where the Governor gets to decide how to carry his residency requirement into effect? Just how tangled up are the courts going to get monitoring the Governor?

The possibilities for the circuit court are both endless and absurd. What if the governor announces that he will reside in the Governor's Mansion, the "official residence" in Charleston? Then he keeps two suits and two pairs of underwear there and loudly declares his intent to return to the Mansion because "it is my residence." Is that sufficient? Can the circuit judge say, no, the Governor needs at least four suits and four pairs of underwear stored at the Mansion to show he is residing there at least four days a week? Can the judge appoint a monitor to inspect the residence to see if the sheets are mussed the required number of days of the week? Can the judge require the Governor to wear an ankle bracelet so his whereabouts are known at all times, and we can know for sure he has a "physical presence" that is "primarily" in Charleston?

The majority opinion's definition of "reside" includes a "physical presence" at the seat of government for the duration of the Governor's term of office. Does that mean the Governor must be physically present in Charleston during the daytime? If he is here during the daytime work hours

Monday through Friday, he can conduct the State's business but I'm not sure that meets the definition of "residing." I drive to work every day from Raleigh County, my daylight hours are spent primarily in Charleston, and I have an intent to return here every day until the end of my term. But I would never say I "reside" in Charleston.

What about the nighttime? If the Governor is in Charleston during the night, at his place of abode, I think he's pretty clearly "living" and "domiciling" and "residing" and "nesting" or whatever it is the majority opinion thinks the Governor is supposed to do. But at night, he's probably sleeping and not conducting the State's business. If the Governor sleeps here at his residence, how are we to say he is actually accomplishing the duties set forth for the executive branch in our Constitution?

The true point that Mr. Sponaugle is trying to make in his case is one of effective and efficient government. Mr. Sponaugle contends that the Governor is not meeting his constitutional duties as efficiently as he could be; the Governor is not as effective at his job as he would be if he just spent some more time eating breakfast in Charleston. Being "for efficient government" is a very persuasive-sounding statement that is hard to disagree with, just like when a politician says he is "against crime" and "for lower taxes." The point he makes is practical and impossible to argue against. Mr. Sponaugle knows this as an elected member of the Legislature.

However, we aren't in a political arena; we are in a courtroom. And the point Mr. Sponaugle is trying to score is purely a political one. His challenge is not to the Governor's residency; it is to the decisions the Governor has made about how he runs his office. Mr. Sponaugle's argument conflates residency with efficient executive management. The argument is that, if the Governor just slept in Charleston more, then the Governor would probably make himself more available to one-on-one visits from members of the Legislature. Mr. Sponaugle clearly concludes that, if a judge would simply tell the Governor to spend more time in Charleston, then he will be a better, more effective leader with better relations to members of the Legislature.

Unlike the majority opinion, I sense that Mr. Sponaugle's "effective government" argument in this case is preempted by the "political question" doctrine. This case is a political spat for the legislative and executive departments to resolve. It should not involve the judiciary. Chief Justice John Marshall recognized early in the existence of our constitutional system of government that courts cannot "enquire how the executive, or executive officers, perform duties in which they have discretion." *Marbury v. Madison*, 5 U.S. 137, 170 (1803). The lesson he made is that "questions, in their nature political can never be made in this court."

Stated simply, the judiciary is powerless to second-guess the quality of decisions by the executive or legislative departments. The efficiency of the Governor's management style, the effectiveness of the efforts of the

Governor toward running the affairs of the State, are not justiciable questions. No court can effectively answer the political question propounded by Mr. Sponaugle. If a court requires the Governor to live in the executive mansion four nights a week, that really will not solve Mr. Sponaugle's true complaint about the way the Governor is managing his office. A court cannot issue a writ of mandamus to say that the Governor must do a better job or exercise discretion in a different way.

The real question then is, to what extent does the Constitution empower a circuit judge to meddle in the day-to-day affairs of an officer of another branch? Even the majority opinion concedes "that, if mandamus were to regulate the comings and goings of the Governor, such action would violate separation of powers principles." If the judge in this case commands the Governor to "reside in Charleston," what does that really mean in the end? In one sentence, the majority opinion concedes that is the limit of the judge's authority. If, as the majority opinion seems to require, the Governor announces that he will make Charleston his principal place of physical presence and his "home base," then the courts can do little more. To go any further and attempt to delineate how the Governor must act so as to achieve efficient or effective governance is clearly a political question that the courts should not be asked to resolve.

The Constitution has two clear penalties if an executive officer fails to live in Charleston: the Legislature can impeach the officer, or the voters can remove him or her from office. The separation of powers doctrine is not merely a suggestion, it is a principle every constitutional officer must strive to enforce. I believe too much mischief abounds when the judicial branch is asked to monitor the day-to-day actions of a state officer and approve how the officer carries out the discretionary obligations entrusted to him by the people. How the executive or legislative branches choose to operate are discretionary political questions beyond the purview of a judge. I appreciate why Mr. Sponaugle *started* this lawsuit over the Governor's residency; I dissent because I cannot see how, or if ever, this ends.

In re REQUEST FOR ADVISORY OPINION FROM HOUSE OF REPRESENTATIVES
961 A.2d 930 (R.I. 2008)

To the Honorable, the House of Representatives of the State of Rhode Island and Providence Plantations:

We have received your request seeking the advice of the justices of this Court, in accordance with the provisions of article 10, section 3 of the Rhode Island Constitution, concerning legislation (2007-H 6266) that is presently pending before the House of Representatives. The questions propounded are as follows:

(1) Would the proposed act, if duly enacted into law, which permits members of the General Assembly to sit as members of the Coastal Resources Management Council (CRMC), violate the constitutional amendment to Article IX, Section 5, so called Separation of Powers Amendment, passed by the electorate on November 2, 2004?

(2) Would the proposed act, if duly enacted into law, permit the Speaker of the House to appoint public members to the Coastal Resources Management Council (CRMC)?

Pursuant to the provisions of article 10, section 3 of the Rhode Island Constitution it is our duty to issue an advisory opinion at the request of the House of Representatives when the question concerns the constitutionality of pending legislation.

In November of 2004, the electorate of the State of Rhode Island approved the so-called separation of powers amendments. These amendments ushered in four fundamental changes to the Rhode Island Constitution and, for the first time in Rhode Island's history, clearly and explicitly established three separate and distinct departments of government. Those fundamental changes may be summarized as follows:

(1) Article 3, section 6 was amended to preclude legislators from serving on state boards, commissions, or other state or quasi-public entities that exercise executive power;

(2) Article 5 was amended to provide that the powers of the Rhode Island government are distributed into "three separate and distinct departments";

(3) Article 6, section 10, which had vested broad "continuing powers" in the General Assembly, was repealed; and

(4) Article 9, section 5 was amended to give the Governor appointment power with respect to members of any state or quasi-public entities exercising executive power, subject to the advice and consent of the Senate.

The doctrine of separation of powers, which is now expressly established in the Rhode Island Constitution, declares that governmental powers at the state level are divided among "three separate and distinct departments." In practice, this doctrine operates to confine legislative powers to the legislature, executive powers to the executive department, and judicial powers to the judiciary, precluding one branch of the government from usurping the powers of another.

While there can be no doubt that the separation of powers amendments constitute an important recalibration of the system of checks and balances within our state government, we do not view the amendments as effectuating a wholesale reallocation of power among the executive and the legislative departments. We emphasize, however, that the pendulum has not now swung to the opposite extreme with the adoption of the 2004 constitutional amendments. While the formal incorporation of the doctrine of separation of powers into the Constitution has established a somewhat different balance of power among the departments from that which existed previously, it would be overly simplistic and patently erroneous to view the amendments as somehow *subordinating* the role of the legislative branch to that of the executive.

It is incontestably true that, for most of its history, the Rhode Island General Assembly enjoyed significantly more power than did the legislatures of most of our sister states. "Unlike the United States Congress, the Rhode Island General Assembly does not look to our State Constitution for grants of power. Accordingly, this court has consistently adhered to the view that the General Assembly possessed all of the powers inhering in sovereignty other than those which the constitution textually commits to the other branches of our state government and that those that are not so committed are powers reserved to the General Assembly."

The proponents and drafters of the constitutional amendments, which were designed to bring about a greater degree of separation of powers in Rhode Island's governmental structure, manifestly carried out their task with precision. Certain powers of the General Assembly were explicitly curtailed, while others were left largely or entirely unaffected by the amendments.

The doctrine of separation of powers does not prohibit some overlapping of functions. The resolution of the problems with which government must grapple requires a certain degree of pragmatism; we are not in the pristine realm of algebraic equations, but rather in the complex and infinitely nuanced real world. Accordingly, administrative agencies may combine, to a certain extent, the functions of all three departments of government.

Nevertheless, as the United States Supreme Court has noted, the principle of separation of powers will be violated where the legislative department tries to control the execution of its enactments directly, instead of indirectly by passing new legislation. Direct legislative control of executive powers would be an impermissible usurpation of the central function of a coordinate branch.

Given the language of the separation of powers amendments, it is now our task to ascertain whether or not the CRMC exercises executive power. If it does exercise such power to any meaningful degree, then, pursuant to the plain language of the separation of powers amendments, two significant conclusions ineluctably result: (1) no member of the General Assembly nor an appointee of that body may sit on the CRMC; and (2) appointments to the CRMC are to be made exclusively by the Governor with the advice and consent of the Senate.

Upon examination of the CRMC's organic statute, chapter 23 of title 46, it appears that the CRMC combines functions that must properly be characterized as executive with functions that are quasi-legislative and quasi-judicial in nature. This is so even though the CRMC is an independent body not subject to direct gubernatorial supervision or control. The

CRMC's organic statute states that its provisions "shall be enforced by the coastal resources management council." The CRMC is authorized to "administer programs" developed pursuant to its quasi-legislative power to develop policy and adopt regulations.

It is clear to us that the above-summarized powers and functions of the CRMC are manifestly executive in nature. To state that *all* of the CRMC's powers and functions are legislative would be to blind oneself to that reality. To do so would be to willfully ignore the language of article 5 of the Rhode Island Constitution, which expressly requires the three departments of government to be "separate and distinct." The duties and functions to be conferred on the CRMC pursuant to the proposed legislation are not unconstitutional; the CRMC may constitutionally combine functions that may best be described as quasi-legislative, executive, and quasi-judicial in nature.

In our opinion, the proposed CRMC legislation, which is the subject of the questions posed to us, cannot be reconciled with our Constitution to the extent that it would permit sitting legislators to serve on the CRMC and would allow the General Assembly to make some appointments to that body. In other words, in view of the fact that the CRMC exercises executive power, the Governor has the right to appoint its members with the advice and consent of the Senate.

Without retreating from the foregoing views with respect to the effect of the separation of powers amendments on the appointment process, we would also emphasize that the General Assembly remains fully empowered to carry out its constitutional duty to protect the natural environment of the state through the vigorous and proactive exercise of its legislative powers. Nothing written in this advisory opinion should be construed as implying that the General Assembly does not retain the fullness of its constitutionally bestowed fact-finding powers and oversight responsibility with respect to the protection of the natural environment. We also note that the legislative branch of our state government also retains an important role in the appointment process due to the fact that the Senate may approve or reject gubernatorial appointments.

It is also important to note that the General Assembly retains without diminution its vast constitutional power to enact, revise, or repeal laws concerning coastal management and preservation of natural resources. In the course of exercising its plenary legislative power, the General Assembly may, for example: (1) provide specific criteria with respect to CRMC membership composition and qualifications; (2) narrow or expand the mandate of the CRMC; (3) adopt more elaborate oversight procedures and safeguards; (4) mandate training for new CRMC members; (5) require periodic reports on CRMC activities; (6) retain the right to review CRMC decisions in discrete areas relating to budget or revenue; (7) create a joint subcommittee to oversee coastal resources management; (8) create procedures for the thorough and rigorous vetting of CRMC nominees (including disclosure statements); (9) limit the Governor's removal power; (10) assume performance of the CRMC's rulemaking functions; or (11) restructure the CRMC in to one or more bodies exercising either purely quasi-legislative or purely executive functions.

We conclude by respectfully urging the Governor and the General Assembly to discuss the various subjects addressed in this advisory opinion with the goal of reaching a mutually satisfactory agreement regarding the rights and duties conferred upon each department by the terms of our Constitution.

Chapter XVI

ADMINISTRATIVE LAW

A. INTRODUCTION

In this chapter, we shift from general separation of powers issues that arise under state constitutions to a specific state separation of powers issue: administrative law. It's worth remembering at this point a difference between state structural limitations and state individual rights limitations. With respect to individual rights protected in the state constitutions and the federal Bill of Rights, such as free speech, free exercise, and so forth, a two-shot opportunity arises. If individuals object, say, to a speech-restrictive state or local law, they usually may challenge the law under the First Amendment's Free Speech Clause and under the free-speech counterpart of that State's constitution. In the context of traditional individual rights, the lawyer customarily has two shots, not one, to attack a law.

Not so with most structural disputes. The U.S. Constitution, generally speaking, does not limit the structure of the States and their state constitutions. The U.S. Supreme Court to date has not treated the republican form of government guarantee in the U.S. Constitution as judicially enforceable. And with respect to the issues discussed in this chapter—delegation of legislative powers and deference to administrative agencies—it will be the rare state law that a party may attack on state *and* federal grounds. For present purposes, the key source of authority usually will be the state constitution.

That still leaves opportunities for inter-governmental dialogue. Here, as elsewhere, state courts and federal courts may borrow historical, pragmatic, living constitutionalist, and other insights from each other. The early state constitutions, particularly those drafted between 1776 and 1786, established the blueprints for our division of government power into legislative, executive, and judicial branches. That gives many state courts a special place in discussing the history and purpose of these guarantees. At the same time, any court—federal or state—may offer useful insights about how best to construe these generally phrased, sometimes implied, limitations on the powers of each branch. That's why we treat this topic in much the same way as we treat the topics in most of the other chapters—as a comparative law inquiry into representative examples of what the federal and state courts have done in the area.

One last thing about state administrative law. This is an area in which the state courts have not been shy about acting independently of federal precedent in construing the structural guarantees in their state constitutions. Take the federal and state courts' treatment of the nondelegation doctrine. At the federal level, one could imagine calling it the "delegation doctrine." Save for two cases decided in the fertile year of 1935, no other U.S.

Supreme Court cases impose a judicially enforceable nondelegation doctrine. At the state level, by contrast, a vibrant judicially enforceable nondelegation doctrine is "alive and well," to borrow from one among several articles about the point. Jason Iuliano & Keith E. Whittington, *The Nondelegation Doctrine: Alive and Well*, 93 Notre Dame L. Rev. 619 (2017); *see also* Douglas H. Ginsburg & Steven Menashi, *Our Illiberal Administrative Law*, 10 N.Y.U. J.L. & Liberty 475, 492–93 (2016); James Rossi, *Institutional Design and the Lingering Legacy of Antifederalist Separation of Powers Ideas in the States*, 52 Vand. L. Rev. 1167, 1195–96 (1999).

A similar story has unfolded in the context of state limitations on judicial deference to administrative agencies. Here, too, many state courts have imposed limitations of their own, either by limiting the settings in which deference applies or by construing state separation of powers to bar judicial deference to agency interpretations of law. A lawyer in state court who blithely invokes *Chevron* deference—the federal doctrine that gives agencies considerable deference over the meaning of ambiguous federal laws—often will leave empty-handed.

B. NONDELEGATION

The United States Supreme Court has not invalidated a law on nondelegation grounds since 1935. That year, the Court invalidated parts of the National Industrial Recovery Act as unconstitutional delegations of legislative power to the executive branch in two cases: *Panama Refining Co. v. Ryan* and *A.L.A. Schechter Poultry Corp. v. United States*. In *Panama Refining*, 293 U.S. 388 (1935), the Court invalidated § 9(c) of the Act, which had given the President power to regulate oil producers. "Congress," the Court reasoned, "has declared no policy, has established no standard, has laid down no rule" to limit the President's authority to issue regulations.

In the second decision, reproduced in part below, the Court invalidated § 3 of the Act.

A.L.A. SCHECHTER POULTRY CORP. v. UNITED STATES
295 U.S. 495 (1935)

HUGHES, C.J.

Petitioners were convicted in the District Court of the United States for the Eastern District of New York on eighteen counts of an indictment charging violations of what is known as the "Live Poultry Code." They contended that the Code had been adopted pursuant to an unconstitutional delegation by Congress of legislative power.

The "Live Poultry Code" was promulgated under § 3 of the National Industrial Recovery Act. That section authorizes the President to approve "codes of fair competition." Such a code may be approved for a trade or industry, upon application by one or more trade or industrial associations or groups, if the President finds (1) that such associations or groups "impose no inequitable restrictions on admission to membership therein and are truly representative," and (2) that such codes are not designed "to promote monopolies or to eliminate or oppress small enterprises and will not operate to discriminate against them, and will tend to effectuate the policy" of Title I of the Act. Such codes "shall not permit monopolies or monopolistic practices." As a condition of his approval, the President may "impose such conditions (including requirements for the making of reports and the keeping of accounts) for the protection of consumers, competitors, employees, and others, and in furtherance of the public interest, and may provide such exceptions to and exemptions from the provisions of such code as the President in his discretion deems necessary to effectuate the policy herein declared." Where such a code has not been approved, the President may prescribe one, either on his own motion or on complaint. Violation of any provision of a code (so approved or prescribed) "in any transaction in or affecting interstate or foreign commerce" is made a misdemeanor punishable by a fine of not more than $500 for each offense.

The "Live Poultry Code" was approved by the President on April 13, 1934. The seventh article, containing "trade practice provisions," prohibits various practices which are said to constitute "unfair methods of competition."

The Constitution provides that "All legislative powers herein granted shall be vested in a Congress of the United States, which shall consist of a Senate and House of Representatives." Art I, § 1. And the Congress is authorized "To make all laws which shall be necessary and proper for carrying into execution" its general powers. Art. I, § 8, par. 18. The Congress is not permitted to abdicate or to transfer to others the essential legislative functions with which it is thus vested. We have repeatedly recognized the necessity of adapting legislation to complex conditions involving a host of details with which the national legislature cannot deal directly. We pointed out in the *Panama Company* case that the Constitution has never been regarded as denying to Congress the necessary resources of flexibility and practicality, which will enable it to perform its function in laying down policies and establishing standards, while leaving to selected instrumentalities the making of subordinate rules within prescribed limits and the determination of facts to which the policy as declared by the legislature is to apply. But we said that the constant recognition of the necessity and validity of such provisions, and the wide range of administrative authority which has been developed by means of them, cannot be allowed to obscure the limitations of the authority to delegate, if our constitutional system is to be maintained.

Accordingly, we look to the statute to see whether Congress has overstepped these limitations, whether Congress in authorizing "codes of fair competition" has itself established the standards of legal obligation, thus performing its essential legislative function, or, by the failure to enact such standards, has attempted to transfer that function to others.

What is meant by "fair competition" as the term is used in the Act? Does it refer to a category established in the law, and is the authority to make codes limited accordingly? Or is it used as a convenient designation for whatever set of laws the formulators of a code for a particular trade or industry may propose and the President may approve (subject to certain restrictions), or the President may himself prescribe, as being wise and beneficent provisions for the government of the trade or industry in order to accomplish the broad purposes of rehabilitation, correction and expansion which are stated in the first section of Title I?

The Act does not define "fair competition." The codes may, indeed, cover conduct which existing law condemns, but they are not limited to conduct of that sort. The Government does not contend that the Act contemplates such a limitation. It would be opposed both to the declared purposes of the Act and to its administrative construction.

For a statement of the authorized objectives and content of the "codes of fair competition" we are referred repeatedly to the "Declaration of Policy" in section one of Title I of the Recovery Act. Thus, the approval of a code by the President is conditioned on his finding that it "will tend to effectuate the policy of this title." § 3(a). The President is authorized to impose such conditions "for the protection of consumers, competitors, employees, and others, and in furtherance of the public interest, and may provide such exceptions to and exemptions from the provisions of such code as the President in his discretion deems necessary to effectuate the policy herein declared." The "policy herein declared" is manifestly that set forth in section one. That declaration embraces a broad range of objectives. Among them we find the elimination of "unfair competitive practices." But even if this clause were to be taken to relate to practices which fall under the ban of existing law, either common law or statute, it is still only one of the authorized aims described in section one. It is there declared to be "the policy of Congress"—"to remove obstructions to the free flow of interstate and foreign commerce which tend to diminish the amount thereof; and to eliminate unfair competitive practices, to promote the fullest possible utilization of the present productive capacity of industries, to avoid undue restriction of production (except as may be temporarily required), to increase the consumption of industrial and agricultural products by increasing purchasing power, to reduce and relieve unemployment, to improve standards of labor, and otherwise to rehabilitate industry and to conserve natural resources."

Under § 3, whatever "may tend to effectuate" these general purposes may be included in the "codes of fair competition." We think the conclusion is inescapable that the authority sought to be conferred by § 3 was not merely to deal with "unfair competitive practices." Rather, the purpose is clearly disclosed to authorize new and controlling prohibitions through codes of laws which would embrace what the formulators would propose, and what the President would approve, or prescribe, as wise and beneficient measures for the government of trades and industries in order to bring about their rehabilitation, correction and development, according to the general declaration of policy in section one. Codes of laws of this sort are styled "codes of fair competition."

The question, then, turns upon the authority which § 3 of the Recovery Act vests in the President to approve or prescribe. If the codes have standing as penal statutes, this must be due to the effect of the executive action. Congress cannot delegate legislative power to the President to exercise an unfettered discretion to make whatever laws he thinks may be needed or advisable for the rehabilitation and expansion of trade or industry. Accordingly we turn to the Recovery Act to ascertain what limits have been set to the exercise of the President's discretion. First, the President, as a condition of approval, is required to find that the trade or industrial associations or groups which propose a code, "impose no inequitable restrictions on admission to membership" and are "truly representative." That condition, however, relates only to the status of the initiators of the new laws and not to the permissible scope of such laws. Second, the President is required to find that the code is not "designed to promote monopolies or to eliminate or oppress small enterprises and will not operate to discriminate against them." And, to this is added a proviso that the code "shall not permit monopolies or monopolistic practices." But these restrictions leave virtually untouched the field of policy envisaged by section one, and, in that wide field of legislative possibilities, the proponents of a code, refraining from monopolistic designs, may roam at will and the President may approve or disapprove their proposals as he may see fit. That is the precise effect of the further finding that the President is to make—that the code "will tend to effectuate the policy of this title." While this is called a finding, it is really but a statement of an opinion as to the general effect upon the promotion of trade or industry of a scheme of laws. These are the only findings which Congress has made essential in order to put into operation a legislative code having the aims described in the "Declaration of Policy."

To summarize and conclude upon this point: Section 3 of the Recovery Act is without precedent. It supplies no standards for any trade, industry or activity. It does not undertake to prescribe rules of conduct to be applied to particular states of fact determined by appropriate administrative procedure.

Instead of prescribing rules of conduct, it authorizes the making of codes to prescribe them. For that legislative undertaking, § 3 sets up no standards, aside from the statement of the general aims of rehabilitation, correction and expansion described in section one. In view of the scope of that broad declaration, and of the nature of the few restrictions that are imposed, the discretion of the President in approving or prescribing codes, and thus enacting laws for the government of trade and industry throughout the country, is virtually unfettered. We think that the code-making authority thus conferred is an unconstitutional delegation of legislative power. We hold the code provisions here in question to be invalid and that the judgment of conviction must be reversed.

NOTE

Over time, 1935 came to look more and more like a good year, the only good year, for federal nondelegation decisions. But in 2019, eighty-four years later, the United States Supreme Court seemed to be on the precipice of accepting a nondelegation argument in *Gundy v. United States*. At issue was a provision of the Sex Offender Registration and Notification Act. A divided Court rejected the claim, but no one opinion captured five votes. Excerpted here are Justice Kagan's plurality opinion (joined by Justices Ginsburg, Breyer, and Sotomayor), Justice Alito's concurrence in the judgment, and Justice Gorsuch's dissent (joined by Chief Justice Roberts and Justice Thomas).

GUNDY v. UNITED STATES
139 S. Ct. 2116 (2019)

KAGAN, J.

The nondelegation doctrine bars Congress from transferring its legislative power to another branch of Government. This case requires us to decide whether 34 U.S.C. § 20913(d), enacted as part of the Sex Offender Registration and Notification Act (SORNA), violates that doctrine. We hold it does not. Under § 20913(d), the Attorney General must apply SORNA's registration requirements as soon as feasible to offenders convicted before the statute's enactment. That delegation easily passes constitutional muster.

The basic registration scheme works as follows. A "sex offender" is defined as "an individual who was convicted of" specified criminal offenses: all offenses "involving a sexual act or sexual contact" and additional offenses "against a minor." An offender must register "before completing a sentence of imprisonment with respect to the offense giving rise to the registration requirement" (or, if the offender is not sentenced to prison, "not later than three business days after being sentenced"). Two provisions down, subsection (d) addresses (in its title's words) the "initial registration of sex offenders unable to comply with subsection (b)." The provision states:

"The Attorney General shall have the authority to specify the applicability of the requirements of this subchapter to sex offenders convicted before the enactment of this chapter and to prescribe rules for the registration of any such sex offenders and for other categories of sex offenders who are unable to comply with subsection (b)."

Subsection (d), in other words, focuses on individuals convicted of a sex offense before SORNA's enactment—a group we will call pre-Act offenders. For the entire group of pre-Act offenders, once again, the Attorney General "shall have the authority" to "specify the applicability" of SORNA's registration requirements and "to prescribe rules for their registration."

The provision, in Gundy's view, "grants the Attorney General plenary power to determine SORNA's applicability to pre-Act offenders—to require them to register, or not, as she sees fit, and to change her policy for any reason and at any time." If that were so, we would face a nondelegation question. But it is not. This Court has already interpreted § 20913(d) to say something different—to require the Attorney General to apply SORNA to all pre-Act offenders as soon as feasible. And revisiting that issue yet more fully today, we reach the same conclusion. The text, considered alongside its context, purpose, and history, makes clear that the Attorney General's discretion extends only to considering and addressing feasibility issues. Given that statutory meaning, Gundy's constitutional claim must fail. Section 20913(d)'s delegation falls well within permissible bounds.

Recall again the delegation provision at issue. Congress gave the Attorney General authority to "specify the applicability" of SORNA's requirements to pre-Act offenders. § 20913(d). And in the second half of the same sentence, Congress gave him authority to "prescribe rules for the registration of any such sex offenders who are unable to comply with" subsection (b)'s initial registration requirement. What does the delegation in § 20913(d) allow the Attorney General to do?

Begin at the beginning, with the "declaration of purpose" that is SORNA's first sentence. § 20901. There, Congress announced that "to protect the public," it was "establishing a comprehensive national system for the registration" of "sex offenders and offenders against children." § 20901. The term "comprehensive" has a clear meaning—something that is all-encompassing or sweeping. That description could not fit the system SORNA created if the Attorney General could decline, for any reason or no reason at all, to apply SORNA to all pre-Act offenders.

Now that we have determined what § 20913(d) means, we can consider whether it violates the Constitution. The question becomes: Did Congress make an impermissible delegation when it instructed the Attorney General to apply SORNA's registration requirements to pre-Act offenders as soon as feasible? Under this Court's long-established law, that question is easy. Its answer is no.

The statute conveyed Congress's policy that the Attorney General require pre-Act offenders to register as soon as feasible. Under the law, the feasibility issues he could address were administrative—and, more specifically, transitional—in nature. Those issues arose from the need to "newly register or reregister a large number of pre-Act offenders" not then in the system. And they arose, more technically, from the gap between an initial registration requirement hinged on imprisonment and a set of pre-Act offenders long since released.

Even for those limited matters, the Act informed the Attorney General that he did not have forever to work things out. By stating its demand for a "comprehensive" registration system and by defining the "sex offenders" required to register to include pre-Act offenders, Congress conveyed that the Attorney General had only temporary authority. That statutory authority, as compared to the delegations we have upheld in the past, is distinctly small-bore.

ALITO, J., concurring in the judgment.

The Constitution confers on Congress certain "legislative powers," Art. I, § 1, and does not permit Congress to delegate them to another branch of the Government. Nevertheless, since 1935, the Court has uniformly rejected nondelegation arguments and has upheld provisions that authorized agencies to adopt important rules pursuant to extraordinarily capacious standards.

If a majority of this Court were willing to reconsider the approach we have taken for the past 84 years, I would support that effort. But because a majority is not willing to do that, it would be freakish to single out the provision at issue here for special treatment.

Because I cannot say that the statute lacks a discernable standard that is adequate under the approach this Court has taken for many years, I vote to affirm.

GORSUCH, J., dissenting.

The Constitution promises that only the people's elected representatives may adopt new federal laws restricting liberty. Yet the statute before us scrambles that design. It purports to endow the nation's chief prosecutor with the power to write his own criminal code governing the lives of a half-million citizens.

The breadth of the authority Congress granted to the Attorney General in § 20913(d) can only be described as vast. As the Department of Justice itself has acknowledged, SORNA "does not require the Attorney General" to impose registration requirements on pre-Act offenders "within a certain time frame or by a date certain; it does not require him to act at all." If the Attorney General does choose to act, he can require all pre-Act offenders to register, or he can "require some but not all to register." For those he requires to register, the Attorney General may impose "some but not all of SORNA's registration requirements," as he pleases. And he is free to change his mind on any of these matters "at any given time or over the course of different administrations." Congress thus gave the Attorney General free rein to write the rules for virtually the entire existing sex offender population in this country—a situation that promised to persist for years or decades until pre-Act offenders passed away or fulfilled the terms of their registration obligations and post-Act offenders came to predominate.

As Chief Justice Marshall explained, Congress may not "delegate powers which are strictly and exclusively legislative." Or as John Locke, one of the thinkers who most influenced the framers' understanding of the separation of powers, described it, "The legislative cannot transfer the power of making laws to any other hands."

Accepting, then, that we have an obligation to decide whether Congress has unconstitutionally divested itself of its legislative responsibilities, the question follows: What's the test?

First, we know that as long as Congress makes the policy decisions when regulating private conduct, it may authorize another branch to "fill up the details." Congress must set forth standards "sufficiently definite and precise to enable Congress, the courts, and the public to ascertain" whether Congress's guidance has been followed.

Second, once Congress prescribes the rule governing private conduct, it may make the application of that rule depend on executive fact-finding.

Third, Congress may assign the executive and judicial branches certain non-legislative responsibilities. While the Constitution vests all federal legislative power in Congress alone, Congress's legislative authority sometimes overlaps with authority the Constitution separately vests in another branch. So, for example, when a congressional statute confers wide discretion to the executive, no separation-of-powers problem may arise if "the discretion is to be exercised over matters already within the scope of executive power."

It's hard to see how SORNA leaves the Attorney General with only details to fill up.

In the end, there isn't a single policy decision concerning pre-Act offenders on which Congress even tried to speak, and not a single other case where we have upheld executive authority over matters like these on the ground they constitute mere "details." This much appears to have been deliberate, too. Because members of Congress could not reach consensus on the treatment of pre-Act offenders, it seems this was one of those situations where they found it expedient to hand off the job to the executive and direct there the blame for any later problems that might emerge.

Nor can SORNA be described as an example of conditional legislation subject to executive fact-finding. Instead, it gave the Attorney General unfettered discretion to decide which requirements to impose on which pre-Act offenders.

Finally, SORNA does not involve an area of overlapping authority with the executive. Congress may assign the President broad authority regarding the conduct of foreign affairs or other matters where he enjoys his own inherent Article II powers. But SORNA stands far afield from any of that. It gives the Attorney General the authority to "prescribe the rules by which the duties and rights" of citizens are determined, a quintessentially legislative power.

The statute here also sounds all the alarms the founders left for us. Because Congress could not achieve the consensus necessary to resolve the hard problems associated with SORNA's application to pre-Act offenders, it passed the potato to the Attorney General. And freed from the need to assemble a broad supermajority for his views, the Attorney General did not hesitate to apply the statute retroactively to a politically unpopular minority.

NOTES

1. *Gundy* may not be the last word on this issue. Three justices, led by Justice Gorsuch, have now offered their reassessment of the doctrine. Justice Alito's concurrence suggests that he remains open to reconsidering the Court's longstanding practice of rejecting nondelegation arguments. Neither Justice Kavanaugh nor Justice Barrett participated in the case.

2. Several state courts already enforce a more robust nondelegation doctrine based on their own state constitutions. The following cases provide a sampling. The state experiences offer at least two insights: (1) They show the various ways in which state separation of powers can work, and (2) they show that many state courts have not had a problem with line drawing—one of the key impediments thus far in enforcing the nondelegation doctrine at the federal level. If state courts can draw principled lines in this area, it's fair to wonder whether the federal courts can do so as well.

McNEILL v. STATE
375 P.3d 1022 (Nev. 2016)

DOUGLAS, J.

In this appeal, we consider whether the State Board of Parole Commissioners may impose conditions not enumerated in NRS 213.1243 on a sex offender subject to lifetime supervision. We conclude that the plain language of NRS 213.1243 does not grant the Board authority to impose additional conditions. We further conclude that this omission was intentional because the Legislature may not delegate its power to legislate. We therefore reverse the district court's judgment of conviction based on violations of conditions of lifetime supervision not enumerated in NRS 213.1243.

Steve McNeill is a convicted sex offender on lifetime supervision. According to McNeill's lifetime supervision agreement, he was required to pay certain fees, submit to a urinalysis, meet a curfew, and maintain full-time employment, among other things.

After five years of lifetime supervision, McNeill was reassigned to Ashley Mangan, a parole and probation officer in the sex offender unit. McNeill reported to Mangan at the Division of Parole and Probation for the first time in March 2013. Mangan established a curfew for McNeill, requiring that he be present near the intersection of two specified streets referred to as his "residence" between 5 p.m. and 5 a.m.

According to Mangan, she was unable to locate McNeill at his residence when she went to visit McNeill to confirm that he was in compliance with his curfew. Thus, when McNeill reported to Mangan in April, Mangan requested that McNeill draw a map of where he was sleeping. McNeill complied and requested an extended curfew. Mangan established a later curfew, requiring that McNeill be at his residence by 8 p.m. rather than 5 p.m.

In August, Mangan requested that McNeill submit to a urinalysis. McNeill refused. Mangan then took McNeill to meet with her supervisor, who was unable to persuade McNeill to comply. McNeill affirmed that he would not submit to urinalyses, had no plans to abide by a curfew, and would sleep where he chose.

The State filed a criminal complaint in March 2014, charging McNeill with violation of conditions of lifetime supervision (count 1) and prohibited acts by a sex offender (count 2).

After a three-day trial, McNeill requested a directed verdict on both charges. The district court dismissed count two, but the jury found McNeill guilty on count one. The district court also denied McNeill's subsequent motion for an arrest of judgment, determining that the Board of Parole Commissioners had authority through the language of NRS 213.1243 to establish conditions of lifetime supervision not enumerated in the statute.

On appeal, McNeill contends that NRS 213.1243 does not delegate authority to the Board to impose additional lifetime supervision conditions that are not enumerated in the statute. Thus, McNeill argues that he did not violate NRS 213.1243, even if he violated the additional conditions imposed by the Board. In contrast, the State argues that the Board may establish additional conditions not specifically enumerated in NRS 213.1243 when supervising a sex offender on lifetime supervision.

Without a doubt, the Legislature may not delegate its power to legislate. And because a violation of a condition of lifetime supervision is a new crime, if the statute is read to mean, as the State suggests, that the Board may create additional conditions, then the Board would effectively have authority to create law. Because we presume that the Legislature is aware that it may not delegate the power to legislate pursuant to the separation of powers, we presume that it acted in accordance.

The State argues that the Legislature may appropriately delegate authority to administrative agencies to facilitate the practical execution of laws it enacts without violating the separation of powers. It is well settled that "although the legislature may not delegate its power to legislate, it may delegate the power to determine the facts or state of things upon which the law makes its own operations depend."

> Thus, the legislature can make the application or operation of a statute complete within itself dependent upon the existence of certain facts or conditions, the ascertainment of which is left to the administrative agency. In doing so the legislature vests the agency with mere fact finding authority and not the authority to legislate. The agency is only authorized to determine the facts which will make the statute effective. Such authority will be upheld as constitutional so long as suitable standards are established by the legislature for the agency's use of its power. These standards must be sufficient to guide the agency with respect to the purpose of the law and the power authorized. Sufficient legislative standards are required in order to assure that the agency will neither act capriciously nor arbitrarily.

In enacting NRS 213.1234, the Legislature did not explicitly provide the Board the authority to create additional conditions. And even assuming that the Legislature had intended to do so, that delegation of power would fail because the Legislature has not provided guidelines informing the Board how, when, or under what circumstances, it may create additional conditions.

Because the Board-imposed conditions were unlawful, and any Board violations cannot be separated from any NRS 213.1243 violations, we reverse the judgment of conviction and remand for a new trial.

In re CERTIFIED QUESTIONS FROM U.S. DISTRICT COURT
958 N.W.2d 1 (Mich. 2020)

MARKMAN, J.

This case concerns the nature and scope of our state's public response to one of the most threatening public-health crises of modern times. In response to a global, national, and state outbreak of the severe acute respiratory disease named COVID-19, Michigan's Governor has issued a succession of executive orders over the past six months limiting public and private gatherings, closing and imposing restrictions upon certain businesses, and regulating a broad variety of other aspects of the day-to-day lives of our state's citizens in an effort to contain the spread of this contagious and sometimes deadly disease.

The ongoing validity of these executive orders has been the subject of much public debate as well as litigation in both state and federal courts. In the interest of comity, the United States District Court for the Western District of Michigan has asked this Court to resolve critical questions concerning the constitutional and legal authority of the Governor to issue such orders. We hereby respond to the federal court in the affirmative by choosing to answer the questions the federal court has certified, concluding as follows: first, the Governor did not possess the authority under the Emergency Management Act of 1976 (the EMA) to declare a "state of emergency" or "state of disaster" based on the COVID-19 pandemic after April 30, 2020; and second, the Governor does not possess the authority to exercise emergency powers under the Emergency Powers of the Governor Act of 1945 (the EPGA) because that act is an unlawful delegation of legislative power to the executive branch in violation of the Michigan Constitution. Accordingly, the executive orders issued by the Governor in response to the COVID-19 pandemic now lack any basis under Michigan law.

The coronavirus (COVID-19) is a respiratory disease that can result, and has resulted, in significant numbers of persons suffering serious illness or death. In response to COVID-19, on March 10, 2020, one day before it was declared a pandemic by the World Health Organization, the Governor issued Executive Order (EO) No. 2020-04, declaring a "state of emergency" under the EPGA and the EMA. On March 20, 2020, the Governor issued EO 2020-17, which prohibited medical providers from performing nonessential procedures. On March 23, 2020, she issued EO 2020-21, which ordered all residents to stay at home with limited exceptions. On April 1, 2020, she issued EO 2020-33, which declared a "state of emergency" under the EPGA and a "state of emergency" and "state of disaster" under the EMA. She then requested that the Legislature extend the state of emergency and state of disaster by 70 days, and a resolution was adopted, extending the state of emergency and state of disaster, but only through April 30, 2020. Senate Concurrent Resolution No. 2020-24.

On April 30, 2020, the Governor issued EO 2020-66, which terminated the declaration of a state of emergency and state of disaster under the EMA. But, immediately thereafter, she issued EO 2020-67, which provided that a state of emergency remained declared under the EPGA. At the same time, she issued EO 2020-68, which redeclared a state of emergency and state of disaster under the EMA. Although the Governor subsequently lifted the ban on nonessential medical procedures, she then issued EO 2020-97, which imposed numerous obligations on healthcare providers, including specific waiting-room procedures, limitations on the number of patient appointments, adding special hours for highly vulnerable patients, and establishing enhanced telehealth and telemedicine procedures.

Plaintiffs in the underlying federal case are healthcare providers that were prohibited from performing nonessential procedures while EO 2020-17 was in effect and a patient who was prohibited from undergoing knee-replacement surgery. Defendants are the Governor, the Attorney General, and the Director of the Michigan Department of Health and Human Services. Although EO 2020-17 has been rescinded, the federal district court held that the case is not moot because at that time EO 2020-114 (now EO 2020-184) continued to impose restrictions on healthcare providers.

The first question before this Court is whether the Governor possessed the authority under the EMA to renew her declaration of a state of emergency and state of disaster based on the COVID-19 pandemic after April 30, 2020. MCL 30.403 of the EMA provides, in pertinent part:

> (3) The governor shall, by executive order or proclamation, declare a state of disaster if he or she finds a disaster has occurred or the threat of a disaster exists. The state of disaster shall continue until the governor finds that the threat or danger has passed, the disaster has been dealt with to the extent that disaster conditions no longer exist, or until the declared state of disaster has been in effect for 28 days. *After 28 days, the governor shall issue an executive order or proclamation declaring the state of disaster terminated, unless a request by the governor for an extension of the state of disaster for a specific number of days is approved by resolution of both houses of the legislature.*
>
> (4) The governor shall, by executive order or proclamation, declare a state of emergency if he or she finds that an emergency has occurred or that the threat of an emergency exists. The state of emergency shall continue until the governor finds that the threat or danger has passed, the emergency has been dealt with to the extent that emergency conditions no longer exist, or until the declared state of emergency has been in effect for 28 days. *After 28 days, the governor shall issue an executive order or proclamation declaring the state of emergency terminated, unless a request by the governor for an extension of the state of emergency for a specific number of days is approved by resolution of both houses of the legislature.* [Emphasis added.]

Critically, MCL 30.403(3) and (4) provide that "after 28 days, the governor shall issue an executive order or proclamation declaring the state of disaster/emergency terminated, unless a request by the governor for an extension of the state of disaster/emergency for a specific number of days is approved by resolution of both houses of the legislature." Because the Legislature here did not approve an extension of the "state of emergency" or "state of disaster" beyond April 30, 2020, the Governor was required to issue an executive order declaring these to be terminated. While the Governor did so, she acted immediately thereafter to issue another executive order, again declaring a "state of emergency" and "state of disaster" under the EMA for the identical reasons as the declarations that had just been terminated—the public-health crisis created by COVID-19. Given that MCL 30.403(3) and (4) required the Governor to terminate a declaration of a state of emergency or state of disaster after 28 days in the absence of a legislatively authorized extension, we do not believe that the Legislature intended to allow the Governor to redeclare under the EMA the identical state of emergency and state of disaster under these circumstances. To allow such a redeclaration would effectively render the 28-day limitation a nullity.

The Governor argues that because MCL 30.403(3) and (4) provide that "the governor shall, by executive order or proclamation, declare a state of disaster/emergency if he or she finds a disaster/an emergency has occurred or the threat of a disaster/an emergency exists," the Governor had no choice here but to redeclare a state of emergency and state of disaster. However, when the cited language is read in reasonable conjunction with the language imposing the 28-day limitation, it is clear that the Governor only possesses the authority or obligation to declare a state of emergency or state of disaster once and then must terminate that declaration after 28 days if the Legislature has not authorized an extension. The Governor possesses no authority—much less obligation—to *redeclare* the same state of emergency or state of disaster and thereby avoid the Legislature's limitation on her authority under the EMA.

The second question before this Court is whether the Governor possessed the authority under the EPGA to proclaim a state of emergency based on the COVID-19 pandemic after April 30, 2020.

MCL 10.31(1) of the EPGA sets forth the circumstances in which the Governor may proclaim a state of emergency and the authorized subject matter of his or her emergency powers:

> During times of great public crisis, disaster, rioting, catastrophe, or similar public emergency within the state, or reasonable apprehension of immediate danger of a public emergency of that kind, when public safety is imperiled, either upon application of the mayor of a city, sheriff of a county, or the commissioner of the Michigan state police or upon his or her own volition, the governor may proclaim a state of emergency and designate the area involved. After making the proclamation or declaration, the governor may promulgate reasonable orders, rules, and regulations as he or she considers necessary to protect life and property or to bring the emergency situation within the affected area under control. Those orders, rules, and regulations may include, but are not limited to, providing for the control of traffic, including public and private transportation, within the area or any section of the area; designation of specific zones within the area in which occupancy and use of buildings and ingress and egress of persons and vehicles may be prohibited or regulated; control of places of amusement and assembly and of persons on public streets and thoroughfares; establishment of a curfew; control of the sale, transportation, and use of alcoholic beverages and liquors; and control of the storage, use, and transportation of explosives or inflammable materials or liquids deemed to be dangerous to public safety.

MCL 10.31(2) of the EPGA sets forth the effectiveness of the emergency powers, including the time at which those powers are no longer in effect:

> The orders, rules, and regulations promulgated under subsection (1) are effective from the date and in the manner prescribed in the orders, rules, and regulations and shall be made public as provided in the orders, rules, and regulations. The orders, rules, and regulations may be amended, modified, or rescinded, in the manner in which they were promulgated, from time to time by the governor during the pendency of the emergency, but shall cease to be in effect upon declaration by the governor that the emergency no longer exists.

MCL 10.32 explains the legislative intentions of the EPGA:

> It is hereby declared to be the legislative intent to invest the governor with sufficiently broad power of action in the exercise of the police power of the state to provide adequate control over persons and conditions during such periods of impending or actual public crisis or disaster. The provisions of this act shall be broadly construed to effectuate this purpose.

Plaintiffs argue that a genuine emergency must necessarily be short-lived and that because our state has been dealing with COVID-19 for more than six months, it is no longer an emergency. We respectfully disagree. Simply because something has been ongoing for some extended period of time does not signify that there is no longer an "urgent need for assistance or relief." That a fire, for example, has been burning for months does not mean that there is no longer an "urgent need for assistance or relief," and the same is obviously true of an epidemic. In short, an emergency is an emergency for as long as it persists as an emergency.

Additionally, both plaintiffs and the Legislature argue that the historical context of the EPGA, enacted in 1945 in response to riots in Detroit in 1943, suggests that it was intended to apply only to local emergencies. However, even if an undisputed or a principal purpose of the EPGA was to enable the Governor to respond to a local emergency such as a riot, that does not indicate that enabling the Governor to respond to a local emergency was the EPGA's *exclusive* purpose. "The remedy of a legal provision often extends beyond the particular act or mischief which first suggested the necessity of the law."

Const. 1963, art. 3, § 2 summarizes the separation-of-powers principle in Michigan as follows:

> The powers of government are divided into three branches: legislative, executive and judicial. No person exercising powers of one branch shall exercise powers properly belonging to another branch except as expressly provided in this constitution.

"The principal function of the separation of powers is to protect individual liberty." "The accumulation of all powers, legislative, executive, and judiciary, in the same hands, whether of one, a few, or many, and whether hereditary, self-appointed, or elective, may justly be pronounced the very definition of tyranny." And as Montesquieu explained, "when the legislative and executive powers are united in the same person, or in the same body of magistrates, there can be no liberty; because apprehensions may arise, lest the same monarch or senate should enact tyrannical laws, to execute them in a tyrannical manner."

Const. 1963, art. 4, § 1 provides that "the legislative power of the State of Michigan is vested in a senate and a house of representatives." "The legislative power has been defined as the power to regulate public concerns, and to make law for the benefit and welfare of the state." "The power of the *Legislative* being derived from the People by a positive voluntary Grant and Institution, can be no other, than what that positive Grant conveyed, which being only to make *Laws*, and not to make *Legislators*, the *Legislative* can have no power to transfer their Authority of making Laws, and place it in other hands." Locke, *Two Treatises of Government*. Accordingly, "one of the settled maxims in constitutional law is, that the power conferred upon the legislature to make laws cannot be delegated by that department to any other body or authority." Cooley, *Constitutional Limitations* (1886).

"Strictly speaking, there is *no* acceptable delegation of legislative power." "The true distinction is between the delegation of power to make the law, which necessarily involves a discretion as to what it shall be, and conferring authority or discretion as to its execution, to be exercised under and in pursuance of the law. The first cannot be done; to the latter no valid objection can be made." "A certain degree of discretion, and thus of lawmaking, *inheres* in most executive or judicial action." "The focus of controversy has been whether the *degree* of generality contained in the authorization for exercise of executive or judicial powers in a particular field is so unacceptably high as to *amount* to a delegation of legislative powers."

We have explained that "challenges of unconstitutional delegation of legislative power are generally framed in terms of the adequacy of the standards fashioned by the Legislature to channel the agency's or individual's exercise of the delegated power." "The preciseness required of the standards will depend on the complexity of the subject." "In making this determination whether the statute contains sufficient limits or standards we must be mindful of the fact that such standards must be sufficiently broad to permit efficient administration in order to properly carry out the policy of the Legislature but not so broad as to leave the people unprotected from uncontrolled, arbitrary power in the hands of administrative officials." "The standards prescribed for guidance must be as reasonably precise as the subject-matter requires or permits."

The scope of the delegation is also relevant when assessing the sufficiency of the standards. "The degree of agency discretion that is acceptable varies according to the scope of the power conferred." Consequently, "the ultimate judgment regarding the constitutionality of a delegation must be made not on the basis of the scope of the power alone, but on the basis of its scope *plus* the specificity of the standards governing its exercise. When the scope increases to immense proportions the standards must be correspondingly more precise."

In other words, it is one thing if a statute confers a great degree of discretion, i.e., power, over a narrow subject; it is quite another if that power can be brought to bear on something as "immense" as an entire economy. Furthermore, "the area of permissible indefiniteness narrows when the regulation invokes criminal sanctions and potentially affects fundamental rights."

Finally, the durational scope of the delegated power also has some relevant bearing, in our judgment, on whether the statute violates the nondelegation doctrine. Of course, an unconstitutional delegation is no less unconstitutional because it lasts for only two days. But it is also true, as common sense would suggest, that the conferral of indefinite authority accords a greater accumulation of power than does the grant of temporary authority.

Simply put, as the scope of the powers conferred upon the Governor by the Legislature becomes increasingly broad, in regard to both the *subject matter* and their *duration*, the *standards* imposed upon the Governor's discretion by the Legislature must correspondingly become more detailed and precise.

Concerning the subject matter of the emergency powers conferred by the EPGA, it is remarkably broad, authorizing the Governor to enter orders "to protect life and property or to bring the emergency situation within the affected area under control." It is indisputable that such orders "to protect life and property" encompass a substantial part of the entire police power of the state. And the police power is legislative in nature. The EPGA "in effect, suspends normal civil government."

To illustrate the breadth of the emergency powers contemplated by the EPGA, we note that during the COVID-19 pandemic the Governor has, by way of executive orders specifically issued under the EPGA, effected the following public policies: *requiring* all residents to stay home with limited exceptions; *requiring* all residents to wear face coverings in indoor public spaces and when outdoors if unable to consistently maintain a distance of six feet or more from individuals who are not members of their household, including requiring children to wear face coverings while playing sports; *requiring* all residents to remain at least six feet away from people outside one's household to the extent feasible under the circumstances; *requiring* businesses to comply with numerous workplace safeguards, including daily health screenings of employees; *closing* restaurants, food courts, cafes, coffeehouses, bars, taverns, brew pubs, breweries, microbreweries, distilleries, wineries, tasting rooms, clubs, hookah bars, cigar bars, vaping lounges, barbershops, hair salons, nail salons, tanning salons, tattoo parlors, schools, churches, theaters, cinemas, libraries, museums, gymnasiums, fitness centers, public swimming pools, recreation centers, indoor sports facilities, indoor exercise facilities, exercise studios, spas, casinos, and racetracks; *closing* places of public amusement, including arcades, bingo halls, bowling alleys, indoor climbing facilities, skating rinks, and trampoline parks; *prohibiting* nonessential travel, in-person work that is not necessary to sustain or protect life, and nonessential in-person business operations; *prohibiting* the sale of carpet, flooring, furniture, plants, and paint; *prohibiting* advertisements for nonessential goods, nonessential medical and dental procedures, and nonessential veterinary services; *prohibiting* visitors at healthcare facilities, residential care facilities, congregate care facilities, and juvenile justice facilities; and *prohibiting* boating, golfing, and public and private gatherings of persons not part of a single household. Each of these policies was putatively ordered "to protect life and property" and/or to "bring the emergency situation within the affected area under control." What is more, these policies exhibit a sweeping scope, both with regard to the subjects covered and the power exercised over those subjects. Indeed, they rest on an assertion of power to reorder social life and to limit, if not altogether displace, the livelihoods of residents across the state and throughout wide-ranging industries.

We accordingly conclude that the delegation of power to the Governor to "promulgate reasonable orders, rules, and regulations as he or she considers necessary to protect life and property," MCL 10.31(1), constitutes an unlawful delegation of legislative power to the executive and is therefore unconstitutional under Const. 1963, art. 3, § 2, which prohibits exercise of the legislative power by the executive branch. The powers conferred by the EPGA simply cannot be rendered constitutional by the standards "reasonable" and "necessary," either separately or in tandem.

We conclude that the Governor lacked the authority to declare a "state of emergency" or a "state of disaster" under the EMA after April 30, 2020, on the basis of the COVID-19 pandemic. Furthermore, we conclude that the EPGA is in violation of the Constitution of our state because it purports to delegate to the executive branch the legislative powers of state government—including its plenary police powers—and to allow the exercise of such powers indefinitely. As a consequence, the EPGA cannot continue to provide a basis for the Governor to exercise emergency powers.

McCORMACK, C.J., concurring in part and dissenting in part.

Every eighth-grade civics student learns about the separation of powers and checks and balances—design features of our government to prevent one branch from accumulating too much power. The principle of separation of powers is fundamental to democracy. As James Madison put it: "The accumulation of all powers, legislative, executive, and judiciary, in the same hands, whether of one, a few, or many may justly be pronounced the very definition of tyranny." The Federalist No. 47.

In this light, the Legislature's delegation of authority to the Governor in the Emergency Powers of the Governor Act may appear concerning at a superficial glance, given that it vests the Governor, and the Governor alone, with the authority to exercise the whole of the state's police power in some emergencies. But our job is to apply the law. And all our precedent vindicates the Legislature's choice to delegate authority to the Governor in an emergency.

That does not insulate the Governor's exercise of that authority from checks and balances. To the contrary, there are many ways to test the Governor's response to this life-and-death pandemic.

We have consistently upheld statutes with broad and indefinite delegations of legislative authority. The bar for what standards qualify as constitutional is low. The delegation in the EPGA plainly has standards that surmount that bar. For the Governor to invoke the EPGA, her actions must be "reasonable" and "necessary," they must "protect life and property" or "bring the emergency situation under control," and they may be taken only at a time of "public emergency" or "reasonable apprehension of immediate danger" when "public safety is imperiled." Those are standards. Reasonable people might disagree about their rigor, but this Court and the United States Supreme Court have consistently held similar standards constitutional. Until today, a delegation was invalid only when there were *no* standards.

It is not my view that only delegations with no standards are unconstitutional. But until today this Court and the United States Supreme Court upheld every delegation that had some standards to guide the decision-maker's discretion. The particular standards in the EPGA are as reasonably precise as the statute's subject matter permits. Given the unpredictability and range of emergencies the Legislature identified in the statute, it is difficult to see how it could have been more specific. Indeed the EPGA contains *multiple* limitations on the Governor's authority, each limitation requiring more of the Governor when exercising authority. Therefore, our precedent holds that it does not violate the nondelegation doctrine.

ASKEW v. CROSS KEY WATERWAYS
372 So.2d 913 (Fla. 1978)

SUNDBERG, J.

The "Florida Environmental Land and Water Management Act" empowers the Division of State Planning to recommend areas of critical state concern to the Governor and cabinet acting as the Administration Commission. In its recommendation, the Division of State Planning must designate the boundaries of the proposed area of critical state concern, explain the reasons for its conclusion that the area is of critical concern to the state or region, the dangers which would result from uncontrolled or inadequate development of the area, and the advantages to be gained from the development of the area in a coordinated manner.

Section 380.05(2) enunciates the criteria which the Division of State Planning shall utilize in determining whether to recommend designation of a particular area as one of critical state concern:

> (2) An area of critical state concern may be designated only for:
>
> > (a) An area containing, or having a significant impact upon, environmental, historical, natural, or archaeological resources of regional or statewide importance.
> >
> > (b) An area significantly affected by, or having a significant effect upon, an existing or proposed major public facility or other area of major public investment.
> >
> > (c) A proposed area of major development potential, which may include a proposed site of a new community, designated in a state land development plan.

Prior to submitting a recommendation with respect to an area of critical state concern to the Administration Commission, the Division of State Planning must give notice to all local governments and regional planning agencies included within the proposed boundaries, including any notice required by the Administrative Procedure Act.

Within 45 days after receiving the recommendations of the Division of State Planning, the Administration Commission must either reject the recommendations or adopt them with or without modification. Thereafter, by rule, the Administration Commission designates the area of critical state concern and approves the principles for guiding development of the designated area. The Administration Commission is statutorily prohibited from designating more than five percent, in the aggregate, of the land within the state (approximately 1.8 million acres) as an area of critical state concern.

The Act affects regulation of virtually all development in an area of critical state concern: all building, mining, and changes in the use or appearance of land, water and air and appurtenant structures; material increases in the density of its use; alteration of shores and banks; drilling; structural demolition; clearing adjunct to construction; and deposit of waste or fill. Excepted are work by road agencies and other utilities; structural maintenance affecting only the interior or the color or exterior decoration of a structure; the use of structures for customary dwelling purposes; changes of usage within the same regulated class of use; changes in ownership; and changes in rights of access, riparian rights, easements and covenants affecting rights and land.

The controversy before us results from actions taken by the Administration Commission of the Department of Administration in designating the Green Swamp area of critical state concern and the Florida Keys area of critical state concern and, in the case of the former, adopting land development regulations.

At contest here are the competing philosophies that underlie two provisions of our fundamental document of government and the attempt by the legislature to accommodate those philosophies. Article II, Section 7, Florida Constitution, enunciates the policy of the State to conserve and protect its natural resources and scenic beauty. Nonetheless, in implementing this policy due regard must be had for the admonition of Article II, Section 3, Florida Constitution:

> Branches of government. The powers of the state government shall be divided into legislative, executive and judicial branches. No person belonging to one branch shall exercise any powers appertaining to either of the other branches unless expressly provided herein.

Appellants urge two propositions upon us. First, that the provisions of Section 380.05(2)(a) and (b) set forth adequate criteria for exercise of the power delegated by Section 380.05(1) when measured against the case law. This argument is bolstered by the decisions from this Court which recognize that the specificity of standards and guidelines may depend upon the subject matter dealt with and the degree of difficulty involved in articulating finite standards. Second, it is asserted that the modern trend in administrative law is to relax the doctrine of unlawful delegation of legislative power in favor of an analysis which focuses upon the existence of procedural safeguards in the administrative process as opposed to standards enunciated by the legislature. Appellants maintain that the broad statement of policy contained in Sections 380.05(1) and 380.05(2)(a) and (b) coupled with the administrative safeguards imposed by Chapter 120, Florida Statutes (1975), alleviates any objection that the Administration Commission will act arbitrarily or capriciously in performing the function assigned by the legislature.

It is the courts, upon a challenge to the exercise or nonexercise of administrative action, which must determine whether the administrative agency has performed consistently with the mandate of the legislature. When legislation is so lacking in guidelines that neither the agency nor the courts can determine whether the agency is carrying out the intent of the legislature in its conduct, then, in fact, the agency becomes the lawgiver rather than the administrator of the law.

The criteria for designation of an area of critical state concern set forth in Section 380.05(2)(a) and (b) are constitutionally defective because they reposit in the Administration Commission the fundamental legislative task of determining which geographic areas and resources are in greatest need of protection.

We emphasize that it is not the legislature's use of the phrases "containing, or having a significant impact upon, environmental, historical, natural, or archaeological resources of regional impact" nor "significantly affected by, or having a significant effect upon, an existing or proposed major public facility or other area of major public investment" which faults the legislation. Such "approximations of the threshold of legislative concern" are not only a practical necessity in legislation, but they are now amenable to articulation and refinement by policy statements adopted as rules under the 1974 Administrative Procedure Act. The deficiency in the legislation here considered is the absence of legislative delineation of priorities among competing areas and resources which require protection in the State interest.

In the cases under review the Administration Commission has in fact exercised the policy role in the first instance of determining which areas of this State and the resources therein are of critical state concern. In contrast, by The Big Cypress Conservation Act of 1973, the legislature conceived the areas of critical state concern and left to the Division of State Planning and the Administration Commission the task of "fleshing out" through adoption of land development regulations.

Our research in other jurisdictions fails to disclose one instance in which the legislative branch has unconditionally delegated to an agency of the executive branch the policy function of designating the geographic area of concern which will be subject to land development regulation by the agency.

The second prong of appellants' argument is based upon a thesis for delegation of legislative power developed and espoused by Professor Kenneth Culp Davis of the University of Chicago College of Law. Professor Davis maintains that there should be a shift in emphasis from legislatively imposed standards for administrative action to procedural safeguards in the administrative process. He supports his rationale by citation to federal decisions as well as decisions from a minority of state court jurisdictions. His premises are that (1) strict adherence to the nondelegation doctrine would stultify the administrative process; (2) the doctrine, in fact, has been used as a label to invalidate legislation of which courts disapprove without any rational distinction between standards approved and those disapproved; and (3) the danger of arbitrary or capricious administrative action is best met through procedural due process safeguards in the administrative process.

Although the Davis view is an entirely reasonable one as demonstrated by its adoption in the federal courts and a minority of state jurisdictions, nonetheless, it clearly has not been the view in Florida. Should this Court, then, accept the invitation of appellants to abandon the doctrine of nondelegation of legislative power which is not only firmly embedded in our law, but which has been so continuously and recently applied? We believe stare decisis and reason dictate that we not.

Regardless of the criticism of the courts' application of the doctrine, we nevertheless conclude that it represents a recognition of the express limitation contained in the second sentence of Article II, Section 3 of our Constitution. Under the fundamental document adopted and several times ratified by the citizens of this State, the legislature is not free to redelegate to an administrative body so much of its lawmaking power as it may deem expedient. In short the primary policy decision of the area of critical state concern to be designated as well as the principles for guiding development in that area are the sole province of an administrative body. From that determination all else follows. Flexibility by an administrative agency to administer a legislatively articulated policy is essential to meet the complexities of our modern society, but flexibility in administration of a legislative program is essentially different from reposing in an administrative body the power to establish fundamental policy.

Accordingly, until the provisions of Article II, Section 3 of the Florida Constitution are altered by the people we deem the doctrine of nondelegation of legislative power to be viable in this State. Under this doctrine fundamental and primary policy decisions shall be made by members of the legislature who are elected to perform those tasks, and administration of legislative programs must be pursuant to some minimal standards and guidelines ascertainable by reference to the enactment establishing the program.

ENGLAND, C.J., concurring.

I sincerely hope that the significance of our decision today is not lost in a debate concerning its effect on the Environmental Land and Water Management Act. Justice Sundberg has revitalized a vastly more important doctrine. One that guarantees that Florida's government will continue to operate only by consent of the governed. He is saying, quite simply, that whatever may be the governmental predilections elsewhere, in Florida no person in one branch of our government may by accident or by assignment act in a role assigned by the Constitution to persons in another branch.

Law giving, the power involved here, is a responsibility assigned to the legislature, and that body is prohibited from relegating its responsibility wholesale to persons, whether elected or appointed, whose duties are simply to see that the laws are observed. The people of Florida placed that restraint on the legislature, as they had every right to do. People in other states may not restrict their public officials to this extent, but their authority to do so, and the effect of their doing so, are readily acknowledged even in states without a similar constitutional limitation.

NOTE

The Florida Supreme Court has continued to enforce its nondelegation doctrine vigorously. In *B.H. v. State*, 645 So.2d 987 (Fla. 1994), the court refused to enforce a statute that criminalized "escape from any secure detention facility of restrictiveness level VI or above" and that allowed the Florida Department of Health and Rehabilitative Services to define and establish up to eight restrictiveness levels. The court emphasized that any redelegation of the power "to declare what the law shall be" violates the Florida Constitution. Likewise, in *Bush v. Schiavo*, 885 So.2d 321 (Fla. 2004), the court invalidated a statute that authorized the Governor to issue a one-time stay to prevent the withholding of nutrition and hydration from a patient on life support. The court reasoned that the statute did not contain any standards that "would serve to limit the Governor from exercising unrestricted discretion in applying the law."

GUILLOU v. STATE OF NEW HAMPSHIRE, DIVISION OF MOTOR VEHICLES
503 A.2d 838 (N.H. 1986)

BATCHELDER, J.

RSA 263:56 states: "The director may order any driver's license issued to any person under the provisions of this title to be suspended or revoked, after due hearing, for any cause which he may deem sufficient."

The plaintiff argues that the statute does not prescribe any policies or standards to guide the director or the superior court in determining whether a suspension or revocation is appropriate, and that it is therefore vague and indefinite. In response, the State argues that the plaintiff has failed to overcome the presumption of constitutionality afforded any State statute, that the statute is necessary to protect the public safety, and that other statutes and regulations offer guidance and set limits for the director and the superior court in determining whether to suspend or revoke a license.

In addressing the presumption of constitutionality, the State relies in part on our statements of the law in two previous cases. In the first, we stated that "a statute will not be construed to be unconstitutional where it is susceptible to a construction rendering it constitutional." In the second case, we stated: "Although guidelines do not appear in a statute, a reviewing court may, by resort to judicial construction, cure an otherwise unconstitutionally vague provision."

Unfortunately, these principles offer little guidance in construing RSA 263:56. One reason is that the statute grants authority to an administrative officer without any express or implied qualifications, and thus provides no aid for judicial construction. A second reason is that this statute is not the type of procedural statute that may be construed in the context of specific constitutional principles, such as due process. Further, the phrase "for any cause which he may deem sufficient" does not provide any legislative guidance for the director in making suspension or revocation decisions. The State argues that the director will look to the statute as a whole for general guidance. The language of RSA 263:56, however, does not mandate, let alone suggest, such a procedure. Even if the director stays within the bounds of the related provisions, the potential for arbitrary and unprincipled decisions is great. In one case, for example, he might determine that the commission of four offenses in a two-year period is cause for revocation. In another, he might determine that five offenses in a two-year period are required. Moreover, as the plaintiff argues, RSA 263:56 does not set any limits on the length of suspension or revocation.

RSA 263:56 provides no guidance, standards, or conditions for the hearing authority to follow. We hold that the statute is an unconstitutional delegation of legislative authority in violation of part I, article 37 of the State Constitution, because it fails to declare a general policy and prescribe standards for administrative action.

Although some delegation of lawmaking authority is necessary, overbroad delegations are to be avoided, and the scope of delegations to administrative agencies should be limited to permitting the agency to fill in the details in order to effectuate the legislative purpose. In the matter before us, we think that the burden placed on the legislature to prescribe specific standards for the director which are consistent with the other motor vehicle statutes is not an onerous one.

TEXAS BOLL WEEVIL ERADICATION FOUNDATION, INC. v. LEWELLEN
952 S.W.2d 454 (Tex. 1997)

PHILLIPS, C.J.

The Anthonomus grandis Boheman, an insect commonly known as the boll weevil, presents a major economic threat to the Texas cotton industry. This pest, which entered Texas from Mexico in 1892, causes an estimated $20 million in crop loss in Texas every year. To aid in the ongoing battle against the boll weevil, the Legislature in 1993 authorized the creation of the Official Cotton Growers' Boll Weevil Eradication Foundation. Instead of directly creating the Foundation, however, the Legislature merely authorized the Commissioner of Agriculture to certify some nonprofit organization representing cotton growers to create the Foundation and propose geographic eradication zones. The Act authorizes the creating organization or the Foundation to conduct referenda in each proposed eradication zone to determine whether those cotton growers desire to establish an official boll weevil eradication zone.

The Foundation exercises broad governmental powers. Besides being authorized to conduct elections in proposed eradication zones, the board may add an area to a zone under certain circumstances if approved by a referendum of cotton growers in the area. The board determines what eradication programs to conduct. The Foundation may impose penalties for late payment of assessments. A cotton grower who fails to pay an assessment within ten days of its due date must destroy his cotton crop. If the grower fails to do so, his crop is automatically declared a public nuisance. On the Foundation's recommendation, and after notice, the Department of Agriculture must destroy it, even if not infested with boll weevils, at the owner's cost. In addition, a cotton grower who violates the statute is guilty of a Class C misdemeanor. Cotton which a delinquent grower has already produced and harvested is subject to a lien. Representatives of the Foundation may enter private property which is subject to eradication without the owner's permission for any purpose under the Act, including "the treatment, monitoring, and destruction of growing cotton or other host plants." Finally, the Commissioner and the Foundation may adopt rules necessary to carry out the purposes of the Act.

While growers in a zone must approve their assessments, they do not approve the type of eradication program or the amount of debt incurred by the Foundation to finance it. These matters are left to the Foundation's discretion. If the eradication program is discontinued for any reason, the Foundation may continue collecting assessments "as necessary to pay the financial obligations of the foundation."

After a referendum has passed, the cotton growers in the zone must be allowed to conduct referenda "periodically" under the terms prescribed in the initial referendum to determine whether to continue their assessments, although the Act says nothing about how often these referenda must occur. In addition, the Foundation must conduct a referendum on whether to discontinue the program on the petition of at least forty percent of the cotton growers in the zone.

We turn to the growers' argument that the Legislature violated Article II, Section 1 of the Texas Constitution, requiring the separation of powers between the legislative, executive, and judicial branches, by improperly delegating governmental authority to the Foundation. In particular, the growers contend that the Foundation is a private entity whose directors are neither constrained before they act by meaningful standards nor made accountable after they act by administrative, judicial, or popular review.

The prohibition on unwarranted delegation of lawmaking power is "rooted in the principle of separation of powers that underlies our tripartite system of Government." The United States Constitution expressly vests legislative power in the Congress, and the Texas Constitution similarly vests legislative power in our Legislature. Thus, "Congress is not permitted to abdicate or to transfer to others the essential legislative functions with which it is vested." *A.L.A. Schechter Poultry Corp. v. United States* (1935). Likewise, in our State "the power to pass laws rests with the Legislature, and that power cannot be delegated to some commission or other tribunal."

Yet, like many truisms, these blanket pronouncements should not be read too literally. Even in a simple society, a legislative body would be hard put to contend with every detail involved in carrying out its laws; in a complex society it is absolutely impossible to do so. Hence, legislative delegation of power to enforce and apply law is both necessary and proper. Such power must almost always be exercised with a certain amount of discretion, and at times the line between making laws and enforcing them may blur.

Even in its heyday, the nondelegation doctrine was sparingly applied. Since the Court retreated from its opposition to New Deal initiatives, it has consistently upheld congressional delegations.

Texas courts have also generally upheld legislative delegations to state or municipal agencies. We most recently did so in *Edgewood Independent School District v. Meno* (Tex. 1995), where we said: "The Texas Legislature may delegate its powers to agencies established to carry out legislative purposes, as long as it establishes reasonable standards to guide the entity to which the powers are delegated." "Requiring the legislature to include every detail and anticipate unforeseen circumstances would defeat the purpose of delegating legislative authority."

But there are some indications that extreme judicial deference to legislative delegation may be declining. In particular, this Court has been especially willing to strike down delegations of legislative authority to the judicial department. And in *Texas Antiquities Committee v. Dallas County Community College District* (Tex. 1977), a plurality of four justices would also have struck down a delegation to an administrative agency.

As difficult as the issue of proper legislative delegation may be, the considerations are even more complex when the delegation is made not to another department or agency of government, but to a private individual or group. While at first blush such delegations might seem manifestly unconstitutional, further reflection demonstrates that they also are frequently necessary and desirable. Presumably no one would argue that the state should not accord the full benefits and responsibilities of a marital union to a couple who was married by a minister, priest, or rabbi rather than a judge. Also, the delegation of authority to private associations to promulgate certain industrial and professional standards has been of immense benefit to the public. For example, a number of states have adopted existing or future versions of the National Electrical Code, promulgated by an industry association, "turning a technical and complex task often quite beyond the competence of many city councils or even state legislatures over to a specialized private group."

Still, private delegations clearly raise even more troubling constitutional issues than their public counterparts. On a practical basis, the private delegate may have a personal or pecuniary interest which is inconsistent with or repugnant to the public interest to be served. More fundamentally, the basic concept of democratic rule under a republican form of government is compromised when public powers are abandoned to those who are neither elected by the people, appointed by a public official or entity, nor employed by the government. Thus, we believe it axiomatic that courts should subject private delegations to a more searching scrutiny than their public counterparts.

We first address whether the Foundation is a public or private entity for purposes of the nondelegation doctrine. Before ever being subject to its authority, any grower will already have had the right to participate in one or more referenda deciding whether to ratify the zone, whom to elect to the board, and what amount is to be assessed on the grower's acreage. These referenda are not purely private affairs, being conducted according to state law, under rather extensive regulations promulgated by the Commissioner of Agriculture. Yet they are not popular elections either, as the suffrage is strictly limited to eligible growers.

Similarly, the statutory provisions as to governmental powers suggest both public and private attributes. The Legislature specifically denominates the Foundation a "governmental unit" for purposes of immunity from suit under the Tort Claims Act. For many purposes, however, the Foundation is not a state agency. Thus, the funds the Foundation collects are expressly "not state funds and are not required to be deposited in the state treasury."

In sum, we do not find it easy to categorize the Foundation as either a public or private agency, a difficulty that may exist with many contemporary bodies. However, courts have universally treated a delegation as private where "interested groups have been given authoritative powers of determination, usually in conjunction with a public administrative agency." Because the Act delegates authoritative power to private interested parties, we conclude that it is a private entity for purposes of applying the nondelegation doctrine.

Now we must determine what standard to apply in determining whether the private delegation was appropriate. Because of the additional risks posed by such delegations to the proper separation of governmental powers, a number of factors should be considered by a reviewing court:

1. Are the private delegate's actions subject to meaningful review by a state agency or other branch of state government?

2. Are the persons affected by the private delegate's actions adequately represented in the decisionmaking process?
3. Is the private delegate's power limited to making rules, or does the delegate also apply the law to particular individuals?
4. Does the private delegate have a pecuniary or other personal interest that may conflict with his or her public function?
5. Is the private delegate empowered to define criminal acts or impose criminal sanctions?
6. Is the delegation narrow in duration, extent, and subject matter?
7. Does the private delegate possess special qualifications or training for the task delegated to it?
8. Has the Legislature provided sufficient standards to guide the private delegate in its work?

We emphasize at the outset that these standards apply only to private delegations, not to the usual delegation by the Legislature to an agency or another department of government. In reviewing a public delegation, we adhere to those factors set forth by this Court in *Housing Authority of City of Dallas v. Higginbotham* (Tex. 1940), and its progeny. Furthermore, nothing in our analysis should be read as suggesting what provisions of the Act would or would not pass muster were this a public delegation.

First, while the Foundation is subject to some oversight by the Commissioner of Agriculture, the review is uneven and incomplete. The Legislature did direct the Commissioner to promulgate rules regarding certain areas of the Foundation's operations. Indeed, the Commissioner's regulations relating to the protection of human life and the environment are fairly extensive. The Commissioner could not, however, adopt any procedure for reviewing such critical decisions as the amount of assessments adopted by the growers, the total amount of funds expended on eradication, the amount of debt incurred by the Foundation, or the repayment terms for such debts. Nor has the Commissioner attempted to do so, either at the Act's inception or after the increase in his rulemaking authority in 1995.

Finally, contrary to the dissenting justices' conclusion, the Commissioner has no general authority to "revoke the Foundation's certification" if it fails to comply with the procedural provisions of the Act. Thus, the first factor weighs against the delegation.

Judging the statute as it is written, rather than as it operated in practice, the second factor militates in favor of the private delegation. The growers in each zone are allowed to vote on whether to participate in the eradication program, and thereby subject themselves to the Foundation's jurisdiction, and are allowed to approve or reject any proposed assessment.

The third factor weighs against the delegation. Far from merely devising eradication guidelines, the Foundation actually applied the programs it devised to all growers in zones where the program was approved. In accordance with its statutory authority, the Foundation collected assessments from individual growers and entered those growers' property to carry out its eradication programs.

The fourth factor also weighs against the delegation. The Foundation board members are cotton growers who have a direct pecuniary interest in the eradication programs implemented by the Foundation.

Under the circumstances of this case, the fifth factor does not weigh in our consideration of whether the statute as a whole is an unconstitutional delegation of authority to the Foundation. The Foundation is vested with authority to impose monetary penalties for late payment of the assessments and to direct the Department to destroy a delinquent grower's crops, and it is further empowered to adopt rules, a violation of which is a criminal offense. While this authority to impose penal sanctions strongly suggests an improper private delegation, principles of severability would allow us to strike down this power and still uphold the Act. Thus, even though the penalty provisions seem to represent an unconstitutional delegation of authority to the Foundation, this should not weigh in judging the validity of the Foundation's core function under the Act, i.e., the levying and collecting of assessments and the expenditure of those assessments on eradication programs.

The sixth factor is inconclusive under the circumstances of this case. While the statute pertains to a specific, narrow purpose—eradication of the boll weevil and other cotton pests—it does not limit the program's cost and duration, other than to provide that the program is subject to the Sunset Act and that it should be discontinued once the boll weevil is eradicated.

The seventh factor, on its face, weighs against the delegation. While the Act is designed to allow those with firsthand experience in the cotton industry to lead the eradication effort, there is no assurance that those elected will actually have special qualifications or training regarding eradication of boll weevils, and there is absolutely no evidence that board actions were "taken for purposes which are independent of the statute," Professor Davis' salient test. The facts are thus quite distinct from a private delegation, say, for the promulgation of a municipal electrical code by an industry association consisting of electrical contractors, inspectors, and manufacturers. There is, of course, some tension between this factor and the second factor. It would ordinarily be difficult for a private delegation both to guarantee adequate representation of those affected by the delegation and to vest decisionmaking authority in a group of experts. Thus, while the Act fails to meet the seventh factor, this failure is excused by the satisfaction of the second factor.

Finally, the eighth factor weighs against the delegation. The Legislature has provided very few statutory standards to guide the Foundation. While the Act provides the procedures for zone referenda and specifies the powers and duties of the board, it provides no guidance as to how assessments are to be set or the amount of debt that the Foundation may incur. Thus, in practice, the Foundation had free rein to incur over $9 million in debt in the Lower Rio Grande Valley Zone to be repaid by the growers there through several years of assessments, even though those growers voted within 21 months to discontinue their eradication program.

We recognize that the judicial branch should defer to the judgment of the people's elected representatives whenever possible, and we by no means suggest that a private delegation must satisfy all eight of these factors. We recognize also that courts should, when possible, read delegations narrowly to uphold their validity. Here, however, the invalidity of the delegation does not hinge on any one provision of the Act that might be narrowly interpreted; rather, the Act as a whole represents an overly broad delegation of legislative authority to a private entity, violating a majority of the eight factors we have set forth. Therefore, the Act cannot stand.

The nondelegation doctrine should be used sparingly, when there is, in Justice Cardozo's memorable phrase, "delegation running riot." Because we believe this is an extraordinary case, we affirm the judgments of the trial courts.

NOTE

Creative legislatures, as the "boll weevil" case confirms, may try to delegate legislative power not just to other agencies but also to private and quasi-private entities. The case also confirms that the line between private and public foundations can be elusive.

Delegation problems also arise at the local level, as the chapter on localism confirms. *See generally* Nestor M. Davidson, *Localist Administrative Law*, 126 Yale L.J. 564 (2017); *see specifically N.Y. Statewide Coal. of Hispanic Chambers of Commerce v. N.Y.C. Dept. of Health & Mental Hygiene*, 16 N.E.3d 538 (N.Y. 2014). The next case involves a delegation of state power to alter the boundaries of local school districts.

In re PETITION TO TRANSFER TERRITORY FROM HIGH SCHOOL DISTRICT NO. 6, LAME DEER, ROSEBUD COUNTY, TO HIGH SCHOOL DISTRICT NO. 1, HARDIN, BIG HORN COUNTY
15 P.3d 447 (Mont. 2000)

HUNT, J.

The dispositive issue on appeal is whether § 20-6-320, MCA, which gives authority to county superintendents of schools to grant or deny petitions to transfer territory among school districts, is an unconstitutional delegation of legislative power.

We have previously held that the authority to alter school district boundaries is legislative in nature. The authority to make school district boundaries is entirely within the power of the legislature. Montana law on this issue is consistent with those of sister states

Section 20-6-320 grants local county superintendents the power to transfer territory from one school district to another. Section 20-6-320, MCA, gives the county superintendents the authority to alter the boundaries of school districts, constituting a delegation of legislative power. The legislature may constitutionally delegate its legislative functions to an administrative agency, but it must provide, with reasonable clarity, limitations upon the agency's discretion and provide the agency with policy guidance.

Article III, Section 1, of the 1972 Montana Constitution provides:

> Separation of powers. The power of the government of this state is divided into three distinct branches-legislative, executive, and judicial. No person or persons charged with the exercise of power properly belonging to one branch shall exercise any power properly belonging to either of the others, except as in this constitution expressly directed or permitted.

In *Bacus v. Lake County* (Mont. 1960), we set the standard for a delegation of legislative power:

> The law-making power may not be granted to an administrative body to be exercised under the guise of administrative discretion. Accordingly, in delegating powers to an administrative body with respect to the administration of statutes, the legislature must ordinarily prescribe a policy, standard, or rule for their guidance and must not vest them with an arbitrary and uncontrolled discretion with regard thereto, and a statute or ordinance which is deficient in this respect is invalid.

A statute granting legislative power to an administrative agency will be held to be invalid if the legislature has failed to prescribe a policy, standard, or rule to guide the exercise of the delegated authority. If the legislature fails to prescribe with reasonable clarity the limits of power delegated to an administrative agency, or if those limits are too broad, the statute is invalid.

This statute's only directive on whether to grant or deny a petition is that "the decision must be based on the effects that the transfer would have on those residing in the territory proposed for transfer as well as those residing in the remaining territory of the high school district." The territory transfer statute does not constrain a county superintendent's discretion in whether to grant or deny a transfer. The decision is left up to the county superintendent's unguided judgment.

While this statute sets forth some criteria, the satisfaction of these conditions does not limit a county superintendent's discretion in granting or denying a petition once the procedural requirements have been met. This statute fails to provide any checks on the discretion of the county superintendent of schools in deciding whether to grant a territory transfer. The statute's only directive is that the county superintendent should make the decision based on the effects felt by those transferred and those remaining. The legislature has provided no criteria for balancing the effects felt by the parties involved in a school district territory transfer. Instead, the decision is left solely to the whim of the local county superintendents.

It is this broad grant of discretion to a county superintendent of schools, unchecked by any standard, policy or rule of decision that renders the territory transfer statute unconstitutional. In *Bacus*, we stated that "the standard must not be so broad that the officer or board will have unascertainable limits within which to act." If the legislature had limited a county superintendent to the role of fact finder or if the legislature had set forth the specific criteria to be weighed when deciding to grant or deny a petition, the statute would have conformed to constitutional requirements.

C. JUDICIAL DEFERENCE TO ADMINISTRATIVE AGENCIES

Separation of powers principles not only may limit delegations of legislative power to executive branch agencies, but they also may limit delegations of judicial power—the power to say what the law means—to executive branch agencies. At stake is this: When, if ever, is it appropriate for federal or state courts to defer to administrative interpretations of a law that the legislature has asked the agency to implement or enforce?

We start, again, with the federal side of the story. In 1984, the United States Supreme Court laid the groundwork for determining when federal courts would defer to an executive agency's interpretation of a statute that it is charged with administering. The approach, now known as the "*Chevron* doctrine," requires federal courts to defer to reasonable interpretations of statutes that Congress has directed the agency to administer.

CHEVRON v. NATURAL RESOURCES DEFENSE COUNCIL
467 U.S. 837 (1984)

STEVENS, J.

In the Clean Air Act Amendments of 1977, Congress enacted certain requirements applicable to States that had not achieved the national air quality standards established by the Environmental Protection Agency pursuant to earlier legislation. The amended Clean Air Act required these "nonattainment" States to establish a permit program regulating "new or modified major stationary sources" of air pollution. Generally, a permit may not be issued for a new or modified major stationary source unless several stringent conditions are met. The EPA regulation promulgated to implement this permit requirement allows a State to adopt a plantwide definition of the term "stationary source." Under this definition, an existing plant that contains several pollution-emitting devices may install or modify one piece of equipment without meeting the permit conditions if the alteration will not increase the total emissions from the plant. The question presented by these cases is whether EPA's decision to allow States to treat all of the pollution-emitting devices within the same industrial grouping as though they were encased within a single "bubble" is based on a reasonable construction of the statutory term "stationary source."

The Court of Appeals observed that the relevant part of the amended Clean Air Act "does not explicitly define what Congress envisioned as a stationary source, to which the permit program should apply," and further stated that the precise issue was not "squarely addressed in the legislative history."

The basic legal error of the Court of Appeals was to adopt a static judicial definition of the term "stationary source" when it had decided that Congress itself had not commanded that definition. Respondents do not defend the legal reasoning of the Court of Appeals. Nevertheless, since this Court reviews judgments, not opinions, we must determine whether the Court of Appeals' legal error resulted in an erroneous judgment on the validity of the regulations.

When a court reviews an agency's construction of the statute which it administers, it is confronted with two questions. First, always, is the question whether Congress has directly spoken to the precise question at issue. If the intent of Congress is clear, that is the end of the matter; for the court, as well as the agency, must give effect to the unambiguously expressed intent of Congress. If, however, the court determines Congress has not directly addressed the precise question at issue, the court does not simply impose its own construction on the statute, as would be necessary in the absence of an administrative interpretation. Rather, if the statute is silent or ambiguous with respect to the specific issue, the question for the court is whether the agency's answer is based on a permissible construction of the statute.

"The power of an administrative agency to administer a congressionally created program necessarily requires the formulation of policy and the making of rules to fill any gap left, implicitly or explicitly, by Congress." If Congress has explicitly left a gap for the agency to fill, there is an express delegation of authority to the agency to elucidate a specific provision of the statute by regulation. Such legislative regulations are given controlling weight unless they are arbitrary, capricious, or manifestly contrary to the statute. Sometimes the legislative delegation to an agency on a particular question is implicit rather than explicit. In such a case, a court may not substitute its own construction of a statutory provision for a reasonable interpretation made by the administrator of an agency.

The 1977 Amendments contain no specific reference to the "bubble concept." Nor do they contain a specific definition of the term "stationary source," though they did not disturb the definition of "stationary source" contained in § 111(a)(3), applicable by the terms of the Act. Section 302(j), however, defines the term "major stationary source" as follows:

> (j) Except as otherwise expressly provided, the terms major stationary source and major emitting facility mean any stationary facility or source of air pollutants which directly emits, or has the potential to emit, one hundred tons per year or more of any air pollutant (including any major emitting facility or source of fugitive emissions of any such pollutant, as determined by rule by the Administrator).

In 1981 a new administration took office and initiated a "Government-wide reexamination of regulatory burdens and complexities." In the context of that review, the EPA reevaluated the various arguments that had been advanced in connection with the proper definition of the term "source." It then set forth several reasons for concluding that the plantwide definition was more appropriate. It pointed out that the dual definition "can act as a disincentive to new investment and modernization by discouraging modifications to existing facilities" and "can actually retard progress in air pollution control by discouraging replacement of older, dirtier processes or pieces of equipment with new, cleaner ones."

In these cases, the Administrator's interpretation represents a reasonable accommodation of manifestly competing interests and is entitled to deference: the regulatory scheme is technical and complex, the agency considered the matter in a detailed and reasoned fashion, and the decision involves reconciling conflicting policies. Congress intended to accommodate both interests, but did not do so itself on the level of specificity presented by these cases. Perhaps that body consciously desired the Administrator to strike the balance at this level, thinking that those with great expertise and charged with responsibility for administering the provision would be in a better position to do so; perhaps it simply did not consider the question at this level; and perhaps Congress was unable to forge a coalition on either side of the question, and those on each side decided to take their chances with the scheme devised by the agency. For judicial purposes, it matters not which of these things occurred.

Judges are not experts in the field, and are not part of either political branch of the Government. Courts must, in some cases, reconcile competing political interests, but not on the basis of the judges' personal policy preferences. In contrast, an agency to which Congress has delegated policy-making responsibilities may, within the limits of that delegation, properly rely upon the incumbent administration's views of wise policy to inform its judgments. While agencies are not directly accountable to the people, the Chief Executive is, and it is entirely appropriate for this political branch of the Government to make such policy choices—resolving the competing interests which Congress itself either inadvertently did not resolve, or intentionally left to be resolved by the agency charged with the administration of the statute in light of everyday realities.

When a challenge to an agency construction of a statutory provision, fairly conceptualized, really centers on the wisdom of the agency's policy, rather than whether it is a reasonable choice within a gap left open by Congress, the challenge must fail. In such a case, federal judges—who have no constituency—have a duty to respect legitimate policy choices made by those who do. The responsibilities for assessing the wisdom of such policy choices and resolving the struggle between competing views of the public interest are not judicial ones: "Our Constitution vests such responsibilities in the political branches." We hold that the EPA's definition of the term "source" is a permissible construction of the statute which seeks to accommodate progress in reducing air pollution with economic growth.

NOTE

Several States reject *Chevron*'s delegation of judicial power to federal administrative agencies. In the following cases, the Wisconsin and Mississippi Supreme Courts reason that the separation of powers principles embedded in their respective state constitutions preclude any such deference.

TETRA TECH v. WISCONSIN DEPARTMENT OF REVENUE
914 N.W.2d 21 (Wis. 2018)

KELLY, J.

The Wisconsin Department of Revenue imposed a tax on the petitioners for the "processing" of river sediments into waste sludge, reusable sand, and water. The petitioners say the statutory term "processing" is not expansive enough to cover the separation of river sediment into its component parts, and so they asked us to reject the Department's interpretation of that term.

Because resolving this question implicates the authoritativeness of an administrative agency's interpretation and application of a statute, we asked the parties to also address this issue: "Does the practice of deferring to agency interpretations of statutes comport with Article VII, Section 2 of the Wisconsin Constitution, which vests the judicial power in the unified court system?"

We conclude that the term "processing" in Wis. Stat. § 77.52(2)(a)11 includes the separation of river sediment into its component parts. Therefore, we affirm the court of appeals. We have also decided to end our practice of deferring to administrative agencies' conclusions of law. However, pursuant to § 227.57(10), we will give "due weight" to the experience, technical competence, and specialized knowledge of an administrative agency as we consider its arguments.

When we review an administrative agency's decision, are there circumstances in which we must defer to the agency's interpretation and application of the law? Our current jurisprudence says there are.

We generally review administrative agency decisions in accordance with chapter 227 of our statutes. As relevant here, § 227.57 contains two specific directions regarding how we are to conduct those reviews. First, it instructs a court to "set aside or modify the agency action if it finds that the agency has erroneously interpreted a provision of law and a correct interpretation compels a particular action, or it shall remand the case to the agency for further action under a correct interpretation of the provision of law." And second, it instructs that, "subject to sub. (11), upon such review due weight shall be accorded the experience, technical competence, and specialized knowledge of the agency involved, as well as discretionary authority conferred upon it."

We have developed, over time, a contextualized methodology of reviewing administrative agency decisions. The provenance of this methodology lies partly with the preceding statute, and partly with our own doctrinal developments. In its modern iteration, this method begins with the principle that "statutory interpretation is a question of law which courts decide de novo." But then we wrap those principles within another, one we have said is of equal gravity: "As important, however, is the principle that courts should defer to an administrative agency's interpretation of a statute in certain situations."

Calibrating this "deference principle" to those "certain situations" resulted in our contextualized, three-tiered treatment of an administrative agency's conclusions regarding the interpretation and application of statutory provisions. When reviewing those conclusions, we give them: (1) great weight deference; (2) due weight deference; or (3) no deference at all.

As the deference doctrine developed, we recognized that its operation allowed the executive branch of government to authoritatively decide questions of law in specific cases brought to our courts for resolution. But nowhere in the journey did we determine whether this was consistent with the allocation of governmental power amongst the three branches. So, as a matter of first impression, we consider whether our deference doctrine is compatible with our constitution's grant of power to the judiciary:

> The judicial power of this state shall be vested in a unified court system consisting of one supreme court, a court of appeals, a circuit court, such trial courts of general uniform statewide jurisdiction as the legislature may create by law, and a municipal court if authorized by the legislature.

Allowing an administrative agency to authoritatively interpret the law raises the possibility that our deference doctrine has allowed some part of the state's judicial power to take up residence in the executive branch of government. To discover whether it did, we must first get our bearings on the nature and extent of judicial power.

We must be assiduous in patrolling the borders between the branches. This is not just a practical matter of efficient and effective government. We maintain this separation because it provides structural protection against depredations on our liberties. The Framers of the United States Constitution understood that "the accumulation of all powers legislative, executive and judiciary in the same hands, whether of one, a few or many, may justly be pronounced the very definition of tyranny." Consequently, "as Madison explained when advocating for the Constitution's adoption, neither the legislature nor the executive nor the judiciary ought to possess, directly or indirectly, an overruling influence over the others in the administration of their respective powers." "The purpose of the separation and equilibration of powers in general," said Justice Antonin Scalia, "was not merely to assure effective government but to preserve individual freedom." *Morrison v. Olson* (1988) (Scalia, J., dissenting). To this day, "after more than two hundred years of constitutional governance, this tripartite separation of independent governmental power remains the bedrock of the structure by which we secure liberty in both Wisconsin and the United States." As United States Supreme Court Justice Joseph Story said, "the three great powers of government should for ever be kept separate and distinct."

The constitution does not, however, hermetically seal the branches from each other. The separation of powers doctrine "envisions a system of separate branches sharing many powers while jealously guarding certain others, a system of separateness but interdependence, autonomy but reciprocity." "The constitutional powers of each branch of government fall into two categories: exclusive powers and shared powers." "Shared powers lie at the intersections of these exclusive core constitutional powers," and "these great borderlands of power are not exclusive to any one branch." Although the "branches may exercise shared power within these borderlands," they "may not unduly burden or substantially interfere with another branch."

Core powers, however, are not for sharing. "Each branch has exclusive core constitutional powers, into which the other branches may not intrude." "For more than a century, this court has been called upon to resist attempts by other branches of government to exercise authority in an exclusively judicial area." These "core zones of authority are to be jealously guarded by each branch of government." The importance of constitutional limitations, Chief Justice Marshall once said, is that they compel restraint when restraint is not desired: "To what purpose are powers limited, and to what purpose is that limitation committed to writing, if these limits may, at any time, be passed by those intended to be restrained?"

The separation of powers prevents us from abdicating core power just as much as it protects the judiciary from encroachment by other branches. "It is fundamental and undeniable that no one of the three branches of government can effectively delegate any of the powers which peculiarly and intrinsically belong to that branch." Even if we truly wished to abandon some aspect of our core power, no other branch may take it up and use it as its own. "As to these areas of authority, *any* exercise of authority by another branch of government is unconstitutional."

The propriety of our deference doctrine, therefore, depends on whether it transfers to a coordinate branch of government a quantum of our core powers. To make that determination, we need to describe those powers well enough that, if they are present in our deference doctrine, we will recognize them.

From the earliest days of our country, we have understood that the judiciary's first and irreducible responsibility is to proclaim the law: "It is emphatically the province and duty of the judicial department to say what the law is." *Marbury v. Madison* (1803). The process of interpreting the law in a specific case is part of that central duty: "Those who apply the rule to particular cases, must of necessity expound and interpret that rule." We agreed with *Marbury* just a few years ago when we described our judicial power as "the ultimate adjudicative authority of courts to finally decide rights and responsibilities as between individuals."

It is fair to say that exercising judgment in the interpretation and application of the law in a particular case is the very thing that distinguishes the judiciary from the other branches:

> The judiciary has no influence over either the sword or the purse, no direction either of the strength or of the wealth of the society, and can take no active resolution whatever. It may truly be said to have neither Force nor Will, but merely judgment; and must ultimately depend upon the aid of the executive arm even for the efficacy of its judgments.

We, too, have said as much: "By vesting the judicial power in a unified court system, the Wisconsin Constitution entrusts the judiciary with the duty of interpreting and applying laws made and enforced by coordinate branches of state government."

Some would argue that the judiciary's law-declaring and law-applying power lies not at the core of what it means to be a court, but somewhere out on the periphery of our powers where we share it with the executive branch. Some of our older cases have spoken in terms that lend this proposition at least some superficial plausibility. For example, in *State ex rel. Wisconsin Inspection Bureau v. Whitman* (Wis. 1929) we said:

> Every executive officer in the execution of the law must of necessity interpret it in order to find out what it is he is required to do. While his interpretation is not final, yet in the vast majority of cases it is the only interpretation placed upon it, and as long as it is acquiesced in it becomes the official interpretation which the courts heed and in which they oftentimes acquiesce as a practical construction.

And even earlier, in *Borgnis v. Falk Co.* (Wis. 1911), we had noted the quasi-judicial nature of some administrative bodies:

> We do not consider the Industrial Commission a court, nor do we construe the act as vesting in the Commission judicial powers within the meaning of the constitution. It is an administrative body or arm of the government which in the course of its administration of a law is empowered to ascertain some questions of fact and apply the existing law thereto, and in so doing acts *quasi*-judicially, but it is not thereby vested with judicial power in the constitutional sense.

But these cases cannot bear the weight their proponents assign them. The executive must certainly interpret and apply the law; it would be impossible to perform his duties if he did not. After all, he must determine for himself what the law requires (interpretation) so that he may carry it into effect (application). Our constitution not only does not forbid this, it requires it. But this comprises interpretation and application *within the executive branch*. We are here concerned with the authoritative interpretation and application of the law as applied to a particular case *within the judicial branch*. "Only the judicial interpretation as opposed to interpretations offered by the other branches would be considered authoritative in a judicial proceeding." Even *Whitman* recognizes that the executive's understanding of the law is provisional, and that it gains a measure of permanence only through habit and inertia. We do not understand *Borgnis* to say anything different. There, we recognized that the work of some administrative agencies looks very similar to that of the courts. We described the power they exercised as "quasi judicial," but it was "quasi" rather than simply "judicial" because they had no power to impose their understanding of the law on the judiciary's resolution of a particular case.

When we distill our cases and two centuries of constitutional history to their essence, the result is a lodestar that leads us directly to the most central of our powers: "No aspect of the judicial power is more fundamental than the judiciary's exclusive responsibility to exercise judgment in cases and controversies arising under the law." Judgment, of course, encompasses interpreting and applying the law to the case *sub judice*. We conclude that only the judiciary may authoritatively interpret and apply the law in cases before our courts. The executive may not intrude on this duty, and the judiciary may not cede it. If our deference doctrine allows either, we must reject it.

We see our core judicial powers lying at the heart of "great weight" deference. When the doctrine's preconditions are satisfied, that is, when an administrative agency meets the four *Harnischfeger* criteria, we cede to the agency the power to authoritatively interpret the law ("an agency's interpretation must then merely be reasonable for it to be sustained"), and apply the law to the case before us ("the courts should not substitute their judgment for the agency's *application* of a particular statute to the found facts.") Because *Harnischfeger Corp. v. LIRC* (Wis. 1995) made this a structural piece of the standard by which we review an agency's decision, we arrive at the legal issues involved in the case with an *a priori* commitment to letting the agency decide them. But our cases say the power to interpret and apply the law in the case at bar is an exclusively judicial power. Therefore, because that power belongs to the judiciary—and the judiciary alone—we may not allow an administrative agency to exercise it.

We provide guardrails for an administrative agency's exercise of our power, to be sure, but they are minimal. Under great weight deference, we simply require that the agency's judgment on the law not overrule our precedents, violate the constitution, contradict legislative history, or be unreasonable. We are concerned here with categories of power, not quantity. Regardless of the circumscriptions we put in place, when we defer we are allowing the agency to exercise what is unmistakably core judicial power.

"Due weight," as a principle, entered our jurisprudence through a statute, but over time our cases grafted it into the administrative deference doctrine. The original statutory foundation, however, is still there, and is just as viable as it was before. Today, we restore the principle of "due weight" to its original form by removing the patina of "deference" with which our cases have covered it.

It is true that due weight deference presents a threat to our core powers that is less extensive than that presented by great weight deference. It has been said that "in most situations, applying due weight deference will lead to the same result as would applying no deference at all." The threat presented by due weight deference is less, however, only in the sense that the preconditions that justify the agency's exercise of our exclusive power are fulfilled more rarely. When the "due weight" preconditions are satisfied, we must defer to the agency when our respective views of the law, while different, are equally reasonable. When there is equipoise, the court cedes its core judicial power just as surely as if great weight deference had applied. Infrequency does not make the cession appropriate.

Nor does cession become acceptable because the agency has less latitude in exercising our power under due weight deference than it does under great weight deference. It is the *fact* of cession, not its frequency or latitude, that implicates separation of powers and due process concerns. The power within the guardrails is part of our core, and so we may not parcel it out in even the smallest of doses. Therefore, due weight deference and great weight deference are structurally unsound for the same reasons.

On the other hand, "due weight"—in its statutory form—presents no such concerns. In § 227.57, we learn we are to give "due weight" to the "experience, technical competence, and specialized knowledge of the agency involved." From our earliest days we have recognized that the state's agencies develop a valuable perspective, unique to them, as they administer the laws within their portfolios. It was, in fact, our appreciation for that collected wisdom that originally led to our deference doctrine.

Recognizing that administrative agencies can sometimes bring unique insights to the matters for which they are responsible, however, does not mean we should defer to them. And there is nothing in § 227.57(10) that suggests we should. We believe the Department accurately described the meaning and effect of this provision. It acknowledged that giving "due weight" to an agency's experience, technical competence, and specialized knowledge will not "oust the court as the ultimate authority or final arbiter" of the law. Instead, it said, "due weight" means giving "respectful, appropriate consideration to the agency's views" while the court exercises its independent judgment in deciding questions of law. We agree. By returning "due weight" to its statutory roots, and ending our erstwhile deference, we honor the requirements of § 227.57(10), the separation of powers, and the parties' due process interests.

Today, the core judicial power ceded by our deference doctrine returns to its constitutionally-assigned residence. Henceforth, we will review an administrative agency's conclusions of law under the same standard we apply to a circuit court's conclusions of law—de novo. As with judicial opinions, we will benefit from the administrative agency's analysis, particularly when they are supplemented by the "due weight" considerations discussed above.

Now that we have identified the proper standard of review, we can address the petitioners' argument that they are not subject to the tax imposed by § 77.52(2).

Understood in this fashion, "processing" encompasses Stuyvesant Dredging's separation of river sediment into its component parts. The petitioners confirm that everything Stuyvesant Dredging receives from them is returned. The only difference is that the property is separated into its components. No new product has been created; no chemical transformation has occurred; and the property is still just as contaminated as when Stuyvesant Dredging received it. The work described by the Commission reflects the performance of a mechanical operation on the river sediments. Therefore, petitioners are subject to the sales and use tax of

§ 77.52(2) because Stuyvesant Dredging received compensation for "processing" river sediment received from the petitioners.

NOTE

Justice Kelly's opinion did not command a majority of the seven-member court. Justice Bradley joined the reasoning set forth in Justice Kelly's lead opinion in full. Justice Ziegler filed a concurring opinion, joined by Chief Justice Roggensack, to emphasize that the court could end Wisconsin's court-created deference practice without relying on the state constitution. Justice Gableman, again joined by Chief Justice Roggensack, filed another concurring opinion, which reasoned that the court could use constitutional avoidance principles to eliminate judicial deference to agency interpretations of Wisconsin statutes.

KING v. MISSISSIPPI MILITARY DEPARTMENT
245 So.3d 404 (Miss. 2018)

COLEMAN, J.

On February 11, 2016, the Adjutant General of the Mississippi Military Department terminated Cindy King's employment with the Department after conducting an investigation into some of King's activities. We hold that, while King may be considered a state service employee as defined by the Legislature, the Adjutant General, by virtue of three statutory provisions, is not subject to review by the Mississippi Employee Appeals Board.

King began working for the Department approximately twenty years ago, and her role was that of a supervisor in the Environmental Office at Camp Shelby. However, in late 2015, Colonel Charles Scott was appointed as an investigating officer to determine whether King "utilized information garnered through her position as the Camp Shelby Environmental Officer to front run the Army Compatible Use Buffer Program for personal gain" by purchasing a specific piece of property located near Camp Shelby. King denied the claim against her, but after concluding the investigation, the Adjutant General terminated King's employment with the Department. The February 2016 letter explained that the investigation "determined that King willfully and knowingly violated Mississippi Code Section 25–4–105. This investigation revealed that you used your position for personal gain." The letter concluded that King's "employment with the Mississippi Military Department Environmental Office is terminated for cause, effective immediately pursuant to Mississippi Code section 33–3–11(a)."

Upon receiving the letter, King appealed her termination from the Department to the Board, and Chief Hearing Officer Michael Watts heard King's and the Department's arguments. The Department's response to King's appeal was to argue that the Board does not have jurisdiction to hear the appeal because King was not a state-service employee and was an at-will employee of the Adjutant General subject to removal at his discretion.

The sole issue is as follows:

> Whether the lower court erred by finding that King was not a state service employee, despite extensive evidence indicating that King was a state service employee, and affirming the Mississippi Employee Appeals Board's decision to dismiss her appeal from an adverse employment action due to lack of jurisdiction.

We have stated that the Court's review of an "agency's interpretation of a rule or statute governing the agency's operation is a matter of law that is reviewed *de novo*, but with great deference to the agency's interpretation." The Court has explained that this "duty of deference derives from our realization that the everyday experience of the administrative agency gives it familiarity with the particularities and nuances of the problems committed to its care which no court can hope to replicate." A caveat being that the agency's interpretation will not be upheld "if it is so plainly erroneous or so inconsistent with either the underlying regulation or statute as to be arbitrary, capricious, an abuse of discretion or otherwise not in accordance with law."

In addition to the contradiction inherent in *de novo* but deferential review, writing on the one hand that we give great deference to agency interpretations of statutes and, then, with the next strike of the computer keyboard, writing that no deference will be given if the agency's interpretation contradicts the best reading of the statute, our approach creates a confusing and vague standard. The same can be said of claiming to give deference while simultaneously claiming that the Court bears the ultimate responsibility to interpret statutes.

Deferential review of executive-branch statutory interpretations gives rise to another problem under Mississippi's strict constitutional separation of powers. Article 1, Section 1 of the Mississippi Constitution of 1890 divides the power of state government into three branches and assigns legislative powers to the legislative branch, judicial powers to the judicial branch, and executive power to the executive branch. While writing and passing statutes is the function of the Legislature, interpreting statutes once enacted is the role of the judicial branch.

If Article 1, Section 1, were not enough to establish the strict separation of powers under Mississippi's Constitution, then Article 1, Section 2, leaves no doubt. It provides as follows:

> No person or collection of persons, being one or belonging to one of these departments, shall exercise any power properly belonging to either of the others.

Executive-branch agencies must follow statutes and, absent a declaration from the judicial branch regarding an interpretation of a statute, must decide what statutes mean. However, when the interpretation of a statute comes before the courts, and when deference is given to an agency interpretation, we share the exercise of the power of statutory interpretation with another branch in violation of Article 1, Section 2.

Pursuant to the foregoing reasoning, we announce today that we abandon the old standard of review giving deference to agency interpretations of statutes. Our pronouncements describing the level of deference were vague and contradictory, such that the deference could be anywhere on a spectrum from "great" to illusory. Moreover, in deciding no longer to give deference to agency interpretations, we step fully into the role the Constitution of 1890 provides for the courts and the courts alone, to interpret statutes. Although not writing of Mississippi's constitutional separation of powers, we find persuasive the reasoning of then-Judge Gorsuch who wrote, in a separate opinion concurring with his own majority in *Gutierrez–Brizuela v. Lynch* (10th Cir. 2016), that, absent judicial deference to administrative agencies' interpretation of statutes, "Courts would then fulfill their duty to exercise their independent judgment about what the law *is*." (Gorsuch, J., concurring)

While the Legislature has not excluded the Department's employees from being defined as "state service," we must affirm the Board's decision to dismiss King's appeal, as the Adjutant General has discretion, given by statute, in the hiring and the termination of the Department's employees; thus, the Board does not have ability to review or adjust his decisions.

PUBLIC WATER SUPPLY CO., INC. v. DIPASQUALE
735 A.2d 378 (Del. 1999)

WALSH, J.

Without reaching the underlying merits of the dispute, we conclude that the standard of review applied by the Superior Court was unduly deferential to the extent it applied a clearly erroneous test to an administrative agency's interpretation of statutory law. Accordingly, we reverse and remand for further proceedings under a *de novo* standard.

The dispute underlying this appeal began with an application to the Secretary of the Department of Natural Resources and Environmental Control (DNREC) by the appellee, Tunnell Companies, L.P. for two potable well permits. The purpose of the application was to allow Tunnell to supply water to tenants of a mobile home project, and an adjacent 18–hole golf course, known as Baywood Greens in the Long Neck area of Sussex County. The application was opposed by the appellant, Public Water Supply Company, Inc. (PWSC), a public utility certificated by the Delaware Public Service Commission (PSC) and DNREC to supply water to the public generally. PWSC's distribution mains adjoin Baywood Greens and it views that area as geographically within its service territory.

The contested application was referred to a Hearing Officer who, after receiving testimony and documentary evidence, ruled that the Baywood Greens water system, as envisioned, did not constitute a water utility and thus did not infringe upon PWSC's certificated area. The Hearing Officer then determined that Tunnell was not precluded from distributing water to its tenants at Baywood Greens. Based on his findings, the Hearing Officer recommended the issuance of the potable well permits to the Secretary who, in turn, approved the Hearing Officer's report and issued the permits.

PWSC then appealed to the Environmental Appeals Board (EAB) which, in effect, adopted the Secretary's affirmation of the Hearing Officer's report and upheld the Secretary's action. PWSC then appealed to the Superior Court alleging that the administrative entities who authorized the issuance of the permits to Tunnell had misconstrued the pertinent provisions of Title 7, Chapter 60 in failing to recognize PWSC's certificated rights to serve water in its service territory.

The Superior Court commenced its review of the EAB ruling by applying the deferential standard of review announced by this Court in *Eastern Shore Natural Gas Co. v. Delaware Public Service Comm.* (Del. 1994). The court then determined that the phrase "for public use" contained in 7 *Del.C.* § 6002(27) was ambiguous and required interpretation. The court further concluded that, "how the EAB reached its decision here is entirely reasonable and not clearly erroneous." In short, the Superior Court affirmed the EAB in all respects.

The question then posed, and critical to this appeal, is whether, on appeal from a decision of an administrative agency, this Court, the Superior Court, and, to a more limited extent, the Court of Chancery should review statutory interpretations of administrative bodies on a *de novo* basis, or, instead, should defer to such interpretations unless shown to be clearly erroneous? This issue was addressed in *Stoltz Management Co. v. Consumer Affairs Bd.* (Del. 1992), in which we stated, as follows:

> On appeal from a decision of an administrative agency the reviewing court must determine whether the agency ruling is supported by substantial evidence and free from legal error. Absent an abuse of discretion, the decision of the agency must be affirmed. However, where, as here, the issue is one of construction of statutory law and the application of the law to undisputed facts, the court's review is plenary.

In this case, the Superior Court did not apply the plenary standard of review for issues of statutory construction suggested by the language in *Stoltz*. Rather, it relied on this Court's later opinion in *Eastern Shore* as stating the appropriate standard for review of the EAB decision. The *Stoltz* affirmation of a plenary standard of review for agency interpretation of statutory law is consistent with this Court's standard of *de novo* review of legal rulings by trial courts. Indeed, it would be anomalous for this Court to accord a higher level of deference to the legal rulings of an administrative agency than that applied to trial courts subject to our appellate jurisdiction.

The language relied upon by the Superior Court, which lies at the root of the issue addressed today, is as follows:

> This Court's standard of review mirrors that of the Superior Court. When the issue is one of agency interpretation of statutory law, and application of that law to undisputed facts, this Court's review of the agency's decision is plenary, and it is not bound by the agency's conclusion. This Court will give substantial weight to the agency's interpretation of a statute it is empowered to enforce, provided that construction is not clearly erroneous. Thus, this Court will not reverse the agency's decision unless we find that its interpretation of 26 *Del.C.* § 102(2) is clearly erroneous.

After quoting from *Eastern Shore,* the Superior Court in this case stated that "if I find that the EAB has not clearly erred in interpreting its statutes, then I will affirm its decision."

PWSC argues that the standard of review described in *Eastern Shore* and applied by the Superior Court in this case is inconsistent with *Stoltz* and unduly deferential to the statutory interpretations of administrative agencies. We agree.

In addition to its questionable case support, the standard of review ruling in *Eastern Shore* appears internally inconsistent. After reciting a plenary review requirement for "agency interpretation of statutory law" this Court created a substantial weight/clearly erroneous level of deference for "interpretation of a statute the administrative agency is empowered to enforce." The two standards cannot co-exist in the same process of statutory review. If there is a distinction to be made in the standard of review of agency decisions it lies in the deference due an agency's interpretation of its own rules or regulations. This may partially explain the holdings in *Nationwide Mutual Ins. Co. v. Krongold* (Del. 1974) (implementing regulations of Insurance Commission, if not clearly wrong, viewed as element supporting statutory interpretation) and *Vassallo v. Haber Electric Co.* (Del. 1981) (regulations of Department of Labor implementing statute given great weight if not clearly erroneous but "the courts ultimately determine the true interpretation or construction of a particular statute or regulation").

We view the standard of judicial review of agency determinations of issues of statutory construction articulated in *Eastern Shore* as overly deferential and confusing. Accordingly, it is overruled. Statutory interpretation is ultimately the responsibility of the courts. A reviewing court may accord due weight, but not defer, to an agency interpretation of a statute administered by it. A reviewing court will not defer to such an interpretation as correct merely because it is rational or not clearly erroneous.

DNREC argues that in the event this Court should disavow *Eastern Shore's* standard of review, we should adopt the standard approved by the United States Supreme Court for federal agencies under *Chevron, U.S.A.,*

Inc. v. Natural Resources Defense Council, Inc. (1984).

We expressly decline to adopt such a standard with respect to review of an agency's interpretation of statutory law and reaffirm our plenary standard of review. While an agency's construction of a regulation promulgated by it may be entitled to some deference, it is unnecessary for this Court to reach the applicability of *Chevron* under the circumstances of this case.

At each level of the administrative process to which Tunnell's application was subjected, from the Hearing Officer through the EAB, the focus was on the interpretation of statutory law, not administrative regulations. Moreover, DNREC has not been charged by the General Assembly with elucidating statutory meaning through implementing regulations. Even if we were invited to consider the merit of *Chevron*'s teaching, this case does not provide an appropriate setting to do so.

NOTE

In recent years, several scholars have written extensively, and incisively, about state administrative law—some of the work focused on nondelegation, some on agency deference, some on still more general topics. *See, e.g.*, Miriam Seifter, *Understanding State Agency Independence*, 117 Mich. L. Rev. 1537 (2019); Miriam Seifter, *Further From the People? The Puzzle of State Administration*, 93 N.Y.U. L. Rev. 107 (2018); Miriam Seifter, *Gubernatorial Administration*, 131 Harv. L. Rev. 484, 521–23 (2017); Keith Iuliano & Keith Whittington, *The Nondelegation Doctrine: Alive and Well*, 93 Notre Dame L. Rev. 619 (2017); Aaron Saiger, Chevron *and Deference in State Administrative Law*, 83 Fordham L. Rev. 555 (2014); Michael Pappas, *No Two-Stepping in the Laboratories: State Deference Standards and Their Implications for Improving the* Chevron *Doctrine*, 39 McGeorge L. Rev. 977 (2008); Jim Rossi, *Dual Constitutions and Constitutional Duels: Separation of Powers and State Implementation of Federally-Inspired Regulatory Programs and Standards*, 46 Wm. & Mary L. Rev. 1343 (2005); Daniel Ortner, *The End of Deference: How States Are Leading a (Sometimes Quiet) Revolution Against Administrative Deference Doctrines* (March 11, 2020), https://ssrn.com/abstract=3552321. *See generally* Jeffery S. Sutton *Who Decides? States as Laboratories of Constitutional Experimentation*, Chapter 6 (Oxford 2021).

Chapter XVII

LOCAL GOVERNMENTS

State constitutions not only set the framework for state governments, but they also set the framework for local governments. Whether one climbs up the ladder of power or down it, the American phenomenon of governments inside of governments rarely disappears—and state constitutions play central roles in both directions. Call it federalism within federalism at the local level. As with federalism, local power allows smaller groups of citizens to embrace and audition innovative fixes to policy challenges and to customize solutions to a discrete group of people who live in one place. As with federalism, local power creates friction over when to keep things local and when to keep things general for the larger government. Just as federalism offers a way to limit friction between disparate positions and a way to avoid winner-take-all options, so the same is true of municipal governments. But just as federalism generates debates about who decides (the national government or a state?), so does local government law (the state or a local government?). Local government offers gears-within-gears benefits and challenges, both a new source of solutions for today's problems and a new line of demarcation about how best to govern. What the U.S. Supreme Court has said in lauding the virtues of federalism applies with equal measure to state and municipal powers. It permits "local policies more sensitive to the diverse needs of a heterogeneous society, permits innovation and experimentation, enables greater citizen involvement in democratic processes, and makes government more responsive by putting the states in competition for a mobile citizenry."

Hamilton's observations about local communities in *The Federalist* 17 offer a good explanation why state and municipal governments have become central to American government. "It is a known fact in human nature, that its affections are commonly weak in proportion to the distance or diffusiveness of the object. Upon the same principle that a man is more attached to his family than to his neighborhood, to his neighborhood than to the community at large, the people of each State are apt to feel a stronger bias towards their local governments than towards the government of the Union." Local attachments often make local governments the most well-suited governments to deal with societal challenges. Local knowledge and local understanding, sometimes conducive to local compromise, lead to greater efficiency and fairness in deciding what each community's local laws should be. Democracy indeed may work most effectively at the local level today.

While local government power has long been important, it has become particularly salient in America's third century. One explanation is a trend that has taken root in most regions of the country. Many large cities have become more politically progressive than other regions of their States. That trend has created tension between progressive cities on the one hand and conservative state legislatures (or less progressive state legislatures) on the other. In both settings, a gap has emerged between the political wishes of state leaders and local leaders.

If any sovereign should appreciate the virtues of local government, it should be the States. A key premise of federalism is localism, the principle of subsidiarity—that some problems are best resolved by a smaller government, one closest to, hence most knowledgeable about, the policy problem of the day. Everything useful about federalism—that it "promotes choice, competition, participation, experimentation, and the diffusion of power," in the helpful words of Heather Gerken—is just as true at the municipal level. Probably more so, as "most of the subnational governance that federalism protects," Richard Briffault adds, "actually occurs at the local level." The push and pull between States and the National Government often turns on answering the same questions about larger geographical units. Which government is best equipped to solve the problem? Is there one best answer to the underlying policy problem? Would experimentation be beneficial? The U.S. Constitution has little to say about how States organize their governments, including whether States delegate power over certain matters to their local governments. That leaves the policy considerations of who's best equipped to solve a problem and how best to try out new approaches to it with state constitutions and state legislation.

At the founding in 1776, with a deeply rooted New England tradition of governing through town meetings, one might have expected the new state constitutions to place considerable constitutional authority in local governments. As a matter of state constitutional structure, that did not happen with the small towns or burgeoning cities, even if local communities largely continued to govern themselves. America, unlike Europe or for that matter ancient Rome or Greece, has no tradition of city-states. The pertinent unit of power relative to Great Britain was the colonial government, and when the colonies became States, that unit of government for the most part and with some variations along the way remained the key one relative to the new national government.

But even if influential cities did not become city-states and even if the key units of sovereignty became the federal and state governments as well as federally recognized tribes, that did not mean the local governments lacked the customary features of a sovereign power. They not only acted like sovereigns in many ways, but they also looked like them. Local governments in most ways mirror the structure of the national and state governments. They have charters, mayors, unicameral (usually) city councils, courts, and agency-like commissions. Separation of powers sometimes applies there too.

States began adding provisions to their constitutions that regulated the relationship between the state and municipal governments in the mid-nineteenth century, as the local governments grew frustrated with twin evils: arbitrary, sometimes petty, oversight of local governments by state legislatures, and negligent, sometimes intentional, neglect of local conditions. In the 1850s, as John Dinan has shown, States began adding constitutional provisions that barred their legislatures from enacting "local or special laws." John Dinan, *State Constitutional Politics* 40 (2018). Michigan wrote the first one at a convention that led to its 1850 Constitution. It dealt just with roads and prohibited the legislature from eliminating "any road laid out by commissioners of highways or any street in any city or village." The Indiana 1851 Constitution created the first general prohibition, which banned the passage of "local or special laws" on a variety of subjects, including "county and township business." *Id.* (quoting Ind. Const., art. IV, § 22 (1851)). It became de rigueur for states to include such prohibitions, and most have them now. The idea behind them was easy to see. They were designed to "protect" "cities of the state against legislative encroachment." The no-special-law principle forced state legislatures to enact general laws, say for cities with more than 50,000 residents, as opposed to parochial legislation designed to tinker with one local charter or overrule one local policy.

Some states added "ripper" laws later in the nineteenth century to similar effect. They prohibited the state from enacting laws that "remove"—rip—"certain tasks from cities and transfer them to state-appointed officials or commissions." By 1900, at least eight states had adopted them: Pennsylvania, New Jersey, Colorado, California, Montana, South Dakota, Wyoming, and Utah. *Id.* They took aim not just at improving government but also at curbing corrupt government. Pennsylvania's prohibition, the first in the country according to Dinan, grew out of a state law that created a "self-perpetuating commission" in Philadelphia that "could require the city council to provide an unlimited sum of money for the construction of public buildings," money spent neither wisely nor honestly too much of the time. *Id.* (quoting David O. Porter, *The Ripper Clause in State Constitutional Law: An Early Urban Experiment: Part 1*, 1969 Utah L. Rev. 307 (1969)).

These laws became a preamble for the key state constitutional innovation in this area: home rule guarantees. Instead of restricting how state legislatures regulated local governments, they licensed local governments to regulate. Instead of "placing restraints" on state legislatures, they "empowered local citizens with the ability to articulate their preferences over institutional forms and functional powers within their local communities." *Id.* (quoting Michael E. Libonati, *Local Government, in 3 State Constitutions for the Twenty-First Century*, 123-24 (G. Alan Tarr & Robert Williams eds., 2006)). *See* Sutton, *Who Decides? States as Laboratories of Constitutional Experimentation*, Chapter 9 (2021).

Let us turn to some concrete disputes about home rule and about how different state courts have handled them.

A. CASES INVALIDATING STATE LAWS ON HOME RULE GROUNDS

Located just outside of Cleveland, Ohio, the hamlet of Linndale has 179 residents and thirty-five residential homes, and occupies less than a tenth of a square mile. Running through Linndale is about 450 yards of Interstate Highway 71, a section of the highway that connects downtown Cleveland to Columbus and many towns in between. For most people, Linndale is a drive-by city, not a destination or home.

The leaders of this municipal government put themselves on the map in an unusual way. With one eye focused on traffic safety and one eye focused on filling the local fisc, Linndale began stationing officers in the 1960s on their modest stretch of Interstate 71. The officers were vigilant—and profitable. Before long, Linndale gained a reputation for an unforgiving speed trap. In some years, Linndale generated nearly $1 million from traffic violations alone.

Some drivers did not appreciate this pilot project of home rule. News of the speed trap made its way to Ed Kasputis, then a representative in the Ohio state legislature. He visited Linndale's municipal court to see for himself, discovering several disgruntled drivers being told to pay up or face consequences. Although Linndale officials did not take ticketed individuals to the county jail for their offenses, Kasputis observed, they threatened to do so and extracted their pound of fines with the threat. Kasputis convinced his colleagues to enact a law in 1994 that prohibited local police from handing out speeding tickets on this highway if fewer than 880 yards of highway cross through their town, a generally written rule but not an ignorantly written rule.

Now it became Linndale's turn to challenge an oppressive government. It sued the state based on the home rule provision of the Ohio Constitution. It grants Ohio municipalities "authority to exercise all powers of local self-government and to adopt and enforce within their limits such local police, sanitary and other similar regulations, as are not in conflict with general laws." Ohio Const. Art. XVIII, § 3. Many of the things that the first part of the guarantee gives to municipalities are potentially taken away by the last words, that local laws may not "conflict with general laws" of the state legislature. According to the Supreme Court of Ohio, "general" laws tend to be "statutes setting forth police, sanitary, or other similar regulations and not statutes which purport only to grant or to limit the legislative powers of a municipal corporation." *West Jefferson v. Robinson*, 205 N.E.2d 382, 386 (Ohio 1965). Another measure of a general law, it said, is one that "operates uniformly throughout the state" and "prescribes a rule of conduct on citizens generally." *Garcia v. Siffrin Residential Ass'n*, 407 N.E.2d 1369, 1377-78 (Ohio 1980). The Ohio Supreme Court agreed with Linndale that the law was not general, reasoning that the law was "simply a limit on the legislative powers of municipal corporations to adopt and enforce specified police regulations." *Village of Lindale v. State*, 706 N.E.2d 1227, 1230 (Ohio 1999). Because the law was "not a part of a system of uniform statewide regulation on the subject of traffic law enforcement," it was unconstitutional. *Id.*

Linndale's victory lasted for a decade, after which the Ohio General Assembly passed another bill. This one said that villages falling under a certain population would be required to dissolve their mayor's courts. The bill originally set the threshold at 150 residents but increased the threshold to 200 after the 2010 census revealed Linndale's population, 179 residents. Without a mayor's court, Linndale still could issue tickets, but the tickets would be processed outside of the municipality. Linndale's ticket revenue went into free fall. Linndale sued again, this time unsuccessfully.

Undaunted, Linndale tried something new. It placed cameras near the town's busiest street, which recorded lots of unsuspecting speeders. After being caught speeding on camera, a motorist would receive a ticket directly in the mail. Because each ticket amounted to a civil infraction, not a criminal one, it did not require a court to enforce it. Linndale made *more* money with the cameras than it did with the speed trap. The Ohio legislature objected to this too. It enacted a law that prohibited the use of traffic cameras unless an officer was "present at the location of the device." *City of Dayton v. State*, 87 N.E.3d 176, 184 (Ohio 2017); *see* Sutton, *Who Decides? States as Laboratories of Constitutional Experimentation* Chapter 9 (2021).

Linndale, little surprise, is not the first or last city in Ohio to use speeding tickets to advance local public safety and local fiscal health. Here is how the Ohio Supreme Court resolved the dispute over the officer-present-with-the-camara law.

CITY OF DAYTON v. STATE
87 N.E.3d 176 (Ohio 2017)

FISCHER, J.

We address whether three statutes regulating local authorities' use of red-light and speed cameras qualify as general laws, such that the statutes do not offend the home-rule powers granted to a municipality in Article XVIII, Section 3 of the Ohio Constitution. We hold that R.C.

4511.093(B)(1), which requires that a law-enforcement officer be present at the location of a traffic camera, infringes on the municipality's legislative authority without serving an overriding state interest and is therefore unconstitutional. We also hold that R.C. 4511.0912, which prohibits the municipality from issuing a fine to a driver who is caught speeding by a traffic camera unless that driver's speed exceeds the posted speed limit by 6 m.p.h. in a school or park zone or 10 m.p.h. in other areas, unconstitutionally limits the municipality's legislative powers without serving an overriding state interest. Finally, we hold that R.C. 4511.095, which directs the municipality to perform a safety study and a public-information campaign prior to using a camera, unconstitutionally limits the municipality's home-rule authority without serving an overriding state interest.

The city of Dayton is an Ohio municipality governed by charter. In 2002, Dayton enacted an ordinance permitting its police department to institute a program using traffic cameras to civilly enforce red-light traffic violations to conserve police resources and to reduce traffic violations and accidents.

Under Dayton's program, cameras take both video and still pictures of vehicles. A police officer then reviews the camera images to confirm that a traffic violation occurred before issuing the owner a "notice of liability." After Dayton established its program using red-light and speed cameras, a new state law became effective in March 2015. It authorizes local authorities to use photo-monitoring devices for traffic-law violations, subject to certain conditions and regulations.

The Home Rule Amendment provides that "municipalities shall have authority to exercise all powers of local self-government and to adopt and enforce within their limits such local police, sanitary and other similar regulations, as are not in conflict with general laws." The Home Rule Amendment provides independent authority to Ohio's municipalities with regard to local police regulations. Nevertheless, a municipal ordinance must yield to a state statute if "(1) the ordinance is an exercise of the police power, rather than of local self-government, (2) the statute is a general law, and (3) the ordinance is in conflict with the statute."

The Dayton ordinances are an exercise of police power. Neither party argues that the Dayton ordinances do not conflict with the statute. The sole issue is whether the contested provisions qualify as general laws.

In determining whether a statute constitutes a "general law" for purposes of the Home Rule Amendment, this court has consistently applied the four requirements laid out in *Canton v. State* (Ohio 2002). To qualify as a general law under the *Canton* test, a statute must

(1) be part of a statewide and comprehensive legislative enactment, (2) apply to all parts of the state alike and operate uniformly throughout the state, (3) set forth police, sanitary, or similar regulations, rather than purport only to grant or limit legislative power of a municipal corporation to set forth police, sanitary, or similar regulations, and (4) prescribe a rule of conduct upon citizens generally.

If a statute meets the *Canton* general-law test, then the statute takes precedence over any conflicting municipal ordinances. However, if the general-law test is not satisfied, then the statute is "an unconstitutional attempt to limit the legislative home-rule powers" of municipalities. Dayton challenges the contested provisions under the third and fourth prongs of the *Canton* test. Because we determine that the contested provisions are unconstitutional under the third prong of the *Canton* test, our analysis will focus solely on that prong. We recognize, however, that the contested provisions may also be unconstitutional under the fourth *Canton* prong.

The third prong of the *Canton* general-law test requires courts to consider whether the statute sets forth police regulations or whether it merely grants or limits municipalities' legislative power to set forth police regulations. In undertaking this analysis, "a statute which prohibits the exercise by a municipality of its home rule powers without such statute serving an overriding statewide interest would directly contravene the constitutional grant of municipal power."

This court confronted the third prong of the *Canton* test in *Ohioans for Concealed Carry, Inc. v. Clyde* (Ohio 2008). In *Ohioans for Concealed Carry*, the court considered whether a municipal ordinance that prohibited licensed gun owners from carrying a concealed gun within a city's parks was constitutional under the Home Rule Amendment. The municipal ordinance conflicted with a state statute that allowed a licensed gun owner to carry a gun anywhere in the state, subject to several exceptions that did not include municipal parks. The court determined that the statute went beyond preventing cities from enacting conflicting legislation because the statute "provided a program to foster proper, legal handgun ownership in this state." The court determined that "the statute therefore represents both an exercise of the state's police power and an attempt to limit legislative power of a municipal corporation to set forth police, sanitary, or similar regulations."

Under the officer-present provision, "a local authority shall use a traffic law photo-monitoring device to detect and enforce traffic law violations only if a law enforcement officer is present at the location of the device at all times during the operation of the device." The state contends that the law represents a legislative compromise: it is not an outright ban on traffic cameras, but it establishes cameras as secondary enforcement tools so that the officers do not have to stop every violator.

However, requiring an officer's presence at a traffic camera directly contradicts the purpose of a traffic camera—to conserve police resources.

Moreover, the law does not require that an officer witness the violation, so the traffic camera is still the primary enforcement tool under the statute; it is not a secondary tool as the state contends. Because the officer-present requirement infringes on municipalities' home-rule authority without serving an overriding state interest, it is unconstitutional.

Under the statute, a local authority also is prohibited from relying on a photo-monitoring device to issue a ticket unless a vehicle exceeds the posted speed limit by 6 m.p.h. or more in a school zone or park or recreation area or, in all other areas, the vehicle exceeds the posted speed limit by 10 m.p.h. or more. With regard to whether the law serves an overriding state interest, the state contends that the speeding-leeway provision accounts for errors in the driver's speedometer or a traffic camera's measuring device, and also creates amnesty for minor speeding infractions. We find the state's arguments unpersuasive. As an initial matter, the state's arguments seemingly contradict its contention that the cameras should be a secondary enforcement tool supplementing police officers. Second, the law provides motorists with an opportunity to challenge violations in which they can contest issues such as speedometer and traffic-camera malfunctions. Third, the speeding-leeway provision would operate as a de facto increase in speed limits in the limited areas covered by a traffic camera. Because the law prohibits the exercise of home-rule powers without also serving an overriding state interest, it is unconstitutional.

The last of the contested provisions requires local authorities to (1) conduct a safety study prior to placing a photo-monitoring device at a location, (2) conduct a public-information campaign about the use of traffic-monitoring devices, (3) inform the public through a local newspaper prior to installing a photo-monitoring device, and (4) once a device is installed, observe a 30–day warning period before issuing a violation.

The statute contains no requirement that the placement of the traffic cameras be instructed by or connected in any way to the results of the traffic study. Thus, the statute does not serve the purpose of directing that the devices be placed in spots where authorities have safety concerns. Nor does the statute restrict the number of cameras in a specified area to serve the purpose of avoiding overconcentration.

Moreover, the public-information campaign, 30–day warning period, and requirement to publish in a local newspaper are of limited scope and duration. The public traveling through municipalities includes motorists who are not members of the local community targeted by the public-information campaign and local-publication requirement. Thus, the statute's requirements do not serve the purpose of ensuring that the public traveling in the area has notice.

Because the statute's alleged purpose is not served by the requirements it creates, the law does not serve an overriding statewide interest. It does not set forth state police, sanitary, or similar regulations but instead merely limits a municipality's legislative power to set forth those regulations.

Home-rule disputes require us to reconcile two competing constitutional provisions. First, Article II of the Ohio Constitution vests legislative power in the General Assembly. Second, the Home Rule Amendment, Article XVIII, Section 3 of the Ohio Constitution, grants municipalities the authority to exercise certain powers of local self-government.

Each home-rule case involves unique facts because no two statutes are exactly alike. When analyzing home-rule issues, we apply the *Canton* test to the statute at issue, which results in a conclusion that is unique to that particular statute. The fact that our conclusions in these fact-intensive cases may vary does not mean that we are being inconsistent or that the *Canton* test is unworkable but rather that varying facts applied to varying statutes compel varying outcomes.

FRENCH, J., concurring in the judgment only.

Although I agree with the lead opinion that the three statutes are not general laws and that they are unconstitutional limits on the home-rule authority of the city of Dayton, I write separately because my analysis differs from the analysis in the lead opinion.

Dayton argues that the contested provisions fail the third and fourth prongs of the *Canton* test. This court has analyzed the third prong of the *Canton* test by considering whether a statute that limits municipal authority also serves an overriding statewide interest, and the lead opinion focuses exclusively on the third prong in this case. The dissents express concern that that analysis steers courts perilously close to legislative policy decisions, which are beyond the judiciary's purview. In my view, however, we can avoid considering whether the contested provisions serve an overriding state interest because those provisions do not prescribe a rule of conduct on citizens generally, as the fourth prong of *Canton* requires.

Under the fourth prong of the *Canton* test, a statute must "prescribe a rule of conduct upon citizens generally" to qualify as a general law. The statute at issue in *Canton*—forbidding political subdivisions from prohibiting or restricting the location of permanently sited manufactured homes in any zone or district in which a single-family home was permitted—did not satisfy that requirement because it "applie[d] to municipal legislative bodies, not to citizens generally." In contrast, a statute that established speed limits and stated, "No person shall operate a motor vehicle at a speed greater or less than is reasonable or proper," prescribed a rule of conduct upon citizens and satisfied the fourth prong of the *Canton* test.

In *Linndale v. State* (Ohio 1999), this court considered a home-rule challenge to former R.C. 4549.17, which prohibited local law-enforcement officers from issuing speeding and excess-weight citations on interstate freeways when (1) less than 880 yards of the freeway were within the locality's jurisdiction, (2) local officers had to travel outside their jurisdiction to enter onto the freeway, and (3) local officers entered the freeway with the primary purpose of issuing the citations. The court held that R.C. 4549.17 was not a general law but was simply a limit on the legislative powers of municipalities to adopt and enforce police regulations. As relevant here, the court stated that the statute did "not prescribe a rule of conduct upon citizens generally."

The contested provisions here do not dictate a rule of conduct applicable to citizens of the state. Indeed, nothing in the law directs citizens' conduct with respect to the operation of a motor vehicle. Driving in excess of the speed limit and running a red light are violations of the law, whether or not a traffic camera exists to record the violation and whether or not a law-enforcement officer has authority to issue a citation. The contested provisions are phrased in terms of what a local authority shall or shall not do. They apply not to citizens but to municipalities. Like the statute in *Linndale*, the contested provisions of S.B. 342 merely limit municipal authority to enforce other substantive laws.

DeWINE, J., dissenting.

Today's decision has the unfortunate effect of further muddling a body of law that is already hopelessly confused. A fractured majority of this court decides that three statutory provisions relating to traffic cameras violate the Home Rule Amendment of the Ohio Constitution. The three justices who join the lead opinion find the provisions unconstitutional because they don't believe the provisions are in the overriding interest of the state. Two other justices say the provisions are lacking because they do not set forth a rule of conduct for citizens generally. But as in many cases in this area, the result today seems to have everything to do with the policy preferences of the majority and nothing to do with the Home Rule Amendment.

Nothing in the Home Rule Amendment makes the constitutionality of a legislative enactment turn upon this court's best guess about what is in the state's interest. Nor does the amendment ask whether a legislative enactment prescribes a rule of conduct for citizens generally. The questions we have to answer are dictated by the language of the amendment: Is the statute a general law? Is the municipal regulation an exercise of police powers? And is there a conflict? Because I determine that all three of the challenged provisions are general laws, and because there is no dispute that the ordinances enacted by the city of Dayton are an exercise of police power that conflicts with these general laws, I would uphold the statutes.

Few areas of our law have proved as troublesome as the application of the Home Rule Amendment. The result is that neither cities nor the legislature can say with any particular degree of certainty—on any particular day—who can do what. The most vexing question has been the one at issue here—what constitutes a general law?

The lead opinion reaches this conclusion by determining that none of the statutes serves an overriding state interest. This overriding-state-interest language appears nowhere in the language of the *Canton* test and nowhere in the language of Article XVIII, Section 3 of the Ohio Constitution. It is hard to discern that the lead opinion is doing anything other than applying the justices' own policy judgments as to the wisdom of the legislation.

For example, in determining that there is no overriding state interest behind the officer-present requirement, it opines that requiring an officer's presence "directly contradicts the purpose of a traffic camera—to conserve police resources." To start with, it is difficult to understand why this matters. The analysis should be about the purpose of the legislation, not the purpose of a traffic camera.

Moreover, the "purpose" of a traffic camera is itself a debatable point. As the state explained in its brief, the legislation was a compromise stemming from a longstanding argument between those who believed that some local authorities were using traffic cameras primarily to generate revenue and others who asserted that traffic cameras were employed for valid safety reasons. Compromises are by their nature often imperfect. Here, the legislature presumably sought a way to deal with concerns that traffic cameras were being misused for revenue purposes while at the same time allowing municipalities some opportunity to use the devices. The lead opinion apparently doesn't share the concern about the misuse of traffic cameras. But that should not make the legislative compromise invalid. The question left unanswered by the plurality is why it is better suited than the legislature to determine what is in the overriding interest of the state.

The General Assembly is not required to tell us its reasons for enacting legislation, so to try to divine its motives, or to require perfection in the motives we divine, is imprudent. Under our precedent, this court should not judge the merits of each statutory section in isolation but rather should evaluate whether the provision is part of a legislative scheme that addresses a subject in which there is an overriding state interest. Here, there can be no question about that state interest—the regulation of traffic. The state furthers that interest by providing a statewide, uniform framework for the use of traffic cameras.

This court has long recognized that the regulation of traffic is a statewide concern. R.C. 4511.13(C) and 4511.21(A) prohibit drivers from running red lights and from exceeding speed limits. The officer-present, safety-study, and speeding-leeway provisions determine how those existing statewide traffic laws will be enforced through the use of photo-enforcement technology. They address the circumstances in which Ohio's drivers are subject to the automated enforcement of those laws and thus are directly connected to state laws regulating the public as part of the state's police power.

NOTE

After the *Dayton* decision, the Ohio legislature passed a nearly identical regulation, but this time in the context of additional requirements. Ohio Rev. Stat. § 4511.093. The new regulation was designed to appear more "general" and, hope springs eternal, withstand the court's scrutiny. Despite this effort, the Court of Appeals of Ohio for the Sixth District held that the regulation still was not a "general" law. *City of Toledo v. State*, 130 N.E.3d 341, 350 (Ohio Ct. App. 2019).

DWAGFYS MANUFACTURING, INC. v. CITY OF TOPEKA
443 P.3d 1052 (Kan. 2019)

STEGALL, J.

The City of Topeka passed Ordinance No. 20099, amending Uniform Public Offense Code § 5.7 (2015) making it unlawful for any person to: "(1) Sell, furnish or distribute cigarettes, electronic cigarettes, tobacco products or liquid nicotine to any person under 21 years of age; or (2) Buy any cigarettes, electronic cigarettes, tobacco products or liquid nicotine for any person under 21 years of age." The day before the Ordinance was to take effect, DWAGFYS Manufacturing, Inc., d/b/a The Vapebar Topeka, sued Topeka seeking to prevent enforcement of the Ordinance. Vapebar argued the Ordinance was unconstitutional under article 12, section 5 of the Kansas Constitution because it impermissibly conflicted with and was preempted by the Kansas Cigarette and Tobacco Products Act. Additionally, Vapebar argued the Ordinance exceeded Topeka's police power authority.

The Ordinance passed by Topeka provided, in part:

(a) It shall be unlawful for any person to:

(1) Sell, furnish or distribute cigarettes, electronic cigarettes, tobacco products or liquid nicotine to any person under 21 years of age; or

(2) Buy any cigarettes, electronic cigarettes, tobacco products or liquid nicotine for any person under 21 years of age.

The Act, in relevant part, provides:

It shall be unlawful for any person:

(l) To sell, furnish or distribute cigarettes, electronic cigarettes or tobacco products to any person under 18 years of age.

(m) Who is under 18 years of age to purchase or attempt to purchase cigarettes, electronic cigarettes or tobacco products.

(n) Who is under 18 years of age to possess or attempt to possess cigarettes, electronic cigarettes or tobacco products.

The preemption and conflict issues raised in this appeal derive from article 12, section 5 of the Kansas Constitution—also known as the home rule amendment. Taking effect in 1961, the amendment empowered local governments to determine their local affairs and government by ordinance. Following the amendment, cities no longer had to rely on the Legislature to specifically authorize the exercise of a particular power or action via statute. The amendment further provided that the "powers and authority granted cities pursuant to this section shall be liberally construed for the purpose of giving to cities the largest measure of self-government."

A city may adopt ordinary ordinances when no state law exists on the subject or when a uniform law applicable to all cities exists on the subject but the Legislature has not expressed a clear intent to preempt the field and there is no conflict between the state and local law.

Thus, to determine whether an ordinary ordinance is a valid exercise of home rule power courts must ask: (1) Is there a state law that governs the subject? (2) If there is a state law, is it uniformly applicable to all cities? (3) If there is a uniform state law, does it preempt further action by cities? and (4) If there is a uniform state law but there has been no preemption, does the local regulation conflict with the uniform state law?

The first two questions are not in dispute. The parties agree that the Act and the Ordinance govern the same subject—i.e., the regulation of cigarettes, electronic cigarettes, tobacco products, and liquid nicotine in Kansas. The parties also agree that the Act is a uniform state law applicable to all cities. Thus, we must resolve the latter two questions—preemption and conflict.

Vapebar asks us to find that the Legislature preempted the field of tobacco regulation when it passed the Act. But there is no express statement of preemption in the Act, and since 1961, we have consistently rejected the doctrine of implied legislative preemption. Instead, we have held that legislative intent to reserve exclusive jurisdiction to the state must be clearly manifested by statute—i.e., by expressly prohibiting cities from enacting any type of ordinance related to the state law.

To avoid application of this caselaw, Vapebar first points us to our decision in *Trimble v. City of Topeka*, 75 P.2d 241 (Kan. 1938), suggesting that the Legislature may implicitly preempt even without an express statement of intent.

Trimble, of course, was decided long before the home rule amendment. Prior to 1961, the general rule was that "the superior power is with the state" and "the city's only power is that delegated to it by the state." In other words, unless the statute expressly granted cities a right to act, it was presumed the state had preempted the field. After the amendment, however, cities no longer need a legislative delegation of power. Rather, cities are "empowered to determine their local affairs" and courts are to construe this power "liberally for the purpose of giving to cities the largest measure of self-government." Kan. Const. art. 12, § 5(b) and (d). Legislative silence is no longer sufficient to imply state preemption. Rather, "legislative intent to reserve to the state exclusive jurisdiction to regulate an area *must be clearly manifested by statute* before it can be held that the state has withdrawn from the cities the power to regulate in the field."

Here, the Act does not manifest a clear intent to preempt cities from action. The language of the Act is plain and unambiguous and we "merely interpret the language as it appears"—we are "not free to speculate and cannot read into the statute language not readily found there." Moreover, the Legislature knows how to expressly preempt city home rule power but did not do so here. *See, e.g.*, K.S.A. 2018 Supp. 75-5174(a) ("The power to regulate, license and tax the management, operation and conduct of and participation in games of bingo and raffles is *hereby vested exclusively in the state*."). In fact, some provisions of the Act seem to contemplate cities enacting ordinances covering at least some of the same conduct. *See* K.S.A. 2018 Supp. 79-3393(c) ("Acts classified as cigarette or tobacco infractions by K.S.A. 79-3322[d], and amendments thereto, shall be classified as ordinance cigarette or tobacco infractions by those cities adopting ordinances prohibiting the same acts. The fine for an ordinance cigarette or tobacco infraction shall be $25.").

Vapebar suggests that perhaps the Legislature's enactment of a "comprehensive scheme" of regulation is sufficient to clearly manifest an intent to preempt the field. We disagree. We have already rejected the idea that the Legislature's adoption of a comprehensive scheme can establish a clear intent to preempt the field. In *Junction City v. Lee*, the defendants relied on a Judicial Council comment that described the state weapons control act as "a comprehensive weapons control act." 532 P.2d 1292 (Kan. 1975). Rejecting this argument for preemption, we held that "legislative intent to preempt is not to be so simplistically found. Absent clear expression to that effect, we cannot conceive that the legislature intended by its enactment, comprehensive though it be, to exclude cities' traditional resources" from protecting its citizens' well-being.

With no language manifesting a clear intent to preempt the field in the Act, the Act does not preempt the Ordinance. But preemption is not the last restriction on a city's home rule power. In order to clear the final hurdle, the Ordinance must not conflict with state law. We have emphasized that "a city ordinance should be permitted to stand unless an actual conflict exists between the ordinance and a statute." In determining whether an actual conflict exists between an ordinance and a statute, we apply the well-cited conflict test articulated in *Lee*: "Whether the ordinance permits or licenses that which the statute forbids or prohibits that which the statute authorizes; if so, there is conflict, but where both an ordinance and the statute are prohibitory and the only difference is that the ordinance goes further in its prohibition but not counter to the prohibition in the statute, and the city does not attempt to authorize by the ordinance that which the legislature has forbidden, or forbid that which the legislature has expressly authorized, there is no conflict."

As with all things home rule, our consideration of whether there is a conflict must be informed with the constitutional command to "liberally construe" the home rule power so as to give "to cities the largest measure of self-government." Kan. Const. art. 12, § 5.

Vapebar argues that the Ordinance conflicts with the Act because the Ordinance prohibits what the Act authorizes. If there was an express authorization in the Act for people under the age of 21 to buy tobacco products, or an express authorization to sell tobacco to those people, Vapebar would have a point. But there is no express authorization. The Act is silent with respect to people who are 18, 19, or 20 years old. In the face of such silence, "where both an ordinance and the statute are prohibitory and the only difference is that the ordinance goes further in its prohibition, there is no conflict."

For example, in *Lee* we found an ordinance outlawing the carrying of both concealed and unconcealed weapons did not conflict with a state statute outlawing only the carrying of concealed weapons. The court found the essential difference to be that "the ordinance denounces carrying on one's person a dangerous knife or firearm while the statute makes such carrying criminal only where the weapons are concealed." The court held that no conflict existed between the statute and ordinance because the ordinance was merely "more restrictive" than the statute. And a more restrictive ordinance will stand as long as "the city does not attempt to authorize by the ordinance that which the legislature has forbidden, or forbid that which the legislature has *expressly authorized*."

More recently in *City of Wichita v. Hackett*, we reiterated the *Lee* test and found an ordinance criminalizing the operation of a bicycle while intoxicated did not conflict with the state law that criminalized motor vehicle DUIs. There, the state statute at issue defined "vehicle" to exclude "*devices moved by human power*." 69 P.3d 621 (Kan. 2003). The City adopted additional traffic regulations that prohibited operation of a bicycle while under the influence of alcohol. In holding this ordinance valid, the court ruled the statute did not expressly authorize the operation of bicycles by those intoxicated. Rather, the statute merely failed to proscribe it.

Similarly, the Ordinance and the Act coexist without conflict. The Act does not "expressly authorize" what the Ordinance prohibits—the selling and buying of tobacco products to and by 18-, 19-, and 20-year-olds. The Act simply fails to proscribe it. Thus, the Ordinance does not conflict with the Act because the Ordinance does not prohibit what the Act expressly authorizes. The Ordinance merely enlarges a provision of the statute by requiring more than the statute—a practice we have repeatedly treated as creating no conflict.

The Ordinance prohibiting retailers from selling, furnishing, or distributing cigarettes, electronic cigarettes, tobacco products, or liquid nicotine to any person under 21 years old is a constitutional exercise of Topeka's home rule power. The Act does not preempt cities from regulating tobacco products, and the Ordinance does not conflict with the Act by imposing greater restrictions. Because the Ordinance is a constitutional exercise of the City's home rule power, we reverse the district court's permanent injunction.

COOPERATIVE HOME CARE, INC. v. CITY OF ST. LOUIS
514 S.W.3d 571 (Mo. 2017)

STITH, J.

On August 28, 2015, St. Louis enacted Ordinance 70078 of its revised city code. The ordinance provides a series of four graduated increases to the minimum wage for employees working within the physical boundaries of St. Louis, beginning on October 15, 2015 at $8.25 per hour and ending on January 1, 2018 at $11 per hour. Beginning January 1, 2021, the minimum wage rate under section 2(B)(2) of the ordinance shall be increased annually on a percentage basis to reflect the rate of inflation. The ordinance further states, "If the state or federal minimum wage rate is at any time greater than the minimum wage rate established by this ordinance, then the greater shall become the minimum wage rate for purposes of this ordinance."

Section 290.502 contains Missouri's minimum wage law, which provides in relevant part that "every employer shall pay to each employee wages at the rate of $6.50 per hour, or wages at the same rate or rates set under the provisions of federal law." The minimum wage rate is subject to yearly adjustments by the Missouri Department of Labor and Industrial Relations, based upon any change in the cost of living. Under Missouri's minimum wage law, the state minimum wage rate is $7.65 per hour.

Section 67.1571 was adopted in 1998 through the enactment of HB 1636. Known as the Community Improvement District Act, HB 1636, as initially proposed, addressed solely the establishment, proper governance, and operation of community improvement districts. It did not address minimum wages or the minimum wage law in any way. Minimum wages were, instead, the subject of another bill, HB 1346, which proposed to "prohibit political subdivisions of this state from establishing or requiring a minimum wage that exceeds the state minimum wage." When HB 1346 failed to pass out of committee, comparable minimum wage language was added as a late amendment to HB 1636. Once HB 1636 became law, the minimum wage provision added to the bill was codified as section 67.1571.

Aware of uncertainties caused by litigation concerning section 67.1571, the General Assembly adopted another minimum wage bill, HB 722, on May 6, 2015. HB 722 provided:

> No political subdivision shall establish, mandate, or otherwise require an employer to provide an employee: (1) a minimum wage or living wage rate; or (2) employment benefits; that exceed the requirements of federal or state laws, rules or regulations. The provisions of this subsection shall not preempt any state or local minimum wage ordinance requirements in effect on August 28, 2015.

A constitutional charter city, such as St. Louis City, derives its charter powers from article VI, section 19(a) of the Missouri Constitution, which states in part:

> Any city which adopts or has adopted a charter for its own government, shall have all powers which the general assembly of the state of Missouri has authority to confer upon any city, provided such powers are consistent with the constitution of this state and are not limited or denied either by the charter so adopted or by statute.

Pursuant to this constitutional provision, if a charter city's power to adopt an ordinance is challenged, the Court will uphold the ordinance upon finding: (1) the ordinance is not preempted by statute, and (2) the locality acted within the constitutional parameters of the authority delegated to it in its charter. Here, Plaintiffs claim that state statutes preempt the ordinance and that the City acted beyond its charter authority.

A charter city is not required to exercise delegated powers in "precisely the same manner as prescribed by the general law of the state," but local legislation cannot create an inconsistent or irreconcilable conflict with state law. If this Court finds such a conflict exists, state statutes preempt the local ordinances.

Preemption of a local law by a statute may be express or implied. Express preemption occurs when the General Assembly has explicitly proscribed local regulation in a specific area.

Implied preemption can occur in either of two ways—through "conflict" preemption or through "field" preemption. Conflict preemption occurs when a local ordinance conflicts with a specific state statute either because it "prohibits what the statute permits" or because it "permits what the statute prohibits." In such cases, the conflict is resolved by giving effect to the state statute rather than the conflicting local law. Yet, while a local ordinance may not directly conflict with the state law, it can supplement the state law by creating additional requirements. By contrast, field preemption occurs when the General Assembly has created a state regulatory scheme that is so comprehensive that it reasonably can be inferred that the General Assembly intended to occupy the legislative field, leaving no room for local supplementation.

Plaintiffs argue that, even if Ordinance 70078 is not specifically preempted by section 67.1571, the entire field of minimum wage regulation is preempted by Missouri's minimum wage law. That law, Plaintiffs say, sets a "standard for authorized conduct," permitting employers to pay employees any wage at or above the statutory minimum. Plaintiffs interpret this to constitute a specific authorization for employers to pay to an employee any wage at or above the statutory minimum, and an ordinance providing for a higher minimum wage "prohibits what the state permits" in that it prohibits employers from paying a wage lower than the local minimum wage standard but higher than the state standard. Plaintiffs argue that Ordinance 70078, therefore, directly conflicts with Missouri's minimum wage law and that the field of minimum wage laws is preempted.

Plaintiffs are incorrect. Their arguments are an amalgam of conflict and field preemption principles and result in a muddied analysis that discusses elements of each interchangeably. This Court addresses these distinct types of preemption separately.

Conflict preemption applies only when a local law prohibits what state law permits or when the local law permits what state law prohibits. For example, in *Page Western, Inc.,* 636 S.W.2d 65 (Mo. 1982), this Court held that an ordinance specifically prohibiting self-service gas pumps directly conflicted with a state regulation expressly permitting self-service gas pumps. The local ordinance prohibited what the state permitted and so was preempted.

By contrast, there is no conflict preemption when a local law simply supplements state law, such as when the locality prohibits more than the state prohibits. That is why this Court found no conflict preemption in *Kansas City v. LaRose,* 524 S.W.2d 112 (Mo. 1975), which involved a municipal ordinance dispensing with a mens rea element that was required by state statute, effectively criminalizing more conduct than the state. It was not preempted because it simply prohibited more than did the state statute.

Similarly, Plaintiffs are incorrect that the Missouri minimum wage law is an affirmative authorization to pay no more than the state minimum wage. To the contrary, it simply sets a floor below which an employee cannot be paid, stating that "every employer shall pay to each employee wages at the rate of the current state minimum wage standard." To conclude that the law was intended to protect *employers* from ever being required to pay a higher wage is at odds with the statute's recognized purpose, which is to ameliorate the "unequal bargaining power as between employer and employee and to protect the rights of those who toil." Its purpose of protecting employees is served by setting a floor for minimum wages; nothing in the law suggests the state also wanted to protect employers by setting a maximum minimum wage. Indeed, that is why section 67.1571 had to be passed in the first instance, because there was no such prohibitory law.

As Ordinance 70078 does not permit the payment of less than the state minimum wage, it is not in conflict with that law. It simply supplements the state law by setting additional local limits on the minimum amount an employer can pay an employee. Its purpose is consistent with that of the state minimum wage law; by its terms, it was enacted "to promote the general welfare, health, and prosperity of the City of St. Louis by ensuring that workers can better support and care for their families and fully participate in the community." Here, the state established a floor for employee wages, and St. Louis simply raised that floor for local employees based on local conditions. Finding no reason to diverge from well-established precedent, this Court holds Ordinance 70078 does not conflict with Missouri's minimum wage law.

While on their face the provisions of the minimum wage law alone do not indicate an intent to preempt all local minimum wage laws, Plaintiffs argue that such preemption becomes evident if Missouri's minimum wage law is read together with section 71.010. Together, they say, these two laws make Missouri's minimum wage law occupy the minimum wage field, preempting any local minimum wage law without regard to the effect of HB 722. Again, this Court disagrees.

Section 71.010 sets out the general and well-recognized principle that municipal ordinances that regulate "matters and things upon which there is a general law of the state shall be in conformity with the state law upon the same subject." This is a general statute ensuring that state and local laws do not conflict. For the reasons just noted, Ordinance 70078 does not conflict with Missouri's minimum wage law. Adding section 71.010 to the analysis, therefore, does not change the result of the preemption analysis.

Plaintiffs seek to add a gloss to section 71.010 by reading it to provide that no locality can adopt ordinances concerning an issue as to which the state has adopted a statute. This is not what section 71.010 says, and it is inconsistent with the long-established rule that local laws may supplement state law so long as they do not conflict with state law. Indeed, local ordinances often enlarge state provisions without creating a conflict between the two. The smoking bans in *Carlson* and the criminal elements in *LaRose* provide perfect examples, as do state and local laws regulating traffic, *City of St. John v. Brockus*, 434 S.W.3d 90 (Mo. App. 2014); zoning, *State ex rel. Teefey & Agri–Lawn, Inc. v. Bd. of Zoning Adjustment of Kansas City*, 24 S.W.3d 681 (Mo. 2000); barber licensing, *Vest v. Kansas City*, 194 S.W.2d 38 (Mo. 1946); engineer licensing, *Bd. of Stationary Eng'rs v. City of St. Louis*, 212 S.W.2d 454 (Mo. App. 1948); hunting and trapping, *Miller v. City of Town & Country*, 62 S.W.3d 431 (Mo. App.

2001); and selling alcohol, *Nickols v. N. Kansas City*, 214 S.W.2d 710 (Mo. 1948). The state has legislated in all of these areas, yet that has never been interpreted to mean that, pursuant to section 71.010, it would conflict with those laws to allow cities and counties to add supplemental regulation.

This conclusion that local minimum wage ordinances may supplement Missouri's minimum wage law because the latter is not intended to preempt the field, is confirmed by the fact that the legislature repeatedly has recognized and authorized local ordinances and additional state laws addressing minimum wages. For instance, section 288.062.6 of Missouri's employment security law specifically acknowledges that local authorities may set a higher minimum wage than that set by the state and requires that this local minimum wage be given effect when considering what employment an injured worker must accept to not violate the worker's compensation laws, stating:

> Extended benefits shall not be denied under subsection 5 of this section to any individual for any week by reason of a failure to accept an offer of or apply for suitable work if: (3) the remuneration for the work offered is less than the minimum wage provided by Section 6(a)(1) of the Fair Labor Standards Act of 1938, as amended, without regard to any exemption *or any applicable state or local minimum wage, whichever is the greater.*

This statutory language recognizes that local minimum wages exist and supplement the state minimum wage law.

HB 722 provides another excellent example of the legislature's recognition of the validity of local minimum wage ordinances. The General Assembly passed both section 67.1571 and HB 722 after it had already passed Missouri's minimum wage law and section 71.010. Plaintiffs say that the legislature may have passed section 67.1571 because it knew localities were improperly passing local minimum wage ordinances and wanted to reinforce that they were not permitted to do so. Nothing in section 67.1571 supports this reading, but even if it were the case, HB 722 cannot be dismissed in this way. Like the employment security law just discussed, HB 722 not only acknowledges that municipalities have adopted minimum wage ordinances, but it also specifically excludes them from the statute's express preemption, stating, "The provisions of this subsection shall not preempt any state or local minimum wage ordinance requirements in effect on August 28, 2015."

As is evident, HB 722 again demonstrates that the legislature was well aware that local minimum wage ordinances supplement the state minimum wage law and that they would not be preempted if in effect before August 28, 2015, the date set out in HB 722. One such law was St. Louis City's Ordinance 65597, which was enacted in lieu of the ordinance that was the subject of litigation in *Missouri Hotel*. Adopted in 2002, Ordinance 65597 requires employers to pay a minimum wage to employees that are performing work pursuant to a contract between the employer and the City at a "Living Wage rate" that is higher than the wage set by the state minimum wage law. Although its adoption was mentioned in *Missouri Hotel*, the General Assembly has made no attempt to invalidate the ordinance or otherwise contest the City's authority to enact it. Instead, HB 722 by its terms provides that such existing ordinances are not preempted, which it would not have done had the legislature intended Missouri's minimum wage law and section 71.010 together to occupy the field and preempt all local laws on this subject.

In a variation on its argument that the Missouri minimum wage law was intended to occupy the field of minimum wage legislation, Plaintiffs argue that what constitutes an appropriate minimum wage is a matter of general state interest and is not within the power of localities to regulate, even when those localities are charter cities.

As noted above, article VI, section 19(a) of the Missouri Constitution provides that "any city which adopts or has adopted a charter for its own government, shall have all powers which the general assembly of the state of Missouri has authority to confer upon any city, provided such powers are consistent with the constitution of this state and are not limited or denied either by the charter so adopted or by statute." The grant of legislative powers to a charter city under this section is limited to those powers incident to the city's affairs and may not "invade the province of the general legislation involving the public policy of the state as a whole."

Plaintiffs do not deny that standards concerning worker wages are linked to the general welfare of the citizens of St. Louis. Instead, they argue that because concern for citizens' welfare extends beyond St. Louis, the state alone has the authority to address it. This argument ignores the fact that the police power is among those powers incident to a city's affairs, so that charter cities have authority to enact ordinances having a substantial and rational relation to the "peace, comfort, safety, health, morality, and general welfare" of its inhabitants. That is the basis on which Missouri courts have upheld local legislation addressing issues such as discrimination, smoking, and similar issues even though those issues also are addressed by state and national laws.

For example, in *Marshall v. Kansas City*, 355 S.W.2d 877 (Mo. 1962), this Court held that Kansas City had not acted beyond its police power by enacting an ordinance designed to prevent racial discrimination in certain businesses, even though the underlying problem of discrimination also is prevalent at the state and national level. "Kansas City has the general power to define, prohibit and regulate acts, practices and conduct of businesses which are detrimental to the health, comfort, safety, convenience and welfare of its inhabitants." Indeed, as discussed above at length, state laws such as HB 722 and the employment security law recognize the authority of municipalities to enact ordinances which address the minimum wage. Local laws such as Ordinance 70078 may address such issues without improperly straying into the province of general legislation regulating statewide concerns. A municipality acting within powers incident to it as a municipality does not prevent the state from passing its own statewide policies on the same subject, and the existence of state laws and local ordinances on that subject is not inherently in conflict. The local ordinance may, as here, supplement state laws. The City did not act outside its home-rule authority in enacting Ordinance 70078.

B. CASES REJECTING HOME-RULE CHALLENGES TO STATE LAWS

CITY OF LAREDO v. LAREDO MERCHANTS ASSOCIATION
550 S.W.3d 586 (Tex. 2018)

HECHT, C.J.

The roving, roiling debate over local control of public affairs has not, with increased age, lost any of its vigor. From public education to immigration policy to fracking to shopping bags, the sides are always deeply divided.

The Texas Constitution states that city ordinances cannot conflict with state law. The Texas Solid Waste Disposal Act provides that "a local government may not adopt an ordinance to prohibit or restrict, for solid waste management purposes, the sale or use of a container or package in a manner not authorized by state law." The sharply contested issue here is whether the Act preempts, and thus invalidates, a local antilitter ordinance prohibiting merchants from providing "single use" plastic and paper bags to customers for point-of-sale purchases.

Both sides of the debate assert public-policy arguments raising economic, environmental, and uniformity concerns. But those arguments are not ours to resolve. "The wisdom or expediency of the law is the Legislature's prerogative, not ours." We must take statutes as they are written, and the one before us is written quite clearly. Its limitation on local control encompasses the ordinance.

As part of a strategic plan to create a "trash-free" city, the City of Laredo adopted an ordinance to reduce litter from one-time-use plastic and paper bags. To discourage use of these bags, the Ordinance makes it unlawful for any "commercial establishment" to provide or sell certain plastic or paper "checkout bags" to customers. The ordinance applies to commercial enterprises that sell retail goods to the general public.

The Ordinance's stated objectives are: (a) To promote the beautification of the city through prevention of litter generated from discarded checkout bags, (b) to reduce costs associated with floatable trash controls and the maintenance of the municipal separate stormwater sewer system, and (c) to protect life and property from flooding that is a consequence of improper stormwater drainage attributed in part to obstruction from checkout bags.

Shortly before the Ordinance's effective date, the Laredo Merchants Association sued the City to forestall its enforcement. The Merchants sought declaratory and injunctive relief, asserting that the Ordinance is preempted by Section 361.0961 of the Act and thus void under the Texas Constitution. That provision expressly precludes a local government from restricting "the sale or use of a container or package" if the restraint is for "solid waste management purposes" and the "manner" of regulation is "not authorized by state law."

As a home-rule municipality, the City of Laredo possesses the "full power of local self-government." But the Texas Constitution provides that home-rule city ordinances must not "contain any provision inconsistent with the Constitution of the State, or of the general laws enacted by the Legislature of this State." While home-rule cities have all power not denied by the Constitution or state law, and thus need not look to the Legislature for grants of authority, the Legislature can limit or withdraw that power by general law. Deciding whether uniform statewide regulation is preferable to a patchwork of local regulations is the Legislature's prerogative. The question is not whether the Legislature *can* preempt a local regulation like the Ordinance but whether it *has*.

A statutory limitation of local laws may be express or implied, but the Legislature's intent to impose the limitation "must appear with unmistakable clarity." The mere "entry of the state into a field of legislation does not automatically preempt that field from city regulation." Rather, "local regulation, ancillary to and in harmony with the general scope and purpose of the state enactment, is acceptable." Absent an express limitation, if the general law and local regulation can coexist peacefully without stepping on each other's toes, both will be given effect.

In this case, legislative intent in the Act to preempt local law is clear. The Act states that "a local government or other political subdivision may not adopt" certain ordinances. The issue is whether the Ordinance falls within the Act's ambit. To decide that, we look to the statutory text and the ordinary meanings of its words.

The Act provides, "It is this state's policy and the purpose of the Act to safeguard the health, welfare, and physical property of the people and to protect the environment by controlling the management of solid waste." To that end, "the state's goal, through source reduction, is to eliminate the generation of municipal solid waste to the maximum extent that is technologically and economically feasible." According to the Act, the state's public policy is that, in disposing of municipal solid waste, the methods listed below are preferred: (1) source reduction and waste minimization; (2) reuse or recycling of waste; (3) treatment to destroy or reprocess waste to recover energy or other beneficial resources if the treatment does not threaten public health or the environment; or (4) land disposal.

The Act thus describes a state interest in "controlling the management of solid waste" that is plenary. The Act's preemption of local control is narrow and specific, applying to ordinances that "prohibit or restrict, [1] for solid waste management purposes, [2] the sale or use of a container or package [3] in a manner not authorized by state law." The City argues that its Ordinance does not meet any of these elements. We address each in turn.

The Act does not define the phrase "solid waste management purposes" but does define its constituent parts. "Solid waste" means "discarded material," including "rubbish," which "consists of combustible waste materials, including paper and plastics." "Management means the systematic control of the activities of generation, source separation, collection, handling, storage, transportation, processing, treatment, recovery, or disposal of solid waste." The term "management" thus refers to institutional controls imposed at any point in the solid waste stream, from generation of solid waste to disposal.

The Ordinance's stated purpose and its intended effect are to control the generation of solid waste by reducing a source of solid waste on the front end so those single-use materials cannot be inappropriately discarded on the back end. The City contends that this is "source reduction," defined by the Act as "an activity or process that avoids the creation of municipal solid waste in the state by reducing waste at the source." The purpose of the Ordinance cannot be "solid waste management," the City argues, because at the moment of regulatory restraint, the bags have not yet been discarded and, therefore, are not yet "solid waste." But "management" includes "the systematic control of the generation of solid waste" as well as its handling after it is created. The Act does not define "generation," so we give the word its ordinary meaning—to generate is "to cause to be: bring into existence." The Ordinance's stated purposes are to reduce litter and eliminate trash—in sum, to manage solid waste, which the Act preempts. The Ordinance cannot fairly be read any other way.

But, the City argues, the Ordinance has other, independent purposes for prohibiting the provision of single-use bags, such as preventing sewer blockages and flooding, promoting beautification, ameliorating the economic impact of this particular form of litter, and protecting water and wildlife. All of these salutary objectives pertain to the ancillary effects of reducing the generation of solid waste, which is a solid waste management purpose. The Ordinance's solid waste management cannot avoid preemption merely because it has other purposes. We think it clear that the Ordinance was adopted for solid waste management purposes.

In the City's view, the Act does not clearly apply to new bags for point-of-sale purchases because the term "bag" is not used in the statute and the statute is contextually focused on trash, not new items. As the City sees it, no matter how likely or expeditiously single-use bags are destined to become trash, the Act's reach is limited to either (1) containers and packages that have already been discarded, or (2) containers and packages that store or transport garbage, like dumpsters. Again, the City's narrow construction is not supported by a plain reading of the statute.

Neither "container" nor "package" is statutorily defined, so we begin by looking to the words' ordinary meanings. A "container" is "an object that can be used to hold or transport something"; "a receptacle (as a box or jar) or a formed or flexible covering for the packing or shipment of articles, goods, or commodities." The term "package" refers to "a commodity in its container: a unit of a product uniformly processed, wrapped, or sealed for distribution; "an object or group of objects wrapped in paper or plastic, or packed in a box"; and "the box or bag in which things are packed." A "bag," commonly understood, is "a container made of paper, cloth, mesh, metal foil, plastic, or other flexible material for properly holding, storing, carrying, shipping, or distributing any material or product." A single-use paper or plastic bag used to hold retail goods and commodities for transportation clearly falls within the ordinary meaning of "container." The Ordinance itself repeatedly characterizes bags as containers. Construing the term "container" to exclude bags is incompatible with the common use and understanding of that word.

The Act is not concerned solely with discarded materials but also includes regulations applicable to the production, retail sale, and distribution of new consumer goods. If consumer products were to be excluded from the preemption provision, the Legislature would have said so, as it did by excluding consumer products elsewhere in the Act. The only reasonable construction of the Act that accords with the statute as a whole is one that affords the terms container and package their ordinary meanings.

Finally, the City argues that the Ordinance escapes preemption because it is "authorized by state law" as shown by its consistency with various state general laws—laws regarding municipal authority to: protect water sources, the municipal water supply, and watersheds; regulate water systems in a manner that protects the municipality's interests; own, construct, operate, and maintain a water system; and establish "a water pollution control and abatement program for the city," including "the development and execution of reasonable and realistic plans for controlling and abating pollution."

But the Act preempts local regulation "in a *manner* not authorized by state law." The question is not whether a municipality has the power to regulate. Home-rule cities already have the power of self-governance unless restricted by state law. If "authorized by law" in the preemption provision referred only to the power municipalities already have, the restriction would have no effect. But the preemption provision applies to local regulation when the *manner* is not authorized by state law. Manner is *how* something can be done, not merely *if* it can be. A manner must be stated by, and not merely implied from, a grant of authority. The stated intent of the Act is to control the manner of regulating the sale or use of containers or packages for solid waste management purposes. To conclude otherwise would render the statute meaningless.

By rescinding local control that would otherwise exist, the Act forbids home-rule cities from regulating that subject matter. By authorizing regulation only when municipalities are told how to permissibly regulate, the Act requires an express authorization. These circumstances are functionally analogous to how general-law municipalities operate under the law. General-law municipalities lack the power of self-government and must look to the Legislature for express grants of power. So too must a home-rule city whose self-governance has been legislatively abrogated.

The Act's exemption does not save the Ordinance because the City has not identified a law authorizing the manner in which the City seeks to regulate. The general grants of regulatory authority the City relies on do not authorize the manner the City has chosen and, more to the point, do not supersede the express directive in the Act.

GUZMAN, J., concurring.

The critical inquiry here is whether the Legislature, through clear and unmistakable language, expressed its intent to preempt local regulation, and it has. Our duty is to enforce the statute as we find it, so we have. Even so, these complex public policy determinations have important ramifications for the environmental legacy the next generation will inherit. And allowing plastic debris—bags, Styrofoam cups, water bottles, and similar pollutants—to migrate unchecked into the environment carries grave consequences that must not be ignored. Though I join the Court's opinion, I write separately to highlight the urgency of the matter. As a society, we are at the point where complacency has become complicity.

Plastic is a miracle material with many beneficial purposes, but the speed at which plastic refuse is proliferating is taxing our waste-management capacities. Improperly discarded plastics have become a scourge on the environment and an economic drain. The optimal solution to the problem of single-use plastics may be unsettled, but the adverse impact of leaving the matter wholly unaddressed is undeniable.

As with many issues of regulatory concern, a solution satisfactory to all is no doubt elusive. But the legislative branch, not the judiciary, bears the unenviable task of making complicated policy decisions that balance the benefits of uniform regulation and the myriad burdens (financial or otherwise) that may be imposed on taxpayers, businesses, and the environment. Having expressly reserved the power to make such decisions, the ball is sequestered in the Legislature's court. I urge the Legislature to take direct ameliorative action or, as Section 361.0961(a)(1) contemplates, create a specific exception to preemption of local control. Standing idle in the face of an ongoing assault on our delicate ecosystem will not forestall a day of environmental reckoning—it will invite one.

ORTIZ v. COMMONWEALTH OF PENNSYLVANIA
681 A.2d 152 (Pa. 1996)

FLAHERTY, J.

The issue raised in this case is whether two home-rule municipalities, Philadelphia and Pittsburgh, may regulate the ownership of so-called assault weapons when the General Assembly has passed a statute prohibiting them from doing so.

Philadelphia Councilman Angel Ortiz and others brought this action in Commonwealth Court. They sought to enjoin the Commonwealth's preemption of Philadelphia's regulation of assault weapons and declare it in violation of the Constitution of Pennsylvania, the home rule charter, and the Home Rule Enabling Act. Pittsburgh filed a petition to intervene, which was granted.

Article 9, Section 2 of the Constitution of Pennsylvania provides:

> Municipalities shall have the right and power to frame and adopt home rule charters. Adoption, amendment or repeal of a home rule charter shall be by referendum. The General Assembly shall provide the procedure by which a home rule charter may be framed and its adoption, amendment or repeal presented to the electors. If the General Assembly does not so provide, a home rule charter or a procedure for framing and presenting a home rule charter may be presented to the electors by initiative or by the governing body of the municipality. *A municipality which has a home rule charter may exercise any power or perform any function not denied by this Constitution, by its home rule charter or by the General Assembly at any time.*

On June 17, 1993, the Mayor of Philadelphia signed and approved Bill No. 508, submitted by the city council, which banned certain types of assault weapons in Philadelphia. In November of 1993, the City of Pittsburgh passed Ordinance 30-1993, which also banned certain specified assault weapons within Pittsburgh's physical boundaries. It is undisputed that these ordinances purport to regulate the ownership, use, possession, or transfer of certain firearms.

After these ordinances were enacted, the General Assembly passed House Bill 185, which amended Title 18 of the Crimes Code, including the Pennsylvania Uniform Firearms Act. The amendment provides:

(a) General rule. No county, municipality or township may in any manner regulate the lawful ownership, possession, transfer or transportation of firearms, ammunition or ammunition components when carried or transported for the purposes not prohibited by the laws of this Commonwealth.

(b) Definition. For the purposes of this section the term "firearms" has the meaning given in Section 5515 (relating to prohibiting of paramilitary training) but shall not include "air rifles" as defined in Section 6304 (relating to sale and use of air rifles).

The sum of the case is that the Constitution of Pennsylvania requires that home rule municipalities may not perform any power denied by the General Assembly; the General Assembly has denied all municipalities the power to regulate the ownership, possession, transfer or possession of firearms; and the municipalities seek to regulate that which the General Assembly has said they may not regulate. The inescapable conclusion, unless there is more, is that the municipalities' attempt to ban the possession of certain types of firearms is constitutionally infirm.

The cities insist that there is more. They argue that the Pennsylvania Uniform Firearms Act is not uniform, and the prohibition against ordinances regulating firearms therefore is invalid. This argument has its basis in the Home Rule Statute governing cities of the first class, namely, Philadelphia:

> No city shall exercise any powers or authority beyond the city limits except such as are conferred by an act of the General Assembly, and no city shall engage in any proprietary or private business except as authorized by the General Assembly. Notwithstanding the grant of powers contained in this act, no city shall exercise powers contrary to or in limitation or enlargement of, powers granted by acts of the General Assembly which are –
>
> (b) Applicable in every part of the Commonwealth.
>
> (c) Applicable to all the cities of the Commonwealth.

The cities assert that they are limited by the acts of the General Assembly only if those acts are applicable in the entire commonwealth, and the firearms statute is not. In particular, they argue that in Philadelphia County, the legislature requires that a person must be licensed to carry weapons openly and not concealed from sight, whereas in all other counties of Pennsylvania, weapons may be carried openly without a license.

This argument is plainly without merit. This act, in limiting municipal regulation of firearms and ammunition, applies in every county including Philadelphia. The fact that one section of the Uniform Firearms Act does not apply in every county is immaterial.

Next, the Philadelphia appellants, joined by the City of Pittsburgh, argue that although the General Assembly may restrict home rule power to some extent, it may not limit "the ability to perform the basic administrative functions of a municipal government and the ability to fulfill a fundamental purpose for which the City government exists." In particular, appellants assert that "the right of a city to maintain the peace on its streets through the regulation of weapons is intrinsic to the existence of the government of that city and, accordingly, an irreducible ingredient of constitutionally protected Home Rule."

In order to prevail in this argument, the cities would have to establish at a minimum that in matters concerning their "fundamental purpose," home rule municipalities may override limitations on their power set by the General Assembly, and that regulating assault weapons concerns this fundamental purpose.

This claim is frivolous. Article 9, Section 2 of the Constitution of Pennsylvania provides: "A municipality which has a home rule charter may exercise any power or perform any function not denied by this Constitution, by its home rule charter or by the General Assembly at any time."

By constitutional mandate, the General Assembly may limit the functions to be performed by home rule municipalities.

Next, the cities claim that various decisions of this court require that home rule municipalities may be restricted in their powers only when the General Assembly has enacted statutes on matters of statewide concern. Although we agree with the cities that the General Assembly may negate ordinances enacted by home rule municipalities only when the General Assembly's conflicting statute concerns substantive matters of statewide concern, this does not help the cities, for the matters at issue in this case are substantive matters of statewide concern. Article 1, Section 21 of the Constitution of Pennsylvania provides: "The right of the citizens to bear arms in defense of themselves and the State shall not be questioned."

Because the ownership of firearms is constitutionally protected, its regulation is a matter of statewide concern. The constitution does not provide that the right to bear arms shall not be questioned in any part of the commonwealth except Philadelphia and Pittsburgh, where it may be abridged at will, but that it shall not be questioned in any part of the commonwealth. Thus, regulation of firearms is a matter of concern in all of Pennsylvania, not merely in Philadelphia and Pittsburgh, and the General Assembly, not city councils, is the proper forum for the imposition of such regulation.

NIGRO, J., dissenting.

I cannot agree with the Majority and therefore must respectfully dissent. In my opinion, whenever the state legislature fails to enact a statute to address a continuing problem of major concern to the citizens of the Commonwealth, a municipality should be entitled to enact its own local ordinance in order to provide for the public safety, health and welfare of its citizens.

Since Philadelphia County is besieged by a multitude of violent crimes which occur involving a variety of hand guns and automatic weapons it is fundamentally essential that the local government enact legislation to protect its citizens whenever the state legislature is unable or unwilling to do so.

BASS v. CITY OF EDMONDS
508 P.3d 172 (Wash. 2022)

GONZÁLEZ, C.J.

Under our system of divided government, many elected bodies hold legislative power, including elected city councils. These councils, however, must legislate within constitutional constraints. One of those constraints is that city ordinances must not "conflict with general laws" that have been enacted by the people of our state by initiative or by our state legislature. Wash. Const. art. XI, § 11. Constitutional general laws that state they explicitly occupy the field, that implicitly occupy the field, or that are otherwise inconsistent with local laws preempt local lawmaking. We are asked today whether a city ordinance that requires that guns be stored safely and kept out of unauthorized hands is preempted by state law. We hold that it is.

After robust debate following a mass shooting at the nearby Marysville Pilchuck High School, the Edmonds City Council adopted an ordinance requiring residents to safely store their firearms when not in use. The ordinance contains two operative provisions. Under the "storage provision,"

> It shall be a civil infraction for any person to store or keep any firearm in any premises unless such weapon is secured by a locking device, properly engaged so as to render such weapon inaccessible or unusable to any person other than the owner or other lawfully authorized user.
>
> Notwithstanding the foregoing, for purposes of this section, such weapon shall be deemed lawfully stored or lawfully kept if carried by or under the control of the owner or other lawfully authorized user.

Under the "unauthorized access" provision,

> It shall be a civil infraction if any person knows or reasonably should know that a minor, an at-risk person, or a prohibited person is likely to gain access to a firearm belonging to or under the control of that person, and a minor, an at-risk person, or a prohibited person obtains the firearm.

At around the same time, Washington voters enacted Initiative 1639. This initiative criminalizes unsafe storage of firearms but in more limited circumstances than Edmonds' ordinance. The initiative specifically did not "mandate how or where a firearm must be stored."

We turn now to whether state law has occupied the field or otherwise preempts this ordinance. Cities have broad police power under article XI, section 11 of our state constitution. Municipal exercises of police power, however, may "not conflict with general laws."

The plaintiffs contend that both operative portions of the ordinance are preempted. "A state statute preempts an ordinance if the statute occupies the field or if the statute and the ordinance irreconcilably conflict." *Watson v. City of Seattle*, 401 P.3d 1 (Wash. 2017). Older cases have held that "a statute will not be construed as taking away the power of a municipality to legislate unless this intent is clearly and expressly stated." We have since found that the intent to occupy the field may be implied. We consider both the specific preemption statute and any related statutes that shed light on legislative intent.

Our legislature has limited local firearm regulation for decades. The current preemption statute says:

> The state of Washington hereby fully occupies and preempts the entire field of firearms regulation within the boundaries of the state, including the registration, licensing, possession, purchase, sale, acquisition, transfer, discharge, and transportation of firearms, or any other element relating to firearms or parts thereof, including ammunition and reloader components. Cities, towns, and counties or other municipalities may enact only those laws and ordinances relating to firearms that are specifically authorized by state law, as in RCW 9.41.300, and are consistent with this chapter. Such local ordinances shall have the same penalty as provided for by state law. Local laws and ordinances that are inconsistent with, more restrictive than, or exceed the requirements of state law shall not be enacted and are preempted and repealed, regardless of the nature of the code, charter, or home rule status of such city, town, county, or municipality.

While the legislature's intent to occupy the entire field of firearm regulation is clear, not every municipal action that touches on firearms is within that field. For example, the law does not prevent a municipality from barring its employees from carrying concealed weapons while on duty. *See Cherry v. Municipality of Metropolitan Seattle*, 808 P.2d 746 (Wash. 1991). After reviewing relevant legislative history, this court concluded that "the Legislature sought to eliminate a multiplicity of local laws relating to firearms and to advance uniformity in criminal firearms regulation" and that "the laws and ordinances preempted are laws of application to the general public." Since the personnel policy was not a law of general application, it was not preempted by the statute.

Similarly, the law did not prevent a city from imposing strict rules on a gun show held at a municipal convention center. *See Pac. Nw. Shooting Park Ass'n v. City of Sequim*, 144 P.3d 276 (Wash. 2006). Not only were the restrictions not laws of general application, cities have specific statutory authority to regulate gun possession in municipal convention centers and general proprietary authority to limit how their convention centers could be used. Accordingly, the city could impose the rules.

Not all rules of general application that touch on firearms are preempted. For example, the law does not prevent a city from taxing firearms and ammunition. While we acknowledge that some regulations could masquerade as taxes, the *Watson* plaintiffs failed to show that the particular tax was a regulation. Since the law preempted only firearm regulations, not taxes, the tax was not preempted.

Similarly, the Court of Appeals found that the law did not preempt a county ordinance requiring shooting facilities to obtain operating permits. *Kitsap County v. Kitsap Rifle & Revolver Club*, 405 P.3d 1026 (Wash. App. 2017). The court noted that on its face, the preemption statute did not reference regulating shooting facilities. The court also noted that the ordinance "imposed requirements only on owners and operators of shooting facilities, not on the individuals who discharge firearms at those facilities." The court also noted that the legislature had explicitly given municipalities the power to "enact ordinances restricting the discharge of firearms where there is a reasonable likelihood that humans, domestic animals, or property will be jeopardized."

Taken together, these cases establish that the law broadly preempts local ordinances that directly regulate firearms themselves, but not necessarily ordinances that have an incidental effect on the use and enjoyment of firearms or exercises of municipal authority that do not establish rules of general application to the public.

The city argues that the legislature intended only to preempt regulation in the nine statutorily enumerated areas: "registration, licensing, possession, purchase, sale, acquisition, transfer, discharge, and transportation of firearms." But the preemption statute begins with "the state of Washington fully occupies and preempts the entire field of firearms regulation." Given that broad introductory phrase, we conclude the list is illustrative, not exclusive.

We decline to limit the preemption statute to firearms' transactions and active use. That limitation is simply not consistent with the words of the statute as a whole. Under that statute, "the state of Washington hereby fully occupies and preempts *the entire field of firearms regulation.*" The key question is whether the ordinance regulates *firearms*—not whether it regulates firearm transactions or active use.

The legislature plainly meant to broadly preempt local lawmaking concerning firearms except where specifically authorized. The city was acting in its regulatory, not proprietary, role and without the sort of explicit or necessarily implied authorization present in *Watson*. Nor was the city acting as an employer as in *Cherry*. Accordingly, we hold that this ordinance is preempted by state law.

STATE ex rel. BRNOVICH v. CITY OF TUCSON
399 P.3d 663 (Ariz. 2017)

PELANDER, J.

The primary issue is whether the state may constitutionally prohibit a city's practice, prescribed by local ordinance, of destroying firearms that the city obtains through forfeiture or as unclaimed property. We conclude that a generally applicable state statute on this subject controls over a conflicting municipal ordinance.

In 2000, the Arizona Legislature passed House Bill 2095, which declared:

> It is the intent of the legislature to clarify existing law relating to the state's preemption of firearms regulation in this state. Firearms regulation is of statewide concern. Therefore, the legislature intends to limit the ability of any political subdivision of this state to regulate firearms and ammunition. This act applies to any ordinance enacted before or after the effective date of this act.

That legislation also provided: "A political subdivision of this state shall not enact any ordinance, rule or tax relating to the transportation, possession, carrying, sale, transfer, purchase, acquisition, gift, devise, storage, licensing, registration, discharge or use of firearms or ammunition in this state."

In 2005, the City of Tucson passed Ordinance No. 10146, which enacted Tucson Code §§ 2–140 to –142. Section 2–142 governs the "disposition of unclaimed and forfeited firearms by the Tucson police department." The Tucson Code permits the Tucson Police Department to keep a forfeited firearm for its own purposes or to transfer it to another law enforcement agency or museum; otherwise, the Code states that the police "shall dispose" of unclaimed and forfeited firearms "by destroying" them.

In 2013, the legislature amended two statutes governing the destruction of firearms. Section 13–3108 was revised to add new subsection (F), which provides: "Any agency or political subdivision of this state and any law enforcement agency in this state shall not facilitate the destruction of a firearm." And § 12–945(B) was amended to state:

> If the property is a firearm, the agency shall sell the firearm to any business that is authorized to receive and dispose of the firearm under federal and state law and that shall sell the firearm to the public according to federal and state law, unless the firearm is otherwise prohibited from being sold under federal and state law.

Between 2013 and October 2016, the City of Tucson destroyed approximately 4,800 unclaimed or forfeited firearms. With certain exceptions, Tucson's Ordinance provides that the City's police department "shall dispose" of unclaimed and forfeited firearms "by destroying" them. State law, in contrast, specifically prohibits any political subdivision or law enforcement agency from "facilitating the destruction of a firearm," and instead, with certain exceptions, requires public agencies to "sell the firearm to any business that is authorized to receive and dispose of the firearm under federal and state law." Thus, the Tucson Code unquestionably conflicts with Arizona law on this subject.

Under state law, a political subdivision may not "enact any ordinance relating to," among other things, the possession, sale, transfer, or use of firearms in Arizona. In no uncertain terms, the Arizona Legislature has declared that "firearms regulation is of statewide concern" and has expressed its intent to preempt "firearms regulation in this state" and thereby "limit the ability of any political subdivision of this state to regulate firearms." We of course respect the legislature's statements, but "whether state law prevails over conflicting charter provisions under Article 13, Section 2 is a question of constitutional interpretation."

Our analysis begins with the "home rule charter" provision in Arizona's Constitution, which from statehood has provided that any city with a population of more than 3,500 "may frame a charter for its own government consistent with, and subject to, the Constitution and the laws of the state." Once adopted and approved, a city's charter is, "effectively, a local constitution." By statute, the roots of which also trace back to statehood, the charter "shall prevail" over any conflicting law relating to charter cities in force when the charter was adopted and approved. "The charter," however, "shall be consistent with and subject to the state constitution, and not in conflict with general laws of the state not relating to cities."

"The purpose of the home rule charter provision of the Constitution was to render the cities adopting such charter provisions as nearly independent of state legislation as was possible." *City of Tucson v. Walker*, 135 P.2d 223 (Ariz. 1943). Consistent with that purpose, we have articulated the following rule:

> Where the legislature has enacted a law affecting municipal affairs, but which is also of state concern, the law takes precedence over any municipal action taken under the home rule charter. But where the legislative act deals with a strictly local municipal concern, it can have no application to a city which has adopted a home rule charter. Whether or not an act of the legislature pertains to a matter of local or state-wide concern becomes a question for the courts when a conflict of authority rises.

Under this state's well-established jurisprudence, whether the City's Code controls over the conflicting state laws essentially hinges "on whether the subject matter is characterized as of statewide or purely local interest." We acknowledge that the extensive Arizona case law in this area is muddled. As we noted in *Tucson II*, "many municipal issues will be of both local and state concern," and thus differentiation is "problematic in application" because it "often involves case-specific line drawing," and "the concepts of local versus statewide interest do not have self-evident definitions."

Our concurring colleague, Justice Bolick, faults *Strode v. Sullivan*, 236 P.2d 48 (Ariz. 1951), as setting Arizona courts on a wayward path that is untethered to article 13, section 2, asserts that *Strode* and similar cases should be overruled, and disavows as irrelevant in cases like this any distinction between matters of statewide interest and those of purely local concern.

The unarticulated but obvious take away from Justice Bolick's concurrence is this: assuming it is constitutional, a state statute on any particular topic will always trump and invalidate a political subdivision's conflicting ordinance, even if the topic indisputably is solely and purely one of local concern. Under that view, one must wonder what is left of charter cities' authority under article 13, section 2.

In the end, we find no need to overhaul our longstanding analytical approach to resolving conflicts between state and local laws. This case does not fall within the "twilight zone separating those matters that are clearly of municipal concern from those that are not."

Unlike municipalities, which have "no inherent police power," the state has broad police power, including "the protection of life, liberty, and property, and the preservation of the public peace and order, in every part, division, and subdivision of the state." Matters involving the police power generally are of statewide concern.

The laws at issue implicate the state's police power in several respects: the disposition of forfeited or unclaimed property, the conduct of law enforcement officers, including their handling of unclaimed property, and the regulation of firearms. The Tucson Police Department's disposition of property is an exercise of police power granted by the state. The state's authority validly extends over the possession and disposition of firearms.

Relatedly, regulating police departments' conduct, including their handling of unclaimed property, is also a matter of statewide concern. Arizona case law recognizes the statewide interest in subjects even tangentially connected to the work of public safety officers and criminal justice.

Regulation of firearms, including their preservation or destruction, also involves the state's police power and is of statewide concern. The legislature has indicated that the disposal of firearms by government agencies is itself a component of firearm regulation by including the disposal restrictions within a comprehensive statutory firearms regulation scheme. Because both the ordinance and the state laws with which it conflicts involve the state's police power and matters "that the entire state is interested in," the matters at issue "are proper subjects for general laws." Accordingly, although the state laws in question undoubtedly "affect municipal affairs," they are also of "state concern" and therefore "take precedence" over the City's conflicting Ordinance.

The City points to the lack of any evidence "of a gun shortage in Tucson, leaving Tucsonans or visitors without access to firearms in the City," or any evidence "that the ordinance impacts anyone or anything outside of Tucson." But as the State observes, "the number of firearms affected by the ordinance has nothing to do with the nature of the regulated subject matter. As this Court has explained, whether general state laws displace charter provisions depends on whether the *subject matter* is characterized as of statewide or purely local interest."

The State and amicus National Rifle Association argue that preserving the right to bear arms under the federal and state constitutions is also a subject of state concern. We agree with that proposition, but even assuming that the Ordinance somehow implicates that right, we need not address this argument inasmuch as the superiority of state law over the Ordinance is clearly established based on the state's police powers discussed above.

The City's contrary arguments are not persuasive. Relying on article 13, section 2 of the Arizona Constitution and a handful of Arizona cases, the City contends that it "has charter authority to dispose of property it owns," including firearms. Because the state statutes address matters of statewide interest, however, whatever powers the City seeks to exercise under its home-rule charter authority and related ordinances must be "consistent with, and subject to, the Constitution and laws of the state." Ariz. Const., art. 13, § 2. Our cases have consistently recognized this significant constitutional restraint on charter cities' powers.

This Court has narrowly limited the concept of "purely municipal affairs," or "local interest or concern," restricting the extent to which charter city ordinances can prevail over state law. In only two areas have we upheld a municipal ordinance that directly conflicts with state law. First, we have held that the "method and manner of conducting elections in the city is peculiarly the subject of local interest and is not a matter of statewide concern." *Strode*, 236 P.2d 48. But the conflict here does not involve municipal elections or "the authority of charter cities to structure how their governing officers are elected." Second, this Court has held that "the manner and method of disposal of real estate of a city is not a matter of state-wide public concern." *City of Tucson v. Arizona ASAE*, 195 P.2d 562 (Ariz 1948). Likewise, this does not support the City's position here.

Because the statutes here involve matters of "statewide concern" and "the legislature has appropriated the field" regarding governmental entities' destruction or disposal of firearms, "its declarations are binding throughout the state, and all cities and municipalities, including charter cities, are precluded" from directly contravening the statutes through local laws.

Other arguments presented by the City and amicus the League of Arizona Cities and Towns are also unpersuasive. The League asserts that "whether the property at issue is real or personal, guns or butter, if it is owned by a charter city, its use or disposition is a matter in which the Legislature is constitutionally proscribed from interfering." *See Luhrs*, 83 P.2d 283 (noting that when the particular activity "is exercised by the city in its proprietary capacity, it is a power incident to home rule"); *cf.* Ariz. Const. art. 13, § 5 ("Every municipal corporation within this State shall have the right to engage in any business or enterprise which may be engaged in by a person, firm, or corporation by virtue of a franchise from said municipal corporation.").

This argument, however, skirts the pivotal inquiry in cases like this: "whether the subject matter is characterized as of statewide or purely local interest." Thus, even if relevant, the City's ownership interest or proprietary capacity is not determinative. In addition, the City does not destroy firearms in a proprietary capacity. Just as a city's wastewater management and disposal are governmental functions, so is the City's destruction of firearms.

Because the proprietary/governmental distinction is murky and unhelpful in resolving disputes of this kind, we do not view it as an appropriate factor in determining whether a state law relates to a matter of "statewide or purely local interest."

The City also proposes a balancing test, under which courts would balance the competing state and municipal interests to determine if the asserted statewide interest is "sufficiently concrete and identifiable to outweigh the local interest of home rule cities in municipal self-government." In support of that concept, the City cites *Johnson v. Bradley*, in which the California Supreme Court stated that "*as a condition of state legislative supremacy*," the state must show "*a dimension demonstrably transcending identifiable municipal interests*," so that the phrase "statewide interest" does not invade areas of intramural concern only, thereby preserving core values of charter city government. 841 P.2d 990 (Cal. 1992). Under California law, if a statewide concern is established, a charter city's contrary law is preempted only if the state law is "reasonably related" to resolving the state's interest and "narrowly tailored" to limit incursion into legitimate municipal interests. *Johnson* was based on California's constitution, which exempts from the control of state law "all ordinances and regulations in respect to municipal affairs." Arizona has no counterpart, and requires a city charter to be consistent with "the laws of the state."

We reject the California approach and the City's proposed balancing test. It would not aid courts in determining if a particular subject is of statewide interest or rather purely local concern. We therefore decline to follow *Johnson* and cases from other states that embrace a balancing approach. In short, we find such a test is neither helpful nor appropriate, and instead would potentially cause confusion and inconsistent results.

BOLICK, J., concurring in part and in the result.

I write separately to address erroneous prior decisions that produced the jurisprudential muddle, from which we can extricate ourselves by aligning our case law with constitutional text. Resort to the Constitution's plain meaning is especially essential where, as the Court freely acknowledges, the state of the law is disarray. In such instances, our fidelity should be to the Constitution rather than to the disarray.

Article 13, section 2, of the Arizona Constitution possesses the virtue of great clarity. It provides cities that meet certain criteria with a mechanism to secure greater self-governance. That section includes two provisions that squarely address the issue presented. An eligible city "may frame a charter for its own government *consistent with, and subject to, the Constitution and the laws of the state.*" Upon approval, the "charter shall become the organic law of such city and *supersede any charter then existing and all ordinances inconsistent with said new charter.*"

That clear language renders simple the dispute here. As the Court amply demonstrates, Tucson's charter provision conflicts with state law regarding the disposition of seized firearms. Tucson's charter is subject to that law and does not supersede it.

Were we construing and applying only the constitutional text as written, we would have no jurisprudential muddle. Charter cities and the state would understand their respective boundaries and taxpayers could save the cost of unnecessary litigation. But the tendency of the law toward complexity over clarity often seems irresistible.

As the Court observes, the law governing conflicts between state and charter cities did not end with the Constitution. Shortly after the Constitution's ratification, the legislature passed an emergency statute. Section 9–284(A) provides that where charter provisions "are in conflict with any law" relating to cities eligible for charter status "in force at the time of the adoption and approval of the charter, the provisions of the charter shall prevail notwithstanding the conflict." Section 9–284(B) provides, "The charter shall be consistent with and subject to the state constitution, and not in conflict with the constitution and general laws of the state not relating to cities."

Two observations about the charter statute are pertinent. First, it established that charter provisions would prevail only as to conflicting statutes "relating to" charter-eligible cities "in force at the time of the adoption and approval of the charter." Thus, the charter statute does not apply here because Tucson's charter was adopted long before the conflicting statute. Second, if article 13, section 2, of the Arizona Constitution itself established supremacy of charters over certain conflicting state statutes, there would have been no need to enact that status through legislation, much less on an emergency basis. The statute's enactment thus implied the legislature's recognition that article 13, section 2 did not, by its own terms, elevate charters over statutes.

Early cases harmonized the charter statute with the Constitution. In *Clayton v. State*, 297 P. 1037 (Ariz. 1931), the Court invalidated local highway laws that conflicted with state statutes. The Court posed the question of who determines whether a matter is of "general statewide concern or of purely municipal concern? Shall the city be permitted to determine this question, or shall the state?" Applying the Constitution, the Court's answer was unequivocal: the state.

The *Clayton* Court continued its analysis, however, by noting that article 13, section 2 was supplemented by statute. The Court explained that *under the statute*, where a conflict exists between preexisting state laws and charter provisions, the latter shall prevail except as to general laws of the state not relating to cities. The Court went on to conclude that the law at issue was a general law not relating to cities, thus it prevailed over the conflicting charter provision. The Court made clear that it was the statute, not the Constitution, that allowed charter provisions to prevail over conflicting state laws in limited circumstances.

In *Mayor & Common Council of City of Prescott v. Randall*, 196 P.2d 477 (Ariz. 1948), the Court struck down a charter city's alcohol regulations that conflicted with state law. The Court cited numerous cases to the effect that "a charter city is sovereign in all of its municipal affairs where the power attempted to be exercised has been specifically or by implication granted in its charter." However, the Court noted that in "practically all of the foregoing cases the effect of section 16–303 [predecessor to § 9–284] has been directly or indirectly considered by this court" as supplementing charter powers conferred by the Constitution.

But only three years later, those statutory considerations vanished from the Court's analysis and the charter statute was grafted onto article 13, section 2. In *Strode v. Sullivan*, the Court held that a charter city's election laws superseded conflicting state law. The Court selectively quoted article 13, section 2, placing emphasis on a city forming a charter "*for its own government*" and omitting any reference to charters superseding inconsistent local laws but not state laws.

Without any overt indication that it was doing so, the Court substituted the charter statute language for the constitutional text. The difference between the constitutional rule announced in *Strode* and the actual constitutional text is so stark that it invites direct comparison:

Article 13, section 2:

Eligible city "may frame a charter for its own government consistent with, and *subject to*, the Constitution and *the laws of the state*. Said charter shall become the organic law of such city and *supersede any charter then existing and all ordinances inconsistent with said new charter*.

Strode Rule:

A city charter becomes the organic law of the city and the *provisions of the charter supersede all laws of the state in conflict with such charter provisions* insofar as such laws relate to purely municipal affairs.

The Court in *Strode* literally rewrote the constitutional provision at issue, which of course it had no power to do. It thus replaced the Constitution's bright line with a judicially manufactured line of constitutional demarcation between matters of statewide concern, over which the state prevails, and matters of purely local concern, over which charter cities have hegemony. That blurry line is entirely the cause of our muddled jurisprudence over the past two-thirds of a century.

Given that *Strode* departed so sharply from constitutional text and has spawned constant litigation to ascertain its contours, I would overturn it along with other decisions holding that charter enactments superseded conflicting state laws. Instead, I would adhere to the Constitution's rule that city charters do not supersede conflicting state laws.

The City protests that such a construction would render charters meaningless. Not at all. As the Court previously observed, "Cities and towns, regardless of how organized, have only such powers as are expressly or by implication conferred upon them." "A municipality has no inherent powers, but only such powers as are expressly conferred by statute or are implied as necessary in aid of those powers which are expressly conferred." By contrast, "a presumption exists that the exercise of power by a home rule municipal corporation is valid if no restriction is found in the constitution, the charter itself, or the acts of the general assembly." In other words, a non-charter municipality generally may do only what the state expressly authorizes; a charter city generally may do anything that the state does not expressly forbid. That is a significant difference in authority. At the same time, it is unsurprising that a subdivision of the state would not have the power to override the powers of the state itself.

Although the Court draws the correct lines here, the Constitution makes that exercise unnecessary and improper. I look forward to the day when we no longer have to draw lines between such conflicting enactments, because we finally accept that our Constitution has drawn that line for us.

NOTES

There are two competing approaches to municipal power. One is skeptical of any local power not expressly granted by the state. The other is open to inherent local power to regulate some matters.

1. The dominant approach in the area owes its origin to a leading scholar and state court judge of the era, John Dillon. He served on the Iowa Supreme Court from 1862 to 1868 (and as chief justice for the last two years) and wrote *Municipal Corporations*, the leading treatise on local government of its time. Dillon wrote several opinions for the Iowa Supreme Court that became the cornerstone of what's now called Dillon's Rule. At issue in *City of Clinton v. The Cedar Rapids & Missouri River R.R. Co.* was another transportation dispute, a classic conflict of the era between a municipal corporation (the city of Clinton) and a private railroad (the Cedar Rapids & Missouri River Railroad Company). In 1859, the Clinton City Council passed an ordinance that barred any "railroad company from constructing its track through or upon any streets within the limits of the city." A railroad company wished to lay tracks between Cedar Rapids and Council Bluffs. In

1867, over the objection of the city, it entered the streets to begin its construction project, relying in part on authority from the state to do so.

What counted: permission of the city to use the land for its railroad tracks? Permission of the state? Or both? In his opinion for the Iowa Supreme Court, Chief Justice Dillon explained that the state grant of permission was all that the railroad needed. He framed the debate this way: "Has the legislature given to the municipality of Clinton such power that it can defeat the construction of a railroad required by public law and demanded by public utility?" *City of Clinton v. Cedar Rapids & Missouri River R.R. Co.*, 24 Iowa 455, 461 (1868). His answer created a *presumption against local power* and turned on the premise that any power of the city came from the state, whether through its constitution or legislation. He expressed the point in this way:

> Municipal corporations owe their origin to, and derive their powers and rights wholly from, the legislature. It breathes into them the breath of life, without which they cannot exist. As it creates, so it may destroy. If it may destroy, it may abridge and control. Unless there is some constitutional limitation . . . the legislature might, by a single act, if we can suppose it capable of so great a folly and so great a wrong, sweep from existence all of the municipal corporations in the State, and the corporation could not prevent it. We know of no limitation on this right so far as the corporations themselves are concerned. They are, so to phrase it, the mere tenants at will of the legislature.

This approach created a predisposition against local power. As he put it in his treatise: "Any fair, reasonable, doubt concerning the existence of power is resolved by the courts against the municipal corporation, and the power is denied." John F. Dillon, *The Law of Municipal Corporations* 173 (2d rev. ed. James Cockroft & Co. 1873). Unless the state legislature clearly gave the city power over the matter, Dillon's Rule said it had none. Under this approach, state law thus determines what independence a local governmental does or does not have. In recent years, thirty-one states follow Dillon's Rule and its presumption against local autonomy and authority. Adam Coester, *Dillon's Rule or Not? National Association of Counties* (Jan. 2004).

2. Another midwestern judge in the nineteenth century took a different approach to the issue. Thomas Cooley was one of the leading state and federal constitutional scholars of the era, maybe *the* leading scholar. Like Dillon, Thomas Cooley served as a chief justice, in his case as the leader of the Michigan Supreme Court. And like Dillon, Cooley was a professor. He was the dean of the University of Michigan Law School and wrote many influential books and treatises, including *A Treatise on the Constitutional Limitations Which Rest Upon the Legislative Power of the States of the American Union*, perhaps the most widely read treatise of its day. Cooley understood state constitutional law and helped to shape it. That makes his concurring thoughts in *People v. Hurlbut*, a case about the power of local

governments to rule themselves, worth examining. Just three years after Chief Justice Dillon's *City of Clinton* decision, Cooley offered another way to look at it. At issue was the authority of the Michigan legislature to select the members of local boards of water commissions in Detroit. The court held that the state legislature could not select the local commissioners.

In his concurring opinion, then-Justice Cooley took on this foundational question: "Whether local self-government in this state is or is not a mere privilege, conceded by the legislature in its discretion, and which may be withdrawn at any time at pleasure?" *People v. Hurlbut*, 24 Mich. 44, 95-96 (1871). In answering the question, Cooley acknowledged the prevailing assumptions: that "the state creates the municipal bodies," that these "corporate entities are mere agencies which the state employs for the convenience of government, clothing them for the time being with a portion of its sovereignty, but recalling the whole or any part thereof whenever the necessity or usefulness of the delegation is no longer apparent." *Id.* at 96. Even so, that did not remove the possibility that such limits could be implied. The Michigan Constitution, like other state constitutions, was adopted in the immediate context of local rule: "a system of local government, well understood and tolerably uniform in character, existing from the very earliest settlement of the country, never for a moment suspended or displaced, and the continued existence of which is assumed" and "the liberties of the people have generally been supposed to spring from, and be dependent upon that system." *Id.* at 98.

His central message? Local governments have inherent power to rule themselves. For the people who "framed our institutions," "it has been an axiom" that "our system was one of checks and balances"—that "each department of the government was a check upon the others, and each grade of government upon the rest." *Id.* at 108. These municipalities, he thought, arose "under the protection of certain fundamental principles which no power in the state could override or disregard." Even if the state legislature "may mold local institutions according to its views of policy or expediency," "local government" remains a "matter of absolute right," and "the state cannot take it away." All in all, "when the state reaches out and draws to itself" those "powers" that "from time immemorial have been locally possessed and exercised, and introduces into its legislation the centralizing ideas of continental Europe, under which despotism, whether of monarch or commune, alone has flourished, we seem forced back upon and compelled to take up and defend the plainest and most primary axioms of free government, as if even in Anglican liberty, which has been gained step by step, through extorted charters and bills of rights, the punishment of kings and the overthrow of dynasties, nothing was settled and nothing established." The "right" of "the state is a right, not to run and operate the machinery of local government, but to provide for and put it in motion."

As Cooley acknowledged, this was not the thinking of a purist, as conventional approaches to municipal power all were grounded in the text of the federal and state constitutions. But "some things," he added, were "too plain to be written" and turned on traditions and common law norm shifting—"usages," "customs," things that "have sprung from the habits of life, modes of thoughts, methods of trying facts by the neighborhood, and mutual responsibility in neighborhood interests." What drove Cooley, says Judge David Barron, was the goal that "every one has a right to be governed by general rules." David J. Barron, *The Promise of Cooley's City: Traces of Local Constitutionalism*, 147 Pa. L. Rev. 487, 513 (1999). Legislative interference with local government, Cooley feared, did the opposite. That orientation "led him to distrust public attempts to empower the private realm." In these ways, "the judicial protection of the local community from state interference served as a means by which the individual right to equal administration of the laws could be protected."

For all of Thomas Cooley's influence on the path of state (and federal) constitutional law as a Michigan Supreme Court chief justice and as a leading constitutional scholar, this was not destined to be one of those areas. The Cooley approach "has been applied by the courts of very few states" and "even in these states its application has been limited." John Dinan, *State Constitutional Politics* 44 (2018). Perhaps that owes to the difficulty of identifying a rule of decision, of identifying a judicially enforceable line between explicit and inherent municipal power. The influence of the Cooley approach does not even extend to Michigan, as it turns out. By 2006, after intervening constitutional conventions and amendments, the Michigan Supreme Court had little good to say about this form of local control. "Local governments have no inherent jurisdiction to make laws or adopt regulations of government; they are governments of enumerated powers, acting by a delegated authority; so that while the State legislature may exercise such powers of government that are not expressly or impliedly prohibited, the local authorities can exercise those only which are expressly or impliedly conferred." But all has not been forgotten in Michigan when it comes to Cooley. Even as the state leaves ultimate control with its legislature, it still says that the broad "powers" of "Michigan's cities and villages" under the Michigan Constitution of 1963 "over municipal concerns, property and government are to be liberally construed."

3. Against the backdrop of the Dillon/Cooley debate, states eventually took matters into their own hands, as the last point above suggests. They added home rule provisions to their state constitutions, provisions that honor Cooley's emphasis on local control and Dillon's perspective that the state should oversee the authority of local government. Missouri gets credit for creating the first of these guarantees. In its Constitution of 1875, it added this provision: "Any city having a population of more than one hundred

thousand inhabitants may frame a charter for its own government consistent with and subject to the Constitution and laws of this State." Mo. Const. of 1875 art. IX § 16. St. Louis prompted the change. The new provision made the city an "imperium in imperio," a government within a government, under the state's home rule amendment.

One explanation for the amendment had little to do with whether Dillon or Cooley was right. It had to do with time and knowledge. The home rule amendment allowed the Missouri legislature to focus on statewide matters and to leave the nitty gritty of local politics to the people of St. Louis. As one speaker at Missouri's 1875 convention put it: "If there is any one thing I would wish to keep out of the Legislature, it is legislation upon St. Louis affairs. It has created more confusion & trouble in the Legislature & has done more to prolong the session than anything else & I am in favor of giving as far as possible to the people of St. Louis the regulation of their whole internal affairs." Dinan, *State Constitutional Politics* 42 (quoting GEORGE BRADFIELD, *from* 12 DEBATES OF THE MISSOURI CONSTITUTIONAL CONVENTION OF 1875, 495 (Isidor Loeb & Floyd C. Shoemaker eds., State Historical Society of Missouri, 1930-44).

Missouri paved a path that others soon followed. Three more states—California, Washington, and Minnesota—added home rule provisions to their constitutions before the end of the century. Nine more states approved them in the first two decades of the twentieth century. Many more were added in the decades that followed, and John Dinan tells us that more than half the states have strong home-rule protections in their constitutions today. *Id.* at 42. "All but three states make some provision for home rule," Richard Briffault says, with home rule "grounded in the state constitution" in "forty-one states." Six more states provide for home rule through statutes. Richard Briffault, *The Challenge of the New Preemption*, 70 Stan. L. Rev. 1995, 2011 n.111.

C. LOCAL SEPARATION-OF-POWERS DISPUTES

The governing challenges of today's cities sometimes create separation-of-powers problems that mirror those that arise in the states and the national government. One example turns on delegation of policymaking power and its cousin—administrative deference—under municipal charters of government. As Nestor Davidson helpfully has shown, a substantial body of administrative law operates in American cities and towns under these charters, an observation confirmed by this example.

A decade or so ago, New York City sought to curb consumption of soft drinks—"soda" to some, "pop" to others, "sugary drinks" to New Yorkers. To that end, the New York City Board of Health adopted a "Sugary Drinks Portion Cap Rule" that prohibited the sale of soft drinks in containers that exceeded sixteen ounces. Claimants challenged the rule on the ground that the board overstepped its power. As they saw it, the city's charter allocated this lawmaking power to the city council or the state legislature, not to agencies of the city. Any "food service establishment," the rule said, "may not sell, offer, or provide a sugary drink in a cup or container that is able to contain more than 16 fluid ounces." The rule thus did not ban soft drinks; it just made it difficult to get super-sized containers of them. Here is how the New York Court of Appeals resolved the dispute.

N.Y. STATEWIDE COAL. OF HISPANIC CHAMBERS OF COM. v. N.Y.C. DEP'T OF HEALTH & MENTAL HYGIENE
16 N.E.3d 538 (N.Y. 2014)

PIGOTT, J.

The New York City Board of Health, in adopting the "Sugary Drinks Portion Cap Rule," exceeded the scope of its regulatory authority. By choosing among competing policy goals, without any legislative delegation or guidance, the Board engaged in law-making and thus infringed upon the legislative jurisdiction of the City Council of New York.

The Portion Cap Rule provides in relevant part that "a food service establishment may not sell, offer, or provide a sugary drink in a cup or container that is able to contain more than 16 fluid ounces." A "sugary drink" is defined as a nonalcoholic beverage that "is sweetened by the manufacturer or establishment with sugar or another caloric sweetener; has greater than 25 calories per 8 fluid ounces of beverage; and does not contain more than 50 percent of milk or milk substitute by volume as an ingredient." The Portion Cap Rule does not apply to establishments, such as supermarkets and convenience stores, that are subject to regulation and inspection by the New York State Department of Agriculture and Markets.

First, we address respondents' claim that the Board, having been created by the state legislature, has legislative powers separate and apart from the City Council. The City Charter unequivocally provides for distinct legislative and executive branches of New York City government. The City Council is the sole legislative branch of City government; it is "*the* legislative body of the city vested with the legislative power of the city." The New York State Constitution mandates that, with an exception not applicable here, "every local government shall have a legislative body elective by the people thereof," and that elective body in New York City is the City Council.

Respondents, however, contend that the Board of Health is a unique body that has inherent legislative authority. We disagree. The provision of the City Charter principally cited by respondents—NY City Charter § 558(b)—reflects only a regulatory mandate, not legislative authority. The Charter contains no suggestion that the Board of Health has the authority to create laws. While the Charter empowers the City Council "to adopt local laws for the preservation of the public health, comfort, peace and prosperity of the city and its inhabitants," the Charter restricts the Board's rulemaking to the publication of a health code, an entirely different endeavor.

Moreover, the language in section 558(c) of the Charter—describing the Board's purview as comprising "all matters and subjects" within the authority of the Department of Health and Mental Hygiene—was included in 1979 to preclude the Board from attempting to regulate areas not related to health. At that time, the City's Committee on Health became concerned that "regulations passed by the Board of Health may be overly broad and so invade the City Council's legislative authority." The Committee proposed a bill to clarify the Board's authority, which was passed by the City Council in February 1979 and approved by the Mayor the following month. Far from indicating a wide legislative jurisdiction, as respondents contend, section 558 (c) was intended to ensure that the Board of Health not regulate too broadly.

Respondents offer no practical solution to the difficulties that would arise from treating the Board and the City Council as coequal legislative bodies. On respondents' theory, it is unclear what the law in New York City would be were the Board to pass a health "law" that directly conflicted with a local law of the City Council. It is no solution to this difficulty that the state legislature could step in to resolve such a conflict. In short, it is clear from the Charter that the Board's authority, like that of any other administrative agency, is restricted to promulgating "rules necessary to carry out the powers and duties delegated to it by or pursuant to federal, state or local law." A rule has the force of law, but it is not a law; rather, it "implements or applies law or policy."

Given our position that the Board's role is regulation, not legislation, the next issue raised in this appeal is whether the Board properly exercised its regulatory authority in adopting the Portion Cap Rule. The parties and the lower courts correctly analyze this question by using the conceptual framework of *Boreali v. Axelrod* (N.Y. 1987). Because a doctrine of "separation of powers is delineated in the City Charter," *Boreali* provides the appropriate framework.

In *Boreali*, the Court initially pointed out that the Public Health Council's scheme for protecting nonsmokers indicated its "effort to weigh the goal of promoting health against its social cost and to reach a suitable compromise." We took this to violate the principle that "striking the proper balance among health concerns, cost and privacy interests is a uniquely legislative function." *Boreali* should not be interpreted to prohibit an agency from attempting to balance costs and benefits. Rather, the *Boreali* court found that the Public Health Council had "not been given any legislative guidelines at all for determining how the competing concerns of public health and economic cost are to be weighed."

Here, instead of an outright ban on sugary beverages, the Board decided to reduce their consumption by the expedient of limiting maximum container size, thus making it less convenient for consumers to exceed recommended limits. The more cautious approach, however, does not save the Portion Cap Rule. By restricting portions, the Board necessarily chose between ends, including public health, the economic consequences associated with restricting profits by beverage companies and vendors, tax implications for small business owners, and personal autonomy with respect to the choices of New York City residents concerning what they consume. Most obviously, the Portion Cap Rule embodied a compromise that attempted to promote a healthy diet without significantly affecting the beverage industry. This necessarily implied a relative valuing of health considerations and economic ends, just as a complete prohibition of sugary beverages would have. Moreover, it involved more than simply balancing costs and benefits according to preexisting guidelines; the value judgments entailed difficult and complex choices between broad policy goals—choices reserved to the legislative branch.

By choosing between public policy ends in these ways, the Board of Health engaged in law-making beyond its regulatory authority. Notably, such policymaking would likely not be implicated in situations where the Board regulates by means of posted warnings (e.g. calorie content on menus) or by means of an outright ban of a toxic substance (e.g. lead paint). In such cases, it could be argued that personal autonomy issues related to the regulation are nonexistent and the economic costs either minimal or clearly outweighed by the benefits to society, so that no policymaking in the *Boreali* sense is involved.

Respondents are unable to point to any legislation concerning the consumption of sugary beverages by the state legislature or City Council that the Portion Cap Rule was designed to supplement. Although "the Legislature is not required in its enactments to supply agencies with rigid marching orders" and the legislative branch may, while declaring "its policy in general terms by statute, endow administrative agencies with the power and flexibility to fill in details and interstices and to make subsidiary policy choices consistent with the enabling legislation," the policy choices made here were far from "subsidiary." Devising an entirely new rule that significantly changes the manner in which sugary beverages are provided to customers at eating establishments is not an auxiliary selection of means to an end; it reflects a new policy choice.

Therefore, it is clear that the Board of Health wrote the Portion Cap Rule without benefit of legislative guidance, and did not simply fill in details guided by independent legislation. Because there was no legislative articulation of health policy goals associated with consumption of sugary beverages upon which to ground the Portion Cap Rule, the adoption of the rule involved policymaking.

Here, inaction on the part of the state legislature and City Council, in the face of plentiful opportunity to act if so desired, simply constitutes additional evidence that the Board's adoption of the Portion Cap Rule amounted to making new policy, rather than carrying out preexisting legislative policy.

In light of *Boreali*'s central theme that an administrative agency exceeds its authority when it makes difficult choices between public policy ends, rather than finds means to an end chosen by the legislature, we need not, in this appeal, address whether special expertise or technical competence was involved in the development of the rule. We do not mean to imply that this will always lack significance. A court might be alerted to the broad, policy-making intent of a regulation, and the absence of any perceived need for agency expertise, by the fact that the rule was adopted with very little technical discussion. Here, regardless of who or which arm of government first proposed or drafted the Portion Cap Rule, and regardless of whether the Board exercised its considerable professional expertise or merely rubber-stamped a rule drafted outside the agency, the Portion Cap Rule is invalid.

NOTES

Home rule ultimately permits more governments within governments. That combines the sweet of local control with the bitter of local separation-of-power imperatives, as the New York City Board of Health now knows. But these three-dimensional division-of-power debates don't change anything in one respect. They take us back to the same question, just on a different plane: Who gets to decide?

What is the state of municipal power today? How, if at all, should it be changed?

1. An oddity of modern political discourse is its obsession with national power and relative ignorance of local power. Short of an attack on our borders, a deep recession, or some other existential threat to the country, most government policy that affects us directly occurs at the local level. But what should matter to us greatly—how local government works—is more often accompanied by a deep reservoir of apathy or a happy-go-lucky attitude. It would be one thing if that is how we also reacted to national or even state politics. But that is assuredly not the case. A few decades ago, a national poll showed that more than half of Americans, 52%, did not know their state had a constitution. Confirming the plight of local government law, the poll did not even ask about cities. The poll thus did not add these questions: Did you know your city has its own constitution, a charter? Or do you know how power is allocated in your city? Yes, the typical American

knows when their property taxes increase, when the sanitation department alters the rules for collecting trash, or when the city council changes the speed limit. But ask who does what at the local level and be prepared to meet an awkward gaze. We tend to understand the electoral college, the Senate's filibuster rules, the president's veto power, and the tenure and health of US Supreme Court justices. But we have little idea how the levers of power and policy work in our backyards. For reasons all our own, Americans "do not think of local governments, such as towns and cities, as important components of the federal constitutional structure." Barron, *The Promise of Cooley's City*.

We care least about what affects us most. Judge David Barron has come to a similar conclusion. "Too much of our daily experience with self-government occurs at the local level for us to dismiss localism as an embarrassing feature of constitutional democracy. Local governments are too central to the lives of too many people to serve as passive administrative agents of state majorities without an independent interest in enforcing constitutional norms." *Id.* at 612. The question on the table is whether that lack of engagement has undermined local government law and whether it needs renewed attention, particularly in its interrelation with state and federal constitutional law.

2. In thinking about the future, it's helpful to recall the Cooley/Dillon debate about the nature of local government and its potential sources of authority. Was the power of a local government merely derivative of a state's delegation of power to the municipality, as Dillon claimed? Were cities, then, merely like other state agencies, able to act only when the state delegated power to them and elsewise engaged in *ultra vires* lawmaking? Or was there a part of local government authority that was inherent, as Cooley claimed?

Framed by two of the most distinguished state court judges and scholars of the nineteenth century, the debate might have been expected to end with a prominent role for judges. It did not. The people by and large sorted out the key rules by themselves, mainly through amendments to state constitutions, in some instances by state lawmaking. With Missouri's passage of a home rule constitutional amendment in 1875, the state lit the way for other states, now almost all states, to resolve the debate in a manner that tipped its hat to Dillon *and* Cooley: Dillon because he thought that state constitutions and legislation were the only legitimate sources of local power, and Cooley because the placement of home rule provisions in state constitutions embraced the virtues of self-government as a treasured component of the American political tradition.

Sky-high consequences surrounded the debate at the start. It would have changed the division of powers equation significantly if, in the last 150 years, the state and federal courts had used the American tradition of local self-government to innovate judicially enforceable safeguards about when cities may act only with the permission of their state and when they have inherent rights to govern themselves. For those unhappy with the position of local power today, "Cooley's City," in Judge Barron's welcoming phrase, is not a bad place to start. With fifty state constitutions to pick from and fifty traditions to consider, it is plausible to think that a state in the future might embrace some of Cooley's insights to sort out a state/municipal conflict. No matter what happens, those insights remain relevant to states that alter this constitutional protection in the future.

3. Even if the people ended up making the key choices about the balance between state and local power through home rule amendments of various sorts to their constitutions, that did not sideline judges from state/local conflicts. Judge Dillon made another contribution in the area—Dillon's Rule—a lasting feature of local government law. Consistent with his view that local power is delegated power, Dillon's Rule creates a presumption against local power. In a case in which it is unclear whether the state has delegated power to a city, the city loses. Here we have a debate that lingers and may be intensifying. Owing to the growing divide between some Republican-controlled state legislatures and some Democrat-controlled cities, there has been an increase in tension between the two forms of government. Some of it is fueled by the growing economic power of cities. As of 2017, ten cities in the country generated "$6.8 trillion in economic value," "more than the collective output of thirty-seven states." Richard Briffault et al., Principles of Home Rule for the Twenty-First Century *National League of Cities* 13 (Feb. 12, 2020). Some of it is fueled by state efforts to preempt local lawmaking on controversial topics: gun regulation; environmental initiatives; taxation; plastic bag restrictions. Pick a public policy topic with any political valence to it, and the odds are high it has generated local preemption debates. Anything that divides the country nationally tends to divide states and cities. *See* Paul Diller, *Intrastate Preemption*, 87 B.U. L. Rev. 1113, 1117-1122 (2007); David Schleicher, *Federalism and State Democracy*, 95 Tex. L. Rev. 763 (2017).

Presumptions often make a difference when turf wars go to the courts. That raises the question of whether we should accommodate local variations by flipping the presumption embedded in Dillon's Rule. Many scholars think so. Eight of the top local government scholars in the country wrote a paper for the National League of Cities, "Principles of Home Rule for the Twenty-First Century," that features the point. Richard Briffault et al., Principles of Home Rule for the Twenty-First Century *National League of Cities* 13 (Feb. 12, 2020). The authors are Richard Briffault, Nestor Davidson, Paul Diller, Sarah Fox, Laurie Reynolds, Erin Scharff, Richard Schragger, and Rick Su. It proposes a model home rule provision for state constitutions (or state legislation) that reinforces home rule and places significant restrictions on states before they may preempt local lawmaking. It converts Dillon's Rule into Cooley's Rule: "The state shall not be held to have denied a home rule government any power or function unless it does so expressly." And it limits state efforts to restrict home rule: "The state may expressly deny a home rule government a power or function only if necessary to serve a substantial state interest, only if narrowly tailored to that interest, and only by general law."

Not all states will embrace this approach. And for now, the long-term neutrality of the approach and its local-customs virtues are apt to get caught up in motivated thinking about what these changes would mean for substantive policy choices. While it's understandably difficult for elected officials facing the ballot box to ignore the current preferences of their constituents on the policy debates that drive them, whether gun regulation, speeding tickets, limits on sugary drinks, or plastic bag bans, it is useful to remember that the same experimental benefits of federalism for a country can work for a state.

Local government law is one of the few areas in which the people largely have taken control of their own fate, leaving little room for significant state and federal court involvement over local structure. Whatever stand one takes on current and past debates in the area, the issues tend to get worked out in democratic ways, not through the courts for the most part. That raises a paradox in American constitutional law. The state and federal courts have innovated least in the area most likely to affect local government and innovated most in the areas least likely to affect our day-to-day affairs. How unusual that we have so much federal constitutional litigation over general phrases that have all kinds of impact on policy and government today. But through it all, we have declined to innovate inherent limitations on state regulation of local power—of perhaps the right that matters most to us, the right of self-government at home. It's not as if this is an obscure area of experience. It happens to be the one form of local help and local limits that people see every day.

4. For additional literature on home rule, see David Barron, *Reclaiming Home Rule*, 116 Harv. L. Rev. 2255 (2003); Richard Briffault, *The Challenge of the New Preemption*, 70 Stan. L. Rev. 1995 (2018); Richard Briffault et al., Principles of Home Rule for the Twenty-First Century *National League of Cities* (Feb. 12, 2020); Heather Gerken, *Foreword: Federalism All the Way Down*, 124 Harv. L. Rev. 4 (2010); Nestor Davidson, *Cooperative Localism: Federal-Local Collaboration in an Era of State Sovereignty*, 93 Va. L. Rev. 959 (2007); Erin Scharff, *Hyper Preemption: A Reordering of the State-Local Relationship?*, 106 Geo. L.J. 1469 (2018).

CHAPTER XVIII

AMENDMENT AND REVISION OF STATE CONSTITUTIONS

A. INTRODUCTION

Constitutions tell us who is in charge. Amendments remind officeholders that it is not them. The circumstances under which the people may amend a constitution raise a host of challenging questions and possibilities.

"Just as little distance (twenty-one miles) separates Monticello and Montpelier, few ideas separated the worldviews of Thomas Jefferson and James Madison. They agreed on most of the key debates at the founding, they became political partners, they became sequential presidents of the United States, and they were two of the most pivotal authors of change at the founding, one given credit for the Declaration of Independence, the other credit for the Bill of Rights. But they did not agree about a signal feature of a constitution: How often should it be amended? If these two Virginians could not agree about the answer, be prepared for a vexing topic." Sutton, *Who Decides? States as Laboratories of Constitutional Experimentation* 331 (Oxford 2021).

Jefferson maintained that constitutions should give each generation an opportunity to choose its own form of government:

> Let us provide in our Constitution for its revision at stated periods. What these periods should be, nature herself indicates. By the European tables of mortality, of the adults living at any one moment of time, a majority will be dead in about nineteen years. At the end of that period then, a new majority is come into place, or, in other words, a new generation. Each generation is as independent as the one preceding, as that was of all which had gone before. It has then, like them, a right to choose for itself the form of government it believes most promotive of its own happiness; and it is for the peace and good of mankind, that a solemn opportunity of doing this every nineteen or twenty years, should be provided by the constitution.

Jefferson to Samuel Kercheval, July 12, 1816, *in* Thomas Jefferson, *Writings* 1402 (Library of America 1984).

Madison took a different view. In *Federalist* No. 49, he argued that a readily amendable constitution would undermine stability. The longevity of a constitution, he thought, would increase the people's veneration of it. For him and for many others, state and federal legislatures were the places to look to accommodate changing norms and changing circumstances.

Jefferson and Madison each won the debate—in part. The lofty threshold for amending the United States Constitution in Article V—the requirement that three-quarters of the States ratify any amendment—

reflects Madison's preference for stability and continuity. In marked contrast, Jefferson's view prevailed in the States.

All state constitutions are easier to amend than the U.S. Constitution. Just one Constitution has existed for the United States, while the States have had 144 constitutions. The U.S. Constitution has been amended 27 times, while the State Constitutions have been amended 7,586 times (as of 2017). John Dinan, *State Constitutional Politics* 23 (2018). No State Constitution has been amended less frequently than the U.S. Constitution. *Id.* at 11. Since 1776, thirty-one States have had two or more constitutions. *See* Kermit L. Hall, "Mostly Anchor and Little Sail: The Evolution of American State Constitutions," *in Toward a Usable Past: Liberty Under State Constitutions* 394–95 (Paul Finkelman & Stephen E. Gottlieb eds. 1991). Although most state constitutions have not been completely revised every generation, as Jefferson would have preferred, the process of periodic amendments between replacements has been constant for nearly two and a half centuries. *See* Donald S. Lutz, *Toward a Theory of Constitutional Amendment*, 88 Am. Pol. Sci. Rev. 355, 359 (1994); *see also* James A. Henretta, *Foreword: Rethinking the State Constitutional Tradition*, 22 Rutgers L.J. 819, 829 (1991); W. Brooke Graves, *State Constitutional Law: A Twenty-Five Year Summary*, 8 Wm. & Mary L. Rev. 1, 36 (1966); G. Alan Tarr, *Constitutional Politics in the States: Contemporary Controversies and Historical Patterns* 3 (1996).

The continual process of state constitution-making often has transformed the short, principle-oriented charters of the early republic into "super-legislative" documents. Henretta, *Rethinking the State Constitutional Tradition*, 829. In 1776, state constitutions contained an average of about 7,150 words. By 1985, the average state constitution contained 26,150 words and the longest, the Alabama Constitution, was almost ten times greater than the national average. Hall, *Mostly Anchor*, 388.

Just as the first state constitutions provided guidance for the United States Constitution, later state constitutions have continued to provide positive and negative examples for each other and the nation. State constitutions have pioneered provisions regarding "popular election of judges, women's suffrage, equal rights for women, black disfranchisement and suffrage, the income tax," prohibition, the line-item veto, and balanced budget requirements. Hall, *Mostly Anchor*, 394–95.

Early state constitutions were relatively succinct frameworks of government. By contrast, most current state constitutions, like Delaware's 1897 Constitution, "contain many of the provisions adopted during the various waves of state constitution-making." Robert F. Williams, *State Constitutional Law: Cases and Materials* 19 (2d ed. 1993). Two exceptions are Vermont and Massachusetts, which have kept their state constitutions of 1793 and 1780, respectively. *Toward a Usable Past*, 14 n.19. Another exception is the 1784 New Hampshire Constitution. But the norm for state constitutions is that they reflect a "layering" of the political, social, and other concerns of each successive generation. Williams, *State Constitutional Law*, 19.

The same evolutionary process has not taken place with the United States Constitution. In a nineteenth century treatise, commented upon favorably by Chief Justice John Marshall, Justice Joseph Story, and Chancellor James Kent, the author noted:

> The convention did not suppose that their production was perfect. Changes in the circumstances of the country, might require corresponding alterations in the government. The Framers of the Constitution were aware of this, and, therefore, wisely provided a method, by which it may be amended, without disturbances of the public tranquility, or injury to the general system.
>
> The Constitution contains within itself a provision for amendment, by which to remedy any defects in its original structure, or such as may occur in process of time. But this power should be used with great caution; and always with the conviction, that *stability* is an important requisite of good government; and that frequent changes are destructive of its utility.

James A. Bayard, *A Brief Exposition of the Constitution of the United States* 3, 135–36, 160 (2d ed. 1838). In reality, the imperatives of Article V have made the United States Constitution nearly impervious to change. Lutz, *Toward a Theory*, 355. The first ten amendments to the United States Constitution, the Bill of Rights, were submitted collectively and became operative with Virginia's ratification in 1791. Following the ratification of the Twelfth Amendment in 1804, the United States Constitution was not amended again until 1865. Roughly 10,000 amendments to the United States Constitution have been proposed. Richard B. Bernstein & Jerome Agel, *Amending America* xii (1993). To date, however, there have only been a total of twenty-seven amendments to the United States Constitution and it contains a total of only approximately 7300 words. For better or for ill, most of the changes to the U.S. Constitution have come through interpretation by the U.S. Supreme Court, not amendment by the People.

B. ALTERING STATE CONSTITUTIONS

Anne Permaloff, *Methods of Altering State Constitutions*
33 Cumb. L. Rev. 217 (2003)

All of the 50 state constitutions in the United States contain provisions outlining the manner in which they may be altered or revised. State constitutions may be altered through legislatively proposed amendments, constitutional conventions, constitutional initiatives, constitutional commissions, and judicial interpretation. This paper examines the methods of alteration that include direct public representation and involvement at some stage in the alteration process, thus limiting the discussion to the first four methods listed.

There is considerable variation among the states in terms of which methods of alteration are allowed by their existing state constitutions. Furthermore, each method varies greatly in terms of the procedures required for its use. This paper will identify and discuss the variations within each method of alteration, which states use a given method, and the positive and negative factors associated with its use. Some of the philosophical, political, and cultural factors that influenced adoption of specific methods will be discussed as well.

The Idea that Constitutions May Be Altered Is Not New

Popular sovereignty or the idea that government is based on popular consent served as the foundation for the Declaration of Independence, the original state constitutions, as well as the U.S. Constitution. Donald S. Lutz who has studied early state constitutional development indicates that an evolutionary process resulted in the gradual adoption of the idea, "that a doctrine of popular sovereignty required that constitutions be written by popularly selected convention, rather than the legislature, and then ratified by a process that elicited popular consent ideally in a referendum."

Lutz notes that this notion quickly led to American expansion of John Locke's concept that replacement of government and the contract upon which it was based (a constitution) could occur only if those exercising power breached their contract. The American version held that if the public created the governing document and could alter its content by amendment, it also could replace the document at any time.

Lutz and others suggest that at least three other ideas reinforced this conception of constitutional change: human nature though imperfect is educable; faith that deliberative processes of decision-making will lead to the public good; and distinct differences between fundamental or constitutional law and legislative enactments.

Popular sovereignty implies that all constitutional matters should be based upon some form of popular consent, which in turn implies a formal, public process. Human fallibility implies the need for some method of altering or revising the constitution. A distinction between normal and constitutional matters implies that constitutional matters require a distinctive, highly deliberative process and thus implies the need for an amendment procedure more difficult than that used for normal legislation. Together these premises require that the procedure be neither too easy nor too difficult.

Robert F. Williams writes of another basis for the notion that constitutions may be altered—the idea that each generation should have the opportunity to refashion government to meet its needs. He and others quote

Thomas Jefferson's views on this point for Jefferson not only advocated amending constitutions through convention, he advocated periodic revisions within set time frames:

> Some men look at constitutions with sanctimonious reverence, and deem them like the arc of the covenant, too sacred to be touched. They ascribe to the men of the preceding age a wisdom more than human, and suppose what they did to be beyond amendment. I knew that age well; I belonged to it, and labored with it. It deserved well of its country. It was very like the present, but without the experience of the present I am certainly not an advocate for frequent and untried changes in laws and constitutions. But I know also that laws and institutions must go hand in hand with the progress of the human mind. Let us, as our sister States have done, avail ourselves of our reason and experience, to correct the crude essays of our first and unexperienced, although wise, virtuous, and well-meaning councils. And lastly, let us provide in our constitution for its revision at stated periods. Each generation is as independent as the one preceding, as that was of all which had gone before. It has then, like them, a right to choose for itself the form of government it believes most promotive of its own happiness; consequently, to accommodate to the circumstances in which it finds itself, that received from its predecessors; and it is for the peace and good of mankind, that a solemn opportunity of doing this every nineteen or twenty years, should be provided by the constitution; so that it may be handed on, with periodic repairs, from generation to generation, to the end of time, if anything human can so long endure.

Jefferson wrote this passage in response to questions about a constitutional convention to revise the original Virginia constitution. Similar comments from other original signers of the U.S. Constitution could be cited to make the point that from the beginning of this nation's history, trust in the public and its ability to grow and learn served as the basis of the argument that constitutions should change over time.

Other contemporaries of Jefferson's such as James Madison and John Adams believed in the ability to alter constitutions by amendment, but they believed that constitutions should not be altered easily. They did not support automatic periodic revision. For Madison the danger to be avoided was use of the amending process to foster factional (interest group) objectives. He believed constitutional change should be reserved for important matters such as the protection of basic rights. He was the major champion of the first amendments to the U.S. Constitution which were proposed by the very first Congress, the Bill of Rights.

Alan Tarr, one of the best known scholars on the development of state constitutions writes:

> The United States has not one constitution but fifty-one. These constitutions were drafted at various stages in the nation's history, and their contents (not surprisingly) reflect the constitutional thought regnant at the time of their adoption. The political theory underlying state constitutions has often diverged from the perspective of 1787.

For Tarr, the states have their own constitutional tradition which encompasses not only the constitutional amendment and constitutional convention processes but constitutional initiative as well:

First, the initiative and direct democracy more generally fit comfortably within the state constitutional tradition. Second, this compatibility derives from the belief, basic to the state constitutional tradition, that the primary danger facing republican government is minority faction—power wielded by the wealthy or well-connected few—rather than majority faction. Third, the state tradition's divergence from Federalist No. 10's diagnosis of the threats to republican government is paralleled by a skepticism about the "republican remedies" proposed in The Federalist Papers. More specifically, the state constitutional tradition is characterized by a distrust of government by elected representatives; representation not only fails to solve the problems afflicting republican government, but it may even aggravate those problems by empowering minority factions. If this is so, of course, then direct democracy—or mechanisms designed to approximate it—become much more attractive.

Tarr also reminds us that:

State constitutions of the eighteenth and early nineteenth centuries tended to concentrate power in the state legislature. In addition to enacting laws and imposing taxes, the legislatures in most states selected the governor and state judges and appointed other state officials (and oftentimes local officials as well). Legislators could also remove officials by impeachment and require the removal of judges by address. Moreover, these broad powers existed virtually without check.

The legislative authority was based on the fact that the legislature was considered the only institution that directly represented the citizenry. Even more important, state constitution-makers sought to approximate direct democracy in their systems of representative government.

Legislatively Proposed Amendments

State constitutions are altered most frequently through legislatively proposed amendments. This process first appeared in state constitutions in the 1770s and was a well established principle by the 1780s. Today all 50 state constitutions allow for such amendment. All but one state (Delaware) requires that amendments proposed by the legislature be ratified by a vote of the electorate.

Conditions of legislative passage vary from state to state. Seventeen states require that the proposal pass by a simple majority of the membership of each house or 50% plus one. Alabama and seven other states set the bar higher at three-fifths or 60% of the membership of each house while 18 states require a two-thirds vote or 67%. Additional requirements may also apply.

Twelve states (including Delaware, Indiana, Iowa, Massachusetts, Nevada, New York, Rhode Island, South Carolina, Tennessee, Virginia, and Wyoming) require that the amendment proposal be passed at two or more separate sessions of the legislature. The conditions of the vote may be different for each session. For example, Connecticut sets the vote at three-fourths (75%) of each house in the first session of passage and then requires passage in two more sessions at a majority level. And, a general election must occur between the two final sessions. South Carolina, Virginia and

CHAPTER XVIII   AMENDMENT AND REVISION OF STATE CONSTITUTIONS   1033

Tennessee, the only southern states that require passage in two sessions, differ in their procedures. Virginia requires a majority vote in both sessions. In South Carolina, initial passage is set at two-thirds of the membership; second passage is set at a majority but occurs only after ratification of the amendment by the electorate. In Tennessee the number on first passage is set at two-thirds of the senate and a majority of the house and then on second passage the figure is set at two-thirds of both houses.

Only six states place limits on the number or types of amendments that may be presented to the electorate. Arkansas, Kansas and Kentucky limit amendments on a ballot to three, five, and four respectively. In Colorado no more than six articles of the constitution may have amendments proposed in the same legislative session. New Jersey does not limit the number of proposed amendments on the ballot, but a proposal that has been defeated by the electorate may not be put on the ballot until three general elections have passed.

State constitutions either set a specified time and type of election for popular ratification (for example, the next general election) or allow the timing of the vote to be determined by the legislature itself. When the legislature is given the power to determine the timing of the vote as it is in Alabama, the type of election at which the vote occurs (for example, primary vs. general election, presidential election year vs. off-year election, regularly scheduled election vs. a special election) and factors such as likely turnout level and the disposition of voters likely to vote may influence the decision-making. High or low turnout may be the goal depending upon the purpose, as well as the beneficiaries, of the proposal.

Because legislatively proposed amendments are not normal legislation, they are not sent to the governor for signature or veto. The governor is important to the process, however. As a political party leader, she may work with legislative leaders to facilitate or block passage. Easy access to the media and interest groups may be part of this effort, particularly in attempting to activate supporters or opponents in legislative lobbying efforts. Sometimes governors lead election style campaigns aimed at activating the electorate to vote. Governors engaged in such campaigns may find their potential opponents working the other side of the issue while testing the waters for the next election.

Almost all (44 out of 49) of the state constitutions require a majority popular vote for ratification of an amendment. Most require a majority vote of those voting on the amendment. Three require a majority of those voting in the election while New Hampshire requires a two-thirds vote of those voting on the amendment. Illinois requires a two-thirds vote on the amendment or a majority of those voting in the election. States may add other requirements to these numbers. For example, in Florida any amendment creating a new tax or fee not in effect on November 7, 1994 must pass by a two-thirds vote, and Louisiana requires that amendments that impact five or fewer political subdivisions (for example, parishes or counties) must pass by a majority vote at the state level and a majority in each impacted subdivision. In New Mexico some amendment votes dealing with the right to vote and with education must be approved by 75% of the electorate; they reach the ballot only after 75% of each house have agreed to the proposals. Georgia's current constitution allows only for amendments that are of a general and uniform applicability throughout the state. This eliminates local purpose amendments and keeps the number of amendments down.

Constitutional Conventions

The constitutional convention is the oldest and traditional method used for creating constitutions and making major changes in existing constitutions. The convention is often referred to as the most democratic of the alteration procedures because it involves the electorate to the greatest extent.

Tarr, in outlining the Nineteenth Century experience with constitutional conventions, suggests at least three ways in which constitutional conventions then (and now) approximate direct democracy:

> First, the membership of state constitutional conventions tended to mirror the populace of the states. Convention delegates were—like state legislators—elected by the people, but unlike legislators, they did not tend to be professional politicians. Second, the people exercised control over the calling of conventions. Whereas the legislature met regularly, a convention came into being only by popular vote, when the people wanted fundamental political issues addressed. Thus when convention delegates met, they had a ready-made agenda of popular concerns to guide their deliberations. Third, ratification by referendum afforded the people an opportunity to approve or reject the measures proposed by constitutional conventions—not an approximation of direct democracy but the real thing. Usually voters considered the proposed constitution as a whole rather than voting on particular provisions. Yet in at least some states the practice developed of submitting controversial proposals as separate items, lest opposition to them doom the entire document.

Tarr also writes that often constitutional conventions were initiated in the 1800s in order to create a balance between the branches of government. As legislative bodies came to be viewed as dominated by specific interest groups, the conventions were used to enhance gubernatorial and judicial authority in order to protect the public. Constitutional initiatives, which will be addressed in a later section, were also used to return power to the people.

Constitutional Convention Procedures Today

Forty-two of the 50 states make provisions in their constitutions for constitutional conventions. Generally legislatures are given the right to initiate the constitutional convention call. That call usually requires voter approval. Then, the electorate selects the delegates to the convention using procedures outlined by the state constitution or by the legislature in enabling legislation. The enabling legislation may be outlined to the electorate at the time of its vote on the convention call. The electorate generally must ratify any document or alterations in the existing constitution that are proposed by the convention. As with the amending process, however, there are many variations in this overall pattern.

The standard convention call requirements are a majority vote or a two-thirds (67%) vote of both houses. South Dakota and Illinois require three-quarters (75%) of each house to call a convention.

Fourteen states require an automatic periodic vote by the electorate on whether to hold a convention. New York's 1846 constitution was the first to include such a mandatory referendum provision. Eight states (Connecticut, Illinois, Maryland, Missouri, Nebraska, New York, Ohio, and Oregon) mandate a vote every 20 years. Michigan requires a vote every 16 years. Four states (Alaska, Iowa, New Hampshire, and Rhode Island) use a 10 year cycle while Hawaii's vote must occur every 9 years. For many of these states if a vote for a convention has been called during the interim period, the mandatory vote cycle starts from the date of that vote.

An important factor to be considered in relation to the mandatory vote is whether the constitution includes a self-executing clause for any convention voted for by the electorate. Self-executing clauses may set up procedures for calling the convention, outline delegate selection procedures and delegate requirements, provide for convention location and staff support as well as operating funds all with no action required by the legislature. Without self-execution clauses, the voters may authorize a convention only to find that the legislature may then fail to enact the enabling legislation required, thus forcing the electorate to seek judicial remedies.

State constitutions vary greatly on whether a popular vote is required to ratify the recommendations made by a constitutional convention. When popular ratification procedures are specified in the constitution, the standard requirement for passage is a majority vote of those voting on the proposal. Nine states including Alabama, Florida, Mississippi, and West Virginia do not have specific ratification requirements in their constitutions. The convention call proposal itself usually outlines the procedures to be used for ratification, but the conditions of the ratification vote may also be left to the determination of the convention itself. Seven state constitutions, including Kentucky's, make no provision at all for popular ratification.

Conventions often are called during crisis periods or periods of major change. For example, the 1968 Florida Constitution was written by a convention called for by the first legislature to take office after reapportionment on a one-person, one-vote basis. One set of political issues its members had to deal with were the tensions between North Florida and South Florida. These tensions not only reflected differences in political party orientations but differences in their economic base. They also were tied to North Florida's domination of the state legislature due to the several decades long failure of the legislature to reapportion itself as the population base grew in South Florida. Similar regional tensions tied to legislative malapportionment aided in making the 1960s the last major decade for state constitutional conventions and total rewriting of state constitutions. The last constitutional convention which was successful in winning voter approval of its recommendations was held in Louisiana in 1974.

The greatest strength of the legislatively called convention process is that it maximizes direct citizen participation in the revision process. Citizens are indirectly represented at the legislative vote stage because they decided through the election process who votes on the proposal. They then vote directly on the proposal. They vote again to select convention delegates. Finally, recommendations from the convention must be ratified by the electorate. There is the potential for increasing citizen attention and interest in politics, governmental problems, and possible solutions. There is also the potential for increasing knowledge levels and developing a true public dialogue and debate process.

Several weaknesses or problems with the convention approach to revision are cited by opponents. First, many recent attempts to call conventions have failed due to public suspicion and distrust of politicians and the political process. Second, interest group activity is likely to be high and to create a divisive atmosphere at the delegate selection stage, during convention operations, and at ratification. Some groups will seek to preserve the protected position they have in the current constitution; they will be competing with those who have a vested interest in seeking special treatment for themselves. This is, of course, the democratic process at work. Third, many fear that the ability to spend money or to attract money from interest groups, not competence or concern for the public interest, will drive delegate selection. Others fear that unless specifically barred by the enabling legislation or the constitution, legislators and other elected officials will predominate among the delegates. The previously mentioned items are viewed as reinforcing this possibility.

A major problem exists in the manner by which conventions usually originate by legislative proposal. If the legislature has been captured by interests seeking to preserve the status quo (for example, rural Alabama's dominance of the legislature until the late 1960s), a proposal for a convention will not pass the legislature, and the will of the people may be thwarted. This is precisely the argument advanced by Progressive and Populist reformers during the late 1800s and early 1900s to justify the use of constitutional initiative as a revision method. An automatic periodic vote to determine if a convention should be held is another mechanism for bypassing a recalcitrant legislature.

Constitutional Initiatives

An initiative is a form of direct legislation that allows individuals or groups to propose public policy through the creation of a constitutional amendment. Currently, 18 states have constitutional initiative powers that allow the public to propose amendments to their constitutions and then submit them to the electorate for ratification. In Florida this process may be used to call a constitutional convention.

Constitutional initiative proposals usually are restricted to single topics and may generally deal with only one article of the constitution. Exceptions include situations where change in one article impacts another article; both may then be changed by the amendment. The general procedures for initiatives begin with the filing of the proposed amendment with the required state office. That office must determine that the amendment and petition meets legal requirements. The sponsors then circulate the petition within the electorate. Numbers of petition signatures required usually are tied to a percentage of the total votes cast in the last gubernatorial election. Currently the numbers range from 3% to 15%. When the requisite number of registered voters have signed the petitions, they are filed with the appropriate state office for review and certification. If the petitions meet all legal requirements, the proposed amendment is placed on the ballot for a vote.

Other requirements than the general format listed above may be set. For example, Mississippi requires petition signatures to be collected within a 12 month period, be equal to at least 12% of the votes for governor in the last gubernatorial election, and have no more than one-fifth (20%) of the signatures from any one congressional district. If a congressional district represents more than one-fifth of the signatures, the Mississippi Secretary of State who must determine whether the petition qualifies for the ballot must eliminate the excess signatures from the signature count.

Direct Initiative

Sixteen states use the direct constitutional initiative process. There is no legislative review or revision of the proposed amendment. Once legal requirements are met, the proposed amendment must be placed on the ballot. The timing of the vote is set by the constitution in relation to the date of formal certification of the petitions as legal. The election is usually specified as a general election.

Many of the direct constitutional initiative states specify that if two conflicting amendment proposals pass in the same election, the one with the highest number of votes will go into effect. The effective date of a newly passed amendment may be immediately or 30 days after the official certification of election results or a constitutionally specified day of the year such as January 1 or July 1, the first day of the budget year for most states.

Indirect Initiative

Two states, Mississippi and Massachusetts, use the indirect constitutional initiative. Indirect initiatives require that once the petition process is complete and certified as meeting all legal requirements, the proposed amendment must be submitted to the legislature for review.

Limitations on Constitutional Initiatives

Constitutional initiatives may be limited by specific provisions of a constitution. What, if any, limitations exist varies greatly from state to state. For example, the Massachusetts constitution places specific restrictions on what portions of the constitution may not be amended through the initiative process. It states that basic citizen rights such as the right to a jury trial, freedom of speech, freedom of the press, the right to peacefully assembly, and religious matters are excluded from initiative action, as are some election related matters. The Massachusetts constitution also protects the independence of the judiciary by disallowing constitutional initiatives that alter judicial appointment procedures, judicial qualifications, and the tenure and removal processes for judges. In addition, constitutional initiatives are barred from creating specific appropriations from the state treasury. Illinois's constitution limits constitutional initiatives to structural and procedural subjects found in the Legislative article. The Mississippi constitution states that the initiative may not be used to alter or repeal the following: the Bill of Rights; Mississippi Public Employees' Retirement System (and laws related to it); right to work provisions; or the constitutional initiative process. California requires that all initiatives must apply to all political subdivisions and be applicable to all subdivisions even if a majority in that jurisdiction voted against the ratified initiative.

Some states may require review of a constitutional initiative by the attorney general of the state for its legality. The opinion that results may be merely advisory in nature or may be given the force of law. Some reviews are accomplished at an initial notice filing that precedes circulation of the petition. This review determines whether all legal requirements have been met for the petition itself, including proper format, especially improper or unclear ballot language; it may also determine whether the proposal itself meets constitutional muster. Both federal and state constitutional issues may be involved. Some states require the reviews at the time signed petitions have been filed. These reviews may be undertaken by a state's supreme court. The proposals may become the subject of court cases both before and after they have been approved by the electorate.

The constitutional initiative process, particularly in the direct initiative form, returns the power to act to the public. This power may be exercised even when a legislature or one of its houses has been captured by interest groups and blocks all efforts to institute a constitutional convention or to propose amendments. For example, the Oklahoma initiative was created to thwart the power that the railroads held over the state legislature. It is often viewed as a form of direct grassroots democracy.

Weaknesses cited for the initiative process are numerous. One set of complaints focuses on the procedures involved in the petition process. Because states may set the number of required signatures high, require signatures from registered voters, and often limit the time period within which the signatures must be collected, organized groups with large memberships and/or money rather than individual citizens have a distinct advantage. Those with the money are increasingly employing professionals who may not even live in the state to generate and circulate the petitions. In other instances, groups from outside the state that have a national agenda may go into several states with their initiative campaigns. At least one state has attempted to deal with these issues by restricting the right to file and circulate petitions to those who are registered voters in the state. Some states passed laws to make the paying of those who circulate a petition illegal, but a Colorado law to this effect was declared unconstitutional by the U.S. Supreme Court in a unanimous vote. Another problem is that unless the statutory or constitutional requirements require a clear and concise petition statement summarizing the proposal and give a court or the attorney general the authority to police these factors, confusing and purposely misleading information may be disseminated. A similar problem can exist for ballot summaries. Another concern is that majorities voting on initiatives may not be sensitive to minority rights. Both conservative rural interests and African American groups in Mississippi opposed the initiative process on this ground. Minority rights issues are one reason state constitutions may specify that basic rights found in their bill of rights are not alterable by initiative. Constitutions are supposed to serve as the fundamental law of the state. Amendments added by initiative increasingly represent policy issues normally dealt with by legislatures using their lawmaking powers.

A final issue centers around extraordinary majorities; it often is cited by those who are concerned by minority rights. A state that uses constitutional initiative may require a majority vote for passage of the initiative or for passage of a legislatively proposed amendment. An initiative proposal may include within it restrictions on how the proposal once adopted may be changed by future initiatives or amendments. The popular restriction is to require a two-thirds or three-fifths vote. Future generations must come to higher levels of agreement to change proposals made today by a majority vote. They lose the flexibility to create change that was part of the original argument for creation of constitutional initiative authority. A constitutional initiative also may be used to place restrictions on how certain laws may be passed by the legislature. An example is the Florida requirement that new tax proposals pass the legislature by supermajority.

Constitutional Commissions

Constitutional commissions serve two major purposes: (1) studying the constitution and proposing changes and (2) preparing for a constitutional convention. They have also been used by legislatures as devices to forestall constitutional convention calls.

Commissions may be authorized by law or state constitution to meet on a periodic basis. They may be established by law, executive order, or other means to meet for a specified period. They generally report the results of their work to the governor, legislature, or other public authority. In the 1990s both California and New York used the commission system. New York's governor in 1992 created the Temporary New York State Commission on Constitutional Reform to prepare for a convention should the public agree to the automatic convention call set for 1997. The electorate rejected the convention call. California used an executively created commission to make recommendations to the legislature and governor.

One example of the successful use of a commission as an advisory group charged with making recommendations to the legislature may be found in Florida in the 1960s. In 1964 a legislatively proposed amendment received majority support from the Florida electorate. The amendment specified:

> Either branch of the legislature, at any regular session, or at any special or extraordinary session called for the purposes, may propose by joint resolution a revision of the entire constitution or a revision or amendment of any portion or portions thereof and may direct and provide for an election thereon.

The Florida legislature used its new authority to create a revision commission by statute. It met in 1965–66 and submitted proposals for major revisions to the legislature in 1966. These proposals, together with legislative revisions, were submitted to the voters in the 1968 general election. On passage they became the 1968 Florida Constitution. This new constitution added not only constitutional initiative but a revision commission unlike that used to develop the new constitution. The Florida Constitutional Review Commission is the only constitutionally established commission with the authority to report its recommendations directly to the electorate for a vote.

The commission system allows for study and careful deliberation. Its work can be done transparently so that the public is fully informed of all its activities and has numerous opportunities to contribute their concerns and recommendation. If the commission must report to the legislature, its recommendations must be translated into legislatively proposed amendments. Only Florida has a commission that reports recommendations directly to the public. Even when the public has voted against this commission's recommendations, public debate has been increased and change has been generated through later legislative actions.

If commissions are dependent upon legislatures or governors for their call rather than automatically established on a periodic basic, they may never be called into existence. Or if called by a governor, the legislature might ignore their work for partisan reasons. A periodic cycle for automatically calling a commission into session can insure that constitutional reviews are accomplished.

C. INITIATIVE

Ronald M. George, *The Perils of Direct Democracy: The California Experience*

Speech to the American Academy of Arts & Sciences (Oct. 10, 2009)

It is an honor to speak as a representative of the new class of Academy members. I would like to share some thoughts with you on a matter that has been of recent and continued professional concern to me, but that I believe may be of general interest to members of the Academy, because it fundamentally implicates how we govern ourselves. This is the increasing use of the ballot Initiative process available in many states to effect constitutional and statutory changes in the law, especially in the structure and powers of government.

A not-too-subtle clue to my point of view is reflected in the caption I have chosen for these remarks—"The Perils of Direct Democracy: The California Experience." Although two dozen states in our nation permit government by voter Initiative, in no other state is the practice as extreme as in California.

By the terms of its Constitution, California permits a relatively small number of petition signers—equal to at least 8% of the voters in the last gubernatorial election—to place before the voters a proposal to amend any aspect of our Constitution. (The figure is only 5% for a proposed non-constitutional statutory enactment.) If approved by a simple majority of those voting at the next election, the Initiative measure goes into effect on the following day.

The legislature (by two-thirds vote of each house) shares with the voters the power to place proposed constitutional amendments before the electorate. California, however, is unique among all American jurisdictions in prohibiting its legislature, without express voter approval, from amending or repealing even a statutory measure enacted by the voters, unless the Initiative measure itself specifically confers such authority upon the legislature.

The process for amending California's Constitution thus is considerably easier than the amendment process embodied in the United States Constitution, under which an amendment may be proposed either by a vote of two-thirds of each house of Congress or by a convention called on the application of the legislatures of two-thirds of the states. It can be ratified only by the legislatures of (or by conventions held in) three-quarters of the states.

The relative ease with which the California Constitution can be amended is dramatically illustrated by the frequency with which this has occurred. Only 17 amendments to the United States Constitution (in addition to the Bill of Rights, ratified in 1791) have been adopted since that document was ratified in 1788. In contrast, more than 500 amendments to the California Constitution have been adopted since ratification of California's current Constitution in 1879.

Former United States Supreme Court Justice Hugo Black was known to pride himself on carrying in his pocket a slender pamphlet containing the federal Constitution in its entirety. I certainly could not emulate that practice with California's constitutional counterpart.

One Bar leader has observed: "California's current constitution rivals India's for being the longest and most convoluted in the world. With the cumulative dross of past voter initiatives incorporated, it is a document that assures chaos."

Initiatives have enshrined a myriad of provisions into California's constitutional charter, including a prohibition on the use of gill nets and a measure regulating the confinement of barnyard fowl in coops. This last constitutional amendment was enacted on the same 2008 ballot that amended the state Constitution to override the California Supreme Court's decision recognizing the right of same-sex couples to marry. Chickens gained valuable rights in California on the same day that gay men and lesbians lost them.

Perhaps most consequential in their impact on the ability of California state and local government to function are constitutional and statutory mandates and prohibitions—often at cross-purposes—limiting how elected officials may raise and spend revenue. California's lawmakers, and the state itself, have been placed in a fiscal straitjacket by a steep two-thirds-vote requirement—imposed at the ballot box—for raising taxes. A similar supermajoritarian requirement governs passage of the state budget. This situation is compounded by voter Initiative measures that have imposed severe restrictions upon increases in the assessed value of real property that is subject to property tax, coupled with constitutional requirements of specified levels of financial support for public transportation and public schools.

These constraints upon elected officials—when combined with a lack of political will (on the part of some) to curb spending and (on the part of others) to raise taxes—often make a third alternative, borrowing, the most attractive option (at least until the bankers say "no").

Much of this constitutional and statutory structure has been brought about not by legislative fact-gathering and deliberation, but rather by the approval of voter Initiative measures, often funded by special interests. These interests are allowed under the law to pay a bounty to signature-gatherers for each signer. Frequent amendments—coupled with the implicit threat of more in the future—have rendered our state government dysfunctional, at least in times of severe economic decline.

Because of voter Initiatives restricting the taxing powers that the legislature may exercise, California's tax structure is particularly dependent upon fluctuating types of revenue, giving rise to a "boom or bust" economic cycle. The consequences this year have been devastating to programs that, for example, provide food to poor children and health care for the elderly disabled. This year's fiscal crisis also has caused the Judicial Council, which I chair, to take the reluctant and unprecedented step of closing all courts in our state one day a month. That decision will enable us to offset approximately one-fourth of the more than $400 million reduction imposed by the other two branches of government on the $4 billion budget of our court system.

The voter Initiative process places additional burdens upon the judicial branch. The court over which I preside frequently is called upon to resolve legal challenges to voter Initiatives. Needless to say, we incur the displeasure of the voting public when, in the course of performing our constitutional duties as judges, we are compelled to invalidate such a measure.

On occasion, we are confronted with a pre-election lawsuit that causes us to remove an Initiative proposal from the ballot because, by combining insufficiently related issues, it violates our state Constitution's single-subject limitation on such measures. At other times, a voter Initiative—perhaps poorly drafted and ambiguous, or faced with a competing or "dueling" measure that passed at the same election—requires years of successive litigation in the courts to ferret out its intended meaning, and ultimately may have to be invalidated in whole or in part.

One thing is fairly certain, however. If a proposal, whatever its nature, is sufficiently funded by its backers, it most likely will obtain the requisite number of signatures to qualify for the ballot, and—if it does qualify—there is a good chance the measure will pass. The converse certainly is true—poorly funded efforts, without sufficient backing to mount an expensive television campaign—are highly unlikely to succeed, whatever their merit.

This dysfunctional situation has led some to call for the convening of a convention to write a new Constitution for California to replace our current 1879 charter, which in turn supplanted the original 1849 document. Yet, although a recent poll reflects that 79% of Californians say the state is moving in the wrong direction, only 33% believe that the state's

Constitution requires "major" changes and approximately 60% are of the view that decisions made by Californians through the Initiative process are better than those made by the legislature and the governor.

Add to this mix a split among scholars concerning whether a constitutional convention, if called, could be limited in the subject matter it is empowered to consider. Some argue that a convention would be open to every type of proposal from any source, including social activists and special interest groups. There also is controversy over the most appropriate procedure for selecting delegates for such a convention.

A student of government might reasonably ask: Does the voter Initiative, a product of the Populist Movement that reached its high point in the early 20th century in the mid-west and western states, remain a positive contribution in the form in which it now exists in 21st century California? Or, despite its original objective—to curtail special interests, such as the railroads, that controlled the legislature of California and of some other states—has the voter Initiative now become the tool of the very types of special interests it was intended to control, and an impediment to the effective functioning of a true democratic process?

John Adams—who I believe never would have supported a voter Initiative process like California's—cautioned that "democracy never lasts long. There is never a democracy that did not commit suicide." The nation's Founding Fathers, wary of the potential excesses of direct democracy, established a republic with a carefully crafted system of representative democracy. This system was characterized by checks and balances that conferred authority upon the officeholders of our three branches of government in a manner designed to enable them to curtail excesses engaged in by their sister branches.

Perhaps with the dangers of direct democracy in mind, Benjamin Franklin gave his much-quoted response to a question posed by a resident of Philadelphia after the adjournment of the Constitutional Convention in 1787. Asked the type of government that had been established by the delegates, Franklin responded: "It would be a republic, if you can keep it." And, as Justice David Souter recently observed in quoting this exchange, Franklin "understood that a republic can be lost."

At a minimum, in order to avoid such a loss, Californians may need to consider some fundamental reform of the voter Initiative process. Otherwise, I am concerned, we shall continue on a course of dysfunctional state government, characterized by a lack of accountability on the part of our officeholders as well as the voting public.

NOTES

1. The people of South Dakota adopted the first state constitutional initiative in 1898, followed by Utah in 1900 and Oregon in 1902. Nineteen States permit citizens to change their state constitutions through initiatives.

2. Often called a form of direct democracy, the initiative process stands in contrast with representative democracy. When the initiative procedure was challenged as violating the United States Constitution's guarantee that each State must have a republic form of government, the Supreme Court held that it raised a political question for Congress to decide, not the Court. *Pacific States Tel. & Tel. v. Oregon* (1912).

3. That does not insulate the initiative process from *other* federal constitutional challenges. In *Romer v. Evans* (1996), for example, the United States Supreme Court held that an initiated amendment to the Colorado Constitution violated the federal Equal Protection Clause.

4. For more on the initiative process in California, see Rudy Klapper, *The Falcon Cannot Hear the Falconer: How California's Initiative Process Is Creating an Untenable Constitution*, 48 Loy. L.A.L. Rev. 755 (2015).

D. CONSTITUTIONAL CONVENTION— REQUIRED FOR COMPLETE REVISION

CITIZENS PROTECTING MICHIGAN'S CONSTITUTION v. SECRETARY OF STATE
921 N.W.2d 247 (Mich. 2018)

VIVIANO, J.

The question in this case is whether the voter-initiated amendment proposed by intervening defendant Voters Not Politicians (VNP) should be placed on the ballot. VNP launched a petition drive to propose an amendment that would reestablish a commission to oversee legislative redistricting. Plaintiffs brought suit to stop the petition from being placed on the ballot, making the now familiar argument that the proposed amendment is actually a "general revision" that can only be enacted through a constitutional convention.

We took this case to determine whether the VNP petition is a constitutionally permissible voter-initiated amendment under Const. 1963, art 12, § 2. To answer this question, we must fulfill our Court's most solemn responsibility: to interpret and apply the pertinent provisions of our Constitution. After closely examining the text, structure, and history of the Constitution, we hold that, to be permissible, a voter-initiated amendment must propose changes that do not significantly alter or abolish the form or structure of the government in a manner equivalent to creating a new constitution.

VNP is a ballot-question committee. It filed with defendant Secretary of State the initiative petition at issue in this case. The initiative proposal would, among other things, amend Const. 1963, art 4, § 6, which established a commission to regulate legislative redistricting. The commission prescribed by our present Constitution is inactive because this Court declared that it could not be severed from apportionment standards contained in the Michigan Constitution that had been held to be unconstitutional, as explained further below. After that ruling, this Court oversaw redistricting until the Legislature took control of the process. VNP's proposal would bring Michigan's constitutional redistricting standards in line with federal constitutional requirements and revive the redistricting commission's authority to set redistricting plans for the state house, state senate, and federal congressional districts.

A sufficient number of registered electors signed the petition for it to be placed on the November 2018 general election ballot. Before the Board of State Canvassers could certify the petition for placement on the ballot, plaintiff Citizens Protecting Michigan's Constitution (CPMC), along with other plaintiffs, filed the present complaint for a writ of mandamus directing the Secretary of State and the Board to reject the VNP proposal. CPMC argued that the proposal was not an amendment of the Constitution that could be proposed by petition under Const. 1963, art 12, § 2; rather, the proposal amounted to a "general revision" of the Constitution and could be enacted only through a constitutional convention under Const. 1963, art 12, § 3.

Our Constitution is clear that "all political power is inherent in the people." The people have chosen to retain for themselves the power to initiate proposed constitutional amendments that, if various requirements are met, will be placed on the ballot and voted on at election time. It has been observed that "there is no more constitutionally significant event than when the wielders of all political power under that document choose to exercise their extraordinary authority to directly approve or disapprove of an amendment thereto." In this case, we must determine the scope of the voters' power to initiate amendments. In answering this question, we do not consider whether the proposed amendment at issue represents good or bad public policy. Instead, we must determine whether the amendment meets all the relevant constitutional requirements. There may be an "overarching right" to the initiative petition, "but only in accordance with the standards of the constitution; otherwise, there is an overarching right to have public policy determined by a majority of the people's democratically elected representatives." In particular, we have stated that the "right of electors to propose amendments is to be exercised in a certain way and according to certain conditions, the limitations upon its exercise, like the reservation of the right itself, being found in the Constitution."

Our inquiry here, then, is to determine the extent of the people's right to initiate constitutional amendments and whether any clear limitations may be found in the Constitution. As with any constitutional provision, the objective of our interpretation "is to determine the text's original meaning to the ratifiers, the people, at the time of ratification."

Three basic procedures allow for alterations of the Constitution. The first, not directly relevant here, provides for "amendments" proposed in the Senate or House and approved by two-thirds of the members in each chamber, then submitted to the voters for approval. Const. 1963, art 12, § 2 provides the second manner of altering the Constitution, which is the one VNP attempted here: "Amendments may be proposed to this constitution by petition of the registered electors of this state." "Every petition shall include the full text of the proposed amendment, and be signed by registered electors of the state equal in number to at least 10 percent of the total vote cast" for Governor in the most recent general gubernatorial election. Once the "person authorized by law to receive such petition" determines that the petition signatures were valid and sufficient, the proposed amendment is placed on the ballot. Finally, under Const. 1963, art 12, § 3, the third manner of changing the Constitution is by constitutional convention. Every 16 years, "and at such times as may be provided by law, the question of a general revision of the constitution shall be submitted to the electors of the state"; if the voters vote in favor of performing a "general revision," a constitutional convention is convened for that purpose. We have explained that the adoption of the initiative power, along with other tools of direct democracy, "reflected the popular distrust of the Legislative branch of our state government."

The scope of the initiative amendment process and its relation to the "general revision" process is at the heart of this case. How extensive can a voter-initiated amendment be, and does the Constitution place any relevant subject matter limitations on such amendments?

The textual analysis begins with examining the meaning of "amendment" as used in the text. "Amendment" is relevantly defined as "an alteration of a legislative or deliberative act or in a constitution; a change made in a law, either by way of correction or addition," or "the correction of an error in a writ, record, or other judicial document." The definition does not directly speak to the breadth of the change that can be made by amendment or provide any substantive limitations on amendments. With regard to limitations on the scope of amendments, the text of the predecessor provision to Article 12, § 2 was meaningfully changed soon after its ratification in 1908. When it was ratified, the Constitution gave the Legislature a veto over voter-initiated amendments before the election at which the proposal would appear on the ballot, and the Legislature could also submit alternative or substitute amendments. Yet despite the

Legislature's considerable oversight, the framers of the Constitution nonetheless thought that "the effect of this will be the submission to a vote of the electors of practically all amendments petitioned-for."

The relevant substantive limitation on the scope of voter-initiated amendments arises from the text of Article 12, § 2 when read together with Article 12, § 3. By adopting these two different procedures for altering the Constitution, the framers intended that the mechanisms must be different in some regard.

Our Constitution tells us what this basic difference is. The result of a constitutional convention called to consider a "general revision" is a "proposed constitution or amendments" adopted by the convention and proposed to the electors. The convention, then, can propose amendments to the existing Constitution or offer a new constitution. By contrast, if approved, a voter-initiated amendment under Article 12, § 2 "shall become part of the constitution, and shall abrogate or amend existing provisions of the constitution." Consequently, an amendment does not replace a constitution in full, but simply adds to or abrogates specific provisions in an existing constitution. Thus, the constitutional text distinguishes between amendments that can be made by petition and new "constitutions." Because only the convention has the power to propose a constitution, by logical implication an initiative amendment cannot do so. And since this limitation would be meaningless if it only required a new constitution to be labeled as an amendment, it follows that an initiative amendment cannot propose changes that are tantamount to the creation of a new constitution.

The phrase "general revision" supports this dichotomy between amendments and "new" constitutions, although the phrase has engendered some confusion. The "purpose" of a convention is to consider "the question of a general revision of the constitution." "General" means "dealing with all or the overall, universal aspects of the subject under consideration." "Revision," in turn, is relevantly defined as "the act or work of revising." Thus a "revision" is not contradistinguished from an "amendment." Rather, as noted, the distinction between the Article 12, § 3 convention process and the Article 12, § 2 amendment process is that the former can produce a proposed constitution, while the latter is limited to proposing less sweeping changes.

Having determined that the relevant substantive limitation is that a voter-initiated amendment cannot be equivalent to a new constitution, we must determine what this limitation entails. As an initial matter, the number of changes is not dispositive, as even a limited number of changes can have the effect of creating a new constitution. A constitution, after all, is more than words on a page. Its most basic functions are to create the form and structure of government, define and limit the powers of government, and provide for the protection of rights and liberties. These are the basic threads of a constitution, and when they are removed, replaced, or radically rewoven, the whole tapestry of the constitution may change.

Therefore, changes that significantly alter or abolish the form or structure of our government, in a manner equivalent to creating a new constitution, are not amendments under Article 12, § 2. It is not necessarily the impact on the operations of government that matters—like the United States Supreme Court, we decline to accept "the narrow-minded assumption" that the only purpose of our constitutional provisions "is to make the government run as efficiently as possible." Further, a change that recalibrates the relative power of the branches of government—such as limiting or taking away a specific power from one branch—is not, absent a significant effect on the structure of government, a change that is tantamount to the creation of a new constitution. Indeed, we have stated that, despite its eliminating power from the judiciary or executive branch, an amendment permitting indeterminate criminal sentences was "the people's exercise of a right inherent in them to adopt a constitutional amendment taking away from, or adding to, the powers of either of the departments of government." In fact, it would be difficult to imagine many amendments that leave the proportionate powers of the branches completely unchanged.

To determine whether VNP's proposal is a permissible amendment, we must ask whether it significantly alters or abolishes the form or structure of our government in a manner that is tantamount to creating a new constitution. One central feature of the VNP amendment is that it sweeps away unconstitutional provisions that have remained in the Constitution for some time. The "weighted land area/population formulae" and the accompanying apportionment factors are gone, and so counties would not be the organizing feature of redistricting plans. But these changes involve no great transformation because these features were held unconstitutional 36 years ago. In their place our state has used federal constitutional requirements and various state "guidelines," enacted in 1996, including that the districts "be areas of convenient territory contiguous by land," "preserve county lines with the least cost to the principle of equality of population," and remain as compact as possible when drawn within a city or township with multiple districts. VNP's proposed standards reflect many of the same principles, including, of course, adhering to federal law, and also requiring contiguous districts, respecting municipal boundaries, and seeking reasonable compactness. The proposal contains a few new items too, such as considerations of partisan fairness. But given their continuities with the current standards, VNP's proposed standards are no revolution in redistricting, and they certainly do not portend a transformation of our form or structure of government.

As noted above, various provisions in VNP's proposal mirror those in the current Constitution. The Secretary of State has substantially the same general responsibilities, being the nonvoting secretary of the commission responsible for furnishing its needs. The Secretary of State has more detailed obligations under the proposal, involving the formation of the commission. But these tasks are ministerial and in line with our current Constitution—requiring the Secretary of State to manage applications or other records is business as usual, not a new way of governing Michigan.

In sum, VNP's proposal leaves the form and structure of the government essentially as it was envisioned in the 1963 Constitution. Consequently, it is not equivalent to a new constitution and is therefore a permissible amendment under Const. 1963, art 12, § 2.

The question we face today has broad significance for the people of this state: what limitations have they placed, in the Constitution they ratified, on their power to put forward voter-initiated amendments? This question implicates some of the oldest and most perplexing problems in political theory, such as the nature of sovereignty, republicanism, and democracy. But it is not a judge's role to philosophize a theory of government. Rather, we are stewards of the people and must faithfully abide by the decisions they make through the laws they adopt. We accomplish this by adhering to the plain meaning of the text of those laws. Here, that approach leads us to conclude that a voter-initiated amendment under Const. 1963, art 12, § 2 is permissible if it does not significantly alter or abolish the form or structure of our government, making it tantamount to creating a new constitution. VNP's proposal surpasses these hurdles and is a permissible voter-initiated amendment under Article 12, § 2.

E. PROCEDURAL REQUIREMENTS

In addition to determining whether a proposed amendment sweeps so broadly as to alter or abolish the existing constitutional structure, courts often adjudicate procedural disputes related to the amendment process. State constitutions regulate everything from how many subjects an amendment may encompass, *see, e.g.*, S.D. Const. art. XXIII, § 1 (imposing a single-subject requirement), to how the amendment must appear on the ballot, *see, e.g.*, Ohio Const. art. XVI, § 1 (requiring that the ballot language identify the substance of the proposal but not requiring the text of the amendment to appear). The following cases illustrate some of the difficult judgments courts must make before the people may vote to change their constitution.

STATE ex rel. VOTERS FIRST v. OHIO BALLOT BD.
978 N.E.2d 119 (Ohio 2012)

PER CURIAM

This is an original action pursuant to the Ohio Constitution, Article XVI, Section 1 for a writ of mandamus compelling respondent Ohio Ballot Board, which includes respondent Secretary of State Jon Husted, to reconvene forthwith to replace ballot language previously adopted with ballot language that properly describes the proposed constitutional amendment. Because relators have established their entitlement to the requested extraordinary relief, we grant the writ.

The proposed amendment would amend the Ohio Constitution, Article XI, Sections 1, 3, 4, 6, 7, 9, 10, and 13, repeal Article XI, Sections 8 and 14, and adopt Article XI, Section 16, to set forth new constitutional standards and requirements to establish federal congressional and state legislative district lines for Ohio. The proposed amendment would establish the Ohio Citizens Independent Redistricting Commission, consisting of 12 members.

Under the proposed constitutional amendment, the commission shall adopt the redistricting plan that, in its judgment, most closely meets the specified factors of community preservation, competitiveness, representational fairness, and compactness, without violating applicable state and federal constitutional provisions, federal statutory provisions, and the requirement that each district shall be composed of contiguous territory. In addition, the commission must consider and make publicly available with each proposed redistricting plan a report that identifies for each district the boundaries, population, racial and ethnic composition, compactness measure, governmental units that are divided, and political party indexes. No plan shall be drawn or adopted with the intent to favor or disfavor a political party, incumbent, or potential candidate. The legislative districts cannot contain a population less than 98 percent or greater than 102 percent of the ratio of representation.

Eight days after the ballot board's approval of the secretary's proposed language, on August 23, relators filed this original action pursuant to the Ohio Constitution, Article XVI, Section 1 for a writ of mandamus to find that the approved ballot language is invalid and to compel the board and the secretary of state to reconvene forthwith to adopt ballot language that properly describes the proposed constitutional amendment for the November 6, 2012 general election.

In determining the applicable duties imposed on the ballot board, we must review the pertinent constitutional and statutory provisions. Under the Ohio Constitution, Article II, Section 1g, the ballot board's language must comply with the Article XVI, Section 1 requirements for issues proposed by the General Assembly. In turn, Article XVI, Section 1 provides that the Ohio Ballot Board shall prescribe the ballot language for proposed constitutional amendments, that the ballot language "shall properly identify the substance of the proposal to be voted upon," and that the ballot "need not contain the full text nor a condensed text of the proposal." The Ohio Constitution, Article XVI, Section 1 vests this court with "exclusive, original jurisdiction in all cases challenging the adoption or submission of a proposed constitutional amendment to the electors."

The question to be decided by this court is not whether the amendment proposed by relators should become part of the Ohio Constitution. Nor is it pertinent "whether the members of this court might have used different words to describe the language used in the proposed amendment, but, rather, whether the language adopted by the ballot board properly describes the proposed amendment."

Under Article XVI, Section 1, the sole issue is whether the board's approved ballot language "is such as to mislead, deceive, or defraud the voters." In *State ex rel. Bailey v. Celebrezze* (Ohio 1981), we adopted the following three-part test for evaluating the propriety of ballot language for a proposed constitutional amendment:

> First, a voter has the right to know what it is he is being asked to vote upon. Second, use of language which is in the nature of a persuasive argument in favor of or against the issue is prohibited. And, third, the determinative issue is whether the cumulative effect of these technical defects in ballot language is harmless or fatal to the validity of the ballot.

We conclude that the ballot language approved by the board omits material provisions concerning the commission-member selection process and the commission's criteria for redistricting.

The board's approved ballot language includes one salient point concerning the selection process—that the proposal calls for a 12-member commission that is politically balanced in its composition, with four members from each of the two largest political parties and the remaining four members not affiliated with those political parties.

But the approved ballot language says nothing about *who* will be selecting the commission members. It is axiomatic that "who does the appointing is just as important as who is appointed." There is a vast difference between, for example, conferring the authority to select commission members on one elected official and authorizing a bipartisan panel of individuals to perform the selection. Without any description of this process even in the most general terms, the ballot language leaves voters to speculate about who selects the commission members.

By not including, at a minimum, *who* would be selecting the commission members, the ballot board's ballot language fails to properly identify one of the key elements of the proposed constitutional amendment.

The ballot language is similarly deficient because it does not state what criteria the commission will use in drawing federal and state legislative districts. A key part of the proposed amendment specifies that the commission must adopt the plan that complies with all applicable federal and state constitutional provisions, federal statutory provisions, and the contiguity requirement and that most closely meets the factors of community preservation, competitiveness, representational fairness, and compactness. And the commission must also not draw or adopt a plan with an intent to favor or disfavor a political party, incumbent, or potential candidate.

Instead of specifying any of the pertinent criteria that the commission must follow in redistricting, the ballot language merely states that if approved, the proposed constitutional amendment would "change the standards and requirements in the Constitution for drawing legislative and congressional districts."

The board's ballot language thus states very generally that the proposed amendment would change the constitutional standards and requirements for creating federal and state legislative districts in Ohio without describing those changes or the pertinent redistricting criteria.

Because this subject matter strikes at the very core of the proposed amendment, the board's condensed ballot statement does not fairly and accurately present the issue to be decided so as "to assure a free, intelligent and informed vote by the average citizen affected."

Relators next claim that the ballot language adopted by the ballot board is defective because it contains inaccurate and prejudicial language concerning the commission-member selection process, commission funding, and challenges to legislative districts.

We agree with relators' contention regarding the language approved by the ballot board in paragraph five of its summary, which states that the proposed amendment would "mandate the General Assembly to appropriate all funds as determined by the Commission." That statement is inaccurate and prejudicial because it indicates that the General Assembly must appropriate all funds to the commission without qualification.

The actual text of the proposed constitutional amendment does not state that the redistricting commission would have—as the ballot board's language indicates—a blank check for all funds as determined by the commission. Rather, the proposed constitutional amendment expressly limits appropriations for the commission to those "necessary to adequately fund the activities" of the commission. Even the language proposed by the group opposing relators' amendment included the limitation that the General Assembly would "provide any and all funds *necessary* to finance operations of the commission." In essence, the omission in the ballot's board's condensed ballot language of the qualifying limitations on commission funding is in the nature of a persuasive argument against its adoption.

The cumulative effect of these defects in the ballot language is fatal to the validity of the ballot because it fails to properly identify the substance of the amendment, a failure that misleads voters. Therefore, for all of the foregoing reasons, the ballot board's approved ballot language is invalid. While we do not suggest that either the board or the secretary was motivated by anything other than honorable intentions in approving the ballot language or that they intended to mislead voters, the language has the effect of misleading.

O'CONNOR, C.J., concurring.

I concur in the judgment and opinion granting the writ of mandamus to compel the Ohio Ballot Board to reconvene forthwith to replace its previously adopted ballot language for State Issue 2 with language that properly describes the proposed constitutional amendment. I write separately, however, to respond to Justice Pfeifer's suggestion in his concurring opinion that we should usurp the ballot board's exclusive constitutional authority to craft the ballot language for the proposed constitutional amendment. To do so would violate the doctrine of separation of powers, the Ohio Constitution, and our precedent. "While Ohio, unlike other jurisdictions, does not have a constitutional provision specifying the concept of separation of powers, this doctrine is implicitly embedded in the entire framework of those sections of the Ohio Constitution that define the substance and scope of powers granted to the three branches of state government."

The Ohio Constitution, Article XVI, Section 1 vests exclusive jurisdiction to prescribe the ballot language for proposed constitutional amendments in the Ohio Ballot Board, which consists of the secretary of state and "four other members, who shall be designated in a manner prescribed by law and not more than two of whom shall be members of the same political party." One of the members of the ballot board shall be appointed by the president of the senate, one shall be appointed by the minority leader of the senate, one shall be appointed by the speaker of the house of representatives, and one shall be appointed by the minority leader of the house of representatives.

Although that same constitutional section vests this court with exclusive, original jurisdiction in all cases challenging the ballot language prescribed by the ballot board, it limits our authority to a determination of whether the contested language is invalid. Nothing in Article XVI, Section 1 or any other constitutional provision authorizes this court to sit as a super ballot board to prescribe ballot language for a proposed constitutional amendment after we have determined that the language prescribed by the board is invalid.

Consistent with the plain language of the Ohio Constitution, Article XVI, Section 1, once this court has exercised its jurisdiction by determining that the language prescribed by the ballot board is invalid, our authority over the matter ends, and it is up to the ballot board to exercise its exclusive constitutional authority to adopt ballot language that properly describes the proposed constitutional amendment.

PFEIFER, J., concurring.

I concur in the judgment granting relators' request for a writ of mandamus but write separately to suggest ballot language that would "assure a free, intelligent and informed vote by the average citizen affected." Given the proximity of the applicable deadlines for boards of elections to have absentee ballots printed and ready to use, it is appropriate for this court to provide specific guidance to the ballot board regarding ballot language.

SAVE OUR VOTE v. BENNETT
291 P.3d 342 (Ariz. 2013)

BALES, V.C.J.

The question presented is whether Proposition 121, a constitutional amendment proposed by voter initiative, complies with the separate amendment rule of Article 21, Section 1 of the Arizona Constitution. This rule requires that when more than one constitutional amendment is proposed, voters must be allowed to vote for or against each one separately. Proposition 121 would amend the Constitution to replace partisan primary elections with an open "top two primary" in which all candidates appear on the same ballot and the two receiving the most votes, regardless of party, advance to the general election.

Since statehood, Arizona's Constitution has provided that "the Legislature shall enact a direct primary election law." This requirement was one way in which the Constitution sought to ensure popular control over government through the electoral process.

Consistent with the constitutional directive, Arizona's first state legislature enacted a law "to provide for primary elections." This law established the framework that remains in place today. A "recognized" party—that is, one entitled to have its candidates appear on the general election ballot—must nominate its candidates through the primary election. In the primary, only voters who are registered with a particular party, or not registered with another recognized party (e.g., independent voters), may vote the party's ballot. The winner of the primary appears on the general election ballot along with the nominees of other recognized parties.

Proposition 121, titled the "Open Elections/Open Government Act," purports to "abolish the existing system of taxpayer-funded primary elections to select nominees for political parties" and to "create in its place an Open Top Two Primary Election." Under this proposal, all candidates for an office, regardless of party, appear on the same ballot and voters may vote for any candidate; the two candidates who receive the most votes then face each other in the general election.

The proposition would replace Article 7, Section 10 of Arizona's Constitution with a new Section 10 containing eight subparts. The new section does not apply to non-partisan or presidential preference elections; it recognizes a right to vote in primary and general elections for the candidate of choice regardless of a voter's party affiliation; and it outlines procedures for the top two primary. New Section 10(D) provides that the number of voter signatures a candidate must obtain to qualify for the ballot shall be the same for all candidates regardless of party affiliation. More generally, new Section 10(H) declares that all qualified voters and candidates shall be treated equally by laws governing elections regardless of party affiliation. Candidates may choose to identify their party affiliation on nomination petitions and the ballot, but government-issued voter education materials and the ballot will prominently note that a candidate's identified affiliation does not indicate a party's nomination or endorsement.

Proposition 121 also contains a proposed Section 10(G) addressing the rights of political parties:

> Nothing in this section shall restrict the right of individuals to join or organize into political parties or in any way restrict the right of private association of political parties. Nothing in this section shall restrict the parties' right to contribute to, endorse, or otherwise support or oppose candidates for elective office. Political parties may establish such procedures as they see fit to elect party officers, endorse or support candidates, or otherwise participate in all elections, but no such procedures shall be paid for or subsidized using public funds.

Opponents of Proposition 121 filed this action seeking to enjoin the Secretary of State from placing the measure on the ballot because it violated the separate amendment rule of Article 21, Section 1 of the Arizona Constitution. That rule provides:

> If more than one proposed amendment shall be submitted at any election, such proposed amendments shall be submitted in such manner that the electors may vote for or against such proposed amendments separately.

The provisions in Proposition 121 are topically related. They concern whether political parties and their candidates should be afforded favored treatment—through taxpayer-funded partisan primaries, the provisions of laws or regulations, or public funding—with regard to Arizona elections.

The common topicality of the provisions is not undermined by the fact that the Supporters identify the Proposition's purpose as replacing the existing system of taxpayer-funded primary elections with a non-partisan top two primary. Eliminating partisan primaries is a particular application of the more general principle that the state should not favor political parties or party-affiliated voters in election-related matters. Moreover, the favored status that recognized parties enjoy under the partisan primary system and other election laws is the reason the state has an interest in regulating internal party governance

We turn to whether the provisions of Proposition 121 are sufficiently interrelated to comply with the separate amendment rule. This rule does not require "that all components of a provision be logically dependent on one another." Instead, we measure the provisions against objective factors, such as whether various provisions are facially related, whether all the matters addressed by an initiative concern a single section of the constitution, whether the voters or the legislature historically has treated the matters addressed as one subject, and whether the various provisions are qualitatively similar in their effect on either procedural or substantive law.

The provisions of Proposition 121 are not only facially related, but also logically related. Section 10(G) declares that public funds shall not be used to pay for or subsidize procedures used by political parties "to elect party officers, endorse or support candidates, or otherwise participate in all elections." This broad prohibition on public funding of party activities logically embraces Section 10(C)'s elimination of partisan primaries. If public monies cannot be used to support a party's endorsement of candidates or participation in elections generally, then such funds cannot be used to pay for partisan primaries to identify a party's official candidate for the general election.

This aspect of Proposition 121 distinguishes this case from *Clean Elections Inst., Inc. v. Brewer* (Ariz. 2004), which found a separate-amendment violation in a ballot measure related to the Citizens Clean Elections Commission. One provision would have prohibited public funding of candidates' political campaigns, thereby displacing provisions of the Clean Elections Act that require such funding. Another provision would have eliminated the statutorily mandated funding for all the Commission's other duties, including voter education and debate programs that were unaffected by the provision barring funding of political campaigns. The Court found no facial relationship between these provisions because they did not advance any "common purpose or principle." That is, the candidate funding prohibition did not logically imply eliminating the Commission's funding dedicated to other purposes.

Clean Elections is also distinguishable because there the Court relied on predictions about the views of a "reasonable voter," noting that "we cannot conclude from any objective factor that voters favoring one proposition would likely favor the other." Although *Clean Elections* followed prior cases in considering the views of a "reasonable voter," we have since abandoned that approach, and now "apply the *topicality* and *interrelatedness* approach to assess whether a common purpose or principle joins the provisions of a proposed amendment."

Applying the interrelatedness approach here, we note the provisions of Proposition 121 all concern Article 7, Section 10 of the Arizona Constitution. Moreover, Arizona's legislature has historically treated the matters addressed in Proposition 121 as one subject, inasmuch as the "direct primary law" enacted by the first state legislature embraced not only the creation of partisan primary elections but also the election of precinct committeemen and other aspects of internal party governance. Finally, the provisions are "qualitatively similar" in their effect on procedural or substantive law. Replacing the partisan primary with an open primary in which candidates and voters participate without regard to party affiliation is qualitatively similar in its effect to the broader provisions in Proposition 121 mandating a level playing field regardless of party and barring public funding for specified political party activities.

In arguing that Proposition 121 does not have sufficient interrelatedness, the Opponents note that two other states have adopted open primaries while preserving state-funded elections of party precinct committeemen. The Opponents, and certain amici supporting their position, agree with the trial court that "there is no good reason" that a vote for or against funding of certain party activities "should be bundled with a vote on an open primary." Opponents also contend that if Proposition 121 were adopted, it would require changes in a large number of Arizona statutes.

We are not persuaded. The fact that the objectives of a constitutional measure could be achieved by an alternative means does not itself establish a violation of the separate amendment rule. The separate amendment rule does not require that a constitutional amendment identify the most narrowly tailored means for achieving identified goals, only that the provisions have a sufficient common purpose or principle. Nor does the fact that a proposition, if adopted, would require extensive statutory changes necessarily suggest that the proposition violates the separate amendment rule. Finally, assertions that there is no "good reason" to combine Proposition 121's different provisions into one ballot measure appear to speculate about the views of hypothetical voters. As noted, our separate amendment analysis no longer turns on whether a reasonable voter would likely support one provision in a proposed constitutional amendment without supporting another, but rather on the topicality and interrelatedness of the provisions.

Because the provisions contained in Proposition 121 share both topicality and interrelatedness, we conclude they are "sufficiently related to a common purpose or principle" and do not violate the separate amendment rule.

Various arguments have been made to this Court whether the proposed top two primary would be desirable or instead detrimental as a matter of public policy. These arguments are misdirected. Our conclusion that

Proposition 121 satisfies the separate amendment rule says nothing about whether the measure should be approved. If a ballot measure meets the statutory and constitutional requirements to appear on the ballot, its wisdom as a policy matter is for the voters to decide.

F. CONSTITUTIONAL COMMISSIONS

Peter J. Galie & Christopher Bopst, *The Constitutional Commission in New York: A Worthy Tradition*
64 Alb. L. Rev. 1285 (2001)

In 1997, when New Yorkers decisively defeated a constitutionally mandated ballot proposition to convene what would have been the state's fourth constitutional convention in the twentieth century, they placed the fate of constitutional reform with the state legislature. Not until the year 2017 will the question be required to appear on the ballot, and the likelihood of the legislature proposing a convention vote in the interim is remote. New York does not permit amendments to be submitted to the electorate through constitutional initiative, and no constitutional commission has the power to submit amendments directly to the voters; constitutional reform can only emanate from either a constitutional convention or the state legislature. Since 1938, legislatively proposed amendments have been the only procedure successfully used for revising the state's charter.

Paradoxically, the latest rejection came at a time when many of the state's political actors agreed that systematic constitutional revision was needed. The League of Women Voters, Civil Service Employees Association, American Federation of Labor—Congress of Industrial Organizations, National Organization of Women, and various environmental groups who opposed the calling of a convention in 1997, were, nevertheless, in agreement with proponents of the convention on the need for constitutional reform. Thus, debate has focused on the means for achieving reform. Constitutional conventions, viewed as cumbersome, expensive, and subject to approval by a suspicious, even dangerous, electorate have fallen from favor with citizen groups and politicians. The alternative, the legislature, may not be the ideal agency for providing systematic, regular revision and, in any case, has not been a successful forum for addressing such serious problems as fiscal integrity and state/local relations. Have we reached an impasse? This article examines the use of the constitutional commission, particularly in New York, as a means of achieving constitutional reform.

A study of the constitutional history of New York reveals that the constitutional commission has a long and vital history as a means of proposing meaningful and necessary reform within the state. Some of the most significant constitutional revision in New York has been the product of such commissions, and the most successful commissions were held in the aftermath of constitutional convention defeats.

This article examines the history and tradition of commissions as mechanisms to effectuate constitutional reform in New York, from its origins in the 1870s, when the state was struggling with issues such as corruption, home rule for burgeoning cities, and African-American suffrage, to the present-day, when the state budget process, debt limitations, and social welfare are issues of concern. Each commission will be analyzed, and placed in the historical context from which it emerged. Although a detailed analysis of the results of each commission is outside the scope of this article, an emphasis will be placed on the accomplishments and failures of each commission, as well as each commission's unique contributions to New York's constitutional history. After analyzing the constitutional commission experience of New York State, this article examines the use of constitutional commissions to provide meaningful constitutional reform in several other states, such as Florida, Utah, and Georgia.

1. The New York State Constitutional Commission Experience

Throughout its history, New York has convened ten constitutional commissions. Of these bodies, five were created specifically to prepare for upcoming constitutional conventions, while five were formed to study and propose changes to the existing constitution. As indicated by the appended table, the majority of constitutional commissions were statutorily created, although some were formed by a resolution of one or both houses of the legislature, and others were the product of executive order. The composition of these commissions, both in the number of members and the method of appointment varies. The largest commission was the forty-two member Constitutional Convention Committee of 1937-1938, while the smallest commission was the five-member 1914-1915 Constitutional Convention Commission. In marked contrast to constitutional conventions, which typically are composed of over one hundred delegates, six of New York's commissions have had twenty or less members. The maximum amount of funding for an individual commission was $800,000 for the Temporary State Commission on the Constitutional Convention, which was in operation from 1965 through 1967. Although this may appear expensive compared to the earlier commissions, the subsequent convention for which this commission prepared cost taxpayers over six million dollars.

2. The Constitutional Commission Experience in Other States

Resort to the use of constitutional commissions has increased throughout the country since mid-century, and approximately two-thirds of the states have resorted to this procedure in the last thirty years. The composition and function of these commissions varies greatly from state to state. Among the several states achieving considerable success in reforming their state constitutions through constitutional commissions, Florida, Utah, and Georgia provide three different, yet effective, models for constitutional reform using a constitutional commission.

a. Florida

Although Florida has utilized constitutional commissions to effectuate constitutional revision since the 1950s, the Florida Constitution of 1968 represented a unique and historical development in the history of constitutional commissions. In contrast to prior Florida constitutions that had allowed constitutional revision only by legislative amendment or constitutional convention, the new constitution provided an independent constitution revision commission.

The Constitution Revision Commission was mandated to convene in 1978, and every twentieth year thereafter. The thirty-seven member body consists of the attorney general, fifteen members appointed by the governor, nine members each selected by the leaders of both houses of the legislature, and three members chosen by the chief justice of the state supreme court. The chairman of the commission is selected by the governor. When the commission was created, its jurisdiction was plenary, although tax and budget matters were subsequently removed from the province of the body. Proposals from the commission must be filed with the secretary of state at least 180 days before the election, and they do not require legislative approval for ballot placement.

In 1988, Florida voters approved a constitutional amendment that "created a major opportunity to revamp Florida's outdated tax structure." The amendment created a Taxation and Budget Reform Commission with the authority to place proposals on the 1992 ballot without obtaining legislative approval. Unlike its counterpart, the Constitution Revision Commission, the Taxation and Budget Reform Commission is appointed by leaders in only two branches of the government. Taxation and budget processes are the only matters over which the commission has authority, and commission approval of amendments requires a two-thirds vote of the entire body and a majority of each appointed group of members. Sitting legislators are prohibited as voting members of the commission. The body is mandated to meet every ten years, beginning in 1990.

The Florida commissions, the first in history to be afforded the power to submit their proposals directly to the voters, have achieved substantial reform in various areas. The first Constitution Revision Commission submitted many proposals to voters in 1978, recommending a total of eighty-seven constitutional changes to various articles of the constitution. Floridians, unwilling to extensively revise a constitution that had been operating less than ten years, rejected all of the proposals, and even one by a margin of three to one.

Following the rejection of the initial commission's work, the Taxation and Budget Reform Commission in 1992 submitted four proposals to the voters. Of these proposals, one was invalidated by the Florida Supreme Court as violating statutory requirements on clarity of ballot language, and two were ultimately approved by voters. These amendments represented the first time proposals that had been submitted directly by a constitutional commission were approved by voters. In 1998, after several months of meetings and public hearings, the Florida Constitution Revision Commission submitted thirteen proposals to voters, many of which addressed multiple subjects. Of these proposals, twelve were subsequently approved by the voters, validating the effectiveness of the commission as a permanent, constitutionally prescribed device for achieving meaningful constitutional reform.

 b. *Utah*

Like Florida, Utah has established a permanent commission to propose constitutional changes. Unlike the Florida commission, the Utah commission may not make proposals directly to the voters. Instead of meeting at fixed intervals, such as every ten or twenty years, the commission operates continuously, allowing it to address issues in need of reform without additional legislative activity or within the limits of a fixed time period.

Although the composition of the commission contains heavy legislative representation, safeguards have been placed in the enacting legislation to avoid, or at least minimize, partisan conflict. The commission is composed of sixteen members: three are appointed from each house of the legislature by the respective leader of the house, but no more than two of the members appointed from each house may be members of the same political party; three members of the commission are appointed by the governor, and no more than two of them may be from the same political party; the director of the Office of Legislative Research and General Counsel serves as an ex officio member of the commission; and the remaining six commissioners are chosen by the ten existing members. The term of a commission member is six years, and no commissioner may serve for longer than twelve years. The commission selects its own officers.

In addition to conducting a comprehensive examination of the state constitution and making recommendations to the governor and legislature as to specific proposed constitutional amendments to implement the commission's recommendations for constitutional change, the commission is authorized to advise the governor and legislature on any proposed constitutional amendment or revision. The commission is directed to consider recommendations from the governor, members of the state legislature, state agencies, and "responsible members of the public." The commission must publish and distribute an annual report of its studies and recommendations.

The Utah commission, a permanent body combining legislative influence with the expertise of independent members in a non-partisan manner, has achieved considerable success. The commission has made recommendations on, and the voters have approved, amendments concerning several articles, including the legislature, the executive, corporations, election and rights of suffrage, revenue and taxation, education, and the judiciary. The ability of this commission to achieve success in reforming articles that have traditionally been difficult to amend was a testament to the success of the Utah approach.

c. Georgia

Although Georgia has not utilized a permanent constitutional commission to provide systemic reform of its state charter, it has used a constitutional commission to propose a new constitution. The Georgia Constitution of 1877 was ratified as an attempt to deal with the problems of Reconstruction, and resembled a legislative code in its length and prolixity. By 1900, it became apparent that the constitution needed major revision, and by 1943 it had been amended 301 times. Although all seven of Georgia's previous constitutions had been the product of constitutional conventions, fear of an attempt to reapportion representation had prevented the legislature from obtaining the two-thirds vote of the total membership of both houses of the legislature necessary to call a constitutional convention.

In March of 1943, as an alternative to a constitutional convention that was not politically feasible at the time, the General Assembly enacted a resolution sponsored by Governor Ellis Arnall for the creation of a twenty-three member constitutional commission. Not only did the creation of this commission circumvent the previous problems with elected conventions, as its proposals would be submitted directly to the General Assembly, but this commission was a product of the belief that constitutional revision could be achieved "more satisfactorily by a small commission than through a constitutional convention." The membership of the commission included:

> the Governor, the President of the Senate, the Speaker of the House of Representatives, three members of the Senate appointed by the President, five members of the House appointed by the Speaker, a justice of the Supreme Court chosen by the members of that court, a judge of the Court of Appeals chosen by the members of that court, the Attorney General, the State Auditor, two judges of the Superior Courts, three practicing attorneys-at-law, and three laymen appointed by the Governor. The resolution creating this commission provided that the commission could submit to the general assembly "proposed amendments to the Constitution or a proposed new constitution."

This commission convened on January 6, 1944, and adjourned on December 9, 1944. However, many of the subcommittees appointed by Governor Arnall, who served as chairman of the commission, met and held public hearings prior to the first full commission meeting. The commission submitted a proposed new constitution in January 1945 to the general assembly. The legislature undertook an extensive study of the document and made several revisions, submitting the new constitution to voters at a special election held on August 7, 1945. At that election, "the new Constitution was approved by a vote of 60,065 to 34,417."

The Georgia Constitution of 1945 represents the first time in American history that a constitution was written by a commission and ratified by popular vote. This action was taken following several unsuccessful attempts to pass a resolution that would have convened a constitutional convention, and represents a method for obtaining a complete revision of the constitution while avoiding the negatives of the convention process.

3. Conclusion

The past quarter century has witnessed the decline of the constitutional convention as a mechanism for achieving constitutional change. Although twenty-six state constitutional conventions were held between 1960 and 1995, thirteen of these were held during the 1960s. Only one state constitutional convention was held between 1988 and 1993. A combination of factors has conspired to make it likely that this trend will continue. Conventions are controversial for a number of reasons: they are viewed as "Pandora's boxes," creating the possibility of dangerous additions to the constitution; they threaten to upset established relationships between the governing institutions and organized interests; and they are viewed as cumbersome, unwieldy and expensive mechanisms. As an example, the rejected convention in New York in 1997 was projected to cost at least fifty million dollars.

The reluctance to resort to conventions, combined with the inability or unwillingness of state legislatures to propose systematic revision, has left states with few options for meaningful constitutional change. The constitutional commission has the potential to break this constitutional logjam. The commission allows an educated, highly specialized group of persons to analyze the problems of the state in a deliberate and relatively nonpartisan manner. When contrasted with constitutional conventions, which in New York have over 150 delegates, it is not surprising that commissions are often viewed as progressive and deliberate in their work. Moreover, the relatively low cost of a commission compared to a constitutional convention makes using a commission a bargain for constitutional reform.

Constitutional reform commissions have played a significant role in New York's constitutional development, providing expertise and impetus for constitutional conventions, the legislature, and the people in the exercise of their respective powers to revise and amend the constitution. Florida, Utah, and Georgia provide models of constitutional commissions that differ from the traditional commission employed in New York. These varied state experiences, and the history of the commission in New York, suggest that a constitutional commission to undertake a comprehensive evaluation of the constitution and provide recommendations to the legislature for its revision, offer the state its best hope for accomplishing needed constitutional reform.

NOTE

For more articles about the amendment and revision of state constitutions, see John Dinan, *State Constitutional Initiative Process and Governance in the Twenty-First Century*, 12 Chap. L. Rev. 61 (2016); Jon M. Philipson, *Second-Order Logrolling: The Impact of Direct Legislative Amendments to State Constitutions*, 41 Nova L. Rev. 23 (2016); John Dinan, *State Constitutional Amendments and American Constitutionalism*, 41 Okla. City U. L. Rev. 27 (2016); and Vikram David Amar, *Evolving State Constitutional Processes of Adoption, Revision, and Amendment: The Path Ahead*, 69 Ark. L. Rev. 553 (2016).

G. LEGISLATING BY VOTER INITIATIVE

Fourteen States have extended the logic of popular sovereignty and direct democracy to the legislative process, permitting ordinary law-making by direct voter initiatives. *See* Ariz. Const. art. IV, § 1; Ark. Const. art. V, § 1; Cal. Const. art. II, §§ 8, 10; Colo. Const. art. V, § 1; Idaho Const. art. III, § 1; Mo. Const. art. III, §§ 50–51; Mont. Const. art. III, § 4; Neb. Const. art. III, §§ 1–2, 4; N.D. Const. art. III; Okla. Const. art. V. §§ 1–3, 6–8; Or. Const. art. IV, § 1; S.D. Const. art. III, § 1; Utah Const. art. VI, § 1; Wash. Const. art. II, § 1. Another seven States allow indirect voter initiatives on ordinary legislation, meaning that state legislatures have an opportunity to act on the petition before it is put to a statewide vote. *See* Alaska Const. art. XI, §§ 1–7; Me. Const. art. IV, Init., pt. 3, § 18; Mass. Const. amend. art. XLVIII, pt. 5, § 1; Mich. Const. art. II, § 9; Nev. Const. art. XIX, § 2; Ohio Const. art. II, § 1b; Wyo. Const. art. III, § 52. The following case considers the nature and limits of *the people*'s legislative power in states that allow direct legislation. For an excellent survey of state initiative and referendum laws, see John Dinan, *State Constitutional Politics* (2018). *See also State I&R*, Initiative and Referendum Institute, http://www.iandrinstitute.org/states.cfm; Sutton, *Who Decides? States as Laboratories of Constitutional Experimentation* Chapter 10 (Oxford 2021).

CARTER v. LEHI CITY
269 P.3d 141 (Utah 2012)

LEE, J.

This case presents questions concerning the scope of the people's initiative power under article VI of the Utah Constitution. Petitioners are Lehi City voters who sought to place on the municipal ballot initiatives regulating salaries and residency requirements for certain city employees. The City refused to accept the initiatives, and this litigation ensued.

Our consideration of this matter has caused us to reexamine our precedents defining the nature and extent of the people's power to legislate by initiative. The framework embraced in those precedents has prompted some misgivings over the years. At the core of our concern has been the difficulty of applying the test in our cases predictably and consistently.

This concern is particularly troubling in a field that implicates the constitutional power of the people to initiate legislation. That power is a fundamental guardian of liberty and an ultimate protection against tyranny. Its preservation cannot be left to the whims of a doctrine whose invocation turns on the discretionary decrees of the judicial branch. Of all the branches of government, we are least suited to decide on the wisdom of allowing the people to supplant their representatives in a particular field of regulation. We are the least representative branch of government. There is a troubling irony in our making discretionary calls on the propriety of acts by the ultimate repository of regulatory power. We must assure that our decisions on such vital matters are dictated by law, not by our individual preferences.

With this in mind, we return to first principles to examine the nature and scope of the people's initiative power. In the paragraphs below, we evaluate the text and structure of article VI of the Utah Constitution and analyze its meaning in historical perspective. From those materials we develop a legal framework for delineating the people's initiative power that is consistent with the text and original meaning of article VI.

This page of history outweighs the volume of logic in our existing precedent. Thus, we abandon the framework set forth in *Citizen's Awareness Now v. Marakis* (Utah 1994), and refined in subsequent cases, replacing it with a standard that defines the people's initiative power on the basis of the nature of the power to effect "legislation," as that term is traditionally understood.

In so doing, we do not envision a fundamental change in the ultimate breadth of the initiative power. Our new framework is not aimed at overturning the results of most of our prior decisions in this area. We aim to clarify the law and to bring it in line with the text and original meaning of the constitution, not to overrule the results of many of our cases. Thus, our decision today is sensitive to and ultimately consistent with the doctrine of stare decisis. That doctrine recognizes that "people should know what their legal rights are as defined by judicial precedent, and having conducted their affairs in reliance on such rights, ought not to have them swept away by judicial fiat." A decision to clarify unworkable precedent does not undermine but advances that goal, particularly where we preserve the results of most of our prior cases.

Applying our new standard, we uphold the initiatives proposed by petitioners as properly legislative and reject Lehi City's various objections to placing them on the ballot.

In December 2010, a group of Lehi City voters sought to amend two city ordinances by submitting to the city recorder two voter initiatives for inclusion in the 2011 municipal election ballot. Initiative One sought to set "maximum salary and total compensation limits" on all salaried city employees. Initiative Two sought to impose a city residency requirement for certain city employees. Each initiative garnered more than the minimum number of registered voter signatures required by statute, and it is undisputed that the initiatives otherwise complied with title 20A, chapter 7 of the election code, which governs the manner and conditions for proposing citizen initiatives.

In a May 2011 council meeting, the Lehi City Council determined that the proposed amendments were not valid exercises of the voters' power to initiate legislation, and adopted a resolution directing the city recorder to refuse to place them on the November 2011 election ballot. The resolution stated the council's conclusions that "both initiatives are legally insufficient in that they: i) are not the proper subject of an initiative petition because they are administrative in nature; ii) may be an unconstitutional impairment of contract; and iii) conflict with state law."

Upon learning of the council's decision, three of the initiatives' sponsors filed a petition for writ of extraordinary relief directly in this court as authorized by Utah Code section 20A–7–507. The petitioners contend that Initiatives One and Two are proper exercises of initiative power under article VI of the Utah Constitution and that the initiatives should be submitted for voter approval in the next municipal election. We agree with the petitioners: The subject matter of Initiatives One and Two is legislative in nature; the initiatives do not conflict with state law because Utah Code section 10–3–818, invoked by the City, does not apply to voter initiatives; and the City's remaining arguments are not ripe for review.

Lehi City's central contention is that Initiatives One and Two are "administrative in nature" and thus not "appropriate for voter participation." We disagree with Lehi and hold that Initiatives One and Two are proper exercises of the people's legislative power.

Article VI, section 1 of the Utah Constitution vests "Legislative power" in "the people of the State of Utah" and provides for its exercise through ballot initiatives and referenda. Under this provision, our cases have long recognized a general limit on the people's initiative power. An initiative is appropriate if it is "legislative," but *ultra vires* if it is "administrative." *Citizen's Awareness*. This legislative/administrative distinction is a reflection of our constitution's explicit and strict separation of powers, which is set forth in article V.

Under article V of the Utah Constitution,

> The powers of the government of the State of Utah shall be divided into three distinct departments, the Legislative, the Executive, and the Judicial; and no person charged with the exercise of powers properly belonging to one of these departments, shall exercise any functions appertaining to either of the others, except in the cases herein expressly directed or permitted.

We begin with some fundamental principles that are evident in the text, structure, and history of our constitution. First, the initiative power of the people is parallel to and coextensive with the power of the state legislature. Second, the constitution accords a similar initiative power to the people on a local level, to be exercised within counties, cities, and towns. From these principles, it follows that the question courts should ask in evaluating the propriety of a proposed initiative is whether the initiative would be a proper exercise of legislative power if enacted by the state legislature.

"The government of the State of Utah was founded pursuant to the people's organic authority to govern themselves." As reinforced in our constitution, "all political power is inherent in the people; and all free governments are founded on their authority." Under this basic premise, upon which all our government is built, the people have the inherent authority to allocate governmental power in the bodies they establish by law.

Acting through the state constitution, the people of Utah divided their political power, vesting it in the various branches of government. Article VI vests "The Legislative power of the State" in two bodies: (a) "the Legislature of the State of Utah," and (b) "the people of the State of Utah as provided in Subsection (2)." On its face, article VI recognizes a single, undifferentiated "legislative power," vested both in the people and in the legislature. Nothing in the text or structure of article VI suggests any difference in the power vested simultaneously in the "Legislature" and "the people." The initiative power of the people is thus parallel and coextensive with the power of the legislature. This interpretation is reinforced by the history of the direct-democracy movement, by constitutional debates in states with constitutional provisions substantially similar to Utah's article VI, and by early judicial interpretations of those provisions.

Utah amended its constitution to provide for ballot initiatives in 1900, the second of twenty-four states to do so. At the time, a Progressive movement had gained widespread support, based on the premise that "only free, unorganized individuals could be trusted and that any intermediary body such as politicians, political parties and legislative bodies were inherently corrupt and distorted the public interest." The thrust of the initiative movement was a sentiment that the people should flex the muscles of their organic governmental power and reserve for themselves the legislative power that had previously been vested solely in the state legislatures. Only by wielding the legislative power could the people govern themselves in a democracy unfettered by the distortions of representative legislatures.

The Progressive movement's nationwide force impelled many states to consider constitutional amendments that provided for direct democracy in the form of initiatives and referenda. These debates addressed the nature of the legislative power that would be exercised directly by the people. Although the legislative history of Utah's initiative amendment is limited, the debates in other states inform the scope of the people's legislative power as it was originally understood.

For example, throughout the debates in Massachusetts and Ohio, delegates acknowledged that the people are the ultimate source of sovereign power and spoke of the initiative amendments as reservations of the same power delegated to the legislature. Indeed, the delegates took for granted that the governmental power to be reserved by the people was legislative power and focused their arguments on the wisdom of sharing that power between the people and the legislature.

The adoption of initiative and referendum amendments raised questions in many state courts regarding the power allocated between the people and the legislature. In early judicial interpretations of article VI and similar constitutional provisions in other states, courts generally understood that the people and the legislature hold parallel and coextensive power.

In one of the first Utah cases interpreting article VI, Justice Larson explained that through ballot initiative, the people are a "legislative body coequal in power" with the legislature. The Supreme Court of Washington stated that "the passage of an initiative measure as a law is the exercise of the same power of sovereignty as that exercised by the Legislature in the passage of a statute." Likewise, soon after becoming the first state to pass an initiative amendment, the North Dakota Supreme Court recognized that "the Legislative Assembly and the people are in effect coordinate legislative bodies with coextensive legislative power." And the Oregon Supreme Court, explaining that the initiative power is parallel to the legislature's power, stated that "laws proposed and enacted by the people under the initiative are subject to the same constitutional limitations as other statutes, and may be amended or repealed by the Legislature at will."

The people's legislative power may be exercised at either a statewide or local level. Article VI, section 1(2) distinguishes statewide and local initiatives but affirms that the initiative power at both levels is coextensive with the power vested in the legislature.

Under subsection (2)(a), "legal voters of the State" are authorized to "initiate *any desired legislation* and cause it to be submitted to the people for adoption," subject only to the "conditions," "manner," and "time provided by statute." Subsection (2)(b) recognizes parallel power of "legal voters of any county, city, or town"—to "initiate *any desired legislation* and cause it to be submitted to the people of the county, city, or town for adoption," again subject only to the "conditions," "manner," and "time provided by statute."

These two provisions recognize a relatively unlimited legislative power reserved by the people. Whether on a statewide or local basis, the people may propose any measure that is "desired"—so long as it is "legislation," and so long as the people follow the conditions and manner prescribed by statute. And though the legislature may prescribe the "manner" and "conditions" for exercising initiative power, article VI nowhere indicates that the scope of the people's initiative power is less than that of the legislature's power, or that the initiative power is derived from or delegated by the legislature. Instead, "under our constitutional assumptions, all power derives from the people, who can delegate it to representative instruments which they create." Therefore a "referendum or initiative cannot be characterized as a delegation of power." And in exercising the initiative power, the people do not act under the authority of the legislature.

Yet while article VI, subsection (2) authorizes the people to exercise their full legislative power by proposing "any desired legislation," its division between statewide and local authority necessarily implies a geographical limit on local initiative power. The voters of a municipality could not adopt, for example, a statewide traffic law. Otherwise, however, the people's legislative power is the same—and is coextensive with the power delegated to the legislature—regardless of whether that power is wielded on a statewide or local level. Therefore, when courts must determine the propriety of a voter initiative, the relevant inquiry must look to the nature and limits of legislative power. The people's initiative power reaches to the full extent of the legislative power, but no further.

The conclusion that the people hold retained, coextensive power to adopt "legislation" leaves unresolved the question of the nature and extent of the legislative power. It may not be possible to mark the precise boundaries of that power with bright lines. But we can describe the essential hallmarks of such power, and in so doing we can prescribe a working standard for judging the propriety of ballot initiatives under the Utah Constitution.

The starting point in our analysis is the constitutional separation of legislative, executive, and judicial powers. Our understanding of the legislative power is informed by its placement in relation to—and separation from—the executive and judicial power. Thus, we proceed to identify the hallmarks of legislative power and to describe its boundaries in part by its separation from the executive and the judicial power.

In the paragraphs that follow, we identify two key hallmarks of legislative power as it has historically been understood. Legislative power generally (a) involves the promulgation of laws of general applicability; and

(b) is based on the weighing of broad, competing policy considerations. This power is different from the executive power, which encompasses prosecutorial or administrative acts aimed at applying the law to particular individuals or groups based on individual facts and circumstances. It is also distinguished from the judicial power, which involves the application of the law to particular individuals or groups based on their particularized circumstances.

In light of the foregoing, a ballot initiative should be deemed an appropriate legislative act where it proposes a law of general applicability. Laws that prescribe rules of conduct for the general population are squarely within the ambit of generally applicable rules, and ballot initiatives proposing such laws are per se legislative.

General application to the population as a whole is a sufficient condition to sustain the legislative propriety of a ballot initiative. But it is not a necessary condition. Legislation usually applies to "more than a few people," but there are circumstances where legislation may properly extend to only one or a few individuals. Such a law could still be "legislative" where it (1) is based on general policy concerns rather than individual circumstances and (2) governs "all future cases falling under its provisions" and not just specified individuals.

In questionable cases at the margins of these standards, it may be useful to consult historical examples of traditional exercises of legislative power. Thus, if a particular initiative seems close to a blurry part of the doctrinal line between the legislative and the executive, a court's decision may be informed by history. An initiative that finds longstanding parallels in statutes enacted by legislative bodies, for example, may be deemed legislative on that basis, while initiatives that seem more like traditional executive acts may be deemed to fall on that side of the line.

Our decision today adopts a new paradigm for evaluating the propriety of ballot initiatives under our constitution. In so doing, however, we do not intend to signal an abrupt change in the scope of the initiative power or in the results that we foresee in the cases that come before us. In fact, the framework articulated above preserves the results of many of our prior cases in this field and is even consistent with some of our prior analysis.

We turn, finally, to the initiatives at issue in this case. In our view, Initiatives One and Two fall comfortably within the constitutional framework set forth above. Initiative One sets salary limits on all city officials who are ineligible for overtime pay. If passed, this initiative would apply generally to any person fitting the definition of a city employee who is ineligible for overtime. All current and future employees coming within the initiative's terms would be subject to the initiative. Rather than applying to one specific person, the salary limits apply generally to the entire class of persons specified by the proposed law. The adoption of salary limits for city offices, moreover, is based on broad policy considerations pertinent to the offices, not the specific circumstances of individual, identified employees. This is classic legislation possessing all of the hallmarks of the legislative power.

Initiative Two is likewise legislative. It imposes a residency requirement for eighteen city officials. This requirement is generally applicable because, for each listed official, all present and future individuals obtaining that office would be subject to the residency requirement. Like the salary cap, the residency requirement applies generally to an entire class of persons, not a specific person. And again a decision whether to impose a residency requirement is based on broad policy considerations pertinent to the office, not the specific circumstances of individual officers. This, too, is classic legislative action within the people's initiative power.

If there were any doubt about the legislative nature of these initiatives, it could easily be resolved by reference to historical uses of similar government power. Here again, history confirms our theoretical analysis. Residency and salary restrictions are hardly novel exercises of legislative power. In fact, the legislature has long adopted residency requirements for various county and municipal government offices by legislation.

As for salaries for government offices, our state constitution tasks the legislature with setting many such salaries, including "the Governor, Lieutenant Governor, State Auditor, State Treasurer, Attorney General, and any other state officer as the Legislature may provide." Following this constitutional mandate, the legislature has—since the founding of our state—enacted legislation setting the extent and limits of public-employee compensation.

This historical pattern confirms that public-employee compensation and residency requirements are subject matters appropriate for legislative control. Initiatives One and Two are properly legislative and should have been accepted by the Lehi City recorder for placement on the municipal ballot.

INDEX

Abortion 6, 258–286, 782–785
Adequacy of school funding 597–627
Advisory opinions 330–331, 816–819, 871, 876–881, 891–901, 919–923
Age, classifications based on 153–161
Altering state constitutions, generally 1027–1041
Amendment and revision 1027–1065
Anti-commandeering principle 9, 39–44
Automobile search 120–124, 409, 465–475
Blaine Amendments 69, 555–560, 563–567, 570, 576, 580, 587–593
Bodily integrity, the right of... 261, 274, 334–346
Certified questions 686, 814, 901–909, 936–937
Clear title rules 767–779, 789–790
Commerce power 10–21, 34–39
Commissions 1029, 1040–1041, 1059–1065
Competency hearing... 253
Confrontation 299, 381–384
Conventions 65, 95, 106–107, 153, 157, 185, 295, 298, 301,
.... 349, 352–353, 356, 403, 501, 512, 517, 590,
.... 611, 736, 977, 1018, 1034–1050, 1059–1064
Counsel.. 34, 253, 255–258, 377–381, 900–901
Cruel and unusual punishment 34, 131, 396–405
Direct democracy 245–247, 1032, 1034, 1041–1045, 1047, 1065–1072
Double jeopardy... 299, 392–396
Dual sovereignty 3, 9–75, 77, 80, 125, 295, 437
Due process of law 29, 34, 251–350, 513–533, 697
Economic rights 513–533
Education, fundamental right to 137, 595–607, 634
Election of judges.. 79, 154–156, 850–864, 1028
Eleventh Amendment immunity 44–57
Equality 133–175, 314, 597–607, 632–637
Establishment of religion 113, 535, 555–593
Evidence, duty to preserve 384–391
Excessive fines 35, 396
Executive power.. 667, 688, 824–850
Extradition.. 56, 64–65
Freedom of religion... 535–554
Full faith and credit 42, 56, 64
Gender, classifications based on 148–153
Gerrymandering 179–221
Good faith exception 418–436
Guarantee Clause 69–75, 241–250
Home Rule 978–1017
Independent and adequate state ground... 113–123
Initiatives... 73, 241, 1037–1045
   Direct constitutional 1037
   Indirect constitutional.. 1038
   Legislative 919–930
   Limitations 1038–1039
   Procedures for 1050–1059
Interstate compacts.. 39, 56
Intimate association, the right of.. 287–304
Judicial branch 850–909
Jury trial 33–34, 94–98, 351, 718

Civil	718–727
Criminal	351–363
Justiciability	865–900
Legislative power	761–766
Life-sustaining support, withdrawal of	334–337
Line-item veto	841–850
Local governments	975–1026
Magna Carta	251, 651–659, 672
Marijuana	10–21, 341–345
Marriage	6, 162, 314–334
Miranda violations	476–481
Open courts	651–700
Organization of state governments	809–924
Original purpose rules	767, 771–772, 774
Parental rights, termination of	255–258
Post-conviction relief	351–360
Preemption	9, 58–61
Privacy	702–706
Privacy (autonomy), right of	258–287
Privileges and immunities	63
Probable cause	409–418
Proportionality	396–405
Public purpose requirements	790–802
Racial classifications	134–148
Religious Freedom Restoration Act	27–33, 538–540, 554
Religious Land Use and Institutionalized Persons Act	538, 546, 549, 554
Reproductive autonomy	258–287
Right to bear arms	34, 79, 727–748
Right to counsel	245–255, 377–381
Right to a remedy	34, 257, 692–699
Search and seizure	80, 84, 113, 125, 338, 409–481, 704
Seizure of individual	459–464
Self-incrimination	118, 363–377
Separation of powers	1, 32–33, 190, 613, 651, 682, 687–689, 809, 823–824, 830–837, 811–822, 829–836, 925–926, 933–934, 936, 940, 943 951–953, 957–958, 961–970, 977, 998, 1018–1025, 1054, 1067, 1070
Sexual orientation, classifications based on	162–164
Single subject requirement	2, 5, 768–789
Speech and expression	706–718
Standing	437–443, 865–891
Suicide, physician-assisted	337–341
Supremacy clause	35, 41–42, 49, 58–64, 77
Taking of private property	486–513
Term limits	58–62, 810–816
Thorough and efficient education, right to	607–627, 632–637
Victims' rights	754–761
Voting	221–250
Vouchers	570–593, 627–632
Warrant requirement	84–88, 409, 418–437, 443–459, 701–706, 756–760